Foundation Flash CS5 for Designers

Tom Green and Tiago Dias

Foundation Flash CS5 for Designers

Copyright © 2010 by Tom Green and Tiago Dias

All rights reserved. No part of this work may be reproduced or transmitted in any form or by any means, electronic or mechanical, including photocopying, recording, or by any information storage or retrieval system, without the prior written permission of the copyright owner and the publisher.

ISBN-13 (pbk): 978-1-4302-2994-0

ISBN-13 (electronic): 978-1-4302-2995-7

Trademarked names, logos, and images may appear in this book. Rather than use a trademark symbol with every occurrence of a trademarked name, logos, or image we use the names, logos, or images only in an editorial fashion and to the benefit of the trademark owner, with no intention of infringement of the trademark.

The use in this publication of trade names, service marks, and similar terms, even if they are not identified as such, is not to be taken as an expression of opinion as to whether or not they are subject to proprietary rights.

Distributed to the book trade worldwide by Springer Science+Business Media LLC., 233 Spring Street, 6th Floor, New York, NY 10013. Phone 1-800-SPRINGER, fax (201) 348-4505, e-mail orders-ny@springer-sbm.com, or visit www.springeronline.com.

For information on translations, please e-mail rights@apress.com or visit www.apress.com.

Apress and friends of ED books may be purchased in bulk for academic, corporate, or promotional use. eBook versions and licenses are also available for most titles. For more information, reference our Special Bulk Sales–eBook Licensing web page at www.apress.com/info/bulksales.

The information in this book is distributed on an "as is" basis, without warranty. Although every precaution has been taken in the preparation of this work, neither the author(s) nor Apress shall have any liability to any person or entity with respect to any loss or damage caused or alleged to be caused directly or indirectly by the information contained in this work.

The source code for this book is freely available to readers at www.friendsofed.com in the Downloads section.

Credits

President and Publisher: Paul Manning

Lead Editor: Ben Renow-Clarke

Technical Reviewers: Cheridan Kerr, Kristian Besley

Editorial Board: Clay Andres, Steve Anglin, Mark Beckner, Ewan Buckingham, Gary Cornell, Jonathan Gennick, Jonathan Hassell, Michelle Lowman, Matthew Moodie, Duncan Parkes, Jeffrey Pepper, Frank Pohlmann, Douglas Pundick, Ben Renow-Clarke, Dominic Shakeshaft, Matt Wade, Tom Welsh

Coordinating Editor: Mary Tobin

Copy Editor: Kim Wimpsett

Compositor: Lynn LHeureux

Indexer: Kevin Broccoli

Artist: April Milne

Cover Designer: Anna Ishchenko

To Sarah and Rory McGrath in Berne, Switzerland. May your marriage be one of peace, love, and joy.

—Tom Green

Contents at a Glance

About the Authors xiv
About the Technical Reviewers xv
Acknowledgments xvi
Preface xviii
Chapter 1: Learning the Flash CS5 Professional Interface 1
Chapter 2: Graphics in Flash CS5 67
Chapter 3: Symbols and Libraries 151
Chapter 4: ActionScript Basics 213
Chapter 5: Audio in Flash CS5 279
Chapter 6: Text 315
Chapter 7: Animation, Part 1 361
Chapter 8: Animation, Part 2 427
Chapter 9: Flash Has a Third Dimension 495
Chapter 10: Video 527
Chapter 11: Building Interfaces with the UI Components 601
Chapter 12: XML (Dynamic Data) 643
Chapter 13: CSS 669
Chapter 14: Building Stuff 695
Chapter 15: Optimizing and Publishing Flash Movies 757

Index 809

Contents

About the Authors xiv
About the Technical Reviewers xv
Acknowledgments xvi
Preface xviii

Chapter 1: Learning the Flash CS5 Professional Interface 1
    Getting started 2
    Creating a new Flash document 5
    Managing your workspace 6
    Setting document preferences and properties 8
        Document preferences 9
        Document settings 10
        Zooming the stage 11
    Exploring the panels in the Flash interface 14
        The timeline 14
        The Properties panel 23
        The Tools panel 29
        The Library panel 31
    Using layers 32
        Layer properties 33
        Creating layers 34
        Adding content to layers 36
        Showing/hiding and locking layers 38
        Grouping layers 40
        Where to get help 40
    Your turn: building a Flash movie 42
        Nesting movie clips 45
        Drawing the fly 47
        Creating the illusion of depth with Flash 48
        Creating an animated fly 55
        Adding audio 59
        Testing and saving Flash files 61
    You have learned 65

Chapter 2: Graphics in Flash CS5 67
- The Tools panel 70
  - The Selection and Subselection tools 72
  - The Free Transform tool 75
  - The Gradient Transform tool 77
  - Object Drawing mode 80
- Drawing in Flash CS5 83
  - The Pencil tool 83
  - The Brush tool 85
  - The Deco tool 88
  - The Spray Brush tool 98
  - The Eraser tool 101
  - The Pen tool 102
- Your turn: let's have a campfire 104
  - Drawing the tree trunk 104
  - Drawing the pine tree 106
  - Adding pine needles 107
  - Build the campfire movie 108
- Working with color in Flash 110
  - The Color palette and the Color Picker 112
  - Creating persistent custom colors 115
  - The kuler Color Picker 117
  - Your turn: playing with color 119
- Using bitmap images in Flash 123
  - Working with bitmaps in Flash 125
  - Your turn: tracing bitmaps in Flash 127
  - JPEG files and Flash 131
  - Using GIF files in Flash CS5 134
  - Importing Fireworks CS5 documents into Flash CS5 137
  - Importing Illustrator CS5 documents into Flash CS5 140
  - Importing Photoshop CS5 documents into Flash CS5 146
- You have learned 149

Chapter 3: Symbols and Libraries 151
- Symbol essentials 152
- Symbol types 155
  - Graphic symbols 155
  - Button symbols 156
  - Movie clip symbols 158
  - Editing symbols 159

9-slice scaling 160
    How 9-slice scaling works 161
    Your turn: frames for an olive seller.. 163
    The 9-slice "gotchas" 166
Sharing symbols 169
    Sharing libraries 171
Filters and blend modes 174
    Applying filters 174
    Applying a Drop Shadow filter... 175
    Adding perspective 177
    Playing with blends 180
Managing content on the stage 184
    Aligning objects on the stage 186
    Stacking order and using the Align panel 189
Masks and masking 194
    A simple mask... 194
    Using text as a mask 201
Your turn: a sunny day on Catalina Island 205
    Adding the clouds 206
    Getting the clouds in motion.. 208
What you've learned... 211

Chapter 4: ActionScript Basics 213

The power of ActionScript... 214
    Actions panel components 216
    The Actions panel vs. the Behaviors panel... 219
Everything is an object 220
    Classes 221
    Properties 222
Setting properties via ActionScript 225
    Methods 226
    Events 229
Coding fundamentals 233
    Syntax 233
    Capitalization matters 233
    Semicolons mark the end of a line 234
    Commenting code.. 235
    Dot notation 237
    Scope... 239
    Variables... 240

Data types	241
Operators	244
Conditional statements	247
Class files and the document class	251
Syntax checking	253
How to read the ActionScript 3.0 Language and Components Reference	257
Getting help	258
Search tactics	259
Using ActionScript	260
Your turn: pause and loop with ActionScript	261
Pausing a timeline	261
Looping the Timeline	265
Using movie clips to control the timeline	266
Using Code Snippets	266
What you've learned	276

Chapter 5: Audio in Flash CS5 279

Flash and the audio formats	280
Bit depth and sample rates	281
Flash and MP3	283
Adding audio to Flash	284
Importing an audio file	284
Setting sound properties	285
Using audio in Flash	288
Choosing a sound type: event or streaming	288
Removing an audio file from the timeline	291
Getting loopy	291
Adjusting volume and pan	293
Your turn: adding sound to a button	296
Controlling audio with ActionScript 3.0	298
Playing a sound from the Library	298
Using a button to play a sound	300
Playing a sound from outside of Flash	301
Turning a remote sound on and off	302
Adjusting volume with code	304
Your turn: storm over Lake Superior	305
Code snippet: visualize audio	309
What you've learned	313

Chapter 6: Text 315
Fonts and typefaces 316
Adobe CoolType 319
Typefaces and fonts 321
Working with device fonts 322
Embedding fonts 324
The two text engines: TLF and Classic 328
Types of text 330
Read-only text properties 331
Container and flow 337
Selectable and editable text 340
TLF and ActionScript 341
Using TLF text as a button 345
Hyperlinks and TLF 349
Using ActionScript to add hyperlinks to TLF text 350
Checking spelling 352
Your turn: scrollable text 355
Using the UIScrollBar component 355
Rolling your own scroller 356
What you have learned 360

Chapter 7: Animation, Part 1 361
Shape tweening 363
Scaling and stretching 363
Modifying shape tweens 368
Altering shapes 369
Shape hints 373
Altering gradients 377
Classic tweening 379
Rotation 379
Classic tween properties 381
Scaling, stretching, and deforming 382
Easing 384
Custom easing 387
Using animation 395
A closer look at the Timeline panel 395
Onion skinning 397
Modifying multiple frames 400
Combining timelines 402

Motion guides	408
Tweening a mask	411
Tweening Filter Effects	413
Programmatic animation	415
Copying motion as ActionScript	416
Using the keyboard to control motion	419
Creating random motion using ActionScript	421
What you have learned	426

Chapter 8: Animation, Part 2 427

Animating with the Motion Editor panel	428
Getting acquainted: scaling and moving	430
Easing with graphs	437
Managing property keyframes	445
Motion paths	450
Manipulating motion paths	450
Motion tween properties	454
Motion presets	455
Inverse kinematics (IK)	458
Using the Bone tool	459
Putting some "spring" in your bones	468
Animating IK Poses	478
Using the Bind tool	480
Your turn: animate a fully rigged IK model	487
Inspiration is everywhere	492
What you have learned	493

Chapter 9: Flash Has a Third Dimension 495

What 3D really means in Flash (and what it doesn't)	496
Understanding the vanishing point	498
Using the 3D tools	501
The 3D Rotation tool	501
The 3D Translation tool	506
Strategies for positioning content in 3D space	512
The parallax effect: traveling through space	512
Use the 3D center point to your advantage	517
Be aware of depth limitations	520
Your turn: simulate a photo cube	522
What you have learned	526

Chapter 10: Video 527

Video on the Web 529
Video formats 530
Encoding an FLV 532
    Using the Adobe Media Encoder 532
    Batch encoding 541
    Creating an F4V file 542
    More Media Encoder Goodness 544
Playing an FLV in Flash CS5 546
    Using the wizard 546
    Using the FLVPlayback component 552
    Playing video using ActionScript 555
    Using the FLVPlayback control components 560
    Navigating through video using cue points 562
    Adding captions with the FLVPlaybackCaptioning component 567
    Preparing and using alpha channel video 572
    Going full-screen with video 574
When video is not video 579
Embedding video 579
    Embedding video as a movie clip 581
    Interacting with video content 582
Adding cue points 583
    An alternate XML format for cue points 584
    Your turn: create XML captions for video 588
Your turn: play with alpha video 593
Your turn: think big, really big! 597
What you have learned 598

Chapter 11: Building Interfaces with the UI Components 601

Button component 603
    Using the Button component 603
    Changing the Button component's appearance 610
CheckBox component 615
ColorPicker component 617
ComboBox component 619
DataGrid component 622
Label component 624
List component 624
NumericStepper component 626
ProgressBar component 628

RadioButton component 630
ScrollPane component 632
Slider component 633
TextArea component 635
TextInput component 636
TileList component 637
UILoader component 638
UIScrollBar component 641
What you have learned 641

Chapter 12: XML (Dynamic Data) 643
Writing XML 645
Loading an XML file 648
Using E4X syntax 649
    Dots and @s 650
    Node types 654
    E4X filtering 656
    Double dots and more 657
    Namespaces 659
    Your turn: time to explore XFL 661
What you have learned 667

Chapter 13: CSS 669
Styling with CSS 671
Loading external CSS 676
    Custom tags 684
    Style inheritance 686
    Styling hyperlinks 688
    Embedded fonts 690
    Selectors vs. the Properties panel 693
What you have learned 694

Chapter 14: Building Stuff 695
Loading content 697
    Are we there yet? 697
    Somebody stole my preloader 701
Building a slide show with components and XML 703
    A tour of the Beijing art district 704

Building an MP3 player with XML	711
Setting up the external playlist	712
Polishing up the symbols	713
Wiring up the MP3 player controls	720
Evaluating and improving the MP3 player	735
Going mobile	737
A quick tour of Device Central	737
Package the game as an Android AIR app	750
Build more stuff	756
What you have learned	756

Chapter 15: Optimizing and Publishing Flash Movies ... 757

Flash's love-hate Internet relationship	758
This "Internet" thing	759
Enter the World Wide Web	760
Bandwidth	760
So, who are these folks we call users?	762
Streaming	763
The Bandwidth Profiler	765
Simulating a download	765
Pinpointing problem content	769
Can I get that in writing?	770
Optimizing and fine-tuning your Flash movies	771
Planning your project	771
Distributing the weight	776
Optimizing elements in the movie	778
Publishing and web formats	783
Flash	784
HTML	785
Animated GIFs	786
QuickTime	790
It's showtime!	791
Publish settings	792
Publishing the butterfly garden	803
Publishing Flash movies containing linked files	805
What you have learned	807

Index	**809**

xiii

About the Authors

Tom Green is currently Professor, Interactive Media through the School of Media Studies at the Humber Institute of Technology and Advanced Learning in Toronto, Canada. He has written numerous books on Adobe technologies and several hundred tutorials for numerous magazines and websites including activetutsplus.com, layersmagazine.com, Community MX, and Computer Arts. Tom is also an Adobe Community Professional and an Adobe Education Leader. He has spoken and lectured at more than 20 conferences and post-secondary institutions internationally including Adobe Max, FITC, SparkEurope, and the Central Academy of Fine Arts in Beijing, China. In his spare time, you can catch him hiking a trail with the Cub Scout group he has led for the past 15 years or paddling a lake in Northern Ontario. You can contact Tom at tom@tomontheweb.ca.

Tiago Dias discovered Flash around the time of Flash 3, after seeing a Flash site for the first time. He started off by doing freelance work on the side from his day job as a network/systems engineer. Today he works as a Senior Flash Platform Developer at Publicis Modem, the digital unit of Publicis. Previously he worked as a video producer and Flash developer at a Corporate Television company in Zurich.

Besides working and writing, Tiago is an Adobe Community Professional and one of the co-managers of the Swiss Flash User Group (SFUG) and has spoken at such conferences as FITC and FATL on various topics.

In his free time, he writes tutorials on Flash, Flex, AS3, and new technologies/libraries for various communities. To relax, he tries to go snowboarding every time the sun is shining in the Swiss Alps or hops on a plane and flies to a sunny and warm destination to go scuba diving. He currently lives and works in Zurich, Switzerland.

About the Technical Reviewers

Cheridan Kerr has been involved in web development and design since 1997 when she began working on a research team for the Y2K Millennium Bug. It was here she learned about the Internet and promptly fell in love with the medium. In her career, she has been responsible for websites in the early 2000s such as Weight Watchers Australia and `Quicken.com.au`, and she has worked as a creative services manager of Yahoo!7 in Australia on clients such as Toyota, 20th Century Fox, and Ford. Currently, she is working as the head of digital for an Australian advertising agency.

Kristian Besley is a Flash and web developer currently working in education and specializing in games/interactivity and dynamically driven content using Flash, PHP, and .NET (not all at the same time, obviously!). He also lectures in interactive media.

Kristian has produced freelance work for numerous clients including the BBC, Heinemann, and BBC Cymru. He has written a number of books for friends of ED, such as working on the Foundation Flash series, *Flash MX Video* (ISBN-13: 978-1-59059-172-7), *Flash ActionScript for Flash 8* (ISBN-13: 978-1-59059-618-0), and *Learn Design with Flash MX* (ISBN-13: 978-1-59059-157-4). He was also a proud contributor to the amazing Flash Math Creativity books and has written for *Computer Arts* magazine.

Kristian currently resides with his family in Swansea, Wales and is a fluent Welsh speaker.

Acknowledgments

In the acknowledgments for the CS3 version of this book, I said, "Working with a coauthor can be a tricky business. In fact, it is a little like a marriage. Everything is wonderful when things are going well, but you never really discover the strength of the relationship until you get deep into it." You may notice there is a new name, Tiago Dias, on the cover, which indicates that David Stiller, my previous coauthor, had to back out of this project because his Flash development business took off, and he simply didn't have the time necessary to devote to this book.

Four years ago Tiago and I explored the intersection of After Effects and Flash when we worked together on another friendsofED title *From After Effects to Flash: Poetry in Motion Graphics*. When Dave graciously stepped aside, who better to step in than Tiago?

Having kept in close touch for the four years between our first book and this one, we had developed a close personal and professional relationship, which made the transition between coauthors seamless. As well, Tiago brought a fresh pair of eyes to the process, and there were several times when I would get e-mails that started off with "Dude, let's try this approach..." when I went sideways instead of forward. Like David, Tiago gave me a good shake when I wasn't understanding a code block or technique; these inevitably started with, "It's really very simple, Tom," and he would lay out exactly what I was missing. When we finished the book, I reflected on the process and discovered that Tiago and I had picked up exactly where we left off four years ago, and that, my friends, is the mark of an amazing partnership.

Next up is our editor Ben Renow-Clark. There seems to be this generalized misconception that the relationship between an editor and a writer is adversarial. Actually, the best work is done when the relationship is the exact opposite, and I am so grateful to have just that relationship with Ben.

Another group of people that have had a profound influence on this book are my students at the college where I teach and those of you I have met at conferences, online or through my tutorial efforts. I am deeply grateful for your patience when I tried out some of the exercises in this book and you reacted negatively or positively. It showed me where I was doing something right or where I needed to start over again. Also, hearing from my education peers around the world who use this book in their classrooms didn't hurt when it came to actually writing the exercises and even determining their order.

Finally, writing a book means I disappear into my office and generally become moody and difficult to live with as I mull over some aspect of an exercise or the order of a chapter. It takes a very unique individual to put up with that, let alone understand why, and my wife, best friend, and life partner for more than 30 years, Keltie, has somehow put up with it.

Tom Green

In 2009, Tom and I got together at Adobe's MAX 2009 for a rather "quick" chat at one of the lunch tables. The whole conversation was relatively short—15 to 20 minutes—and over that space of time we reviewed all the chapters of this book, their content, and who was doing what. The result of that conversation is the book you are holding. Now you might think that is crazy—our having one brief chat. It might seem like that to you, but for us it was normal. The real discussions happened when we switched on our webcams and saw each other—one in his home office and me in my living room, garden, office, or wherever I was at that time. It was fun, and we laughed a lot during our Skype conversations.

As Tom already mentioned, we worked on a book together four years ago, and since then we have developed a great partnership. We understand each other quite well, and, when one side knows what the other is thinking or wants to accomplish, that leads to an awesome workflow. But as it is, life is not a piece of cake; sometimes things don't go the way they should, and that's where your good friends, and in this case especially Tom, come in. He backed me up during the course of this book, something that I was a bit scared of, and, because of my job, I couldn't always be there for him. If I were asked again to write a book, I think I would only do it with this old man! No one else managed to wake my creativity while writing books. Tom, you are a great person and a great mentor.

Next up I would like to thank Mischa Plocek and Pascal [P] Baumann for donating some of their work to be used in this book. Thank you guys for all your work and time invested doing what you guys can do best! Marcel, thanks for giving me the spare time I needed and providing me with some ideas; I don't know how to thank you for this, but I think I can come up with something.

Last, but not least, writing books can be a challenge. You constantly think day and night of what you have to deliver the next day. Thanks to the time zones, I always had a few more hours to work on until Tom woke up. I normally close myself in a state of writing in the morning, writing during lunch, and writing any time when I'm home. There is not really a break, and I become very impatient and difficult to be around. It needs lots of nerves and time to handle me during that time, and I can't thank my girlfriend, Anjanee, enough for supporting me and trying to handle my difficult moods during the process of the book and all the other situations in life. Thank you!

Tiago Dias

Preface

I can remember the day as clear is if it were just yesterday. I was walking by my boss's office late one winter afternoon at the college where I teach, and he called me into his office. Sitting on his desk was a thin white box with some sort of weird swirl on it. He slid the box across to me and asked, "You know anything about Flash?"

To be honest, as a Director user, what I knew was filtered through the eyes of a Director guy, which meant I didn't know much and what I did know convinced me it was a wind-up toy compared to Director. I replied, "A bit." The boss leaned back in his chair and said, "Well, learn a lot more because you are teaching it in four weeks." This was the start of one of the longest, strangest, and most exhilarating trips I have ever been on. The version was Flash 3, and I have been using and teaching Flash ever since.

What I didn't expect is to be writing books, articles, and tutorials around Flash for the past 10 years. I also didn't expect that my fascination with Flash would take me around the world speaking at conferences or lecturing at universities from Amsterdam to Wu Han on the subject of Flash and web-based media. It has been quite the experience, and Flash CS5 makes things even more fascinating.

Flash CS5 is one of the more important versions in the history of the product. Flash CS5 has evolved into a serious design tool able to handle everything from simple motion graphics to broadcast-quality animations. It also marks the point where Flash is fully integrated into the Adobe product line up. The Motion Editor, a rejigged Media Encoder, the TextLayoutFramework, and a fist full of sophisticated animation tools are evidence of that.

This book is also a bit different from any Flash book you may have read or considered purchasing. From the very start of the process, we put ourselves in your shoes and asked a simple question: "What do you need to know and why?" This question led us into territory that we didn't quite expect. As we were grappling with that question early in the process, we kept bothering our network of Flash friends to be sure we were on the right track. At some point, both of us simultaneously came to the conclusion, "Why not just let them explain it in their own words?" This is why, as you journey through this book, you will encounter various experts in the field telling you why they do things and offering you insights into what they have learned. The odd thing is, at some point in their careers, they were no different from you.

One other aspect of this book that we feel is important is we had a lot of fun developing the examples and exercises in the book. The fun aspect is important because, if learning is fun, what you learn will be retained. Anybody can show you how to apply the new Springs feature to a rectangle on the Flash stage. It is more effective when you do exactly the same thing to bend trees. Anybody can dryly explain 9-slice scaling, but it becomes less techie when you apply it to a Chinese olive seller. Nested movie clips are a "yawner" at best, but, when they are related to a Hostess Twinkie, the concept becomes understandable. Shared libraries are an important subject. Instead of filling a library with circles and text, the concept becomes relevant when the library is populated with "Bunny Bits." Interested in going out on the bleeding edge of Flash and preparing a project for an Android-based device? Whack-A-Bunny makes it interesting and fun.

As you may have guessed, we continue to exhibit a sense of joy and wonder with Flash, and we hope a little bit of our enthusiasm rubs off on you as well.

Book structure and flow

To start, this is not a typical Foundation book. There is no common project that runs throughout the book. Instead, each chapter contains a number of exercises to help you develop some "Flash chops," and then we turn you loose in the "Your turn" section of each chapter.

We start by dropping you right into the application and creating a small Flash movie located in a "butterfly garden" (told you we were having fun). This chapter familiarizes you with the Flash workspace and the fundamentals of using Flash Professional CS5. Chapter 2 introduces you to working with the graphic tools and with graphics files and finishes with your creating a banner ad for an ice hotel.

Chapter 3 introduces you to symbols and libraries in Flash CS3. In this chapter, you learn how to create and use symbols, and we even let an olive seller explain how 9-slice scaling works. With those fundamentals under your belt, we show you how to share symbols and libraries between movies and how to manipulate symbols with filters and blend effects, and along the way you travel from a park bench in Paris to a wall in Adobe's San Jose headquarters, discovering how to create some rather powerful effects in your Flash movies. The chapter finishes by showing you how to use masks to your advantage in Flash.

At this point in the book, you have pretty well mastered the fundamentals. The rest of the book builds upon what you have learned. Chapter 4 picks you up and throws you into the ActionScript 3.0 pool. Chapter 5 starts by explaining how to use audio in Flash and finishes with your constructing an MP3 player. Chapter 6 reinforces the message that "text isn't the gray stuff that surrounds your animations." We show you how it is both serious and fun by stepping through how to create scrolling text and how to use the TextLayoutFramework to bring professional-level typography into your work.

Chapter 7 is one of the more important chapters in the book because Flash's roots were as an animation application. You are going to learn the basics here, but don't expect to be shoving boxes and circles around. You will be banging hammers, eating apples, dropping rabbits, fixing a neon sign and lighting it up, and setting a butterfly in motion. Did we mention we believe in having fun? Chapter 8 continues the motion theme by getting you deep into the new Motion Editor, and Chapter 9 walks you through the 3D tools introduced in Flash CS4 and improved upon in Flash CS5.

From animation, we move into video in Flash. In Chapter 10, we show the entire process from encoding to upload. In fact, the chapter finishes with your adding captions and a full-screen capability to a Superman movie. Along the way, you will visit heaven and meet a "Girl with Stories in Her Hair."

Chapters 11, 12, and 13 give you the chance to play with all of the Flash user interface components, actually style a Flash movie using Cascading Style Sheets, and explore how XML gives you a huge amount of flexibility when it comes to adding dynamic data to your movie.

Chapter 14 is where you get to pull it all together and build everything from a simple preloader to a full-bore game designed to be played on an Android device.

The final chapter focuses on the end game of the design process. It shows you a number of the important techniques you need to know that will keep your movies small and efficient, how to create the SWF that will be embedded into a web page, and how to keep that process as smooth as possible.

Finally, Tiago and I are no different from you. We are learning about this application and what it can and cannot do at the same time as you. Though we may be coming at it from a slightly more advanced level, there is a lot about this application we're still learning. If there is something we have missed or something you don't quite understand, by all means contact us. We'll be sure to add it to the book's site.

Our final words of advice for you are these:

The amount of fun you can have with this application should be illegal. We'll see you in jail!

Layout conventions

To keep this book as clear and easy to follow as possible, the following text conventions are used throughout.

Important words or concepts are normally highlighted on the first appearance in **bold type**.

Code is presented in `fixed-width font`.

New or changed code is normally presented in **`bold fixed-width font`**.

Pseudocode and variable input are written in *`italic ixed-width font`*.

Menu commands are written in the form `Menu` ➤ `Submenu` ➤ `Submenu`.

Where we want to draw your attention to something, we've highlighted it like this:

> *Ahem, don't saw we didn't warn you.*

Sometimes code won't fit on a single line in a book. Where this happens, we use an arrow like this: ↪

```
This is a very, very long section of code that should be written all ↪
on the same line without a break
```

Chapter 1

Learning the Flash CS5 Professional Interface

Welcome to Flash Professional CS5 Professional. We suspect you are here because you have seen a lot of the great stuff Flash can do and it is now time for you to get into the game. We also suspect you are here because you have discovered Flash is more complex than you originally thought. The other reason you may be here is because you are an existing Flash user and CS5 is suddenly a lot different from Flash 8 or even Flash CS3 or CS4, and you need to get a handle on this new stuff in relatively short order. Whatever your motivation, both of us have been in your shoes at some point in our careers, which means we understand what you are feeling. So, instead of jumping right into the application, let's go for walk.

What we'll cover in this chapter:

- Exploring the Flash interface
- Using the Flash stage
- Working with panels
- The difference between a frame and a keyframe

CHAPTER 1

- Using frames to arrange the content on the stage
- Using layers to manage content on the stage
- Adding objects to the Library
- Testing your movie

If you haven't already, download the chapter files. You can find them www.friendsofED.com/download.html?isbn=1430229940.

These are the files used in this chapter:

- `Magnify.fla` (Chapter01/Exercise Files_CH01/Exercise/Magnify.fla)
- `Leaf.fla` (Chapter01/Exercise Files_CH01/Exercise/Leaf.fla)
- `Properties.fla` (Chapter01/Exercise Files_CH01/Exercise/Properties.fla)
- `Layerss.fla` (Chapter01/Exercise Files_CH01/Exercise/Layers.fla)
- `Garden.fla` (Chapter01/ExerciseFiles_CH01/Exercise/Garden.fla)
- `FliesBuzzing.mp3` (Chapter01/ExerciseFiles_CH01/Exercise/FliesBuzzing.mp3)
- `XFL_Example` (Chapter01/ExerciseFiles_CH01/Exercise/XFL_Example/)

What we are going to do in this chapter is take a walk through the authoring environment—called the **Flash interface**—pointing out the sights and giving you an opportunity to play with some of the stuff we will be pointing out. By the end of the stroll, you should be fairly comfortable with Flash and have a good idea of what tools you can use and how to use them as you start creating a Flash movie.

As we go for our walk, we will also be having a conversation that will help you understand the fundamentals of creating a Flash movie. Having this knowledge right at the start of the process gives you the confidence to build upon what you have learned. So, let's start our walk right at the beginning of the process, the `Start` page.

Getting started

A couple of seconds after you double-click the application icon to launch Flash, the `Start` page, shown in Figure 1-1, opens. This page, which is common to all the CS5 applications, is divided into six discrete areas.

LEARNING THE FLASH CS5 PROFESSIONAL INTERFACE

Figure 1-1. The `Start` page

- **Create from Template:** This category is a bit misleading. Double-clicking one of the choices actually opens the `New from Template` dialog box shown in Figure 1-2. If you have used previous versions of Flash, you will immediately notice that the variety and utility of the offered templates—more than 50 of them—has greatly expanded.

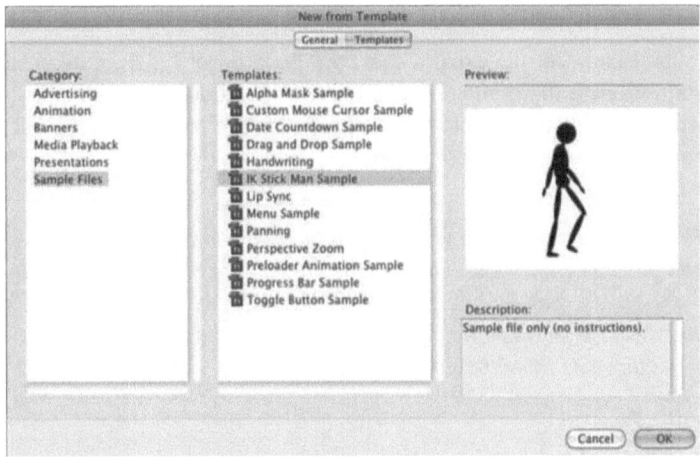

Figure 1-2. Flash Professional CS5 contains a new lineup of templates designed to help you become more productive.

CHAPTER 1

- **Open a Recent Item:** The documents listed in this category are the ones you have opened recently. Provided you haven't moved them to another location or deleted them, clicking one will open the document. The **Open** link at the bottom of the list lets you browse for files not contained in this list

- **Create New:** The middle area of the page is where you can choose to create a variety of new Flash documents. Your choices include a blank Flash document, which is the ActionScript 3.0 choice and is called a **flah**; a project aimed at a tablet, cell phone, or other mobile device; an AIR file; a series of code-based documents; and a Flash project, which is used to organize multiple .fla files in a given project.

> *The key to the* **Start** *page is the ability to select a new document based upon which version of ActionScript will be used in the document. The current version of ActionScript is 3.0, which was introduced in Flash CS3. The previous version of this language, used in Flash MX 2004 and Flash 8, was ActionScript 2.0. We will be digging into ActionScript 3.0 in greater depth in Chapter 4. From this point on, unless otherwise stated, you will be selecting the* **ActionScript 3.0** *option when opening new documents throughout this book.*

- **Extend:** Click this, and, providing you have an Internet connection, you will be taken to the Adobe Exchange. This is a location where Flash designers and developers offer a variety of small applications, called **extensions**, that add to or improve upon Flash's functionality. These extensions can either be purchased or are offered for free.

- **Learn:** The right area of the page is reserved for a variety of links that are designed to help you discover more about a specific aspect of Flash.

The items at the bottom allow you to explore the new features of Flash, explore the Flash Developer Center where experts (including the authors of this book) write about the code side of Flash, and explore the Design Center where the artistic aspects of the application are presented and discussed. The last link, **Adobe TV**, is a rather extensive set of video tutorials.

> *We are willing to bet those of you who have used Flash in the past missed a sweet little change when you launched Flash. In previous versions of Flash, when you launched the app, the* **Welcome** *screen appeared and took over the computer. You couldn't do anything else while Flash was loading. That annoyance is a thing of the past, so feel free to return to Twitter while Flash boots.*

Creating a new Flash document

Let's continue our stroll through Flash by creating a new Flash document. To do this, simply click the `ActionScript 3.0` button in the `Create New` area of the `Start` page. This opens the interface shown in Figure 1-3.

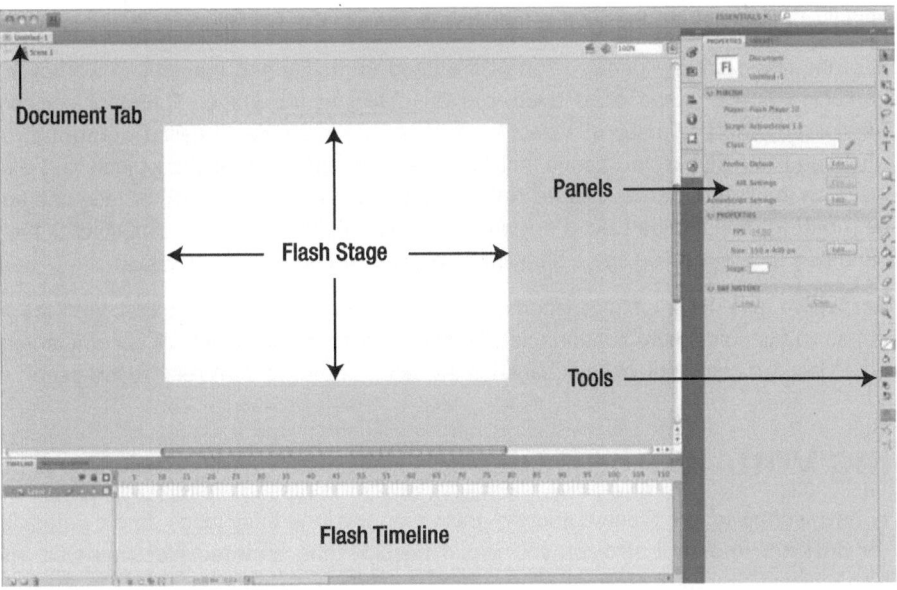

Figure 1-3. The Flash authoring environment

This interface is the feature-rich authoring environment that is the heart and soul of Flash. The Object Windows Library (OWL) first introduced in the CS4 lineup is now common to practically all Adobe applications in the CS5 lineup from Adobe. If you are a Mac user and, depending upon your "rabidity" of all things Mac, you are going to either love this interface or hate it. The reason is that Adobe has dispensed with the floating panels that tended to drive Flash developers and designers who worked "cross platform" up the wall, across the ceiling, and down the other wall.

Let's now step into that big white area on the screen and take a moment to look around. The **stage**, that large white area in the center of the screen, is where the action happens. A good way of regarding the stage in relation to Flash is this: if it isn't on the stage, the user isn't going to see it. There will be instances where this last statement is not *exactly* true, but we'll get into those later in this book.

On the far-right edge of the screen is a set of tools that will allow you to draw, color, and otherwise manipulate objects on the stage. Just to the left of these tools is the `Properties` panel.

At the bottom of the interface is the `Timeline` panel, which longtime Flash users simply refer to as the **timeline**. This is the place where action occurs. As you can see, the timeline is broken into a series of boxes called **frames**. The best way of regarding frames is as individual frames of a film. When you put something on the stage, it will appear in a frame. If you want it to move from here to there, it will start in one frame and move to another position on the stage in another frame a little further along the timeline. The box with the vertical red stem draped over the timeline is called the **playhead**. Its purpose is to show you the current frame being displayed. When a Flash movie is playing through a browser, the playhead is in motion, and the user is seeing the frame where the playhead is located. This is how things appear to move in Flash. Another thing you can do with the playhead is drag it across the timeline while you are creating the Flash movie. This technique is known as **scrubbing** the timeline and has its roots in film editing.

To the right of the stage are the panels. Panels are used to modify and manipulate whatever object you may have selected on the stage or to even add an object to the stage. These objects can be text, photographs, line art, short animations, video, or even interface elements called **components**. You can use the panels and the menus to change not only the characteristics of the objects but also how the objects behave on the stage. Panels can be connected to each other (**docked**), or they can float freely in the interface (**floating**) and can be placed anywhere you like. To move a panel simply, click the `Panel` tab and drag it to a new location. If you see a blue line, the panel will dock to that location.

From our perspective, one of the more indispensable panels is the `Properties` panel. We'll talk about this a little later, but as you become more comfortable with the application, this panel will become a very important place for you. In fact, we can't think of any chapter in this book where we don't refer to this panel.

Managing your workspace

As you may have surmised, the Flash authoring environment is one busy place, and if you talk to a Flash developer or designer, they will also tell you it can become one crowded place as well. As you start creating Flash projects, you will discover that screen real estate is a valuable commodity because it fills up with floating panels and other elements. This has all changed in Flash Professional CS5. Here's how you manage the panels:

- **Collapse panels:** At the top of the `Tools` panel and the `Panels` area on the right side of the screen is an icon that looks like a double arrow (see Figure 1-4). Click it, and the panels will collapse and become icons. If you click the arrow above the tools, the `Tools` panel changes from a single strip to an icon. The process is called **panel collapse**, and it is designed to free up screen space in Flash.

Figure 1-4. Panels can be collapsed to give you more screen space.

- **Show collapsed panels as icons only:** Sometimes you need the extra interface room taken up by the panel's name. Roll the mouse pointer to the left or right edge of the panel strip. When the mouse pointer changes to a double-sided arrow, click and drag to expand and show the panel's name, or shrink to the width of the icons in the strip.
- **See tooltips for panel icons:** When a panel is collapsed to nothing more than its icon, you only need to place the mouse pointer over an icon, and a tooltip showing the panel name will appear. This is especially handy when you see an icon and wonder, "What panel is that?"
- **Open and close drawers:** Click an icon, and the contents of that panel will fly out, as shown in Figure 1-5. Click it again, and it will slide back. These panels that fly out and slide back are called **drawers**.

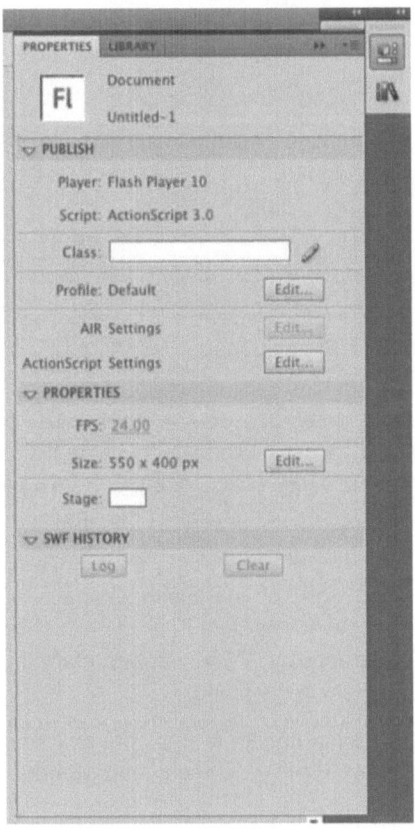

Figure 1-5. Click a panel icon, and the contents slide out. Click the icon again, and they slide in.

- **Minimize panels**: Another method of buying screen real estate is to minimize panels you aren't using. Double-click the tab with the panel's name, and the panel collapses upward. Double-click it again, and it expands to its original dimensions.

- **Close panels:** Right-click (Windows) or Control+click (Mac) a panel, and select `Close` from the context menu. This not only closes the panel but also removes it from your workspace. To get it back, simply open the `Window` menu, and click the name of the panel you closed to restore it.
- **Add panels to sets:** A collection of panel icons, as shown in Figure 1-6, is called a **panel set**. To create a customized panel set, drag one panel icon onto another panel. When you release the mouse, the panel will expand to include the new panel added. To remove a panel from a set, just drag the panel icon to the bottom of the stack.

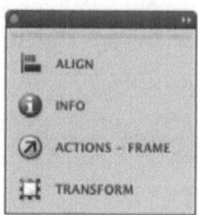

Figure 1-6. A typical panel set

> Though not a technique, this tip falls squarely into the "Well, it's about time" category of new stuff. If you drag a floating panel over another interface element, the floating panel will become somewhat transparent and let you see what is under the panel.

To save your customized workspace, select `Window ➤ Workspace ➤ New Workspace`, and enter a name for your custom workspace into the New Workspace dialog box. Click OK to add the workspace. If you want to delete one of your workspaces, select `Window ➤ Workspace ➤ Manage Workspaces`. When the `Manage Workspaces` dialog box opens, select the space to be deleted, and click the `Delete` button.

Speaking of workspaces, at the top right of the Flash interface is a drop-down list of "prerolled" workspaces that came with the application. The default is `Essentials`. If you click and hold down that button, a drop-down list of the choices appears. If you want to return the workspace to its "out-of-the-box" look, select the `Reset Essentials` item in the menu.

Now that you have learned to become the master of the work environment, let's take a look at how you can also become the master of your Flash document and wander over to the `Preferences` and `Properties` areas of Flash.

Setting document preferences and properties

Managing the workspace is a fundamental skill, but the most important decision you will make concerns the size of the Flash stage and the space it will take up in the browser. That decision is based upon a number of factors, including the type of content to be displayed and the items that will appear in the HTML document beside the Flash movie. These decisions all affect the stage size and, in many respects, the way the document is handled by Flash. These two factors are managed by the `Preferences` dialog box and the `Document Properties` panel.

Document preferences

To access preferences, select `Edit` ➤ `Preferences` (Windows) or `Flash Professional` ➤ `Preferences` (Mac). This will open the Flash `Preferences` dialog box. There is a lot to this dialog box, and we'll explore it further at various points throughout this book. For now, we are concerned with the general preferences in the `Category` area of the window. Click `General`, and the window will change to show you the general preferences for Flash, as shown in Figure 1-7.

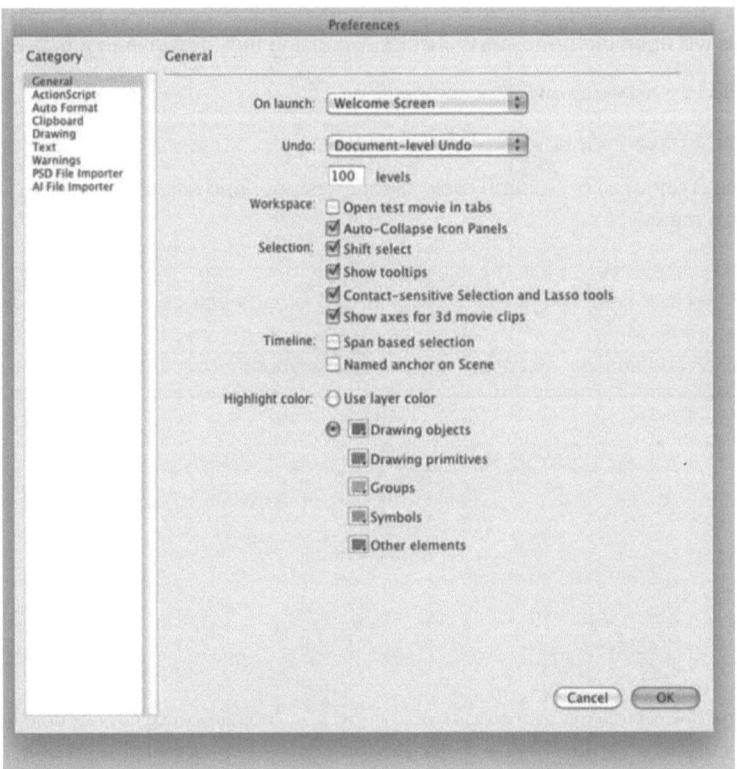

Figure 1-7. The general preferences can be used to manage not only the workspace but also items on the stage.

If you examine the selections, you will realize they are fairly intuitive. You can choose to see the `Welcome` screen when the application starts, to see tooltips when the mouse pointer is over a tool or object, and to have a test movie appear in a tabbed window or float. You can determine how items are selected on the stage and the timeline and even the colors that will be used to tell you what type of object has been selected on the stage.

CHAPTER 1

> *If you have been using Flash for a few years, the expansion of the* `Highlight color` *list to include a variety of objects is a welcome addition.*

Now that you know how to set your preferences, let's take a look at managing a document's properties. Click the Cancel button to close the `Preferences` dialog box. When it closes, let's wander back to the stage and explore how a document's properties are determined.

Document settings

To access the `Document Settings` dialog box, use one of the following techniques:

- In the `Properties` panel, click the `Edit` button in the `Properties` area—not the `Publish` area. This will open the `Document Settings` dialog box shown in Figure 1-8.
- Select `Modify` ➤ `Document`.
- Press Ctrl+J (Windows) or Cmd+J (Mac).
- Right-click (Windows) or Control+click (Mac) the stage, and select `Document Properties` from the context menu.

> *As you have just seen, there are a number of methods you can use in Flash to obtain the same result. In this case, it is opening the* `Document Settings` *dialog box. Which one is best? The answer is simple: whichever one you choose.*

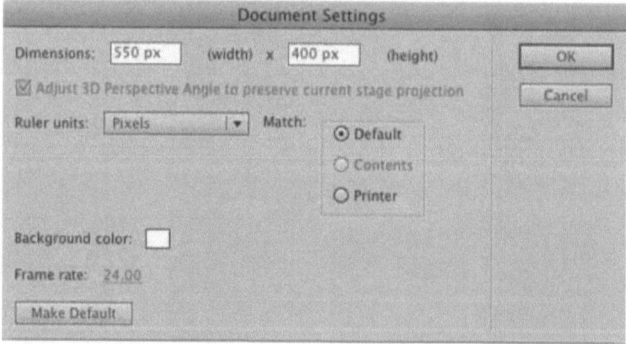

Figure 1-8. Set the stage size through the `Document Settings` dialog box.

Now that the `Document Settings` dialog box is open, let's look around. The `Dimensions` input area is where you can change the size of the stage. Enter the new dimensions, press the Enter (Return) key, or click the `OK` button, and the stage will change. The `Match` area is commonly used to shrink the stage to the size of the content on the stage. The `Contents` radio button is currently grayed out because the stage is empty.

> *For those of you wondering about the* `Adjust 3D Perspective Angle` *... selection, sit tight. This is better explained in Chapter 9.*

For example, if you change the `Dimensions` setting to a width of 400 pixels and height of 300 pixels, set the `Background color` option to `#000099`, and then click `OK`, the stage will shrink to those dimensions and change color to the dark blue chosen. The changes, as shown in Figure 1-9, are also reflected in the `Properties` panel.

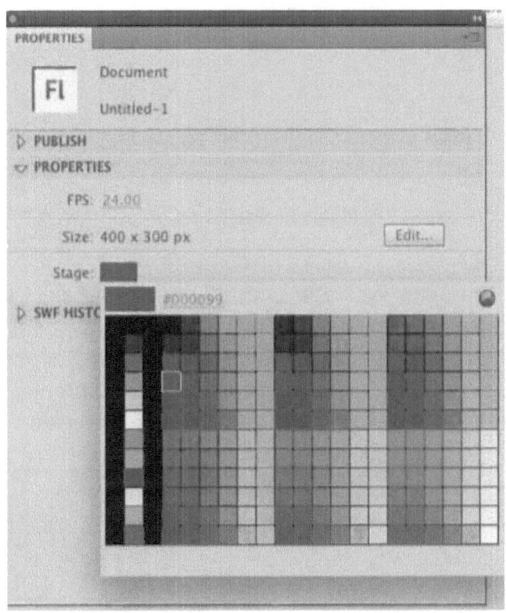

Figure 1-9. Changes made to the document properties are shown in the `Properties` panel.

> *The only two document properties that can be directly changed through the* `Properties` *panel are the frame rate (*`FPS`*) and the stage color (*`Stage`*).*

Zooming the stage

There will be occasions when you discover the stage is a pretty crowded place. In these situations, you'll want to be sure that each item on the stage is in its correct position and is properly sized. Depending on the size of the stage, this could be difficult because the stage may fill the screen area. Fortunately, Flash allows you to reduce or increase the magnification of the stage through a technique called **zooming**. (Note that zooming the stage has no effect upon the actual stage size that you set in the `Document Settings` dialog box.)

To zoom the stage, click the `Magnification` drop-down menu near the upper-right corner of the stage. The drop-down menu shown in Figure 1-10 contains a variety of sizes ranging from `Fit in Window` to `800%` magnification. For example, click the `400%` option, and the stage will most likely fill your screen, as shown in Figure 1-11. Just keep in mind you are not scaling the image on the stage. You are actually magnifying the stage and its contents. Click the `25%` option, and you will see not only the stage but the entire pasteboard, that grey area surrounding the stage, as well.

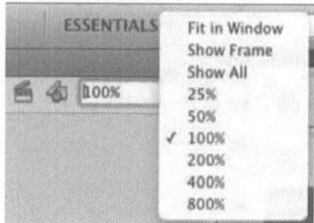

Figure 1-10. Select a zoom level using the `Magnification` drop-down menu.

If you want more zoom, you can get a lot closer than 800 percent. Select `View ➤ Zoom In` or `View ➤ Zoom Out` to increase the zoom level to 2000 percent. If you want a real bird's-eye view of the stage, `Zoom Out` allows you to reduce the magnification level to 8 percent. For you keyboard junkies, `Zoom In` is Ctrl+= and `Zoom Out` is Ctrl+ -. If you are a control freak, you can enter your own value. Just keep in mind the maximum zoom level is 2000 percent, and the minimum zoom level is 8 percent.

Figure 1-11. Selecting a 400 percent zoom level brings you close to the action.

If you want a side-by-side comparison in which one image is at 100 percent view and the other is at 400 percent or 800 percent, follow these steps:

1. Open the `Magnify.fla` file in the `Chapter 1 Exercise` folder.
2. Select `Window ➤ Duplicate Window`. The current document will appear in a separate tab.
3. Set the new window's magnification level to `400%`.
4. Undock the 100 percent window, as shown in Figure 1-12, and let it float.
5. Select the image in the floating window by clicking the image and dragging it around the stage. You will see the zoomed-in version in the docked window also moves. This is a really handy feature if precise positioning of elements on the stage is critical.
6. Click each window's close button to close the window. Don't save the changes.

Figure 1-12. Duplicating a window gives you a bird's-eye view and a detailed view of your work simultaneously.

Exploring the panels in the Flash interface

At this point in our stroll through the Flash interface, you have had the chance to play with a few of the panels. We also suspect that by this point you have discovered that the Flash interface is modular. By that we mean that it's an interface composed of a series of panels that contain the tools and features you will use on a regular basis, rather than an interface that's locked in place and fills the screen. You have also discovered that these panels can be moved around and opened or closed depending upon your workflow needs. In this section, we are going to take a closer look at the more important panels that you will use every day. They include the following:

- The timeline
- The `Library` panel
- The `Properties` panel
- The `Motion Editor`
- The `Tools` panel
- The `Help` panel

The timeline

Here's the secret behind how one becomes a proficient Flash designer: master the timeline, and you will master Flash.

When somebody visits your site and an animation plays, Flash treats that animation as a series of still images. In many respects, those images are comparable to the images in a roll of film or one of those flip books you may have played with when you were younger. The ordering of those images on the film or in the book is determined by their placement on the film or in the book. In Flash, the order of images in an animation is determined by the timeline.

The timeline, therefore, controls what the user sees and, more importantly, when they see it. To understand this concept, let's go for a walk in a Canadian forest while the leaves are falling from the trees.

At its most basic, all animation is movement over time, and all animation has a start point and an end point. The length of your timeline will determine when animations start and end, and the number of frames between those two points will determine the length of the animation. As the author, you control those factors.

For example, Figure 1-13 shows you a simple animation. It is a maple leaf that falls from the top of the stage to the bottom of the stage. From this, you can gather that the leaf will move downward when the sequence starts and will continue to its finish position at the bottom of the stage once it has twisted in the middle of the sequence.

LEARNING THE FLASH CS5 PROFESSIONAL INTERFACE

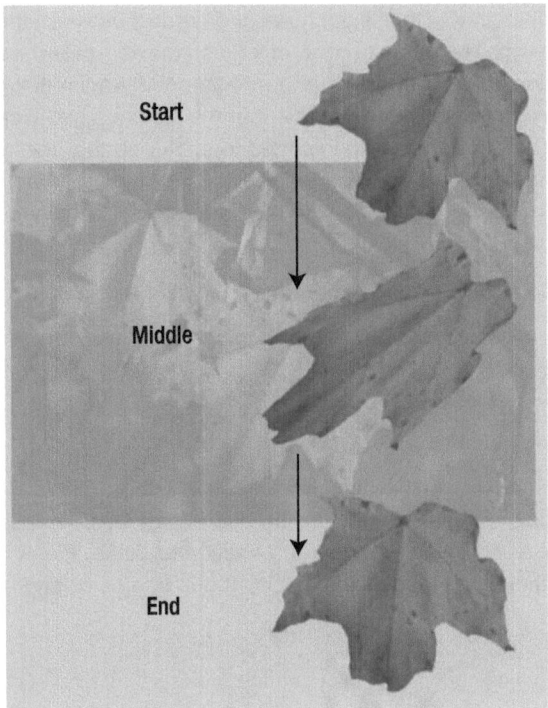

Figure 1-13. A simple animation sequence

Figure 1-14. Animation is a series of frames on the timeline.

15

CHAPTER 1

So, where does time come into play? Time is the number of frames between the start and middle or middle and end points in the animation. The default timing in a Flash movie—called **frame rate**—is 24 frames per second (fps). In the animation shown previously, the duration of the animation is 48 frames, which means it will play for 2 seconds. You can assume from this that the leaf's middle location, where it twists, is the 24th frame of the timeline. If, for example, you wanted to speed up the animation, you would reduce the length of the timeline to 12 frames; if you wanted to slow it down, you would increase the number of frames to 72 or decrease the frame rate. If you would like to see this animation, open the Timeline.swf file in the 01_Complete folder.

So much for a walk in the woods; let's wander over to the timeline and look at a frame.

Frames

If you unroll a spool of movie film, you will see that it is composed of a series of individual still images. Each image is called a **frame**, and this analogy applies to Flash.

When you open Flash, your timeline will be empty, but you will see a series of rectangles—these are the frames. You may also notice that these frames are divided into groups. Most frames are white, and every fifth frame is gray (see Figure 1-15), just to help you keep your place. Flash movies can range in length from 1 to 16,000 frames, although a Flash movie that is 16,000 frames in length is highly unusual.

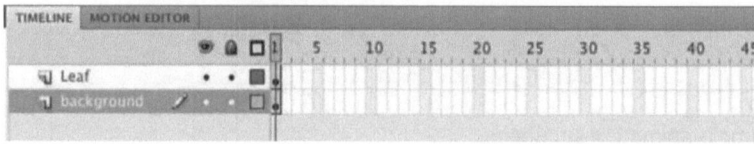

Figure 1-15. The timeline is nothing more than a series of frames.

A frame shows you the content that is on the stage at any point in time. The content in a frame can range from one object to hundreds of objects, and a frame can include audio, video, code, images, text, and drawings either singly or in combination with each other.

When you first open a new Flash document, you will notice that frame 1 contains a hollow circle. This visual clue tells you that frame 1 is waiting for you to add something to it. Let's look at a movie that actually has something in the frames and examine some of the features of frames:

1. Open the Leaf.fla file located in the Chapter 1 Exercise folder. When the file opens, you will see a yellow leaf, in frame 1, sitting on the stage. You should also note the solid dot in the **Leaf** layer. This indicates that there is content in the frame. The empty layer above it has a hollow dot, which indicates there is no content in that frame.

2. Place the mouse pointer on any frame of the timeline, and right-click (Windows) or Control+click (Mac) to open the context menu that applies to frames (see Figure 1-16).

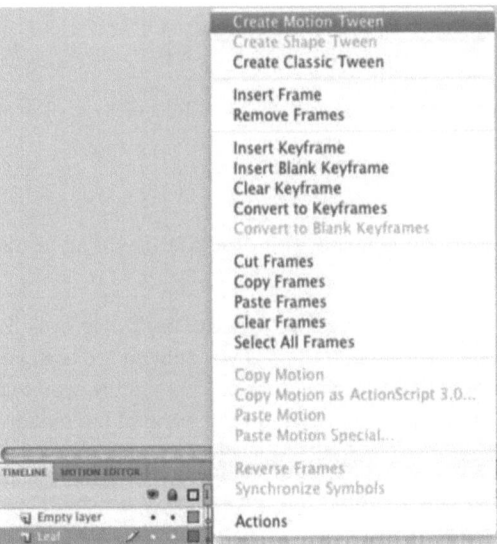

Figure 1-16. The context menu that applies to frames on the timeline

As you can see, quite a few options are available to you. They range from adding motion to the timeline to adding actions (code blocks) that control the objects in the frame. We aren't going to dig into what each menu item does just yet, but be assured, by the time you finish this book, you will have used each menu item.

3. Place the mouse pointer at frame 36 of the `Leaf` layer, open the context menu, and select `Insert Keyframe`. Repeat this step at frame 72 as well. What you will notice is that the timeline changes to the series of gray frames and three black dots, as shown in Figure 1-17. These gray rectangles represent a span of frames separated by keyframes.

> *If you prefer to use the keyboard, place the mouse pointer at frame 36, and press F5. With that frame selected, press F6. The F5 command adds a frame, and F6 converts the selected frame to a keyframe. If you just want to add a keyframe, select frame 36, and press F6.*

An obvious question at this point is, "So, guys, what's a keyframe?" Remember when we talked earlier about animations and how they had a start point and an end point? In Flash, those two points are called **keyframes**; any movement or changes can occur only between keyframes. In Flash, there are two types of keyframes: those with stuff in them (indicated by the solid dot shown in frame 1 of Figure 1-17) and those with nothing in them. The latter are called **blank keyframes**, and they are shown as frames with a hollow dot. The first frame in any layer, until you add something to that frame, is always indicated by a blank keyframe.

CHAPTER 1

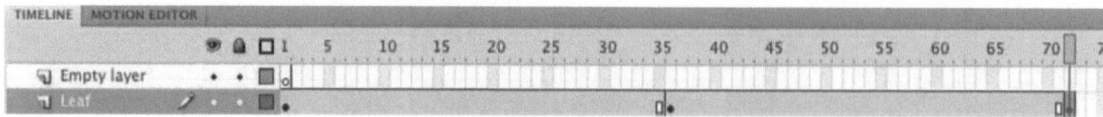

Figure 1-17. The timeline contains three keyframes.

To navigate to specific frames in the timeline, you drag the playhead to the frame. It is the red rectangle with the line coming out of it.

4. Drag the playhead to frame 36, use the `Selection` tool to click the leaf on the stage, and move the leaf down to the middle of the stage. As you moved the leaf, you may have noticed there was a "ghosted" version of the leaf on the screen. This feature was introduced in Flash CS4. What it does is to give you a reference to the starting position of the motion.

> As mentioned earlier in the chapter, the technique of dragging the playhead across the timeline is called **scrubbing**. As you scrub across the timeline, you will also see the values in the `Current Frame` and `Elapsed Time` areas at the bottom of the timeline change. This is quite useful in locating a precise frame number or time in the animation.

5. Drag the playhead to the keyframe in frame 72, and drag the leaf off the bottom edge of the stage.
6. Scrub the playhead across the stage. The leaf doesn't do much other than to snap to its new positions as you encounter the keyframes. Let's fix that right now.
7. Right-click (Windows) or Control+click (Mac) between the first two keyframes of the leaf layer, and select `Create Classic Tween` from the context menu. An arrow will appear between the two keyframes. Scrub across the timeline again, and the leaf's movement is much smoother. Repeat this step for the next two keyframes

A **motion tween** is how simple animations are created in Flash. Flash looks at the locations of the objects between two keyframes, creates copies of those objects, and puts them in their positions in the frame. If you scrub through your timeline, you will see that Flash has placed copies of the leaf in frames 2 through 35 and in frames 36 through 71 and put them in their final positions to give the illusion that the leaf is falling.

That was interesting, but we suspect you may be wondering, "OK, guys, do tweens work only for stuff that moves?" Nope. You can also use tweens to change the shapes of objects, their color, their opacity, and a number of other properties. We'll get to them later on in the book.

8. Drag the playhead to frame 36, and click the leaf on the stage. Drag the leaf toward the center of the stage to the bottom of the stage. If you scrub through the timeline, you will see the leaf move quite a distance to the right. This tells you that you can change an animation by simply changing the location of an object in a keyframe.
9. Close the file without saving it.

Using the Motion Editor panel

As you get deeper into working with Flash, you will find there is a reason why the `Timeline` and `Motion Editor` panels are docked beside each other in the interface; motion is created in the timeline and manipulated in the `Motion Editor`. Make a change in one panel, and it is instantly reflected in the other.

In previous versions of Flash, the `Property Inspector`, which is now the `Properties` panel, could be used to change the properties of an animation. This would include techniques such as "ramping" the speed of an animation, called **easing**, or even changing how an animation occurs such as adding or removing rotation. This is still true for shape tweens and classic tweens, but the true power of motion is realized in the `Motion Editor`.

Though we are going to get deeper into using this panel's features in Chapters 7 and 8, now would be a good time to stroll over to it and take a peek at it. Open the `MotionPath.fla` file. When the file opens, the first thing you will notice is there is an icon, as shown in Figure 1-18, beside the layer name. This "zooming square" icon indicates the layer is a tween layer. The term **tween** indicates that something is changing at some point in the layer—we'll get into tweening in more detail later. The other thing you may have noticed, especially if you have used Flash, is there are no arrows between the keyframes. The tween span is indicated in blue, and because of the icon, the use of the arrow is not necessary. The dotted line you see on the stage indicates a tween path.

> *If you are an After Effects user, you may be looking at that tween path and thinking, "Nah, it can't be!" Yes, it is a motion path, and just like an After Effects motion path, you can adjust that path by clicking and dragging one of the dots. Each dot represents a frame of the animation.*

Drag the playhead across the timeline, and you will see the leaf tumble, grow, and shrink as you move the playhead from left to right. Select the `Leaf` layer name on the timeline, and click the `Motion Editor` tab to open the `Motion Editor`, as shown in Figure 1-18.

You may have noticed us mentioning After Effects when we talk about tweens and this panel. This is deliberate because this feature of Flash can trace its roots in a straight line back to After Effects. In that application, objects put in motion or otherwise manipulated over time have a full set of properties and guides for each layer of content in an After Effects project. The major property is motion. Flash users who use After Effects to create motion graphics for their Flash projects find the "After Effects way of doing things" to be relatively compact and simple. The result over the years has been Flash designers wondering why Flash didn't have this feature. Obviously enough of you asked the question because it was introduced in Flash CS4 and has been broadly accepted by the Flash community.

CHAPTER 1

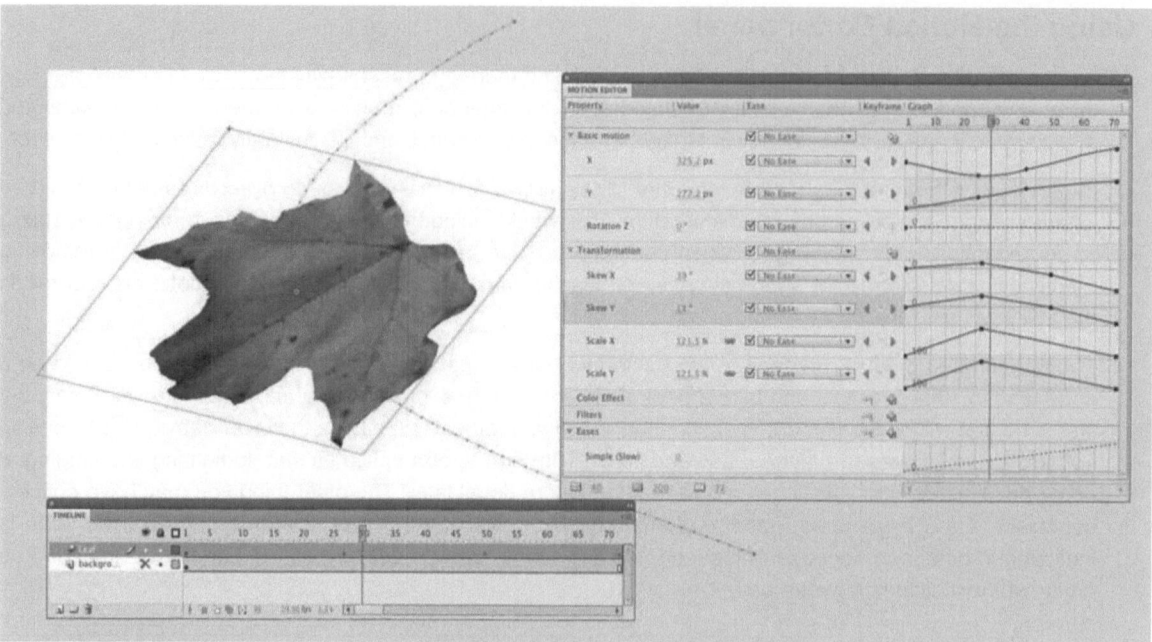

Figure 1-18. A motion layer, tween path, and the `Motion Editor` panel

> *Time for a history lesson. Back in 2000, one of us attended FlashForward 2000. That event is regarded by many of the old Flash hands as being Flash's "Woodstock." It was at this conference that Adobe introduced its "Flash killer": LiveMotion. LiveMotion used the same timeline as the `Motion Editor`. At the time, we (and many people at the conference) thought the timeline was a "sweet" idea, and eight years later, three years after it purchased Macromedia (which owned Flash), Adobe added this feature to Flash.*

If you have never used After Effects, now would be a good time to start easing you into the application, and we'll start with terminology. See those triangles beside the property names in Figure 1-18? If you click one, it rotates down, and the area is revealed. After Effects users call those triangles **twirlies**, and the term used to describe clicking one of them to reveal the contents of the area uses is **to twirl down**. We will be using these terms quite extensively when we talk about the `Motion Editor` panel.

LEARNING THE FLASH CS5 PROFESSIONAL INTERFACE

The `Motion Editor` panel is broken into five distinct areas:

- **Basic Motion:** If you twirl down Basic Motion, you will see that it controls the movement of the object on the x- and y-axes and rotation on the z-axis.
- **Transformation:** Think of this panel as a "by-the-numbers" version of the `Free Transform` tool, which allows you to slant (**skew**) and resize (**scale**) the selected object.
- **Color Effect:** This panel—click the + sign to open it—allows you to manipulate alpha (transparency), color, brightness, and tint.
- **Filters:** This is where you apply one of the filters—Drop Shadow, Blur, Glow, Bevel, Gradient Glow, Gradient Bevel, Adjust Color—to the object on the stage.
- **Eases:** This area is where you affect the starting or stopping motion of an animation.

When you twirl down an area of the panel, all of the properties it can affect are revealed.

> The `Color Effect` and `Filters` areas are also available in the `Properties` panel. Why? These are the properties of an object that can be changed, but they can also be "tweened." For example, you could have the leaf change from yellow to red if you tween its `Tint` property.

At the bottom of the panel there are three icons, and each one, as shown in Figure 1-19, has a blue number beside it. These values allow you to control how the graph and frames will appear in the `Motion Editor`.

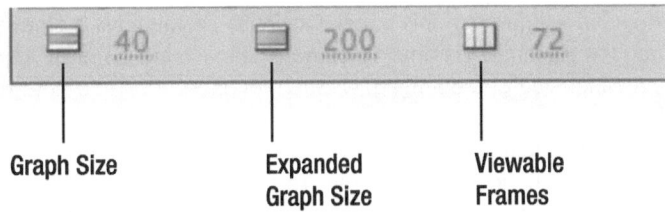

Graph Size   **Expanded Graph Size**   **Viewable Frames**

Figure 1-19. You can manage the look of the `Motion Editor` panel.

If you place the mouse pointer over one of the numbers, notice how the mouse pointer changes to a double arrow. This tells you the number can be changed because it is "hot text." One way to change the value is to double-click the number and enter a new value. Another is to click and drag across the number; as you do so, the value changes. This click-and-drag method is called **scrubbing**. Hold down the Shift key when you scrub, and the values will increase by increments of 10; or, simply scrub the numbers to increment by single digits. Scrubbing in this area of the `Motion Editor` works as follows:

CHAPTER 1

- Scrub across the `Graph Size` value, and the side of the graph in the panel gets larger or smaller.

- Scrub across the `Expanded Graph Size` value, and just the graph for the selected property gets larger or smaller. This one, at first, is a bit tricky. Changing the value doesn't result in an immediate change. What you need to do to see the graph is to click the solid color area of the strip. When you do this, the property strip expands to full size, and you can now make the change.

- Scrub across the `Viewable Frames` value, and you will see the frames in the graph get larger or smaller. The maximum value for this feature is the current number of frames in the tween span, not the Flash movie. Notice how you can't get a number larger than the 72 frames in the animation.

Twirl down the `Basic motion` section. If you scrub across any of the values, the object in that particular frame will change.

> Be careful with that blue back arrow on the title strip. This is the `Reset Values` button, and it doesn't simply reset the values to their original values. Click it, and the tween is removed.

Click the twirlie in the `Eases` area to open it, and you see that you can remove any "eases" or apply a `Simple (Slow)` ease to the entire area or to individual properties. We aren't going to explain a `Simple (Slow)` ease because you are, for now, just passing by. We'll cover this in greater depth in the animation chapters.

You will notice that you have a timeline in this panel. Obviously, if you have a timeline, you should be able to add a keyframe. Drag the playhead to frame 15 of the timeline in the `Motion Editor`. In the keyframe area are two arrows on either side of a diamond. Click the diamond to add a new keyframe, which is now visible as a dot on the graph, and if you look up at the main timeline, you will see a keyframe has also been added in frame 15 of the main timeline. The diamond also turns golden. If you move the playhead to another position, the keyframe changes back to gray. This should tell you a golden diamond, as shown in Figure 1-20, means there is a keyframe in the frame. If you click the arrows on either side of the diamond, you will jump to the previous keyframe or the next keyframe. When one of those arrows is grayed out, you are essentially being told there are no further keyframes beyond the current position of the playhead.

LEARNING THE FLASH CS5 PROFESSIONAL INTERFACE

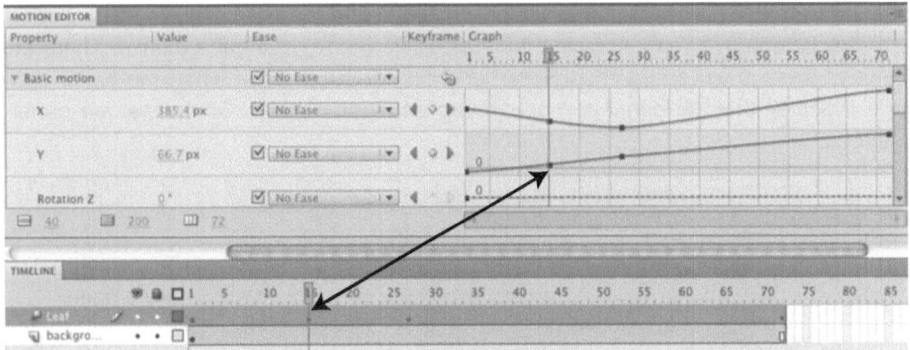

Figure 1-20. Key frames added in the `Motion Editor` also appear on the main timeline.

The `Colors`, `Filters`, and `Eases` strips are treated a bit differently. Instead of an arrow, they have plus and minus signs. Click the + in the `Filters` area. A drop-down menu containing a list of the filters, as shown in Figure 1-21, appears. To remove a filter, click and hold the – sign. A drop-down list of the filters applied to that object will appear. Click a filter in that list, and it will be removed.

Figure 1-21. Filters can also be added and tweened.

The Properties panel

We have been mentioning the `Properties` panel quite a bit to this point, so now would be a good time to stroll over to it and take a closer look. Before we do that, let's go sit down on the bench over there and discuss a fundamental concept in Flash: everything has **properties**.

What are properties? These are the things objects have in common with each other. Tiago and Tom share the Author property of this book. We are both males. We both have a common language property, English, but we also have properties we don't share. For example, our location properties are Zurich and Toronto. Tiago is a bit taller than Tom. At our most basic, we are humans on the planet Earth. In Flash terms, though, we are objects on the stage. Click the Tiago object, and you will instantly see that, even though he and Tom share similar properties, they also have properties that are different. The properties of any object on the Flash stage will appear in the `Properties` panel, and best of all, any properties appearing on the panel can be changed.

23

The panel, as shown in Figure 1-22, is positioned, by default, to the right of the screen. You can move it elsewhere on the screen by simply dragging it into position and releasing the mouse. There are locations on the screen where you will see a shadow or darkening of the location when the panel is over it. This color change indicates that the panel can be docked into that location. Otherwise, the panel will "float" above the screen.

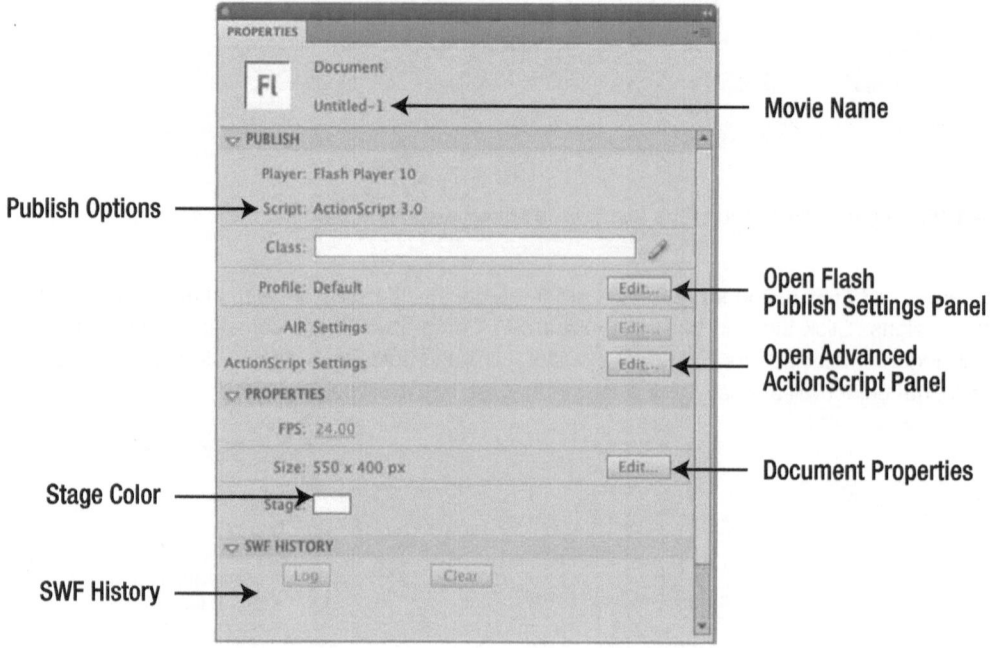

Figure 1-22. The `Properties` panel

New to the `Properties` panels in Flash Professional CS5 is the `SWF History` area. This handy little feature tracks the changes in SWF size and the date and times when the SWF was tested. In Figure 1-23, you can see how this feature works. The latest changes or tests are shown in the `Properties` panel. If you click the `Log` button, the full history appears in the `Output` panel. Tracing changes really isn't necessary with this project. In this case, click the `Clear` button, and the entries in the `Properties` and `Output` panels will be deleted.

LEARNING THE FLASH CS5 PROFESSIONAL INTERFACE

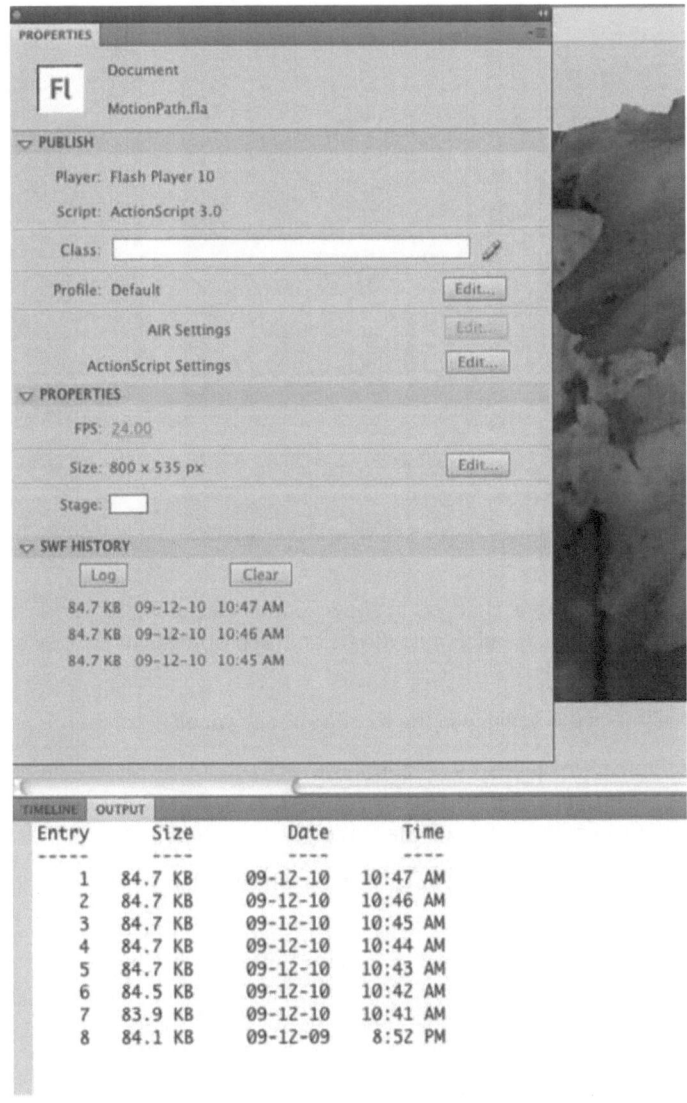

Figure 1-23. SWF History is a useful addition to the application.

When an object is placed on the stage and selected, the Properties panel will change to reflect the properties of the selected object that can be manipulated. For example, in Figure 1-24, a box has been drawn on the stage. The Properties panel shows you the type of object that has been selected and tells you the stroke and fill colors of the object can also be changed. In addition, you can change how scaling will be applied to the object and the treatment of the red stroke around the box.

25

CHAPTER 1

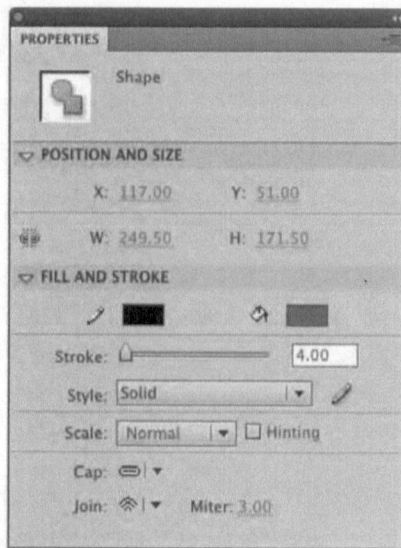

Figure 1-24. The `Properties` panel changes to show you the properties of a selected object that can be manipulated (in this case, the size, location, and stroke and fill properties of the box on the stage).

Let's experiment with some of the settings in the `Properties` panel:

1. Open the file named `Properties.fla` in the `Exercise` folder. When the file opens, you will see an image of the Summer Palace in Beijing over a black background and the words `Summer Palace, Beijing` at the bottom of the stage.

2. In the `Tools` panel, click the `Selection` tool, which is the solid black arrow at the top of the `Tools` panel (see Figure 1-25).

> *Clicking tools is one way of selecting them. Another way is to use the keyboard. When you roll the mouse pointer over a tool, you will see a tooltip containing the name of the tool and a letter. For example, the letter beside the `Selection` tool is V. Press the V key, and the `Selection` tool will be highlighted in the `Tools` panel.*

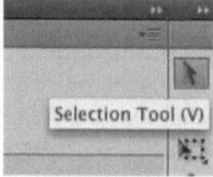

Figure 1-25. Click a tool or use the keyboard to select it.

3. Using the **Selection** tool, click once white area of the stage. The **Properties** panel will change to show you that you have selected the stage and can change its color.

4. In the **Properties** panel, click the **Background Color** chip to open the **Color Picker**, as shown in Figure 1-26. Click the medium gray on the left (#999999), and the stage will turn gray. You have just changed the color property of the stage.

Figure 1-26. Color and stage dimensions are properties of the stage.

5. Click the text. The **Properties** panel will change to show you the text properties, as shown in Figure 1-27, that can be changed. Click the color chip to open the **Color Picker**. When it opens, click the white chip once. The text turns white.

Figure 1-27. Color is just one of many text properties that can be manipulated.

6. Click the black box surrounding the image. The `Properties` panel will change to tell you that you have selected a shape and that the fill color for this shape is black. It also lets you know that there is no stroke around the shape. In the `Position and Size` areas are four numbers that tell you the width, height, and x and y coordinates of the shape on the stage. Select the `Width` value, and change it from `500` to `525`. Change the `Height` number from `380` to `400`. **Finally, change the X and Y values for the selection to 5 and 23**, as shown in Figure 1-28. Each time you make a change, the selected object will get wider or higher.

> *If you are an After Effects user, then seeing properties as links (or, as they are known in Flash, **hot text**) is not new. If you want to quickly change any value, simply click and drag a value to the left or the right. As you drag, the numbers will change, and the selected object on the stage will reflect these new values as you drag.*

Figure 1-28. The size and the location of selections can also be changed in the `Properties` panel.

The Tools panel

The `Tools` panel, as shown in Figure 1-29, is divided into four major areas:

- **Tools**: These allow you to create, select, and manipulate text and graphics placed on the stage.
- **View**: These allow you to pan across the stage or to zoom in on specific areas of the stage.
- **Colors**: These tools allow you to select and change fill, stroke, and gradient colors.
- **Options**: This is a context-sensitive area of the panel. In many ways, it is not unlike the `Properties` panel. It will change depending upon which tool you have selected.

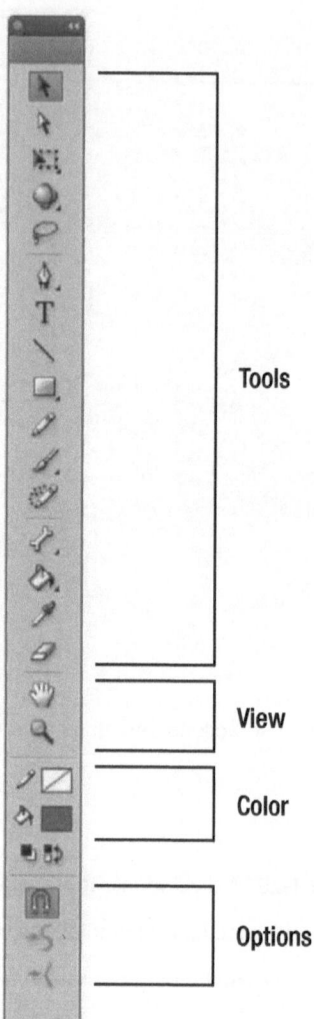

Figure 1-29. The Tools panel

LEARNING THE FLASH CS5 PROFESSIONAL INTERFACE

If there is a small down arrow in the bottom-right corner of a tool, this indicates additional tool options. Click and hold that arrow, and the options will appear in a drop-down menu, as shown in Figure 1-30.

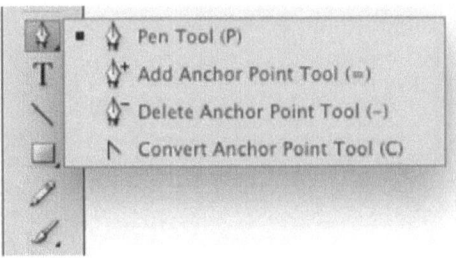

Figure 1-30. Some tools contain extra tools, which are shown in a drop-down list.

The Library panel

The `Library` panel is one of those features of the application that is so indispensable to Flash developers and designers that we simply can't think of anybody who doesn't use it . . . religiously.

In very simple terms, it is the place where content, including video and audio, that is used in the movie is stored for reuse later in the movie. It is also the place where symbols and copies of components that you may use are automatically placed when the symbols are created or the components are added to the stage.

Let's wander over to the `Library` and take a look. If the `Properties.fla` file isn't open, open it now. Click the `Library` icon on the right side of the screen, or click the `Library` tab if the panel isn't collapsed. The `Library` will fly out, as shown in Figure 1-31. Inside the `Library`, you will see the Summer Palace image is actually a library asset. Drag a copy of the image from the `Library` to the stage. Leave it selected, and press the Delete key. Notice that the image on the stage disappears, but the `Library` item is retained. This is an important concept. Items placed on the stage are, more often than not, instances of the item and point directly to the original in the `Library`.

To collapse the `Library` panel, click the stage. Panels, opened from icons, are configured to collapse automatically. If, for some reason, you want to turn off autocollapse, select `Edit ➤ Preferences` (Windows) or (`Flash ➤ Preferences`) to open `Preferences`. Click `General`, and deselect `Auto-Collapse Icon Panels` when the preferences open. Another way of opening and closing the `Library` is to press Ctrl+L (Windows) or Cmd+L (Mac).

CHAPTER 1

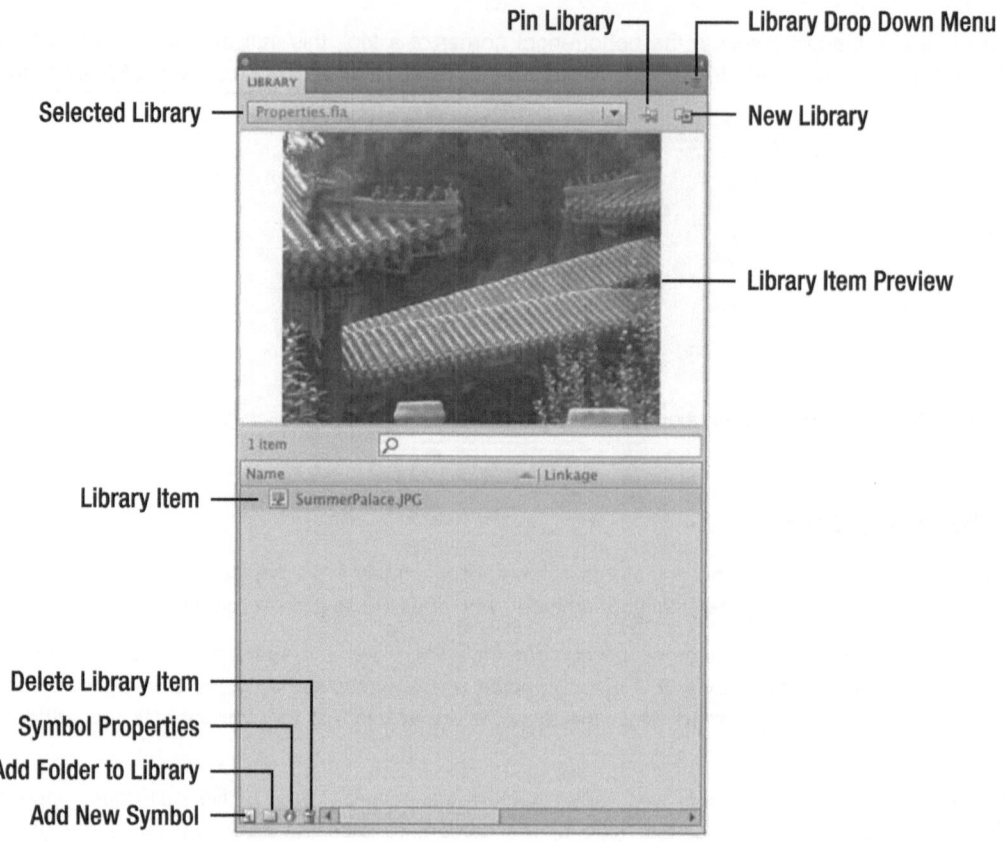

Figure 1-31. The Library panel

Using layers

The next stop on our walkabout is found under the stage: the layers feature of the timeline. There are a few things you need to know regarding layers:

- You can have as many layers in a Flash movie as you need. They have no effect upon the file size.

- Use layers to manage your movie. Flash movies are composed of objects, media, and code, and it is a standard industry practice to give everything its own layer. This way, you can easily find content on a crowded stage. In fact, any object that is tweened must be on its own layer.

- Layers can be grouped. Layers can be placed inside a folder, which means you can, for example, have a complex animation and have all the objects in the animation contained in their own layers inside a folder.

- Layers stack on top of each other. For example, you can have a layer with a box in it and another with a ball in it. If the ball layer is above the box layer, the ball will appear to be above the box.
- Name your layers. This is another standard industry practice that makes finding content in the movie very easy.

> *Screen real estate is always at a premium. If you need to see more of the stage, double-click the `Timeline` tab to collapse the layers. Double-click the `Timeline` tab again, and the layers are brought back.*

Layer properties

Layers can also be put to very specific uses, and this is accomplished by assigning one of five layer properties, as shown in Figure 1-32, to a layer. Though they are called **properties**, they really should be regarded more as layer modes than anything else. We will be covering these in great depth in Chapter 3 and Chapters 7 and 8, which focus on animation, but this is a good place to start learning where they are and what they do. The modes, accessed by right-clicking (Windows) or Control+clicking (Mac) a layer name and clicking `Properties`, are as follows:

- **Normal layer:** This is the layer you have been working with to this point in the book. Objects on these layers **are** always visible, and motion is more or less governed by the `Motion Editor`. You can always identify a normal layer; its icon looks like a folded sheet of paper.
- **Mask layer:** The shape of an object on a masking layer is used to hide anything outside the shape and reveals only whatever is under the object. For example, place an image on the stage and add a box in the layer above it. If that layer is a masking layer, only the pixels of the part of the image directly under the box will be seen. The icon for a mask layer is a square with an oval in the middle of it.
- **Masked layer:** If you have a mask layer, you will also have one of these. Like Siamese twins, mask layers and masked layers—any layer under a mask—are joined together. The icon for a masked layer **looks** like a folded sheet of paper facing the opposite direction as the icon for a normal layer. In addition, the layer name for a masked layer is indented.
- **Folder layer:** The best way of thinking of this mode is as a folder containing layers. They also provide quick access to layer groupings you may create. The icon for a folder layer is a file folder with a twirlie. Click the twirlie, and the layers in the folder are revealed. Click the twirlie again, and the layers collapse.

- **Guide layer**: A guide layer contains shapes, symbols, images, and so on, that you can use to align elements on other layers in a movie. These things are really handy if you have a complex design and want a standard reference for the entire movie. What makes guide layers so important is that they aren't rendered when you publish the SWF. This means, for example, that you could create a comprehensive design (or **comp**) of the Flash stage in either Fireworks CS5 or Photoshop CS5, place that image in a guide layer, and not have to worry about an overly large SWF being published and bloating the SWF with unnecessary file size and download time. The icon for a guide layer is a T-square.

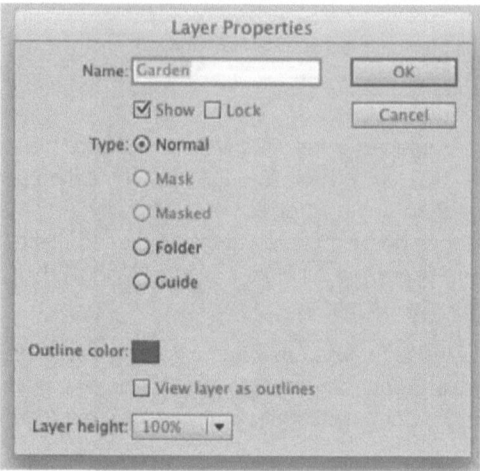

Figure 1-32. The `Library` panel

> Flash Professional CS5, by default, omits layers that are hidden—we get into hiding layers in a couple of minutes—when the SWF is eventually published. The result is a reduction in the size of the SWF.

Creating layers

Let's start using layers. Here's how:

1. Open the `Layers.fla` document. When it opens, you will see the garden and a couple of butterflies, as shown in Figure 1-33. If you look at the timeline, you could logically assume this is a simple photograph sitting on a single layer named `Garden`.

2. Open the `Library`. You will notice that there is an object named `Butterfly` contained in the `Library`. That object is a movie clip. We'll get into movie clips in a big way in Chapter 3.

LEARNING THE FLASH CS5 PROFESSIONAL INTERFACE

Figure 1-33. We start with what appears to be a photograph of flowers and butterflies.

3. Click the keyframe in the `Garden` layer. Three objects—the two Monarch butterflies and the image—are selected. What you have just learned is how to select everything on a layer. Click the pasteboard to deselect the objects.

4. Each object should be placed on its own layer. Click the `New Layer` button—it looks like a page with a turned-up corner—directly under the `Garden layer` strip. A new layer, named `Layer1`, is added to the timeline.

5. Select `the Garden layer by clicking it,` and add a new layer. Notice how the new layer is placed between `Garden` and `Layer 1`. This should tell you that all new layers added to the timeline are added directly above the currently selected layer. Obviously, `Layer 2` is out of position. Let's fix that.

6. Drag `Layer 2` above `Layer 1`, and release the mouse. Now you know how to reorder layers and move them around in the timeline. Layers can be dragged above or below each other.

7. Add a new layer, Layer 3. Hold on—we have four layers and three objects. The math doesn't work. That new layer has to go.

8. Select `Layer 3`, and click the `Trash Can` icon under the `Garden` strip. `Layer 3` will now be deleted, and now you know how to get rid of an extra layer.

35

CHAPTER 1

9. Double-click the `Layer 1` layer name to select it. Rename the layer `Butterfly`. Now that you know how to rename a layer, select `File ➤ Revert` to revert the file to its original state. It's now time to learn how to put content on layers.

Adding content to layers

Content can be added to layers in one of two ways:

- Directly to the layer by moving an object from the `Library` to the layer
- From one layer to another layer

Let's explore how to use the two methods to place content into layers:

1. Create a new layer, name it `Butterfly01`, and drag the `Butterfly` movie clip from the `Library` to cover the flower, as shown in Figure 1-34, in the bottom-right corner of the stage. The hollow dot in the layer will change to a solid dot to indicate that there is content in the frame. When moving objects from the `Library` to the stage, be sure to select the layer, sometimes called a **target layer**, before you drag and drop. This way, you can prevent the content from going in the wrong layer. Let's now turn our attention to getting the two other butterflies into their own layers.

Figure 1-34. Objects can be dragged directly from the `Library` and added to specific layers.

2. With the Shift key held down, click the two butterflies in the center and upper-left corner of the stage. This will select them, and the blue box around each one indicates they are movie clips.

3. Select `Modify` ➤ `Timeline` ➤ `Distribute to Layers`, or press Ctrl+Shift+D (Windows) or Cmd+Shift+D (Mac). The butterflies will appear in the new `Butterfly` layers that appear under the `Garden` layer. Rename these layers `Butterfly02` and `Butterfly03`, and move them, as shown in Figure 1-35, above the `Butterly01` layer.

Figure 1-35. Multiple selections can be placed in their own layers using the `Distribute to Layers` command.

The next technique is one that addresses a very common issue encountered by Flash designers: taking content from one layer and placing it in the exact same position in another layer. This is an issue because you can't drag content from one layer to another.

1. Click the `Butterfly` movie clip in the center of the stage, and press Ctrl+X (Windows) or Cmd+X (Mac) to cut the selection out of the layer.

2. With the layer still selected in the timeline, select `Edit` ➤ `Paste in Place` (see Figure 1-36). A copy of the butterfly will appear in the precise location at which you cut it.

CHAPTER 1

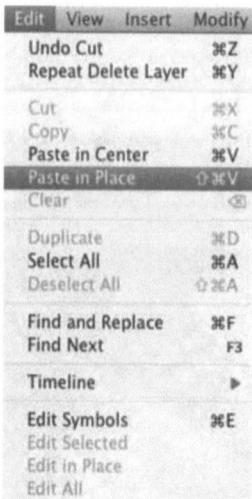

Figure 1-36. `Paste in Place` pastes objects in the precise location of the original object that was either cut or copied to the clipboard.

> *Whatever happened to a simple paste command in the `Edit` menu? The `Paste in Center` command replaces it. It has always been a fact of Flash life that any content on the clipboard is pasted into the center of the stage. The name simply acknowledges this.*

Showing/hiding and locking layers

We are sure the three icons—an eyeball, a lock, and a hollow square (shown in Figure 1-37)—above the layers caught your attention. Let's see what they do.

Figure 1-37. The `Layer Visibility`, `Lock`, and `Show All Layers As Outlines` icons. Note the `Pencil` icon in the `Butterfly02` layer, which tells you that you can add content to that layer.

Click the eyeball icon. Notice that everything on the stage disappears, and the dots under the eyeball in each layer change to a red *x*. This eyeball is the `Layer Visibility` icon, and clicking it turns off the visibility of all the content in the layers. Click the icon again, and everything reappears. This time, select the `Butterfly02` layer, and click the dot under the eyeball. Just the butterfly in the center of the stage disappears. What this tells you is that you can turn off the visibility for a specific layer by clicking the dot in the visibility column.

When you click a layer, you may notice that a pencil icon appears on the layer strip. This tells you that you can add content to the layer. Click the `Butterfly02` layer, and you'll see the pencil icon. Now, click the dot under the lock in the `Butterfly02` layer. The lock icon will replace the dot. When you lock a layer, you can't draw on it or add content to it. You can see this because the pencil has a stroke through it. If you try to drag the `Butterfly` movie clip from the `Library` to the `Butterfly02` layer, you will also see that the layer has been locked because the mouse pointer changes from a tan arrow to a circle with a line through it. Also, if you try to click the butterfly on the stage, you won't be able to select it. This is handy to know in situations where precision is paramount and you don't want to accidentally move something or, god forbid, delete something from the stage.

> *OK, we sort of "stretched the truth" there by telling you that content can't be added to a locked layer. ActionScript is the only thing that can be added to a locked layer. This explains why many Flash designers and developers create an ActionScript-only layer—usually named `scripts` or `actions`—and then lock the layer. This prevents anything other than code from being placed in the layer.*

The final icon is the `Show All Layers As Outlines` icon. Click it, and the content on the stage turns into outlines. This is somewhat akin to the wireframe display mode available in many 3D modeling applications. In Flash, it can be useful in cases where dozens of objects overlap and you simply want a quick "X-ray view" of how your content is arranged. With animation, in particular, it can be helpful to evaluate the motion of objects without having to consider the distraction of color and shading. Like visibility and locking, the outlines icon is also available on a per-layer basis.

> *You can change the color used for the outline in a layer by double-clicking the color chip in the layer strip. This will open the `Layer Properties` dialog box. Double-click the color chip in dialog box to open the Color Picker; then click a color, and that color will be used.*

Grouping layers

You can also group layers using folders. Here's how:

1. Click the `Folder` icon in the `Layers` panel. A new unnamed folder—`Folder 1`—will appear on the timeline. You can rename a folder by double-clicking its name and entering a new name.
2. Drag the three `Butterfly` layers into the folder. As each one is placed in the folder, notice how the name indents. This tells you that the layer is in a folder.
3. Next, remove the layers from the folder. To do so, simply drag the layer above the folder on the timeline. You can also drag it to the left to unindent it.
4. To delete a folder, select it, and click the `Trash Can` icon.

> *Step away from the mouse, and put your hands where we can see them. Don't think you can simply select a folder and click the `Trash Can` icon to remove it. Make sure that the folder is empty. If you delete a folder that contains layers, those layers will also be deleted. If this happens to you, Adobe has sent a life raft in your direction. An alert box telling you that you will also be deleting the layers in the folder will appear. Click `Cancel` instead of OK.*

Where to get help

In the early days of desktop computing, software was a major purchase, and nothing made you feel more comfortable than the manuals that were tucked into the box. If you had a problem, you opened the manual and searched for the solution. Those days have long passed. This is especially true with Flash, because as its complexity has grown, the size of the manuals that would need to be packaged with the application would also need to have grown. In this version of Flash, the user manuals are found in the `Help` menu. Here's how to access `Help`:

1. Select `Help` ➤ `Flash Help`, or press the F1 key. The `Help` panel that opens (see Figure 1-38) is one of the most comprehensive sources of Flash knowledge on the planet; best of all, it's free. The `Help` panel is driven by an Adobe AIR application—Adobe Help—that is installed when you install the CS5 applications. The `Help` menu is more generically known as Adobe Community Help.

   The panel is divided into two areas. On the left side you can enter your criteria for very specific topics and choose to have the result drawn from Adobe Help on your computer—`Local`—or from a variety of web sources, `Online`. The right side of the window allows you to choose a more general topic.

LEARNING THE FLASH CS5 PROFESSIONAL INTERFACE

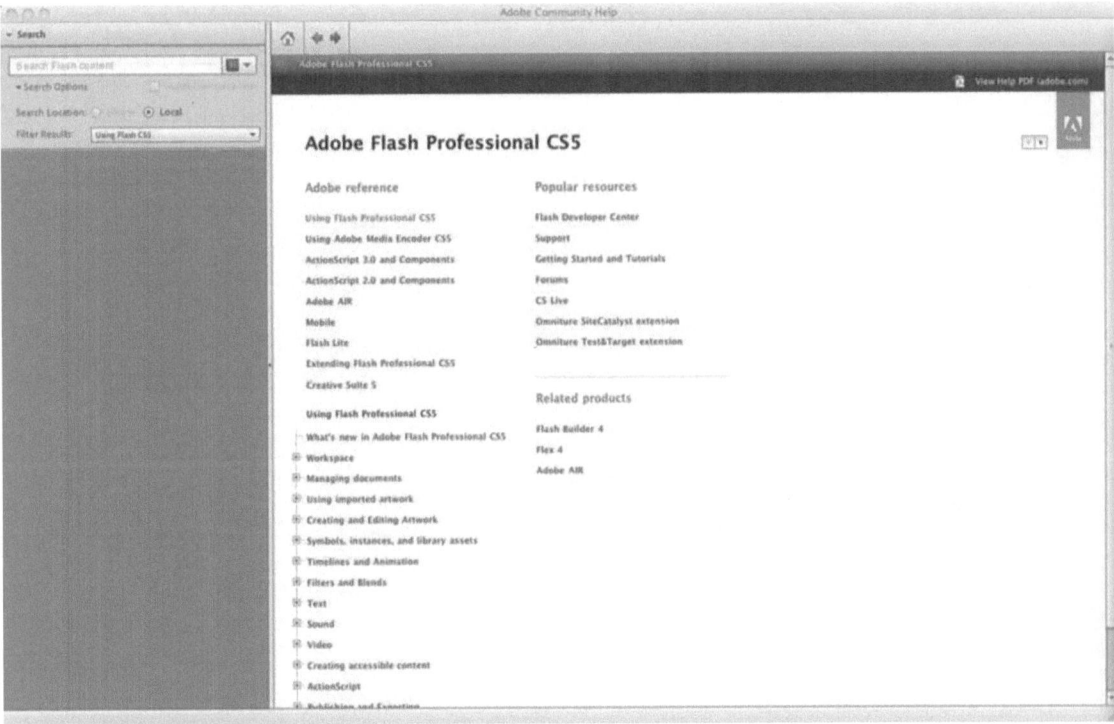

Figure 1-38. The Flash `Help` panel is extensive.

2. Click the `What's new in Adobe Flash professional link` to open it. As you can see, the `Help` topics are actually collections of individual documents designed to help you learn what you need to know, along with practical examples of specific techniques.

3. To go to a specific topic, just type the word into the text input box at the top of the interface, and click the `Search` button. For example, enter **video** into this area, and press the Return (Enter) key. The results are presented directly under your search criteria.

4. Click the first link, `Create video for use in Flash`, and the right pane will fill with the selected page (as shown in Figure 1-39).

CHAPTER 1

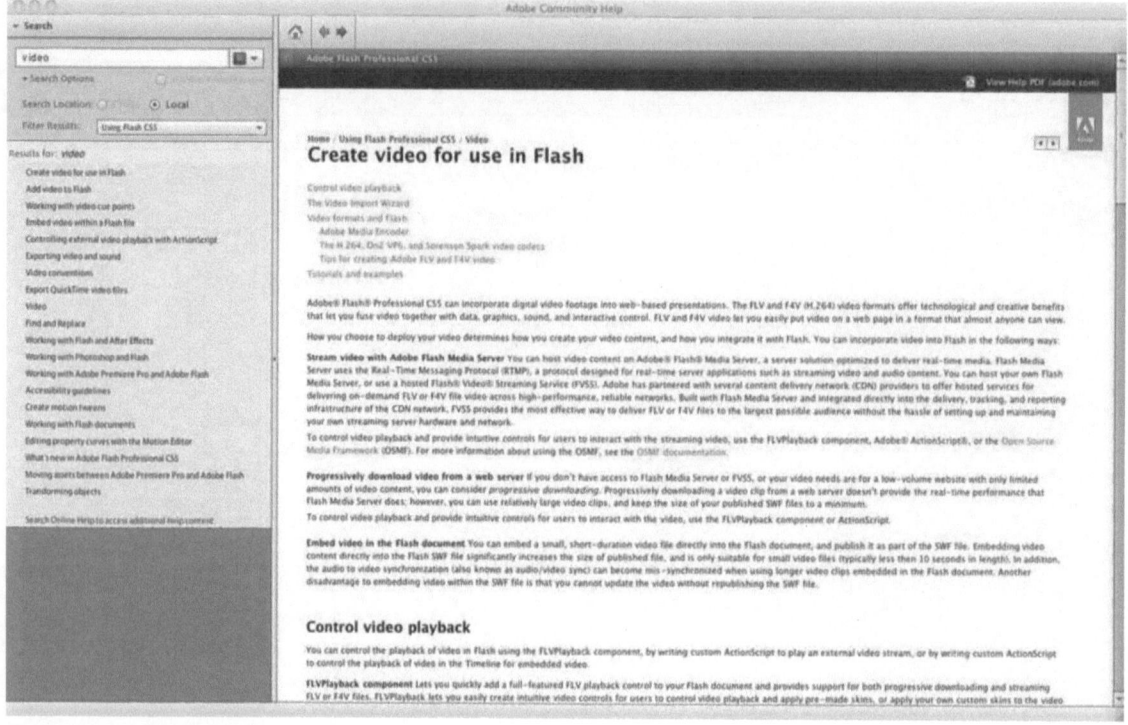

Figure 1-39. Searching a term in the Flash Help documents

So much for the walkabout. It is time for you to put into practice what you have learned.

Your turn: building a Flash movie

In this exercise, you are going to expand on your knowledge. We have shown you where many of the interface features can be found and how they can be used, so we are now going to give you the opportunity to see how all these features combine to create a Flash movie.

You will be undertaking such tasks as the following:

- Using the `Properties` panel to precisely position and resize objects on the stage
- Creating layers and adding content from the `Library` to the layers
- Using the drawing tools to create a shape
- Creating a simple animation through the use of a tween
- Saving a Flash movie
- Testing a Flash movie

By the end of this exercise, you will have a fairly good understanding of how a Flash movie is assembled and the workflow involved in the process.

1. Open the `Garden.fla` file.

2. When the file opens, if it isn't already open, open the **Library** by selecting **Window ➤ Library** or pressing Ctrl+L (Windows) or Cmd+L (Mac). As you can see in Figure 1-40, you are starting with a background image and a few movie clips.

Figure 1-40. The assets are in place. It is your job to turn them into a movie.

3. The **Library** is still a bit messy. Let's do a little tidying. Click the **New Folder** icon—it looks like a file folder—at the bottom of the **Library** panel. A new, untitled folder will appear in the **Library**. Double-click the folder name, not the icon, to select the name. Change the folder's name to `MovieClips`.

4. Drag all the movie clips—the blue files with the "gear" in the upper-right corner of the icon—into the new folder. A **movie clip** is an animation with its own timeline. We get into that topic in Chapter 3.

5. Create a new folder, and name it `Audio`.

43

6. Let's bring the audio file for this movie into the `Library`. To start, select `File` ➤ `Import` ➤ `Import to Library`. Navigate to this chapter's Exercise folder, and select the `FliesBuzzing.mp3` file, as shown in Figure 1-41. Click the `Import to Library` button, and when the file appears in the `Library`, move it to the `Audio` folder.

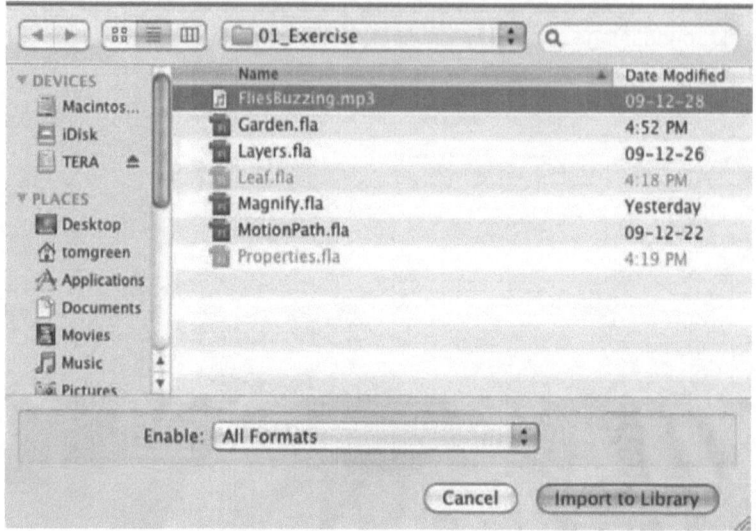

Figure 1-41. Importing a file to the `Library`

> *Though you are given the choice of importing content into the timeline or the `Library`, it is considered a best practice in Flash to import everything directly into the `Library`. The only file without the option of importing its content to the stage is an audio file.*

With the assets in place, we can now turn our attention to the project.

The plan is to have a fly merrily buzz through the flowers and around the butterflies in the garden. The key words are *buzz* and *through*. "Buzz" indicates there is an audio file, and you have brought that into the `Library`. You will be adding that file to the project near the end of the process.

The "through" part may at first appear to be a no-brainer. Of course, a fly is going to buzz through the flowers in the image. No, it isn't. As the movie is currently set up, the fly will buzz above the flat image of the flowers on the stage. It won't go behind the flowers and butterflies because it can't. What this should tell you is that we are going to create the illusion of depth by using the layers in the Flash timeline and creating a butterfly and some flowers for the fly to fly behind.

To accomplish this, we need to first create the butterfly by using movie clips inside a movie clip to create an object. That, of course, was a mouthful, and there is a term for it: **nesting**. Here's how to create a nested movie clip.

Nesting movie clips

Before we start, it is important for you to know we are not going to get into a long discussion on the subject of movie clips, animation, and so on. We are saving those discussions for Chapters 3 and 7. What we want to do here is to get you used to working with the interface, so to start, let's build a butterfly.

1. With the `Library` panel open, click the `New Symbol` button—the turned-up piece of paper—at the bottom of the `Library` panel. The `Create New Symbol` dialog box shown in Figure 1-42 will open.

2. Select the text in the `Name` area, and enter the word `Butterfly`. Select `Movie Clip` from the `Type` drop-down menu. Click `OK`. The dialog box will close, and what looks like a blank stage will open.

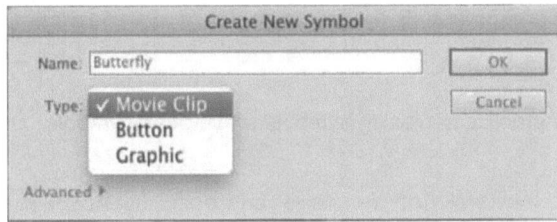

Figure 1-42. Creating a new Flash symbol

The blank stage you are looking at is called the `Symbol Editor`. If you look at the top-left corner of the interface, you will see buttons for `Scene 1` and `Butterfly`. The last symbol you see is the one currently open. In many respects, these are breadcrumbs that enable you to follow your path back to the main timeline, which is always `Scene 1`. The + sign you see in the center of the stage is actually the upper-left corner of the main stage in your Flash movie.

3. Select `Layer 1`, and add two more layers. Starting with the bottom layer, name the layers `Body`, `RightWing`, and `LeftWing`.

4. Select the `LeftWing` layer, open the `MovieClips` folder in the `Library`, and drag the `WingL` movie clip to the selected layer.

5. Select the `RightWing` layer, and drag the `WingR` movie clip to the stage. These last two steps did exactly the same thing; they put something on the stage in a specific layer. Use whichever technique works for you.

6. Select the `Body` layer, and drag the `Body` movie clip to the stage. You have just placed (**nested**) three movie clips by placing them on separate layers (Figure 1-43) inside a single movie clip. Let's get the `Butterfly` assembled.

45

Figure 1-43. Nesting is the practice of placing symbols within other symbols.

7. Select the `WingL` movie clip on the stage, and open the **Properties** panel. Twirl down the **Position and Size** strip, and set the `X` and `Y` positions for the selection to `0,0`, as shown in Figure 1-44.

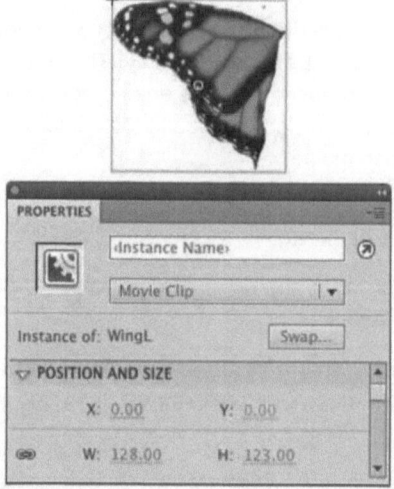

Figure 1-44. Use the hot text feature to accurately position selections on the stage.

LEARNING THE FLASH CS5 PROFESSIONAL INTERFACE

8. Click the `Body` movie clip, and drag it into position against the right edge of the left wing. Drag the right wing to the right edge of the `Body` movie clip, as shown in Figure 1-45.

9. Click the `Scene 1` link to save the `Butterfly` movie clip and to return to the main timeline.

> *Here's a little "teacher trick" you might find useful. Use the `Magnifying Glass` tool to zoom in on an object like the butterfly, as shown in Figure 1-45. Then select an object, and use the arrow keys on your keyboard to nudge the selected object into place.*

Figure 1-45. The butterfly you will be using in the movie has been assembled.

Drawing the fly

Having discovered how to create a movie clip using existing objects, let's now create one from "scratch." We need a fly to buzz through the garden, and if you poke through the `MovieClips` folder in the `Library`, you will notice the fly is missing.

Before we start, we aren't going to ask you to draw a fly or create a cartoon version of one. Instead, you are going to create a shape that is somewhat "flylike" and have it buzz through the flowers. Follow these steps to create the fly:

1. Select `Insert` ➤ `New Symbol`, or press the Ctrl+F8 (Windows) or Cmd+F8 (Mac) keys to open the `Create New Symbol` dialog box. In the previous exercise, you used the `New Symbol` button in the `Library` to create a new symbol. This is another method of creating a symbol. Which is best? Who cares? Use what works for you.

2. Name the symbol `Fly`, and select `Movie Clip` as its `Type`. Click `OK` to open the `Symbol Editor`.

3. When the `Symbol Editor` opens, select `400%` from the `Zoom` drop-down menu. This lets you create a rather small object but still be able to see what you are doing.

4. Select the `Pencil` tool, and in the `Stroke` color area of the `Tools`, select `Black` as the stroke color. Draw a shape that looks somewhat flylike.

47

5. In the tools, set `Fill Color` to `Black`. Select the `Paint Bucket` tool, and click once inside your shape to fill it (Figure 1-46) with black.
6. Click the `Scene 1` link to return to the main timeline. When the main timeline appears, put your `Fly` movie clip into the `MovieClips` folder in the `Library`.

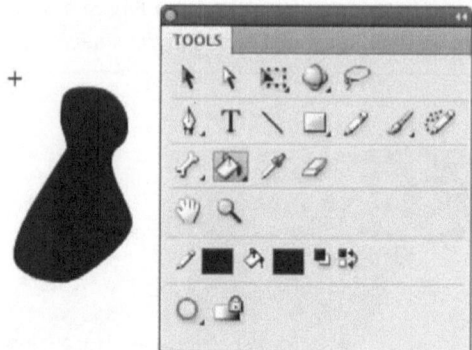

Figure 1-46. The fly shape is filled with a color using the `Paint Bucket` tool.

Creating the illusion of depth with Flash

If you spend any time creating Flash movies, you will inevitably be asked, "How did you do that?" Though you can give a long explanation of how you created the movie to develop the technique, the short answer is always, "Magic!"

In this exercise, the "magic" involves manipulating a flat space in such a way that the "illusion" of depth is created. This illusion can be created in a few ways:

- **Use layers to your advantage:** Objects in layers are either above or below the objects contained in the layers above them or below them.
- **A Blur filter can be used to show depth:** Use blurs to provide depth of field much like you do with your camera.
- **The z-axis can be used as the depth axis:** Objects on the Flash stage can be moved or positioned either up and down (y-axis), to the left or right (x-axis), or closer or farther away (z-axis).
- **Tweens are great for creating depth:** Resizing objects over time can create the illusion of objects receding into the distance or moving toward the viewer.

In this part of the exercise, we are going to use all four methods to create depth. Let's start this process by using the first one: layers. Here's how:

1. Add three new layers to the Garden.fla file. Name the layers FrontGarden, MiddleGarden, and Butterfly. Make sure the FrontGarden layer is above the MiddleGarden layer.

2. Select the MiddleGarden layer, open the Library, and drag the BottomFlower movie clip from the MovieClips folder to the stage.

3. With the BottomFlower movie clip selected on the stage, move it into position in the bottom-right corner of the stage.

4. Select the Butterfly layer, and drag the Butterfly movie clip to the stage.

5. Select the FrontGarden layer, and drag the Front movie clip to the stage. Place it at the bottom-left corner of the stage, as shown in Figure 1-47.

Figure 1-47. Layers are a quick way of adding depth to a movie.

Now that the objects are in place, let's further add to the illusion of depth by adding some depth of field and blurring the background image. Here's how:

1. Drag the playhead to frame 50 of the timeline, and unlock the **Background** layer.

2. Right-click (Windows) or Control+click (Mac) frame 50 of the **Background** layer to open the context menu. Select **Insert Keyframe** from the menu. The black dot that appears in the frame, as shown in Figure 1-48, tells you this is a keyframe.

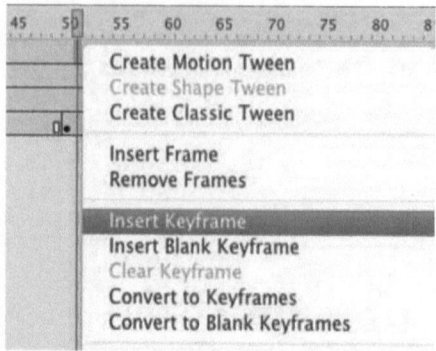

Figure 1-48. Adding a keyframe to a layer

3. Move the playhead to frame 1 of the timeline, and click the background image on the stage to select it.

4. Open **the Properties** panel, and twirl down the **Filters** strip.

5. Click the **Add Filter** button—it looks like a turned-up piece of paper—at the bottom of the panel, and select **Blur** from the pop-up menu. The **Blur** filter's parameters, as shown in Figure 1-49, appear in the panel. Set the **Blur X** and **Blur Y** values to 10, and select **High** from the **Quality** drop-down menu. The image blurs, and the three layers above it remain in sharp focus.

6. Save the file.

> *What's with the keyframe? We are eventually going to require the background to return to sharp focus. Adding the keyframe gives us the flexibility to have the image slowly come into focus through the use of a motion tween.*

LEARNING THE FLASH CS5 PROFESSIONAL INTERFACE

Figure 1-49. Use of a `Blur` filter can provide depth of field.

The next technique uses the z-axis to provide depth. Introduced in Flash CS4, the z-axis is becoming a vital 3D tool in the hands of Flash designers and animators. What the z-axis does is to essentially move a camera closer to or farther away from an object. As the camera moves closer to the object, it appears to grow, and as it moves farther away from the object, it shrinks. Let's try it:

1. Lock the `Background` layer. Move the playhead to frame 50, and with the Shift key pressed, click in frame 50 of the layers on the timeline. Press the F6 key to add a keyframe to each of the selected frames.

   > *In the previous exercise, you used the context menu to add a key frame, and in this one you pressed F6. Which is the best way? Who cares? You have created a keyframe. Having said that, use of the F6 key is more common throughout the Flash community.*

2. Select the `Front` movie clip on the stage, and click the `Properties` tab to open the `Properties` panel.

3. Twirl down the `3D Position and View` strip, and set the `Z` value to -100. The selection, as shown in Figure 1-50, appears to get larger.

4. Use the following 3D position values for the flower and the butterfly in the other two layers:
   - `Flower`: X = 475, Y = 428, Z = -50
   - `Butterfly`: Z = -20

5. Save the file.

Figure 1-50. Negative values on the z-axis make selections look bigger.

Did the image get larger when we applied the negative z-axis value? Not quite. When thinking of the z-axis, regard the surface of the computer's screen as being the 0 value. Moving away from the screen toward you, using negative z-axis values, actually pulls the object closer to the camera. In this case, the camera is located at a position of about -500 pixels away from the screen. If you change the `Z` value of the selection to `-503`, the image seems to disappear. In fact, the image is now behind the camera, and because you can't swivel the camera, it is essentially out of the movie.

Don't go crazy with this effect. It is processor-intensive, and there are limits to how far you can go without an error message. The reason is this effect is achieved through scaling.

As you change the `Z` values in the `Property` panel, notice how there is a corresponding change in the `W` and `H` values. This is because, as shown in Figure 1-51, as you move along the positive values on the z-axis, you start approaching the object's vanishing point.

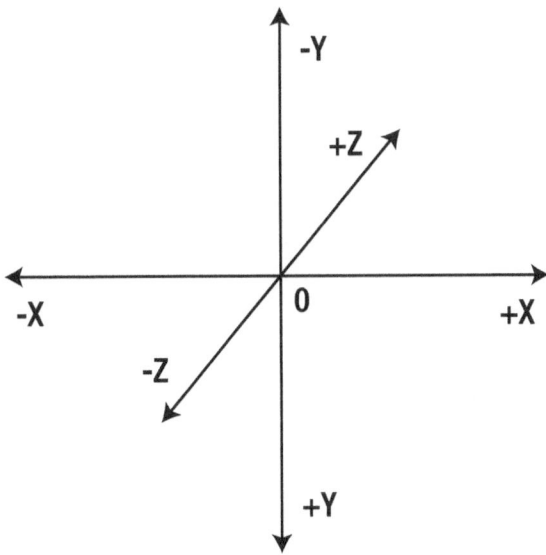

Figure 1-51. Move along positive side of the z-axis, and you approach the vanishing point.

Now that we have the first three methods of creating depth in place, the time has arrived to put those keyframes in frame 50 to good use. What we are going to do is to have the three layers with z-axis values move back to a value of 0, and at the same time, the blurred image will come back into focus.

This can all be done because each of the objects to be affected is a movie clip. Here's how:

1. Right-click (Windows) or Control+click (Mac) between the two key frames in the **FrontGarden** layer. Select **Create Motion Tween** from the context menu. Two things will happen. The first is that the span of frames between the two keyframes turns blue, and the icon for the layer changes from a piece of paper with a turned-up corner to a piece of paper with a comet tail. Both, as shown in Figure 1-52, are graphic indications that you have created a motion layer.

2. Unlock the **Background** layer, and add motion tweens to the remaining layers.

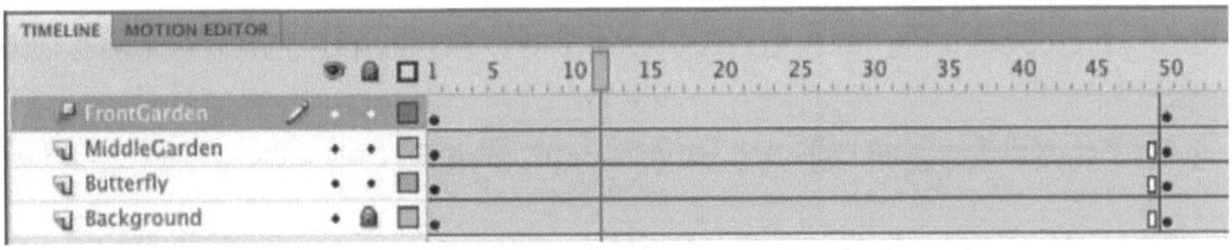

Figure 1-52. The layer icon and the powder blue color indicate a motion layer.

3. Click anywhere on the tween in the **FrontGarden** layer to select the span. Click the **Motion Editor** tab to open the **Motion Editor**, as shown in Figure 1-53.

4. Drag the playhead to the end of the timeline in the **Motion Editor**. Twirl down **Basic Motion**, and change the **Z** value from **-100** to **0**. Notice how the graph changes from a straight line to one that moves upward across the span.

Figure 1-53. Tweens are created by changing property values in the **Motion Editor**.

5. Repeat step 4 for the **MiddleGarden** and **Butterfly** layers. When finished, click the **Timeline** tab to close the **Motion Editor**.

6. Select the object in the **Background** layer, and move the playhead to the last frame of the motion tween.

7. In the **Properties** panel, change the **Blur** amount to **0**. Notice the addition of a keyframe to the layer.

8. The flower in the **MiddleGarden** layer, thanks to the 3D positioning, may be out of position. To fix that, move the playhead to the last frame of the motion tween, select the flower, and move it into position.

9. Scrub the playhead across the tweens, as shown in Figure 1-54, to preview the effect.

10. Save the project.

Figure 1-54. Z-axis and blur properties can be tweened to create the illusion of depth.

Creating an animated fly

If you look at the project so far, you should feel pretty good about what you have been able to accomplish with a few mouse clicks. The animation in the garden looks pretty good, and the blur tween is a pretty nifty technique. Naturally, Flash designers are rarely satisfied with their projects when there is something else that could be added to make it even more effective. In this case, the fly needs to buzz among the flowers, butterflies, and bees in the images on the stage. The fly will reinforce the illusion of depth and provide some visual interest to the viewer.

Before we start, let's take a moment and have a brief chat about those last two sentences.

When people first start using this application, there is a real tendency to load up projects with all manner of effects. In many cases, there is no rationale for the inclusion of these effects apart from the designer telling his friends, "Aren't I clever?"

CHAPTER 1

Flash is a powerful tool, and some of the most interesting Flash movies out there are ones where the effects are subtle. They quietly support the design rather than overpower it. In this case, the effect will be a small fly buzzing around the stage. The purpose of the fly is to reinforce the illusion of depth and to provide a subtle animation in an otherwise static image. To create a fly buzzing among the flowers, follow these steps:

1. Select the `Background` layer, and click the `New Layer` button to add a layer directly above the `Background` layer. Name this layer `Fly`.

2. With the `Fly` layer selected, drag the `Fly` movie clip to the stage. Obviously, as shown in Figure 1-55, the fly is a bit large for the garden.

Figure 1-55. The fly is in its own layer and on the stage.

3. Click the fly on the stage, and select the `Free Transform` tool from the `Tools` panel. Click a corner handle, and drag the handle inward to shrink the fly.

4. The fly is still a bit too distinct. With the fly still selected on the stage, apply a `Blur` filter to the selection. Set the `Blur X` and `Blur Y` values to `3 px` and the `Quality` value to `High`. Now that the fly's physical characteristics have been dealt with, let's put the fly in motion.

Using a motion guide

Putting the fly in motion is easy. The hard part is determining how to do it. That may seem a bit odd, but there are several methods for putting the fly in motion. These methods range from frame-by-frame animation to a purely code-driven approach. Picking the one best suited to the task at hand will make or break the project.

If you have ever watched flies, you will see that they move around in an erratic manner. Mimicking this using a frame-by-frame approach would be too time-consuming to be worth it, and coding the movement with changes in directions, loopbacks, and so on, would require some hard-core coding chops. The solution is to draw the path for the fly to follow. Here's how:

1. Lock all of the layers except the **Fly** layer, and move the **Fly** movie clip to the left of the stage on the pasteboard. Scrub over to frame 721, and add a key frame on the **Fly** layer. Return the playhead to frame 1.

2. Right-click (Windows) or Control+click (Mac) the label of the **Fly** layer. When the context menu opens, select **Add Classic Motion Guide**, as shown in Figure 1-56. When you release the mouse, a new layer named **Guide:Fly** appears above the **Fly** layer, and the **Fly** layer indents.

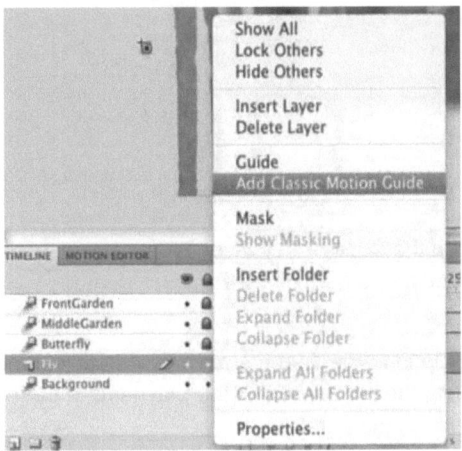

Figure 1-56. Adding a motion guide layer

3. Select the first frame of the **Guide:Fly** layer.

4. Select the **Pencil** tool, and starting where your fly is located, draw a meandering path, as shown in Figure 1-57, around the stage and finishing on the pasteboard on the other side of the stage.

> *Don't forget that you can smooth out the path after you have drawn it. Simply switch to the **Selection** tool, and double-click the path to select it. With the path selected, click the **Smoothing** button at the bottom of the **Tools** panel to make angular changes a bit more rounded.*

Figure 1-57. The path is drawn in the `Guide:Fly` layer. Note that the path starts on the pasteboard to the left and finishes on the pasteboard to the right of the stage.

5. Select the `Fly` movie clip in frame 1, and snap it to the start of the path by dragging it to the start of the path and releasing the mouse. Move the playhead to the end of the timeline, and snap the `Fly` movie clip to the end of the path.

6. Right-click (Windows) or Control+click (Mac) anywhere between the key frames on the `Fly` layer, and select `Create Classic Tween` from the context menu. An arrow, as shown in Figure 1-58, will appear on the `Fly` layer, and if you scrub the playhead, the `Fly` movie clip will travel along the path you drew with the `Pencil` tool.

7. Save the movie.

> If your fly doesn't follow the path, it may not have snapped to the end points of the guide. If this is the case, zoom in on the fly with the magnifying glass tool, and select it. With the fly selected, place the mouse pointer over the fly's registration point—the hollow dot in the selection—and drag the fly to the tip of the line. It should snap into place when you release the mouse.

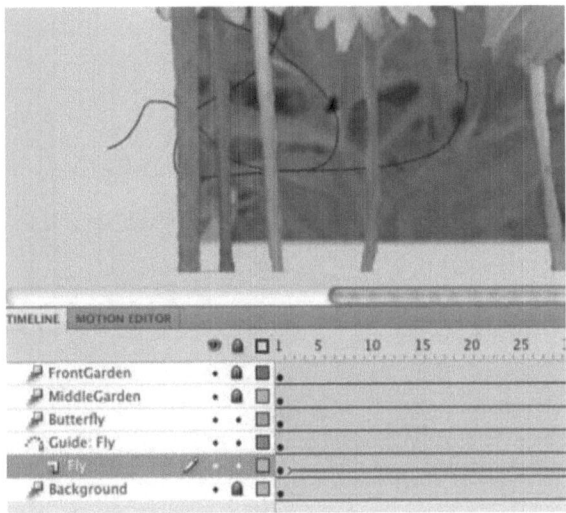

Figure 1-58. The classic tween snaps the movie clip to the path in the `Guide:Fly` layer.

Adding audio

Nothing mystifies us more than Flash designers who regard audio as an afterthought. In many respects, this a huge mistake because audio can actually "seal the deal" when it comes to Flash movies. In this case, it's nice to have a fly buzzing around the movie, but the sound of the fly is what makes this whole thing even more believable. Let's add some audio:

1. Add a new layer above the `FrontGarden` layer, and name it `Audio`.

2. Open the library, and locate the `FliesBuzzing.mp3` file in the Audio folder. Double-click it to open the `Sound Properties` dialog box.

3. Click the `Advanced` button to reveal all the features of this dialog box, as shown in Figure 1-59. Click the `Test` button to preview the audio file. The fly is buzzing, but you can also hear birds and the wind blowing through the garden.

> We would like to thank dobroide at freesound.org for permission to use this clip—20060620.ambiance.forest.summer01.flac—in this project. This clip and others are available at http://www.freesound.org/samplesViewSingle.php?id=20026.
>
> For those of you who are interested, the file was downloaded from freesound.org as a .flac (Free Lossless Audio Codec) file. It was renamed and converted to an .mp3 file using xAct for Macintosh. We are telling you this just in case you are a Mac user and you can't get .flac files from freesound.org to convert to another format.

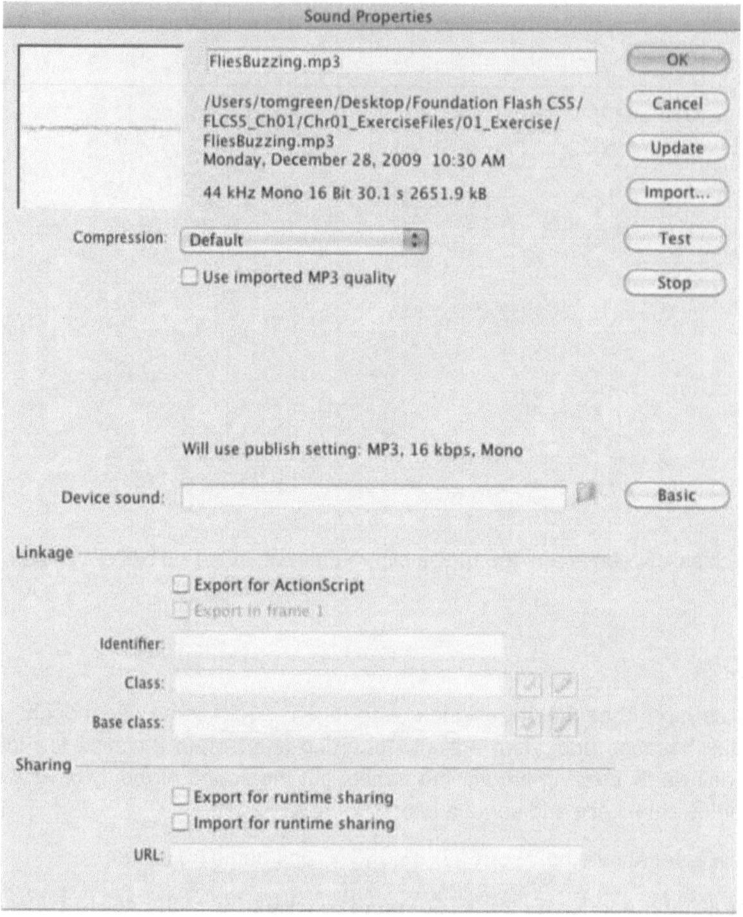

CHAPTER 1

Figure 1-59. Audio can be previewed by clicking the `Test` button.

4. With the `Audio` layer selected, drag the audio file from the `Library` to the stage. When you release the mouse, the audio waveform appears in the layer.

> *Dragging audio from the library and sticking it on the stage is not a good habit to develop. Audio files can be rather large, and when they are in the `Library`, they increase the size of the SWF, which increases the download time, and it gets ugly from there. We have a whole chapter on audio, Chapter 5, devoted to best practices, so for now let's just content ourselves with simply being able to get sound into a presentation and getting it to play.*

5. Click anywhere on the waveform, and you will see the `Properties` panel change to show you the sound properties. If you don't see them, click the `Sound` twirlie.

6. Click the `Sync` drop-down menu, and select `Stream`, as shown in Figure 1-60.

Figure 1-60. Audio waveform on the timeline and the `Sound` properties in the `Properties` panel

7. Scrub across the timeline, and you will hear the audio playing. This is possible because of the use of the `Stream` syncing in the `Sound` properties. Return the playhead to frame 1, and press the Return (Enter) key. The sound will start playing and stop only when the playhead reaches the end of the timeline.

8. Save the file.

> *Noticing a pattern here? Get into the habit of saving your work every time you do something major with your movie. Do this, and it isn't a big deal should your computer crash. Don't get into the habit, and prepare to reconstruct entire files from the point of your last save when the computer crashes.*

Testing and saving Flash files

The fly is merrily buzzing among the flowers. The audio are playing, and the birds are singing. Maybe.

Even though you have created this animation and scrubbed through bits and pieces of it, you still haven't seen the whole project play from start to finish much as it would on a Web page. Now would be a really good time to test the movie in Flash Player. We can't stress enough the importance of test, test, test, and test again! The procedure is, as one of us tells their students, rather simple: "Do a bit. Test it. Do a bit more. Test it." As you have seen, Flash movies can be complex. Each element or feature you add also increases the complexity of the movie. This is why it is so important that you develop the habit of regularly testing your work because, regardless of how simple it may appear to you, this is the place to identify and fix any errors, mistakes, or problems you may see. What it comes down to is this: do you really want to examine the entrails of each frame of a completed movie along with hundreds of lines of code, or do you want to catch simple errors early in the process? Your call.

To test a Flash movie, all you need to do is to press Ctrl+Enter (Windows) or Cmd+Return (Mac), and the movie will start playing in Flash Player. If you prefer to use a menu, select `Control` ➤ `Test Movie`. You will see an alert box telling you the movie is being exported and, when that finishes, the movie, as shown in Figure 1-61, will open in Flash Player. What you should see is the flowers move into place, the fly buzzing around the garden, and you will hear the audio track.

If you open the folder where the file has been saved, you will see that a SWF has been added to the folder. A SWF (pronounced "swiff") is the compact version of your animation that will be placed in a Web page.

Figure 1-61. Testing the movie in Flash Player

The final part is a look at a feature that is new to Flash CS5: the end of the `.fla` format.

A couple of years ago, Richard Galvan, the Flash product manager, made it pretty clear to one of us over lunch that the FLA format was being placed on the "Threatened Species" list. This wasn't too much of a shock because Adobe was starting to concentrate on the fact that data and presentation were two separate entities and data was pretty sexy.

LEARNING THE FLASH CS5 PROFESSIONAL INTERFACE

The FLA format moved onto the "Endangered Species" list in the CS4 release of the product. A new output format—XFL—was introduced to After Effects, and Flash CS4 could read an XFL file but couldn't write one. The release of Flash CS5 marks the start of the old FLA format on its progress toward extinction as the new XFL format takes over. In Flash CS5, the default FLA file you'll save is now created in the XFL format, with the old style of FLA file being relegated to an option for backward compatibility—¡Viva la revolución!

XFL? We know it sounds like an American Football league, but think of the XFL container format as a folder that contains an XML file and all the assets referred to in the XML file. The assets and the XML are the files used to build the FLA. Until this release of Flash, that container has, essentially, been sealed. Not anymore.

1. With your **Garden.fla** file open, select **File ➤ Save As** to open the **Save As** dialog box. Navigate to the **XFL_Example** folder in your Chapter 1 Exercise folder.

2. Click the **Format** drop-down menu, as shown in Figure 1-62, to open it. You now have three choices:

    - **Flash CS5 Document (*.fla)**: Select this, and you create the usual document that can be opened only by Flash CS5.
    - **Flash CS4 Document (*.fla):** Select this, and the file will be saved in a format that can be read by Flash CS4. Just be aware that any features available only in Flash CS5 won't be available.
    - **Flash CS5 Uncompressed Document (*xfl):** Select this, and you create an "exploded" view of the file or what many are calling a **folder of files**.

Figure 1-62. The XFL format is the new kid on the block.

CHAPTER 1

3. Name the file **Garden**, and select the `.XFL` format. Click the **Save As** button. A progress bar will appear as the files are created, and when finished, the progress bar and the **Save As** dialog box will close. Minimize Flash, and open the XML_Example folder.

When the folder opens, you will see that your simple Flash project is now a folder named **Garden**. When you open that folder, you will see your simple file consists of a number of separate XML and Flash files, as shown in Figure 1-63. Now you understand what we meant by the terms *exploded* and *folder of files*.

Name	Date Modified	Size	Kind
▼ Garden	Today, 9:40 AM	--	Folder
▼ bin	Today, 9:39 AM	--	Folder
M 1 1262100258.dat	Today, 9:39 AM	1....B	Microsoft Excel 97-2004 workbook
M 2 1262100258.dat	Today, 9:39 AM	8 KB	Microsoft Excel 97-2004 workbook
M 3 1262100258.dat	Today, 9:39 AM	29 KB	Microsoft Excel 97-2004 workbook
M 4 1262100258.dat	Today, 9:39 AM	29 KB	Microsoft Excel 97-2004 workbook
M 5 1262100258.dat	Today, 9:39 AM	5...KB	Microsoft Excel 97-2004 workbook
M 8 1262554723.dat	Today, 9:39 AM	2....B	Microsoft Excel 97-2004 workbook
M 10 1262219047.dat	Today, 9:39 AM	98 KB	Microsoft Excel 97-2004 workbook
SymDepend.cache	Today, 9:39 AM	4 KB	SimpleText Format
DOMDocument.xml	Today, 9:39 AM	86 KB	eXtensible Markup Language (XML) document
Garden.xfl	Today, 9:39 AM	4 KB	Adobe Flash Document
▼ LIBRARY	Today, 9:40 AM	--	Folder
▶ Audio	Today, 9:39 AM	--	Folder
▶ Fireworks Objects	Today, 9:39 AM	--	Folder
FliesBuzzing.mp3	Today, 9:39 AM	2...KB	MP3 Audio File
▼ MovieClips	Today, 9:39 AM	--	Folder
Background.xml	Today, 9:39 AM	4 KB	eXtensible Markup Language (XML) document
Body.xml	Today, 9:39 AM	4 KB	eXtensible Markup Language (XML) document
BottomFlower.xml	Today, 9:39 AM	4 KB	eXtensible Markup Language (XML) document
Butterfly.xml	Today, 9:39 AM	4 KB	eXtensible Markup Language (XML) document
Fly.xml	Today, 9:39 AM	8 KB	eXtensible Markup Language (XML) document
Front.xml	Today, 9:39 AM	4 KB	eXtensible Markup Language (XML) document
WingL.xml	Today, 9:39 AM	4 KB	eXtensible Markup Language (XML) document
WingR.xml	Today, 9:39 AM	4 KB	eXtensible Markup Language (XML) document
▼ PNG	Today, 9:39 AM	--	Folder
BFlyFlowers.png.xml	Today, 9:39 AM	4 KB	eXtensible Markup Language (XML) document
BottomFlower.png.xml	Today, 9:39 AM	4 KB	eXtensible Markup Language (XML) document
Flowers01.png.xml	Today, 9:39 AM	4 KB	eXtensible Markup Language (XML) document
▼ META-INF	Today, 9:39 AM	--	Folder
metadata.xml	Today, 9:39 AM	12 KB	eXtensible Markup Language (XML) document
MobileSettings.xml	Today, 9:39 AM	Z...KB	eXtensible Markup Language (XML) document
PublishSettings.xml	Today, 9:39 AM	8 KB	eXtensible Markup Language (XML) document

Figure 1-63. The contents of an uncompressed XFL document folder

We are not going to get any deeper into this subject until Chapter 12. Having said that, you need to know the important files are `Garden.xfl` and the `DOMDocument.xml` files. If you double-click the `.xfl` file, the project will open in Flash, and the only difference will be the `.xfl`, not `.fla`, file extension in the document tab.

The XML document is where all the information about the project is kept. This includes pointers to embedded fonts, audio, images, and anything else pertaining to the project including the layering order and the contents of the layers.

> *If you create an uncompressed XFL file or are handed the XFL folder, make sure that you always work in that folder and that you don't, for obvious reasons, delete or remove any files used in the project from the folder.*

You have learned

- How to customize your Flash workspace
- A number of methods of manipulating objects on the Flash stage
- How to dock, undock, and minimize panels
- The importance of the `Properties` panel in your daily workflow
- The difference between a frame and a keyframe
- The process involved in using frames to arrange and animate content and the properties of content on the stage using the `Motion Editor`
- How to add, delete, nest, and rearrange layers
- How to test a Flash movie
- How to create an uncompressed XFL document

That's a lot of stuff you've learned by taking a casual stroll through Flash Professional CS5. In the next chapter, you'll learn how to use the tools to create content in your movies and how Fireworks CS5, Photoshop C4, and Illustrator CS5 are important elements in your workflow.

Chapter 2

Graphics in Flash CS5

In the previous chapter, we handed you a bunch of images and essentially said, "Here, you toss them on the stage." In this chapter, you'll dig into how those objects were created, and in fact, you are going to be drawing trees, drawing the moon, creating Venetian blinds, and playing with Chinese dancers and T-shirts, among other things. You will be looking at the new Illustrator and Photoshop file importers and also playing with JPEG and GIF images. There's a lot to cover. Let's get started.

What we'll cover in this chapter:

- Flash graphic fundamentals
- Using the drawing tools
- Managing and working with color
- Working with fills, strokes, and gradients
- Tracing bitmap images
- Image file formats and Flash
- Importing Illustrator documents into Flash
- Importing Photoshop documents into Flash

If you haven't already, download the chapter files. You can find them at www.friendsofED.com/download.html?isbn=1430229940.

CHAPTER 2

Files used in this chapter:

- FreeTransform.fla (Chapter02/Exercise Files_CH02/Exercise/FreeTransform.fla)
- ObjectDrawing.fla (Chapter02/Exercise Files_CH02/Exercise/ObjectDrawing.fla)
- Deco.fla (Chapter02/ExerciseFiles_CH02/Exercise/Deco.fla)
- DecoCow.fla (Chapter02/ExerciseFiles_Ch02/Complete/ DecoCow.fla)
- DecoCow.swf (Chapter02/ExerciseFiles_Ch02/Complete/ DecoCow.swf)
- Deco02.fla (Chapter02/ExerciseFiles_Ch02/Exercise/ Deco02.fla)
- SprayBrush.fla (Chapter02/ExerciseFiles_Ch02/Exercise/ SprayBrush.fla)
- Campfire.fla (Chapter02/ExerciseFiles_Ch02/Complete/Campfire.fla)
- ImageFill.fla (Chapter02/ExerciseFiles_Ch02/Exercise/ ImageFill.fla)
- CanoeBurnside.jpg (Chapter02/ExerciseFiles_Ch02/Exercise/ CanoeBurnside.jpg)
- Trace.fla (Chapter02/ExerciseFiles_Ch02/Exercise/Trace.fla)
- JPGCompression.fla (Chapter 02/ExerciseFiles_CH02/Exercise/JPGCompression.fla)
- JPGCompression.swf (Chapter 02/ExerciseFiles_CH02/Exercise/JPGCompression.swf)
- GIF.fla (Chapter 02/ExerciseFiles_CH02/Exercise/GIF.fla)
- Counterforce.gif (Chapter 02/ExerciseFiles_CH02/Exercise/Counterforce.gif)
- Banner.png (Chapter 02/ExerciseFiles_CH02/Exercise/Banner.png)
- Mascot.ai (Chapter 02/ExerciseFiles_CH02/Exercise/Mascot.ai)
- IglooVillage.psd (Chapter 02/ExerciseFiles_CH02/Exercise/IglooVillage.psdi)

Before we start, let's take a look at what you have to work with.

Graphics in Flash CS5 come in two flavors: vector or bitmap. **Vector images** are usually created in a drawing application such as Illustrator CS5 or Fireworks CS5. When you draw an object on the Flash stage, you are using the drawing tools to create a vector image. **Bitmap images** are created in such applications as Photoshop CS5 and Fireworks CS5.

At its heart, Flash is a vector drawing and animation tool. The great thing about vectors is their relatively small file size compared to their bitmap cousins. The other thing to keep in mind is that Flash's roots were as a vector animation tool (FutureSplash) for the Web. When it was introduced, broadband was just establishing itself, and the ubiquitous 56KBps modem was how many people connected to the Internet. In those days, size was paramount, and vectors, being extremely small, loaded very quickly.

What makes vectors so appealing is they require very little information and computing power to draw. In very simplistic terms, a circle of 100 pixels in diameter contains five points—four on the circle and one in the center—and those points are used in a mathematical calculation that results in the diameter of the circle. The computer might also need to know whether there is a stroke around the circle and whether the circle is being filled with a solid color. If you assume the circle is yellow and the stroke is 1 point wide and colored black, this circle needs only a small amount of data: the five points, fill color, stroke width, and stroke color. This explains why vectors are best used in situations requiring clean lines and areas of color.

Its bitmap counterpart is treated a lot differently. Instead of requiring a limited amount of information to draw the circle, each pixel's location in the circle is charted and remembered. Not only that, but each pixel will require three units of color information to produce the red, green, and blue values for that pixel. On top of that, the computer also needs to map and draw each pixel in the background the circle is sitting on. Let's assume the circle has a diameter of 100 pixels and is sitting on a white background. The entire image measures 200 by 200, which means each one of the white pixels in the background needs to be mapped as well. This means that producing a simple yellow circle requires thousands of bits of information, which explains why bitmap images add weight to a SWF's file size. This weight is critical because bitmaps best preserve the fine details of an image such as a photograph.

> *All is not "sweetness and light" with vector images. Some of this art can be phenomenally complex with thousands if not millions of points. The best way of deciding whether to go vector or bitmap is to test the movie. Create a test SWF with the original vector artwork and nothing else. Then create a test SWF with the vector art in other formats, such as JPEG, PNG, TIFF, or the like. Go with the one that gives you the smallest SWF.*

Vectors are also device independent. This means they can be scaled to 200 percent and still maintain their crisp edges. Scale a bitmap by that percentage, and the pixels become twice their original size. The image degrades because the pixels are "tied" to the device displaying them, which in this case is a computer monitor. If you've ever printed a photograph and seen a series of blocks in it, as if a mesh had been laid over the image, you've experienced what can happen when a device-dependent format is handled by another device.

What types of graphic objects can Flash use? Flash uses four types of graphic objects:

- **Shapes**: These are usually vector drawings created using the Flash drawing tools or files imported into Flash from Illustrator CS5 or Fireworks CS5.

- **Drawing objects**: These are another sort of shape you draw using the Flash drawing tools. They behave differently from shapes when combined in the same layer, thanks to Object Drawing mode, which you will learn about later in this chapter.

- **Primitives**: These are created by using the `Rectangle Primitive` and `Oval Primitive` tools in the `Tools` panel. These are vector shapes with a difference: they can be modified in nondestructive ways even after they are drawn.

- **Bitmaps**: These are pixel-based images usually created in Photoshop CS5 or Fireworks CS5 an imported into Flash.

So much for the raw material—let's dig into Flash's drawing tools.

The Tools panel

The `Tools` panel, shown in Figure 2-1, is where all your drawing tools are located. Used along with Flash's `Properties` panel, effects, blends, and `Color` panels, Flash's drawing tools put a pretty powerful and high-end graphics package at your disposal.

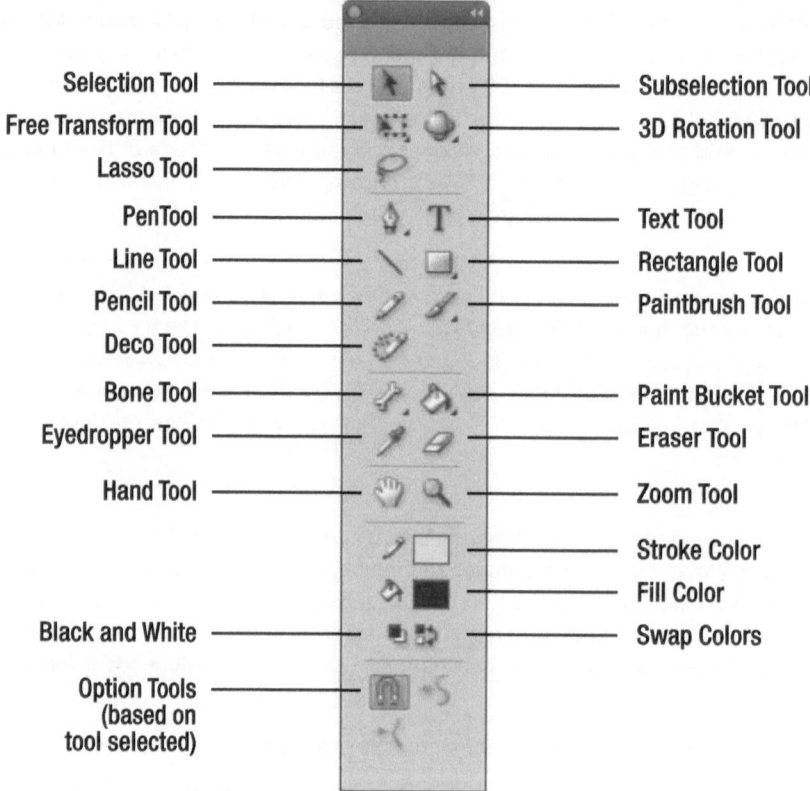

Figure 2-1. The Flash `Tools` panel

The tools can be roughly grouped into six distinct categories. The groupings, from top to bottom, are `Selecting`, `Drawing`, `Modification`, `Viewing`, `Color Modification`, and `Options`.

- **Selecting**: The first two tools and the `Lasso` tool allow you select objects, select points within objects, and even select a piece of an object. The `3D Rotation` and `Free Transform` tools, thematically, fit better into the `Modification` grouping.

- **Drawing**: The seven tools in this section—`Pen` to `Deco`—can be used to draw images, create graphics and text elements, and draw shapes and lines.

- **Modification**: These four tools—**Bone** to **Eraser** along with the **Free Transform** and the **3D Rotation** tools—allow you to select strokes and fills, manipulate shapes and angles, choose a specific color, or even remove a color or piece of an object. For example, you use the **Ink Bottle** tool to change the color of a stroke around a circle and the **Paint Bucket** tool to fill the circle or change its color. These four tools are traditionally used in conjunction with the **Color Modification** tools.

- **Viewing**: The **Grabber Hand** and **Zoom** tools allow you to move around the stage or zoom in on it while you are working.

- **Color Modification**: The four tools in this section—**Stroke Color** to **Swap Color**—allow you to change the colors of selected shapes or set the colors used by other modification tools.

- **Options**: These options change based upon the tool selected. For example, select the **Lasso** tool and the options, as shown in Figure 2-2, change to a **Magic Wand** and **Polygon Lasso**.

> If you have used previous versions of Flash, you may notice that not only have the tools been regrouped, but also the names for the grouping sections have been removed.
>
> Certain tools—**Free Transform**, **3D Rotation**, **Pen**, **Rectangle**, **Paint Bucket**, and the **Stroke** and **Fill** color chips—have a small triangle that looks like an arrow at the bottom right. Clicking this opens a drop-down menu that offers you a subselection of related tool choices. Color chips open the **Color Picker**.

Figure 2-2. Select the Lasso tool, and the tool options change.

The Selection and Subselection tools

The odds are that the `Selection` and `Subselection` tools are the ones you will use most frequently in your everyday workflow. Along with the `Free Transform` and `Gradient Transform` tools, you will use these tools, at least once, in practically any Flash design situation.

1. Open a new Flash ActionScript 3.0 document. Click the `Rectangle` tool, and make sure the `Object Drawing` button (the circle in the `Options` area at the bottom of the toolbar) is deselected. (We aren't going explain why at this point because we have devoted a section of this chapter to that very subject.) Draw a rectangle on the stage. Choosing a color for the stroke and fill is not important right now.

2. Switch to the `Selection` tool, as shown in Figure 2-3, by either clicking it or pressing the V key. When you roll the tool over the square, a cross with arrows appears under the mouse pointer. This means you are hovering over an object that can be moved by clicking and dragging.

> *All tools can be selected using the keyboard. If you roll the mouse pointer over a tool, a tooltip, as shown in Figure 2-3, will appear, and the letter between the brackets is the key that can be pressed to select the tool. If you find tooltips annoying, open `Preferences ▶ General` and deselect `Show tooltips` in the `Selection` section of the `Preferences` dialog box.*

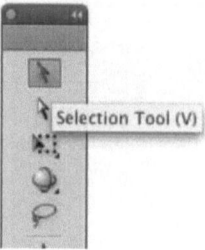

Figure 2-3. Select a tool, and a tooltip will appear.

3. Click the square, and drag to the right. Holy smokes, you just pulled the fill out of the square (see Figure 2-4)! Press Ctrl+Z (Windows) or Cmd+Z (Mac) to undo that last action.

GRAPHICS IN FLASH CS5

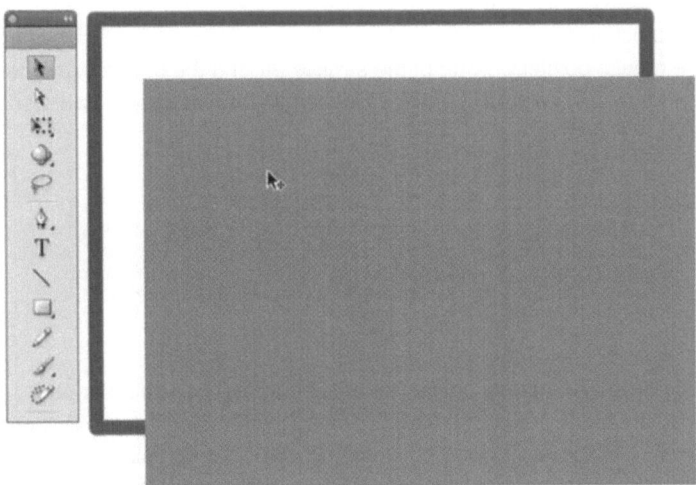

Figure 2-4. Selections in Flash aren't always what they seem.

You have just discovered that Flash regards all objects you draw as being composed of two things: a stroke and a fill. If you are an Illustrator, Photoshop, or Fireworks user, this may strike you as being a bit odd because in a vector universe separating the stroke from its fill is not a common behavior. Give us a minute, and we'll ease you back into more familiar territory. We have a square to move.

4. To select the entire square, you have two choices. The first is to double-click the item. The second is to "marquee" the stroke and the fill by drawing a selection box around the object. To draw your selection box, click outside the rectangle near one of its corners, and then drag toward the opposite corner. Go ahead—try both methods of selection, and drag the square. You'll see the whole square move this time.

5. Now that you know objects drawn on the stage are actually composed of a stroke and a fill, we'd like to mention a third approach to selecting and moving them as a unit. Marquee the object, and select **Modify ➤ Group**. Now, when you click the object, it is regarded as a single entity and can be dragged at will.

You can use the **Selection** tool for more than simply dragging objects around the stage. You can also use it to modify the shape of an object. The square on the stage, as you know, is composed of two vector objects—a stroke and a fill. This means not only can they be moved around the stage, but they also be reshaped and still retain their crisp strokes and fills.

73

6. Select your object on the stage, and select **Modify ➤ Ungroup**. Deselect the objects, and place the tip of the mouse pointer on one of the strokes around the square. Do you see the little quarter circle, as in Figure 2-5, below the arrow? That symbol indicates you can reshape the stroke.

Figure 2-5. The shape under the mouse pointer means the stroke can be reshaped.

7. Click and drag the stroke. When you drag the stroke, it actually bends. This tells you that the stroke is anchored, and, as in Illustrator CS5 or Fireworks CS5, if you drag a point on a line between two anchor points, the line changes its shape. The stroke uses the location of the point where you released the mouse as the apex of the curve. The other thing you may have noticed is, as shown in Figure 2-6, the fill also updates to reflect the new shape.

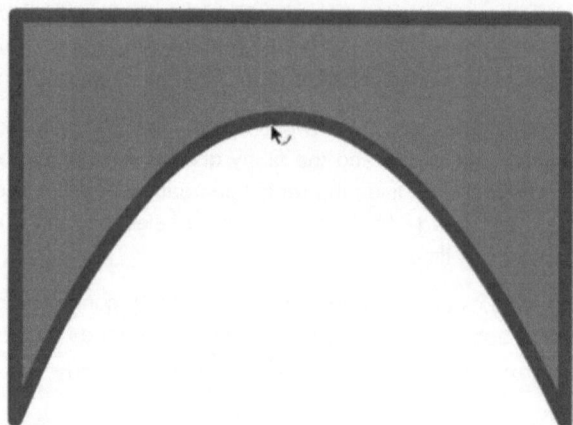

Figure 2-6. Both the stroke and the fill will change to reflect the new shape.

8. Select the **Subselection** tool, or press the A key to switch to this tool. Double-click one of the corner points for the curve you have just created. The points and the handles, as shown in Figure 2-7, become visible. You can further adjust the curve by moving either the handles or the points. These handles are available only on curves.

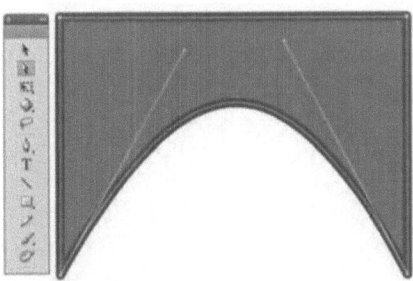

Figure 2-7. Change a shape by dragging a handle or corner point.

Another tool that allows you to manipulate objects on the stage is the `Free Transform` tool, which you will learn about next.

The Free Transform tool

If there is such a thing as an indispensable drawing tool in Flash, this one may just be it. It scales, skews, and rotates objects on the stage. Here is how to use it:

1. Open the `FreeTransform.fla` file in the `Chapter02/Exercises` folder. When it opens, you will see an image of some apple blossoms. They are in a movie clip named **Blossoms**. If you test the movie by pressing Ctrl+Enter (Windows) or Cmd+Return (Mac), you will see the image fade in and out.

2. Select the movie clip on the Flash stage, and select the `Free Transform` tool by either clicking it or pressing the Q key. The selected object sprouts a bounding box with eight handles and a white dot in the center.

3. Move the mouse pointer near each of the corner handles. Notice how, as in Figure 2-8, the mouse pointer develops a rotate icon. This tells you that if you click and drag a corner, you can rotate the object. Try it—you should also see a ghosted representation of the original position of the movie clip, which is a handy feature to ensure the rotation is correct.

4. Test the movie. The movie clip has rotated and fades in and out. This tells you that it isn't only objects that can be transformed. Symbols with tweens and motion and other movie elements can also be transformed with this tool. Close the SWF to be returned to the Flash stage, and let's try something else.

Figure 2-8. Rotating an object using the `Free Transform` tool

5. This time place the mouse pointer on the bounding box. The mouse pointer changes to split arrows. This tells you that clicking and dragging will skew (or slant) the object in the direction in which you drag. Go ahead, give it a try.

6. Now place the mouse pointer directly over one of the handles. It changes to a double-headed arrow, meaning you can scale the object from that point.

The key to mastering the `Free Transform` tool is to master that white dot in the middle. It is the transformation point of the object. Rotations use that dot as a pivot, and any of the other transformations applied using this tool are based on the location of that dot when you hold down the Alt key. Holding down the Alt (Windows) or Option (Mac) key while using the `Free Transform` tool changes the location of the transformation point. For example, if you rotate a corner, the transformation will rotate around the white dot. Hold down the Alt (Windows) or Option (Mac) key, and the rotation will occur around the corner diagonally across from the corner being dragged.

7. Click the white dot, and drag it over the upper-left corner handle. Rotate the object using the handle in the lower-right corner. The rotation occurs around that white dot. Undo the change, and this time scale the object using the bottom-right corner. Again, as shown in Figure 2-9, the upper-left corner is used as the anchor for the transformation.

8. Now try another skew. With the white dot close to one of the corners, place the mouse pointer on the bounding box to see the split arrows icon. Click and drag, and then hold down the Alt (Windows) or Option (Mac) key and drag again. See the difference? Do the same with a scale transform.

GRAPHICS IN FLASH CS5

To constrain the proportions of an object when using the mouse to scale the object, hold down the Shift key before you drag the handle. You can use Shift at the same time as the Alt (Windows) or Option (Mac) key, as described previously, to both constrain and use the white dot as a pivot.

Figure 2-9. The transformation point is moved to the upper-left corner of the image.

> *Applied a couple of transformations and don't want to use them? To remove transformations, select* `Modify` ➤ `Transform` ➤ `Remove Transform` *or press Ctrl+Shift+Z (Windows) or Cmd+Shift+Z (Mac). All transform actions applied to the object will be removed.*

The Gradient Transform tool

To the novice, gradients in Flash can be a little tricky. The reason is you can create the colors in the gradient, but moving them around and changing their direction is not done at the time the gradient is created. This is done using a separate tool.

Let's try a couple of gradient exercises:

1. Open a new ActionScript 3.0 document. Select the `Oval` tool found in the Rectangle drop-down, and deselect the stroke by opening the `Stroke` color swatch panel and selecting the top-right swatch with a diagonal red line through it. Draw a circle on the stage now, and you'll see it has only a fill.

2. With the circle selected, change the width and height values of the circle to `120` and `120` in the **Properties** panel.

3. Click the `Fill` Color chip to open the `Color Chip` panel, and select the blue gradient, shown in Figure 2-10, at the bottom of the panel.

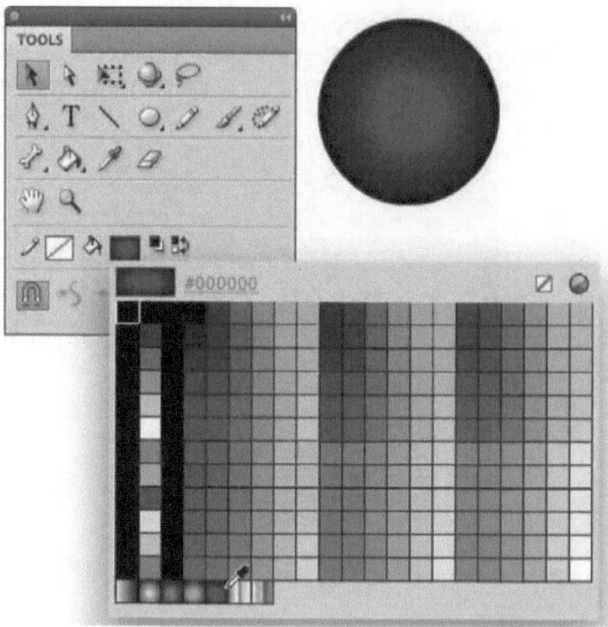

Figure 2-10. Selecting a preset gradient using the Fill color in the Tools panel

There are a couple of ways of changing this gradient in order to position the centered highlight elsewhere in the graphic. The first is to use the Paint Bucket tool. This tool simply fills a selected shape with the color in the Fill color chip, but it does something really interesting when the color is a gradient. Follow these steps:

4. Choose a gradient, and click the Paint Bucket tool to select it (or press the K key to switch to this tool).

5. Click in the upper-left corner of the circle. The center of the gradient moves to the point, where you clicked the mouse, as you can see in Figure 2-11. How this occurred is that the paint pouring out of the tool's icon is the hot spot for the tool. The center of the gradient will be the point where the "pour" is located.

6. Click again somewhere else on the shape to move the center point of the gradient.

The other technique for changing a gradient is to use the Gradient Transform tool, which is more precise than using the Paint Bucket.

7. Click and hold on the Free Transform tool to open the drop-down menu. Select the Gradient Transform tool from the menu. Alternatively, simply press the F key to switch from the current tool to the Gradient Transform tool.

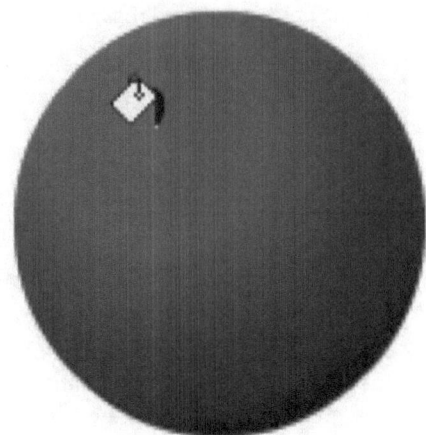

Figure 2-11. The tip or "pour" point of the Paint Bucket's icon is its hot spot.

8. Click the object on the stage. When you do, it will be surrounded by circle, a line will bisect the selection, and three handles will appear, as shown in Figure 2-12. The circle represents the area of the gradient fill.

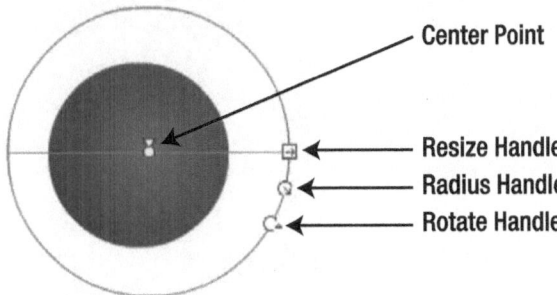

Figure 2-12. The Gradient Transform tool allows you to precisely control a gradient.

Let's look at each of these controls:

- **Center point**: This is actually composed of two features. The white dot is the center point of the gradient and can be moved around in the usual manner. The triangle, which can only move along the line, determines the focus of the center point, which is where the first color, the bright blue, in the gradient first appears.

- **Resize handle**: Dragging this handle resizes and distorts the gradient without affecting the shape of the filled object.

CHAPTER 2

- **Radius handle**: Moving this one inward or outward resizes the gradient proportionally.
- **Rotate handle**: Drag this handle, and the gradient rotates around the center point. The effect can be quite subtle with a radial gradient, but you'll see a difference if you squeeze the gradient into a lozenge shape with the resize handle.

Now that you know how to use the tool on a radial gradient, give it a try on a linear gradient. Here's how:

1. Select one of the linear gradients from the `Fill` color chip in the `Tools` panel.
2. Select the `Rectangle` tool, and draw a square. Click the square with the `Gradient Transform` tool.
3. As you can see in Figure 2-13, the same controls are in place. This time two lines, which indicate the range of the gradient, appear. If you click the resize handle and drag it downward toward the top of the box, the colors in the gradient become more compressed. The rotate and center point handles work in the same manner as their radial gradient counterparts.

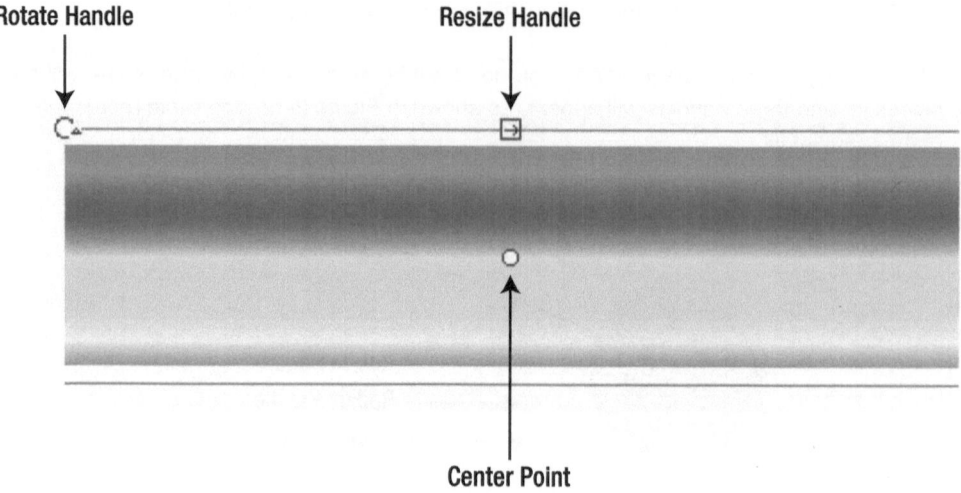

Figure 2-13. The `Gradient Transform` tool can be used on linear gradients as well.

Object Drawing mode

Introduced in Flash 8, the addition of the Object Drawing mode feature was greeted with wild cheering and dancing in the streets. Well, it didn't exactly happen that way, but a lot designers became seriously "happy campers" when they discovered this feature.

Prior to the release of Flash 8, shapes that overlapped each other on the stage were, for many, a frustrating experience. If one shape was over another—in the same layer—and you selected and moved it, it would cut a chunk out of the shape below it. This is not to say it was flaw in the application. This behavior is quite common with painting applications. In Flash, once you understand the "one piece eats the other" phenomenon, it becomes a great construction tool. It can be much simpler to throw down a base shape and purposefully "take bites" out of it to achieve a complex figure than to draw the same figure from scratch. Object Drawing mode uses the opposite concept. You get the best of both worlds, and the choice is yours.

When you select a drawing tool, the `Object Drawing` icon, shown in Figure 2-14, appears in the `Tools` panel. Click it, and the oval you are about to draw will be drawn as a separate object on the stage and will not automatically merge with any object under it, even on the same layer. Let's see how it works.

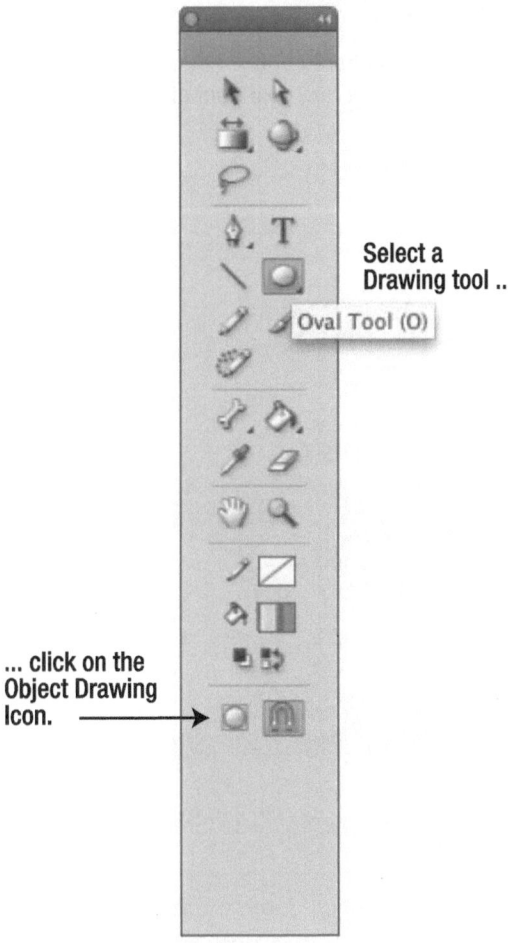

Figure 2-14. Click the `Object Drawing` icon to turn on this feature.

CHAPTER 2

1. Open the `ObjectDrawing.fla` file in your Chapter 2 `Exercise` folder.
2. Select the **Oval** tool, turn off the stroke in the **Tools** panel, and draw a circle over the shape on the stage.
3. Select the circle, and drag it off of the shape. When you release the mouse, you will see that your circle has bitten off a chunk of the shape.
4. Select the **Oval** tool, click the **Object Drawing mode** button in the **Tools** panel, and draw another circle over the shape. Drag it away and nothing happens, as shown in Figure 2-15. Hooray for Object Drawing mode!

When you drew that second circle, Flash offered you a visual clue that you were in Object Drawing mode. When you selected the shape, it was surrounded by a bounding box.

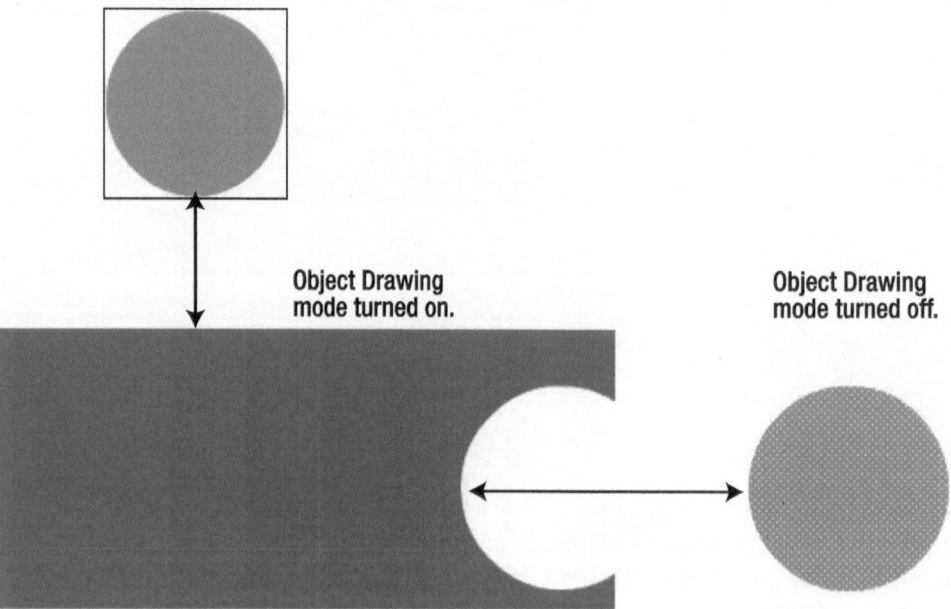

Figure 2-15. The effects of having Object Drawing mode turned on or turned off

> Here's a little trick you can use to edit a single object in Object Drawing mode: double-click the second circle you just drew. Everything but the object you just double-clicked fades, and the words `Drawing Object` appear beside the `Scene 1` link. This allows you to edit the object in place without disturbing anything else on the stage. To return to the stage, click the `Scene 1` link or double-click outside the shape to go back a layer.

Drawing in Flash CS5

In this section, you will review the four primary drawing tools:

- `Pencil`: Use this tool to draw free-form lines and shapes. It is also draws strokes.
- `Brush`: Use this tool to paint in fill colors. A variant of this tool will appeal to the inner delinquent in all of us: the `Spray Brush`.
- `Eraser`: The opposite of the `Brush` tool. It erases and removes rather than fills.
- `Pen`: Use this one to draw Bezier curves.

The Pencil tool

Think of the `Pencil` tool as being a mechanical pencil with a huge number of leads and colors, all of which are available with a simple click. Select the `Pencil` tool, and the `Properties` panel changes (Figure 2-16) to allow you to set properties for the lines you will draw such as line thickness, style, and color.

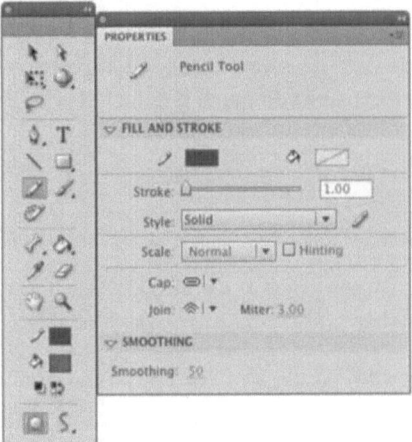

Figure 2-16. The `Pencil` tool and its properties

This tool also has a modifier that appears at the bottom of the `Tools` panel. Click it, and a drop-down menu, as shown in Figure 2-17, gives you three modes to choose from. These modes are important because they control how the line behaves when you draw. Also, when you select this tool, you can choose to use the Object Drawing mode.

Figure 2-17. The Pencil tool has three drawing modes.

Let's try the modes:

1. Open a new Flash document, and select the **Pencil** tool or press the Y key.

2. Using the **Pencil** tool, draw three squiggly lines. Use one of the following three modes for each line. The results, as shown in Figure 2-18, will be slightly different for each. Here's what the modes do:

   - **Straighten**: Use this if you want curves to flatten.
   - **Smooth**: Use this mode to round out kinks or otherwise smooth awkward curves.
   - **Ink**: This is the mode that gives you exactly what you draw. If you use this mode, make sure that **Hinting** in the **Properties** panel is selected. This will ensure crisp, nonblurry lines.

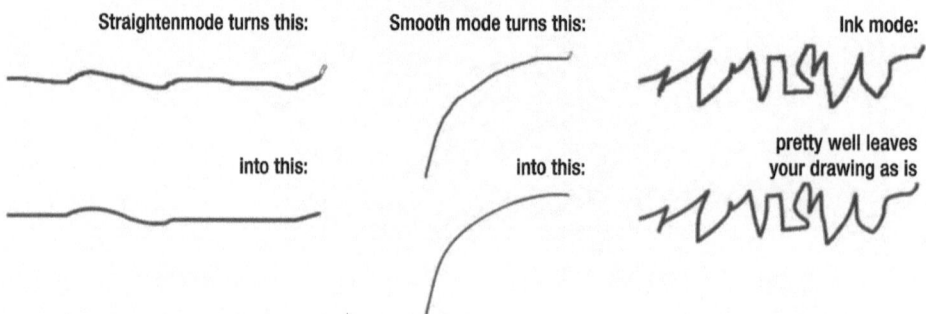

Figure 2-18. The Smooth and Straighten modes can remove awkward angles.

3. Switch to the **Selection** tool, and click the top line. Notice how you selected just a piece of it. The lines you draw with the **Pencil** tool are vectors.

4. Deselect the line segment, and this time roll the mouse over the line. When you see a small curve appear under the mouse, click and drag. This tells you that you can change the shape of the lines you draw by simply moving their segments.

5. Double-click one of the lines, and change the thickness and line type from the drop-down menu in the `Properties` panel. As shown in Figure 2-19, your choices are `solid`, `dashed`, `dotted`, `ragged`, `stippled`, and `hatched`.

Figure 2-19. Choose a line style in the `Properties` panel.

6. Draw a circle using the `Pencil` tool in `Smooth` mode. Select the shape with the `Selection` tool, and in the `Tools` panel click the `Smooth` button. Notice how the awkward edges of your circle become rounded. Now click the adjacent `Straighten` button a couple of times. Your awkward circle actually becomes a round circle. Double-click one of your lines. The `Pencil` options change to show you separate `Straighten` and `Smooth` buttons. Click the `Smooth` and `Straighten` buttons to see how they work on nonclosed shapes. As you can see, these buttons work independently of the `Straighten` and `Smooth` options available through the `Pencil` tool's drop-down menu.

> *Flash has preferences that will help you with your drawing chores. If you select `Edit` ➤ `Preferences` (Windows) or `Flash` ➤ `Preferences` (Mac), you will open the `Preferences` panel. Click the `Drawing` category, and the panel will change to show you how Flash handles the drawing tools, lines, and shapes. The `Recognize shapes` drop-down list can be set to take your hand-drawn approximations of circles, squares, triangles, and the like, and replace them with truer shapes, as if drawn by the `Oval` or `Rectangle` tool.*

The Brush tool

You have discovered that all objects drawn on the stage are separated into strokes and fills. The `Pencil` and `Brush` tools follow that separation. The `Brush` tool feels quite similar to the `Pencil` tool in how it is used. The difference between the two is that the `Brush` tool works with fills while the `Pencil` tool works with strokes, which is a subtle but also quite profound difference.

When you select the `Brush` tool or press the B key to select the tool, a number of options will appear at the bottom of the `Tools` panel, and the `Properties` panel will change, as shown in Figure 2-20.

CHAPTER 2

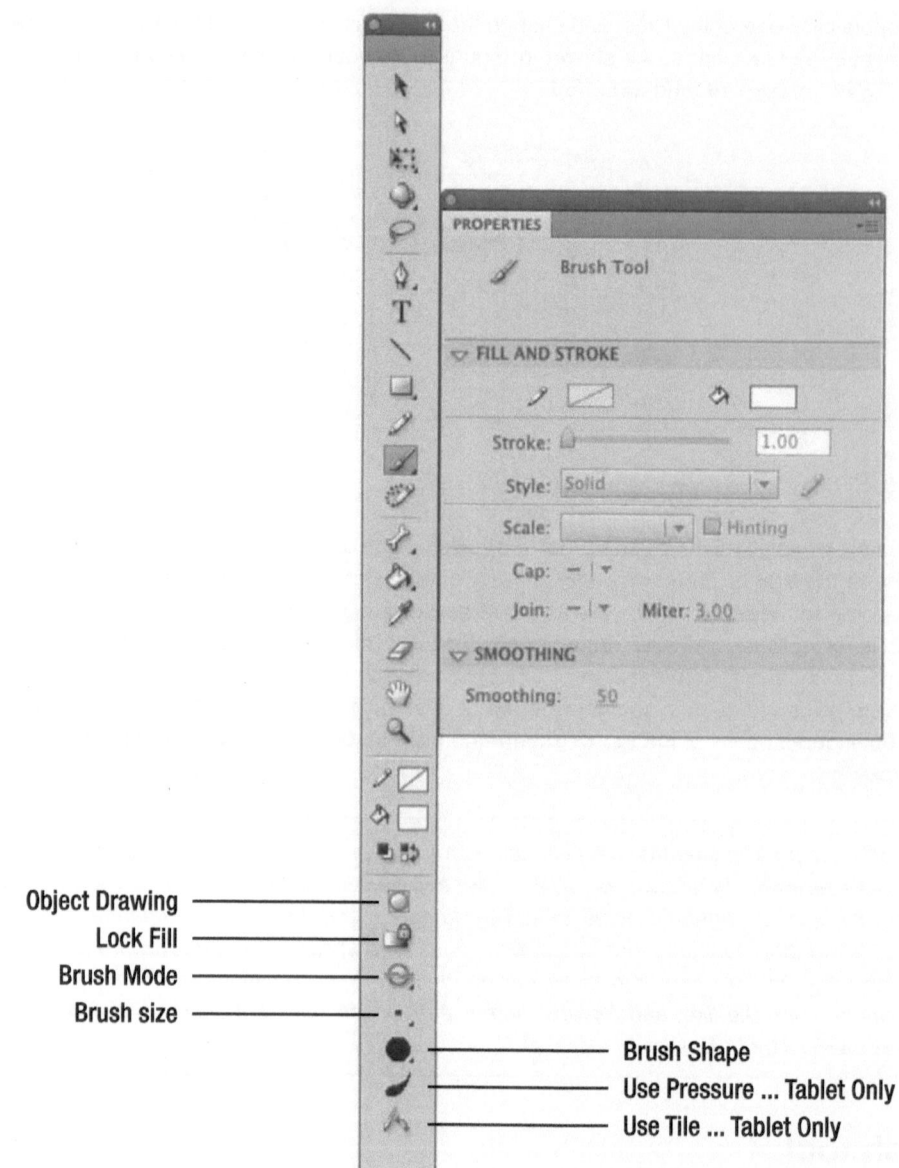

Figure 2-20. The Brush tool options and properties

- **Object Drawing**: You saw this earlier in the chapter. It's the button that toggles Object Drawing mode on and off.
- **Lock Fill**: Select this to fill multiple objects with a single gradient or some other fill. This can be useful in cases where the gradient implies a highlight, because the "lighting" will be applied evenly across all selected objects.
- **Brush Mode**: This controls how the strokes are painted, and the drop-down menu contains the following five modifiers:
  - **Paint Normal**: Paints over anything on the screen providing they are on the same layer and not in Object Drawing mode. These caveats apply to the other mode options as well. If your content is a drawing object, use **Modify ➤ Break Apart** to turn it into a shape. When you finish, you can put it all back together as a single object by selecting **Modify ➤ Combine Objects**.
  - **Paint Fills**: Paints the fills and leaves the stroke alone.
  - **Paint Behind**: Paints only on the empty areas of the layer.
  - **Paint Selection**: Paints only on the selected areas of the object.
  - **Paint Inside**: Paints only inside the area surrounded by a stroke. This mode works only if the **Brush** tool starts inside the stroke; otherwise, it acts like **Paint Behind**.
- **Brush Size**: Use this to change the width and spread of the brush strokes.
- **Brush Shape**: This drop-down menu offers a number of brush shapes ranging from round to square.
- **Use Pressure and Use Tilt**: These two appear only if a tablet is attached to the computer. They allow you to use the pressure and angle settings of a graphics tablet's pen. This is a piece of hardware with a special drawing surface and "pen" that translates your actual hand motions into drawings on the screen.

The final control is the **Smoothing** option on the **Properties** panel. This option determines the amount of smoothing and sharpness applied to an object drawn with the **Brush** tool. In many respects, it is the same as the **Smooth** mode of the **Pencil** tool. Try it:

1. Select the **Brush** tool, and select a fill color.
2. Turn off Object Drawing mode, and make sure the **Brush** mode is set to **Paint Normal**.
3. In the **Properties** panel, set the **Smooth** value to 0, and draw a squiggle on the screen.
4. Set the **Smooth** value to 50, and draw another squiggle on the screen. Repeat this step with a value of 100. As you can see in Figure 2-21, the edges move from rough to smooth and flowing.

If these strokes don't look all that different from each other, take a look at Figure 2-22. The number of vector points used to create the object reduces significantly as the **Smoothing** value increases. To see for yourself, select the **Subselection** tool, and click the edge of each scribble. The vector points become visible. Remember, vector points require processing power to draw on the screen at runtime. Which will appear quicker: the squiggle on the left or the one on the right?

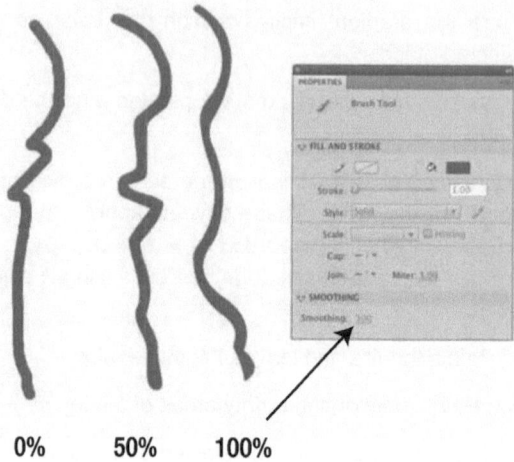

Figure 2-21. Smoothing brush strokes

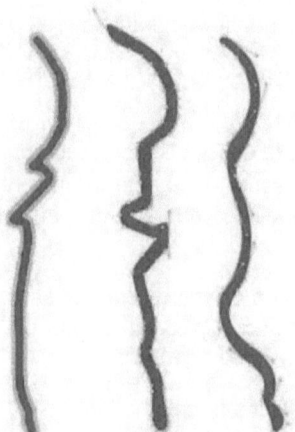

Figure 2-22. Smoothing reduces a haze of points on the left to a manageable number toward the right.

The Deco tool

When it was first introduced in Flash CS4, Flash designers greeted the `Deco` tool with a resounding, "I don't get it." This was quite understandable because all it seemed to do was draw vines, and their clients weren't exactly overwhelming them with requests for vines. If you think we are kidding, try it for yourself:

1. Open a new Flash document, and select the `Deco` tool.

2. Click anywhere in the upper-left corner of the stage to watch Flash draw a bunch of vines and flowers, as shown in Figure 2-23.

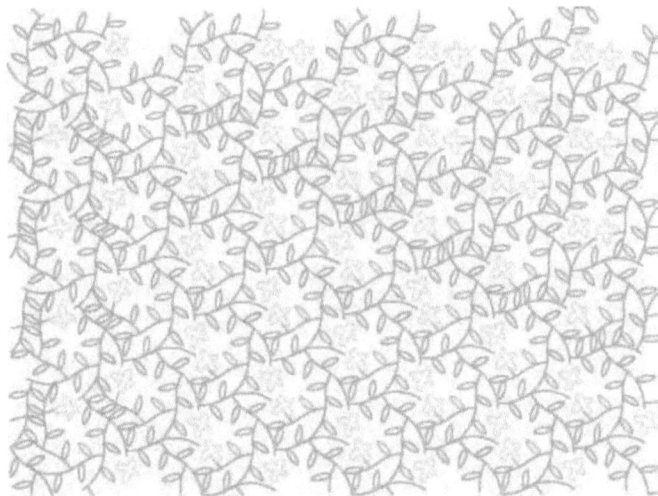

Figure 2-23. The Deco tool's default value is a tangle of vines and flowers.

If you need a stage full of vines, now you know where to go. Unfortunately, this is where many Flash designers stop. This tool's value isn't in its default setting but in its purpose: it is a JavaScript-based drawing tool that allows you to create new drawing tools. This tool, and its counterpart the Spray Brush tool, were introduced in Flash CS4 as part of a new infrastructure called **procedural modeling**, which is "techie talk" for using the computer code to draw.

> For those of you just itching to see the code that drives these things, they can be found in the following location from where you installed Flash: Adobe Flash CS5/Common/First Run/ ProcScripts. The .jsx files you see drive the brushes, and the visual assets used by those files can be found in the svg folder. If you do want to make changes, we can't stress strongly enough how important it is to make any changes to a copy of the file. At the time this book was being written, there wasn't any documentation regarding the Deco scripting APIs. Adobe tells us it is in the process of creating this documentation, but there is no date for its release.

So, how can you properly use this tool? Read on:

1. Open the Deco.fla file in the Chapter 2 Exercise folder. When it opens, you will see a blank stage, and in the **Library** there is a movie clip named **Box**.

2. Reselect the Deco tool, and take a look at the Drawing Effect area in the Properties panel. There is a drop-down menu. That's your ticket to fun and a chance for you to explore a major change to this tool in Flash CS5. Change the drop-down from Vine Fill to Grid Fill.

At this point, you could play around with the Deco tool, but it really becomes interesting when it has something to play with. When you selected Grid Fill, the Properties panel changed to show four tile strips with Edit buttons and a color fill, as shown in Figure 2-24.

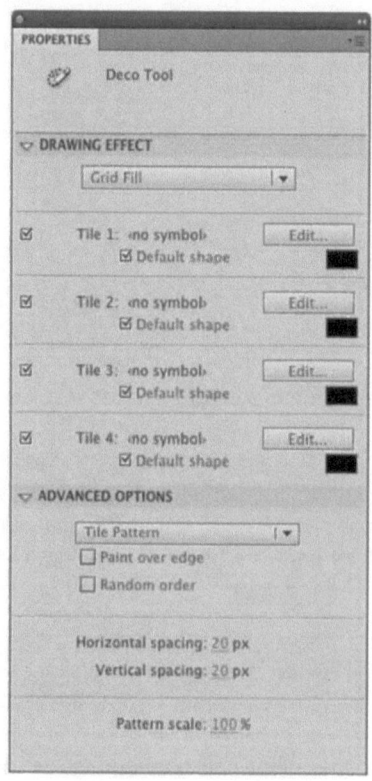

Figure 2-24. The Deco tool's Grid Fill properties

3. Change the Tile 2 color to yellow, and click the stage once. The stage fills with a bunch of black and yellow boxes spaced according to the Horizontal and Vertical spacing values in the Advanced Options. Double-click the Eraser tool to clear the stage.

4. Deselect Tiles 2, 3, and 4. Click the Edit button in Tile 1 strip to open the Select Symbol dialog box. Click the Box symbol once, and click the OK button to close the dialog box.

5. Twirl down the Advanced Options, and set the Horizontal and Vertical spacing values to 0. This will tighten up the spacing between the repeated Box symbols you are about to see.

6. Click once near the upper-left corner of the stage, and you will get the pattern shown in Figure 2-25. If you switch to the **Selection** tool and click the pattern, you will discover the pattern is a single object, which means it can be moved around the stage. This tool doesn't just cover the stage with a pattern; it can be used as a fill brush.

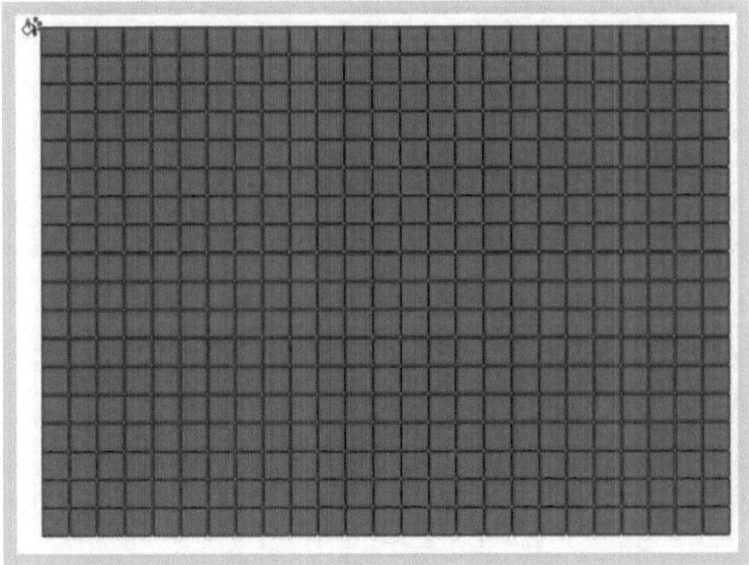

Figure 2-25. The Deco tool's Grid Fill options can be used to create grids.

7. Double-click the **Eraser** tool to clear the stage. Select the **Rectangle** tool, and set its fill to none. Draw a rectangle on the stage.

8. Click the **Deco** tool once, and in the **Advanced Options**, select **Floor Pattern** from the new **Pattern** drop-down menu. Click once inside the rectangle, and, as shown in Figure 2-26, the object looks like it is filled with floor tiles.

> *Keep in mind the important aspect of this section is not the tool. It is the fact you can use a movie clip to create the drawing. One of the authors demonstrated this in a seminar. Rather than use squares, he used a movie clip of a cow that was scaled and rotated. If you open the DecoCow.fla or DecoCow.swf file in the Completed folder, you can see the example used in the presentation.*

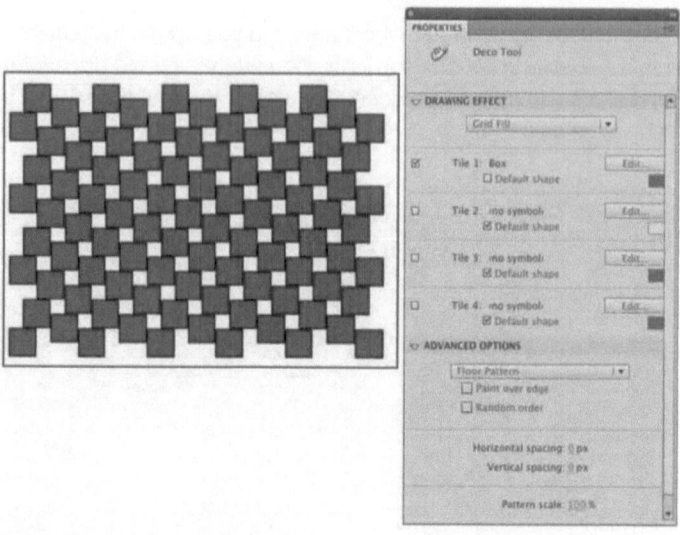

Figure 2-26. Deco tool patterns can be used to fill objects you draw in Flash.

As you can see, you can use the tool to create interesting backgrounds, flags, quilts, or whatever else you may create that requires a grid layout. Using the Deco tool is a lot less work than placing these elements by hand.

Ready for a truly versatile Deco tool option?

1. Open the Deco02.fla file in you Chapter 2 Exercise folder. You will see, in the Library, a movie clip containing an image of a lake in northern Ontario.

2. Click the Deco tool, and select Symmetry Brush from the drop-down list in the Drawing Effect area of the Properties panel.

3. Using the Edit button, make sure that Lake is the selected symbol.

4. In the Advanced Options, select Reflect Across Line in the drop-down list.

5. Start clicking the stage with the Deco tool. When you click, don't immediately release the mouse. Instead, click and hold and drag around a bit to see how that affects the Lake symbol. Being in Reflect Across Line mode means you see a mirror image, as shown in Figure 2-27, on the other side of the line of where you placed the Lake movie clip.

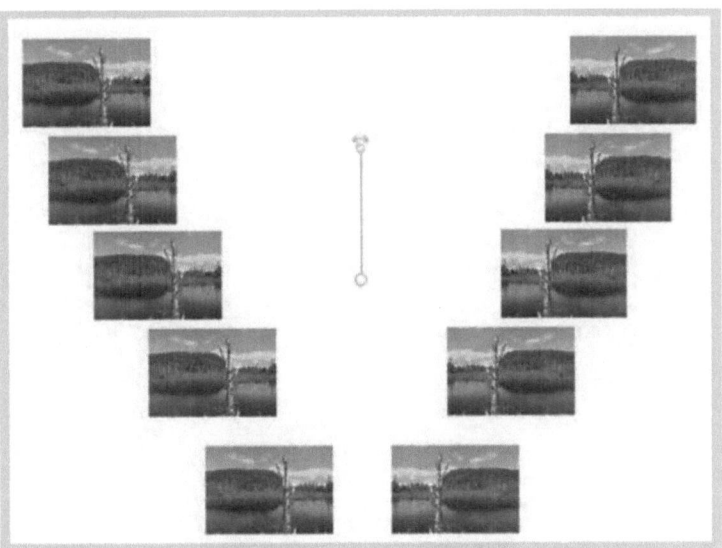

Figure 2-27. The `Reflect Across Line` option lets you create mirrored artwork.

6. Place the mouse pointer over the pivot handle (it is the one with curved double-headed arrow), and drag it in an arc. As you drag, two things happen: the pattern rotates, and each movie clip rotates. Drag the handle back to the start position.

7. In the **Properties** panel, switch the `Advanced Option` to `Reflect Across Point`. One of the arms will disappear because the mirroring is now up and down as well as left and right.

8. In the **Properties** panel, switch to `Rotate Around`. This time, the content looks like a kaleidoscope because of the mirroring increase.

9. If you move the double-curved arrow, the artwork rotates, and the circle in the center lets you move the whole shebang around the stage. The handle with the + sign lets you change the number of arms in the "pinwheel." Click and drag that handle clockwise or counterclockwise, and you can, as shown in Figure 2-28, have quite a few copies of the movie clip appear on the stage.

10. Let's finish this part up with a look at the `Grid Translation` option. Double-click the `Eraser` tool to clear the stage, and select the `Deco` tool. Make sure the `Symmetry Brush` is chosen from the `Drawing Effect` drop-down menu, and select `Grid Translation` from the `Advanced Options` drop-down menu.

11. Click once in the graph area and a couple of copies of the movie clip will appear on the stage. Drag the handles with the + sign up and out to add more copies of the movie clip and to fill the stage with a pattern, as shown in Figure 2-29.

Figure 2-28. The Rotate Around option lets you create kaleidoscopic artwork.

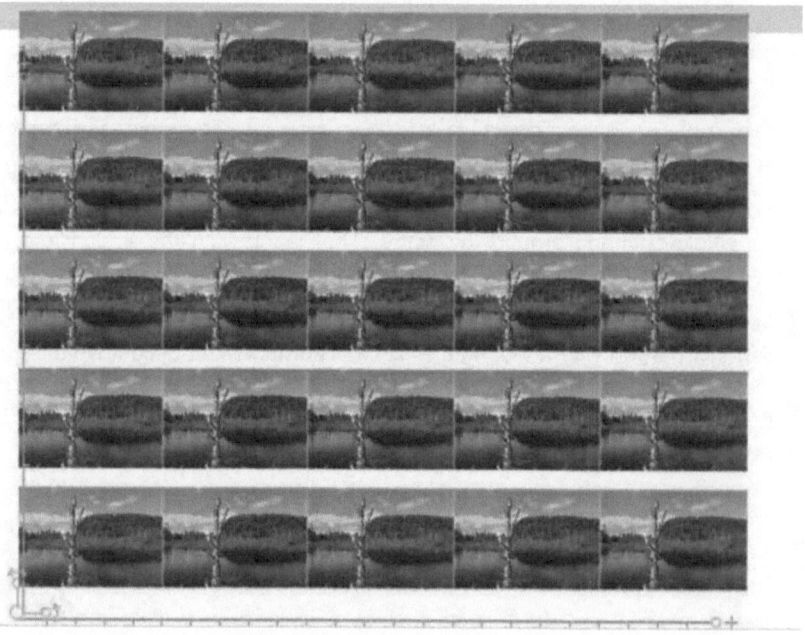

Figure 2-29. The Grid Translation option gives you dynamically modifiable grids.

The major difference between this and the `Grid Fill` option is the fact that, with `Grid Translation`, you can actually modify the grid's characteristics dynamically. By this we mean you can drag and rotate the handles to change the look of the grid.

We are going to finish our exploration of the `Deco` tool by trying a couple of the new brushes in the `Drawing Effect` drop-down. Before we start, it is important for you to understand that these brushes demonstrate the concept of procedural modeling; they aren't professional-grade drawing brushes, but they are fun to use. Here's how:

1. Open the `Deco03.fla` file from your Chapter 2 `Exercise` folder, and select the `Deco` tool.

2. In the `Drawing Effect` drop-down, select the `3D` brush. Click the `Edit` button in the Object 1 strip, and select the `Lake` movie clip. This tool works best if you use a movie clip with the brush.

3. Twirl down the `Advanced Options`, and use these settings:

    - `Max objects`: 1000
    - `Spray area`: 50 px
    - `Perspective`: Selected
    - `Distance scale`: 10%
    - `Random scale range` : 50%
    - `Random rotation range`: 45 deg

4. Click and drag the brush around stage. When you stop, you will see, as shown in Figure 2-30, that quite a few copies of the movie clip are on the stage and that they recede, thanks to the `Perspective` selection, into the distance as you drag away from your starting point.

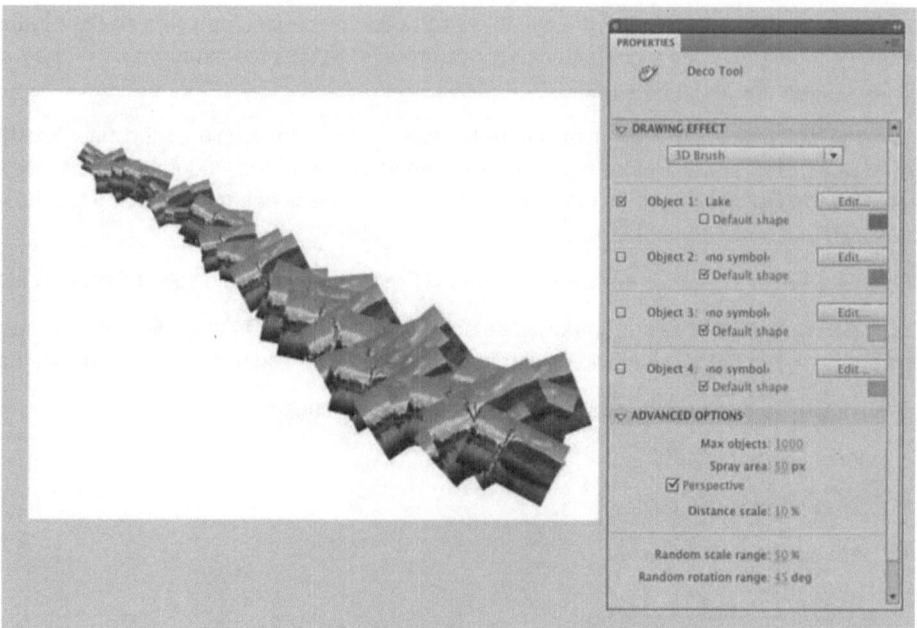

Figure 2-30. The 3D brush uses perspective to give the effect of distance.

What is not commonly known is that the "official" name for the group of tools comprising the `Deco` and `Spray Brush` tools is **Decorative drawing tools**. Their description in the Adobe Flash CS5 documentation is quite succinct: "The Decorative drawing tools let you turn graphic shapes that you create into complex, geometric patterns. The Decorative drawing tools use algorithmic calculations—known as procedural drawing. These calculations are applied to a movie clip or graphic symbol in the `Library` that you create. In this way, you can create a complex pattern using any graphic shape or object." Follow these steps to use the `Deco` tool to create a cityscape.

1. Open a new Flash document.
2. Select the `Deco` tool, and click the `Properties` panel. In the `Drawing Effect` drop-down, select the `Building Brush`, and in the `Advanced Options`, select `Random Building` and set `Building Size` to 5.
3. Don't simply click the mouse to draw a building. Click where you want the building to start and drag upward. When you release the mouse, a building will appear. Draw a few more buildings, as shown in Figure 2-31. If you want a bit more variety, change the `Building Size` value before drawing a building.

GRAPHICS IN FLASH CS5

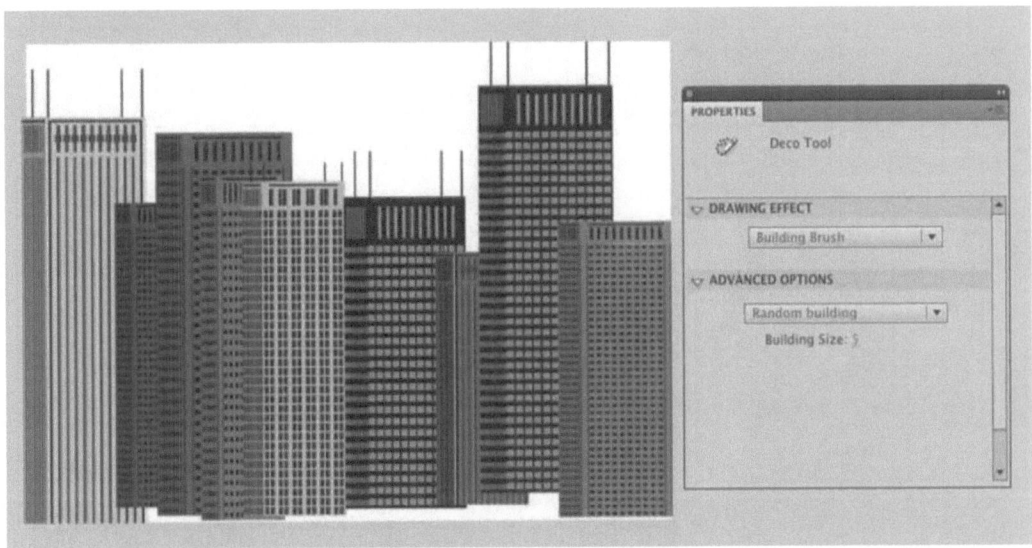

Figure 2-31. Using procedural drawing to create a block of skyscrapers

Let's add some trees. Here's how:

4. Add a new layer to the document.

5. Select the `Deco` tool, and select `Tree Brush` from the `Drawing Effect` drop-down. In the `Advanced Options`, select `Poplar Tree` from the drop-down.

6. Place the brush where you want the tree to grow, and click and drag upward. As you "draw," the trunk will appear and then the foliage. If you want a "bushier" tree, hold the mouse button down for a second before releasing it. Branches, as shown in Figure 2-32, will be added.

CHAPTER 2

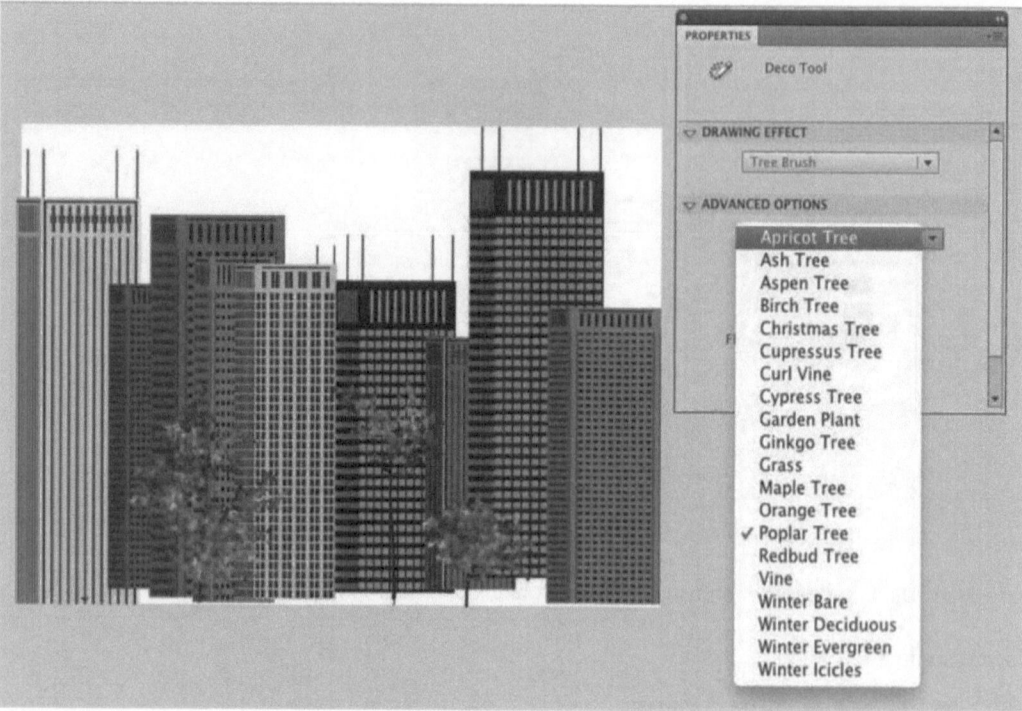

Figure 2-32. Pick a tree...any tree.

The Spray Brush tool

There is a tool in the CS5 lineup that is seriously fun to use. The tool? Introduced in Flash CS4, it is called the `Spray Brush` tool, and, like the `Deco` tool, it is part of the procedural modeling framework. Here's how to use it:

1. Open the `SprayBrush.fla` file in the `Exercise` folder. When it opens, you will notice there is a movie clip symbol named `Figurine` in the `Library`.

2. Click the drop-down menu for the `Brush` tool, and you will see the `Spray Brush` tool. Select it. The tool's icon looks like a can of spray paint. This should tell you that you are about to become a graffiti artist.

GRAPHICS IN FLASH CS5

3. .Open the **Properties** panel shown in Figure 2-33, and the tool's properties are available to you. The properties are as follows:

   - **Default Shape**: You can spray with a symbol in the **Library** or a series of dots by selecting **Default Shape**. Click the color chip under the **Edit** button, and you can change your paint color.
   - **Scale width**: Scrub across this to make the paint drops wider. This is available only if you spray using a **Library** symbol.
   - **Scale height**: Scrub across this to make the drops higher.
   - **Random scaling**: Select this to have nonuniform paint drops.
   - **Rotate symbol**: Select this, and the symbol being sprayed onto the canvas will rotate. This is available only if you spray using a **Library** symbol.
   - **Random Rotation**: Select this, and the symbol will rotate in a random manner.

4. So much for the theory; let's have some fun.

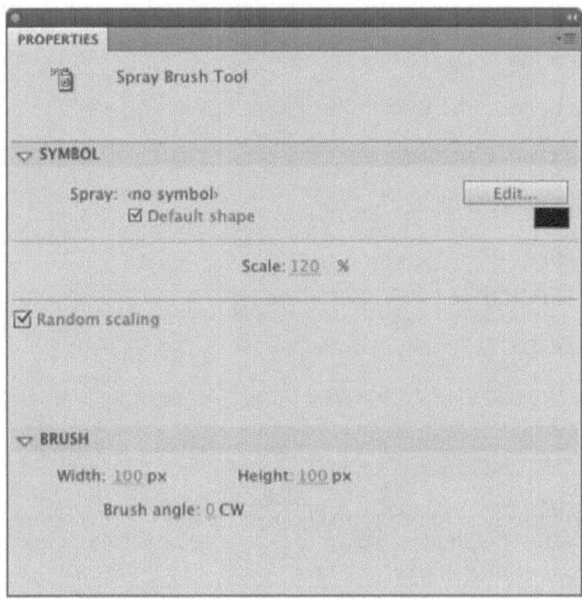

Figure 2-33. Spray Brush tool properties

5. With the `Spray Brush` tool selected in the `Tools` panel, open the `Properties` panel, and use these settings:
   - `Default shape`: Selected
   - `Color`: #000099 (Blue)
   - `Scale width`: 200%
   - `Random scaling`: Selected

6. Click the mouse a couple of times on the stage. Now click and drag the mouse. Having fun? Double-click the `Eraser` tool to clear the stage.

7. Change the brush's `width` and `height` values in the `Properties` panel to `85`, and change the angle to `150 CW`. Click and drag. As you can see, you can create some pretty interesting effects by changing the properties of the brush.

Where this tool moves from neat to really cool is its ability to spray `Library` items onto the stage. If you open the `Library`, you will see we have included a `Figurine` movie clip symbol in the `Library`.

8. With the `Spray Brush` selected, click the `Edit` button in the `Properties` panel. This will open the `Select Source Symbol` dialog box. Click the `Figurine` symbol once, and click `OK`.

9. Use these values in the `Properties` panel:
   - `Scale width and height`: 150%
   - `Random scaling`: Selected
   - `Random rotation`: Selected
   - `Brush Width`: 53 px
   - `Brush Height`: 100 px
   - `Brush angle`: 0 CW

10. Click the mouse. Holy figurines! Click and drag. You have just created a bunch of figurines, as shown in Figure 2-34.

> Here's a really neat trick. If you use a movie clip symbol, you can spray paint animated artwork onto the stage. Need twinkling stars in a night sky? Create the twinkling star in a movie clip and paint it into the sky.

GRAPHICS IN FLASH CS5

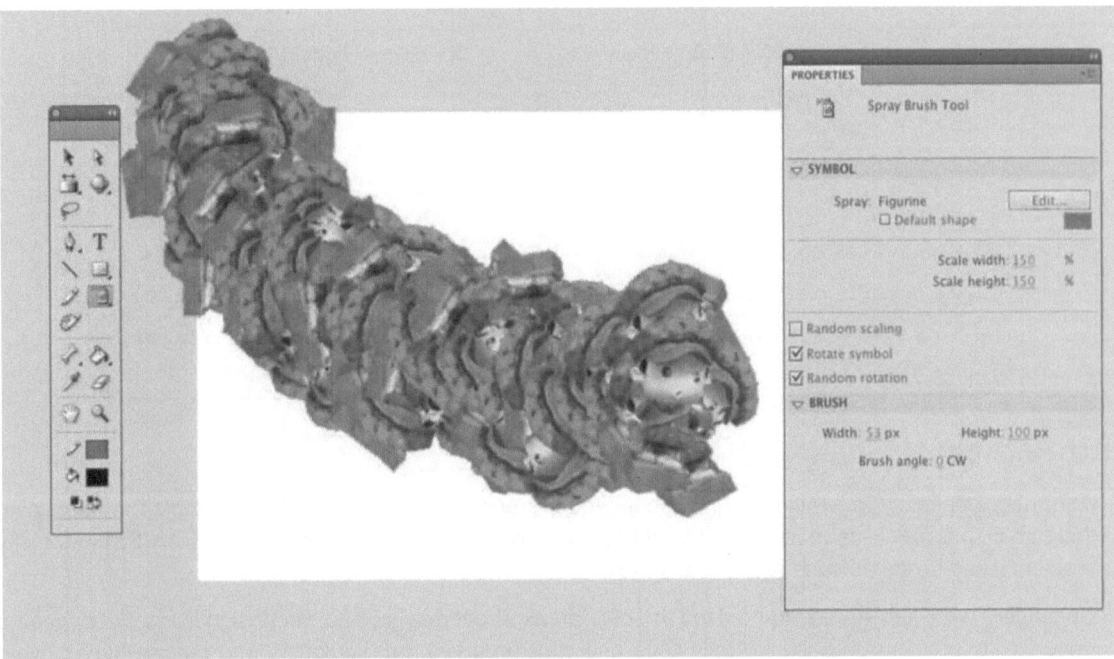

Figure 2-34. `Spray Brush` properties

The Eraser tool

The `Eraser` tool is quite similar to the `Brush` tool, only it erases rather than paints. Select the `Eraser` tool or press the `E` key, and the following three modifiers, shown in Figure 2-35, appear in the `Tools` panel:

- **`Eraser Mode`**: There are five choices in this drop-down menu, and they match those in the `Brush` tool.

- **`Eraser Shape`**: The choices in this drop-down menu let you select from a number of shapes for the eraser.

- **`Eraser Faucet`**: Select this, and you can erase an entire fill or line with one click. The hot spot is the drip on the faucet.

101

CHAPTER 2

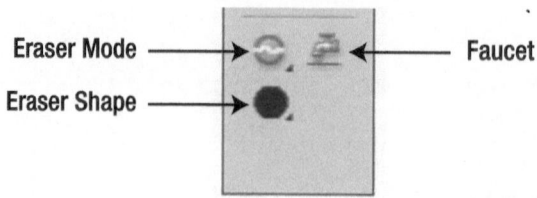

Figure 2-35. The Eraser options

> Here's a quick way to erase the contents of an entire layer: double-click the Eraser tool to clear your layer.

The Pen tool

If you use Illustrator, Fireworks, or Photoshop, you are accustomed to using the Pen tool. The interesting thing about this tool is its roots aren't found in the graphics industry. It started out as a solution to a tricky problem faced by the auto industry in the 1970s.

Computers were just starting to be used in some areas of car design, and the designers involved faced a rather nasty problem: they could draw lines and simple curves, but squiggles and precise curves were completely out of the question. The solution was to use a calculation developed by the mathematician Pierre Bezier to produce what we now know as **Bezier curves**.

A simple curve is composed of a number of points. A Bezier curve adds two additional pieces of data called **direction** and **speed**. These two data bits are visually represented by the handle that appears when you draw a curve with the Pen tool. Here's how to create a Bezier curve:

1. Open a new Flash document, and select the Pen tool or press the P key. When you place the mouse pointer on the stage, it changes to the pen, and a small *x* appears next to it.

2. Click and drag. As you drag, you will see three points on the line, as shown in Figure 2-36. The center point, called the **anchor point**, is the start of the curve, and the two outer points, called **handles**, indicate the direction and degree of the curve.

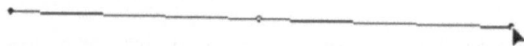

Figure 2-36. The start of a Bezier curve

3. Roll the mouse to another position on the screen, and click and drag the mouse. As you drag, the mouse handles and the curve get longer, and the curve follows the direction of the handle, as shown in Figure 2-37.

4. Click and drag a couple of more times to add a few more points to the shape.

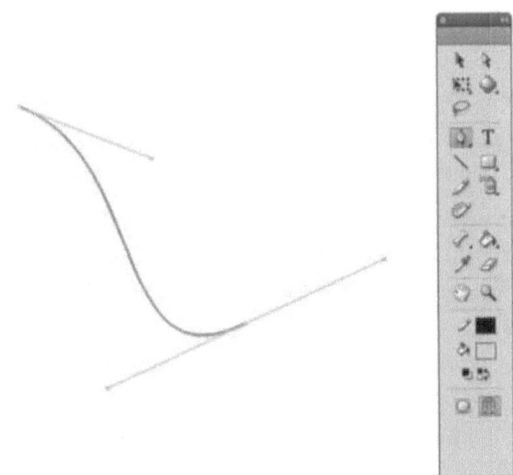

Figure 2-37. The curve shape changes based on the length and direction of the handle.

5. Roll the mouse over the starting point of the shape. Notice the little o under the `Pen` tool, as shown in Figure 2-38? This tells you that you are about to create a closed shape. Click the mouse.

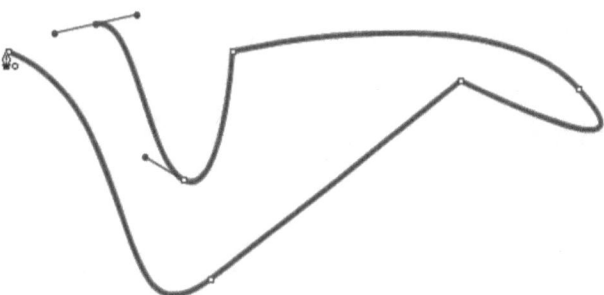

Figure 2-38. The shape is about to be closed.

A couple other options are available to you with the `Pen` tool that will allow you to edit your curves. If you click and hold the `Pen` tool in the `Tools` panel, you will see there are three extra choices:

- `Add Anchor Point`: Select this tool, and click anywhere on the line to add an extra point.
- `Delete Anchor Point`: Click an anchor point to remove it. The shape will change.
- `Convert Anchor Point`: Click an anchor point, and the point will be converted to a corner point. Unfortunately, this conversion does not go both ways. To get your curve back, switch to the `Selection` tool, and hover near a line that extends from the corner point. When you see the curve mouse pointer, drag out a bit of curvature yourself, and then switch back to the `Pen` tool.

Prior to Flash CS3, these alternate `Pen` tool modes were not available as separate tools, so the distinction is a great addition. You can, however, access the functionality of each tool from the main `Pen` tool. Here's the wrapped-up-in-one approach:

- **Adding an anchor point**: Using the `Pen` tool, hover over an existing line. Note how the normal `x` under the mouse pointer becomes a `+`. Click to add a new anchor.

- **Deleting an anchor point**: Hover over a corner point, and you'll see the mouse pointer acquire a little `-`. Click to delete the anchor. Hover over a normal anchor, and you'll have to click twice: once to convert the anchor to a corner point and a second time to delete it.

- **Converting an anchor point**: Well, you just saw this in the previous bullet point. But note, in addition, that the Alt (Windows) or Options (Mac) key temporarily converts the `Pen` tool into the `Convert Anchor Point` tool.

Your turn: let's have a campfire

It's time to try what you have been experimenting with. In this little exercise, you are going to draw a small campfire in the woods. Along the way, we are going to introduce you to a couple of new tools. Let's get to work:

1. Open a new Flash document file, and save it to your Chapter 2 `Exercise` folder.

2. Select `Insert` ➤ `New Symbol`. When the `New Symbol` dialog box opens, name the symbol `Trees`, and select `Graphic` as its `Type`. Click `OK` to accept the changes and to open the `Symbol Editor`. The tree you are about to draw will form the basis for this entire exercise.

Drawing the tree trunk

You'll start by drawing the trunk of the tree.

1. Select the `Pencil` tool, and in the `Smooth` mode, draw a stretched oval shape. Don't worry about the stroke or fill. We'll get to that in a moment. This will be the tree trunk. Select the shape on the stage, and click the `Smooth` button.

2. Select the `Zoom` tool, which looks like a magnifying glass, and click and drag over your shape. When you release the mouse, the shape will be larger, and you will be able to manipulate it more easily.

3. Switch to the `Subselection` tool, and click your shape. You will see the vector nodes and handles. Manipulate the nodes and handles to change the shape of the trunk. Refine the shape by rolling the mouse pointer over it, and when you see the curved line under the mouse pointer, drag the line segment you are over inward or outward to refine the shape.

4. When you finish, double-click the `Zoom` tool on the `Tools` panel to zoom out to `100 percent` view.

GRAPHICS IN FLASH CS5

5. Switch to the `Selection` tool, click your shape, and in the `Properties` panel specify these values:

   - `Width`: 20
   - `Height`: 45
   - `X`: 35
   - `Y`: 104.5
   - `Stroke Color`: #480000 (dark brown)

   If you really need to see the decimal values while scrubbing, hold down the Ctrl key (Windows) or Control (Mac), and you will be able to scrub using decimal values.

6. In the `Tools` panel, set the `Fill` color to `#480000`, and select the `Paint Bucket` tool or press the `K` key. Place the tip of the bucket in the hollow part of the shape, and click the mouse. The tree trunk, as shown in Figure 2-39, will fill with the dark brown color. (An alternative would be to select the `Brush` tool and, using the `Paint Inside` mode, paint the fill color into the shape.)

   You are probably looking at the `Hex` color value in the panel and thinking, "Hey, it's blue. I can scrub it to get the color." Be our guest. Give it a shot. Not easy, is it? When choosing color values, forget about scrubbing and directly input them instead. Why? You have more than 16 million colors to scrub through.

7. Right-click the shape you have just drawn, and select `Convert To Symbol` from the context menu. Name the symbol `Log`, and select `Graphic` from the `Type` menu. Click `OK` to close the dialog box and return to the `Symbol Editor`.

8. Name the layer `Trunk`, and lock the layer.

Figure 2-39. The tree trunk is filled using the `Paint Bucket` tool.

CHAPTER 2

Drawing the pine tree

Think back to your youth and how you drew a pine tree. It was nothing more than a triangle. You will do the same thing here, but you will fill it with a gradient color.

1. Add a new layer named `Fir`.
2. Select the new layer, and select the `Line` tool in the `Tools` panel or press N on your keyboard. The `Line` tool draws straight lines and is great for drawing things like triangles.
3. Click and drag the tool on the stage to draw a line at an angle. Release the mouse, and the line is drawn. Repeat this step two more times to draw the three lines to form a triangle. Move your triangle over the tree trunk.
4. When you reach the start point of the first line, a circle will appear, indicating you are about to close the path. Click the mouse.
5. Select the `Subselection` tool, and click the triangle. Notice how the anchor points become visible. Select an anchor point with the `Subselection` tool, as shown in Figure 2-40, and using either the mouse or the arrow keys on your keyboard, move the points until the triangle takes on the shape of a pine tree.

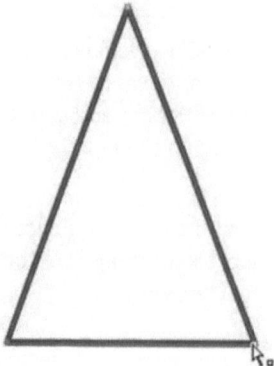

Figure 2-40. Use the `Subselection` tool to select and move anchor points.

6. Switch to the `Selection` tool, and roll the mouse to the bottom line of your triangle. When you see the small curve under the pointer, drag the line slightly downward. Your triangle should now look like a cone. Select the `Paint Bucket` tool, and click once inside the shape to fill it with a color.
7. Double-click the stroke, and press the Delete key to remove the stroke around the shape.
8. Switch to the `Selection` tool, double-click the shape to select it, and in the `Properties` panel set its width to `81` and its height to `114`.
9. With the object selected, open the `Color` panel, and select `Linear` from the `Type` drop-down menu.

GRAPHICS IN FLASH CS5

10. Click the left crayon, and set its color value to #002211 (dark green). Set the color value of the right crayon to #004433, which is a lighter green.

11. Select the Paint Bucket tool, and fill the triangle. The gradient, as shown in Figure 2-41, gives the tree a bit of depth.

12. Lock the layer.

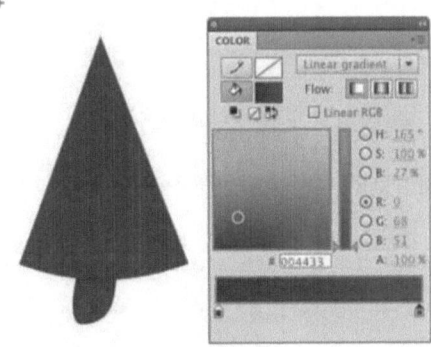

Figure 2-41. Use a gradient to give the tree some depth.

Adding pine needles

The final step in the process is to give your pine tree some needles. The key to this technique is to match the gradient on the tree. It is a lot easier than you may think.

1. Add a new layer named Needles.

2. Open the Color panel, select the Stroke color chip, and select Linear from the Type drop-down menu. The gradient you just created is now in the Stroke area of the Tools panel.

3. Select the Pencil tool, and set the stroke width to 20 pixels in the Properties panel.

4. Click the Edit stroke style button (the pencil to the right of the Style drop-down) in the Properties panel to customize your stroke. In the Stroke Style dialog box shown in Figure 2-42, specify the following settings:

    - Type: Hatched
    - Thickness: Medium
    - Space: Very Close
    - Jiggle: Wild
    - Rotate: Medium
    - Curve: Medium Curve

107

- Length: Random

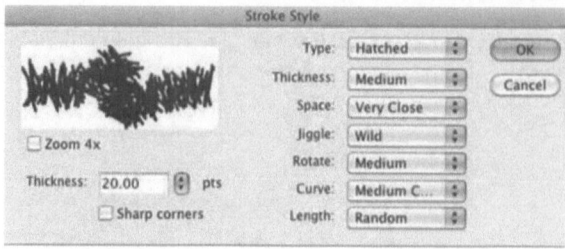

Figure 2-42. You can set the stroke style for the `Pencil` tool.

5. Use the `Zoom` tool to zoom in on the tree. Draw four lines across the tree, as shown in Figure 2-43.

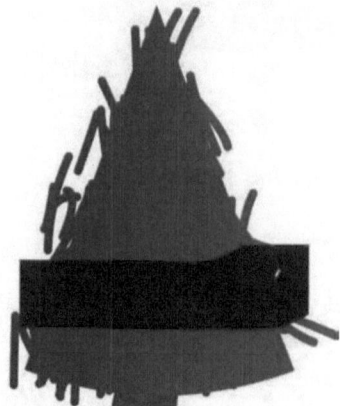

Figure 2-43. Drawing the lines on the tree

> A number of preset strokes are available from the `Property` panel's drop-down menu to the left of the `Edit stroke style` button.

Build the campfire movie

Now that you have created the assets for the movie, let's put them to work. Follow these steps:

1. Click the `Scene 1` button to return to the main timeline. Change the stage color to a medium gray color: `#666666`.
2. Add two more layers. From the top layer down, name the layers `Trees`, `Logs`, and `Fire`.
3. Select the `Spray Brush` tool, load the `Trees` symbol into the brush, and click and drag across the `Trees` layer to add the forest.

4. Select the Logs layer, and drag three copies of the Log graphic symbol to the stage.

5. Create a TeePee fire by manipulating each Log symbol with the Free Transform tool's rotate and resize features. Move the logs into place, as shown in Figure 2-44.

Figure 2-44. Building the campfire with the Log symbol

6. Click the Fire layer once. Select the Deco tool, and select Fire Animation from the Drawing Effect drop-down menu.

7. If you need to, in the Advanced Options, change the Fire duration value to 50 frames.

8. Click the stage once just above the log stack. The tool, as shown in Figure 2-45, will build the entire animation of the fire across 50 frames. When you have finished, save and test the movie.

CHAPTER 2

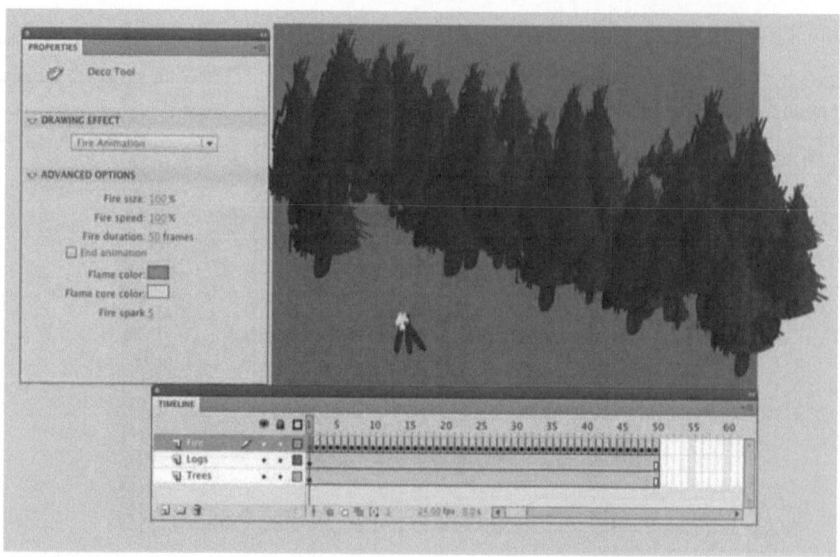

Figure 2-45. The `Fire Animation Deco` brush builds an animated fire with one click.

Working with color in Flash

So far you have spent some time filling objects or strokes with either a solid color or a gradient color. The purpose of this section is to dig a bit deeper into the color models available to you as a Flash designer and to show you a couple of really snazzy color techniques you can use in your day-to-day workflow. What we *aren't* going to do is get into color theory or take color down to its molecular level. Entire books have been written on those subjects.

In Flash, you have three basic color models available to you: RGB, HSB, and hexadecimal. Let's briefly look at each one.

The **RGB model** is the computer color model. Each pixel on your computer monitor is composed of a mixture of red, green, and blue lights. The value for each color is actually based on the old black-and-white model for computers where there were 256 shades of gray that were able to be displayed. The values started at 0 and ended at 255. The best way to imagine this is to think of 0 as being "no light," which means the color is black. This means 255 is pure white. When it comes to the RGB model, each pixel can have a color value that ranges from 0 to 255. If you are looking at a pixel with values of 0 for red, 0 for green, and 255 for blue, you can assume the pixel is pure blue. The A value you see is the opacity value.

The letters in the **HSB model** represent hue, saturation, and brightness. Hue is the color, saturation is the amount of the color or its purity, and brightness is the intensity of the color. The ranges for each value differ in this model. Hue goes from 0 to 360; that's one of 360 degrees around an imaginary wheel of color. Red starts at 0 (the same as 360). Green is one third of the way around the wheel, 120. Blue is two thirds around, 240. To see your secondary colors, shift your travel around the wheel by 60 degrees: yellow is 60, cyan is 180, and magenta is 300. Saturation and brightness are percentages. That pure blue value from the RGB model would here be as follows: hue = 240, saturation = 100, brightness = 100.

The **hexadecimal model** is the one commonly used on the Web. In this model, the red, green, and blue values for a pixel can be either a letter ranging from A to F, a number from 0 to 9, or a combination of the letters and numbers. In the case of a blue pixel, the hexadecimal value would be #0000FF.

The six characters in any hexadecimal color are actually three pairs of values: red, green, and blue. We humans, with ten fingers, count in decimal notation. We start with nothing and keep adding 1 to the "ones column" until we hit 9—that's a range of ten values, 0 to 9. Add one more, and the ones column can't go any higher, so it resets to 0, while the "tens column" advances by 1.

Computers aren't so simple. They have 16 fingers on each hand, so their ones column goes from 0 to 15. Columns can hold only one character at a time, so after 9, the value 10 is represented by...a letter—the letter A. For example, 11 is represented by B, and so on, until 15, which is F. Add one more, and the ones column can't go any higher, so it resets to 0, while the tens column—actually, the "sixteens column"—advances by one. If your brain hasn't already turned to jelly, good, because even though this doesn't feel normal to us humans, it's not so hard.

CHAPTER 2

That 1 in the sixteens column and 0 in the ones column look like 10, but in hexadecimal notation, that value is 16. For example, 17 would be 11, 18 would be 12, and so on. A 10 in the ones column, as you now know, would be A. So, what we would call 26 in decimal—that is, a 1 in the sixteens column and a 10 in the ones column—would be 1A. Follow that through, and you'll see that FF refers to what we call 255 (that's 15 in the sixteens column, a total of what we call 240, plus a 15 in the ones column).

So, hexadecimal notation is just another way to represent a range from 0 to 255 in each of the primary colors.

The Color palette and the Color Picker

When you click a color chip in Flash, the current `Color` palette, shown in Figure 2-46, opens. The color chips are all arranged in hexadecimal groupings. As you run your mouse pointer across them, you will see the hex value for the chip you are currently over. The colors on the left side of the `Color` palette are referred to as the **basic colors**. These are the grays and solid colors used most often.

> *There is a reason for the pink and turquoise colors being there. The left column in that `Color` palette goes like this, from top to bottom: six even distributions of gray, from black to white. Then are the three primaries (red, green, blue) and finally the three secondaries (yellow, cyan, magenta). These colors, by the way, follow this hex pattern: red = #FF0000; green = #00FF00; blue = #0000FF; yellow = #FFFF00; cyan = #00FFFF; magenta = #FF00FF.*

Another really useful feature of this panel is the ability to sample color anywhere on the computer screen. When the `Color` palette opens, your mouse pointer changes to an eyedropper, and if you roll the mouse pointer across the screen, you will see the hex value of the pixels you're over appearing in the `Hex` edit box, and the color will appear in the preview box. This is a relatively dangerous feature because if you click the mouse over a pixel on your screen, that will be the selected color.

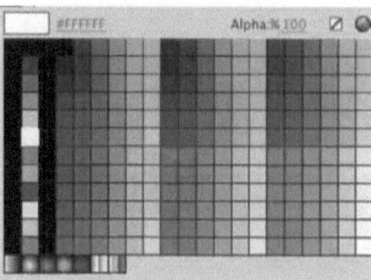

Figure 2-46. The current `Color` palette

The color wheel in the upper-right corner, when clicked, opens the Flash `Color Picker` shown in Figure 2-47. The swatches in the top left are the basic system colors, and you probably noticed the pane on the right with all of that color that sort of looks like the Northern Lights gone haywire. This pane, called the `Color` window, contains all the color you can use in your movies. Click a color, and you will see its RGB and HSB values as well as a preview of the color chosen. You can adjust that color by moving the `Luminance` slider up or down.

How many individual colors are available to you in the `Color` window? The answer is more than 16 million. One of the authors once answered this question, and the student who asked the question remarked, "Is that all?" The author told him that was one seriously large number of crayons in his box, and the student responded, "What if I want more?" The author thought about that one for a couple of seconds and asked the student to imagine a crayon box with 16 million crayons. "If you have a box of crayons, are they all given a color name on the label?" asked the author. The student replied, "Of course." The author then said, "OK, you have in your hands a box containing 16 million crayons. None is labeled. Start naming them." That ended that discussion.

How do we get 16 million colors? First, the exact number is 16,777,216. At rock bottom, computers use base 2 notation (aka binary), and millions of colors is referred to as being 24-bit color. Each pixel is comprised of three primary colors, and each color is defined by 8 bits (8 to the 2nd power is 256—a-ha, a number we already understand!). So, that's where the 24 comes from: 3 times 8, which is the same as saying 256 to the 3rd power ($256 \times 256 \times 256$)—or 2 to the 24th power.

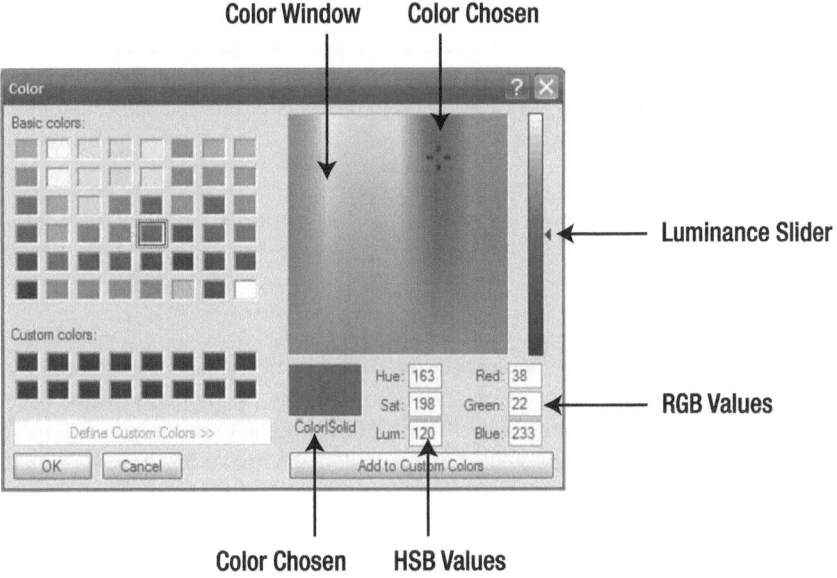

Figure 2-47. The Flash (Windows) `Color Picker`

Things are a bit different on the Mac, as shown in Figure 2-48. Though the `Color Picker` may look different, it works in almost the same manner.

CHAPTER 2

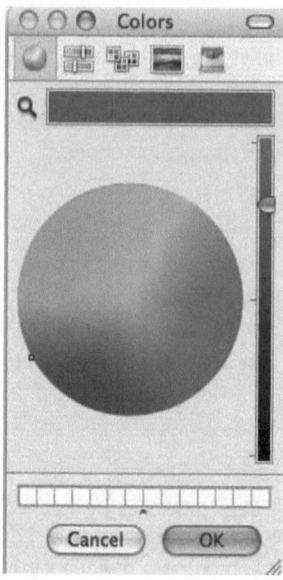

Figure 2-48. The Macintosh Color Picker

In the Mac-only color wheel, a color is chosen by clicking it in the wheel. If you want to adjust the RGB values, click the Color Sliders button at the top, and select RGB Sliders, as you see in Figure 2-49, from the drop-down menu. The color picking options, to be honest, are far superior to those on Windows and well out of the scope of this book. What the Mac can't do is create multiple custom colors. You will have to mix those individually.

> To save a color on the Mac, you just drag and drop a color from the preview area into the Custom Color boxes at the bottom of the dialog box.

To add the color to your palette, either click the Add to Custom Colors button (Windows) or click OK (Mac). Of course, things are not always wonderful for Windows users. The custom color you just added appears in the Custom Colors area of the Color Picker. That's the good news. The bad news is if you add enough (more than 16) custom colors, Flash will wrap back to the beginning and overwrite your first color. If you are creating a number of custom colors, select the empty box before you pick your color.

So, you have a created a bunch of custom colors; are you ready to use them in all of your projects? Not quite. They aren't automatically saved when you close Flash. If you create a bunch of custom colors and then close Flash, they will be gone—forever—when you return to Flash. The question, therefore, is how do you save your custom colors?

GRAPHICS IN FLASH CS5

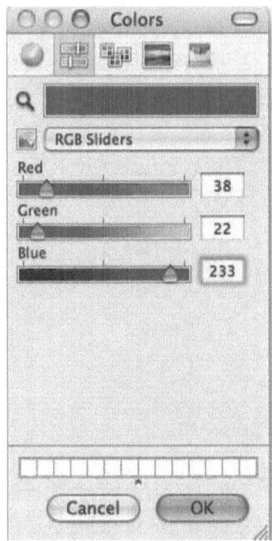

Figure 2-49. Choosing the sliders to change a color value

Creating persistent custom colors

Saving custom colors in Flash is not exactly up there in the category of "dead simple." After you have created your custom color, you need to add it to the main Color palette and then save it as a color set. Here's how:

1. Open the Color panel, select the Fill color, and select Solid Color as the fill type. Create this color—#B74867 (dusty rose)—and make sure it is now the Fill color by pressing the Enter (Windows) or Return (Mac) key.

2. Click the menu in the upper-right corner of the panel to open the panel's drop-down menu. Select Add Swatch, as shown in Figure 2-50.

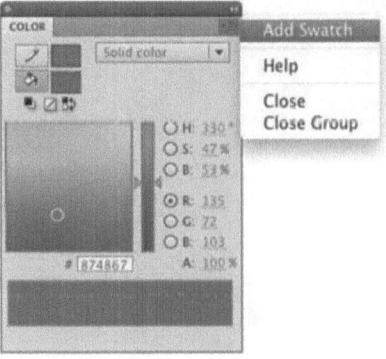

Figure 2-50. You start by selecting Add Swatch from the panel menu.

115

CHAPTER 2

3. Click the `Fill` drop-down menu to open the current `Color` palette. Your new swatch will appear, as shown in Figure 2-51, in the bottom-left corner of the swatches. You can add as many colors as you want, but we'll stay with the one we are using here.

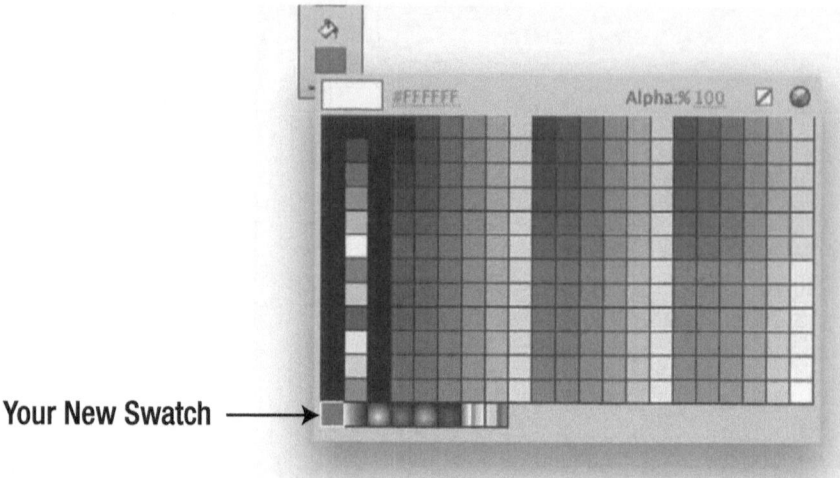

Figure 2-51. Your custom color now appears on the current `Color` palette.

4. Open the `Swatches` panel by selecting `Window ➤ Swatches` or pressing Ctrl+F9 (Windows) or Cmd+F9 (Mac).

5. When the panel opens, click the panel menu, shown in Figure 2-52, and select `Save Colors`. The `Save As` dialog box will open.

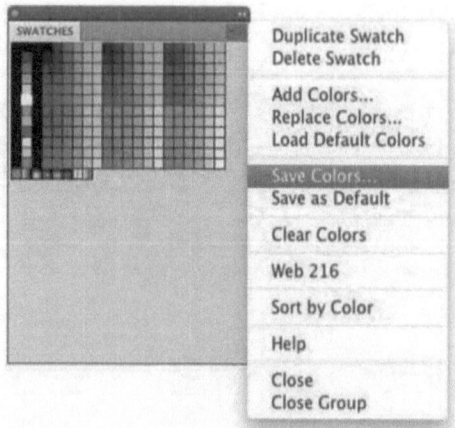

Figure 2-52. Saving a swatch

If you pay attention to the Save As dialog box, you will notice the file is being saved as a **Flash Color Set** or `*.clr` file.

6. Name your file `myFirstSet.clr`, and as shown in Figure 2-53, save it to `C:\Program Files\Adobe\Adobe Flash CS5\Common\First Run` (Windows) or `<Hard Drive> / Users / <User Name> / Library/ Application Support / Adobe / Flash CS5 / en / Configuration / Color Sets` (Mac). Click OK to create the CLR file and close the dialog box.

> *You don't have to use the Flash application folder for these. Just put them in a location where they will be handy. Some Flash designers stick them in their My Documents folder, and others put them in the project folder.*

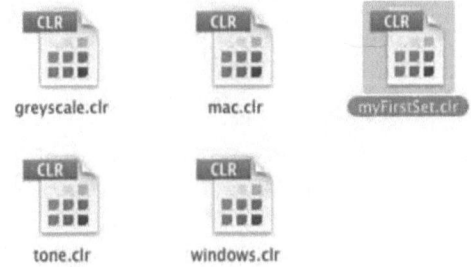

Figure 2-53. A color set

7. To load the color set, simply open the Swatches panel, and select Add Colors from the panel menu. Navigate to the folder containing the set, and double-click it to add the set to Flash.

Yes, we agree that is a lot of work. Is there an easier way? In fact, there is. Why not do what the print guys do and attach a color swatch directly to the file? Let's assume you have a client who has six specific corporate colors that must always be used. Create a movie clip containing squares filled with those colors, and then simply put that movie clip on the pasteboard, which is the area just outside the stage that doesn't show in the published SWF by default. Any time you need the color, select the Eyedropper tool and sample it. If you are really lazy, don't add it to the pasteboard, and simply sample the color using the Library Preview pane. If you use the colors in a lot of projects, you might even consider adding it to a shared library along with the client's logos and other common elements used in the client's Flash projects.

The kuler Color Picker

A couple of years ago, Adobe introduced a small web-based color picker named **kuler**. The whole premise behind the application was to give designers the opportunity to freely share custom color schemes with each other. Needless to say, the application was a hit, and it has quietly been added to practically every Adobe application that contains a color palette. Flash is no exception.

To access the Kuler panel shown in Figure 2-54, select `Window` ➤ `Extensions` ➤ `Kuler`. Scroll through the list in the panel. If you a see a combination (they are called **themes**) you like, just click the arrow to the right of the set's name, and select `Add to swatches panel`. When you open the `Swatches` panel, you will see the set has been added to the bottom color chips.

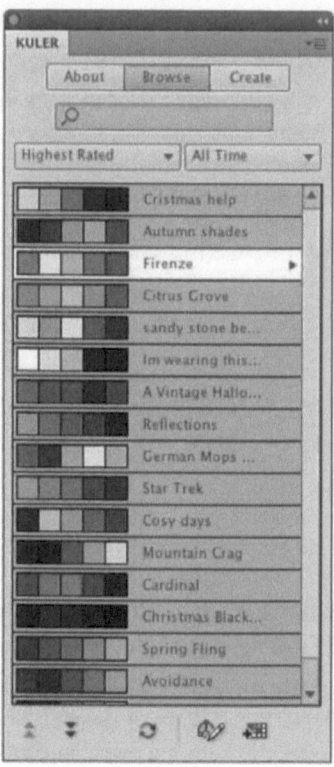

Figure 2-54. The `Kuler` panel

You can also edit a swatch in the panel. Click the right arrow that appears when you select a theme, and select `Edit This Theme` from the drop-down menu. The `Create` area of the `Kuler` panel, as shown in Figure 2-55, will open. Select a swatch, and start making changes. Once you have a color or theme that works for you, click the `Save Theme` button to name your theme. If you want to return to the main panel, click the `Browse` button.

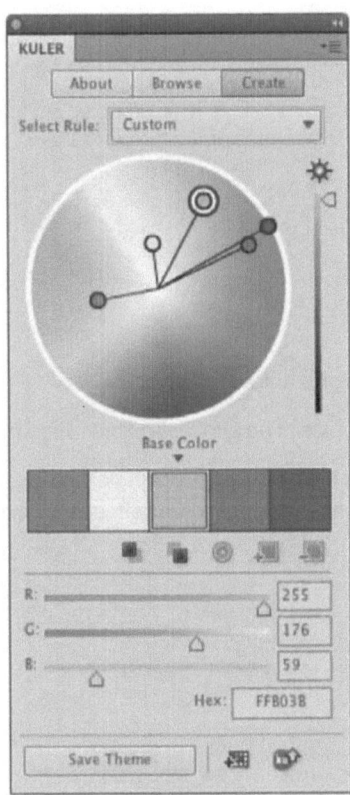

Figure 2-55. Editing a kuler theme

Your turn: playing with color

Here are a few tricks you can do with color. Two involve the standard use of a tool, but the other is right up there in the realm of "That is waaay cool."

The first trick involves a gradient. Did you know Flash allows you to create a variety of gradient effects with the click of a mouse? Here's how:

1. Open a new Flash document, and create a big rectangle filled using the leftmost gradient in the bottom-left corner of the fill `Color Picker`.

2. Switch to the `Gradient Transform` tool, and resize the fill so it is much smaller than the rectangle. When you shorten the gradient, the black and white areas of the gradient become larger. This is because Flash is filling the rectangle with the end colors. This process is called **overflowing**.

3. Open the `Color` panel, and click the middle chip in the `Flow` area of the panel (Figure 2-56).

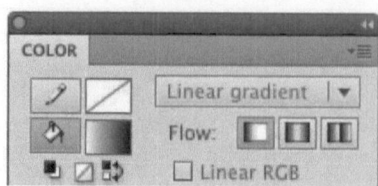

Figure 2-56. The `Gradient Overflow` options

4. These choices, from left to right, are as follows:

- **Extend**: The default choice. The two last colors in the gradient extend to fill the shape.
- **Reflect**: The overflow area of the rectangle will be filled with repeating versions of the gradient. Every other version is mirrored/reflected. Select this, and the rectangle looks like stacked pipes (see Figure 2-57).

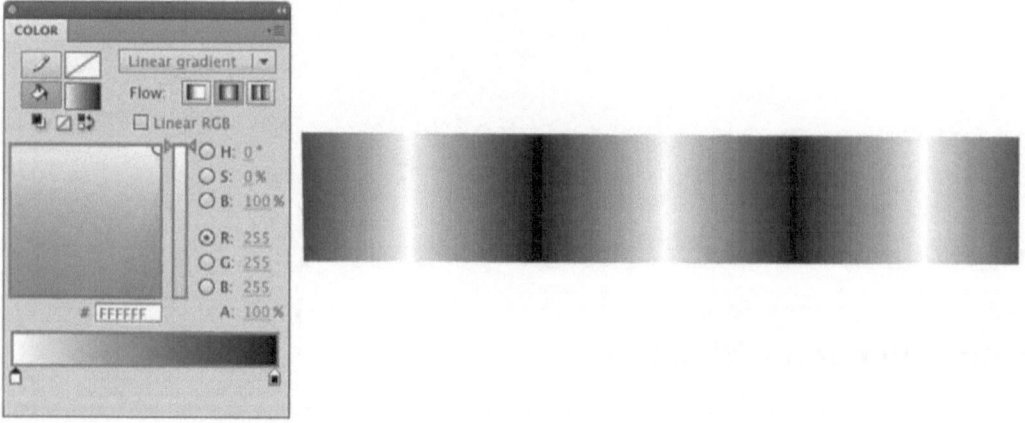

Figure 2-57. The `Reflect` overflow

- **Repeat**: The gradients aren't reflected. The result is the "Venetian blind" look in Figure 2-58.

Figure 2-58. The Repeat overflow

If you really want to rock 'n' roll with this technique, change the gradient type to **Radial**, reduce the size of the gradient with the **Gradient Transform** tool, and select the **Repeat** option. As shown in Figure 2-59, the result resembles the Looney Tunes logo background.

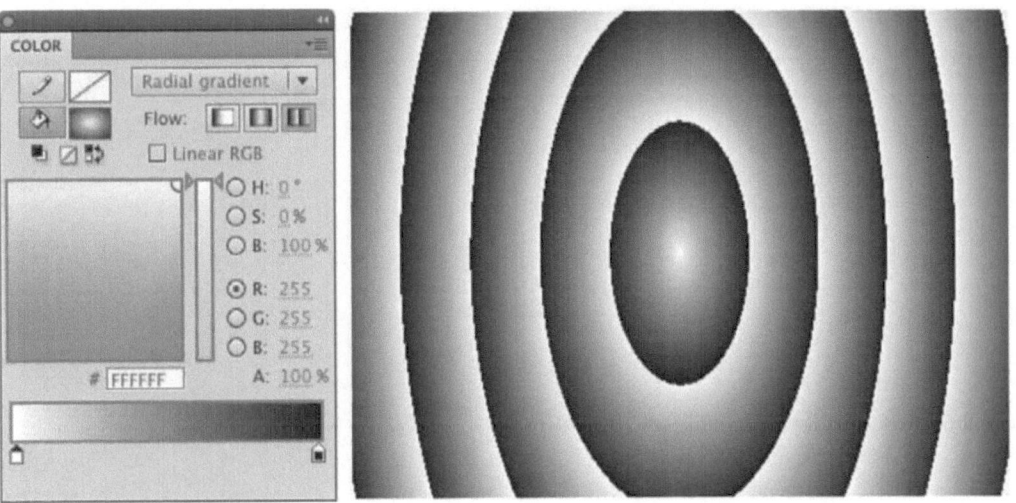

Figure 2-59. That's all, folks!

The next technique is one a lot of Flash designers tend to overlook: using an image, not a gradient or a solid color, to fill an object. There are two methods of accomplishing this, and they each have a different result. Let's try them:

1. Open the ImageFill.fla file, and open the Color panel.

2. Select Bitmap as the fill type. In cases where the FLA does not yet contain imported images, an Import to Library dialog box will open at this point. In this sample file, an image already exists in the Library panel, so you'll see the Import button instead.

3. Click the Import button, if you like, to import an image of your own. If you go this route, use the Import to Library dialog box to navigate to an image. Select the image, and click OK to close the dialog box. Of course, you're welcome to use the already-imported Lake.jpg.

4. If you take a look at the Fill chip in the Color panel, the image is in the chip and in the Fill area of the Tools panel.

5. Select the Paint Bucket tool, and click once inside the object on the stage. It fills, as shown in Figure 2-60, with the image.

6. Select the Gradient Transform tool to adjust the tiled image in various ways. Given the minuscule size of the tiles, you may want to zoom in first.

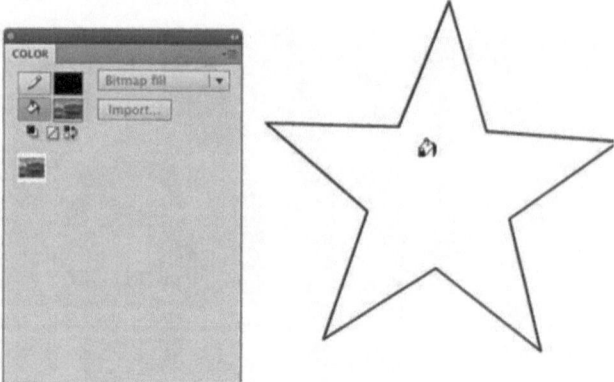

Figure 2-60. Using a bitmap as a fill

Here's the second method:

1. Add your image or the one we supplied in the `Library` to the stage. Click the photo on the stage, and select `Modify` ➤ `Break Apart` or press Ctrl+B (Windows) or Cmd+B (Mac). The image looks crosshatched because the image has changed from a bitmap instance to a shape with a fill.

2. Select the `Eyedropper` tool, and click once in the photo. The image will appear in the `Fill` color chip of the `Tools` panel.

3. Select the `Paint Bucket` tool, and click the object on the stage. The image, shown in Figure 2-61, fills the object.

Figure 2-61. Another way of using a bitmap as a fill

Now that you have finally had a chance to use a bitmap, let's take a closer look at how such images are used in Flash.

Using bitmap images in Flash

To this point in the book, you have been working with vectors. Though we have been telling you they are the most wonderful things in the Flash universe, we are sure our photographer friends are not exactly "happy campers." Let's face it—you are going to be using bitmaps in your workflow. You can't avoid them, and they are just as important as vectors. In fact, Adobe has really improved how Flash manages images and integrates with Photoshop CS5, Illustrator CS5, and Fireworks CS5.

In this section of the chapter, we are going to look at how you can use bitmap images in your workflow. We are going to talk about the image formats you can use; cover how to import images from Photoshop, Illustrator, and Fireworks into Flash; and even show you how to convert a bitmap image to a vector image in Flash. Let's start with the formats that can be imported.

As an Adobe application, it is not surprising that Flash can import the following formats:

- **AI**: Adobe Illustrator. This is the native Illustrator file format. This format allows Flash to preserve the layers in your Illustrator document. The good news is the Illustrator-to-Flash workflow has had its molecules rearranged and turned inside out—in a good way.

- **GIF**: Graphic Interchange Format. This is the former standard for imaging on the Web. The upside of this format is the real small file size. The downside is the color palette is limited to 256 colors. These files come in two flavors: transparent and regular. The increasing use of Flash banner ads, with their strict file size requirements, has resulted in a resurgence of this format on websites.

- **PNG**: Portable Network Graphic. This is the native format for Fireworks. Think of PNG files as a combination vector/bitmap file. This format supports variable bit depth (PNG-8 and PNG-24) and compression settings with support for alpha channels. PNG files imported into Flash from Fireworks arrive as editable objects and will preserve vector artwork in the file.

- **JPEG or JPG**: Joint Photographic Experts Group. This is the current standard for web imaging, and any image arriving in Flash will be converted to this format when the SWF is published.

- **PDF**: Portable Document Format. PDF is a cross-platform standard used in the publishing industry.

- **EPS**: Encapsulated PostScript. Think of this as a raw vector file.

- **PSD**: Photoshop Drawing. This is the native Photoshop file format. A PSD image usually contains multiple layers. Again, the workflow between Flash CS5 and Photoshop CS5 has undergone a profound change for the better.

- **PICT**: This is a Macintosh format comparable to a BMP file on Windows computers.

- **TIF or TIFF**: Tagged Image File Format. This is usually a high-resolution CMYK document.

A bitmap or raster image is nothing more than a collection of pixels. The reason bitmap images have taken a bit of a "bum rap" in the Flash community is because the image file needs to map and remember the location of each pixel in the image. The result is a large file size, which tends to go against the grain in a community that chants, "Small is beautiful. Small loads fast."

Use bitmaps when you need photos or lifelike images, when you need a screenshot, or when you need pictures of drawings or artwork. In fact, a good rule of thumb is to look at a bitmap image and ask, "Could I draw this in Flash?" If the answer is yes, you might want to consider that route instead.

The best advice we can give you about bitmaps is to make them as small as possible—a process called **optimization**—in the originating application. For example, Fireworks CS5 contains an `Optimize` panel, shown in Figure 2-62, which allows you to compare the effects of various image settings upon an image. In Illustrator CS5, see whether you can reduce the number of points in your shapes, and make sure you have removed all the stray points that aren't connected to anything. In Photoshop CS5 and Fireworks CS5, reduce the image size to fit the image size in Flash. These applications were designed to perform these tasks; Flash wasn't.

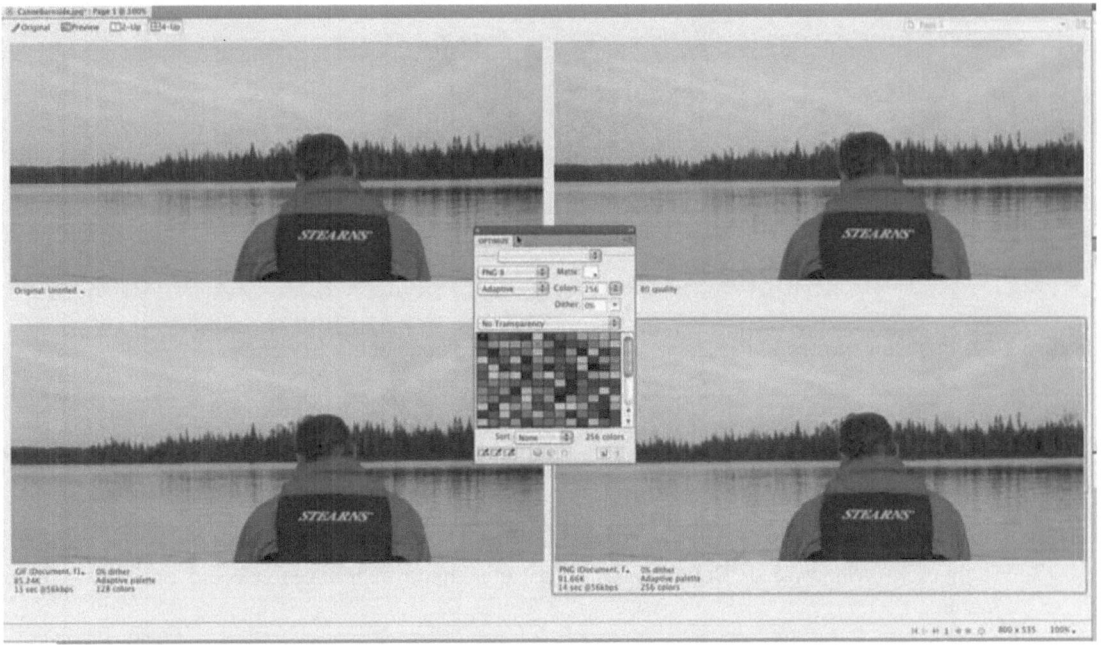

Figure 2-62. Four-up image optimization in Fireworks CS5 allows you to balance quality against image size.

Working with bitmaps in Flash

The decision is final. You need to use a bitmap and place it in Flash. Then you discover the color is all wrong or something needs to be cropped out of the image. It needs to be edited. How do you do it? Follow these steps:

1. Open a new Flash document, and select `File ➤ Import ➤ Import to Stage`. When the `Import` dialog box opens, navigate to the `CanoeBurnside.jpg` file.

2. Select the file, and click `Open` to close the `Import` dialog box. The image will appear on the stage and in the `Library`, as shown in Figure 2-63.

Figure 2-63. Images imported to the stage are automatically placed in the Library.

> *Do not delete the image from the Library. This is the original bitmap, and deleting it will ripple through an entire project. If you screw something up on the stage, delete the image on the stage.*

3. Right-click (Windows) or Control+click (Mac) the image in the Library to open the context menu.

4. Select Edit With. This will launch the Open dialog box, allowing you to navigate to the application folder containing the application you will be using to edit the image. If you select Photoshop CS5, the image will launch in Photoshop. When you make your changes, select Edit ➤ Save. When you return to Flash, the change made in Photoshop CS5 will be reflected both in the image on the stage and in the Library.

> *Fireworks CS5 and, for that matter, practically every other application in the Creative Suite has a rather cool feature called **round-tripping**. If you launch Fireworks CS5 as your editor, the image will open, and you will see a Done button, as shown in Figure 2-64, at the top of the canvas as well as notification you are, indeed, "Editing from Flash." Make your changes, and click the Done button. Fireworks will close, you will be returned to Flash, and the change will be visible on the stage and in the Library.*

Figure 2-64. Round-trip editing between Fireworks and Flash

Your turn: tracing bitmaps in Flash

Tracing converts an image to a series of vectors. On the surface, this sounds like a win-win for everybody. Not quite. Yes, you get a vector image with all the benefits of scalability and so on, but you also inherit a load of potential problems along the way.

Tracing an image

There are no hard-and-fast rules in this area, so it is best to experiment. Let's fire up the Bunsen burner:

1. Open the `Trace.fla` file. You will see two images of temple painting from a small temple in the Chinese village of Hougou.

2. Click the image over the `Trace Image` text, and select **Modify ➤ Bitmap ➤ Trace Bitmap** to open the **Trace Bitmap** dialog box. Specify the values shown in Figure 2-65.

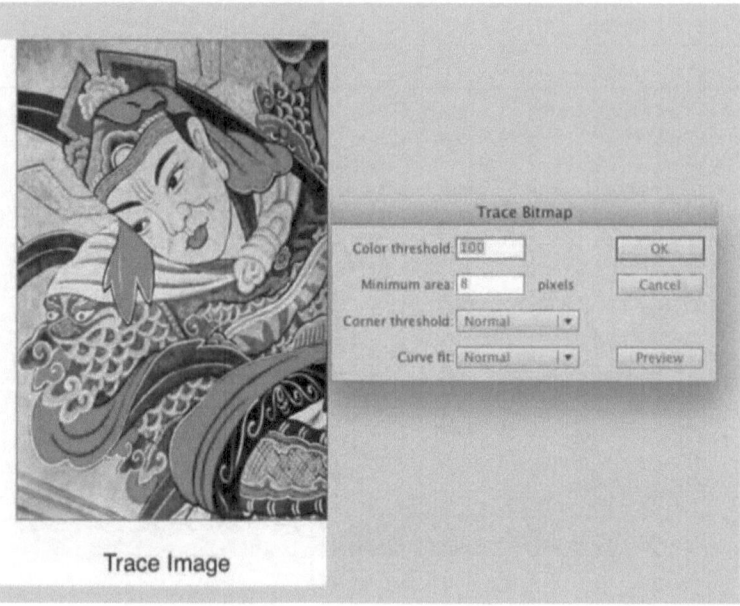

Figure 2-65. The Trace Bitmap dialog box

The settings aren't all that mysterious:

- **Color threshold**: The higher the number, the more colors are considered a match and the fewer the vectors. Set this value to 100.

- **Minimum area**: The number entered here defines the smallest size for a vector shape. If you want a really detailed image, use a low number. Just keep in mind that the smaller the number, the more shapes and therefore the larger the file size. In fact, extremely complex vectors can, and often do, carry a greater file size penalty than the bitmap images they're based on. Set this value to 8 pixels.

- **Curve fit**: Think of this as being a smoothing setting. Select **Pixels**, and you get a very accurate trace. Select **Very Smooth**, and curves really round out. Again, the fewer the curves, the smaller the file size.

- **Corner threshold**: This value determines how much a line can bend before Flash breaks it into corners. The fewer the corners, the smaller the file size. (Picking up a theme here?)

3. Click the **Preview** button to see the effect of your choices, as shown in Figure 2-66.

GRAPHICS IN FLASH CS5

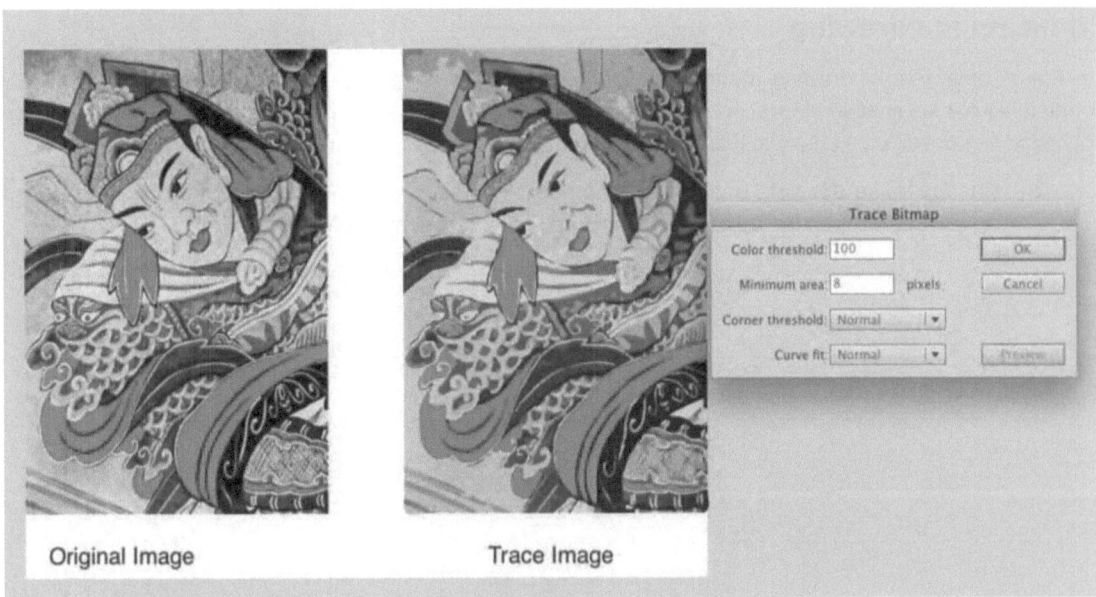

Figure 2-66. A traced bitmap is on the right, and the original image is on the left.

> *If you have used previous versions of Flash, you will find the* `Preview` *button in the* `Trace Bitmap` *dialog box a welcome addition to Flash CS5.*

4. Click `OK` to apply the change and close the dialog box.

5. Now you'll see what happens when you use even closer tolerances. Select the image on the right of the stage, and open the `Trace Bitmap` dialog box. Specify these values:

    - `Color threshold`: 5
    - `Minimum area`: 2
    - `Corner threshold`: `Many corners`
    - `Curve fit`: `Pixels`

6. Click the `Preview` button. The progress bar will take a bit longer this time, and when it finishes, the difference between the original image and the vector image is not readily evident. Click `OK` to apply the changes.

You are about to find out that there is indeed a major difference between the original bitmap and the traced image. The difference becomes evident when you optimize the image. Let's get real clear on one aspect of tracing: Flash should be your last resort. Illustrator CS5's Live Trace feature is far superior and more accurate.

129

Optimizing the drawing

In Flash, optimizing a drawing means you are reducing the number of corners in a traced image and smoothing out the lines in the traced image to give you a smaller and less-precise image. Though you can optimize any drawing you have in Flash, this technique is best applied to traced images. Here's how:

1. Change to the Selection tool, and marquee the image you traced. Select Modify ➤ Shape ➤ Optimize to open the Optimize Curves dialog box shown in Figure 2-67.

Figure 2-67. The Optimize Curves dialog box lets you reduce the size of a traced image.

2. Drag the Smoothing slider up to the Maximum value of 100, and click OK. The process starts, and when it finishes, you will be presented with an Alert box telling you how many curves have been optimized (see Figure 2-68).

The downside is the image loses a lot of its precision, and some of the curves become spiky because Flash converted all the pixelated smoothness to vectors. If you repeat the process on the second image but only move the Smoothing slider to the midpoint, the process will take a lot longer than the previous one, and the curve reduction will be minimal. This is because you essentially created a high-resolution vector image, so there are a lot more curves to check out. The bottom line here is the decision regarding using a bitmap, tracing it, and optimizing the curves is up to you.

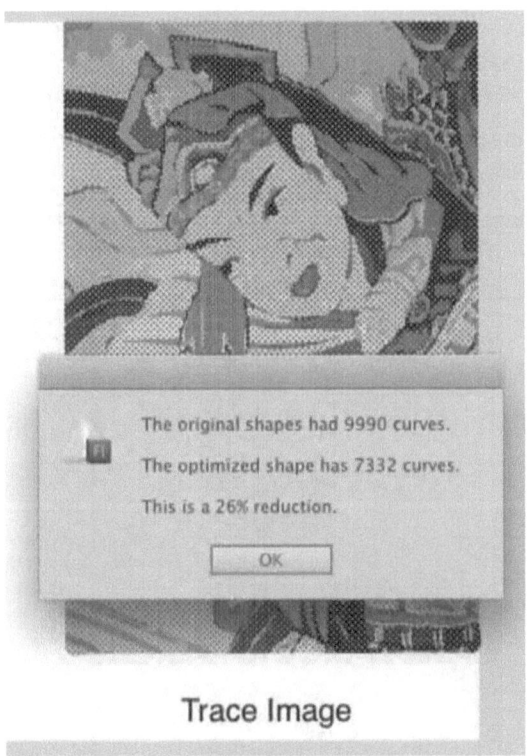

Figure 2-68. A 26 percent curve reduction means a hefty file size reduction.

JPEG files and Flash

The JPG/JPEG file format is the one used for photos. As mentioned earlier, JPEG stands for Joint Photographic Experts Group and is a method of compressing an image using areas of contiguous color. The file size reductions can be significant with minimal to moderate image quality loss. This explains why this format has become a de facto imaging format for digital media. In this exercise, you are going to learn how to optimize a JPEG image in Flash.

Before you do this, it is extremely important you understand that the JPEG format is **lossy**. This means each time a JPEG image is compressed in the JPEG format, the image quality degrades. The point here is you have to make a decision regarding JPEG images before they arrive in Flash. Will the compression be done in Photoshop or Fireworks, or will Flash handle the chores? If the answer is Flash, always set the `JPG Quality` slider in Photoshop or Fireworks to 100 percent to apply minimal compression. If you don't know where the image came from or what compression was used, don't let Flash handle the compression.

1. Open the `JPGCompression.fla` file in your `Chapter 2 Exercise` folder. When it opens, you will notice the movie contains nothing more than a single JPEG image, and the stage matches the image dimensions. In short, there is no wasted space that can skew the results of this experiment.

2. Minimize Flash, and open the Chapter 2 Exercise folder. Inside the folder is a file named JPGCompression.swf. It is the compiled version of the FLA file, and if you check its file size, you will see it comes in at about 176KB. Let's see whether we can shed some weight from this file.

3. Return to Flash, and save the open Flash file to your Exercise folder by selecting **File ➤ Save As** and naming the file JPGCompression2.fla.

4. Double-click the image in the **Library** to open the **Bitmap Properties** dialog box shown in Figure 2-69.

> *Be aware that any changes made in this dialog box ripple through the entire movie and will override the defaults used in the* Publish *dialog box.*

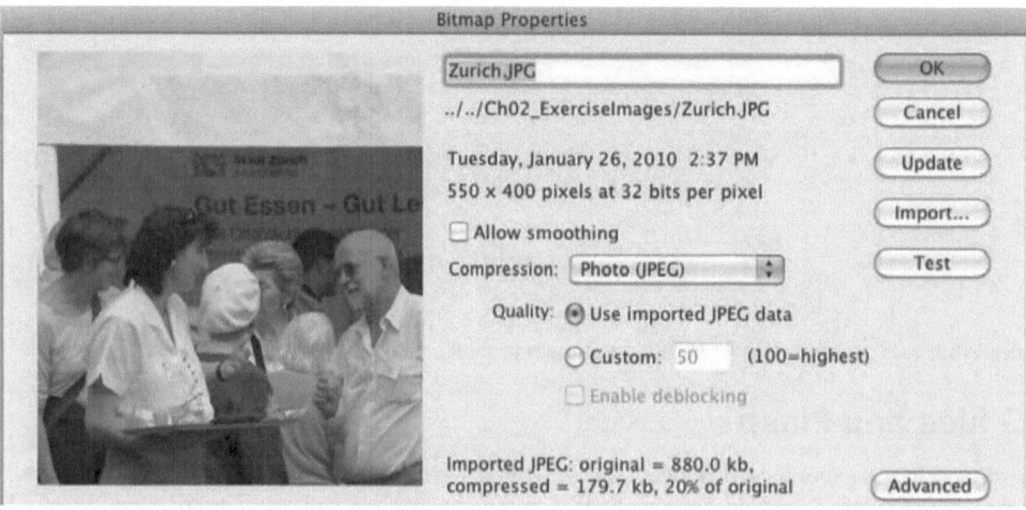

Figure 2-69. The Bitmap Properties dialog box

Let's examine this dialog box. To start, the image on the left side is the preview image. As you start playing with some of the settings, this image will show you the final result of your choices. This is a good thing because changes you make in this dialog box are visible only when the SWF file is running; they won't be reflected in the image on the stage. The other areas are as follows:

- **Name**: This is the name of the file. If you want to rename the file, select it and enter a new name. This only changes the name by which Flash knows the file—it does not "reach outside of Flash" and rename the original image.

- **Path, date, dimensions**: These are fairly self-explanatory. There will be the odd occasion where this information will not be displayed. The reason is the image was pasted in from the Clipboard.

- **Update button**: If you have edited the image without using the `Edit with` feature, clicking this button will replace the image with the new version. This button will not work if you have saved or moved the original image to a new location on the computer. To "reconnect" such a broken link, respecify the image file's location with the `Import` button, explained next.
- **Import button**: Click this, and you open the `Import Bitmap` dialog box. When using this button, the new file will replace the image in the `Library`, and all instances of that image in your movie will also be updated.
- **Allow smoothing option**: Think of this as anti-aliasing applied to an image. This feature tends to blur an image, so use it judiciously. Where it really shines is when it is applied to low-resolution images because it reduces the dreaded jaggies.
- **Compression drop-down menu**: This allows you to change the image compression to either `Photo (JPEG)` or `Lossless (PNG/GIF)`. Use `Photo (JPEG)` for photographs and `Lossless (PNG/GIF)` for images with simple shapes and few colors, such as line art or logos. To help you wrap your mind around this, the image in the dialog box uses `Photo (JPEG)` compression, and if you click the `Test` button, the file size is about 2.4KB. Apply `Lossless` compression and click the `Test` button, and the file size rockets up to 142KB.
- **Use Imported JPEG data option**: Select this check box if the image has already been compressed or if you aren't sure whether compression has been applied. Selecting this avoids the nasty results of applying double compression to an image.
- **Quality option**: If you deselect the `Use Imported JPEG data` check box, you can apply your own compression settings. In fact, let's try it.

5. Make sure your compression setting is `Photo (JPEG)` and that you have deselected the `Use Imported JPEG Data` check box. Change the `Quality` value to `10 percent`, and click the `Test` button. The image in the preview area, shown in Figure 2-70, is just plain awful. The good news is the file size, at the bottom of the dialog box, is 4.6 KB.

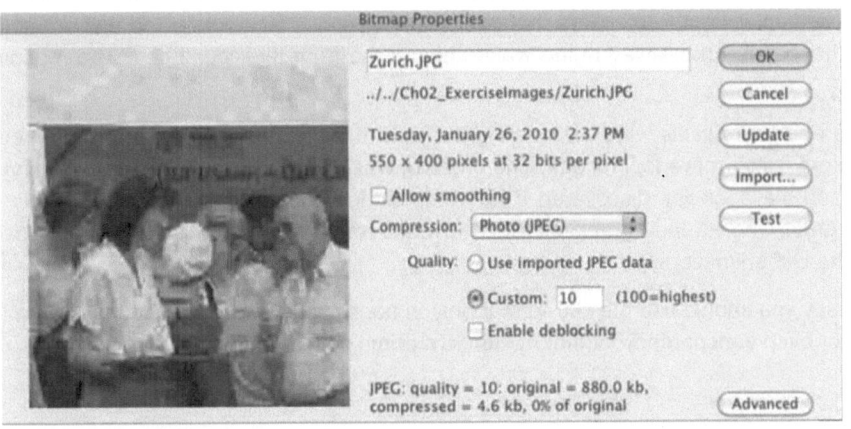

Figure 2-70. At 10 percent quality, the image is terrible.

6. Change the `Quality` setting to `40 percent`, and click the `Test` button. Things are a little better, but the text in the banner a bit looks pixelated, and the file size has gone up to 16KB.

7. Change the `Quality` value to the normal `80 percent` value used by imaging applications, and click the `Test` button. The text issue is resolved, but the file size has risen to 43.1KB. As you are seeing, there is an intimate relationship between the `Quality` setting and file size.

8. Knowing the quality between 50 percent and 80 percent is a vast improvement; let's see if we can maintain quality but reduce the file size. Set the `Quality` value to `65 percent`, and click the `Test` button. The difference between 65 percent and 80 percent is minimal, but the file size has reduced to 3KB. Click `OK` to apply this setting and close the dialog box.

9. Save the movie, and press Ctrl+Enter (Windows) or Cmd+Return (Mac) to test the movie. This will create the SWF you need. Minimize Flash and the SWF window, and navigate to your `Exercise` folder. The results are, to say the least, dramatic. The file size, as you see in Figure 2-71, has reduced to 29KB from 176KB. Save and close the open movie.

Figure 2-71. Applying compression in Flash can result in seriously smaller and more efficient SWF files.

Using GIF files in Flash CS5

There was point a few years back where many web and Flash designers were preparing to celebrate the death of the GIF image and the GIF animation. The reason was simple: in a universe where bandwidth is plentiful and every computer on the planet is able to display 16-bit color, the limited color range and small file size of a GIF image that made the format so important were irrelevant. GIF images were developed for a time of limited color depth—monitors that could only display 256 colors—and dial-up modems. Then a funny thing happened on the way to the wake; they arose from their deathbed. The reason was banner advertising.

Ad agencies and their clients were discovering the Web really was a viable advertising medium and that Flash was a great interactive tool for ads. The problem was, standards for banner advertising appeared on the scene, and the agencies discovered they were handed a file size limit of 30KB. This tended to go against the grain, and as they grappled with the requirement for small files, they rediscovered the GIF image and the GIF animation.

This isn't to say you should use the GIF format only in banner ads. It can be used in quite a few situations where size, or even transparency for that matter, is a prime consideration.

Working with GIF images

Here's how to use GIF images and GIF animations in Flash:

1. Open the `GIF.fla` file in your Chapter 2 Exercise folder. When the file opens, open the `Library`. There are two GIF files in the `Library`.

2. Drag the `Figurines` image from the `Library` to the stage. Notice how you can see the stage color behind the image. This image is a transparent GIF. When it comes to GIF transparency, you have to understand it is an absolute. It is either on or off. There are no shades of opacity with this format. GIFs may contain up to 256 colors, and one of those colors may be transparent.

3. Drag the `FigurinesNoTrans` file to the stage, and place it under the image already there. This image is a GIF image with no transparency applied.

4. Select the image you just dragged onto the stage, and press the Ctrl+B (Windows) or Cmd+B (Mac) combination to break the image apart. Hold on, that isn't right. Only the figurines in the image break apart (see Figure 2-72). That is an expected behavior. Remember what we said in the previous step? The background in a GIF image is either on or off. If it is on, it can't be removed in Flash.

When you break apart an image like this, here's what's really going on. That image is simply translated into a shape with a bitmap fill. It is the same thing as drawing a shape and filling it with that bitmap. This is why file size is identical between the white and transparent versions of this image. The GIF is the same in all respects—except that the color slot in one file's color table is white and in the other file the color table is transparent. But both GIFs have the same number of colors and weigh the same.

5. To "get rid of" the white background, you can drag in the edges of the shape that contains the white version, just like the star shape from the earlier bitmap fill example. Obviously, this would be nearly impossible by hand with an image of this complexity, but any portion of the bitmap fill can be hidden by changing the shape hat contains it.

6. Close the file, and don't save the changes.

CHAPTER 2

Figure 2-72. Transparent and regular GIFs are treated differently in Flash.

Working with GIF animations

Animated GIFs are a bit different. They are a collection of static images—think of a flip book—that play, one after the other, at a set rate, all stored inside a single GIF file. These flip book "pages" can be imported either directly into the main timeline (not a good idea) or into a separate movie clip. Here's how:

1. Open a new Flash document, and create a new movie clip named `Counterforce`. The `Symbol Editor` will open.

2. Select `File` ➤ `Import` ➤ `Import to Stage`, and when the `Open` dialog appears, locate the `Counterforce.gif` file, select it, and click the `Open` button.

GRAPHICS IN FLASH CS5

3. When the import is finished, you will see that each frame of the animation has its own Flash frame, and each image in the animation, as shown in Figure 2-73, has its own image in the `Library`.

4. Press the Enter key to test the animation or click the `Scene 1` link to return to the main timeline, add the movie clip to the stage, and test the movie.

> *A good habit to develop is to place the images in the `Library` in a folder. This way, your `Library` doesn't end up looking like what your mom would call "a pigsty."*

Figure 2-73. Importing GIF animations into a movie clip

Importing Fireworks CS5 documents into Flash CS5

When Macromedia was acquired by Adobe in 2006, the betting in the Macromedia community was that Fireworks, Macromedia's web imaging application, would simply not make the cut. The reason was the market regarded Fireworks as a competitor to Photoshop—it wasn't—and, as such, the application was doomed to extinction.

What the Macromedia community failed to comprehend was that Adobe, prior to the acquisition, had quietly announced it was no longer supporting ImageReady, which was the web imaging application for Photoshop. When the acquisition was settled, Fireworks did indeed make the cut, and in fact Adobe had decided to reposition Fireworks as a rapid prototyping application for web designers. Along the way, Adobe improved how Fireworks PNG files integrate with Flash CS5 along with Illustrator CS5, Flex Builder 2, and Photoshop CS5, and the movement of files from Photoshop and Illustrator into Fireworks. The end result is Flash designers now have a tool that will seriously improve their workflow.

We will be showing you elsewhere in this book techniques in which Fireworks integration will be a huge timesaver. For now, though, let's concentrate on getting a PNG image—the native file format used by Fireworks—into Flash.

As you can see in Figure 2-74, the Fireworks file we will be working with is composed of one layer, **Background**, and three sublayers. When you import this PNG image into Flash, you will see these layers move, intact, into the movie.

Figure 2-74. We start with a Fireworks CS5 PNG image.

To import the PNG image, follow these steps:

1. Open a new Flash document. When the **New Document** dialog box opens, click the **Templates** button, select **Advertising** from the **Category** list, and select **728 x 90 Leaderboard** from the **Template** list, as shown in Figure 2-75. Click **OK** to open the template.

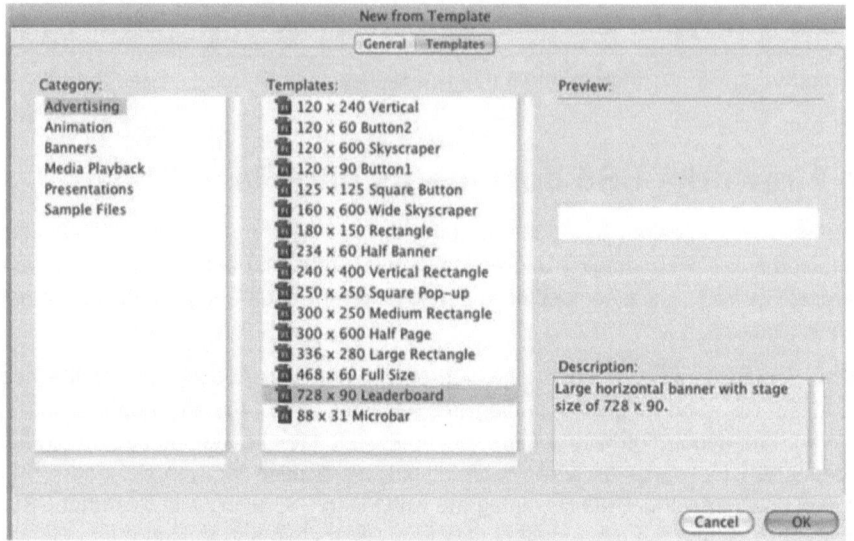

Figure 2-75. Opening a Flash CS5 template

2. Select **File ➤ Import to Library**, and navigate to the Banner.png image in the Chapter 2 Exercise folder.

3. When you click the Open button, the dialog box will close, and the Fireworks PNG Import Settings dialog box, shown in Figure 2-76, will open.

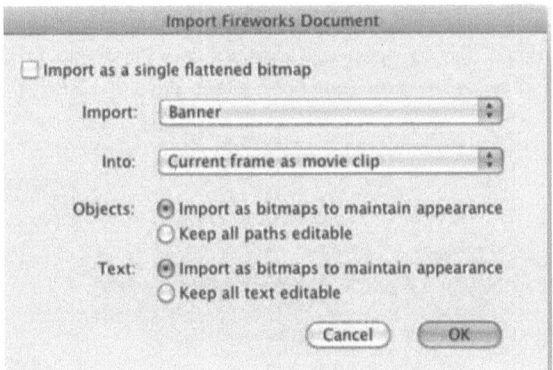

Figure 2-76. The Fireworks import dialog box

Let's review the options:

- **Import**: The important aspect of this is not the scene but the fact you are being asked to import pages. This feature was first introduced to Flash CS3. Because it is a rapid prototyping application, Fireworks CS5 is able to create multipage documents for websites. If the PNG file contains multiple pages, you can select the page to be imported from the drop-down menu.

- **Into**: Select Current frame as movie clip so all the layers in the Fireworks image are placed into separate layers in the movie clip. When this occurs, Flash creates a new folder in the Library named Fireworks Objects and places the movie clip in this folder. The second choice allows you to add the selected page as a new layer on the main timeline.

- **Objects**: The choices are to flatten everything on the Fireworks layer or keep each object editable.

- **Text**: This has the same choices as objects. We tend to keep text editable just in case there is a typo.

- **Import as a single flattened bitmap**: This option flattens all the layers into a bitmap.

4. Go with the default values for this example. Click OK to import the image into Flash.

5. When the import finishes, you will see the `Fireworks Objects` folder in the **Library**. Open it, and you will see that Flash has created a folder for the page just imported, and if you open that folder, you will see the movie clip and a flattened bitmap of the file.

6. Double-click the movie clip to open it. Compare the Flash file (shown in Figure 2-77) to the Fireworks file in Figure 2-74. You can now either save the file or close it without saving the changes.

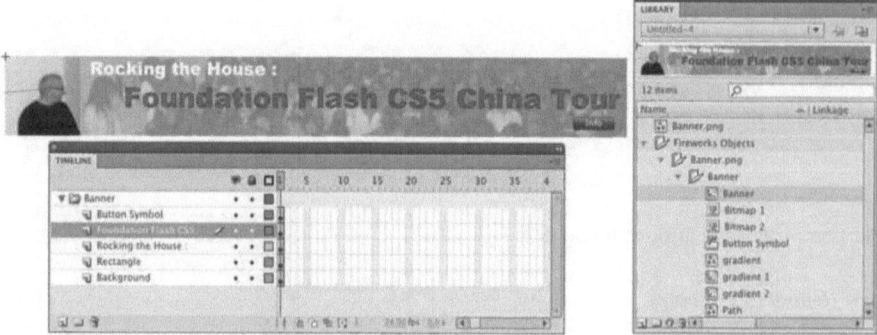

Figure 2-77. The Flash movie clip layers match those in the Fireworks PNG image.

Importing Illustrator CS5 documents into Flash CS5

Flash lets you import Illustrator AI files directly into Flash and generally allows you to edit each piece of the artwork when it is in Flash. The Illustrator file importer also provides you with a great degree of control in determining how your Illustrator artwork is imported into Flash. For example, you can now specify which layers and paths in the Illustrator document will be imported into Flash and even have the Illustrator file be converted to a Flash movie clip.

The Flash Illustrator file importer provides the following key features:

- Preserves editability of the most commonly used Illustrator effects such as the Flash filters and blend modes that Flash and Illustrator have in common.

- Preserves the fidelity and editability of gradient fills.

- Imports Illustrator symbols as Flash symbols.

- Preserves the number and position of Bezier control points; the fidelity of clip masks, pattern strokes, and fills; and object transparency.

- Provides an improved copy-and-paste workflow between Illustrator and Flash. A copy-and-paste dialog box provides settings to apply to AI files being pasted onto the Flash stage.

To many Flash designers, that list is "nirvana," but there are two critical aspects of the Flash-to-Illustrator workflow that must be kept in mind:

- Flash supports only the RGB color space. If the Illustrator image is a CMYK image, do the CMYK-to-RGB conversion in Illustrator before importing the file into Flash.
- To preserve drop shadow, inner glow, outer glow, and Gaussian blur in Flash CS5, import the object to which these filters are applied as a Flash movie clip. In Flash, these filters can be applied only to movie clips.

Let's import an Illustrator CS5 drawing to see what is causing all of the joy. The file we will be using, `Mascot.ai`, contains a number of Illustrator layers and paths (see Figure 2-78). One path—in the Head layer—contains a drop shadow.

Figure 2-78. The Illustrator CS5 file for this example contains a number of layers and paths.

> The authors would like to thank Mischa Plocek for the use of the `Mascot.ai` file. Mischa is a flash developer/artist based in Zurich, Switzerland, and his work can be seen at `www.styleterrorist.com`.

Follow these steps to import an Illustrator CS5 document into Flash CS5:

1. Open a new Flash document, and import the `Mascot.ai` file into the Flash `Library`. The `Import` dialog box, shown in Figure 2-79, will appear. Keep in mind the `Head` layer contains a `Drop Shadow` filter, and as you can see, Flash will import that layer as a movie clip in order to retain the drop shadow.

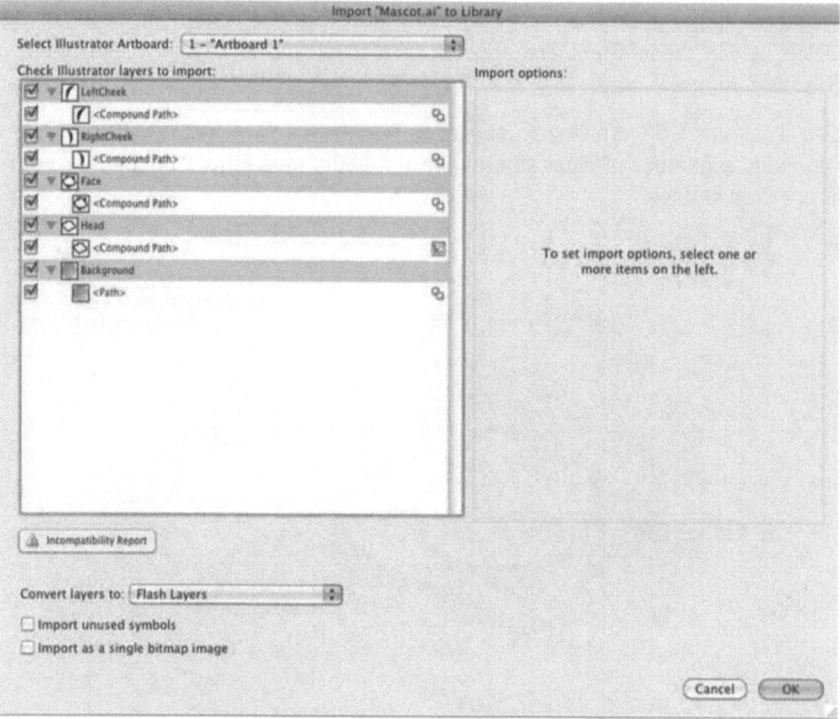

Figure 2-79. The `Import` dialog box used for an Illustrator CS5 image

> If you select `File ▶ Import to Stage`, the `Import` dialog box will contain a couple of choices not shown here. You will be asked whether you want the images in each layer to be placed at their original position in the Illustrator document, and you will also be asked whether you want to trim the stage to the dimensions of the Illustrator document.

2. Select the remaining layers, not the paths, and select `Create movie clip`, as shown in Figure 2-80. Don't bother with instance names because there is no need for ActionScript here. The `Convert layers to` drop-down menu allows you to convert your Illustrator layers to Flash layers or to a series of Flash keyframes (this is handy if they are animated) or allows you to put the whole image into one Flash layer. You are also given the opportunity to import unused symbols created in Illustrator or to flatten the image and bring it in as a bitmap.

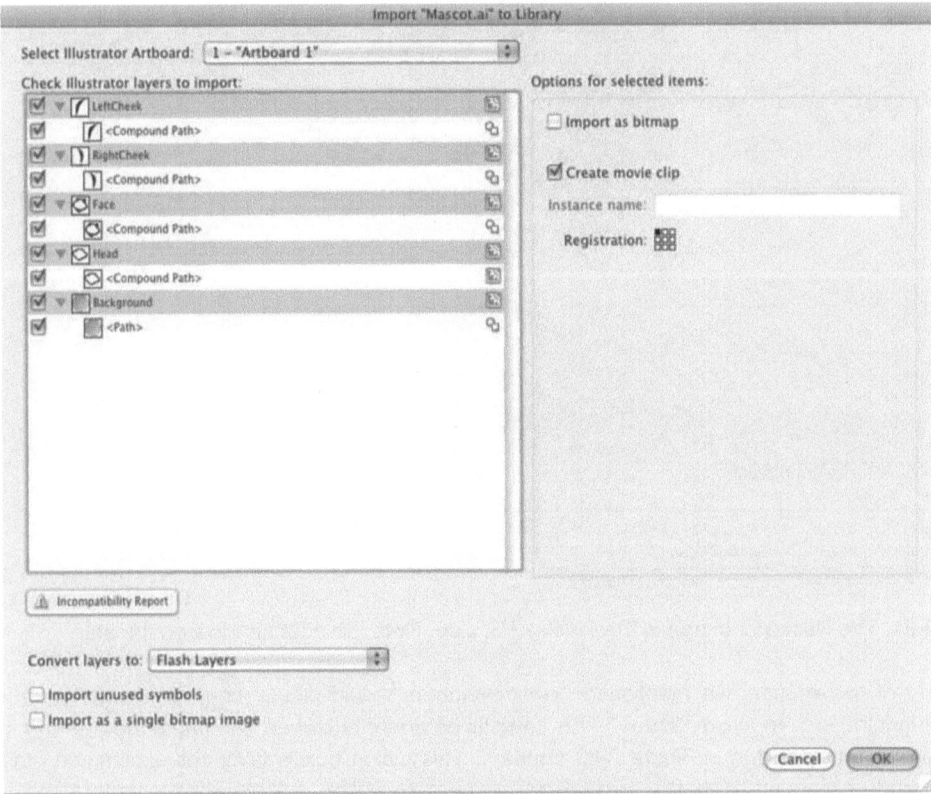

Figure 2-80. Illustrator layers can be converted to movie clips.

> The `Import unused symbols` option may be a bit confusing. Illustrator allows you to create symbols, and these symbols can be imported directly into Flash from Illustrator. We will show how this works in the next chapter.

3. Click `OK`, and when the import process finishes, open the `Library`, as shown in Figure 2-81. The image has been directly imported to the stage, but each of the layers has its own folder containing the movie clip you created in the `Import` dialog box.

Figure 2-81. The Illustrator image in the Flash `Library`. Note the drop shadow on the star.

At the top of this section, we mentioned how developers would simply copy Illustrator documents and paste them into Flash to avoid "issues." This can still be done, but when you paste the drawing into Flash CS5, the dialog box shown in Figure 2-82 appears. This dialog box is fairly self-explanatory, though you may be wondering about the **Paste using AI File Importer preferences** choice.

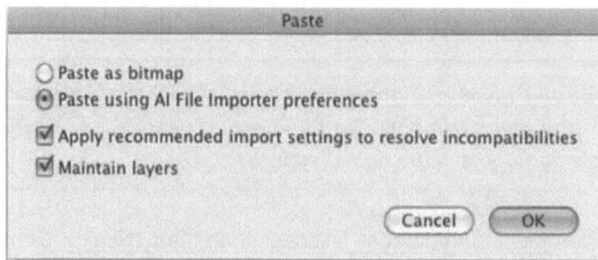

Figure 2-82. Pasting a drawing from Illustrator to Flash will open this dialog box.

You can get to the preferences by selecting **Edit** ➤ **Preferences** (Windows) or **Flash** ➤ **Preferences** (Mac). When the **Preferences** dialog box opens, click the **AI File Importer** selection at the bottom of the **Category** list. This will open the **AI File Importer** preferences, as shown in Figure 2-83. As you can see, many of the choices are also available in the **Import** dialog box.

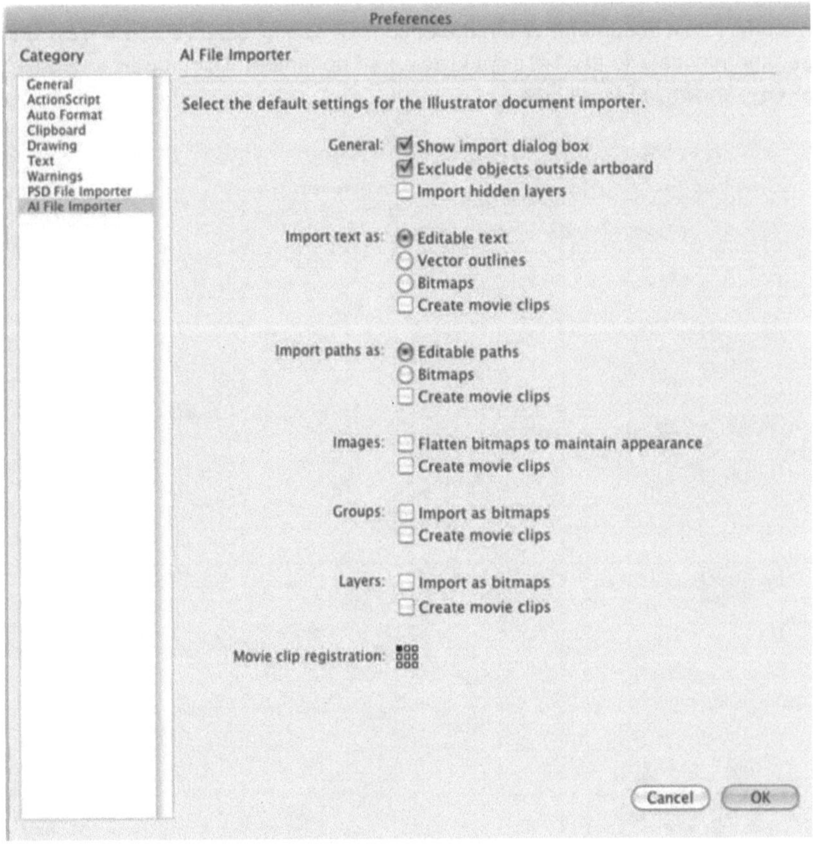

Figure 2-83. The AI File Importer preferences

You are most likely looking at the Mascot image in the **Library** and thinking, "That's all well and good, but how do I get the dang document onto the Flash stage and play with it?" Here's how:

1. Drag the Mascot.ai file from the **Library** to the Flash stage.

2. Double-click the image on the stage. When the **Symbol Editor** opens, you will see the image is actually composed of the movie clips in the Mascot.ai.Assets folder from the **Library** and that each movie clip is on a separate named layer.

Importing Photoshop CS5 documents into Flash CS5

We'll wind up this overview of Flash's drawing features with the import of Photoshop CS5 images into Flash. As you saw with Illustrator CS5, the process has been streamlined, and you are in for a rather pleasant surprise. Follow these steps to import a Photoshop document into Flash:

1. Open a new Flash document. When the document opens, select `File ➤ Import ➤ Import to Stage`, and navigate to the `IglooVillage.psd` document. Click `Open` to launch the `PSD File Importer`, shown in Figure 2-84.

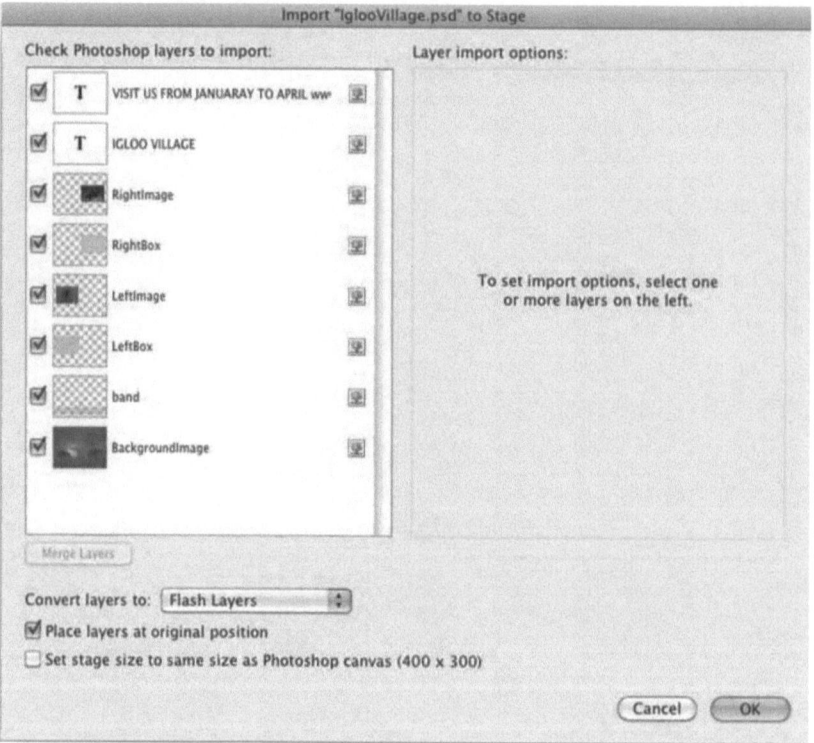

Figure 2-84. The PSD file importer

The dialog box looks similar to its Illustrator counterpart. Still, there are a couple of major differences. The inclusion of a `Place layers at original position` check box option ensures the contents of the PSD file retain the exact position that they had in Photoshop. For example, if an object was positioned at X = 100, Y = 35 in Photoshop, it will be placed at those coordinates on the Flash stage. If this option is not selected, the imported Photoshop layers are centered on the stage.

The other check box option, `Set stage to same size as Photoshop canvas`, is a real godsend. In the case of this image, the canvas size is not the default Flash size—500 by 400—but 468 by 146. When the file imports, the Flash stage will be resized to the dimensions of the Photoshop document.

> *The manner in which PSD files are imported into Flash is set in the Preferences. You can reach them by selecting* `Edit` ➤ `Preferences` *(Windows) or* `Flash` ➤ `Preferences` *(Mac) and selecting* `PSD File Importer` *in the* `Category` *listing.*

2. Hold down the Shift key, and click the first two layers to select them. The **Merge Layers** button lights up. This means you can combine the selected layers into one layer. This works for selected adjacent layers only. Deselect the layers.

3. Select the check box beside the first layer. What you have just done is to tell Flash to ignore importing that layer. Reselect the check box.

4. Click the name of the first layer. The import options, as shown in Figure 2-85, appear on the right side of the dialog box. The first thing you should notice is the Importer has figured out you clicked a text layer. You have three choices as to how the text will be handled, and if you want, you can put the selection in its own movie clip. Select the `Editable text` import option.

> *If the text in the PSD file is PostScript or TrueType, always select* `Editable text`. *If you select the other two options, typos move, cemented, into Flash.*

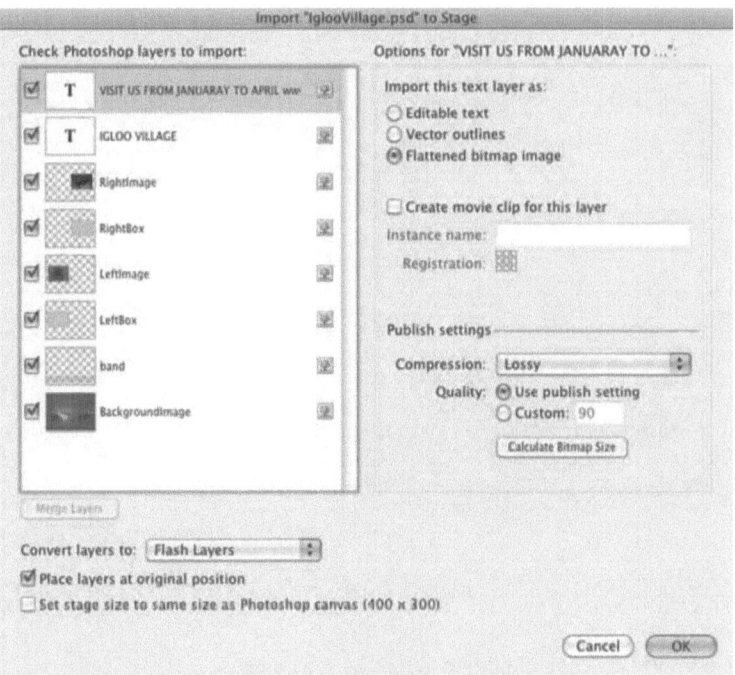

Figure 2-85. The text import options

CHAPTER 2

5. With the layer still selected, select the `Create movie clip for this layer` check box option, and enter `Headline` as the instance name. Notice the placement of a movie clip icon on the layer strip.

6. Click the `BackgroundImage` layer. Pay attention to how, as shown in Figure 2-86, the import options change to reflect the selection of a bitmap. You can choose to put the layer in a movie clip—`Bitmap image with editable layer styles`—or import a flattened bitmap image. It makes sense with this image to choose the first option to maintain the layer transparency.

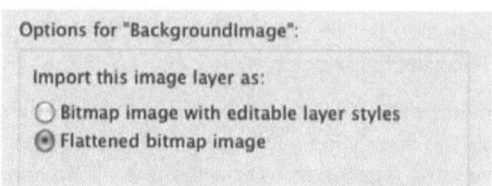

Figure 2-86. The text import options for a bitmap image

Hold on, does this mean you have to repeat this step with the remaining five layers? No. Shift-click each layer to select all of them, and click the first option. A movie clip icon, as shown in Figure 2-87, will appear beside each layer.

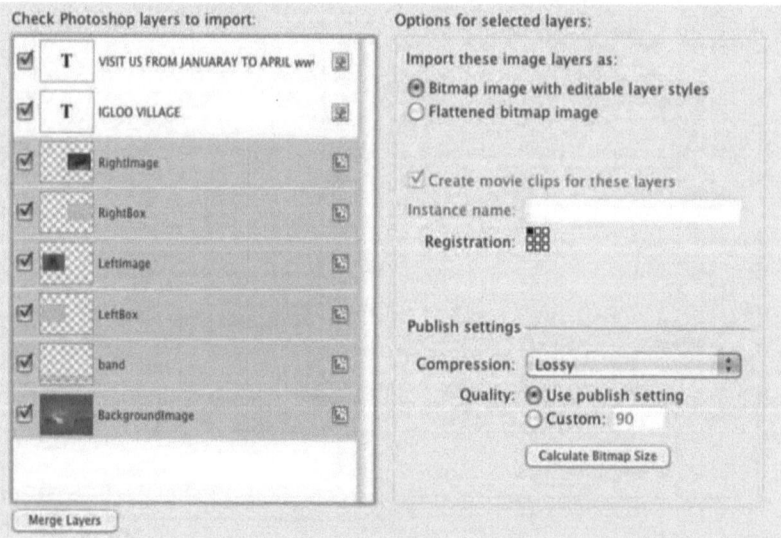

Figure 2-87. How to import a series of bitmap layers as movie clips

7. With all the layers selected, click OK to import the image. The layers are placed on the main timeline, and the movie clips requested appear in the `Library`, as shown in Figure 2-88. Save the file as `BannerEx.fla`.

Figure 2-88. The Photoshop file is imported and placed on the Flash stage and in the `Library`.

You have learned

This has been a fairly intense chapter but, along the way, you have learned the following:

- How to use the drawing tools in the `Tools` panel
- How to create and customize gradients
- How to create custom strokes and fills
- The various color features in Flash and how to create and save a custom color
- How to trace a bitmap in Flash
- How to import and optimize graphics in Flash
- How to use the new Illustrator and Photoshop file importers in Flash CS5

CHAPTER 2

We aren't going to deny this has been a pretty intense chapter. Even so, all the topics covered here will ripple through the remainder of this book. Most important of all, you have learned how graphic content is created, added to Flash, and optimized in Flash. The next step is making that content reusable in Flash movies or available to different Flash movies. That is the subject of the next chapter. See you there.

Chapter 3

Symbols and Libraries

Symbols, the topic of this chapter, are one of the most powerful features of Flash. This is because they allow you to create reusable content. You need only one copy of a symbol. Once it is on the stage, you can then manipulate that symbol in any number of ways without those changes affecting the original piece of content.

We'll cover the following in this chapter:

- Creating and using symbols
- Creating, using, and sharing libraries
- Adding filters and blends to symbols
- Grouping and nesting symbols
- Using rulers, stacking, and alignment to manage content on the Flash stage
- Creating masks
- Creating soft masks

If you haven't already, download the chapter files. You can find them at `www.friendsofED.com/download.html?isbn=1430229940`.

These are the files used in this chapter:

- GraphicSymbol.fla (Chapter03/Exercise Files_CH03/ GraphicSymbol.fla)
- ButtonSymbol.fla (Chapter03/Exercise Files_CH03/ ButtonSymbol.fla)
- MovieClip.swf (Chapter03/Exercise Files_CH03/ MovieClip.swf)
- MovieClip.fla (Chapter03/Exercise Files_CH03/ MovieClip.fla)
- SymbolEdit.fla (Chapter03/Exercise Files_CH03/ SymbolEdit.fla)
- 9Slice.fla (Chapter03/Exercise Files_CH03/9Slice.fla)
- Olives.fla (Chapter03/Exercise Files_CH03/ Olives.fla)
- 9Slice2.swf (Chapter03/Exercise Files_CH03/9Slice2.swf)
- 9SliceGotchas.fla (Chapter03/Exercise Files_CH03/9SliceGotchas.fla)
- SharedLibrary.fla (Chapter03/Exercise Files_CH03/SharedLibrary.fla)
- Filter.fla (Chapter03/Exercise Files_CH03/Filter.fla)
- Blends.fla (Chapter03/Exercise Files_CH03/Blends.fla)
- NuttyProfessor.fla (Chapter03/Exercise Files_CH03/ NuttyProfessor.fla)
- Stacks.fla (Chapter03/Exercise Files_CH03/ Stacks.fla)
- AlignPanel.fla (Chapter03/Exercise Files_CH03/ AlignPanel.fla)
- SimpleMask.fla (Chapter03/Exercise Files_CH03/ SimpleMask.fla)
- Seasons.fla (Chapter03/Exercise Files_CH03/ Seasons.fla)
- Seasons02.fla (Chapter03/Exercise Files_CH03/ Seasons02.fla)

Symbols are also the building blocks of everything you will do in Flash (other than ActionScript). They are inevitably created when you come to the realization that the piece of content you are looking at will be used several times throughout a movie. In fact, the same content may appear in a number of movies, or even have a single use, such as a movie clip that plays a particular video or sound. The most important aspect of symbols is they keep the file size of a SWF manageable. The end result of a small SWF is fast load times and users who aren't drumming their fingers on a desk waiting for your movie to start.

Symbol essentials

Reduced to its basics, a **symbol** is something you can use and reuse. It could be an image, an animation, a button, or even a movie used within the main movie. When a symbol is created, it is placed in the `Library`, and any copy of that symbol on the stage at any point in the movie is said to be an **instance** of that symbol. Let's create a symbol and start examining how these things work. Follow these steps:

SYMBOLS AND LIBRARIES

1. Launch Flash, and when a new document opens, select the **Rectangle**, and draw a rectangle on the stage. Don't worry about stroke and fill at this point. You are simply concentrating on creating a symbol.

2. Right-click (Windows) or Cmd+click (Mac) the shape, and select **Convert to Symbol** from the context menu (as shown in Figure 3-1). You can also select the object on the stage and press the F8 key, or you can select the object and choose **Modify ➤ Convert to Symbol**.

Figure 3-1. Creating a symbol

3. When the **Convert to Symbol** dialog box opens, name the symbol **Box**, and select **Movie clip** as its **Type** (see Figure 3-2). Click **OK**; the dialog box will close, and the new symbol will appear in the **Library**.

If you are new to Flash, you may notice a button named **Advanced** in the **Convert to Symbol** dialog box. When you click it, a number of extra options will open. Let's look at each element in the dialog box:

- **Name**: The name you enter here will be the name for the symbol as it appears in the **Library**.

- **Type**: You select the symbol type here. Symbol types will be explained in even greater depth in the next section.

- **Registration**: Each of the nine dots represents a possible location for the symbol's registration point. The registration point (also known as the **transformation** or **pivot point**) is used for alignment with other objects on the stage and for movement along a motion guide or for objects put into motion using ActionScript.

- **Folder**: This was new to Flash CS4. Click the `Library root` link to open a `Move to folder` dialog box, which lets you specify the `Library` folder for your new symbol. You can even create and name a new `Library` folder in the same step, if desired, which is a huge productivity booster. In the dialog box, select the `New folder` radio button, and you can name a folder. Select the `Existing folder` radio button, and you can save the symbol to any folder in the `Library`.

- **Enable guides for 9-slice scaling**: Select this, and the guides for this special scaling will appear. We'll deal with this important topic in a separate section of this chapter.

- **Linkage**: You can use ActionScript to pull symbols and other assets out of the `Library` and either put them on the stage or use them for another purpose, such as playing audio. To do this, you need to assign an instance name, called a **linkage identifier**, for ActionScript to be able to find it in the `Library`. The `Linkage` check boxes allow the symbol to be used by ActionScript and to load the symbol into the first frame of the movie when the movie plays.

- **Sharing**: This area allows you to share symbols with other Flash movies or to import symbols from other Flash movies into your project. This used to be bundled into the `Linkage` area but Adobe, recognizing that symbols are the cornerstones of Flash, have made this its own little configuration in Flash CS5.

- **Source**: This area allows you to identify external content in a shared library or elsewhere to be used as a symbol. This comes into play in cases where you've dragged an asset from one FLA into another. For example, a Flash animator might build a character's body parts in one FLA, save it, and then use that external library in a completely different series of movies. If he changes the color of a shirt in the original library from blue to red, the shirt can be configured to change in the current movie as well. Note that you can select `Always update before publishing`, which makes the change in each FLA to which it is linked, minimizing duplicated effort.

4. Click OK. If you look at the box on the stage, you will see it now surrounded by a thin blue line. This tells you that the object just selected is a symbol. The `Properties` panel will also change to show that you have, indeed, selected a symbol.

5. Open the `Library`, and drag another copy of the symbol to the stage. Click the symbol to select it. Select the `Free Transform` tool, and scale and rotate the object. As you can see, changing one instance of a symbol does not affect any other instance of that same symbol on the stage.

6. Close the movie without saving it.

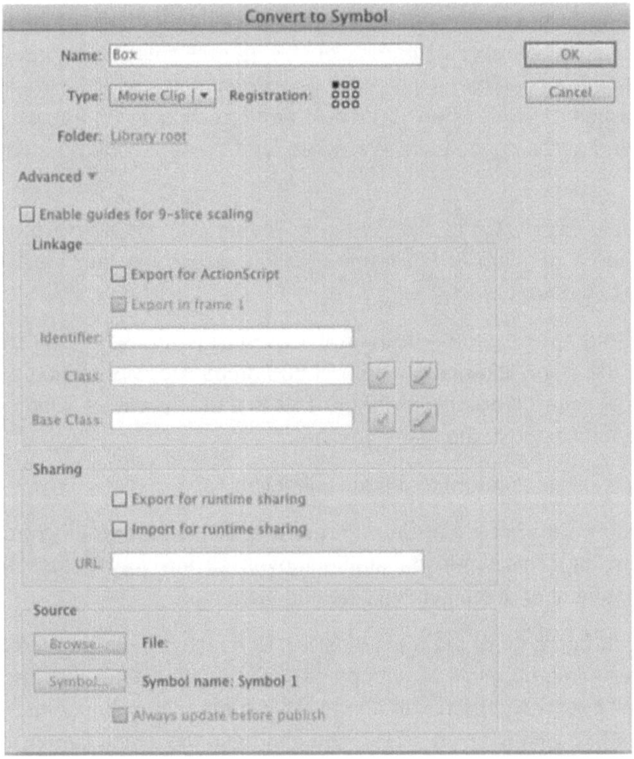

SYMBOLS AND LIBRARIES

Figure 3-2. The `Convert to Symbol` dialog box

Symbol types

You have three basic symbol types to choose from: graphic, button, and movie clip. Each one has specific capabilities, and the type you choose will be based upon what needs to be done. For instance, say you have a logo that will be used in several places throughout a movie and not be required to move. In this case, the graphic symbol would be your choice. If the need is for a racing car zooming across the screen with the engine sounds blasting out of the user's speakers, then the movie clip symbol is the choice. Need a button? Well, that one is a bit obvious. Let's briefly review each symbol type.

Graphic symbols

Graphic symbols are used primarily for static images or content used in a project. They can also be used as the building blocks for complex animations. Though we say they are primarily static, they can be put into motion on the main timeline or the timelines of other symbols.

CHAPTER 3

Graphic symbols, unlike their movie clip cousins, do not play independently of the timeline they are in. This is why they need a matching number of frames on the parent timeline in order for each frame of the graphic symbol to display. For example, if a graphic symbol animates over 60 frames and you want it to be on the main timeline for half of its life, then you would need to allocate 30 frames on the main timeline for this task. That may sound a little convoluted. We agree, and have provided a small movie that shows you what we mean:

1. Open the `GraphicSymbol.fla` file. When it opens, you will see a bronze Mao statue on the timeline that has a duration of ten frames. Scrub across the timeline, and the statue moves a short distance to the right.

2. Double-click the graphic symbol—**Mao**—in the **Library**, and when the **Symbol Editor** opens, you'll see that the animation has a length of 60 frames. Double-clicking a symbol on the stage to open the symbol is called **editing in place**. This is a handy way of fixing symbols and seeing how the changes are reflected in the main timeline.

3. Click the **Scene 1** link to return to the main timeline.

4. Select frame 60 on the main timeline, and add a frame (not as keyframe, just a frame). Scrub across the timeline. This time, the statue moves all the way across the stage because it is matching the movement of the symbol's nested animation.

5. Insert a frame at frame 61 of the main timeline. Because the statue's internal timeline loops back to frame 1 after frame 60, the statue pops back to the left side of the stage. If you keep inserting frames, you will eventually finish with a loop. This is an extremely useful technique to know. If you were to have a bird with flapping wings, you can have the wings flap inside the graphic symbol's timeline while the main timeline manages the motion of the bird flying from side to side of the stage.

6. Select the statue on the stage, and open the **Properties** panel.

7. Twirl down the **Looping** area in the **Properties** panel. The drop-down menu in the **Options** area lets you choose **Loop**, **Play Once** and **Single Frame**. The field labeled **First** lets you choose which frame of the graphic symbol's timeline to display first. We'll dig into this interesting feature in Chapter 7.

8. Close the file without saving the changes.

Button symbols

Button symbols are rather interesting in that they are able to do a lot more than you may think. Button symbols have a four-frame timeline in which each frame is the state of the button (up, over, down, and hit), as shown in Figure 3-3. The button states can be created using graphic symbols or movie clips or drawn directly into the frame using the tools. The key to a **Button** symbol, as you will see, lies in telling Flash where the mouse has to be to activate the various states of the button. Let's look at a typical button:

SYMBOLS AND LIBRARIES

1. Open the ButtonSymbol.fla file, and select **Control ➤ Enable Simple Buttons**. This menu item brings the button to life on the Flash stage. If you roll over a button and click it, you will see that the button changes in relation to whether it has been clicked or rolled over and whether the mouse is off of the button. In this case, nothing happens. Let's see why.

> *If you use the* **Enable Simple Buttons** *menu item, do your sanity a favor, and deselect it after you have tested the button. This menu item puts the button into its "live" state, meaning that you can't select it or move it to another location on the stage.*

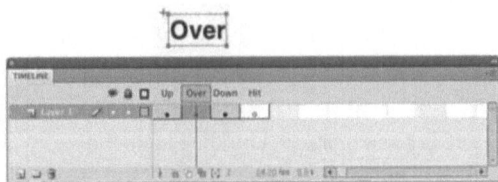

Figure 3-3. The button symbol timeline

2. Double-click the button symbol named **Button** in the **Library**. When the **Symbol Editor** opens, you will see that each state of the button is in its own keyframe. Select the **Hit** keyframe.

The button didn't work in step 1 because the **Hit** frame is empty. Flash doesn't have a clue where the mouse should be to make the button work. We are fixing this by defining a "hot" area in the **Hit** frame.

3. Select the **Rectangle** tool, and draw a large square or rectangle that covers most of the stage.

4. Click the **Scene 1** link, turn on **Enable Simple Buttons**, and drag the mouse across the stage. The over state will appear even though the mouse pointer is not over the button. This is the hit state coming into play. The area of the shape determines the active area for an event. This should tell you that you can have a button composed only of a hit state. If you do, what you have created is a hotspot, sometimes referred to as an invisible button, on the stage.

5. Close the movie, and don't save the changes.

> *You can add layers to a button symbol. A common use of this feature is adding a sound to a button. For example, you could have something explode only when the mouse is over a button. Drag the* **BlowUp** *button to the stage and try it. The explosion sound is on the* **Audio** *layer of the symbol and is triggered only when the mouse is over the button on the stage.*

157

Movie clip symbols

Movie clips can be thought of as movies within movies. These symbols, unlike their graphic counterparts, actually run independent of the timeline in which they are placed. They can contain code, other symbols, and audio tracks. Movie clips can also be placed inside other movie clips—the term for this is **nesting**—and they have become so ubiquitous and useful among Flash designers that they are, in many cases, replacing graphic and button symbols on the stage.

A major aspect of their timeline independence is that movie clips continue to play even if the parent timeline is stopped, which explains why they are often placed in a single frame on the main timeline. In cases where, for example, a movie clip fades in over a period of time, it may extend across a number of frames to accommodate this effect, but, technically, movie clips need only a single frame on whatever timeline they are placed into. The other major feature of movie clips is they can be controlled using ActionScript. We are going to get into this in a big way later in the book. In the meantime, let's explore that concept of timeline independence:

1. Double-click the `MovieClip.swf` file to launch Flash Player. You will see a sports car come roaring onto the screen and drive off the right edge of the stage. Close the SWF, and let's look at how this was put together.

2. Open the `MovieClip.fla` file. If you drag the playhead across the timeline, you will see that the car starts moving across the stage in frame 6 and is off the stage by frame 45.

3. Open the **Library** panel, and you will see the car is actually composed of several symbols. The `Car` graphic symbol doesn't contain a rear wheel. Why is it a graphic symbol? It is simply a picture The `Rear` movie clip contains the wheel that is rotated over a series of frames in its timeline. Why is this one a movie clip? The answer is the rotating wheel on the movie clip's timeline.

4. Double-click the `Race` movie clip in the **Library** to open the **Symbol Editor**. You will see that the car is composed of two layers; and each layer contains a symbol. This is what is meant by *nesting*. Movie clips can be placed inside other movie clips. This is also true of graphic symbols, but again, the key difference, in terms of animation, is that the timelines for the movie clips aren't controlled by the main timeline. Notice that each symbol resides in a single frame of its own layer. Even though the `Rear` movie clip gets one frame of the timeline, it still spins when the SWF is published.

5. Click the `Scene1` link to return to the main timeline. Select the car anywhere between frames 6 and 45 on the stage, and open the **Properties** panel. You will see that the `Race` movie clip, as shown in Figure 3-4, is used for the animation.

6. Scrub the playhead across the timeline. You'll see that the car gets larger and smaller, thanks to a tween. The key aspect of this is that movie clip properties can be changed, and in the case of nested movie clips, this change is reflected throughout the entire symbol, including the movie clips nested inside the main movie clip.

SYMBOLS AND LIBRARIES

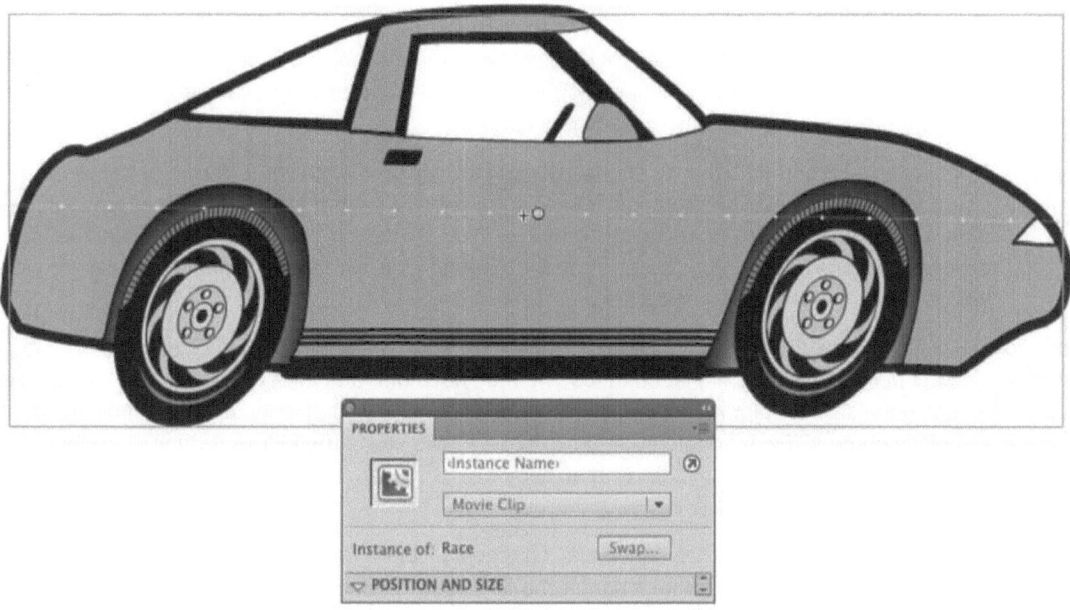

Figure 3-4. The `Race` movie clip is selected on the stage.

> Yes, we agree this is not exactly a well-designed piece. In fact, one of the authors saw it and said, "Dude, what's with that?" Sometimes the technique is more important than the actual content. This is an important concept for those of you who are new to Flash: get it to work, understand why it works, and then start playing with it. Everything you will do in Flash starts with a basic concept, and everything else in the movie builds upon that concept. For example, Joshua Davis, one of the more influential characters in the Flash community, started one project by simply watching how a series of gray squares rotated on the Flash stage. Once he got the squares to rotate in a manner that worked for him, he simply swapped out the squares for shapes he had drawn in Illustrator.

Editing symbols

There will be occasions where you will want to edit a symbol. This is where the `Symbol Editor` becomes an invaluable tool. There are two ways of opening the `Symbol Editor`:

1. Open the SymbolEdit.fla file in your Exercise folder.

2. Open the **Library**, and double-click the **Circle** movie clip symbol in the **Library**. The **Symbol Editor** will open. This technique is also known as **entering the timeline** of a symbol. Click the **Scene 1** link to return to the main timeline.

3. Double-click the squashed circle on the stage. This will also open the **Symbol Editor**, but, as you may have noticed, the other instances of any symbol on the stage are visible but look to be dim. If you try to select the instance of the box, you will notice you can't. This technique, called **editing in place**, allows you to see how the change to a symbol or instance affects, or works with, the rest of the content on the stage.

The edit in place technique often provides the designers with a helpful sense of context. The other important aspect of this technique is that changes you may have made to the symbol on the main timeline, such as changing the size or color of the squashed circle, are only reflected in the symbol's timeline thanks to the edit in place context. If you double-click the **Circle** movie clip in the Library, you will see that it isn't squashed. What you can learn from this is that symbols can be manipulated on the timeline without affecting the original symbol in the **Library**.

4. In the **Symbol Editor**, you can make changes to the symbol. Click the squashed circle to select it and, in the **Tools** panel, change the fill color to a different color. When you do this, both instances of the circle symbol on the stage will change color.

5. Close the file without saving the changes.

What you can gather from this is that instances of symbols can be changed without affecting the original symbol in the **Library**. Change the symbol in the **Symbol Editor**, and that change is applied to every instance of the symbol in the movie.

9-slice scaling

Until the release of Flash 8, Flash designers essentially had to put up with a rather nasty design problem. Scaling objects with rounded or oddly shaped corners was, to put it mildly, driving them crazy. No matter what they tried to do, scaling introduced distortions to the object. The release of Flash 8 and the inclusion of 9-slice scaling solved that issue. To be fair, there are still a few quirks with this feature, but it was so welcome in Flash that this feature is now appearing in Fireworks and Illustrator CS5. The best part of this addition to those two applications is that symbols created in these applications that are destined for Flash can have 9-slice scaling applied to them that carry over into Flash as well.

As we pointed out at the start of this chapter, 9-slice scaling is applied to movie clips when the **Convert to Symbol** dialog box opens. If you create a movie clip and decide to apply this feature later during the production process, select the movie clip in the **Library** and right-click (Windows) or Control+click (Mac) the symbol to open the context menu. Select **Properties**, and add 9-slice scaling by selecting this option at the bottom of the symbol **Properties** dialog box. Movie clips with 9-slice scaling applied will show a grid in the **Library** panel's preview window,

How 9-slice scaling works

What the heck is 9-slice scaling?

That question is not as dumb as it may sound because it is a hard subject to understand. What happens is that the symbol in question—in Flash it can only be a movie clip—is overlaid with a three-by-three grid. This grid divides the movie clip into nine sections (or slices) and allows the clip to be scaled in such a way that the corners, edges, and strokes retain their shape.

Figure 3-5 shows the actual grid that Flash places over the object. The object is broken into the nine areas. The eight areas surrounding the center area—the area with the 5—will scale either horizontally or vertically. The area in the middle—area 5—will scale on both axes. The really interesting aspect of this feature is that each section of the grid is scaled independently of the other eight sections.

Figure 3-5. The 9-slice scaling grid

The best way of understanding how all of this works is to actually see it in action.

1. Open the 9Slice.fla file. When it opens, you will see two movie clips on the stage. The upper movie clip doesn't have 9-slice scaling applied; the lower one does (see Figure 3-6). The key to both of these objects is they are the identical size, and the stroke width around both shapes is also identical.

2. Click the upper movie clip, and open the **Transform** panel (**Window ▶ Transform**).

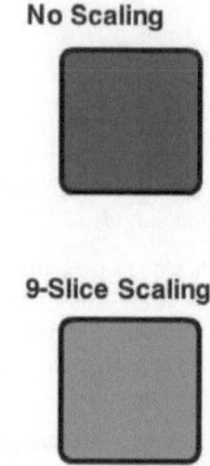

Figure 3-6. You start with two movie clips on the stage.

3. When the `Transform` panel opens, change the `Horizontal` scaling value to `300 percent`. When you press the Enter (Windows) or Return (Mac) key, the shape scales along the horizontal axis, but as you can see, the corners flatten out and distort, and the stroke gets fatter.

4. Click the lower movie clip, open the `Transform` panel, and change the `Horizontal` scaling value to `300 percent`. When you press the Enter (Windows) or Return (Mac) key, the shape scales along the horizontal axis, and the corners don't distort (as shown in Figure 3-7). You can see why by looking at Figure 3-5. The areas numbered 2, 5, and 8 are scaled horizontally, and the corner areas are unaffected.

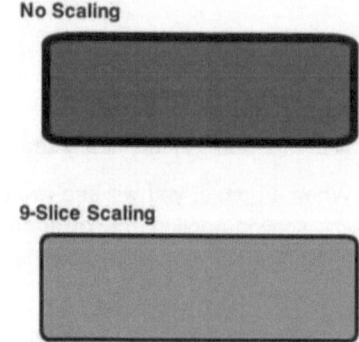

Figure 3-7. Both movie clips are scaled at 300 percent along the horizontal axis; the movie clip without 9-slice scaling is distorted.

SYMBOLS AND LIBRARIES

Additionally, the guides are adjustable. They can be moved, which allows you to control how the scaling will be applied. Here's how:

5. Double-click the `9Scale` movie clip in the `Library` to open the `Symbol Editor`. You will see the grid.

6. Roll the mouse pointer over one of the slice guides, and it will change to include a small arrow pointing to the right if you are over a vertical guide, or pointing downward if you are over a horizontal guide (see Figure 3-8).

7. Click and drag the selected guide to its new position. When you release the mouse and return to the main timeline, you will see the change in the `Library`'s preview window.

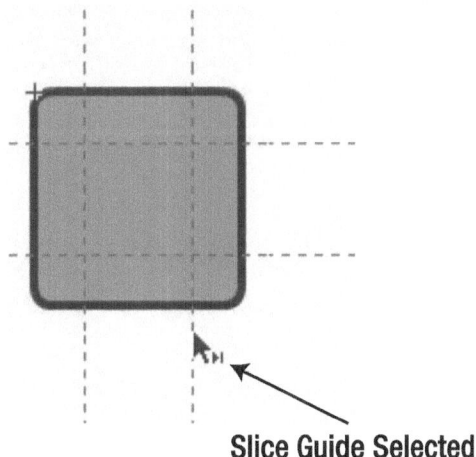

Slice Guide Selected

Figure 3-8. The guides can be repositioned.

So far, so good. You have applied the slice guides to a geometric object. OK, we hear you. You are probably muttering, "Not exactly a real-world project." We thought about that, and agree with you. What about occasions where the corners are irregular? Let's go visit an Olive Seller in Guang Zhou to give you some "real-world" experience with that issue.

Your turn: frames for an olive seller

When we approached this exercise, the question was, "What could we put in a picture fame that would be memorable?" Flowers and other images are interesting, but they really don't make the point. Then one of the authors said, "How about a picture of an olive seller?" The reply was, "Yeah, right." To which the author who made the original suggestion said, "No. No. No. There is a guy in Guang Zhou, China, who sells olives on the street. He wears a rooster suit and blows a horn. Maybe we can use it?"

1. Open Olives.fla. When the file opens, you will notice that the images of the olive seller don't exactly fit their frames (see Figure 3-9). Let's fix that.

Figure 3-9. The picture frames don't fit the images.

2. Right-click the **Frame** movie clip in the **Library**, and select **Properties** from the context menu.

3. When the **Symbol Properties** dialog box opens, click the **Enable guides for 9-slice scaling** check box, as shown in Figure 3-10.

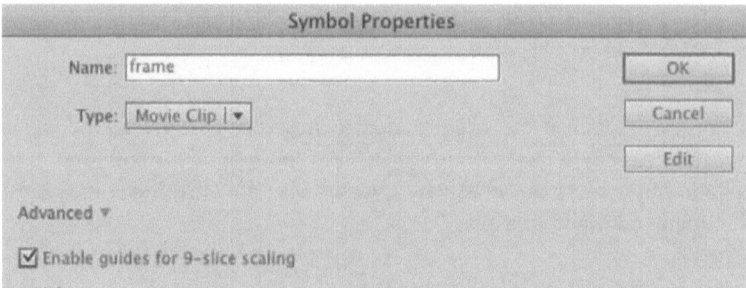

Figure 3-10. Enabling 9-slice scaling for a symbol

4. Open the movie clip in the **Symbol Editor**, and adjust the guides to match those shown in Figure 3-11. Note that the guides are positioned to encompass the extent of each corner olive.

SYMBOLS AND LIBRARIES

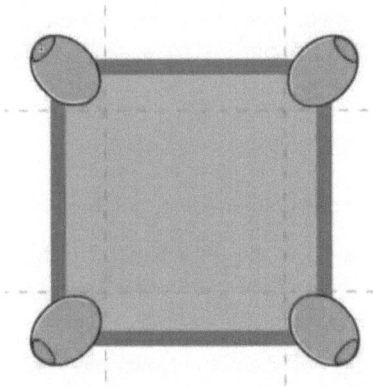

Figure 3-11. Applying 9-slice scaling and adjusting the guides

5. Click the `Scene 1` link to return to the main timeline.
6. Select the `Free Transform` tool, and adjust the picture frames found in the `frame1` and `frame2` layers to fit the image, as shown in Figure 3-12. Even though each photo has its own width, the same symbol can now be used to neatly frame these different dimensions.

Figure 3-12. 9-slice scaling allows us to put a frame around the olive seller.

Now that you have seen how 9-slice scaling works, how it is applied, and how to use it, don't get lulled into thinking it is especially easy to use. That is a real danger with books of this sort, where everything appears rosy, wonderful, and trouble-free. In many cases, it is. In this one, it isn't.

When we started working on olive seller's picture frame, things started "blowing up." The corner images started distorting when they shouldn't have. This caused us to halt the process and really dig into this

165

particular feature. The next section gives you the unrosy, "it ain't all that wonderful and easy to use" rundown regarding what we discovered about 9-slice scaling. Thankfully, our pointers should help you steer clear of the mines.

The 9-slice "gotchas"

You need to know that there are a handful of interesting "gotchas" involved with 9-slice scaling.

The first concerns the area in the middle of the 9-slice grid, which scales across both the horizontal and the vertical axes. If you have content in the center area of the grid (area 5), such as a gradient or image, it will distort if the scaling is uneven. Take a look for yourself.

Open the `9Slice2.swf` file, and drag out a corner. Notice how the flower distorts. This is because the frame and the flower are both in the area 5 slice (see Figure 3-13). Depending on your needs, this makes 9-slice symbols useful only as background borders, layered behind content that simply must not be distorted. In the `Olives.fla` file, the photos are on layers of their own.

Figure 3-13. The center area of a symbol containing 9-slice scaling scales on two axes. The area in the middle will distort.

The second involves maintaining the integrity of any drawings or objects used in the corners. Shapes, drawing objects, primitives, or graphic symbols can be used. Movie clips or rotated graphic symbols, such as the graphic symbol of the olive originally destined for the frame's corners, can't be used. That would be easy enough to remember, but an interesting quirk rears its head with graphic symbols: if you use graphic symbols that are rotated, they will not display correctly as specially scaled 9-slice elements in the Flash interface. Rest assured, they work just fine in the SWF—you just can't see that they're working until you test your movie. If this annoys you, bear in mind that Flash 8 didn't show 9-slice scaling in the authoring environment at all, so this is an improvement!

SYMBOLS AND LIBRARIES

You can see what we are talking about in Figures 3-13 and 3-14. Instead of the drawing of the olive, it was placed into a graphic symbol, which was then rotated to meet the design. When we applied the 9-slice scaling to the movie clip, the result was Figure 3-14. The boxes and olives looked like something had gone horribly wrong.

Figure 3-14. Rotating a simple graphic symbol can cause issues.

When the movie was tested in Flash Player, as shown in Figure 3-15, everything looked normal.

167

CHAPTER 3

Figure 3-15. Testing in Flash Player. Problem? What problem?

Stretching objects along the horizontal axis is another issue that will jump up and bite the unwary. Figure 3-16 demonstrates this. We started with nothing more than a rounded rectangle with a square in the upper-left corner. If you open `9SliceGotchas.fla`, you will see that a shape, a drawing object, a primitive, a graphic symbol, a movie clip, and an imported bitmap representing the square. These objects were all wrapped in a movie clip to which 9-slice scaling is applied.

We did nothing more than select the `Free Transform` tool and stretched the selection along the horizontal axis. The results were, to be gentle, rather surprising.

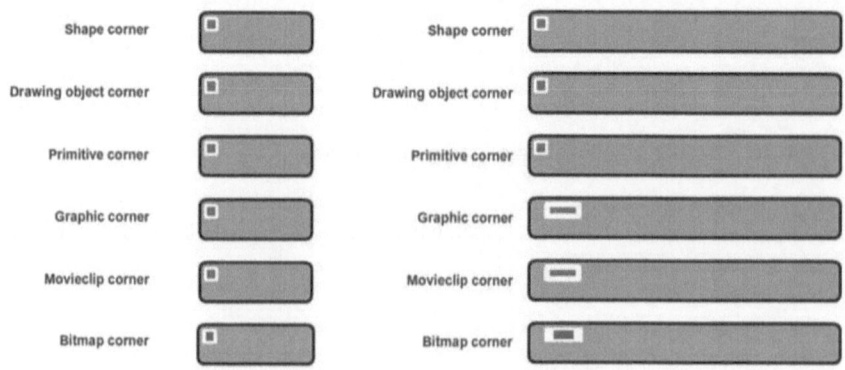

Figure 3-16. Horizontal scaling can introduce distortions.

SYMBOLS AND LIBRARIES

The bottom line is: use 9-slice scaling with care. The idea is a good one, but don't go nuts with it. Keep it simple! Avoid nesting symbols in the corners and sides. If you insist on using bitmaps, bear in mind that they'll stretch in ways that may not be predictable. We encourage you to experiment on your own, but by all accounts, the simpler, the better.

> It is OK to rotate symbols that are not movie clips in 9-slice corners, but they look correct only when your FLA is configured for ActionScript 3.0. You can do this by selecting `File ➤ Publish Options` and clicking the `Flash` tab. The change is made by selecting `ActionScript 3.0` from the `Script` drop-down menu.

Sharing symbols

One of the really useful features of symbols in a `Library` is that they are available to files other than the current movie. Symbols in a Flash `Library` can be shared with other Flash movies. This is extremely helpful if you are working on a number of movies and need to use the same symbol or symbols in numerous Flash documents.

Animators make extensive use of this feature. An animator will, for example, create a character composed of a number of symbols—eyes, arms, legs, and hands, for instance—that are used to put the character in motion. As the animations are built in a given movie, the animator will use symbols that were created in a separate character `Library` movie instead of redrawing them. Here's how to use symbols from another movie:

1. Create a new Flash document, and open the new document's `Library`. As you can see, it is empty.

2. Select `File ➤ Import ➤ Open External Library` or press Ctrl+Shift+O (Windows) or Cmd+Shift+O (Mac), as shown in Figure 3-17. When the `Open` dialog box appears, navigate to the Chapter 3 Exercise folder, and open SharedLibrary.fla.

Figure 3-17. Importing a `Library` from one Flash document into another

3. The `Library` for the selected movie will open, but there are a couple of things missing from that `Library`. There is no drop-down menu, the pushpin is missing, and the `Open New Library` buttons are missing. As well, the `Library` looks grayed out. All of these are visual clues that the SharedLibrary.fla file isn't open.

4. Drag the `arrowLeft` symbol to the empty `Library`. When you release the mouse, the symbol and the bitmap that it comes from will appear in the empty `Library` and become available for use in the movie (see Figure 3-18).

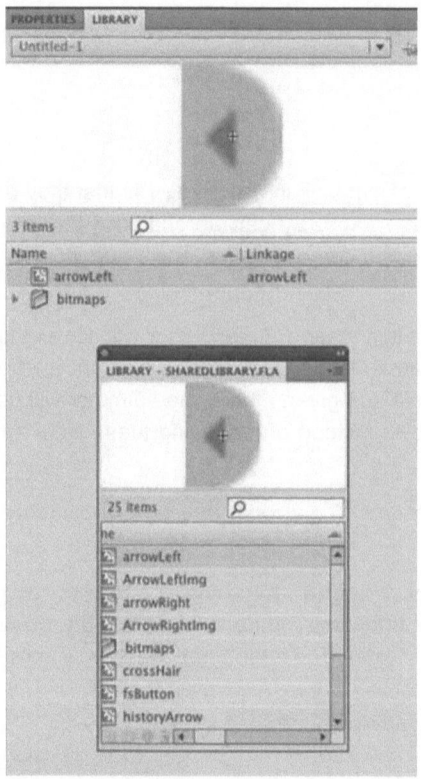

Figure 3-18. Drag a symbol from the imported `Library` to the empty `Library`.

> You can also share font symbols between movies. We'll get into that subject in Chapter 6.

Sharing libraries

Since the introduction of Flash 5, Flash designers and developers have had the ability to link symbols, sounds, animations, bitmaps, and other `Library` symbols within external SWF files to other Flash movies. These external SWF files are called **shared libraries**.

Why would you want to create a shared `Library`? The reason is that it only needs to be downloaded once, even though several other Flash movies may need to access the same symbol. For example, you may be creating a character animation that uses the same image background in ten of the movies that comprise the animation. Rather than adding it in each of the ten movies that use it—not a good idea because the file size of the image will be added to the final SWF for each movie—you can have that symbol reside in a shared `Library` SWF file. This way, the file is loaded only once but used by several movies.

The other thing that sets a shared `Library` SWF apart from a regular SWF is that it doesn't load into a movie clip. Instead, you create the `Library` as you would any other `Library`, but none of the content in that `Library` is put on the Flash stage. Then, each item in the `Library` is given a class identifier, which allows ActionScript to access that item. The file is saved, and the SWF is published.

The key is the **class identifier**. When you select an item in the `Library` and select `Linkage` in the `Symbol Properties` dialog box, you will see a `Linkage` area (shown in Figure 3-19). If a `Library` is to be shared at runtime, then you must select `Export for runtime sharing` and enter the location of the shared `Library`. In the case of Figure 3-16, the URL indicates that the shared `Library` SWF will be located in the same folder as the other SWFs that use it. If the shared `Library` were in a different location, you would enter a full path, such as http://www.myMostExcellentSite.com/excellentMovie/SharedLibrary.swf.

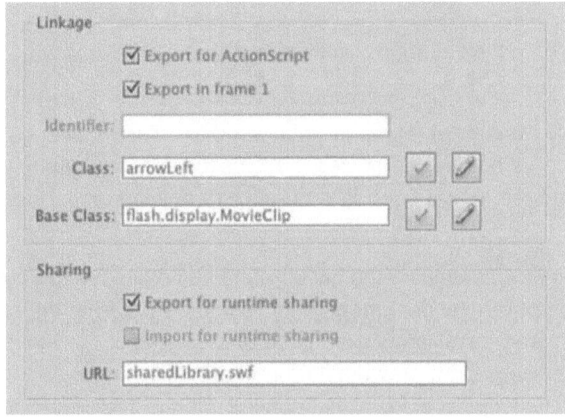

Figure 3-19. Adding items to a shared `Library` using the `Linkage Properties` dialog box

Items in shared libraries can also be created when the symbol is created (see Figure 3-20) or by selecting **Properties** from the **Library** drop-down menu.

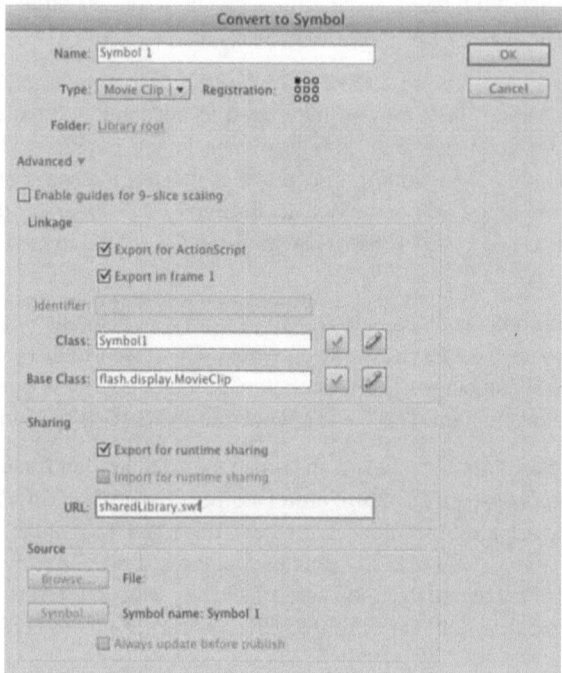

Figure 3-20. Symbols can be added to shared libraries when they are created.

Obviously, things will rarely remain the same in your workflow. Things change and, more often than not, these changes ripple through a number of movies. Let's assume, for example, you need to add or remove something from the background image used in a number of animations in the movie. This is quite easily accomplished.

The first step is to open the FLA containing the background and make the change in the **Symbol Editor**. When you finish, save and publish the document, and close the FLA. With the change made, open a Flash document that uses the shared asset and open its **Library**. Select the symbol that was changed, and select **Update** from the **Library** drop-down menu or, alternatively, right-click (Windows) or Control+click (Mac) on the item and select **Update** from the context menu. This will open the **Update Library Items** dialog box (shown in Figure 3-21). Select the check box next to the item's name, and click the **Update** button.

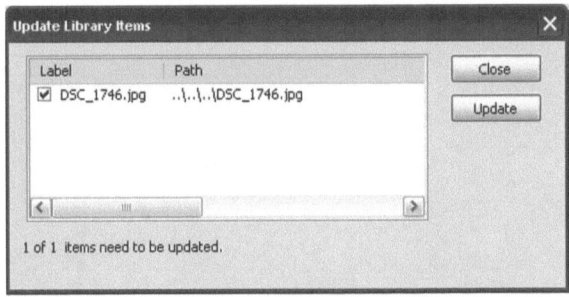

Figure 3-21. Symbols that have changed in a shared `Library` can quickly be updated wherever they are used.

If you have been carefully going through the chapter to this point, you are probably thinking, "Man, there is a lot of serious stuff that I have to know." We can't deny that, but once you understand the serious stuff, you can then start having fun with symbols. In fact, let's start.

A WORD FROM THE BUNNIES

Jennifer Shiman has created what is arguably one of the funniest sites on the Web (`www.angryalien.com/`). On a regular basis, she releases a Flash movie that uses the following premise: the movie is a 30-second synopsis of a popular film, and the actors are bunnies. Drawing and animating each bunny would be a daunting task. Jennifer's solution is the use of a shared `Library` containing all of the "bunny bits" needed to create the animations (see Figure 3-22). This is what Jennifer says about how she does it:

> "This is my library of 'bunny bits,' which I incorporate into each of my 30-Second Bunnies Theatre cartoons. I've compiled a bunch of the symbols I use most commonly in animating the bunnies, and I grouped them into folders. For instance, within the 'bun mouths' folder are subfolders of different mouth shapes for lip sync; mouths smiling and frowning; mouths in color and black and white; mouths of differing line thickness. The 'bkgds' folder contains background symbols I frequently use, such as standardized clouds, grass, and trees. At the beginning of production, I'll open the bunny bits library and drag the folders into the library of my current cartoon file. Then I import the additional artwork specifically pertaining to that cartoon.
>
> "During the course of production, if I create new bunny-related artwork I want to use in future files (such as a new version of a bunny mouth shape or a bunny arm position I'll use often), I drag those symbols into the bunny bits library file. It saves time to have one central location for these types of reusable elements."

CHAPTER 3

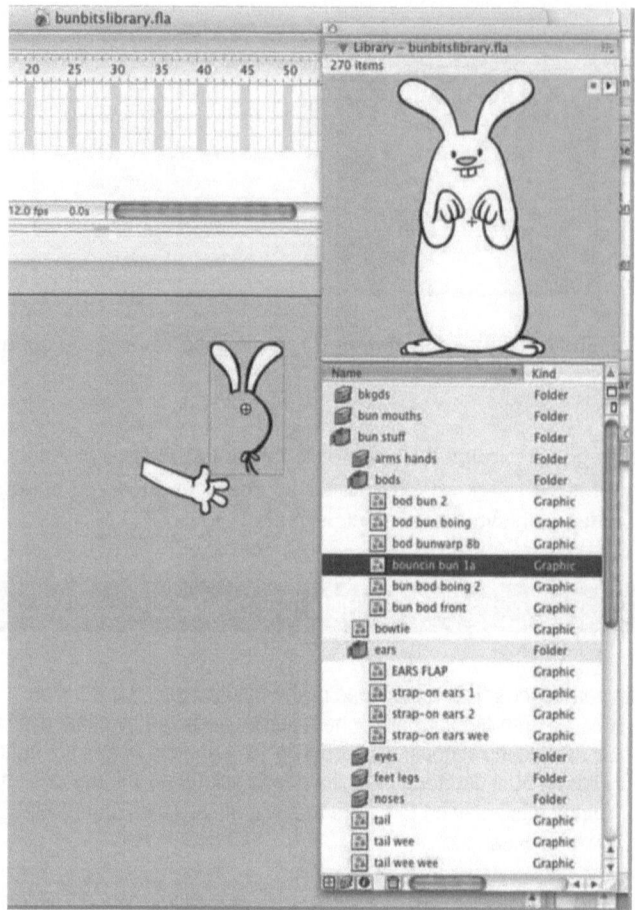

Figure 3-22. Shared libraries help Jennifer manage complex animations.

Filters and blend modes

The introduction of filters and blend modes in Flash 8 was a direct response to Flash designers looking for more eye candy. Since then, they have become indispensable tools for animators and designers.

Applying filters

In the years prior to Flash 8, Flash designers were quite comfortable using Photoshop filters or Fireworks Live Effects. Back in those days, if you needed to add a blur, drop shadow, or glow, you would leave Flash, open an imaging application containing the needed effect, export a PNG, and import the bitmap into

Flash. If the effect wasn't quite right, you made the round-trip again. Those days are over, and, thankfully, these same filters have become part of Flash. The ability to use filters directly in the Flash authoring environment (and animate them, to boot) has handed you a quick-and-easy method to create some fascinating visual effects.

The filters that are available in Flash are as follows:

- `Drop Shadow`: Places a gray or colored shadow beneath an object, which gives it the appearance of floating over the background.
- `Blur`: Takes the subject out of focus, making it look smudged or out of the depth of field.
- `Glow`: Creates a faint glowing outline around an object by following its curves.
- `Bevel`: Gives an object a 3D look by creating shadows and highlights on opposite edges.
- `Gradient Glow`: Quite similar to the Glow filter, except that the glow follows a gradient of colors from the inside to the outside edges of the object.
- `Gradient Bevel`: Comparable to the Bevel filter, except that a gradient is applied to the shadow and the highlights of the bevel.
- `Adjust Color`: Allows you to adjust the brightness, contrast, hue, and saturation of an object.

> *There are also three filters that can be applied only through the use of ActionScript: `Color Matrix`, `Displacement Map`, and `Convolution`. Their use is out of the scope of this book, but check out the ActionScript dictionary in the `Help` menu for explanations and demonstrations of how to use these filters.*

Before you start playing with them, understand filters can't be applied to everything you see on the Flash stage. Filters can be applied only to buttons, text, and movie clips. This makes a lot of sense because the bulk of the movie clips that will receive a filter arrive in the `Library` as either bitmaps from Photoshop and Fireworks or line art from Illustrator. As you saw in Chapter 2, they inevitably get imported as movie clip symbols. Even neater is, if an imported image has transparent areas, the filter—such as a Drop Shadow—is applied only to the opaque edges of the symbol.

Applying a Drop Shadow filter

In Flash, you can apply filters using a couple of methods. The most common is to select the object on the stage and then click the `Filters` twirlie on the `Properties` panel. Filters can also be applied through ActionScript.

To get started, let's get creative with a simple drop shadow:

1. Open the `Filter.fla` file. You will see that a cartoon of one of the authors has been placed over an image of a couple of people asleep on a park bench in Paris (see Figure 3-23). The cartoon is a Fireworks image that was imported into the `Library` as a movie clip.

CHAPTER 3

Figure 3-23. We start with a Fireworks image imported into Flash.

> *The authors would like to thank Chris Flick of Community MX and Capes & Babes (www.http://www.capesnbabes.com/) for allowing us to use this caricature of Tom. Chris is a colleague at Community MX, where he produces the weekly strip CMX Suite every Tuesday at www.communitymx.com/.*

2. Select the character on the stage, and click the **Filters** twirlie in the **Properties** panel. Click the **Add** Filter button in the bottom-left corner of **Properties** panel to open the **Filters** drop-down menu. Select **Drop Shadow**.

3. The **Properties** panel will change to show the various options for this filter, and the selection on the stage will also develop a drop shadow using the current default values for the Drop Shadow filter.

4. Change the **Blur X** and the **Blur Y** values to **8** to make the shadow a little bigger and change the **Distance** value to **11** to make the shadow a bit more pronounced. Also change the **Quality** setting to **High**. The shadow should now look a lot better (see Figure 3-24).

The lock joining the **Blur X** and **Blur Y** values ensures that the two values remain equal. Click the lock if you want the **Blur X** and **Blur Y** values to be different.

The first rule of "Flash physics" states: for every action, there is an equally opposite and ugly implication. Selecting **High** quality results in a great-looking shadow. The ugly implication is that this setting requires more processing power to apply when the SWF is playing in the browser. This is not a terrible thing if the image is static. For objects in motion, however, keep the setting at **Low**.

176

SYMBOLS AND LIBRARIES

Figure 3-24. The filter is applied to the selection.

The result is acceptable, but we can do a lot better than what you see. The problem is the shadows in the image. Notice how they are at a different angle than the one used for the character? Let's fix that.

Adding perspective

What we are going to do is to make this effect look a little more realistic. Applying the `Drop Shadow` filter in the previous steps resulted in a character that looks flat and has no perspective. Yet, if you closely examine the image, the shadows all move away from the character in the foreground. In this exercise, you are going to add the perspective. Follow these steps:

1. Select the object on the stage, select the `Drop Shadow` filter in the `Properties` panel, and click the `Trash` can at the bottom of the `Filters` area of the `Properties` panel to remove the `Drop Shadow` filter. With the object selected on the stage, copy it to the clipboard.

2. Add a new layer, give it a name, and with the new layer selected, select `Edit ➤ Paste in Place`. A copy of the character is pasted into the new layer. Turn off the layer's visibility.

> You also have the ability to copy the contents of a particular frame in the timeline. Right-click (Windows) or Control+click (Mac) the frame or sequence of frames, and select `Copy Frames` from the context menu. You can then select the frame where the content is to be placed, open the context menu again, and select `Paste Frames`.

177

3. Select the character on the stage and apply a `Drop Shadow` filter. Use these settings:
   - `Blur X`: `30`
   - `Blur Y`: `7`
   - `Strength`: `70 percent` (this is an opacity value)
   - `Quality`: `High`
   - `Angle`: `87 degrees`
   - `Hide Object`: `Selected`

What you should see is nothing more than a somewhat transparent shadow on the image due to your selecting `Hide Object` (see Figure 3-25). This opens you up to some rather creative applications. For example, just a shadow appearing over something adds a bit of a sinister feeling to a scene.

Figure 3-25. Hiding the object allows you to only show the shadow.

4. To add the perspective, select the object with the `Free Transform` tool, and scale, rotate, and skew the selection.

5. Turn on the visibility of the hidden layer. Select the shadow on the stage and, using the arrow keys, move the shadow to align with the foot that is on the ground.

6. Select the copy on the stage and apply the `Drop Shadow` filter.

7. This time leave the values alone, but select **High** as the **Quality** setting, and select **Inner shadow**. The character takes on a bit of a 3D look to go with the shadow he is casting, as shown in Figure 3-26.

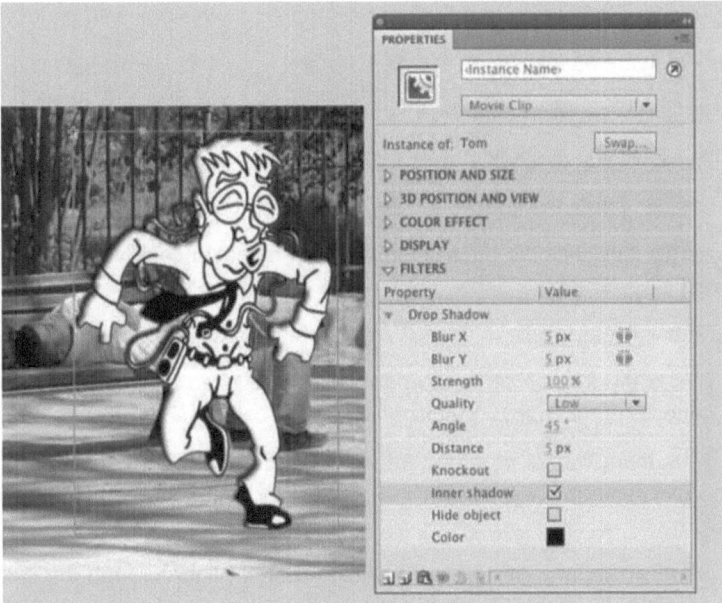

Figure 3-26. Apply an inner shadow to add some depth.

Some filter facts

Before we move on to applying a blend, here are a few things you should know about adding and using filters:

- You can apply multiple filters to an object. The character can, for example, have the **Drop Shadow**, **Glow**, and **Bevel** filters applied to it. If you need to remove one, select the filter name and click the **Trash** icon in the **Filters** area.

- You cannot apply multiple instances of a filter to an object. You saw this in this exercise. Each movie clip has a **Drop Shadow** filter applied to it.

- Filters do result in a hit on the user's processor when the movie plays in the browser. Use them judiciously.

- Filters applied to layers in Photoshop will be visible in Flash but will not be editable in Flash when the image is imported into the Flash **Library** or to the stage.

- Alpha channel video in a movie clip can have filters applied to it.

- Filters can be applied to objects using ActionScript.

CHAPTER 3

Playing with blends

The blend modes operate quite differently from the filters. If you are a Fireworks or Photoshop user, you may already be familiar with the concept. In applications like those two, such modes are commonly used to manipulate the colors of pixels to create new colors based on combinations with underlying pixels.

The blend modes in Flash are as follows:

- `Normal`: No blend is applied, and the selection isn't affected. Use this one to remove a blend.
- `Layer`: This allows you to stack movie clips on top of each other with no effect upon their color.
- `Darken`: This compares the foreground and background colors and keeps the darkest one.
- `Multiply`: This multiplies the base color value by the blend color value and divides the result by 256. The result is inevitably a darker color.
- `Lighten`: This is the opposite of darken with the result always being a lighter color.
- `Screen`: This is the inverse of the blend color is multiplied by the base color. Think of this as being the opposite of `Multiply` resulting in a lighter color.
- `Overlay`: This multiplies, or **screens**, the colors depending on the base color. The base color is not replaced. Instead, it is mixed with the blend color to reflect the lightness or darkness of the original color.
- `Hard Light`: This mimics the effect of shining a bright light through the selection. If the blend color is darker than 50 percent gray, the image is darkened as if it were multiplied. This is another way of adding shadows to a selection.
- `Add`: The blend and base colors are added together resulting in a lighter color.
- `Subtract`: The blend and the base colors are subtracted from each other resulting in a darker color.
- `Difference`: Depending upon their brightness values, either the base color is subtracted from the blend value or vice versa. The result looks like a color film negative.
- `Invert`: This inverts the base color.
- `Alpha`: The blend color is converted to an alpha channel, which, essentially, turns transparent.
- `Erase`: This is the base color including those of the background image are erased.

Blend modes, once you grasp that they are math-driven, work like this: the pixel colors values are considered from two separate layers of an image and mathematically manipulated by the blend mode to create the effect. An excellent example of this manipulation is the `Multiply` mode. This mode will multiply the color values of a pixel in the source layer with the color values of the pixel directly below it in the destination layer. The result is divided by 256 and is always a darker shade of the color. In Flash, these calculations are performed on overlapping movie clips or buttons on the stage.

When applying a blending mode in Flash, keep in mind that it is not the same task as it is in Photoshop or Fireworks. Flash lets you place multiple objects in a layer. When a blend mode is applied to a movie clip or button in Flash, it is the object, which could be a photo, directly under the movie clip or button, which will supply the color for the change in the movie clip or the button.

Blend modes are extremely powerful creative tools in the hands of a Flash artist. Though they can be applied only to movie clips and buttons, applied judiciously, the blend modes can provide some rather stunning visual effects. To apply a blend mode, you simply select the movie clip to which it is to be applied and select the mode from the **Blend** drop-down menu in the **Properties** panel. Let's look at a few of the blend modes and learn some blend fundamentals along the way.

1. Open the Blend.fla file. When the file opens, you will see we have put two movie clips on the stage (see Figure 3-27). The movie clips are also in separate layers named **Source** and **Destination**. In this example, the **Source** layer contains some text filled with a neutral gray color. The **Destination** layer contains an image of autumn leaves that were blurred using the **Gaussian Blur** filter in Photoshop. Those layers have been given those names for a reason: *blending modes are applied in a top-down manner*. This means that the effect will do the manipulation using the source layer's pixels and apply the result to the movie clip on the destination layer. That's right, anything visible under the source (including the stage) will be affected by the transformation.

Figure 3-27. The pixels in the **Source** layer—the text—are used to create the effect with the pixels in the destination layer—the blurred autumn leaves.

2. Select the movie clip in the `Source` layer—the text—and click the twirlie in the `Display` area of the `Properties` panel. Then select `Normal` from the `Blending` drop-down menu, as shown in Figure 3-28. The `Normal` mode does not mix, combine, or otherwise play with the color values.

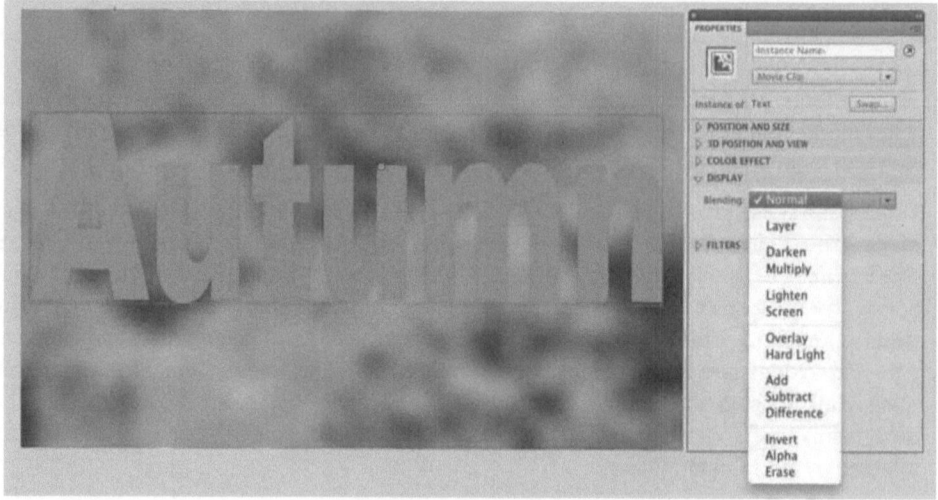

Figure 3-28. Blend modes are applied through the `Properties` panel.

3. With the text still selected, apply the `Multiply` mode. As you can see, Figure 3-29, the colors have mixed, and the darker colors make the `Source` image darker. The important thing to notice here is how the medium gray of the stage is also being used where the `Source` image overlaps only the stage. If you return the mode to `Normal`, select the image in the `Destination` layer, and apply the `Multiply` mode—the image will darken because of the dark gray color (#606060) of the stage. Nothing happens to the text in the `Source` layer.

SYMBOLS AND LIBRARIES

Figure 3-29. The `Multiply` mode

4. Set the blend mode of the `Destination` layer to `Normal`. Select the text in the `Source` layer, and apply the `Lighten` mode. In this example, as shown in Figure 3-30, the lighter color of both the `Source` and `Destination` images is chosen. As you can see, the lighter pixels in the `Destination` image are replacing the darker pixels in the `Source` image.

Figure 3-30. The `Lighten` mode

183

5. Finally, select the image in the `Source` layer, and apply the `Difference` mode. This mode is always a surprise. This one works by determining which color is the darkest in the `Source` and `Destination` images and then subtracting the darker of the two from the lighter color. The result, as shown in Figure 3-31, is always a vibrant image with saturated colors.

Figure 3-31. The `Difference` mode

Managing content on the stage

Now that you have had some fun, playtime is over. It is now time to get back to the serious issue of managing your work. Though we have talked about using folders in layers and in the `Library`, we really haven't addressed the issue of managing the content on the stage.

As we have been telling and showing you to this point, you can determine the location of objects on the stage by dragging them around. We look upon that practice, in many respects, as attempting to light your BBQ with an atom bomb. You will light the BBQ, but taking out the neighborhood is a lot less precise than striking a match and lighting a burner. This is why we have been doing it by the numbers. We enter actual values into the `Properties` panel or use menus to precisely place items on the stage, and we resize and otherwise manipulate content.

We'll start by showing you how to group content:

1. Open the NuttyProfessor.fla file in the Chapter 3 Exercise folder. When the file opens, head over to the **Library**, and open the **Professor** movie clip.

2. Click the **Professor** layer, and you will see that the drawing is composed of quite a few bits and pieces (see Figure 3-32). If you wanted to move that drawing over a couple of pixels, you would have to select each element to be moved. There is an easier method.

Figure 3-32. Line art, in many cases, is the sum of its parts.

3. Select **Modify ➤ Group**, or if you are a keyboard junkie, press Ctrl+G (Windows) or Cmd+G (Mac). The pieces become one unit, as indicated by the square surrounding them.

4. Deselect the group by clicking the stage, and then click the image of the professor on the stage. Again, you will again see the box indicating that the selection is grouped, and you will also be given the same information in the **Properties** panel, as shown in Figure 3-33.

5. To ungroup the selection, select **Modify ➤ Ungroup**, or press Ctrl+Shift+G (Windows) or Cmd+Shift+G (Mac).

6. Close the file without saving the changes.

Figure 3-33. A group is indicated both on the stage and in the `Properties` panel.

Aligning objects on the stage

Now that you know how to make your life a little easier by grouping objects, let's turn our attention to how objects can be aligned with each other on the stage. Reopen the `NuttyProfessor.fla` file.

The first technique is the use of `Snap Align`. You can switch on this very handy feature on and off by selecting `View` ➤ `Snapping` ➤ `Snap Align`. When `Snap Align` is switched on, the default, dragging one object close to another object, will show you a dotted line. This line shows you the alignment with the stationary object.

Click the words on the stage and slowly drag them toward the bottom-left corner of the movie clip. You will see the `Snap Align` indicator line (see Figure 3-34) telling you that the left edge of the text is aligned with the left edge of the movie clip. By dragging the text up and down the indicator line, you can align objects at a distance. Release the mouse, and the text will snap to that line.

SYMBOLS AND LIBRARIES

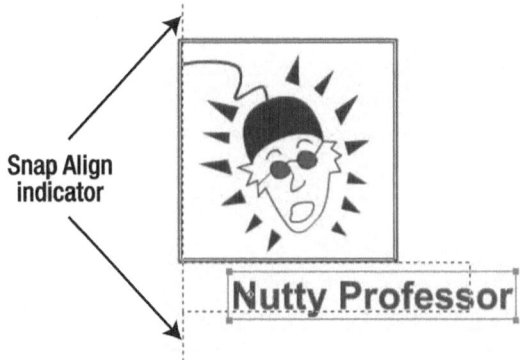

Figure 3-34. Using `Snap Align`

Snapping to the grid

You can also align objects on the stage through the use of a grid. This is a handy way of precisely positioning objects on the stage. You can turn on the grid by selecting `View ➤ Grid ➤ Show Grid`. When you release the mouse, a grid will appear on the stage. This grid is what we call an **authortime** feature. That means that the grid won't appear when you publish the SWF and put it up on a web page.

You can also edit the grid by selecting `View ➤ Grid ➤ Edit Grid.` The `Grid` dialog box, shown in Figure 3-35, will appear. Here you can change the color of the grid lines, determine whether items snap to the grid, and change the size of the squares in the grid. The `Snap accuracy` drop-down menu lets you choose how snapping to the grid lines will be managed by Flash.

Figure 3-35. Adding a grid and managing it on the stage

187

CHAPTER 3

> *Take another look at the* Grid *panel in Figure 3-35. There is a* Show over objects *option that was added in Flash CS4. This option allows you to show the grid over everything on the stage, meaning you now have the ability to be super accurate in snapping objects to grid lines. As we said in the previous edition of this book, this option is "super cool."*

Aligning with guides

Another method for aligning objects or placing them in precise locations on the stage is to use guides. You can add guides by dragging them off either a horizontal or a vertical ruler. The ruler isn't shown by default in Flash; to turn it on, select View ➤ Rulers. At 100 percent view, the rulers are divided into five-pixel units. If you need even more precise placement, zooming in to 2,000 percent view allows you to work in units of .5 pixels.

To add a guide, drag it off of either the horizontal or vertical ruler, and when it is in position, release the mouse. To remove a guide, drag it back onto the ruler.

Once a guide is in place, you can then edit it by selecting View ➤ Guides ➤ Edit Guides. This will open the Guides dialog box (see Figure 3-36), which is quite similar to the Grid dialog box. The Snap accuracy drop-down menu allows you to determine how close an object needs to be to a guide before it snaps to the guide. You can also choose to lock the guides in place. Locking guides once they are in position is a good habit to develop. This way, you won't accidentally move them.

If you need to turn off the guides, select View ➤ Guide ➤ Show Guides; reselect it to turn them on again. If you no longer need the guides, you can remove them with a single click of the mouse by selecting View ➤ Guides ➤ Clear Guides.

Figure 3-36. Rulers, guides, and the Guide dialog box

Snapping in a guide layer and to pixels

Finally, you can snap objects to items in a guide layer—not to be confused with the guides we just discussed—and even to individual pixels.

Snapping to an object in a guide layer is nothing more than a variation of the **Snap to Objects**, except the layer in question has been converted to a guide layer by right-clicking (Control+clicking) the layer name and selecting **Guide**. What's the difference? As you saw in Chapter 1, the lines drawn in a guide layer aren't included in the SWF.

Snapping to pixels is best-suited to ultra-precise positioning and control freaks. This is extremely useful with the placement of bitmaps and text fields. In fact, you won't even see the pixel grid until you have zoomed in to at least 400 percent. The pixel grid is not the same grid we demonstrated earlier.

Stacking order and using the Align panel

Layers are effective tools for managing content, but there is another related concept you need to be aware of: **stacking**. When multiple objects are in a layer, the objects also have a front-to-back relationship with each other, appearing to be placed on top of each other, which is called the **stacking order**.

Symbols, drawing objects, primitives, text fields, and grouped objects can be stacked. Everything else essentially falls to the bottom of the pile in the layer. To accomplish this, each new symbol or group added to a layer is given a position in the stack, which determines how far up from the bottom it will be placed. This position is assigned in the order in which the symbols or objects are added to the stage. This means that each symbol added to the stage sits in front, or above, the symbols or objects already on the stage. Let's look at this concept:

1. Open the `Stacks.fla` file. You will see four photos on the stage.

2. Drag the objects on top of each other, and you will see, as shown in Figure 3-37, a stack; the location of each object in this stack is a visual clue regarding when it was placed on the stage.

CHAPTER 3

Figure 3-37. Objects stacked in a layer

Stacking order is not fixed. For example, suppose you wanted to move the bread image to the top of the stack and move the stairs image under the fountain image.

3. Select the bread image on the stage, and select `Modify` ➤ `Arrange` ➤ `Bring to Front`. The image moves to the top of the stack. This tells you that the `Bring to Front` and `Send to Back` menu items are used to move selected objects to the top or the bottom of a stack.

4. Right-click (Windows) or Control-click (Mac) on the stairs image to open the context menu.

5. When the context menu opens, select `Arrange` ➤ `Send Backward`, as shown in Figure 3-38. The stairs move under the fountain image. This tells you that the `Bring Forward` or `Send Backward` menu items can be used to move objects in front of or behind each other. What you have also learned is the `Arrange` menu is available in the `Modify` menu or by opening an object's context menu.

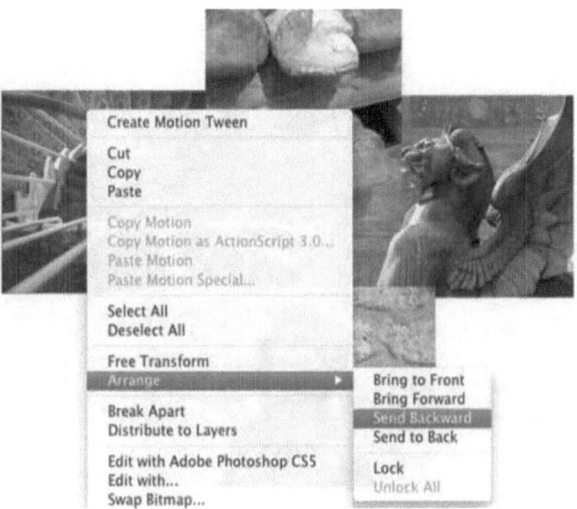

Figure 3-38. You can also use the context menu to change the stacking order of selected objects.

Throughout this book, we have talked about the use of layers to manage content. Obviously, stacking objects on top of each other flies in the face of what we have said. Not so fast. There is an incredibly useful menu item that actually allows you to bring a bit of order to the chaos.

1. Select all the items on the stage.
2. Select **Modify ➤ Timeline ➤ Distribute to Layers**. When you release the mouse, the order of the objects in relation to each other doesn't change, but each object has been removed from the original layer—**Layer 1**—and is now on its own named layer, as shown in Figure 3-39. This is extremely useful, for example, when you import Photoshop layer folders as movie clips and then you see that you need to break them into Flash layers.
3. Close the file, and don't save the changes.

Now that you see what you can do with this powerful menu item, you also need to understand some rules regarding its use:

- Symbols, shapes, drawing objects, primitives, text fields, and grouped objects will be placed on their own individual layers.
- For symbols, layer names are based upon either the instance name in the **Properties** panel or the symbol name in the **Library**. If both the symbol name and the instance name are the same, instance names take precedence.
- For text fields the name of the layer is based on the text content—or the text field's instance name in the **Properties** panel. Again, instance names take precedence.

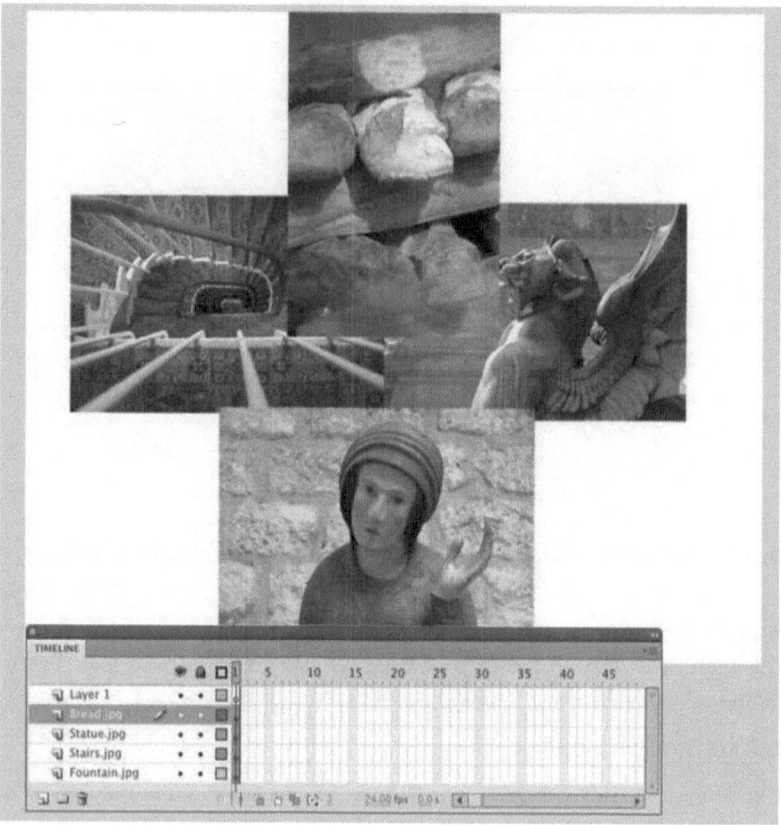

Figure 3-39. `Distribute to Layers` places each selected object on its own layer.

Using the Align panel

The `Align` panel allows you to line up and center objects and otherwise bring order to chaos with a click or two of the mouse.

You can access the `Align` panel either by selecting `Window` ➤ `Align` or pressing Ctrl+K (Windows) or Cmd+K (Mac) to open the panel shown in Figure 3-40. When the panel opens, you are presented with a number of alignment options—there are 17 options available and a button labeled `Align to stage`. The `Align to stage` button allows you to either align objects with each other or, if it is selected, align them with the stage.

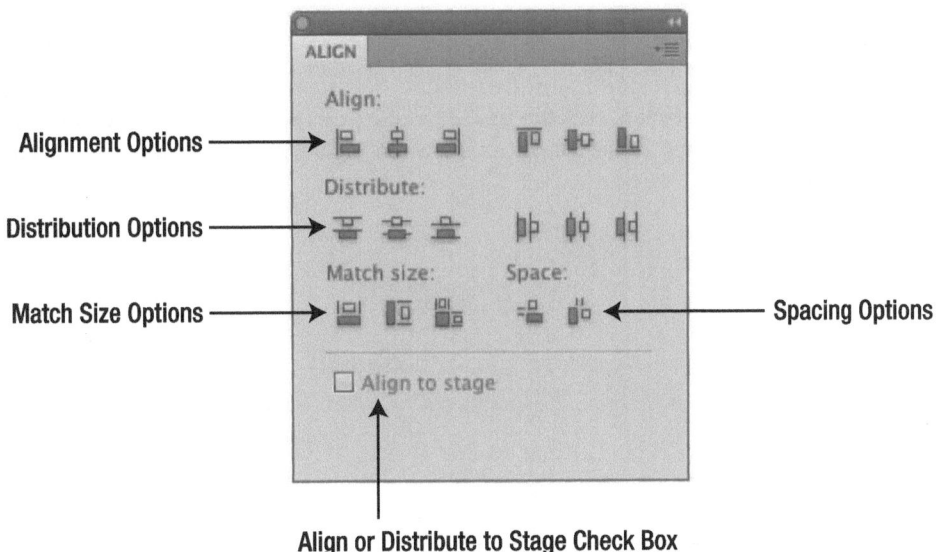

Figure 3-40. The `Align` panel

Let's see how all of this works:

1. Open the `AlignPanel.fla` file in the Chapter 3 Exercise folder. As you can see, the file consists of a number of button components scattered across the stage. Open the `Align` panel.

2. Select all the components, and being sure the `Align to stage` check box is not selected, click the `Left Align` button in the panel. The buttons all line up along their left edges.

> The addition of a check box to the `Align to stage` feature is a welcome change. Up to this version of the application designers and developers constantly complained about not knowing when the button was selected.

3. Click the `Vertical Spacing` button in the `Space` options, and the components will be spaced evenly on the vertical axis. Click the `Distribute Top Edge` button to even out the spacing.

Now let's use the panel to create a button bar across the top of the stage.

4. Click the `Align to stage` check box on the `Align` panel.

CHAPTER 3

5. Select all the buttons and click the `Align Top Edge` button. The buttons will all pile on top of each other at the top of the stage.

6. With the buttons still selected, click the `Distribute Horizontal Center` button. The buttons spread out along the top of the stage, as shown in Figure 3-41. Not bad—two clicks, and you have a button bar.

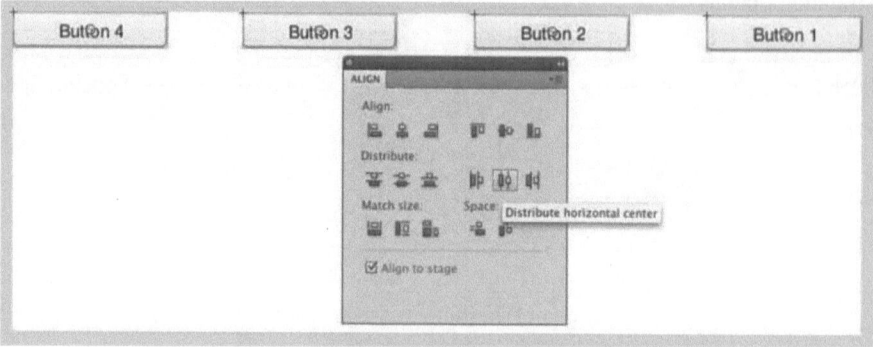

Figure 3-41. Two clicks is all it takes to create a button bar.

Masks and masking

Before we turn you loose on a project, the final subject we will be examining is the issue of masking in Flash. As you know, masks are used to selectively show and hide objects on the Flash stage. The value of a mask is, in many respects, not clearly understood by Flash designers. They tend to regard masking as a way to hide stuff. They see it as an overly complicated method of doing something that could be more easily done in an imaging application. This is not exactly incorrect, but what they tend to miss is that masks in Flash can be animated and can even react to events on the stage. For example, one of the authors connects a webcam to his computer and, using Flash, is able to broadcast himself peering out of billboards in Times Square, waving at people walking by in Piccadilly Circus in London, or looking out of the porthole of a sensory deprivation tank. When the camera is not connected, the images used revert to their normal states.

Here you will learn to create simple mask, create a masked animation, and use text as a mask. Finally, you'll tackle creating a soft mask, an exercise designed to pull together much of what you have discovered in this chapter.

A simple mask

In this exercise, we are going to show you the basic steps involved in a creating a mask in Flash. Once you have the fundamentals under your belt, you can then apply what you have learned in a rather creative manner. Let's start:

SYMBOLS AND LIBRARIES

1. Open the SimpleMask.fla file.
2. Add a new layer named **Mask**, and draw a circle with no stroke on the new layer.
3. Right-click (Windows) or Cmd+click (Mac) on the **Mask** layer to open the **Layer** context menu. Select **Mask**. When you release the mouse, the image of the frozen pond will look like it is circular. You should also notice that the appearance of the layers has changed and that they are locked (see Figure 3-42). The icon beside the **Mask** layer name (the rectangle with a cutout) indicates that the layer is a mask, and the indent for the **Cycle** layer name indicates that it is the object being masked.

Figure 3-42. Applying a mask

CHAPTER 3

What you see is the image showing through the circle in the `Mask` layer, with the stage color visible. One thing you need to know about masks is that you need to be careful dragging other layers under them. Do that, and they, too, will be masked—depending on how you are doing the dragging. The following steps explain what we're getting at:

4. Add a new layer above the mask, and name it `Square`. Select the `Rectangle` tool, and draw a rectangle on this new layer.

5. Drag the `Square` layer under the `Blue Springs` layer. When you release the mouse, the circle and the square are visible. Click the `Lock` icon in the `Square` layer, and the square will disappear because it is under the photograph.

> *The locks turn the masks on and off and allow you to edit or manipulate the content in the layers, including the masks. When you finish making your changes, click the locks to reapply the mask. When all layers are locked (the masked layers and the mask), the mask goes into a preview mode.*

6. Unlock the `Square` layer, and drag it back above the `Mask` layer. This time, drag the `Mask` layer above the `Square` layer. When you release the mouse, you will see that both the `Mask` and `Cycle` layers have moved above the `Square` layer and that the shape in the layer is visible, as shown in Figure 3-43.

7. Drag the `Square` layer below the `Blue Springs` layer again, this time keeping to the left. When you release the mouse, the `Square` layer is no longer associated with the mask. This is an alternative method of toggling between the `Normal` and `Masked` (or `Mask`) layer options seen when you right-click (Windows) or Control-click (Mac) a layer and select `Properties`.

8. Close the file without saving the changes.

Figure 3-43. Masking layers can be moved around.

Now that you understand the fundamentals, let's get a little more complex.

Creating a masked animation

The art of Flash is, in many respects, the art of illusion. In this exercise, you'll create the illusion of the Dancing Fool from the `Drop Shadow` example earlier in the chapter sliding across six panels on a wall in Adobe's San Jose Headquarters building. The problem to contend with is the fact the panels are large, and each panel has its own shape. How do you get the Dancing Fool to slide out from behind one panel, across a few more and slide behind another as he exits the stage?

You think a bit differently.

The effect you want to create is shown in Figure 3-44. Instead of using the panels as the mask, you need to use the colored area in each panel as the mask. The following steps show you how to accomplish this.

CHAPTER 3

Figure 3-44. The Dancing Fool slides across colored panels.

1. Open the `Wall.fla` file. All of the items you will need for this exercise are located in the **Library**.
2. Select the `Magnifying Glass` tool, and zoom in on the bottom six panels by clicking and dragging the `Magnifying Glass` across them.
3. Select the `Pen` tool, and draw a shape that matches the colored area without the triangle with the dot in the bottom-right corner of each panel.
4. Fill each shape drawn with the `Pen` tool with black by clicking inside it with the `Paint Bucket` tool.
5. Holding down the Shift key, select each of the shapes you have just drawn, and convert the selection to a movie clip named `Mask`.
6. Open the `Mask` movie clip in the `Symbol Editor`. Change `Layer 1`'s name to `Panels`, and add a new layer named `DancingFool` to the timeline. Drag the `DancingFool` layer under the `Panels` layer.
7. Select frame 1 of the `DancingFool` layer, and drag a copy of the `DancingFool` movie clip to the stage. Place the movie clip to the left of shapes in the `Panels` layer, as shown in Figure 3-45.

SYMBOLS AND LIBRARIES

Figure 3-45. Place the movie clip to the left of shapes in the `Panels` layer.

With the assets in place, you can now concentrate on creating the animation. The plan is to have the Dancing Fool slide through the frames. Here's how you do that:

1. Select frame 80 of the `Panels` layer, and insert a frame.

2. Select frame 80 of the `DancingFool` layer, and add a frame. Right-click (Windows) or Control+click (Mac) anywhere between the two frames, and select `Create Motion Tween` from the context menu.

3. Select frame 80 of the `DancingFool` layer, and move the movie clip to the right of the panels. You will see a keyframe in frame 80 of the `DancingFool` layer and the motion path, shown in Figure 3-46.

4. Right-click (Control+click) the `Panels` layer, and select `Mask` from the context menu. If you scrub across the timeline, you will see the mask you just applied.

5. Click the `Scene 1` link to return to the main timeline. The `Mask` movie clip just created is the white dot shown in Figure 3-47 that is located just above the panels being masked.

6. Save the movie and test it.

199

CHAPTER 3

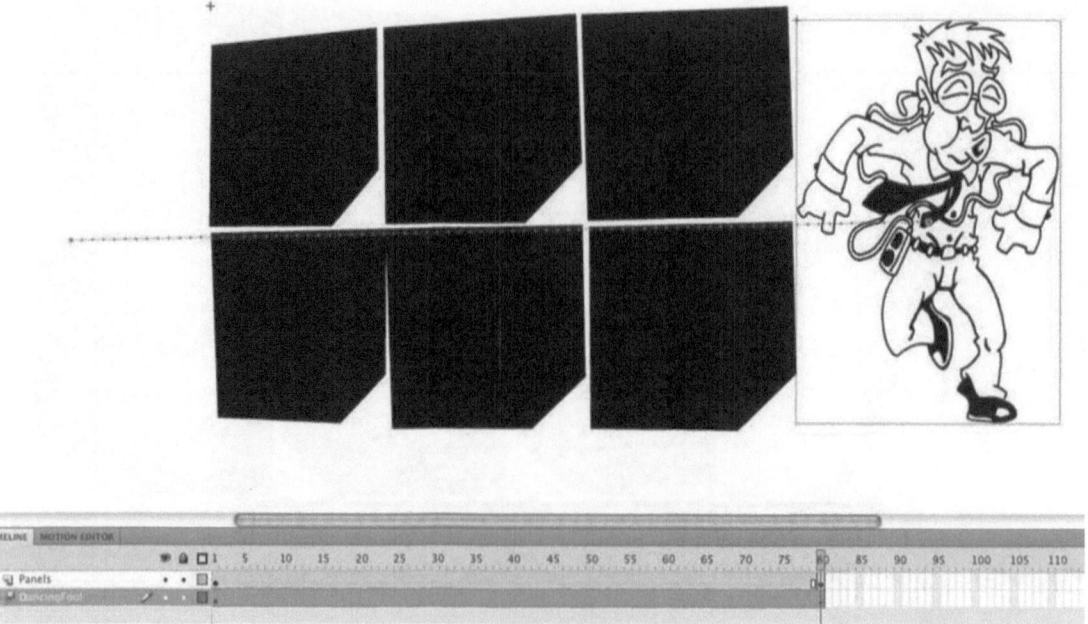

Figure 3-46. The assets are in place, and you can now move on to creating the movie.

Figure 3-47. The movie clip with the mask appears as a white dot on the main timeline.

Using text as a mask

Though we are going to fully explore the use of text in Flash in Chapter 6, we can't overlook the power of using text as a mask. If you are going to be using text for this purpose, use a font that has a separate bold version, such as Arial Black, or another font that has the words *Heavy*, *Black*, *Bold*, or *Demi* in its name. These fonts are traditionally used as headline fonts, which makes them ideal for use as a mask.

Let's have some fun with a text mask and create an intro screen for a site named `Places`.

1. Open the `Seasons.fla` file. Add a new layer and name it `Text`.

2. Select the `Text` layer, and then select the `Text` tool. Open the `Properties` panel, and select `Classic Text` from the `Text` type drop-down.

3. Click in the `Text` layer, and enter the word `Winter`. Select the word with the `Text` tool.

4. In the `Properties` panel, change the font to a strong sans serif—we chose `Arial Black`—and set the point size for the text to `150` and the `Letter spacing` to `-7.0` and the color to `white`, as shown in Figure 3-48. The font size slider in the `Properties` panel only goes up to a value of 96, so double-click the value and enter `150` from the keyboard. The objective is to get the letters to run across the image. If you use a different font, you will need to use different values for `Size` and `Letter spacing`.

5. Select the `Text` layer, and turn it into a mask layer. The shadows on the snow will appear through the characters in the text.

CHAPTER 3

Figure 3-48. Use a strong font as the mask.

Now let's add a bit of motion to this movie. To start, turn off the mask in the `Text` layer by unlocking the `Text` layer.

6. Select the text on the stage, and convert it to a movie clip named `Text`.

7. Add a frame to frame 60 of the Image layer.

8. Right-click frame 1 of the `Text` layer, and select `Create Motion Tween` from the context menu. Drag the last frame of the blue Motion Tween to frame 60.

9. Right-click the last frame of the `Text` layer, and select `Insert Keyframe ➤ Scale`. A small blue diamond will appear in the last frame. This sets the end size for the animation.

10. Drag the playhead to frame 1 of the `Text` layer. Select the text on the stage, and select the `FreeTransform` tool. Scale the text down to a very small size.

11. Click the `Timeline` tab, lock the `Text` layer to reapply the mask, and scrub across the timeline. The text, as shown in Figure 3-49, will grow as you drag the playhead.

Figure 3-49. Masks are not static; they can be animated.

You can also add a bit of graphic interest to the mask by applying a filter to the text. If you intend to go this route, keep in mind that filters can't be applied to text that's being used as a mask. Instead, the filter needs to be applied to a copy of the text and its layer moved under the mask to give the illusion that a filter has been applied. Here's how:

1. Open the `Seasons02.fla` file in your `Exercise` folder. When it opens, add a new layer named `Filter` to the timeline.
2. Unlock the `Text` layer, select the text on the stage, and copy the text to the clipboard.
3. Relock the `Text` layer to apply the mask. Select frame 1 of the `Filter` layer, and select `Edit` ➤ `Paste in Place` to position the text directly over the mask.

4. Select the text in the `Filter` layer, and apply the `Gradient Glow` filter using the following settings in the `Properties` panel (see Figure 3-50):

   - `Blur X`: 9
   - `Blur Y`: 9
   - `Strength`: 100 percent
   - `Quality`: High
   - `Angle`: 300
   - `Distance`: 10
   - `Knockout`: Selected (this will turn the text transparent and apply the glow to the edges)
   - `Type`: Outer
   - `Start Color`: #FFFFFF (white)
   - `End Color`: #CCCCCC (Light gray)

5. Drag the `Text` layer above the `Filter` layer. Notice how both layers in the mask move. As you can see, as shown in Figure 3-50, the effect gives the mask a bit of a 3D look. Feel free to save the changes before moving on.

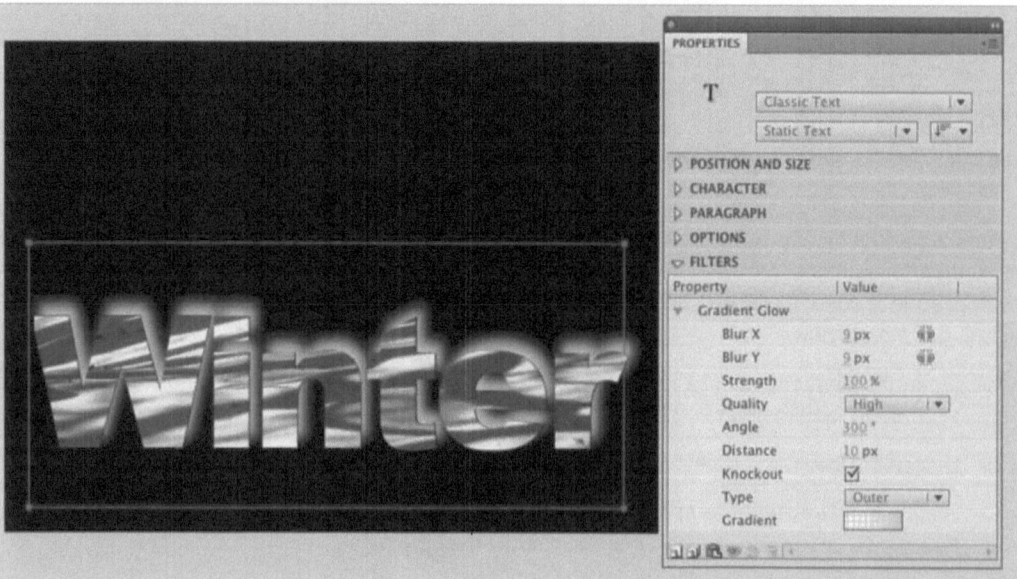

Figure 3-50. Filters can add a bit of zing to mask effects.

Your turn: a sunny day on Catalina Island

In this final exercise, you will let you turn a fog bank rolling in on Catalina Island just west of Los Angeles into a blue sky and clouds. Here's how:

1. Open `Catalina.fla`. When it opens you will see, as shown in Figure 3-51, the foggy image is already on the stage, and the clouds image is in the **Library**.

The plan for this project is simple. Replace the fog bank in the sky with the clouds image and, to give it a bit of eye candy, to put the clouds in motion. You may be thinking why not simply pop open Photoshop or Fireworks, pull out the fog, heave in the clouds and save it as a `.psd` or `.jpg` image? The answer is sometimes all you get is a `.fla` and you don't have the extra time to manipulate the image elsewhere. Also, this is as good a time as any for you to start getting comfortable with the tools in Flash.

Figure 3-51. You can do amazing stuff with only two images and Flash's tools.

2. There is obviously a lot more stage than there is image. Click the stage, and in the Properties **panel**, click the **Edit** button to open the **Document Properties** dialog box. Click the **Contents** radio button to shrink the stage to the size of the image, and click **OK**.

> *If you are designing Flash movies and the stage is larger than the stuff on it, get into the habit of reducing the stage size. Wasted space, in the Flash universe, translates into increased download times. Remember, when you think Flash, think small.*

3. Add a new layer to the timeline, and name it **FogMask**.
4. Select the **Pen** tool in the toolbox. Turn off the stroke, and draw a shape that follows the tops of the mountains and covers the bottom of the image as shown in Figure 3-52.
5. Select the **Paint Bucket** tool and fill the shape with a color of your choosing.
6. Right-click (Control+click) the **FogMask** layer, and convert it to a mask. The clouds will disappear, and the harbor will reappear.

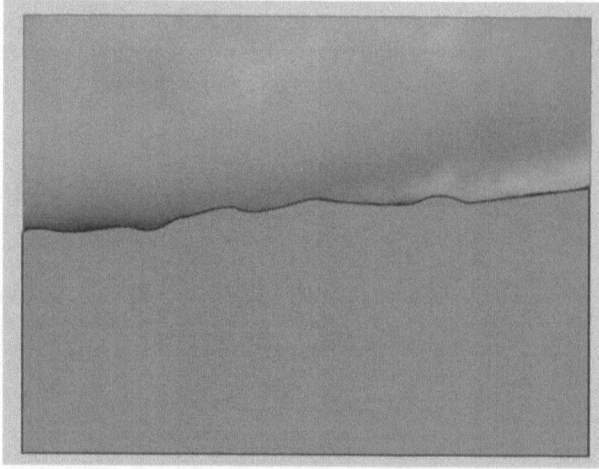

Figure 3-52. Draw a shape that covers the mountains and the harbor.

Adding the clouds

With the fog bank masked out, you can now turn your attention to the sky and making the day a lot brighter.

1. Add a new layer named **Clouds**, and drag it under both layers on the timeline.
2. Drag the cga_Clouds.png image from the **Library** into the **Clouds** layer. Line the right edge of the clouds image against the right edge of the stage, as shown in Figure 3-53.

SYMBOLS AND LIBRARIES

Figure 3-53. The clouds are added.

As you can see in Figure 3-53, there is a problem. The clouds image is huge, and you have no idea where the top of the stage is located. This is a "nonissue" if your intention is to go no farther. All of the excess will be "trimmed off" when you test the movie because content that isn't on the stage isn't visible at runtime. We intend to put the clouds in motion, so let's solve the issue:

3. Select the `Clouds` layer, and add a new layer named `CloudsMask` above it.
4. Turn off the visibility of the `Clouds` layer to turn off the image, which lets you see the top of the stage.
5. Select the `CloudsMask` layer, and draw a rectangle that covers the white area of the stage.
6. Turn on the visibility of the `Clouds` layer, select the image, and convert it to a movie clip.
7. Turn the `CloudsMask` layer into a mask. As shown in Figure 3-54, the image is looking a lot better.

CHAPTER 3

Figure 3-54. Two masks and the day is looking brighter.

Getting the clouds in motion

In this, the final part of the exercise, you are going to put the clouds in motion. There are any number of ways of doing this, but the issue you will be dealing with has to do with something one of the authors tells his students: "Pay attention to the world around you." In the case of the clouds, the image is flat, and the clouds won't look quite right because, even though they can move sideways or up and down they will still look flat. Instead, let's have the clouds move toward the viewer. Here's how:

1. Scrub over to frame 200 of the main timeline, and add a frame to all of the layers. This tells you the animation will occur over 200 frames.

2. Unlock the `Clouds` layer, right-click the image, and convert it to a movie clip named `Clouds`.

3. Right-click anywhere in the `Clouds` layer's timeline between frames 1 and 200 and select **Create Motion Tween**.

4. Select the Clouds movie clip on the stage, and select **Window ➤ Transform**. This opens the **Transform** panel shown in Figure 3-55.

SYMBOLS AND LIBRARIES

We are going to get a lot deeper into this panel in Chapter 9 for now, though, pay attention to the 3D `Rotation` settings. These settings allow you to rotate objects on the x-, y-, and z-axes in 3D space.

5. With the `Clouds` movie clip selected on the stage, set the `X` value in the `Transform` panel's `3D Rotation` area to 60 degrees. The clouds will "tilt." Close the `Transform` panel.

6. With the `Clouds` movie clip still selected, move the playhead to frame 200.

Figure 3-55. Tilt the clouds to add a degree of realism.

7. Click the `Clouds` movie clip, and in the `Properties` panel twirl down the `3D Position and View` area.

8. In the `3D Position and View` area, change the `Z` value to `-260`. If you scrub across the timeline, the clouds will look like they are moving towards you.

9. To complete the effect, lock the `Clouds` layer to reestablish the mask.

10. Save and test the movie. The cloud motion (Figure 3-56) looks a lot more realistic.

Figure 3-56. The small value change on the z-axis makes the clouds move lazily across the sky.

Bonus round

Before we start, you are probably wondering, what's a bonus round? We have thrown a few of these into the book in order to give you the opportunity to play and further extend your skills. What we don't do is give you detailed instructions. Instead, we tell you how to do it in much the same way a colleague would talk about how he or she did something cool. It's like when you learned to ride a bike. Eventually the person teaching you takes their hand off of the bike seat and lets you go solo. We just let go of your bike seat.

Here are a couple of things you might want to try with the Catalina Island project you just completed.

If you think the harbor is too dark, here's a way to brighten it up. Add a new layer above the Layer 1 layer containing the Catalina harbor image. Copy and paste the Catalina image into that new layer, and convert it to a movie clip. Apply the `Subtract` blend mode to the movie clip you just created. Reapply the mask, save, and test.

The purpose of this exercise was to not only let you play with the tools but to reinforce the fact that effects where *subtlety* is used are, more often than not, the most effective ones. Still, you can have a blast with this exercise.

Here's another idea. Slide another copy of the `Clouds` movie clip into a new layer under the masked clouds layers. If you unlock the layer, select the distorted movie clip, and apply a variety of `Blends` from the `Properties` panel, you can get a number of different effects ranging from a softer sky (`Overlay`) to a post nuclear blast sky (`Subtract`). Have fun.

What you've learned

In this chapter, you learned the following:

- How to create and use symbols in Flash animations and movies
- How to create and share libraries among Flash movies
- The power of filters and blends
- A variety of methods for managing on-stage content
- How to create and use a mask
- How to use masks and the 3D tools in Flash to create a realistic sky.

In the next chapter, you will be exposed to ActionScript 3.0, the current version of Flash's programming language.

Chapter 4

ActionScript Basics

Programming is a discipline all its own. In fact, Flash has grown so much over the ten years of its existence that people are actually earning fairly decent incomes as ActionScript programmers, or, as they are known in the industry, Flash developers. This is not to say our intention is to turn you into a programmer outright, but an understanding of the ActionScript 3.0 language and the fundamentals of its use will make your day-to-day life easier.

Here's what we'll cover in this chapter:

- Using the `Actions` panel
- Understanding the fundamentals of objects
- Commenting code
- Creating and using variables
- Using data types, operators, and conditionals
- Using the new Code Snippets feature
- Getting help

The following files are used in the exercises in this chapter (located in `Chapter04/ExerciseFiles_Ch04`):

- `Instance.fla`
- `Events.fla`

CHAPTER 4

- twinkie.fla
- PauseTimeline.fla
- carRace.fla
- AddSnippet.fla
- CodeHint.fla

Additionally, we've provided completed versions of several exercises for your reference (located in Chapter04/ExerciseFiles_Ch04/Complete/).

The source files are available online at www.friendsofED.com/download.html?isbn=1430229940.

Using ActionScript is a lot like owning a car. Our hunch is that most of you own one, or have at least thought about owning one. We also suspect that some of you (including one of the authors) find the mechanics of a car so mystifying that you prefer to let a mechanic handle routine maintenance. Others of you won't be happy unless the hood is up and you're covered in grease up to your elbows. Whichever way you lean, it's hard to argue against acquiring at least the basic skills necessary to change the oil and maybe fix a flat tire. You never know when you'll be stuck on the side of the road without a cell phone!

This chapter gives you an introduction to programming as it relates to Flash CS5. We trust the following information will guide you past the first few mile markers.

> *This chapter has been acknowledged by many as one of the better introductions to ActionScript that is available. It appeared in both the Flash CS3 and Flash CS4 editions of this book and was largely written by our former coauthor, David Stiller. Other than minor tweaks here and there and the inclusion of a couple of new CS5 features, this chapter is intact because, as David would say, "It would be like drawing a moustache on the Mona Lisa." Thanks, David.*

The power of ActionScript

When Flash first appeared on the scene (first as FutureSplash Animator and then later as Flash), web designers were quite content to populate sites with small movies that moved things from here to there. The result was the rise of bloated Flash movies and, inevitably, the infamous `Skip Intro` button. But once ActionScript was introduced into the mix, Flash started its march forward.

Today, Flash is a mature application, and Adobe now refers to the use of Flash CS5 as part of the **Flash Platform**, an umbrella term that includes industrial-strength programming tools like Flex and AIR. This means that SWF files are no longer the exclusive property of the Flash authoring environment. Flash Builder 4 also produces SWFs. They're fundamentally the same as SWFs built in Flash—they all run in the same Flash Player 9 or newer—but Flex is geared toward programmers who normally work in applications like Microsoft Visual Studio or Borland JBuilder—not at all the domain of artsy types! As you have seen in the preceding chapters, Flash can still be used to move things from here to there. On one hand, you have an animation tool for building scalable, lightweight motion graphics that renders animated GIFs extinct, and many Flash designers are using the application to create broadcast quality cartoons for display on the Web and television.

On the other hand, even without Flash Builder, Flash developers have plenty of room to spread their wings. They use the platform for everything from building online banking applications to fully realized clones of Super Mario Brothers. In between is a wealth of content ranging from interactive banner ads to MP3 players, from viral e-cards to video-enhanced corporate multimedia presentations. How far you go, and the directions you take, are up to you—that's an exciting prospect! These are all possible thanks to ActionScript.

Put simply, ActionScript brings your movies to life. No matter how impressive your sense of graphic design, the net result of your artistry gets "baked," as is, into a published SWF. What's done is done—unless you introduce programming to the picture. With ActionScript, your opportunities extend beyond the bounds of the Flash interface. You can program movies to respond to user input in orderly or completely random ways.

ActionScript also has a pragmatic side. You can reduce SWF file size and initial download time by programming movies to load images, audio, and video from external, rather than embedded, files. You can even make things easier for yourself by loading these files based on information stored in XML documents and styled with CSS (these topics are covered in Chapters 12 and 13).

ActionScript 3.0 is the latest and most mature incarnation of the programming language used by Flash. As a point of interest, it was supported a full year before Flash CS3 came to market by two related, but distinct, Adobe products: Flex Builder 2 and Flash Player 9. This was an all-time first in the history of Flash. The decision to do so was a wise one on the part of Adobe. What it meant was that Flash developers had already become familiar with the new features and improvements of ActionScript 3.0 by hearing about it around the watercooler. If you were in an academic or office setting during the release of Flash CS3, chances were good that a kind and wise soul had already forged ahead and cleared the path. With the release of Flash CS5, few are looking back. Numerous tutorials and articles on ActionScript 3.0 are already available online at the Adobe Developer Connection (www.adobe.com/devnet/). All of the examples in this book use the ActionScript 3.0 language.

> *Flash CS5 is perfectly capable of using ActionScript 2.0 and even older versions of the language. But do note that ActionScript 1.0, the first iteration, is on its last legs, and ActionScript 2.0 is heading for that status as well. The adoption of ActionScript 3.0 has become more rapid than in the past because of the introduction of Flex and the fact that the Flash developer community was exposed to the language so far in advance of Flash CS3.*

So, where did ActionScript come from? Before Macromedia joined the Adobe family, it looked at the programming languages used for web interactivity and realized JavaScript was predominant. Rather than add yet another language, the decision was made in Flash 5 to stay within the parameters of something called the ECMA-262 specification. This makes ActionScript a close cousin of JavaScript, so if you're already comfortable with that, you may find ActionScript encouragingly familiar.

CHAPTER 4

> *Ecma International (formerly the European Computer Manufacturers Association) is an industry standards association that governs a number of specifications for data storage, character sets, and programming languages, including specs for C++ and C#. It's something like the World Wide Web Consortium (W3C), which manages the specifications for HTML, XML, and CSS.*

So much for history. Let's roll up our sleeves and get covered in electrons up to our elbows by getting to know the interface for ActionScript: the `Actions` panel.

Actions panel components

Let's take a look at what the `Actions` panel has to offer. Create a new Flash File (ActionScript 3.0) document. When the document appears, select Window ➤ Actions or press F9 (Option+F9) to open the `Actions` panel. As shown in Figure 4-1, this panel has three distinct zones: the `Actions` toolbox, the script navigator, and the `Script` pane.

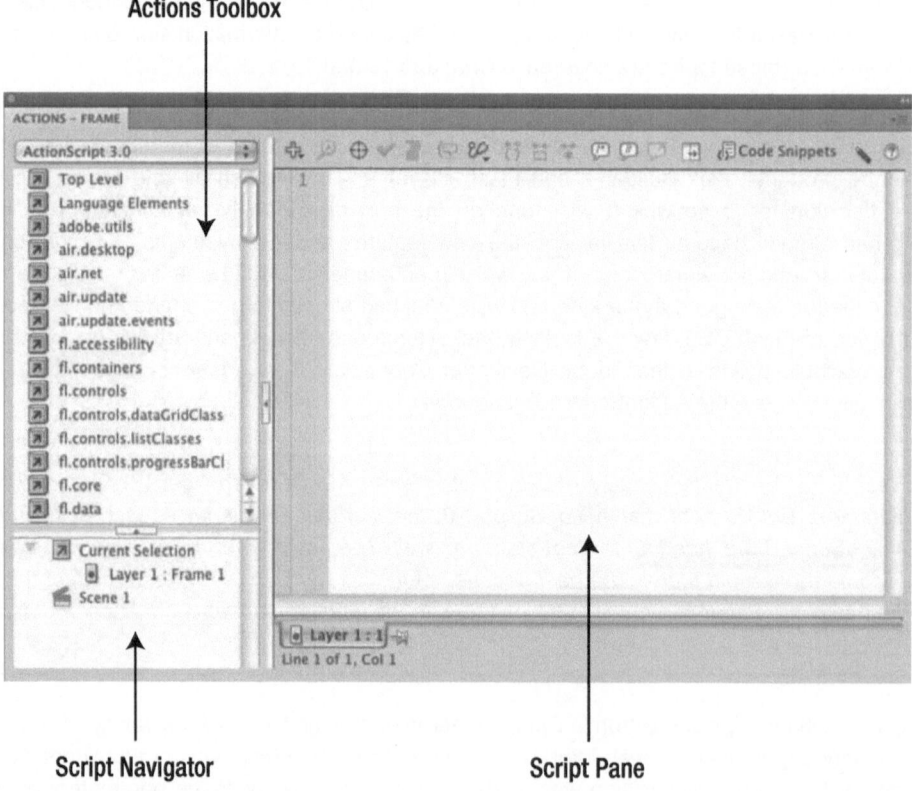

Figure 4-1. The `Actions` panel

216

Of the script editors mentioned, the `Actions` panel has been around the longest. It has evolved through significant changes since its introduction in Flash 4, and it even reveals a handful of new features since Flash 8.

Actions toolbox

The `Actions` toolbox provides a kind of "card catalog" for the default available scripting functionality in Flash. Clicking one of the little book icons with arrows opens that book to reveal either more books—in an extensive, cascading organization of categories—or a circle icon that lets you add that particular bit of ActionScript to your code. You may do this by double-clicking the desired circle icon or by dragging it to the `Script` pane at the right. In theory, this gives you a helpful point-and-click mechanism for building complex expressions without having to memorize the whole language. In practice, however, this is like using alphabet magnets to compose sonnets on the refrigerator...with a spatula. It's much easier and quicker to simply type the code you need by hand. ActionScript 3.0 is significantly larger in scope than previous versions of the language, and no one has the full application programming interface (API) memorized, so don't worry if you find yourself looking up code all of the time.

Script navigator

ActionScript may be placed in any frame on any movie clip timeline. The script navigator area shows which frames have scripts, and it allows you to quickly jump to the desired code.

Selected scripts may be "pinned" beneath the `Script` pane. Each pinned script is displayed as a new tab, which provides an alternative navigation method.

Script pane

The `Script` pane is the high-traffic zone of the panel, because it's where you type your code. Along the top of the pane, you'll find the following buttons for working with your code (see Figure 4-2). Note that you may have to increase the size of the code panel to see all of these buttons:

- `Add a New Item to the Script`: Provides functionality equivalent to the `Actions` toolbox.
- `Find`: Lets you find and replace text in your scripts.
- `Insert a Target Path`: Helps you build dot-notation reference paths to objects.
- `Check Syntax`: Provides a quick "thumbs up" or "thumbs down" on whether your code is well formed.

> *If you relied on the `Check Syntax` feature back in Flash 8, be prepared for a bit of disappointment. This button behaves very differently for ActionScript 3.0 documents, though it still works the same for ActionScript 2.0 documents. For details, see the "Syntax checking" section later in this chapter.*

CHAPTER 4

- `Auto Format`: Sweeps through your code to correct its posture, based on your own formatting preferences. In a pinch, this can act as a backup `Check Syntax` button, because it applies formatting only to legal code.

- `Show Code Hint`: Summons a tooltip that suggests what you might want to type next.

- `Debug Options`: Lets you set and remove breakpoints, which are used to help debug ActionScript.

- `Collapse Between Braces`, `Collapse Selection`, and `Expand All`: Allow you to "fold up" long stretches of code to reduce clutter, and then open them again.

- `Apply Block Comment`, `Apply Line Comment`, and `Remove Comment`: Allow you to add code comments in two different ways, and then remove them again.

- `Show/Hide Toolbox`: Opens and closes the books in the `Actions` toolbox.

- `Open Code Snippets`: Holds pieces of code you use on a regular basis. It is new to Flash CS5, and you'll be getting to it later in the chapter.

- `Script Assist`: Puts the `Actions` panel into a special line-by-line mode that provides programming hand holding.

- `Help`: Opens the ActionScript section of the Flash documentation.

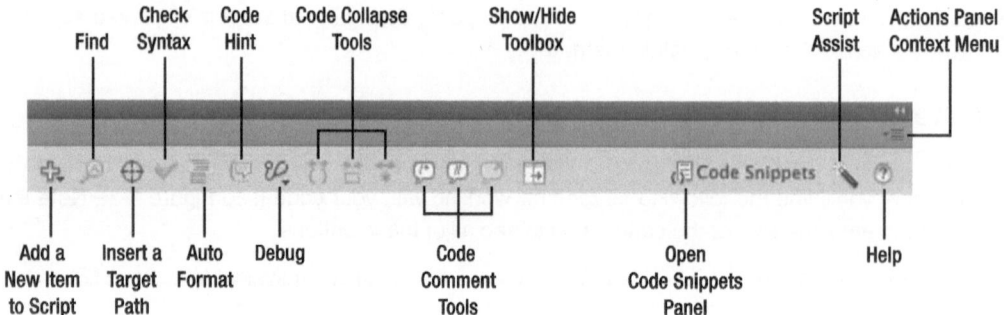

Figure 4-2. The `Script` pane buttons

Panel context menu

The `Actions` panel's context menu, shown in Figure 4-3, resides in the upper-right corner of the panel. Many of its choices repeat functionality already discussed—`Pin Script`, `Auto Format`, and `Check Syntax`—but a good handful of choices show features unavailable anywhere else. These include the ability to import in, export out, and print script from the `Actions` panel; show and hide hidden characters and line numbers; and wrap text.

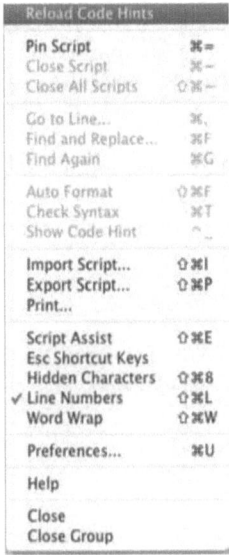

Figure 4-3. The Actions panel context menu

> *A really good habit to develop is to keep* Line Numbers *selected in the context menu. Code can get very long, and if there is a mistake, Flash usually tells you the line number where the mistake can be found.*

The Actions panel vs. the Behaviors panel

If you're not new to Flash, you may be familiar with the Behaviors panel. This panel allows you to select an object with the mouse, such as a button symbol, and apply a prewritten script—a *behavior*—to it. Behaviors include common functionality such as pausing and playing embedded video, sending the playhead to a particular frame, dragging a movie clip, and so on. The Behaviors panel is still available in Flash CS5—under Window ➤ Behaviors—but behaviors are not compatible with ActionScript 3.0 documents.

That's right. If you're using ActionScript 3.0, you need to write your own code. This is partly because the on() and onClipEvent functions, which allowed earlier ActionScript to be attached directly to objects, are no longer part of the language. Is this a big loss? Not really. The truth of the matter is that code written through the Behaviors panel is of the canned, one-size-fits-all variety. This means that it is often more complicated than it needs to be, which can make your code harder to maintain or customize. In fact, many Flash developers avoid behaviors completely because, as they rightly claim, it produces "bloated code." By that, they mean that a behavior may need six lines to accomplish what could otherwise be done using one or two lines.

CHAPTER 4

Are behaviors a bad thing? No, but they frequently give you a false sense of freedom. As soon as you find yourself in a position where you "just need this one part to act a bit differently," you're stuck, because you haven't the foggiest idea where to begin. That isn't the **Behaviors** panel's job. Its purpose is to write the code for you, not tell you what it is doing.

It is a lot like buying coffee from a vending machine in the office. Coffee from a vending machine might seem convenient at first, but it is never as good as a pot you have attentively brewed on your own. When you finish this chapter, you'll be well equipped to explore ActionScript on your own and use much more of it than the **Behaviors** panel offers.

Why are we exposing you to it if it is to be avoided? Because it is to be avoided.

Before you start entering code in the **Actions** panel, let's step back and understand exactly what it is you are working with when you enter code. It is called an *object*.

Everything is an object

Your first step in using ActionScript, and possibly the most important, is to think in terms of **objects**. This concept is fundamental to ActionScript's object-oriented environment and ties the whole language to an elegant, unifying metaphor. So, what is an object? Well, that's just it: you already know what an object is! An object is a *thing*—something you can look at, pick up, and manipulate with code.

The Flash interface allows you to "physically" manipulate certain objects—movie clips, text fields, and so on—by means of the **Free Transform** tool, the **Properties** panel, and other tools and panels. But that's only the tip of the iceberg, and merely one way of looking at the "reality" of the parts of a Flash movie.

In ActionScript, objects aren't physical things, but if you place yourself mentally into Flash territory, you'll find it helpful to imagine them that way. With programming, you're dealing with an abstract world. In this world, objects "live" in the parallel universe determined by the binary information stored in a SWF. That information may be governed by tools and panels or by ActionScript, or both.

Every movie clip in a SWF is an object. So is every text field and button. In fact, everything you use, interactive or not, is an object. For visual elements, this is generally an easy concept to grasp—you can see them on the stage—but it goes further. Things you might not think of as objects, such as the characteristics of the **Glow** effect or changes in font settings, can be described in terms of objects. Even nonvisual notions—such as math functions, today's date, and the formula used to move an object from here to there—are objects. Thinking of these in this way may seem disorienting at first, but the concept should ultimately empower you, because it means you can manipulate everything of functional value in a SWF as if it were a tangible thing. The best part is that all objects are determined by something called a **class**. In many respects, classes provide a kind of owner's manual for any object you encounter, which is a big tip on how to approach the documentation.

Before we move on to the owner's manual, let's look at two objects: Tiago and Tom. The authors of this book, in object terms, are human beings. We'll refine this analogy in just a moment, but for now, let's say our class is `Male`. You can look at either one of us and say, with certainty, "Yep, those are two guys." But drill deeper, and you'll discover that even though we are of the same class, we are also quite different, which is where the owner's manual comes into play.

Classes

Think of a class as a sort of blueprint or recipe for a given object. If you're a fan of pizza, all you need is a single pizza recipe, and you're good to go. As long as you follow the recipe, every pizza you make will be as good as the one that came before it. Some pizzas will be larger than others, some will be square, some round, and the toppings will certainly change, but there's no mistaking what's on your plate. It's the same with objects.

A movie clip symbol is defined by the `MovieClip` class. Any given movie clip will have its own width and height, and it might have a longer or shorter individual timeline, but all movie clips *have* dimensions, and all movie clips *have* a timeline. Along the same lines, every type of object in ActionScript has its own unique qualities. These are generally defined by some combination of three facets:

- Characteristics the object has
- Things the object can do
- Things the object can react to

In programming terms, these facets are known respectively as **properties**, **methods**, and **events**. Collectively, these are called **members of a class**. This also explains why even though Tiago and Tom fit into the class `Male`, we are also different. We feature the same properties across the board—height, fishing license, Moose Lodge membership, and, say, hair—but each has his own unique values for those properties. For example, Tom's Moose Lodge membership expires next year, but Tiago's has only begun. Someday, one of us might have the value `bald` for his `hair` property—but not yet. It's the same with methods and events. Both of us can kick a football, and because our `singleMale` properties are set to `false`, both of us respond to the `sheIsCalling` event.

It's time to refine the analogy in which Tiago and Tom are instances of the `Male` class. Both of the authors have a dog, and it's immediately clear these dogs aren't instances of the `Male` class. So, let's reshuffle our thinking a bit.

In a broader sense, the authors are instances of a class that could be called `Human`. That means our dogs aren't part of our class, which is obvious. But here is where it gets interesting. As it turns out, the `Human` class, in turn, fits into an even broader category called `Mammal`, which fits into a broader category still, called `Vertebrates`, then `Animal`, and so on. The broader you go, the more the members of these groups have in common. It's when you get narrower—down to the `Human` branch, for example—that specifics come into play. Mammals, for example, don't lay eggs (with *very few* exceptions!); they feed their young milk, and so forth. This distinguishes mammals from other vertebrates, such as fish or amphibians; and yet, as vertebrates, all backbone animals at least have a spine in common, which explains how our dogs and their authors can share a class.

It works the same way in ActionScript. The `MovieClip` class defines movie clip symbols. You learned about movie clips in Chapter 3, but at the time, we didn't clue you in to the fact that movie clips belong to a larger family tree. The reason we withheld this information earlier is because the ancestors of movie clips are available only in ActionScript, not something you can create with drawing tools. Just as `Human` is a sort of `Mammal`, `MovieClip` is a sort of `Sprite`. Where mammals—the authors and their dogs—are a particular sort of vertebrate, the `Sprite` class is a particular sort of `DisplayObjectContainer`. The list continues. Further down the family tree, the `DisplayObjectContainer` class is simply one branch of the `InteractiveObject` class, which itself is a particular branch of the `DisplayObject` class.

If your eyes are already starting to glaze over, don't worry. You won't see a quiz on this stuff—not in this book. The important part is that you get a general sense that classes define only the functionality that's specific to the type of object they represent. The `Mammal` class wouldn't define what a spine is, because all mammals are vertebrates—along with fish and amphibians—so it would be redundant for each group of animal to restate that definition. All of these animals share a spine, and therefore all of their classes rely on the definition of "spine" from the `Vertebrate` class, from which they all inherit information. Bearing that in mind, let's take a closer look at properties, methods, and events.

> Do you want to know the name of the absolute rock-bottom object—the class used as the starting point of all classes, inherited by them all? You'll smile when you hear it. The mother of all objects is...the `Object` class.

Properties

Properties might be the easiest class members to conceptualize, because they seem the most concrete. For example, Tiago and Tom both live in cities, but the value of our `city` property is different. Tiago's `city` value is `Zurich`; Tom's is `Toronto`. Now wrap your mind around a movie clip on the Flash stage. That movie clip symbol clearly exists at a particular position on the stage. Its position is apparent during authoring because you establish it yourself, perhaps by dragging the movie clip by hand or by setting its coordinates with the **Properties** panel. To access these same properties with ActionScript, you'll need to be able to call the movie clip by name, so to speak.

Using instance names

As you learned in Chapter 3, you may drag as many instances of a symbol to the stage as you please. So that an instance is set apart from the others—at least in terms of ActionScript—each instance needs a unique instance name. Recall that the two authors are unique instances of the `Human` class. You tell us apart by giving each of us an `instance name`.

A symbol's library name and its instance name are not the same thing, so they can overlap if you like. But the instance name must be unique from other instance names in the same scope. What's scope? We'll touch on this later in the "Scope" section of this chapter, but think of scope as ActionScript's take on the concept of *point of view*. Tiago and Tom can both have a dog named Guinness, and those names do count as unique from the point of view that refers to each dog as "Tiago's dog Guinness" and "Tom's dog Guinness." But there's another point of view—in Tom's head, for example—that simply refers to the dog as "Guinness." From Tom's point of view, he can have only one dog by that name; otherwise, he won't know which of his dogs is which. In the same manner, two movie clips on the main timeline can't share the same instance name.

You name an instance through the appropriately named Instance Name field of the **Properties** panel. Once a movie clip has an instance name, you can access its MovieClip class members in terms of that particular movie clip instance. Here's how:

1. In your Chapter 4 Exercise folder, open Instance.fla.
2. Rename **Layer 1** to **content**, add a new layer named **scripts**, and then lock it.

> *A standard practice in Flash development is to put scripts in a separate, locked layer named **scripts**, **actions**, **Actions** or some other meaningful description. This way, all the code is in one place, and nothing else but scripts can be added to the layer. This has become an "unofficial" naming convention throughout the Flash industry.*

3. Open the **Library**, and drag a copy of the Guinness.jpg image into the **content** layer.
4. Convert the image to a movie clip symbol named **Guinness** so that it appears in the **Library** by that name. Select the movie clip on the stage, and give it the instance name **guinness** in the **Properties** panel (as shown in Figure 4-4).

 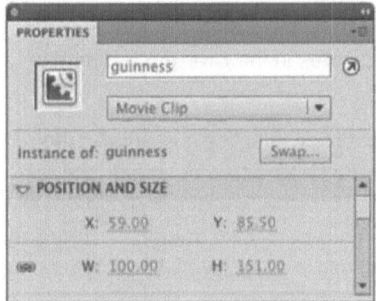

Figure 4-4. Instance names are added in the **Properties** panel.

5. Use the **Selection** tool to drag the **guinness** instance to the upper-left corner of the stage—not flush with the corner, just in the vicinity. Note its x and y coordinates as indicated by the **Properties** panel. You're about to see ActionScript tell you these same figures.
6. Open the **Actions** panel by selecting **Window ▶ Actions**. Select frame 1 in the **scripts** layer. This directs the **Actions** panel to that frame—this is where your script will be stored. Type the following ActionScript into the **Script** pane:

```
trace(guinness.x, guinness.y);
```

7. Close the **Actions** panel, and test your movie.

After the SWF has been created, locate the `Output` panel, which will have opened automatically (it should appear in the area where the `Timeline` and `Motion Editor` panels are docked, but you can always show and hide it by selecting `Window` ➤ `Output`). In the `Output` panel, you'll see two numbers, as shown in Figure 4-5. They will be the same numbers you noted in your `Properties` panel. These numbers appear as a result of the `trace()` function you just typed. They are the horizontal and vertical coordinates—the `MovieClip.x` and `MovieClip.y` properties—of the `guinness` instance of the `MovieClip` class. In fact, they match the x and y coordinates shown in the `Properties` panel.

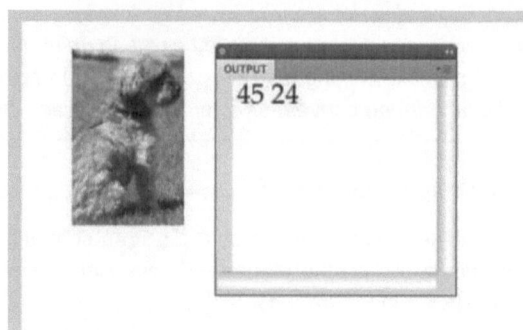

Figure 4-5. The `guinness` movie clip on the stage shows its coordinates in the `Properties` panel. In the SWF, it shows its coordinates in the `Output` tab thanks to the `trace()` function.

How does this work? The `trace` function accepts something called *parameters*, and these parameters affect the way the `trace` function acts. Whatever values—called *expressions*—you place between its parentheses, separated by a comma, are displayed in the `Output` panel. In this case, the two expressions are `guinness.x` and `guinness.y`. Like methods, functions are coding keywords that do things, but functions aren't associated with a class. We'll show you some additional examples of functions later in the chapter.

> *You'll find the `trace()` function to be a useful tool in experimenting with ActionScript. Its sole purpose is to display information normally under wraps, such as the value of an object property, an expression, or a variable. In actual practice, you might use a movie clip's position or the value of a property of an object to determine the outcome of some goal. For example, you might want a movie clip to stop being draggable after it has been dragged to a certain location on the stage. You wouldn't need the `trace()` function to accomplish such a task, but it could certainly help you test your code along the way.*

For interest's sake, the x and y properties of this movie clip don't originate with the `MovieClip` class. This is where the concept of inheritance, touched on earlier, comes into play. Movie clips certainly aren't the only objects that can be positioned on the stage. The same is true of button symbols, text fields, and many other objects. The classes that define these objects, many in their own offshoot branches of the family tree, all inherit x and y properties (and more, besides) from the `DisplayObject` class. If you look up the

`MovieClip` class entry in the *ActionScript 3.0 Language and Components* reference, you might not see the x and y properties at first. The documentation features headings for properties, methods, and events, and each heading has a hyperlink that lets you see inherited functionality. We'll talk more about the documentation in the "How to read the ActionScript 3.0 Language and Components Reference" section later in this chapter.

Setting properties via ActionScript

In addition to being retrieved, or read, in this manner, many properties (but not all) can also be set via ActionScript. Here's how:

1. Save your current file as `Instance2.fla`.
2. Select frame 1 of the `scripts` layer, if it isn't already selected, and return to the `Actions` panel. Delete the existing line of ActionScript. Enter the following new lines, and test your movie again:

```
guinness.x = 300;
guinness.y = -50;
```

This time, you'll see the `image` positioned at 300 pixels in from the left and 50 pixels past the top of the stage, just as if you had placed it there yourself. Want to adjust something else? How about width?

1. Save your current file as `Instance3.fla`.
2. Replace the existing ActionScript to make it look like the following code, and then test your movie:

```
guinness.x = 200;
guinness.y = 100;
guinness.width = 300;
```

See what happens? Not only does the movie clip change position—this time to 200 pixels in from the left and 100 pixels down from the top—but it also stretches to a new width of 300 pixels.

> *Changing the code and then testing it to this point may seem a bit mundane in these simple examples. There is a very good reason why we are doing this. What you have been doing is changing the code and adding to it. ActionScript can get pretty complex. This is why now would be a good time to get into the habit of "Do a bit. Test it." This way, if there is a problem or an unexpected result, you can easily fix it because you know exactly where the change was made.*

There are dozens of `MovieClip` properties, and we mentioned that not all are settable. One example is the `MovieClip.totalFrames` property, which indicates the number of frames in a movie clip's timeline. Another is `MovieClip.mouseX`, which indicates the horizontal position of the mouse in reference to a given movie clip. Some things simply are what they are. The documentation tells you at a glance what the full set of an object's properties is and which of them are read-only. Later in the chapter, we'll discuss how to best approach the documentation, in particular the ActionScript 3.0 Language and Components Reference, but for now, let's keep rolling.

Methods

Methods are the "verbs" of an object—things the object can do. You can spot them right away, because they usually end in parentheses (()), which is the punctuation that actually runs the method or function in question. Staying with the Tiago and Tom metaphor, both of us can walk, but Tiago may decide to take a left turn at the corner, while Tom takes a right. Like functions, methods can accept parameters that alter the way the method is carried out.

As with properties, each unique object type has its own set of methods. The TextField class, for example, provides for the selection of text in various ways. These methods are absent in the MovieClip class, which makes perfect sense because movie clips do movie clip things and text fields do text field things. The Loader class provides for the loading of files and data from outside a SWF. It makes equally good sense that its methods are unique to instances of Loader and that neither text fields nor loader objects can send the playhead to the frame of a movie clip's timeline.

> *ActionScript 3.0 is much better organized in this regard than previous versions of the language. In ActionScript 1.0 and 2.0, movie clips were responsible for loading external SWFs and images. There was also a class called MovieClipLoader that did the same thing but in a more useful way. Thanks to the new virtual machine introduced in Flash Player 9, ActionScript 3.0 slices through such legacy ambiguity.*

Let's keep exploring our movie clip instance, because movie clips are arguably the most important object in Flash to learn. Why? Because the main timeline itself is a MovieClip instance, which means SWF files are functionally equivalent to movie clip symbols. If you're interested in controlling the main timeline, you'll want to know where to look for the necessary methods, and those are found in the MovieClip class. Some advanced developers will tut-tut this by pointing out that the main timeline *can* be configured as its immediate ancestor class, Sprite. Technically, they're right, but that's not the sort of hairsplitting we'll get into in this book. You could also say that binoculars are actually a pair of telescopes strapped together. The bottom line is that if you're planning to send the playhead from frame to frame on the main timeline, it means you're *using a timeline*, which means you're using the MovieClip class.

As you learned in previous chapters, timelines have frames. By default, the playhead runs along those frames, displaying whatever visual assets they contain. In other words, the natural tendency of a movie clip is to move, rather than stand still. As you'll see, the MovieClip class provides methods to stop the playhead, send it to a specified frame (skipping frames in between), and stop or play from there, plus plenty more.

1. Save your current file as Instance4.fla.
2. Delete the existing three lines of ActionScript, and close the **Actions** panel for now.

3. Click frame 50 of the content layer. Select **Insert ➤ Timeline ➤ Frame**, which spans out the guinness instance over a series of 50 frames.

4. Right-click (Windows) or Control+click (Mac) anywhere inside the span of frames, and select **Create Motion Tween**.

5. In frame 50, use the **Selection** tool to reposition the box instance to the right side of the stage, and use the **Free Transform** tool to increase its size.

6. Test your movie. You should see the **Guinness** instance move from the left side of the stage to the right, increasing in size as it goes. So far, this is nothing new. This is the same sort of tweening done in Chapter 1.

In the previous section, we referred to the guinness instance to access its MovieClip properties. Here, we could access its methods in essentially the same way—and we will in the next section, "Events"—but for the time being, let's refer to the main timeline instead. Ah, but wait a moment! The main timeline doesn't have an instance name. How is this going to work? The solution depends on a special, flexible keyword: this. The meaning of the this keyword changes depending on context. Since your ActionScript is in a keyframe of the main timeline, it refers, in this context, to the main timeline.

> *The this keyword is one of a small selection of special statements in ActionScript that stand apart from all the classes that make up the language's objects. When you see this in code, recognize it as a reference to the timeline in which it appears or to the object in which it appears.*

7. Click in frame 1 of the **scripts** layer, and open the **Actions** panel.

8. Type the following ActionScript, and test your movie:

```
trace(this);
```

9. Test your movie. The movie will animate as before, but this time you'll see a new message in the **Output** panel: "[object MainTimeline]." Bingo!

As the movie naturally loops, the message will repeat itself whenever the playhead enters frame 1. So, because you know the main timeline is a movie clip, you now have your reference to a MovieClip instance. At this point, you simply follow that reference with a dot and refer to the desired MovieClip method.

10. Replace the existing code with the following ActionScript, and then test your movie:

```
this.stop();
```

11. Test your movie. This time, the movie stays put at frame 1. Visually, that's pretty boring, but the fact is, you just used ActionScript to direct the course of a SWF! Let's do something a little more interesting.

12. Comment out the existing ActionScript by putting two forward slashes at the beginning of line 1. You may either type them yourself or use the **Actions** panel's **Apply line comment** button. To use this button, either position your cursor at the beginning of the line or highlight the entire line, and then click the button. If code coloring is active, you'll see your ActionScript change color.

```
//this.stop();
```

For some of you the term *commenting* might seem a bit odd. In fact, commenting is a standard coding best practice. The most common use for comments is to let others know what something does. For example, your comment for the previous line would be as follows:

```
// This code stops the timeline on frame 1
```

Don't forget to add the slashes. Omit them, and Flash's **Output** panel will give you this rather cryptic message:

Scene 1, Layer 'Layer 1', Frame 1   1071: Syntax error: expected a definition keyword (such as function) after attribute This, not code.

That message translates to this: "I don't have a clue what this is." Use code coloring as your visual clue. If a comment is gray, it is a comment. We get deeper into this subject later in this chapter.

> *What's code coloring? Certain words, phrases, and other terms that ActionScript recognizes will be colored black, blue, green, or gray. The words* this *and* stop *are reserved for ActionScript and are blue by default, though you can customize these colors by selecting* **Edit (Flash)** ➤ **Preferences** ➤ **ActionScript***. Gray is the default color for commented code, which is nonfunctional as long as it remains a comment. Keep an eye on the code color. If the word* stop*, for example, is not blue, you may have a problem (maybe a typo). As you can imagine, code coloring is especially helpful with longer words and expressions.*

13. Click frame 50 of the **scripts** layer, and add a blank keyframe (**Insert** ➤ **Timeline** ➤ **Blank Keyframe**). Select this keyframe, and notice that the **Actions** panel goes blank. That's because no code exists on this frame. You're about to add some.

14. Type the following ActionScript into this frame:

```
this.gotoAndPlay(25);
```

> The keyword `this` isn't always needed, strictly speaking. If you drop the reference to `this` in these examples, Flash understands that you're referring to the timeline in which the code appears.

15. Test your movie. You'll see that, because the ActionScript in frame 1 is commented out, it's ignored.

The playhead breezes right on past frame 1. When it reaches frame 50, the `MovieClip.gotoAndPlay()` method is invoked on the main timeline, and the movie jumps to frame 25, where it eventually continues again to 50. At frame 50, it will again be invoked and send the playhead to frame 25, and the cycle will repeat—sort of like a dog chasing its tail. The only difference between ActionScript and a dog is that a dog will eventually stop. The only way to stop this movie is to quit Flash Player.

What makes the playhead jump to frame 25? The number inside the method's parentheses determines that. Like the `trace` function we used earlier, some methods accept parameters, and `MovieClip.gotoAndPlay` is one of them. If you think about it, the idea is reasonably intuitive. A method like `MovieClip.stop` doesn't require further input. Stop just means "stop," but `gotoAndPlay` wouldn't be complete without an answer to the question "go where?"

To be fair, it isn't always obvious when parameters are accepted. In fact, in many cases, when they are, they're optional. Some methods accept many parameters; others accept none. What's the best place to find out for sure? The answer, once again, is the documentation. Seriously, it's is your quickest source for definitive answers to questions about class members.

Events

Events are things an object can react to. Yell at Tiago, and he will turn his head in your direction. Push Tom to the right and, if he is walking, he will veer in that direction. It is no different in ActionScript. Events represent an occurrence, triggered either by user input, such as mouse clicks and key presses, or by Flash Player itself, such as the playhead entering a frame or the completion of a sound file. Because of this dependence on outside factors, your response to events—called **event handling**—requires an additional object.

It's something like you see in physics: for every action (event), there is a reaction (event handling)—and it applies only if you want Flash to do something when an event occurs. On its own, Flash doesn't actively respond to anything. You have to tell it to respond. At this point, you may want to roll up your pant legs a few twists, because we're going to wade a little deeper here.

CHAPTER 4

Event handling in ActionScript 3.0 requires an instance of the `Event` class or one of its many derivatives, including `MouseEvent`, `ScrollEvent`, `TimerEvent`, and others listed in the `Event` class entry of the ActionScript 3.0 Language and Components Reference. The handling itself is managed by a custom function, written to perform the response you want to see when the event occurs. Before this begins to sound too complex, let's return to our movie clip instance.

1. Open `Events.fla` in your Chapter 4 `Exercise` folder.
2. Double-click the `box` instance on the stage to open the `Symbol Editor`.
3. Select frame 2, and select `Insert` ▶ `Timeline` ▶ `Blank Keyframe` to add a blank keyframe.
4. Use the `Oval` tool to draw a circle that is approximately 75 × 75 pixels in frame 2. If you like, use the `Properties` panel to adjust these dimensions precisely and to position the shape at coordinates 0,0.
5. Test the movie. You will see the `box` instance animate from left to right, increasing in size. This time, however, that second frame inside box's timeline causes it to naturally loop, fluttering between the square and circle—something like an abstract artist's impression of a butterfly. It's a neat effect, but let's harness that and make it act in response to the mouse instead.
6. Click the `Scene 1` link to return to the main timeline.
7. Select frame 1 of the `scripts` layer, and open the `Actions` panel.
8. After the existing ActionScript, type the following new line:

```
box.stop();
```

9. Test your movie. You will see that the fluttering has stopped, and only the square shape (the first frame of the `box` instance) is visible on the stage, even though the main timeline continues, which means the box moves to the right and increases in size. This happened because you invoked the `MovieClip.stop()` method on the box instance, which told *that* movie clip—as opposed to the main timeline—to stop. Now let's use the mouse to manage some events and make this even more interactive.
10. Open the `Actions` panel, and click at the end of line 2 of the code. Press the Enter (Windows) or Return (Mac) key, and add the following code block:

```
box.addEventListener(MouseEvent.CLICK, clickHandler);
box.addEventListener(MouseEvent.MOUSE_OVER, mouseOverHandler);
box.addEventListener(MouseEvent.MOUSE_OUT, mouseOutHandler);

box.buttonMode = true;

function clickHandler(evt:MouseEvent):void {
  trace("You just clicked me!");
}
```

```
function mouseOverHandler(evt:MouseEvent):void {
  box.gotoAndStop(2);
}

function mouseOutHandler(evt:MouseEvent):void {
  box.gotoAndStop(1);
}
```

That may seem like an awful lot of complicated code, but it really isn't. We'll go over it in a moment.

11. Test the movie. You'll see that the cursor now controls the action. In fact, just place the cursor in the path of the box moving across the stage and watch what happens.

> *If you get errors or the code doesn't work, don't worry. You can use the* `Event.fla` *file we've provided in the* `Chapter 4 Complete` *folder. We'll talk about checking for coding mistakes a little later in the chapter.*

In the code, you are essentially telling Flash to listen for a series of mouse events (the three `addEventListener()` lines) and do something in response to them (the three blocks of code beginning with the word `function`). The events happen, regardless. It's your call when you want to handle an event. The first three lines do just that. Let's dissect the first line, which will illuminate the other two.

In plain English, the line first tells the box to listen up (`box.addEventListener`) and then says, "When the mouse clicks (`MouseEvent.CLICK`) the object on the stage with the instance name `box`, perform the action called `clickHandler`."

It's a lot like visiting the local fire station. Let's assume you're in a fire station for the first time. Suddenly, there is a bell sound and the firefighters slide down a pole, jump into their suits, and pile onto the truck. The truck, with the firefighters aboard, goes roaring out of the front door of the station. This is all new to you, so you just stand there and watch. The firefighters, trained to react to the bell (`addEventListener`), did something completely opposite from what you did. The difference is that the firefighters knew what to do when the bell rang. You did not. The firefighters knew what to listen for—a bell and not the phone or an ice cream truck driving past (either one of which could be considered an event)—and they knew what to do when that event occurred (execute an event handler). What you are doing with this movie is telling Flash how to behave when the bell rings (`MouseEvent.CLICK`), when the phone rings (`MouseEvent.MOUSE_OVER`), or when the ice cream truck arrives (`MouseEvent.MOUSE_OUT`).

You might be curious why the function references—`clickHandler`, `mouseOverHandler`, and `mouseOutHandler`—don't end in parentheses in the first three lines. They're functions, right? Functions and methods are supposed to end in parentheses. Well, this is the exception. It's the parentheses that kick a function or method into gear, and you don't want the functions to actually do anything quite yet. In those three lines, you're simply referencing them. You want them to *act* when the event occurs, and `addEventListener()` does that for you. (Incidentally, the `addEventListener()` method *does* feature parentheses in those lines precisely because that method *is being asked* to perform immediately: it's being asked to associate a function reference to a specific event.)

The fourth line essentially tells Flash to treat the box like a button:

`box.buttonMode = true;`

This means the user is given a visual clue—the cursor changes to the pointing finger shown in Figure 4-6—that the box on the stage can be clicked.

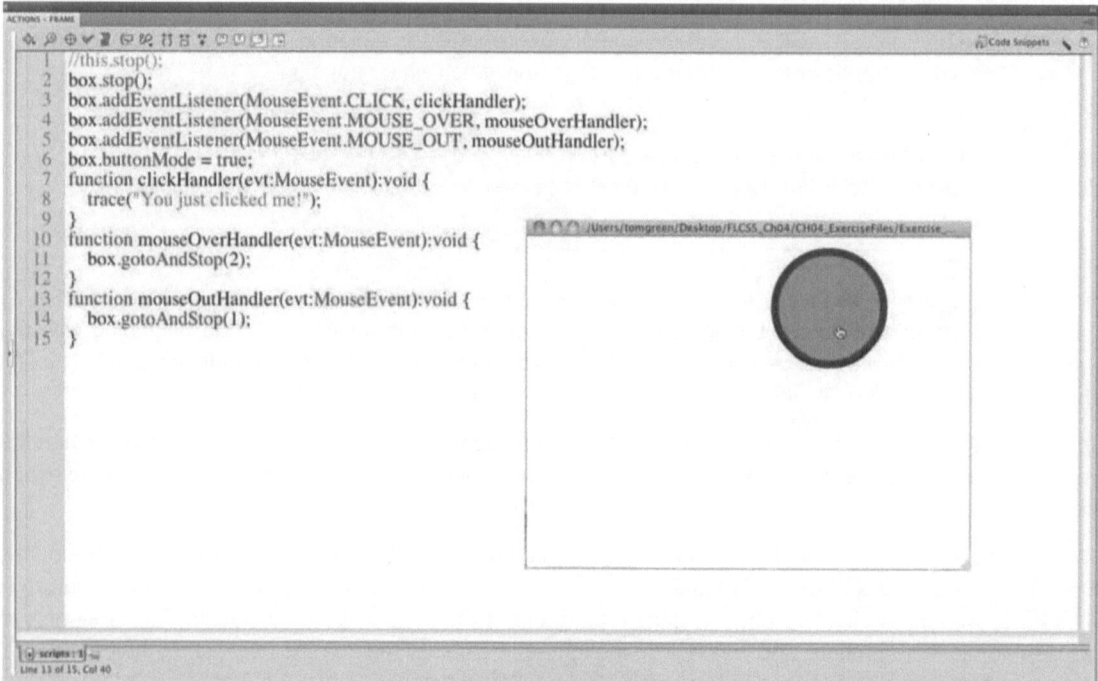

Figure 4-6. The `mouseOverHandler` function is what changes the box into the circle.

The remaining functions tell Flash to put some text in the **Output** panel if the box is clicked, to go to frame 2 of that movie clip (showing the circle) when the mouse moves over the box, and to go to frame 1 of that movie clip (showing the square) when the mouse moves off it.

So, what about the parameters inside the event handler functions? What's the `:void` for, and what's `evt:MouseEvent`? We'll get into `:void` in the "Data types" section later in this chapter, but it basically means these functions don't return a value; they simply do something without reporting. In contrast, the `Math.round` method, for example, does return a value; if you feed in `4.2` as a parameter, you get back `4`.

The expression `evt:MouseEvent` represents the mouse event itself—literally, an instance of the `MouseEvent` class—that gets fed to the event handler automatically. It isn't being used in the functions as shown, but it must be present or the compiler complains (you'll see error messages if you leave the parentheses blank). Using the mouse event is pretty easy. The `MouseEvent` entry of the *ActionScript 3.0 Language and Components* reference lists a number of properties for this class. One is called `shiftKey`, which lets you know if the Shift key was pressed while the mouse event was dispatched. To see this in action, revise the `clickHandler` function so that it looks like this:

```
function clickHandler(evt:MouseEvent):void {
  trace("You just clicked me!");
  if (evt.shiftKey == true) {
    trace("The Shift key was pressed while that happened.");
  }
}
```

As you can see, the `MouseEvent` instance is referenced by the arbitrarily named `evt` parameter. This object features a number of properties, which can be accessed by referencing the object first (`evt`), followed by a dot (`.`), and then naming the desired property (`shiftKey`). If the value is `true`—because the user is holding down Shift while clicking—then a second `trace` statement is sent to the `Output` panel. Test the movie again, and see for yourself. Pretty neat!

Coding fundamentals

Now that you understand the idea of objects and what can be done with them, let's look at how to write ActionScript code. We'll begin with the most basic language rules.

Syntax

Just like English, ActionScript has a set of grammatical rules that governs its use. In English, for example, sentences begin with a capital letter and end with a period, exclamation point, or question mark. Of course, it gets much more complicated than that, but we assume you know most of the important stuff, even if you don't have an English degree. ActionScript's grammar is called *syntax*, and it's easier than you might think. In fact, there are two major rules when working with ActionScript. The first rule of grammar is this: *capitalization matters*.

Capitalization matters

ActionScript 3.0 is a case-sensitive language. If you want to know which frame a movie clip is currently on, you must reference its `MovieClip.currentFrame` property, spelled just like that—not `currentframe` or any other combination of uppercase and lowercase letters.

If the thought of memorizing arbitrary capitalization has you worried, have no fear. ActionScript follows a manageably small set of conventions. As a general rule of thumb, just imagine a camel. Those humps will remind you of something called *camel case*, a practice in which spaces are removed from a group of words, and each letter that begins a new word (other than the first word) is capitalized. So "current frame" becomes `currentFrame`, "track as menu" becomes `trackAsMenu`, and so on.

Add to this the observation that class names begin with a capital letter. The class that defines text fields is `TextField`, the class that defines movie clips is `MovieClip`, and the class that defines the stage display state is `StageDisplayState`. Still camel case, but with an initial cap.

Constants are the exception to this rule, because they always appear in full uppercase, with underscores where the spaces should be. For example, in the `StageDisplayState` class just mentioned, the constant that refers to "full screen" is `FULL_SCREEN`, and the constant that refers to "normal" is `NORMAL`. You've already seen a few constants in the "Events" section, such as `MouseEvent.CLICK`.

Semicolons mark the end of a line

As you've already seen, every line of ActionScript code terminates with a semicolon (;). Adding semicolons is optional, but if you omit them, Flash will make the decision on your behalf as to when a given statement has ended. It's better to place them yourself.

Mind your keywords

Certain words belong to you, and certain words belong to ActionScript. The ones that aren't yours are called **keywords** or **reserved words**. You've run into some of these already. For example, `function` is a keyword that means something to Flash (it declares a function); the term `true` is a Boolean value that tells you whether something is true; the term `this` gives you a reference to the current scope. These words aren't part of the class structure that defines ActionScript's objects, but they're essential to the language, so you can't commandeer them for your own uses. For example, you can't create a custom function named `new()`, because `new` is used to create instances of a class (as in, `var mc:MovieClip = new MovieClip();`). To find the full list, as shown in Figure 4-7, select `Help` ➤ `Flash Help`. When the Help menu opens, click `Learning ActionScript 3.0`, and click the `Syntax` link.

What, only three rules of syntax? Truthfully, no. But these three rules will help you ward off some of the most common beginner errors. Offshoots of the syntax concept are discussed in the following sections.

Additionally, the `Actions` panel provides help in the form of code coloring. Correctly typed ActionScript keywords are displayed in color, as opposed to plain old black and white, which is reserved for words and so on that aren't in Flash's dictionary. In fact, different categories of ActionScript are colored in different ways. You may configure these colors as you please, or turn them off completely, under the ActionScript user preferences (select `Edit (Flash)` ➤ `Preferences` ➤ `ActionScript` or the `Preferences` choice under the `Actions` panel's context menu).

You also might have noticed the `Check Syntax` button of the `Actions` panel's toolbar. We'll talk about that after we cover some other coding essentials.

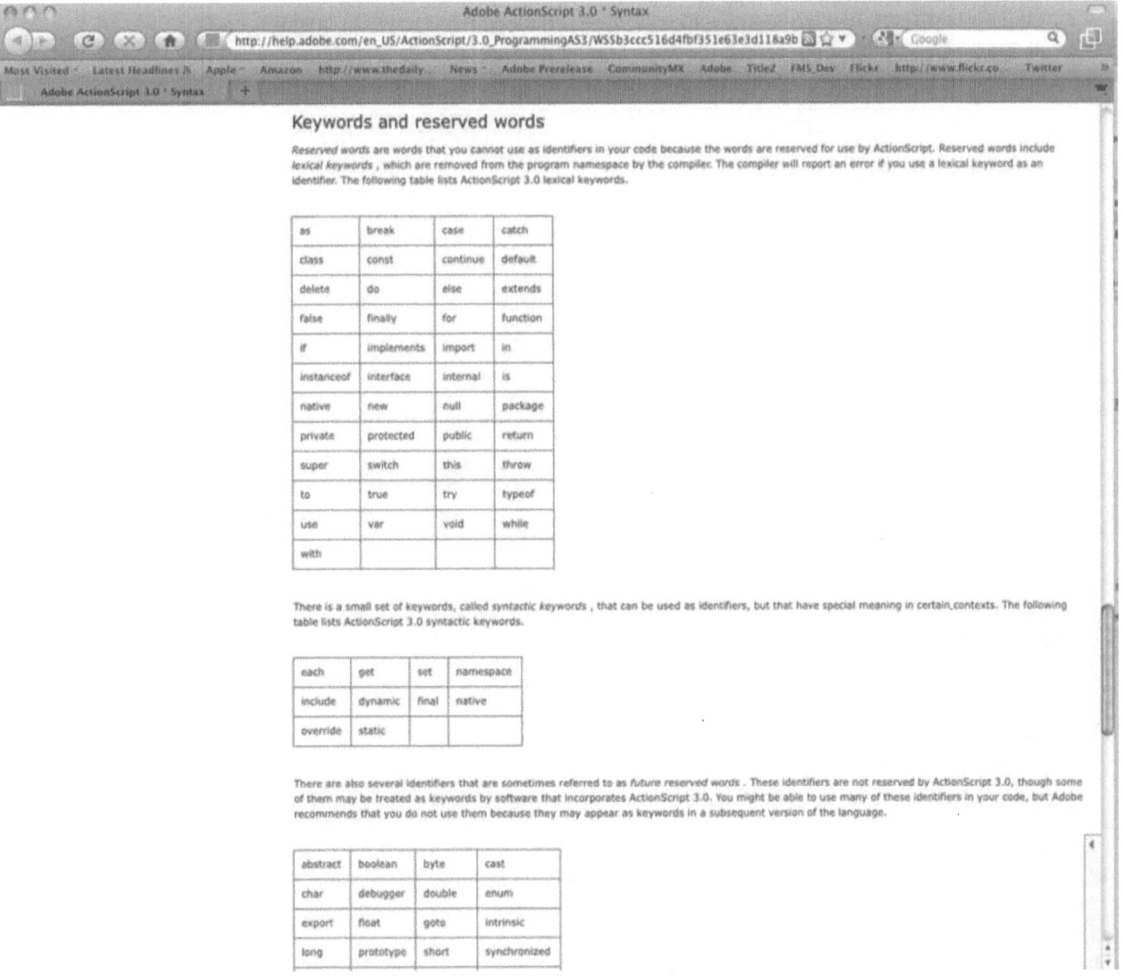

Figure 4-7. The documentation spells out all of ActionScript's keywords and reserved words.

Commenting code

Now that you are aware of the major grammar rules, you should also be aware of a coding best practice: **commenting**.

In the previous exercise, we asked you to enter a lot of code. We are willing to bet that when you first looked at it on the page, your first reactions was, "What the hell does this stuff do?" A major use of commenting is to answer that question. Flash developers heavily comment their code in order to let others know what the code does and to make it easy to find all of the functions in the code.

A single-line comment always starts with a double back slash (//), which tells the Flash compiler to ignore everything that follows in the same line. If we had added comments to the earlier code, you might not have wondered what was going on. For example, doesn't this make your life easier?

```
// Tell the box what events to listen for and what to do and
// when an event is detected

box.addEventListener(MouseEvent.CLICK, clickHandler);
box.addEventListener(MouseEvent.MOUSE_OVER, mouseOverHandler);
box.addEventListener(MouseEvent.MOUSE_OUT, mouseOutHandler);

// Treat the box as though it were a button to let user know it is live

box.buttonMode = true;

// Put a message in the Output panel when the object is clicked

function clickHandler(evt:Object):void {
trace("You just clicked me!"");
}

// Go to frame two and show the ball movie clip
// when the mouse is over the box

function mouseOverHandler(evt:Object):void {
box.gotoAndStop(2);
}

// Go to frame one and show the box
// when the mouse is outside of the object

function mouseOutHandler(evt:Object):void {
box.gotoAndStop(1);
}
```

You can even put the two slashes at the end of line, if you like:

```
someObject.someProperty = 400; // These words will be ignored by Flash
```

You may also use a comment to temporarily "undo" or "hold back" a line of ActionScript. For example, you might want to experiment with a variety of possible values for a property. Single-line comments make it easy to switch back and forth. Just copy and paste your test values, commenting each one, and remove the slashes for the desired value of the moment.

```
//someObject.someProperty = 400;
someObject.someProperty = 800;
//someObject.someProperty = 1600;
```

You can comment whole blocks of ActionScript by using a block comment. Rather than two slashes, sandwich the desired code or personal notes between the special combination of /* and */ characters. Regardless of how you do them, comments are easy to spot in code: they are gray.

```
/*someObject.someProperty = 400;
someObject.someProperty = 800;
someObject.someProperty = 1600;*/
```

Dot notation

Objects can be placed inside other objects, just like those Russian stacking dolls, *matryoshki*. Actually, that analogy gives the impression that each object can hold only one other object, which isn't true. A better comparison might be folders on your hard drive, any of which might hold countless files and even other folders. On Windows and Macintosh systems, folders are usually distinguished from one another by slashes. In ActionScript, object hierarchies are distinguished by *dots*. As you have already seen, class members can be referenced by a parent object followed by a dot, followed by the desired member.

Nested movie clips can be referenced in the same way, because, after all, movie clips are just objects. All you need is a movie clip with an instance name.

Junk food is a great example of this concept. Imagine a nested set of movie clips in the main timeline that, combined, represent the Hostess Twinkie in Figure 4-8. The outermost movie clip is made to look like the plastic wrapper. Inside that is another movie clip that looks like the yellow pastry. Finally, the innermost movie clip represents the creamy filling.

Figure 4-8. Real-world dot notation

CHAPTER 4

If each movie clip is given an instance name that describes what it looks like, the innermost clip would be accessed like this from a keyframe of the main timeline:

`plasticWrapper.yellowCookie.creamyFilling`

Note the camel case. Because `creamyFilling` is a `MovieClip` instance, it contains all the functionality defined by the `MovieClip` class. If the innermost movie clip—`creamyFilling`—has a number of frames in its own timeline and you want to send the playhead to frame 5, you would simply reference the whole path, include another dot, and then reference a relevant `MovieClip` method, like this:

`plasticWrapper.yellowCookie.creamyFilling.gotoAndPlay(5);`

This linked series of objects is known as a **path**. The extent of a path depends on the "point of view" (scope) of the ActionScript that refers to it. In Flash, this point of view depends on where the ActionScript itself is written. In this case, it's written inside a keyframe of the main timeline, and you're aiming for the innermost object; therefore, the full path is required. If ActionScript is written inside a keyframe of the innermost movie clip's timeline—then the `this` keyword would suffice. The `creamyFilling` instance would simply be referring to itself:

`this.gotoAndPlay( );`

It wouldn't make sense to mention `yellowCookie` or `plasticWrapper` in this case unless you needed something in those movie clips. From the point of view of `creamyFilling`, you could reference `yellowCookie` via the `Movieclip.parent` property, like this:

`this.parent;`

But bear in mind, it's usually best to keep your point of view in the main timeline. Why? Well, when all of your code is on one place—in the same layer or even in the same frame—it's much easier to find six months from now, when you have to frantically update your movie.

The most important thing to realize is that you're the one in control of what you build. If it's easier for you to drop a quick `MovieClip.stop` method into some keyframe of a deeply nested movie clip—as opposed to "drilling down" to it with a lengthy dot-notated path—then do that. Just keep in mind that paths are fundamentally important, because they serve as the connection between objects.

If you want to actually see how movie clips are nested using dot notation, open `twinkie.fla`. We have constructed the image on the stage as a series of movie clips from the **Library**. This is the code in the **scripts** layer:

`trace(plasticWrapper.yellowCookie.creamyFilling);`

This essentially asks, "What is the object at the end of the path?" If you test the movie, the **Output** panel will tell you the object is a `MovieClip`.

> *If you consult the `MovieClip` class entry in the ActionScript 3.0 Language and Components Reference, you'll find the built-in class members that ship with Flash. Obviously, it won't list whatever instance names you might assign on your own. This example works because the `MovieClip` class is a dynamic class, which means you can add members to it right in timeline code. Not all classes are dynamic; in fact, most are not.*

Scope

Movie clips aren't the only objects that can be nested. And just as `plasticWrapper`, `yellowPastry`, and `creamyFilling` in the previous example each has its own point of view, so do all objects. These points of view can be thought of as special compartments that manage the availability of variables, class members, and other information to the code currently being executed.

If you trace x, for example, from the scope of `creamyFilling`—that is, if you put code inside a keyframe of the `creamyFilling` timeline that says `trace(x);`—you'll get the horizontal position of that movie clip in relation to its parent, `yellowPastry`. You won't get the position of any other movie clip, and that makes sense. `creamyFilling`'s scope reports its own x value when asked because that scope looks into its own private world first. When it sees that it has such a property, it says so. If `creamyFilling` didn't have an x value, its scope would look "up the chain" to `yellowPastry` and try to find an x value there. This tells you that outer scopes are visible to inner scopes, but it doesn't go the other way around.

Here's a quick hands-on example:

1. Create a new Flash document, and rename **Layer 1** to **scripts**.
2. In frame 1, open the **Actions** panel, and type the following ActionScript:

```
var loneliestNumber:int = 1;
trace(loneliestNumber);
```

3. Test the movie. You'll see 1 in the **Output** panel. You've created a numeric variable named `loneliestNumber`, set it to 1, and traced its value. Close the SWF.
4. Beneath the existing ActionScript, add the following new code:

```
function quickTest():void {
  trace(loneliestNumber);
}
quickTest();
```

5. Test the movie again. You'll see 1 in the **Output** panel twice: once from the original trace and once from the trace inside the custom `quickTest()` function. Close the SWF.

The idea is a bit harder to grasp, but try to wrap your head around the notion that `quickTest()` is an instance of the `Function` class. Remember that everything is an object! Just like `creamyFilling` is a

MovieClip instance nested inside yellowPastry, this is a Function instance nested inside the main timeline. Because quickTest() doesn't have its own loneliestNumber value, it looks outside its own scope to find that value in the scope of its parent.

   6. Replace the existing ActionScript altogether with this variation:

```
trace(loneliestNumber);

function quickTest():void {
  var loneliestNumber:int = 1;
  trace(loneliestNumber);
}
quickTest();
```

   7. Test this movie one last time. You'll see an error in the **Compiler Errors** panel: **1120: Access of undefined property loneliestNumber**. Close the SWF.

This time, the variable is declared inside the function. The function's scope can see it, but the main timeline's no longer can. Why? Outer scopes can't look in; the process moves only from inside out. You got an error because, when the main timeline looks into its own private world, it doesn't see anything named loneliestNumber. There's nothing above it that has that value either, so it gives up.

You've seen that scope has the potential to trip you up with variables. Now let's dig deeper into variables.

Variables

Variables are often described as buckets. It's not a bad analogy. Like buckets, **variables** are containers that temporarily hold things. Like buckets, variables come in specific shapes and sizes, and these configurations determine what sorts of things, and how many of them, a given variable can hold. In fact, variables are practically the same as properties.

A great way of understanding the concept of a variable is to consider a trip to the supermarket. You pay for a bunch of tomatoes, a can of soup, a box of Twinkies, a head of lettuce, and a package of paper towels. The clerk puts them in a bag, you pay for them, pick up the bag, and walk out of the store. If someone were to ask you what you carrying, the answer would be "groceries." The word describes all of the objects you have purchased, but it doesn't describe any item in particular, and the contents of your bag certainly might change. The word *groceries* is a suitable placeholder.

Essentially, variables are properties that aren't associated with a particular class, which means you can create a variable in any timeline and access it from that timeline without needing to refer to an object first. The formal term for creating a variable is **declaring** a variable. This is done with the var keyword, like this:

```
var theGreatStoneFace:String = "Buster Keaton";
```

or this:

```
var groceries:Array = new Array("tomatoes", "soup", "Twinkies", "lettuce", "toweling");
```

From that point forward, the variable `theGreatStoneFace` is a stand-in, or placeholder, for the phrase "Buster Keaton," referring to the deadpan comedian of early silent films. If you type `trace(theGreatStoneFace);` after the variable declaration, you'll see **Buster Keaton** in the Output panel. The variable `groceries` is a placeholder for an instance of the `Array` class, which lets you store lists of things.

To summarize, the `var` keyword dictates, "All right folks, time for a variable." `theGreatStoneFace` and `groceries` are arbitrary names provided by you, used to set and retrieve the contents of the variable. The `:String` or `:Array` part is interesting. Although not strictly necessary, its presence declares the variable as efficiently as possible, as explained in the next section. Just because we said the class declaration is not "strictly necessary," not using it is not suggested or recommended—by using it you are letting Flash know exactly what you mean, and in return Flash can help you by giving you more accurate code hinting in the **Actions** panel and better error reporting in the Output panel when something goes wrong. Finally, the equality operator (=) sets the value of the variable. In the first example, its value is set to a string, delimited by quotation marks. In the second, the variable value is an array, with its elements in quotation marks, separated by commas, and enclosed in parentheses.

> *One of the authors, in order to get his students to understand variable naming, tells them they can use any name they want, and then he creates a variable named scumSuckingPig. A few years back, Macromedia asked for a video tape of one of his lessons, and not even thinking while the camera was rolling, he wrote "scumSuckingPig" on the white board, pointed to it, and asked the class, "What is this?" Thirty voices answered, "a variable." To this day, those Macromedia people who saw the tape never forget to mention this to him.*

You pick the names for your variables, but remember the third grammar rule: you can't name your own variable after an existing keyword in ActionScript. That makes sense—how is Flash supposed to know the difference between a variable named `trace` and the `trace()` function? As noted earlier, search the phrase *keywords and reserved words* in the documentation, and you'll find the full list. Also, your variable names can contain only letters, numbers, dollar signs ($), and underscores (_). If you decide to use numbers, you can't use a number as the first character.

Data types

Arguably, data types are just another way to describe classes. When used with variable declarations, however, they provide a useful service. Specifying a variable's data type not only helps you avoid code errors but, in ActionScript 3.0, can also reduce memory usage, which is always a good thing. Many of the people who have been test-driving ActionScript 3.0 have discovered that this also is a factor in the speed of playback in Flash Player 9 and 10. Adobe is not shy about claiming speed boosts of an order of magnitude, and we aren't disputing that claim.

Thanks to the way Flash Player 10 is built, strongly typed variables in ActionScript 3.0 can reduce memory usage because they allow variables to be only as big as they need to be. When it creates a variable, what's actually going on is that Flash Player asks the computer to set aside a certain amount of memory (RAM) to hold whatever information needs to be stored in the variable. Some data types require more memory than others, and when ActionScript knows what type you intend to use, it requests the minimum amount necessary.

Another important result of using data types is that you avoid coding errors. The more Flash knows about your intentions, the better it's able to hold you accountable for them. If a variable is supposed to hold a number and you accidentally set it to a bit of text, Flash will let you know about it. Mistakes like that happen more often than you might think, and to be honest, it will happen to you. Let's make a mistake and see how Flash reacts.

1. Create a new Flash ActionScript 3.0 document, and save it as DatatypeError.fla. Rename **Layer 1** to **text field**.

    Use the **Text** tool to draw a text field somewhere on the stage. Select the text field, and use the **Properties** panel to set its type to **Input Text** (as shown in Figure 4-9). Give it the instance name **input**.

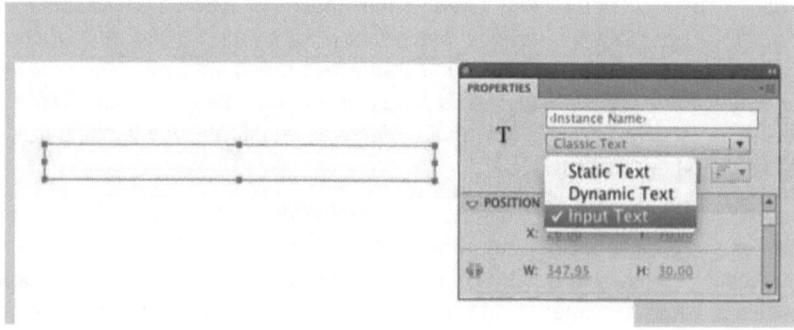

Figure 4-9. Setting the text field to **Input Text**

2. Create a new layer and name it **scripts**. Select frame 1, and open the **Actions** panel. Type the following ActionScript into the **Script** pane:

```
var num:Number = 0;
num = input.text;
```

Another way of writing the first line would be as follows:

```
var num:Number = new Number(0);
```

The keyword new is normally used when creating new instances of complex data types, such a Sound object or a NetStream used to play a video. Less complex data types, including simple stuff like numbers and strings, really don't require the new keyword for them to be instantiated.

ACTIONSCRIPT BASICS

3. Test the SWF and keep your eye on the `Compiler Errors` tab in the `Properties` panel group. You'll see a helpful error warning that lets you know the num variable, a Number data type, doesn't like the idea of being fed a String data type, which is what the `TextField.text` property provides (see Figure 4-10).

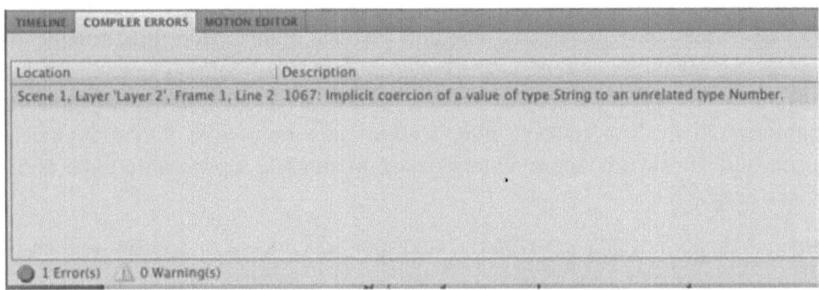

Figure 4-10. Trying to call `Apples` as numbers results in an error, thanks to data typing.

> *You can double-click the error in the `Compiler Errors` tab, and it will take you to the exact line in the `Actions` panel that contains the error.*

4. For extra credit, use the Number() function to convert the String to a Number on the fly. This is known as **casting**.

```
var num:Number = 0;
num = Number(input.text);
```

Besides indicating the sort of variable something is, data typing can also specify the return value of functions and methods. If a function returns a string, for example, it can (and should) be typed like this:

```
function showMeTheMoney():String {
  return "$$$";
}
trace(showMeTheMoney());
```

Many functions don't return anything, which means they get to use :void.

```
function manipulateAMovieclipSomewhere():void {
  // movie clip manipulation code here
  // notice the function doesn't return anything
}
manipulateAMovieclipSomewhere();
```

For further detail on available data types, search the topic *Data type descriptions* in the *Programming ActionScript 3.0* book of the `Help` panel.

243

Operators

"Hello, operator? Connect me with Grand Central, will ya?" Actually, that's not the sort of operator we're talking about here. Whether you are a casual ActionScript programmer making things move from here to there or a hard-core coder, you will use operators—they can't be avoided.

In ActionScript, **operators** are special characters—usually punctuation but sometimes words—that evaluate or change the value of an expression. Some of those most commonly used look and act just like mathematical symbols. For example, the addition operator, +, adds numbers together; the subtraction operator, -, subtracts them. The multiplication and division operators, * and /, multiply and divide numbers, respectively. These are appropriately called **arithmetic operators**. Let's use our old friend `trace` to see these in action.

Type the following ActionScript into a keyframe, and test your movie to see the results of these simple math problems:

```
trace(5 + 5);
trace(7 - 2);
trace(5 * 5);
trace(7 / 2);
```

The `Output` panel shows `10, 5, 25,` and `3.5`, as you would expect. The thing about operators is they deal with complexity in a very different manner than they deal with simplicity. For example, consider this:

```
trace(5 + 5 / 2 * 3 - 1);
```

Now, what number would that expression produce? If you answered 14, you are wrong. The answer is 11.5, and it is vitally important to your sanity that you understand how Flash arrives at this answer. The result depends on something called **operator precedence**. Generally speaking, expressions are evaluated from left to right. However, certain calculations take priority over others. This is the concept of precedence. The rule is simple: *multiplication and division take priority over addition and subtraction*. A good way to remember this is to think of how multiplication and division problems quickly reach higher (or lower) numbers than addition and subtraction do. Let's slowly walk through that calculation to help you grasp the precedence concept.

In the preceding expression, various pairings are considered in the order in which they appear, and operator precedence determines which pairings are evaluated in which order. For example, the first pairing is 5 + 5, and, sliding over one "slot," the next pairing is 5 / 2. Between those first two pairings, the division operation wins. Under the hood, the division is done before the addition, and the "new" expression reads as follows:

```
5 + 2.5* 3 - 1
```

Now the process starts again. The first two pairings at this point are 5 + 2.5 and 2.5 * 3. Of those, which one wins? Multiplication. The process continues, with the "newest" expression now reading as follows:

```
5 + 7.5 - 1
```

Here, the pairings have been simplified to 5 + 7.5 and 7.5 - 1. Neither trumps the other in this case, so the 5 is added to 7.5, making 12.5; and 12.5 has 1 removed, which leaves 11.5.

```
5 + 7.5 - 1
12.5 - 1
11.5
```

As you can see, precedence can get pretty complex. Thankfully, there happens to be a way to override the natural precedence of operators. Unless you aim to specialize in operators (and there's nothing wrong with that), we recommend that you use parentheses to group expressions. For example, 3 + 5 * 4 is 23, because 5 * 4 takes priority and evaluates to 20, and then 3 plus 20 is 23. However, 3 + 5) * 4 is 32, because (3 + 5) now takes priority and evaluates to 8, and then 8 times 4 is 32.

> Here's another way of wrapping your mind around precedence. It's one of those tricks you learn in high school, and the good ones stick. Although the word doesn't mean anything on its own, the acronym PEDMAS (Please Excuse My Dear Aunt Sally) is easy to remember. It spells out the order of operations:
>
> P: Parentheses
>
> E: Exponents
>
> D: Division
>
> M: Multiplication (D and M in the order they appear)
>
> A: Addition
>
> S: Subtraction (A and S in the order they appear)
>
> Thanks to Adam Thomas for the tip!

The addition operator also works for text, in which case it does what's called **concatenation**, which is a fancy word for joining things. For example, the concatenation of the strings "Twin" and "kie" is the complete word Twinkie, as illustrated here:

```
trace("Twin" + "kie");
// Outputs the value Twinkie, which is a string
```

Numbers concatenated with text become text, so be careful of your data types!

```
trace(5 + 5); // Outputs the value 10, which is a number
trace(5 + "5"); // Outputs the value 55, which is a string
```

Even though the 55 in the output generated by that second line looks like a number, it's actually stored by Flash as a string of two characters that, by coincidence, happen to be numerals.

Another operator you'll see frequently is the assignment operator (=), which we've already used several times in this chapter. The assignment operator assigns a value to a variable or property. It is an active thing because it changes the value. In the following lines, the value of the `looseChange` variable is updated repeatedly:

```
var looseChange:Number = 5;
looseChange = 15;
looseChange = 99;
```

Here, it happens with a string:

```
var author:String = "Carlos";
author = "Tom";
author = "Tiago";
```

In plain English, the assignment operator could be described as "equals," as in "`looseChange` now equals 99" (hey, that's almost a dollar!) or "`author` now equals Tom Clancy."

Contrast this with the equality operator (==), which is used for checking the value of a variable. Don't confuse the two! When you see something like this:

```
if (looseChange = 67) {
  // buy a Twinkie
}
```

you're actually changing the value of that variable, `looseChange`, to 67. When you want to *see if it equals 67*, use this:

```
if (looseChange == 67)
```

If you want to check for any number but 67, use the inequality operator (!=, think of it as "not equal to"), like this:

```
if (looseChange != 67) {
  // buy something else
}
```

These are examples of a group called **comparison operators** (as well as conditional statements, which are discussed in the next section). These particular comparison operators are narrow, though. The equality operator seeks a very specify value, not a range. The inequality operator seeks a very specific value too, just from the opposite angle.

What if you don't know the exact value you're looking for? As often as not, you'll find yourself in a position to make decisions on whole sets of numbers. Think of it in terms of those restriction signs at the theme park: "You must be at least 42 inches tall to ride this roller coaster." They're not looking for people exactly 3.5 feet tall; they're looking for people greater than or equal to that number. ActionScript offers quite a few ways to compare values in this manner, including the following:

- < (less than)
- > (greater than)
- <= (less than or equal to)
- >= (greater than or equal to)

In the next section, you'll see some of these in action. But be aware there are plenty more operators than we've touched on here. To see the full list, search the term *Operators* in the documentation.

Conditional statements

One of the cornerstones of programming is the ability to have your code make decisions. Think about it. You make decisions every day. For example, if you want to visit the authors of this book, you have a decision to make: do I go to Canada to visit Tom, to Switzerland to visit Tiago, or do I go to England to visit Ben?

ActionScript provides a handful of ways to make this determination, and the most basic is the `if` statement. An `if` statement is structured like this:

```
if (condition is true) {
  do something
}
```

Thus, in ActionScript terms, the decision to visit an author might look somewhat like this (remember, `==` checks for equality):

```
if (visitBen == true) {
  bookflightToEngland();
}
```

The condition between the parentheses can be relatively simple, like this:

```
if (fruit == "apple")
```

This might mean something like "if the fruit is an apple" (hand it over to Snow White). On the other hand, it might be a little more complex, such as the following:

```
if (beverage == "coffee" && dairy == "milk" || dairy == "cream")
```

This may seem to mean "if the beverage is coffee and the dairy is either milk or cream" but actually means something quite different. In the preceding expression, two new operators, && and ||, represent "and" and "or," respectively. Because of the way precedence works, the expression hinges on the ||. We're checking whether the beverage is coffee and the dairy is milk (both must be true) *or* simply if the dairy is cream. As stated, the full expression doesn't actually care what the beverage is (if there even is a beverage). Contrast that with this:

```
if (beverage == "coffee" && (dairy == "milk" || dairy == "cream"))
```

CHAPTER 4

In the revision, the nested parentheses group the || elements together, and the full expression now requires that beverage not only be present but be coffee and that dairy be present and be either milk or cream.

As you may have guessed by now, the only decision an `if` statement ever makes is whether something is true or false. Let's just jump in and take a look at this concept.

In the following example, you're going to make a draggable star that dims when it's moved too close to the moon. The determination will be made by an `if` statement. Here's how:

1. Start a new Flash document. Change the name of `Layer 1` to `sky stuff`.

2. Select the `Polystar` tool—it's under the same button as the `Rectangle` and `Oval` tools—to draw a polygon or star.

3. Before you draw the shape, click the `Options` button in the `Properties` panel to open the `Tool Settings` dialog box. In the `Style` drop-down, list select `star`, as shown in Figure 4-11. Then set the `Stroke` to `None` and click `OK`.

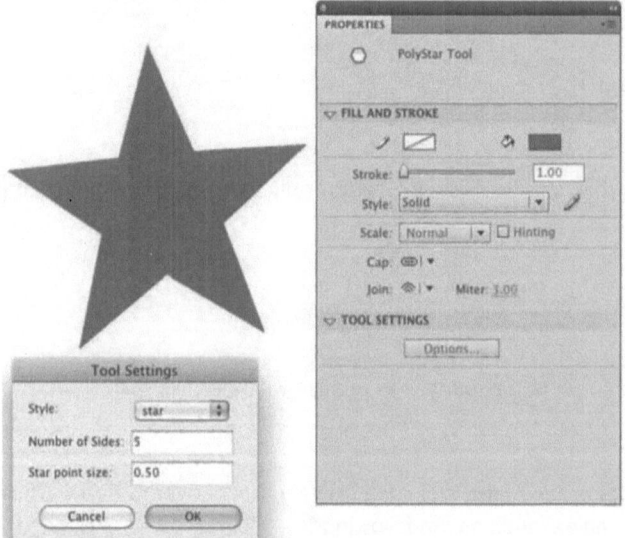

Figure 4-11. Click the `Options` button in the `Properties` panel to draw a star.

4. Click and drag to create the star shape. Convert this shape into a movie clip, and give it the instance name `star`. Position it on the left side of the stage.

5. Use the `Oval` tool to draw a circle with no stroke and filled with the solid color or gradient of your choice. Convert it into a movie clip named `Circle` and, in the `Properties` panel, give it the instance name `moon`. Position it on the right side of the stage.

6. Create a new layer, and name it **scripts**. Select frame 1 of the **scripts** layer, open the **Actions** panel, and type the following ActionScript:

```
star.addEventListener(MouseEvent.MOUSE_DOWN, mouseDownHandler);
star.addEventListener(MouseEvent.MOUSE_UP, mouseUpHandler);

star.buttonMode = true;

function mouseDownHandler(evt:Object):void {
  star.startDrag();
  star.addEventListener(MouseEvent.MOUSE_MOVE, mouseMoveHandler);
}

function mouseUpHandler(evt:Object):void {
  star.stopDrag();
  star.removeEventListener(MouseEvent.MOUSE_MOVE, mouseMoveHandler);
}

function mouseMoveHandler(evt:Object):void {
  if (star.x > moon.x) {
  star.alpha = 0.4;
  } else {
    star.alpha = 1;
  }
}
```

7. Test your movie. When the SWF opens, drag the star, and see it turn semitransparent when you drag it to the right of the moon, as shown in Figure 4-12.

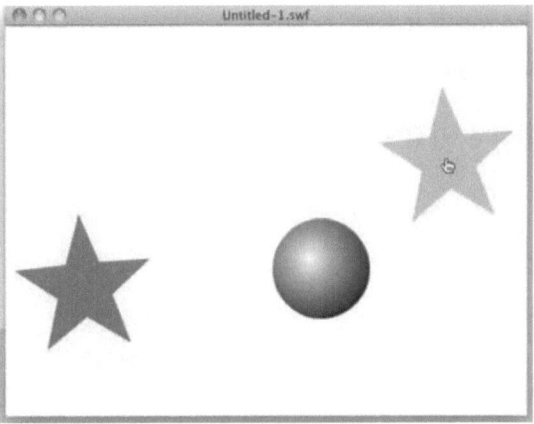

Figure 4-12. An opaque star turns semi-transparent when dragged to the other side of the moon.

CHAPTER 4

We've used what may look like a lot of code, but there really isn't a whole lot that's new. Just as you saw earlier in the "Events" section, you're calling the star instance by name and assigning a couple event listeners: one for when the mouse is down (the user presses the mouse button) and one for when the mouse is up (the user releases the mouse button). Once again, the buttonMode property supplies the visual clue that star is clickable.

The function that handles the MouseEvent.MOUSE_DOWN event does an interesting thing. First, it invokes the MovieClip.startDrag method on the star instance. This causes the movie clip to follow the mouse. (If you poke around the documentation, you'll find that the startDrag method is inherited from the Sprite class. This inheritance business happens all over the place.) Second, it adds a new event listener to the star instance—this time for an event that occurs while the mouse is moving. Just like the other event handlers, this one has its own function, and that's where the if statement appears. The event handler assigned to MouseEvent.MOUSE_UP stops the dragging and tells star to stop listening for the MouseEvent.MOUSE_MOVE event. So, pressing down starts the dragging, and letting go stops it. That's pretty straightforward.

The third event handler is where the decision making occurs. An if statement evaluates the expression star.x > moon.x by asking whether star's horizontal position is greater than moon's horizontal position. The answer, as you know, can only be true or false. This question is asked every time you move the mouse inside the SWF. When the star instance moves beyond the right side of the moon instance, as determined by the registration point of each movie clip, the comparison expression evaluates to true. In this case, the MovieClip.alpha property (or transparency) of the star instance is set to 0.4 (40 percent), which makes it partially see-through.

Now, try one more thing with your open SWF file. While the SWF is open, drag the star back to the left side of the moon. It's still semitransparent! With the current if statement, the opacity of star is reduced the first time its path crosses that of moon, but once dimmed, it will never go back. Depending on your goals, that might suit you just fine, but if you want the star to repeatedly change between both transparencies, you need to add an else clause to your if statement. An else clause essentially says, "Do this other thing if the condition is *not* met."

   8. Close the SWF and update your mouseMoveHandler() function to look like this:

```
function mouseMoveHandler(evt:MouseEvent):void {
  if (star.x > moon.x) {
    star.alpha = 0.4;
  } else {
    star.alpha = 1;
  }
}
```

Now, when the expression inside the if statement evaluates to false—that is, when star's x property is no longer greater than moon's x property—star's alpha property is set back to 1 (100 percent).

In cases where you want to test several conditions in a row, you may want to consider a switch statement. From a practical standpoint, switch and if do the same thing, so it's really up to you which you use. Compare the two to settle on which looks cleaner or more compact to you. Here's an example that demonstrates the use of both (note that `else` and `if` can be combined in the same line):

```
var favoriteColor:String = "deep purple";
if (favoriteColor == "red") {
  // do something reddish
} else if (favoriteColor == "blue") {
  // do something blueish
} else if (favoriteColor == "green") {
  // do something greenish
} else {
  // do something else, because no one guessed
}

var favoriteColor:String = "deep purple";
switch(favoriteColor) {
  case "red":
    // do something reddish
    break;
  case "blue":
    // do something blueish
    break;
  case "green":
    // do something greenish
    break;
  default:
    // do something else, because no one guessed
}
```

What are all those `break` statements? In the context of `switch` statements, `break` tells ActionScript to ignore the rest of the list as soon as it matches one of the `case` values.

Class files and the document class

With all this talk of objects and classes, you may be wondering if it's possible to create classes of your own. The answer is yes and is squarely in the realm of "advanced ActionScript not covered in this book." Still, be aware that ActionScript allows you to come up with completely new objects of your own design.

In Flash, classes are stored in external text files and imported as needed during the compile process. There are many benefits to writing code in this way, not the least of which is that classes allow you to separate your visual design from your programming design. An experienced programmer might, for example, program a game in a series of classes—a `SpaceShip` class, a `LaserBeam` class, and so on—which would allow new laser beam objects to be created as needed, regardless of which library assets might be used to visually portray those lasers. Artwork could be given to a designer and later "married" with the code with relative ease, because external class files aren't spread among dozens of keyframes.

It is, in fact, entirely possible to produce a heavily coded SWF without any ActionScript touching the FLA at all. This is accomplished via something called the **document class**.

CHAPTER 4

Click somewhere on the stage or work area to put the `Properties` panel into stage mode. You'll see a `Class` field in the `Publish` area of the `Properties` panel, as shown in Figure 4-13. This field allows you to associate a class file with the Flash document. Technically, it's how you can redefine the main timeline, making it more than just a movie clip (or configuring it to be a `Sprite` and then optionally making it more than just a sprite).

> *New to Flash CS5 is the `Edit` button in the `ActionScript Settings` area. Click this, and you will be taken to the `Advanced ActionScript 3.0 Settings` panel, which was commonly found in the Flash area of the `Publish Settings` dialog box. You can also open this panel by selecting `File` ➤ `ActionScript Settings`.*

Figure 4-13. Document class files are accessed through the `Publish` area of the `Properties` panel.

Think of a document class as the main script that creates all the other ActionScript objects necessary to do the developer's bidding. Prior to Flash CS3, and even in Flash CS4 in anything other than ActionScript 3.0, this sort of association wasn't possible. Developers could get close, by typing a line or two of ActionScript into frame 1 and importing the main class there, but ActionScript 3.0's document class concept allows a fully programmed FLA file to be code-free in the FLA itself.

On migrating to ActionScript 3.0: the pain and the joy

Kristin Henry is president and lead developer at GalaxyGoo (www.galaxygoo.org), a nonprofit organization dedicated to increasing science literacy. She specializes in developing educational applications and interactive visualizations of scientific data using Flash. She has also contributed to Flash books and has presented at both industry and academic conferences including Flashforward and the Gordon Research Conference on Visualization in Science and Education. To the authors of this book, it was a no-brainer to ask such an accomplished developer for an "in the trenches" glimpse at what it's like to migrate from ActionScript 2.0 to 3.0. We're grateful to Kristin for sharing a few of her impressions. Here is what she had to say:

"Learning AS3, after years of working with Flash, was both exciting and frustrating for me. At first, I was going back and forth between the versions. That didn't work well for me. So I jumped in with both feet and started coding everything in AS3. Once I'd gone through deep immersion in the new language, it was easier for me to go back and forth to earlier versions when needed.

"The syntax is very similar to previous versions of ActionScript, but subtle differences took some getting used to. For a while, my fingers twitched into habitually typing an underscore for properties like `this._x`. In AS3, most of these properties have lost the underscore and are now `this.x`.

"In my projects, I use XML to format external data all the time. The way AS3 handles XML is fantastic! It's so much simpler to work with, and it's wonderful for searching and moving through an XML structure. [Note: This is covered in Chapter 13 of this book.]

"One of my favorite things about AS3 is the display list concept. Instead of attaching a movie clip to the stage and then building up its content, you can now prepare your movie clip first, build up any content and computational graphics, assign property values, and then add it to the display list, by way of the `addChild()` method, when you're ready. [Note: This is true not only of movie clips, but also of any class that extends the `DisplayObjectContainer` class, including dynamic text fields. You can see an example in Chapter 6.]

"I'm a bit of a foodie, and to me this is a lot like preparing mise en place before firing up the pots and pans. Get everything ready first; then add it. It can be much more elegant and clean to code in that style. After coding with AS3 for a while now, I'm not sure how I got by without it for so long."

Syntax checking

In Flash 8, and even earlier, the **Check Syntax** button of the **Actions** panel's toolbar was a little more reliable than it is today. Even in Flash CS5, if you set the document's publish settings to ActionScript 2.0 (**File ➤ Publish Settings ➤ Flash**), you can get a taste of the "good old days." But ActionScript 3.0 documents represent a new era, where all is not as it seems, and the **Actions** panel hasn't entirely caught up yet. Here's a look at what we mean:

1. Create a new Flash File (ActionScript 2.0) document—that's right, 2.0; we're going retro—and save it as `AS2Syntax.fla` in the `Exercise` folder for this chapter. Rename **Layer 1** to **scripts**.

2. Open the **Actions** panel, and type the following ActionScript into frame 1:

```
var str:String = 5;
```

Can you spot the error?

3. Click the **Check Syntax** button at the top of the **Script** pane. Boom! Flash fires up the **Compiler Errors** panel, shown in Figure 4-14, which tells you about a "type mismatch" error: Flash was looking for a string value in that `str` variable, but you gave it a number instead.

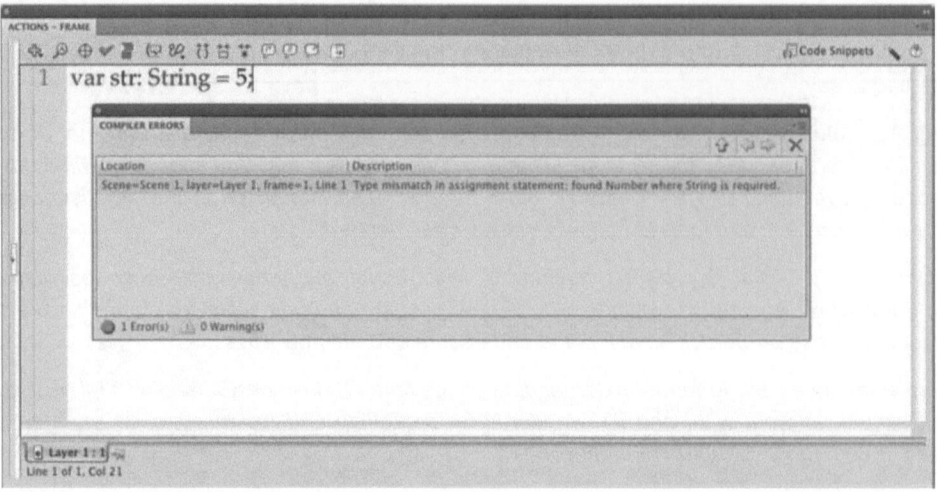

Figure 4-14. In ActionScript 2.0 documents, the `Check Syntax` button helpfully provides even the most basic syntax checking.

4. Click OK, and then save and close the document.

5. Create a new Flash File (ActionScript 3.0) document—yes, this time 3.0—and save it as AS3Syntax.fla in the Exercise folder for this chapter. You're about to perform the same experiment, so rename **Layer 1** to **scripts**.

6. Open the **Actions** panel, and type the following identical ActionScript into frame 1:

```
var str:String = 5;
```

> *Syntax doesn't necessarily carry over so easily from one version of the language to another, but in this case, the variable declaration in question is indeed the same in both ActionScript 2.0 and 3.0.*

7. Click the `Check Syntax` button. Nothing happens. Obviously the code is wrong. How do you find out?

8. As you saw in the "Data types" section, Flash does check syntax during a compile, but you must go as far as creating the SWF before you see the error. To prove it here, select **Control ▶ Test Movie**. Keep an eye on the **Compiler Errors** panel. Sure enough, you get the expected "type mismatch" error (see Figure 4-15). It's worded a bit differently, but the gist is the same.

ACTIONSCRIPT BASICS

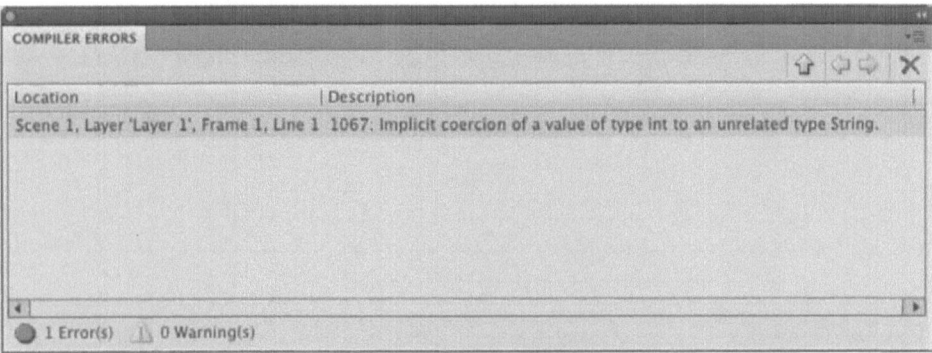

Figure 4-15. Thankfully, syntax is checked when a movie is tested.

The trouble with testing a movie in order to "proof" your syntax becomes clear as soon as your movie takes on any complexity. There will be times you simply want to "check your bearings" in place, without having to go to the trouble of generating a SWF file. Does this mean the `Check Syntax` button is useless in ActionScript 3.0 documents? Well, the word *useless* might be a little harsh. To be fair, the `Check Syntax` button does report on certain kinds of errors; it's just that you won't find them nearly as often.

You have two documents handy, so let's tag-team between them and look at a few more examples. We recommend you keep both AS2Syntax.fla and AS3Syntax.fla open and flip back and forth as you test the following code.

9. Delete the existing code in your ActionScript 3.0 document, and type the following into the **Actions** panel in frame 1:

```
var d:Date = new Date();
d.setMillennium(3);
```

As you do, you'll see some code hinting when you get to line 2. Thanks to the strongly typed variable d in line 1 (the strong typing is provided by the :Date suffix), Flash knows that d is an instance of the Date class. As a courtesy, the **Actions** panel gives you a context-sensitive drop-down menu as soon as you type the dot after the variable. The drop-down menu suggests Date class members (see Figure 4-16).

10. Type **s**, and the drop-down menu jumps to class members that start with that letter, such as setDate(), setFullYear(), and so on.

11. Type as far as **setM**, and you'll see setMilliseconds(). At this point, you're going to be a rebel. Rather than go with any of the suggestions, type **setMillennium(3);** to complete line 2 of the code shown previously. As you can see from the drop-down menu, the Date class features no such method. Does **Check Syntax** agree?

12. Click the **Check Syntax** button to find out. The ActionScript 3.0 document will beep at you. That sound is a bit of a shady poker face because that beep means is, "This script contains no errors." Shucks, we know better than that ourselves!

255

CHAPTER 4

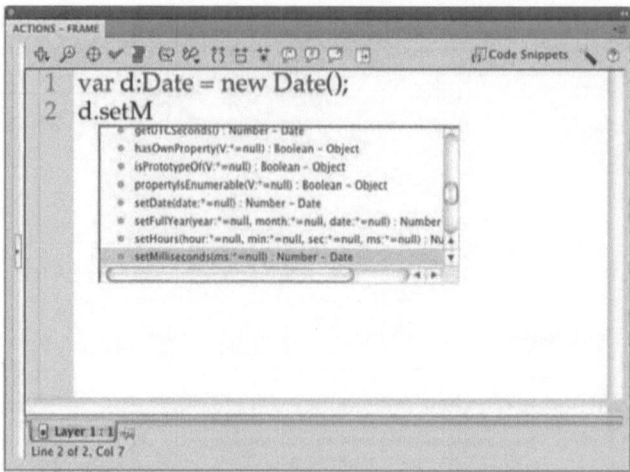

Figure 4-16. Using strongly typed variables gives you useful code hinting.

> *In this version of Flash, Flash CS5, Adobe has in its "wisdom" removed the alert box that used to tell you things were fine. In our humble opinion, replacing an alert box with a beep is a huge usability error. When a button named* `Check Syntax` *is clicked, it should not beep at you. It should actually tell you, "This script contains no errors."*

13. Repeat the same steps in the ActionScript 2.0 document. Once you've replaced the existing code with the two-line `Date`-related ActionScript—complete with the made-up `setMillennium()` method—click the `Check Syntax` button. Here, the alert sends you to the `Compiler Errors` panel, which slams you with the hard truth: `There is no method with the name 'setMillennium'`. Hey, even if the truth hurts, it's good to know.

14. Return one last time to the ActionScript 3.0 document. Delete the last two characters in your code so that it looks like this:

```
var d:Date = new Date();
d.setMillennium(2000
```

15. Click the `Check Syntax` button. Are you holding your breath? Go ahead and exhale. Ahhh, the `Compiler Errors` panel fires up and gives you a message, which reads as, `1084: Syntax error: expecting rightparen before end of program`. Sure, it sounds a little stilted. You can imagine it intoned by the colossal WOPR computer from the 1980s nerd classic *WarGames*, just before it asks Professor Falken about a nice game of chess. But it's an error message, and that's a good thing. Click OK to close the alert box.

16. For good measure, make a final visit to the ActionScript 2.0 document, and remove the closing);
characters there, too. Click the **Check Syntax** button. What do you get? You get an alert box
that tells you to check out the error message in the **Compiler Errors** panel: `')'` or `','`
expected. It's more or less the same message, just stated more succinctly. Honestly, the
ActionScript 3.0 version is a bit more helpful. Click **OK** to close the alert box.

What can you learn from this? In ActionScript 3.0 documents, the **Actions** panel's **Check Syntax**
button reports on gross structural problems. If you have a missing parenthesis or bracket, such as in this
expression:

```
if ((2 + 2) == 4) {
  trace("Yes, 2 + 2 is 4.");
} else
  trace("Oddly, it isn't.");
}
```

you'll be warned about it. In the preceding code, the else clause is missing a curly bracket ({) to its right.
This sort of error reporting, even if it's all you get, is a positive asset. In the words of our mothers, "Be
thankful for what you have." To that, we add this: if you need a bit of something to lean on in your
programming, use the resources at hand. They include the ActionScript 3.0 Language and Components
Reference and code hinting, at the very least.

Even the **Script Assist** feature of the **Actions** panel, which will step you through code writing line by
line, only catches the sort of errors found by the **Check Syntax** button in ActionScript 3.0 documents. So,
tuck your feet, pretzel-like, beneath you, and then up again over your legs. This is the lotus position. It
encourages breathing and good posture and is said to facilitate meditation. Don't lose heart! The very best
syntax checker is sitting closer than you think—it's right there between your shoulders.

How to read the ActionScript 3.0 Language and Components Reference

Have you ever had to give a presentation in front of a room full of people? If you're not used to that, it can
be pretty nerve-wracking. In spite of hours of preparation, people have been known to draw a complete
blank. The authors have seen many newcomers to Flash react in the same way to the **Help** panel,
especially when faced with the ActionScript 3.0 Language and Components Reference. You may have
been following along just fine in this chapter—nodding your head, because things seem to make sense—
but then, when you find yourself sitting in front of an empty Flash document...gosh, where to begin?

The **Help** panel isn't especially larger than the other panels you've seen, but it contains immeasurably
more information. You may be feeling a sense of the old "dictionary catch-22"—how are you supposed to
look up a word to find out how it's spelled...if you don't know how it's spelled?

Let's get you past **Help** panel stage fright.

CHAPTER 4

Getting help

There are several places where you can access the Help files. If you are working in the Flash interface, select `Help` ➤ `Flash Help`. If you have the `Actions` panel open and want to quickly jump to code-specific documentation, select `Help` from the panel's upper-right menu (see Figure 4-17), or click the `Help` button in the `Actions` panel toolbar. If you really need help in a hurry, press the F1 key or use the search field in the upper-right corner of the authoring environment (see Figure 4-18).

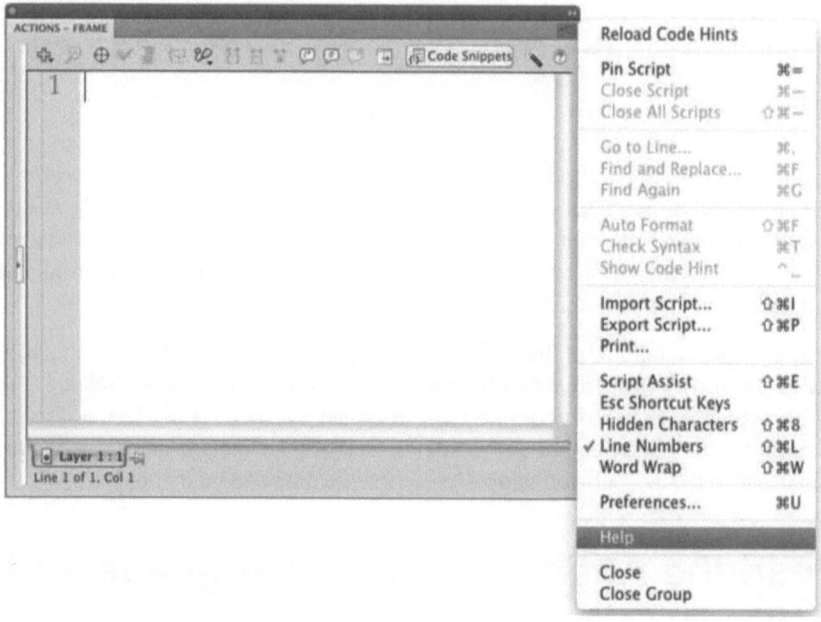

Figure 4-17. Access help through the `Action` panel's context menu.

> *If you want quick help regarding a specific term in the code, highlight that term in the* `Actions` *panel's* `Script` *pane—in other words, select a keyword in your actual code—and then press the F1 key, click the* `Actions` *panel's* `Help` *button, or select* `Help` *from the panel's menu. Flash automatically detects which version of ActionScript you're using and opens the documentation to the keyword you highlighted. Be aware that if you go this route, results can sometimes go astray. For example, the* `TextField` *class and the* `Label` *class (a component) both feature an* `htmlText` *property. In one particular test, one of the authors highlighted the* `htmlText` *property of a* `TextField` *instance and pressed F1. The documentation jumped to the* `Label.htmlText` *entry.*

258

ACTIONSCRIPT BASICS

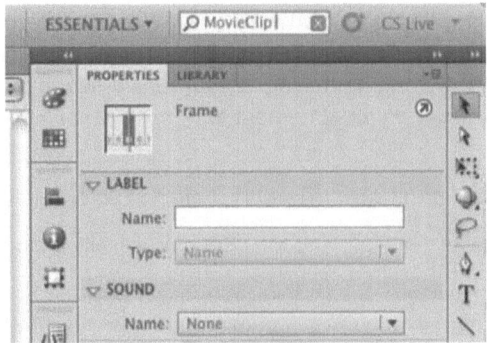

Figure 4-18. A search field in the upper-right corner gives you quick access to documentation.

Search tactics

Browsing the ActionScript 3.0 Language and Components Reference is a good thing. We heartily encourage the practice. Flip open a section, even at random, and dig in; there's always plenty to learn, even for the expert. That said, busy schedules often mean that spare moments come at a premium. Flash's search field can be a speedy assistant when your manager is breathing down your neck.

Your number-one strategy at all times is to reduce the number of places you need to look. If a book filter is available, use it to filter the books in which you're interested. If you're not looking for ActionScript-related information, select a choice that doesn't include ActionScript in the title. If you're tracking down programming information, select **ActionScript 3.0**. If a product filter is available, make sure to filter results for Flash only, as opposed to Flash and Flex Builder. This prevents Flash from looking at books you don't need, which means you won't need to wade through unnecessary search results, including results that might steer you down a very wrong path. In fact, the best path is to stay put and select **Local** as your search location. This way you don't get "carpet bombed" with results from the Internet. For example, remember that if your movie's publish settings are configured for ActionScript 3.0, you can't put code from any other version of ActionScript into the mix.

> *For the last several versions of Flash, advanced developers have had access to something called the Flash JavaScript API, also known as JSFL. This special language is different from ActionScript altogether, because it allows the Flash interface itself to be manipulated programmatically. For example, you can automate repetitive tasks with JSFL or even build new drawing tools from scratch. But this language can be used only with the authoring environment and Flash documents, not SWF files. The last thing you want to do is search and discover some exciting "new feature" in JSFL and spend hours trying to figure out why it doesn't work in your movie.*

Take the time to learn two important descriptive ActionScript terms. Write them on a sticky note, if you like, and keep it taped to your monitor. Why? Because a number of ActionScript keywords match common

English words used in everyday language. You won't get anywhere searching the word *if*, for example, because although `if` is an important ActionScript statement, it's also used all over the place in help documents that have nothing do with programming. If you want to see the entry on `if`, `if..else`, and the like, look up the *sort* of ActionScript an `if` statement is: a *conditional*. Here's that helpful two-item cheat sheet:

- Conditionals, which include `if`, `if..else`, `switch`, and so on
- Operators, which include `<`, `>`, `+`, `-`, and tons more practically impossible to find otherwise

Perhaps the biggest tip we can give you is this: think in terms of objects. Sounds familiar, right? We hit that topic pretty hard early in the chapter, so why is it coming up again here? Well, remember that objects are defined by classes, and the class entry gives you all the owner's manuals you'll need. If you're dealing with a movie clip instance, think to yourself, "Which class would define this object?" Nine times out of ten, the answer is a class of the same name. Search *MovieClip* or *MovieClip class*, and you're ushered pretty quickly to the `MovieClip` class entry.

A class entry will show you the properties, methods, and events relevant to any instance of that class. No more hunting and pecking! If you're dealing with a text field and stumble across a question, search *TextField*. If you're having trouble with audio, look up the `Sound` class. If your problem involves any of the user interface components—such as `CheckBox`, `ColorPicker`, or `ComboBox`—look up the class for that component. The only common object whose class name doesn't match the item it represents is the class that defines button symbols. In ActionScript 3.0, button symbols are instances of the `SimpleButton` class. (There's always an exception, right?)

Once you get to a class entry, use the hyperlinks in the upper-right corner to quickly jump to the class member category you need. Remember that properties are an object's characteristics, methods are things the object can do, and events are things it can react to. When you get to the desired category, make sure to show the inherited members in that category.

Edgar Allen Poe once mentioned something about a "dream within a dream." It was actually a pretty tormented poem about not being able to hold onto life or perhaps time. Fortunately for you, it's not so bad with Flash. The documentation is in a self-contained AIR application.

Using ActionScript

You are going to be using ActionScript throughout the rest of the book. Ideally, if you have made it to this point of the chapter, you should feel pretty confident about facing it. In fact, once you have coded a few projects, you will actually be able to read code. Once you arrive at that point, you are on your way to mastering the application.

Flash has come a long way from its vector animation roots and has improved significantly with ActionScript 3.0. It's a more powerful language than ever. The really neat thing about ActionScript is it is relatively accessible for navigational programming of the sort used in presentations, banner ads, and other interactive projects you may undertake.

Here's a recap of our recommendations:

ACTIONSCRIPT BASICS

- Get into the habit of creating a `Scripts` or `Actions` layer in the main timeline and movie clip timelines, if you choose to add code to nested symbols. When everything has its place, it's easier to find, which means it's easier to update.

- Take a pragmatic approach. Hard-core programmers may insist that you put all your code in a single frame, or better, in external files. In complex situations, that may be the best way to go. When you're ready to undertake complex coding and the circumstances require it, go for it. In the meantime, don't lose any sleep over doing this the old-fashioned way in Flash, which amounts to little snippets of code among many keyframes. Remember, *nobody cares how it was done. They only care that it works.*

- Strongly type your variables.

- Use comments to leave footnotes through your code. Even if you are the only one working on your files, you'll appreciate your efforts later, when the client asks for a change. Comments help you get your bearings quickly.

- Use the `trace` function to help yourself see where you are in a published SWF.

> *ActionScript has matured to the point where there are a lot of people making a very good living from writing ActionScript code. If code isn't your thing, learn it anyway. The odds are almost 100 percent that you will eventually work with an ActionScript programmer, and being able to speak the language will make your design efforts even smoother.*

With the advice out of the way, let's look at two practical uses for ActionScript by applying it to two very popular requests on the Adobe support forums.

Your turn: pause and loop with ActionScript

People often want to know how to pause the main timeline for a certain amount of time before moving on, and they often want to know how to loop a movie a certain number of times before stopping at the end. Let's wire them up.

Pausing a timeline

Here's an example of how a small bit of ActionScript can really make your life easier. Let's say you're building a presentation in which numerous photos advance from one to the next. You have 20 of these on the main timeline and have added visual interest by tweening the symbols' `alpha` property to make each photo fade in and out. Your instructions are these: after an image fades in, make it hold for 5 seconds before moving on. Assuming your movie frame rate is the default 24 fps, you'll need 120 frames for each hold. Considering the 20 photos, that's a lot of frames! And what are you going to do when the boss says, "Ehh, you know what? Change the pause to 10 seconds"? That's a lot of manual keyframe wrangling. As

CHAPTER 4

soon as you redo those tweens, just watch...your boss will come back with, "Sorry, make it 3 seconds." (We guarantee something like this will happen to you in a real-life office setting. Really, it will.)

The key to a quick solution is understanding Flash's wristwatch. If you have an analog wristwatch, the minutes are marked around the dial, and the second hand ticks around the face. Flash doesn't have a second hand; it has a millisecond hand. And the watch face is not divided into minutes or seconds; it sports 1,000 little division marks. This gives you quite a bit of control, which is a good thing.

You've already seen how Flash can pay attention to mouse-related events. You've seen event handlers for mouse clicks, rollovers, and the like. Now, you're going to see an event handler for a timer-related event. In this exercise, you are simply going to tell Flash, "When you hit this point on the timeline, hang around for 5 seconds (actually, 5,000 milliseconds) before moving on."

1. Open the `PauseTimeline.fla` file. If you scrub the playhead across the timeline, images in each layer fade in and fade out.

2. Click frame 1 of the **scripts** layer, and open the **Actions** panel. Enter the following code into the **Script** pane:

```
var timelinePause:Timer = new Timer(5000, 1);
timelinePause.addEventListener(TimerEvent.TIMER, timerHandler);
```

> *Did you notice something interesting when you entered that first line of code? Your code got shifted down to line 3 and a line of code—import flash.utils.Timer;— "magically" appeared in line 1. All this line says is, When this project flames up, import the Timer class. This automatic class import feature for "internal" and "external" class files is new to Flash CS5.*

This is new stuff, but the gist should start to look familiar. In the first line, you're declaring a variable, -timelinePause, which points to an instance of the `Timer` class. Think of timer objects as triggers. They nudge other functions into action at a given (and adjustable) interval. The constructor for the `Timer` class—that is, the mechanism that actually creates the object, `new Timer()`—accepts two parameters. The first tells `timelinePause` how long its interval is. In other words, it tells `timelinePause` to consider itself a 5,000-millisecond timer. The second parameter tells the timer to trigger its associated function once and then quit. If you define the second parameter as 0, the timer will trigger its function on an endless loop, once every interval. If you define the second parameter as 3 (or 10, or 300), the timer will trigger its function that many times and then quit.

In this case, the associated function is determined in line 4, thanks to `addEventListener()`. You've seen this method before. Here, it instructs `timelinePause` to listen for a `TimerEvent.TIMER` event, and then perform the `timerHandler` function when it encounters that event. You haven't written `timerHandler` yet, but you will in just a few milliseconds.

ACTIONSCRIPT BASICS

> *In ActionScript 3.0, nearly every object you'll use can be created with a constructor (new SomeClassName()), but a few objects can alternatively be created with the drawing tools, such as movie clips, buttons, and text fields. When such objects are created by hand, ActionScript has no reference to them, which explains the need for instance names. Instance names are nearly interchangeable with the variables, in that both give you a reference to a class instance.*

3. Add the following new ActionScript after the existing code:

```
function timerHandler(evt:TimerEvent):void {
timelinePause.removeEventListener(TimerEvent.TIMER, timerHandler);
 play();
}
```

This function is written like any other event handler you've seen in this chapter. In this case, the function simply invokes the `MovieClip.play` method on the timeline in which this code appears. As mentioned earlier in the chapter, you could precede the `play` method with the `this` keyword (`this.play`), but even in its absence, Flash understands that you're referring to the main timeline. The scope of this function tells Flash to look in the current object (the main timeline) and see whether it has a `play` method—and it does. Obviously, this is the part that restarts the timeline after it's been halted. To complete the equation, you'll need to hit the proverbial pause button a few times.

4. In the **scripts** layer, add keyframes to frames 5, 14, and 23. These are the frames in which each symbol's `alpha` property is fully opaque (the image is fully visible). Type the following ActionScript into each of those keyframes (see Figure 4-19):

```
stop();
timelinePause.start();
```

Here's the breakdown. When you test this movie, the playhead begins in frame 1. When it encounters the ActionScript there, it takes note of its instructions, sets up a timer named `timelinePause`, and commits a `timerHandler` function to memory. Then it notices a graphic symbol with an alpha set to 0 and renders that. Since nothing tells the playhead to stop, it continues to frame 2, and so on. Until it hits frame 5, the playhead doesn't see anything new, code-wise, so it continues updating the alpha of the symbol in each frame.

In frame 5, it sees the `MovieClip.stop` method. "Sure thing," says Flash, and stops the main timeline. It also sees `timelinePause.start`, which tells Flash to invoke the `Timer.start` method on the `timelinePause` instance declared in frame 1. Five seconds later, the timer dispatches its event, which is handled by the `timerHandler` function, and the playhead restarts. It doesn't matter that the timer and the event handler were declared in frame 1: they're still available afterward to any frame of this timeline.

Figure 4-19. Pausing the Flash timeline

5. Test your movie to verify that each image pauses for 5 seconds. After frame 28, the timeline naturally loops and the process repeats.

Has the boss told you yet to change the timer interval? You have two ways to do it. Either revise the 5000 parameter in frame 1 to some other number—10 seconds would be 10000, 2.5 seconds would be 2500—or set the Timer.delay property of the timelinePause instance in later frames. The first approach updates the interval across the board. The latter approach lets you tweak each frame's pause individually. For example, to make frame 5 pause for 5 seconds, leave it as is. To make frame 14 pause for only 1 second and then frame 23 pause for 5 seconds again, change the code in frame 14 to this:

```
stop();
timelinePause.delay = 1000;
timelinePause.start();
```

and change the code in frame 23 to this:
```
stop();
timelinePause.delay = 5000;
timelinePause.start();
```

Any way you slice it, using ActionScript has considerably reduced the horizontal expanse of your timeline, and timing changes are easy to make.

ACTIONSCRIPT BASICS

Looping the Timeline

We've all seen banner ads that play two or three times and then stop. As you witnessed in the previous section, timelines loop on their own without any help. The trouble is that they do it forever. It's easy enough to add a quick `stop` method to the very last frame of the **scripts** layer. That would keep the timeline from looping at all. But what if you want to control the looping?

To loop a timeline three times (a popular number for banner ads, but it could be any number), declare a counting variable in frame 1 (call it `loop` if you like), and initialize it to 0. Then increment that value in the last frame, and use an `if` statement to decide when to quit. Here's how:

1. Open the `LoopTimeline.fla`. File in your Exercise folder.

2. Select frame 1 of the **scripts** layer, and open the **Actions** panel. You'll see the Timer code already in place. Add the following new variable declaration after the existing ActionScript:

```
var loop:int = 0;
```

This just introduces a variable, `loop`, whose data type is `int` (integer) and whose value is currently 0.

3. In the **actions** layer, add a keyframe at frame 28. Select that frame, and enter the following new code. Then save and test the movie.

```
loop++;
if (loop < 3) {
  gotoAndPlay(2);
} else {
 stop();
}
```

In the first line, the `loop` variable is incremented by one. That's what the increment operator (++) does. If you prefer, you can swap the expression `loop` with its longhand equivalent—`long = long + 1`—but that's the nice thing about operators: ActionScript has tons of them, and they make light work of your efforts.

Next is an `if` statement that checks if the value of `loop` is less than 3. Naturally, this is true during the first pass (you declared `loop` as 0 in step 3). It was just incremented, so at this point, its value is , but that's still less than 3. Therefore, Flash sends the playhead back to frame 2, where it plays through the tweened animation (complete with scripted pauses) until it hits frame 28 again.

Why go back to frame 2 instead of 1? Frame 1 declares the value of `loop` as 0, so if the playhead enters frame 1 again, you negate the increment gained at frame 28. Going back to frame 2 leaves the value of `loop` as is. On the playhead's second visit to frame 28, the value of `loop` increments again. Now its value is 2. That's still less than 3, so it loops for a third pass. This time, when it increments, its value climbs to 3. At that point, the `if` statement's condition no longer evaluates as `true` (3 is not less than 3), which means the `else` clause tells the playhead to stop.

265

Using movie clips to control the timeline

Movie clips, as you know, can be thought of as Flash movies with timelines independent of the main timeline. The interesting aspect of this concept is you can use actions in a movie clip to kick off actions outside of their timeline on the main timeline or another movie clip's timeline. Here's how:

1. Open the carRace.fla file in your Chapter 4 **Exercise** folder. When the file opens, you will see a truck on the stage. If you scrub across the timeline a car on the right side of the stage replaces the truck on the left side of the stage.

2. Test the movie. The truck moves from left to right, and then the car takes over and moves, from right to left, across the stage. If you close the SWF and look at the main timeline, there is nothing to indicate the motion of either vehicle. In fact, open the code in frame 1 of the actions layer, and you will see a stop(); action, which essentially stops the playhead of the main time dead in its tracks. So, where does the motion come from?

3. Open the **car1** movie clip in the **Library**. The motion tween between frames 1 and 35 solves the mystery of the moving truck but offers no clue as to how that car roars across the stage.

4. Open the code in frame 35 of the actions layer. When it opens you will see:

```
MovieClip(root).gotoAndStop( 10 );
```

This line says when the truck hits the last frame of the animation in this movie clip, go to frame 10 of the main timeline—root—and stay put. So, where does the car come into the picture?

5. Click the **Scene 1** link to return to the main timeline. The car is sitting in frame 10. If you test the movie, the truck roars across the stage and then the car, thanks to the code in the previous step, keeps moving across the stage. Let's loop this animation and have the truck roar across the screen.

6. Open the **car2** movie clip, select the last frame in the **actions** layer, and open the **Actions** panel.

7. Click once in the **Script** pane, and enter the following code:

```
MovieClip(root).gotoAndStop( 1 );
```

8. Test the movie. The animation now loops. The truck zooms across the stage, and the car zooms across the stage in the opposite direction.

Using Code Snippets

New to Flash CS5 is a rather cool panel named **Code Snippets**. Code snippets are pieces of code you save and reuse on a regular basis. Code snippets have been a feature of Dreamweaver for years, and there were a lot of Flash developers who have wondered why this was never introduced to Flash. The wait is over. Here's how use a snippet and add one to the panel and delete one that you no longer need:

1. Open the Snippet.fla file in your Chapter 4 **Exercise** folder. You will see one of the images from the **Pause and Loop** exercise is on the stage.

   In that exercise, you essentially had to reenter the same code:

```
stop();
timelinePause.start();
```

   three times in three different frames on the timeline. That's a lot of typing. The **Code Snippets** panel allows you to save code for subsequent reuse. In this case, we want the image on the stage to fade in, and when it is clicked, the playhead advances to the next frame. On the surface, especially if you are new to ActionScript, this could be a daunting challenge. Code snippets to the rescue.

2. Click the **Images** layer to select it, and open the **Code Snippets** panel either by clicking the **Code Snippets** button, as shown in Figure 4-20, in the panel strip on the right side of the interface or by selecting **Window ➤ Code Snippets** to open the panel.

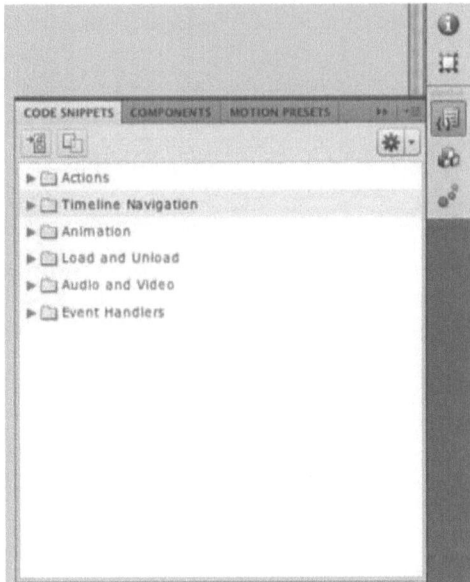

Figure 4-20. The **Code Snippets** panel

When the panel opens, it is not terribly difficult to figure out what snippets are available and the purpose of the buttons in the upper-right corner. The button on the far right, **Add to current frame**, is how a snippet is added to the timeline, and the one beside it copies the snippet to the clipboard and allows you to paste the code into the **Script** pane, if this is what you need to do.

CHAPTER 4

In this case, you need to do a couple of things:

- Stop the timeline
- Fade the image in
- Allow the user to click the image and go to the next frame in the movie

To accomplish this, follow these steps:

3. Select the image on the stage (it is the `Cambridge` movie clip in the Library and has the instance name `boston`). Then open the `Code Snippets` panel, and twirl down the `Timeline Navigation` folder. You will see a list of code snippets.

4. Click the `Stop at this Frame` snippet to select it, and click the `Add to current frame` button. When you click the button, an `Actions` layer will be added to the timeline, the code will appear in frame 1 of the `Actions` layer, and the `Actions` panel will open, as shown in Figure 4-21.

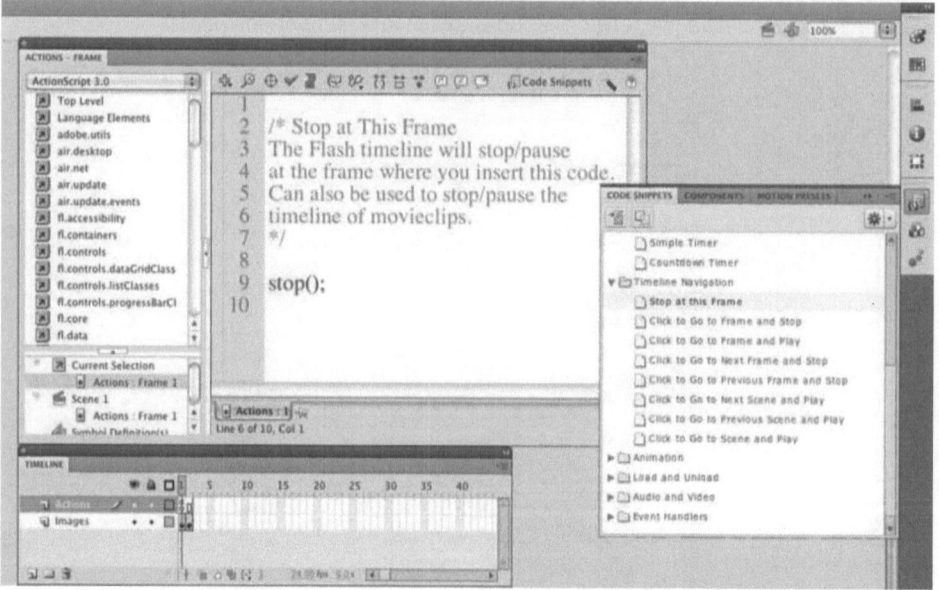

Figure 4-21. A code snippet is added to the movie.

> *If you don't select the object to which the snippet will be attached, you will be prompted to make the selection before applying the snippet. This does not apply the code directly to the selection—not a best practice or good coding habit—but to the instance of the selected object on the stage within the `Actions` panel.*

5. With the image selected, open the `Code Snippets` panel, and twirl down the `Animation` folder. Select the `Fade In a Movie Clip` snippet, and click the `Add to current frame` button. If you check out the code, you will see that an alpha fade has been applied to the `boston` instance.

6. With the image still selected, twirl down the `Timeline` navigation folder, and apply the `Click to Go to Next Frame and Stop` snippet.

7. Test the movie. The image will fade in, and when you click it, the playhead is sent to the next frame of the movie and stops dead thanks to the snippet that sent it there.

> *Now that you have discovered how to use code snippets, you need to know that developing a reliance on them is not exactly going to help you learn how to use ActionScript. In fact, those who develop Flash movies using a blank stage and nothing but code are not exactly thrilled with this feature because it does not foster "best coding practices." We agree. Use code snippets as a way of learning how ActionScript works, not as the way to code a movie.*

Adding a snippet into the Code Snippets panel

Though we have said a reliance on snippets in the last Focus Point is not exactly a best practice, within the world of coders, "snippets" are a fact of life. These are blocks of code that developers realize they can reuse, or need, and instead of entering them into the `Actions` panel, they save them to the `Snippets` panel for reuse. Here's how:

1. Open the `AddSnippet.fla` file found in your Chapter 4 `Exercise` folder. If you test the file, you will see it does nothing more than add 60 randomly placed balls on the stage.

2. Select the first frame of the `Actions` layer, and open the `Actions` panel. Select all of the code in the `Script` pane.

3. Open the Code `Snippets` panel, click the `Options` button, and select `Create New Code Snippet` from the drop-down menu. This will open the `Create New Code Snippet` dialog box shown in Figure 4-22.

4. Enter `Random Balls` into the `Title` area, and in the `Tooltip` area enter `Creates a series of random balls on the stage`.

5. Click the `Auto-fill` button where it says `Use code selected in Actions Panel?` The code will appear in the `Code` area. Click `OK` to accept the snippet and close the dialog box.

CHAPTER 4

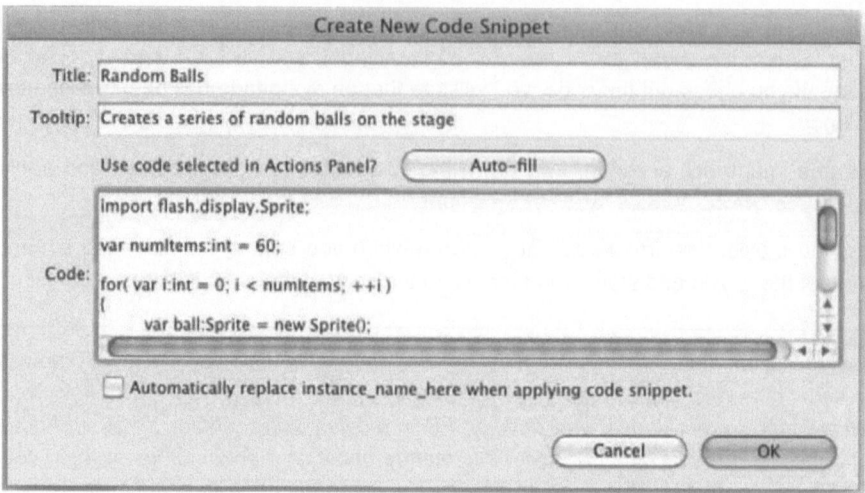

Figure 4-22. A code snippet is created.

6. Open the `Code Snippets` panel, and you will see that a folder named `Custom`, as shown in Figure 4-23, has been created; your snippet is in the folder.
7. Delete the selected code in the `Script` pane, and close the `Actions` panel.

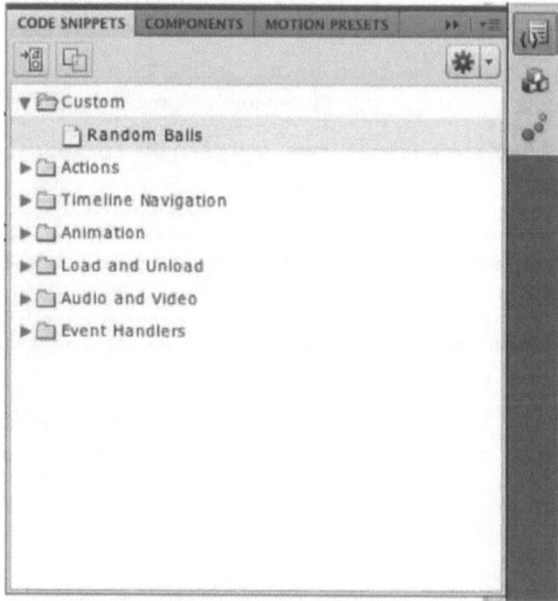

Figure 4-23. An imported snippet has been added to the panel.

8. Select the new snippet, add the snippet to the timeline, and test the movie. A series of randomly placed balls, as shown in Figure 4-24, will appear in the SWF.

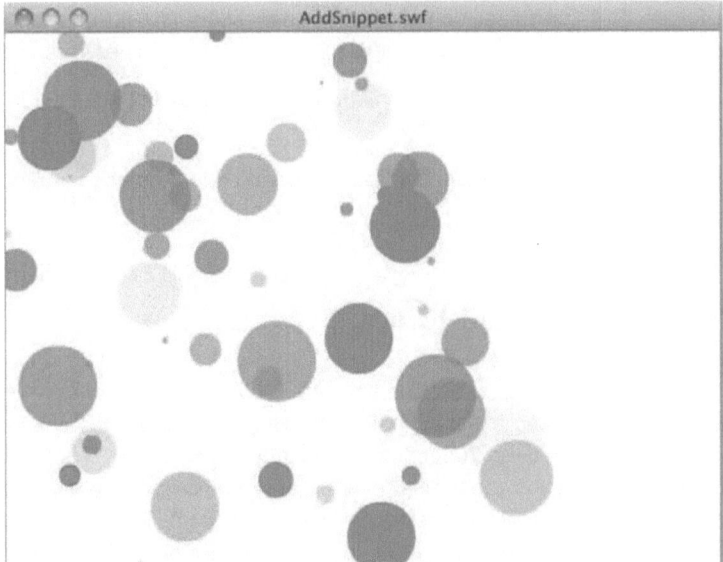

Figure 4-24. The new snippet plays in the SWF.

What if you no longer need the snippet? Here's how to remove it:

1. Open the `Code Snippets` panel, and select the snippet you just created.
2. Click the `Options` button, and select `Delete Code Snippet` from the menu.
3. A dialog box will open, asking whether you really want to do this. Click OK, and the snippet is gone.

Code completion for custom classes

As we pointed out at the start of this chapter, "think of a class as a sort of blueprint or recipe for a given object." Also, in the section on class files, we briefly mentioned how these documents are stored as `.as` documents outside of the Flash file. In this final exercise, we are going to give you the opportunity to try one and discover a new feature of Flash CS5: code hints for custom classes.

As ActionScript has matured over the past few years, a rather robust industry has sprung up. It is the creation and distribution of custom class files that perform a variety of tasks not bundled into Flash's own set of class files. In this exercise, you are going to be using using a custom class than handles tweens—TweenMax—from Greensock Software. To start, you need to point your browser to www.greensock.com/tweenmax/ and download the AS3 version of the file. When the download finishes, follow these steps:

CHAPTER 4

1. Uncompress the greensock-as3.zip file.

2. Open the uncompressed file, and copy the com folder to the TweenMax folder in your Chapter 4 Exercise folder. The com folder contains all the necessary files to use this class and must be kept, intact, in this folder. As well, don't change the name of the folder from com to another name.

3. Open a new Flash ActionScript 3.0 document, and save it as CodeHint.fla to your TweenMax folder.

4. Rename Layer 1 as **Actions**, select the first frame, and open the **Actions** panel.

5. Click in the **Script** pane, and enter the following:

```
import flash.display.Sprite;
import com.greensock.TweenMax;
import com.greensock.easing.*;
```

You start by importing the necessary classes. The first line imports the Sprite class from Flash because you are going to be creating a movie clip without a timeline, which is a good way of thinking about a sprite. The next line loads tells Flash to load the TweenMax.as file in the com folder. This file is the class file. The final line tells Flash to bring in all the properties, events, and methods of the **TweenMax** easing class. Without getting overly technical, think of the easing folder as a package. The wildcard character (*) is how all of the .as files in the easing folder/package are loaded into the Flash Player when you run the SWF either on your hard drive or on a website.

> *That first line of code is actually optional. It will get added when you enter the next block of code and create a Sprite object. This automatic adding of the classes to the Script pane is new to Flash CS5.*

6. Press the Enter (Windows) or Return (Mac) key twice, and enter the following code:

```
var numItems:int = 60;

for( var i:int = 0; i < numItems; ++i )
{
var ball:Sprite = new Sprite();
ball.graphics.beginFill(0xff0000, Math.random() * 1 );
ball.graphics.drawCircle( Math.floor( Math.random() * 400 ), Math.floor(
Math.random()↵
 * 400 ) , Math.floor( Math.random()* 32 ) );
ball.graphics.endFill();
addChild( ball );
ball.name = "ball" + i;
}
```

In this exercise, you are going to create 60 balls of various sizes, color them red, put them on the stage, and then put them in motion. The only thing this code block doesn't do is put them in motion. `TweenMax` will manage that task.

The first line sets a limit to the number of balls that can be created. If you want more balls or fewer balls, feel free to change the number. The `for` loop tells Flash that ball creation starts at 0 and says to keep an eye on the number of balls being created and when it hits 60—++1—to stop creating them. To this point, all we have done is answer Flash's first question: "How many balls do you want me to make?"

The rest of the code block answers the next logical question Flash will ask: "What do these balls you want look like?" Your answer would be somewhat like this:

"First off, Flash, I know you don't have a clue what a ball is so the first thing I need you to create is a `Sprite` named `ball`.

"This thing named `ball` will actually be a graphic filled with the color red—`0xff0000`—and the alpha value will be a `random` number between 0 and 1 that I'll let you pick and assign as a percentage of the red color. Got that?

"This graphic thing named `ball` will be a circle that you will draw—`drawCircle`. This `circle` is to be randomly placed anywhere on the stage as a percentage of 400 pixels on the x-axis and 400 pixels on the y-axis. As well, I want to you change up the sizes of the ball in a random manner as long as they aren't more than 32 pixels in diameter. You want to write this down?

"When you figure out what the balls look like and where they will be placed, you can stop creating them.

"I know that's a lot to remember, so use the `addChild` method to put them on the stage so I can see them.

"There are a lot of balls on the stage, and your trusty assistant `TweenMax` needs to know their names. Please go ahead and name them by putting the word `ball` and the ball's number—`i`—together." Before we put them in motion, here's a little background regarding what you are about to do and what you will be asked to look for.

Prior to this release of Flash CS5, if you were a developer needing to use an external class file from a third party, you had a bit of an issue. Though Flash would gleefully use them, you had to spend an hour or so pawing through the documents, as shown in Figure 4-25, and learning how the properties, methods, and events for this custom class were used. Even then, the odds were pretty good that you would make a mistake, and another trip back to the documentation was called for. This wasn't a case of developers being unable to grasp what the class did; it was simply trying to remember what went where and how it was spelled. This resulted in developers watching how Flash displayed the code hints in its own classes and wondering, "Wouldn't this be neat for non-Flash classes?" The wait is over.

CHAPTER 4

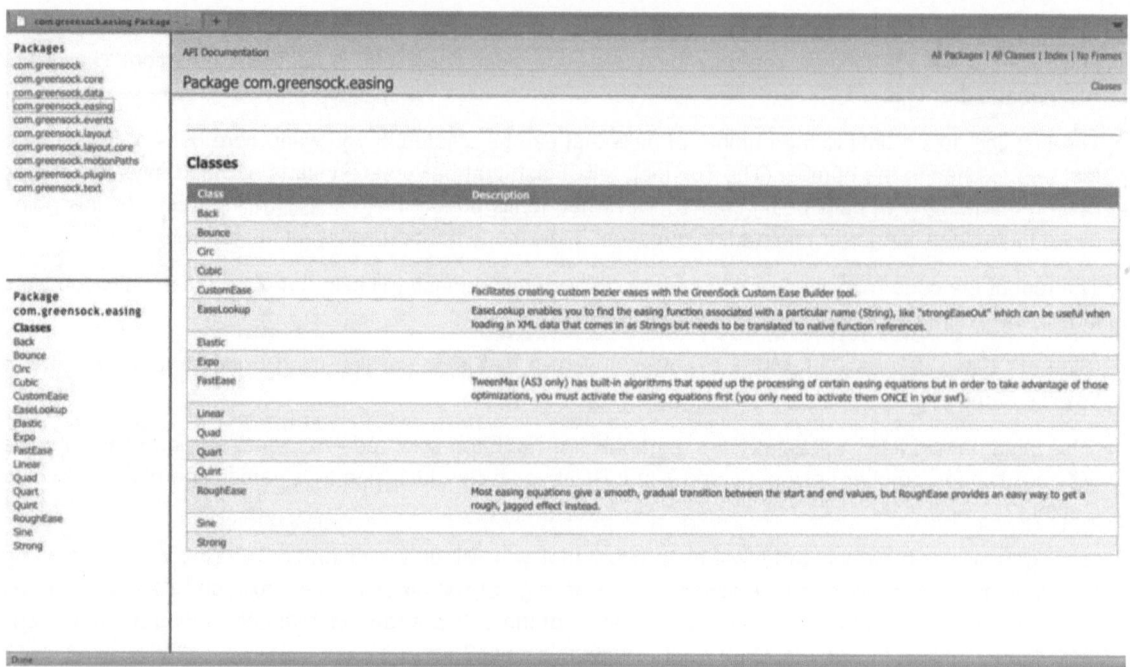

Figure 4-25. The classes in the TweenMax easing package

7. Press the Enter (Windows) or Return (Mac) key twice, and enter the following code:

animateBalls();

function animateBalls():void {

Did you notice something when you pressed the Enter (Windows) or Return (Mac) key after typing that curly brace? Flash skipped a line and entered the closing brace on the next line on your behalf. Just like the automatic class entry, this feature is new to Flash CS5 and is a gift to you if you are new to coding in Flash. Apart from spelling errors the next, most common ActionScript mistake you will make is forgetting to close off brackets.

8. Press the Enter (Windows) or Return (Mac) key, and enter the following code into the `Script` pane:

var randNum:Number = Math.floor(Math.random() * numItems);

The first thing you need to do is to create a variable that assigns each ball created a random number.

ACTIONSCRIPT BASICS

9. Press the Enter (Windows) or Return (Mac) key twice, and enter the following line:

```
var tweenmax:TweenMax = new TweenMax( getChildByName( "ball" + randNum), 2, 
{ scaleX:2, scaleY:2, onComplete:animateBalls } );
}
```

If you are new to Flash, you may have missed the importance of what happened when you entered the class name, TweenMax. If you are a longtime developer, you are probably smiling and thinking, "At last!" The code hint shown in Figure 4-26 actually contains the TweenMax class.

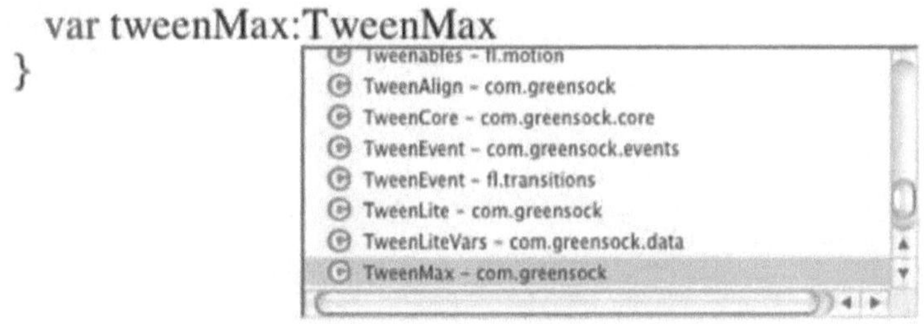

Figure 4-26. Custom classes now appear in the code hints.

What will really put a smile on your face is what happened next. When you entered the first bracket after starting the new TweenMax object, a small code hint, as shown in Figure 4-27, appeared. What this code hint does is show you the parameters that need to go between the brackets. Again, this is completely new to Flash CS5 and a welcome addition.

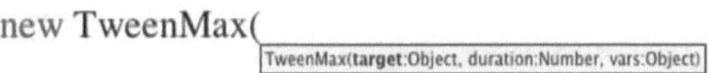

Figure 4-27. You are now shown the methods, properties, and events used by custom classes.

10. Save and test the movie. When the SWF opens, as shown in Figure 4-28, you will see the balls on the stage are randomly placed and, thanks to the alpha value, have differing shades of red. Also, the balls are put into motion courtesy of TweenMax.

275

CHAPTER 4

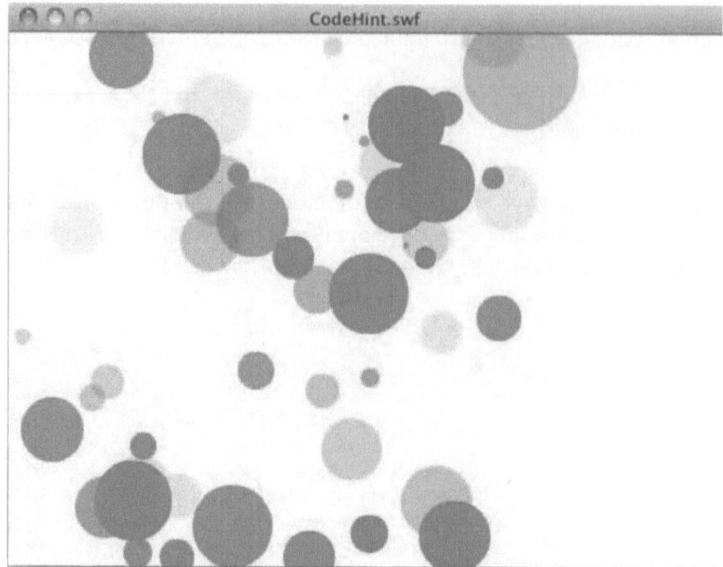

Figure 4-28. Watch the circles move around thanks to TweenMax.

What you've learned

In this chapter, you learned the following:

- The basics of ActionScript
- The anatomy of the `Actions` panel
- Why objects are so important and what a class is
- The roles of properties, methods, and events
- Why instance names are needed to reference objects on the stage
- Some syntax rules of thumb
- How to comment your code
- How dot notation and scope help you locate objects
- How to strongly type your variables

- How precedence affects operators
- How to use conditional statements
- How to check syntax
- Tips on using the ActionScript 3.0 Language and Components Reference

A lot of ground has been covered in this chapter. We hope that you are eager to start learning how to use ActionScript in your everyday workflow.

In fact, every chapter from here on out will use it, so feel free to keep returning here to refresh your knowledge. Also, we recommend that you continue to learn about ActionScript in other reference books. As noted at the beginning of the chapter, two helpful books are *Foundation ActionScript 3.0 with Flash and Flex* and *Object-Oriented ActionScript 3.0* (both published by friends of ED).

In Chapter 1, we told you we would get you deep into using audio in Flash. With the basics of ActionScript under your wing, let's see what we can do with audio in Flash and how ActionScript and audio make an ideal pairing.

Chapter 5

Audio in Flash CS5

If you're one of those who treat audio in Flash as an afterthought, think again. In many respects, audio is a major medium for communicating your message. In this chapter, we dig into audio in Flash: where it comes from, what formats are used, and how to use it in Flash. Regardless of whether you are new to Flash or an old hand, you are about to discover the rules regarding audio in Flash have changed—for the better.

We'll cover the following in this chapter:

- Audio file formats used in Flash
- Adding and previewing audio in Flash
- Playing audio from the `Library`
- Playing remote audio files
- Using ActionScript 3.0 to control audio

If you haven't done so already, download the chapter files. You can find them at www.friendsofED.com/download.html?isbn=1430229940.

The following are the files used in this chapter:

- `PreachersAndThieves.aif (Chapter05/Exercise Files_CH05/Exercise/PreachersAndThieves.aif)`
- `Bang.fla (Chapter05/Exercise Files_CH05/Exercise/Bang.fla)`
- `FrogLoop.fla (Chapter05/Exercise Files_CH05/Exercise/FrogLoop.fla)`
- `FrogPan.fla (Chapter05/Exercise Files_CH05/Exercise/FrogPan.fla)`
- `ButtonSound.fla (Chapter05/Exercise Files_CH05/Exercise/ButtonSound.fla)`
- `kaboom.mp3 (Chapter05/ExerciseFiles_CH_05/Exercise/kaboom.mp3`
- `CodeButtonSound.fla (Chapter05/Exercise Files_CH05/Exercise/CodeButtonSound.fla)`
- `On Borrowed Time.mp3 (Chapter05/Exercise Files_CH05/Exercise/On Borrowed Time.mp3)`
- `RemoteSound.fla (Chapter05/Exercise Files_CH05/Exercise/RemoteSound.fla)`
- `RemoteSound2.fla (Chapter05/Exercise Files_CH05/Exercise/RemoteSound2.fla)`
- `RemoteSound3.fla (Chapter05/Exercise Files_CH05/Exercise/RemoteSound.fla)`
- `Pukaskwa.jpg (Chapter05/Exercise Files_CH05/Exercise/Pukaskwa.jpg)`
- `Rain.flv (Chapter05/Exercise Files_CH05/Exercise/Rain.flv)`
- `RainStorm.mp3 (Chapter05/Exercise Files_CH05/Exercise/RainStorm.mp3)`
- `AudioVisualization.fla (Chapter05/Exercise Files_CH05/Exercise/CodeSnippets/AudioVisualization.fla)`

Flash and the audio formats

When it comes to sound, Flash is a robust application in that it can handle many of the major audio formats, including the more common formats listed here:

- **MP3 (Moving Pictures Expert Group Level-2 Layer-3 Audio)**: This cross-platform format is a standard for web and portable audio files. In many respects, the growth of this format is tied to the popularity of iPods and audio players on cell phones. Though you can output these files in a stereo format, you really should pay more attention to bandwidth settings for your MP3s.

- **WAV**: If you use a computer to record a voice-over or other sound, you are familiar with the WAV format. WAV files have sample rates ranging from 8 kilohertz (the quality of your home phone) up to 48 kilohertz (DAT tapes) and beyond. These files are also available with bit depths ranging from 8 bits right up to 32 bits. Just keep in mind that a file with a sample rate of 48 kilohertz and a 32 bit depth will result in a massive file size that simply shouldn't be used with Flash.

- **QuickTime**: These files have a `.qt` or `.mov` extension and can contain audio in many formats. If you create a QuickTime audio file, you need to make the movie self-contained in QuickTime Pro.
- **AIFF (Audio Interchange File Format)**: AIFF is the standard for the Macintosh and offers the same sample rates and bit depths as a WAV file. Many purists will argue that the AIFF format is better than the WAV format. This may indeed be true, but to the average person, the difference between this format and WAV is almost inaudible.
- **AAC (Advanced Audio Coding)**: AAC is the new "audio kid on the block" when it comes to working with audio in Flash. It is another lossy codec but is regarded as being far superior to its MP3 cousin. In fact, AAC was developed as the successor to the MP3 standard. Though you may not be familiar with the format, if you have ever downloaded a song from iTunes, used the Sony PlayStation, the Nintendo Wii, or even an iPhone, you have "heard" an AAC-encoded audio file.
- **ASND (Adobe Sound Document)**: In very simple terms, an ASND file is a stereo audio file that you can use in Premiere Pro CS5, After Effects CS5, or Flash CS5. The format was introduced in Soundbooth CS4 as a way of easily moving audio between Premiere Pro, After Effects, and Flash while at the same time saving audio edits in a nondestructive manner. For example, you can launch Soundbooth CS5 from the ASND file in the Flash CS5 `Library` and not only make changes to the stereo audio but get an entire "multitrack environment" as well as the ability to save multiple versions of your audio edits and move between them. You can even reference video/animation exports from Flash.

> *Take this obscure fact to a trivia contest, and you will clean up: AIFF also has a sample rate of 22,254.54KHz. Why the odd sample rate? This was the original Macintosh sample rate and was based on the horizontal scan rate of the monitor in a 128KB Mac.*

Bit depth and sample rates

We traditionally visualize sound as a sine wave—when the wave rises above the vertical, the sound gets "higher"; where it runs below the vertical, the sound gets "lower." These waves, shown in Figure 5-1, are called the **waveform**. The horizontal line is silence, and the audio is "measured" from the top of one "blip" to the top of the next one along the waveform. These blips are called **peaks**, and the sampling is done from peak to peak.

For any sound to be digitized, like a color image in Fireworks or Photoshop, the wave needs to be sampled. A **sample** is nothing more than a snapshot of a waveform between peaks at any given time. This snapshot is a digital number representing where, on the waveform, this snapshot was taken. How often the waveform is sampled is called the **sample rate**.

CHAPTER 5

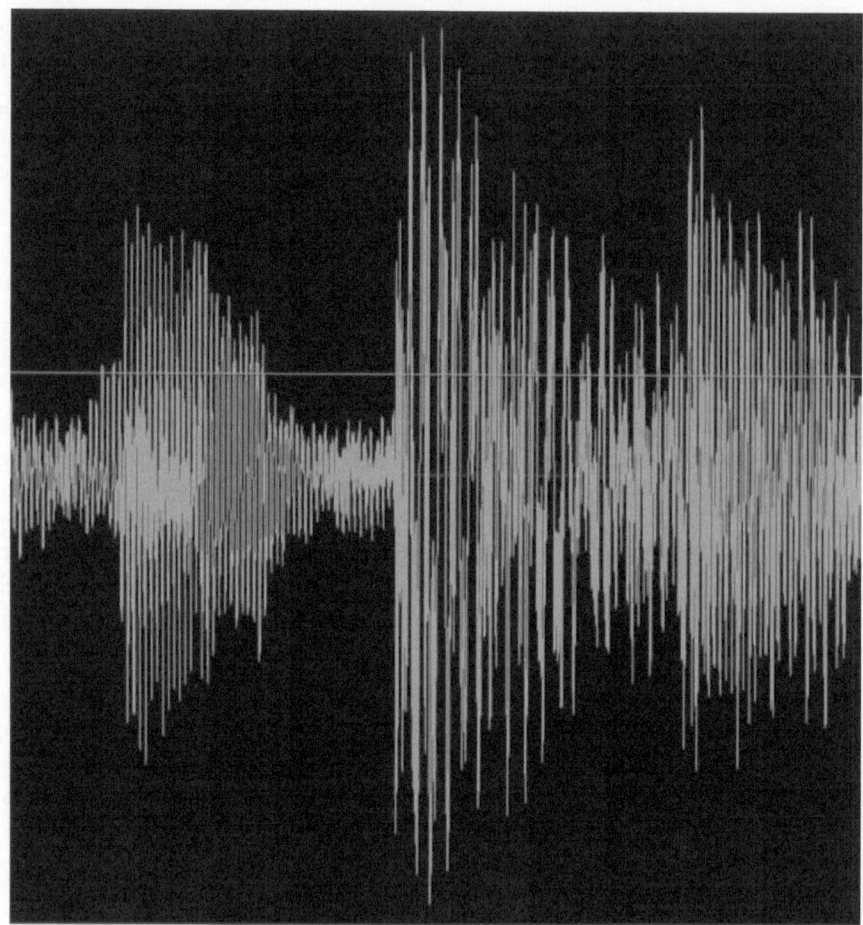

Figure 5-1. A typical waveform from Soundbooth CS5

Bit depth is the resolution of the sample. A bit depth of 8 bits means that the snapshot is represented as a number ranging from –128 to 127. A bit depth of 16 bits means that the number is between –32,768 to 32,767. If you do the math, you see that an 8-bit snapshot has 256 potential samples between each peak, whereas its 16-bit counterpart has just over 65,000 potential samples between the peaks. The greater the number of potential samples of a wave, the more accurate the sound. The downside to this, of course, is the more samples on the wave, the larger the file size. These numbers represent where each sample is located on the waveform. When the numbers are played back in the order in which they were sampled and at the frequency they were sampled, they represent a sound's waveform. Obviously, a larger bit depth and higher sample rate mean that the waveform is played back with greater accuracy—more snapshots taken of the waveform result in a more accurate representation of the waveform. This explains why the songs from an album have such massive file sizes. They are sampled at the highest possible bit depth.

One wave cycle in 1 second is known as a **hertz**, which can't be heard by the human ear, except possibly as a series of clicks. Audible sound uses thousands of these waves, and they are crammed into a 1-second time span and measured in that span. A thousand waveform cycles in 1 second is called a **kilohertz** (KHz), and if you listen to an audio CD, the audio rate is sampled at the frequency of 44.1 thousand waves per second, which is traditionally identified as 44.1KHz. These waves are the sample rate.

The inference you can draw from this is the more samples per wave and the more accurate the samples, the larger the file size. Toss a stereo sound into the mix, and you have essentially doubled the file size. Obviously, the potential for huge sound files is there, which is not a good situation when dealing with Flash. Large files take an awfully long time to load into a browser, which means your user is in for a painful experience. One way of dealing with this is to reduce the sample rate or number of waves per second.

The three most common sample rates used are 11.025KHz, 22.05KHz, and 44.1KHz. If you reduce the sample rate from 44.1KHz to 22.05KHz, you achieve a significant reduction, roughly 50 percent, in file size. You obtain an even more significant reduction, another 50 percent, if the rate is reduced to 11.025KHz. The problem is reducing the sample rate reduces audio quality. Listening to your Beethoven's *Ninth Symphony* at 11.025KHz results in the music sounding as if it were playing from the inside of a tin can.

As a Flash designer or developer, your prime objective is to obtain the best quality sound at the smallest file size. Though many Flash developers tell you that 16-bit, 44.1KHz stereo is the way to go, you'll quickly realize this is not necessarily true. For example, a 16-bit, 44.1KHz stereo sound of a mouse click or a sound lasting less than a couple of seconds—such as a whoosh as an object zips across the screen—is a waste of bandwidth. The duration is so short that average users won't realize it if you've made your click an 8-bit, 22.05KHz mono sound. They hear the click and move on. The same holds true for music files. The average user is most likely listening through the cheap speakers that were tossed in when they bought their computer. In this case, a 16-bit, 22.05KHz soundtrack will sound as good as its CD-quality rich cousin.

Flash and MP3

The two most common sound formats used in Flash are WAV and AIFF. Both formats share a common starting point—they are both based on the Interchange File Format proposal written in 1985 by Electronic Arts to help standardize transfer issues on the Commodore Amiga. Like video, sound contains a huge amount of data and must be compressed before it is used. This is the purpose of a **codec**. Codec is an acronym for enCODer/DECoder, and the format used by Flash to output audio is the MP3 format, although you can import both AIFF and WAV files (and others) into Flash.

From your perspective, the need to compress audio for web delivery makes the use of AIFF or WAV files redundant. The MP3 format is the standard, which explains why WAV and AIFF files are converted to MP3 files on playback. If you are working with an audio-production facility, you will often be handed an AIFF or a WAV file. Even if you have the option of receiving an MP3, you are better off with the AIFF or WAV file, for the same reason that you wouldn't want to recompress a JPG file: because they are both lossy compression schemes.

Why are MP3 files so small but still sound so good? The answer lies in the fact that the MP3 standard uses perceptual encoding. All Internet audio formats toss a ton of audio information into the trash. When information gets tossed, there is a corresponding decrease in file size. The information tossed when an MP3 file is created includes sound frequencies your dog may be able to hear but you can't. In short, you hear only the sound a human can perceive (and this sort of explains why animals aren't huge fans of iPods).

All perceptual encoders allow you to choose how much audio is unimportant. Most encoders produce excellent-quality files using no more than 16Kbps to create voice recordings. When you create an MP3, you need to pay attention to the bandwidth. The format is fine, but if the bandwidth is not optimized for its intended use, your results will be unacceptable, which is why applications that create MP3 files ask you to set the bandwidth along with the sample rate.

So much for theory; let's get practical.

Adding audio to Flash

Knowing that you can bring all of these formats into Flash and that MP3 is the output format for Flash is all well and good. But how do they get into Flash, and, more importantly, how does an AIFF or WAV file get converted to an MP3 file when it plays in Flash? Let's explore that right now starting with an import.

Importing an audio file

To see what happens when you import an audio file, open a new Flash document, and import `PreachersAndThieves.aif` (in the `Exercise` folder for this chapter) to the `Library`. Because of the unique manner in which sound files are added to a Flash movie, they simply cannot be imported to the stage.

> If you select `Import to Stage` when importing an audio file, it won't be placed on the stage. Instead, it will be placed directly into the `Library`.

When you open the `Library` and select the file, you will see the file's waveform in the preview area, as shown in Figure 5-2. You can click the `Play` button, which is the triangle located above the waveform in the preview area, to test the sound file.

Figure 5-2. Select an audio file in the `Library`, and its waveform appears in the preview area.

Setting sound properties

To set the sound properties for an audio file, double-click the speaker icon next to the audio file's name in the `Library`. Figure 5-3 shows the `Sound Properties` dialog box for `PreachersandThieves.mp3`.

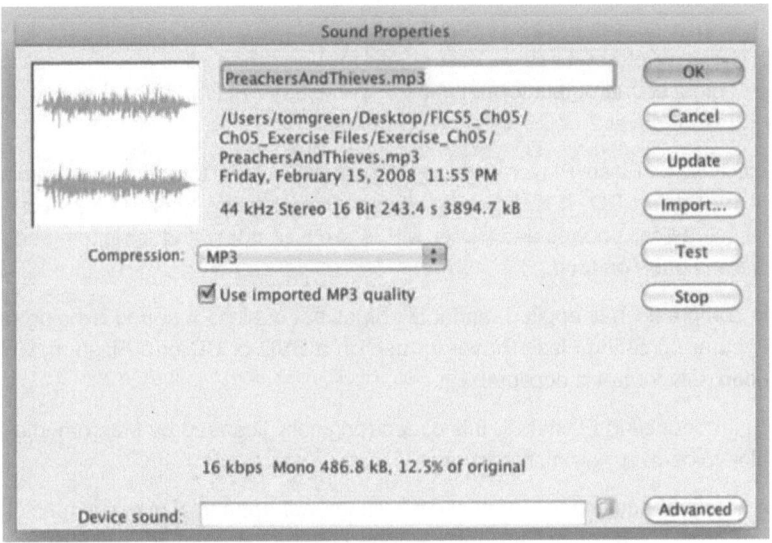

Figure 5-3. The `Sound Properties` dialog box is opened when you double-click an audio file in the `Library`.

This dialog box is a really useful tool. You can use it to preview and stop an audio file: click the `Test` button to preview the sound file, and then click the `Stop` button to stop the sound playback. The `Update` button is also handy. If an audio file has been edited after being placed into Flash, you can click the `Update` button to replace the imported copy with the edited version—as long as its original location on your hard drive hasn't changed since the file was imported. If the file has moved, use the `Import` button to find it again, or replace this `Library` asset with a new file.

> *Speaking of editing an audio file, if you right-click (Windows) or Control+click (Mac) the file in the `Library`, the context menu that opens allows you to edit the file directly in Soundbooth. Though Soundbooth is positioned as an entry-level audio editor, it is widely regarded as the audio editor for Flash. Once you make your edits in Soundbooth, simply save the file, and the changes will be reflected in Flash.*

Notice the audio information under the path and date. This file—at over 4.0 minutes in duration (243 seconds) and around 3.9MB (3894.7KB)—is rather large.

Don't worry about the `Device sound` input field at the bottom. Device sounds are used in PDAs and other devices that employ Flash Lite.

From our perspective, the `Compression` drop-down list is of major importance. In this drop-down, you are asked to pick a codec. In Flash, the default is to export all sound in the MP3 format. Still, the ability to individually compress each sound in the `Library` is an option that shouldn't be disregarded. Your choices are as follows:

- `ADPCM`: This type of sound file is best suited for very short clips and looped sound. This format was the original sound output format in older versions of Flash. If, for example, you are outputting for use in Flash Player 2 or 3, ADPCM is required.

- `MP3`: Use this for Flash Player versions 4 or newer. This format is not compatible with Flash Player 4 for Pocket PC. It is, however, compatible with the Flash Lite player, which is used in devices such as cell phones and PDAs. MP3s are also not suited for looping sounds because the end of a file is often padded.

- `Raw`: No compression is applied, and it is somewhat useless if sound is being delivered over the Web. If you are creating Flash Player for use on a DVD or CD or a Flash movie for incorporation into a video, this format is acceptable.

- `Speech`: Introduced in Flash MX, this codec (originally licensed by Macromedia from Nellymoser) is ideal for voice-over narrations.

Once you select a codec, additional compression settings will appear. For our example, select `MP3` from the `Compression` drop-down menu, and the settings change, as shown in Figure 5-4. Click the `Test` button and listen to the sound. What you may notice is how flat the audio is compared to the original version. If you take a look at the `Bit rate` and `Quality` settings in the `Preprocessing` area, you will see why. That 3.9MB file is now sitting at about 12 percent of its original size, or 487KB.

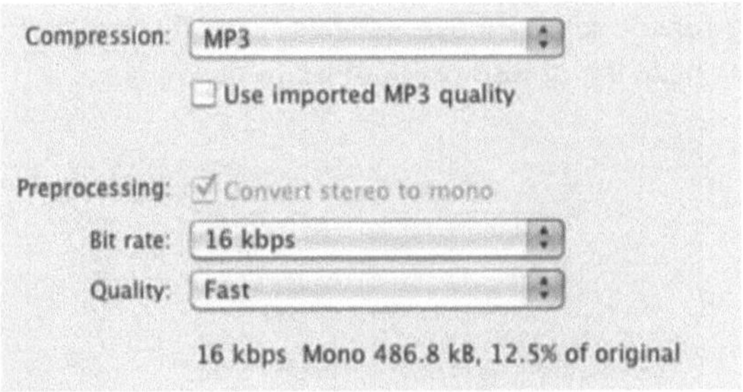

[Figure showing MP3 compression settings dialog with Compression: MP3, Use imported MP3 quality unchecked, Preprocessing: Convert stereo to mono checked, Bit rate: 16 kbps, Quality: Fast, 16 kbps Mono 486.8 kB, 12.5% of original]

Figure 5-4. Setting MP3 compression

Change the bit rate to `48 kbps`, and select `Best` in the `Quality` drop-down menu. Also make sure that `Convert stereo to mono` is selected. If you click the `Test` button, you will hear a marked improvement in the audio quality.

> *Unless your audio includes specialized panning or there is some other compelling reason for using stereo, feel free to convert the stereo sound to mono. The user won't miss it, and the audio file size will plummet. Flash even allows mono sounds to be panned.*

Asking you to compare the audio quality to the original in the previous two steps is a bit disingenuous on our part. Our intention was to let you "hear" the quality differences, not compare them with the original audio. In the final analysis, comparing compressed audio against the original version is a "fool's game." Users never hear the original file, so what do they have as a basis for comparison? When listening to the compressed version, listen to it in its own right and ask yourself whether it meets your quality standard.

> *No, you can't "supersize" an audio file. If the MP3 being used has bit rate of 48Kbps in the original file imported into Flash, you can never increase the bit rate above that level in Flash. "Up-sampling" audio will more often than not decrease, not increase, the audio quality.*

One other place where the sound output format can be set is through the `Publish Settings` panel. To access these settings, select `File` ➤ `Publish Settings`, and click the `Flash` tab in the panel. Near the top of this panel, shown in Figure 5-5, are preferences for `Images and Sounds`, which include `Audio stream` and `Audio event` settings. We'll get into these two in the next section, but the important thing to note for now is the `Override sound settings` check box. If you select this check box, the audio settings shown for the `Audio stream` and `Audio event` areas will override any settings applied in the `Sound Properties` dialog box. Think of this as the ability to apply a global setting to every sound in your movie. Unless there is a compelling reason to select this choice, we suggest you avoid it. It's better to spend time with each file rather than apply a setting that may actually degrade quality for a couple of files.

If you do have a compelling reason to use these settings, click the relevant `Set` button, and you will be presented with the same options in the `Sound Properties` dialog box.

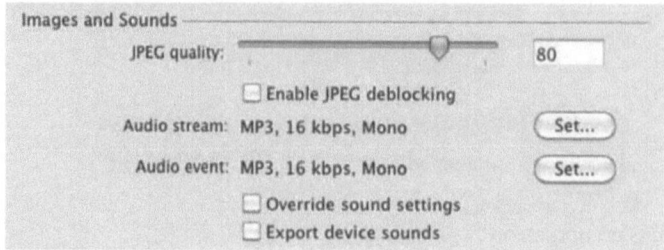

Figure 5-5. The `Images and Sounds` settings

Now that you know what the properties do, let's move on to using a sound file in Flash. If you have been following along, close any documents you might have open, and don't save the changes.

Using audio in Flash

In Chapter 1, you added an audio file of a buzzing fly to enhance the ambience of the movie and to add a bit of realism to it. We asked you to do a couple of things in that chapter, but we didn't tell why you were doing them. The purpose was to get you hooked on Flash, and it obviously worked because you are now at this point of the book. The time has arrived to give you the answers to the "Why?" questions.

Choosing a sound type: event or streaming

Flash has two types of sound: event and streaming. **Event sound** tells Flash to load a sound completely into memory—as soon as the playhead encounters the frame with this audio—before playing it. Once loaded, the sound continues to play, even if the movie's playhead stops, which means event sounds are not locked to the timeline. (Audio can be forced to stop, but that takes specific action on your part.)

In a 24 fps Flash movie, a file like `PreachersandThieves.aif` from the previous section takes about 5,760 frames to play completely. If you're hoping to synchronize that with animation in the same timeline, think again. If the resultant SWF is played back on a slower machine than yours, it's almost certain the audio will not conclude on the frame you expect. Also, a movie would take a long time to start playing, because Flash must load the sound fully before playback can begin.

Event sound is ideal for pops, clicks, and other very short sounds or in situations where the audio will be played more than once or looped. If you want to synchronize extended audio with timeline animation, use streaming sound.

Streaming sound is a sound that can begin playing before it has fully loaded into memory. The trade-off is that it must be reloaded every time you want to play it. This sound type is ideal for longer background soundtracks that play only once. Because it is locked in step with the timeline, streaming sound is the only realistic option for cartoon lip-syncing or any scenario that requires tight integration between audio and visuals.

Now that you know what to expect, let's work with both types:

1. Open the Bang.fla file. When it opens, you will see we have included the kaboom.mp3 audio file in the **Library**.

2. Rename the layer in the timeline to **Audio**, and drag the kaboom file from the **Library** onto the stage. Audio files are added to the Flash timeline by dropping them on the stage or the pasteboard where they seemingly vanish—but not by dragging them onto the timeline. When you release the mouse, you may see a line running through the middle of frame 1 in the timeline. This line is the start of the waveform.

3. Insert a frame in frame 97 of the timeline. You can now see the entire waveform on the timeline.

4. Right-click (Windows) or Control+click (Mac) the layer name, and select **Properties** from the context menu.

5. When the **Layer Properties** dialog box opens, as shown in Figure 5-6, select **300 percent** from the **Layer height** drop-down menu, and click **OK**. When you release the mouse, the layer view is three times larger, and you can see the full waveform.

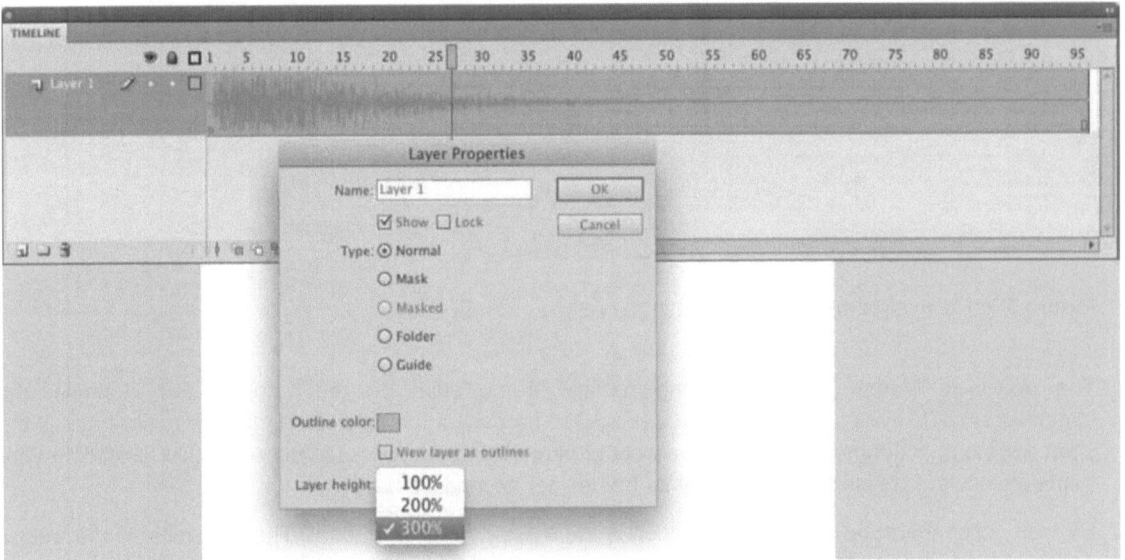

Figure 5-6. Use the layer properties to "zoom in" on the timeline.

Being able to see the waveform on the timeline is a huge advantage to you because you can now use the waveform's peaks or valleys to time animation of other events to the audio file in Stream mode.

6. Click once in the waveform on the timeline anywhere but frame 1, and in the `Sync` area of the `Properties` panel, select `Event` from the drop-down menu. Press Enter (Windows) or Return (Mac). The playback head moves, but the sound doesn't play. Drag the playback head to frame 1 or frame 96, and press Enter (Windows) or Return (Mac).

What you have just heard is a fundamental truth of an event sound: you can only preview event sounds by playing them in their entirety.

> *Being the nice guys we are, you can thank us for not using the* `PreacherAndThievesmp3` *audio file. If it were an event sound, you would be sitting here listening to the full four minutes of the file. Event sounds play for their entire duration, and you can't stop playback by pressing Enter (Windows) or Return (Mac). All that does is to start playing another copy of the sound over the one that is currently playing. To stop an event sound from playing on the timeline, press the Esc key.*

7. Change the `Sync` setting to `Stream`, as shown in Figure 5-7. This time, drag the playhead across the timeline. Notice you can hear the sound as you scrub across it. Drag the playback head to frame 2, and press Enter (Windows) or Return (Mac). The sound plays from that point and, for longer audio files, pressing the Enter (Windows) or Return (Mac) key stops playback.

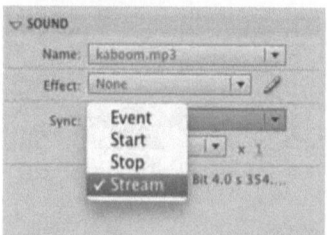

Figure 5-7. Using stream or event sound in the `Properties` panel

The downside is the playback is only for the frame span on the timeline. For example, the `PreachersAndThieves.mp3` file would require 5,760 frames on the timeline to play the entire track. If the span were only 50 frames, you would be able to play only about two seconds of the file, assuming your frame rate is set to Flash's default rate of 24 frames per second.

Did you notice the `Stop` and `Start` choices in the `Sync` drop-down menu? They're similar to the `Event` option with the addition that they keep sounds from overlapping. Let's try them:

8. Add a new timeline layer, and name it `audio2`. Add a keyframe to frame 20 of the new layer, select that frame, and drag `kaboom.mp3` from the `Library` to the stage. Now you have two layers associated with the explosion sound.

9. In the `audio2` layer, set the `Sync` property to `Event` for the audio in frame 20. Drag the playhead to frame 1, and press Enter (Windows) or Return (Mac). You'll hear two explosions.

10. Change the `Sync` property in frame 20 to `Stop`. The first thing to notice is that the audio file in the audio2 layer disappears. Press Enter (Windows) or Return (Mac) again from frame 1, and you'll hear only one explosion. Not only that, but the explosion gets cut off right at frame 20. That's the playhead encountering the `Stop` keyframe. It's important to understand that a `Stop` keyframe doesn't halt all sounds. The halted sound must be specified.

11. Select frame 20, and choose `None` from the `Properties` panel's `Name` drop-down list. Now you merely have a keyframe set to `Stop`, but without an associated sound. Press Enter (Windows) or Return (Mac) from frame 1, and you'll hear the full explosion.

12. Reselect `kaboom.mp3` from the `Name` drop-down list.

13. Select frame 20 one last time, and change the `Sync` property to `Start`. Press Enter (Windows) or Return (Mac) from frame 1, and you might be surprised to hear only one explosion. Didn't you just tell two of the sounds to play (one as `Event` and one as `Start`)? You did, but the `Start` option waits until the specified sound has finished before it starts another copy of it.

14. Drag the keyframe at frame 20 until you move it past the waveform in the `audio` layer—frame 98 should do it. Now that the `Start` keyframe has moved beyond the previous sound, you should hear two explosions again when you press Enter (Windows) or Return (Mac) from frame 1. Users on a slower computer might hear only one explosion, because the first sound may not have finished by the time the playhead hits frame 98. Like the `Stop` option, `Start` relies on an explicit sound file reference in the `Name` drop-down list.

Before finishing up with the `bang.fla`, let's get an interesting quirk out of the way.

Removing an audio file from the timeline

Audio files simply can't be deleted from the timeline. Go ahead, try it:

1. Hold down the Shift key, and select frames 1 and 97 on the timeline to select the audio file. Press the Delete key. Nothing happens.

2. To remove an audio file from the timeline, select a frame in the audio waveform, and in the `Properties` panel, select `None` from the `Name` drop-down menu. The sound is removed.

3. To put the `kaboom.mp3` audio file back on the timeline, open the `Name` drop-down menu, and select `kaboom.mp3`. If you have a number of audio files in your `Library`, they will all be listed in this drop-down menu, and you can use it to add or change audio files without deleting them or dragging them onto the timeline.

4. Close `Bang.fla` without saving the changes.

Getting loopy

If you want to loop your audio, the `Properties` panel puts a couple choices at your disposal. Here's how to set up looping:

1. Open FrogLoop.fla in the Exercise folder for this chapter. Press the Enter (Windows) or Return (Mac) key, and you will hear a frog croak. The waveform shows that the croaking happens only once, even though the timeline spans 60 frames. Surely, the frog has more to say than that. Let's give it something to really sing about.

2. Select anywhere inside the waveform, and change the 1 next to the **Repeat** drop-down list to **4**, as shown in Figure 5-8. Notice that the waveform now repeats four times.

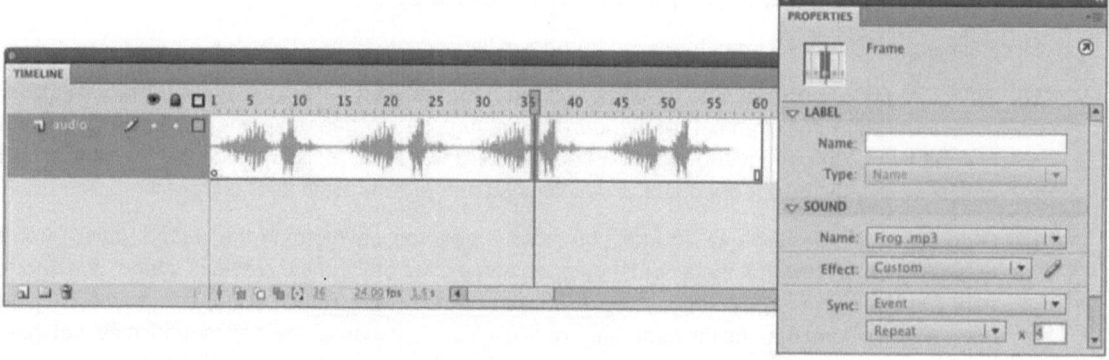

Figure 5-8. Use the **Sync** area's **Repeat** drop-down list to configure looping.

3. Scrub the timeline to verify that, as an event sound, the audio does not preview until you press Enter (Windows) or Return (Mac) from frame 1.

4. Change the **Sync** property to **Stream** and scrub again. As expected, you can now hear the audio as you drag the playhead. This tells you that streaming sound can be looped just like event sound.

5. Change the **Repeat** property value to **Loop**. The **x 4** value next to the drop-down list disappears, and the waveform changes visually to what looks like a single play-through. In spite of its looks, this sound will repeat forever unless you stop it with a **Stop** keyframe later in the timeline—or until your user closes Flash Player or flees the web page out of desperation. The **Loop** setting repeats a sound indefinitely.

6. Close the file without saving the changes.

> Be very careful with the **Loop** setting! If a sound is set to **Event** and **Loop**, you can accidentally cause instant psychosis if the timeline has more than one frame. Timelines naturally loop when they hit the end of their frame span. If the timeline cycles back to frame 1 while the audio is still playing, you can quickly produce an unwanted echo torture chamber.

Adjusting volume and pan

Flash lets you adjust the volume of audio files even after they've been imported to the `Library`. Because of the way Flash outputs its internal audio mix, this also means you can pan your sounds by adjusting each speaker's volume separately. In effect, you can bounce audio back and forth between the two speakers, even if those audio files were recorded in mono.

> *Ideally, you'll want to set a file's overall volume with audio-editing software, such as Adobe Audition or Soundbooth. Flash can't magnify a file's volume; it can only reduce the volume. So, the volume of your file as recorded is the volume it plays back in Flash when the settings are turned all the way up.*

You'll be surprised how easy it is to slowly pan the frog serenade from left to right in the timeline. Here's how:

1. Open the `FrogPan.fla` file in the Chapter 5 Exercise folder. Click into frame 1 of the `audio` layer, and verify that the `Sync` property is set to `Event` and `Repeat x 4`.

2. Select `Fade to right` in the `Effect` drop-down list in the `Properties` panel, as shown in Figure 5-9. Test the SWF so far.

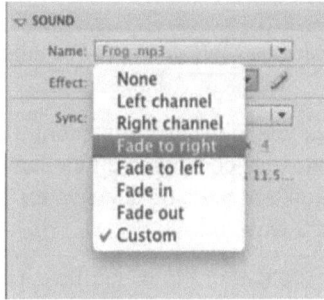

Figure 5-9. The `Effect` drop-down list lets you change volume and panning.

You'll hear that the effect works, but the panning moves to the right almost immediately, rather than spread over the four "ribbits." This happens because Flash evaluates the actual length of an audio file when assigning one of its effects presets. It's easy enough to tweak.

3. Click the `Edit` button, which looks like a pencil, next to the `Effect` drop-down list. This opens the `Edit Envelope` dialog box, as shown in Figure 5-10.

CHAPTER 5

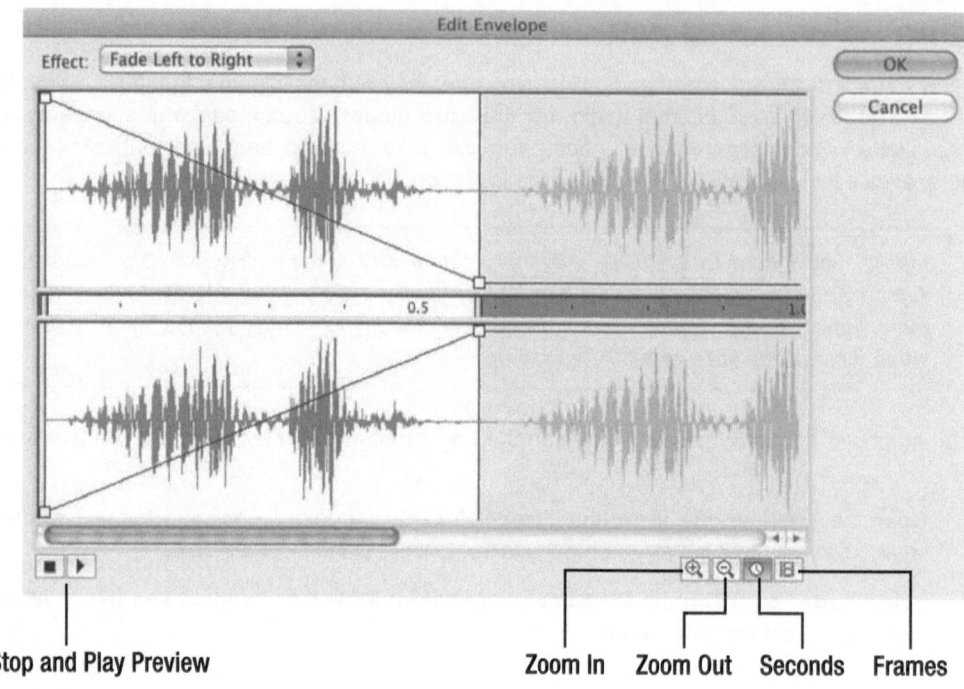

Figure 5-10. The `Edit Envelope` dialog box lets you apply volume changes to audio files.

In the `Edit Envelope` dialog box, the diagonal lines represent a change in volume in the left (top) and right (bottom) speakers. The volume steadily decreases on the left (moves down) while increasing on the right (moves up), which gives the illusion that the croaking sweeps across the screen. Note that the effect applies to only the first occurrence of the waveform.

Notice the series of buttons along the bottom of the dialog box. You can preview your effect settings by clicking the `Play` and `Stop` buttons on the left. On the right, you can zoom in and out to show less or more of the waveform span. The `Seconds` and `Frames` buttons affect how the horizontal number line in the middle looks: seconds or timeline frames.

4. Click the `Zoom Out` button until all repeats of the waveform are visible. Drag one of the right-side squares on the diagonal lines toward the end of the fourth repeat, as shown in Figure 5-11. It doesn't matter if you drag in the top or bottom—both will move. The `Effect` field in this dialog box changes to show `Custom`, because you've altered one of the presets.

5. Click the `Play` button to preview the updated effect. Now the panning happens more slowly, arriving fully in the right speaker only after the fourth "ribbit" ends.

AUDIO IN FLASH CS5

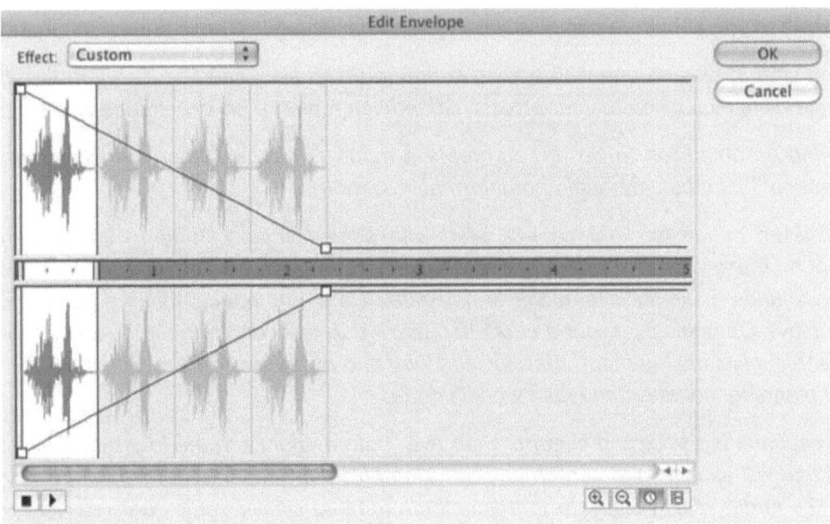

Figure 5-11. The `Edit Envelope` dialog box lets you apply custom audio effects.

6. Experiment with other **Effect** drop-down presets. Play around with altering them. Here's a hint: you can add new draggable white squares by clicking anywhere along one of the diagonal lines. Remove white squares by dragging them off the dialog box.

7. Click OK, and save your movie.

A note from a master

Dave Shroeder is regarded by many in this industry as being a master when it comes to the use of audio in Flash. He has spoken at a number of very important industry conferences, and his company, Pilotvibe (www.pilotvibe.com), has developed a solid international reputation for supplying the industry with high-quality sound loops and effects for use in Flash. In fact, his homepage, shown in Figure 5-12, can be regarded as a master class in the effective use in audio to set the "mood" in a Flash movie.

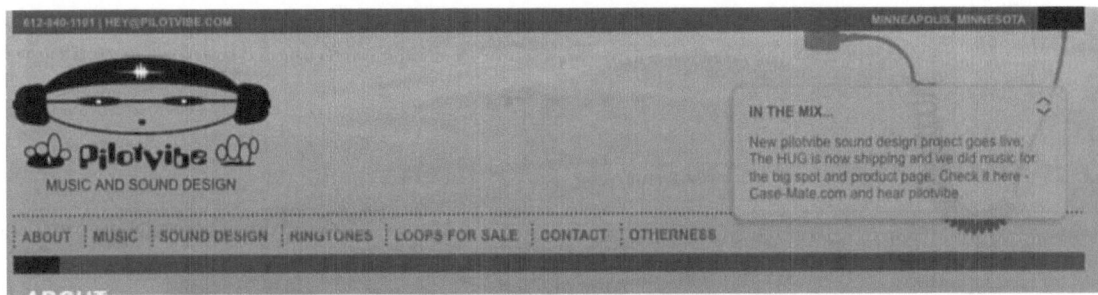

Figure 5-12. The Pilotvibe homepage is a master class in the effective use of sound in Flash.

295

CHAPTER 5

Who better to talk to you about the use of audio in Flash than the guy who is setting the standard?

"Once you start to play around with adding sound to Flash files, you'll probably realize that it can add an incredible dimension to your project. Sound can really tie an experience together.

"It can bring an animation to life. It can create a mood or suggest characteristics that reinforce your message. It can be entertaining or informative or both.

"If sound is an option for your project, start with some simple planning. First determine why adding sound makes sense. What purpose does it serve? Does voice-over communicate a story? Do button sounds make the site easier to navigate? Do sound effects make a game more fun or easier to play? Does music give it a cool character? Use answers to these questions to generate a short "sonic mission statement" that outlines why and how you plan to use sound. Do this early in project planning, not after the Flash work is done.

"Sourcing sounds is easier and cheaper than ever before, thanks to the Internet. There are many websites that will allow you to search and download files for reasonable fees. Once you've found sounds, use audio-editing software to adjust them to have similar sonic qualities. You want them to sound like they're in the same room or in the same canyon or the same secret underground lair, and so on. Adjust their volumes and equalization (EQ) to achieve this. Use your ears, listen, and you'll do fine. Do they sound close or far, light or heavy, fast or slow? Also, trim the heads and tails of the sound files to be as short as possible without cutting the sound off. The shorter the file, the better it syncs, and the smaller the file size.

"When you're picking music, try to find a piece that fits the mood or reinforces the story. Don't just use death metal because you like death metal or techno for techno's sake. Music has emotional power that transcends genre, and you want to leverage it to make your project as engaging as possible. If you're working with loops, trying to use as long a loop as possible given your file size considerations. Anything under 10 seconds gets old pretty fast unless it's something minimal like a drumbeat. Look into layering loops to create the illusion of a longer track with more variation.

"A sound on/off button is a courtesy I always recommend. Compress your sounds so they sound good. A little bit bigger file is worth it if it means people will listen to it. A tiny file that sounds lousy is worse than no sound. Also, compress each sound so it sounds good by itself and in relation to the other sounds. A combination of hi-fi and lo-fi sounds wrecks the illusion of the sounds existing together."

Thanks, Dave, and also thank you for supplying our readers with the Pilotvibe clips in the `Exercise` folder.

Your turn: adding sound to a button

Now you'll put what you have learned to practical use. Let's blow some stuff up. Follow these steps to accomplish this task:

1. Open the `ButtonSound.fla` file in your `Exercise` folder, and import the `kaboom.mp3` file into your **Library**.

2. Double-click the `Blam` button symbol in the `Library` to open it in the `Symbol Editor`.
3. Add a new layer named `Audio`, and add a keyframe to the `Down` area of the `Audio` layer.
4. With the keyframe selected, drag a copy of the `kaboom` audio file to the stage. Your timeline should now resemble that shown in Figure 5-13.

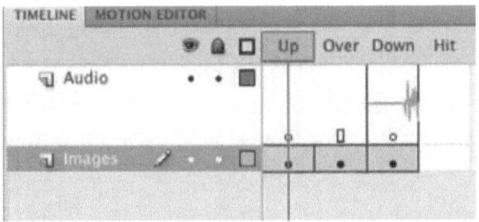

Figure 5-13. You can add sound to buttons.

5. Click in the waveform, and in the `Properties` panel select `Event` in the `Sync` drop-down menu.

> *This may seem like an odd instruction because all sounds added to the stage are event sounds by default. We have been around this silly business long enough to embrace the wisdom of the following rule: trust no one and nothing, especially yourself. Get into the habit of double-checking everything and never assuming everything is correct.*

6. Click the `Scene 1` link to return to the main timeline.
7. Select `Control ▶ Enable Simple Buttons`. Click the button on the stage, and you will hear an explosion. Deselect `Enable Simple Buttons`.
8. Test the file. When the SWF opens, click the button. You will hear an explosion every time you click the button.

So far, so good. If you stopped here, you would have a competent Flash movie—basically a C on your report card—which isn't bad. If you want the A, though, you'll refine this button just a tad, based on what you've already learned in this chapter.

So, what's wrong with it? Click the button in rapid succession, like a double-click. Heck, click it five times in a row (you'll be surprised at what users do when playing with your content). What do you hear? Because of the numerous triggering of that `Event` keyframe, you end up with an artillery barrage of explosions. This may not be what you want. Fortunately, the remedy is simple.

9. Double-click the button symbol to open it again in the `Symbol Editor`. Change the audio keyframe's `Sync` property from `Event` to `Start`.
10. Reselect `Enable Simple Buttons`.

11. Return to the main timeline, and test the button with repeated clicks. Even though you click a few times, you hear the explosion only once.

12. Save the file as `ButtonSound01.fla`, and publish the SWF file. Just as in testing mode, the explosions don't overlap when you click the button.

Be careful with this technique, because when you create a SWF file that contains audio, the audio files in the `Library` are embedded into the SWF file. The result, depending upon the audio files and their length, could be an extremely large SWF file that will take a long time to load.

Now that you understand how audio files can be used in Flash, let's take that knowledge to the next level and actually control sound using ActionScript. This is where the full power of audio in Flash is handed to you.

Controlling audio with ActionScript 3.0

Before we start, let's really get clear on the following: you aren't going to be fully exploring the nuances and features of audio controlled by code. We are going to give you the basics in this section:

- Playing a sound in the `Library` without adding it to the timeline
- Using movie clips and buttons to turn audio on and off
- Using movie clips and buttons to load sound dynamically—from your HTTP server—into your Flash movie

Still, if you are familiar with controlling sound through ActionScript 2.0, you need to know there have been some renovations. For example, the `Sound.attachSound()` method is no longer around, and even familiar things like creating linkage identifiers have fundamentally changed. Just keep in mind that change is a good thing. It just takes a bit of getting used to.

Playing a sound from the Library

This technique is ideal for sounds that need to play in the background. Be aware that any sound played through ActionScript is treated as a streaming sound.

1. Open a new Flash document, and import the `PreachersAndThieves.mp3` file into the `Library`. The plan is to have this sound play, almost as background audio, when the movie starts.

2. Select the `PreachersAndThieves.mp3` file in the `Library`. Right-click (Windows) or Control+click (Mac) the audio file, and select `Properties` from the context menu. When the `Sound Properties` dialog box menu opens, click the `Advanced` button to open the `Advanced` properties.

3. When the panel expands, you will see the `Linkage` area shown in Figure 5-14. If you are going to play audio files contained in the `Library` and control them through ActionScript, they must be given a special label to let ActionScript find them in the `Library`.

> In ActionScript 2.0, "linkage" was accomplished with a linkage identifier. In fact, you'll see a disabled *Identifier* field in the dialog box. What gives? In ActionScript 3.0, the rules are different. You need to create a custom class that extends the native Sound class. Fortunately, Flash handles the entire process for you, though advanced developers may, if they want, go to the expense of writing the actual external text file normally needed.

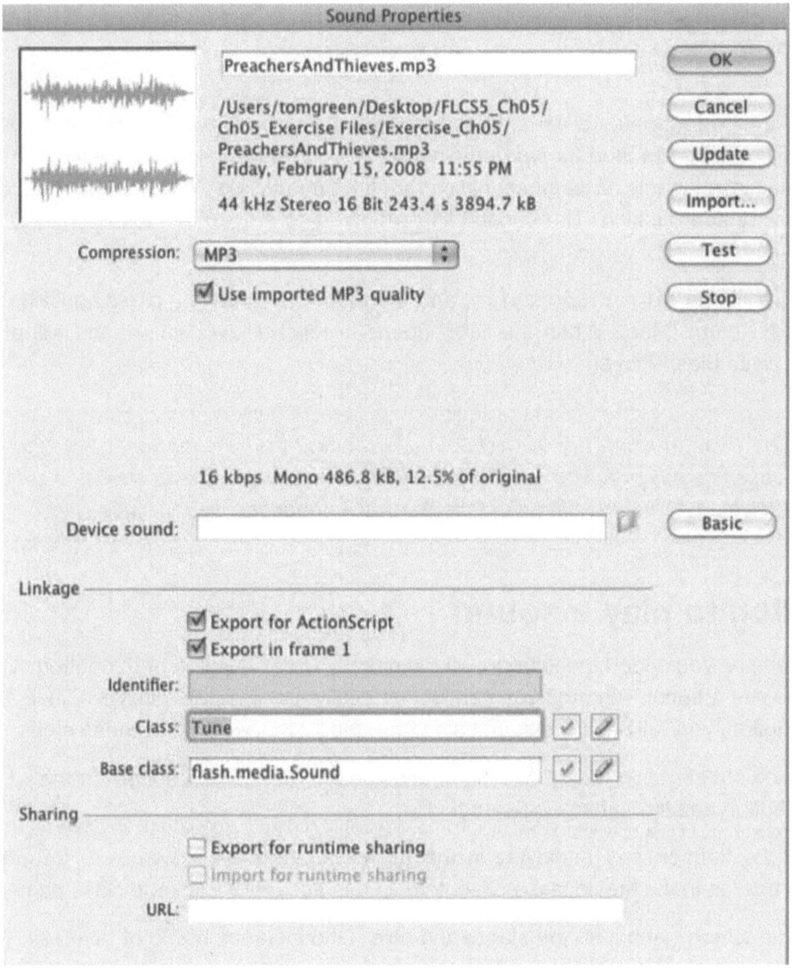

Figure 5-14. Establishing a linkage identifier

4. Select **Export for ActionScript**, and replace the name of the audio file with the word **Tune** in the **Class** area of the dialog box. Click **OK** to close the dialog box.

5. You will get a warning dialog box telling you there is no such thing as a Tune class. Click **OK** to close it. By clicking **OK**, you are telling Flash to go ahead and create this class on your behalf. (The name Tune is arbitrary. but because our audio file is a song, Tune makes good sense.)

6. Rename **Layer 1** to **Actions**, select the first frame in the layer, and open the **Actions** panel. Enter the following code:

```
var audio:Tune = new Tune();
audio.play();
```

The first line of the code creates a variable named `audio` and uses the Tune class—from the **Linkage Properties** dialog box—as its data type. In Chapter 4, you learned about classes and inheritance, and this custom Tune class inherits all its functionality from the Sound class. This means it is a bona fide Sound instance, but a very specific kind. The second line simply uses the Sound class's `play()` method to play the audio file.

7. Save the file as `LibrarySound.fla`, and then test the movie by pressing Ctrl+Enter (Windows) or Cmd+Return (Mac). When the SWF opens in Flash Player, the sound will play. To stop the audio, close Flash Player.

> *If you are used to using the `attachSound()` method from ActionScript 2.0, understand that it doesn't apply in ActionScript 3.0. All you need to do now is to specify a subclass—Tune (or whatever name suits your fancy)—that extends the Sound class.*

Using a button to play a sound

In an earlier example, you added the kaboom sound directly to the timeline of the button symbol. This time, you are going to use a button—though you can just as easily use a movie clip. Also, instead of embedding a sound in the button, you will have the sound play from the **Library**. Follow these steps:

1. Open the `CodeButtonSound.fla` file in this chapter's **Exercise** folder. In the **Library**, you will see a button and the `kaboom.mp3` audio file.

2. Select the `kaboom.mp3` audio file in the **Library**. Use the **Advanced Sound Properties** dialog box, as in the previous exercise, to give this audio file a linkage class named `Blam`.

3. Click the button symbol on the stage, and give it the instance name of `btnPlay`. (Remember that symbols controlled by ActionScript need an instance name.)

4. Add a new layer named **scripts** to the timeline. Lock the **scripts** layer, select the first frame, and open the **Actions** panel. Enter the following code:

```
var audio:Blam = new Blam();

btnPlay.addEventListener(MouseEvent.CLICK, clickHandler);
function clickHandler(evt:MouseEvent):void {
  audio.play();
};
```

The first line creates an instance of the `Blam` class—actually a `Sound` instance that has been extended by an automatically generated custom class—and stores a reference to that instance in a variable named `audio`. After that, an event handler function, `mouseUpHandler()`, is associated with the `MouseEvent.CLICK` event for the `btnPlay` button.

The event handler works the same as you saw in Chapter 4, even though the object in question—an instance of the `Blam` (Sound) class—is different from movie clips and buttons. In ActionScript 3.0, event handling is consistent across the board (with very few exceptions, and you'll see those in the chapter on video). When the `MouseEvent.CLICK` event occurs, the `clickHandler()` function is triggered. In turn, the `clickHandler()` function makes a reference to the `Blam` instance, by way of the `audio` variable, and invokes the `Sound.play()` method on it. The result is that you hear an explosion when you click the button.

5. Save the file and test the movie.

Playing a sound from outside of Flash

You know that embedding sound into a SWF file adds to its file size. Is there a way to play a sound that isn't inside the SWF file? The answer is absolutely.

The best use for this technique is to play any audio file that is longer than a couple of seconds. In this case, we will be using a ten-minute radio documentary produced by two radio broadcast students from the School of Media Studies at the Humber Institute of Technology and Advanced Learning in Toronto. This track, created by Andre Jeremiah and Shauna McCreedy, won Best of Show – Radio at the 2009 Media Advisors Convention in New York and is quite typical of the type of audio podcasts that Flash is now delivering on the Web.

1. Open the `RemoteSound.fla` file in this chapter's **Exercise** folder. You will see that we have placed a button symbol on the stage and given it the instance name of `btnPlay`.

2. Add a new layer named **actions**, select the first frame in the **actions** layer, open the **Actions** panel, and enter the following code (we'll review it after you test the movie):

```
var audio:Sound = new Sound();
var req:URLRequest = new URLRequest("On Borrowed Time.mp3");
audio.load(req);
audio.play();
```

CHAPTER 5

3. Test the movie to create your SWF. The audio starts to play.

The second and third lines of the ActionScript you entered handle the external sound. In ActionScript 3.0, you can't simply tell Flash, "There's an audio file in this folder that you need to play." Instead, you need to use an instance of the URLRequest class to specify the file's location. That object, referenced by a variable named req, gets passed as a parameter to the load() method of the Sound instance created in the first line of the code.

In ActionScript 3.0, most things brought into a Flash movie—audio, images, and even SWF files—need to be "called in" through a URLRequest instance (one notable exception is video, which is covered in Chapter 10).

If the MP3 is in the same folder as the HTML document that contains the SWF, you can simply name the MP3 without a file path. Of course, you can just as easily use an absolute path to a folder on your server. In that case, the syntax would be something like this:

```
var req:URLRequest = new URLRequest("http://www.domain.com/audio/On Borrowed Time.mp3");
audio.load(req);
```

> The authors would like to thank both Andre and Shauna for permission to use this file in our book. We would also like to acknowledge William Hanna, dean of the School of Media Studies, and Jerry Chomyn, who manages the college's radio station for their assistance in allowing us to include this file in the book.

Turning a remote sound on and off

The previous exercise contained a rather nasty usability flaw. The audio file played, and there was no way, other than closing the SWF, to turn it off. Let's address this oversight. In this exercise, you will code up two buttons: one button will play the sound, and the other will turn it off. The really neat thing about these buttons is that they aren't buttons. You are about to learn how movie clips can be used as buttons instead. Let's get started:

1. Open the RemoteSound2.fla file. Again, we have provided you with the raw material, as shown in Figure 5-15. The **start** button with the instance name **playMC** will be used to turn the sound on. The **Stop** button, **stopMC**, will be used to turn the sound off.

> The choice of instance names is deliberate. Many Flash designers and developers try to use contractions that tell the coder what type of object is being used. This explains why you may see code elsewhere and the instance names somehow contain an indication of exactly what object is being used. For example, **playMC** could also be written as **Play_mc** or **mcPlay**. The key is the **mc**, which indicates it is a movie clip.

AUDIO IN FLASH CS5

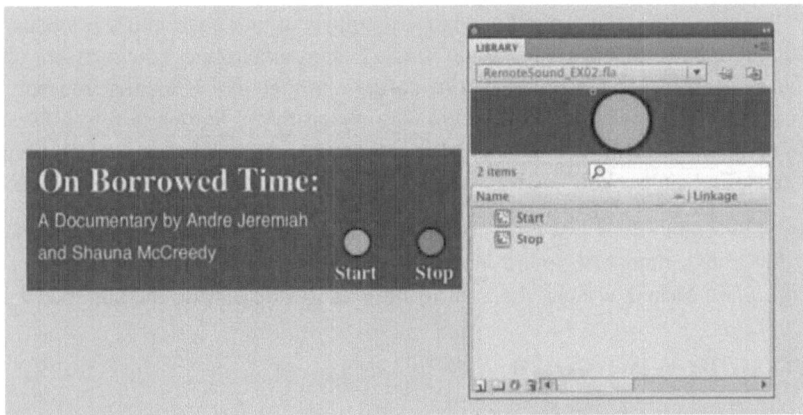

Figure 5-15. Two movie clips are used to turn a sound on and off.

The plan for this project is to have the user click the **Start** button to have the audio file play and then click the **Stop** button to turn off the audio.

2. Create a new layer named **actions**, click the first frame in the **actions** layer, and open the ActionScript Editor. When the **Script** pane opens, enter the following code:

```
var audio:Sound = new Sound();
audio.load(new URLRequest("On Borrowed Time.mp3"));

var channel:SoundChannel = new SoundChannel();

playMC.buttonMode = true;

playMC.addEventListener( MouseEvent.MOUSE_UP, playIt);
function playIt (evt:MouseEvent):void {
  channel = audio.play();
};
stopMC.buttonMode = true;

stopMC.addEventListener(MouseEvent.MOUSE_UP, stopIt);
function stopIt(evt:MouseEvent):void {
  channel.stop();
};
```

3. Save and test the movie by clicking the **Start** and **Stop** buttons.

The first thing to notice is the use of the `buttonMode()` method to change a movie clip to a button. This doesn't "change" it to a button when the movie plays. What it does is to turn the cursor to the "Pointing Finger" icon, which tells the user, "Hey, you can click this to make stuff happen."

303

CHAPTER 5

Other than that, the only major difference between this code and that used in the previous example is the addition of a `SoundChannel` object. The `SoundChannel` class controls a sound in an application. Each sound playing in a Flash movie now has its own sound channel, which means you can have up to 32 concurrent sound channels playing different audio files. Flash mixes them down to a two-channel stereo mix (or a mono mix) for you that can be mixed together. The `SoundChannel` class features a `stop()` method for turning sound off, but you need to assign the sound to a `SoundChannel` instance first.

In this case, the **Play** button does just that. When clicked, its event handler associates the remote sound represented by the `audio` object (a `Sound` instance) with the `SoundChannel` instance named `channel`. The **Stop** button, when clicked, will use the `stop()` method to stop playing the sound in that channel.

Adjusting volume with code

What if you don't want to stop the audio but simply allow the user to temporarily mute it? Providing your users with this option is a courteous thing to do. Fortunately, it's not very hard to do.

To see how muting is accomplished, open the `RemoteSound3.fla` file in this chapter's Exercise folder. By this point, you should be feeling a sense of *déjà vu*. The file looks nearly the same as in the previous exercise, but the instance names have changed. The buttons now have instance names `muteMC` and `unmuteMC`. The code has also changed, but not by much.

1. Click into frame 1 of the **scripts** layer, and take a look in the **Actions** panel. You'll see the following code:

```
var audio:Sound = new Sound();
var req:URLRequest = new URLRequest( "On Borrowed Time.mp3");
audio.load(req);
var channel:SoundChannel = audio.play();
var xform:SoundTransform = new SoundTransform();

muteMC.buttonMode = true;

muteMC.addEventListener(MouseEvent.CLICK, muteSound);
function muteSound (evt:MouseEvent):void{
        xform.volume = 0;
        channel.soundTransform = xform;
}

unmuteMC.buttonMode = true;

unmuteMC.addEventListener(MouseEvent.CLICK, unmuteSound);
function unmuteSound (evt:MouseEvent):void{
        xform.volume = 1;
        channel.soundTransform = xform;
}
```

This time, the `channel` instance is associated with the `audio` instance right away in line 4. No button click is needed to play this song; it just plays. Just as before, the `Sound.play()` method, as invoked on `audio`, lets `channel` know which `sound` it controls.

The new part is an instance of the `SoundTransform` class, stored in a variable named `xform`. Check out the `muteSound()` function, which acts as the event handler for the `btnMute` button's `MouseEvent.CLICK` event. The `SoundTransform` class features a `volume` property, and this property is referenced in terms of the `xform` instance. It is given a value of 0 (silence). In the next line, the `xform` instance is assigned to the `SoundChannel.soundTransform` property of the `channel` instance. That's all there is to it.

In the `unmuteSound()` function, the same process takes place, except that the `volume` property is set to 1 (full volume). Want to turn down the volume instead of muting it? That's easy.

2. Inside the `muteSound()` function, change the 0 to 0.5. Your code should now look like this:

```
btnMute.addEventListener(MouseEvent.CLICK, muteSound);
function muteSound(evt:MouseEvent):void {
  xform.volume = 0.5;
  channel.soundTransform = xform;
};
```

3. Test the movie, and click the buttons. Then close the SWF. Change the 0.5 back to a 0, and test again. Neat stuff!

> *For those of you wondering why we stop with this exercise and don't get into using a slider to adjust the volume, the reason is simple: you need a bit more ActionScript experience before you tackle that. You will add such a slider to a full-bore MP3 player in Chapter 14.*

Your turn: storm over Lake Superior

One of the really neat aspects of being a Flash designer is that you get to bring otherwise static media to life. A great example of this is turning a photograph into a motion graphics piece and then using audio to "seal the deal" and bring it to life. You are going to do just that in this exercise.

One of the authors is an avid hiker and camper. Living in Canada, he has lots of opportunities to indulge in his passion. On the North Shore of Lake Superior is a National Park named Pukaskwa (pronounced "puck-ah-squaw"). In this exercise, you are going to stand with him on the top of a cliff and "experience" a thunderstorm that rolled in off of the lake during his hike. Let's get started:

1. Open a new Flash document, and import the `Pukaskwa.jpg` image in the `Chapter 5 Exercise` folder to your **Library**. Save the file to your Chapter 5 Exercise folder.

2. Add two more layers to the movie, and name them **Rain** and **actions**. Rename **Layer 1** to **Image**.

3. Select the first frame of `Layer 1`, and drag the image from the `Library` to the stage. Select `Modify` ➤ `Document` to open the `Document Properties` dialog box, and select `Contents`. Click `OK`, and the stage resizes to fit the image. Lock the `Image` layer.

The rest of this project will be assembled "over" the image on the stage. The next step will involve adding the rainstorm to the movie, and before we start, there are a couple of things you need to know. The first is we are going to import an FLV, which is a Flash Video file, directly into Flash. This is not exactly regarded as a best practice in the industry because these files can be quite large in file size. We tend to agree, but in the Flash universe, rules can be broken. In this case, if the FLV were a couple of seconds in length and physically small, this is not an issue. In this case, we wouldn't do what we are asking you to do if the project were destined for the Web. The next thing you need to know is you don't always need code to obtain some rather interesting effects. In this case, the rainstorm was created in After Effects CS5. So much for the chat; we standing on a cliff overlooking Lake Superior, and there is a rainstorm headed our way. Let's add the rain:

4. Select `File` ➤ `Import` ➤ `Import Video`, as shown in Figure 5-16. This will open the `Import Video` dialog box.

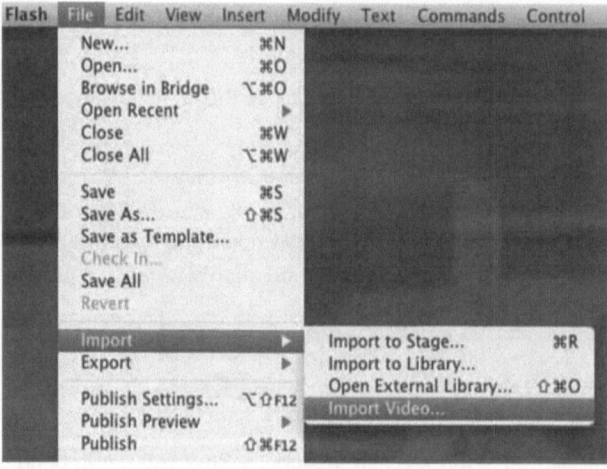

Figure 5-16. Video files can be imported directly into Flash.

5. When the `Import` dialog box opens, click the `Browse` button, and navigate to your Chapter 5 `Exercise` folder. Locate the `Rain.flv` file, and click `Open`.

6. The next decision you need to make is how the file will be handled. Select the `Embed FLV in SWF and play in timeline` option. This will add the rather stern warning shown at the bottom of the `Import Video` dialog box, as shown in Figure 5-17. Click `Continue` to open the `Embedding` options.

AUDIO IN FLASH CS5

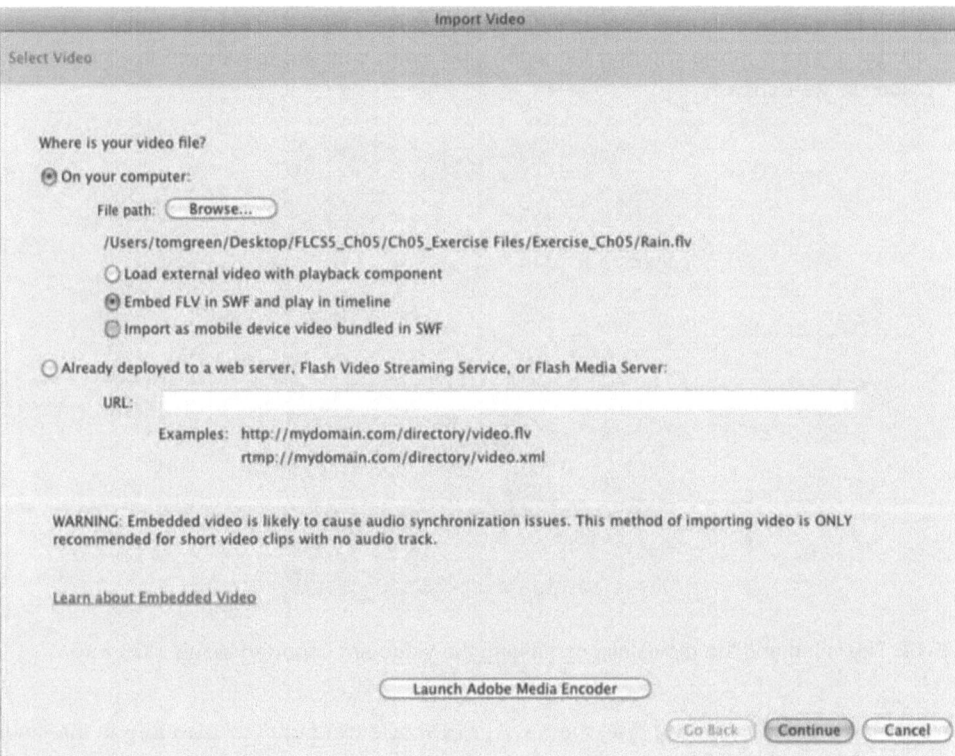

Figure 5-17. The stern warning is not be taken lightly.

7. When the **Embedding** options opens, select **Movie clip**, as shown in Figure 5-18, from the **Symbol Type** drop-down, and deselect **Place instance on stage**. Click the **Continue/Next** button to open the **Finish Video Import** section of the **Import Video** dialog box.

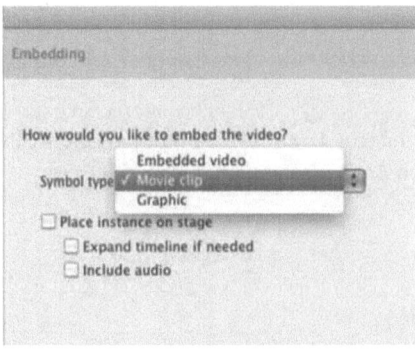

Figure 5-18. The video is to be imported into a movie clip.

307

8. When the `Finish Video Import` dialog box closes, click the `Finish` button. The dialog box will close, and a movie clip and the video (the video camera), as shown in Figure 5-19, will be placed in the `Library`.

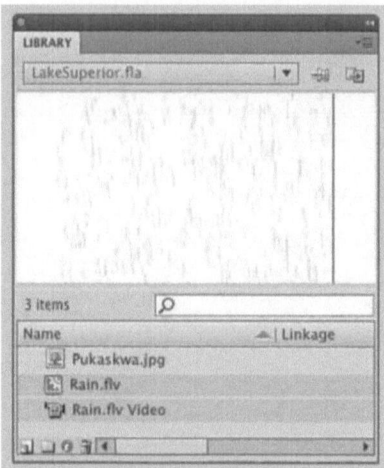

Figure 5-19. The video and the movie clip containing the video are imported to the `Library`.

9. Select the `Rain` layer, and drag the `Rain.flv` movie clip from the `Library` to the stage. Save and test the movie. Welcome to our rainstorm.

> This will be the first and last time we will be visiting the `Import Video` feature of Flash CS5. As we said, embedding video directly into the timeline of a Flash movie is a rather dangerous habit to develop. It is ideal for techniques such as this where the video is very short and physically small, but other than that, professional Flash designers rarely, if ever treat video in this manner. We'll show you how the pros work with video in Chapter 10.

Now that we are standing on a cliff overlooking Lake Superior and getting wet, let's add that last little bit of realism: rain and thunder.

10. Select the first frame of the `actions` layer, and open the `Actions` panel. When it opens, enter the following code into the `Script` pane:

```
import flash.media.Sound;
import flash.net.URLRequest;

var audio:Sound = new Sound();
var req:URLRequest = new URLRequest("RainStorm.mp3");
audio.load(req);
audio.play();
```

11. Save and play the movie. As you may have noticed, the simple addition of an audio track makes this project much more powerful.

Code snippet: visualize audio

In the previous chapter, we introduced you to code snippets. As you may recall, these are pieces of code that, once added to the panel, can be reused on a regular basis. From this point on in this book, we will be adding the occasional code snippet that allows you add functionality, or **widgets**, to your movies. These snippets will be heavily commented, and we will explain which values you can change to "customize" the snippet to your needs.

This snippet creates an audio visualization movie clip and puts it on the stage. As shown in Figure 5-20, a series of bars rise or fall based upon the loudness (amplitude) of the audio track. This feature was added to Flash CS3 and falls squarely into the realm of intermediate to advanced ActionScript. The addition of code snippets gives us the opportunity to let you try some advanced techniques without getting yourself into trouble. To add the snippet, follow these steps:

Figure 5-20. Create a snippet that adds the audio visualization bars on the right of the stage.

1. Open the `AudioVisualization.fla` file in your Chapter 5 in the `CodeSnippet` folder found in your Chapter 5 `Exercise` folder.

2. Select the first frame of the **actions** layer, and open the **Actions** panel to see the following code:

```
import flash.net.URLRequest;
import flash.media.Sound;
import flash.media.SoundChannel;
import flash.utils.ByteArray;
import flash.display.Sprite;
import flash.utils.Timer;
import flash.events.Event;
import flash.events.TimerEvent;

var url:String = "On Borrowed Time.mp3";
var req:URLRequest = new URLRequest(url);
var audio:Sound = new Sound();
```

CHAPTER 5

```
audio.addEventListener(Event.COMPLETE,completeHandler);
audio.load(req);

var track:SoundChannel = audio.play();
audio.addEventListener(Event.SOUND_COMPLETE,soundCompleteHandler);
var ba:ByteArray = new ByteArray();

var gr:Sprite = new Sprite();
gr.x = 300;
gr.y = 100;
addChild(gr);

var time:Timer = new Timer(50);
time.addEventListener(TimerEvent.TIMER,timerHandler);
time.start();

function completeHandler(evt:Event): void{
        evt.target.play();
}

function soundCompleteHandler (evt:Event):void{
        time.stop();
}

function timerHandler(evt:TimerEvent):void {
  SoundMixer.computeSpectrum(ba,true);
  var i:int;
  gr.graphics.clear();
  gr.graphics.lineStyle(0, 0xFFFFFF);
  gr.graphics.beginFill(0xFFFFFF);
  gr.graphics.moveTo(0, 0);
  var w:uint = 2;
  for (i=0; i<512; i+=w) {
    var t:Number = ba.readFloat();
    var n:Number = (t * 25);
    gr.graphics.drawRect(i, 0, w, -n);
  };
};
```

3. Select the code, and open the **Code Snippets** panel.

4. Click the **Options** button, and select **Create New Code Snippet** to open the **Create New Code snippet** dialog box.

5. Name the snippet **Audio Visualizer**, and enter **Create an audio visualization widget** in the **Tooltip** area.

6. Click the `Auto-fill` button to add the selected code to the snippet, and click `OK` to add it to your `Code Snippets` panel.
7. To use the snippet, add it to the timeline or your `Script` panel if you are already there and simply make the changes regarding audio file, color, location, and size where indicated in the code.

If you are new to ActionScript, you may be looking at all of that code and be wondering: what does it do?

The whole thing starts with the declaration of a bunch of variables:

```
var url:String = "Chill.mp3";
var request:URLRequest = new URLRequest(url);
var tune:Sound = new Sound();

tune.addEventListener(Event.COMPLETE,completeHandler);
tune.load(request);

var song:SoundChannel = tune.play();
song.addEventListener(Event.SOUND_COMPLETE, soundCompleteHandler);
var ba:ByteArray = new ByteArray();
```

The first three lines identify the audio file that will play and where the file is located and creates the `Sound()` object that will play it. The next two lines tell Flash to reload the audio file when it finishes. The final three lines start the audio file playing, tell Flash what to do when the sound ends, and create a `ByteArray()`.

That last line may have you scratching your head, but it is how the sound is eventually turned into the bouncing bars. A `ByteArray()` is a series of numbers between -1 and 1 that can contain up to 512 values. The first 256 values represent the left audio channel, and the remaining 256 values represent the right channel. These are the numbers that put the graph in motion. High frequencies are on the right side of the graph, and the low frequencies are on the left side. As we move deeper into this code, you will discover the spikes are strictly a function of the values in that array.

The next code block starts by creating the movie clip that you are seeing and puts it on the stage:

```
var gr:Sprite = new Sprite();
gr.x = 20;
gr.y = 200;
addChild(gr);

var time:Timer = new Timer(50);
time.addEventListener(TimerEvent.TIMER, timerHandler);
time.start();

function completeHandler(evt:Event):void {
  evt.target.play();
};
```

```
function soundCompleteHandler(evt:Event):void {
  time.stop();
};
```

The movie clip is a special type of object called a Sprite. Sprites are nothing more than movie clips without a timeline. The next chunk tells Flash how often to update the graph. In this case, the Timer() object will check what is going on every 50 milliseconds and run the final function, timerHandler, as long as the song is playing. If it isn't playing, the soundComplete handler turns off the timer, which is why things flat line at the end of the documentary.

The final function is where the magic happens:

```
function timerHandler(evt:TimerEvent):void {
  SoundMixer.computeSpectrum(ba,true);
  var i:int;
  gr.graphics.clear();
  gr.graphics.lineStyle(0, 0x000000);
  gr.graphics.beginFill(0x000000);
  gr.graphics.moveTo(0, 0);
  var w:uint = 2;
  for (i=0; i<512; i+=w) {
    var t:Number = ba.readFloat();
    var n:Number = (t * 100);
    gr.graphics.drawRect(i, 0, w, -n);
  };
};
```

Audio visualization is accomplished through the SoundMixer() class introduced into ActionScript 3.0. One of the methods in this class is the computeSpectrum() method, which takes a snapshot of the sound wave every 50 milliseconds and places it in a ByteArray(ba) object.

The computeSpectrum() method has three parameters:

- **outPutArray**: This is the **ByteArray** that is used to create the spikes.
- **FFTMode**: This Boolean value indicates whether a Fourier transform is performed on the sound data. Like you, we really didn't have a clue what a Fourier transform was. It took a quick side trip to Wikipedia to learn it is simply a bunch of math that turns the audio into a frequency graph instead of a sound wave. The default value is **false**. This is how the graph bounces up and down. Change it to **false**, and the graph, as shown in Figure 5-16, is turned into a wave that bounces up and down on both sides of the line.
- **stretchFactor**: This is a number that sets the resolution of the audio. The default value is 0, meaning the audio will be sampled at a rate of 44.1KHz. Use a value of 1, and the sound is sampled at 22.05KHz, and so on, as you slice the proverbial salami.

The balance of the code uses Flash's Drawing API to draw the black lines—gr.graphics.lineStyle(0, 0x000000);—and to fill them with black—gr.graphics.beginFill(0x000000); . From there, the lines are positioned within the sprite—`moveTo()`—and used to create the boxes through the use of the `drawRect()` method.

> *This will be the only place in this book where we present a basic use of the Drawing API in Flash. It is a rather complex subject and is well out of the scope of this book. Still, exposing you to it should give you an idea of the creative possibilities open to you. If you want to learn more about this feature, we suggest you check out our sister volumes,* Foundation ActionScript 3.0 for Flash and Flex *by Darren Richardson and Paul Milbourne and* Foundation ActionScript 3.0 Animation *by our good friend Keith Peters.*

What you've learned

In this chapter, you learned the following:

- How to add audio to Flash
- The difference between an event and a streaming sound
- How to set the preferences for sound output in Flash CS5
- Various approaches to playing a sound in the Flash `Library` and one located outside of Flash
- The various classes, properties, and methods ActionScript 3.0 uses to control and manage sound in Flash
- How to create a simple audio visualization in Flash.

As you discovered, there is a lot more to audio in Flash than simply tossing in some sort of electronica beat and becoming a "cool kid." Audio in Flash is a powerful communications tool, and savvy Flash designers and developers who realize this are leveraging audio in Flash to its full potential. Speaking of communications tools, text is no longer that gray stuff that goes around your animations. To find out more, turn the page, because text is the focus of the next chapter.

Chapter 6

Text

"Letterforms that honor and elucidate what humans see and say deserve to be honored in their turn. Well-chosen words deserve well-chosen letters; these in their turn deserve to be set with affection, intelligence, knowledge and skill. Typography is a link, and it ought, as a matter of honor, courtesy and pure delight, to be as strong as the others in the chain."

—Robert Bringhurst

This quote from Bringhurst's master work, *The Elements of Typographic Style, Second Edition* (Hartley and Marks, 2002), sums up the essence of type in Flash. The words we put on the stage and subsequently put into motion are usually well chosen. They have to be, because they are the communication messengers, providing the user with access to understanding the message you are trying to communicate. In this chapter, we focus on using type to do just that.

The introduction of the Adobe CS5 product line puts some powerful typographic tools in your hands, such as a new application programming interface (API) called the Text Layout Framework (TLF). In addition, as more tools in the Adobe lineup nudge closer to a confluence point with Flash, the field of typographic motion graphics on the Web is about to move into territory that has yet to be explored. To start that exploration, you need to understand what type is in Flash and, just as importantly, what you can do with it to honor the communication messengers of your content.

CHAPTER 6

We'll cover the following in this chapter:

- The basics of type
- The new Text Layout Framework
- Creating multicolumn text
- How to flow text between containers on the stage
- Using ActionScript to create, format, and present text
- Creating hyperlinks
- Using the spell checker
- Creating scrollable text blocks

The following files are used in this chapter:

- Containers.fla (Chapter06/Exercise Files_CH06/Exercise/Containers.fla)
- TLF_hyperlink_AS.fla (Chapter06/Exercise Files_CH06/Exercise/TLF_Hyperlink_AS.fla)
- SpellItOut.txt (Chapter06/Exercise Files_CH06/Exercise/SpellItOut.txt)
- ScrollComponent.fla (Chapter06/Exercise Files_CH06/Exercise/ScrollComponent.fla)
- TLF_Scrollable_AS.fla (Chapter06/Exercise Files_CH06/Exercise/TLF_Scrollable_AS.fla)

The source files are available online at www.friendsofED.com/download.html?isbn=1430229940.

Fonts and typefaces

Before we define what a font is and what a typeface is, let's get really clear on one point: type is not that gray stuff that fits around your "whizzy" Flash animations. It is your primary communications tool.

Reading is hardwired into us. If it wasn't, you wouldn't be looking at this sentence and assimilating it in your brain. You have a need for information, and the printed word is how you get it. The thing is, the choice of font and how you present the text not only affects the message but also affects the information. You can see this in Figure 6-1. The phrase "Flash rocks" takes on a different meaning in each instance of the phrase. Using the same Times typeface but with the bold and italic variants, the message "changes" depending on the style applied.

Flash rocks
Flash rocks
Flash rocks
Flash rocks

Figure 6-1. It is all about the message.

You can take this to the next level and see that not only variants but typeface has an effect upon the message. Figure 6-2 shows five examples of the same information presented using different typefaces. You can see how the message changes even more dramatically.

Times .... Flash Rocks

Futura Book .... Flash Rocks

Party .... Flash Rocks

Brush Script .... Flash Rocks

Rockwell .... Flash Rocks

Figure 6-2. It is all about the message and the typeface chosen.

When choosing your fonts, you also have to be aware of their impact upon readability and legibility. Both are achieved by an acute awareness of the qualities and attributes that make type readable. These attributes include the typeface, the size, the color, and so on.

To illustrate this point, take a look at a small exercise one of the authors uses in his classes. What word is shown in Figure 6-3? Don't be too hasty to say *legibility*. What are the sixth, seventh, eighth, and ninth characters? What letters are the first and second letters? Suddenly things become a bit disorienting.

CHAPTER 6

legibility

Figure 6-3. What word is this?

This disorientation is important for you to understand. Our visual clue to legibility and readability, as shown in Figure 6-4, is the flow along the tops of the letters. This is why text that consists of all capital letters is so hard to read.

legibility

Figure 6-4. We get our clues to letterforms from the tops of the letters.

We include this exercise because there is a huge temptation on the part of people new to Flash to prove they're one of the "cool kids" and use font and color combinations that make otherwise legible text impossible to read. A good example of this is Figure 6-5. The word is set in a medium gray color on a dark gray background, and the size for the text is 10 pixels. The text is very difficult to read, and yet somehow the "cool kids" think this is some sweet action. Wrong! They just killed all access to the information contained in the text. The next figure, Figure 6-6, goes in the opposite direction. Type is used as a clear communications vehicle for the message.

Even though paying attention to design is critical, from a type perspective, font-rendering technology in Flash was a huge issue until the introduction of CoolType in Flash CS4.

Figure 6-5. It is all about the message and the font chosen.

Figure 6-6. The message—"Opel drives on natural gas"—comes through loud and clear.

Adobe CoolType

Flash CS5 contains a rather major change "under the hood" that was introduced in Flash CS4, and we suspect that not a lot of people will pay much attention to it. The change? The inclusion of CoolType technology.

Designers are an odd bunch. They can pick out something that doesn't "look quite right" with what seems to be a cursory glance at the page or the screen. For years, designers have noted that type in Flash just doesn't "look right," and as strange as this may seem, they were correct. This was an odd situation because Adobe has always been in the lead with font technologies, and yet one of its flagship applications seemed to be lagging in this important area. We won't get into the reasons why—they are complex and tediously technical—but font rendering and management in Flash has always been a sore point with designers. CoolType may have just put that one to rest.

To understand how big a deal this is, you have to go back into the gray mists of time to around 1984 and the introduction of the Macintosh. For many of you, 1984 is a murky year in your childhood. For some of us, especially one of the authors, it was the year that graphic layout started its move from art boards, waxers, and X-Acto knives to the computer screen. Two players—Apple and Adobe—made this possible. Apple supplied the computer and the LaserWriter printer, while Adobe supplied PostScript.

To that point, layout on a computer was interesting, but the problem was that stuff called **type**. A letter would show up on the computer screen, but it would be blocky. There was essentially no way to differentiate a capital letter A using Garamond from its Times counterpart. This was because of the way computers rendered on-screen type. Essentially, the letters were constructed in a grid of pixels that gave them the rather blocky, pixelated look we have come to call the **jaggies**. PostScript, developed by Adobe, somewhat solved this problem by creating a language—PostScript—that, in very simple terms, "drew" the letter over the pixels and gave designers what they wanted: Garamond As that actually looked like Garamond As on the screen. The fact that they looked even crisper when run through the LaserWriter was also a huge factor in moving the graphics industry to computers.

Still, designers spent a lot of time complaining about on-screen resolution and font crispness. They had a point because, no matter how you cut it on the screen, text had some serious readability issues because pixels were still being lit up to create letters. As the Web took hold and Flash took off, designers noticed the fonts they used still didn't look "quite right" because the text was being displayed on-screen and subject to the lingering problems inherent in on-screen text.

As we have stated, the relatively poor readability of text on-screen compared to its paper counterpart has been a significant sticking point with designers almost from the word "Go." The source of the problem is low-resolution computer screens. While the resolution of the typical printer is often 600 dots per inch (dpi) or more, the resolution of the average laptop, PDA device, or desktop screen is only 72 (Macintosh) or 96 (Windows) dpi on a screen. This means type that looks crisp and smooth on paper appears coarse and jagged on-screen.

To combat the jaggies, traditional grayscale font **anti-aliasing** (also called **font smoothing**) buffs out the corners in text by filling in the edges of bitmapped characters with various shades of gray pixels, which can make text at small point sizes appear blurry. Flash attempted to address this issue when it introduced a number of anti-aliasing features into Flash in 2004. Though a huge improvement, Flash designers were still unhappy because their text still didn't look "quite right." They looked at the introduction of CoolType to Acrobat in 2000 and asked, "Uh, what about us?" The thing is, a lot of our work was in color, and adding fuzzy gray pixels around colorful letters wasn't making life easier for either party.

CoolType to the rescue

What CoolType does is create clearer, crisper type using a font-rendering technique Adobe calls **color anti-aliasing**, which works on digital liquid crystal display (LCD) screens such as those in laptops, handheld devices, and flat-panel desktop monitors. Unlike conventional anti-aliasing, which manipulates only whole pixels, CoolType controls the individual red, green, and blue subpixels on a digital LCD screen. The key word here is *subpixels*. The hundreds of thousands of squares on the screen, which are the pixels, are actually further subdivided into even more squares. These are the subpixels, which are something like quarks in the realm of the formerly indivisible atom.

According to Adobe, by adjusting the intensity of the subpixels independently, the strokes of a character can be aligned on any subpixel boundary, thus achieving sharper, more precise smoothing along the edges of characters. Using this subpixel technique, CoolType can dramatically increase horizontal resolution for improved readability. Again, the keyword in that last sentence is *horizontal*. We read text across the page, which means the characters are even sharper, which, in turn, makes them even more legible and readable. Figure 6-7, taken from the Adobe CoolType web page, shows you how subpixels reinterpret character display.

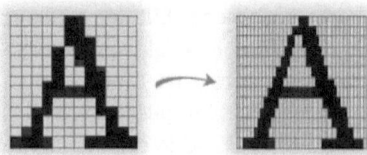

Figure 6-7. On the left is regular pixelated type, and on the right is the same character using subpixels.

Typefaces and fonts

What is a typeface, and what is a font? Technically speaking, a **typeface** is an organized collection of glyphs (usually letters, numbers, and punctuation) that shares stylistic consistency. A **font** is one particular size or variety of a typeface. So, Arial 10 and Arial 12 represent two distinct fonts but belong to the same typeface. The same goes for Arial and Arial Bold or the fonts—Times, Times Italic, Times Bold, Times Bold Italic—used in Figure 6-1: separate fonts that belong to the same font family. In everyday talk, for better or worse, most people simply use the word *font* for all the of preceding.

Flash offers an interesting advantage when it comes to typography: although HTML is capable only of displaying fonts that are installed on the viewer's computer, Flash can display whatever font you like. Want to use some zany dingbat characters or an extravagant cursive font you designed yourself? Have at it. Even input text fields—the sort typed into by the user—can be displayed in whatever font suits your fancy. Flash text fields even support the filters encountered in Chapter 3.

Does this sound too good to be true? Well, everything has a price. Fonts can add to a SWF's file size—the more ornate, the greater the penalty. Take a moment to consider what fonts are, and you'll see that this makes sense. Most fonts store a mathematical description of the lines and curves that define each glyph. Simple shapes require less description than complex shapes.

> *Does that sound oddly familiar? It should because most fonts today are drawn in a PostScript drawing application. In fact, Illustrator CS5 is rapidly becoming the tool of choice among the type design community.*

Flash CS5 supports the following font formats: TrueType, OpenType, PostScript Type 1, bit (Macintosh), and device fonts.

Staying with PostScript, you know the more complex the shape (that is, shapes with a lot of points), the larger the file size. Let's try a little experiment to prove it:

1. Head over to `www.lipsum.org`, a terrific site for generating placeholder text, and copy a paragraph of *Lorem Ipsum* (we'll call it *lipsum* for fun) to the clipboard.

2. Open a new Flash document, and select the `Text` tool. In the `Properties` panel, choose a simple sans-serif font, like Arial, and confirm that `Classic Text` is being used and the type of text is `Static Text`. Click in the upper-left corner of the stage, and, with the mouse still down, drag to the other side of the stage and let go.

3. Paste the `lipsum` text into this text field.

4. Test your movie; when the SWF opens, select **View ➤ Bandwidth Profiler** to see the file size information. Your SWF should be in the neighborhood of 4KB to 8KB.

5. Close the SWF, and change your text field's font to something more elaborate, such as **Blackadder ITC**, **Brush Script**, or whatever decorative typeface in your font list catches your fancy. Test again, and compare file sizes. Your mileage will vary, of course, but experiment a bit to see how different fonts carry different weights. You also might want to try this using more than one font in the text field. This is very common practice, and this is a good place to start learning how fonts affect the "weight" of a SWF.

> *Where did Lorem Ipsum originate? Being a wealth of absolutely useless information, we are glad to oblige you with an answer. The earliest known example of its use is from an unidentified type specimen produced in the 1500s. A printer jumbled up the text from Cicero's* de Finibus Bonorum et Malorum, Liber Primus, *sections 1.10.32 and 1.10.33, and used it to show off his typefaces. It stuck and has been used ever since.*

By the end of this chapter, you'll know what your options are and will be equipped to make informed choices. For starters, let's look at how to dial back to zero the weight that a font adds to a SWF.

Working with device fonts

If you want, you certainly can go with fonts that are installed on the user's machine, just like HTML does. The benefit is that your SWF's weight will be completely unaffected by text content. The drawback is that you have to count on your audience having the same font(s) installed as you do (not a good idea) or choose among three very generic font categories: **_sans** (sans-serif), **_serif**, and **_typewriter** (monospace). These are the device fonts, and they are ideal for use on mobile devices.

In the **Properties** panel, take a look at your font choices in the font drop-down list. The top two, shown in Figure 6-8, are preceded by an underscore. That's the tip-off. If you select one of these fonts, Flash will choose on your behalf whatever it thinks is the closest fit on the viewer's computer. **_sans** will probably be Arial or Helvetica, **_serif** will probably be Times New Roman or Times, and **_typewriter** will probably be Courier New or Courier—but who knows for sure?

> *If you used Flash prior to this release, you may have had the same reaction we did when we saw the font menu: "Whoa!!!" This reorganized font menu is part of the inclusion of CoolType.*

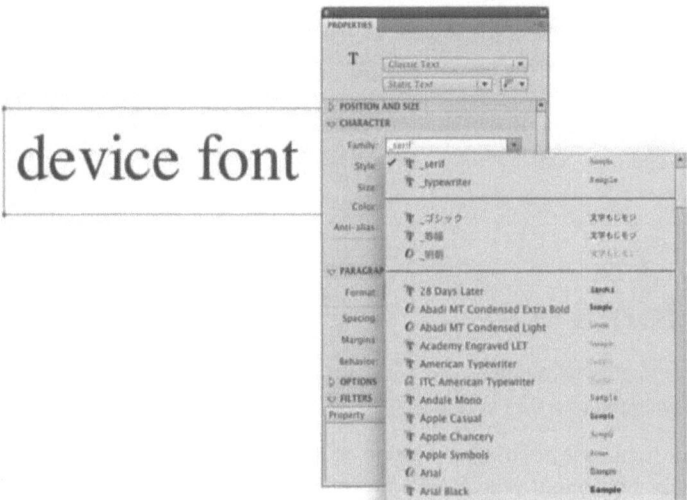

Figure 6-8. The device fonts work everywhere but have limitations.

Another place where you can use device fonts is in those situations where you choose a font, such as Helvetica, and you aren't sure whether the user has the font. As shown in Figure 6-9, you can select `Use device fonts` in the `Anti-alias` pop-down menu, and the fonts will be substituted at runtime.

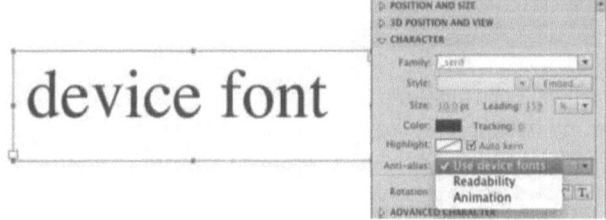

Figure 6-9. Device fonts can be used to override the fonts in the movie at runtime.

Currently Flash can't treat device fonts as graphics. Tweening stuff containing a device font is going to be unpredictable.

Also realize the term *device font* is a "weasel word" for "pick the closest approximation." This means you lose all control over the spacing and length of the text on the screen at runtime. Depending on the font chosen by the user's machine, you may wind up having the user view your work through a font that has a bigger x-height than your font. If you need an exact match, device fonts aren't the way to go.

CHAPTER 6

> *X-height? What's that? It is the height of the letter X in the font, and this proportional characteristic can vary widely in different typefaces of the same size. Tall x-heights are two-thirds the height of a capital letter and short when they are one-half the height of a capital letter. Staying with our useless information theme, the trend to the larger x-height in the sans category was sparked by a Swiss typographer, Adrian Frutiger, when he released Univers 55.*

Embedding fonts

We need to deal with this subject before we dive into the Text Layout Framework and Classic Text. The reason is both types will embed a font into a SWF.

As you have learned, fonts are PostScript outlines of the letters and glyphs contained in a font. You buy fonts, and as such, it is a copyright violation if you were to hand the user the opportunity to install a font in order to see your amazing work. This is one of the reasons Matthew Carter designed the classic web fonts. They were automatically installed on practically every computer on the planet in order to give designers a bit of typographic variety and to keep them out of court. Apart from the web fonts, device fonts are one solution and embedding is the other.

> *Matthew Carter may have designed the web fonts—Arial, Verdana, Georgia, and so on—but it was Microsoft that put them into play when they asked Matthew to design them. The fonts were released when Microsoft introduced Internet Explorer 4 in 1997.*

How does embedding work? Let's assume you are creating a rather grunge-looking design for a skateboard company and the design specification calls for the use of a font named 28 Days Later. Your decision is to use `TLF Text`, and the `Anti-alias` option chosen is `Readability`. You click the text tool and enter `Check out our decks`. Just the letters in those four words will get embedded into the SWF. Duplicates, in this case *o*, *e*, *c*, *u*, and *k*, will be ignored, which means a smaller SWF. Let's try it:

1. Open a new Flash ActionScript 3.0 document, and select the `Text` tool. Click the stage, open the `Properties` panel, select `TLF Text` from the `Text Engine` drop-down, and select `Read Only` from the `Text Type` drop-down.

2. Choose a font in the family drop-down—we chose `28 Days Later`, but you can use any font in your list. Set the size to `48` points and the color to black (`#000000`). Make sure the `Anti-alias` drop-down shows `Use Device Fonts`.

3. Click, and enter `Check out our decks`, as shown in Figure 6-10.

TEXT

Figure 6-10. We start with a simple line of text that uses a grunge-type font.

4. With the text box selected, choose `Readability` from the `Anti-alias` drop-down menu. The alert shown in Figure 6-11 will appear. You actually have a couple of choices. Clicking the `Not now` button will dismiss the alert, and Flash won't embed anything into the SWF. Click the `Embed` button, and the characters will be embedded into the SWF once you finish with the `Font Embedding` dialog box that will open. Click the `Embed` button.

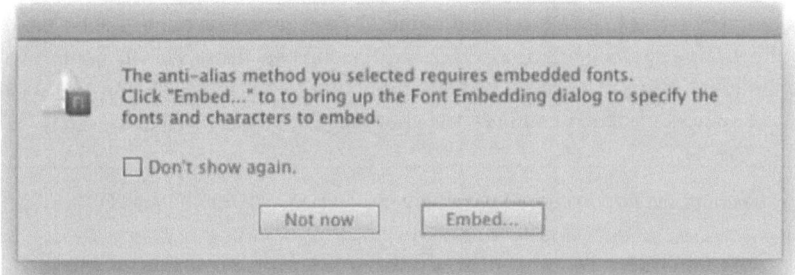

Figure 6-11. You make the decisions regarding embedding.

5. The `Font Embedding` dialog box that opens, as shown in Figure 6-12, may, at first, appear to be a bit overwhelming. Let's go through various bits and pieces of this dialog box.

CHAPTER 6

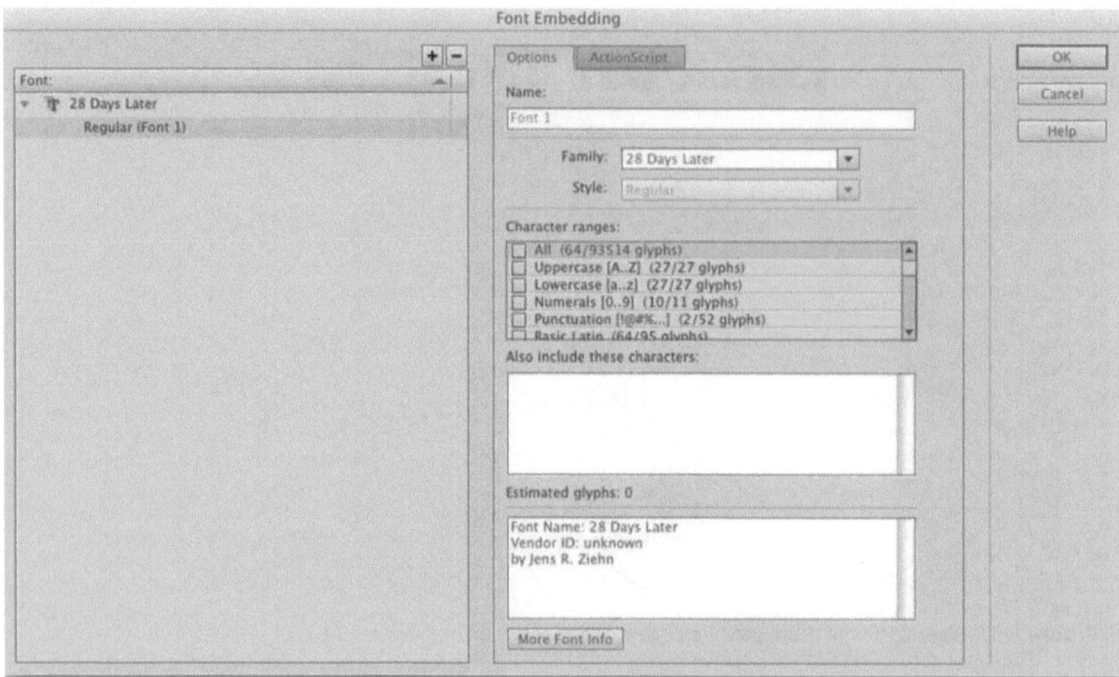

Figure 6-12. The `Font Embedding` dialog box

On the left side of the dialog box is the name of the font. Click it, and everything on the right side grays out. This is because, as we pointed out earlier, the name of the font is the family name. The fonts in the family or style—`Regular (Font 1)`—are listed underneath. Select it, and the right side lights up.

The `Options` area allows you to give the font a name. Do this, and that name will be used in the resulting font symbol in the `Library`. Your `Character range` choices allow you to control which glyphs are embedded into the font symbol. The more glyphs added, the larger the SWF. As you make your choices, the number in the `Estimated Choices` area will change.

> *Glyph? Each character in the font is called a **glyph**. In some fronts, the number of characters can range into the hundreds. A good example of this concept are these two glyphs: e and é. Notice the accent? That letter, with the accent, is a variation on the letter e and is a character in the font set.*

You can skip the selections and include only selected letters. For example, if you use the contents of the text just entered, you would type `chekoutrds`, which, according to the `Estimated glyphs` total, would add only ten characters to the embedded font.

326

TEXT

The bottom box gives you information regarding the font. This information is pulled from the font's metadata. Clicking the `More Font Info` button will launch the browser, take you to the Adobe site, and open a `Font License` page. This page gives you a bit of information regarding the end user license agreement (EULA) of the font. This would include whether the font can or cannot be embedded into a SWF. This works really well for Adobe fonts, but fonts such as the one used here will result in the page telling you, in a nutshell: "We can't find the font, so you make the licensing call." Why this legal stuff? It is there to ensure that copyright is obeyed.

> *Here's a little Mac trick if you want to remain "purer than pure" with embedding. Open Font Book, select your font, and `select Preview ► Show Font Info`. If there is a `Yes` in the `Embeddable` category, you are good to go.*

If you click the `ActionScript` tab, a rather familiar area opens. The `Linkage` area should tell you that the resulting font symbol can be used by ActionScript.

> *The `Outline format` area at the top of the `ActionScript` area lets you choose the format used to draw the screen outlines of the glyphs. There are now two methods that are tied to the Classic or TLF text engines. Select the `Outline` method that matches your chosen text engine.*

6. Click OK to accept the changes, and close the `Font Embedding` dialog box. Open your `Library`, and you'll see that a font symbol, as shown in Figure 6-13, has been added to your `Library`.

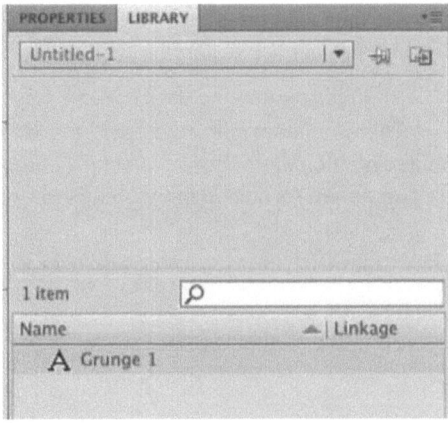

Figure 6-13. A font symbol in the `Library` tells you a font has been embedded.

327

The two text engines: TLF and Classic

If you clicked the `Text Engine` drop-down, you were presented with two choices: `TLF Text` and `Classic Text`. Let's deal with each one before moving on to how to use them.

If there has been one issue around Flash that designers have found frustrating, it would be how Flash handles text. Considering that Adobe has always been a huge name in the font universe—both on the print and digital sides of the fence—it was a mystery to designers as to how typography was so inconsistently handled by Flash. These were things like ligatures, character formatting, text flow, and other typographic nuances that were relatively unimportant to the casual user but a never-ending source of frustration for designers who understood the importance of typography.

Flash CS5 marks the first major step to finally getting this issue out of the way. The Text Layout Framework allows you to use ActionScript or the `Properties` panel in such a way as to make the old way of managing text—Classic Text—look like a creaking machine on its last legs. You can do the following with TLF Text:

- Highlight text
- Underline text
- Use strikethroughs, superscript, and subscript
- Control case, ligatures, and baseline shift
- Flow text between text containers to create columns
- Have text run from left to right or right to left depending upon the alphabet used
- Apply padding, borders, and background colors to the columns

Just keep in mind that TLF Text works only with projects aimed at Flash Player 10 or newer and only with TrueType and OpenType fonts. If your project scope targets any player older than this version or uses a PostScript font, you have to use Classic Text.

The best way of regarding Classic Text is to consider it as being the way text was formatted in previous versions of Flash. Another way of seeing the differences is to simply compare the differences in formatting options presented in the `Properties` panel. As shown in Figures 6-14 and 6-15, they are significant.

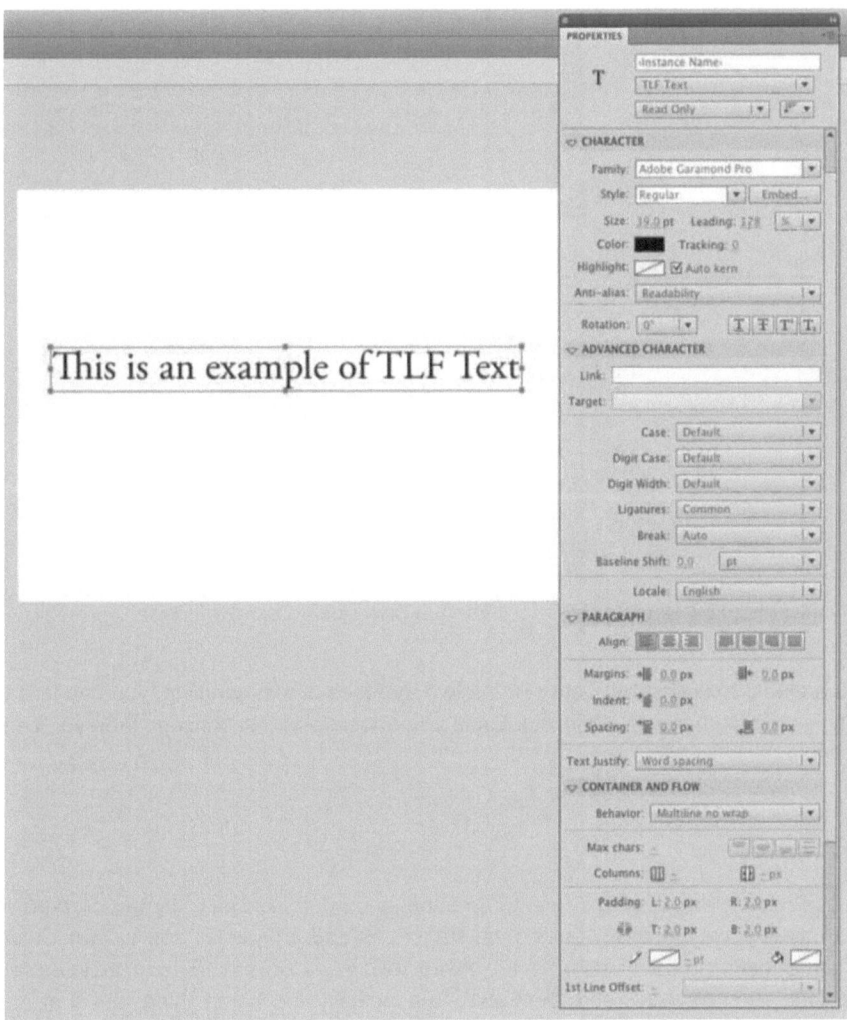

Figure 6-14. TLF Text puts some powerful typographic tools in your hands.

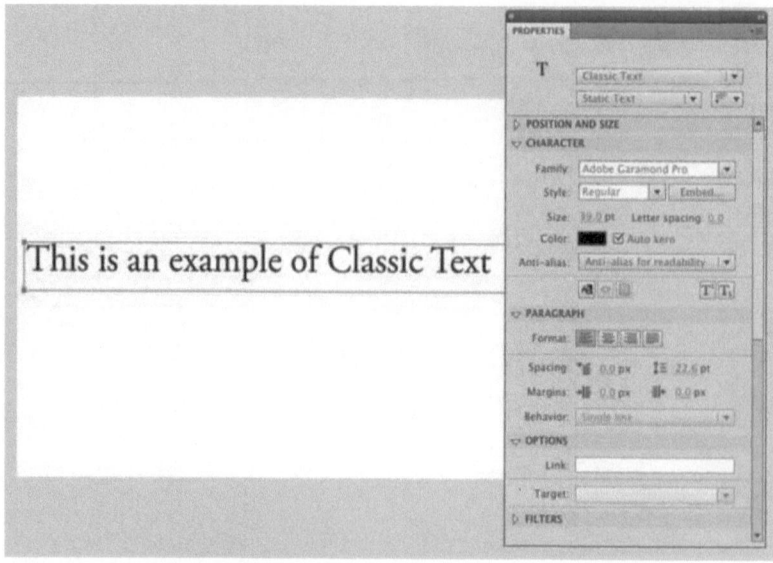

Figure 6-15. Classic Text is how text was formatted in previous versions of Flash.

Now that you are able to distinguish between the two methods of text handling, you can turn your attention to the three types of text that both work with. Once you understand this concept, then you can start playing with text.

Types of text

If you select `Classic Text` in the `Properties` panel and open the `Text Types` drop-down, you will be presented with three ways to classify text on the stage: `Static`, `Dynamic`, and `Input`. Select `TLF Text` and do the same thing, and your choices are `Read Only`, `Selectable`, and `Editable`. In a sense, `Dynamic`, `Input`, `Selectable`, and `Editable` are actually the same thing, but that only matters in terms of ActionScript. In relation to the `Properties` panel, static and read-only text fields contain text that won't be edited after the SWF is published, dynamic text fields contain text that will (or can), and input text fields contain text that is entered by the user. Each classification carries its own characteristics, much of which is shared among all three. Let's get to our penmanship!

> *From this point onward in this chapter, we are going to work with the TLF feature rather than Classic Text. This is not because TLF is so "cool." It is strictly because TLF is so new that dealing with both Classic and TLF text would require more than one chapter in the book.*

Read-only text properties

Read-only text is the least powerful sort of text in Flash, but don't let its humble nature fool you. If you're into racing, it's also true that horses run slower than cheetahs, but why split hairs?

As with most other tools in the `Tools` panel, the `Properties` panel, shown in Figure 6-16, controls text field properties in a big way, so let's take a look at each configurable item outside of the already familiar `Position and Size` properties.

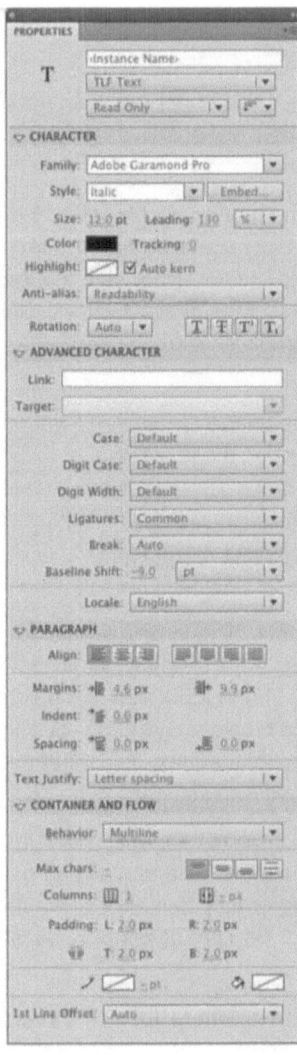

Figure 6-16. The `Properties` panel and read-only text

Character properties

The following properties are in the `Character` category:

- **Family**: This lets you select from the list of fonts installed on your computer. With static text, in most cases, font outlines are included with the SWF. For that reason, it doesn't matter whether your audience has the same font installed. The only exception is when you use the first three device fonts (the ones with the underscores). This setting marks the first of many that may be applied more than once, and in various ways, in the same text field.

> *TLF Text does not support PostScript Type 1 fonts. It only supports TrueType and OpenType fonts. If you choose a PostScript font, Flash will substitute the PostScript font for a device font such as _sans.*

- **Style**: Most typefaces contain Regular, Bold, Italic, and other variants. To apply a style to the whole text field, choose the `Selection` tool, click the text field, and then make your selection. To apply a style to individual words or characters, use the `Text` tool to select the text field, highlight the desired glyphs, and then select the desired variant. Bold and italic versions of the chosen font must exist on your computer for this styling to occur.

> *The Style drop-down menu replaces the B and I buttons traditionally used to specify bold or italic variants. It also groups the font families. Prior to this release, each font was its own entry in the Font drop-down list. If you are a font junkie, this resulted in a font list that seemed to stretch for meters. Now the variations of the font, such as the Italic shown in Figure 6-16, are in one neat, tidy package.*

- **Size**: This sets the selected font's size, in points. Multiple font sizes are allowed within the same text field. The scrubber ranges from 8 points to 96 points, but you may type in other values directly, anywhere from 0 (invisible) to 2,500 (jaw-droppingly way huge). This includes noninteger values, such as 12.75. In cases between 1,800 points and 2,000 points, the glyphs of most fonts "jump outside" the bounding box of their text fields, but this doesn't seem to affect text rendering; it merely makes the text field harder to select.

- **Leading**: This determines the uniform distribution of space between lines of text. The higher the number, the wider apart the lines, and vice versa. You get to choose between specifying leading as a percentage of the type size or as points. For example, you can choose to add 2 points or 20 percent leading to 10-point text. Be careful with this because the values between the two options can be different.

- **Color**: Want fuchsia text? Here's where to make that statement. Multiple colors are allowed within the same text field.

- **Highlight Color**: Think of this as being able to choose the color of a highlighter pen.

- **`Tracking`**: Also known as **letter spacing**, this value determines the uniform distribution of space between glyphs. The higher the number, the wider apart the characters, and vice versa. If you want, you can even squish letters together by using a negative number. Typographers have a term for this: **crashing text**. Multiple `Letter Spacing` settings may be applied to the same text field.

- **`Auto kern`**: This check box toggles auto-kerning. What is **kerning**? This is in the same ballpark as letter spacing, except kerning refers to individualized spacing between pairs of glyphs. Consider the capital letters *A* and *V*: the bottom of the *A*'s right side extends out, which fits neatly under the "pulled-in" bottom of the *V*. Kerning reduces the space between these and other glyphs that "fit together" in this way, which tends to provide greater visual balance.

- **`Anti-alias`**: Flash Player 8 introduced a number of new visual effects, and one of those was improved text rendering. This enhancement lives on in Flash Player 10, the player that corresponds to the default publish settings for Flash CS5. You have three anti-aliasing choices for font rendering:

    - **`Use device fonts`**: This relies on the user having your chosen font installed. Unlike the three device fonts mentioned earlier (`_sans`, `_serif`, and `_typewriter`), this setting uses exactly the font you specify—provided it is available on the computer playing the SWF file. If not, Flash makes the choice.

    - **`Readability`**: New since Flash 8, this format improves readability of small- and regular-sized fonts. Text animates smoothly because alignment and anti-aliasing are not applied while the text animates (it is reapplied when animation stops). This advanced anti-aliasing is not supported in Flash Player 7 or earlier SWFs, in skewed or flipped text (rotated is OK), in printed text, or in text exported as PNG. Under these circumstances, the normal anti-aliasing (`Anti-alias for animation`) is applied.

    - **`Animation`**: This provides normal text anti-aliasing. Glyphs appear smooth (no jaggies) and may be applied to text fields in older versions of Flash Player.

- **`Rotation`**: You get three choices: `Auto`, `0`, and `270`. This feature is not exactly what you would assume it is used for. It is to be used where there is a combination of Roman and Asian text where characters must be rotated to display properly in a vertical layout. Referred to as **tate-chu-yoko** (also called **kumimoji** and **renmoji**), this feature makes it easier to read half-width characters such as numbers, dates, and short foreign words in vertical text.

- **`Underline`, `Strikethrough`, `Superscript`, and `Subscript`**: Select a word or glyph, and click one of these buttons to apply these styles.

To see a `Read Only` text field in action, start a new Flash document, select the `Text` tool, choose `TLF` as the `Text type` in the `Properties` panel, and click somewhere on the stage. Type your name. Select the second letter of your name by dragging the mouse from one side of the letter to the other. Change the font. Select the third letter, and change the font again.

Notice that the text field automatically widens as you type. The indicator for this is the little white circle in the bottom-right corner of the text field, as you can see in Figure 6-17. If you keep typing, the text field will eventually extend past the stage and off into the wild blue yonder. To set a specific width, which causes text to wrap, hover over that white circle until you see the double-headed arrow cursor. Click and drag to the desired width. The white circle turns into a white square. To switch back to auto-widen mode, double-click that square.

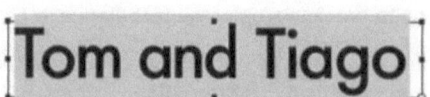
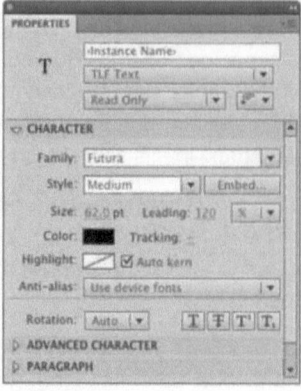

Figure 6-17. A white dot tells you the text field will widen as you type.

Advanced character properties

These choices, with one exception, are new to Flash CS5. Here's what they do:

- **Link and Target**: These settings, which have been around for a very long time, allow you to create hyperlinks inside text fields. Either select the whole text or use the mouse to select individual glyphs or words, and then type a URL into the **Link** field (such as `http://www.VisitMe.com/`). Entering anything at all into the **Link** field activates the **Target** field below it, which gives you the same four choices available to HTML anchor tags (`<a>`):

  - **_blank**: Opens the URL in a new browser window.
  - **_parent**: Opens the URL in the parent frameset of an HTML frameset (this assumes the SWF is embedded in an HTML page that appears in multiple framesets).
  - **_self**: Opens the URL in the same window or frame as the current HTML document that holds this SWF. This is the default behavior.
  - **_top**: Opens the URL in the topmost window of a frameset, replacing the frameset with the new URL.

Hyperlinks in the **Link** field do not change the appearance of the text in any way, even though a dashed line appears under hyperlinked text during authoring. This differs from HTML hyperlinks, which are traditionally differentiated by an underline and a change in color. Flash hyperlinks are primarily meant for loading HTML documents, which may or may not contain additional Flash content. As a general rule, this is not the place to load external SWFs into the current movie.

- **Case, Digit Case, Digit Width**: These three choices allow you to format numbers. When used with OpenType fonts (the ones with an O in the **Family** drop-down) that offer both *lining* and *oldstyle* numbers, you choose the style to apply in the **Case** drop-down and whether to use proportional or tabular numerals using the **Digit Case** and **Digit Width** options in their respective drop-down menus. So, how does all of this work?

Oldstyle figures, shown in Figure 6-18, are a type of numeral, which approximates lowercase letterforms by having an x-height and varying lengths in their ascenders and descenders. They are considerably different from the more common "lining" (or "aligning") figures shown in Figure 6-18 that are all-cap height and typically monospaced in text faces so that they line up vertically on charts. Oldstyle figures have what is considered to be a traditional, classic, almost calligraphic look. They are available only for certain typefaces, sometimes as the regular numerals in a font, but more often within a supplementary or expert font. The figures are proportionately spaced, eliminating the white spaces that result from monospaced lining figures, especially around the numeral one.

Oldstyle – Goudy Old Style:

0123456789$

Lining – Minion Pro

0123456789$

Figure 6-18. The fundamental differences between oldstyle and lining numerals are evident in the numbers 4 and 7.

- **Ligatures**: This moves into the realm of advanced typography for people new to the subject. Ligatures are typographic replacement characters for certain letter pairs, such as **fi** and **fl**, when they are available in a given OpenType font. With OpenType fonts, when you choose **Common** from the **Ligatures** drop-down menu, you will see the standard ligatures built into the font, as determined by the font designer. However, some fonts, such as **Hypatia Pro**, shown in Figure 6-19, include more ornate, optional ligatures, which can be produced when you choose the **Minimum**, **Uncommon**, or **Exotic Ligatures** options. As you can see from Figure 6-19, the ligature style chosen tends to tighten up or appear to condense a line of text.

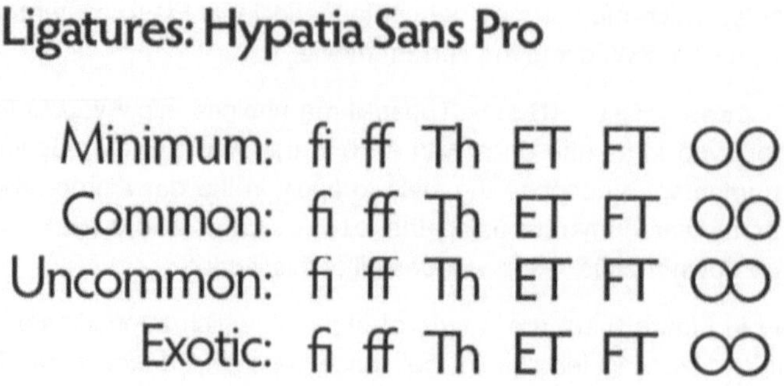

Ligatures: Hypatia Sans Pro

Minimum: fi ff Th ET FT OO
Common: fi ff Th ET FT OO
Uncommon: fi ff Th ET FT ∞
Exotic: fi ff Th ET FT ∞

Figure 6-19. A selection of ligatures and how the various `Ligature` options affect the ligatures

- `Break`: You can prevent words from breaking at the end of lines—for example, proper names or words that could be misread when hyphenated. You can also keep multiple words or groups of words together—for example, clusters of initials and a last name. To use the options in the drop-down menu, select the word or group of words you don't want to break and select an option.

> *Be very careful with this option. If you apply the No Break choice to too many adjacent characters, the text may wrap in the middle of a word.*

- `Baseline Shift`: Select a range of letters or an entire line of text, and by changing the value, the selection moves above or below the baseline. The drop-down menu allows you to choose points or a percentage for the amount as well as to treat the selection as superscript or subscript text.
- `Locale`: This has absolutely nothing to do with spelling or localization. The language chosen will set the typographic rules that apply to the language chosen.

Paragraph properties

These are the `Paragraph` properties:

- `Align Left`, `Align Center`, `Align Right`, `Align Justify`: These buttons in the `Format` area only make practical sense when applied to fixed-width text fields. In cases where your words wrap, this determines how they do it. `Align Left` means the left edge of your lines of text will be even. `Align Center` means your lines will be centered inside the text field. `Align Right` means the right edge will be even. `Align Justify` means both the left and right edges will be even. The four justification buttons to the right let you determine how the last line or word of a paragraph will be justified. Different alignments may be applied to each line of text in a text field.
- `Margins`: Scrub across these values, and you can add space to the right and the left of a text block.

- **Indent**: Select the first line of a text block and scrub across the indent value, and the selection will move inward (positive values) or outward (negative values).

- **Spacing**: Scrub across the spacing values to add spacing between paragraphs to the top or bottom line of the paragraph. This adds space between paragraphs to make the text look less cramped.

- **Text Justify**: Your two choices are **word** and **letter** spacing if text is to be justified. Letter spacing spreads all the letters out across the text block. Word spacing adds the space between the words. Both are dangerous choices, and our advice is to apply text justification with care and to keep the added spacing between words or letters to a minimum.

Container and flow

If any one aspect of text management in Flash hits the proverbial "sweet spot," this just may be it. This feature of the Text Layout Framework allows you to create multicolumn text and flow text between the columns. The really neat thing is you can create your own columns or break a single text box into multiple columns. Here's how:

1. Open the Containers.fla document in your Chapter 6 Exercise folder. When it opens, you will see a text block containing the first three paragraphs that opened this chapter.

2. Select the **Selection** tool, click the text block to select it, and, in the **Properties** panel, twirl down the **Container and Flow** options, as shown in Figure 6-20.

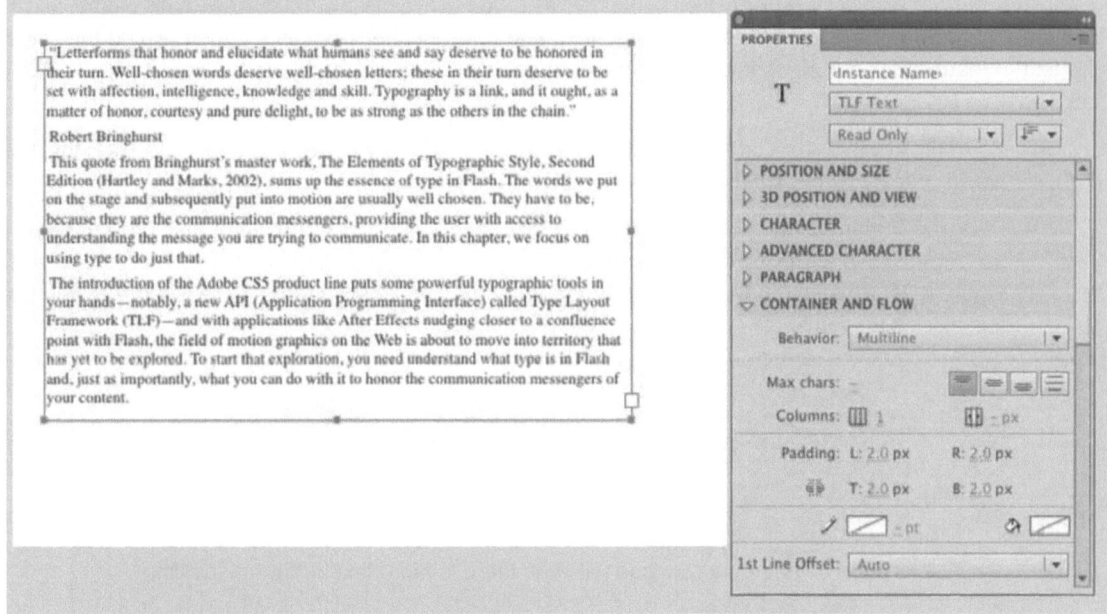

Figure 6-20. A single block of text is about to become a single block of multicolumn text.

3. Open the `Behavior` drop-down. The three choices—`Single Line`, `Multiline`, and `Multiline no break`—determine how the text will flow within the text box. Select each one, and see what it does. When you finish, make sure you have `Multiline` selected.

4. Double-click the hot text in the `Columns` category, and enter 2. Press the `Enter` key, and the text is now in two columns. Notice, too, that the `Gutter Width` now sports a value of 20 pixels. This value is the space between the columns.

5. Click the `Link` icon in the `Padding` area to apply the changes uniformly. Scrub across the `Left` padding hot text to see how padding affects the flow of the text in the columns.

6. Click the `Stroke` and `Fill` color chips, and select different colors. A stroke color is added to the edge of the text box, and you can scrub across the hot text to make the stroke thicker or thinner. The fill choice fills the text box or container. Set both the `Stroke` and `Fill` colors to `None`.

7. The final area is `1st Line Offset`, and the drop-down menu offers you a variety of choices ranging from manually setting a value to letting the software handle the duties for you. If you select `pt` from the drop-down menu and scrub across the hot text, you will see the top line of each column move down. This should tell you this feature lets you set the distance between the top edge of the container and the text. When you finish, select `Auto` from the drop-down.

8. Select `File ➤ Revert` to revert to the original one-column version of this file.

Now that you have had a chance to try this new feature, let's explore another, even cooler aspect of working with columns in Flash.

If you are familiar with InDesign or even QuarkXPress, you are quite aware of how multicolumn text is created. You draw out the text boxes, add some text, and then link them together. When you do this, all of the text in that first column flows into the other linked columns. This is exactly how it now works in Flash. Let's give it a try:

9. You should have the `Containers.fla` file open. Click the `Selection` tool, and click the text box. The text box or container sports those familiar handles.

10. Click the bottom-center handle of the text box, and drag it up to a point just under `Robert Bringhurst` in the text block. When you release the mouse a red box, the `Flow` icon shown in Figure 6-21, appears on the left edge of the text box. This tells you that there is more text in this text block than you see.

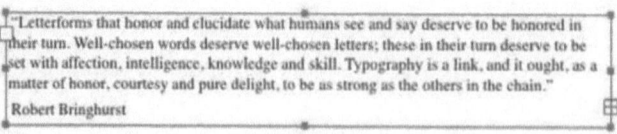

Figure 6-21. The location of that red `Flow` icon tells you there is more text below the last line.

11. Click the `Flow` icon. Your cursor will change from the pointer to what looks like a text box. Click the stage just under the text box. That new icon told you the text was "loaded," and when you clicked the mouse, another text box appears. Inside that new box is the loaded text, and an arrow, shown in Figure 2-22, appears, which shows you the text is flowing from the top container to the new one.

> *To remove a link, double-click the `Flow` icon on either side of the connecting line.*

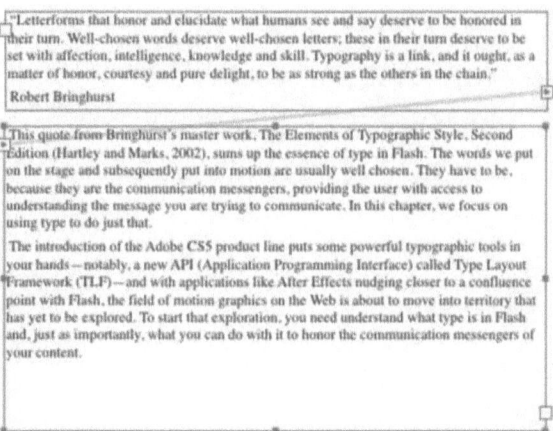

Figure 6-22. An arrow indicates how the text flows from one container to another.

12. Click the new text box, and in the `Container and Flow` options choose 2 columns. You now have the quote in a single text box and the paragraphs after it spanning two columns. Let's make the quote in the top text container a little prettier.

13. Select the quote (including the quotation marks), twirl down the `Character` properties, and choose `Italic` from the `Style` drop-down. Change the size to `14` points, and set `Leading` to `120%`.

> *If text moves between linked containers, expand or contract the containers by clicking and dragging one of the resize handles. The text that shifted will move back into its proper location.*

14. Twirl down the `Paragraph` settings, and set the `Indent` value to 3 pixels and the `Space after paragraph` value to `4.5`.

15. Twirl down `Container and Flow`. Click the `Lock` icon in the `padding` area, and change the `Left` value to 10 pixels. Set the `1st Line Offset` value to 10 points.

16. Select the words `Robert Bringhurst`, and in the `Character` area, choose `Bold Italic` from the `Style` drop-down. The entire text block shown in Figure 6-23 is a lot more inviting than the one we started with in Figure 6-22.

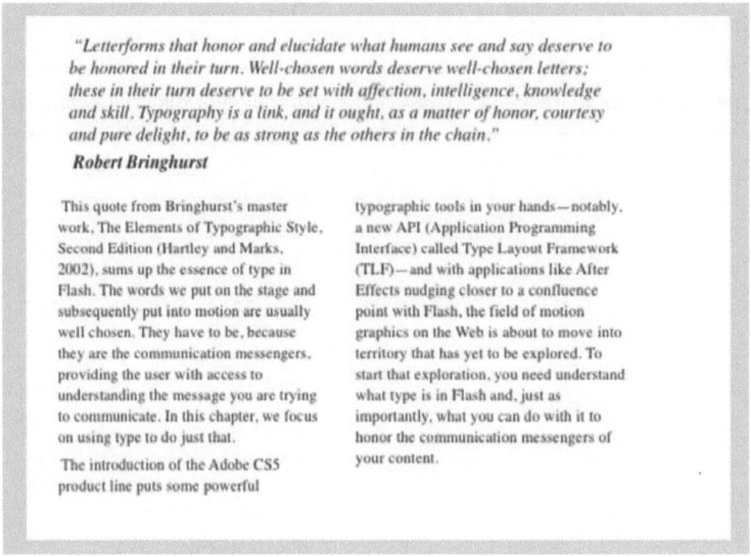

"*Letterforms that honor and elucidate what humans see and say deserve to be honored in their turn. Well-chosen words deserve well-chosen letters; these in their turn deserve to be set with affection, intelligence, knowledge and skill. Typography is a link, and it ought, as a matter of honor, courtesy and pure delight, to be as strong as the others in the chain.*"

Robert Bringhurst

This quote from Bringhurst's master work, The Elements of Typographic Style, Second Edition (Hartley and Marks, 2002), sums up the essence of type in Flash. The words we put on the stage and subsequently put into motion are usually well chosen. They have to be, because they are the communication messengers, providing the user with access to understanding the message you are trying to communicate. In this chapter, we focus on using type to do just that.

The introduction of the Adobe CS5 product line puts some powerful typographic tools in your hands—notably, a new API (Application Programming Interface) called Type Layout Framework (TLF)—and with applications like After Effects nudging closer to a confluence point with Flash, the field of motion graphics on the Web is about to move into territory that has yet to be explored. To start that exploration, you need understand what type is in Flash and, just as importantly, what you can do with it to honor the communication messengers of your content.

Figure 6-23. The Text Layout Framework drops some amazingly powerful tools into your hands.

Selectable and editable text

What makes selectable text and editable text different from their read-only counterpart? From the point of view of the `Properties` panel, not a whole lot. Change the text type setting to `Dynamic Text`, and nothing really changes. Change it to `Editable`, and the `Link and Target` areas of the `Advanced Character` properties area of the `Properties` panel disappears.

The major difference is not when you create the text; it becomes evident at runtime when the SWF is playing. **Selectable text** lets your user select the text in the container and copy it to the clipboard. All of the formatting applied in the `Properties` panel is in play when you run the SWF, but it is lost when the text is copied from the container to the clipboard. Use selectable text when you want the user to be able to grab text from your SWF and use it elsewhere. A good example would be tutorial sites where you can copy the code presented, paste it into a text document, and get back to it later.

Editable text is text that can be edited in the SWF. The best way of thinking of this type is as an input box in a form. This means you can enter text, change words, and so on, while the SWF is running. That's the good news. The bad news is changes are hardwired into the SWF, which means you can't choose Undo or use Ctrl+Z (Windows) or Cmd+Z (Mac) if you make a mistake.

TLF and ActionScript

A lot has changed between how text was handled in Flash CS4 and Flash CS5. We think now is a good time to pull up a stool, sit down, and review, in very broad terms, what one needs to know before "wiring up" an exercise or project using ActionScript.

As you have seen, text is found in these things called **containers**. They either can be physically drawn on the stage using the **Text** tool and given an instance name or, as is more common, can be created at runtime. You also know that the text can be formatted and manipulated using the **Properties** panel. The neat thing here is the word *properties*. If there is a property in the panel, its counterpart is found in ActionScript. The bad news is, ActionScript is stone, cold stupid. It doesn't have a clue, for example, what a container is until you tell it to create one. It won't format text until you tell it what to do. It won't even put the text on the stage until it is told to do so.

Most projects will start with you telling Flash to create a Configuration() object, which is used to tell Flash there is a container on the stage and how to manage the Text Layout Framework for the stuff in the container. The actual appearance is handled by the TextFlow() class, which takes its orders, so to speak, from the Configuration() object.

Naturally, being stupid, the Configuration() object needs to be told exactly how to manage the text in the container. The default format is set through a property of the Configuration class called textFlowInitialFormat. To change it, you simply use the TextlayoutFormat () class to set the fonts, colors, alignment, and so on, and then tell the boss—Configuration ()—that its textFlowInitialFormat has changed to the ones you set using TextLayoutFormat().The boss will get that, but he isn't terribly bright, so you next need to tell him to hand the actual work to another member of the management team, the TextFlow() class. This class has overall responsibility for any words in a container. Being just as dim as the boss, TextFlow() needs to be told what a paragraph is (ParagraphElement), how wide the paragraph is (SpanElement), whether any graphics are embedded in the paragraph (InLineGraphicElement), whether any of the text contains links (Link Element), and so on. Not only that, but it needs to be told what text is being added to the container so it can handle the line length and to add any children (addChild) that contain that formatting so the user can actually see it.

The TextFlow() class, again not being too terribly bright, will then hand the job over to another member of the management team, the IFlowComposer() class, whose only job is to manage the layout and display of the text flow within or among the containers. The flow composer finishes the process by deciding how much text goes into a container and then adds the lines of text to the sprite. This is accomplished through the use of the addController() method, which creates a ContainerController() object whose parameters identify the container and its properties.

The usual last step is to tell the FlowComposer to update the controllers and put the text on the stage according to how the other members of the team have told the Configuration() object how their piece of the project is to be managed.

With this information in hand, let's move on to working with TLF in ActionScript.

Creating a column of text with ActionScript

To create a column of text with ActionScript, follow these steps:

1. Open a new Flash ActionScript 3.0 document, rename `Layer 1` to `actions`, select the first frame of the `actions` layer, and open the `Actions` panel.

2. Click once in the `Script` pane, and enter the following:

```
var myDummyText:String = "The introduction of the Adobe CS5 product line puts some powerful typographic tools in your hands-notably, a new API (Application Programming Interface) called Type Layout Framework (TLF)-and with as more tools in the Adobe line up nudge closer to a confluence point with Flash, the field of typographic motion graphics on the Web is about to move into territory that has yet to be explored. To start that exploration, you need understand what type is in Flash and, just as importantly, what you can do with it to honor the communication messengers of your content.";
```

You need some text to add to the stage. This string is the third paragraph of this chapter.

3. Now that you have the text to go into the container, you need to load the class that will manage it. Press the Enter (Windows) or Return (Mac) key, and add the following line of code:

```
var config:Configuration = new Configuration();
```

As you may have noticed, as soon as you created the `Configuration()` object, Flash imported the class—`flashx.textLayout.elements.Configuration`—whose primary task is to control how TLF behaves. The next code block tells TLF how the text will appear on the stage.

4. Press the Enter (Windows) or Return (Mac) key twice, and enter the following:

```
var charFormat:TextLayoutFormat = new TextLayoutFormat();
charFormat.fontFamily = "Arial, Helvetica, _sans";
charFormat.fontSize = 14;
charFormat.color = 0x000000;
charFormat.textAlign = TextAlign.LEFT;
charFormat.paddingLeft =100;
charFormat.paddingTop = 100;
```

The `TextLayoutFormat` class, as we said earlier, is how the text in a container is formatted. The properties in this class affect the format and style of the text in a container, a paragraph, or even a single line of text. In this case, we are telling Flash which fonts to use, the size, the color, how it is to be aligned (note the uppercase used for the alignment), and the padding that moves it off the edges of the container.

> *Before you move on, you need you to do something. There is a coding issue. Scroll up to the import statements. If you see this line—`import flashx.textLayout.elements.TextAlign;`—proceed to the next code block. If you don't, delete this line in the code block just entered: `charFormat.textAlign = TextAlign.LEFT;`. Reenter `charFormat.textAlign =`. Type in the first two letters of the class (Te), press Ctrl+spacebar, and the code hint should appear. Find TextAlign, and double-click it. This should add the missing `import` statement. To preserve your sanity, we will be providing a list of the `import` statements that should appear at the end of each exercise. We strongly suggest that you compare your list of `import` statements against the list presented and, if you are missing any, add them into your code.*

5. Now that you know how the text will be formatted, you need to tell the `Configuration()` object to use the formatting. If you don't, it will apply whatever default setting it chooses. Press the Enter (Windows) or Return (Mac) key twice, and enter the following:

```
config.textFlowInitialFormat = charFormat;
```

6. Press the Enter (Windows) or Return (Mac) key, and enter the following code block:

```
var textFlow:TextFlow = new TextFlow( config );
var p:ParagraphElement = new ParagraphElement();
var span:SpanElement = new SpanElement();
span.text = myDummyText;
p.addChild( span );
textFlow.addChild( p );
```

The `TextFlow ()` object needs to be here because its job is to manage all the text in the container. The constructor—`TextFlow (config)`—lets TLF know that it is to use the `config` object created earlier so it now knows how to format the contents of the container and even the container itself.

The next constructor—`ParagraphElement()`—essentially tells Flash how a paragraph is to be handled. There is only one here, so it really doesn't need a parameter.

7. The final step is to get all the formatting and layout into the container on the stage. Press the Enter (Windows) or Return (Mac) key, and add these final two lines:

```
textFlow.flowComposer.addController( new ContainerController( this, 500, 350 ) );
textFlow.flowComposer.updateAllControllers();
```

The first line adds the `ContainerController` and tells Flash the container being managed is the current `DisplayObject` (`this`), which currently is the stage, and to set its dimensions to 500 pixels wide by 350 pixels high.

8. Save the project, and test the movie. The text, as shown in Figure 6-24, appears using the formatting instructions you set.

Import statements for this exercise

These are the `import` statements for this exercise:
```
import flashx.textLayout.elements.Configuration;
import flashx.textLayout.formats.TextLayoutFormat;
import flashx.textLayout.formats.TextAlign;
import flashx.textLayout.elements.TextFlow;
import flashx.textLayout.elements.ParagraphElement;
import flashx.textLayout.elements.SpanElement;
import flashx.textLayout.container.ContainerController;
```

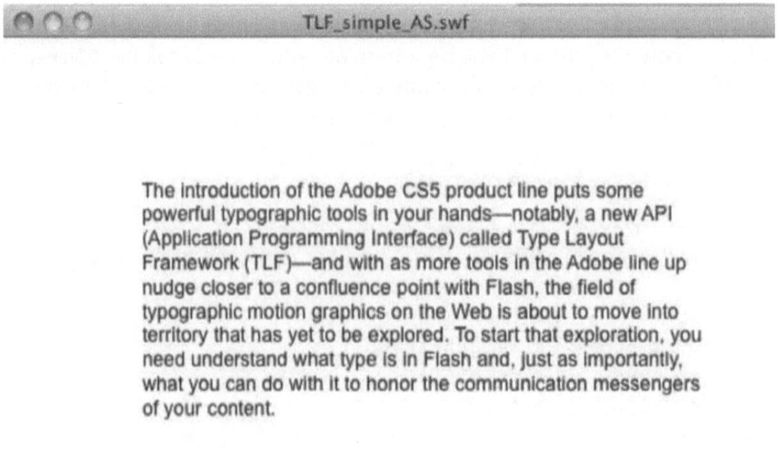

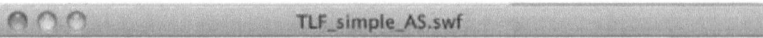

The introduction of the Adobe CS5 product line puts some powerful typographic tools in your hands—notably, a new API (Application Programming Interface) called Type Layout Framework (TLF)—and with as more tools in the Adobe line up nudge closer to a confluence point with Flash, the field of typographic motion graphics on the Web is about to move into territory that has yet to be explored. To start that exploration, you need understand what type is in Flash and, just as importantly, what you can do with it to honor the communication messengers of your content.

Figure 6-24. Using ActionScript to create and format the container and its text

> *The completed file for this exercise—TLF_simple_AS.fla—can be found in the Complete folder in this Chapter's Exercise folder.*

Though this coding task may, at first, appear to be a rather convoluted process, we can assure it isn't; it will become almost second nature as you start using ActionScript to play with text in the containers.

With the introduction of the Text Layout Format, your ability to create text, format text, put it in columns, and generally manipulate it using ActionScript has greatly expanded your creative possibilities. Before you get all excited about this, you need to know that the word *Framework* is there for a reason.

Any TLF text objects you create will rely on a specific TLF ActionScript library, also called a **runtime shared library** (RSL). When you work on the stage in the Flash interface, Flash provides the library. This is not the case when you publish the SWF and place it in a web page. It needs to be available, much like Flash Player, on the user's machine. When the SWF loads, it is going to hunt for the `Library` in three places:

- **The local computer**: Flash Player looks for a copy of the library on the local machine it is playing on. If it is not there, it heads for Adobe.com.

- **Adobe.com**: If no local copy is available, Flash Player will query Adobe's servers for a copy of the library. The library, like the Flash Player plug-in, has to download only once per computer. After that, all subsequent SWF files that play on the same computer will use the previously downloaded copy of the library. If, for some reason, it can't grab it there, it will look in the folder containing the SWF.

- **In the folder containing the SWF**: If Adobe's servers are not available for some reason, Flash Player looks for the library in the web server directory where the SWF file resides. To provide this extra level of backup, manually upload the library file to the web server along with your SWF file. We provide more information around how to do this in Chapter 15.

When you publish a SWF file that uses TLF text, Flash creates an additional file named `textLayout_X.X.X.XXX.swz` (where the Xs are replaced by the version number) next to your SWF file. You can optionally choose to upload this file to your web server along with your SWF file. This allows for the rare case where Adobe's servers are not available for some reason. If you open the file where you saved this exercise, you will see both the SWF and, as shown in Figure 6-25, the SWZ file.

Figure 6-25. The `.swz` file contains the Text Layout Framework.

Using TLF text as a button

It should come as no surprise that you can use TLF text as a button to kick off an event in your movie. For example, you could have a text block on the stage that talks about a visit to Times Square in New York, and when the user clicks the phrase `Times Square`, a photo appears on the stage. In this example, you are going to click some text, and a yellow star you will create on the stage starts spinning. Here's how:

1. Open a new Flash ActionScript 3.0 document, and save it to your Chapter 6 Exercise folder as `TLF_eventLink_AS.fla`. Change the name of `Layer 1` to `Star`, and add a new layer named `actions`.

CHAPTER 6

2. Click once in the first frame of the `Star` layer. Click and hold on the `Rectangle` tool on your toolbar, and select the `PolyStar` tool.

3. In the `Properties` panel, twirl down the `Fill and Stroke` properties and set the `Stroke` value to `None` and the `Fill` value to `Yellow` (`#FFFF00`).

4. Twirl down the `Tool Settings`, and click the `Options` button to open the `Tool Settings` dialog box shown in Figure 6-26. Select `Star` from the `Style` drop-down, and enter 5 for the `Number of Sides`. Click OK to close the dialog box.

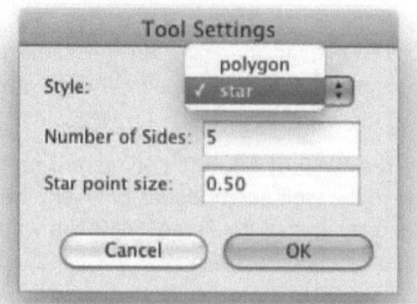

Figure 6-26. Use the `PolyStar` tool to create stars.

5. Draw a star somewhere in the bottom half of the stage, convert it to a movie clip named `Star`, set its registration point to `Center`, and in the `Properties` panel give the `Star` movie clip the `Instance name` of `starMC`.

6. Click the first frame of the `actions` layers, and open the `Actions` panel. When the panel opens, click once in the `Script` pane, and enter the following code block:

```
var containerSprite:Sprite = new Sprite();
this.addChild( containerSprite );
containerSprite.x  = 25
containerSprite.y = 50;
```

As we pointed out in Chapter 4, a `Sprite` is a virtual movie clip with no timeline. We start by creating a `Sprite` named `containerSprite`, which will be used to hold the text. The reason we need this is because there is going to be some interactivity involved. This `Sprite` is placed 25 pixels from the left edge of the stage and 50 pixels from the top.

7. Press the Enter (Windows) or Return (Mac) key twice, and enter the following code:

```
var container :ContainerController = new ContainerController( containerSprite, 400, 300);
var config :Configuration = new Configuration();

var charFormat:TextLayoutFormat= new TextLayoutFormat();
```

```
charFormat.fontFamily= "Arial, Helvetica,_sans";
charFormat.fontSize = 14;
charFormat.color = 0X000000;
charFormat.textAlign = TextAlign.LEFT;
config.textFlowInitialFormat = charFormat;
```

Nothing new here. The container for the text is created along with the `Configuration()` object, and the formatting for the text to be placed in the container is created.

   8. Press the Enter (Windows) or Return (Mac) key twice, and enter the following:

```
var textFlow :TextFlow = new TextFlow();
var p :ParagraphElement  = new ParagraphElement();
p.linkHoverFormat  = { color:0XFF0000 };
p.linkNormalFormat = { color:0x0000FF,textDecoration:TextDecoration.NONE };
```

The last two lines are new, and their purpose is to let you change the color of a word or group of words when the user rolls over them. The `linkHoverFormat` property belongs to the `TextFormat` class and is used to tell Flash what color the text identified as a link will be when the mouse rolls over it. In this case, the color will change to Red.

As you may have guessed, the second line tells Flash what color the link is to be when the mouse rolls off. In this case, it will be blue. Naturally, links are traditionally underlined. The way the underline is removed is to use the `NONE` constant, which is part of the `TextDecoration` class. If you want the underline, it would be `TextDecoration.UNDERLINE`.

   9. The next step in the process is to tell Flash what to do when the colored text is clicked. Press the Enter (Windows) or Return (Mac) key twice, and enter the following:

```
var link:LinkElement = new LinkElement();
link.addEventListener(FlowElementMouseEvent.CLICK, linkClicked);
```

   10. There is, of course, nothing to click. Let's deal with that issue. Press the Enter (Windows) or Return (Mac) key a couple of times, and add the following:

```
var linkSpan:SpanElement = new SpanElement();
linkSpan.text = "Click here" ;
link.addChild(linkSpan);

var span:SpanElement = new SpanElement();
span.text = " to see your star spin on the stage";
p.addChild(link);
p.addChild(span);
```

11. The next step is to get the text flowing into the container. Press the Enter (Windows) or Return (Mac) key, and add the following:

```
textFlow.addChild(p);
textFlow.flowComposer.addController(container);
textFlow.flowComposer.updateAllControllers();
```

12. The final code bit is the function that gets the star spinning when the text is clicked. Enter the following:

```
function linkClicked(evt:FlowElementMouseEvent) :void{
      evt.preventDefault();
      var tween :Tween = new Tween( starMC, "rotation", Elastic.easeOut, 0, 180, 2, true);
}
```

The first line of code tells Flash to ignore any default settings there might be in regards to the mouse and the text in the container.

The magic happens in that second line. The parameters tell the Tween class to work with the rotation property of the star (starMC) and to apply an easeOut to the star when it finishes rotating. Naturally, Flash, being stupid, needs to be told that the rotation starts with the star at 0 degrees and to rotate across 180 degrees. It does this two times and uses seconds as the measure of time.

13. Click the **Check Syntax** button as your first skim through the code looking for errors. If there are none, your computer will ding. If errors are found, they will be shown in the Compiler panel. The most common error will be spelling or a missing import statement.

> Here's a quick tip. If a class doesn't show up as an import, the Compiler panel will tell you the property is **undefined**. Select the class in the code where it appears, and delete the text. Type in the first two letters of the class, and press Ctrl+spacebar. The class will appear in the resulting code hint. Double-click the class to add it back into the code. This also creates the missing import statement.

14. Save and test the movie. The text, as shown in Figure 6-27, is colored. When you click the mouse, the star spins. A completed version of this file—TLF_eventlink_AS.fla—can be found in the Complete folder located in your Chapter 6 Exercise folder.

TEXT

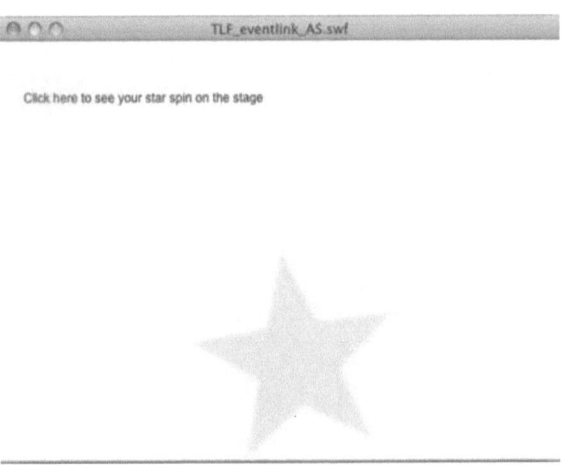

Figure 6-27. Text can be used to initiate events on the Flash stage.

Import statements for this exercise

These are the import statements for this exercise:
```
import flash.display.Sprite;
import flashx.textLayout.container.ContainerController;
import flashx.textLayout.elements.Configuration;
import flashx.textLayout.formats.TextLayoutFormat;
import flashx.textLayout.elements.TextFlow;
import flashx.textLayout.elements.ParagraphElement;
import flashx.textLayout.elements.LinkElement;
import flashx.textLayout.elements.SpanElement;
import flashx.textLayout.events.FlowElementMouseEvent;
import fl.transitions.Tween;
import flashx.textLayout.formats.TextDecoration;
import fl.transitions.easing.Elastic;
import flashx.textLayout.formats.TextAlign;
```

Hyperlinks and TLF

Every type of TLF text in Flash—`Read Only`, `Selectable`, and `Editable`—supports hyperlinks. All it takes to add a link in a text container is to type in your text, select a few words, and enter the desired URL into the `Properties` panel, as shown in Figure 6-28. Optionally, you can enter a target as well. If you want the whole text container hyperlinked, use the `Selection` tool to select the container itself, and then use the `Link` and `Target` properties in the `Advanced Character` options area of the `Properties` panel in the same way.

CHAPTER 6

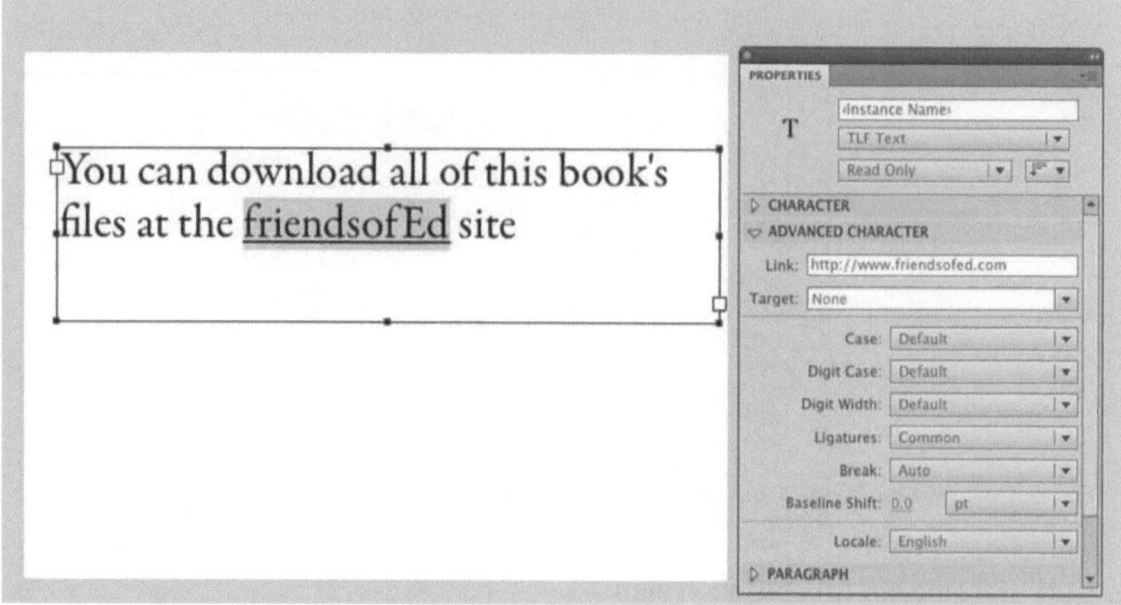

Figure 6-28. Applying a hyperlink to text

As easy as this approach is, a downside is the hyperlink underline added to the text. It simply can't be removed. Still, hyperlinks may be absolute, such as `http://www.SuperSite.com/thisPageHere.html`, or relative, such as `../thisOtherPage.html`. For relative paths, it's important to know that the path will be determined not from the point of view of the SWF, but from the HTML file that contains it. For example, you may choose to keep all your HTML files in the root of your website. Because you're an organized developer, you may choose to put all your image files in their own subfolder of the root, and you may just do the same with your Flash content. From a SWF's point of view, the relative path to all HTML files requires stepping back one folder. So, if a SWF links to one of those pages, you might be tempted to precede the destination's filename with `../`, but don't! The HTML file that contains the SWF in question is already in the same folder as the destination page, and it's the containing HTML file's point of view that matters.

Using ActionScript to add hyperlinks to TLF text

As you saw in the previous example, you can use a piece of text in a container to trigger an event on the Flash stage. It goes without saying that the same piece of text can be used to launch a web page. Rather than rehash everything done previously, open the `TLF_Hyperlink_AS.fla` file in your Chapter 6 `Exercise` folder, and let's see how this is accomplished.

1. Scroll down to line 32 of the `Script` pane. Select the word NONE, and change it to UNDERLINE. The result of this change is to actually have the clickable text look like a common HTML hyperlink that uses an underline.

2. Press the Enter (Windows) or Return (Mac) key twice, and enter the following code block:

```
var link:LinkElement = new LinkElement();
link.href = "http://www.friendsofed.com";

var linkSpan:SpanElement =new SpanElement();
linkSpan.text = "Click here ";
link.addChild( linkSpan);

var span:SpanElement = new SpanElement();
span.text = " to download the files for this book.";

p.addChild(link);
p.addChild(span);
textFlow.addChild(p);
```

As you may have gathered, all items in a TLF container are influenced or managed by elements. The first two lines establish that a variable called `link` will be managed by a `LinkElement` and will be placed in a `LinkElement()` object. The next line uses the common `href` tag from HTML to identify the link.

Now that you have established where the link is going—to the friends of ED website—you create a span for the text that will be clicked, put the text into the span, and use the `addChild()` method to put the `linkSpan` on the stage.

The rest of the code adds the remaining text, associates the link to the text in the sentence (p), puts the sentence on the stage, and flows it into the `textFlow` container.

3. Save the file, and test the movie. The text containing the link, as shown in Figure 6-29, is blue and sports a rather spiffy underline. Click the link, and the friends of ED homepage opens.

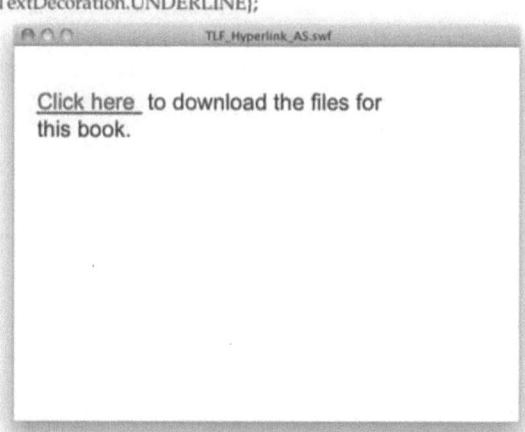

Figure 6-29. Using the **UNDERLINE** constant adds the common HTML underline users are used to.

Import statements used for this exercise

These are the `import` statements used for this exercise:
```
import flash.display.Sprite;
import flashx.textLayout.container.ContainerController;
import flashx.textLayout.elements.Configuration;
import flashx.textLayout.formats.TextLayoutFormat;
import flashx.textLayout.formats.TextAlign;
import flashx.textLayout.elements.TextFlow;
import flashx.textLayout.elements.ParagraphElement;
import flashx.textLayout.edit.EditManager;
import flashx.undo.UndoManager;
import flashx.textLayout.formats.TextDecoration;
import flashx.textLayout.elements.LinkElement;
import flashx.textLayout.elements.SpanElement;
```

Checking spelling

We'll admit it: if we enter text, we will inevitably use the wrong spelling for a word or two. Flash CS5 contains a tool that checks the spelling of all the text in a document. You don't have heartless editors peering over your shoulders as we do, so spell checking your work before sending it to the Web is a really good idea. It should therefore not come as too much of a surprise to discover that the spell-checking feature of Flash is quite robust. It allows you to check not only the spelling of the text in your text fields but also the spelling in your layer names.

If you have never used the spelling features of Flash CS5, you need to set up the spelling checker before you undertake your first spell check. Open a new Flash document, and select **Text ▶ Spelling Setup** to open the **Spelling Setup** dialog box, as shown in Figure 6-30. The **Document options** area sets up what spelling is to be checked, including any strings you may use in ActionScript. You can choose from a number of dictionaries and even create your own for commonly used words not found in a dictionary. The **Checking options** area permits you to decide which words or groups of words will be included or omitted from any spell checks.

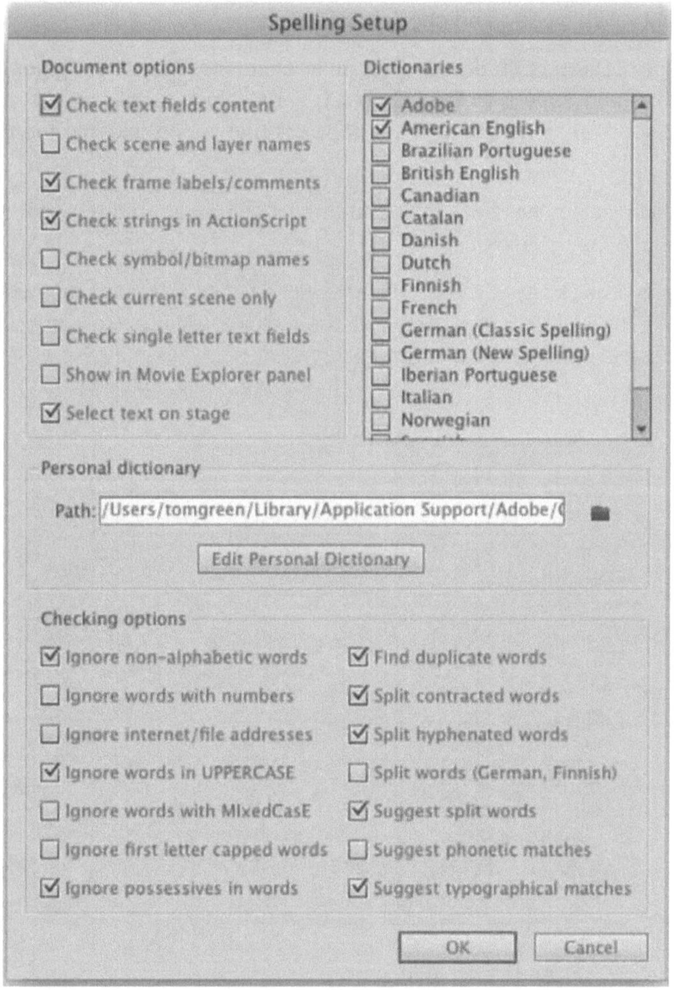

Figure 6-30. The `Spelling Setup` dialog box

> It is heartening for one of the authors to see a Canadian dictionary and a British English dictionary. Canadian and British English are understandably similar, but writing for publishers based in the United States can be a bit disorienting. For example, the word *color*, which is used extensively throughout this book, is not correct in the United Kingdom or Canada, where it is spelled colour. Another word used in the American English dictionary is the word check. This important method of payment is spelled cheque *in the Queen's English.*

Let's bring in some text—with typos—and check the spelling:

1. Open the `SpellItOut.txt` document in this chapter's `Exercise` folder in a word processor, select the text, and copy it to the clipboard. Large amounts of text are pasted into Flash. For better or worse, there is no ability in the application to import text into the library. Close the word processor.

2. Return to Flash, select the `Text` tool, and draw a container on the stage. Select `Edit ➤ Paste` to add the text to the container.

3. Select `Text ➤ Check Spelling`. The `Check Spelling` dialog box will appear, as shown in Figure 6-31. If the word is not recognized, the checker will provide you with a suggestion, which you can choose to either change or ignore.

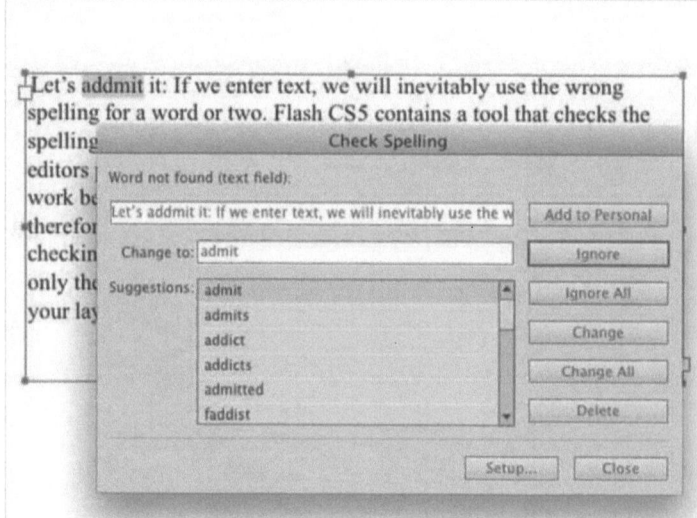

Figure 6-31. Using the `Check Spelling` dialog box

4. When you complete your spell check, click the `Close` button.

> *Although there is no language known as `Adobe`, the Flash dictionary is full of terms exclusively used by the Adobe products. A great example of an "Adobian" word is ActionScript. It wouldn't be flagged by the Adobe spelling checker but will be considered an error by most other spelling checkers.*

Your turn: scrollable text

The final two exercises in the chapter deal with one of the more frequently asked questions regarding text: "How do I scroll a large amount of text?" In fact, there are several ways of approaching this one. We'll look at two. The first is to use the `UIScrollBar` component, which, to quote a friend of ours, is "easy-peasy." The second is to "roll your own" scroller using ActionScript.

Before you start, let's get clear on the fact that the TLF container using a `ScrollBar` component will require you to embed all the fonts into the SWF if your `Anti-alias` option is `Readability`. This is ignored if the `Anti-alias` option is `Use device fonts`.

Using the UIScrollBar component

Let's start with the "easy-peasy" method: using the `UIScrollBar` component. We will talk about components in great depth in Chapter 11. For now, just work with us. In this particular case, no ActionScript is involved, which is why we're showing you the `UIScrollBar` component early. Components usually require a bit of programming.

1. Open the `ScrollComponent.fla` file in the Chapter 6 Exercise folder. You will see we have put some formatted text on the stage in a TLF container.

2. Select `Window ▶ Components`. From the `Components` panel, open the `User Interface` components, and select the `UIScrollBar` component, as shown in Figure 6-32. Drag a copy of it onto the text.

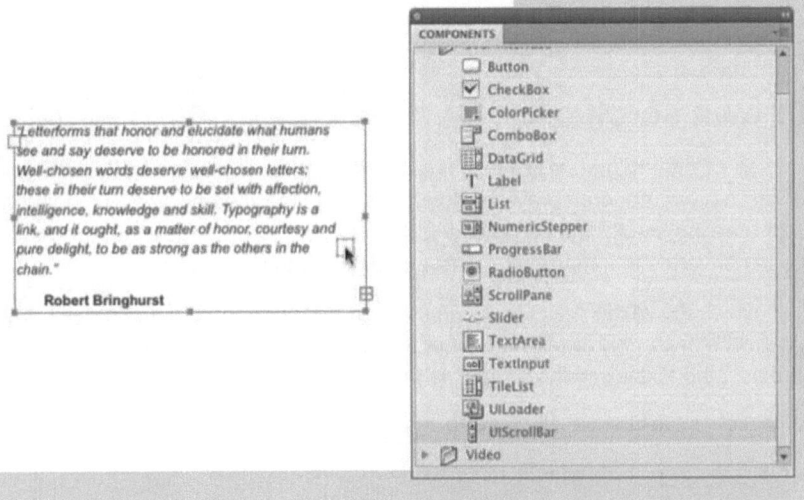

Figure 6-32. The `UIScrollBar` component is found in the `User Interface` components.

CHAPTER 6

3. Depending on which side of the text field you chose, the component will spring to the closest side of the text field. Switch to the `Selection` tool, and move it to the opposite side of the field. Now move it back to the right side of the field, and release the mouse.

4. Save and test the movie. You will see that you can scroll the text up and down, as shown in Figure 6-33.

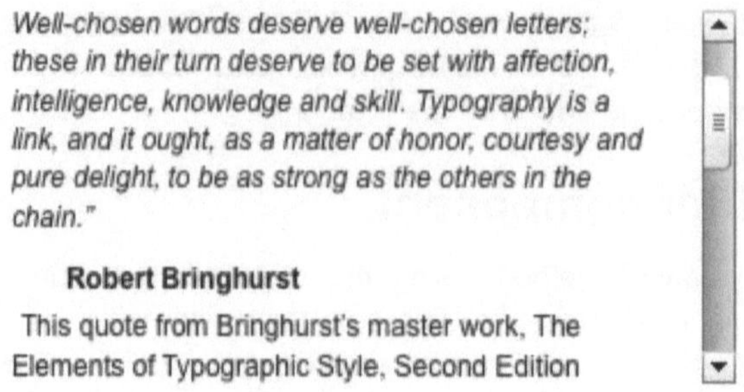

Well-chosen words deserve well-chosen letters; these in their turn deserve to be set with affection, intelligence, knowledge and skill. Typography is a link, and it ought, as a matter of honor, courtesy and pure delight, to be as strong as the others in the chain."

Robert Bringhurst

This quote from Bringhurst's master work, The Elements of Typographic Style, Second Edition

Figure 6-33. The `UIScrollBar` component in action

> *It would be a really good idea, if you are using this component to use the `Padding` and/or `Margins` options in the `Properties` panel, to pull the text away from the edges of the component. Select the text on the stage, and check out how we did it in the `Properties` panel.*

Rolling your own scroller

In this final exercise of the chapter, you are going to wire up a scroller using ActionScript. Just keep in mind that there are several hundred ways of doing this, and the method you are going to use is a very basic example of creating scroll buttons. In this example, you use a simple button created in Fireworks CS5 that has been converted to a movie clip. This button is found in the `Library`.

In this example in which the whole process is managed by ActionScript, the text moves up or down a short distance (one line) with each mouse press. Others may have the text move up or down until the mouse is released. Regardless, the text is scrolling, which is the point of this exercise. Let's get busy:

1. Open the `TLF_scrollable_AS.fla` file in this chapter's `Exercise` folder.

2. Open the `Library`, and right-click the `arrow` movie clip. When the context menu opens, select `Properties` to open the `Symbol Properties` dialog box.

3. Twirl down the **Advanced** options, and select **Export for ActionScript**. The word **arrow** should appear in the **Class** area. Click OK, and when Flash tells you there isn't such a thing as an **arrow** class, just click OK. By doing this, you have given the movie clip an instance name and let Flash know that it can be pulled out of the **Library** and used.

4. Select frame 1 of the **actions** layer, and open the **Actions** panel. Being the nice guys that we are, we have entered the text that will appear in the container. Everything else, though, is up to you. Click once in line 1 of the **Script** pane, and enter the following code that creates the sprites that will hold the arrow movie clip in the **Library**:

```
var upArrow:Sprite = new arrow();
var downArrow:Sprite = new arrow();
```

5. Next up you have to create the sprite that will hold the text container and put it on the stage. Click at the end of the text string, press the Enter (Windows) or Return (Mac) key twice, and enter the following:

```
var containerSprite: Sprite = new Sprite();
this.addChild(containerSprite);
containerSprite.x = 25;
containerSprite.y = 50;
```

6. Now that you have a sprite to hold the container, you need to put that container under the control of the ContainerController class and to set the size of the container. Press the Enter (Windows) or Return (Mac) key twice, and enter the following:

```
var container:ContainerController = new
ContainerController(containerSprite,400,300);
```

7. Scrolling can be accomplished by having the text move up and down (vertically) or from side to side (horizontally). You have to tell Flash that the text is to scroll vertically. Enter this line of code to accomplish that task:

```
container.verticalScrollPolicy = ScrollPolicy.ON;
```

8. With the ScrollPolicy out of the way, the next task is to let the Configuration class take over the management of the text in the container. Enter the following code:

```
var config:Configuration = new Configuration();
var myEditManager :EditManager = new EditManager( new UndoManager());
```

The second line is optional but answers a question that may have occurred to you as you went through these exercises: how does TLF text controlled by ActionScript switch from **Read Only** to **Selectable** or **Editable**? This line is how that task is accomplished.

9. Press the Enter (Windows) or Return (Mac) key twice, and let's format the text going into the container:

```
var charFormat: TextLayoutFormat = new TextLayoutFormat();
charFormat. fontFamily = "Arial,Helvetica,_sans";
charFormat.fontSize = 14;
charFormat.lineHeight = "160%";
charFormat.color = 0x000000;
charFormat.textAlign = TextAlign.LEFT;
config.textFlowInitialFormat = charFormat;
```

That fourth line is new. One of the TLF **Character** properties in the **Properties** panel is **Leading**. By setting the lineHeight property to 160%, you are essentially spreading out the lines of text by 22 points and making the text more readable.

10. With the text formatted, it needs to be treated as a paragraph. Enter the following code to accomplish that task:

```
var textFlow:TextFlow = new TextFlow(config);
textFlow.interactionManager = myEditManager;
var p:ParagraphElement = new ParagraphElement();
var span:SpanElement = new SpanElement();
span.text = myDummyText;
p.addChild(span);
textFlow.addChild(p);
textFlow.flowComposer.addController (container);
textFlow.flowComposer.updateAllControllers();
```

With the text out of the way, you can now turn your attention to the **arrow** movie clip and give it the ability to handle the vertical scrolling. Enter the following code:

```
createScrollButtons();
function createScrollButtons() :void{
     addChild(upArrow);
     upArrow.rotation = 180;
     upArrow.x = 500;
     upArrow.y = 75;
     upArrow.buttonMode = true;
     upArrow.addEventListener (MouseEvent.CLICK,downScroll);
     addChild(downArrow);
     downArrow.x = 500;
     downArrow.y = 325;
     downArrow.buttonMode = true;
     downArrow.addEventListener (MouseEvent.CLICK, upScroll);
};
```

```
function downScroll(evt:MouseEvent) : void{
      container.verticalScrollPosition -= 15;
}
function upScroll(evt:MouseEvent) : void{
      container.verticalScrollPosition += 15;
}
```

There isn't much new here except for one little "trick" and how to set how much the text scrolls with a mouse click.

The "trick" involves the upArrow sprite. The actual movie clip in the **Library** has the arrow pointing down. The rotation property applied to the upArrow sprite created in the first code line simply flips the arrow by rotating it 180 degrees.

The upScroller and downScroller functions that finish off the code use the verticalScrollPosition property to move the text up (+=15) or down (-=15) by 15-pixel increments each time the arrow is clicked. If you need larger or smaller increments, simply change the number.

11. Save and test the movie. When the SWF opens, as shown in Figure 6-34, note how much space there is between the lines of text and how it moves up or down when the arrow is clicked.

Import statements used for this exercise

The following are the import statements used for this chapter:
```
import flash.display.Sprite;
import flashx.textLayout.container.ContainerController;
import flashx.textLayout.container.ScrollPolicy;
import flashx.textLayout.elements.Configuration;
import flashx.textLayout.edit.EditManager;
import flashx.undo.UndoManager;
import flashx.textLayout.formats.TextLayoutFormat;
import flashx.textLayout.formats.TextAlign;
import flashx.textLayout.elements.TextFlow;
import flashx.textLayout.events.TextLayoutEvent;
import flashx.textLayout.elements.ParagraphElement;
import flashx.textLayout.elements.SpanElement;
import flash.events.MouseEvent;
```

CHAPTER 6

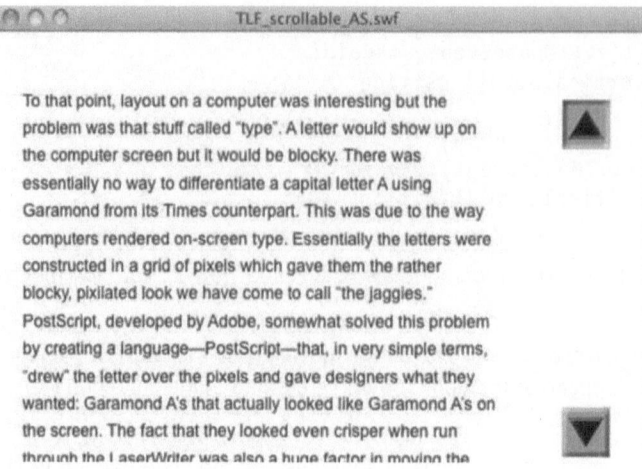

Figure 6-34. The `UIScrollBar` component in action

What you have learned

In this chapter, you learned the following:

- How to add text to Flash
- The various text-formatting features available to you in Flash CS5
- How to choose and work with the Text Layout Format
- The ActionScript necessary to create, format, and provide interactivity through the use of text
- When to embed font outlines into a SWF and how to accomplish that task
- How to create scrolling text in Flash

We suspect you are more than a little confounded at the possibilities open to you when it comes to using text in Flash. If you are one of those who saw text as the gray stuff hovering around your animations, we hope you have seen the error of your ways. And, if you are one of those who want to get going and turn out really cool motion graphics pieces, we hope you paid close attention to what Bringhurst was saying in the quote that opened this chapter. Regardless of which camp you fall into, we know that you are now aware that adding text to a Flash CS5 animation doesn't stop with a click of the `Text` tool and the tapping of a few keys on the keyboard.

Now that you know how to work with text and put it in motion, the time has arrived to put objects in motion. Animation in Flash is covered in the next two chapters, and to find out more, turn the page.

Chapter 7

Animation, Part 1

Ah, animation! Where would we be without the likes of Disney, Warner Bros., Walter Lanz, Hanna-Barbera, and dozens more like them? For many people, animation is *the* reason to get involved with Flash as a creative outlet. This makes perfect sense, because Flash began life more than a decade ago as an animation tool. Supplemental features like ActionScript, XML parsing, and video integration—every one of which is a tremendous addition—all followed. What hasn't changed in all these years is Flash's increasingly productive ability to help you create high-quality, scalable animation for the Web, and even for television and film.

You caught the faintest whiff of tweening in Chapters 1, 2, and 3. It gets considerably more complex—read *considerably more fun!*—because Flash CS5 gives you a double-dose of animation apparatus. You now have two independent tweening models to work with, the newer of which will make users of Adobe After Effects feel right at home. Each of these tweening models gets its own chapter in this book.

The original Flash approach, now called *classic tweening*, is covered here in Chapter 7. Chapter 8 delves into the new stuff. To get the most out of animation in Flash, you should read both chapters, starting with this one. As you'll discover, you can use both models in the same movie. You'll learn enough in these chapters to help you comfortably choose which approach, or combination of approaches, works best for your particular needs.

Here's what we'll cover in this chapter:

- Shape tweening
- Shape hinting

CHAPTER 7

- Classic motion tweening
- Easing
- Using the `Custom Ease In/Ease Out` editor
- Animating symbols
- Combining timelines
- Applying motion tween effects
- Using ActionScript to create and manage animations

The following files are used in this chapter (located in `Chapter07/ExerciseFiles_Ch07/Exercise/`):

- `PepperShape.fla`
- `StarStar.fla`
- `StarCircle.fla`
- `Ant.fla`
- `LogoMorphNoHints.fla`
- `FlowerWeed.fla`
- `GradientTween1.fla`
- `GradientTween2.fla`
- `BitmapFillTween.fla`
- `PepperSymbol.fla`
- `MalletNoEasing.fla`
- `MalletCustomEasing.fla`
- `CustomEasingComparison.fla`
- `CustomEasingMultiple.fla`
- `CuriousRabbit.fla`
- `SyncPropertyGraphic.fla`
- `EditMultipleFrames.fla`
- `CombineTimeline.fla`
- `Grotto.fla`
- `MotionGuide.fla`
- `MaskTween.fla`

- `MaskTweenMotionGuide.fla`
- `BlueMoon.fla`
- `CreateMotionAS3.fla`
- `KeyboardControl.fla`

The source files are available online at www.friendsofED.com/download.html?isbn=1430229940.

Because this chapter has a lot of moving parts, let's cut straight to the "without further ado" and jump directly into the fray!

Shape tweening

As useful as symbols are, both in organizing artwork and reducing SWF file size, they shouldn't overshadow the importance of shapes. After all, unless a symbol is the result of text or an imported image file, chances are good it was constructed from one or more of Flash's most basic of visual entities: the shape.

Shapes differ significantly from symbols, although many of their features overlap. Like symbols, shapes are tweened on keyframes. Tweening may be finessed by something called **easing** and can affect things such as position, scale, distortion, color, and transparency. The difference comes in how these changes are achieved. In addition, shapes can do something symbols can't: they can actually morph from one set of contours to another!

Scaling and stretching

Let's start with the basics:

1. Open the `PepperShape.fla` file in the Chapter 7 Exercise folder. You'll notice that there is nothing in the **Library**. This is because the hot pepper on the stage is composed entirely of shapes.

2. Select **Insert ➤ Timeline ➤ Keyframe** to insert a keyframe at frame 10. This effectively produces a copy of the artwork from frame 1 in frame 10 and makes the copy available for manipulation. Any changes you make to frame 10 will not affect the shapes in frame 1, so you can always remove that second keyframe (**Modify ➤ Timeline ➤ Clear Keyframe**) and start again from scratch if you desire.

> *If you prefer, you can insert a blank keyframe at frame 10 (**Insert ➤ Timeline ➤ Blank Keyframe**) and then copy and paste the artwork from frame 1. It makes no practical difference, but clearly the approach in step 2 requires less effort. You may even draw completely new shapes into frame 10, and Flash will do its best to accommodate—but that's skipping ahead. There's more on that in the "Altering shapes" section.*

CHAPTER 7

> *All of these menu choices have right-click (Windows) or Control+click (Mac) equivalents, available from the context menu of any timeline frame.*

3. With frame 10 selected, choose the `Free Transform` tool, and drag the right side of the pepper's bounding box to the right. As you do this, you'll see a live preview of the shapes—stem, leaves, and pepper—in their new stretched size, as shown in Figure 7-1.

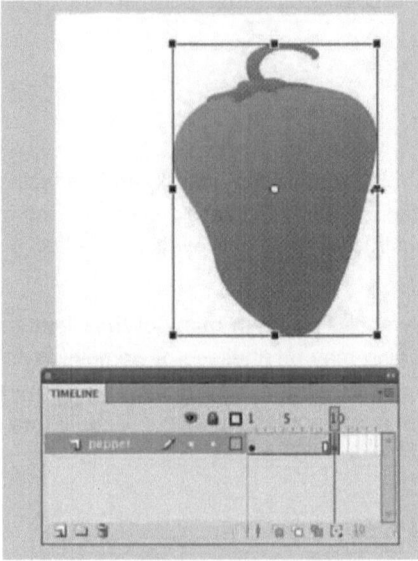

Figure 7-1. Changing a shape's shape in preparation for a shape tween

> *You might find that you have accidentally selected either only the pepper or only its cap. The `Free Transform` tool's bounding box will let you know at a glance which shape(s) you have selected, because either it will encompass the full surface area of the artwork or it won't. To ensure you've grabbed all the shapes, use the `Selection` tool to first draw a marquee (that is, a selection) around the whole pepper. An even simpler technique is to click the keyframe at frame 10, which selects everything on that layer in that keyframe.*

4. Select `Edit` ➤ `Undo Scale` to undo. (You might need to undo twice: once to reselect and once to remove the widen transform.)
5. Reapply the transform and hold down the Alt (Windows) or Option (Mac) key while dragging to the right. Notice how the artwork now scales out from the center.

ANIMATION, PART 1

This feature often comes in handy, but it's important to understand what's really going on. When the Alt (Windows) or Option (Mac) key is used, it's not the center of the artwork that becomes the pivot, but rather the **transformation point**, which is that small white circle in the middle of the pepper. You can drag this circle where you like, even outside the confines of the shape's bounding box. With or without the Alt (Windows) or Option (Mac) key, the transformation point acts as the fulcrum of your modifications, but using the key changes how the fulcrum is applied.

Because you're dealing with shapes, you can even use the `Free Transform` tool's `Envelope` and `Distort` options (shown in Figure 7-2), which aren't available for symbols. Right-click (Windows) or Control+click (Mac) the object selected by the `Transform` tool, and the options are shown in the `Context` menu. If you do, just be aware that things can quickly fall apart with such transformations unless you use shape hints, which are covered later in the chapter.

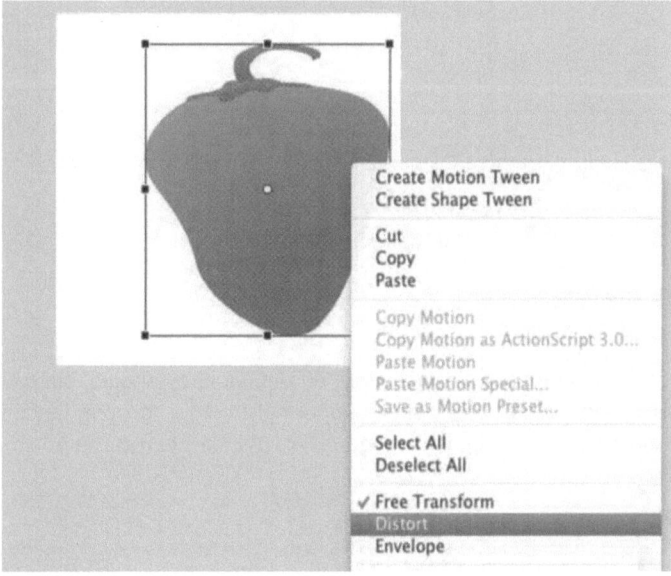

Figure 7-2. Shape transformations include `Envelope` and `Distort`.

6. Now that you have two keyframes prepared, it's time for the magic. Make sure the pepper is changed in frame 10 (for example, the widening applied in step 5). Right-click (Windows) or Control+click (Mac) anywhere in the span of frames between both keyframes, and select `Create Shape Tween` from the context menu (see Figure 7-3). Two things will happen:

    - The span of frames will turn green, which indicates a shape tween. They will also gain an arrow pointing to the right, which tells you the tween was successful.
    - The pepper will update to reflect a visual state between the artwork in either keyframe, depending on where the playhead is positioned.

7. Drag the playhead back and forth to watch the pepper seem to breathe.

CHAPTER 7

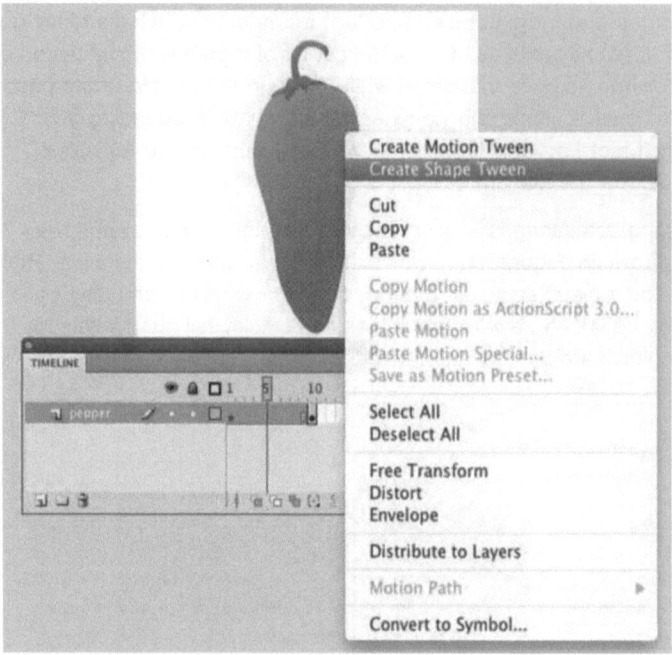

Figure 7-3. Applying a shape tween

If your tweened frames fail to turn green, don't worry. By default, they should, but crazier things have been known to happen. Click in the `Timeline` panel's upper-right corner to open its context menu and make sure `Tinted Frames` is selected, as shown in Figure 7-4. (All the hot rods have 'em.)

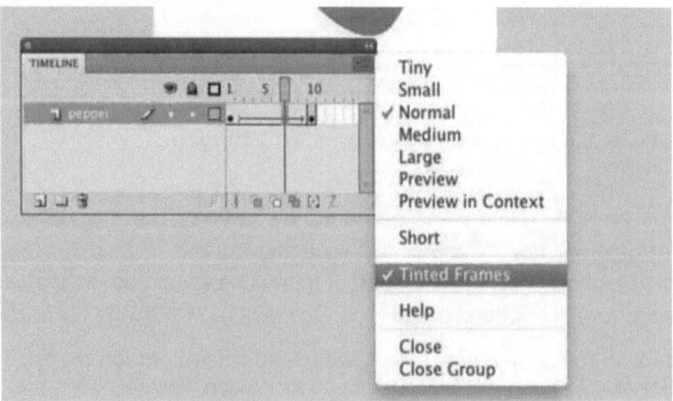

Figure 7-4. The `Tinted Frames` option helps you recognize tweened frames.

> *If you applied the tween while in frame 1—a perfectly legal choice, by the way—you wouldn't immediately see the pepper change. Why? Because the tweening is applied between the two keyframes, and frame 1 still represents the artwork as it was before tweening changed it. Drag the playhead back and forth, and you'll see the tween.*

8. Right-click (Windows) or Control+click (Mac) anywhere between the two keyframes, and choose `Remove Tween`. The tween goes away.

9. Let's try another tween. Right-click (Windows) or Control+click (Mac) your frame span, and choose `Create Motion Tween`. Motion tweening is not supported for shapes, and Flash gives you an unmistakable sign that you've gone wrong. You'll see an alert box that offers to convert your shape into a symbol, as shown in Figure 7-5. Click `OK`, and you'll see most of your frame span turn blue, along with the appearance of a new movie clip in the `Library`.

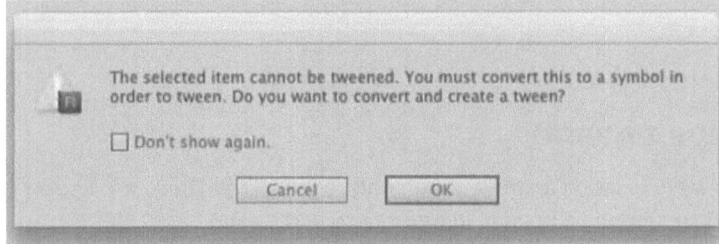

Figure 7-5. Tweens other than the shape variety require symbols.

It's nice that Flash does this for you, but generally speaking, you'll want to decide on your own what sort of symbol to create: movie clip, graphic, or button. Unfortunately, this automated process does the choosing for you.

Motion tweens are part of the new After Effects–like tweening model you'll learn about in Chapter 8. Motion tweens are nothing like shape tweens; they are an altogether different concept.

10. Select `Edit ➤ Undo Create Motion Tween` to step back. That sets the frames back and automatically removes the `Library`'s movie clip.

11. Time for another mistake. Right-click (Windows) or Control+click (Mac) your frame span, and choose `Create Classic Tween`.

Instead of green, the span of frames will become purple, and you'll see *two* new symbols in the `Library` (this time, graphic symbols)—without even a warning! Purple frames indicate a classic tween, which you'll learn about later in this chapter. These, too, are nothing like shape tweens.

12. Perform an undo, and the frames will revert to a nontweened state. You'll need to delete the graphic symbols by hand, though. Go ahead and do that by selecting them in the `Library` and clicking the `Trash Can` icon at the bottom of the `Library` panel.
13. Reapply a shape tween, and scrub to frame 10.
14. Select the `Free Transform` tool, and drag around one of the bounding box corners to change both the horizontal and vertical scales. If you like, hold down Shift to constrain the aspect ratio, and Alt (Windows) or Option (Mac) to apply changes from the center of the transformation point. Make the pepper a good bit bigger than the original size. This shows that it's possible to adjust keyframes even after they're already part of a tween.

> *Another way to apply shape tweens is to click between two keyframes and select* `Insert` ➤ `Shape Tween`. *To remove a shape tween, select* `Insert` ➤ `Remove Tween`. *You'll see that you can do the same with motion and classic tweens.*

Modifying shape tweens

There are a couple ways to refine a shape tween once it's applied. These are shown in the `Properties` panel when you click in a tweened span of frames: `Ease` and `Blend`.

Easing tends to make tweens look more lifelike because it gradually varies the amount of distance traveled between each frame. If an astronaut throws a golf ball in outer space, the ball flies at a constant rate until...well, until it hits something. That's not how it works on a planet with gravity. The ball flies faster at first and then gradually slows down. This deceleration is called **easing out**. A ball dropped from a tall building begins its descent slowly and then gradually increases speed. This acceleration is called **easing in**.

Click anywhere between two key frames of a tween, and adjust the `Ease` hot text in the `Properties` panel to see how easing affects the shape tween applied to the pepper in the previous exercise. Supported values range from `100` (strong ease out), through `0` (no easing), to `-100` (strong ease in). As shown in Figure 7-6, easing can have a profound effect upon an object in motion. We'll cover easing in greater detail in the "Classic tweening" section.

> *If you don't see much of a difference after experimenting with easing, try lengthening the duration of your shape tween. To do so, click somewhere in the tween span between the two keyframes, and then press the F5 key several times to insert new frames.*

ANIMATION, PART 1

Figure 7-6. Examples of easing, from top to bottom

The **Blend** pop down, directly under the **Ease** hot text, is a much subtler matter. There are two **Blend** settings: **Distributive** (the default) and **Angular**. According to Adobe, **Distributive** "creates an animation in which the intermediate shapes are smoother and more irregular," and **Angular** "creates an animation that preserves apparent corners and straight lines in the intermediate shapes." In actual practice, the authors find this distinction negligible at best. In short, don't worry yourself over this setting. Feel free to use the one with which you are most comfortable. We're willing to bet our hats you won't be able to tell one from the other.

So far, so good. These tweens have been pretty straightforward. In fact, as you'll find later in the chapter, everything you've seen to this point can be accomplished just as easily with classic tweens. This raises a good question: what makes shape tweens so special? Why not just use classic tweens or the motion tweens you'll learn about in Chapter 8?

The answer comes in two parts: gradients and shape. Let's tackle shape first, because it has the potential to set your teeth on edge if you aren't prepared for it.

Altering shapes

The compelling reason to use shape tweens is their ability to manipulate the actual form of the artwork itself, beyond scaling and stretching. Let's keep playing:

1. Continuing with `PepperShape.fla`, use the **Free Transform** tool at frame 10 to rotate the pepper about 90 degrees in either direction.

2. You should still have a shape tween applied (if not, add one). Drag the playhead back and forth to see a result that may surprise you. Rather than rotating, the pepper temporarily deforms itself as it changes from one keyframe to another (see Figure 7-7).

CHAPTER 7

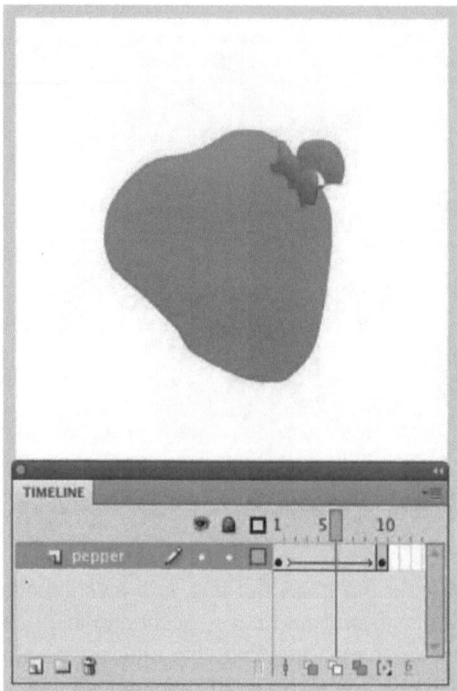

Figure 7-7. Sometimes shape tweens perform unexpected transformations.

What on Earth is going on here? Though it may look like an absolute mess, what you are seeing is the key distinction between shape tweening and the other kinds of tweening. Believe it or not, this behavior can be a very useful thing. You'll see an example in just a moment. First let's take a quick field trip to frame 10 in order to illustrate a point.

> *In case you're worried, we'll put your mind at ease without further ado: it is entirely possible to rotate artwork with tweens in Flash. In fact, it's easy. In contrast to shape tweens, classic and motion tweens maintain a strict marriage between the vector anchor points of one keyframe and the next. We'll show you why later in this chapter and in Chapter 8. When you understand what each approach does best, you'll know which one to use for the task at hand.*

3. Choose the `Subselection` tool, and click the edge of the pepper in frame 10. You'll see dozens of tiny squares that act as anchor points among the various lines and curves that make up the pepper's shape. All those points exist in frame 1 as well, of course, but they're in different positions relative to one another.

ANIMATION, PART 1

With shape tweens, Flash does not think of artwork in terms of a whole; instead, it manipulates each anchor point separately. What seems like a rotation to you is, to a shape tween, nothing more than a rearrangement of anchor points—sometimes a chaotic one, at that!

Think of it like a square dance. If a particular point happens to be in the upper-left corner on frame 1, it has no idea that its corresponding point may be in the upper-right corner on frame 10. It simply changes a partner—do-si-do!—and moves to a new spot during the tween. Like square dancing, there are sophisticated rules at play, and movement across the dance floor may appear unpredictable. It's possible, for example, that two keyframes may even present a completely different number of anchor points. Let's look at that next.

Examining anchor points

Open the StarStar.fla file in this chapter's Exercise folder, and examine the 22-point star in frame 1. Use the **Subselection** tool, if you like, to see the individual anchor points (there are 44). Click in frame 20 to see a seven-point star (14 anchor points). Note that a shape tween has already been applied between these two keyframes. Drag the playhead back and forth to watch the promenade (shown in Figure 7-8). Flash handles the reduction in anchor points in a neat, organized way. In this case, by the way, the star in the second keyframe was drawn as new artwork into frame 20.

Figure 7-8. The 44 anchor points artfully become 14.

Now open the StarCircle.fla file in this chapter's Exercise folder and run through the same steps to see a 22-point star become an 8-point circle. These are some nifty transformations that are simply not possible with classic tweens.

> *In Chapter 2, we described a vector circle as having five points: four on the perimeter and one in the center. So, why does the circle in this exercise have eight perimeter points? Frankly, because the Flash engineers know more about vectors than we do. Our discussion in Chapter 2 was for illustrative purposes.*

This opens up a whole avenue of vector-morphing possibilities, from sunshine gleams to water ripples to waving hair and twitching insect antennae.

Shape changing

For anything where you need the actual shape of an item to change—where anchor points themselves need to be rearranged—shape tweens are the way to go. Keep in mind that tweens happen on a keyframe basis, and timeline layers are distinct. If you have a complex set of shapes and you want to tween only some of them, move those shapes to a separate layer. In fact, you may want to put every to-be-tweened shape on its own layer, because that reduces the number of anchor points under consideration for each keyframe. Let's try it by setting some antennae in motion:

4. Open the Ant.fla file in this chapter's Exercise folder, and insert a keyframe in frames 15 and 30 of the **antenna1** layer.

5. Select the **Subselection** tool, and change the shape of the antenna in frame 30 of the antenna 1 layer.

6. Add a shape tween between the keyframes, and scrub through the timeline. The antennae move around (see Figure 7-9).

Figure 7-9. Need to change the shape of those antennae? Shape tweens to the rescue!

As you've seen, Flash can make some fairly stylish choices of its own in regard to the repositioning of anchor points. Well, that's true most of the time. The earlier pepper rotation demonstrates that Flash's choices aren't always what you might expect. Fortunately, Flash provides a way to let you take control of shape tweens gone awry. The solution is something called **shape hints**.

Shape hints

What are shape hints? Often overlooked or misunderstood, these useful contraptions allow you to specify a partnership between a vector region of your choosing from one keyframe to the next. They are a means by which you can guide an anchor point, curve, or line toward the destination you've determined is the correct one. Let's take a look.

1. Open the `LogoMorphNoHints.fla` file in this chapter's `Exercise` folder. Take a look at frame 1 to see a lowercase *i* that has been broken apart from a text field into two shapes. In frame 55, you'll see an abstract shape that represents a hypothetical logo.

2. The aim here is to morph between the shapes in an appealing way, but something has gone horribly wrong (see Figure 7-10). Drag the playhead along the timeline, and note the atrocities committed between frames 20 and 35.

Figure 7-10. Something has gone horribly wrong.

This looks as bad as (if not worse than) the hot pepper rotation, but why? On the face of it, this should be a basic shape tween. Seemingly, the letter and logo shapes aren't especially intricate, and yet, the timeline doesn't lie.

> At this point, the authors look deftly side to side, and with a sly, "Hey, pssst," invite you to step with them into a small, dimly lit alley. (Don't worry, we're here to help.) "The thing is," begins the first, "honestly, there's often a bit of voodoo involved with shape tweens, and that's the truth." "That's right," chimes in the other, lowering his voice. "To be frank, if I may"—you nod—"we don't know why these anchor points sometimes go kablooey. It's just a thing, and you have to roll with it." There is a slight pause, and suddenly a cappuccino machine splooshes in the distance. The first author draws a finger across his nose. "Keep that in mind as we continue," he says. Another pause. "You wanna see the shape hints?" You nod again.

CHAPTER 7

3. Click in frame 20, and select Modify ➤ Shape ➤ Add Shape Hint (see Figure 7-11). This puts a small red circle with the letter a in the center of your artwork. Meet your first shape hint.

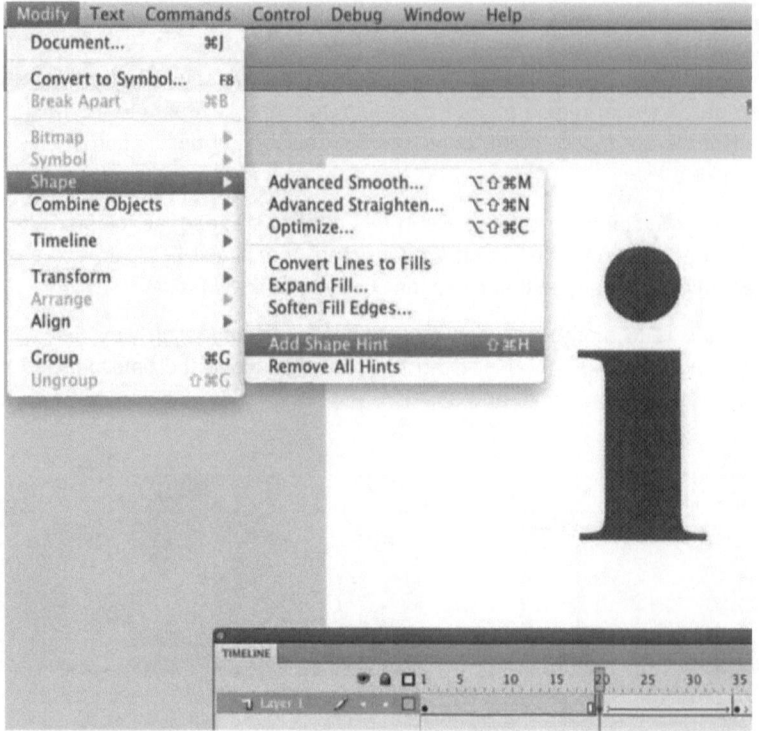

Figure 7-11. Inserting a shape hint

4. You can check to ensure object snapping is on, either by selecting Snap to Objects in the Tools panel or by ensuring that a check mark is present under View ➤ Snapping ➤ Snap to Objects. Snapping helps the placement of shape hints significantly.

5. Drag and snap a circle to the lower-left corner of the letter's upper serif, as shown in Figure 7-12. If you are a stickler for detail, feel free to zoom the stage before you try snapping the circle.

ANIMATION, PART 1

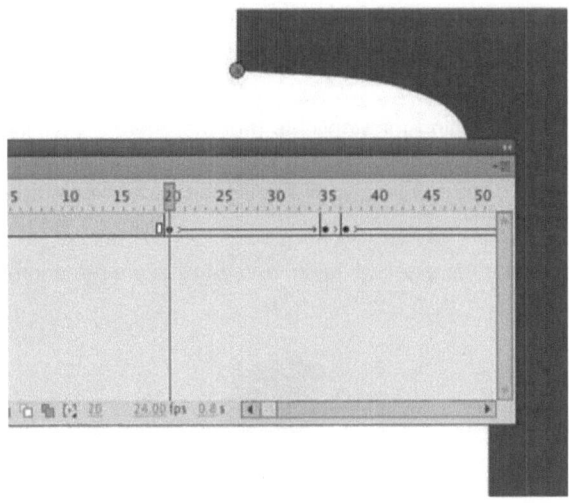

Figure 7-12. Positioning a shape hint

This next point is important: what you've done is placed *one half* of a shape hint *pair*. The other half—the partner—is on the next keyframe, frame 35.

6. Drag the playhead to frame 35, and position the second **a** circle on the corresponding serif on this keyframe's shape, as shown in Figure 7-13.

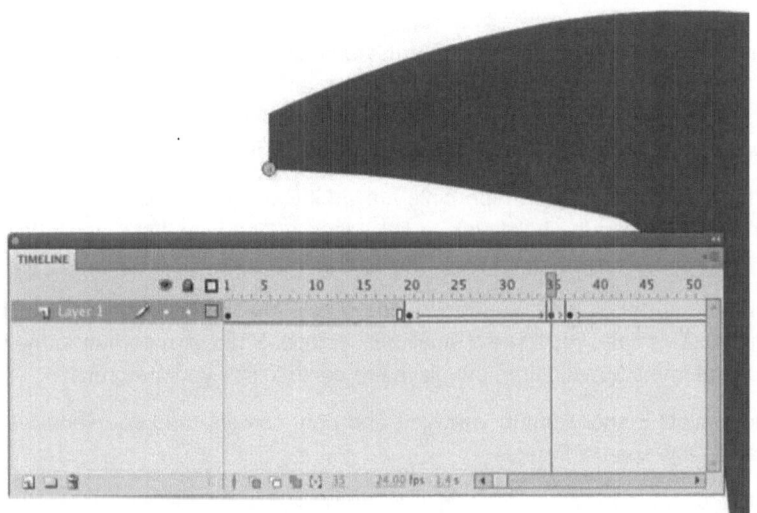

Figure 7-13. Positioning the shape hint's partner

375

CHAPTER 7

7. When this partner snaps into place, it will turn green. Return to frame 20, and notice that the original shape hint has turned yellow. It's a dramatic improvement, but there are still a few trouble spots.

It may be that shape hints have a thing for stoplights (not that there's anything wrong with that), but the point is that the color change indicates something. It tells you that this shape hint pair has entered into a relationship. You have now indicated to Flash your intentions that these paired regions now correspond to each other.

8. Slide the playhead along the timeline again, and you'll see a remarkable improvement (as shown in Figure 7-14).

Figure 7-14. It's a dramatic improvement, but there are still a few trouble spots.

The improvement is so remarkable, in fact, that the authors look deftly side to side, wink, and silently mouth the word "voodoo." To be frank, if we may, the placement of shape hints often makes a noticeable difference, but the decision on placement is something of a dark art. We encourage you to reposition your first shape hint pair at other corners to see how the remaining trouble spots ripple to other areas.

You should get the idea by now that shape hints are a bit like cloves (you know, the star-shaped things you poke into your ham during the holidays)—a little goes a long way. Let's add a few more, but do so sparingly.

9. To get rid of the kink in the upper curve, add a new shape hint to the upper-right corner of the **i** on frame 20. This time, you'll see a small **b** in a circle. Snap its **b** partner to the upper-right corner of the logo at frame 35, and drag the playhead again to see your progress.

10. Add shape hints **c** and **d** to the lower-left and right corners, and you should see a very smooth morph along this span of frames.

11. The only problem remaining, if you're a perfectionist, is a slight wrinkle along the bottom of the "egg" between keyframes 37 and 55. Remedy this by adding a new shape hint at frame 37. It will start again at **a**, because this is a new pair of keyframes, and snap in place to the corresponding curve at frame 55.

Compare your work with the `LogoMorph.fla` file in this chapter's `Complete` folder, if you like. When you open a file that already contains shape hints, you'll need to take one small step to make them show, because they like to hide by default. To toggle shapes hints on and off, select **View ➤ Show Shape Hints**.

Even with the benefit of shape hints, we caution you to keep simplicity in mind. Certain collections of shapes are simply too intricate to handle gracefully. Remember that not every website visitor will have as powerful a computer as yours. It is entirely possible to choke Flash Player through the use of an overwhelming number of anchor points. To see what we mean, open the `FlowerWeed.fla` file in this chapter's `Exercise` folder, and drag the playhead along the timeline. The morph isn't especially polished (see Figure 7-15), but it certainly doesn't count as a complete eyesore. Test the SWF (**Control ➤ Test Movie**), and—depending on the power of your computer—you may see that playback slows or skips during the most complex portions of the tween. If that doesn't happen for you, count yourself lucky! But generally speaking, try to avoid asking this much of your users. Why do we mention this? The reason is because it is a "bad experience" for the user. In the case of this exercise, you are the only user. Now extrapolate this out to the flower being in a banner ad and your bad experience is now being shared by thousands of others.

Figure 7-15. Moderation in all things! Although this transformation doesn't look awful, it nearly chokes Flash Player.

Altering gradients

If you want to animate gradients, shape tweens are the only way to do it. You may not immediately think of gradients as shapes, but when you select the **Gradient Transform** tool and click into a gradient, what do you see? You see the handles and points shown in Figure 7-16.

That center point, to Flash, is not much different from an anchor point. The resize, radius, and rotate handles are not much different from Bezier control point handles. In effect, you are manipulating a shape—just a special kind. When animating a gradient, you simply change these gradient-specific features from keyframe to keyframe, rather than a shape's corners, lines, and curves.

CHAPTER 7

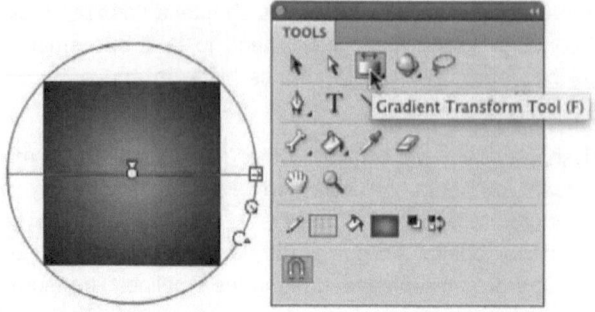

Figure 7-16. Gradients, like anything else, can be edited on keyframes, and those keyframes are tweenable.

Open the `GradientTween1.fla` file in this chapter's `Exercise` folder, and drag the playhead along the timeline to see an example in action. Frame 1 contains a solid red fill. Frame 10 contains the built-in rainbow gradient, which is rotated 90 degrees in frame 20. Frames 20 through 30 provide a bit of interest because they demonstrate a limitation of gradient shape tweens: it is not possible to tween one type of gradient to another. Well, we take that back. You certainly can, but the results are unpredictable. Flash tries its best to convert a linear gradient into a radial one, but between frames 29 and 30, the gradient pops from one type to the other.

Next, open the `GradientTween2.fla` file in this chapter's `Exercise` folder. This example shows a combination of a gradient and a shape change at the same time. Not only does the gradient fill transform, but anchor points move, and even stroke color (and thickness!) changes from keyframe to keyframe. Experiment with solid colors as well as the **Color** panel's **Alpha** property. When you finish, close the file without saving the changes.

Even bitmap fills are tweenable, which makes for some interesting visual possibilities, as shown in Figure 7-17. Open the `BitmapFillTween.fla` file in this chapter's `Exercise` folder, and press the Enter (Return) key to see some roller-coaster camera work using an image of a sculpture sitting on a window sill in Bern, Switzerland. As with other types of gradients, use the **Gradient Transform** tool to manipulate gradient control handles at each keyframe, and then let the shape tween handle the rest. Easing works the same way.

Figure 7-17. Shape tween your bitmap fill transformations for some real zing!

Classic tweening

When we left that hapless hot pepper hanging, it had been hoping to rotate. It didn't and instead found its molecules tumbling in a frenzied jumble. We told you there was a much easier way to handle that rotation, and classic tweening is one of them. Shape tweens are for rearranging anchor points and animating gradients. Classic tweens and motion tweens are for everything else, from enlivening text and imported photos to animating vector artwork drawn directly in Flash or imported from another application like Illustrator CS5 or Fireworks CS5. As we've said, we'll cover motion tweening in Chapter 8. Here, we'll continue with classic tweens only, but keep in mind that you'll have additional choices.

In contrast to shape tweens, classic tweens require self-contained entities. These include symbols, primitives, drawing objects, and grouped elements, which many designers find easier to work with than raw shapes. Open `PepperSymbol.fla` in this chapter's `Exercise` folder, for example, and you'll see that it's easier to select the whole pepper without accidentally omitting the cap.

> *Be aware that primitives and drawing objects blur the lines somewhat between what constitutes a shape and what constitutes a symbol. It is possible to apply both shape tweens and motion tweens to primitives and drawing objects. However, many properties, such as color, alpha, and the like—and in primitives, shape—are properly animated only with shape tweens. These "gotchas" tend to steer the authors toward a path of least resistance: use shapes for shape tweens and symbols for classic tweens. Within those symbols, use whatever elements you like.*
>
> *One fundamental point: when it comes to classic tweens, always put each tweened symbol on its own layer. If you apply a classic tween to keyframes that contain more than one symbol, Flash will try to oblige—but will fail. It's a simple rule, so abide by it, and you'll be happy.*

Rotation

Let's pick up with that rotation, shall we?

1. Open the `PepperSymbol.fla` file in this chapter's `Exercise` folder. You'll see a pepper symbol in the **Library** (the shapes from the earlier `PepperShape.fla` example have been placed inside a graphic symbol).

2. Add a keyframe in frame 10. Then select the **Free Transform** tool, and rotate the artwork 90 degrees in either direction in that keyframe you just added in frame 10. Sounds familiar, right? Here comes the difference.

3. Right-click (Windows) or Control+click (Mac), and select **Create Classic Tween** from the context menu. There it is!

4. Drag the playhead back and forth to see a nice, clean rotation of the pepper. As you saw with shape tweens, the span of frames between the two keyframes changes color (to purple this time), and a solid arrow appears within the span to indicate a successful tween, as shown in Figure 7-18.

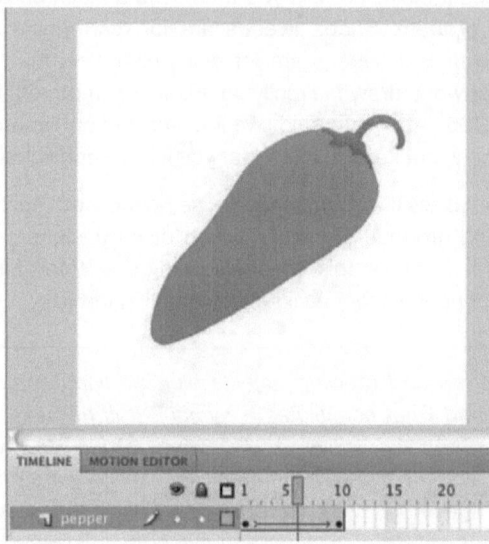

Figure 7-18. Classic tweens, indicated by purple and an arrow between the keyframes, make rotations a snap.

Now, let's think about *real* rotation: topsy-turvy—a full 360-degree spin. How would you do it? (Hint: This is something of a trick question.) In a full spin, the pepper ends up in the same position at frame 10 as it starts with in frame 1, so there's not really a transformation to tween, is there?

Rotation is set through the `Rotate` drop-down menu in the `Tweening` area of the `Properties` panel. Notice that the `Rotate` drop-down is currently set to `Auto`, as shown in Figure 7-19. This is because you have already rotated the pepper somewhat by hand. The choices are `CW` (clockwise) and `CCW` (counterclockwise). The hot text immediately to the right of the drop-down menu specifies how many times to perform the rotation.

ANIMATION, PART 1

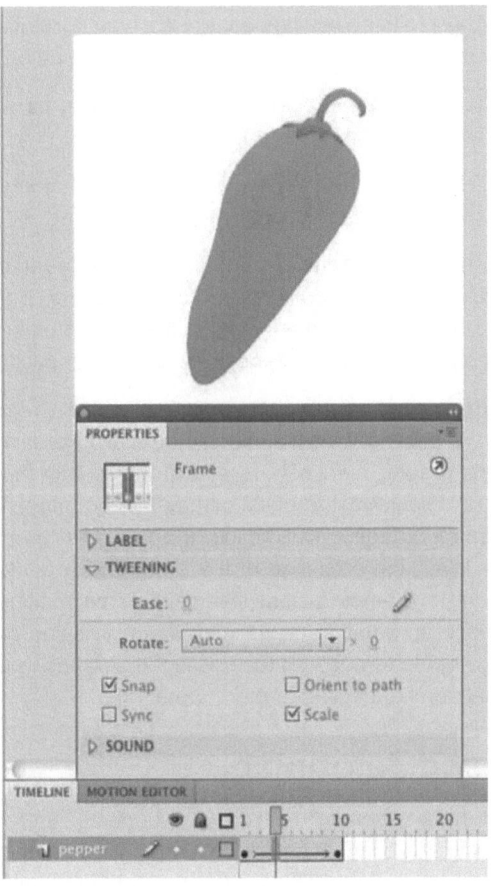

Figure 7-19. The `Rotate` property makes quick work of rotations.

5. Click the pepper in frame 10, and select **Modify ➤ Transform ➤ Remove Transform** to reset the symbol's rotation.

6. Click once in frame 1. In the `Rotate` drop-down menu, change the setting to CW (clockwise), and drag the playhead back and forth. Pretty neat!

Classic tween properties

While we're looking at the `Tweening` area of the `Properties` panel, let's go through the other settings. Here's a quick overview of classic tween properties:

- **Ease** and **Edit**: These settings apply a range of easing to the tween. The **Edit** button (a pencil icon) allows for advanced, custom easing. More on this in the "Easing" section of this chapter.

CHAPTER 7

- `Rotate` and `x [number]`: These settings control the type of rotation and the number of times the rotation occurs. Only `CW` and `CCW` support the `x [number]` setting.

- `Snap`: This `Snap` check box helps position a symbol along its motion guide (discussed in the "Motion guides" section later in this chapter).

- `Orient to path`: This check box applies only to tweens along a motion guide. It determines whether a symbol points toward the direction in which it moves.

- `Scale`: If a check mark is present, tweening for the current span of frames will include a transformation in scale (size), *if such a transformation exists*. If you haven't scaled anything, it doesn't matter what state the check mark is in. If scaling and other transformations are combined in a given classic tween, only the other transformations will show if the check mark is deselected.

- `Sync`: In our experience, most people don't even realize this property exists, but it can be a real time-saver when you're dealing with graphic symbols. Unlike movie clips, which have their own independent timelines, graphic symbols are synchronized with the timeline in which they reside. Even so, there is a bit of flexibility: graphics can be looped, played through once, or instructed to rest on a specified frame of their own timeline. If a particular graphic symbol has been tweened numerous times in a layer, the presence of the `Sync` check mark means you can update these timeline options for all keyframes in that layer simply by making changes to the first graphic symbol in the sequence. In addition, `Sync` allows you to swap one graphic symbol for another and have that change ripple through all the synced keyframes in that layer. More on this feature in the "Editing multiple frames" section of this chapter.

Scaling, stretching, and deforming

We visited this topic in the "Shape tweening" section, and honestly, there's not a whole lot different for classic tweens. The key thing to realize is that scaling, stretching, and deforming a symbol is like doing the same to a T-shirt with artwork printed on it. Even if the artwork looks different after all the tugging and twisting, it hasn't actually changed. Shake it out, and it's still the same picture. Shape tweening, in contrast, is like rearranging the tiles in a mosaic. For this reason, the `Free Transform` tool disables the `Distort` and `Envelope` options for symbols. These transformations can't be performed on symbols and therefore can't be classic tweened.

> *Symbol distortion can be performed with the 3D tools (Chapter 9) and can even be animated, but the animation requires motion tweens (Chapter 8), not classic tweens.*

Let's take a quick look at the other transform options:

1. Return to the `PepperSymbol.fla` file, select frame 1, and set the `Rotation` setting for the tween to `None`.

2. Use the `Free Transform` tool to perform a shear transformation at frame 10.

Shear? What's that? Something you do with sheep, right? Well, yes, but in Flash, shearing is also called **skewing**, which can be described as tilting.

3. With the `Free Transform` tool active, click the `Rotate and Skew` option at the bottom of the `Tools` panel, and then hover over one of the side transform handles (not the corners) until the cursor becomes an opposing double-arrow icon. Click and drag to transform the pepper (see Figure 7-20).

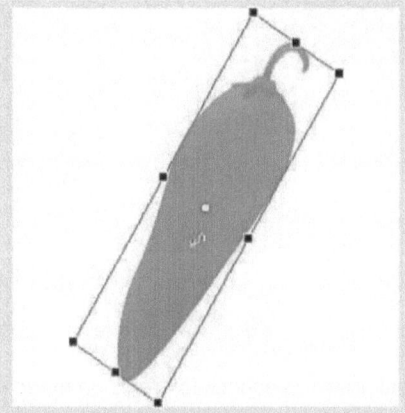

Figure 7-20. Classic tweening a symbol transformation. The "shear" cursor is just under the transformation point.

The live preview gives you an idea what the symbol will look like before you let go of the mouse. Note that the skew occurs in relation to the transformation point, indicated by the small white circle.

4. Drag the white circle around inside or even outside the bounding box of the pepper, and then skew the pepper again to see how its placement affects the transformation. Hold down Alt (Windows) or Option (Mac) while skewing to temporarily ignore the transformation point and skew in relation to the symbol's opposite edge.

We've been using the `Free Transform` tool quite a bit, so let's try something different.

5. Open the `Transform` panel (`Window` ➤ `Transform`) and note its current settings. You'll see the skew summarized near the bottom and, interestingly, the change in scale summarized near the top (see Figure 7-21). From this, it becomes clear that skewing affects scale when applied with the `Free Transform` tool.

6. To see the difference, select `Modify` ➤ `Transform` ➤ `Remove Transform` or click the `Remove Transform` button in Figure 7-21 at the bottom right of the `Transform` panel to reset the symbol. The scale area of the `Transform` panel returns to `100 percent` horizontal and `100 percent` vertical.

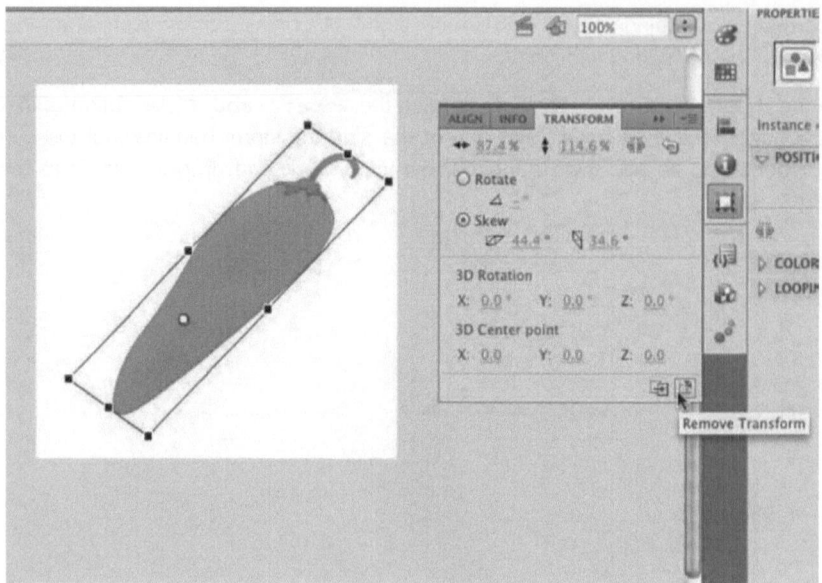

Figure 7-21. The `Transform` panel provides access to precision measurements.

7. Click the `Skew` radio button, and scrub the hot text of either skew value to `38`. Notice that the scaling stays at `100 percent`, which subtly changes how the skew looks.

8. Enter `200` into the scale input fields at the top. (The `Constrain` check mark means you need to enter this number into only one of them.) Slide the playhead back and forth to see two transformations tweened at once.

Easing

Here's where classic tweening begins to pull ahead of shape tweening. Easing is much more powerful for classic tweens, thanks to the `Custom Ease In/Ease Out` editor. Before we delve into that, though, let's look at a sample use of the standard easing controls for a classic tween, so you can see how much easier things are with the custom variety.

1. Open the `MalletNoEasing.fla` file in this chapter's `Exercise` folder. You'll see a hammer graphic symbol in the `Library` and an instance of that symbol on the stage. Select the hammer, and note that the transformation point—the white dot in the handle—is located in the center of the symbol.

2. We're going to make this hammer swing to the left, so select the `Free Transform` tool. Selecting this tool makes the transformation point selectable. Click and drag that point to the bottom center of the mallet (see Figure 7-22).

ANIMATION, PART 1

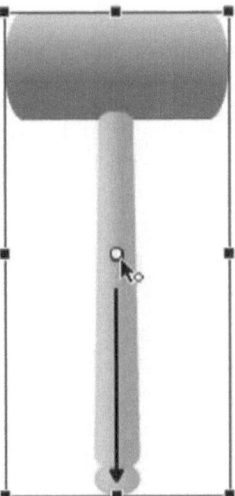

Figure 7-22. You'll need to move that transformation point to make the movement realistic.

3. Insert a keyframe at frame 10 (**Insert ➤ Timeline ➤ Keyframe**), and rotate the mallet at frame 10 to the left by 90 degrees.

4. Apply a classic tween to the span of frames between 1 and 10, and scrub the timeline to see the effect. That's not bad but not especially realistic. How about some easing and bounce-back?

5. In the **Tweening** area of the **Properties** panel, scrub the **Ease** hot text all the way to the left to specify a full ease in. The number should be **-100**. This causes the hammer to fall slowly as it begins to tip and increase speed as it continues to fall (see Figure 7-23).

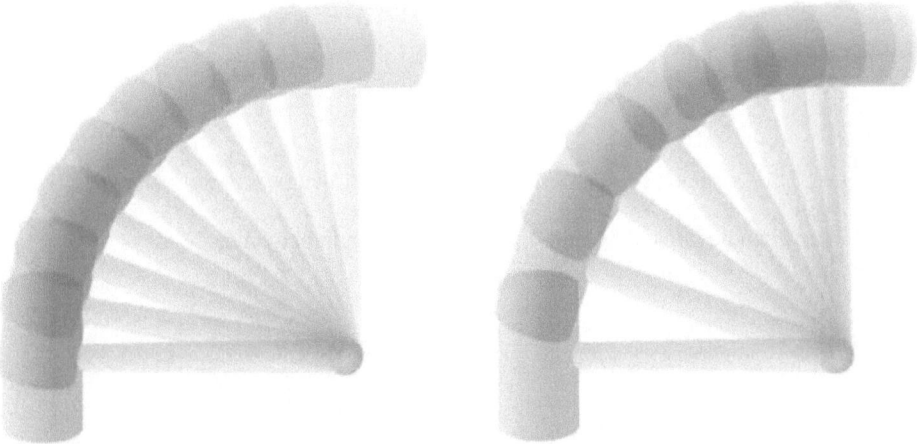

Figure 7-23. Ease in (right) vs. no easing (left). On the right, the hammer falls in a more natural manner.

385

This is a good start. To push the realism further, let's embellish the animation. We're going to provide some tweening that makes the hammer rebound on impact and bounce a few times.

6. Add new keyframes at frames 15, 20, 23, and 25. At frame 15, use the **Free Transform** tool or the **Transform** panel to rotate the hammer to approximately northwest; in the **Transform** panel, this could be something like -55 in the **Rotate** area. At frame 23, set the rotation to roughly west-northwest (something like -80 in the **Rotation** area). A storyboard version of the sequence might look like Figure 7-24.

Figure 7-24. Using several keyframes to make the hammer bounce

> *The fading image trails—visual echoes of the mallet—are the result of something called* **onion skinning**, *which is very helpful in animation work. It's used here for illustrative purposes and is covered later in the chapter.*

7. Now that the mallet has been positioned, it just needs to be tweened and eased. You can click separately into each span of frames and apply a classic tween, or you can click and drag across as many spans as you need (as shown in Figure 7-25). That way, you can apply the tweens all in one swoop.

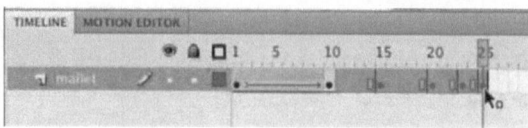

Figure 7-25. Tweens can be applied to more than one frame span at a time.

8. Click into each span of frames to apply easing, for the final touch. Remember that span 1 through 10 already has -100. Apply the following easing to the remaining spans:

- Span 10 to 15: 100 (full ease out)
- Span 15 to 20: -100 (full ease in)
- Span 20 to 23: 100
- Span 23 to 25: -100

9. Drag the playhead back and forth to preview the action, and then test the movie to see the final presentation. If you like, compare your work with MalletNormalEase.fla in the Complete folder.

This exercise wasn't especially arduous, but wouldn't it be even cooler if you could perform all the preceding steps with a single classic tween?

Custom easing

Introduced in Flash 8, the Custom Ease In/Ease Out dialog box unleashes considerably more power than traditional easing. Not only does it provide a combined ease in/out—where animation gradually speeds up *and* gradually slows down, or vice versa—but it also supports multiple varied settings for various kinds of easing, all within the same classic tween. Let's take a look.

To perform custom easing, select a span of motion-tweened frames, and then click the Edit button (a pencil icon) in the Tweening area of the Properties panel. You'll see the Custom Ease In/Ease Out dialog box, as shown in Figure 7-26. This dialog box contains a graph with time along the horizontal axis, represented in frames, and percentage of change along the vertical axis.

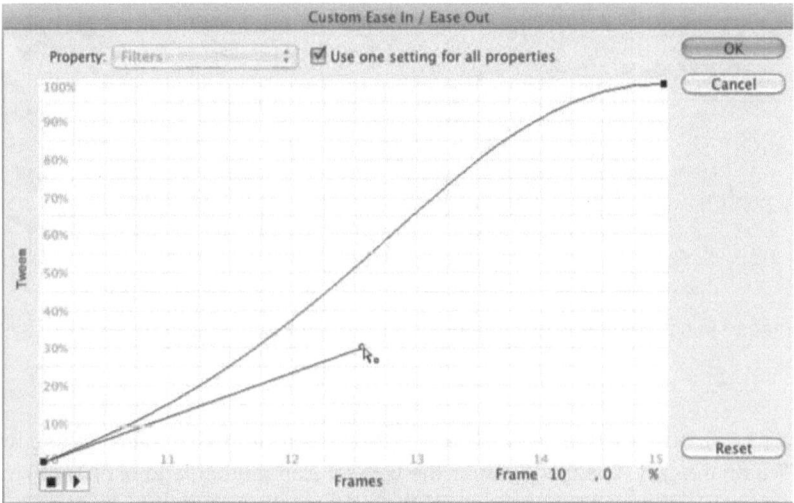

Figure 7-26. The Custom Ease In/Ease Out dialog box

Here's a quick rundown of the various areas of the dialog box:

- **Property**: By default, this is disabled until you deselect the check mark next to it. If the check mark is present, custom easing—as specified by you on the grid—applies to all aspects of the tween symbol. If the check mark is absent, this drop-down menu lets you distinguish among **Position**, **Rotation**, **Scale**, **Color**, and **Filters**.
- **Use one setting for all properties**: When selected, this allows multiple properties to be eased individually.
- **Grid**: The Bezier curves on this grid determine the visual result of the custom easing applied.
- **Preview**: Click the two buttons in this area to play and stop a preview of the custom easing.
- **OK**, **Cancel**, and **Reset**: The **OK** and **Cancel** buttons apply and discard any custom easing. **Reset** reverts the Bezier curves to a straight line (no easing) between the grid's opposite corners.

So, how does the grid work? Let's look at a traditional ease in to see how the **Custom Ease In/Ease Out** dialog box interprets it.

1. Open the CustomEasingComparison.fla file in the Chapter 7 Exercise folder, and set the **Ease** property to -100 (a normal full ease in) for the tween in the top layer.
2. Scrub the timeline to confirm that the upper symbol starts its tween more slowly than the lower one but speeds up near the end. The lower symbol, in contrast, should advance the same distance each frame (see Figure 7-27).

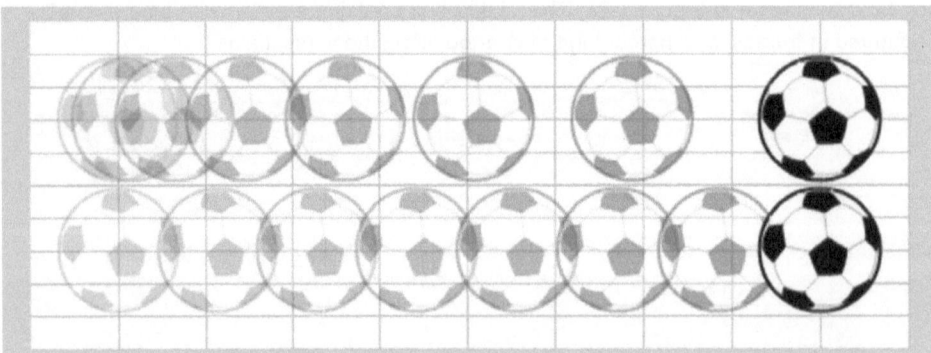

Figure 7-27. An ease in causes the upper symbol to start slower and speed up (artwork by Steve Napiersk).

3. Click the **Edit** button in the **Tweening** area of the **Properties** panel to see what an ease out looks like on the grid. The curve climbs the vertical axis (percentage of change) rather slowly and then speeds its ascent near the end of the horizontal axis (time in frames). Hey, that makes sense!

ANIMATION, PART 1

4. Click `Cancel`, apply a full ease out (`100`), and then click the `Edit` button to check the grid again. Bingo—the opposite curve.

It follows that a combination of these would produce either a custom ease in/out (slow, fast, slow) or a custom ease out/in (fast, slow, fast). Let's do the first of those two.

5. Click the upper-right black square in the grid to make its control handle appear. Drag it up to the top of the grid and about two-thirds across to the left, as shown in Figure 7-28.

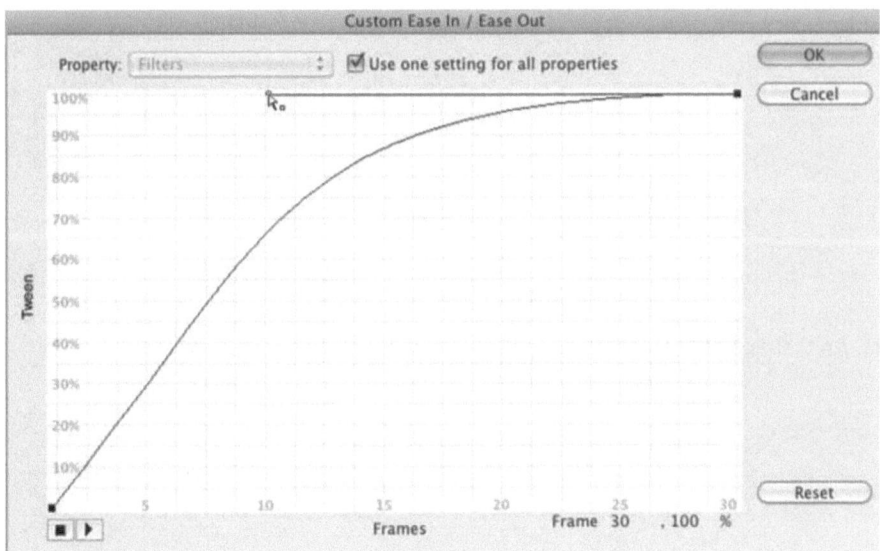

Figure 7-28. Dragging a control handle to create a custom ease

6. Click the bottom-left black square, and drag its control handle two-thirds across to the right. The resulting curve—vaguely an *S* shape—effectively combines the curves you saw for ease in and ease out (see Figure 7-29).

7. Click OK to accept this setting, and scrub the timeline or test the movie to see the results.

8. Let's inverse this easing for the lower symbol. Select the lower span of frames, and click the `Edit` button. This time, drag the lower-left control handle two-thirds up the left side. Drag the upper-right control handle two-thirds down the right side to create the inverted *S* curve shown in Figure 7-30. Click OK, and compare the two tweens.

CHAPTER 7

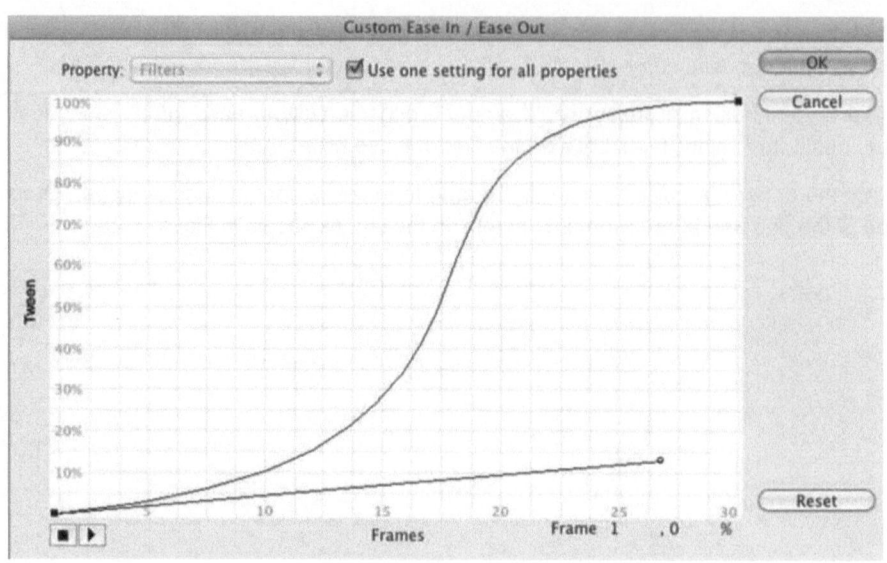

Figure 7-29. An *S* shape produces an ease in/out (slow-fast-slow) tween.

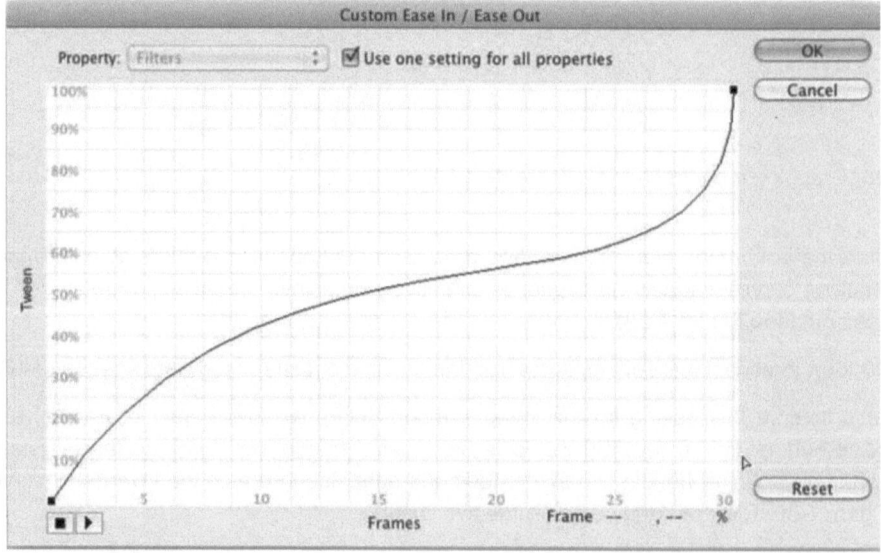

Figure 7-30. An inverted *S* shape produces an ease out/in (fast-slow-fast) tween.

Think this is cool? We're just getting started!

ANIMATION, PART 1

Adding anchor points

By clicking anywhere along the Bezier curve, you can add new anchor points. This is where you can actually save yourself a bit of work.

1. Open the `MalletNoEasing.fla` file in this chapter's `Exercise` folder again. If you saved your work earlier, remove the tween, and delete all frames except for frame 1. To do this, click and drag from frame 2 to the right until you've selected all the frames, and then use `Edit` ➤ `Timeline` ➤ `Remove Frames`.

2. Confirm that the mallet's transformation point is positioned at the bottom center of its wooden handle. Now add a new keyframe at frame 25, and apply a classic tween to the span of frames between 1 and 25.

3. Using the `Free Transform` tool at frame 25, rotate the mallet 90 degrees to the left. Because a tween is already applied, you can preview the falling mallet by scrubbing the timeline.

This may seem like déjà vu, but things are about to change. You're going to emulate the same bounce-back tween you did earlier, but this time, you'll do it all in one custom ease.

4. Click in frame 1—or anywhere inside the tween span—and click the `Edit` button in the `Tweening` area of the `Properties` panel.

5. In the `Custom Ease In/Ease Out` dialog box, click the Bezier curve near the middle, and you'll see a new anchor point with control handles. Click that new anchor point and press the `Delete` key—it disappears. Add it again and straighten the control handles so that they're horizontal, as shown in Figure 7-31.

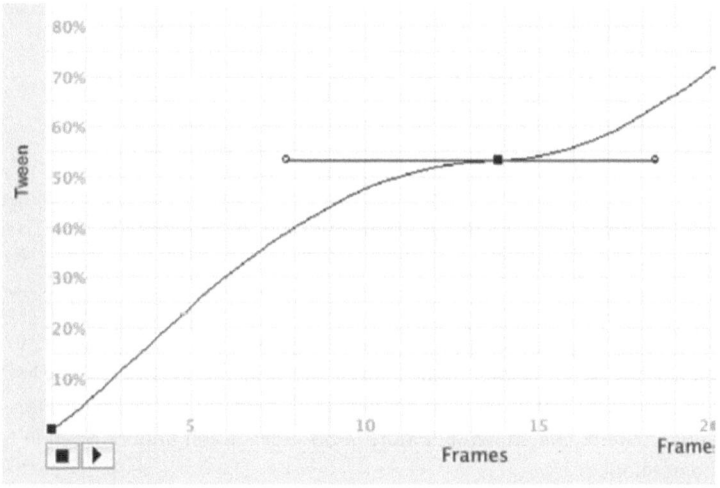

Figure 7-31. Starting a more complex custom ease

6. Repeat this process three more times, up the hill, as shown in Figure 7-32. This prepares the way for the sawtooth shape you'll create in the next step.

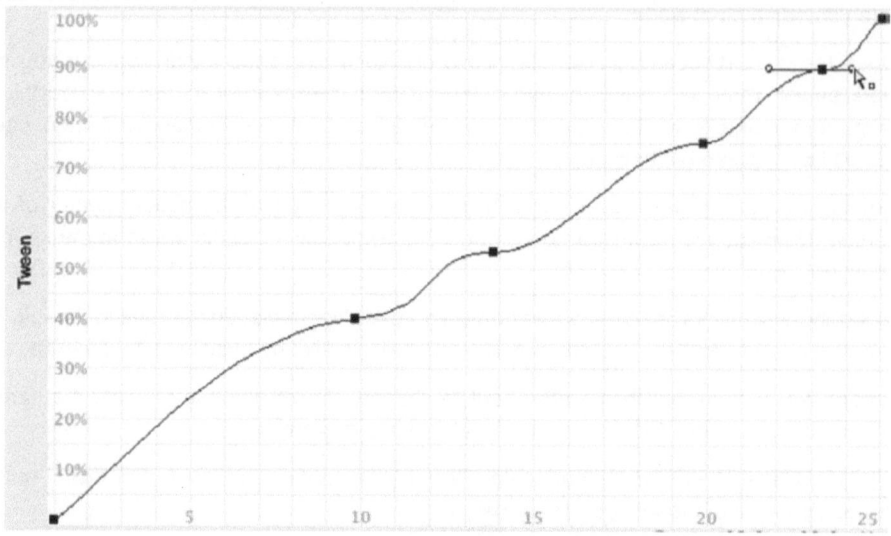

Figure 7-32. Continuing to add anchor points for a sawtooth curve

7. Leave the corner anchor points where they are. Position the four new anchor points as follows:
    - `100%, 10`
    - `60%, 15`
    - `100%, 20`
    - `85%, 23`

> *You'll notice that the anchor points gently snap to the grid while you drag. To temporarily suppress this snapping, hold down the X key.*

8. You've probably heard of certain procedures described as more of an art than a science. Well, we've come to that point in this step. Here's the basic idea, but it's up to you to tweak these settings until they feel right to you. To achieve the sawtooth curve we're after—it looks very much like the series of shark fins shown in Figure 7-33—click each anchor point in turn and perform the following adjustment:
    - If it has a left control handle, drag that handle in toward the anchor point.
    - If it has a right control handle, drag that handle out a couple of squares to the right.

You should get something like the shape shown in Figure 7-33.

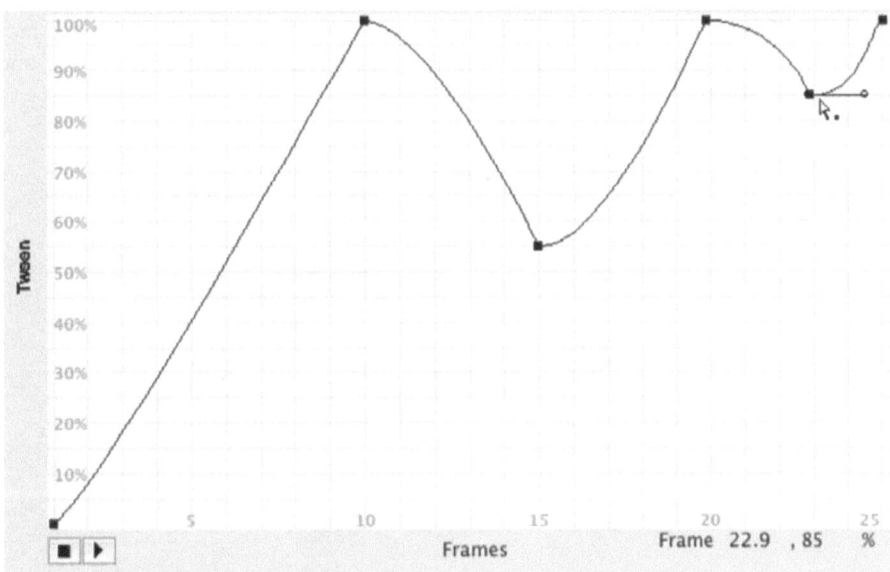

Figure 7-33. Shark fins produce a bounce-back effect.

9. Click the `Preview` play button to test your custom ease. It should look similar to the original series of mallet bounce-back tweens, but this time you saved yourself a handful of keyframes.

How does this work? As depicted in the grid and following the horizontal axis, you have an ease-in curve from frames 0 to 10, an ease-out curve from 10 to 15, an ease-in curve from 15 to 20, and so on—just like your series of keyframes from earlier in the chapter. The mallet moves from its upright position to its leaned-over position in the very first curve. From frames 10 to 15, the vertical axis goes from 100 percent down to 60 percent, which means that the mallet actually rotates clockwise again toward its original orientation, but not all the way. With each new curve, the hammer falls again to the left, and then raises again, but never as high. Compare your work with `MalletCustomEasing.fla` in this chapter's `Complete` folder.

Easing multiple properties

On the final leg of our custom easing expedition, let's pull out all the stops and examine a tween that updates multiple symbol properties at once. You'll be familiar with most of what you're about to see, and the new parts will be easy to pick up.

1. Open the `CustomEasingMultiple.fla` file in this chapter's `Exercise` folder. Select frame 1, and note that a movie clip symbol of an apple shape appears in the upper-left corner of the stage. It is solid green. Scrub across to frame 55, and note the changes to the starting state of the apple that occur as you move the playhead.

At this point, frame 55, the apple is positioned in the center of the stage, is much larger and more naturally colored, and has a drop shadow (see Figure 7-34). From this, you can surmise that color and filters are tweenable—that's the new part.

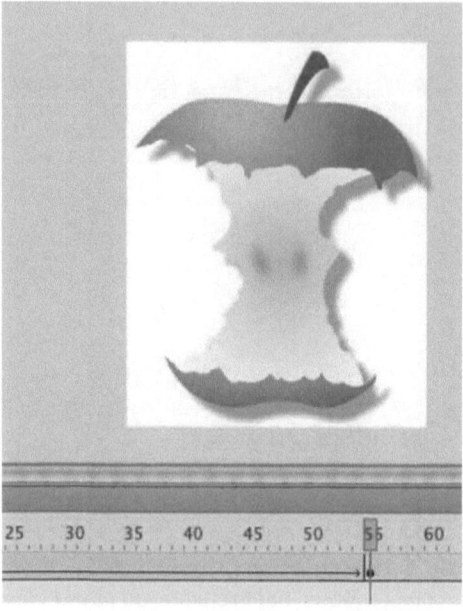

Figure 7-34. You are about to discover that it isn't only rotation that can be tweened.

2. In frame 1, select the apple symbol to see that a `Tint` has been applied in the `Properties` panel, which is replaced by `None` in the other keyframe. Next, twirl down the `Filters` at frame 55, and click the apple to see that a drop shadow has been applied that is not present in frame 1. The `Filters` properties are no different from `Position` and `Scale` as far as tweens are concerned.

3. Click into the span of tweened frames, and note that a `CW` (clockwise) rotation has been specified for `Rotation` and `Scale` is enabled (without it, the apple wouldn't gradually increase in size). The `Ease` property reads ---, which means custom easing has been applied. That's what we're after. Click the `Edit` button.

4. Thanks to the empty `Use one setting for all properties` check box, the `Property` drop-down menu is now available. Use the drop-down menu to look at the grid curve for each of five properties, all of which are depicted in the tween: `Position`, `Rotation`, `Scale`, `Color`, and `Filters`. Each property has its own distinct curve, which translates into five individual custom ease settings for their respective properties (see Figure 7-35).

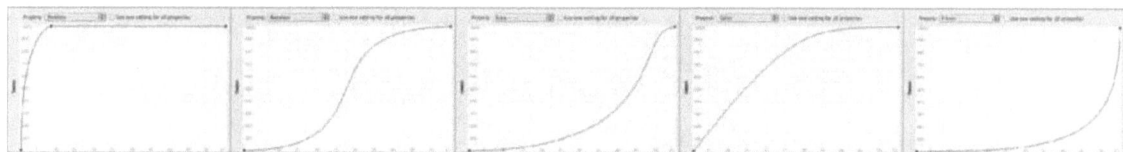

Figure 7-35. The `Custom Ease In/Ease Out` dialog box lets you specify distinct easing for five different tweenable properties.

5. Click the `Use one setting for all properties` check box to disable the drop-down menu.

Ack! Have you lost your custom settings? Thankfully, no. Flash remembers them for you, even though they're hiding.

6. Click the `Preview` play button to preview the tween with no easing (the default lower-left to upper-right curve).

7. Click the check box again to see that the custom ease settings are still intact. Preview the tween again, if you like.

Using animation

So far, we've shown you a hefty animation toolbox. We've opened it up and pulled out a number of powerful tools to show you how they work. In doing so, we've covered quite a bit of ground, but there are still a handful of useful animation features and general workflow practices to help bring it all together. Let's roll up our sleeves, then, shall we?

A closer look at the Timeline panel

Whether you use shape, classic, or motion tweens, the `Timeline` panel gives you a pint-sized but important dashboard (see Figure 7-36). Don't let its small size fool you. This strip along the bottom of the timeline helps you quickly find your bearings, gives you at-a-glance detail on where you are, and even lets you time travel into both the past and the future, to see where you've been and where you're going.

CHAPTER 7

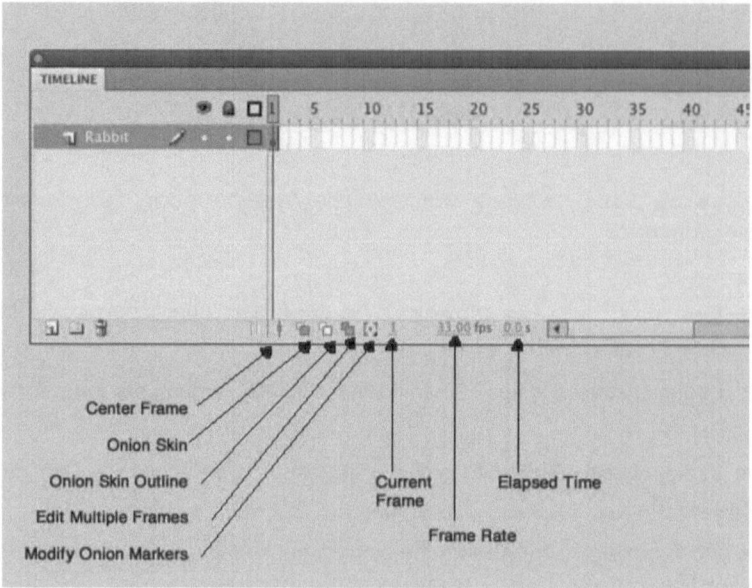

Figure 7-36. The bottom edge of the timeline provides a collection of useful tools.

Let's take an inventory of this useful, if small, real estate.

- **Center Frame**: In timelines that are long enough to scroll, this button centers the timeline on the playhead.

- **Onion Skin** and **Onion Skin Outlines**: These buttons toggle two different kinds of onion skinning, which give you a view of your work as a series of stills.

- **Edit Multiple Frames**: This button allows you to select more than one keyframe at the same time, in order to edit many frames in one swoop.

- **Modify Onion Markers**: Click this button to see a drop-down menu that controls the functionality of the onion skin buttons.

- **Current Frame**: This indicates the current location of the playhead. Scrub or enter a value to move the playhead to that frame.

- **Frame Rate**: This indicates the movie's frame rate. Scrub or enter a value to change it.

- **Elapsed Time**: Given the current frame and the movie's frame rate, this indicates the duration in seconds of the playhead's position. For example, in a movie with a frame rate of 24 fps, this area will say `1.0s` at frame 24. Scrub or enter a value to move the playhead to the frame that closely matches your specified elapsed time.

Onion skinning

Traditional animators—those wonderful people who brought us Mickey Mouse and Bugs Bunny—often drew the motion of their characters on very thin paper over illuminated surfaces called **light boxes**. This paper, called **onion skin**, allowed the artist to see through the current drawing to what had occurred in the previous drawings or frames. In this way, animators could control the motion of someone's head or the speed and shape of the anvil about to land on a coyote's head.

Flash offers you this same capability with a lot more flexibility than flipping through sheets of paper. In Flash, you can choose to see through as many frames as you want, moving backward and forward looking at solids or outlines. Let's take a look at how you do this:

1. Open the CuriousRabbit.fla file in this chapter's Exercise folder. Pay particular attention to the movie's frame rate of 30 fps.

2. All of the animation happens in the Rabbit movie clip found in the Library. Double-click this movie clip in the Library to open its timeline. Drag the playhead to frame 60 where the rabbit begins to move its head closer to you. Take a look at the Elapsed Time indicator at the bottom of the panel. It should, as shown in Figure 7-37, read about 2.0 seconds. This makes sense: 60/30 = 2.0.

Figure 7-37. Now you know why it is called a timeline.

3. Change the movie's fps to 60, and note the `Elapsed Time` changes, as expected, to 1 second. Now change the frame rate to 15 fps. The fps shows 4.1 seconds. What's with the discrepancy? Shouldn't it be 4 seconds? We aren't sure, but it is close enough to the expected value to satisfy us. Change the time back to the original 30 fps.

4. Place the playhead at frame 60, and, using the bar at the bottom of the timeline, scroll all the way to the left until you see frame 1 and the playhead is hidden. This is a common issue faced by Flash designers. You have a long timeline, and it suddenly hits you: where's the playhead? Click the `Center Frame` button (shown in Figure 7-36), and you will pop right over to frame 60. This is a great "you are here" panic button that's really shines with especially long timelines.

5. Position the playhead at frame 70, and click the `Modify Onion Markers` button. Choose `Onion 5` from the drop-down menu. This puts two markers on frames 65 and 75 on either side of the playhead, as shown in Figure 7-38. If you aren't seeing them, return to the `Modify Onion Markers` menu, and select `Always Show Markers`.

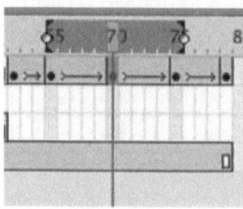

Figure 7-38. Onion skinning adds markers to either side of the playhead.

These markers extend five frames back from and ahead of the current position, which explains the name of the `Onion 5` setting. What they show are semitransparent views of those frames fading as they get farther from the playhead—just like artwork on thin paper! Not only do they let you see back in time at previous frames, but they also show artwork on future frames, which provides practical sequential context for any moment in time.

6. To actually see these onion skins, click the `Onion Skin` button. In this case, you're seeing 11 "sheets," including the one under the playhead (which is the darkest) and then five ahead and behind.

7. Click `Modify Onion Markers` again, and choose `Onion 2`, as shown in Figure 7-39. This reduces your view to five "sheets," as opposed to the previous 11. Drag the playhead slowly to frame 65 and back. Notice that the onion markers move with you.

ANIMATION, PART 1

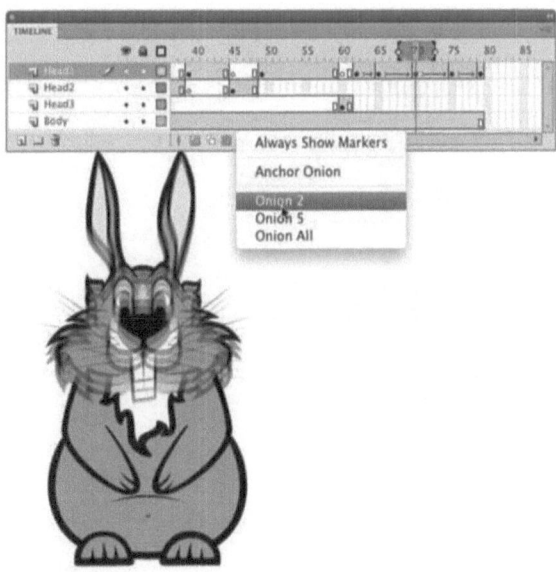

Figure 7-39. Various onion skin settings

What are the other choices on this drop-down menu? `Always Show Markers` keeps the onion markers visible, even if you toggle the `Onion Skin` button off. `Anchor Onion` keeps the onion markers from following the playhead. `Onion All` spreads the onion markers along the whole timeline. You can try it with this file. The result is overwhelming (and also makes it hard to drag the playhead around), but with timelines of little movement, it probably has its place. If you do select `Onion All`, be aware that the selected frames—the "all" part of `Onion All`—will move along with the playhead unless you select `Anchor Onion` in the `Modify Onion Markers` menu. If you want some setting besides `2`, `5`, or `All`, drag the markers along the timeline yourself. If you like, you can look eight frames back and two frames forward, or any combination that suits your animation.

8. Choose `Onion 5`, and drag the playhead to frame 70. Click the `Onion Skin Outlines` button. Note that the same sort of onion skinning occurs, but that the tweened areas are shown in wireframe format (see Figure 7-40). This makes it even clearer to see what's moving and what isn't.

Onion skinning is just as relevant to shape and motion tweens as it is to classic tweens. Use it to help you whenever you get the notion.

399

CHAPTER 7

Figure 7-40. Onion skin outlines show tweened artwork in a wireframe format.

Modifying multiple frames

Timeline animation can be painstaking work, no doubt about it. Even if you're using onion skinning, chances are good that you're focused on only a handful of frames at a time. There's nothing wrong with that, just as long as you remember to keep your eye on the big picture, too. Sooner or later, it happens to everyone: artwork is replaced, your manager changes her mind, or you find that you've simply painted yourself into a corner and need to revise multiple keyframes—maybe hundreds—in as few moves as possible.

Fortunately, the timeline has a button called `Edit Multiple Frames`, which allows you to do just what it describes. That's the obvious answer, of course, and we'll cover that in just a moment, but it's worth noting that the concept of mass editing in Flash extends into other avenues.

Because of the nature of symbols, for example, you can edit a `Library` asset and benefit from an immediate change throughout the movie, even if individual instances of that symbol have been stretched, scaled, rotated, and manipulated in other ways. For example, if an imported graphic file, such as a BMP, has been revised outside Flash, just right-click (Windows) or Control+click (Mac) the asset in the `Library`, select either `Update` (if the location of the external image hasn't changed) or `Properties`, and then click the `Import` button to reimport the image or import another one.

Sometimes it's not that easy. Sometimes you will have finished three days of meticulous classic tween keyframing only to learn that the symbol you've tweened isn't supposed to be *that* symbol at all. Time to throw in the towel? Well, maybe time to roll the towel into a whip. But even here, there's hope...if you're using graphic symbols.

Swapping graphic symbols

It's easy enough to swap out symbols of any type for any other type at a given keyframe, but the swap applies only to the frames leading up to the next keyframe. With graphic symbols, it's possible to apply a swap across keyframes, but you need to know the secret handshake. Let's try it.

   1. Open the `RabbitSwap.fla` in this chapter's `Exercise` folder.

You have decided to get in touch with your inner "Looney Tunes" and drop an anvil on the rabbit's head. Your co-workers all think this is rather cool except for the guy who is a "comic book" fan. He points out that the animation doesn't do a thing for him. "In fact," he says, "shouldn't the rabbit react to an anvil dropping on its head?" Tell him to give you a minute to fix that oversight, and you'll call him back. He wanders off to his cubicle at the other side of the office.

   2. Scrub over to frame 30, and click the rabbit's head on the stage.
   3. Open the **Properties** panel, and click the **Swap** button to open the **Swap Symbol** dialog box shown in Figure 7-41. A list of all the symbols in the movies appears; the selected symbol is indicated with a black dot, and a preview of the selected rabbit head appears on the left.

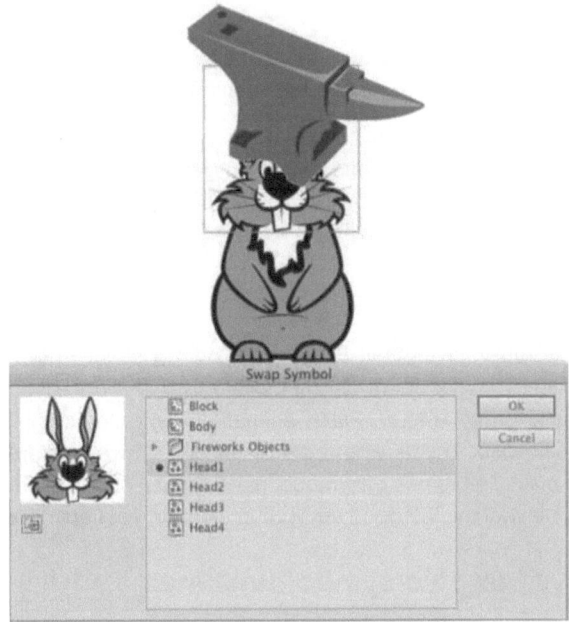

Figure 7-41. Swapping symbols is a great way to create animation effects.

   4. Select the **Head4** graphic symbol, and click **OK**. The new symbol, as shown in Figure 7-42, appears on the stage. Move it into position.

CHAPTER 7

Figure 7-42. One rabbit head has been swapped for another in the `Library`.

5. Select the rabbit head in Frame 33, and swap the `Head4` graphic symbol with the `Head3` graphic symbol. Scrub across the timeline to see the rabbit wince, close its eyes, and then open them as the anvil leaves the stage.

This technique a great productivity booster, and once you get the hang of it, you can make changes like these well before the "comic guy" makes it back to his cubicle. When he asks how you did it, look knowingly at him with a faint smile and say, "Magic."

Combining timelines

Pat your head. Good! Now rub your tummy. Excellent. Now do those both at the same time. Until the undertaking snaps into place, it might seem an impossible feat, but once you manage to pull it off, you know you've done something pretty snazzy. Flash animations get interesting in the same way when you combine techniques and timelines. This is where the distinction between graphic symbols and movie clip symbols really comes into play. Both types of symbols have timelines, but each behaves in a different way. Understanding this paves the way toward good decision making in your animations.

Movie clip timelines vs. graphic symbol timelines

Movie clips operate independently of the timelines they occupy. You can create a 500-frame animation on the main timeline and then transfer all those frames into a movie clip symbol, and everything will run the same, even if that movie clip occupies only a single frame on the main timeline. This is not so with graphic symbols. Graphic symbols are synchronized with the timelines that contain them. So if you transfer all those frames into a graphic symbol, that symbol will need to span a length of 500 frames in the main timeline in order for its own timeline to play fully.

ANIMATION, PART 1

Although movie clips can be instructed by ActionScript to stop, play, and jump to various frames, graphics can only be told to hold their current position, play through once, or loop. This instruction comes not from ActionScript but from the **Properties** panel settings. ActionScript within the timelines of graphic symbols is not performed by a containing timeline. Sound in graphic symbols is also ignored by parent timelines. Let's see this in action:

1. Open the CombineTimeline.fla file in this chapter's Exercise folder, and select the symbol at frame 1.

2. Look in the **Properties** panel's **Looping** area, and you'll see that the **Options** drop-down menu is set to **Single Frame**. Below it, the **First** field is set to **1**, which refers to the timeline of this graphic symbol. Change this number to **20**, and press Enter (Return). Doing so changes the graphic: the rabbit's eyes close, as shown in Figure 7-43.

Figure 7-43. Changing the displayed frame of a graphic symbol

3. Double-click the **Rabbit** symbol in the **Library**, and you'll see why this change occurs. The **Rabbit** symbol has a timeline, and the **Head** symbol changes every 10 frames. You can see this by selecting the head on the stage in frame 1. The instance name in the **Properties** panel is **Head1**. Scrub over to frame 10, click the head on the stage, and the instance name changes to **Head2**.

4. Select the symbol again in the main timeline. Change the **Single Frame** setting to **Play Once**, and change the **First** input field to **10**. This changes the rabbit's head and instructs the graphic symbol to play through the end of its timeline a single time.

5. Drag the playhead slowly to the right to see the heads change while the symbol moves across the stage. At the top, the symbol continues to move but no longer updates the rabbit head. The reason for this is that the symbol's timeline has reached its end but does not repeat.

6. Change the **Play Once** setting to **Loop**, and change **First** to **1**. Scrub again, and you'll see the heads change.

403

CHAPTER 7

You might also want to select `Synch` in the `Looping` properties. When `Sync` is selected for the various spans in a multiple-keyframe classic tween, `Looping` properties are applied to all spans. When `Sync` is deselected, `Looping` properties apply to only the current span. Selecting this option for a nested animation ensures the nested frames in the graphic symbol will be synchronized with the main timeline.

Nesting symbols

Designer and animator Chris Georgenes (www.mudbubble.com) has lent his talents to numerous cartoons on television and the Web, including *Dr. Katz, Professional Therapist*; Adult Swim's *Home Movies*, and, well, more online animation than either of us could shake a stick at. One of the giants in the field, Chris uses combined timelines to great effect in practically all of this Flash work. From walk cycles to lip-syncing, Chris builds up elaborate animated sequences by organizing relatively simple movement into symbols nested within symbols. The orchestrated result often leaves viewers thinking, "Wow! How did he do that?" Luckily for us, Chris was kind enough to share one of his character sketches, which provides a simplified example.

Open the `Grotto.fla` file from the `Example` folder for this chapter. Note that the main timeline has only one frame and only one symbol in that frame (see Figure 7-44). This base symbol is a movie clip, because Chris wanted a slight drop shadow effect on the friendly monster, and graphic symbols don't support filters.

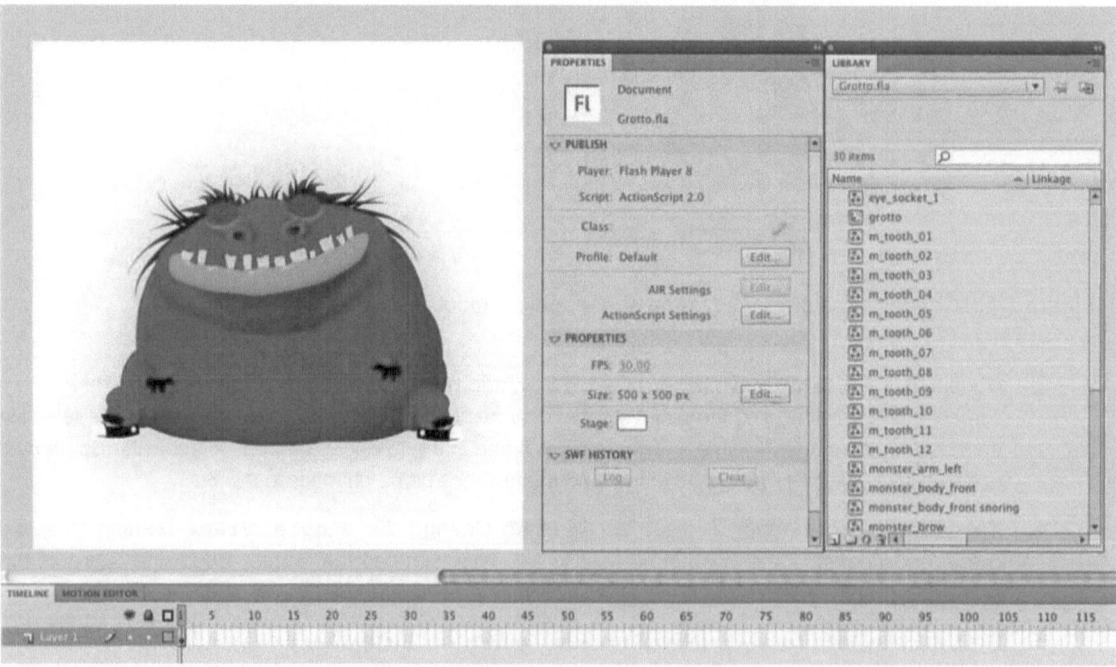

Figure 7-44. Nested symbols allow you to take the most useful features of each symbol type.

Double-click this movie clip to enter its timeline. Even with a basic example like this one, you may be surprised by the number of layers inside. Try not to feel overwhelmed! The layers are neatly labeled, as shown in Figure 7-45. (Now that you see how a pro does it, start labeling your layers as well.) Also, although there are many of them, they all have a purpose. If you like, temporarily hide a number of layers to see how each layer adds to the complete picture. What we're interested in is the mouth.

Figure 7-45. Complex images and animations are built up from simple pieces.

Double-click the `mouth` symbol to enter its timeline. Here, too, there is a handful of layers, comprising the lips, teeth, and a few shadows on this monster. There are 115 frames of animation here—mostly classic tweens, but also a shape tween at the bottom. If you scrub the timeline, you'll see the mouth gently move up and down. This is Grotto breathing (see Figure 7-46). Because the mouth itself is a graphic symbol, its movement can be made to scrub along with the timeline of its parent.

CHAPTER 7

Figure 7-46. Nesting timelines is a way to compartmentalize complexity.

Return to the `grotto` timeline by clicking the `grotto` movie clip icon in the breadcrumbs area of the `Timeline` panel (shown above the monster in Figure 7-46). Drag the playhead to a keyframe, such as 11, and click the `mouth` symbol. Note that it's set to `Loop` in the `Properties` panel and starts at frame 11. Because the `mouth` symbol loops, the mouth itself can be tweened to various locations and rotations during the course of the `grotto` symbol's timeline. The complexity of the mouth's inner movement is neatly tucked away into the `mouth` symbol.

At any point, you can pause this breathing movement by adding a keyframe in the `grotto` symbol's timeline and changing the mouth symbol's behavior setting from `Loop` to `Single Frame`.

The phenomenon you've just seen can be nested as deeply as you like. Even limited nesting, like that in `Grotto.fla`, can, for example, be used to animate a bicycle—the wheels rotate in their own timeline while traveling along the parent timeline—or twinkling stars. Just keep in mind that if a given graphic symbol's timeline is, say, 100 frames long, and you want *all* of those frames to show, the symbol will need to span that many frames in the timeline that contains it. Of course, you may purposely want to show only a few frames.

Graphic symbols as mini-libraries

Between the rabbit and grotto, we are sure you are slowly coming to the conclusion that animation projects can get rather complicated, rather quickly. There are a lot of tweens and symbols, and the odds for becoming quickly entangled in a project seem to be rather significant. Our answer is, "Not really." The graphic symbol's timeline is your life ring.

To understand what we are getting at, open the `TalkingPanda.fla` file found in your `Exercise` folder. (This file is actually a template that ships with Flash CS5. It can be found in `File ➤ New Templates ➤ Sample Files ➤ Lip Synch`).

Lip syncing, when one is first introduced to Flash, is one of those techniques one will avoid because...well...because it looks so hard. Let's get over that right now.

ANIMATION, PART 1

To start, simply press the Return/Enter key to see the project in action. As the playhead moves, the panda says: "Sweet and sour chicken." This is accomplished through the use of the ten graphic symbols you see on the pasteboard and in the Mouth shape with graphic symbols folder in your Library. Each symbol represents a sound or range of sounds, which means you won't need one symbol for each letter of the alphabet.

As you have seen, there are a couple of methods of swapping out the symbols. If you look at the mouth layer, the first conclusion you may come to is that each key frame in the layer represents a symbol from the collection on the pasteboard. This looks complicated because just the word *sweet* looks like you need to use three of the symbols. You could if you are into beating yourself in the head with a board.

Click the first mouth symbol on the stage and open the Properties panel. The first thing you will notice, as shown in Figure 7-47, is it isn't one of the symbols on the pasteboard. It is the mouth symbol. Twirl down the Looping parameter in the Properties panel, and you will immediately see why this example falls smack into the category of "Work smart. Not hard." The Looping Option is set to Single Frame, and each key frame or swap is accomplished by shooting the playhead to a specific frame in the mouth symbol and letting it play from there.

Figure 7-47. Graphic symbols can be used as mini-libraries to keep the real Library from overcrowding.

This is a perfect example of how a graphic symbol's timeline can be used to reduce clutter in the Library. Sure, you can use the Swap button to replace any symbol with another at any keyframe, but it is much less hassle to update the First field in the Properties panel for graphic symbols. This technique is one of those hidden gems that becomes a favorite once you realize it, and we thank Chris Georgenes for sharing such a useful trick.

CHAPTER 7

> *For more information about character design, advanced tweening, and lip-syncing techniques, search* Chris Georgenes *on the Adobe website (http://www.adobe.com/). You'll find a number of Chris's articles and Macrochats (Flash-based recordings of live tutorial presentations).*

Motion guides

Tweening in a straight line is effortless, and we've shown how easing can make such movement more realistic. But what if you want to tween along a curve? Wouldn't it be great if we could tell you that it's only marginally more difficult? Well, we can, and we'll even show you. The trick is to use something called a **motion guide**, which requires its own layer. You were first introduced to this feature at the end Chapter 1, but now is the time to really look at it. When you get to Chapter 8, you'll see an even easier way to do this for motion tweens, but for classic tweens, motion guides are the way to go.

1. Open the MotionGuide.fla file in this chapter's Exercise folder. You'll see a butterfly graphic symbol in one layer and a curvy squiggle in another. If you scrub the timeline at this point, you'll see the butterfly tween in a straight line with a slight rotation between frames 240 and 275. Butterflies don't really fly like that, so let's fix the flight pattern.

2. Right-click (Windows) or Control+click (Mac) the **flutter by** layer, and choose **Guide** from the context menu, as shown in Figure 7-48. Its icon turns from a folded page to a T-square.

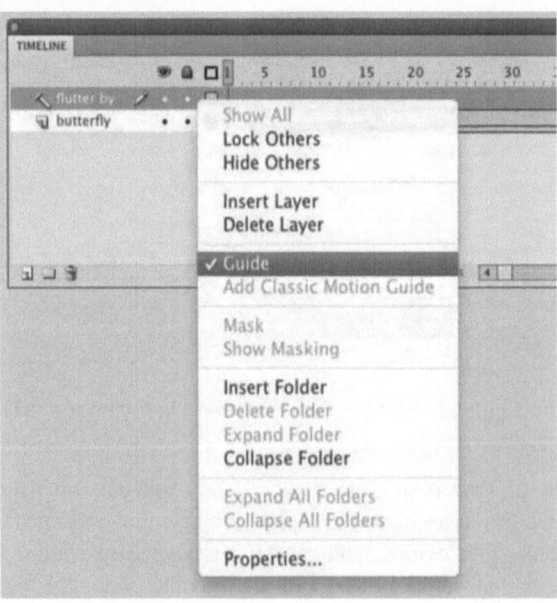

Figure 7-48. Changing a normal layer into a guide layer

ANIMATION, PART 1

You've changed the flutter by layer into a guide layer, which means anything you put into it can be used as a visual reference to help position objects in other layers. Depending on your snap settings (View ➤ Snapping), you can even snap objects to drawings in a guide layer. Artwork in guide layers is not included in the published SWF and does not add to the SWF's file size. In this exercise, the squiggle is your guide—but setting its layer as a guide layer isn't enough. It must become a motion guide. Let's make that happen.

3. Gently drag the **butterfly** layer *slightly up* and then to the right, as shown in Figure 7-49. Drag too high, and you simply swap layer positions. Do it right, and the T-square icon changes into a shooting comet.

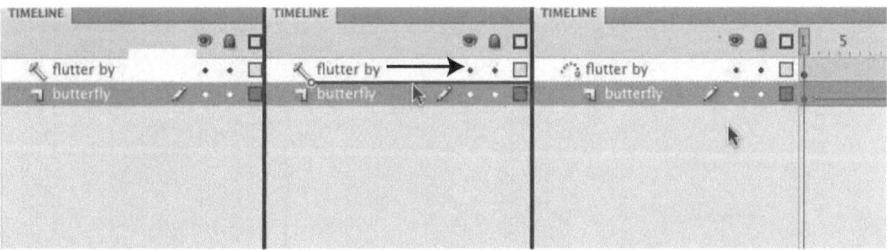

Figure 7-49. Changing a guide layer into a motion guide layer by dragging a layer slightly up and to the right.

To undo this association, simply drag the **butterfly** layer slightly down and to the left again. Practice this a few times, and when you're finished, make sure the **butterfly** layer is reassociated (the T-square has turned into the comet).

> *Motion guides must have a clear beginning and end point, as does the squiggle shown. Guides that cross over each other may cause unexpected results, so take care not to confuse Flash. Also, make sure your motion guide line extends the full length between two keyframes, including the keyframe at either end.*

4. Thanks to the **Snap** setting in the tweened frames (see the **Properties** panel while clicking anywhere inside the tween), the butterfly should already be snapped to the closer end point at the last keyframe. Scrub to make sure. The butterfly should follow the squiggle along its tween (as shown in Figure 7-50). If it doesn't, make sure to snap the **butterfly** symbol to the squiggle's left end in frame 1 and snap it again to the right end in frame 240.

5. Click anywhere inside the tween, and put a check mark in the **Orient to Path** check box in the **Tweening** area of the **Properties** panel. Scrub the timeline to see how this affects the butterfly's movement. The butterfly now points in the direction described by the squiggle.

CHAPTER 7

Figure 7-50. A motion guide affects the tweened path of a symbol.

For more realism, let's add some complexity, as described earlier in the "Combining timelines" section.

6. Double-click the `Butterfly` asset in the `Library` to enter its timeline. Add a keyframe to the `LeftWing` and `RightWing` layers in frames 10 and 20.

7. In the Body layer, click in frame 20, and extend the frames to that point (`Insert` ➤ `Timeline` ➤ `Frame`).

8. Select both `wings` symbols at frame 10, and use the `Free Transform` tool to reduce their `width` by about two-thirds. Use the Alt (Windows) or Option (Mac) key to keep the transformation centered.

9. Add classic tweens to the `LeftWing` and `RightWing` layers, as shown in Figure 7-51. Make sure to add your tweens between keyframes 1 and 10 and also between keyframes 10 and 20.

410

ANIMATION, PART 1

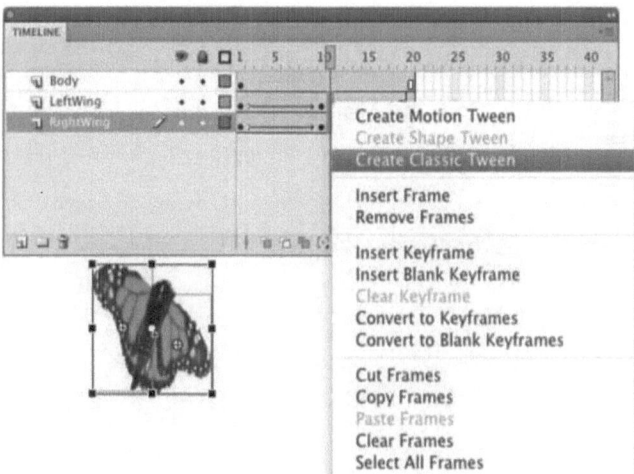

Figure 7-51. Tweening a timeline inside the butterfly graphic symbol

10. Test your movie to see the combined effect.

> *Did you notice an alternate way to create a motion guide in Figure 7-51? The context menu features a selection called* **Add Classic Motion Guide** *just beneath the* **Guide** *selection discussed in step 2. If you choose that instead, Flash handles the gentle dragging described in step 3 for you.*

Tweening a mask

Animating masks is no more difficult than animating normal shapes or symbols. In fact, the only difference is the status of the layer that contains the mask.

Animating a mask

In Chapter 3, you used text to create a mask. In this exercise, you'll use a shape for a mask, and you'll apply a shape tween to it to produce an iris-wipe transition, like in the old movies.

1. Open the `MaskTween.fla` file in this chapter's `Exercise` folder. You'll see three layers: a photo of a doorway in Guangzhou, China, plants in a garden to provide some background texture, and a small yellow dot.

2. Use the **Free Transform** tool to increase the size of the dot in the keyframe in frame 30 so that it matches the width and height of the photo.

411

CHAPTER 7

3. Because the dot is a shape, apply a shape tween between the keyframes in the `dot` layer.
4. Right-click (Windows) or Control+click (Mac), and select **Mask** to convert the `dot` layer to a mask layer.
5. Scrub the timeline to see the result, as shown in Figure 7-52. Easy as pie!

Figure 7-52. Masks can be tweened just as easily as regular shapes or symbols.

Using motion guides with masks

Often, once new designers get comfortable with motion guides and masks, they come to the realization that a layer can be converted to either a guide or mask layer, but not both. Naturally, the question arises, "Is it possible to tween a mask along a motion guide?" The answer is yes, and yet again, combined timelines come to the rescue. Let's see how it's done:

1. Open the `MaskTweenMotionGuide.fla` file in this chapter's `Exercise` folder. The setup here is very similar to the `MaskTweenk.fla` file, except that the `dot` layer is now named **guide mask**.

2. Double-click the guide mask symbol to enter its timeline. Confirm that a dot symbol is classic tweened in association with a motion guide. Return to the main timeline.

3. Right-click (Windows) or Control+click (Mac) the **Dot** layer, and select **Mask** from the context menu. This nested combination gives you a motion-guided mask!

Tweening Filter Effects

It may come as a bit of a surprise, but not only can objects—graphic symbols, text, and movie clips—be tweened but so can filters. Just keep in mind that filters can be applied only to movie clips or text.

In this example, we visit a lounge in Las Vegas and, using filter tweens, fix an obviously broken neon sign. What we are going to do is to have that broken tube flicker on and off as neon is wont to do on occasion. Here's how:

1. Open the `BlueMoon.fla` file in your `Exercise` folder, and take a gander at the timeline. It is quite obvious from Figure 7-53 that the **M** in the sign is not working. To fix it, we started by using the **Pen** tool to trace out the shape of the tube, filled it with a 2-point white stroke, and converted the shape to a movie clip.

Figure 7-53. We start with a broken neon sign.

2. Click the movie clip on the stage, and apply a **Glow** filter with these settings:
   - **Blur X**: 5
   - **Blur Y**: 5

- **Strength**: 100%
- **Quality**: High
- **Color**: F0FDF8

> *How did we know what color to use? We zoomed in on the lights, clicked the filter's* `Color` *chip to open the* `Color Picker`, *and, when you move the cursor over the image, it changes to the Eyedropper. We found a color we liked, clicked it, and that became the color for our glow.*

3. Add a keyframe in frame 60 of the `M` layer, and add a classic tween between the two key frames.
4. Add eight more randomly placed key frames between the two keyframes.
5. Select each new keyframe, and change the `Blur` and `Strength` values of the filter. The objective here is to create the effect of a flickering neon sign.
6. When finished, return to frame 1, and press the Return/Enter key to see your attempt, as shown in Figure 7-54, at a neon repair. If you really want to "rock" this sign, try tweening the alpha from the `Color effect` drop-down to fade the letter in and out.

Figure 7-54. *Repairing a neon sign is easy with filter tweens.*

Programmatic animation

To this point in the chapter, we have explored physically moving things from "here" to "there" using tweens. In this, the final section, we are going to let ActionScript shove things around. This is a rather large subject because, as you have discovered, animation involves a lot more than motion. Everything you have done to this point—move, distort, swap, change—can just as easily be done using ActionScript.

Our intention is to show you how this is accomplished. That's the good news. The bad news is we can't cover the subject in any great depth because it is massive. Still, once you understand, in broad terms, how ActionScript moves stuff around, you can start to fully explore how games are created, slide shows are pulled together, and interface elements such as sliders are constructed.

Prior to Flash CS5, the coauthors of this volume would spend a quite a bit of time prior to writing the book discussing how we could approach this subject in a very short space. We inevitably gave it a pass, not because we were lazy, but because we felt we couldn't do the subject justice in the space allotted. Flash CS5 changed that equation. The application contains code snippets and templates that are ideal learning tools, and we strongly urge you to fully explore them and to take from what you learn with them and apply it to your projects.

> *For those of you who become inspired with this section and want to learn more, look no further than* Foundation ActionScript 3.0 Animation: Making Things Move *written by our colleague here at friends of ED, Keith Peters.*

In this section, you are going to do the following:

- Let Flash convert motion to ActionScript
- Create a small game that uses the keyboard to control an object's motion
- Create random motion that simulates particles jiggling around in a suspension.

Again, these are very simple projects, using very simple code to accomplish some very basic tasks. Even so, if you are new to this, you have to start somewhere, and this is as good a place as any. Let's start by bouncing that rabbit around the screen.

CHAPTER 7

Copying motion as ActionScript

You'll start with a really neat option, introduced in Flash CS3, that fits this chapter like a glove. The option is called `Copy Motion as ActionScript 3.0`. Here's how it works:

1. Open the `CreateMotionAS3.fla` file in the Chapter 7 Exercise folder. You will see that we have added an animated ball and a parrot to the stage, as well as an `actions` layer (see Figure 7-55).

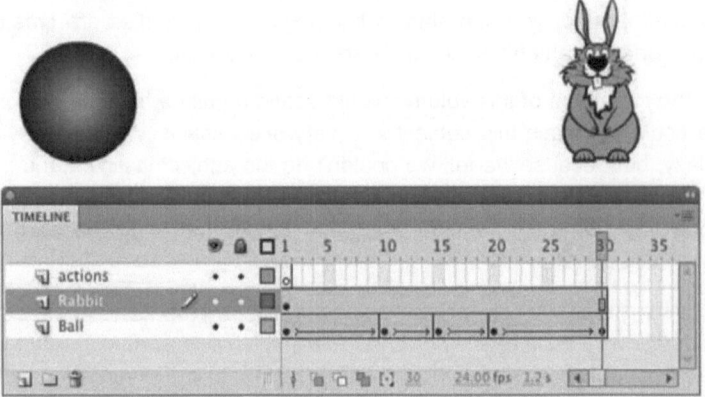

Figure 7-55. We start with a ball and one really dumb rabbit.

2. Scrub the playhead across the timeline. You will see the ball fall to the bottom of the stage, squash, stretch, and bounce back up to the top of the stage. Let's apply that animation to the rabbit.

3. Select the rabbit on the stage, and in the `Properties` panel, give it the instance name of `Rabbit`.

4. Select the first frame of the `ball` layer, press the Shift key, and then select frame 28. This selects all but the last frame of that layer. Why all but the last? Because only the first 28 frames will contain a classic tween.

5. With the frames selected, either select `Edit ➤ Timeline ➤ Copy Motion as ActionScript 3.0`, as shown in Figure 7-56, or right-click (Windows) or Control+click (Mac) and select `Copy Motion as ActionScript 3.0` from the context menu.

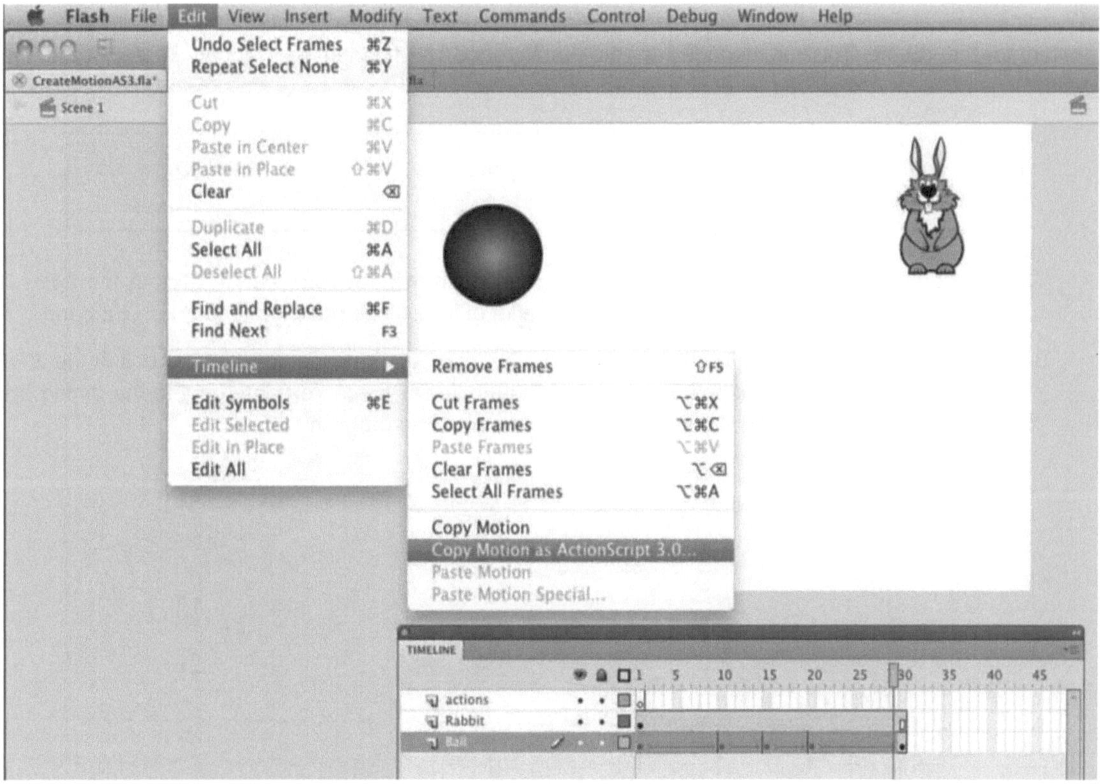

ANIMATION, PART 1

Figure 7-56. You can access the command through the `Edit` menu item or the context menu.

6. When you select that menu item, a dialog box will open asking you for the name of the symbol to which the motion will be applied (see Figure 7-57). Enter `Rabbit`, and click `OK`.

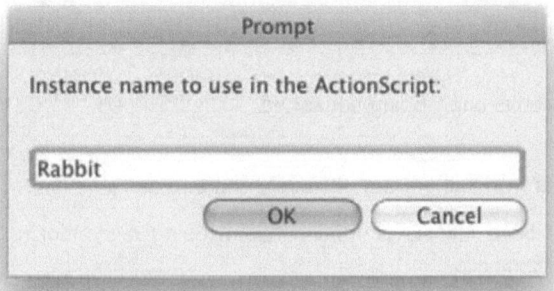

Figure 7-57. You must identify the instance to which the ActionScript will be applied.

417

What you have done is ask Flash to translate the motion of the ball into ActionScript and apply that same motion to the rabbit. This all happens in the background, and when the motion is translated into ActionScript, the code is placed on the clipboard.

> *Be careful not to paste anything to the clipboard at this point! You'll erase the ActionScript that was copied there in step 6.*

7. Select the first frame of the `actions` layer, and open the `Actions` panel. Click in the `Script` pane, and select `Edit ▶ Paste`. The code—a lot of it!—will be pasted into the `Script` pane.

8. Save and test the movie. The rabbit takes on the animation and distortion of the ball in the SWF (see Figure 7-58). This happens because of the instance name you entered into the dialog box (`Rabbit`), which matches the instance name you gave the rabbit in step 3.

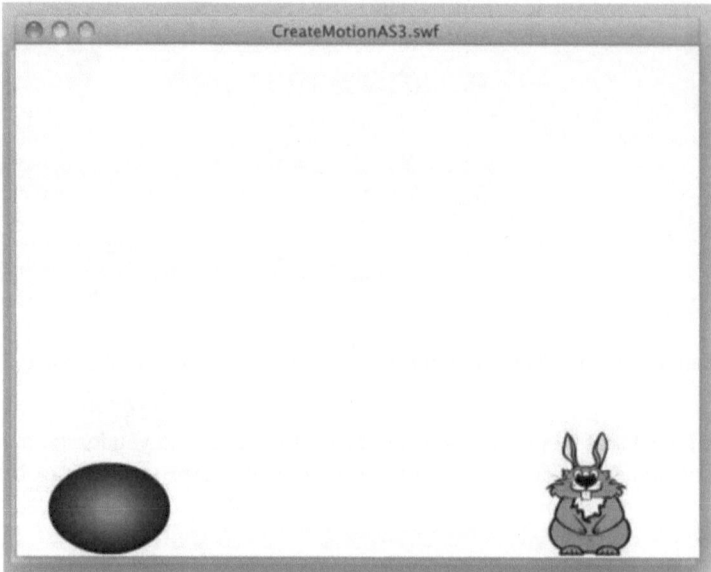

Figure 7-58. Only stupid rabbits enjoy being squashed.

Now that you know how this works, there are obviously some rules:

- The motion must be a classic or motion tween using a symbol (any symbol will do; the ball happens to be a movie clip).
- The code can be applied only to a movie clip, because you'll need to supply an instance name, and graphic symbols don't allow for that.

ANIMATION, PART 1

The great thing about this feature is that the tween can contain the following properties and features (many of which we've talked about in this chapter):

- Position
- Scale
- Skew
- Rotation
- Transformation point
- Color
- Blend modes

- Orient to path
- Cache as bitmap
- Frame labels
- Motion guides
- Custom easing
- Filters

The bottom line is that you can create, transfer, and reuse some pretty amazing scripted animation effects without writing a single line of ActionScript.

Using the keyboard to control motion

In this very simple example, we are going to use the arrow keys on your keyboard to move a ball along path. Though a very simple example, it is a starting point for many games requiring a user to move something from here to there using the keyboard. Let's get started:

1. Open the `KeyboardControl.fla` file found in your `Exercise` folder. When it opens, you will see, as shown in Figure 7-59, a ball and the white path the ball must follow. The ball is a movie clip and has been given the instance name of **Ball** in the **Properties** panel.

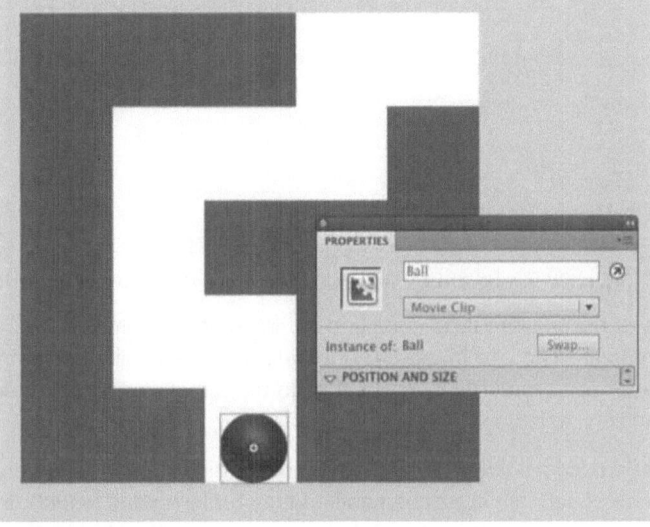

Figure 7-59. You start with a simple path and assign the object to be moved an instance name.

419

CHAPTER 7

2. Select the ball on the stage, open the **Code Snippets** panel, and select **Move with Keyboard Arrows** found in the **Animation** folder.

3. Click the **Add to Current frame** button in the **Code Snippets** panel. An **Actions** layer will be added to your timeline, and **Actions** panel will open. Let's take a look at the code:

```
stage.addEventListener(KeyboardEvent.KEY_DOWN, fl_PressKeyToMove_2);

function fl_PressKeyToMove_2(event:KeyboardEvent):void
{
        switch (event.keyCode)
        {
                case Keyboard.UP:
                {
                        Ball.y -= 5;
                        break;
                }
                case Keyboard.DOWN:
                {
                        Ball.y += 5;
                        break;
                }
                case Keyboard.LEFT:
                {
                        Ball.x -= 5;
                        break;
                }
                case Keyboard.RIGHT:
                {
                        Ball.x += 5;
                        break;
                }
        }
}
```

The code block starts by having the stage listen for keyboard input and, when it detects it, executes the fl_PressKeyToMove_2 function. That's a rather long name, and if it doesn't make sense to you, rename it to something like moveIt. If you do, be sure to change the name after the word function in the next line.

The rest of the code essentially tells Flash: "Don't do a thing unless one of the four arrow keys—UP, DOWN, RIGHT, or LEFT—is pressed." The use of the Switch statement makes life easier for you because it tests for a condition—Is the UP arrow pressed?—and if it is, to do something. The break statement tells Flash there are no other conditions to test for.

Each of the key presses is contained in a case statement, which is how things are done when a switch statement is in play. The beauty of case statements is they replace what would otherwise be your sitting down and writing out a separate function for each key press. It puts all of that in one tidy package.

ANIMATION, PART 1

The magic is found in how the `Ball` instance moves—Ball.x+=5 or Ball.y-= 5. Remember, all on screen motion can occur on only two axes: the x-axis for left to right motion and the y-axis for up and down. The operator (+= or - =) tells Flash which direction to move. If a minus sign is used, the ball moves to the left or up. Use the plus sign, and the opposite occurs. The number, 5, tells Flash how many pixels the ball will move each time a key is pressed.

   4. Save and test the movie.

Creating random motion using ActionScript

The final exercise in this section has its roots with a Scottish botanist named Robert Brown who worked out the math around the random movement of particles suspended in a solution such as water or air. When ActionScript arrived in Flash, it was only a matter of time before such Flash wizards as Jared Tarbell (http://levitated.net/) and James Patterson (http://presstube.com/project.php?id=259) started using math to create particles and jaw-dropping programmatic art such as Jared's example in Figure 7-60.

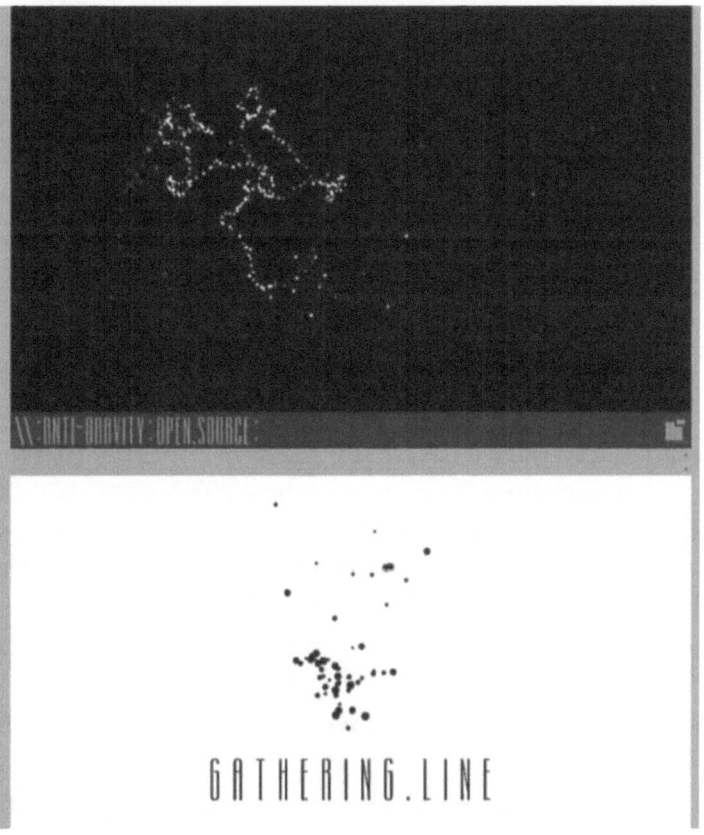

Figure 7-60. Gathering line from levitated.net

CHAPTER 7

In this example, we are going to move into the realm of Flash heresy and actually use a template that comes packaged with Flash CS5. Many Flash developers regard these things with disdain, claiming "real Flash designers don't use templates." Though there is some truth to this, we also might add the templates that ship with Flash CS5 are invaluable teaching and learning tools. Let's get started:

1. Select `File` ➤ `New`, and click the `Templates` button in the `New Document` dialog box.

2. Select the `Animation` category, and select `Random Movement Brownian` (Figure 7-61) in the `Templates` area. On the right side, you will see a preview of the template's stage and a brief description of what the template does underneath it. Click `OK` to open the template.

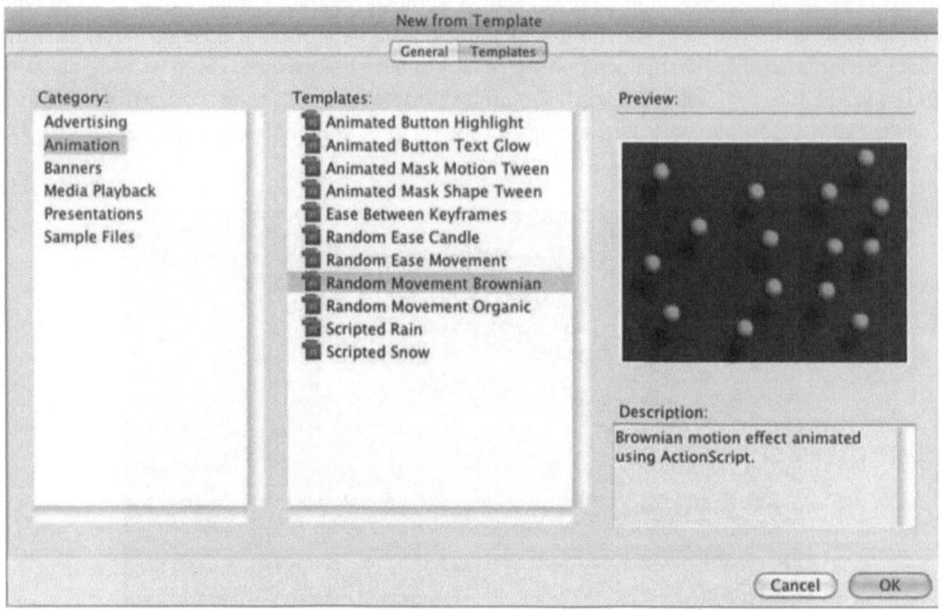

Figure 7-61. Choosing a template in Flash CS5

3. All templates open as an `Untitled` document. When the template opens, feel free to save it to your `Exercise` folder. In this case, Adobe has told us how to check out the code by putting the instruction in a guide layer, which will be ignored when the SWF is created.

4. To start, test the movie. You will see the little green balls jiggling and moving around on the stage. Close the SWF, and let's see how that happens.

5. Double-click any of the balls on the stage to open the `Particle Movie Clip` symbol found in the `Library`.

6. Select the first frame of the `Actions` layers, and open the `Actions` panel. When it opens, you will see this code:

ANIMATION, PART 1

```
var moveAmount:Number = 12;

addEventListener(Event.ENTER_FRAME, fl_randomParticleMove);
function fl_randomParticleMove(evt:Event):void
{
        var xChange:Number = Math.round( Math.random()*moveAmount - (moveAmount/2)
);
        var yChange:Number = Math.round( Math.random()*moveAmount - (moveAmount/2)
);
        x += xChange;
        y += yChange;

        if(x > 550) { x = 0; }
        if(x < 0) { x = 550; }
        if(y > 400) { y = 0; }
        if(y < 0) { y = 400; }
}
```

Your first reaction to the code most likely was "Come on, there's got to be more to this." That is quite understandable considering you saw all of those balls jittering around the stage in the SWF. What you need to understand is that each ball on the stage is a copy of this movie clip, and the ball in the movie clip is managed by this simple code. Let's go through it.

The code starts off by setting a number for how far the ball will move. In this case, the distance is 12 pixels. To change the effect, feel free to play a "what if?" game and change the number. "What if?" games are wonderful ways of learning how things work in ActionScript. In this case, it would be "What if I change the number to 24. What would that look like?" Do that, and the balls, when you test the SWF, move into jitter overdrive. Reduce the number to 6, and things slow down. The rest of the code explains how that happens.

This is a one-frame movie, so the next line listens for the playhead to come back into the frame—ENTER_FRAME—and when it does, the function is executed. This is a way of looping a one-frame timeline.

The function uses math to change the x and the y position of the ball, each time the playhead comes back into the frame. This is accomplished by first using the Math.round() method to strip off any decimal points that result from the calculation between the bracket. The calculation creates a random number between 0 and 1, multiplies it by the moveAmount set in line 1, and multiplies that result by half of the moveAmount variable. To wrap your mind around this, let's walk through the math assuming the random number chosen is .92:

```
var xChange:Number = Math.round( .92*12 - (12/2) );
var xChange:Number = Math.round( .92*12 - (6) );
var xChange:Number = Math.round( 11.04 - (6) );
var xChange:Number = Math.round(5.04);
var xChange:Number = 5;
```

That result is then used to move the ball over and down on the x- and y-axes by 5 pixels.

423

The `if` statement keeps an eye on the location of the ball on the stage. Obviously there is a potential for the number to eventually move the ball off the stage. This statement checks its location and, if it does indeed move outside of the stage's 500 by 450 boundary, yanks it back on to the stage.

Brownian bonus round

If you are new to ActionScript, this is a great place to start the process of understanding that, when it comes to code, you usually play with numbers. Just because this is the code you were given doesn't mean you don't have permission to change it. Try the following, and see what happens in the SWF when you make the change:

- Change the `moveAmount` number.
- Change the `moveAmount/2` calculation to `moveAmount*.3` or any other number or operator such as -, * and +.
- Reduce the values in the `if` statement to see how a more confined space will affect the movie.
- Add a few more copies of the movie clip to the stage.

NOGGIN NUGGETS OF GOLD FROM A VISIONARY RASCAL

Back in high school, one of the former authors of this book, David Stiller, fancied himself a poet. As often happens in those formative years, the subject was introduced in terms of rhyme schemes. To be sure, there's nothing essentially wrong with that. The usual Romantic role models—Byron, Wordsworth, Keats, Longfellow, Emerson, and so on—wallowed in rhyme. It's a long-standing custom in many artistic disciplines to "study the masters" first, and for good reason. The masters figured out where all the pebbles were, which toughened their feet. Walk in their shoes, and you benefit in the same way.

Of course, once traditions are in place, the path is cleared for visionaries: inventive weirdos who see things differently, who dash off into the brush and break the rules. People who find new pebbles. Think ee cummings. What we've shown you in this chapter are a number of well-worn trails. Shape tweening and shape hints, classic tweening and easing...these are familiar corridors for many a Flash master. We encourage you to tramp along these paths until your shoes are good and comfortable, and then be at the ready to kick off your shoes and sprint with the visionaries.

If you can keep up with him, you'll want to chase the flapping longfellows of John Kricfalusi (http://johnkstuff.blogspot.com/), creator of *The Ren & Stimpy Show* and pioneer of Flash-animated cartoon series. A full decade ago, John broke new ground with the "The Goddamn George Liquor Program," which had cartoon fans laughing until...well, until milk gushed from their noses. For Flash cartooning, that was an Internet first. What's John's rhyme scheme? Enjoy Flash for the useful tool it is, but pile up most of your eggs in that basket called your brain. Here's what he had to say:

ANIMATION, PART 1

"I have been asked to write up some tips about how to creatively use Flash. I guess my best advice is to lean on it as little as possible, to not use it as a creative crutch. Flash isn't inherently a creative tool. It's not like a pencil or a brush or talent.

"I use it mainly as an exposure sheet to quickly test my drawings and animation to see if they work. Your best Flash tool is your drawing skill. You will always creatively be limited by your ability to make interesting drawings and movement. I see many animators using Flash mainly for its in-betweens, or **tweens** *as they are now called. This little tool makes every movement look smooth. But if you want to compete against the best animators, whether in Flash or in traditional animation, you will be competing with drawings, acting, and real motion [see the following illustration]. Real motion has nonmathematical in-betweening. Every in-between looks different and conveys information that mere tweening can't. Tweening just moves the same drawing from one place to another, and it's completely obvious when you watch most Flash cartoons that you are watching tricks, not animation.*

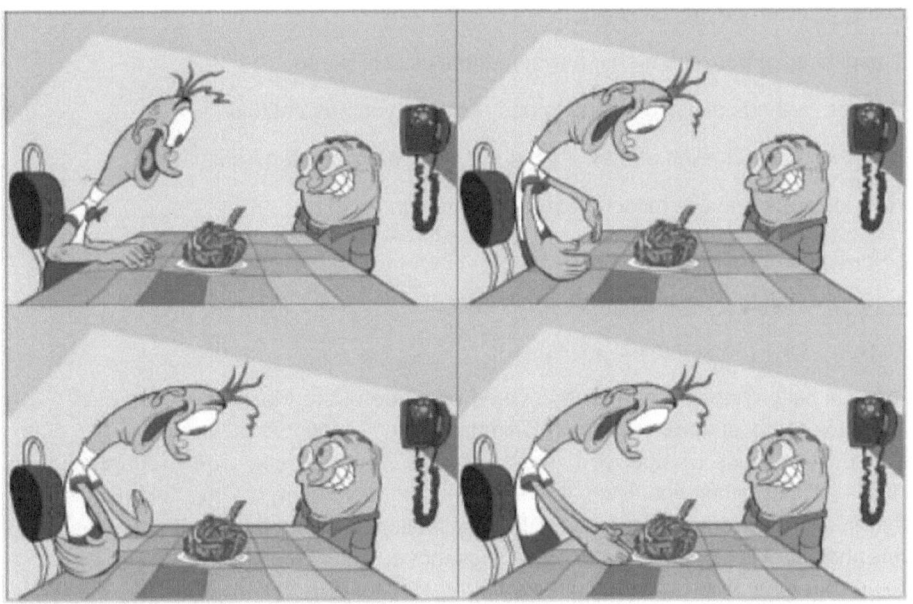

No amount of tweening can accomplish such joyous hand clapping: those are frame-by-frame drawings.

"Since I started using Flash back in caveman times, I've been trying to find ways to make it not look like Flash, to try to undermine all its computery tricks. I've tried different approaches. It's hard for me to draw my key poses directly on the computer, so I usually draw them in pencil and scan them in. Once they are in, I time them in the timeline to musical beats. When I'm satisfied with the rough timing, I then draw breakdown poses directly on a Cintiq

(www.wacom.com/cintiq/) in the timeline. I constantly roll across the animation to see if the motion is smooth. If I'm animating to a dialogue track, I draw the mouth positions in Flash and, again, roll back and forth to see if the animation is working.

"I am always trying new ways to beat Flash's limitations and don't have a perfect solution. The best thing about Flash, to me, is that you can instantly see if your animation works, because you can play it back right after you do it. But Flash isn't doing the creative part. The drawings are. My best advice for how to be good at Flash is to learn as much about drawing and traditional animation as you can. That'll put you ahead of every Flash animator who just drags around some simple primitive pictures. More and more real animators are starting to use Flash, so the competition is going to get tougher for those who are lacking in drawing skills."

What you have learned

In this chapter, you learned the following:

- The difference between a shape tween and a classic tween
- Various methods of using easing to add reality to your animations
- How to use the timeline and the `Properties` panel to manage animations
- How to create and use motion guides in animation
- How to animate a mask
- How to translate an animation into ActionScript
- How to create programmatic animation

This has been a busy chapter, and we've covered one side of the Flash animation coin. The path so far has led from tweening shapes to turning animations into ActionScript. In many respects, this is an important chapter, because whether you care to admit it, Flash is quite widely regarded as an animation program first—all that other cool stuff it does is secondary. Many of the techniques and principles presented in this chapter are the fundamentals of animation in Flash. If there is one message you should get from this chapter, it is pay attention to how things move.

Thanks to the motion tweening model, that concept—how things move—has been flipped on its head, just like a coin, in a really cool way. The new approach doesn't negate any of the techniques you've seen here. It's just that your kitchen has gotten bigger, and there are a lot of new gadgets! Whenever you're ready to continue cooking, just turn the page.

Chapter 8

Animation, Part 2

What you saw in the previous chapter was a compendium of traditional animation techniques—traditional not in the Flash animation pioneer John Kricfalusi sense, but in the sense that they represent the basic tools Flash animators have used since time out of mind. Some tools don't change simply because they don't have to; *they're that useful*. The exciting part is that Flash CS4 introduced a new set of tools in addition to the time-tested tools. This double-whammy puts you in charge of the workflow that makes the most sense to you. Use one set or the other or combine them—the choice is yours. The best part is that because this is animation, you pretty much have to drink a broth of lukewarm poisonwood oils to not have fun while you're working.

Here's what we'll cover in this chapter:

- Motion tweening, using both the **Motion Editor** panel and the **Timeline** panel
- Advanced easing with the **Motion Editor** panel's graphs
- Manipulating motion paths
- Using motion presets and copying motion from one symbol to another
- Applying inverse kinematics (IK), including the **Bone** and **Bind** tools
- IK tweening

The following files are used in this chapter (located in `Chapter08/ExerciseFiles_Ch08/Exercise/`):

- `Mascot.fla`
- `MascotEasing.fla`
- `MascotCustomEasing.fla`
- `MascotMultipleEasing.fla`
- `ManagingKeyframes.fla`
- `ChangingDuration.fla`
- `MotionGuideSimple.fla`
- `MotionGuideComplex.fla`
- `MotionPreset.fla`
- `Bones.fla`
- `BonesRigged.fla`
- `IK_Poses.fla`
- `badBinding.fla`
- `Spring.fla`
- `SteamEngine.fla`
- `betterBinding.fla`
- `Bind.fla`
- `WaveCanadian.fla`
- `WaveAmerican.fla`
- `Richard.fla`
- `jumping.jpg`

The source files are available online at `www.friendsofED.com/download.html?isbn=1430229940`.

Animating with the Motion Editor panel

Before there were websites like Digg and Delicious and before the term *viral marketing* became a cliché, people actually e-mailed hyperlinks to each other. Some of the earliest must-share Flash animations include Alex Secui's "Nosepilot" (`http://animation.nosepilot.com/`) and JoeCartoon.com's "Frog in a Blender" (`http://joecartoon.atom.com/cartoons/67-frog_in_a_blender`), shown in Figure 8-1. These are classics that still entertain after more than a decade, and they were created with shape tweens and what are now called classic tweens, along with a good dose of elbow grease.

ANIMATION, PART 2

Clearly, the existing animation tool set—the `Timeline` panel and its trusty sidekicks, the `Free Transform` tool, the `Transform` panel, and a handful of others—is perfectly adequate to get the job done. But just as it can be good in a relationship to agree on acceptable word pronunciations *(toe-may-toe* and *toe-mah-toe* come to mind), it will be good for your relationship with Flash to consider other ways to animate content. You're about to start flirting with the `Motion Editor` panel.

Figure 8-1. A scene from Joe Cartoon's infamous "Frog in a Blender" from 2000, which was among the first Flash animations to go viral.

Introduced in Flash CS4, the `Motion Editor` panel provides a second non-ActionScript paradigm for moving things from here to there. It's an alternate mechanism to the classic tweens and shape tweens that are carried out in the `Timeline` panel. In Chapter 1, we gave you a drive-by `Motion Editor` overview, and you've seen glimpses of it in a handful of other chapters. Now that you have read Chapter 7 and have experimented with the various details and nuances of the traditional tweening model, the differences between the old and the new will become abundantly clear.

We suspect there will be a surge of interest in the new-style motion tweens—and there's good reason for that, as you'll see. People will begin to ask, "Which approach is better?" We'll be compelled to reply with the only legitimate answer there is: the best approach depends entirely on whatever works best for the project at hand.

Think of it like this: you've been using a conventional oven for years, when suddenly a newfangled microwave shows up on your doorstep. It's small and sleek and even has a rotating platter. Grinning, you carry it into the kitchen, plug it in, and slide in some of the goulash leftovers from last night. Two minutes and 20 seconds later—*ding!*—you have an instant lunch. "Let's try that again," you think, and put in a glass of milk with Hershey's syrup—45 seconds later, instant hot chocolate. Does it get any better? From this day forward, it takes you only 3 minutes to get fresh popcorn. In many ways, life has gotten easier, but

CHAPTER 8

you can bet your bottom BBQ that the conventional oven isn't leaving its venerable perch. There's no way the microwave bakes a loaf of homemade bread, for example. Then again, a medium rare steak done on the BBQ is far better than one done in a skillet.

Clearly, you'll want the best of both worlds. And your kitchen is big enough for it.

Getting acquainted: scaling and moving

Let's take a comprehensive tour of the Motion Editor panel, covering all the basics. Portions of this will feel like a review after Chapter 7, but it's important to understand how the mechanics of motion, scaling, and distortion are distinct from the machinery of classic tweens. You won't be seeing any shapes, by the way, until much later in the chapter. The Motion Editor panel deals exclusively in symbols and text fields, just as is the case with classic tweens.

In this case, you'll be creating **motion tweens**, which look and behave like their classic cousins. The differences come in how they're made and how you can edit them, as you'll see in the following steps:

1. Open the Mascot.fla file found in the Chapter 8 Exercise folder. When it opens, you will notice the Turtle mascot from Chapter 2 has made a guest appearance. The object you see on the stage is the Turtle movie clip found in the Library.

2. Click the symbol on the stage to select it. Now open the Motion Editor panel by clicking its tab or selecting Window ➤ Motion Editor.

What you see is an inactive panel, as shown in Figure 8-2, which tells you a fundamental principle of motion tweens: they must exist on a **tween layer**, which is a particular mode of a normal layer, as opposed to a mask or guide layer.

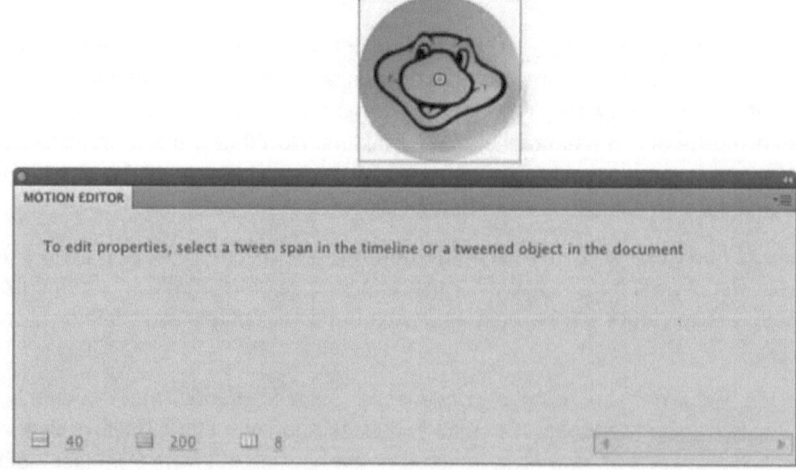

Figure 8-2. The Motion Editor panel is useless without a tween layer.

3. Switch back to the timeline, right-click (Windows) or Control+click (Mac) frame 1, and select **Create Motion Tween** from the context menu. This converts the layer into a tween layer and makes it available to the **Motion Editor** panel. (Alternatively, you can click frame 1 and select **Insert ▶ Motion Tween**.)

When you apply the motion tween, several things happen at once: the single frame stretches out to a 24-frame span, the span turns light blue, and the **Motion Editor** panel becomes active. Why 24 frames? The default length is 1 second, so what you are seeing is one second of animation on the timeline. If you need more time, roll the mouse pointer to the end of the span. When the mouse pointer changes to a double-arrow, click and drag to the right.

4. Open the **Motion Editor** panel again. This time—provided you haven't deselected the tween layer—you'll see the various grids and input controls shown in Figure 8-3. If you see the same message displayed in Figure 8-2, it means you've somehow clicked away from the layer. Either click the layer in the **Timeline** panel to reselect it or click the symbol itself.

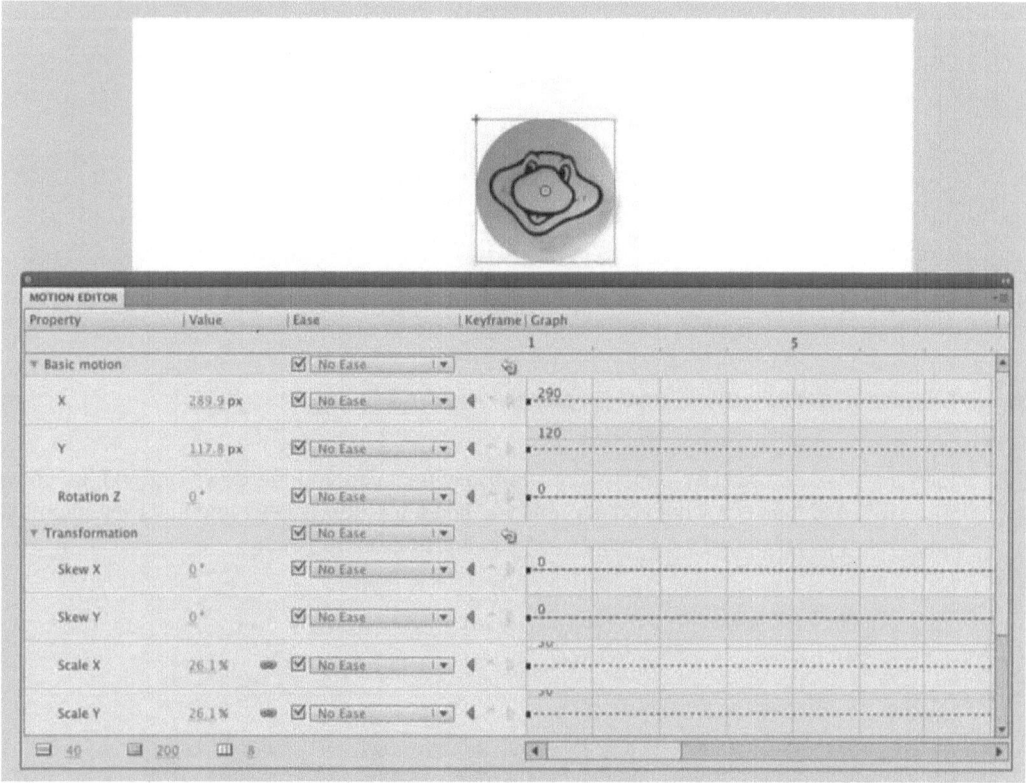

Figure 8-3. Applying a motion tween activates the **Motion Editor** panel for that layer.

CHAPTER 8

5. Removing a motion tween is as easy as applying one. Switch back to the **Timeline** panel, and right-click (Windows) or Control+click (Mac) the tween layer. Select **Remove Tween**, and the layer turns gray again.

It's time to take a look at the some of the differences between motion tweens and classic tweens. The key is to be aware that the **Timeline** and **Motion Editor** panels are fond of each other. You might even say they're connected at the hip. When you apply changes to a tween layer in one panel, you'll see the changes are instantly reflected in the other.

6. In the **Timeline** panel, drag the playhead to frame 20. Use the **Free Transform** tool or the **Transform** panel to make the symbol much wider than it should be.

When you widen the symbol, you'll see a black diamond appear under the playhead in frame 20, as shown in Figure 8-4. Notice the diamond is a tad smaller than the dot that represents the default keyframe in frame 1. The difference in shape and size tells you this is a *property keyframe*, which is just tween-layer–speak for a keyframe.

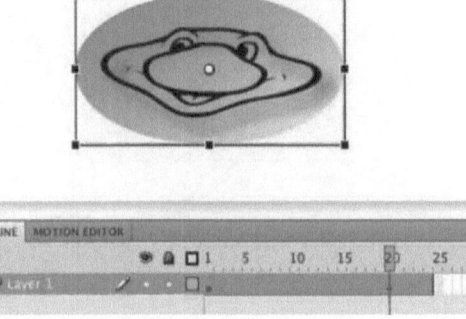

Figure 8-4. Tween layer changes are stored in property keyframes.

7. Open the **Motion Editor** panel. Scroll vertically until you find the **Scale X** grid, as shown in Figure 8-5, and then scroll horizontally until you find the property keyframe that was automatically added when you changed the symbol's width in the **Timeline** panel.

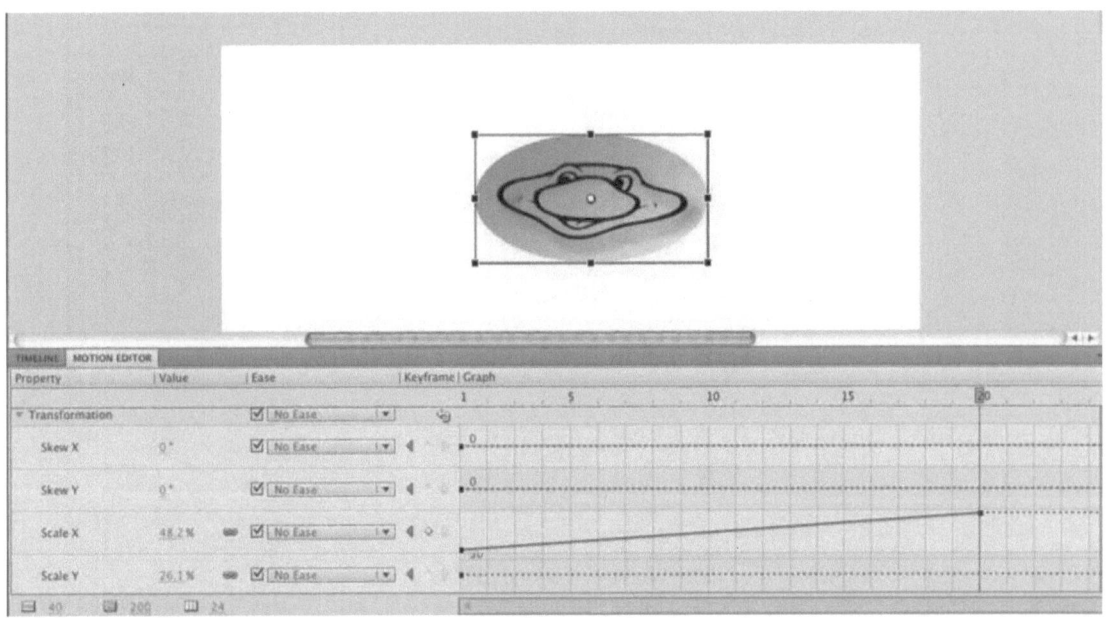

Figure 8-5. The `Motion Editor` panel shows property changes in detailed, collapsible graphs.

8. Click the left side of the `Scale X` grid—somewhere that isn't a word, check box, drop-down list, or other input widget. For example, click in the blank area between the `Scale X` label and the percentage hot text. You'll see the grid snap open to reveal the taller view shown in Figure 8-6.

The particular graph depicted shows a change in x-axis scale; that is—assuming the symbol isn't rotated—the width. The numbers along the left side stacked vertically show values that pertain to this property, which are percentages of scale. The numbers along the top show frames, which equate to changes over time. The text in the yellow box shows you the scale value at that precise point in the graph.

9. Follow the slanted line in the graph from bottom left up toward the upper right. It shows that the selected symbol began at a 100 percent width—the 100 is partially obscured by the slanted line's left point—and was stretched to 200 percent over a span of 20 frames

This is considerably more detail than you get with classic tweens. We'll come back to this graph concept in just a moment. First, back to the kissin' cousin.

10. Open the `Timeline` panel and, with the playhead still in frame 20, drag the `Mascot` symbol to the upper-right corner of the stage, as shown in Figure 8-7. At this point, you've tweened three distinct properties: `Scale X`, the `X` position, and the `Y` position.

CHAPTER 8

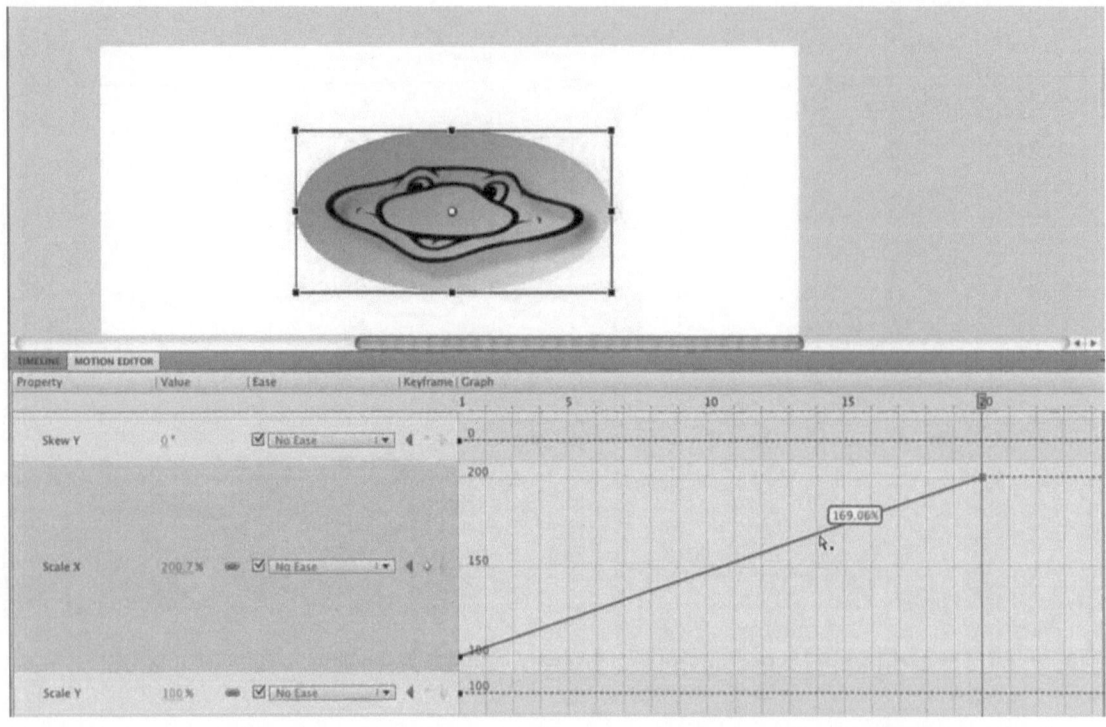

Figure 8-6. Expanded graphs in the `Motion Editor` panel can make data easier to see.

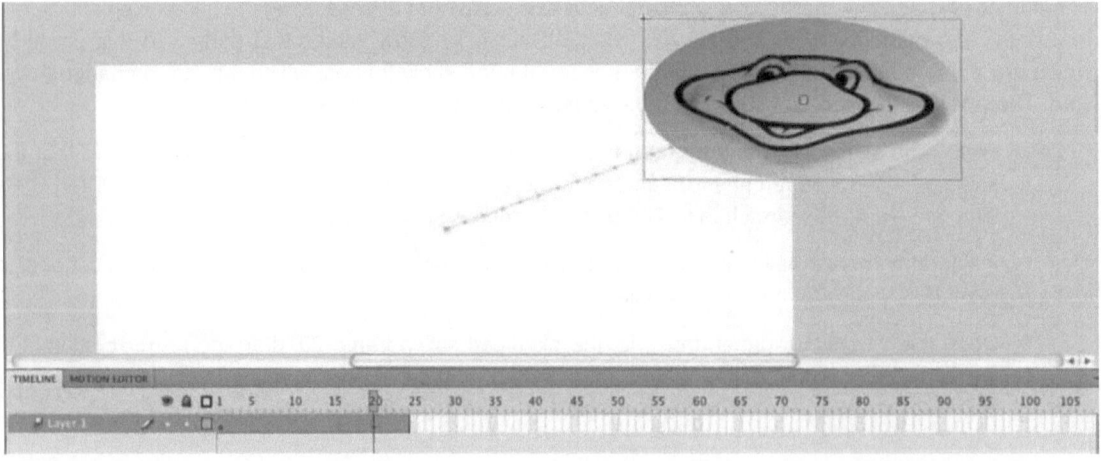

Figure 8-7. Multiple properties aren't shown in the `Timeline` panel but do update the graphs in the `Motion Editor` panel.

ANIMATION, PART 2

Note that the property keyframe, from this view, is still just a small diamond at frame 20 in the timeline. All you can tell at a glance is that something has changed. But even if there's less detail here, the two panels are in agreement, and the `Timeline` panel does give you a summary. Later in this chapter, in the "Changing duration nonproportionally" section, you'll see how the `Timeline` panel's abridged view actually makes it easier to update numerous property keyframes at once.

Naturally, you can *see* the changed properties directly on the stage, not only because the symbol itself is stretched and moved but also because of that green dotted line that connects the current position of the symbol (specifically, its transformation point) to the position it held in frame 1. If you count them carefully, you'll see 20 dots along the line, which represent the 20 frames in this tween span. The dots are all evenly spaced apart, which tells you the tween has no easing applied. Let's check back with the `Motion Editor` panel again before we apply easing.

11. Open the `Motion Editor` panel. You'll see the `Scale X` graph as it was before, but in addition, you'll also see the new changes reflected in the `X` and `Y` graphs, as shown in Figure 8-8.

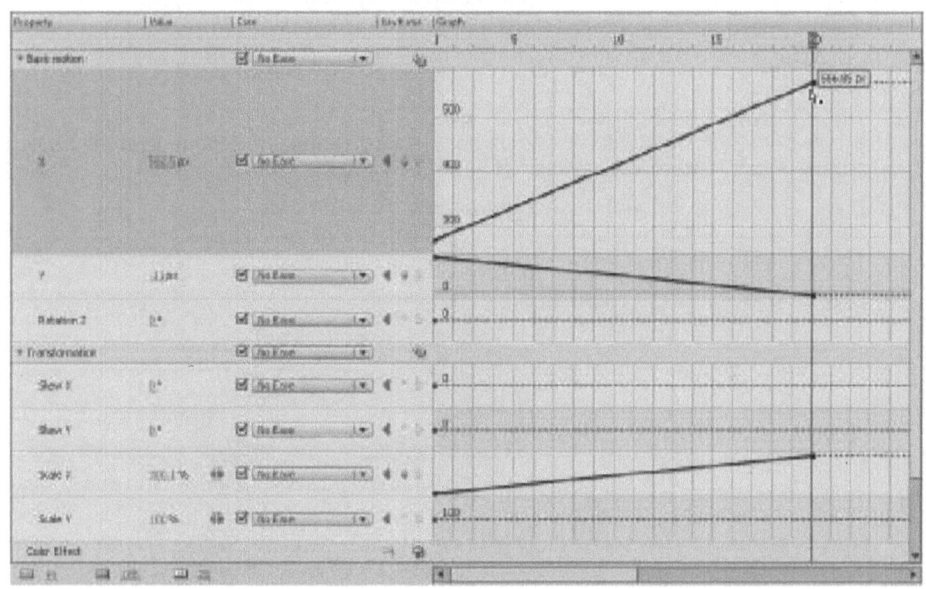

Figure 8-8. In the `Motion Editor` panel, multiple tweened properties can be viewed at once.

The vertical values in these graphs, along with the tooltips, change depending on the property represented. For example, the `X` graph starts at just above 200 on the left side (not 100, like the `Scale X` graph), because the symbol is positioned at 216.4 pixels on the x-axis in frame 1. On the right side of the slanted line, the tooltip reads `555.94 px`, because that's where the symbol is positioned on the x-axis in frame 20. The point to take away from this is that these graphs are adaptable, and they change to suit the values of the property at hand. The `X` graph shows pixels, `Scale X` shows percentages, `Rotation Z` and `Skew X` show degrees, and so on.

435

CHAPTER 8

> *If any of these graphs seem cramped to you, use the three hot text areas at the bottom left of the panel to fine-tune your view. From left to right, they adjust the vertical height of collapsed graphs (`Graph Size`), the vertical height of expanded graphs (`Expanded Graph Size`), and the horizontal width of the graphs themselves (`Viewable Frames`). These values apply across all graphs in the `Motion Editor` panel.*

12. Open the `Timeline` panel, and select the keyframe at frame 20 of the timeline.
13. In the `Properties` panel; twirl down the `Ease` twirlie, if necessary; and scrub the hot text value—`0`, by default—slowly toward the left. Scrub it to approximately `-10`, and then let go. Scrub again to `-20` or so, and then let go. Scrub again to `-30`, `-40`, and so on, until `-100`, which is a full ease-in.

As you scrub and release in small increments, you'll see that the dots, which were evenly distributed after step 12, begin to cluster toward the lower left, as shown in Figure 8-9, which represents the beginning of the tween. You just applied an ease in, so it makes sense that the dots are packed more closely at the beginning of the tween.

> *In classic tweens, easing takes effect only between keyframes. In motion tweens, easing is distributed over the frame span of the whole tween, independent of property keyframes. This is a significant departure from the classic model.*

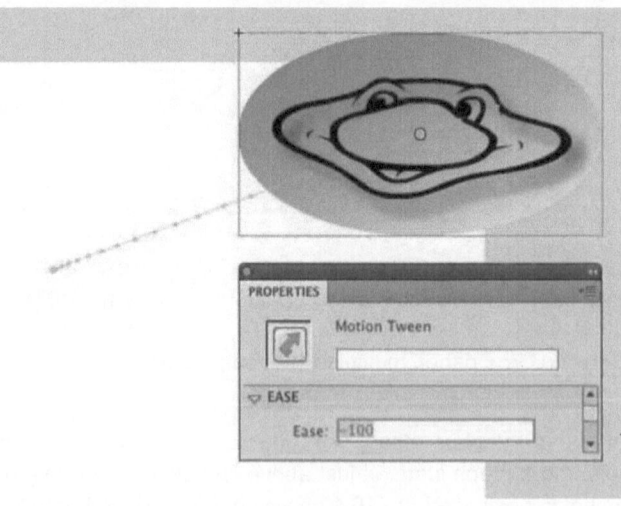

Figure 8-9. Tween layer changes are stored in property keyframes.

14. Close your file without saving it.

Easing applied to a motion tween with the `Properties` panel is the same sort of easing applied to classic tweens, excluding the special-case `Custom Ease In/Ease Out` dialog box, discussed in Chapter 7. To get to the exciting stuff, you'll need the `Motion Editor` panel, and advanced easing merits its own section.

Easing with graphs

When it comes to the `Motion Editor` panel, the concept of easing ascends to a whole new level. For classic tweens, the `Custom Ease In/Ease Out` dialog box is the only thing that came close to sharing similar functionality, yet it provides little more than an introduction. The `Custom Ease In/Ease Out` dialog box associated with a classic tween, while it does get you wet, is a skateboard. It has nothing on the robust flexibility and depth of the `Motion Editor` panel's graphs. In contrast, those are a Lamborghini.

A powerful feature of the `Motion Editor` panel is that it overcomes a subtle, but significant, limitation of the `Custom Ease In/Ease Out` dialog box: classic easing, for whatever property is under consideration, begins at a starting point of 0 percent and ends at a destination point of 100 percent. If you're moving a symbol from left to right—for example, from 25 pixels to 75 pixels—a classic tween begins at its starting point of 25 pixels (0 percent of the destination) and ends at 75 pixels (100 percent of its destination). Normal easing lets you adjust the acceleration and deceleration between those two immutable points. The `Custom Ease In/Ease Out` dialog box lets you adjust the velocity with greater control, thanks to Bezier curve handles. In fact, by adding anchor points, you can even opt to arrive at the destination point early, then head back out again and return later, as demonstrated in Chapter 7 with the bouncing mallet exercise. But in the end, there must always be a final anchor point. With classic easing, the final anchor point is always tethered to the 100 percent mark (see Figure 8-10).

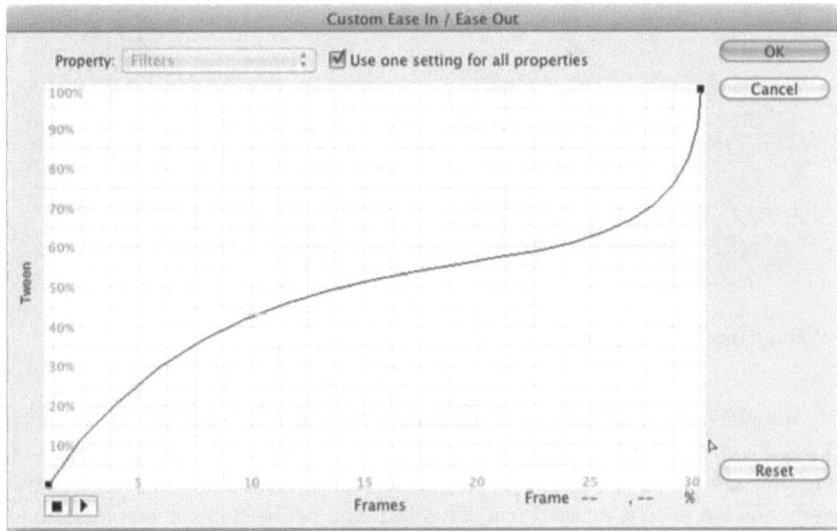

Figure 8-10. With classic tweens, the final easing anchor point (in the upper right here) always ends at 100 percent.

CHAPTER 8

Unimpeded in this regard, the graphs of the **Motion Editor** panel can end up where you like. A custom ease can start at its beginning point of 0 percent, travel three quarters of the way to its destination, dance around a bit, and then return all the way to the beginning.

This freedom within the property graphs is a powerful tool, which is generally a good thing. But as anyone into *Spider-Man* will tell you, "With great power comes great responsibility." Everything comes at a cost, and the price here is that the banished 100 percent restriction can occasionally be disorienting, especially when eases continue past the last property keyframe in a tween span. Let's take a look.

Built-in eases

If you'll pardon the pun, we're going to *ease* into this. Let's start with the built-in eases:

1. Open the `MascotEasing.fla` file in the `Exercise` folder for this chapter. Our cute mascot is back, and this time the symbol has been given a 60-frame motion tween that moves it from the left side of the stage (frame 1) to the right side (frame 30) and then lets it sit in place until frame 60.

2. Select the tween layer or the symbol by clicking it, and then open the **Motion Editor** panel. Find the **X** graph and notice the straight line from the beginning point (bottom left) to the destination point (upper right), as shown in Figure 8-11. Because no other **X** changes occur after frame 30, there are only two property keyframes in the graph.

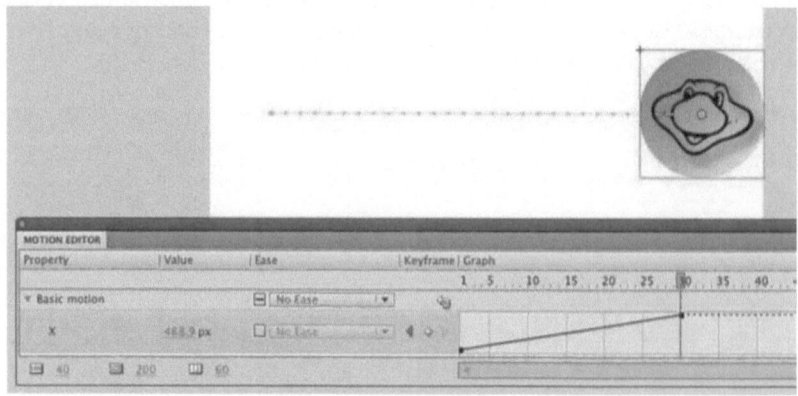

Figure 8-11. Without easing, the graph shows a straight line.

3. Notice the setting on the left side of the graph that currently says **No Ease**. Let's change that. Click the check box to enable easing, and from the drop-down list select **Simple (Slow)**, which is your only choice. At this point, you've applied an ease, and the check mark next to the drop-down means the ease is active. (You can select and deselect this check mark to toggle the ease on or off.)

4. Press Enter (Windows) or Return (Mac), and watch the lunatic move from left to right.

If that doesn't look like easing to you, you're right. Selecting `Simple (Slow)` isn't enough. You need to choose a percentage for that ease, which affects its strength. Think of it as a faucet—applying the ease means you've paid the water bill, but you won't see water until you turn on the faucet.

5. Scroll down to the bottom of the `Motion Editor` panel, and you'll see an `Eases` twirlie. Twirl that down, if necessary, and you'll see the reason why `Simple (Slow)` appeared in the X graph's easing drop-down list.

6. Scrub the hot text as far right as it will go, changing the default 0 to 100. As you scrub, you'll see a dashed line, representing the ease, begin to curve in the graph, as shown in Figure 8-12.

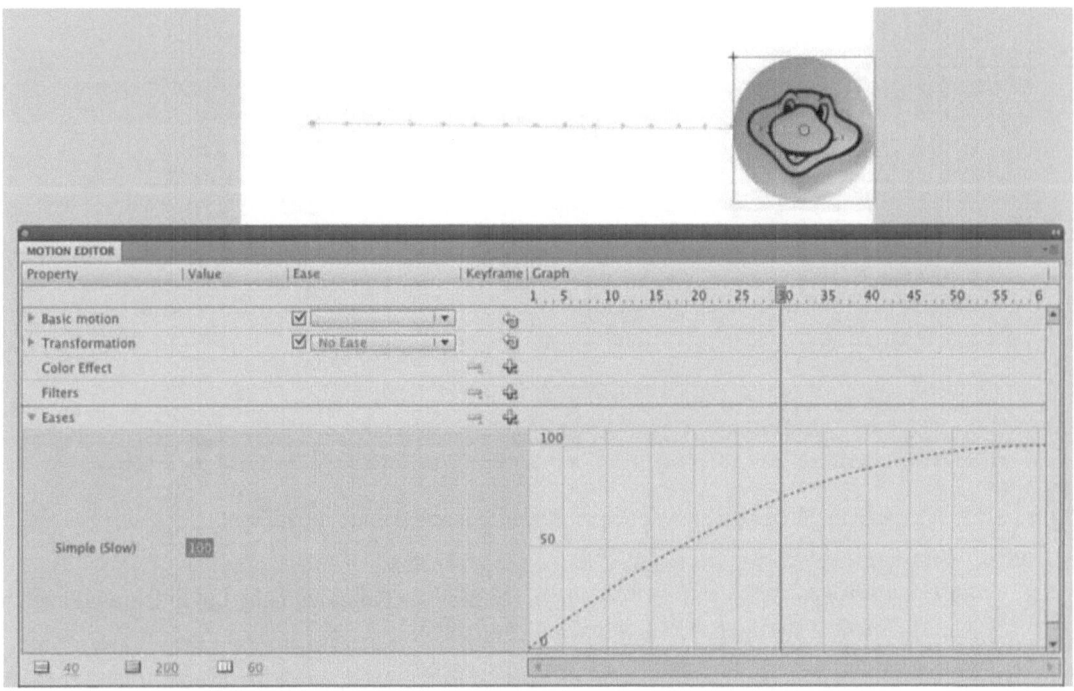

Figure 8-12. Change the default from 0 to 100, and the curve appears.

This particular graph changes the `Simple (Slow)` ease itself, which is comparable to changing a symbol inside the `Library`. As you learned in Chapter 3, changing a `Library` symbol means that every instance of it is changed on the stage. The same goes for these eases. You also might have noticed the mascot shift around on the stage as the ease is applied to the motion.

7. Scroll back up to the **x** graph, and you'll see that the ease is now superimposed over the line that represents the symbol's x-axis movement. To get a better view, click the left side of the **x** graph, and scrub the `Viewable Frames` hot text until all 60 frames are displayed in the graph, as shown in Figure 8-13.

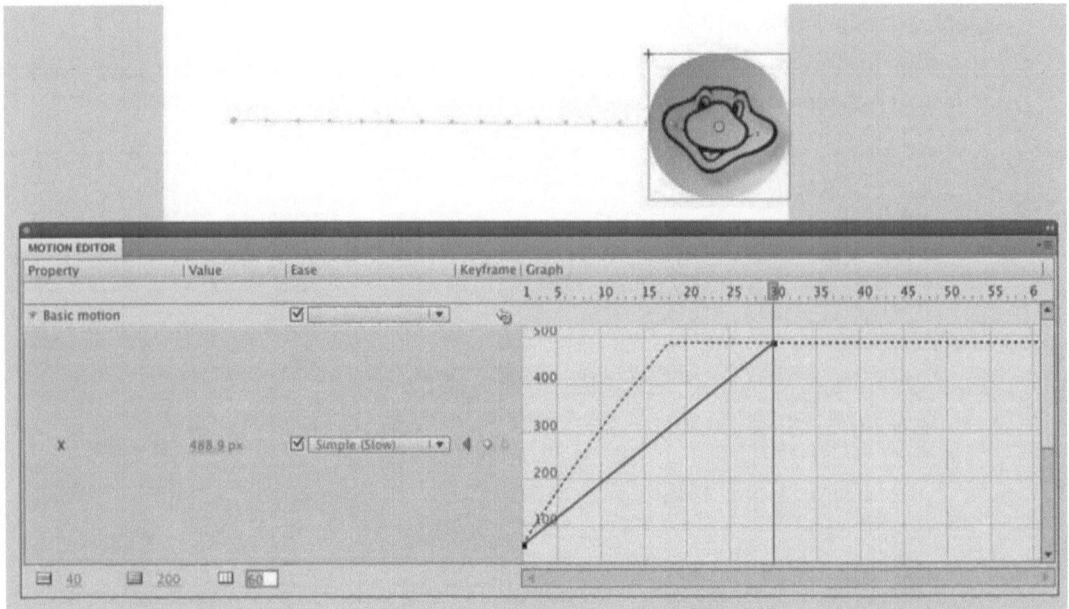

Figure 8-13. With easing, the graph shows actual movement and easing movement.

8. Press Enter (Windows) or Return (Mac) again to preview the movement, but prepare yourself for disappointment: it still doesn't look like much of an ease.

The reason for this is that motion tween eases are applied to the full span of the tween. In this case, the full span is 60 frames, while the only visible change occurs between frames 1 and 30.

9. Click the upper-right property keyframe, and holding down the Shift key, drag the keyframe to the right until you hit frame 60. Doing so brings the solid line and the dashed line into agreement, as shown in Figure 8-14. The tooltip lets you know which frame you're on, and the Shift key constrains your movement.

ANIMATION, PART 2

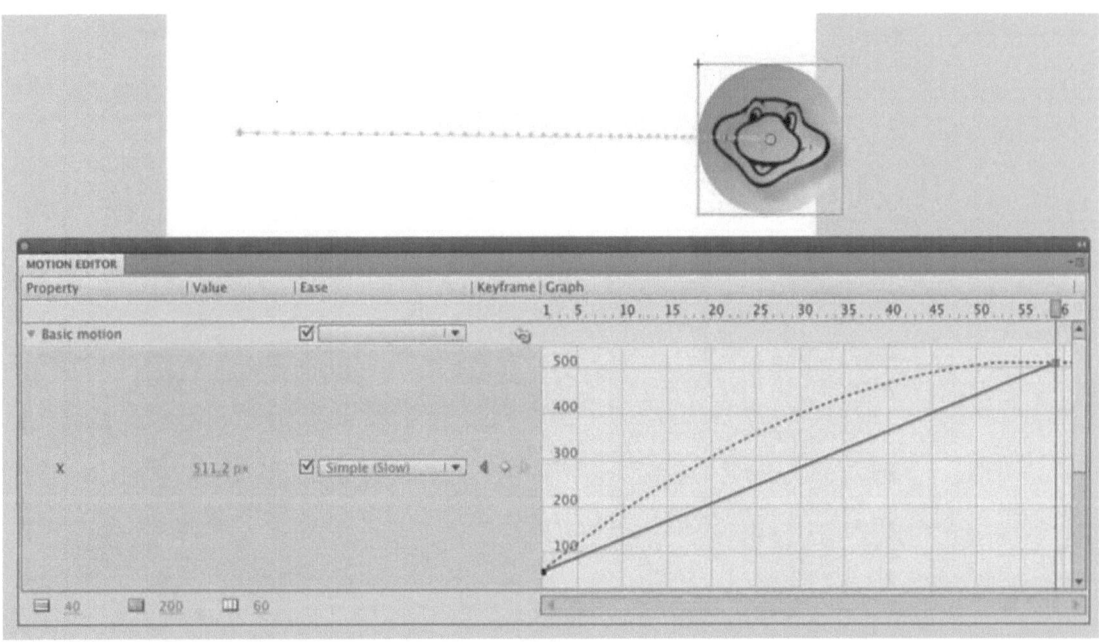

Figure 8-14. Keyframes can be moved from inside a graph.

If you don't use the Shift key while you drag, it's easy to slide the keyframe up and down, even if you intend to move only to the right, which increases the duration between this keyframe and the one before it. Why is it a bad thing to slide up and down? Actually, it isn't. Sometimes, you might *want* to do that, and it's good to know you have the option. Sliding up and down changes the property's destination point. In this case, because you're dealing with x-axis movement, it means that even from this graph, you could push the symbol farther to the right on the stage (slide the keyframe higher) or back toward the left (slide the keyframe lower).

> *The visual result of a property's destination point depends entirely on what the property represents. In the* `Y` *graph, the destination point affects the symbol's vertical position. In the* `Rotation Z` *graph, it affects the symbol's rotation. If you add a color effect or filter, the destination point determines how much of that effect is applied.*

10. Press Enter (Windows) or Return (Mac) again. Because the solid and dashed lines' final anchor points meet, you'll see the full `Simple (Slow)` ease.

11. Using the Shift key again, drag the right property keyframe back to frame 30.

12. Scroll down to the **Eases** area in the **Motion Editor** panel, and click the + button. This opens a context menu offering more than a dozen built-in eases. Choose **Bounce**, as shown in Figure 8-15.

441

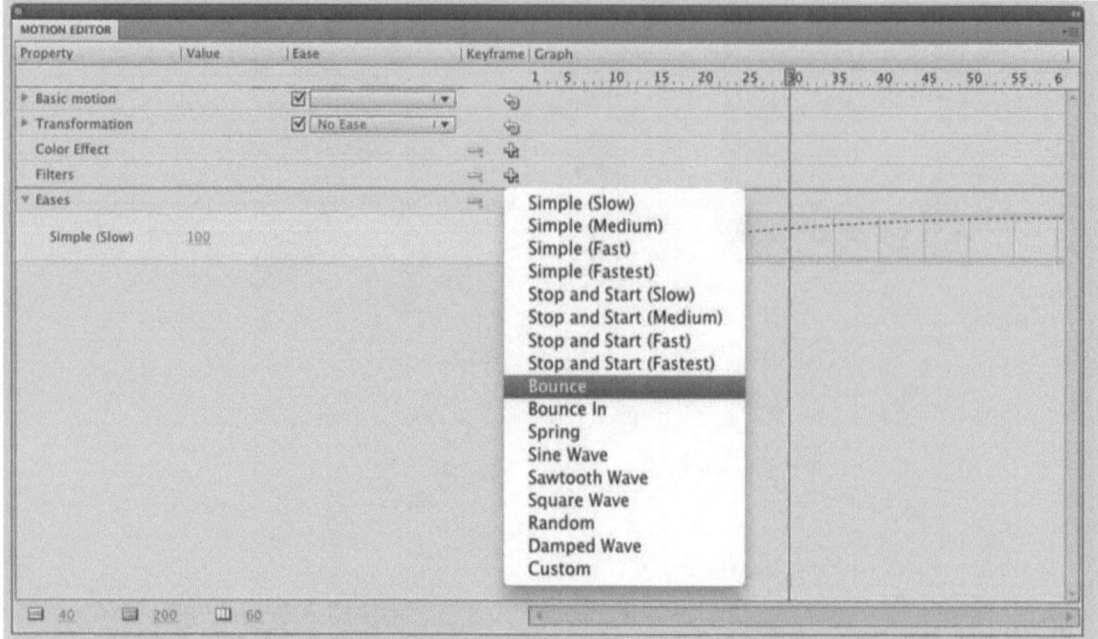

Figure 8-15. Use the + button to add new built-in eases.

13. Scroll down a bit to see the new ease beneath the graph for `Simple (Slow)`. By default, the `Bounce` ease's hot text is set to 4, which makes the four bounces depicted in its graph. Change the hot text to 3 to reduce the number of bounces to three.

Adding an ease to the `Eases` area makes that ease available to all the property graphs in the `Motion Editor` panel. Eases can be applied and changed for each property individually by using that property's drop-down menu and/or check mark. Eases can be applied and changed for whole groups of properties by using the drop-down menus in the `Basic motion` and `Transformation` twirlies. Add as many eases as you like, including multiple custom eases.

As you may have guessed, you can use the – button at any time in the `Eases` area to remove an ease from consideration for all drop-downs.

14. Scroll back up to the `x` graph, and use the drop-down list to change the easing from `Simple (Slow)` to `Bounce`.

Three interesting things happen when you make this change, First, because you moved the property keyframe back to frame 30, part of the `Bounce` ease is clipped, as you can see in the flattened hump of the first bounce—between frames 6 and 27—in Figure 8-16. The second interesting thing is, though the graph may have developed "bumps," they are only on the x-axis, meaning the bumps represent lateral movement, which explains why the motion path on the stage doesn't change. The third interesting thing becomes apparent when you preview the ease.

ANIMATION, PART 2

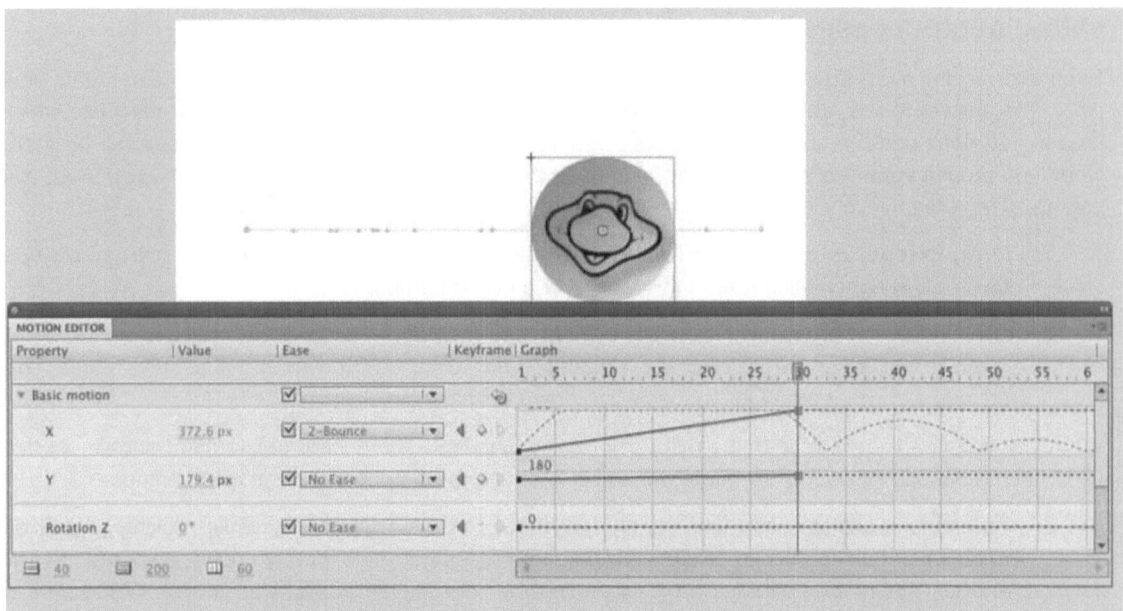

Figure 8-16. Eases can clip when the last property keyframe isn't the last frame in the span.

15. Press Enter (Windows) or Return (Mac) , and watch the mascot slam to the right side, pause for a moment (that's the clipped first bounce), then resume its rebounding course, and finally end up back on the left side of the stage!

With motion tweens, easing can completely override the actual property represented by the solid line in the graph. Without the ease, this is a simple left-to-right movement. With easing, this *could be that*, but as you've seen, it can just as easily change the destination point to one quite outside of Kansas.

> *We chose physical movement to illustrate the mechanics of motion tween easing, because a change in position correlates well with the lines and curves on the graph. Be aware that this concept applies in exactly the same way to rotation, scaling, skewing, color effects like alpha and tint, and filters like Drop Shadow and Blur.*

16. Shift-drag the right property keyframe back to frame 60. Verify that all three bounces are now visible in the **x** graph.
17. Press Enter (Windows) or Return (Mac) to view the full, smooth three-bounce easing of the lunatic.

443

Creating custom eases

Even after seeing more than a dozen built-in eases, you might be wondering whether you can create your own. The answer is yes, and it's pretty easy. Best of all, custom eases are saved with the FLA, which means you don't need to commit all your easing finagling to memory. Your custom eases will be there when you reopen your files in the morning, and even better, once they are added to the `Eases` area, you can apply (and reapply) custom eases to any property, just like built-in eases. Here's how:

1. Open `MascotCustomEasing.fla` in this chapter's `Exercise` folder. Again, we start you with a basic left-to-right motion tween, this time over a full 60 frames.

2. Click the tween layer (layer 1) or the symbol, and then open the `Motion Editor` panel. Scroll down to the `Eases` area, click the `+` button, and select `Custom` from the context menu. This creates a `Custom` graph for you, so scroll down to take a look.

What you see is a line with run-of-the-mill Bezier curve handles. The anchor points and handles operate very much like those for normal drawings with the `Pen` tool, and we encourage you to experiment.

3. To create a custom ease use the Ctrl (Windows) or Cmd (Mac) key while clicking to add an anchor point along the line or curve. The same procedure removes any anchor point but the first and last (there must always be a beginning and destination point). Use the Alt (Windows) or Option (Mac) key while clicking to convert a curve anchor point to a corner anchor point, and vice versa.

4. When you finish, scroll to the `x` graph, and select your custom ease from the `x` property's drop-down menu. Press Enter (Windows) or Return (Mac) to preview the effect.

5. Close your file without saving the changes.

Applying multiple eases

It may not immediately sound ambiguous, but the phrase "applying multiple eases" can actually be interpreted in a variety of ways. To be sure, you can apply numerous eases to a given motion tween—one separate ease for each tweenable property is perfectly acceptable. Give your `x` a bounce, your `y` a `Simple (Slow)`, your `Rotation z` a custom ease, and so on, down the line. What you can't do is to apply more than one ease between property keyframes. If you've used previous versions of Flash, this may take some getting used to, which is why we've stressed that motion tween easing applies to the full tween span, not to the span between property keyframes.

To follow one sort of easing with another sort within the same tween layer, you'll need to use more than one tween span. Here's how:

1. Open `MascotMultipleEasing.fla` in this chapter's `Exercise` folder. This time, to mix it up, we prepared a vertical motion tween for you.

2. Click the tween layer or the symbol, and then open the `Motion Editor` panel. Scroll down to the `Eases` area, click the `+` button, and select `Stop and Start (Medium)`. When its graph appears, scroll down and scrub its hot text to the right until it says `100`.

3. Scroll up to the Y graph, and select `Stop and Start (Medium)` in the easing drop-down menu. Press Enter (Windows) or Return (Mac) to preview the ease, which makes the mascot look as if it were being dragged upward with two heaves of a rope.

4. Select the `Timeline` layer. Right-click (Windows) or Control+click (Mac) the tween span, and select `Copy Frames` from the context menu. Now right-click (Windows) or Control+click (Mac) frame 31, and select `Paste Frames`. Just like that, you've created a twin of the original animation, complete with its easing.

5. Right-click (Windows) or Control+click (Mac) the second tween span, and select `Reverse Keyframes`. Preview the animation again, and this time, the lunatic gets heaved up and then heaved down again. Even though the motion is reversed, the tween is still the same for both tween spans.

6. Head back to the `Motion Editor` panel, and use the `Eases` area's + button to add a `Spring` ease. Scroll up to the Y graph, and change the second span's Y easing from `Stop and Start (Medium)` to `Spring`. Preview the animation, and you'll see the lunatic getting heaved up and then suddenly fall and "sproiiing" to a halt.

Same tween layer, two tween spans—that's how you get two or more types of easing in the same layer. As an aside, notice that the mascot doesn't come to a rest at the bottom of the stage. That's because the `Spring` ease is one of those whose destination point doesn't stop at 100 percent.

Managing property keyframes

Before we turn you loose on a rather interesting project, there is one final issue to cover: property keyframes. The small diamonds you see on a motion layer are called **property keyframes**, and they can be managed in one of two areas: the `Timeline` or the `Motion Editor`. The thing you need to know is that each one has its own way of handling the details. When it comes to exercising fine control of keyframes, the `Motion Editor` is your best bet, but there are a few circumstances where using the `Timeline` panel definitely makes your life simpler. We'll get to that in a moment, but let's start with a diamond:

1. Open the `PixelDisposal.fla` file from the `Exercise` folder for this chapter. When it opens, you will see a character on a sign tossing a red pixel into the trash. If you scrub across the timeline, the property keyframe at fame 35 is where the pixel changes direction, rotates, and starts to shrink.

2. While you are in the `Timeline` panel, the only way you have to move from keyframe to keyframe is to scrub the playhead. Go ahead and scrub to frame 40.

3. Right-click the tween layer at frame 40, and select `Insert Keyframe ➤ Position` from the context menu, as shown in Figure 8-17. A property keyframe will appear at frame 40.

CHAPTER 8

Figure 8-17. Property keyframes can be added from the `Timeline` panel.

4. Select the `Red cube` symbol, and move it downward. As you saw earlier in the chapter, property keyframes are created for you automatically in the current frame when you change a symbol's position, scale, rotation, or the like. What you learned from step 3 is that it's still perfectly OK to create your keyframe first.

5. Switch back to the `Timeline` panel, and right-click (Windows) or Control+click (Mac) again on frame 40. Note that you have options for clearing keyframes and also determining which property keyframes to display in the `Timeline` panel.

Don't be fooled by the `Clear Keyframe` choice! You would think, because `Insert Keyframe` inserts the desired keyframe(s) in the current frame, that `Clear Keyframe` would, like its `Classic Tween` brother, follow suit and remove only keyframes in the current frame. This is not so. By choosing `Clear Keyframe`, you're removing *all property keyframes* in the current tween span. If you select `Clear Keyframe` ▶ `Rotation`, for example, you remove all property keyframes in the `Motion Editor` panel's `Rotation Z` graph, regardless of in which frame they appear.

446

ANIMATION, PART 2

Once you see these features and understand them for what they are, you'll surely find them useful, but the `Motion Editor` panel does more.

6. Open the `Motion Editor` panel, and scrub the playhead of along the `Motion Editor`'s timeline. You get the same sort of preview as the `Timeline` panel. The difference is that the `Motion Editor` panel also gives you a pair of arrows and a diamond, as shown in Figure 8-18.

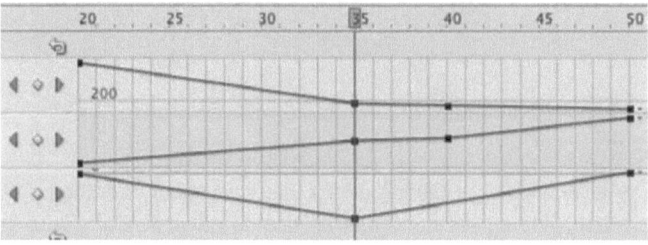

Figure 8-18. In the `Motion Editor` panel, keyframes can navigated, added, and removed with this widget.

Keep an eye on the diamond as you scrub. When you drag the playhead to a frame that already contains a keyframe, the diamond turns yellow. Use the left and right arrows to jump from keyframe to keyframe. Arrows will temporarily become disabled, as appropriate, at the first and last keyframes.

7. Scrub to frame 45, and click the `Y` graph's diamond. It turns yellow, and a new anchor point appears in the `Y` and `X` graphs at frame 15. (The `Y` and `X` graphs are synchronized, but this isn't the case with most property graphs.) Click the diamond again, and the keyframe disappears. Click it a third time to bring the keyframe back.

8. With the new keyframe in place, use the mouse to drag the anchor point in the `Y` graph downward, which correspondingly moves the cube upward on the stage. Note how the anchor point snaps to frames if you slide it left and right. That makes sense, because you can't have a keyframe between two frames.

9. Move your mouse elsewhere in the `Y` graph, and then hold down the Ctrl (Windows) or Cmd (Mac) key while you hover over one of the line segments. As shown in Figure 8-19, the cursor turns into a pen with a plus sign, which indicates you can click to add a new keyframe. Hover over an existing keyframe while holding the Ctrl (Windows) or Cmd (Mac) key, and you'll see a pen cursor with a minus sign. Click to remove the keyframe.

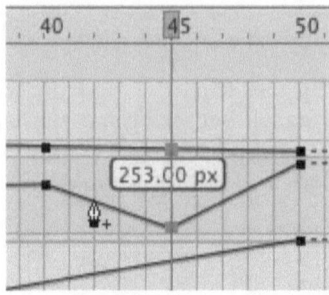

Figure 8-19. Keyframes can also be added and removed with the mouse.

10. Hold down the Alt (Windows) or Option (Mac) key, and hover over the keyframe in frame 45 in the `Rotation Z` graph. The cursor turns into an upside down V. Click, and this converts the anchor point into a curve anchor, which can be adjusted with Bezier handles (Figure 8-20). The effect of these handles on the `x` and `y` graphs isn't always obvious, but for many properties, it gives you a "quick-and-dirty" custom ease.

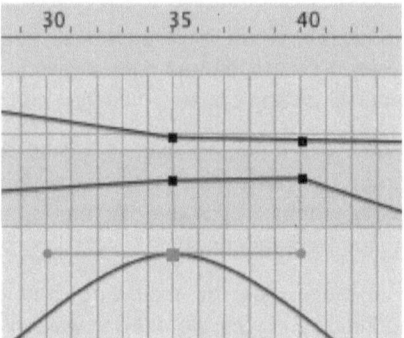

Figure 8-20. Anchor points can be converted from corner points to smooth with the Alt (Windows) or Option (Mac) key.

11. Grab the right Bezier curve handle, and drag it up and to the right so that the curve rises above its 100 percent mark, as shown in Figure 8-21. As you drag the point watch the rotation of the cube as you move the anchor point up or down on the graph and as you move the handles on the curve.

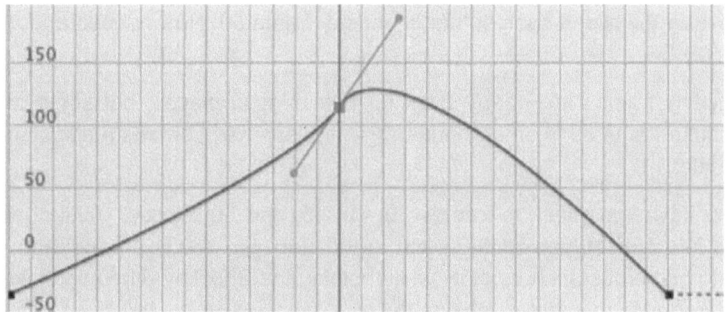

Figure 8-21. Anchor points can be manipulated with Bezier curve handles.

12. Press Enter (Windows) or Return (Mac) to preview the animation, and you'll see that the symbol rotates farther than it did before—you've pushed it past its original destination, to approximately 160 percent—and then eases back the `Rotation Z` setting in the property keyframe at frame 50. Don't close this file just yet; we are going to work some further "magic" on it in the next exercise.

As helpful as the `Motion Editor` panel is, sometimes less is more. When you want to compress or expand the duration of a tween span, for example, the `Timeline` panel is the only way to do it, if you want to do it proportionally. If not, you could use either panel, but the `Timeline` panel makes it easier.

Changing duration proportionally

The animation in the `PixelDisposal.fla` you were just using spans 60 frames. At 24 fps, that's approximately 2.5 seconds, which may or may not be what you want. To change a tween span's duration proportionally, you'll need to use the `Timeline` panel. Here's how:

1. Move your mouse to the right edge of the tween span. You'll see the cursor turn into a double-headed arrow, as shown in Figure 8-22. Click and drag toward the left. For example, shorten the tween span so that it ends at frame 50. Notice that all four property keyframes are still in place, and, proportionately speaking, are the same relative distance from each other as before.

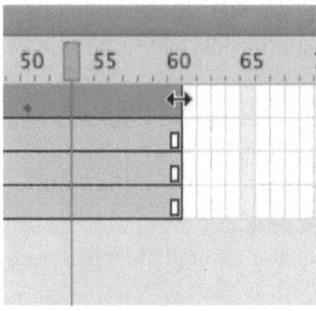

Figure 8-22. Drag the tween span to shorten or increase a tween's duration.

2. Click and drag the tween span so that it ends at frame 59. Now release and drag the tween span to frame 60.

This time, the property frames are *nearly* back to their original places, but some are slightly off. That makes sense, because frame 59 is an odd number, and Flash had to make a decision on how to shift the frames to compensate.

To get the property keyframes back to frames 30, 40, 45, and 50 exactly, you'll need to use a different approach. If you're into tedium, you could switch to the `Motion Editor` panel and visit every property graph in turn, sliding numerous anchor points while holding the Shift key. The middle keyframe, especially, would give you a headache, because it affects the `X`, `Y`, `Rotation Z`, `Scale X`, and `Scale Y` graphs. There's an easier way, and we describe it in the very next paragraph.

Changing duration nonproportionally

Sometimes you'll want to change the duration *between* property keyframes, which may or may not incorporate a change in span duration. You could do this with the `Motion Editor` panel, visiting each relevant graph and moving property keyframes individually, or you can update the keyframes in several graphs at the same time. For that, use the `Timeline` panel. Here's how:

1. Continuing with `PixelDisposal.fla` file you have been working on and still in the `Timeline` panel, hold down the Ctrl (Windows) or Cmd (Mac) key and click the keyframe closest to frame 35. Notice that holding down Ctrl (Windows) or Cmd (Mac) allows you to select a single frame in the tween span, rather than the whole span.

2. Now that you have a single property keyframe selected, release the Ctrl (Windows) or Cmd (Mac) key, and then click and drag the selected keyframe left or right along the timeline. Doing this effectively selects all the anchor points for the current frame in the `Motion Editor` panel and lets you move them as one.

Motion paths

In Chapter 7 we showed you how to animate a butterfly along a special kind of layer called a **motion guide**. As you discovered, it was a path that could be as intricate as you wanted and allows a symbol to appear to meander around the screen following loops and curves that you drew with the pen tool. This capability is also possible in the `Motion Editor`. When you go this route, you don't use a guide, you use a path that is hardwired right into the motion layer. In fact, you have already seen this feature but never really got a chance to use it. Your opportunity has arrived.

Manipulating motion paths

The most fascinating thing about this feature of the `Motion Editor` is you don't need to use the `Motion Editor`. Motion paths are best manipulated through the `Timeline` panel. Here's how:

1. Open the MotionGuideSimple.fla file from this chapter's Exercise folder. When it opens, you will see that our pixel disposer has three pixels to toss into the trash bin. Turn off the visibility of the Green and Blue layers by clicking the eyeball icon on the layer strip.

2. Scrub through the timeline, and you will see that red cube fall to the bottom of the wastebasket. Did you catch the problem? The cube seems to move over the bin before hitting the bottom. You can see this in Figure 8-23 if you follow the motion path. Let's fix that.

Figure 8-23. The Motion Path shows you the "line" an object in motion will follow.

3. Drag the playhead somewhere between the two keyframes, and switch to the Selection tool. Hover near the motion path, and a curve will appear under the arrow. Click and drag the path to the left. As you do the path will curve, and as shown in Figure 8-24, a representation of the original path will be visible.

Figure 8-24. Motion paths can be manipulated on the stage.

4. Turn on the visibility of the `Green` layer, and switch to the `Subselection` tool.

5. Click on either anchor point and drag the Bezier curve handles, as shown in Figure 8-25, to increase the range of the curve. As you can see, motion paths can be treated as vector objects.

> *This technique works only if the path has a curve.*

Figure 8-25. Use the `Subselection` tool to treat the path as a vector line.

Not only can you reshape the motion path, but you can also move it, rotate, skew it, and treat it like any other shape or object on the stage. Let's keep experimenting.

6. Turn on the visibility of the `Blue` layer, and select it. Now turn your gaze to the `Properties` panel. Twirl down the `Path` options. Scrub across the `X`, `Y`, `W`, and `H` values, and you will see that you can move and resize the path. Impressed? Hang on…it gets better.

7. Open the `Transform` panel. Get your hand off the mouse because this one is a bit trickier. You need to select the path here, not the object, or Flash will think it has to transform the blue cube instead.

8. Use the `Selection` tool to click anywhere along the path. Now scrub across the `Transform` panel's `Rotate` value. The path will, as shown in Figure 8-26, rotate around its start point.

9. Experiment with the `Width`, `Height`, and `Skew` properties in the `Transform` panel.

10. If you want to do it yourself and not use numbers, switch to the `Free Transform` tool and select the path. The bounding box shown in Figure 8-26 appears, and you can manipulate the path just as you would with a movie clip of graphic symbol. If you don't want to switch tools and do this strictly with the mouse, select the path with the `Subselection` tool and press Ctrl (Windows) or Cmd (Mac).

ANIMATION, PART 2

> *Don't forget the Alt (Windows) or Option (Mac) key while you make these transformations with the mouse. Without it, transformations pivot around the bounding box's center. With Alt (Windows) or Option (Mac), transformations pivot along the opposite corner or edge. In either case, the Ctrl (Windows) or Cmd (Mac) key is required to produce the bounding box.*

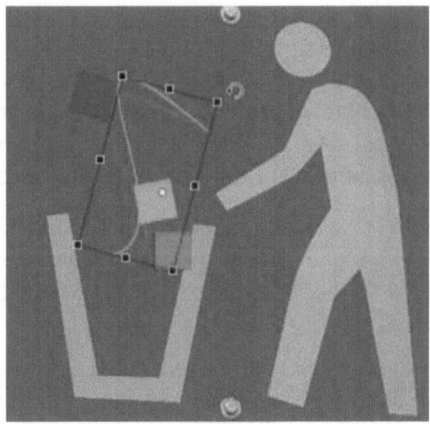

Figure 8-26. Use the free `Transform` tool or press Ctrl (Windows) or Cmd (Mac) to transform a motion path with your mouse.

Using advanced motion paths

In Chapter 7, the butterfly went on a pretty wild ride—nothing like the tame Bezier curves you've seen so far in this chapter. You can do the same thing with the new tweening model, and you still don't need a motion guide layer. Here's how:

1. Open `MotionGuideComplex.fla` in this chapter's `Exercise` folder. You'll see a slightly different finished version of the butterfly `MotionGuide.fla` exercise from Chapter 7, including a classic tween directed by a motion guide layer. Your job—and it's an easy one—is to convert that complex motion guide into a motion path.

2. Right-click (Windows) or Control+click (Mac) the `flutter by` (motion guide) layer, and deselect `Guide` from the context menu. This converts that layer back to a normal layer.

3. Using the `Selection` tool, double-click the wavy line to select the whole thing, and then cut the curves to the clipboard (`Edit ▶ Cut`).

4. Right-click (Windows) or Control+click (Mac) the classic tween, and select `Remove Tween` from the context menu.

5. Right-click (Windows) or Control+click (Mac) again, and select `Create Motion Tween`.

6. With the tween layer selected, paste the wavy line into the layer by selecting `Edit ➤ Paste in Place`. That's all there is to it! If you like, delete the now-empty `flutter by` layer.

7. Click the tween layer again. Use the `Properties` panel to select or deselect `Orient to path`, which behaves as it did for the classic tween version.

Motion tween properties

As you've seen throughout this book, the `Properties` panel is the most versatile panel in your arsenal, simply because it changes to reflect whatever object is selected. When you're dealing with motion tweens, there are two things the `Properties` panel lets you manipulate: the symbol and the tween itself (that is, the motion path). Some of these properties are the ones you see for classic tweens, but they don't all apply for motion tweens.

Let's take a look. Open any of the files you've used to far, and make sure a motion tween is applied to at least one symbol. Select the tween span, and you'll notice the following properties in the `Properties` panel:

- `Ease`: This applies the `Motion Editor` panel's `Simple (Slow)` ease to the full frame span selected. You can adjust this ease's hot text to a value from -100 (ease in) through 0 (no ease) to 100 (ease out).

- `Rotate [x] time(s) + [y]°`: This is comparable to the `Rotate` drop-down for classic tweens and manages symbol rotation. The two hot text values let you specify the number of full rotations (`[x]`) and degrees of partial rotation (`[y]`).

- `Direction`: Once rotation numbers are configured with the previous property, you can choose clockwise (`CW`), counterclockwise (`CCW`), or `none` to determine the direction of those settings or cancel them.

- `Orient to path`: This check box applies only to orientation along a motion path.

- `X, Y, W (Width) and H (Height)`: These reposition or transform a tween span's motion path.

- `Sync graphic symbols`: Human beings still have an appendix, but modern science can't figure out what it's good for, and the same goes for this property. Given its name, it's presumably the motion tween equivalent to the classic tween `Sync` property discussed in Chapter 7. With motion tweens, symbol synchronization happens automatically, whether or not this property is selected. As you'll see in the next section, this feature is moot in any case, because motion paths can be reassigned to any symbol you like.

The other motion tween–related `Properties` panel settings depend on the symbol itself. For movie clips, your configuration options for motion tweens are the same as those for classic tweens. Some properties—such as `position`, `scale`, and `rotation`, and even color effects such as `alpha`—are tweenable. Others, such as blend modes, are not. These are consistent across the board when you're dealing with movie clips. It's when you're using graphic symbols that you need to be aware of a few limitations.

The limitations involve the `Loop`, `Play Once`, `Single Frame`, and `Frame` options in the `Properties` panel's `Looping` area. These properties apply to classic tween keyframes as discussed in Chapter 7. For motion tweens, they apply only to the tween span's first keyframe. They're ignored for property keyframes. The long and short of it is that you can set the `Loop`, `Play Once`, and `Single Frame` drop-down options and `Frame` input field once for a given motion tween—and Flash will obey your command—but only once for that tween span. Change these settings at any frame along the span, and the settings are changed for the whole span.

> *Even though we're focusing on symbols in these paragraphs, bear in mind that motion tweens can also be applied to text fields.*

One final note. Like classic tweens, motion tweens can accommodate only one symbol per tween span. In fact, motion tweens are a bit stricter about this constraint. Once you've applied a classic tween between two keyframes, Flash won't let you draw a shape or add a symbol to any of the frames between the keyframes. Interestingly enough, it will let you draw or add symbols to tweened *keyframes*, but doing so breaks the classic tween, whose "I'm a tween" indicator line then becomes a dashed line. With motion tweens, Flash won't let you draw or add a symbol to *any frame* of the tween span, keyframe or not. The moral of this story is that you should give each of your tween spans its own layer.

Motion presets

Here's another good example of letting the computer do the work for you. Flash CS5 takes advantage of one of the major facets of motion tweens—that you can copy and paste motion paths—by providing you with a panel with more than two dozen prebuilt *motion presets*. These are reusable motion paths, complete with motion changes, transformations, and color effects, which you can apply to any symbol or text field. Here's how:

1. Open `MotionPreset.fla` from the `Exercise` folder for this chapter. You'll see our old friend, the mascot, along with the dancing fool.

2. Select the `Dancing Fool` symbol, and open the `Motion Presets` panel (`Window` ▶ `Motion Presets`, or click the `Code Snippets` button on the toolbar and click the `Motion Presets` tab).

3. Open the `Default Presets` folder, if it is not already open, and click among the various choices to see a preview of the animation in the `Motion Presets` panel's preview (see Figure 8-27). You'll see wipes and zooms, blurs and bounces, and all manner of helter-skelter. When you find a preset you like—we chose `bounce-smoosh`, the third one—click the panel's `Apply` button to copy that motion path to the `Dancing Fool` symbol.

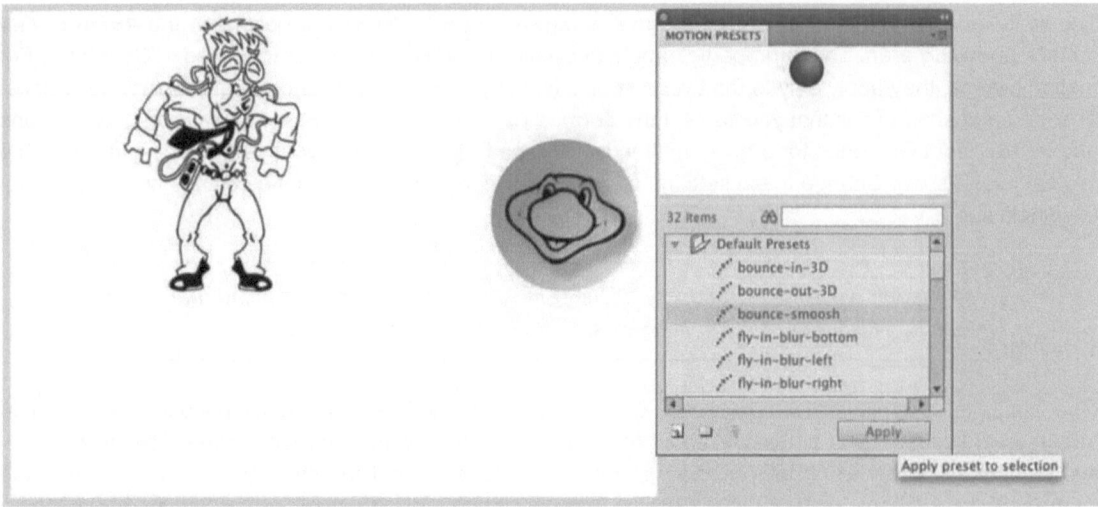

Figure 8-27. The Motion Presets panel gives you 30 stock motion paths.

Applying the motion preset automatically inserts a motion tween on the dancing fool's layer and then adds the relevant property keyframes to reproduce the animation in question

4. Using the Subselection tool, click the motion path, and then use the Align panel to center the animation vertically on the stage.

As you may have guessed, it's just as easy to apply the same (or different) motion preset to the other symbol, but we would like to draw your attention to a related feature instead. That related feature is that motion paths can be edited, or created completely from scratch, and then saved to the Motion Presets panel. How? Glad you asked.

5. Shorten the duration of the dancing fool's animation by dragging the right edge of the tween span slightly to the left. In our file, we shortened the tween span from 75 frames to 50. Drag the playhead to one or more of the property keyframes and use the Properties panel, Transform panel, or Free Transform tool to alter the symbol's antics along the existing motion path. Also, the Dancing Fool goes off stage. You might want to scrub to the end of the tween and move him so that his feet are on the bottom of the stage

6. Click the tween span, and in the Motion Presets panel, click the Save selection as preset button (Figure 8-28). You'll be prompted to give the new preset a name. Enter whatever you like (we used bounce-smoosh-alt), and click OK. Scroll to the Custom Presets folder to find your preset.

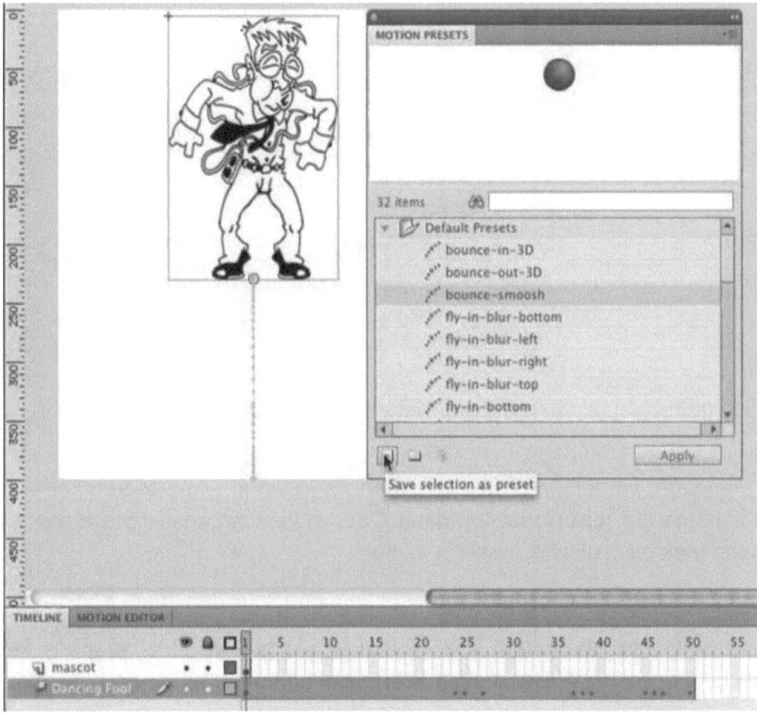

Figure 8-28. Motion paths, whether made from scratch or based on presets, can be saved for later reuse.

The other buttons in the `Motion Presets` panel let you create new folders and delete folders or presets.

Naturally, you could select the `Dancing Fool` symbol and apply your newly minted custom preset, but there's another way you can share motion paths.

7. Right-click (Windows) or Control+click (Mac) the `Dancing Fool`'s tween span, and select `Copy Motion` from the context menu. Now right-click (Windows) or Control+click (Mac) frame 1 of the `Mascot` layer, and select `Paste Motion`.

Because you used the `Align` panel to change the position of the original motion path, you'll need to do the same for the copied path, assuming you want the lunatic and the cartoon mouse to fall in sync. It's easy as pie. Although you could certainly use the `Edit Multiple Frames` workflow discussed in Chapter 7—that does still work here—you've learned in this chapter that motion tweens can be repositioned by way of their motion paths.

8. Using the `Subselection` tool, click the mascot's motion path to select it. Use the `Align` panel, again, to center the animation vertically to the stage.

9. Preview the animation. You'll see that both symbols perform the same movements (see Figure 8-29).

Figure 8-29. Motion paths can be shared even without the `Motion Presets` panel.

That's impressive enough, but let's redo the last demonstration in a more dramatic way. These last few steps should drive home the notion that, in Flash CS5, motion tweens—specifically, motion paths—are entities that stand on their own, distinct from the symbol.

    10. Select the `Dancing Fool` symbol at any point along its tween span, and delete the symbol.

When you delete the symbol, the tween span remains, along with all its property keyframes. Visually speaking, the only difference in the tween span is that its first frame, usually a black dot, is now an empty white dot.

    11. Click the empty tween span to select it.

    12. Drag a copy of the `Turtle` symbol from the `Library`, and drop it somewhere on the stage. Location doesn't matter—it can even be on the right side of the existing mascot on the stage.

Because you selected the tween span first, the symbol will immediately adopt that span's motion path when you release the mouse to drop the symbol. You can't do that with a classic tween!

Inverse kinematics (IK)

In one of the happiest sequences in Disney's 1940 classic, *Pinocchio*, the wooden-headed puppet, once freed from the apparatus that formerly helped him move, bursts into song, proudly declaring, "I got no strings on me!" In Flash CS5, the authors suspect that you, too, will burst into song—but for the opposite reason—when you see the tools for a feature introduced in Flash CS4 called *inverse kinematics* (IK).

What is this academic, vaguely sinister-sounding term? In simple words, IK lets you string up your artwork like a train set, like sausages, or, if you prefer, like a marionette. And when you pull the strings, so to speak, or move one of the connected symbols, your artwork responds like a bona fide action figure. You can use IK to make poseable models and then animate them.

Seriously, this feature is way cool, and we think you're going to love playing with it. That said, it's one of the more complicated feature sets in Flash CS5. Stringing up your symbols is easy enough. The official terminology calls for creating an *armature* and populating it with *bones*, which can then be dragged around. Adobe engineers have made this dead simple.

The tricky part is a question of *how*. To a certain extent, you'll find armatures and bones immediately intuitive, but just when you think they make sense, they'll behave in a way that might just strike you as utterly wrong. You'll see what we're talking about in the following exercises, and we'll show you an approach that should give you what you expect.

It all starts with something called the `Bone` tool.

Using the Bone tool

The `Bone` tool is your key to the world of poseable armatures in the authoring environment. Using it will give you an inkling of the satisfaction experienced by a certain famous Victor Frankenstein, without anywhere near the hassle he went through or the illegal outings. You won't be visiting any actual graveyards, for example.

Let's see how the `Bone` tool works.

1. Open the `Bones.fla` file from the `Exercise` folder for this chapter. You'll be greeted by a more or less anatomically correct hand, sans flesh. Go ahead and wave! The wrist and hand bones are all part of the same graphic symbol, named `hand` in the `Library`. The knuckles are also graphic symbols, named by finger and knuckle number—for example, `ring1`, `ring2`, and `ring3`. All of these symbols happen to be on the same layer, but that doesn't need to be the case.

2. Select the `Bone` tool from the `Tools` panel. It's the one in Figure 8-30 that looks like a bone, just above the `Paint Bucket`. Click over the bottom-center portion of the skeleton's wrist, and drag toward the bottom of the thumb's first knuckle, as shown in Figure 8-30. When you release the mouse, you'll see your very first armature, which includes a single IK bone.

> *Bones can only be rigged between graphic symbols, movie clips, or artwork that has been broken apart. Trying to run a bone, for example, from one photo to another will result in an error message telling you, essentially, "Nope you can't do that!"*

Notice the new layer in the `Timeline` panel, called `Armature_1`. That's your armature, and as you continue to connect your symbols together with IK bones, those symbols will automatically be pulled to this new layer. Just like a motion tween layer, this layer has distinctive properties. For example, you can't right-click (Windows) or Control+click (Mac) an armature layer to tween it, even though IK poses can be tweened (more on this later in the chapter, in the "Animating IK poses section"). You can't draw shapes on or drag symbols to an armature layer.

Bones have two ends, and it's helpful to know their anatomy. The larger end of the bone, where you started to drag, is called the **head**. The smaller end of the bone, where you released the mouse, is called the **tail**. The tail is pointing up and to the left in Figure 8-31. A string of connected bones is called an **IK chain** or a **bone chain**.

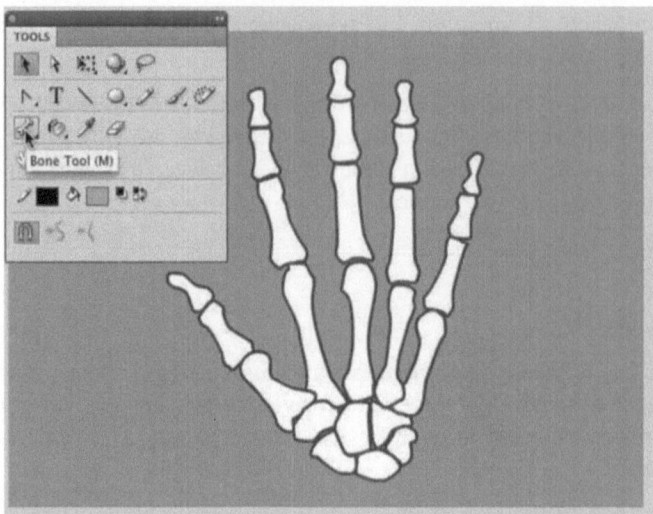

Figure 8-30. The `Bone` tool lets you connect symbols the way bones are connected in real life.

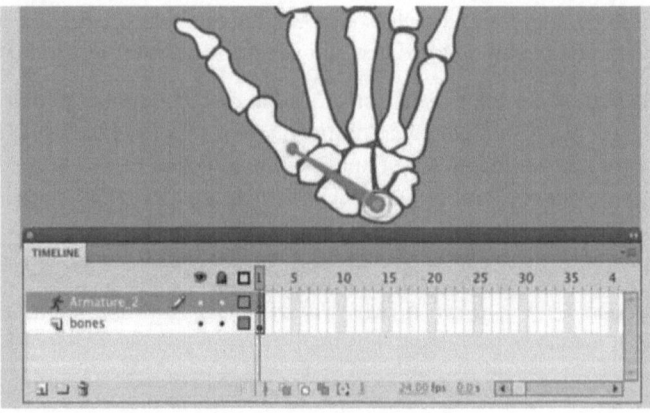

Figure 8-31. Drawing your first bone creates the armature.

3. Still with the `Bone` tool, hover somewhere inside the symbol that represents the first knuckle. You don't need to be exact—just within the symbol's bounding box. Then click and drag toward the bottom of the second knuckle. You'll notice that even if you don't begin the second drag directly over the tail of the first armature bone, Flash will automatically snap it into place for you. Release when you're over the bottom of the second knuckle.

4. To finish the thumb, hover anywhere inside the second knuckle's symbol. Click and drag upward to the bottom of the third knuckle. When you release, you'll have the simple bone rigging shown in Figure 8-32.

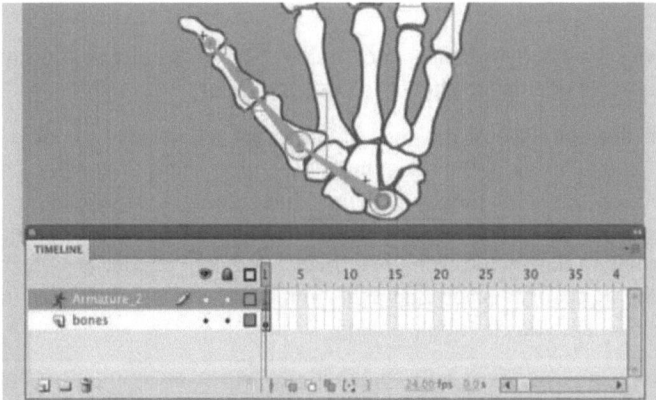

Figure 8-32. As you connect symbols with bones, the symbols are pulled to the armature layer.

If you're anything like the authors, you're just *dying* to try these bones, so let's take a quick *break* and do just that.

5. Switch to the `Selection` tool, grab that third knuckle, and give it a shake.

We fully expect you'll have fun, but all the same, you'll also see that it's pretty easy to arrange the hand into what looks like an orthopedic surgeon's dream (see Figure 8-33). It may surprise you, for example, that the wrist pivots, and those knuckles are bending into contortions that make even our yoga buddies wince. We'll fix those issues in just a moment. First, let's get acquainted with the `Bone` tool properties.

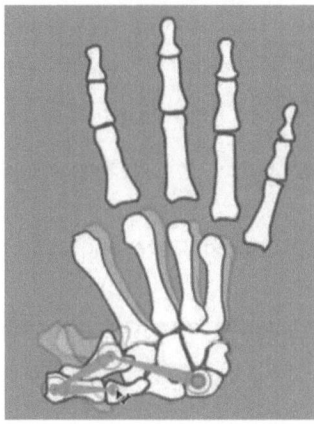

Figure 8-33. Ouch! Bones are easy to connect, but the results aren't always what you might anticipate.

Bone tool properties

There are two ways to nudge the `Properties` panel into showing bone-related properties: by clicking an IK bone on the stage and by clicking the armature itself, which is represented by an armature layer. Let's start with the armature.

1. Continuing with the `Bones.fla` file, click frame 1 of the `Armature_2` layer. When you do, the `Properties` panel updates to show two twirlies:

    - `Ease`: In this area, you'll find a drop-down list for selecting easing from a list of prebuilt choices and a `Strength` value that lets you specify intensity, just as you saw in the `Properties` panel for motion tweens. These settings configure easing for the span of an armature layer (you can drag out an armature span to encompass as many frames as you like). Armature layers provide their own tweening capability, which is discussed in the "Animating IK poses" section and again in the last exercise of this chapter. For now, just note that this is where you can apply easing.

    - `Options`: The area gives you something to see even without tweening. The `Style` drop-down list lets you specify how you want the IK bones to look. You have three choices: `Solid` (the default), `Wire`, and `Line`, which are illustrated in Figure 8-34 from left to right. When working with numerous or very small symbols, consider using the `Wire` or `Line` styles. Why? Because the `Solid` view can obscure symbols that appear under the IK bones.

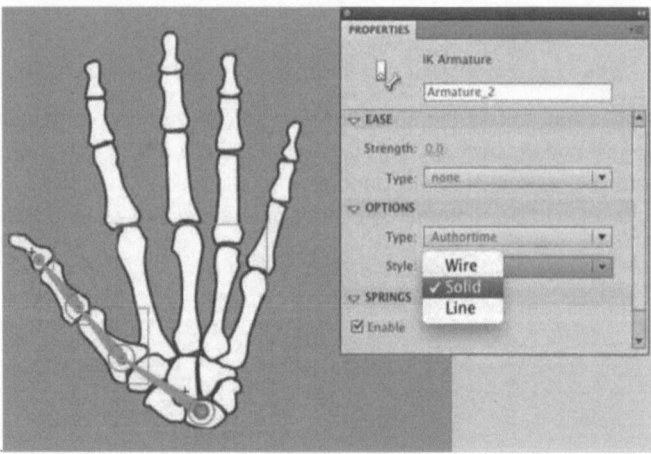

Figure 8-34. Bones can be configured as `Solid`, `Wire`, and `Line`.

2. Change the `Type` drop-down selection from `Authortime` to `Runtime`. You'll see the warning message shown in Figure 8-35.

ANIMATION, PART 2

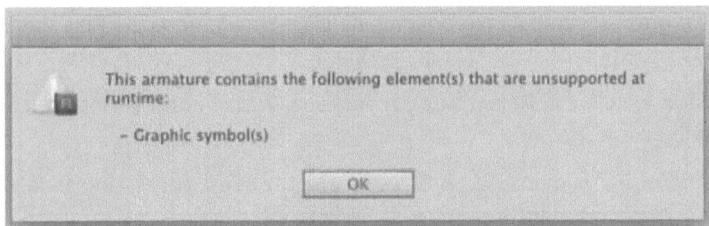

Figure 8-35. Only movie clip bones can be interactive at runtime.

The reason for the warning is that, although bones can be made interactive for the user, Flash requires that the boned symbols be movie clips when `Type` is set to `Runtime`. Fortunately, this is easy to change in Flash CS5, even if there are numerous symbols in play.

3. Click OK to close the warning dialog box.
4. Open the `Library`, and click the first symbol, named `hand`, to select it. Press and hold the Shift key, and then select the last symbol. Now everything in your `Library` is selected.
5. Right-click (Windows) or Control+click (Mac) any one of the symbols and choose `Properties` from the context menu.

What you get is a feature introduced in Flash CS4, which is an incredible time-saver. The `Symbol Properties` dialog box opens—not just for the symbol you clicked, but for all selected symbols.

6. In the `Symbol` Properties dialog box, place a check mark in the `Type` property, and change the drop-down choice to `Movie Clip`, as shown in Figure 8-36. Then click OK.

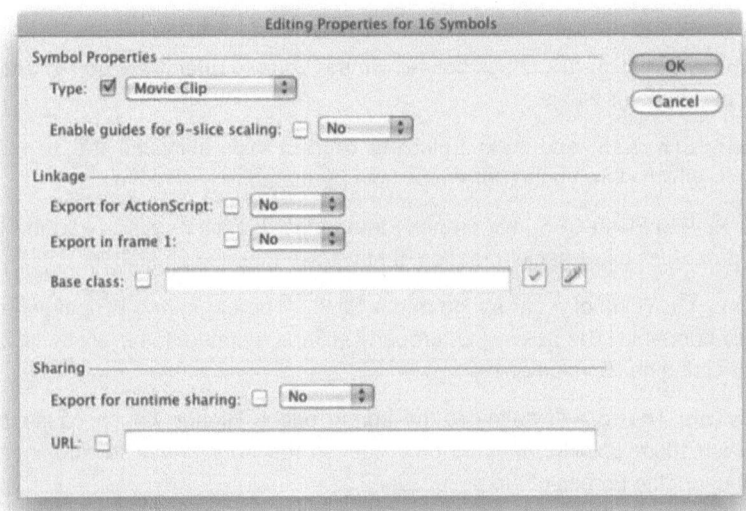

Figure 8-36. Flash CS5 lets you change multiple symbol properties at once in the `Library`.

463

All of your `Library`'s graphic symbols become movie clips simultaneously. This used to take a separate visit to each asset. However, you still need to let the stage know what you've done.

7. Click the stage to select it. Select `Edit ➤ Select All`. In one swoop, you just selected all your symbols on the stage.
8. Click any one of the symbols to update the `Properties` panel, and then select `Movie Clip` from the drop-down list at the top of the `Properties` panel.
9. Click frame 1 of the `Armature_2` layer, and change the `Type` drop-down selection to `Runtime`.
10. Test the movie and wiggle those thumb knuckles inside Flash Player. Pretty neat!
11. Close the SWF, and click one of the IK bones to update the `Properties` panel.

Now you see bone-specific properties. Let's go over those:

- `Position X, Y, Length`, and `Angle`: These are read-only properties, which means you can look, but don't touch. Thankfully, the names are self-explanatory.
- `Speed`: Think of this as friction, or how much "give" the selected bone has in the armature. A higher number means faster movement, and your range is `0` (no movement) to `200` (fast movement).
- `Joint: Rotation`: Here, you have the following choices:
  - `Enable`: Selecting this check box allows the bone to pivot around its head. In contrast, deselecting it means the bone won't act like a hinge.
  - `Constrain, Min`, and `Max`: Selecting `Constrain` activates the `Min` and `Max` hot text values, which allow you to determine how wide an arc your hinge can pivot on.
- `Joint: X and Y Translation`: The choices for this property are as follows:
  - `Enable`: Selecting this check box allows the bone to effectively pop in and out of its socket, in either the x- or y-axis.
  - `Constrain, Min`, and `Max`: Selecting `Constrain` activates the `Min` and `Max` hot text values, which allow you to determine how far the bone can move.
- `Spring`: New to Flash CS5, this property integrates dynamic physics into the Bones IK system. The two properties allow easier creation of physics-enhanced animation.
  - `Strength`: Think of a car spring and a Slinky. The car spring is rigid, whereas the Slinky is totally bendable. The `Strength` property stiffens a spring. If the Slinky has a value of 0, then a car spring has a value of 100.
  - `Damping`: The rate of decay of the spring effect. Higher values cause the springiness to diminish more quickly. A value of 0 causes the springiness to remain at its full strength throughout the frames of the pose layer

ANIMATION, PART 2

Of the properties available, `Rotation`, `Translation`, and `Spring` will give you the biggest bang for your buck. Let's see how easy it is to fix that misshapen hand! While we're at it, you'll learn some helpful subtleties on manipulating the symbols in an armature.

Constraining joint rotation

IK bone rigs are as much an art as a science. The science facet derives from the `Properties` panel, which gives you have some configuration settings. The art facet depends on your sense of the appropriate range of motion for a given armature. Let's jump in:

1. Continuing with the `Bones.fla` file, use the `Selection` tool to drag the hand itself—not any of the fingers or the thumb—and carefully pivot the hand so that it realigns again under the fingers.

2. Select the first IK bone (the one closest to the wrist), and deselect the `Enable` check box in `Properties` panel's `Joint: Rotation` area.

3. Drag the thumb's third knuckle again, and note that the wrist no longer moves.

If you ever change your mind, just reselect the first IK bone, and put a check mark back in the `Enable` property. Now let's make sure the thumb doesn't look so double-jointed.

4. Select the second IK bone and, in the `Properties` panel, enable the `Constrain` check box in the `Joint: Rotation` area, as shown in Figure 8-37.

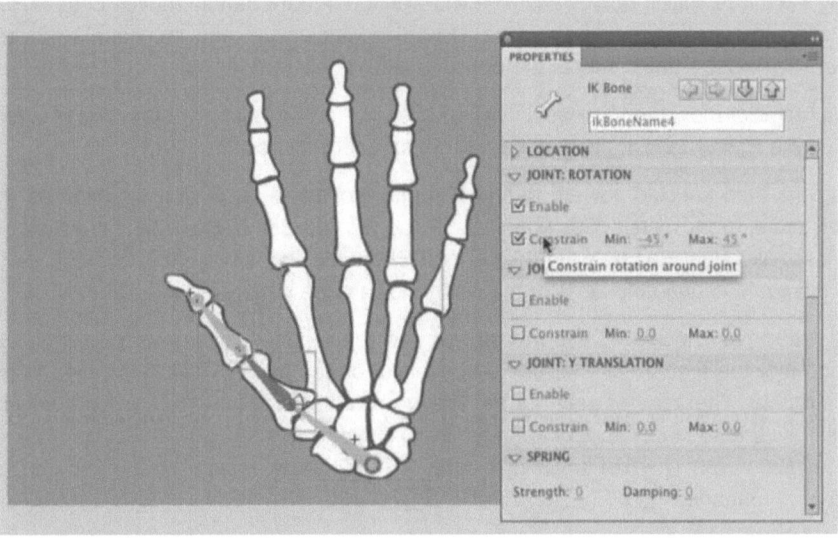

Figure 8-37. The `Constraint` check box lets you constrain a joint's range of motion.

Choosing `Constrain` adds a new component to the IK bone, which you can see in Figure 8-38. Suddenly, the bone's head sprouts a wedge shape, with a line in the middle that separates the wedge into

465

two pie pieces. The line has a square handle on its outside end. (If you're in a Robin Hood mood, it may look like a bow and arrow.) This wedge represents the joint's range of movement. By default, you get a 90-degree sweep.

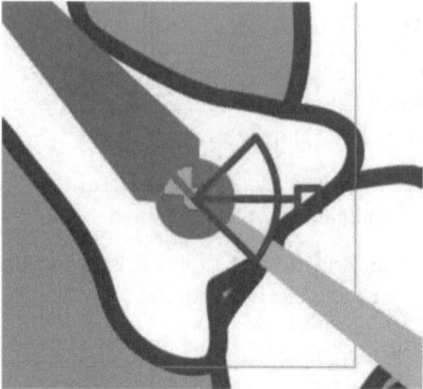

Figure 8-38. Select `Constrain` in the `Joint: Rotation` area of the `Properties` panel, and joints sprout a range-of-movement icon.

5. Drag the third knuckle downward. The line with the square handle moves counterclockwise until it rests against that side of the wedge. Drag the knuckle up, and the handle moves to the other side—clockwise—until it meets the opposite side of the wedge.

Adjusting this range of movement is easy. The workflow we prefer is to pivot the IK bone into position first and then scrub the `Min` or `Max` hot text as necessary to meet that position.

6. Drag the third knuckle upward until the thumb moves as far in that direction as you like. If you need more room, select first knuckle's IK bone, and scrub the `Max` value toward the right to increase its value. Readjust the thumb, and when you like how it sits, scrub the `Max` value toward the left again to bring the edge of the wedge toward the square-handled line.

7. Drag the third knuckle all the way down, and repeat this process for the other extreme. You'll notice that the first knuckle appears above the bones of the wrist, as shown in the left side of Figure 8-39. That may or may not be what you want. If you want to send the knuckle behind the wrist, use the `Selection` tool to select that knuckle's symbol, and select `Modify` ➤ `Arrange` ➤ `Send to Back`. The first knuckle is done. You can now move onto the second, which isn't any harder to manage.

8. Add a `Joint: Rotation` constraint to the second knuckle and configure the `Min/Max` values in whatever way suits you.

As you move the skeleton bones around, you can use the Shift key to temporarily change the way the IK bones respond. For example, drag the third knuckle up and down, and then hold down Shift and drag again. When Shift is pressed, only the third knuckle moves. This works with any other bone. Drag the second knuckle with and without Shift to see what we mean.

While you're at it, experiment with the Ctrl (Windows) or Cmd (Mac) key as well. If you ever want to reposition a symbol without having to redo an IK bone from scratch, hold down Ctrl (Windows) or Cmd (Mac) while you drag. This temporarily releases the dragged symbol from its IK chain. When you release the key, the IK bones are reapplied.

The third knuckle is the interesting one, because although it's attached to an IK bone, it's only associated with that bone's tail. This means you can't constrain its rotation. (Give it a try!) So, what to do? Since we're dealing with so many kinds of bones, we think it's fitting that the answer relies on the presence of a ghost—not a real ghost, of course, but a stand-in "ghost" movie clip.

9. In the `Timeline` panel, select the non-armature layer (the one labeled `bones`).

10. Use the `Oval` tool to draw a small circle—say, 20 pixels × 20 pixels—no stroke, and color doesn't matter.

11. Convert that circle to a movie clip. Name the symbol `ghost handle`, and position it just past the thumb's third knuckle.

12. Using the `Bone` tool, add a fourth IK bone between the third knuckle and the `ghost handle` movie clip, as shown in Figure 8-39.

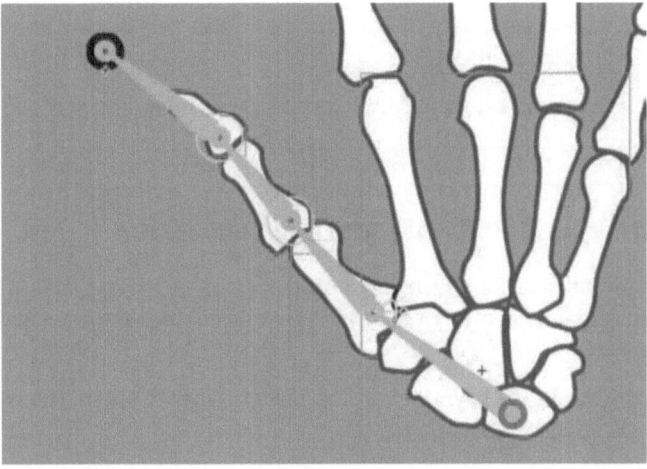

Figure 8-39. Use a stand-in movie clip to let you constrain the previously end-of-the-line IK bone.

13. Select the newest IK bone, and constrain its `Joint: Rotation` property.

14. Save your file.

Sure, the "ghost" movie clip may look a little silly, but its presence allows you to configure your IK bones from start to finish.

Here's the best part: whenever you need another stand-in IK bone, make sure to keep reusing that same `ghost handle` movie clip. Why? Because when you're ready to publish the SWF, all you have to do is open that symbol in the `Library` and change its fill color to `0% Alpha`. Just like that, your extra handles become invisible, and they still do their job.

Deleting bones

We showed you how to create IK bones, but you'll also want to know how to delete them. It couldn't be easier:

1. After saving your `Bones.fla` file, and use the `Selection` tool to select the fourth IK bone from the previous exercise. Press the `Delete` key. Badda bing, badda boom...the bone is gone.

2. Skip the third IK bone, and select the second one. Press the Delete key.

This time, both the second and third bones disappear. This tells you that deleting an IK bone automatically deletes any other bones attached to its tail.

3. Right-click (Windows) or Control+click (Mac) frame 1 in the `Armature_1` layer, and select `Remove Armature` from the context menu.

As expected, the last IK bone disappears. If you had made this selection in step 1, all of the IK bones would have disappeared from the start.

4. Select `File ➤ Revert`, and then click the `Revert` button in the alert box to undo all the deletions.

Putting some "spring" in your bones

New to Flash CS5 is the addition of a `Spring` option for bones. Adobe calls it a "physics engine for Inverse Kinematics" and, regardless of what you call it, we think it's a pretty neat way of bending stuff in an animation. Let's take a look:

1. Open the `Springs.fla` file in your `Exercise` folder. When it opens you will see two trees on the stage, and if you scrub across the timeline, you will see them bend in a gust of strong wind.

2. Springiness works best when the object containing the bones is put into motion. This is done using poses, which we will get into later in this chapter.

3. Click the tree on the left, and click the bone at the bottom to select it.

4. Open the `Properties` panel, and you will notice the bone, as shown in Figure 8-40, has a `Strength` value of `100` and a `Damping` value of `5`. `Strength` is the stiffness of the spring. Higher values create a stiffer spring effect. `Damping` is the rate of decay of the spring effect. Higher values cause the springiness to diminish more quickly. A value of `0` causes the springiness to remain at its full strength throughout the frames of the pose layer.

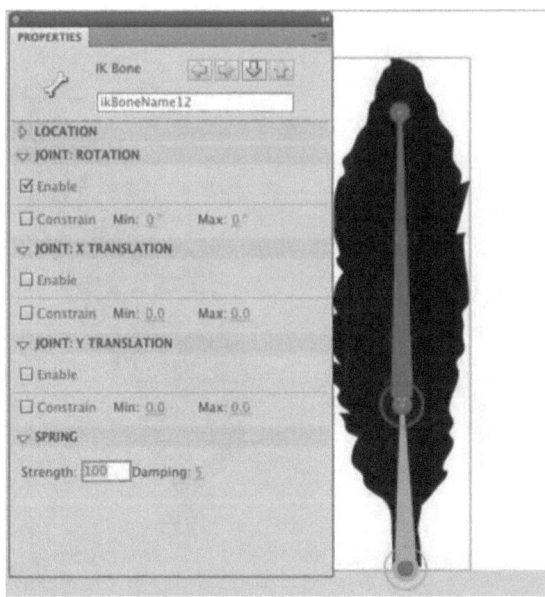

Figure 8-40. Adding spring to a bone using the `Strength` and `Damping` properties

5. Now that you know what the values mean, scrub across the timeline to the first keyframe and compare the shapes of the trees. The tree on the right does not have springiness applied to it. As shown in Figure 8-41, the tree that has been "stiffened" looks a lot more natural than its counterpart on the right which has had springiness disabled.

> There is something else you need to know: Spring properties are applied to bones. Springiness is applied to layers. If you click any frame of the `NoSpring` layer and open the `Properties` panel, you will see that the `Enable` check box is deselected.

CHAPTER 8

Figure 8-41. Springs, used in the tree on the left, add realism to objects in motion.

Applying joint translation

Another way to control the movement of joints is called **joint translation**. This affects movement of an IK bone along its x- or y-axis (or both). To illustrate, we'll leave our skeleton at the chiropractor's for a while and turn our attention to a rudimentary steam engine.

   1. Open the `SteamEngine.fla` file from the `Exercise` folder for this chapter. The symbols are already in place for you.

In Figure 8-42, we've labeled the engine's anatomy to assist you in the next steps, so you can focus your attention entirely on the IK rigging. You're going to connect three horizontal symbols from left to right. Ignore the wheel for the time being.

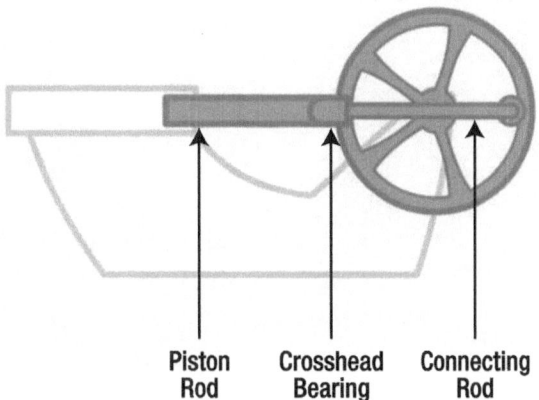

Figure 8-42. The movement of this steam engine will include joint translation.

2. Select the `Bone` tool, and then add a bone that starts on the left side of the `piston rod` symbol and ends on the `crosshead bearing` symbol (the center symbol).

3. Add another bone from the `crosshead bearing` symbol to the right side of the `connecting rod` symbol, as shown in Figure 8-43. This is no different from the bone rigging you did for the knuckles.

Figure 8-43. Two bones connect three symbols.

Joint translation doesn't require ActionScript, but we're going to use some programming to demonstrate it in this particular case. Because we'll be using ActionScript, let's give the bones and armature meaningful instance names.

4. Using the Selection tool, select the bone on the right, and use the Properties panel to give it the instance name connectingRod, as shown in Figure 8-44.

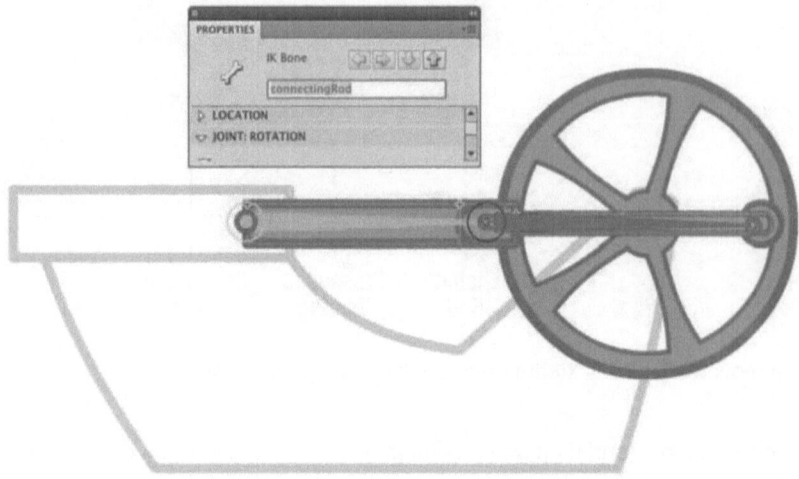

Figure 8-44. Bones and armatures support instance names, just like movie clip symbols.

> *Pay close attention to the Properties panel when making your selections. It's easy to accidentally click the symbol to which a bone is applied, rather than the bone itself. In this context, the symbol is listed as an IK Node in the Properties panel. If you select an IK node, this exercise won't work properly. Figure 8-44 shows the correct selection of a bone, which displays IK Bone in the Properties panel.*

5. Select the other bone, and give it the instance name pistonRod.
6. Select the armature itself by clicking frame 1 of its layer in the Timeline panel. Use the Properties panel to give the armature the instance name engine. The armature's layer name will update to the same name.

Now it's time for the joint translation, but first, let's keep this bone from rotating. It's possible for bones to translate *and* rotate, but that isn't what we want here. Our aim is to let the piston rod slide left and right when the armature moves.

7. Select the pistonRod bone, and use the Properties panel to disable its rotation (that is, deselect the Enable check box in the Joint: Rotation area).
8. To achieve the left-and-right motion, select the Enable check box in the Joint: X Translation area. The bone's head gets a horizontal double-headed arrow, as shown in Figure 8-45.

ANIMATION, PART 2

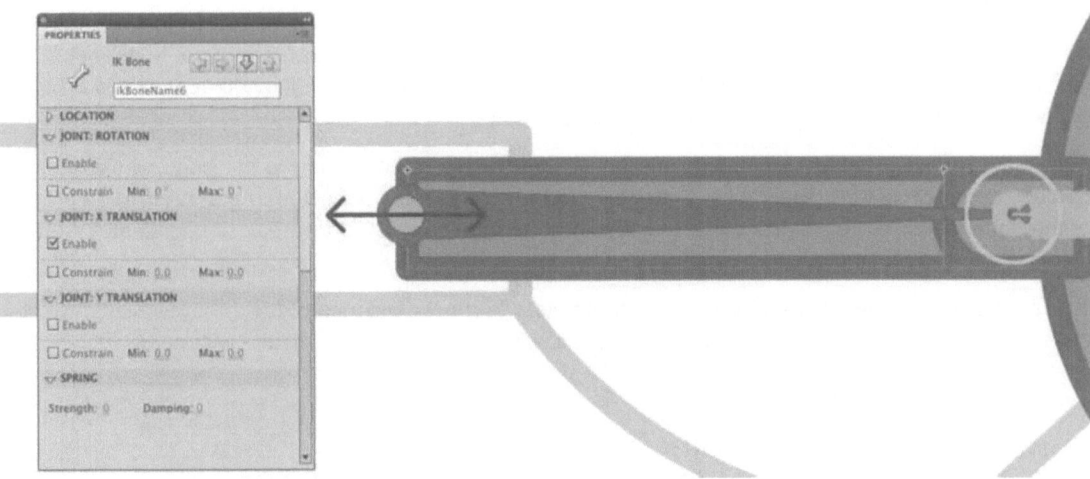

Figure 8-45. Joint translation is indicated by a double-headed arrow along the relevant axis.

You could optionally constrain this translation by selecting the **Constrain** check box and configuring **Min** and **Max** values, just as with joint rotation, but that isn't necessary here. Note, too, that you could optionally translate (and constrain) along the y-axis, but we'll also omit that step.

Time to get this steam engine moving!

9. Click frame 1 of the armature's layer (**engine**) to select the armature. In the **Options** area of the **Properties** panel, and change the **Type** drop-down selection to **Runtime**. Now this rigging is ready for ActionScript.

10. Select frame 1 of the **scripts** layer, and open the **Actions** panel. Type the following ActionScript:

```
import fl.ik.*;

var pt:Point = new Point();
var arm:IKArmature = IKManager.getArmatureByName("engine");
var bone:IKBone = arm.getBoneByName("connectingRod");
var tail:IKJoint = bone.tailJoint;
var pos:Point = tail.position;

var ik:IKMover = new IKMover(tail, pos);
```

The first line imports all the classes in the fl.ik package, which includes classes necessary for identifying and manipulating armatures created in the authoring tool. The next line declares a variable, pt, set to an instance of the Point class. (The Point class doesn't reside in the fl.ik package, but in just a moment, you'll see that something called the IKMover class needs a Point instance.)

CHAPTER 8

From the third line on, the code unfolds like the lyrics in that old catchy tune, "Dry Bones" ("the knee bone's connected to the...thi-i-igh bone"). How so? A variable, arm, is declared and set to an instance of the IKArmature class. This variable takes its value from a method of the IKManager class, which connects it to the armature whose instance name is engine.

After that, a bone variable—an instance of the IKBone class—is connected to the bone whose instance name is connectingRod. Then a tail variable (IKJoint class) is connected to the tailJoint property of the bone instance. Finally, a new Point instance (pos) is connected to a pair of coordinates from the position property of the tail instance.

The tail and pos variables are passed as parameters to a new instance of the IKMover class, which is stored in the variable ik. That ik variable is what allows you to move the armature with code.

11. Add the following new ActionScript after the existing code:

```
wheel.addEventListener(Event.ENTER_FRAME, spin);
function spin(evt:Event):void {
  wheel.rotation += 5;
  pt.x = wheel.crank.x;
  pt.y = wheel.crank.y;
  pt = wheel.localToGlobal(pt);
  ik.moveTo(pt);
}
```

The basic premise here is something you've already seen in other chapters: a custom function, spin(), is associated with the Event.ENTER_FRAME event of an object with the instance name wheel. In this case, wheel is the instance name of the wheel-shaped movie clip symbol. (We've already configured the instance name for you in the sample file, and the **wheel** symbol contains another movie clip inside it with the instance name crank.)

So, what's going on in this event handler? First, the MovieClip.rotation property of the wheel instance is incremented by five. That gets the wheel rolling continuously. After that, it's just a matter of updating the pt variable declared earlier. Being an instance of the Point class, the pt variable has x and y properties, which are set to the **crank** movie clip's x and y properties, respectively. Because crank resides inside wheel, the object path to the desired x property is wheel.crank.x. The same goes for y.

This updates pt's properties to the current position of crank, but that isn't quite enough. From the **wheel** symbol's point of view, crank never actually moves—it's wheel that does the rotating!—so the coordinates need to be considered from the point of view of the stage. That's what the second-to-last line does by invoking the DisplayObject.localToGlobal() method on the wheel instance. In plain English, it tells pt to reset itself in from crank's local coordinates inside wheel to the crank's global coordinates shared by all objects on the stage.

Finally, pt is passed as a parameter to the IKMover instance represented by the ik variable.

12. Test your movie so far to see the result.

It's close to being correct, and the `pistonRod` bone does perform its horizontal joint translation, but if you look carefully, you'll notice that the armature occasionally "slips" from the crank movie clip. That's easy to fix, and it's nothing more than a matter of priorities.

The armature isn't updating as quickly as the wheel turns, so let's fix that by limiting the number of calculations it has to make.

13. Use the `Actions` panel to insert the following two lines after the `ik` variable declaration and the event listener (new code shown in bold):

```
. . .
var ik:IKMover = new IKMover(tail, pos);
ik.limitByIteration = false;
ik.iterationLimit = 5;

wheel.addEventListener(Event.ENTER_FRAME, spin);
function spin(evt:Event):void {
. . .
```

14. Test the movie again, and everything should run fine.

A note about bone preferences

Let's return to our friendly skeleton hand. We mentioned earlier in this chapter that IK poses can be animated, even without the use of a motion tween layer. You'll see how in the next section. First, it's time for a quick field trip.

1. Open the `BonesRigged.fla` file in this chapter's `Exercise` folder. You'll see the fingers and thumb pointing upward, and the thumb has a ghost handle.

2. Use the `Selection` tool or the `Free Transform` tool to click the first knuckle of the pointer finger. As Figure 8-46 shows, the symbol's transformation point (the small white circle) is dead center.

3. Noting the transformation point, select `Edit (Flash)` ➤ `Preferences`, and click the `Drawing` choice in the `Category` area. Find the `IK Bone tool: Auto Set Transformation Point` check box and deselect it, as shown in Figure 8-47. Click `OK` to close the `Preferences` dialog box.

CHAPTER 8

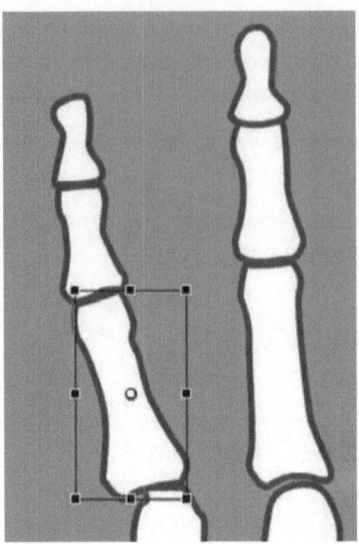

Figure 8-46. This symbol's transformation point is horizontally and vertically centered.

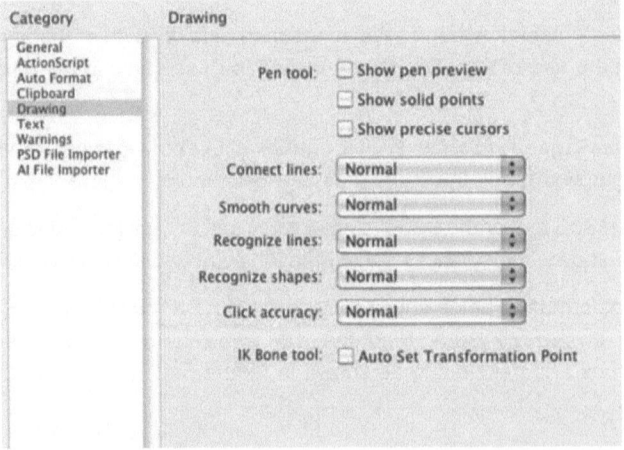

Figure 8-47. The `Auto Set Transformation Point` setting affects how bones are applied to symbols.

4. Using the `Bone` tool, hover over the `hand` symbol, and then click and drag a new IK bone toward the first knuckle of the pointer finger. As you do, notice that the tail of the IK bone snaps to the transformation point of the first knuckle. Note, also, that the armature is perfectly capable of handling more than one chain of bones.

ANIMATION, PART 2

5. Repeat this process to rig up the remaining knuckles of the pointer finger.

6. Using the `Selection` tool, grab the third knuckle and give the finger a wiggle. As shown in Figure 8-48, the pivots occur on the transformation points, which just doesn't work for this scenario. We want the knuckles to line up end to end.

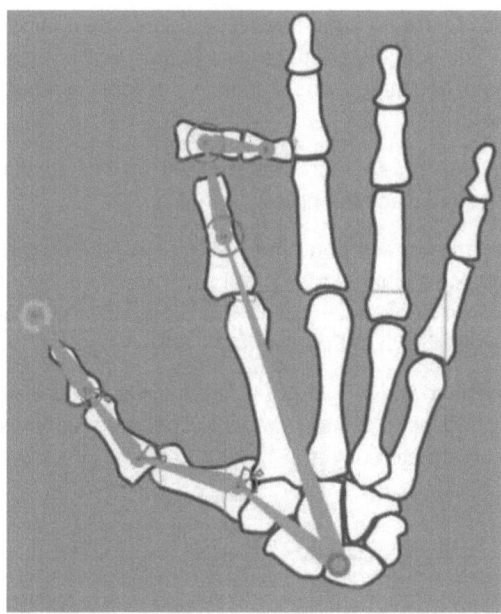

Figure 8-48. If you want, IK bones can snap to a symbol's transformation point.

7. Return to the `Preferences` dialog box, and reselect the `IK Bone tool` check box.

8. Select `File ➤ Revert`, and then click the `Revert` button to roll the file back to its original state.

We brought up the `IK Bone tool` preference setting because it's hard to spot unless you happen to be poring through the `Preferences` dialog box. We chose a silly example because silly visuals tend to stick.

> By leaving the `Auto Set Transformation Point` check box selected in the `Preferences` dialog box's `Drawing` section, you're telling Flash to move a symbol's transformation point for you automatically. If you prefer to maintain that control on your own, deselect that check box, and then use the `Free Transform` tool to make your symbol selections. When selected with the `Free Transform` tool, a symbol lets you move its transformation point with an effortless click-and-drag operation. If the symbol already belongs to an IK chain, any heads or tails connected to it will reposition themselves to the new location of the symbol's transformation point.

CHAPTER 8

Animating IK Poses

As you saw earlier with the springs example, to get those trees to bend in the wind, we needed to animate the IK poses. In this section, we show you how to do that but rather than bend trees, let's slip on our hard hats and visit a construction site.

1. Open the `IK_Poses.fla` file in your `Exercise` folder. You will see we have placed a Steam Shovel on the stage. The image started life as a multilayer Photoshop image imported into Flash. Each layer of the Photoshop image was placed in a graphic symbol, and each symbol has its own layer on the main timeline.

2. Select the `Magnifying Glass` tool, and zoom in on the machine. You are going to need a closer view of the pieces to place the bones.

3. Select the `Bone` tool, and draw a bone from the back of the `MainArm` symbol to the top joint of the `ShovelArm` symbol. Keep in mind that `Bones` links symbols only to each other. Bones within a symbol will kick out an error message. In this case, run the bone between the `MainArm` and `ShovelArm` symbols, as shown in Figure 8-49.

4. Draw another bone, as shown in Figure 8-49, from the top of the `ShovelArm` symbol to the joint where the shovel is attached to the `ShovelArm`. The three symbols have been moved from their respective layers to the armature layer.

Figure 8-49. The bones used in the animation are in place.

5. Right-click (Windows) or Control+click (Mac) frame 70 of the `Cab` layer, and select `Insert Frame`. The `Cab` symbol now spans 70 frames. Lock the `Cab` layer.

6. We are going to start the animation by establishing its finish position. Right-click (Windows) or Control+click (Mac) frame 70 of the armature layer, and, as shown in Figure 8-50, select `Insert Pose` from the `Context` menu.

That green strip across the armature layer tells you that you have created a pose layer. Pose layers are quite different from motion layers. They can only be created by adding a pose at a frame and they only work with armature layers. The little keyframe icon in the pose layer tells you where the poses are located.

ANIMATION, PART 2

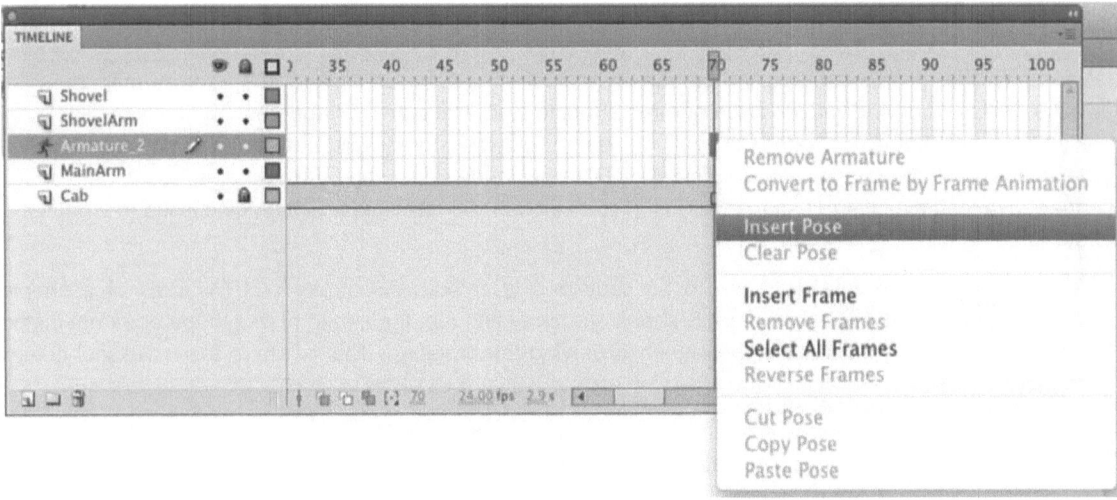

Figure 8-50. Poses are added through the context menu.

7. Scrub back to frame 1. Switch to the **Selection** tool, and move the arms and the shovel to the position shown in Figure 8-51. If you scrub across the timeline the two arms and the shovel lower to the ground. This tells you that poses in an armature layer can be tweened only in the armature layer.

Figure 8-51. Use the **Selection** tool to change a pose.

8. Move the playhead to frame 15. Switch to the **Selection** tool, and extend the shovel arms. What you need to know about this is that by changing the positions of the bones in an armature layer, a keyframe is automatically added. There is no need to insert a pose. This may sound rather familiar because this is exactly what happens when you change the properties of an object in a motion layer.

9. At this point you can continue moving through the timeline and having the machine scoop up and dump some dirt to you can close this example and not save the changes.

479

CHAPTER 8

Using the Bind tool

We expect that IK has sparked the creative center of your brain enough to keep you happily busy for weeks. Believe it or not, you still have one more tool to see. The team at Adobe has made IK available not only to symbols but also to shapes! You'll be using the **Bone** tool for this exercise, but the **Bind** tool will make an appearance as an important sidekick. The best way to describe IK for shapes is to consider it a super-advanced evolution of shape tweens in combination with the shape hinting discussed in Chapter 7. Let's jump right in.

When it comes to IK, the distortion to be controlled is in both the stroke and fill areas of a shape. Depending on the configuration of an IK shape, you may find that the stroke of the shape does not distort in a pleasing way or joints move around when moving the armature. This is where the **Bind** tool comes into play.

By default, the control points of a shape are connected to the bone that is nearest to them. The **Bind** tool allows you to edit the connections between individual bones and the shape control points. The upshot is you control how the stroke distorts when each bone moves.

Before we start, it might not be a bad idea to simply take a look at what effect "binding" has on a drawing. This way, you can see, in a rather dramatic fashion, what it does and learn what to look for.

1. Open the `badBinding.fla` file in your `Exercise` folder. When it opens, you will see two people preparing to arm wrestle.

2. Click the pink character's arm to see the bones.

3. Switch to the **Selection** tool and move the arm. You will notice two things, as shown in Figure 8-52. First, the elbow moves off of the table and some rather disturbing distortions occur around the elbow joint.

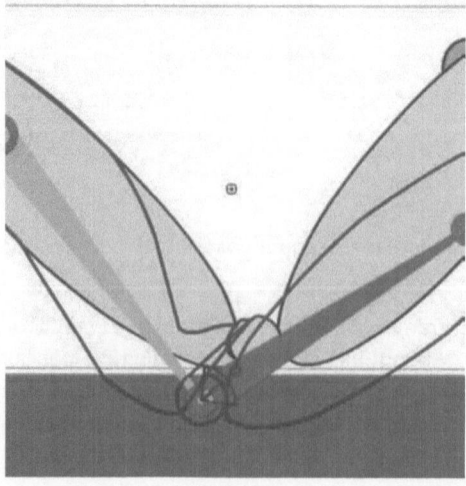

Figure 8-52. Moving a bone in a shape causes distortions and unlifelike movement.

480

4. Open the betterBinding.fla file in your Exercise folder, and give the arm a wiggle. As you can see, Figure 8-53, the elbow stays put, and the distortions are not as severe.

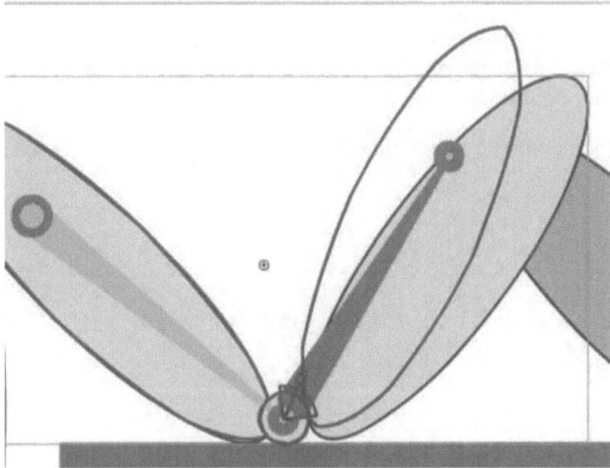

Figure 8-53. Binding, when properly applied, can add realism to movement.

Now that you have seen how binding can affect and armature, let's get to work and start learning how to use the **Bind** tool.

1. Open the Bind.fla file in the Exercise folder for this chapter, and say hello to an earthworm, as shown in Figure 8-54. (The correlation between a worm, bones, steam shovels, and graveyards is purely coincidental, we assure you.) The **Library** for this FLA is empty, because the worm is nothing more than a handful of shapes.

Figure 8-54. IK for shapes is brought to you by a worm.

2. Assuming you want to drag the worm around by its head, you'll want to draw the bones of your armature from the opposite side of the worm. Select the `Bone` tool and starting from the bottom of the shape, drag a small IK bone upward.

3. With that first bone in place, hover over the tail of the IK bone. When the tiny black bone icon inside the mouse cursor turns to white, you'll know you've hit the right spot. Click and drag upward to add another bone.

   In this manner, keep adding small IK bones until you reach the top of the worm (see Figure 8-55).

Figure 8-55. IK bones can easily be applied to shapes.

4. Before you give the worm a wiggle, switch to the `Bind` tool, and click the bottommost IK bone.

5. This is where it gets interesting. To see we're talking about, switch to the `Zoom` tool, and using the `Bind` tool, marquee the bottom several bones in the tail. Now you're ready for action.

Using the `Bind` tool is a bit like using the `Subselection` tool in that it reveals a shape's anchor points. In Figure 8-56, you can see anchor points represented in three different ways. At the top of the figure, they look like the sort you've seen in previous chapters—just small squares. At the bottom, they're considerably larger and thicker and appear in the form of triangles as well as squares.

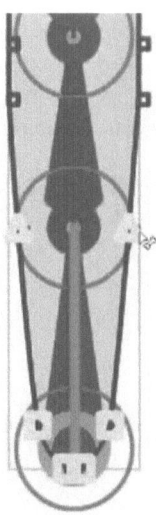

Figure 8-56. The `Bind` tool lets you manipulate anchor points.

When you select an IK bone with the `Bind` tool, Flash shows you which of the shape's anchor points are associated with that particular bone. Squares indicate an association with a single bone; triangles indicate an association with many bones.

In this case, the bottom four anchor points—the heavy squares—are associated with the bottommost bone only. The upper two anchor points—the heavy triangles—are associated with the bottommost bone and with the bone immediately above it. The triangle anchor points are affected when either of their associated bones moves.

Click any of the other IK bones in this armature, and you'll see that Flash has done a great job of automatically deciding which associations to make. This won't always be the case. Thankfully, you can override Flash's decisions.

6. Hold down the Ctrl (Windows) or Cmd (Mac) key, and click one of the bottom four heavy squares. This makes it look like a normal anchor point (smaller and not bold). Still holding Ctrl (Windows) or Cmd (Mac), click one of the heavy triangles, which also becomes a normal anchor point.

7. Select the next IK bone, and you'll see that the triangle anchor is back. but now it's a heavy square. That makes sense: before step 6, this anchor was associated with two bones (triangle), but now it's associated with only this one (square).

8. Select the bottommost bone again, and, without holding down Ctrl (Windows) or Cmd (Mac), click the anchor point that was previously a heavy square. Drag it toward the bone (see Figure 8-57) and release. That anchor point is now reassociated with the bone.

9. Click another bone, and then click this one again. You'll see the heavy square as it originally was, along with its companions.

10. To reassociate the formerly triangle anchor point, use the **Bind** tool to select the appropriate anchor, and then press and hold Ctrl (Windows) or Cmd (Mac) while you drag it to the bottommost bone. As you do, you'll see an association line in the upper bone as well as the diagonal association line created by your dragging (see Figure 8-58).

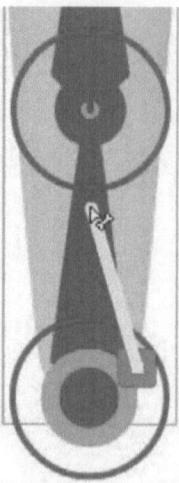

Figure 8-57. Click and drag an anchor point to associate it with a bone.

Figure 8-58. Press Ctrl (Windows) or Cmd (Mac) while dragging to associate an anchor point with more than one bone.

11. Save the file. (You're going to continue with it in the next exercise.)

Use the `Bind` tool to fine-tune your shape armatures, just as you would use shape hints to fine-tune a shape tween. Any anchor points not associated with an IK bone are ignored when the armature is manipulated.

You can animate shape armatures in the same way as symbol armatures—and you're about to do just that—which will introduce you to two "gotchas" of this feature.

When it comes to IK with shapes, two limitations leap to mind:

- Shape armatures don't manipulate gradient and bitmap fills.
- Complex shapes cannot be boned, so keep your overall anchor point count to a minimum.

Let's explore these limitations before moving on to a full-scale IK animation exercise.

Shape IK and fills

To see what we mean about fills, continuing with the `Bind.fla` from the previous exercise, use the `Selection` tool to give your worm a wiggle. It's fun to do, because the shape responds in a very worm-like way. When you're finished, click the stage to deselect the bones and the shape's bounding box.

The shape looks great, but as you can see in Figure 8-59, the gradient fill, which gave the worm a slightly rounded look, hasn't bent along with the shape. This tells you to stick with solid fills for shape armatures.

Figure 8-59. Shape armatures don't affect gradient or bitmap fills.

Shape IK and anchor points

Let's see how the number of anchor points affects shape IK:

1. Open the `WaveSwiss.fla` file in this chapter's `Exercise` folder. You'll see a drawing of the Swiss flag with a shape armature in place.

2. Drag the right side of the armature up and down to wave the flag (see Figure 8-60).

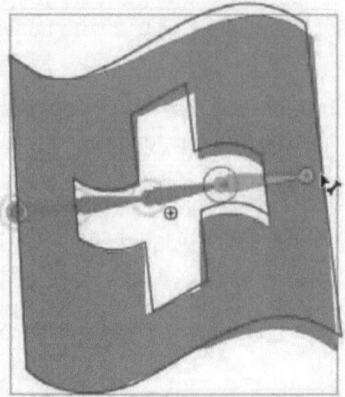

Figure 8-60. There is a definite relationship between armatures and vector points when it comes to IK in Flash.

3. Open the `WaveAmerican.fla` file from the same folder. In this file, the armature hasn't been added yet.
4. Use the `Selection` tool to select the whole shape, and then switch to the `Bone` tool and try to add an IK bone.

Instead of a new armature, you'll see the alert box in Figure 8-61 telling you the shape is too complex. Want to know the culprit?

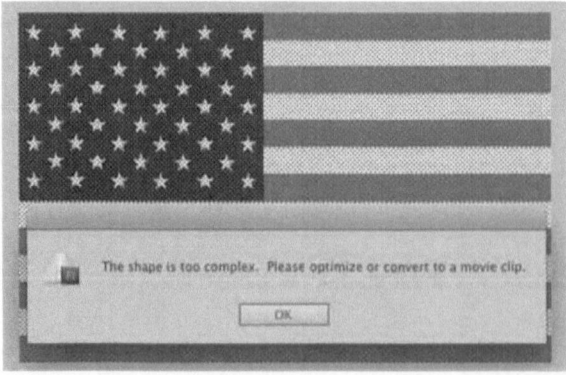

Figure 8-61. Shape complexity also comes into play when it comes to IK in Flash.

5. Switch to the `Subselection` tool, and draw a selection around the whole shape.

ANIMATION, PART 2

Each of those 50 stars is composed of 10 anchor points. That's 500 points already, and that doesn't include the stripes. We're not sure where the official line is drawn, but 500+ anchor points is too much. Your solutions are to either optimize the graphic, which we cover in Chapter 15, or convert the entire flag to a movie clip. Our suggestion is go the movie clip route because optimizing will reduce the number of vector points but not sufficiently to avoid a repeat of this warning.

Your turn: animate a fully rigged IK model

We figure you appreciate worms, bending trees, steam shovels, and skeleton hands as much as the next designer (and so do we!). But surely, your thoughts have already wandered toward more complex implementations. We suspect you're wondering if the IK tools are useful for more than a few fingers. What about a whole body? The answer to these questions is yes, and you're about to find out firsthand. In this final exercise of the chapter, you'll expand on what you learned in previous sections by rigging up a character with arms and legs and then animating it against a backdrop of hand-sketched poses. Let's do it.

1. Open the `Richard.fla` file from the `Exercise` folder for this chapter. You'll see an assembled collection of symbols in the likeness of Richard (see Figure 8-62), one of the regular characters in Steve Napierski's web comic "The Outer Circle" (www.theoutercircle.com/).

> *The authors would like to give Steve a hearty thanks for letting us use his artwork! See more at www.pierski.com/.*

Figure 8-62. Meet Richard. Give him a hug. You're going to make Richard jump.

2. Select **Edit (Flash) ➤ Preferences**, and click the **Drawing** choice in the **Category** area. Deselect the **IK Bone tool: Auto Set Transformation Point** check box. As described in the "A note about bone preferences" section earlier, this means you'll be the one deciding where to place your bone heads and tails, and you'll adjust them afterward.

3. Select the **Oval** tool and, in the **Richard** layer, draw a small circle about 22 pixels × 22 pixels near one of the character's hands. Select the shape and convert it to a graphic symbol named **handle**. This is going to be your "ghost handle," which lets you constrain the hands, feet, and head.

4. Drag additional instances of the **handle** symbol from the **Library** to the stage, positioning them near the Richard's other hand, his feet, and his head, as shown in Figure 8-63. In this exercise, Richard's chest will act as the starting point for every new chain of bones, just as the skeleton's palm did in earlier exercises.

Figure 8-63. Make sure to include extra symbols to allow for rotation constraints.

5. Select the **Bone** tool, and then click and drag a bone from the torso symbol to one of the upper leg symbols. Be sure to release the bone's tail low enough on the upper leg that it clears the bounding box of the torso (see the bounding box in Figure 8-64, and note how the bone tail falls below it). Even though this puts the bone tail lower than it should on the leg symbol—effectively moving the "hip" into the thigh—you'll be able to readjust it in just a moment.

ANIMATION, PART 2

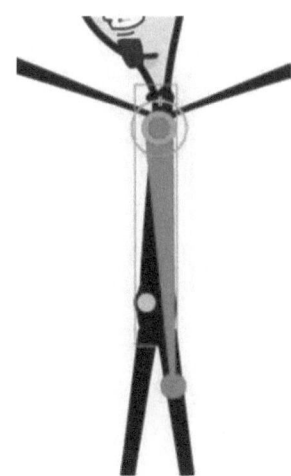

Figure 8-64. Make sure the bone's tail clears the bounding box of the torso symbol.

The fact that these symbols overlap is part of the reason we had you deselect `Auto Set Transformation Point` in step 2. Although not always a problem, in this case, the obscured symbol rotation points make it harder for Flash to decide on its own where new chains of bones should begin.

6. Just as you did earlier for the knuckles, continue adding a new bone that connects the upper leg to the lower leg, the lower leg to the ankle, the ankle to the foot, and finally the foot to the foot's ghost handle. Feel free to zoom the stage—particularly for the ankle! —if necessary.

7. Select the `Free Transform` tool, and then click the stage to deselect the armature itself.

8. Click each symbol in turn, from the ghost handle back up to the torso, and adjust the transformation point so that it sits over the symbol's registration point. To do this, click the white circle (transformation point), drag it to the small plus sign (registration point), and then release. Selecting `Snap to Objects` in the `Tools` panel will make this task easier for you.

9. After you've adjusted the transformation point for each boned symbol, select the `Bone` tool again, and click the head of the torso's existing bone to begin a new chain of bones down the other leg. Follow this with a repeat of the `Free Transform` tool adjustments of the relevant symbols' transformation points.

10. Obviously, the arms need the same treatment, as does the head. Starting from the same gathering of torso bones each time, use the `Bone` tool to create new bone chains from the torso to upper arm, lower arm, hand, to ghost handle on both sides, and then from torso to head to ghost handle at the top of the character. When you're finished, revisit all relevant symbols with the `Free Transform` tool to reposition transformation points over their corresponding registration points. Your armature should look like the one shown in Figure 8-65.

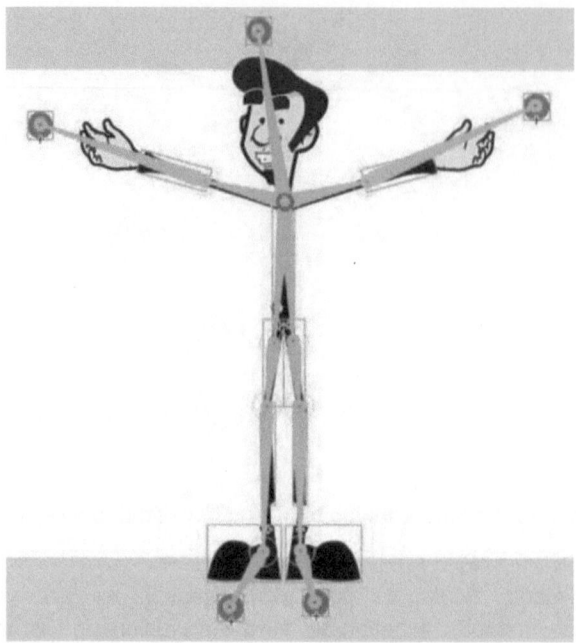

Figure 8-65. A complete IK rig

At this point, Richard is nearly ready for his calisthenics. First, we need a few rotation constraints.

11. Using the `Selection` tool, click any of the torso bones and deselect the `Enabled` option in the `Joint: Rotation` area of the `Properties` panel. Because all the torso bones share the same head, this action will disable rotation for the whole body.

12. Zoom the stage, if necessary, and disable rotation for the ankle bones.

13. Add rotation constraints to the remaining bones according to your preferences. For example, select the lower leg's bone, and in the `Properties` panel, select the `Constrain` option and adjust the `Min` and `Max` values to keep the knee from bending backward.

When you're finished, the `Timeline`'s original `Richard` layer will have long since been emptied, because every symbol was moved to the automatically created armature layer as it was associated with a bone.

14. Rename the `Richard` layer to `poses`.

15. Select `File` ➤ `Import` ➤ `Import to Stage`, and import the `jumping.jpg` file in this chapter's `Exercise` folder. This JPG features a number of hand-drawn poses you can use as guides to manipulate the armature. Position the imported JPG slightly to the right, so that it appears behind Richard, and then lock the `poses` layer.

16. Select `Edit` ➤ `Select All` to select the armature's symbols.

ANIMATION, PART 2

17. Open the `Transform` panel (`Window ▶ Transform`). Make sure the `Constrain` option in the `Transform` panel is selected (the chain icon is not broken), and resize the fully selected armature to approximately 75 percent, as shown in Figure 8-66. This matches the character's size with the hand-drawn poses.

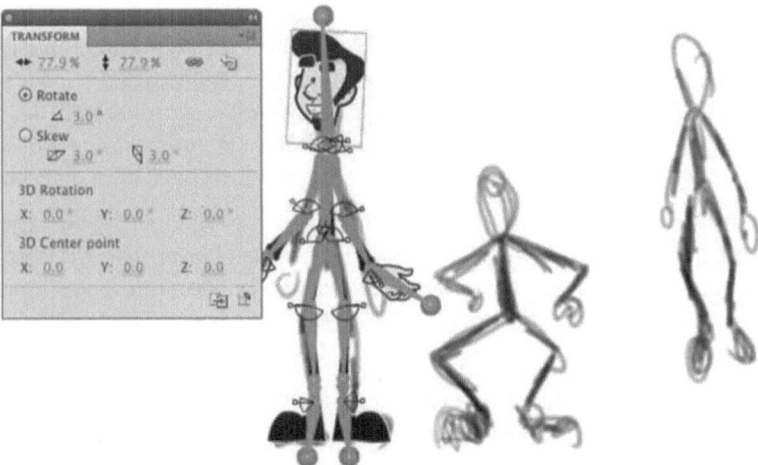

Figure 8-66. Resize the armature, and all its symbols, to the hand-drawn guides, and you're set.

When you release the mouse after scrubbing, the `Transform` panel will seem to indicate that the armature is still scaled to 100 percent, but if you select each symbol individually, the `Transform` panel will correctly show the smaller scale you chose in step 18.

Richard's jump should take about one second. Because the movie's frame rate is 24 fps, that means 24 frames is fine.

18. Hover near the right edge of the of the armature's single frame until the icon turns into a double-headed arrow. Drag out the armature span until it reaches frame 24.

19. Right-click (Windows) or Control+click (Mac) the `poses` layer at frame 24, and select `Insert Frame` from the context menu. This matches up the JPEG to the time span of the armature layer.

20. We're about to cut you loose, so here's the basic gist of what you'll repeat until the sequence is finished:

    a. Unlock the `poses` layer and slide the JPG to the left in order to position the next pose under the armature. Once the JPEG is moved, lock the `poses` layer again.

    b. Drag the playhead six frames to the right (one-fourth of the armature span, because there are four poses after the first drawing).

    c. Use the `Selection` tool to manipulate the character's body parts so they match the hand-drawn pose.

Here are two important tips:

- Depending on how you might have constrained your joints, you may not be able to match the drawing perfectly. Treat the drawings as *rough guides*. In Figure 8-63, for example, you can see that our elbows don't match the pose at all—they're bent in the opposite direction! Just have fun with it.

- You will often need to move the whole armature at once. To accomplish this, hold down the Ctrl (Windows) or Cmd (Mac) key, and click the current frame of the armature layer. Doing so simultaneously selects all the armature's symbols in the chosen frame. At this point, slowly tap the keyboard's arrow keys to move the armature. If you hold down Shift while pressing the arrow keys, you can move in 10-pixel increments, which makes it go faster.

21. After you've finished posing the armature at frames 6, 12, 18, and 24, right-click (Windows) or Control+click (Mac) the `poses` layer and convert it to a guide layer. This will keep it from showing when you publish the SWF. (Alternatively, you could hide the `poses` layer and configure your preferences to omit hidden layers from the SWF—see the "Using layers" section of Chapter 1—or simply delete the `poses` layer.)

22. Double-click the `handle` symbol in the `Library` to open it in the `Symbol Editor`. Change the opacity of its fill color to `0%`, to make the ghost handles invisible when you publish.

23. Save your file, and test the movie. If you like, compare your work with the completed `Richard.fla` file in this chapter's Complete folder.

Inspiration is everywhere

We started this chapter with a mention of some inspirational early Flash animation, so it's fitting to finish with a few more current resources.

- Chris Georgenes (http://mudbubble.com) is one of the most talented Flash animators we know and a friendly guy to boot! His http://keyframer.com forum has become an immensely popular meeting place for Flash cartoonists and animators, from beginner to pro. So, visit his forum, sign up (it's free), and bring along your artwork, demo reels, and questions. You'll find literally thousands of eager participants ready to share their Flash-based tips and tricks.

- For a look at some jaw-droppingly amazing, multiple award-winning Flash cartoons, check out the "Animation" section of Adam Phillips's http://biteycastle.com website. Adam was happy to lend us a screenshot from "Waterlollies" (see Figure 8-67). He draws and animates all his artwork directly in Flash. When you see what's possible with the authoring tool, you might just think (as one of the authors does), "When I grow up, I want to be Adam Phillips."

ANIMATION, PART 2

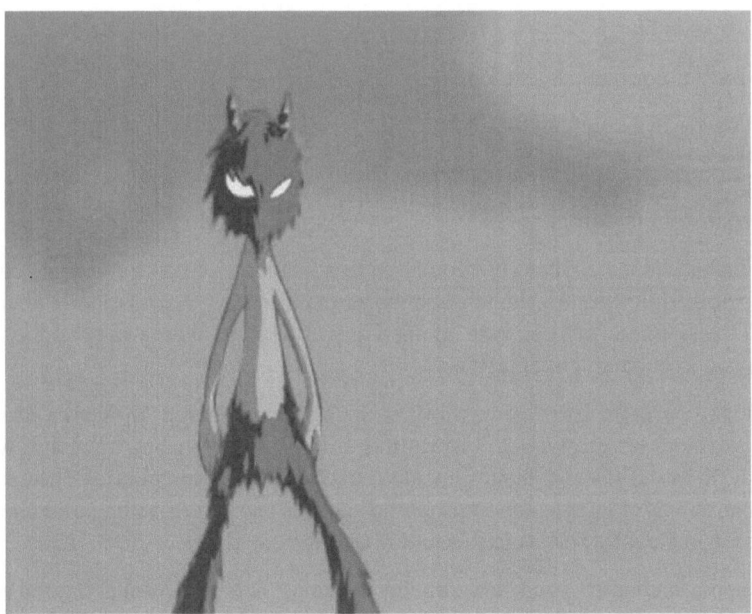

Figure 8-67. A scene from Adam Phillips's "Waterlollies" (www.biteycastle.com)

- For an additional 360 pages of top-notch Flash animation how-to, check out *Foundation Flash Cartoon Animation* (friends of ED, 2007), by Tim Jones, Barry Kelly, Allan Rosson, and David Wolfe (www.friendsofed.com/book.html?isbn=9781590599129). This book was written for Flash CS3, so it covers only the technical content discussed in Chapter 7, but it goes on to elaborate on industry practices, including `Library` organization, storyboarding and animatics, frame-by-frame animation, and integration with After Effects.

What you have learned

In this chapter, you learned the following:

- How to use the `Motion Editor` panel
- That even though the new tweening model is intended for the `Motion Editor` panel, the `Timeline` panel continues to be useful for motion tweens
- How to use and configure advanced easing graphs and how to create your own
- How to navigate property keyframes in the `Motion Editor` and `Timeline` panels
- How to change the duration of a tween span
- How to manipulate and reuse motion paths, with or without the `Motion Presets` panel

CHAPTER 8

- How IK works in Flash
- How to use the **Bone** and **Bind** tools
- How to use the **Spring** feature
- Tips on improving your IK bone rigging workflow
- How to animate an IK armature

This has been a rather intense chapter, but you have to admit there is some seriously cool animation stuff in Flash CS5. We started by walking you through the **Motion Editor**, including motion paths. Up to this point in the book, the **Motion Editor** was something you "visited." Now you have learned how valuable a tool it will be as you strengthen your Flash skills.

From there, we took you deep into the new inverse kinematics features of Flash CS5. Starting with the **Bone** tool and a skeleton, we guided you through this subject. By animating trees in a wind storm, steam shovels, flags waving in the breeze, steam engines, and an honest-to-goodness real cartoon character, you discovered the power of inverse kinematics and quite a few of the gotchas and workarounds being developed as the Flash industry adjusts to this new animation capability.

As you went through this chapter, you were probably thinking, "This is all well and good in a flat space, but where's the 3D?" Great question. Why don't you turn the page and find out.

Chapter 9

Flash Has a Third Dimension

Designers had been asking for 3D manipulation tools in Flash for a long time. In fact, this feature has been requested in some form or another since the beginning of the product line. That makes sense if you consider that the mid-1990s promise of Virtual Reality Modeling Language (VRML) gave web surfers a taste of 3D before Flash ever hit the market. VRML was a great idea, but it was ahead of its time and, sadly, didn't go very far. In any case, it was more of a programmer's pursuit than something a designer would want to grapple with.

Then came Flash, which sparked an explosion of stylish 2D designs that began to reshape what the web experience meant. Over the years, intrepid designers began experimenting with ways to simulate three dimensions in their SWFs. They used centuries-old techniques to accomplish these goals—for example, increasing the size of an object to "move it forward"—which were the same practices used in real-life painting and sketching. Nothing in the Flash interface provided direct assistance. This all changed in Flash CS4. The requested tools arrived, and they're here to stay in CS5. If you'll pardon the pun, they open a whole new dimension in creative potential.

Here's what we'll cover in this chapter:

- Understanding the 3D environment
- Using the 3D tools
- Positioning symbols in 3D space

The following files are used in this chapter (located in Chapter09/ExerciseFiles_Ch09/Exercise/):

- Amsterdam.fla
- FigurineSmall.jpg
- Figurine.jpg
- Amsterdam01.jpg
- SpaceFinal.png
- Space.fla
- swingDoors.fla
- AirheadMail.fla
- 3DCube.fla

The source files are available online at www.friendsofED.com/download.html?isbn=1430229940.

What you'll learn in this chapter pertains to the 3D-related tools in the Flash CS5 `Tools` panel, along with some workflow suggestions to help you get the most out of them. This will be enough to introduce you to a new playground.

If you want to supplement the benefits of the new 3D tools with older techniques, consider checking out *Flash 3D Cheats Most Wanted* by Aral Balkan, Josh Dura, et al. (friends of ED, 2003). To learn about simulating 3D with ActionScript 3.0, see Chapters 15 through 17 of *Foundation ActionScript 3.0 Animation: Making Things Move!* by Keith Peters (friends of ED, 2007). For the perfect introduction to using a 3D engine (Away3D) to create "real" 3D in Flash, see *The Essential Guide to 3D in Flash* by Richard Olsson and Rob Bateman (friends of ED, 2010).

What 3D really means in Flash (and what it doesn't)

When it comes to 3D in Flash, consider this feature as you would pizza. No matter what the server brings from the kitchen, you're going to love it. *Capisce?* Good. Now that you're thinking of a delicious pie with all your favorite toppings, tease your mind back to Flash for a moment. Between bites, wrap your brain around three levels of wow factor:

- Good ("Hey, this is super cool!")
- Better ("My jaw just hit the floor!")
- Best ("Somebody bring me oxygen!")

Game consoles like the Wii, PlayStation 3, and Xbox 360 have redefined what consumers expect in terms of 3D interactivity. This is the bring-me-oxygen stuff—the Best level—which isn't available in Flash. We need to mention that right out of the gate. (Hey, are you going to eat that pepperoni?)

On the design side of things, you would need specialized 3D modeling software to produce that sort of content for game consoles, television, or film. We're talking about software like Maya, 3Ds Max, Blender, or Cinema 4D. These industrial-strength powerhouses are designed specifically for the task and are capable of turning out extremely complex, high-resolution output. Examples include everything from Hollywood aliens, dragons, and virtual stunts, all the way to vehicle mock-ups, such as the Hot Rod created by Belgian CG artist Laurens Corijn for `cg.activtutsplus.com`, shown in Figure 9-1.

Figure 9-1. Highly complex 3D models are created in software designed for the task, which doesn't include Flash (car modeled by Laurens Corijn).

For better or worse, advanced 3D modeling is not the sort of field trip you'll be taking in Flash CS5—at least, not with the new drawing tools. Don't let that get you down, though. For you code jockeys, be aware that ActionScript does give you a surprising range of possibilities, but you'll probably want to use third-party code libraries to pull it off.

For the jaw-dropping stuff—the Better level—you'll want to check out Papervision3D (`www.Papervision3D.org/`). This is open source software (created by core team members Carlos Ulloa, Ralph Hauwert, John Grden, Tim Knip, and Andy Zupko) consisting of a framework of ActionScript 3.0 and 2.0 class files. Papervision3D allows programmers to create a range of *3D primitives* (basic shapes, from which other shapes can be built), and even import COLLADA (an open XML standard) data files from external modeling applications, and then bring those models to life in complex ways, as shown in Figure 9-2. Yup, that's Flash, and every fish, including the shark, is interactive. In addition, the entire scene gives you a complete 360-degree view of the reef when you drag the mouse. Interactive. In many ways, this is comparable to VRML.

CHAPTER 9

Figure 9-2. An example of Papervision3D content

If you're experienced with previous versions of Flash, you may have heard of Swift 3D (www.erain.com). Swift 3D is a best-of-breed, low-cost modeler closely integrated with Flash in that it exports models as SWFs. These SWFs can then be loaded or imported into your normal work files and used to simulate three-dimensional objects. The latest version of Swift 3D even exports to Papervision3D, so you're in good hands with this product. Designers typically import Swift 3D assets as elements of otherwise two-dimensional layouts. That workflow is every bit as useful in Flash CS4 as it has been in the past, but it's not the topic we're covering here.

What you'll learn about in this chapter is the super-cool stuff—the Good level—and a great place to start if you're new to nonscripted 3D in Flash (which pretty much means anyone using Flash CS5 for the first time). We won't be covering 3D in terms of ActionScript. It's simply a topic that merits its own book (such as *The Essential Guide to 3D in Flash*, mentioned earlier), and we again direct your attention to www.Papervision3D.org or www.away3d.com. What you are about to discover, behind that heavenly melted mozzarella, is a pair of shiny tools that first appeared in Flash CS4 that give you direct three-dimensional manipulation of your symbols. But first, we need to cover a bit of theory.

Understanding the vanishing point

When you open your eyelids and cast your gaze ahead, even if all you can see are the tweed walls of your cubicle, you have a horizon in front of you. Turn your head, and it's still there. The horizon might be hidden, but the principles of perspective still apply, just as gravity still applies even when you climb a tree or take a dive in the swimming hole. In a theoretical sense, this horizon holds something called a **vanishing point**, which is a special location, usually off in the distance, where the parallel lines in your view seem to converge. It's a natural optical illusion, and you see it every time you stare down a length of railroad tracks. In linear perspective drawings, you can have as many as three vanishing points, but Flash keeps things manageable for you by providing one. Here's how it works.

Imagine you are in a huge square in front of a museum. The square is paved with square paving stones, and you take a picture from where you are in the square to the front door of the museum. If you drawn lines along the surface of the square that follow the parallel lines in the pattern of the paving stone, those lines will eventually intersect at a place, as shown in Figure 9-3, called the vanishing point.

Figure 9-3. The vanishing point is the location where parallel lines appear to converge on the horizon.

That vanishing point is your key to understanding how the `3D Rotation` and `3D Translation` tools, coupled with the `Transform` panel and `Properties` panel, give you access to 3D manipulation in Flash. Without this concept, you can still experiment with these tools and have plenty of fun. But if you want to actually wallpaper a three-dimensional cube with movie clips or project a photo on to a wall that isn't displayed head-on, you should keep a firm grip on the notion of those perspective lines. By actually drawing them as temporary guides over your artwork, you'll find the new 3D tools a ton easier to work with.

Consider the real-world example of the Amsterdam street scene shown in Figure 9-4. You're going to use this photo to get acquainted with the new tools, so let's put those perspective lines in place. Here's how:

1. Open the Amsterdam.fla file from the Exercise folder for this chapter. Note the already-imported photo in a layer named **background**.
2. Create a new layer, and name it **perspective**. Right-click (Windows) or Control+click (Mac) the new layer's name, and select Guide from the context menu. This converts the layer into a guide layer, which means you can see its contents during authoring, but anything on this layer will disappear in the published SWF, which is exactly what you want.
3. Select the Line tool, and make sure the Object Drawing button is not selected in the Tools panel. Use the Line tool to draw some lines, like those in Figure 9-4, into the **perspective** layer. Start from the lower-right corner, and follow the edge where the garage door meets the street.

Figure 9-4. Use perspective lines in a guide layer to assist with the 3D drawing tools.

4. Repeat this process with another line that follows the top of the garage door, until you can pin down the vanishing point to the far left.
5. Save your file, because you're going to revisit it later in the chapter. You can compare your work with the completed Amsterdam.fla in the Complete folder, which shows the two lines already in place.

Now, let's have some fun with the 3D tools themselves.

Using the 3D tools

As we've mentioned, Flash CS5 provides two 3D tools: the `3D Rotation` tool and the `3D Transformation` tool.

The 3D Rotation tool

In terms of visual cool factor, the `3D Rotation` tool falls into the realm of "wicked cool." This tool allows you to quickly and intuitively rotate a movie clip in 3D space. In previous versions of Flash, this was possible only with shapes, and even that technique required a bit of careful nudging with the `Free Transform` tool. You simply couldn't do this with a symbol. Now you can, and that means you can perform perspective transforms on complex artwork, imported photos, and, yes, even video. Kind of makes the corners of the mouth go up, doesn't it?

To illustrate how groundbreaking this is, let's start with how it used to be.

Old-school 3D rotation

Prior to this release of Flash, 3D perspective was not exactly up there in the realm of "really easy to accomplish." You needed to actually draw in perspective by hand or use the `Free Transform` tool to simulate 3D rotation. Let's go "old school" and see how that technique works:

1. Create a new FLA file, and select the `Rectangle` tool. Make sure the `Object Drawing` button is not selected so that your shape is nothing more than a fill, with an optional stroke. Color settings don't matter. Draw a square approximately 300 × 300 pixels.

2. Once you've drawn your shape, double-click to select it, and then change to the `Free Transform` tool. You'll see a number of buttons appear in the options area of the `Tools` panel.

3. Click the `Distort` button—it looks like a paper airplane at the bottom of the `Tools` panel, which lets you make perspective distortions by individually clicking and dragging each corner of your square. Go ahead and do precisely that. With a bit of practice, you can reshape the square to appear as if you're standing above it, looking slightly down on it, as shown in Figure 9-5.

4. Click away from the reshaped square to deselect it. Now double-click the shape to select it again. When you do—assuming that `Free Transform` is still your current tool—you'll notice that the shape's bounding box no longer follows the contours of the shape. That's to be expected, since the bounding box represents the full area required to contain the shape.

Figure 9-5. The `Distort` option of the `Free Transform` tool lets you simulate perspective with shapes.

At this point, if you want to adjust your perspective distortion (see Figure 9-6), you'll find it much harder to accomplish with precision, simply because the bounding box no longer matches the corners or edges of the shape. Worse, you can't do a thing with imported photos, if that's your aim. Let's see the problem with photos.

Figure 9-6. Adjusting already-distorted shapes quickly becomes a challenge.

5. Import the `FigurineSmall.jpg` included in the `Exercise` folder for this chapter to your `Library`, and set it as the bitmap fill for the reshaped square. Notice that the bitmap simply tiles inside the shape and doesn't "play along" with this distortion game in the least (see Figure 9-7). After all, this is a simulation of perspective, not the real thing.

FLASH HAS A THIRD DIMENSION

> *If bitmap fills have you scratching your head, flip back to Chapter 2 for a quick refresher.*

Figure 9-7. Bitmaps are not affected by perspective distortion.

Using 3D rotation

If you want to turn your world around—practically speaking, and in a good way—you'll need to step over to the `3D Rotation` tool. This is where it gets really neat, folks.

1. Start a new Flash document, and import the `Figurine.jpg` image from your `Exercise` folder to the stage.
2. Select the photo, and convert it to a movie clip symbol.

Step 2—converting to a movie clip—is the deal maker. Without it, the 3D drawing tools are useless. They work with movie clips, period. Keep that in mind, whatever artwork you intend to spin around in 3D space. Fortunately for you, movie clips are a supremely useful symbol.

3. Select the `3D Rotation` tool, and click the movie clip. You'll see a somewhat complex looking bull's-eye.

Figure 9-8 shows the same bull's-eye repeated four times, with the mouse pointer moving from area to area. Notice how the mouse pointer changes. Each of those lines and circles has a meaning. Hover near the vertical red line (far left in the figure), and the mouse pointer turns into a black arrow with an **x** next to it. This line controls the x-axis rotation, which you'll see in just a moment. Hover near the horizontal green line—the second bull's-eye in Figure 9-8—and you'll see the letter **y**, which controls y-axis rotation. Hover near the inner large blue circle, and you'll see a **z**, which controls the z-axis. The outer orange circle (far right in the figure) isn't associated with a letter, because it affects all three axes at once. The tiny circle in the middle represents the 3D rotation center point, and it's basically the pivot for this sort of rotation.

503

Figure 9-8. Four views of the same interactive bull's-eye, showing x-, y-, z-, and all-axis rotation

4. To see what an x-axis rotation does, hover near the vertical red line, and then click and drag sideways, slowly back and forth. You'll see a pie chart–like wedge appear inside the bull's-eye (see Figure 9-9), which gives you an idea of the current size of the angle. In the figure, the angle is approximately 45 degrees.

5. To adjust y-axis rotation, hover near the horizontal green line, and then click and drag slowly up and down. For z-axis and all-axis rotation, click and drag in any direction you please.

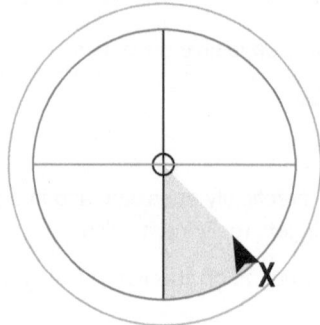

Figure 9-9. A wedge shape tells you how far you're rotating.

The visual effect on the movie clip is easy to see. As shown in Figure 9-10, the rotations work as follows:

- X-axis rotation (left) moves like a head nodding "yes."
- Y-axis rotation (center) moves like a head shaking "no."
- Z-axis rotation (right) moves like a doorknob, which is effectively the same as rotating with the `Free Transform` tool.

FLASH HAS A THIRD DIMENSION

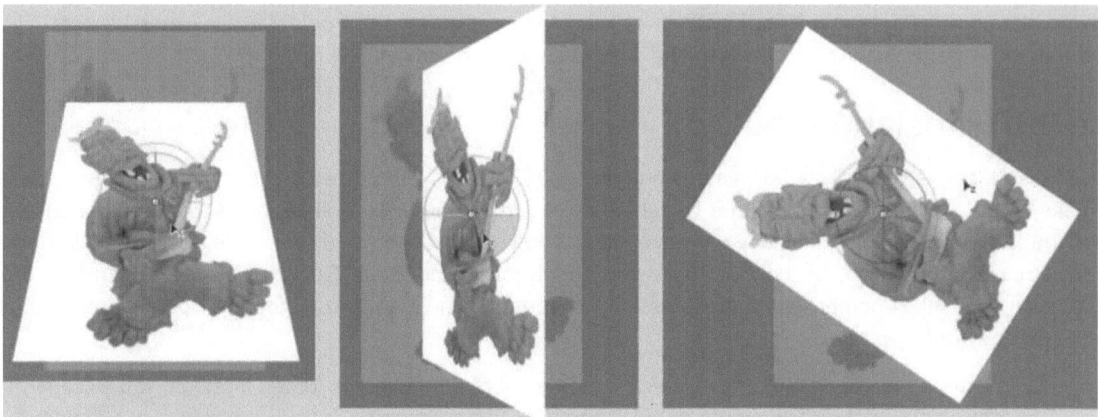

Figure 9-10. Three axes of rotation: x moves like a head nod, y moves like a head shake, and z moves like a doorknob.

6. Experiment with rotation, keeping an eye on the `Transform` panel (`Window ➤ Transform`). It's easy to get disoriented when rotating numerous axes at once—for example, by dragging the outer orange circle—or when rotating any particular axis after others are set to nonzero values. If dragging ever gets out of hand, click the `Transform` panel's `Remove Transform` button (see Figure 9-11). In fact, do that now to see the movie clip return to its default flat appearance.

7. Still in the `Transform` panel, scrub each of the hot text values in the `3D Rotation` area. They provide an alternate way to rotate along the x, y, and z axes—with the added benefit that you can enter exact values by hand.

8. Feel free to save your file.

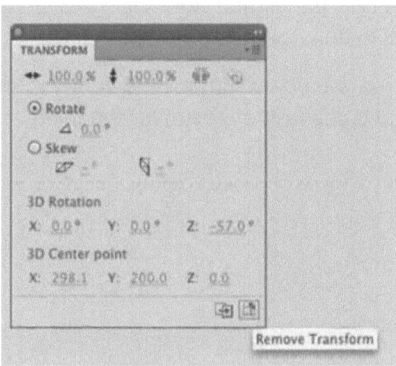

Figure 9-11. Use the `Transform` panel to reset 3D rotations.

Now that you understand rotation, it's time to learn how to position your object in Flash's 3D space. This sort of movement is called **translation**, and it features a tool all its own.

The 3D Translation tool

Because Flash is primarily a two-dimensional interface, the `3D Translation` tool may not immediately make sense. Without the context of a vanishing point, it may seem like nothing more than another version of the `Selection` tool. It lets you move things, but the way it works is more restrictive than the `Selection` tool, which, by contrast, lets you simply click and drag. So what gives? To answer that question, let's take another visit to that street in Amsterdam. The plan is to project the figurine image on to that garage door.

1. Open the `Amsterdam01.fla` file you saved earlier in the chapter. When it opens, you will see the vanishing point guides created earlier and the figurine image, which is a movie clip, sitting in the photo layer.

2. Select the figurine. Use the `Free Transform` tool or the `Transform` panel to resize the photo to about 65 percent of its actual size (approximately 100 × 100 pixels). Try to have the top and bottom corners on the right edge of the photo somewhat align with the guides. An easy way of doing this is to move the transform point to the bottom-right corner of the movie clips.

> *According to recommended best practices, you would normally import a photo that doesn't require such a change in scale, because even though it looks small in the SWF, the actual imported file is big, which adds to the SWF's file size. In this exercise, you're giving yourself leeway as you experiment.*

3. At this point, it's time to make use of the perspective lines in the guide layer. Using the `Selection` tool, click the figurine movie clip to select it. Twirl down the `3D Position and View` area of the `Propert`ies panel, and note the `Vanishing point` values at the bottom of that area, next to a `Reset` button, as shown in Figure 9-12.

4. Until you adjust it otherwise, the vanishing point is centered on the stage. Click and scrub the `x` value slowly to see a set of crosshairs appear over the photo.

FLASH HAS A THIRD DIMENSION

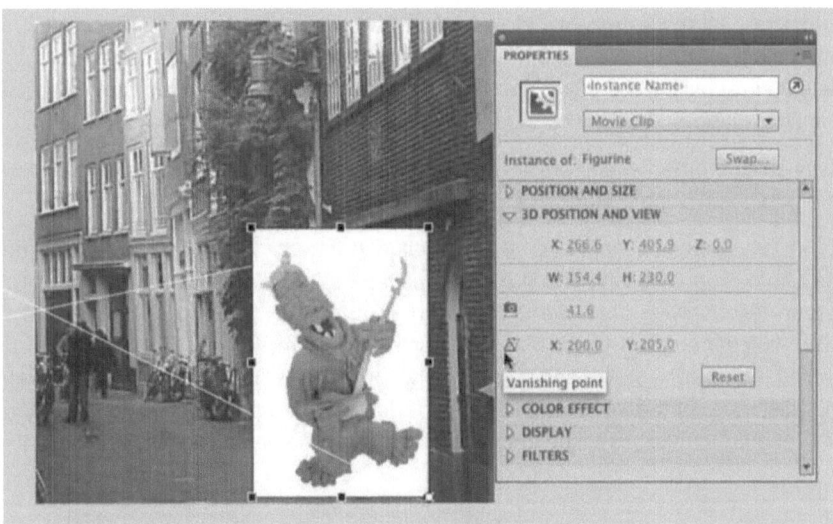

Figure 9-12. The vanishing point can be adjusted in the `Properties` panel.

The crosshairs represent the official vanishing point Flash uses to position 3D objects. When your goal involves matching up assets to actual background images, you'll find that helps to match Flash's vanishing point with the real-world vanishing point in your reference artwork. Let's do it.

5. Scrub the **x** value far to the left so that the horizontal portion of the crosshairs lines up with the point where the perspective lines intersect. When you're satisfied, do the same with the **y** value to lift it a bit higher

6. Click the figurine to select it, and switch to the **3D Translation** tool. You'll see a pair of arrows arranged in an L shape on the image.

Figure 9-13 shows the same set of arrows repeated four times, with the mouse pointer moving from area to area, changing as it does. The arrows and the heavy dot each have their own meaning. Hover near the horizontal red line (far left in the figure), and the mouse pointer turns into a black arrow with an **x** next to it. This arrow controls the x-axis position. Hover near the vertical green line, and you'll see the letter **y**, which controls the y-axis position. You'll use this in just a moment.

Figure 9-13. Four views of the same interactive L shape, showing x-, y-, and z-axis position

The heavy dot takes a bit more dexterity. Hover in the center of the dot, and you'll see a `z`, which controls movement along the z-axis. Hover near the edge of the dot, and you won't see any letters. Why? Dragging at this point lets you reposition the 3D center point for this object, which affects how translation is applied (the center point's position isn't nearly as obvious with translation as it is with rotation).

7. Hover near the green y-axis arrow, and then click and drag down until the photo appears to rest on the perspective line that runs along where the door meets the street.

8. Use the `Transform` panel to scrub the `Y` value in the `3D Rotation` area until the bottom edge of the photo roughly follows the line of the pavement as it meets the buildings (see Figure 9-14). You can alternatively use the `3D Rotation` tool to accomplish the same task, but the `Transform` panel gives you a bit better control. If you're surprised at how much the image gets stretched, don't worry. We'll show you how to fix that later in the chapter. The stretch is because of the "distance" of the vanishing point, off to the side. What you need to pay attention to is how the top and bottom edges of the image roughly follow the vanishing point guides.

Figure 9-14. Use the `Transform` panel for finer rotation control.

9. With the `Transform` panel open, scrub across the `Resize` values at the top to shrink the image. Be sure that the link icon is selected to ensure uniform scaling. As you scale the image, notice how the `x` and `y` values shown in Figure 9-15 aren't the same. This is because of the 3D translation applied to the image that aligns it to the perspective.

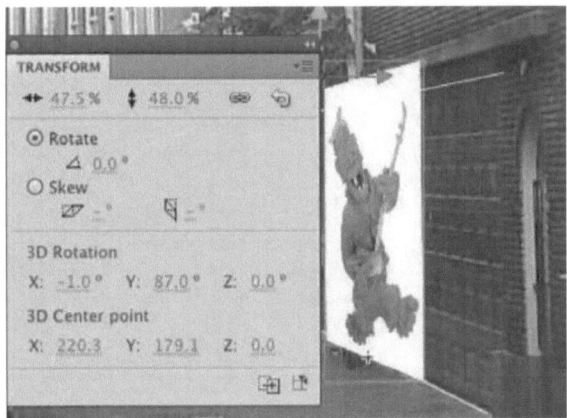

Figure 9-15. Scale the image in the `Transform` panel and use the `Y Translation` arrow to move it into position.

10. Use the `Y Translation` arm to move the image so that its bottom edge sits on the bottom vanishing point guide.

With the image somewhat in place and resized, you are now going to put it into its final position. What you won't be doing here is changing over to the `Selection` tool and pulling and pushing the image into place. You will need to use the `3D Translation` tool, the `Transform` panel, and the `Properties` panel to "slide" the image into position on the x-axis and to "push" it into the door on the z-axis.

To understand X and Z movement—at least in the current scenario—think of those perspective lines in terms of the ones shown in Figure 9-3 in the square in front of the museum. In that earlier figure, the line seems to be growing out of the image toward you, because its vanishing point is at the "back" of the square. In that case, or when the vanishing point is centered on the stage, Z movement causes the object to get bigger or smaller as it moves "out" or "in." The apparent scaling is a perspective effect that happens because the z-axis is pointing at you. In this case, the z-axis is pointing somewhere over your right shoulder. It's as if you're looking at the figurine image from the side. Why? Because the vanishing point is over to the left.

Let's illustrate this.

11. Hover over the heavy dot until you see the letter z appear in the mouse pointer. Slowly drag up and down. The image still changes scale, but more important, it moves sideways, zooming along the pavement. That's because the "front" of the z-axis is pointing toward the right, and the back is pointing toward the vanishing point at left.

12. Now hover over the horizontal red line until you see the mouse pointer acquire an X. Click and drag slowly left and right. At first, the movement might look similar to Z movement, but there's an important difference. Yes, there is some left-and-right movement, but because of the position of the vanishing point, the photo seems to be moving "onto the street" or "into the door," as depicted in Figure 9-16.

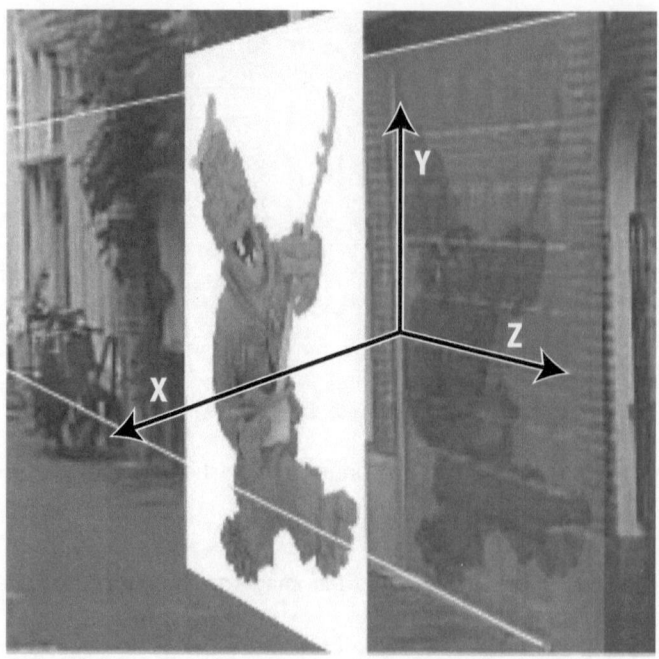

Figure 9-16. The orientation of the x-, y-, and z-axes depends on the position of the vanishing point.

As you are most likely discovering, using the arrows on the `3D Translation` tool to move a selection can be a bit tricky. Here's a more precise method:

1. Select the image on the stage and open the `Properties` panel.
2. Twirl down the `3D Position and View` options.
3. Switch to the `3D Translation` tool, and scrub across one of the handles. Pay attention to how the values in the X, Y, and Z areas, as shown in Figure 9-17, in the `Properties` panel change as you drag the arrow. Now scrub across the values in the `Properties` panel. The selection moves on the axis you are scrubbing.
4. What does that little camera in the `3D Position and View` properties do? Scrub across the value. That little gem is the `Perspective Angle`, and as, you have seen, it moves the selection along the sight line of the vanishing point.

FLASH HAS A THIRD DIMENSION

Figure 9-17. Use the `Properties` panel to "do it by the numbers."

5. To finish, get the image into position as shown in Figure 9-17. To get the bottom to line up with the road, open the `Transform` panel, and adjust the Y value in the 3D rotation area.
6. With the image selected, twirl down the `Color Effect` properties and select `Alpha` from the `Style` drop-down. Reduce the `Alpha` value to `50%`.
7. Turn off the visibility of the guide layer, and deselect the image. It now looks, as shown in Figure 9-18, like someone is projecting the image onto that garage door.

Figure 9-18. The image "projected" on to a wall in Amsterdam

Strategies for positioning content in 3D space

The orientation of movement along any of the three axes (x, y, and z) depends entirely on the location of the vanishing point. When the vanishing point is centered on the stage, the z-axis is pointing nearly straight at you. This means z-axis movement will increase and decrease the size of the object, as it apparently moves closer and farther from you. As illustrated in the previous exercise, this orientation can change.

Without ActionScript, it isn't possible to point the x- or y-axis directly at you, but you can approximate these orientations by setting a very high number, such as `10000`, for the `X` and `Y` values in the `Vanishing point` setting in the `Properties` panel's `3D Position and View` area. Extreme positions for the vanishing point result in the following orientations:

- **Significantly high or low X value**: Z movement becomes horizontal.
- **Significantly high or low Y value**: Z movement becomes vertical.
- **Significantly high or low X and Y values**: Z movement becomes diagonal.

Fiddle enough with these settings, and you'll get seasick! Just remember that you can always start from scratch very easily by selecting your movie clip and clicking the `Reset` button in the `Properties` panel and the `Remove Transform` button in the `Transform` panel. In spite of the utility of this tip, you can quickly find yourself in a pickle when positioning numerous objects—not just one—in the 3D space of the stage. We hope the following suggestions make your journey a bit easier.

The parallax effect: traveling through space

Parallax is an optical illusion that gives an otherwise flat 2D image the illusion of depth. We have all experienced this effect. Imaging you are sitting in your car zipping along the highway. The line in the road seem to be a blur, whereas the cows in the field move across your line of sight rather slowly and the forest in the distance behind the cows appears to hardly move at all.

Though the technique has been liberally used by science-fiction movies for years, it really didn't catch massive attention until Ken Burns, in his Public Broadcasting Service (PBS) movie *The Civil War* (www.pbs.org/civilwar/), used it to bring grainy black-and-white civil war photos to life. In the movie, the camera would slowly pan across an image seeming to move forward into the image or backward across the image.

The introduction of the 3D tools in Flash hands you the opportunity to create your own parallax effects in your movies. In this exercise, we are going to put a series of 2D images into motion to create the effect. Along the way, you will discover how objects can be animated in 3D space and how important movie clips are to the process of creating the illusion of parallax. Let's get started.

> *The files used in this exercise are freely available from the NASA website (www.nasaimages.org/). The images on this site are stunning and, because they are part of the Internet archive, are available, for free, to anybody who chooses to use them for whatever purpose.*

1. Open the SpaceFinal.png image in your Exercise folder in Fireworks CS5 or Photoshop CS5. When the image opens, as shown in Figure 9-19, you will see that we have created the scene to be used in this project. Each of the images has been placed on its own layer, and the background for the images is transparent. Feel free to move things around. When you finish, save the file as a PNG image, and quit Fireworks or Photoshop.

Figure 9-19. You start with a multilayer composite image using images downloaded from NASA.

2. Open the Space.fla file in your Exercise folder. When the file opens, you will see we have imported the Fireworks image into the **Library**.

3. In the **Properties** panel, change the stage color to black (#000000).

4. Open the **SpaceComposition** movie clip found in the **Fireworks Objects** folder. We are going to do a little house cleaning before we start moving stuff around.

5. Select layer 1, and delete it from the timeline. There is nothing n this layer, so it isn't needed.

6. Select each object on the screen—**Astronaut**, **Earth**, and each of the four planets—and convert them, as shown in Figure 9-20, to a movie clip.

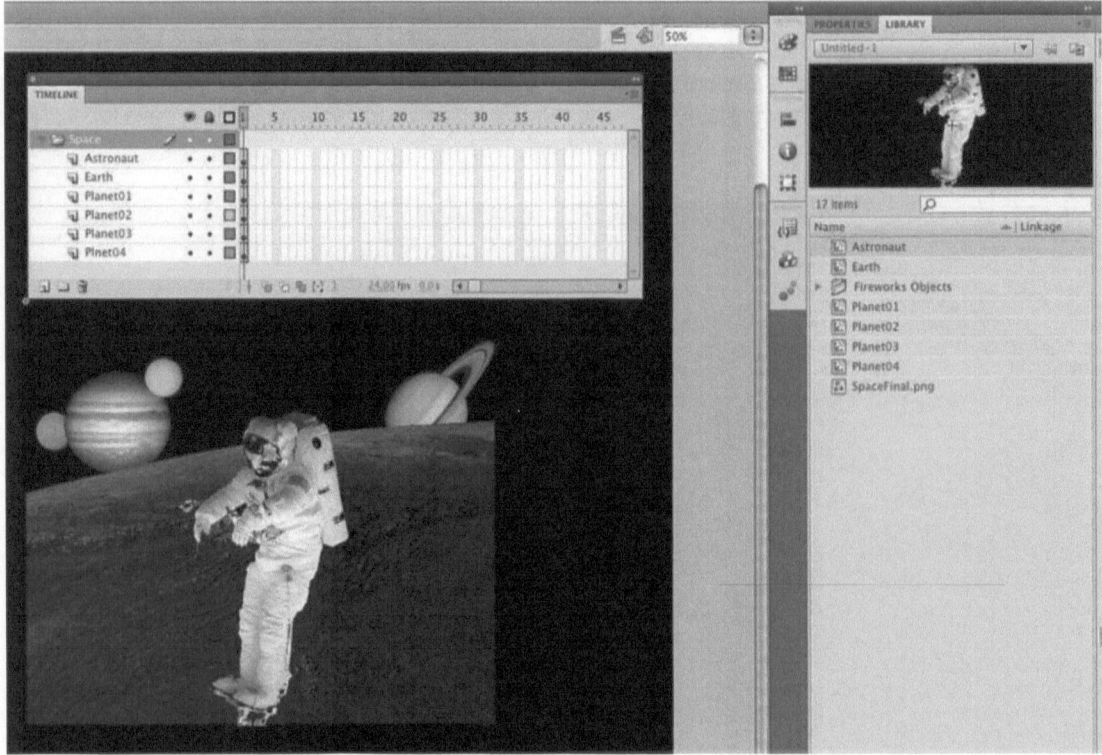

Figure 9-20. The images are converted to movie clips.

The next step in the process is to get each image positioned in 3D space. We will accomplish this by adjusting each movie clip's screen position using the z-axis. To wrap your mind about what you are going to do, think of the monitor's screen as being position zero. As you move deeper into the screen—positive numbers—the objects will appear to get smaller, and if you move away from the screen—negative numbers—the objects will appear to get bigger. This isn't the case. The objects don't resize; they either recede into the distance or appear closer to you. Let's get started:

7. Open the `Properties` panel, and twirl down the `3D Position and Size` properties. Select each object on the screen, and use the following `z` values:

    - `Astronaut: -10`
    - `Earth: 10`
    - `Planet 01: 350`
    - `Planet 02: 450`
    - `Planet 03: 550`
    - `Planet 04: 700`

FLASH HAS A THIRD DIMENSION

When you finish, the scene will look a bit different, as shown in Figure 9-21, because you have used depth to move the objects in the movie clip closer to or farther away from the surface of your computer screen.

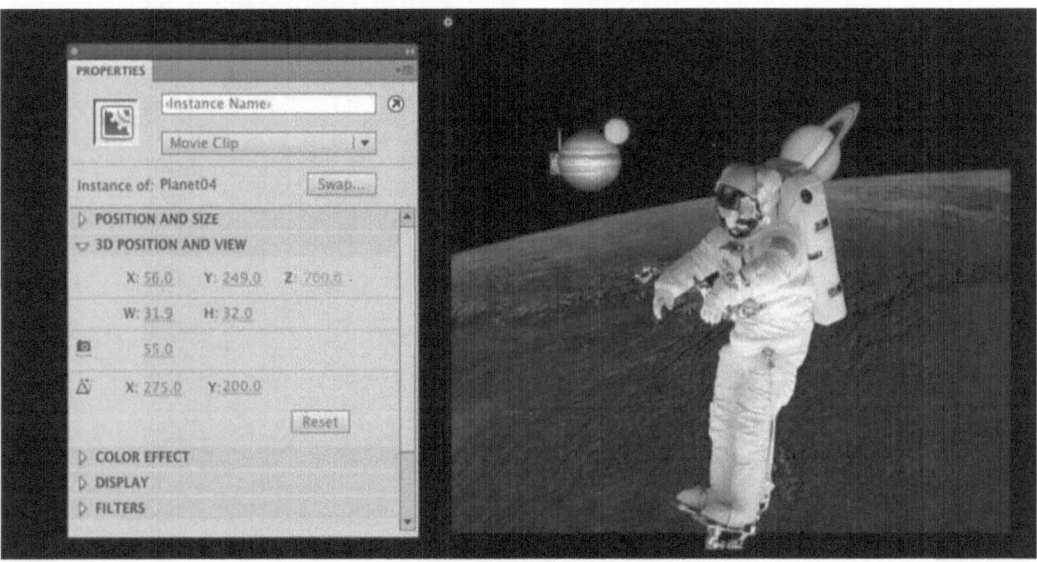

Figure 9-21. Each movie clip is positioned in 3D space by changing its z-axis value.

The next step is to get the whole thing into motion and give the project the appearance of a camera panning through space.

8. Click the `Scene 1` link to return to the main timeline. When the timeline opens, right-click frame 1, insert a motion tween, and drag the span out to frame 350.

9. The "magic" happens here. Select the movie clip on the stage, open the `Properties` panel, and change the `X,Y` and `Z` axis settings in the `3D Position and View` area to bring the movie clip "closer" to the viewer.

10. Open the `Transform` panel, and in the `3D Rotation` area change the `X`, `Y`, and `Z` values, as shown in Figure 9-22, to create the illusion of a "fly through" and rotation.

11. Test the movie.

CHAPTER 9

Figure 9-22. Use 3D Rotation to give the illusion of motion and distance.

A WORD FROM THE AUTHORS ABOUT FIREWORKS CS5

You may have noticed throughout this book that Photoshop CS5 seems to be missing in action. It isn't that the authors have a distinct dislike for Photoshop. Far from it, but we are firm believers in the adage "Use the right tool for the job at hand." In many cases, Fireworks CS5 is that tool. Though we briefly touched on the subject in Chapter 2, now would be a good time to answer the inevitable question Why Fireworks?

Fireworks tends to be the red headed child in the family of blondes when it comes to imaging in the Adobe line up. This is primarily because there is a certain attitude —"Why use anything else but Photoshop?"—that has developed over the years within the design community. There is also a huge misconception that Fireworks is more of a "wind-up toy" than anything else when it comes to imaging and compositing for the Web. Whichever camp you fall into is irrelevant. What is important is that you is you start using Fireworks CS5.

Up until the release of Fireworks CS4, Macromedia and then Adobe had never quite dispelled the notion that Fireworks is a competitor to Photoshop. In fact, when Macromedia was acquired by Adobe, the betting was that Fireworks was a doomed product. It wasn't until the release of the CS4 collection that Fireworks finally found its niche as the imaging application for screen-based media. This is an important distinction

If you need power, high resolution, and effects galore, then Photoshop is the choice. If you live in Flash's world—the world of small—then you need to start using Fireworks. Fireworks does two things really well:

- Compresses images for the Web
- Is a rapid prototyping tool for websites, AIR applications, Flash movies, and so on

The native file formats for Flash are primarily PNG and JPEG. The advantage to you, as a Flash designer, is that PNG images contain transparency and can be, as you see in the earlier example, used in layers. If the image needs to be flattened or further optimized for use in Flash's "World of Small," the JPEG kicked out by Fireworks is actually smaller and more efficient than the one kicked out by Photoshop. Don't take our word for it. Greg Rewis is a Creative Suite Evangelist for Adobe, and his job is to travel the world talking about the Adobe products. As Greg puts it, one of the most common "Oh, wow" moments he encounters in his travels is when he does a side-by-side JPEG optimization of the same image in Photoshop and Fireworks. Needless to say, the Fireworks image is significantly smaller than its Photoshop counterpart, and you can see for yourself by traveling to his blog (http://blog.assortedgarbage.com/?p=387) and carefully following exactly how he does it.

The rapid prototyping usage is just starting to catch on. We are going to let David Hogue, tell you all about that one in Chapter 14 when you build an AIR application. In this example, though, the entire image can be imported into Flash as a fully functional movie clip with its layering and transparency intact. As well, the Fireworks `Pages` feature allows you to design the various screens and so on used in a Flash site by putting those designs on separate pages and then importing those pages as separate movie clips, as needed, into Flash. On top of that, you can actually turn those pages into interactive PDF files, which can then be submitted, for client approval, before you even light up one pixel in Flash.

Use the 3D center point to your advantage

Up to this point in the chapter, we haven't properly illustrated what the 3D center point does. Let's remedy that by showing you how to animate a pair of swinging doors. Ready to make your grand entrance?

1. Open the `swingDoors.fla` file from the `Exercise` folder for this chapter. You'll see three layers in the main timeline—**image**, **Door Right**, **Door Left** —and a handful of items in the **Library**.

2. Select the **3D Rotation** tool, and click the movie clip that contains the left door. Hover over the center of the bull's-eye so that no letters show in the mouse pointer, and drag the bull's-eye—or use the **Transform** panel—to move the 3D center point to the middle of the left side of the door, as shown in Figure 9-23.

Why the left side? Because this door naturally swings on its hinges, and the 3D center point is roughly analogous to a hinge. Why the middle, rather than a corner? That's just an arbitrary choice. Given the angle of the doors, there really is no perspective. In this case, hinging the middle is the way to go. Click the movie clip that contains the right door. Reposition this movie clip's 3D center point in the upper right. This time, the hinge is on the other side, which makes sense. If you leave the 3D center point at its default value for each movie clip, the doors will spin like ballerinas.

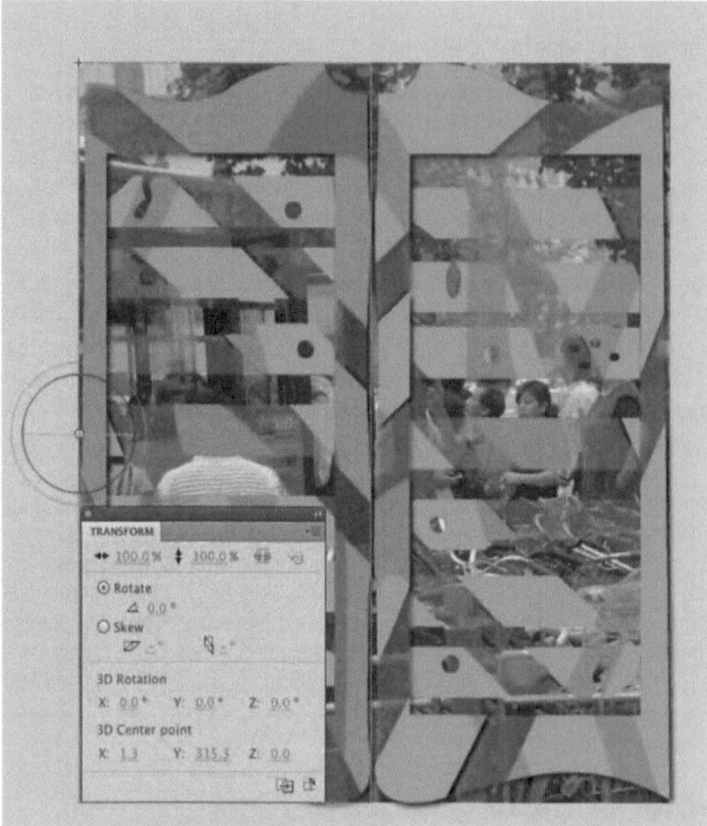

Figure 9-23. Changing the 3D center point alters where an object rotates

3. Right-click (Windows) or Control+click (Mac) frame 1 of the `Door Left` layer, and select `Create Motion Tween`. This converts the layer to a tween layer, but it's not quite enough.

4. Right-click (Windows) or Control+click (Mac) the `Door Left` layer again, and select `3D Tween`, which puts a check mark in that choice whenever you open the context menu again. (You can remove the check mark if you ever change your mind.)

5. Repeat steps 2, 3, and 4 for the `Door Right` layer.

6. Extend the two tween layers to frame 30, and add a frame to frame 30 of the Image layer. Select the left door's movie clip, and use the `3D Rotation` tool or the `Transform` panel to "swing the door in" about 90 degrees (see Figure 9-24). Do the same thing for the right door.

FLASH HAS A THIRD DIMENSION

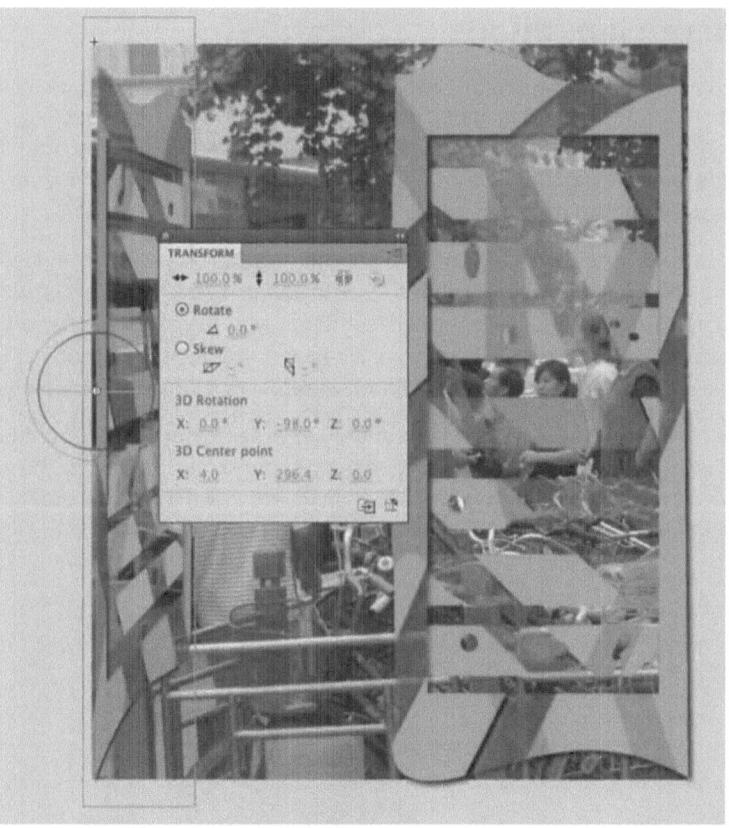

Figure 9-24. Swinging the door inward toward 90 degrees

7. To improve the illusion, darken the doors while they're swinging in. Still at frame 30, use the **Selection** tool to select each door in turn. In the **Properties** panel, choose **Brightness** from the **Style** drop-down list of the **Color Effect** area, and set its value to -34%.

8. To add some polish, add a new layer, and name it **Audio**.

9. Select **Window ➤ Common Libraries ➤ Sounds** to open a panel of audio files that are installed when you install Flash. Drag the file named **Household Door Wood Door Squeak 01.mp3** to frame 1 of the **Audio** layer.

10. Using the **Selection** tool, click into frame 80 of each layer, and press the F5 key to pad out the frame span of each layer. This allows the audio to fully play out, without looping too early, when you test your movie.

11. Select **Control ➤ Test Movie** to see the SWF. Close the SWF, and compare your work with the finished version of swingDoors.fla in this chapter's Complete folder.

Be aware of depth limitations

As cool as the 3D tools are, they do have a limitation in terms of how three-dimensional depth (generally the z-axis) corresponds to the stacking order of your layers, and even the stacking order of numerous symbols inside a single layer. In short, stacking order overrides 3D depth. If you drag the layer of one 3D movie clip above the layer of another 3D movie clip, the movie clip on the higher layer will always appear on top, no matter how you adjust its z index.

There are pros and cons to everything, and the pro here is that layers and in-layer symbol stacking continue to operate the way they always have. For longtime Flash users, this will feel familiar and comfortable. If you're new to Flash, this behavior may throw you for a loop, but you can work around it. The challenge arises when you want to perform a 3D tween that moves one object in front of another, when its original position was behind (and therefore obscured). Let's look at a hands-on example:

1. Open the `AirheadMail.fla` file from the `Exercise` folder for this chapter. You'll see an envelope with a couple postage stamps above it, one stacked behind the other, as shown in Figure 9-25. There's another stamp in a hidden layer behind the envelope, but we'll get into that in a moment. Just be aware that both of the visible stamps are located in the same timeline layer.

Figure 9-25. Depth is determined more by layer and stacking order than z index (envelope photo by Cris DeRaud).

2. Select the `3D Translation` tool, and click the unobscured stamp (the one on top) to select it. Adjust its z index to scale the stamp smaller and larger.

In terms of 3D space, a higher z-index value seems to "push the stamp away," making it smaller. No matter how far you "push," you'll find that you cannot move the upper stamp behind the lower one. To do that, you'll have to use the old-fashioned approach.

3. Right-click (Windows) or Control+click (Mac) the upper stamp, and select **Arrange ➤ Send Backward** (or **Send to Back**). You'll see the upper stamp pop behind its partner.

4. Unhide the bottom timeline layer (named `stamp`, just like the top timeline layer). This reveals a third stamp partially obscured by the envelope.

5. Using the `3D Translation` tool again, adjust the z index of either stamp in the upper `stamp` layer. As in step 2, nothing you do moves either stamp behind the envelope or the stamp in the bottom `stamp` layer.

6. To bring the lowest stamp above the other two, you'll need to move its layer. Click the lower `stamp` layer, and drag it above the other `stamp` layer, as shown in Figure 9-26.

Figure 9-26. Drag layers to move lower content above higher content.

This is all well and good for still compositions, but how does it work for animation? You can't very well drag layers around in the middle of a tween. The trick is to split your animation over two layers, as shown in

CHAPTER 9

Figure 9-27. Check out AirheadMailAnimated.fla in this chapter's Complete folder to see the animation in action.

Figure 9-27. Splitting an animation between separate layers

In what appears to be one smooth motion, the stamp emerges from behind the envelope, flies in front of it, and settles into place for mailing. In actuality, the magic happens at frame 14, where the movie clip abruptly ends in the lower stamp layer and reappears in the upper stamp layer to continue its above-the-envelope movement.

Your turn: simulate a photo cube

We began the theory part of this chapter with a cube and thought it fitting to come to a close with the same shape. (We wanted so badly to describe that as "coming full circle," but it felt like we were mixing metaphors!) For this final exercise, we're going to show you how to build a box out of a series of square movie clips. What you do with the box is up to you. We certainly hope it will spark some inspiration. In any case, we're pretty confident you'll find it motivating that you can—sort of—rotate the thing after it's built.

To really stay with the theme, we are going to use a series of images featuring the work of Toronto-based architect Will Alsop. If you ever visit Toronto and you visit the Art Gallery of Ontario, you will see what looks like a box supported on a series of colored pencils. This building is the work of Alsop and was designed as an addition to the Ontario College of Art.

Ready to be there or be square? Let's jump in:

1. Open 3DCube.fla from the Chapter 9 Exercise folder. We've done the tedious part for you. The **Library** contains five imported JPGs, already converted to movie clip symbols.
2. Select the five movie clips in the **Library**, and drag them to the stage. Open the **Align** panel and, with all five movie clips selected, align them to the center of the stage.

Now you have five copies of the same movie clip stacked on top of each other in the same layer. Why? It's because we're about to make like Henry Ford and run an assembly line. This approach will make things come together more quickly, and the precision of doing the next few steps "by the numbers" will help considerably.

3. Select the top movie clip, and use the **Transform** panel to change the **3D Rotation** area's **Z** value to **90**. Now scrub the **Y** rotation value until it hits **90**. This "stands up" the top movie clip and faces it west. In the **Properties** panel's **3D Position and View** area, scrub the **X** value down to **75** (that's 200 pixels to the left, or half the movie clip's width).

You're going to repeat this process—with different values—for the next three movie clips.

4. Select the next movie clip and configure it like this:
   - `Transform Panel :3D Rotation Z= -90`
   - `Transform Panel: 3D Rotation Y = -90`
   - `Properties Panel: 3D Position X = 475`

This movie clip now faces east and has moved half its width to the right.

5. Select the next movie clip and configure it like this:
   - `Transform Panel: 3D Rotation Z = -180`
   - `Transform Panel : 3D Rotation X = -90`
   - `Properties Panel: 3D Position Y= 0`

This movie clip now faces north (yes, this sounds like an REM song) and has moved half its height to the top.

6. Select the next movie clip and configure it like this:
   - `Transform Panel : 3D Rotation Z= 0 (no change)`
   - `Transform Panel: 3D Rotation X = 90`
   - `Properties Panel: 3D Position Y= 400`

This movie clip now faces south and has moved half its height to the bottom.

At this point, you're essentially looking down into the cube (see Figure 9-28). Although it may not appear to be, the image at the bottom of the cube is already halfway up the cube. The reason the depth looks wrong is because of the stacking order of these movie clips.

CHAPTER 9

Figure 9-28. One result of rotating and translating by the numbers

7. Right-click (Windows) or Control+click (Mac) the right (east) movie clip, and select **Arrange ➤ Bring to Front**. Do the same thing to the other movie clips in the following order: bottom (south), left (west), and finally center.

Why restack them in that particular order? It's because we're about to tilt the box forward, which means we'll be looking at what's currently the south wall. The movie clip currently on top of the stack—building above the trees—needs to be moved "toward you" first, though.

8. Select the movie clip that appears to be "inside the stack, and set its **3D Position Z** value to **-200**.

9. Click frame 1 in the timeline to select all the 3D objects simultaneously. With all the movie clips selected, click the one showing (this puts the **Properties** panel where you want it), and change the **3D Position Z** value to **0**. This moves the whole collection "back" toward the stage.

10. In the **Transform** panel, change the **3D Rotation X** value to **-46** and the **3D Rotation Y** value to **-28**.

524

FLASH HAS A THIRD DIMENSION

11. In the **Properties** panel, just above the **Vanishing point** values, you'll see a setting we visited on our trip to that street in Amsterdam. It has a camera icon, and if you hover over that, you'll get a tooltip that says **Perspective angle**. Scrub the **Perspective angle** value from its default **55** down to **38**. See how that relaxes the slight fish-eye lens effect?

12. Change the **3D Rotation Z** value to **-20** to straighten out your box. You'll get something like the cube shown in Figure 9-29.

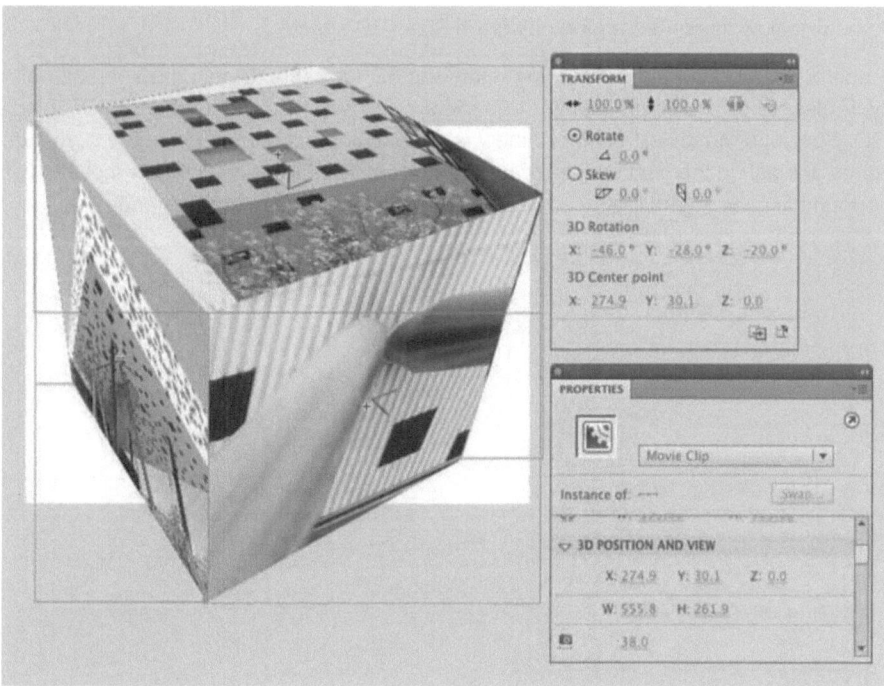

Figure 9-29. A way-too-cool photo cube

Whatever angle you approach it from, 3D manipulation in Flash is a ton of fun! While you still have your 3DCube.fla file open, we encourage you to keep experimenting. With all the movie clips selected, use the **3D Rotation** tool to see what happens when you spin that cube all the way around (you'll see the stacking order limitation again).

What happens if you scrub **Perspective angle** all the way down to 1? How about over a 100? How does the **Vanishing point** setting affect things? Can you convert the selected movie clips—all five of them—into a new movie clip? (Hint: Absolutely!) When you do, can you arrange two or more movie clips of the completed box on the stage? (You betcha.)

We could keep going, but we hope you're excited enough to take it from here.

CHAPTER 9

What you have learned

In this chapter, you learned the following:

- The rudiments of perspective drawing, including the concept of the vanishing point
- How to use the `3D Rotation` and `3D Translation` tools
- How to use the `Property inspector` and `Transform` panel in conjunction with the 3D tools
- Some workflow tips on arranging objects in Flash 3D space

One of the authors has been fond of anything related to 3D for years. In fact, he keeps a pair of red-and-blue anaglyph glasses on top of his monitor—you know, for watching those cheesy 1950s science fiction movies in 3D. Speaking of movies, sci-fi or otherwise, Flash is pretty hip on cinema too. In fact, one of the hottest features of Flash in the past couple years is its video capabilities, which now include high-definition, full-screen support. Ready to jam like Cecil B. DeMille? You just have to turn the page.

Chapter 10

Video

When Macromedia, now Adobe, launched Flash 8 Professional and included the Flash Video (FLV) Encoder and playback component with the application, a valid argument could be made that this marked the final acceptance of Flash as a viable web video medium. As more and more sites started featuring Flash video, there was a corresponding decline in the number of sites that used the web video solutions provided by QuickTime, Windows Media, and Real Player. By that time, Flash Player could be found on more than 90 percent of all computers on the planet.

Flash video's success actually has had more to do with cunning than with market acceptance. Most people didn't see Flash as a media player. They thought of it as being this "cute thing" that played animations. When they suddenly realized they could stream audio (Chapter 5) and video through Flash Player without excessive wait times or downloading an additional plug-in, it was basically "game-set-match" for the others.

Flash CS5 continues to firmly entrench video into the application. In early 2008, Flash Player 9 was updated to allow the inclusion of high-definition (HD) video, and this feature is in Flash CS5 and Flash Player 10.1. You also get a totally "rejigged" encoder, now called the Adobe Media Encoder. With Flash CS5, you have been handed a full video encoding and playback suite of tools that makes it dead simple to add video to your Flash projects.

CHAPTER 10

Here's what we'll cover in this chapter:
- Streaming video
- Encoding an FLV
- Playing an FLV in Flash
- Playing full-screen video
- Adding captions to Flash video
- Adding filters and blend effects to video

The following files are used in this chapter (located in the `Chapter10/ExerciseFiles_Ch10/Exercise/` folder):
- `Rabbit.mov`
- `Vultures.mp4`
- `Rabbit.flv`
- `ThroughADoor.flv`
- `Controls.fla`
- `ASCuePoints.fla`
- `Captions.flv`
- `captionsFLV.xml`
- `Alpha.mov`
- `AlphaEx.fla`
- `FilmTV.mov`
- `Apparition.flv`
- `RainFall.fla`
- `Rain.flv`
- `BlobEffect.fla`
- `CuePoints.xml`
- `SupermanNoCuePoints.flv`
- `VideoJam.fla`

The source files are available online from either of the following sites:

- www.FoundationFlashCS4.com
- www.friendsofED.com/download.html?isbn=1430229940

> *The authors would like to thank William Hanna, Dean of the School of Media Studies, at the Humber Institute of Technology and Advanced Learning in Toronto, and Robert O'Meara, a faculty member with the Film and Television Arts program at Humber, for permission to use many of the videos in this chapter. The videos were produced by students of Humber's Interactive Multimedia program and Film and Television program. We also want to thank Phoebe Boswell for letting us use her student project—The Girl With Stories In Her Hair—and to her instructor, Birgitta Hosea, at Central Saint Martins College of Art and Design in London, UK, for introducing us to Phoebe.*

Video on the Web

Before we turn you loose with creating and playing Flash video, it is critically important that you understand how it gets from the server to the user's machine.

The Flash video format uses the .mp4, .mov, .flv, or .f4v extension. The first two must be encoded using the H.264 codec and AAC encoding for the audio track. It plays only in Flash, Adobe Bridge, or Adobe Media Player (a free AIR application available from www.adobe.com/products/mediaplayer/). The key thing about this format is that the data is sent to the user's computer from the server, and then Flash Player plays it. To help you understand this process, let's go visit the Hoover Dam in the United States.

The Hoover Dam was built in the 1930s to control the Colorado River. When the dam was completed, the water behind it backed up to form Lake Mead. Now the water flows along the Colorado River into Lake Mead, and the dam releases that water, in a controlled manner, back into the Colorado River. That means if the water rushes to the dam and overwhelms it, or the dam operator releases too much water, the people downstream from the dam are in for a really bad day.

Streaming video is no different from the water flow to the Hoover Dam and beyond (see Figure 10-1). The data in the FLV is sent, at a data rate established when the video was encoded, from the server to Flash Player. The video is then held in a buffer and released, in a controlled manner, by Flash Player to the browser. If the flow is too fast—the data rate is too high for the connection—the browser is overwhelmed, and the result is video that jerkily stops and starts. This is because the buffer constantly emptying and having to be refilled. In many respects, your job is no different from that of the crew that manages the flow of water from the buffer behind the Hoover Dam back into the Colorado River. When you create the FLV, the decisions you make will determine whether your users are in for a really bad experience.

Figure 10-1. When it comes to Flash video, you control the Hoover Dam.

Video formats

The first step in the process of creating the FLV file that will be used in the Flash movie is to convert an existing video to the FLV format. This means you will be working with digital videos that use the following formats:

- **AVI (Audio Video Interleave)**: A Windows format that supports a number of compression schemes but also allows for video without any compression
- **DV**: The format used when video moves directly from a video camera to the computer
- **MPG/MPEG (Moving Pictures Experts Group)**: A lossy standard for video that is quite similar to the lossy JPG/JPEG standard for still images
- **MOV**: The QuickTime format

> *For those of you wondering about the WMV (Windows Media Video) format, yes, you can encode it. However, the encoding can be done only on a Windows computer. This book is somewhat platform-agnostic, which explains why WMV didn't make the video format list here.*

Do yourself and your users a favor, and check out the compressor used to create the video. If a lossy compressor was used, you are going to have a serious quality issue. The compressors used to create FLV files are also lossy, meaning you will be compressing an already-compressed video.

Both the QuickTime player and Windows Media Player show you compressor information. In the QuickTime player, select `Window ➤ Show Info`. You will see a dialog box with movie information, including the compressor used, as shown in Figure 10-2.

VIDEO

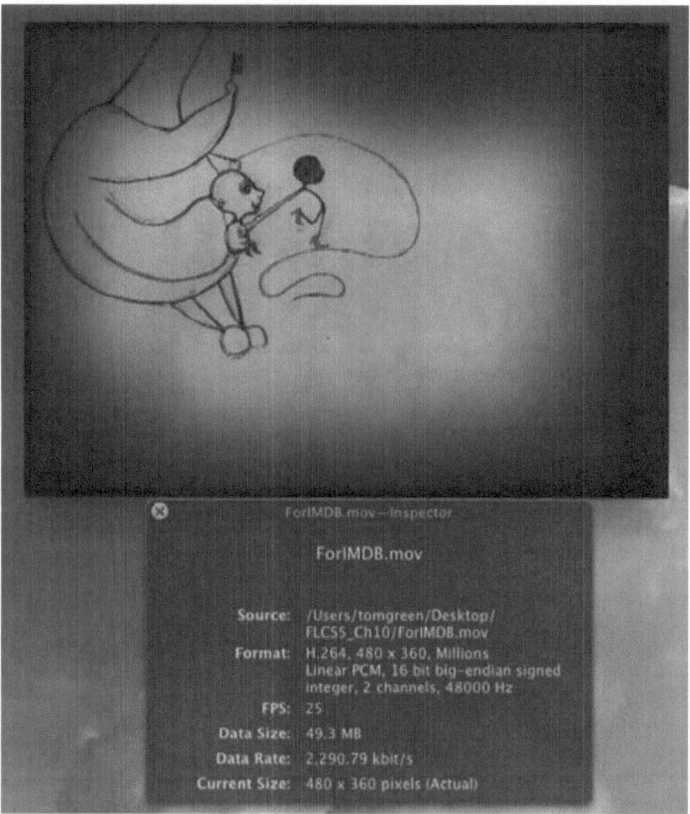

Figure 10-2. QuickTime's Movie info dialog box shows that the H.264 compressor was used for the *The Girl With Stories In Her Hair* video.

Windows video files playing through the Windows Media Player are a bit different. Open a file in the Media Player, right-click the file's name, and select `Properties` from the context menu. You will see the `Properties` dialog box, which identifies the video codec. Now that you know which file formats you can use, you also need to know that three output formats are available to you:

- **FLV**: This is the common format used on the Web, which can be played by Flash Player 6 and higher.

- **F4V**: This is the new kid on the block and was primarily developed to manage HD files that will need to be converted to a format that is used by Flash Player 9,0,115,0 or higher. Think of this as being an MP4 video for Flash, and you will be on the right track.

- **H.264**: This is a common format that you might know better as MPEG-4 or MP4. It is an international standard (MPEG4 H.264) developed by the Moving Pictures Expert Group (MPEG) and is also recognized by the International Standardization Organization (ISO).

CHAPTER 10

From a Flash designer's perspective, the H.264 format has some rather profound implications. The biggest one is that video, for all intents and purposes, has become untethered—it is not device-dependent. The file handed to you by your video producer can just as easily be played on a website as it can on an iPod, Sony's PlayStation Portable, or high-definition television (HDTV). It also means that, thanks to the addition of hardware acceleration and multithreading support to Flash Player, you can play back video at any resolution and bitrate, including the full HD 1080p resolution you can watch on HDTV.

Encoding an FLV

Surprisingly, the first step in the conversion process has absolutely nothing to do with Flash. Instead, open the video in your player of choice and watch the video twice. The first time is to get the entertainment/coolness factor out of your system. The second time you watch it, ask yourself a few questions:

- Is there a lot of movement in this video?
- Is the audio of major importance?
- Is there a lot of color in the piece?
- Is the video in focus, or are there areas where the image becomes pixelated?

The answers to these questions will determine your approach to encoding the video.

To demonstrate encoding, we will use the Rabbit.mov file, located in this chapter's Exercise folder. Go ahead and open this file in QuickTime, and watch it twice.

Yes, the file is huge: just over 70MB. There is a reason. When creating Flash video, you need every bit of information contained in the video when you do the conversion. Uncompressed video is about as big as it gets. When you finish converting the video into an FLV, you will be in for a rather pleasant surprise.

Using the Adobe Media Encoder

To encode video, you use the Adobe Media Encoder CS5. This used to be known as the Adobe Flash Video Encoder. The name change is deliberate. Adobe came to the conclusion that the Flash brand name was being attached to a lot of stuff, and there was understandable concern that the brand was becoming diluted. The release of Creative Suite 4 started the process of Adobe's refocusing of the Flash brand. If you have used Flash to encode video in previous, pre-CS4, iterations of the application, you will find that things have really changed.

To begin, open the Adobe Media Encoder, found in C:\Program Files\Adobe\Adobe Media Encoder CS5 on a Windows computer or Macintosh HD\Applications\Adobe Media Encoder CS5 on a Mac. Then drag a copy of the Rabbit.mov file from your Exercise folder into the render queue, as shown in Figure 10-3. Alternatively, you could click the **Add** button or select k**File ▶ Add**. Then, using the **Open** dialog box, navigate to your Exercise folder for this chapter, select the video, and click the **Open** button to add the video to the queue. Just be aware that once a video is added to the queue, the clock starts running. If you do nothing within the couple of minutes you get, the video will be created using the default settings.

VIDEO

The drop-down lists in the **Format** and **Preset** areas actually aren't as complicated as they may first appear. The **Format** drop-down list offers the format choices **FLV/F4V** and **H.264**. The **Preset** list includes presets for a variety of situations and formats. To keep this chapter manageable, we aren't going to go deep into the choices and formats. Instead, let's just create a simple FLV file that will allow you to explore this application.

Click the **Preset** drop-down arrow, and select **Edit Export Settings** at the bottom of the menu. This will open the **Export Settings** window, as shown in Figure 10-4. At the left is a preview area. The area underneath the video preview is where cue points can be added. We'll talk about cue points later in this chapter. The right side of the window consists of a series of tabs that allow you to choose a preset encoding profile, select a filter, choose an output format, set the video compression, and set the audio compression.

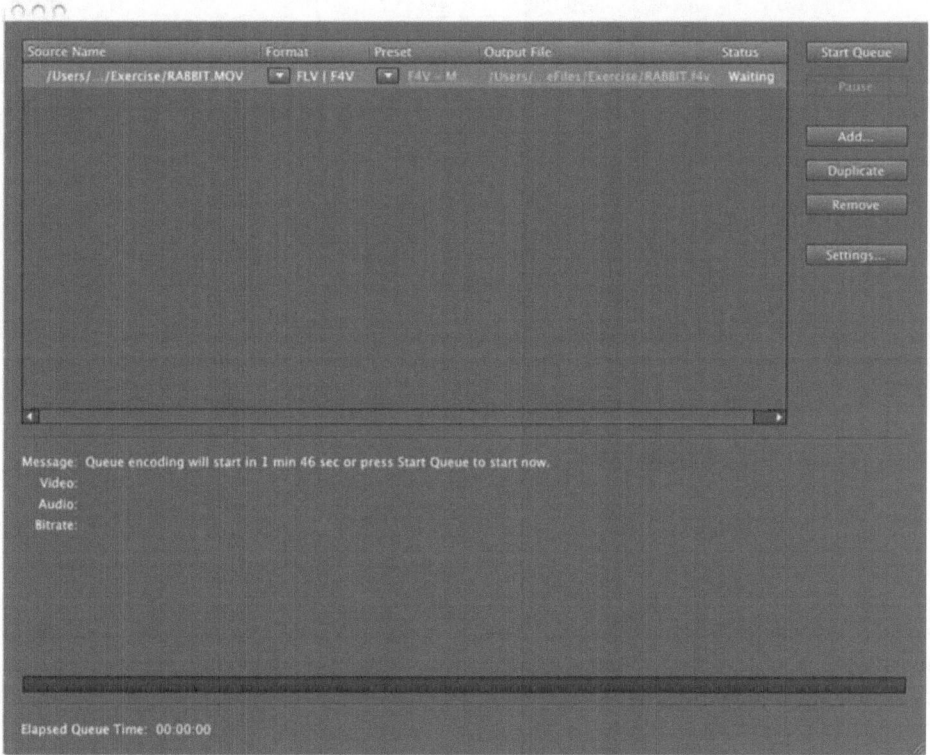

Figure 10-3. A file is in the render queue waiting to be encoded.

533

CHAPTER 10

Figure 10-4. The Export Settings window

We are not huge fans of the encoding presets in the `Preset` drop-down list. The problems with the presets are that they assume the lowest common denominator, tend to be wrong, and result in files that are unnecessarily large. For example, many of the presets have the audio track encoded to stereo, which, as we explain later, usually just increases the file size and bandwidth demand, without adding any quality to the audio. Making your own choices for the encoding, rather than using presets, puts you in control of the process and allows you to produce files that meet your specific design needs, instead of satisfying a broad, homogenous audience.

Previewing and trimming video

Under the preview area is the current time indicator. It displays time in the format *hours*: *minutes*: *seconds*: *milliseconds*. The triangle at the top of the line is the *jog controller*. If you drag it back and forth, the video will follow along.

Underneath the jog controller are two other triangles. The one on the left is the `In` point, and the one on the right is the `Out` point. You can use these to trim the video. For example, assume there are two seconds of black screen and no audio at the end of the video. If you drag the Out point to the start of the stuff you don't need, it will be removed when you create the FLV.

> *Here's a neat little trick that can help with setting `In` and `Out` points. The preview controls are very precise, and reaching an exact point in time can be an exercise in tedium. Assume you want the current video to last 4 minutes and 14 seconds instead of `04:14:53`. Drag the playhead slider rightward to the end of the video. Press and hold the left arrow key. When the key is down, the milliseconds measure will reduce. When you are close to the `000` milliseconds point, release the key, and then click the Out point slider. The video will now have an Out point at that precise point in time.*

Video settings

On the right side of the `Export Settings` window, click in the `Format` tab, and click the `FLV` radio button. Then click the `Video` tab to open the `Basic Settings` area, as shown in Figure 10-5. This is where you set the all-important video data rate.

> *If you want to change the name of the video, double-click the `Output Name` on the right side of the `Export Settings` window to open the `Save As` dialog box. All this does is save the filename. It does not create the FLV.*

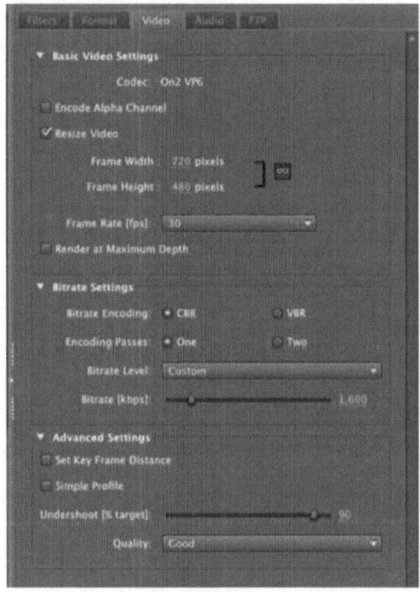

Figure 10-5. Setting the encoding values for the video portion of the movie

The various areas of the `Video` pane are as follows:

- **`Codec`**: The job of the *codec* (short for **CO**mpressor/**DEC**ompressor or en**CO**der/**DEC**oder) is to reduce the data rate while maintaining image quality. In simple terms, there are two types of codecs: lossy and lossless. Lossless codecs, like QuickTime's Animation codec, add minimal compression to preserve data, which explains why these files are massive and inappropriate for direct web playback. The two codecs that are available for your selection here—`Sorenson Spark` and `On2 VP6`—are lossy. They preserve playback quality while tossing out a ton of information, which explains how a 1MB video file becomes an 800KB FLV or F4V file. Note that If your target is Flash Player 7 or lower, your only choice is the `Sorenson Spark` codec. For our example, select `On2 VP6`.

- **`Encode Alpha Channel`**: If your video contains an alpha channel, select this. Alpha channel video can be encoded using the `On2 VP6` codec only. For our example, this option should not be selected.

- **`Resize Video`**: If this is selected, deselect it. This is not the place to resize video. If you really need to resize a video, do it in Adobe Premiere, After Effects, Final Cut Pro, or another video-editing application.

> *If you need to resize a video, be sure to maintain the video's aspect ratio. When digital video is created for your television, it is created at a 4:3 ratio. This ratio is called the video's aspect ratio and fits most computer monitors. Other common examples would be widescreen television video, which has an aspect ratio of 6:5, and HDTV, which uses a 16:9 aspect ratio.*
>
> *For example, the video you are encoding has a physical size of 320 pixels wide by 240 pixels high. The width is easily divisible by 4, and the height is divisible by 3. By maintaining the aspect ratio, you avoid introducing artifacts (blocky shapes and other nastiness) into the video when it is resized.*
>
> *While we are on the subject of resizing video, never increase the physical size of the video. If you need to change the size, use this area to reduce, not increase, the width and height values. Increasing the physical dimensions of the video from 320 × 240 to 640 × 480 will only make the pixels larger, just as it does in Photoshop and Fireworks when you zoom in on an image. The result is pixelated video, and it will also place an increasing strain on the bandwidth, or flow of data into Flash Player.*
>
> *In spite of our having said to never increase the size of a video, Flash Player 9,0,115,0 (and higher) now permits full-screen video playback. We'll review this feature later in the chapter. It changes video size in an exception-to-the-rules way.*

- **Frame Rate [fps]**: This is how fast a video plays, measured in frames per second (fps). If you are unsure of which frame rate to use, a good rule of thumb is to choose a rate that is half that of the original file. If the original was prepared using the NTSC standard of 29.97 fps (close enough to 30), select 15 fps. If the PAL standard was used (25 fps), rates of 12 or 15 fps are acceptable. Of course, with the improvements to Flash Player, the industry is steadily moving toward 24 fps. For this example, set **Frame Rate** to **15**.

- **Bitrate Encoding**: Your choices are **CBR** (for constant bitrate) and **VBR** (for variable bitrate). If you are streaming video through Flash Media Server 3 or using the Flash Video Streaming Service, choose **CBR**, which, as the name implies, provides a level bitrate into Flash Player. Choose **VBR** if you are intending to use a web server making standard HTTP requests. For this example, select **VBR**.

- **Encoding Passes**: **One** pass means the video analysis and encoding are done at the same time. **Two** passes means the encoder analyzes the video in the first pass looking for major changes, and the second pass encodes the video to accommodate those changes. So, what's the difference? Two-pass encoding is the best for videos with numerous bitrate changes. For example, you could have a video with a narrator who stays put for the first few seconds of the video and, when he finishes, race cars go roaring by. The narration doesn't require much to play, but the cars zipping by will require a higher bitrate to display accurately. Encoding in two passes allows the bitrate savings at the start of the video to be passed on to the action sequence. So, **Two** is the right choice for our example.

- **Bitrate [kbps]**: This slider sets the bitrate for the video portion of the encoding process in kilobits per second (kbps). Be very careful when choosing a **Bitrate** setting. For example, don't think you can supersize the quality and set the data rate to, say, the maximum of 10,000 kbps. Do that, and you can guarantee that residents downstream from the Hoover Dam are in for a day that involves scuba gear. The data rate for an FLV is the sum of the audio and the video data rates. What should you choose? Until you become comfortable with creating FLV files, consider a combined audio and video data rate of around 350 kbps to 400 kbps as being a fair target. For the example, use **300** kbps.

- **Set Key Frame Distance**: This is in the **Advanced** area for a reason. Unless you have mastered video, it is best to let the software do the work and leave this option unselected.

- **Key frame interval**: Enter a value here, and the **Key frame placement** selection will change to **Custom**. Remember that first question we asked you to consider at the start of the chapter: is there a lot of movement? The answer determines key frame placement. If you are recording paint drying, having a key frame every 300 frames of the video would work. If you are encoding a video of a Formula One race from trackside, you will want the key frames to be a lot closer to each other, such as every 30 frames or so.

After you've set the video values, click the **Audio** tab, not the **OK** button, to continue.

Audio settings

The `Audio` pane, shown in Figure 10-6, is where you manage the audio quality. As we pointed out in Chapter 5, the default format for all audio in Flash is MP3. This explains why you have only that one choice in the `Audio` pane.

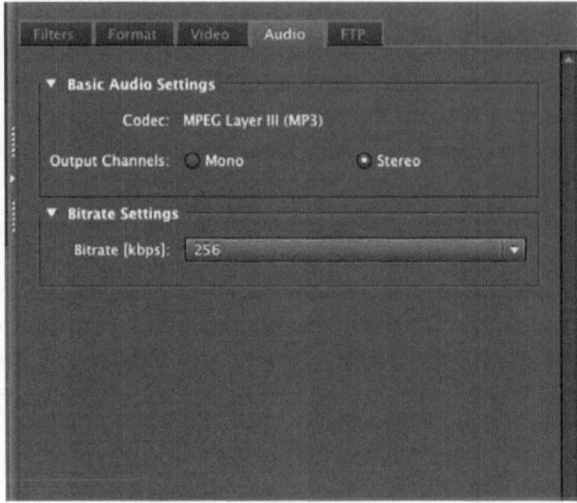

Figure 10-6. Setting the data rate for the audio portion of the movie

You need to make two decisions here:

- Will it be stereo or mono?
- What will the data rate be?

Unless there is a persuasive reason—you are encoding a band's video, for instance—stay with a `Mono` setting for `Output Channels`. Don't think you can improve the audio track by outputting it as a stereo track if it was originally recorded in mono. You can't change mono to stereo. All that does is double the size of your audio by playing two synchronized mono tracks. Outputting stereo will only serve to increase the final file size of the FLV.

Twirl down the `Bitrate Settings`. `For Bitrate [kbps]`; you should generally choose either `48` or `64`. Anything lower results in an increasing degradation of audio quality. Anything higher only serves to increase the demand on the bandwidth, with no appreciable quality gain. Still, 32 kbps is a good choice if the soundtrack is nothing more than a voice-over, and 16 kbps is ideal if the soundtrack is composed of intermittent sounds such as the buzzing fly sound used in the Butterfly project that started this book. For this example, select `64` from the `Bitrate [kbps]` drop-down menu.

Cropping video

Let's now turn our attention to the left side of the `Export Settings` window, as shown in Figure 10-7. The top of the pane contains a `Crop` tool. You can use this tool to eliminate unwanted areas of the video. When you click the tool, handles are added to the sides of the video, and you can use them to crop. If you want to do it by the numbers, scrub across the values. The `Crop Proportions` drop-down list is very important. It helps you to not only crop a video but also to maintain the all-important aspect ratio.

Figure 10-7. The left side of the panel allows you to crop the video, set the In and Out points, and generally manipulate the final output.

Click the `Output` tab. You get one choice: `Crop Setting`. Provided you have selected the `Crop` tool in the `Source` pane, the drop-down menu offers three choices. These choices have nothing to do with physically cropping a video. They specify how to deal with the dead area once an aspect ratio has been applied during the actual crop, as follows:

- `Scale To Fit` will scale the video to fit the area.
- `Black Borders` will keep the original aspect ratio of the video and fill areas on the sides where there is no video with black.
- `Change Output Size` will change the size of the video to the dimensions of the crop.

> You can toggle between the `Source` and `Output` panes by clicking the toggle button—`Switch To Output`—to the right of the `Crop Setting` drop-down list.

CHAPTER 10

Running the render process

After you've set your export settings, click OK to return to the render queue. Then click the `Start Queue` button to start the process.

You will see the progress bar move across the screen as the video is being rendered, and you will also see the video being rendered in the preview area, as shown in Figure 10-8. If you click the `Stop Queue` button, you will see a dialog box asking you whether you want to stop the process or finish the render. If you have a number of videos in the queue, clicking the `No` button in the dialog box will stop the process, and an `Errors` dialog box will appear, telling you that you stopped the render process. If you want to make changes to the settings or restart the render process, select the video—its status will be set to `Skip` in the `Status` area—and select `Edit ► Reset Status`.

Don't be terribly surprised if you see your video look like it is being encoded twice. New to Flash CS5 is a little message that tells you which pass of the two passes selected with the encoder is currently being undertaken.

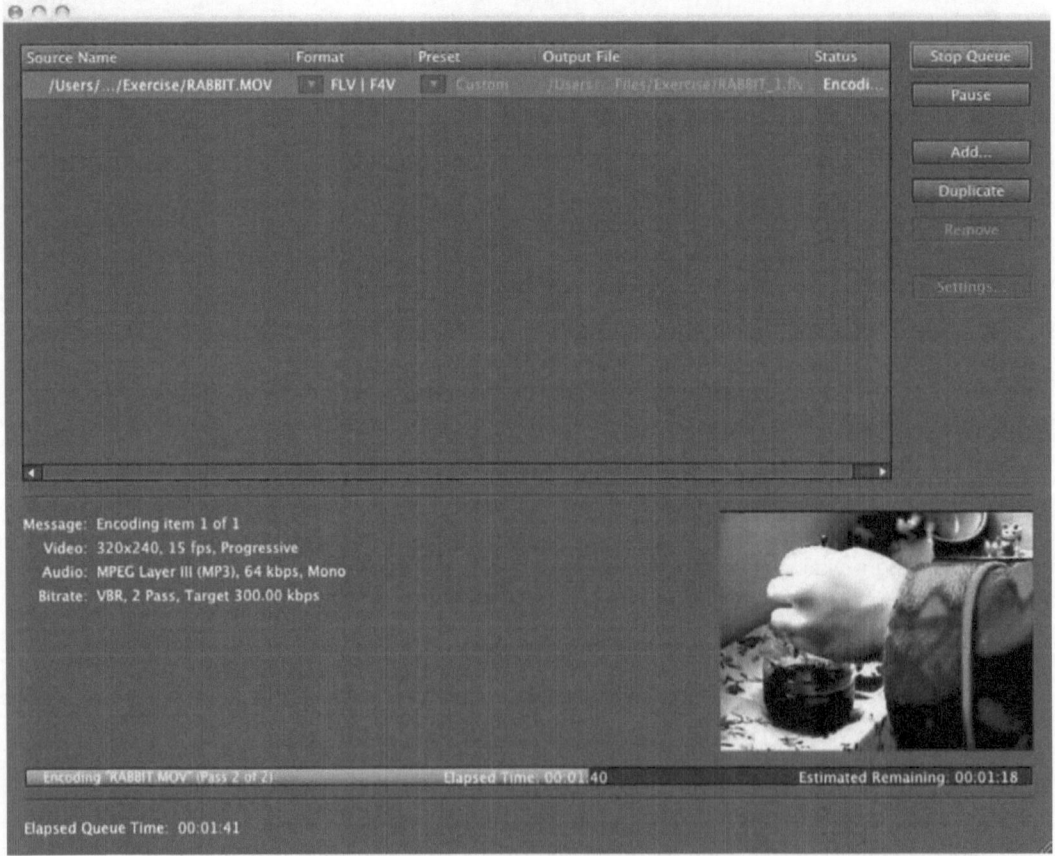

Figure 10-8. Rendering an FLV

VIDEO

> *Here's a little-known technique that will make your life much less stressful. Selecting a video in the render queue and clicking the* Remove *button will remove it from the render queue. What if you have made a mistake and need to make a simple change to the video or audio settings? If the video is still in the render queue and its status is set to either* Skip *or* Completed, *you can select the video and choose* Edit ➤ Reset Status *to put it back into the render queue and then click the* Settings *button to return to the original video and audio settings. This is really handy in situations where you have messed up a cue point or two. For this to work, though, you can't move the video from its original folder or delete the video from the render queue.*

When the encoding is complete, a green check mark will appear in the Status area. Close the Adobe Media Encoder, and open the Chapter 10 Exercise folder. If this is the first time you have used the Adobe Media Encoder, you had better sit down. You will notice the FLV and the QuickTime movie are in the same folder. Check out the file size of the FLV. The size has plummeted from around 59MB to 13MB, as shown in Figure 10-9. Don't panic—this is common with the Adobe Media Encoder. Remember that the On2 VP6 codec is lossy, and it really spreads out the keyframes. Both of these combine to create significant file-size reductions. This also explains why it is so important that the source video not be encoded using a lossy codec.

Figure 10-9. It is not uncommon to have an FLV shrink to 20 percent or less of the original file size.

Batch encoding

If there was one common complaint about encoding videos for Flash, it was that there was no way of encoding a bunch of them all at once. Third-party software, such as Sorenson Squeeze and On2's Flix Pro, allowed for batch processing, but this feature was unavailable in Flash—that is, until now. Here's how to encode a folder full of videos:

1. Create a folder on your desktop named WatchMe or something like that.
2. Add a bunch of MOV and/or AVI files to this folder.
3. Open the Adobe Media Encoder.
4. Select File ➤ Create Watch Folder to open the Browse for Folder dialog box.

5. Navigate to the folder you just created, select it, and click Choose. When you return to the Adobe Media Encoder, the folder and the files in it will appear, as shown in Figure 10-10.

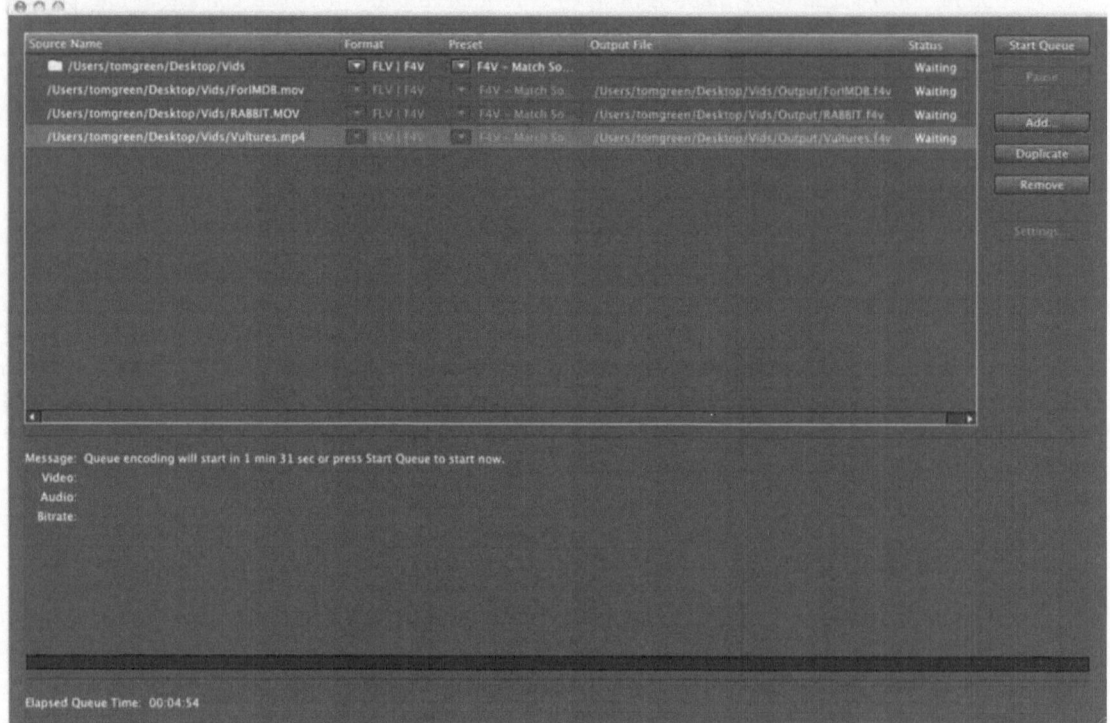

Figure 10-10. You can do batch encoding.

6. Select a preset, including a custom one you may have created. This preset will be applied to all the files in the folder. For better or worse, you can't apply different encoding settings to each of the files in the folder. It is sort of: "One setting for all."
7. Click the Start Queue button to encode all the files.

When the encoding finishes, open your folder. You will see that the Adobe Media Encoder has created a folder named Output and placed the encoded files in that folder. It has also created another folder, Source, and moved the original files into it.

Creating an F4V file

The F4V format was introduced in conjunction with Flash Player's ability to play H.264-encoded files. Even though .mov files encoded with the H.264 compression can be played directly out of Flash Player, the F4V format offers one significant difference: these files can't be played anywhere but through Flash Player and can't be converted to another format and subsequently edited. Based on the ISO base media format, F4V is becoming a secure format for HD video because the video track is encoded using H.264 and the audio is compressed using the AAC compression standard. As well, it is ideally suited to video with the 16:9 aspect ratio, whereas FLV has always been the choice for video with a 4:3 aspect ratio. Here's how to create an .f4v file:

1. Open the Adobe Media Encoder, and add the Vultures.mp4 file in your Exercise folder to the **Render Queue**.

2. Click the **Settings** button to open the **Export Settings** dialog box shown in Figure 10-11. Click the **Format** tab, select the **f4v** option, and then click the **Video** tab to open the video settings.

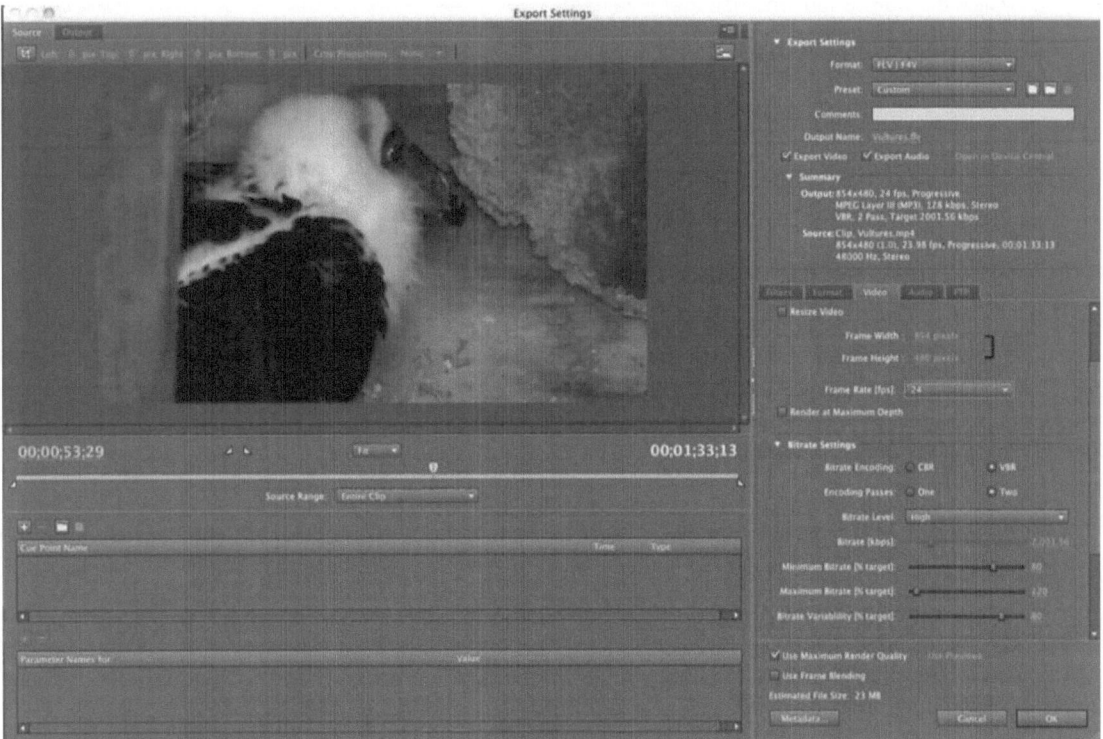

Figure 10-11. Creating an .f4v file

3. In the `Video settings` area, use these values:
    - `Frame Rate`: Select `24`. According to the summary, the original's frame rate is 23.98 fps.
    - `Bitrate Encoding`: Select `VBR`.
    - `Encoding Passes`: Select `Two`.
    - `Bitrate Level`: Select `High` from the drop-down. The plan for this video is to play it from the desktop so data rate is not an issue.
    - `Quality`: Select `Best`.
4. Click the `Audio` tab, and use these values:
    - `Output Channels`: Select `Stereo`.
    - `Bitrate`: Select `128 kbps`.
5. Click `OK` to return to the render queue. Click the `Start Queue` button to start encoding the video. Close the encoder when you finish.

More Media Encoder Goodness

The changes between the Adobe Media Encoder CS4 and its CS5 reincarnation are rather startling. In many respects, the CS5 version is a sleek, well-oiled machine dedicated to a sole purpose: create video for Flash Player. For example, if you were to click the `Export formats available` box for the `Vultures.mp4` file in the CS4 render queue, you would be presented with a list of 16 potential formats ranging from Audio Interchange File Format to MPEG2 Blu-ray. The CS5 version gives you two choices: H.264 and FLV/F4V.

The H.264 format is the most important because it is the most ubiquitous. You can find it playing video on everything from an iPod to a 60-inch HD screen and from YouTube and Vimeo to your cell phone.

Another really interesting aspect of the Adobe Media Encoder can be found in the `Export Settings` dialog box. If your output format is H.264, the preset drop-down list shown in Figure 10-12 appears. As you can see, your choices range from the TV in your home to the formats preferred by Vimeo, YouTube, and Apple's iPod and Apple TV devices.

If you select one of the `3GPP` choices—a common video format for cell phones—the `Open in Device Central` area lights up. With the advent of Flash Player 10.1 and the increasing growth of the Android platform, the Adobe Media Encoder CS5 is destined to be the device workhorse when it comes to video. When you select the format and encode the video, it will be placed into a letterbox if the video's and device's aspect ratios aren't similar. When the encoding finishes, Device Central launches, and, as shown in Figure 10-13, the video starts playing in the device chosen.

VIDEO

```
Apple iPod, Apple iPhone Audio
Apple iPod, Apple iPhone Video
Apple iPod, Apple iPhone Widescreen Video
Apple TV 480p
Apple TV 720p
HDTV 1080p 24 High Quality
HDTV 1080p 25 High Quality
HDTV 1080p 29.97 High Quality
HDTV 720p 24 High Quality
HDTV 720p 25 High Quality
HDTV 720p 29.97 High Quality
NTSC DV High Quality
NTSC DV Widescreen High Quality
PAL DV High Quality
PAL DV Widescreen High Quality
TiVo® Series3™ (NTSC)
TiVo® Series3™ HD
Vimeo HD
Vimeo SD
YouTube SD
YouTube Widescreen HD
YouTube Widescreen SD
3GPP 176 x 144 15fps Level 1
3GPP 176 x 144 15fps
3GPP 220 x 176 15fps
3GPP 320 x 240 15fps
• 3GPP 352 x 288 15fps
3GPP 640 x 480 15fps
```

Figure 10-12. H.264 is the way to go when a video is destined for more than web playback.

Figure 10-13. You can preview the file in Device Central.

545

Playing an FLV in Flash CS5

After encoding the video, you're ready to have it play in Flash. There are three ways to accomplish this task:

- Let the wizard do it for you.
- Use the `FLVPlayback` component.
- Use a video object.

The first two are actually variations on the same theme. Both will result in the use of the `FLVPlayback` component, but they approach the task from opposite angles. The final method is the most versatile but involves the use of ActionScript. Regardless of which approach you may choose, the end result is the same: you are in the Flash video business.

Using the wizard

We'll begin with an example of using the wizard. We'll cover the steps involved in actually adding video to Flash. If you have never used Flash video, this is a great place to start. Let's get going:

1. Create a new Flash document, and select `File ➤ Import ➤ Import Video`. This will open the `Import Video` wizard.

2. The first step in the process is to tell the wizard where your file is located. Click the `Browse` button, and navigate to the folder where you placed the FLV created in the previous exercise, or use the `Rabbit.flv` file in your Chapter 10 `Exercise` folder.

There are only two possible locations for a video: your computer or a web server. If the file is located on your computer, the `Browse` button allows you to navigate to the file, and when you select it, the path to the file will appear in the `File path` area, as shown in Figure 10-14. This rather long path will be trimmed, by Flash, to a relative path when you create the SWF that plays the video.

3. Click the `Load external video with playback component` radio button. This tells Flash it needs to stream the video into Flash Player.

If you have a lot of videos, you may have put them in a folder on your website. In this case, you need to add an absolute path to the file. The path to Rabbit.flv would be www.mySite.com/FLVfile/Rabbit.flv. The path to the Flash Video Streaming Service or Flash Media Server would be a bit different—something like rtmp://myHost.com/Rabbit. (We won't be getting into the use of the Flash Video Streaming Service or Flash Media Server in this book. All videos will be played back either locally or through an HTTP site.)

VIDEO

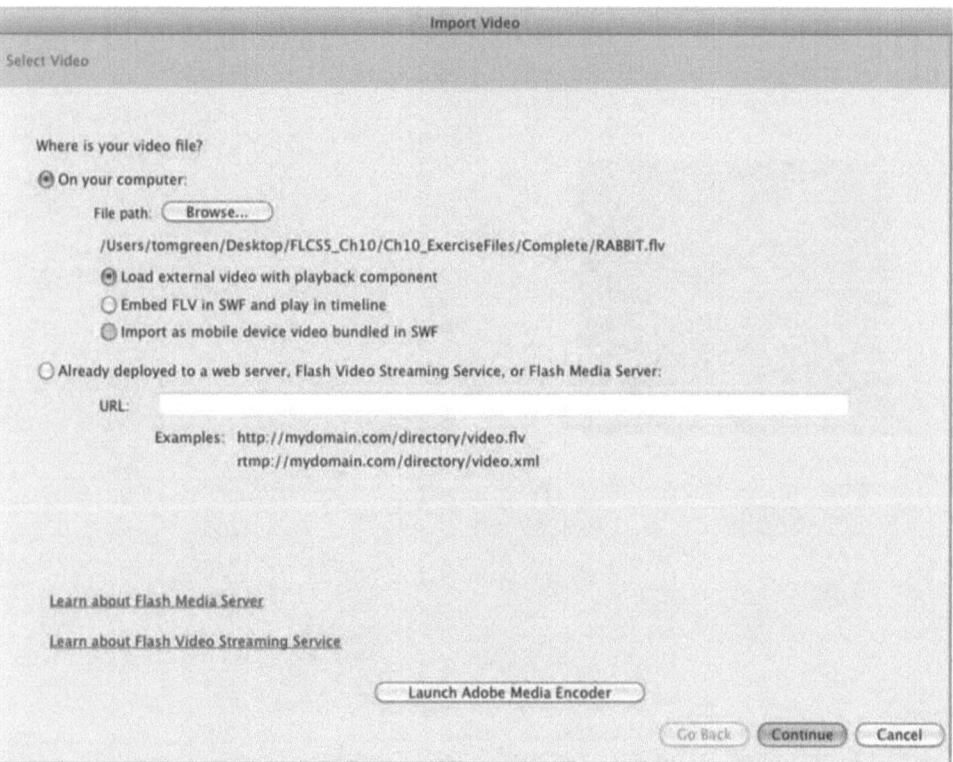

Figure 10-14. Setting the path to an FLV using the wizard

> *If you are into beating yourself in the head with bricks, then by all means, be our guest and select the* `Embed FLV in SWF and play in timeline` *option. This will place the entire video into the SWF. If that FLV is, say, 7MB, the user will need to wait as that 7MB makes the timeline creep along. The other danger is the tendency for video to last several minutes. Flash has a maximum timeline length of 16,000 frames. If the video is substantially long, the odds are almost 100 percent Flash will run out of timeline. We'll talk more about embedding video in the "When video is not video" section later in this chapter.*

4. When the path is established, click the `Next` (`Continue`) button to move to the `Skinning` page.
5. Click the `Skin` drop-down menu to see the choices available to you. Click a skin style, and the preview area will change to show the chosen skin, as shown in Figure 10-15.

547

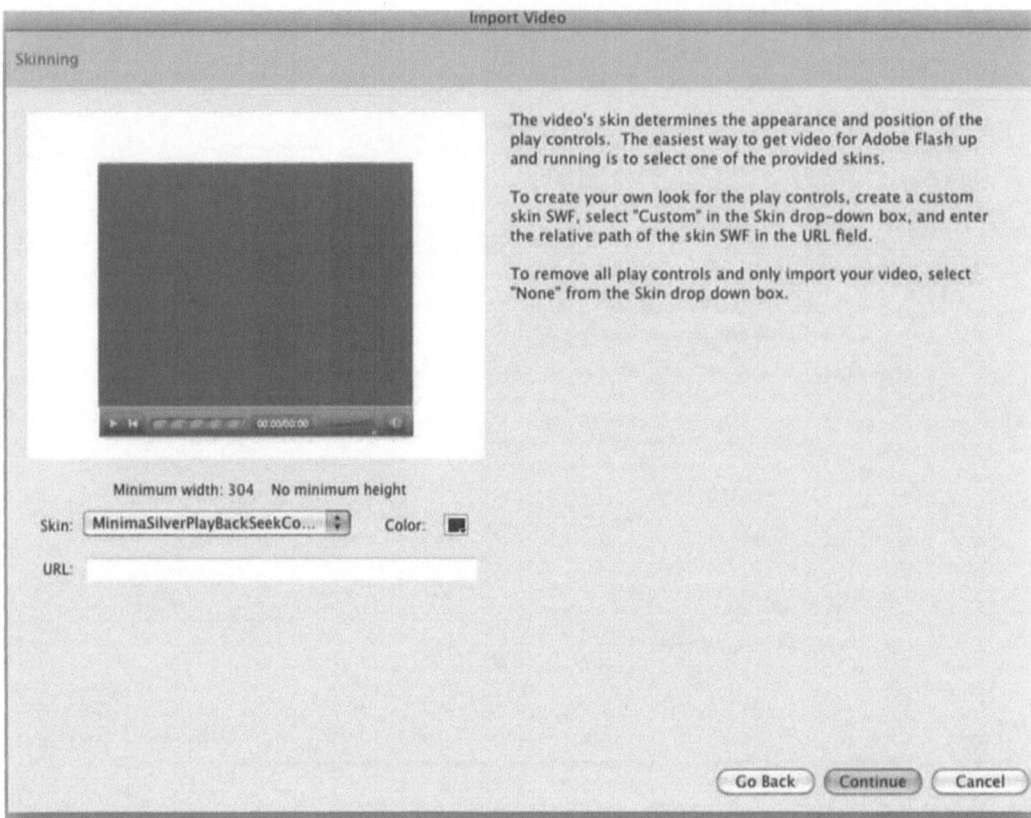

Figure 10-15. What skin or control style will be used?

Skin? Think of it as a techie word for video controls.

You are presented with two major skin groupings: `Over` and `Under`. Skins containing the word `Over` will overlay the controls directly on top of the video, which means you may want to configure the skin to automatically hide until the user moves the mouse cursor over the video. You can do this later by selecting the component and using the `Properties` panel to set the `skinAutoHide` parameter to `true`. Skins containing the word `Under` place the controls below the video.

Pay close attention to the minimum width for each skin. For example, selecting `SkinUnderAll.swf` requires a video that is at least 330 pixels wide. So, if your video is 320 pixels wide, the skin is going to hang off the sides of the video. You can see this in the preview.

Selecting `None` in the `Skin` drop-down menu means no skin will be associated with the video. Choose this option if you are going to create your own custom controls, use the components in the `Video` area of the `Components` panel, or display the video without allowing for user interaction.

If you select `Custom Skin URL` in the `Skin` drop-down menu, you will be prompted to enter the path to this skin. Use this feature if you have created a custom skin, such as one containing a client's branding. The path to this is best set as an absolute path.

The `URL` input area is used if you place the skin SWFs in a location on your site other than the folder containing the FLV and the Flash SWF.

6. Select `MinimaFlatCustomColorPlayBackSeek.CounterVolume.swf`. Click the color chip to open the Color Picker, choose a color, and the skin will change to that color.

The ability to add a custom color to a skin is rather neat. This way, you can, for example, easily use a client's corporate color in the controls. You can even make the color semitransparent—extremely useful in an `Over` skin—by setting the alpha to less than 100 percent.

7. Click the `Continue (Next)` button to move to the `Finish Video Import` page. This page simply tells you what will happen when you click the `Finish` button at the bottom of the page.

8. Click the `Finish` button. You will see a progress bar showing the progress of the video being added to the Flash stage. When it finishes, the `FLVPlayback` component will be placed on the Flash stage, as shown in Figure 10-16.

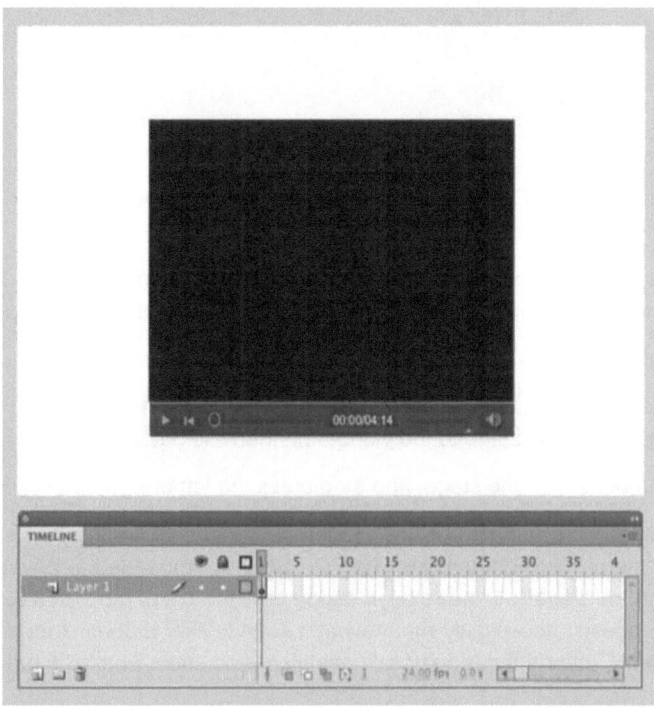

Figure 10-16. The video is "good to go."

9. Click the video on the stage, and in the Properties panel, set its x and y coordinates to 0.

Now this is where it gets really neat. If you have used previous versions of the component, you found yourself starting at a black box with an FLV icon in the middle of the black box. In many respects, this was a placeholder, and if you wanted to see if you had the correct video, you would have to save and test the file. No longer. The controls in the component are now "live." Click the Play button, and the video plays. Drag the scrubber, and you can move through the video. Click the volume button, and the audio track mutes. Drag the Scrubber button left and right, as shown in Figure 10-17.

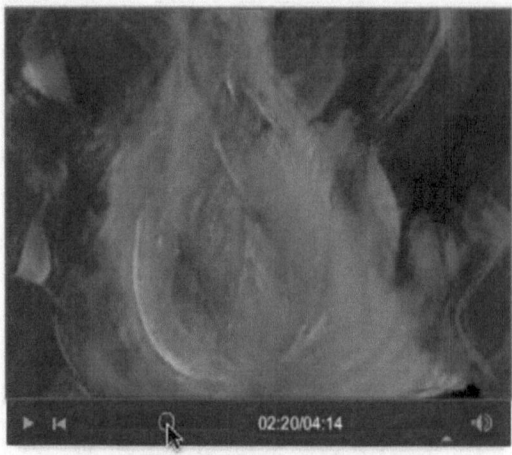

Figure 10-17. The controls in the FLVPlayback component are now "live."

10. Save the movie. It's important to save the FLA file to the same folder as the FLV you linked to. The FLVPlayback component needs this path to ensure playback of the video.

11. Close the video in the SWF to return to the Flash movie.

12. Select Modify ➤ Document. In the Document Properties dialog box, click the Contents radio button to shrink the stage to the video, and then click OK.

13. Select the component on the stage, and then press the left or right arrow key a few times.

Holy smokes—the controls are hanging off the stage! Depending on your publish settings, chances are good that this means the skin will not display when the SWF is embedded in a web page, which renders the controls useless. In the Publish Settings dialog box, the HTML tab's Scale setting is set to Show all by default, which doesn't necessarily mean what it sounds like. It doesn't mean "show everything on the stage and pasteboard," but rather, "don't scale anything, and show what's on the stage."

You're seeing a "gotcha" applicable only to the Under skins. When you use the FLVPlayback component, only the component is seen when you shrink the stage. The controls, which are a separate SWF added at runtime, aren't visible. If you are shrinking the stage and the only content on the stage is the FLVPlayback component, do yourself and your sanity a favor, and manually change the stage

VIDEO

dimensions. The width can be set to the width of the FLV, but add about 35 to 45 pixels to the height of the stage to accommodate the skin.

   14. Change the stage dimensions to 320 × 270.

   15. Save the movie and test it.

There is one last thing you need to know before we move on. Open the Exercise folder containing the FLV. As you see in Figure 10-18, the folder contains a number of files: the FLA, the SWF, another SWF containing the name of the skin, the original MOV, and the FLV. Not everything needs to be uploaded to your server. Leave the FLA and MOV on your local computer. If you are going to be embedding this particular project into a web page, make things easy for yourself by putting the two SWFs and the FLV in the same directory on your website. If they are not in the same folder, default settings will cause the video, the controls, or both to be unavailable.

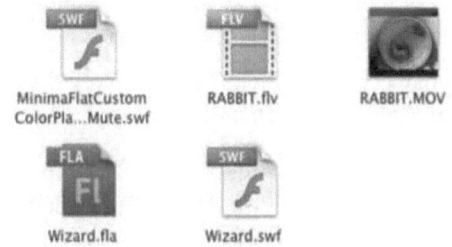

Figure 10-18. The two SWF files and the FLV must be in the same directory if you are uploading to a web page.

A word about file paths

It's certainly possible to put every single file into a separate directory—the HTML page, each SWF, and the FLV—but it means you'll need to meticulously specify the paths for all these files. Not only that, but it gets even crazier if you use relative paths (paths without the http:// or your website's domain name).

If you do find yourself in a situation where relative paths are a must and your files are scattered—this often happens with automated content management systems (CMS)—keep in mind that relative paths depend on the location of files in relation to each other, which hinges on the "point of view" of the document making the request.

Most files requested by a SWF, such as the video player's skin, must be requested from the point of view of the HTML document that embeds the SWF. Let that thought sink in. *When it comes to relative paths, the point of view belongs to the HTML document, not the SWF.* You may need to use the Custom Skin URL setting, mentioned between steps 3 and 4 of the previous exercise, to specify the location of the skin SWF, as follows:

   1. Choose the desired skin.

   2. Test the movie to generate the actual movie SWF as well as the SWF that represents the skin.

3. Move the skin SWF where it belongs on the server.
4. Return to the authoring environment, and select the component on the stage.
5. Using the `Properties` panel, modify the `skin` parameter's `Custom Skin URL` setting to instruct Flash where to locate the skin SWF. You'll specify the relative path as if the HTML page, rather than the movie SWF, were looking for it.

FLV files are an exception. When a SWF requests an FLV, the point of view belongs to the SWF making the request. Regardless of where the HTML document is, if the FLV is in a different directory from the movie SWF, specify your relative path as if the movie SWF were looking for the video.

Using the FLVPlayback component

In the previous exercise, you used the wizard to connect an FLV to the `FLVPlayback` component. In this exercise, you'll be doing the process manually. Once you are comfortable with it, you will discover this method to be a lot quicker than the previous one. Follow these steps:

1. Create a new Flash document, and save it to your Chapter 10 `Exercise` folder. Remember that the FLA needs to be in the same folder as the FLV.

2. In the `Components` panel (`Window` ➤ `Components`), click the `Video` category. Drag a copy of the `FLVPlayback` component onto the stage, as shown in Figure 10-19.

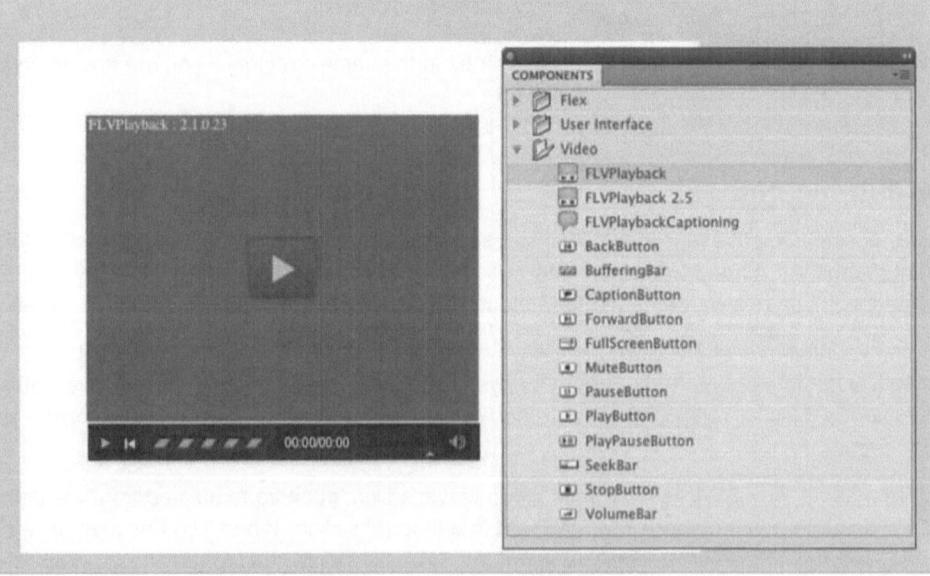

Figure 10-19. The `FLVPlayback` component is found in the `Video` section of the `Components` panel.

You will notice that the component has the same skin color from the previous exercise. This is normal. Also, if you open the **Library**, you will see a copy of the component has been added to the **Library**. This is a handy feature, because you can use the **Library**, rather than the **Components** panel, to add subsequent copies of the **FLVPlayback** component to the movie.

3. Click the component on the stage, and open the **Properties** panel. The parameters, as shown in Figure 10-20, for the component are set here. The parameters, listed here, allow you to determine how the component will function:

   - **align**: The choices in this drop-down list have nothing to do with the physical placement of the component on the Flash stage. The choices you make here will determine the position of the FLV in the playback area of the component if the component is resized.

   - **autoPlay**: When the check box is selected, the default, the video plays automatically. Deselect it, and the user will need to click the **Play** button in the component to start the video. In either case, the FLV file itself starts downloading to the user's computer, so keep this in mind if you put several FLV-enhanced SWFs in a single HTML document.

   - **cuePoints**: If cue points are embedded in the FLV, they will appear in this area.

   - **preview**: If you select this and an FLV is connected to the component, you can see the video without needing to test the movie. This feature, you discovered, is a bit redundant. It is ideal for capturing a frame of the video.

   - **scaleMode**: Leave this at the default value—**maintainAspectRatio**—if video is to be scaled.

   - **skin**: Select this, and the **Select Skin** dialog box will appear.

   - **skinAutoHide**: Adding a check to this means the user will need to place the mouse over the video, at run time, for the skin to appear.

   - **skinBackgroundAlpha**: Your choice is any two-place decimal number between 0 to 1. **0** means the background is totally transparent, and **1** means there is no transparency.

   - **skinBackgroundColor**: Select this, and the Flash color chip appears.

   - **source**: Double-click this area, and the **Content Path** dialog box opens. From here, you can either set a relative path to the FLV or enter an HTTP or RTMP address path to the FLV.

   - **volume**: The number you enter—any two-place decimal number between 0 and 1—will be the starting volume for the video.

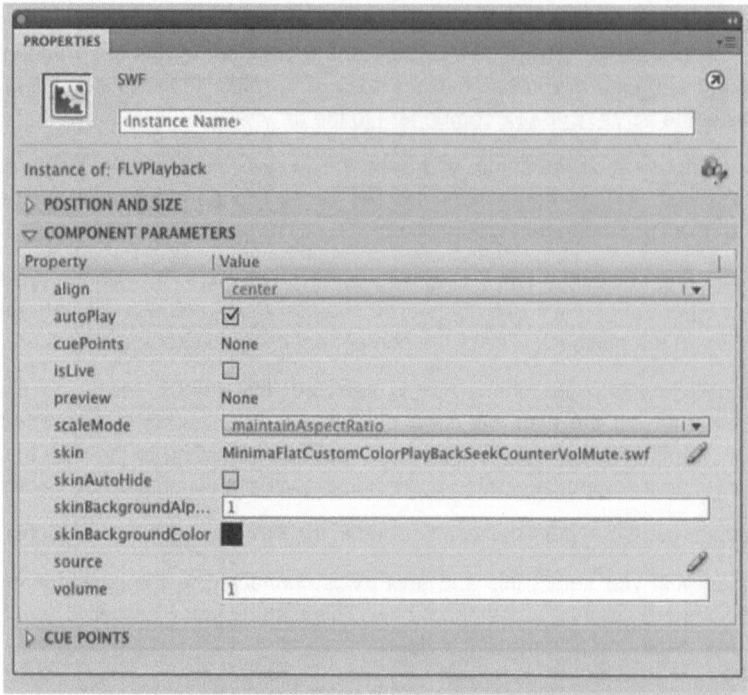

Figure 10-20. The `FLVPlayback` component now relies on the `Properties` panel to determine its look and functionality.

4. With the component selected on the stage, set `autoPlay` to `false` by deselecting it, and change the `skinBackgroundColor` to `#999999` (medium gray).

5. Double-click the `source` parameter to open the `Content Path` dialog box, as shown in Figure 10-21.

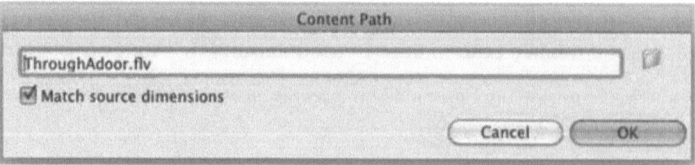

Figure 10-21. Setting the content path to the FLV to be played in the component

VIDEO

6. In the `Content Path` dialog box, click the `Navigate` button—the file folder icon—to open the `Browse for source file` dialog box. Navigate to the Chapter 10 Exercise folder, select the `ThroughADoor.flv` file, and then click the `Open` button.

7. The relative path to the FLV will appear in the `Content Path` dialog box. Select the `Match source dimensions` check box. This will size the component to the exact dimensions of the FLV file. Then click `OK`.

8. Save the movie.

9. Test the movie in Flash Player. Alternatively, click the `Play` button on the skin to start playing the video. When you have finished, close the SWF to return to the Flash stage.

Playing video using ActionScript

In the previous two exercises, you have seen different ways of getting an FLV file to play through the `FLVPlayback` component. In this exercise, you won't be using the component; instead, you'll let ActionScript handle the duties. This is also the point where you are going to get the opportunity to play with some of the new video stuff. The video you will be using is an MP4 file that was "ripped" from a DVD. The ability to use HD-quality video was added to Flash Player 9 in late 2007.

Playing video using ActionScript is a lot like connecting your new television to the cable in an empty room. There are essentially three steps involved: connect, stream, and play.

When you walk into the room where you are about to hook up the television to the cable, the television is sitting on a shelf, and there is a spool of coaxial cable lying on the floor. When you screw the cable into the wall outlet, you are establishing a connection between the cable company and your home. When you screw the other end of the cable into the television, the television is now connected to the cable company. When you turn on the television, the show that is flowing from the cable company to your television starts to play. Let's connect our television to an FLV:

1. Create a new Flash document, and save it as `Vultures.fla` in this chapter's Exercise folder. Set its stage dimensions to `845 × 480`.

2. Open the Flash `Library`. (If you don't have the `Library` in your panel group, select `Window ➤ Library` to open it.) Click the `Library` drop-down menu in the upper-right corner of the panel, and select `New Video` to open the `Video Properties` dialog box.

3. In the `Video Properties` dialog box, make sure the `Video (ActionScript-controlled)` radio button is selected, as shown in Figure 10-22. Click `OK` to close the dialog box.

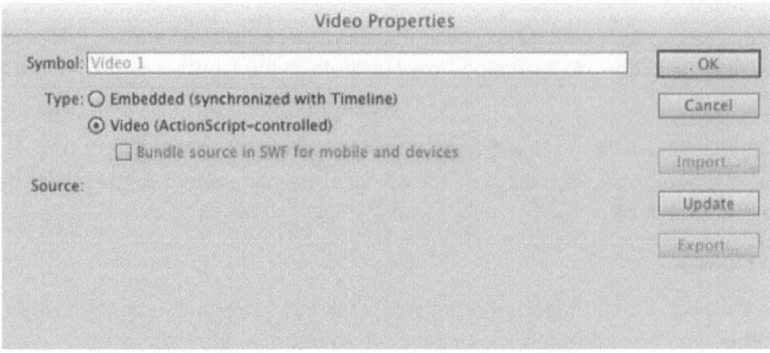

Figure 10-22. Creating a video object that will play an FLV

4. In the `Library`, you will see a little video camera named `Video 1` sitting in your `Library`. This camera is called a **video object**. It's a physical manifestation of the Video class, just as movie clip symbols are instances of the MovieClip class. Drag your video object from the `Library` to the stage. When you release the mouse, it will look like a box with a big X through it, as shown in Figure 10-23.

5. Click the video object, and specify these values in the `Properties` panel:

    - `Instance name`: myVideo
    - `Width`: 854
    - `Height`: 480
    - `X`: 0
    - `Y`: 0

> When you add a video object to the stage, its default dimensions are 160 × 120. This is why you need to physically set the object's dimensions to match those of the video playing through it.

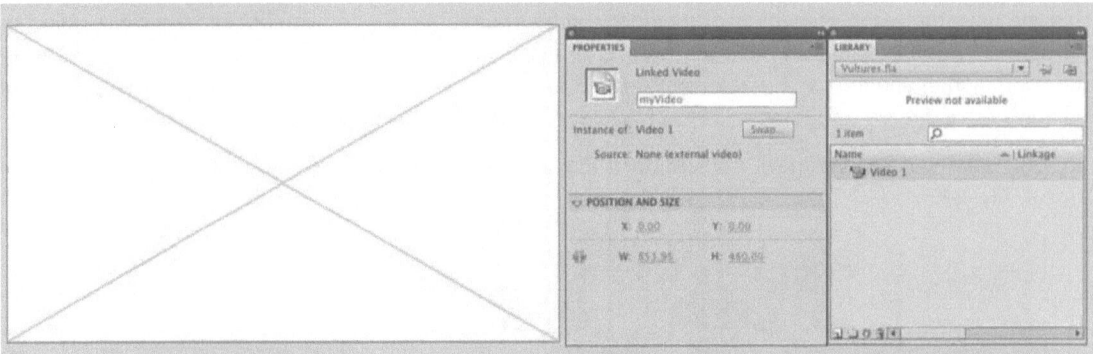

Figure 10-23. The new video object on the stage

6. Save this file to the Chapter 10 Exercise folder.
7. Add a new layer named **Actions**. Select the first frame of the **Actions** layer, open the **Actions** panel, and enter the following code:

```
var nc:NetConnection = new NetConnection();
nc.connect(null);

var ns:NetStream = new NetStream(nc);
myVideo.attachNetStream(ns);
```

The first line declares an arbitrarily named variable, nc, and sets it to an instance of the NetConnection class. This provides the network connection between the player and the server. The second line (nc.connect(null);) tells the player this is an HTTP connection, not an RTMP connection, which requires Adobe's Flash Media Server installed on your web server. Any requested video files, such as the SWF itself or typical web page assets like JPEGs or GIFs, will download progressively. The third line declares another variable, ns, and sets it to an instance of the NetStream class. This establishes the stream—that is, the flow of video data. The fourth line connects the video object, with the instance name myVideo, to the stream that is connected to the server.

8. Press Enter (Windows) or Return (Mac) twice, and enter the following code:

```
ns.client = {};
```

The client is the object that will hold such stuff as the metadata inside the video file. If this isn't there you are going to some rather bizarre messages in the compiler.

9. Press Enter (Windows) or Return (Mac) twice, and enter the following code:

```
ns.play("Vultures.mp4");
```

This line uses the NetStream.play() method to actually stream the video content into the video object on the stage. The important thing to note here is that the name of the video is a string (it falls between quotation marks) and the .mp4 extension is added to the name of the video. The important thing you need to know here is the file extension—.flv, .f4v, .mp4, or .mov—must be included in the file's name.

10. Save and test the movie. When Flash Player opens, the video starts to play, as shown in Figure 10-24.

Figure 10-24. Eight simple lines of ActionScript code drive the playback of this HD video.

To recap, if you want to play video using ActionScript, here is all of the code you will need to get started:

```
var nc:NetConnection = new NetConnection();
nc.connect(null);
var ns:NetStream = new NetStream(nc);
myVideo.attachNetStream(ns);

ns.client = {};

ns.play("Vultures.mp4");
```

The only thing you will ever need to do to reuse this code is to make sure the video object's instance name matches the one in line 4, and change the name of the FLV, F4V, or MP4 file in the last line.

> *Now that you've seen how easy it is to play a* NetStream *instance, what about stopping the video? Check out the* NetStream *class entry in the ActionScript 3.0 Language and Components Reference, and you'll see the answer: you have a number of methods to tinker with, including* pause()*,* resume()*, and* close()*. We'll talk more about these methods in Chapter 14.*

You might be thinking, "Hey, I have the **FLVPlayback** component. Why do I need code?" The answer can be summed up in one word: size. The size of a code-driven SWF is about 1KB, and its FLV counterpart weighs in at more than 55KB. The difference is simply because of the ActionScript involved with the component under the hood.

The increasing use of video in banner advertising is forcing developers to think small, because the maximum size of a banner ad SWF is often no more than 30KB. Obviously, the **FLVPlayback** component is simply too "heavy" for use in banner ads.

Additionally, there is going to come a point in your life when the **FLVPlayback** component simply isn't going to cut it any longer. When you reach this point, you will be creating your own ActionScript-driven controllers, as shown in Chapter 14, and this will require the use of a video object. The real payback for you will come when you discover you can create your own custom controllers that weigh in at under 10KB.

There's a snippet for that

In the previous exercise we asked you to enter the code that makes a video play in a video object. If you found that to be a bit tedious, you can always use a code snippet that does exactly what you just did…with a twist. You don't even need to create the video object. This begs the obvious question: "So, why did you make me type that code before showing me this?

The answer is simple: anybody can add a snippet, but, as you are about to discover, it's better to know what it does rather than blindly heave it in. Let's get started:

1. Create a new Flash document, and save it as VultureSnippet.fla in this chapter's Exercise folder. Set its stage dimensions to **845 × 480**.

2. Open the **Code Snippets** panel, and select **Audio and Video ➤ Create a NetStream Video**.

3. Click the **Add to current frame** button in the panel. An Actions layer will appear on the timeline, and the **Script** pane will open.

4. Review the code:

```
var fl_NC_2:NetConnection = new NetConnection();
fl_NC_2.connect(nullvar fl_NS_2:NetStream = new NetStream(fl_NC_2);
fl_NS_2.client = {};
```

```
var fl_Vid_2:Video = new Video();
fl_Vid_2.attachNetStream(fl_NS_2);
addChild(fl_Vid_2);

fl_NS_2.play("http://www.helpexamples.com/flash/video/water.flv");
```

This code is really no different from that in the previous exercise other than Adobe heaves the creation of the `NetStream` object as the parameter for the `NetConnection`'s connect method.

The three lines in the middle are how the video object is created and used. The first line—`var fl_Vid_2:Video = new Video();`—creates the video object. The second line attaches the `NetStream` to the object. The last line—`addChild(fl_Vid_2)`—puts the object on the stage and makes it visible.

5. Change the path in the `fl_NS_2.play` method to (`"Vultures.mp4"`).

6. Save and test the movie. We'll bet you didn't expect to see the video jammed into a small area. The reason is, the snippet uses the default size for a video object, which is 320 x 240. In many respects we set you up for that one to show you that an unhealthy reliance on "prerolled code" can have unforeseen consequences. Let's fix this.

7. Select the first frame of the Actions layer, and open the **Actions** panel.

8. Click once at the end of line 18, press the Return (Windows) or Enter (Mac) key, and add the following:

```
fl_Vid_2.width = 845;
fl_Vid_2.height = 480;
```

9. Save and test the movie. That's better.

Using the FLVPlayback control components

In the **Video** components area of the **Components** panel, you'll find a bunch of individual buttons and bars. They are there for those situations when you look at the skin options available to you and think, "That's overkill. All I want to give the user is a play button and maybe another one to turn off the sound." This is not as far-fetched at it may sound. There are a lot of websites that use custom players that are nothing more than a series of the individual controls. In this exercise, you will build a custom video controller using these video-specific user interface components.

1. Open the `Controls.fla` document in this chapter's `Exercise` folder. You will see the only thing on the stage is beveled box with a bit of branding on it. If you want, feel to change the text in the **Text** layer to your name.

2. Select the **Video** layer, and drag an **FLVPlayback** component to the stage.

3. Open the **Properties** panel. Set the **skin** to **None** and the **source** to **ThroughADoor.flv**.

4. In the **Properties** panel, set the **X** and **Y** values of the **FLVPlayback** component to 0.

5. Select the `Controls` layer, and drag the following components to the stage:
   - `BackButton`
   - `PlayPauseButton`
   - `SeekBar`
   - `VolumeBar`
6. Hold down the Shift key, and select each of the controls on the stage.
7. Open the `Align` panel, and make sure `To stage` is not selected. Then click the `Align Vertical Center` button. When you finish, your stage should resemble Figure 10-25.

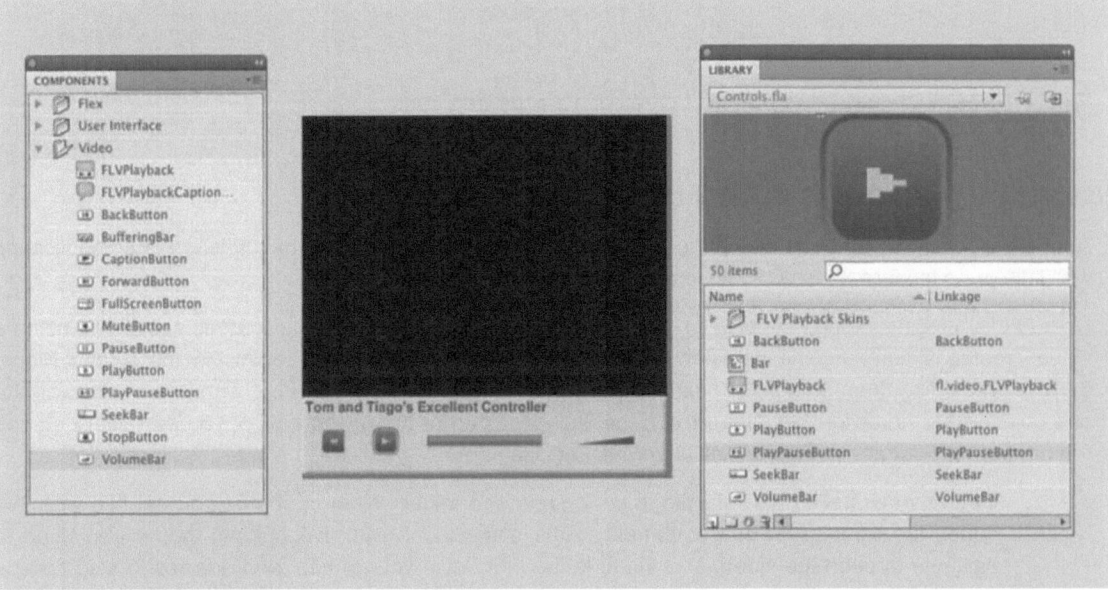

Figure 10-25. The video control components, when added to the stage, are also added to the `Library`.

If you open the `Library`, you will see separate `Play` and `Pause` buttons. Don't panic. The `PlayPauseButton` is actually a combination of both of them.

This is the point in this exercise where what you have done is about to shift from interesting to way too cool. With all of those components on the stage, you are probably preparing yourself, especially if you used them in Flash 8, to start writing a bunch of code. But you can relax. As long as the components are in the same frame as the `FLVPlayback` component, they become fully functional. Think about it—you have just created a custom video controller in a "code-free zone." Don't believe us? Check it out yourself.

8. Save and test the movie. Drag the `Seek` control to the right and left, as shown in Figure 10-26. See...we told you.

CHAPTER 10

Figure 10-26. A custom video controller created in a code-free zone

Navigating through video using cue points

Adobe has this amazing habit of enhancing the functionality of a feature in a new release of an application with little or no fan fare. Flash CS5 is no exception.

Prior to this release adding ActionScript, cue points that allowed the user to navigate to specific points in a video created a cumbersome workflow. It involved either adding the cue points in the Adobe Media Encoder or adding them in the cue points area of the `Component Inspector`. The issue here was the cue points were "hardwired" into the FLV. If the timing was off or there was a typo, you essentially started the process all over again. This has all changed. Let's see how:

1. Open the `ASCuePoints.fla` file in your `Exercise` folder. When it opens, you will see we have added the `FLVPlayback` component to the stage along with five buttons that will be used to navigate through the video. The video is the story of a young man who decides to skip college and become a cartoon character. The neat thing about the video is it is broken into five sections. Feel free to click the `Play` button on the component to review the video. We think you will find it to be rather hilarious.

2. Scrub back to the start of the video, and with the component selected on the stage, twirl down the `Cue Points` area of the `Properties` panel. This is where the magic happens.

3. Click the + sign to add a cue point. When you do you will, as shown in Figure 10-27, see the `Name`, `Time`, and `Type` areas contain values. Click the cue point's name, and change it from `Cue Point 1` to `Decision`. The other really "slick" feature here is the `Time` parameter is hot text, meaning you can scrub across it to change the timing for the cue point if you think the time needs to change. Also, take a look at the `cuePoints` area of the component. Notice how the cue point now appears there?

VIDEO

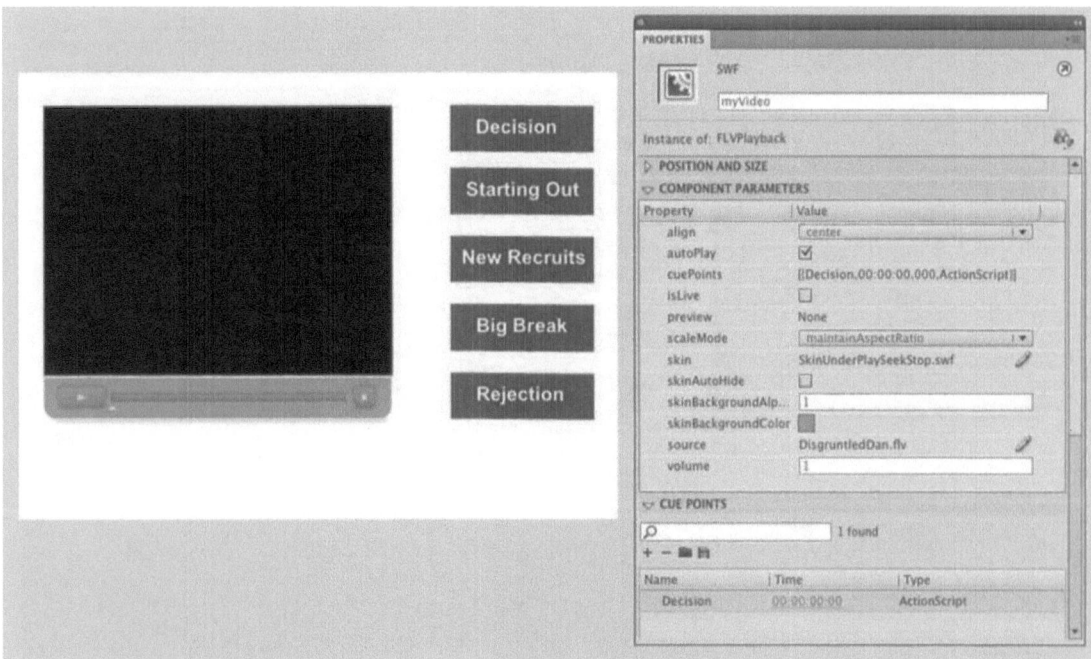

Figure 10-27. Adding an ActionScript cue point just got a ton easier.

Before we move forward with this exercise, let's get really clear about these things. Cue points can be added to a video's metadata and can be read by any application that understands metadata. The neat thing about metadata and cue points is they stay with the video file. The bad news is ActionScript cue points work only with Flash Player. The good news is they can be added or removed without affecting the video.

Cue points can be embedded into the FLV or can be contained in external files, usually XML documents. We are not huge fans of embedding because XML offers a degree of flexibility you simply can't obtain with cue points embedded in an FLV. For example, many video sites will pop up little advertising messages while the video plays. Putting these things into an XML document means they can be changed regularly without having to open the FLA.

There are also two types of cue points: navigation and event. Navigation cue points let you "skip" to sections of a video, whereas event cue points will trigger something in Flash Player when the cue point is reached. A good example of this are those little ads we talked about in the previous paragraph.

4. Click the scrub bar of the video on the stage, and scrub to the point where the words **starting out** appear. If the video won't scrub to that point, click the **Play** button on the component, and when the words appear, pause the video. Add a cue point named **StartingOut** at this point by simply clicking the + sign to add it.

5. Scrub thorough the video, and add three more cue points when, as shown in Figure 10-28, you see the words on the screen. Name them **Recruits**, **Break**, and **Rejection**.

563

CHAPTER 10

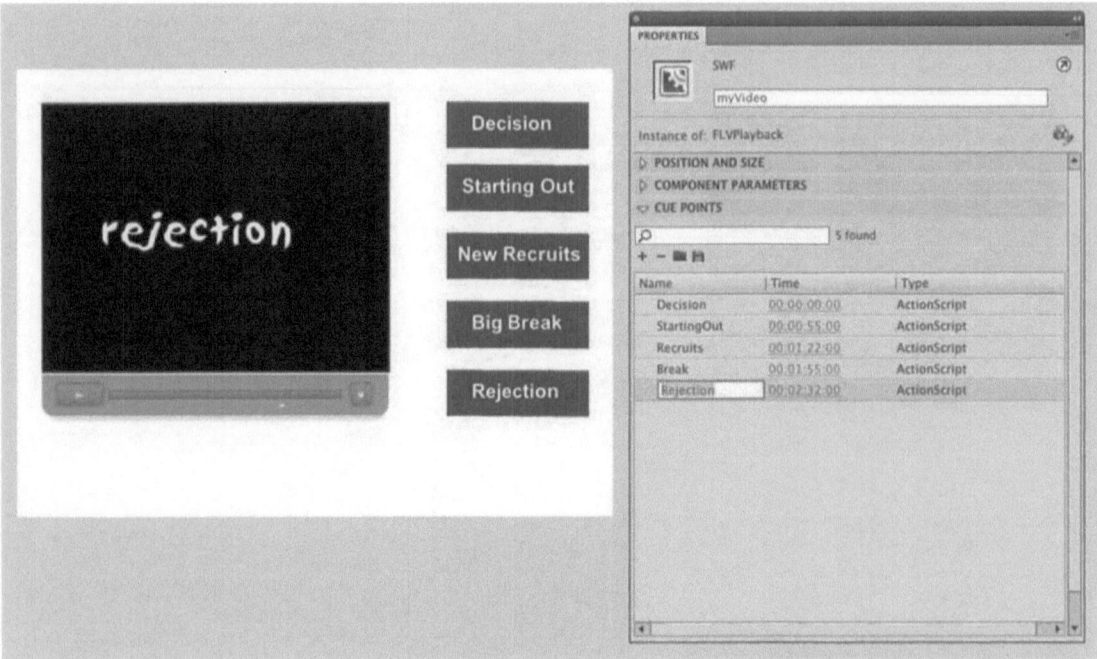

Figure 10-28. Get to the point in the video where you need a cue point and simply add it.

Next up is "wiring up" the buttons on the stage with the ActionScript that pops you through the video. If you click the component, you will see we have given it the instance name of `myVideo` in the **Properties** panel. As well, each button has been given an instance name. Let's get wiring:

6. Select the `Decision` button on the stage, and open the `Code Snippets` panel. As you may have guessed, "There is a snippet for that."

7. In the `Code Snippets` panel, twirl down the `Audio and Video` folder, select the `Click to Seek to Cue Point` snippet, and click the `Add to current frame` button at the top of the panel. An Actions layer will be added to your timeline, and the `Script` pane will open.

> *If you are lazy like us, simply double-click a snippet to add it to the movie.*

8. You need to make a couple of changes to the code. In line 10, change `fl_ClickToSeekToCuePoint_3` to `fl_ClickToSeekToCuePoint_1`. Don't forget to make this change in the next line as well. Line 16 needs a couple of changes too. Change `video_instance_name` to `myVideo` and `Cue Point 1` to `Decisions`. Make sure the word appears between the quotation marks. Also, change the video instance name in line 17 to `myVideo`.

VIDEO

You are most likely looking at this code:

```
btn01.addEventListener(MouseEvent.CLICK, fl_ClickToSeekToCuePoint_1);

function fl_ClickToSeekToCuePoint_1(event:MouseEvent):void
{
var cuePointInstance:Object = myVideo.findCuePoint("Decision");
        myVideo.seek(cuePointInstance.time);
}
```

...and wondering "What does it do?"

The first line tells the button to listen for a mouse click and, when it "hears" that CLICK, to execute the fl_ClickToSeekToCuePoint_1 handler.

The function tells Flash to poke through the video and look for a cue point named Decision. When it finds that cue point, it is to shoot the video's playhead to the time parameter associated with the video in the **Properties** panel. There are four more buttons to wire up. We can do it the "ugly" way or the "elegant" way. Let's get the ugly way out of the way:

9. Select lines 10 to 18 of the code block, and copy them to the clipboard.

10. Click in line 19, and paste the code into that line. Feel free to delete the comments. They aren't needed. Make the following changes:

    - Change the instance name of the button to bthn02.
    - Change the number in fl_ClickToSeekToCuePoint_ 1 to a 2.
    - Change the number in the function.
    - Change the cue point name to StartingOut.

11. Repeat steps 9 and 10 for the remaining three buttons. When finished, your code will have a separate handler for each button.

12. Save and test the movie. Click a button, and you go to that point in the video.

The elegant way is the approach a coder would use. Instead of separate handlers for each button, a coder wraps the function kicked out by the snippet into a case statement. Here's how:

13. Open the **Actions** panel, and delete all of the code in the **Script** pane.

14. Enter the following code block:

```
var cuePointInstance:Object;

// Add Event Listeners to all buttons on the stage
btn01.addEventListener(MouseEvent.CLICK, seekToCuePoint);
btn02.addEventListener(MouseEvent.CLICK, seekToCuePoint);
```

```
btn03.addEventListener(MouseEvent.CLICK, seekToCuePoint);
btn04.addEventListener(MouseEvent.CLICK, seekToCuePoint);
btn05.addEventListener(MouseEvent.CLICK, seekToCuePoint);
```

We create an object to hold the cue points and then tell each button to listen for a CLICK event and, when it hears it, to execute the seekToCuePoint function.

15. Press the Return (Windows) or Enter (Mac) key twice, and add the following code:

```
function seekToCuePoint( evt:MouseEvent ):void
{
        switch ( evt.target.name )
        {
                case "btn01":
                        cuePointInstance = myVideo.findCuePoint("Decision");
                        myVideo.seek(cuePointInstance.time);
                break;
                case "btn02":
                        cuePointInstance = myVideo.findCuePoint("StartingOut");
                        myVideo.seek(cuePointInstance.time);
                break;
                case "btn03":
                        cuePointInstance = myVideo.findCuePoint("Recruits");
                        myVideo.seek(cuePointInstance.time);
                break;
                case "btn04":
                        cuePointInstance = myVideo.findCuePoint("Break");
                        myVideo.seek(cuePointInstance.time);
                break;
                case "btn05":
                        cuePointInstance = myVideo.findCuePoint("Rejection");
                        myVideo.seek(cuePointInstance.time);
                break;
        }
}
```

The key here is to note you haven't really wasted that snippet. It was used in a more efficient manner. A case statement simply checks to see whether the button has been clicked. If it hasn't, then move on looking for which one has been clicked. The break simply tells Flash where it has reached the end point of that statement.

16. Save and test the movie.

Adding captions with the FLVPlaybackCaptioning component

A couple of years ago, one of the authors had written a piece about Flash video and how easy it was to get video onto a website. The thrust of the article was that this was a wondrous technology and that video was about to sweep the Web. The reaction to the article was strongly positive, and the author was feeling pretty good about himself—that is, until he received the following e-mail:

> *Love your books and tutorials! They are very well explained. I have a question. Have you done any tutorials on how to add captions to videos? For example, there is a CC button in your "Talking Head" video box. I would love to learn how to write CC for that. I am deaf and would strongly advocate for all websites that have videos to have captions, but that won't happen right away due to $ and timing. I will be making a small "Talking Head" video introducing myself in sign language, but I want to have captions for hearing people to know what I am saying :-)*

In our zeal to get video out there, we tend to forget that accessibility is a major factor in our business. And accessibility is now the law around the world. Up until Flash CS3, video was often partially or totally inaccessible to those with hearing impairments. What also caught our attention was the last line of the e-mail. It is obvious captioning is a two-way street, and those of us without disabilities rarely see it that way.

This isn't to say captions couldn't be added to video in Flash 8. They could, but it required quite a bit of effort on the designer's or developer's part to get them to work properly. It usually involved XML, cue points in the FLV, and an understanding of how to use XML in Flash and to write the proper ActionScript to make it all come together. Flash CS3 streamlined this process with the inclusion of the `FLVPlaybackCaptioning` component, and it's still right here in Flash CS5.

Before we get going, it is important that you understand this is not a point-and-click workflow. Entering cue points by hand into the `Video Import` dialog box in Flash is a tedious business. For all but the shortest of video clips, it makes best sense to use a special XML document to make it all work—easier to edit later, too—and then you need to "connect" that document to the `FLVPlaybackCaptioning` component.

The `FLVPlaybackCaptioning` component allows for the display of captions in the `FLVPlayback` component through the use of a Timed Text (TT) XML document. If you open the `captionsF4V.xml` document in this chapter's `Exercise` folder, you will see the Timed Text XML code used in this exercise:

```
<?xml version="1.0" encoding="UTF-8"?>
<tt xml:lang="en" xmlns-"http://www.w3.org/2006/04/ttaf1
xmlns:tts="http://www.w3.org/2006/04/ttaf1#styling">
    <head>
        <styling>
            <style id="1" tts:textAlign="right"/>
            <style id="2" tts:color="transparent"/>
            <style id="3" style="2" tts:backgroundColor="white"/>
            <style id="4" style="2 3" tts:fontSize="20"/>
        </styling>
    </head>
```

```
    <body>
        <div xml:lang="en">

<p begin="00:00:3.0" dur="00:00:10.0">Audio: Sound of man walking.</p>
<p begin="00:00:14.0" dur="00:00:02.0">Audio: A bell rings </p>
<p begin="00:00:18.0" dur="00:00:02.0">Audio: A bell rings </p>
<p begin="00:00:22.0" dur="00:00:02.0">Audio: A bell rings </p>
<p begin="00:00:26.0" dur="00:00:04.0">Stale cologne, sweat and smoke on cheap
crimson velour</p>
<p begin="00:00:30"dur="00:00:03.0">Pot bellied foul men drink on the bottom
floor</p>
<p begin="00:00:33.0" dur="00:00:3.00" >They say "petal "and "flower" and stroke us
in our beds</p>
<p begin="00:00:37.0" dur="00:00:04.00">And then run home to kiss the tops of their
wives' heads.</p>
<p begin="00:00:41.0" dur="00:00:03.5">And I sit in my room ...  she detangles my
hair</p>
<p begin="00:00:45" dur="00:00:02.5">To prepare for the next waiting in his
underwear</p>
<p begin="00:00:48.0"dur="00:00:03.5">Where am I? What is this. It must all be in
my head.</p>
<p begin="00:00:52.0" dur="00:00:1.50" >I was young once and pure.</p>
<p begin="00:00:54.0" dur="00:00:09.00">And my mother she said, "All stories on
earth exist in your scribbled hair. If you comb out the tangles you can be
anywhere! "</p>
<p begin="00:01:04.0" dur="00:00:02.5">And she placed me on her lap and she started
to comb.</p>
<p begin="00:01:07.0" dur="00:00:04.0"> And it hurt but she said, "With one stroke
you're in Rome</p>
<p begin="00:01:11.0"dur="00:00:04">With another you are dancing with a prince by
a lake</p>
<p begin="00:01:15.0" dur="00:00:3.00" >Or dining with flamingos eating sunflower
cake</p>
<p begin="00:01:18.0" dur="00:00:03.00">Or skipping on tight ropes all slathered
with gold</p>
<p begin="00:01:21.0" dur="00:00:03.5">You can run fast with leopards and never get
old.</p>
<p begin="00:01:25.0" dur="00:00:04.5">If you do as you're told and always comb
your hair."</p>
<p begin="00:01:30"dur="00:00:04.5">And I combed ... and I combed ... and I combed
ever since.</p>
<p begin="00:01:35.0" dur="00:00:3.50" >But I have only met toads and not once a
prince.</p>
```

```
<p begin="00:01:39.0" dur="00:00:04.50">I've not seen a flamingo. Sunflowers never↪
bloom.</p>
<p begin="00:01:44.0" dur="00:00:04.5">But I did see a rope though, hung in another↪
girl's room.</p>
<p begin="00:01:49.0" dur="00:00:03.5">But I am getting old and I can't help but↪
worry</p>
<p begin="00:01:53.0" dur="00:00:04.5">That my mother was wrong and then I think↪
…</p>
<p begin="00:01:58"dur="00:00:02.5">Sorry… no …no… it can't be</p>
<p begin="00:02:01.0" dur="00:00:3.50" >I need to believe that this hell that I'm↪
in is just a story </p>
<p begin="00:02:05.0" dur="00:00:04.50">Retrieved from a tangle straightened by a↪
stroke of the comb</p>
<p begin="00:02:10.0" dur="00:00:10.0">So tomorrow, with another, I just might wake↪
up in Rome </p>

      </div>
    </body>
</tt>
```

> *We get into XML in a big way in Chapter 13, so if the Timed Text XML code doesn't look especially meaningful to you yet, don't worry. You'll see some similarity to HTML, which may give you a sense of familiarity. In this case, you're looking at a document that adheres to the Timed Text specification set by the W3C, the same folks who wrote the HTML specification. The* `FLVPlaybackCaptioning` *component follows that standard. If you really want to dig into the specification, you can find it at* www.w3.org/AudioVideo/TT/*.*

You will notice that you can set the styling for the text and that each caption needs to have a start point and an end point. This means each caption must have a `begin` attribute, which determines when the caption should appear. If the caption does not have a `dur` or `end` attribute, the caption disappears when the next caption appears or when the FLV file ends. The `begin` attribute means "This is where the caption becomes visible." The `dur` attribute means "This is how long the caption remains visible." Alternatively—and this is really a matter of taste—you can omit `dur` and replace it with `end`, which means "This is where the caption stops being visible."

Where do you get those numbers? You can use the time code in the Adobe Media Encoder to find them, or you can use the time code displayed in the QuickTime or Windows Media Player interfaces. Another place would be in the video-editing software used to create the video in the first place.

Follow these steps to apply the captions in the preceding XML example to a video:

1. Open a new Flash document, and save it to the `CaptioningVideo` folder in your Chapter 10 `Exercise` folder.

2. Drag the **FLVPlayback** component to the stage. In the **Properties** panel, set its **source** to **Stories.f4v** (make sure the **Match source dimensions** check box is selected) and the **skin** parameter to **SkinUnderAll.swf**. Name the layer **video**.

3. Set the stage dimensions to **480 × 450**; in the **Properties** panel, set the component's **x** and **y** position to **0,0**.

4. Add a new layer named **text**. Select the **Text** tool, and draw a text box under the **FLVPlayback** controls. In the **Properties** panel, give the text box the Instance name of **txtCaption**, change the **Text Engine** to **Classic** text, and select **Dynamic Text** from the **Text Type** drop-down.

5. Set the font to one of your choosing, the text size to 16 points, and the color to black (**#000000**).

6. Twirl down the **Paragraph** settings, and select **Multiline** from the Behavior drop-down.

7. Add a new layer named **Captions**. Drag a copy of the **FLVPlaybackCaptioning** component to this new layer. Move the component to the pasteboard.

8. Select the **FLVPlaybackCaptioning** component, and open the **Properties** panel. Twirl down **Component Parameters**, and you will see the following parameters (Figure 10-29):

    - **autoLayout**: The check mark, which is the default, lets the **FLVPlayback** component determine the size of the captioning area.

    - **captionTargetName**: This parameter identifies the movie clip or text field instance where the captions can be placed. The default is **auto**, which means the component will make that decision and run the captions over the video using a font of its choosing. If you are using one of the **Over** skins, this is a dangerous choice because the skin will cover the captions. In steps 4 to 6 you added a text box, and this is the place to explain what was going on.

The captions between the <p> </p> tags will be pulled out of the XML document and placed over the video. We are not huge fans of this practice, which explains the text box. The captions are going to appear in it. You may have also noticed that we select **Classic Type** as the text engine in the **Properties** panel. The **Captioning** component can't use TLF text without the use of ActionScript. That's the reason for the decision regarding the text engine and the **Dynamic Text** text type.

- **flvPlaybackname**: This is the instance name for the **FLVPlayback** component, which is set in the **Properties** panel. If there is only one instance of the component, leave the value at the default of **auto**.

- **showCaptions**: If this is set to **false**, deselected, the captions will not display (they can be turned on with ActionScript or by clicking the captions button on the skin).

- **simpleFormatting**: If you have no formatting instructions in the XML document, set this to **true** by not turning off the check mark.

- **source**: The location of the Timed Text XML document used to supply the captions.

VIDEO

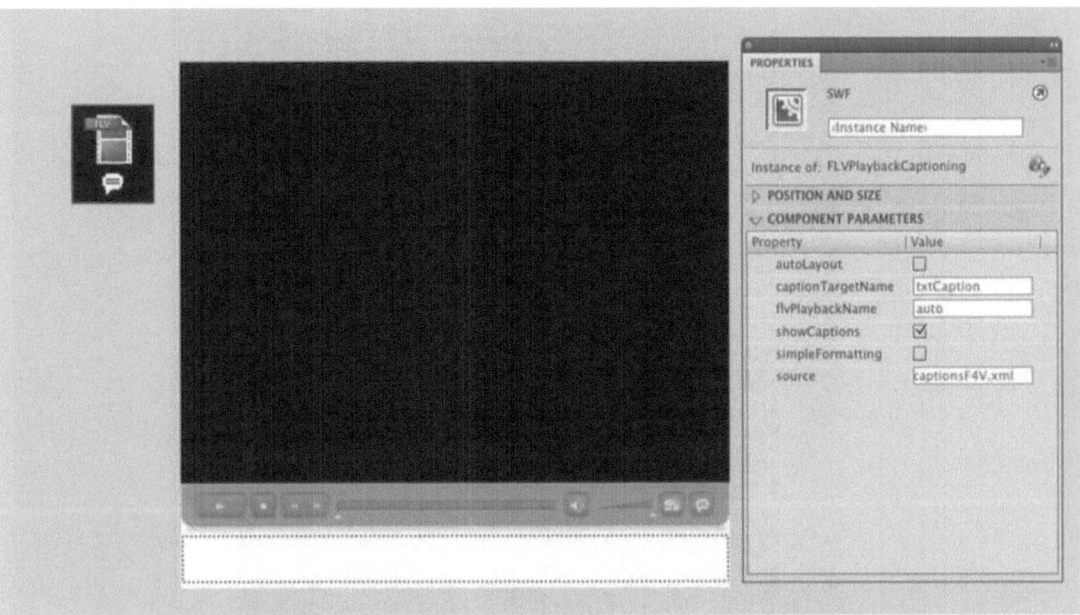

Figure 10-29. The `FLVPlaybackCaptioning` component and its parameters

9. Use these settings for the `Captioning` component:
   - `autoLayout`: Deselected
   - `captionTargetName`: txtCaption
   - `showCaptions`: Selected
   - `source`: captionsF4V.xml

10. Save and play the video. The captions will appear, as shown in Figure 10-30.

> *The authors want to thank Phoebe Boswell for letting us use her student project—The Girl With Stories In Her Hair—in this exercise and her instructor, Birgitta Hosea, at Central Saint Martins College of Art and Design in London, UK, for introducing us to Phoebe. Phoebe did all of the work on this amazing video including the animation, writing, and narration. Every now and then we bump into students who make us stop in our tracks and say, "Wow." Phoebe is one of those students.*

CHAPTER 10

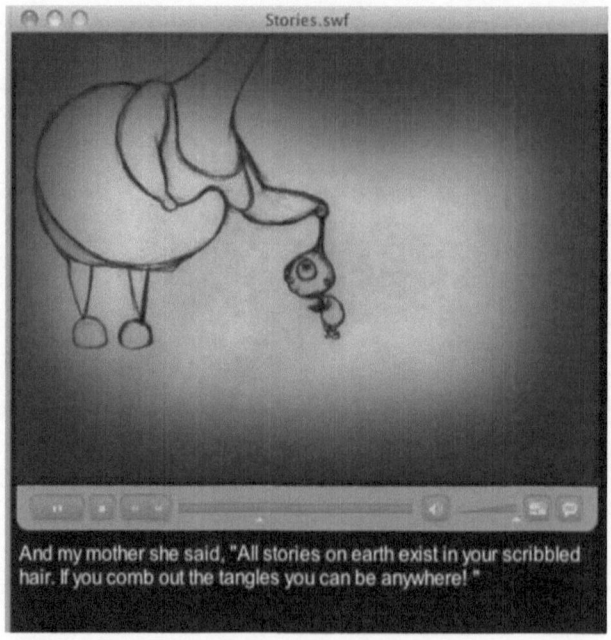

Figure 10-30. The captions appear in the text box, not over the video.

Preparing and using alpha channel video

There will be times when you need a talking head video or you want to move the subject of the video from the studio to another location. These are the instances where an alpha channel video fits the bill. If you watch the weather on your local television station, you are seeing this in action. The weather reporter stands in front of a green wall and starts pointing to fronts and cloud formations. But the stuff being pointed at isn't actually on the wall. To create the scene, the weather reporter is pulled out of the green background location and superimposed on the radar image.

The type of video where a green or blue background is removed, or **keyed**, is called **alpha channel video**. If you are a Photoshop CS5 or Fireworks CS5 user, you are quite familiar with the concept of an alpha channel or masking channel. The difference in a video-editing application is that the channel or mask is in motion.

How do you know you have been handed a video containing an alpha channel? Open it in the QuickTime player, and check the movie information. If the codec used to prepare the video is `Animation` and the number of colors is `Millions+`, the channel is there.

The ability to use this type of video was introduced in Flash 8 Professional. To use this feature in Flash CS5, you need to select the On2 VP6 codec in the Adobe Media Encoder. This means that if your target Flash Player is Flash Player 7 or older, you can't use alpha video.

VIDEO

To see alpha channel video In action, let's try it with a short video. You will encode a small clip of a young adult who has just been informed by his friend that he is dead as the result of being hit by a bus. Then you will place the video over an image in Flash.

1. Open the Adobe Media Encoder, and import the `Alpha.mov` file from this chapter's `Exercise` folder into the render queue.

2. Click `Settings` ... in the Adobe Media Encoder to open the `Export Settings` window. Click the `Format` tab, and select `FLV`. The F4V and H.264 formats do not support alpha channels.

3. Click the `Video` tab. Select the `On2 VP6` codec and the `Encode Alpha Channel` option, as shown in Figure 10-31. If you fail to select this check box, you will lose all transparency in the background.

Figure 10-31. Make sure you select the `Encode Alpha Channel` option.

4. Twirl down the `Bitrate Settings`. Select `VBR` encoding and `Two` encoding passes. Reduce the `Bitrate` setting to 400 kbps, and change the frame rate to 15 fps.

5. Click the `Audio` tab, and change the `Output Channels` setting to `Mono` and `Bitrate` to 80 kbps.

573

6. Click OK to return to the render queue.

7. Click the Start Queue button. When the render process is finished, quit the Adobe Media Encoder.

8. Open the AlphaEx.fla file in Flash. You will see we have tossed an image of a store—Dead Betty's Dyes—into the Background layer.

9. Select the Video layer, and drag an FLVPlayback component to the stage. In the Properties panel, set the source parameter to your alpha video, and set the skin parameter to None. With the component selected, in the Properties panel, set its X and Y values to 0,0.

10. Save and test the movie. The video appears as if filmed over the background image, as shown in Figure 10-32.

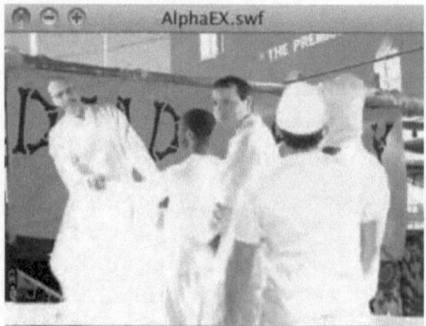

Figure 10-32. Alpha video in action

Going full-screen with video

In the autumn of 2006, Adobe quietly announced that full-screen Flash video was no longer a dream. Full-screen video was released as a part of the Adobe Flash Player 9 beta. But even though it was well received, many thought the process was a bit too convoluted. Between its introduction and Flash CS5, full-screen video became easier to add to you movies and deploy on the Web.

Depending on how you want to approach the application of full-screen video, it can be either dead simple or require a bit of poking around with ActionScript and in the web page's HTML. Let's explore both methods.

Full-screen video the ActionScript/HTML way

In this example, we are going to let Flash write the necessary HTML and JavaScript code. Here's how:

1. Open a new Flash movie, and save it to the FullScreen folder in your Chapter 10 Exercise folder.

2. Set the stage size to 400 × 300 pixels, and set the stage color to #006633 (dark green).

3. Drag an **FLVPlayback** component to the stage, and specify the following parameters:
   - **skin**: SkinOverAllNoCaption.swf
   - **skinAutoHide**: **true**
   - **skinBackGroundColor**: #999999 (medium gray)
   - **source**: FilmTV.mov
4. Save the file as FullScreenSkin.fla.
5. Select **File ➤ Publish Settings** to open the **Publish Settings** dialog box, as shown in Figure 10-33.

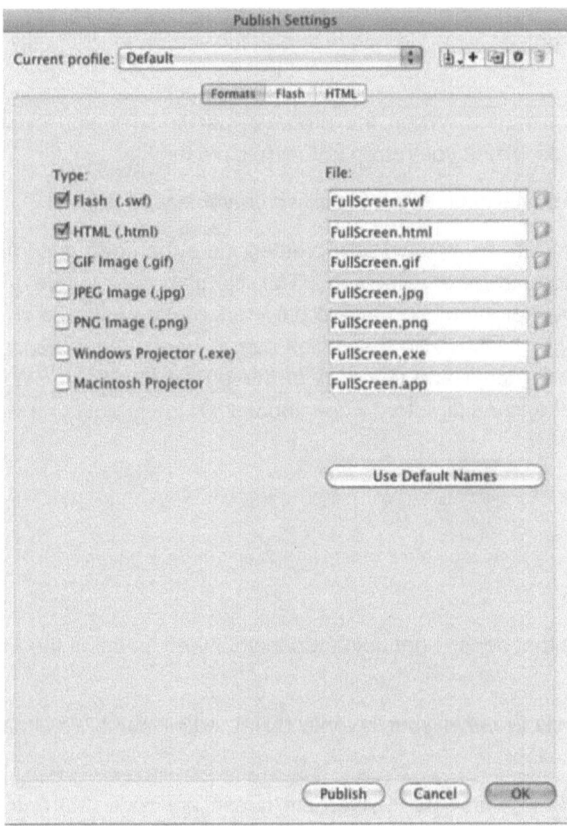

Figure 10-33. The **Publish Settings** dialog box

6. Make sure the **Flash** and **HTML** options are selected.

7. Click the **HTML** tab. In the **Template** drop-down, select **Flash Only-Allow Full Screen**, as shown in Figure 10-34.

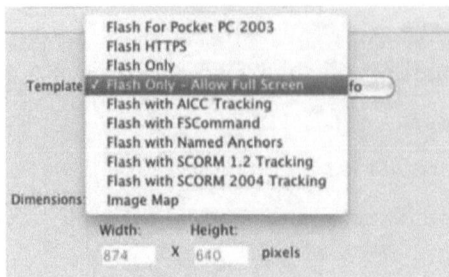

Figure 10-34. Choose the proper HTML template to add full-screen functionality.

8. Click the **Publish** button. When the progress bar finishes and closes, click the **OK** button to close the dialog box. When you return to Flash, save the file.
9. Minimize Flash, and navigate to the folder where you saved the SWF and HTML files.

When you published the HTML file, you actually created more than one document: the HTML file and the SWF file, which is embedded in the HTML. The HTML file also contains JavaScript that allows Flash to play in the browser without user interaction (some browsers require users to click in order to indicate their intent to play active content). Technically, these files can all be placed in separate folders, but it requires custom coding. Do yourself a favor and place all of these files (the FLV, SWFs, and HTML documents shown in Figure 10-35) in the same directory when you upload the project to a web server.

Figure 10-35. The only file that doesn't get uploaded to your web server is the FLA.

10. Open the HTML file in either your favorite HTML editor (such as Dreamweaver CS5) or a word processing application.

As you can see, Figure 10-36, Flash has written the necessary code that enables the button in lines 26 and 41 of the code block.

11. Double-click the HTML file to open it in a browser.
12. When the video starts, click the **Full Screen** button in the bottom-right corner of the controller. The video fills the screen, as shown in Figure 10-37. You can either press the Esc key or click the **Full Screen** button again to reduce the video to actual size.

VIDEO

```
13    <div id="flashContent">
14      <object classid="clsid:d27cdb6e-ae6d-11cf-96b8-444553540000" width="874" height="640" id="FullScreen" align="middle">
15        <param name="movie" value="FullScreen.swf" />
16        <param name="quality" value="high" />
17        <param name="bgcolor" value="#ffffff" />
18        <param name="play" value="true" />
19        <param name="loop" value="true" />
20        <param name="wmode" value="window" />
21        <param name="scale" value="showall" />
22        <param name="menu" value="true" />
23        <param name="devicefont" value="false" />
24        <param name="salign" value="" />
25        <param name="allowScriptAccess" value="sameDomain" />
26        <param name="allowFullScreen" value="true" />
27        <!--[if !IE]>-->
28        <object type="application/x-shockwave-flash" data="FullScreen.swf" width="874" height="640">
29          <param name="movie" value="FullScreen.swf" />
30          <param name="quality" value="high" />
31          <param name="bgcolor" value="#ffffff" />
32          <param name="play" value="true" />
33          <param name="loop" value="true" />
34          <param name="wmode" value="window" />
35          <param name="scale" value="showall" />
36          <param name="menu" value="true" />
37          <param name="devicefont" value="false" />
38          <param name="salign" value="" />
39          <param name="allowScriptAccess" value="sameDomain" />
40          <param name="allowFullScreen" value="true" />
41        <!--<![endif]-->
```

Figure 10-36. Set two `allowFullScreen` attributes in the HTML's `<object>` and `<embed>` tags to `true` to allow full-screen playback.

Figure 10-37. Full-screen video is a reality with Flash CS5.

CHAPTER 10

Full-screen video using Dreamweaver CS5

The previous exercise contained a "fatal flaw." If you are a web designer, you probably looked at that exercise and said, "That ain't the way a designer does it." We agree. More often than not, the web designer is going to only require the SWF, and they will put it into place in a predesigned layout. Let's assume the designer already has a Dreamweaver CS5 page prepared and needs to add the SWF and the full-screen capability. Here's how:

1. Open a new Dreamweaver CS5 HTML page, and save it to your FullScreen folder in this chapter's Exercise folder.

2. Switch to Design View, and click once on the page.

3. Select Insert ➤ Media ➤ SWF (Figure 10-38), and when the Select Swf dialog box opens, navigate to the SWF you created in the previous exercise. Select it, and click OK to close the dialog box. When you return to the Dreamweaver page, you will see the SWF is nothing more than a great big gray box. If you test the page in a browser (File ➤ Preview in Browser ➤ Choose a browser), you will discover that the Full Screen button doesn't work. You need to tell Dreamweaver to make that button operative.

Figure 10-38. You insert the SWF, not the FLV/F4V, file into Dreamweaver.

4. Select the SWF on the page, and click the Parameters button in the Dreamweaver Properties panel. This will open the Parameters dialog box.

5. Click once on the + sign, which is the **Add parameter** button, and enter **AllowFullScreen** as the parameter. Press the Tab key to go to the **Value** area of the parameter just entered and enter **true**. As shown in Figure 10-39, this parameter is now added to the lineup. Click **OK** to close the **Parameters** dialog box, and test the page in a browser.

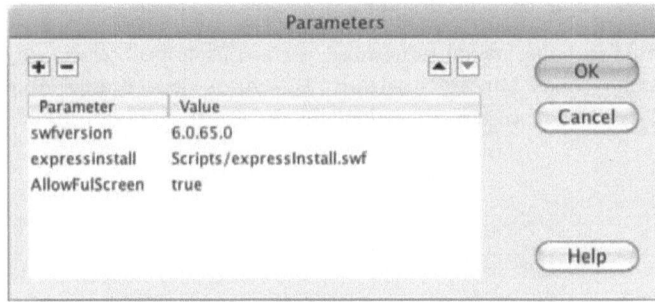

Figure 10-39. Dreamweaver needs to be told that the **Full Screen** button is live.

When video is not video

Up to this point in the chapter, we have treated video as entertainment. The user simply watches it. In this case, video is a rather passive medium. However, sometimes video becomes content and does not require a player, captions, or even full-screen capability. In this case, video can be imported directly into a Flash movie clip, which makes it fully accessible to Flash as content on the stage.

Before we start, we want you to be real clear on a fact of video life: video files are large, and importing any of the files you have worked with so far in the chapter directly onto the Flash timeline would be a major error. When considering working with video content on the Flash timeline, think short—loops of about two seconds—and think small. The physical size of the video should match precisely the area of the stage where it will be used.

> The FLV files used in this exercise were all created in Adobe After Effects. For details about creating such videos, see From After Effects to Flash: Poetry in Motion Graphics by Tom Green and Tiago Dias (friends of ED, 2006).

Embedding video

Earlier, we told you that embedding video in the timeline was, well, evil. Now we are going to show you when this can actually be a good thing. The following exercise demonstrates how this works:

1. Create a new Flash document, and change the stage size to 468 pixels wide by 60 pixels high, which is a common banner ad size.

2. Select **File ▶ Import ▶ Import Video**. This will launch the **Import Video** wizard.

3. On the Select Video page, navigate to the Apparition.flv file in your Chapter 10 Exercise folder.

4. On the same page, select Embed video in SWF and play in timeline. You will see a missive at the bottom of the dialog box warning you of the evils of this technique, but don't worry—the file isn't that big. Click the Continue button to open the Embedding page.

5. On the Embedding page, select Embedded video from the Symbol type drop-down menu. Also be sure the check boxes for Place instance on stage, Expand timeline if needed, and Include audio are selected, as shown in Figure 10-40. Click the Continue button.

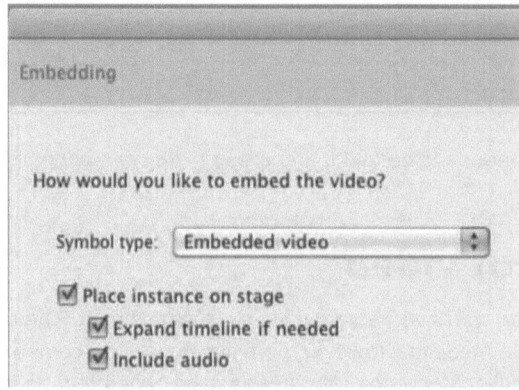

Figure 10-40. Embedding an FLV file in the Flash timeline

6. On the Finish Video Import page, click the Finish button to return to the Flash stage. You will see a progress bar, and when it finishes, the video will be on the stage, and the timeline will expand to accommodate the number of frames in the video.

7. Select the video, and in the Properties panel, set its X and Y values to 0. If you open the Library, you will also see the video is in a video object.

8. Add a new layer to the timeline and enter your name.

9. Save and test the movie. The weird ghostlike apparitions move around behind your name (see Figure 10-41).

Figure 10-41. Embedded video can be used as content.

Embedding video as a movie clip

In this next exercise, you are going to create a rainy day in the mountains of Southern California. In this example, you will discover the power of matching Flash's blend modes with video.

1. Open the `Rainfall.fla` file in your Chapter 10 Exercise folder. You will see that we have placed an image of the mountains on the stage.

2. Click the first frame of the `Video` layer. Select `File` ➤ `Import to stage`. In the Import dialog box, select the `Rain.flv` file, and click `Open`. This will launch the Import Video wizard.

3. Embed the video in the timeline, as in this previous exercise, but this time, when you reach the `Embedding` page, select `Movie clip` as the symbol type, as shown in Figure 10-42. This is a good way to go, because it routes all the necessary timeline frames into a movie clip timeline, rather than expanding the main timeline off a mile to the right.

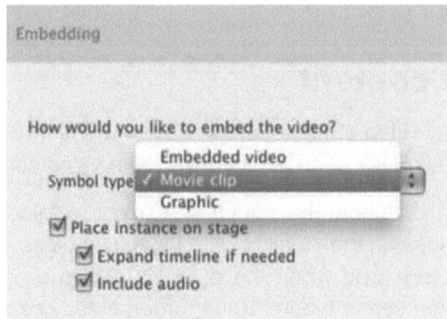

Figure 10-42. Embedded video can be turned into a Flash movie clip.

4. The new movie clip will appear in the first frame of the `Video` layer. Using the `Properties` panel, set its `X` and `Y` values to `0`. Obviously a big, black movie clip that hides the mountains isn't doing the job. Let's fix that.

5. Select the movie clip on the stage, and in the `Properties` panel, set the movie clip's `Blending` option to `Add`. The rain becomes visible, as shown in Figure 10-43.

6. Save and test the movie. Sit back and enjoy the rain fall.

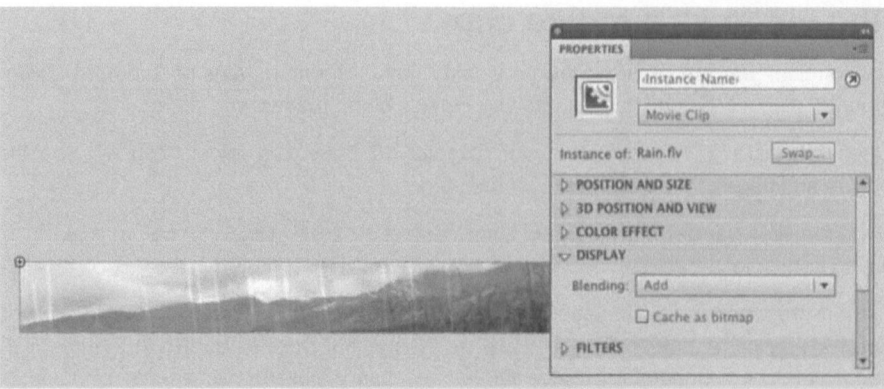

Figure 10-43. Use the `Add` mode to remove the black background in the FLV.

Interacting with video content

So far, you have discovered how video content can interact with Flash content. In the next exercise, you are going in the opposite direction: Flash content interacting with video content.

1. Open the `BlobEffect.fla` file in this chapter's `Exercise` folder. You will see we have already placed an embedded video on the timeline. The video is a blobs effect. To see it, open the **Blobs** movie clip in the **Library**, and when the **Symbol Editor** opens, press Enter (Windows) or Return (Mac). As you can see in Figure 10-44, green blobs ooze from the top of the window and coalesce into a giant blob, which then splits apart into smaller blobs.

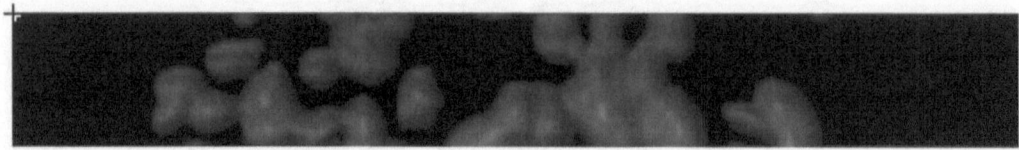

Figure 10-44. We start with some green blobs, which is an FLV file embedded into a movie clip.

2. Click in the **Text** layer, select the **Text** tool (or press T), and enter your name. Use a font and size of your choosing. In the **Properties** panel, change the color of the text to `#FFFF00` (bright yellow).

3. With the text selected, convert the text to a movie clip symbol named **Name**.

4. With the **Name** movie clip symbol selected, select **Overlay** from the **Blending** drop-down menu.

The text will disappear. This is because the `Overlay` mode either multiplies or screens the colors, depending on the destination color, which is the color immediately under the text. In this case, the yellow text is against a black background, so you can't see the effect.

5. Save and play the movie. Notice how the text changes and becomes visible as the blobs pass under it, as shown in Figure 10-45.

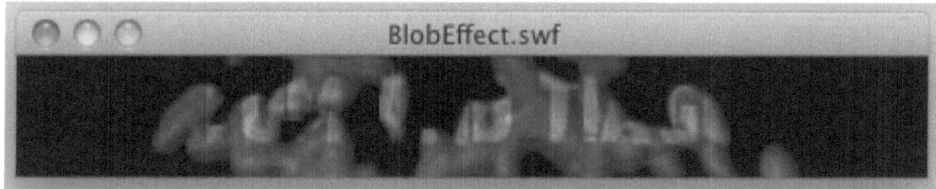

Figure 10-45. A classic example of Flash content interacting with video content

Adding cue points

You can add cue points to an FLV file in four ways:

- Add them when you create the FLV file in the Adobe Media Encoder.
- Add them using the `FLVPlayback` component's parameters.
- Add them using the `addASCuePoint()` method in ActionScript.
- Add them using an XML document.

The first two methods are what we call **destructive**. Once you add a cue point using those two methods, it can't be removed. This means if your timing is off, the video will need to be reencoded and new cue points added. Here's some self-defense if you go with either of those methods: don't remove the video from the render queue until the video is approved for play. In this circumstance—and it works only for cue points added in the Adobe Media Encoder—you select the video in the render queue and choose `Edit ➤ Reset Status`. When you return to the `Cue Points` tab, all the cue points will be there, and they can be removed and changed.

The second method is one we showed you earlier in the chapter. You can use the cue points feature of the `Properties` panel to add them. The downside to this is if changes need to be made you need to have ready access to the original FLA.

The last two ways are the most flexible because, if the timing is off, you simply open the code and change a number.

Here, we will concentrate on using an XML document to insert the cue points. Before we dig into the XML, you should know that in Flash video, there are three flavors of cue points:

- **Navigation cue points**: These cue points do exactly what the name implies: they are used to navigate, seek, and trigger ActionScript methods. If you create a navigation cue point, Flash will actually insert a keyframe at that point in the video.
- **Event cue points**: These are the most common. They tell Flash and/or ActionScript to do something when they are encountered.
- **ActionScript cue points**: These can be used only if you are using the `Cue Points` area in the `Properties` panel. They can be used either for navigation or to initiate events while the video plays.

In the upcoming exercise, you will create event cue points that will be used to tell Flash to display a caption.

An alternate XML format for cue points

We tend to think the Timed Text format described earlier in this chapter is the way to go for cue points, if only because it's a nonproprietary specification. However, it's good to know your options. You may just decide to use the alternate approach described in this section instead. If you do, there is a very specific format you must follow. Let's look at it.

Open the `CuePoints.xml` document in this chapter's `Exercise/YourTurn` folder. You can use Dreamweaver CS5, a simple text editor, or even a word processor for this purpose. Just make sure that when you save the file, you save it as plain text. When the document opens, the first "chunk" of code you will encounter is the following:

```
<?xml version="1.0" encoding="UTF-8" standalone="no" ?>
<FLVCoreCuePoints>
 <CuePoint>
  <Time>9000</Time>
  <Type>event</Type>
  <Name>fl.video.caption.2.0.0</Name>
  <Parameters>
  <Parameter>
  <Name>text</Name>
    <Value><![CDATA[<font face="Arial, Helvetica, _sans"
 size="12">Look ... up in the sky ... look...</font>]]></Value>
  </Parameter>
  <Parameter>
  <Name>endTime</Name>
  <Value>11.0</Value>
  </Parameter>
  </Parameters>
 </CuePoint>
</FLVCoreCuePoints>
```

This is the syntax that must be used. Deviate from it at your own peril. The first line specifies the encoding for the document, and the second line tells Flash that anything between the `<FLVCoreCuePoints>` tags is to be considered within the context of a cue point.

Each cue point you will add must be enclosed between `<CuePoint>` and `</CuePoint>` tags. The `<Time>` tag is the start of the cue point, and this number must be expressed in milliseconds. The next tag, `<Type>`, tells Flash that the cue point is to be an event cue point, and the tag following it, `<Name>`, is the name of the cue point.

The rules regarding naming are rigid. The `<Name>` tag must be `fl.video.caption.2.0` followed by a series of sequential numbers to guarantee unique values. In our sample XML, it goes `fl.video.caption.2.0.0`, `fl.video.caption.2.0.1`, and so on.

The parameters contain the styling data for the text that will appear in the caption and an end time for the caption. Later in the actual XML document, you'll see that we used the `<i>` tag to identify who is speaking by setting the person's name in italics.

The `endTime` property, which must be expressed in seconds, will be the time when the caption disappears from the screen. This number can be an integer (no decimals) or can contain up to three decimal places.

Finally, you may optionally contend with using color in captions, and there are a couple of rules involving this as well. If you scroll down to `caption 2.0.7` in the file, you will see the text in the caption uses `#FF0000`, which is a bright red. A couple of lines later, the `backgroundColor` parameter changes the background color of the caption to `0x01016D`, which is a dark blue.

The key here is how the colors are identified. Colors are specified by hexadecimal values, but the *indication* that the color is in hexadecimal notation—# or 0x—depends on where it's being stated. The first change to the red uses the pound sign, #, as traditionally used in HTML. Why? It's because it appears within HTML-formatted content. The second change—to the dark blue—uses the format for specifying hexadecimal notation in ActionScript, 0x.

If you do change the background color of a caption, that color will "stick." This means all subsequent captions will use this background color. If you need only a single change, as in our example, change the `backgroundColor` parameter back in the next cue point. In our case, we changed it to black again (0x000000), as seen in `caption 2.0.8`.

Do your sanity a favor and separate each caption with an empty line or two in the XML. This makes the captions easier to read and locate. The blank space, called **whitespace**, will be ignored by Flash.

What does all of this have to do with cue points and FLV files? You are about to find out. First, though, you need to download a cartoon.

HTML TAGS AND FLASH

HTML tags may be used only if they're supported by Flash. They are as follows:

- **Anchor tag** (`<a>`): If you want to make a hyperlink without using the **Properties** panel, this is your tag. This tag supports two attributes:
    - `href`: An absolute or relative URL, up to 128 characters in length. This attribute corresponds to the **Link** setting of the **Properties** panel and is required if you want the hyperlink to actually do something. If you're opening a web document, use the `http:` or `https:` protocol. If you want to trigger ActionScript instead, use the `event:` protocol. More on this in the section "Hyperlinks and Flash text."
    - `target`: One of four values that correspond to the **Target** setting of the **Properties** panel: `_blank` (opens the URL in a new browser window), `_parent` (opens the URL in the parent frameset of an HTML frameset), `_self` (opens the URL in the same window or frame as the current HTML document that holds this SWF; this is the default behavior), and `_top` (opens the URL in the topmost window of a frameset, replacing the frameset with the new URL).
- **Bold tag** (`<b>`): Makes text bold, if the current font supports it. Yes, even though HTML jockeys are all using `<strong>` nowadays, Flash Player doesn't support it. Use the `<b>` tag.
- **Break tag** (`<br>`): Represents a line break.
- **Font tag** (`<font>`): Provides three ways to format the styling of text, by way of the following attributes:
    - `color`: A hex value representing a color.
    - `face`: The name of a font.
    - `size`: The size of the font in pixels. You may also use relative sizes, such as +2 or –1.
- **Image tag** (`<img>`): Displays a graphic file, movie clip, or SWF inside a text field. Supported graphic formats are JPEG, GIF, and PNG. This tag may be configured by way of quite a few attributes:
    - `src`: This, the only required attribute, specifies the URL of an external image or SWF, or the linkage class for a movie clip symbol in the **Library** (see the "Symbol essentials" and "Sharing assets" sections of Chapter 3). External files do not appear until they are fully loaded, so depending on your needs, you may want to embed content in the SWF itself. To refer to embedded **Library** content, simply use the linkage class as the value for the `src` attribute—`<img src='MyLinkageClass' />`—instead of the path to an external file.
    - `id`: If you want to control the content of your image tag with ActionScript, you'll need to know the instance name of the movie clip that contains that content. This is where you provide that instance name.
    - `width` and `height`: These specify the width and height of the image, SWF, or movie clip in pixels. If you like, you may scale content along the x axis and y axis by setting these attributes arbitrarily.

- **align**: This determines how text will flow around the image, SWF, or movie clip. The default value is `left`, and you may also specify `right`.
- **hspace** and **vspace**: Just as with HTML, these values determine how much "padding" appears around the image, SWF, or movie clip. Horizontal space is controlled by `hspace`, and vertical space is controlled by `vspace`. The default is 8 pixels. A value of 0 gets rid of the padding, and negative numbers bring in the edges, pulling in adjacent content with them.
- **checkPolicyFile**: This instructs Flash Player to check for a cross-domain policy file on the server associated with the image's or SWF's domain.

- **Italic tag** (`<i>`): Makes text italicized, if the current font supports it. Like our note for the `<b>` tag, use `<i>` for italics in text field HTML, as opposed to the `<em>` tag generally preferred by web developers nowadays.

- **List item tag** (`<li>`): Indents text and precedes it with a round bullet. In the case of normal HTML, `<li>` tags may be further managed by parent list tags. The bullets of unordered lists (`<ul>`), for example, may be specified as circle, disk, or square. The bullets of ordered lists (`<ol>`) may be specified as numbers, roman numerals, or letters. This is not the case in the microcosm of Flash HTML. Lists require neither a `<ul>` nor an `<ol>` tag, are unordered only, and feature only round bullets.

- **Paragraph tag** (`<p>`): Our good, old-fashioned paragraph tag. Paragraphs come with a built-in line break, and you get two attributes with this tag:
  - **align**: This affects the text alignment. Valid settings are `left`, `right`, `center`, and `justified`—the same alignments available in the **Properties** panel.
  - **class**: This specifies the name of a CSS class selector, which can be used to stylize content.

- **Span tag** (`<span>`): This tag doesn't do anything on its own, but it accepts a class attribute that supports CSS, and that attribute is `styling`.

- **Text format tag** (`<textformat>`): In many ways, this is the HTML version of the `TextFormat` class. Use the following parameters to stylize text content:
  - **blockindent**: Determines block indentation.
  - **indent**: Determines indentation of the first line only and accepts both positive and negative values.
  - **leading**: Affects line spacing. It accepts both positive and negative values.
  - **leftmargin**, **rightmargin**: Determines the left and right margins of the text.
  - **tabstops**: Specifies tab stops.

- **Underline tag** (`<u>`): Makes text underlined. This tag is the easiest way to underline text in Flash (other than through CSS styling).

Your turn: create XML captions for video

In the 1940s, the original Superman cartoons were produced by a gentleman named Max Fleischer. A small number of these cartoons have entered the public domain, which means that they are free for you to download and use. One of them, "Superman: the Mechanical Monsters," is the cartoon you will be captioning. To remain purer than pure, we aren't including the cartoon in the `Exercise` downloads. We would respectfully ask that you head over to www.archive.org/details/superman_the_mechanical_monsters. The download options are on the left side of the page, offering files in different compressions and sizes. In theory, it doesn't matter which file you download. We used the `256Kb MPEG4 (27MB)` version.

> *We find it rather fascinating that the copy of the video that plays on the page is Flash video. It's a low-quality one, but it's Flash video all the same.*

Now that you have downloaded the source video, proceed as follows:

1. Open the Adobe Media Encoder, and drag the video from its location into the render queue.
2. Open the `Export Settings` window. Enter `Superman` as the output filename, and select `FLV` as the format.
3. Click the `Video` tab. Ensure you are using the `On2 VP6` codec, Deselect `Resize Video` if it is selected; in the `Bitrate` settings, use `VBR` and `Two` encoding passes. Reduce the `Bitrate` value to `300`.
4. Click the `Audio` tab. Change `Output Channels` to `Mono`, and reduce `Bitrate` to `64` kbps.

Let's now turn our attention to the cue points area under the preview. This is where all of the pain, sweat, and aggravation that went into creating the XML document comes into play. The care and diligence you put into ensuring all of the tags in the XML document are correct are about to pay off. How so? Let's add the first cue point manually to give you the idea.

5. Scrub the playback head of the FLV to the `00:00:09;500` mark of the video.
6. Click the + button (which is the `Add Cue Point` button). Enter `fl.video.caption.2.0.0` as the name of the cue point. Notice how the default value for `Type` is `Event`.
7. Click the `Add Parameter` button, and enter `Text` into the name area. Click in the `Value` area, and enter `<font face="Arial, Helvetica, _sans" size="12">Up in the sky, look!</font>`.
8. Click the `Add Parameter` button, and enter `endTime` as the name and `10.9` as the value. The cue point appears in the cue point area, as shown in Figure 10-46.

Now repeat steps 6, 7, and 8 about 30 more times to add the remaining cue points. (Yeah, we are kidding.)

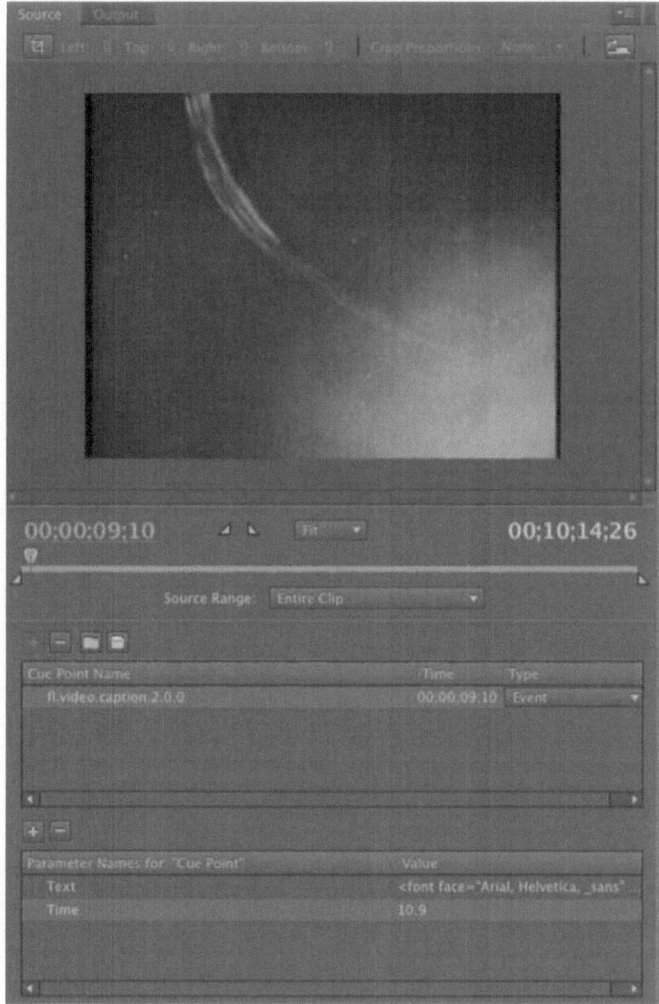

Figure 10-46. Manually adding cue points to an FLV

Obviously, going the manual route is tedious at best. Surely there must be an easier method. There is: embed the CuePoints.xml document directly into the FLV file. Let's use that technique.

9. Select the cue point, and click the **Remove Cue Point** button (the – sign) to remove the cue point you just added.

10. Click the file folder icon (the **Navigate** button) in the cue points area. This will open the **Load Cue Points File** dialog box. Navigate to the 15_YourTurn_CuePoints folder, select the CuePoints.xml file, and click the **Open** button.

In the cue points area, you will notice all the cue points in the XML document have been added. If you select the first one, you will see that the parameters have also been added, as shown in Figure 10-47.

> *Seeing the cue point parameters can be a little tricky. Don't click the cue point's name. That will select the name. Click in the gray area of the strip between the* Cue Point Name *and* Time *areas, and the parameters for that cue point will appear.*

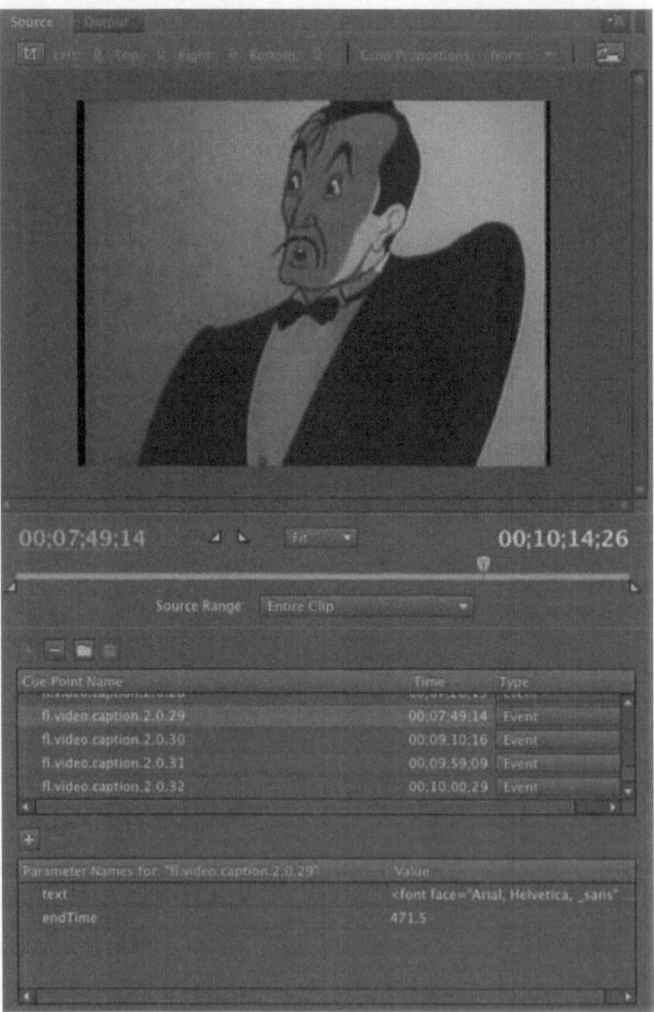

Figure 10-47. Load the XML, and the cue points and their parameters are added in less than one second.

VIDEO

11. Click the OK button to return to the render queue. Click the **Start Queue** button to encode the cartoon.

12. Return to Flash CS5 and create a new document. Save this document to the YourTurn folder.

13. Drag an **FLVPlayback** component to the stage, add a skin (we used **SkinUnderAllNoFullScreen.swf**), and set the **source** parameter to the FLV file you just created. When the dialog box closes, you will see all of the event cue points from the XML document are listed.

14. Drag a copy of the **FLVPlaybackCaptioning** component anywhere onto the pasteboard or stage (it doesn't really matter where, because the component is invisible in the published SWF).

You will notice you don't need to add the CuePoints.xml document as a parameter in the **FLVPlaybackCaptioning** component. All it has to do is be present in the SWF. You only need to do configure the parameter when using Timed Text captions.

15. Save and test the movie. Notice how the captions automatically appear, as shown in Figure 10-48.

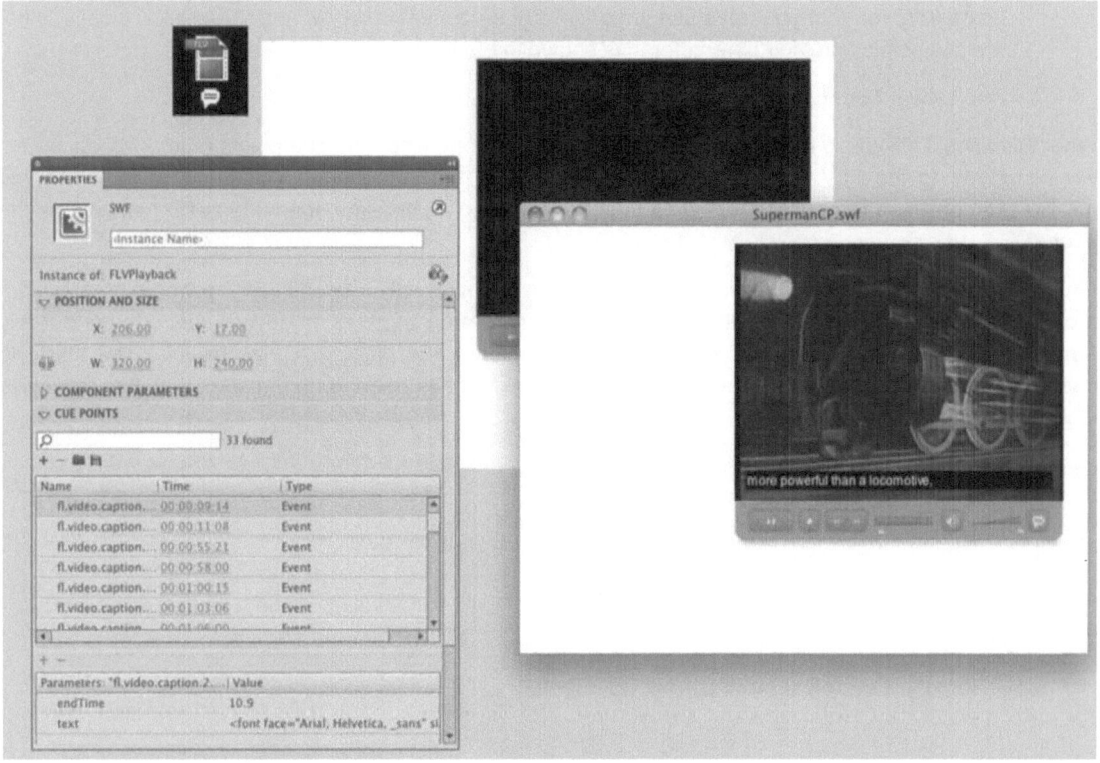

Figure 10-48. The **FLVPlaybackCaptioning** component only needs to be in the SWF and doesn't require configuration.

591

Bonus round

You don't need to add the cue points in the XML document in the Adobe Media Encoder. There is a new way of doing it. Here's how:

1. Open the `CuePoints.xml` document in Dreamweaver CS 5 or a text editor.
2. Select the word event in the first `<type></type>` tag, and using the **Search and Replace** feature of your software, change the word from event to **actionscript**.
3. Save the file as `Superman.xml`.
4. Open a new Flash document, save it to the `15_YourTurn_CuePoints` folder. Heave an FLVPlayback component onto the stage, and set the source to the `SupermanNoCuePoints.flv` file in that folder.
5. Select the component on the stage, and in the **Cue Points** area of the **Properties** panel, click the **Import ActionScript Cue Points** button, which opens the **Import ActionScript Cue Points** dialog box.
6. Navigate to the `Superman.xml` file you just created, and click **Open**. You will see a small **Alert** box telling you that you have just imported 33 cue points. Click **OK**. When the alert closes, all of the cue points and their parameters, as shown in Figure 10-49, will appear.
7. Add a **Captioning** component to the pasteboard and test your movie.

What this should tell you is that you need to determine, up front, when the cue points in an XML document will be added to the FLV. If it is during the encoding of the video, then you need to put event or navigation between the `<type>` `</type>` tags. If it is during author time, then use actionscript as the `<type>`.

Finally, if you think these two exercises are nothing more than "mildly interesting," you would be making a profound error in judgment. One of the reasons Flash video rarely appears on government or other publicly funded/subsidized websites is that video was, for all intents and purposes, inaccessible. The ability to easily add captioned video and to turn the captions on and off has opened up a market that was otherwise closed to Flash designers and developers.

VIDEO

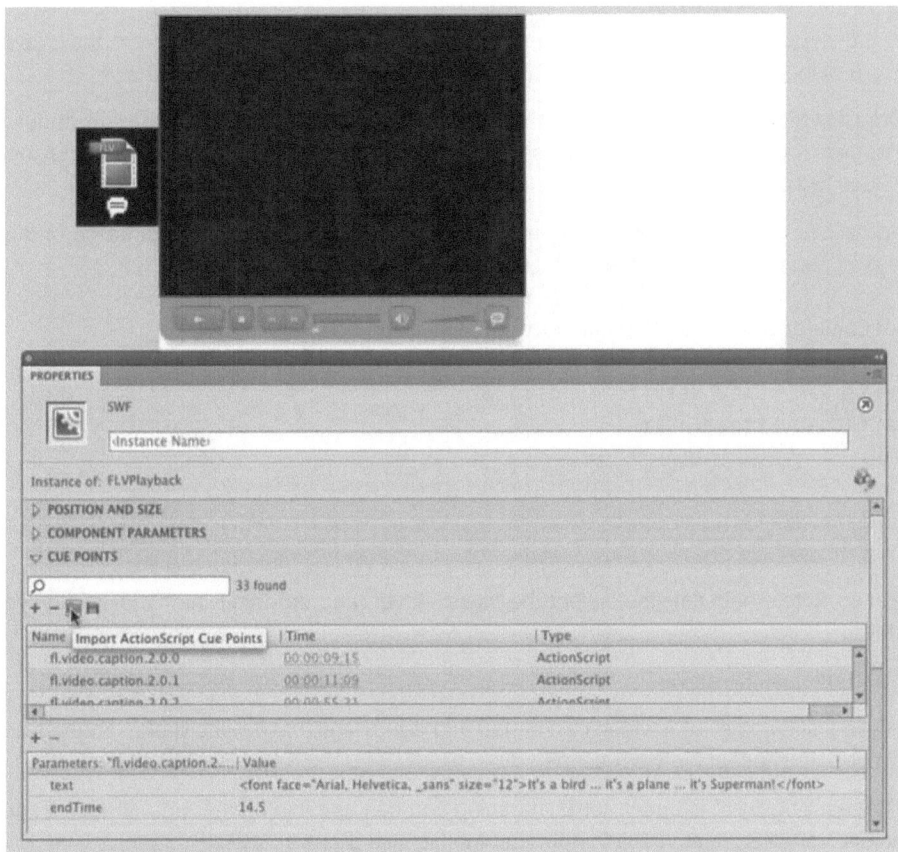

Figure 10-49. The XML cue points can be added using the `Properties` panel.

Your turn: play with alpha video

In this exercise, we introduce you to a couple of new concepts. The first is that video doesn't necessarily need to use the `FLVPlayback` component and reside on the main timeline for it to work. The second concept is that just because it is video is no reason for not having fun with it. Let's start jamming with video:

1. Open the `VideoJam.fla` file in the Chapter 10 `Exercise` folder. You will notice we have provided the background image.
2. Create a new movie clip symbol, and name it `Video`.

3. In the **Symbol Editor**, open the **Library**, and select **New Video** from the **Library** drop-down menu. Just click **OK** when the **Video Properties** dialog box opens.

4. Drag the video object from the **Library** onto the stage. In the **Properties** panel, give it the instance name of **myVideo**, set its **X** and **Y** values to **0**, and change its **Width** and **Height** values to **320** and **214**.

5. Add a new layer to the movie clip, and name it **Actions**. Select the first frame of the **Actions** layer, open the **Actions** panel, and enter the following code:

```
var nc:NetConnection = new NetConnection();
nc.connect(null);
var ns:NetStream = new NetStream(nc);
myVideo.attachNetStream(ns);

ns.client = {};
ns.play("Alpha.flv");
```

6. Return to the main timeline, select the **Video** layer, and drag your new movie clip symbol to the stage.

7. Save and test the movie.

What you have just discovered is video can be put into a movie clip and will still play on the main timeline. This is an important concept for two reasons:

- The resulting SWF is under 30KB, meaning you can use it in banner ads. In fact, if you want it to be even smaller, remove the image, and the file size drops to 1KB.
- Objects contained in movie clips are open to creative manipulation.

Let's continue and check out that last point.

8. Select the movie clip on the stage, and twirl down the **Filters** area of the **Properties** panel. Add a **Drop Shadow** filter, and apply these values:

    - **Blur X**: 15
    - **Blur Y**: 15
    - **Strength**: 75%
    - **Quality**: High
    - **Distance**: 10

9. Test the movie.

You'll see that the people in the video have all developed shadows, as shown in Figure 10-50. This is because the video, like a box drawn in a Flash file, a Fireworks PNG, or a Photoshop image, contains an alpha channel. In the case of video, this channel moves, and Flash applies the drop shadow to the channel. This looks OK, but let's give the subjects a bit of depth.

Figure 10-50. Filters can be applied to video contained in a movie clip.

   10. Select the movie clip on the stage, and add a `Bevel` filter to the video with these values:
       - `Blur X`: 6
       - `Blur Y`: 6
       - `Quality`: High
       - `Distance`: 3
   11. Save and test the movie.

The subjects take on a bit of depth, and you have also added a hint of backlighting, as shown in Figure 10-51. Don't get aggressive with filters; subtlety counts.

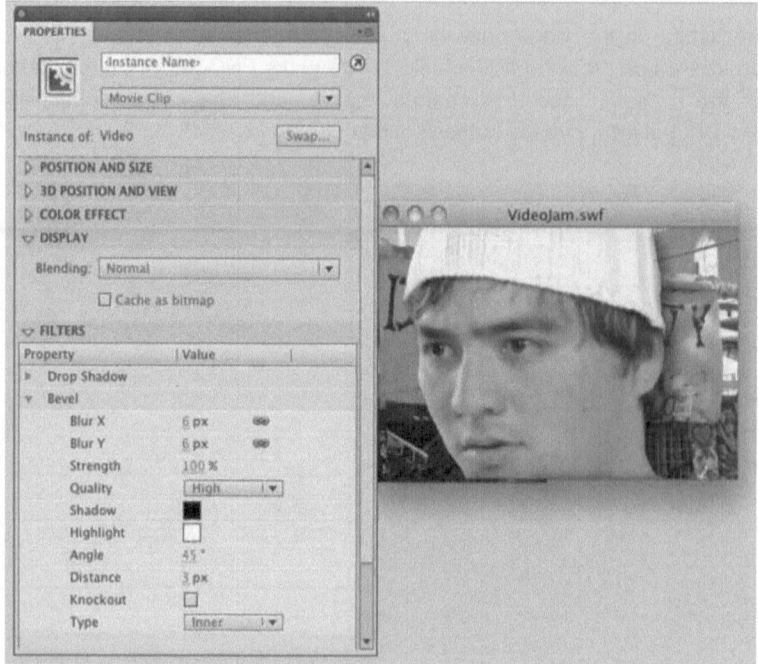

Figure 10-51. Multiple filters can be applied to video.

Hang on, these guys are ghosts. Can you turn them into ghosts? You bet.

12. In the `Filters` area, select the `Drop Shadow` filter, and select `Knockout`, `Inner Shadow`, and `Hide Object`.

13. Test the movie.

You have a 3D ghost. Interesting, but can you do better, of course.

14. In the `Filters` area, select the `Drop Shadow` filter and deselect `Knockout`, `Inner Shadow`, and `Hide Object`.

15. Twirl down `Display` in the `Properties` panel.

16. Select the video on the stage, and select `Overlay` from the `Display` area's `Blending` drop-down menu.

17. Test the video.

You'll see that the subjects take on a "ghost-like" appearance, as shown in Figure 10-52.

Figure 10-52. Don't be afraid to use the blend modes to create some interesting effects.

Your turn: think big, really big!

In this final exercise in this chapter, we want you to think big, and we mean really big. We are talking full-screen, HD video. Using the `FLVPlayback` component to go full-screen has one small issue: the stage is what goes full screen. That means the content on the stage scales up with it. With HD content—720p and higher—this put a huge strain on the computer. The solution, which has been part of Flash Player since Flash Player 9.0.115.0 quietly switched on HD, is to use hardware acceleration.

Hardware acceleration is applied through Flash Player. Simply right-click (Windows) or Control+click (Mac) any video playing in a web page to open the `Flash Player` dialog box. Click the `Display` icon (It looks like a monitor), and you will see the dialog box shown in Figure 10-53. Select `Enable hardware acceleration`, and you are good to go.

CHAPTER 10

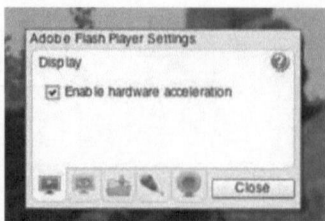

Figure 10-53. Enabling hardware acceleration

We suggest you open the fullScreenRect.fla file in your Exercise folder, and take a peek at the code. The "magic" is found in the in the goFullScreen function at the end of the code:

```
function goFullScreen( e:MouseEvent ):void
{
        stage.fullScreenSourceRect = screenRect;
        stage.displayState = StageDisplayState.FULL_SCREEN;
}
```

The first line of the function—stage.fullScreenSourceRect = screenRect;—essentially tells Flash to create a rectangle that will hover over the stage. This rectangle, in extremely simplistic terms, will be filled with the video object and the button. The next line tells the stage to pop out to full screen, and when it does, only the rectangle and its contents are scaled out to full-screen, and hardware acceleration takes over to play the video.

What we suggest you do is to add this code to your **Code Snippets** panel and to make the changes indicated in the comments.

Finally you can use the HTML template—**Flash Only: Allow Full Screen**—in the **Publish Settings** or use Dreamweaver to tell the HTML page to permit full-screen video.

If you want to try it, open the fullScreenRect.html page in your Exercise folder in a browser.

What you have learned

In this chapter, you learned the following:

- How video can be streamed from your web server
- How to use the Adobe Media Encoder
- How to encode video containing an alpha channel
- Several methods of embedding and streaming video without using the **FLVPlayback** component
- How to display HD content in Flash Player

- How to add Timed Text captions to a video and how to use the `FLVPLaybackCaptioning` component
- An alternate XML captioning approach
- The power of the creative use of filters and blend effects that can be applied to video

This has been quite the chapter, and we suspect you are just as excited about the possibilities of Flash video as we are. The key to the use of Flash video is really quite simple: keep an eye on the pipe. The Adobe Media Encoder is one of the most powerful tools in the Flash video arsenal, and mastering it is the key to Flash video success. From there, as we showed you in several exercises, the only limit to what you can do with Flash video is the one you put on your creativity. Just don't overdo it. Video need to be regarded as content not entertainment and just because "I can do it" is no reason to use it. Video, now, is nothing more than a JPEG image on the stage, and there must be a valid reason for its inclusion.

As you started working with the Flash video components, we just know you were wondering, "How do those user interface components work?" Great question, and we answer it in the next chapter.

Chapter 11

Building Interfaces with the UI Components

Since early in its life, Flash has proven itself the leader in web animation. In recent years, that dominance has nudged into the realm of online applications as well. For user-facing applications, you need user interface (UI) elements, plain and simple—something to receive input from the person viewing your content or display information in a specific way, such as in a grid or selection box. Sure, you've already seen how button symbols work, and you're aware that input text fields accept hand-typed content. They are a good start, but they are really nothing more than the tip of the iceberg.

The UI components that ship with Flash CS5 are a major improvement over the set that first appeared in Flash 8, in a number of ways: they are smaller (much smaller), they perform better, (faster), and they are much easier to customize.

> *As a bonus, Flash CS5 even gives you the previous set, known as the v2 components, but those work only with ActionScript 2.0. That's an important point! They're for publishing older movies if you find that necessary. Choosing the Flash document type or changing your publish settings between ActionScript 3.0 and 2.0 automatically updates the* `Components` *panel to offer the correct set. You cannot mix and match components designed for different versions of ActionScript. If you were to use ActionScript 1.0, you would lose the UI components altogether!*

CHAPTER 11

Here's what we'll cover in this chapter:

- Using the Flash CS5 UI components
- Using ActionScript 3.0 to control components
- Changing component skins

The following files are used in this chapter (located in Chapter11/ExerciseFiles_Ch11/Exercise/):

- Button02.fla
- ButtonTarget.fla
- StyleComponent.fla
- CheckBox.fla
- ColorPicker.fla
- ComboBox.fla
- DataGrid.fla
- Label.fla
- List.fla
- NumericStepper.fla
- ProgressBar.fla
- RedLeaves.jpg
- RadioButton.fla
- ScrollPane.fla
- Slider.fla
- TextArea.fla
- TextInput.fla
- TileList.fla
- Mug01.jpg–Mug08.jpg
- UILoader.fla
- Canoe.jpg

The source files are available online at www.friendsofED.com/download.html?isbn=1430229940.

Anyone familiar with HTML development knows how easy it is to add a check box, radio button, or other form element into a document. These are usually used in "Contact Us" pages, online surveys, and other application scenarios. Flash components provide you the same set of "widgets," but you also get a whole lot more, including components not possible in a browser alone. A smidgen of ActionScript is required to wire up components, but for the most part, adding them is a drag-and-drop operation.

Out of the box, the Flash UI components are styled in a modest, attractive manner that comfortably fits a broad range of designs. Of course, Flash being what it is—free from the relative constraints of HTML—you may want to customize their appearance, and you can. Designers and developers familiar with Flash 8 might warn you with a shudder that you're in for a barrel of headaches. Tell the old-timers they can breathe easy. Things have improved considerably in Flash CS5.

We'll start our exploration with the `Button` component and spend a bit more time with it than the others, simply because once you "get it," you get it. To be sure, certain components are more complex than others, and we certainly won't skimp as we visit each one. But if you're a complete newcomer, you may want to read through the "Button component" section first, and then breeze through the other headings until you find components of interest to you.

Button component

At first glance, the `Button` component is just another button symbol, but the two shouldn't be confused. As discussed in Chapter 3, button symbols have a specialized timeline, made of `Up`, `Over`, `Down`, and `Hit` frames. As such, button symbols are very flexible: `Over` artwork can be made to spill over the button's `Up` shape, paving the way for quick-and-dirty tooltips and other tricks. `Hit` artwork can make the button invisible—but still clickable—if it is the only frame with content. In contrast, the `Button` component has no discernable timeline. It's a self-contained component and is much more conservative (at first glance) than its wild, partying cousin the button symbol. Figure 11-1 shows an example of the `Button` component.

We also need you to prepare yourself. We are going to be spending what may, to you, seem to be an inordinate amount of time on something so simple. In actual fact, much of what we are going to talk about applies to all of the components. It is time well spent.

Figure 11-1. The `Button` component—pretty conservative, even without the tie

> Using one or more instances of the `Button` component in your movie will add 15KB to the SWF if no other components share the load.

Using the Button component

What makes the `Button` component so special? In two words, *consistency* and *toggleability*. The first of those, *consistency*, will be evident in each of the components we visit. If you accept the default skin for every component, you'll get a reliable uniformity among your UI widgets. The second word (OK, *toggleability* isn't actually a word) means that you get a button that optionally stays enabled after you click it and releases when you click it a second time. This useful feature is possible without a lick of ActionScript knowledge. Here's how:

1. Create a new Flash document, and click the **Components** button on the toolbar to open the **Components** panel.

2. In the **Components** panel, twirl down the **User Interface** branch. When it opens, you'll see the list of available UI components. Drag an instance of **Button** to the stage, as shown in Figure 11-2.

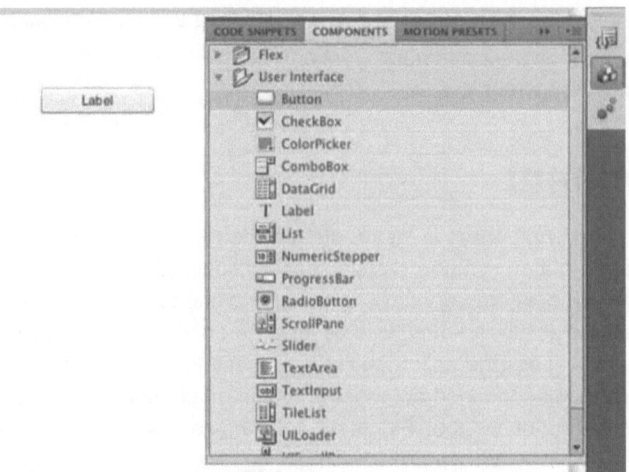

Figure 11-2. Adding a UI component to the stage is as easy as dragging and dropping.

Doing this drops a copy of the **Button** component and a folder named **Component Assets** into your **Library**. You can ignore the **Component Assets** folder for the time being. Any time you want additional **Button** instances from this point forward, drag them from your **Library**.

3. To give your button an instance name, click it on the stage, and then type **myButton** into the **Instance Name** field of the **Properties** panel.

Under normal circumstances, you should make your instance name something more meaningful—say, btnContact or submitForm—but for now, myButton will do.

4. If you like, use the **Free Transform** tool to change the dimensions of the button. Note that it resizes much like any symbol, but its text label stays the same size.

> *Skewing or rotating the button makes its label disappear because font outlines in components are not embedded by default. See Chapter 6 for more information font embedding.*

5. Out of the box, the button's label is the self-descriptive term `Label`. Let's change that. Open the **Properties** panel, twirl down **Component Parameters**, and double-click the right column in the `label` row. Change the word `Label` in the **Value** column to `Activate`, as shown in Figure 11-3. When this button becomes a toggle, you'll make it actually activate something. For now, leave the `toggle` parameter at its default setting of deselected.

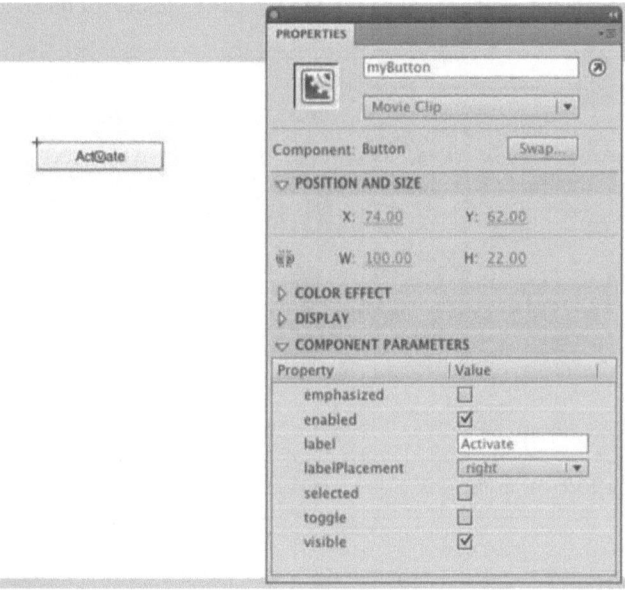

Figure 11-3. Instance names and parameters are now found in the **Properties** panel.

6. Rename your button's layer from `Layer 1` to `button`, and create a new layer. Name the new layer `scripts`, and lock that layer.

Wait a minute! Wasn't this exercise supposed to happen "without a lick of ActionScript knowledge"? In fact, it does. The configuration of your button—even the toggling part you'll see in step 9—all takes place within the **Properties** panel. The following code simply demonstrates that the button actually works (for an explanation of what this ActionScript does, see Chapter 4). ActionScript isn't required to get the toggle to do its thing.

7. Click inside frame 1 of the `scripts` layer. Open the **Actions** panel (**Window ➤ Actions**), and enter the following ActionScript:

```
myButton.addEventListener(MouseEvent.CLICK, clickHandler);
function clickHandler(evt:MouseEvent):void {
  trace("By George, I've been clicked!");
}
```

CHAPTER 11

8. Test your movie (to verify that a button click sends the message "By George, I've been clicked!" to the `Output` panel).

9. To make this button a toggle, return to the `Properties` panel's `Component Parameters` area, and click the `toggle` parameter to add a check mark. Test the movie again, if you like, to confirm that the button now stays in when you click it and pops out again when you click it a second time. Compare your work with `Button01.fla` in the `Complete` folder for this chapter.

> *The parameters available in the `Component Parameters` tab are also available via ActionScript. They're simply properties of the component's class. For example, instead of using the `Properties` panel to change the toggle parameter, you could have referenced the component's instance name:*
>
> ***myButton.toggle = true;***
> ```
> myButton.addEventListener(MouseEvent.CLICK, clickHandler);
> function clickHandler(evt:MouseEvent):void {
>   trace("By George, I've been clicked!");
> }
> ```
>
> *Note the use of the assignment operator (=), which sets a value, rather than the comparison operator (==), which consults a value. Properties set with ActionScript override parameters set in the `Properties` panel.*

Adding button events

To actually make use of this toggled/untoggled state, you will need to use the `BaseButton.selected` property of the `Button` component instance on the stage. Many button-like components, including `Button`, `CheckBox`, and `RadioButton`, inherit from the `BaseButton` class family tree. This means they support a `selected` property, just as their ancestor does. The button's instance name lets you access this property easily.

1. Open the `Button02.fla` file in this chapter's `Exercises` folder. This file picks up where we left off in the previous exercise. The only difference is a movie clip containing a JPEG image has been added to the `Library`. You're going to make this movie clip draggable, but only when the button is enabled.

2. Create a new layer, and name it `Weird Viking`. Select the new layer, and drag an instance of the movie clip `viking` to the stage. Give this movie clip the instance name `dude`.

3. In the `scripts` layer, select frame 1, and add the following new ActionScript beneath the existing code:

```
dude.addEventListener(MouseEvent.MOUSE_DOWN, dragViking);
function dragViking(evt:MouseEvent):void {
  if (myButton.selected == true) {
```

```
      dude.startDrag();
  }
};
dude.addEventListener(MouseEvent.MOUSE_UP, dropViking);
function dropViking(evt:MouseEvent):void {
  dude.stopDrag();
};
```

The key here is the if statement in the MouseEvent.MOUSE_DOWN handler, which is a custom function named dragDude(). The if evaluates the button's selected property as described previously. When it's set to true, dragging commences by way of the MovieClip.startDrag() method, as shown in Figure 11-4; otherwise, dragging is ignored. In the MouseEvent.MOUSE_UP handler, dragging is stopped.

Figure 11-4. Checking the button's selected property means that you can perform actions only when the button is clicked.

> To see the full list of events available to the **Button** component, look up the BaseButton class in the ActionScript 3.0 Language and Components Reference. Don't forget to select the **Show Inherited Styles** hyperlink beneath the **Events** heading!

4. For extra credit, let's handle the MouseEvent.CLICK event to add a bit of polish. Press the Enter (Windows) or Return (Mac) key a couple times after the existing code and type the following additional ActionScript:

```
myButton.addEventListener(MouseEvent.CLICK, clickHandler);
function clickHandler(evt:MouseEvent):void {
  if (myButton.selected == true) {
    dude.buttonMode = true;
  } else {
    dude.buttonMode = false;
  }
};
```

What's going on? This is nothing more than a third event handler. This one listens for a click and then triggers a custom function named `clickHandler()`. The function uses an `if` statement, just as you saw in the previous step, but this time, the evaluation sets the `MovieClip.buttonMode` property of the `dude` instance to `true` or `false`, depending on the toggled state of the button. When the button is toggled, the mouse cursor turns into a finger pointer as it rolls over `dude`. When the button is not toggled, the cursor remains in its default state: an arrow.

Referencing components in event handlers

In the previous code example, the **Button** component was referenced directly by its instance name in the event handler function. Here's another look, just as a reminder, with the instance name in bold:

```
function clickHandler(evt:MouseEvent):void {
if (myButton.selected == true) {
   dude.buttonMode = true;
  } else {
    dude.buttonMode = false;
  }
};
```

There's another way to get to that button—another way to make that same reference—and it can come in handy when you have numerous instances of a given component on the stage. Why? Because although you *could* write a separate function to handle events for each component, you might want to consolidate your functions in order to reduce complexity in your code.

First, consider a scenario with three **Button** components. Their **label** parameters are set to **Apples**, **Bananas**, and **Pears** in the **Properties** panel, and their instance names, respectively, are set to **btn1**, **btn2**, and **btn3** in the **Properties** panel. If you want to populate a dynamic text field whose instance name is output with the most recently clicked **Button**'s label, you could do it like this:

```
btn1.addEventListener(MouseEvent.CLICK, clickHandler1);
btn2.addEventListener(MouseEvent.CLICK, clickHandler2);
btn3.addEventListener(MouseEvent.CLICK, clickHandler3);

function clickHandler1(evt:MouseEvent):void {
  output.text = btn1.label;
};
function clickHandler2(evt:MouseEvent):void {
  output.text = btn2.label;
};
function clickHandler3(evt:MouseEvent):void {
  output.text = btn3.label;
};
```

So far, nothing new—and ultimately, nothing wrong. The code works, but it could be written in a more compact way. Consider the following abbreviated version:

```
btn1.addEventListener(MouseEvent.CLICK, clickHandler);
btn2.addEventListener(MouseEvent.CLICK, clickHandler);
btn3.addEventListener(MouseEvent.CLICK, clickHandler);

function clickHandler(evt:MouseEvent):void {
  output.text = evt.target.label;
};
```

In this case, all three buttons are associated with the same function, `clickHandler()`, rather than the individualized `clickHandler1()`, `clickHandler2()`, and `clickHandler3()`. So, how does the `Button` referencing work? The individual instance names are no longer part of the picture.

It all hinges on the `evt` variable between the function's parentheses. That variable, `evt`, points to an instance of the `MouseEvent` class—namely, the event triggered (`MouseEvent.CLICK`) when the user clicks any of the `Button` components. The click itself is an object. As such, `evt` features whatever properties and other class members are defined by the `MouseEvent` class. One of those properties is `target` (inherited from the `Event` class), which points to the object that dispatched the event in the first place. Here, the dispatcher is going to be `btn1`, `btn2`, or `btn3`, and the expression `evt.target` is as good a reference as any of those instance names. Because the expression `evt.target` points to an instance of the `Button` class, you can tack `label` onto the end of it. See the `ButtonTarget.fla` file in this chapter's `Complete` folder for a working example of the code just discussed.

Considering UI component weight

One final note before we start playing with the look of this component. Unlike normal `Library` assets, UI components add to the weight of your movie whether or not they're used. This is why seasoned Flash developers regard these things in much the same way Dracula regards garlic. The reason for this is that components are set to export for ActionScript. Right-click (Windows) or Control+click (Mac) any component in your `Library`, and choose `Properties` to see for yourself in the `Linkage` area of the `Symbol Properties` dialog box.

The first UI component in your movie usually adds the most weight, proportionately speaking, to the SWF. Some components weigh more than others, but all of them rely on a base framework that provides functionality for the whole set. For this reason, your first instance of `Button` will add 15KB. The second and third instances won't add anything. Your first `CheckBox` instance, on its own, will add 15KB, and additional `CheckBox` instances will add nothing. However, if you *already have* a `Button` instance in the movie and *then* add a `CheckBox`, the combined total of both components is only 16KB.

> *To remove the weight of these components—in case you change your mind and decide to omit them from your design—delete the component(s) and* Component Assets *folder from the* Library.

Changing the Button component's appearance

What you're about to see can be achieved with most of the UI components, not just `Button`. (Some components have little or no visual element, so there are exceptions.) This is good news, because it means you'll get the basic gist right off the bat.

There are two ways to alter a UI component's appearance:

- **Skinning**, which generally deals with the material substance of the component, such as the shape of the clickable surface of a button or the drag handle of a scrollbar
- **Styling**, which generally deals with text, style, and padding

Skinning

Before Flash CS3, the practice of skinning UI components was an exercise in alchemy. Only the wisest and purest of wizards would trust themselves to toss mysterious ingredients into the frothing cauldron. All of that changed when the components were rewritten for ActionScript 3.0, and the improvement remains intact in Flash CS5. In fact, it couldn't get much easier. Here's how:

1. Create a new Flash document, and drag an instance of the `Button` component to the stage. Double-click the button, and you'll see a convenient "buffet table" of the various visual states available to the button, as shown in Figure 11-5.

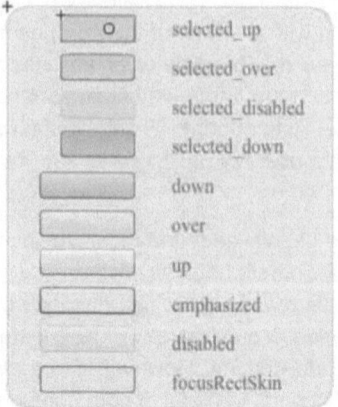

Figure 11-5. Skinning UI components is really easy.

2. The `up` skin is the button's default appearance. Double-click that, and you'll come to the symbol that represents the `up` skin for this component, complete with 9-slice scaling, as shown in Figure 11-6. This particular skin happens to be made of three layers.

BUILDING INTERFACES WITH THE UI COMPONENTS

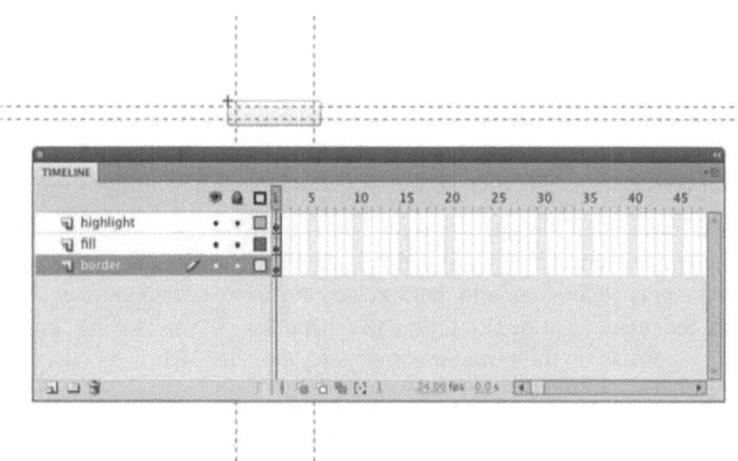

Figure 11-6. A mere two levels in, and you're ready to change the appearance of the button.

3. Select an area in one of these layers, and change the button's appearance, perhaps like Figure 11-7. The choice is yours. Make sure that the existing shapes, or any new ones, align to the upper left (0,0) of the symbol's registration point. Adjust the 9-slice guides as necessary.

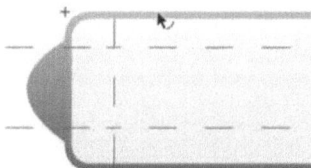

Figure 11-7. Adjust the existing shapes or create new ones.

4. Select **Edit ➤ Edit Document** or click the **Scene 1** link to return to the main timeline. What the...? In the authoring environment, your button hasn't changed. Folks, this is a fact of life with skins in Flash: there is no preview mode for skinning.

5. Test your movie to see that your alteration appears, for both buttons, as the new **up** skin in the published SWF. Click any button to verify that the remaining skins (for example, **down**) function as before. To see this in action, we have included an `SkinButton.fla` file in this chapter's `Complete` folder.

> To reskin a component completely, every skin symbol must be edited or replaced.

611

Styling components

As you've seen, components are easy enough to customize, even if a complete job takes some effort. You may have noticed an important omission, however, while poking around the skin symbols. Even though the `Button` component features a text label, none of the skins contains a text field. What if you want a different font in there, or at least a different color? ActionScript to the rescue.

Each component has its own list of styled elements. Many overlap, but you can see the definitive list for each in the class entry for that component. For example, find the Button class entry in the ActionScript 3.0 Language and Components Reference, and then browse the `Styles` heading, as shown in Figure 11-8. Don't forget to click the `Show Inherited Styles` hyperlink to see the full listing. Remember, the Button class gives you details on the `Button` component; the SimpleButton class gives you details on button symbols.

Components that include text elements, such as the `Button` component, support the inherited UIComponent.textFormat style, which lets you make changes to the button's text label. Other button styles include the inherited LabelButton.icon, which lets you specify an optional image for the button in addition to text.

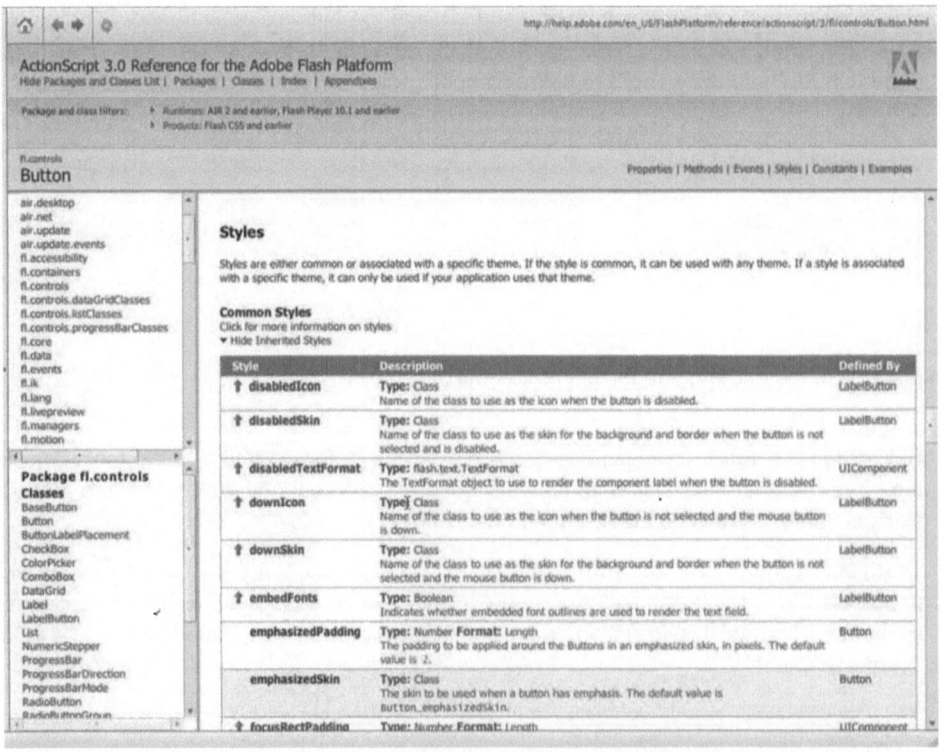

Figure 11-8. The full list of the `Button` component's styles can be found in the `Help` menu.

For this sort of styling, ActionScript allows you to affect the following:

- All components in a document
- All components of a certain type (for example, all **Button** components)
- Individual component instances

Let's see it in action:

1. Open the `StyleComponents.fla` file in the Chapter 11 Exercise folder. You'll see three instances of the **Button** component and one of the **CheckBox** component, as shown in Figure 11-9. Note that each has its own label.

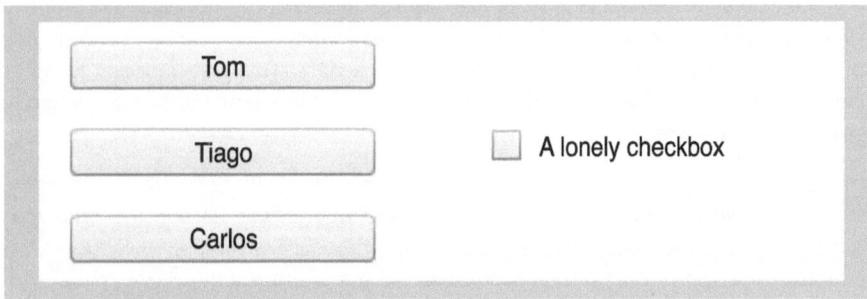

Figure 11-9. Styling is about to change these components.

2. Click once in the first frame of the **scripts** layer. Open the **Actions** panel, and type the following ActionScript into frame 1 of the **scripts** layer:

```
import fl.managers.StyleManager;
import fl.controls.Button;

var fmt1:TextFormat = new TextFormat();
fmt1.bold = true;
fmt1.color = 0xFF0000;

var fmt2:TextFormat = new TextFormat();
fmt2.bold = false;
fmt2.color = 0x0000FF;

StyleManager.setStyle("textFormat", fmt1);
StyleManager.setComponentStyle(Button, "textFormat", fmt2);
btn2.setStyle("icon", "star");
```

3. Test the movie.

You'll notice the following changes:

- The check box's label is red and bold.
- The buttons' labels are blue and not bold.
- The second button contains an icon.

Chapter 6 discusses the `TextFormat` class in detail, but there are a few twists here that deserve some clarification.

First up are the opening two lines, which use the `import` statement. We've been sidestepping this one so far because the `import` statement isn't often necessary in timeline code. In ActionScript 3.0 class files—that is, code written outside Flash altogether—the `import` statement is not only more prevalent, but it's actually *required* in order let the compiler know which other classes you intend to use. In contrast, Flash takes care of this for you—for the most part—in keyframe scripts. This just happens to be an exception. Without those first two lines, Flash will get confused about what you mean later when you mention `StyleManager` and `Button` directly.

> *These hierarchical class arrangements are called* **packages**. *To find the package for other components so that you can carry the preceding styling knowledge to other scenarios, look up the component's class in the ActionScript 3.0 Language and Components Reference. When you're looking at the component's class entry, you'll see a number of headings immediately beneath the name of the class, including* `Package`, `Class`, *and* `Inheritance`. *The* `Package` *heading is the one you want. Most components, including* `Button`, *belong to the* `fl.controls` *package. As an example of the oddball,* `ScrollPane` *belongs to the* `fl.containers` *package. In keyframe scripts, you only need to import classes outside the* `flash` *package, such as* `fl.managers`, `fl.controls`, `fl.containers`, *and the like.*

Two variables, `fmt1` and `fmt2`, are declared and set to instances of the `TextFormat` class, and each is given its own styling. Here's where it gets interesting.

The `StyleManager` class has two methods you can use to apply styling to components. The first of these, `StyleManager.setStyle()`, applies formatting to all components. In this case, we're setting the `textFormat` style of all components—specifically, all components that have a `textFormat` property—to the `fmt1` instance of the `TextFormat` class. We programmed this style to make text red (`0xFF0000`) and bold, and it is indeed applied to all three buttons and the check box. You can specify any styling you like, and the `textFormat` style is common to many components.

"Wait a minute, guys," you may be saying. "Only the check box is red!" This is true. The reason for this is the other method, `StyleManager.setComponentStyle()`. That one applies styling to all components *of a certain type*, which explains why it accepts three parameters. Here, we've specified `Button` and then set the `textFormat` style of all `Button` instances to `fmt2`. This overrides the red, bold formatting of `fmt1` applied in the previous line. Comment out the second `StyleManager` line:

```
StyleManager.setComponentStyle(Button, "textFormat", fmt2);
```

And now test your movie again to prove it.

A good way to tell which style will take effect is to remember this: the more specific the style—for example, `Button` components vs. all components—the higher priority it takes. If you holler to everyone in the room (`StyleManager.setStyle()`), giving instructions to wear green scarves, then everyone will do so. If you holler a second time, telling only the tall people to change their scarves to purple (`StyleManager.setComponentStyle()`), then only the tall people will comply. The instruction you've given the tall people is *more specific*—it applies only to people taller than six feet—and because of that, you can rest assured that, given the choice between two sets of instruction, the tall folks will follow the more specific set and wear purple.

This precedence goes a step further: the `UIComponent.setStyle()` method is invoked directly and specifically on *a particular instance* of the `Button` class, which in this case is the component whose instance name is `btn2`. It works just like `StyleManager.setStyle()` in that it accepts two parameters: the style to change and its new setting. Here, the `LabelButton.icon` style, which `Button` inherits, is set to `"star"`, which refers to the linkage class of the **star** asset in the **Library**. Right-click (Windows) or Control+click (Mac) the **star** asset, and choose **Properties** to verify this.

And now you've had a quick tour of the lobby and one of the rooms here at the UI Component Hotel. There are other rooms, of course, some more elaborate than others, but the layout for each is basically the same.

CheckBox component

You met `CheckBox` briefly in the "Button component" section, but let's take a closer look. This component is essentially a toggle button with its label on the side. Click the box or its label, and the box gets a check mark, as shown in Figure 11-10. Click again, and the check mark goes away.

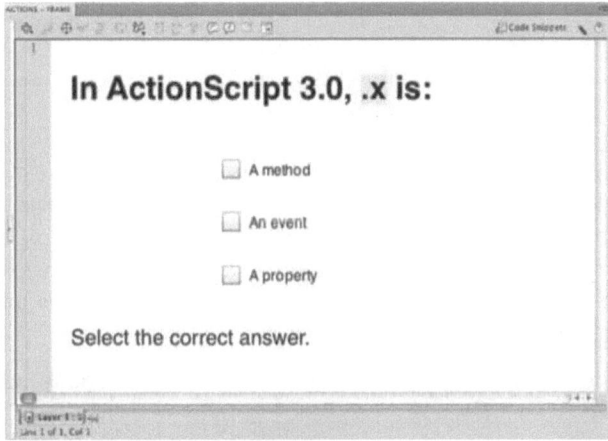

Figure 11-10. The `CheckBox` component is essentially a toggle button with its label on the side.

The `Component Parameters` tab of the `Properties` panel is fairly light for `CheckBox`:

- `label`: Sets the text label
- `labelPlacement`: Determines the position of the label (left, right, top, or bottom)
- `selected`: Lets you display an instance with the check mark showing by default

Double-click any `CheckBox` instance to change the skinning for all. Styling works as described in the "Button component" section.

> *Using one or more instances of the `CheckBox` component in your movie will add 15KB to the SWF if no other components share the load.*

Let's take a look at how to interact with check boxes via ActionScript:

1. Open the `CheckBox.fla` file in this chapter's `Exercise` folder. Note that each `CheckBox` instance has its own label and instance name.

2. Open the **Actions** panel, and enter the following ActionScript into frame 1 of the `scripts` layer:

```
addEventListener(Event.CHANGE, changeHandler);

function changeHandler(evt:Event):void {
  var str:String = "";
  if (cb1.selected == true) {
    str = "Wrong. Try again." + "\n";
  }
  if (cb2.selected == true) {
    str = "Wrong. Try again." + "\n";
  }
  if (cb3.selected == true) {
    str = "Correct!";
  }
  output.text = str;}
```

This assigns an event handler to the main timeline, listening for `Event.CHANGE` events. This event handler could have been attached to each `CheckBox` instance individually, but by doing it this way, the events of all three can be handled at the same time. When any of the three `CheckBox` instances is changed by clicking, each member of the group is checked in turn—via the `CheckBox.selected` property—to see whether it is selected. If so, the value of its label is added to a string that is ultimately assigned to the `Textfield.text` property of a text field beneath them.

3. Save and test the movie. Click the boxes, and see how the code adds the associated text.

ColorPicker component

`ColorPicker` is a fun component, because nothing like it exists in the realm of HTML—at least, not without a swarm of complicated JavaScript! But of course, color pickers are common in applications like Microsoft Word, Adobe Photoshop, and even Flash itself. In a nutshell, the `ColorPicker` component is a clickable color chip that reveals an assortment of colors when selected, as shown in Figure 11-11. It allows the user to choose one of the presented colors or optionally to type in a hexadecimal value, and then the chosen color is available for use.

> Using one or more instances of the `ColorPicker` component in your movie will add 19KB to the SWF if no other components share the load.

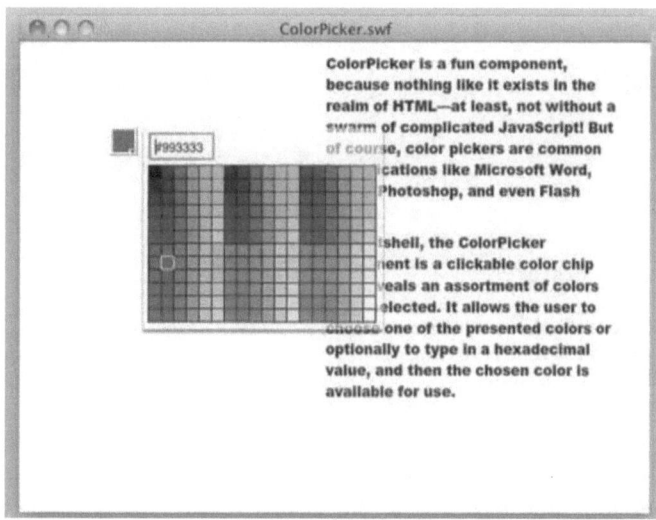

Figure 11-11. The `ColorPicker` component lets users choose from a range of colors.

Double-clicking a `ColorPicker` instance inside the authoring environment makes its skins editable, and styling works the same as it does for the `Button` component. The palette of colors displayed by this component is also editable but requires just a bit of ActionScript, as shown in the following example:

1. Open the `ColorPicker.fla` file in this chapter's `Exercise` folder, and note that the component itself has the instance name `cp`. The text field next to it has the instance name `paragraph`, and the text in the container consists of the first paragraph of this section.

2. Click into frame 1 of the `scripts` layer, and open the `Actions` panel. You will see the following ActionScript:

```
var fmt:TextFormat = new TextFormat();
```

```
cp.addEventListener(Event.CHANGE, changeHandler);
function changeHandler(evt:Event):void {
  fmt.color = cp.selectedColor;
  paragraph.setTextFormat(fmt);
};
```

Here, a variable, `fmt`, is declared and set to an instance of the `TextFormat` class. An `Event.CHANGE` event listener is assigned to the `ColorPicker` instance, `cp`. This event listener does two things. First, it sets the `TextFormat.color` property of the `fmt` instance to the selected color of the `cp` instance (see Chapter 6 for more information about the `TextFormat` class). Second, it applies that format to the text field with the instance name `poem`.

3. Let's determine which colors to display. Update the existing ActionScript to look like this (new code in bold):

```
var fmt:TextFormat = new TextFormat();

cp.colors = new Array(
  0x6E1E46,
  0xA12F1C,
  0xD47565,
  0x557A40,
  0x79A11C
);
cp.selectedColor = cp.colors[0];

cp.addEventListener(Event.CHANGE, changeHandler);
function changeHandler(evt:Event):void {
  fmt.color = cp.selectedColor;
  paragraph.setTextFormat(fmt);
};
```

Specifying your own color palette couldn't be easier. Just provide the desired hexadecimal values—up to 1,024 individual colors—as array elements to the `ColorPicker.colors` property of your component instance (note the `0x` prefix for each color that indicates the hexadecimal format). If you specify your own colors, as shown, the default palette is replaced altogether, and your chosen colors run left to right, wrapping if necessary, as seen for the default colors in Figure 11-11. To see the color chip display color, set the `ColorPicker.selectedColor` property. (Here, it's set to the first element in the `colors` array.)

4. Drag the `ColorPicker` instance to the lower-right corner of the stage.

5. Test the movie to see that the pop-up color palette is smart enough to position itself to the upper left of the color chip.

Note that in the **Component Parameters** tab of the **Properties** panel, the color palette's text field can be hidden by deselecting the **showTextField** parameter. You'll also see that you can set the component's **selectedColor** property as a parameter.

ComboBox component

The `ComboBox` component is similar to the `<select>` element in HTML, except that it doesn't have the `<select>` element's optional `size` and `multiple` attributes. `ComboBox` gives users the ability to make one selection at a time from a drop-down list, as shown in Figure 11-12. In addition, the component can be made editable, which lets the user manually type in a custom selection.

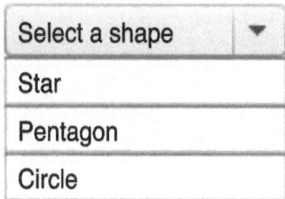

Figure 11-12. `ComboBox` lets users make one selection at a time from a drop-down list.

`ComboBox` skinning is a little more complicated than `Button` skinning, but the basic approach is the same. The complexity stems from the fact that the `ComboBox` combines two other components: `List` and `TextInput` (which are described later in this chapter).

Adding a `ComboBox` instance to your movie puts three components into your `Library`—`ComboBox`, `List`, and `TextInput`—plus the `Component Assets` folder used by all UI components. Double-clicking a `ComboBox` instance in the authoring environment opens the first tier of skins (see the left image in Figure 11-13). Double-clicking the `List` element in this tier opens the skins for the embedded `List` component (the right image in Figure 11-13).

> *Using one or more instances of the `ComboBox` component in your movie will add 35KB to the SWF if no other components, other than the automatically included `List` and `TextInput`, share the load.*

In turn, the skins for `List` include a third tier for scrollbars. In spite of this nesting, individual skins are nothing more than symbols, usually with 9-slice guides, such as the `up` and `over` skins for the `Button` component. Styling works the same as it does for the `Button` component.

CHAPTER 11

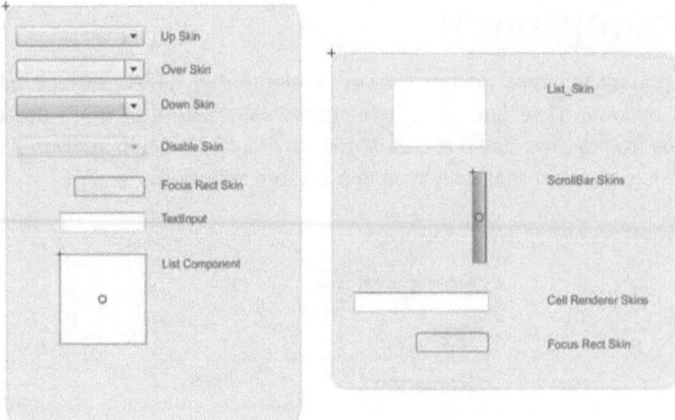

Figure 11-13. `ComboBox` skins (left) include nested elements, such as `List` skins (right).

Let's experiment with `ComboBox`:

1. Open the `ComboBox.fla` file in this chapter's Exercise folder, and select the `ComboBox` instance on the stage. Note that in the **Component Parameters** tab of the **Properties** panel, some information has already been entered into the `dataProvider` parameter, as shown in Figure 11-14. This is an array of objects, each of which represents the visible portion of a drop-down choice (`label`) and the hidden value each label contains (`data`).

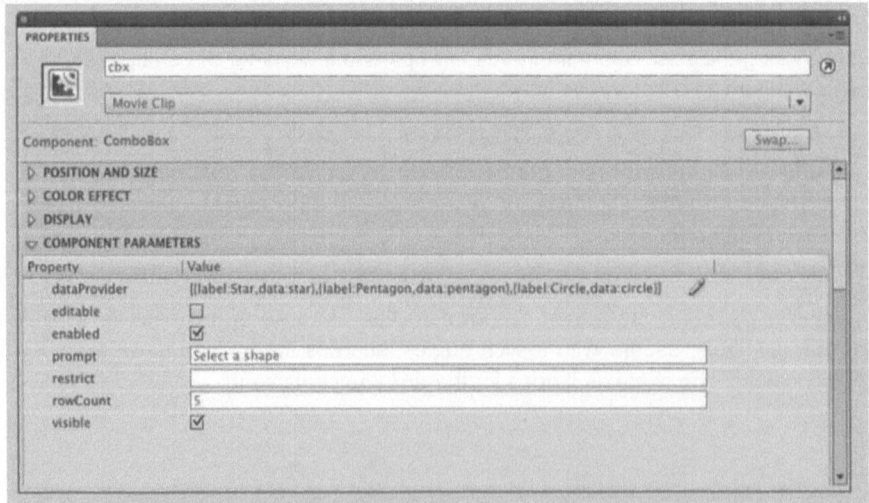

Figure 11-14. An array of objects defines the labels and data that populate a `ComboBox`.

2. Double-click the right column of the `dataProvider` row to open the `Values` dialog box, as shown in Figure 11-15.

Figure 11-15. The `Values` dialog box lets you specify the content and order of a `ComboBox` instance.

3. Click the + button at the top left of the `Values` dialog box to create a new entry, which will appear below the existing `Circle` entry.

4. Double-click the right column of the `label0` row, and change the existing stand-in label to `Square`. Double-click the right column of the `data` row, and enter the value `square`. Pay attention to the capitalization. Click OK to close the `Values` dialog box.

5. Test your movie to verify that the combo box now includes a `Square` choice that changes the shape to its right.

How does this work? Let's take a look. The shapes symbol in the `Library` contains a series of shapes drawn every few frames of its own timeline. Frame labels are provided for each shape, and it is these frame labels that are represented by the data row in the `Values` dialog box.

6. Click into frame 1 of the `scripts` layer to see the ActionScript that pulls this off:

```
cbx.addEventListener(Event.CHANGE, changeHandler);
function changeHandler(evt:Event):void {
  shapes.gotoAndStop(cbx.selectedItem.data);
};
```

The `ComboBox` instance is referenced by its instance name, cbx. An `Event.CHANGE` event triggers a custom function, changeHandler(), that tells the shapes instance—a movie clip—to stop at a particular frame label. The frame label is determined by the `data` property of the `ComboBox` component's currently selected item. How? This is accomplished by way of the `ComboBox.selectedItem` property, which features the `label` and `data` parameters supplied in the `Component Parameters` area of the `Properties` panel.

621

7. To populate the `ComboBox` component by way of ActionScript, add the following line before or after the existing code:

```
cbx.addItem({label:"Triangle", data:"triangle"});
```

This is pretty straightforward! The other parameters in the `Component Parameters` area are just as intuitive:

- `editable`: Determines whether the user can type in a custom selection (if so, check for this value by referencing the `ComboBox`'s instance name and then the `text` property)
- `prompt`: Determines the default text (in this example, the phrase "Select a shape")
- `rowCount`: Determines how many selections to show in the drop-down list (if there are 15 selections and the value of `rowCount` is 5, only five will show, but the rest will be available with a scrollbar).

DataGrid component

The `DataGrid` component is the one of the more complex components in the UI arsenal. Its purpose falls almost entirely in the realm of ubergeek interface programmers, but we're going to give you a cursory look, including a basic sample file. In short, the `DataGrid` component gives you a spreadsheet-like, sortable display for tabular data, as shown in Figure 11-16.

Numeric	English	German	French
1	one	eins	un
2	two	zwei	deux
3	three	drei	trois
4	four	vier	quatre
5	five	fünf	cinq

Figure 11-16. `DataGrid` displays scrollable, sortable tabular data.

> Using one or more instances of the `DataGrid` component in your movie will add 40KB to the SWF if no other components share the load.

BUILDING INTERFACES WITH THE UI COMPONENTS

Open the `DataGrid.fla` file in this chapter's `Exercise` folder for a working demonstration. Click into frame 1 of the `scripts` layer to see the ActionScript. Here's a bird's-eye view of that code:

```
dg.addColumn("num");
dg.addColumn("eng");
dg.addColumn("ger");
dg.addColumn("fre");
```

These first lines reference the `DataGrid` component's instance name, `dg`, and instruct the component to add four columns. These column names are arbitrary and, here, represent a column for numbers and then their English, German, and French equivalents.

```
dg.addItem({num:1, eng:"one", fre:"un", ger:"eins"});
dg.addItem({num:2, eng:"two", fre:"deux", ger:"zwei"});
dg.addItem({num:3, eng:"three", fre:"trois", ger:"drei"});
dg.addItem({num:4, eng:"four", fre:"quatre", ger:"vier"});
dg.addItem({num:5, eng:"five", fre:"cinq", ger:"fünf"});
dg.addItem({num:6, eng:"six", fre:"six", ger:"sechs"});
dg.addItem({num:7, eng:"seven", fre:"sept", ger:"sieben"});
dg.addItem({num:8, eng:"eight", fre:"huit", ger:"acht"});
dg.addItem({num:9, eng:"nine", fre:"neuf", ger:"neun"});
dg.addItem({num:10, eng:"ten", fre:"dix", ger:"zehn"});
```

You cannot populate the `DataGrid` from the `Component Parameters` area of the `Properties` panel, and we're sure you can see why. It's much easier to type in the data in the relatively spacious environs of the `Actions` panel. Here's how to give each column a name:

```
dg.getColumnAt(0).headerText = "Numeric";
dg.getColumnAt(1).headerText = "English";
dg.getColumnAt(2).headerText = "German";
dg.getColumnAt(3).headerText = "French";
```

These lines make the header text a bit "friendlier" to the eye.

Test the movie to see how it all comes together. Click the headers to sort each column. When you sort the **Numeric** column, you'll see something odd. By default, sorting is alphabetical, which puts the numbers 1 and 10 right next to each other. To fix that for columns that contain numerical data, remove the comment (`//`) from the final line of ActionScript so that it looks like this:

```
dg.getColumnAt(0).sortOptions = Array.NUMERIC;
```

> *What about retrieving which cell has been selected? The `selectedItem` property for the `DataGrid` component returns the contents of the whole row you click, not just the clicked cell. It is possible to return the selected cell, but it requires something called the `CellRenderer` class and more ActionScript, and frankly, it rockets way out of the atmosphere that makes this book breathable.*

623

Label component

`Label` is something of an oddball in the UI components collection. Unless you're an avid programmer, we're almost certain you'll want to forego `Label` in favor of a text field (covered in Chapter 6). Why? Practically speaking, from a designer's point of view, `Label` doesn't really *do* anything that can't be accomplished with a text field—and besides, by using a text field, you'll save the 14KB that an instance of `Label` would have brought to the table.

Labels don't really have skins, and double-clicking an instance will tell you as much. Styling works the same as for `Button`, but again, trust us on this one...just use a text field. If you still want to see a `Label` component in action, check out `Label.fla` in the `Exercise` folder.

List component

The `List` component is akin to the `<select>` element in HTML when its optional `size` and `multiple` attributes are specified. This component is basically a `ComboBox` component without the drop-down aspect—it's always dropped down—and it allows multiple selections, as shown in Figure 11-17.

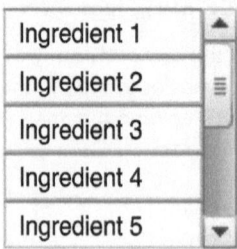

Figure 11-17. The `List` component is scrollable and optionally allows multiple selections.

Like `ComboBox`, the `List` component has nested skins, so when you double-click an instance in the authoring environment, the skins become available for editing in tiers. Styling is handled the same way as described in the "Button component" section.

> *Using one or more instances of the `List` component in your movie will add 29KB to the SWF if no other components share the load.*

The `Component Parameters` area in the `Properties` panel is relatively hefty for the `List` component, as shown in Figure 11-18. Most of the choices pertain to scrolling (the distance to scroll horizontally and vertically, whether scrolling should be automatic or constant, and so on). The important parameters are `allowMultipleSelection` and `dataProvider`.

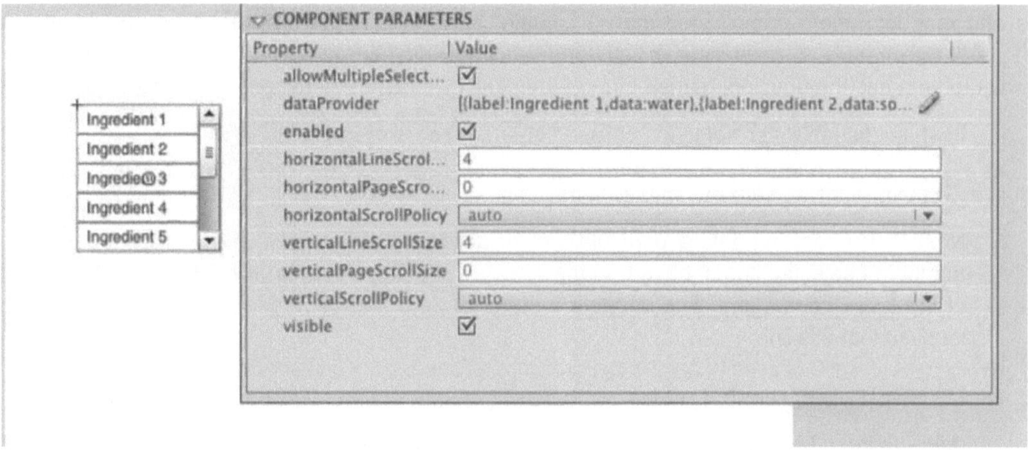

Figure 11-18. The data and the labels are added in the `dataProvider` area.

To populate your user's choices in a given **List** instance, double-click the right column of the **dataProvider** row, and use the **Values** dialog box, as described in the "ComboBox component" section. Selecting **allowMultipleSelections** (the default value is does not have the check mark) lets your users hold down Ctrl (Windows) or Cmd (Mac) while they click in order to select more than one of the listed choices (this is like the multiple attribute in HTML).

To see how **List** works, open the List.fla file in this chapter's Exercise folder. Note that the instance name for the **List** instance is list, which works only because ActionScript is a case-sensitive language—you couldn't call it List, because that's the name of the class that defines this object. In your own work, you'll want to use an instance name that describes the list's use (in this case, that might be the word **ingredients**). Note that the dynamic text field, next to the List instance, has the instance name output.

Click into frame 1 of the **scripts** layer, and type the following ActionScript:

```
list.addEventListener(Event.CHANGE, changeHandler);
function changeHandler(evt:Event):void {
  var str:String = "The secret ingredient(s): ";
  for (var i:uint = 0; i < list.selectedItems.length; i++) {
    str += list.selectedItems[i].data;
    if (i < list.selectedItems.length - 1) {
      str += ", ";
    } else {
      str += ".";
    }
  }
  output.text = str;
};
```

This one may look more complicated than it actually is, so let's break it down. As always, we're using addEventListener() to associate a custom function with an event. In this case, the event is Event.CHANGE, and the function, named changeHandler(), does three things.

1. First, the variable str holds the phrase "The secret ingredient(s): ".

```
var str:String = "The secret ingredient(s): ";
```

2. Next, a for loop repeats a particular set of actions. The duration of the loop depends on the number of selected items, based on the Array.length property of the selectedItems property of the **List** component. The variable i starts at zero and increments at each "lap" around the loop, so that this line:

```
str += list.selectedItems[i].data;
```

refers to the first selected item (item 0) on the first lap, then the second selected item (item 1) on the second lap, and so on. There's a .data tacked onto the end because **List** items are made up of two parts: label and data, which are—bingo!—the elements that make up the **dataProvider** parameter described previously. An if statement adds a comma between items in the middle and a period after the item at the end.

3. Finally, the str variable, which has continuously been updated by this process, is set to the TextField.text property of the output instance.

The net result is that **List** selections populate a dynamic text field with the ingredients of Kraft Cucumber Ranch salad dressing.

For extra credit, add the following line after the existing ActionScript:

```
list.addItem({label:"Ingredient 11", data:"natural flavor"});
```

This shows that it's also possible to populate a **List** instance programmatically.

NumericStepper component

NumericStepper is a compact little gadget that lets the user specify a numeric value, either by typing it in or by clicking up and down arrow buttons, as shown in Figure 11-19. For example, let's assume you have 10 widgets for sale. The numeric stepper component restricts a user from ordering 11 widgets. You, as a designer, can specify your own desired minimum and maximum values, as well as the size of each increment (count by ones, by twos, by tens, and so on). These values can be set via the **Component Parameters** area of the **Properties** panel.

Figure 11-19. The **NumericStepper** component

BUILDING INTERFACES WITH THE UI COMPONENTS

`NumericStepper`'s skins can be edited by double-clicking an instance, and styling can be applied as described in the "Button component" section. This component carries with it the `TextInput` component, so you'll see both in your `Library` if you add `NumericStepper` to your movie.

> Using one or more instances of the `NumericStepper` component in your movie will add 18KB to the SWF if no other components (other than the automatically included `TextInput`) share the load.

Let's play with the `NumericStepper` component:

1. Open the NumericStepper.fla file in the Chapter 11 Exercise folder. Note that the `NumericStepper` instance has the instance name `ns` and that the `thermometer` movie clip has the instance name `thermometer`.

2. In the `Library`, double-click the `thermometer` movie clip to enter its timeline, and you'll see a red rectangle (masked by a green shape) with the instance name `mercury`, as shown in Figure 11-20. You're going to set the height of this nested movie clip based on the value of the `NumericStepper`.

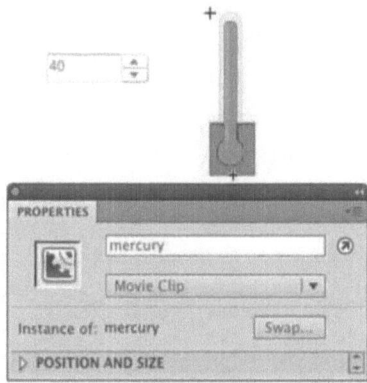

Figure 11-20. The mercury will rise and fall in response to `NumericStepper` clicks.

3. Select **Edit ➤ Edit Document**, or double-click the `Scene 1` link to return to the main timeline.

4. Click into frame 1 of the `scripts` layer, and type the following ActionScript:

```
ns.addEventListener(Event.CHANGE, changeHandler);
function changeHandler(evt:Event):void {
  thermometer.mercury.height = ns.value;
};
```

627

5. Test your movie. Click the up and down arrow buttons to see the component in action. Close the SWF when you are finished experimenting.

The `MovieClip.height` property of **mercury** is set to the value of **NumericStepper**—`ns.value`—as referenced in terms of the `ns` instance. The **mercury** movie clip is nested inside **thermometer**, which explains the matching hierarchical reference `thermometer.mercury`.

ProgressBar component

Used often for preloading, the **ProgressBar** component gives you a rising thermometer-style animation to display load progress when loading files of known size and gives you a barber pole–style animation to indicate that the user must wait (for example, for files of unknown size to load or for processes to finish). Figure 11-21 shows an example.

This component doesn't have a whole lot to skin, but you can access what's there by double-clicking a **ProgressBar** instance. Styling works as it does for the **Button** component, but **ProgressBar** doesn't even have text, so your styling choices are fairly slim.

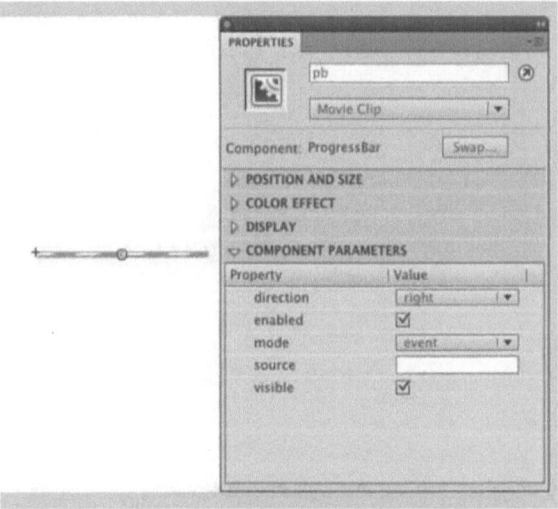

Figure 11-21. The **ProgressBar** component and its parameters

> *Using one or more instances of the **ProgressBar** component in your movie will add 16KB to the SWF if no other components share the load. That means 16KB of nonpreloadable content (the preloader itself!), so don't put much else into the frame that contains the **ProgressBar** component.*

BUILDING INTERFACES WITH THE UI COMPONENTS

Here's an exercise designed to show you how the `ProgressBar` component works:

1. Open the ProgressBar.fla file in this chapter's Exercise folder. Note that a `ProgressBar` instance exists in frame 1 with the instance name pb, as well as a text field with the instance name output. In frame 5, you'll find a fairly heavy image of red leaves on a tree branch, snapped by one of the authors. In the scripts layer, there's a MovieClip.stop() method in frames 1 and 5.

2. Click into frame 1 of the scripts layer. Note the existing stop() method. Type the following ActionScript after that method (new code in bold):

```
stop();

root.loaderInfo.addEventListener(Event.COMPLETE,
↪completeHandler);
function completeHandler(evt:Event):void {
  play();
};

pb.source = root.loaderInfo;
```

Here, first, the playhead stops at this frame. Next, an Event.COMPLETE handler is assigned to the LoaderInfo instance associated with the root property of the main timeline. Say again? Yeah, this one is a bit different from what you've seen.

In the same way that the stop() method is invoked here on the main timeline—appearing, as it does, without an object reference prefix—the root property is also being invoked implicitly on the main timeline. (root is a property of the DisplayObject class, which means MovieClip and other classes have it by inheritance.) The root property refers to the topmost display object in a given display list. In this context, it essentially refers to the display list of the main timeline (everything that's visible—or will be visible—on the main timeline, including that onion photo on frame 5).

The main timeline, being a movie clip, features a loaderInfo property, which points to an instance of the LoaderInfo class that (as its name suggests) manages loading information for the object at hand. In this case, when the movie itself has completed loading, the Event.COMPLETE event is dispatched, and the completeHandler() function invokes MovieClip.play() on the main timeline, causing the playhead to resume play until it encounters the second stop() method on frame 5. It's frame 5 that reveals the image.

Notice that, so far, none of this yet touches the `ProgressBar` component. That happens only at this point. Immediately after the event handler, the ProgressBar.source property, by way of the pb instance, is associated with the root.loaderInfo reference. As if by magic, that's all it takes to set the thermometer-style movement in motion.

3. Test the movie. When the SWF launches, select **View ➤ Simulate Download** from the SWF's menu bar to see the `ProgressBar` component in action. Selecting **View ➤ Download Settings** lets you select the speed of the simulated Internet connection.

4. Close the SWF.

5. Let's also display a text message indicating a percent loaded. In the **Actions** panel, add a few more lines below the existing code:

```
pb.addEventListener(ProgressEvent.PROGRESS,
↪progressHandler);
function progressHandler (evt:ProgressEvent):void {
  output.text = Math.floor(pb.percentComplete).toString() + "%";
};
```

The `ProgressBar` component features a `percentComplete` property, which we're using here. The `addEventListener()` method is invoked against the `pb` instance, listening for a `ProgressEvent.PROGRESS` event. The function it performs sets the `output` text field's `text` property to a rounded-down string version of the progress percentage, with the percent sign tacked onto the end for good measure.

RadioButton component

Radio buttons are gregarious. They belong in groups and courteously defer to each other as each takes the spotlight. What are we talking about? We're talking about a component identical in functionality to radio buttons in HTML. Groups of `RadioButton` components are used to let the user make a single selection from a multiple-choice set, as shown in Figure 11-22.

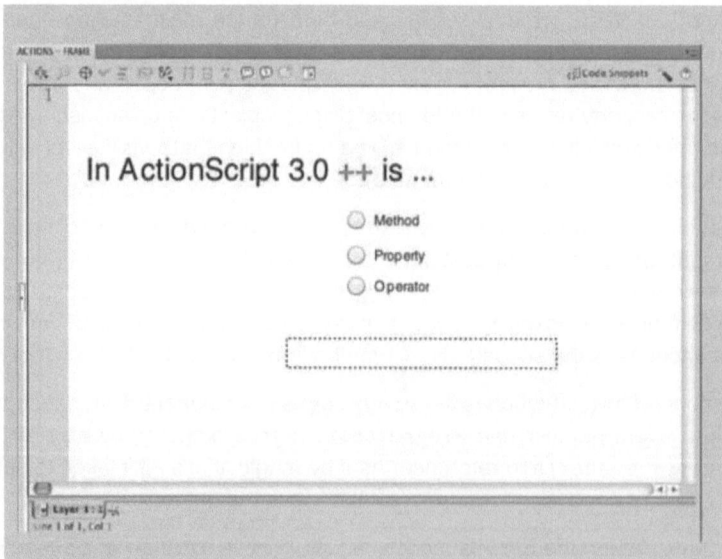

Figure 11-22. The `RadioButton` component lets the user make a single selection from a multiple-choice set.

Double-clicking a `RadioButton` instance provides access to its skins, which you can edit as described in the "Button component" section. Styling works the same way.

> Using one or more instances of the `RadioButton` component in your movie will add 16KB to the SWF if no other components share the load.

To see `RadioButton` components in action, open the `RadioButton.fla` file in this chapter's Exercise file. Because radio buttons work in groups, the **Component Parameters** tab of the **Properties** panel has a "collective consciousness" parameter we haven't seen with other components: `groupName`. Select each of the three radio buttons in turn, and verify that each belongs to the same group, `syntax`, even though each has its own distinct label: **Method**, **Property**, and **Operator** (see Figure 11-23). Note also the empty dynamic text field whose instance name is `output`. You're about to wire up the radio buttons to that text field.

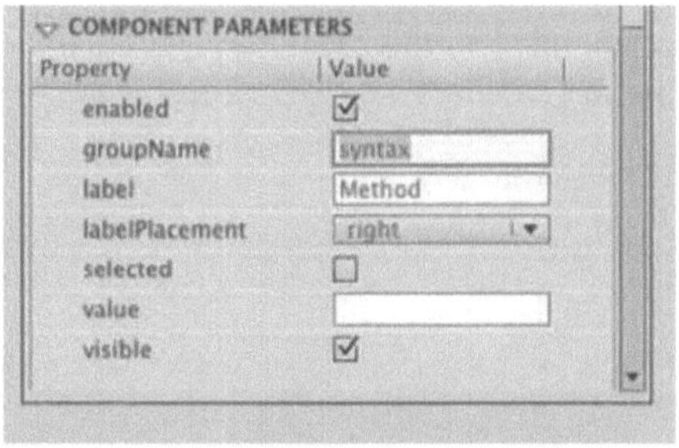

Figure 11-23. `RadioButton` instances must be associated with a group name.

Click into frame 1 of the `scripts` layer, and type the following very condensed but interesting ActionScript:

```
rb1.group.addEventListener(Event.CHANGE,
↪changeHandler);
function changeHandler(evt:Event):void {
  output.text = rb1.group.selection.label;
};
```

What makes this interesting? In most of the event-handling samples in this chapter, you've invoked the `addEventListener()` method on an object that you personally gave an instance name. Here, that might have been `rb1`, but that's not the focal point in this case. You're not adding an event listener to a particular radio button but rather to the *group* to which these buttons belong. The `RadioButton` class provides a group property, which means that each instance knows to which group it belongs. It's the group that dispatches the `Event.CHANGE` event, which occurs when any one of these radio buttons is clicked.

It doesn't matter which radio button's group property you use, because all of them point to the same `RadioButtonGroup` instance. The associated function updates the `output` text field by sending it the selected button in this group—in particular, that button's `label` property, which is either `Method`, `Property`, or `Operator`.

> *Note that the `Component Parameters` area gives you the option to supply a value for each radio button. This allows you to say one thing and do another, just as in the `List` example. The difference is that the `List` choices were `label` and `data`, and here they are `label` and `value`, and the data type of `value` is typed as `Object`, not `String`. The text field wants a string, so you would change that line of ActionScript to `output.text = rb1.group.selection.value.toString();`. For example, if you change the `value` of the `Operator RadioButton` to `Correct`, you turn this exercise into a quiz.*

ScrollPane component

The `ScrollPane` component lets you have eyes bigger than your stomach. If you want to display a super-large image—so large that you'll need scrollbars—`ScrollPane` is your component; Figure 11-24 shows it in action.

Figure 11-24. `ScrollPane` provides optional scrollbars to accommodate oversized content.

`ScrollPane` has nested skins because of its scrollbars, so double-clicking an instance during authoring will open its skin elements in tiers. Styling works the same as described in the "Button component" section, although with no text elements, most of your customization work will probably center around skins.

BUILDING INTERFACES WITH THE UI COMPONENTS

> Using one or more instances of the `ScrollPane` component in your movie will add 21KB to the SWF if no other components share the load.

In this example, there's no need for ActionScript.

1. Open the `ScrollPane.fla` file in this chapter's Exercise folder. Select the `ScrollPane` instance, and click the **Parameters** tab of the **Component Inspector** panel.

2. In the **Component Parameters** area, double-click the right column of the **source** row. Type `Redleaves.jpg`.

3. Test the movie. Pretty slick! The **source** parameter can be pointed to any file format that Flash can load dynamically, including JPEGs, GIFs, PNGs, and other SWFs.

Slider component

The `Slider` component is conceptually the same thing as `NumericStepper`, except that instead of clicking buttons to advance from one number to the next, the user drags a knob along a slider, as shown in Figure 11-25. You, as designer, are responsible for setting the minimum and maximum values, and this component lets you specify whether sliding is smooth or snaps to increments specified by you.

Figure 11-25. `Slider` lets the user drag a handle back and forth to specify a value.

`Slider` has no text elements, so styling is fairly light. What's there works as it does for the `Button` component. Skinning also works as it does for `Button`: double-click a `Slider` instance in the authoring environment to change the knob and track skins.

> Using one or more instances of the `Slider` component in your movie will add 17KB to the SWF if no other components share the load.

To see how the `Slider` component works, open the `Slider.fla` file in this chapter's Exercise folder. Note that the instance name for the `Slider` instance is `slider`, which works only because ActionScript is a case-sensitive language. You couldn't call it `Slider`, because that's the name of the class that defines this object. Also note the instance names `circle1` and `circle2` on the two circles. You're about to wire up the `Slider` component to adjust their width and height.

Click into frame 1 of the **scripts** layer, and type the following ActionScript:

```
slider.addEventListener(Event.CHANGE, changeHandler);
function changeHandler(evt:Event):void {
  circle1.scaleX = slider.value / 100;
  circle2.scaleY = slider.value / 100;
};
```

When the `Event.CHANGE` event is dispatched—this happens as the knob moves along the track—the slider's `value` property is used to update scaling properties of the `circle` movie clips. Why divide by 100? In movie clip scaling, 0 percent is 0 and 100 percent is 1. Because the `Slider` instance happens to have its `maximum` parameter set to `100`, the division puts `value` into the desired range, as shown in Figure 11-26.

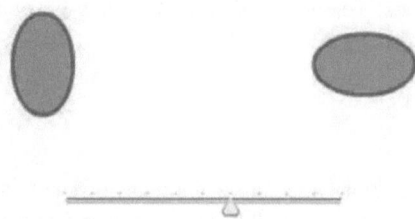

Figure 11-26. A single `Slider` instance can adjust many objects. Hey, that looks like a face!

Be sure to experiment with the parameters in the **Properties** panel's **Component Parameters** area. Most of them are intuitive, but `liveDragging` and `snapInterval` might not be. The `liveDragging` parameter tells `Slider` whether to update its `value` property as the knob moves, as opposed to when it is released. When you set `liveDragging` to `false` (deselected), the circles will resize only after you reposition the knob and then release it. The `snapInterval` parameter tells `Slider` how often to update its `value` property. To demonstrate, set `liveDragging` to `true` (a check mark), and then change `snapInterval` to a small number, such as 1. When you drag the knob, you'll see the circles resize smoothly. Change `snapInterval` to 10 and test again, and the circles resize less smoothly, because you're asking `value` to count by tens.

You may be surprised to find a `direction` parameter (its values are `horizontal` and `vertical`). Why not just use the **Free Transform** tool to rotate this slider? Well, try it. We'll wait...that's kind of weird, right? It doesn't work. Components are a sophisticated phenomenon, even though they look so simple.

Now, what if you want a slanted slider, not horizontal or vertical? Here's a trick: select the `Slider` instance, convert it to a movie clip (**Modify ▶ Convert to Symbol**), and give that movie clip an instance name such as `sliderClip`. When both the movie clip and its nested `Slider` have instance names, you're set.

```
sliderClip.slider.addEventListener(Event.CHANGE, changeHandler);
function changeHandler(evt:Event):void {
  circle1.scaleX = sliderClip.slider.value / 100;
  circle2.scaleY = sliderClip.slider.value / 100;
};
```

TextArea component

Chapter 6 introduced you to text fields and containers. Consider the `TextArea` component a text field in a tux. It has an attractive, slightly beveled border, lets you limit how many characters can be typed into it (like input text fields), and is optionally scrollable (see Figure 11-27). This component is akin to the `<textarea>` element in HTML.

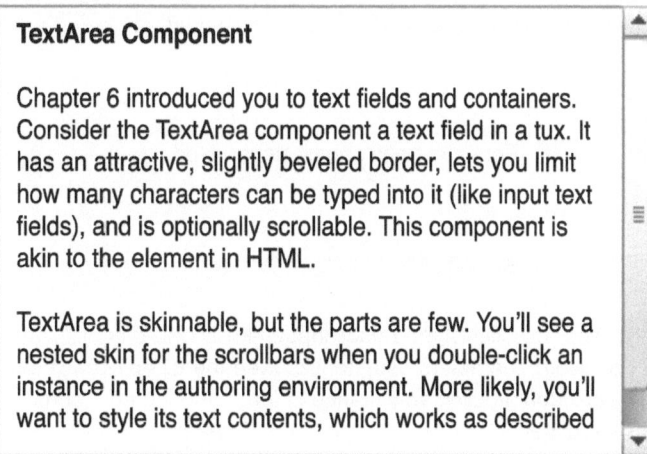

Figure 11-27. `TextArea` is the James Bond of text fields.

`TextArea` is skinnable, but the parts are few. You'll see a nested skin for the scrollbars when you double-click an instance in the authoring environment. More likely, you'll want to style its text contents, which works as described in the "Button component" section.

> *Using one or more instances of the `TextArea` component in your movie will add 21KB to the SWF if no other components (other than the automatically included `UIScrollBar`) share the load.*

Open the `TextArea.fla` file in this chapter's `Exercise` folder to see an example of populating a `TextArea` instance with text. (We figured it would be cruel to make you type in a lengthy bit of sample text on your own.) Note that the `TextArea` component can display HTML text, as shown in the sample file, or plain text. Use the component's ActionScript `htmlText` or `text` properties accordingly.

Notice that the `Component Parameters` tab of the `Properties` panel shows only a `text` parameter for supplying text. We can't imagine anyone using that tiny space to enter more than a sentence, so reference that parameter as a property in your ActionScript. Assuming `ta` is the `TextArea` component's instance name, here's the code:

```
ta.htmlText = "<p>HTML text here, with styling.";
```

or it could look like this:

```
ta.text = "Plain text content here.";
```

TextInput component

The `TextInput` component is the single-line kid brother of `TextArea`. For this reason, to trump it up, we'll show it displaying one of the shortest short stories in the world, attributed to Ernest Hemingway (see Figure 11-28).

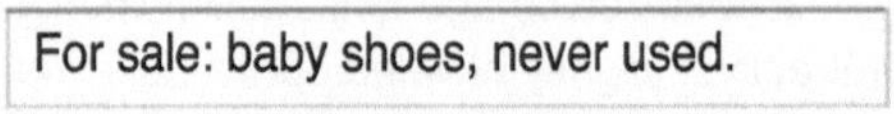

> For sale: baby shoes, never used.

Figure 11-28. `TextInput` is a single-line component, mainly used for user input.

`TextInput` is primarily used to collect typed user input, like HTML-based "Contact Us" forms, and can even be set to display password characters as asterisks (see the `displayAsPassword` parameter). The component is skinnable—just double-click an instance in the authoring environment—but there's not much to skin. Styling works as described in the "Button component" section.

> Using one or more instances of the `TextInput` component in your movie will add 15KB to the SWF if no other components share the load.

To see the `TextInput` component in action, open the TextInput.fla file that accompanies this chapter. Note the two `TextInput` instances, with instance names input (top) and output (bottom). Select each component in turn, and look at the **Parameters** tab of the **Component Inspector** panel as you do. For the top `TextInput` instance, the `displayAsPassword` and `editable` parameters are set to `true`. For the bottom one, both of those parameters are set to `false`. You're about to make the upper component reveal its password to the lower one.

Click into frame 1 of the `scripts` layer, and type the following ActionScript:

```
input.addEventListener(Event.CHANGE, changeHandler);
function changeHandler(evt:Event):void {
  output.text = input.text;
};
```

As text is typed into the upper `TextInput` instance, the `Event.CHANGE` handler updates the lower instance's text content with that of the upper instance's content. Because of the parameter settings, the text content is hidden above but clearly displayed below.

TileList component

`TileList` is not unlike the `ScrollPane` component. Both load files for display, optionally with scrollbars, but `TileList` displays numerous files—JPEGs, SWFs, and so on—in the tiled arrangement shown in Figure 11-29.

Double-click a `TileList` instance to edit its skins. You'll see a second tier of skins for the scrollbars. Styling may be accomplished as described in the "Button component" section.

> Using one or more instances of the `TileList` component in your movie will add 32KB to the SWF if no other components share the load.

Figure 11-29. `TileList` displays a tiled arrangement of content, optionally scrolling as necessary.

Quite a few parameters are listed in the `Component Parameters` area of the `Properties` panel for this component, but they're all easy to grasp. For example, there are settings for the width and number of columns, height and number of rows, direction or orientation (`horizontal` or `vertical`), and scrolling settings (`on`, `off`, and `auto`, the last of which makes scrollbars show only as necessary). The `dataProvider` parameter is the most important, because that's where you define the content to show. It works the same as the `dataProvider` for `ComboBox`, except that instead of `label` and `data` properties, `TileList` expects `label` and `source`.

If you find the `Component Parameters` a bit confining, you can always use ActionScript to add items to the `TileList`. To try this, open the `TileList.fla` file in the Chapter 11 Exercise folder. Note that the

`TileList` instance has the instance name tl, and the dynamic text field below it has the instance name output.

Click into frame 1 of the `scripts` layer, and type the following ActionScript:

```
tl.addItem({label:"Mug 6", source:"Mug06.jpg"});
tl.addItem({label:"Mug 7", source:"Mug07.jpg"});
tl.addItem({label:"Mug 8", source:"Mug08.jpg"});

tl.addEventListener(Event.CHANGE, changeHandler);
function changeHandler(evt:Event):void {
  output.text = tl.selectedItem.label;
};
```

The first three lines use practically the same approach we used for adding an additional item to the `ComboBox` instance in that section of the chapter. Mugs 1 through 5 are specified in the **Properties** panel. Here, these three lines of code give us a few more mug shots (heh, mug shots—we love that joke). In the event handler, the changeHandler() function updates the output text fields' text property with the label value of the `TileList`'s selected item.

> *`TileList` also supports multiple selections, like the `List` component. The sample code in the "List component" section provides the same basic mechanism you would use here, except instead of targeting the data property, you'll probably want to target label, as shown in the preceding single-selection sample.*

UILoader component

If the Flash CS5 UI components all went to a Halloween party, `UILoader` would show up as the Invisible Man (see Figure 11-30).

Figure 11-30. Practically speaking, `UILoader` has no visual elements (and yes, this figure is empty; being able to include it cracks us up).

BUILDING INTERFACES WITH THE UI COMPONENTS

So, what's the point? Ah, but `UILoader` is such a selfless, *giving* component! Its purpose is to load and display content other than itself. This lets you avoid using the `Loader` class (which you'll encounter in Chapter 14), just in case the thought of ActionScript makes you feel like you discovered half a worm in your apple. Simply enter a filename into the `source` parameter of the `Properties` panel's `Component Parameters` area, and you're set (see Figure 11-31).

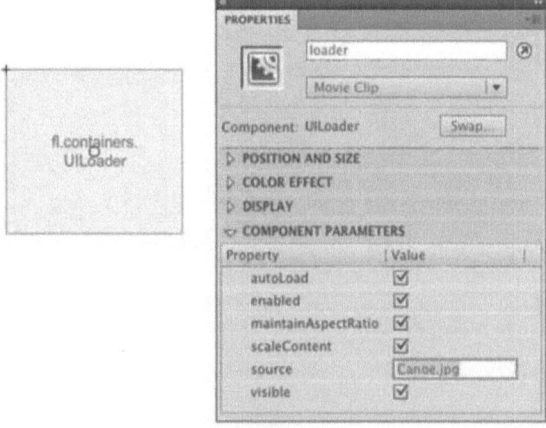

Figure 11-31. Just enter in the name of a supported file format, and Flash will load it.

> Using one or more instances of the `UILoader` component in your movie will add 15KB to the SWF if no other components share the load.

Here's a `UILoader` component exercise:

1. Open the `UILoader.fla` file that accompanies this chapter. Double-click the `UILoader` instance, and you'll see message that no skins are available. Since we aren't speaking to this component with ActionScript (yet), it doesn't need an instance name.

2. In the `Parameters` tab of the `Component Inspector` panel, enter the filename `Redleaves.jpg` into the right column of the `source` row. This references a JPG file in the same folder as your FLA.

3. Test your movie, and you'll see the leaves load into its `UILoader` container.

4. Deselect the `maintainAspectRatio` parameter and test again. This time, the image loads a bit squished. Our personal preference is usually to maintain aspect ratio. The `scaleContent` parameter determines whether the loaded content is scaled or cropped in its container.

639

5. Our friend **ProgressBar** is about to make a cameo appearance. Drag an instance of the **ProgessBar** component to the stage below the **UILoader** instance, and give the **UILoader** instance the instance name `loader`.

6. Select the **ProgressBar** instance, and in the **Parameters** tab, set its **source** parameter to `loader`—that's the instance name you just gave the **UILoader** instance (see Figure 11-32). You're associating the two and telling the **ProgressBar** component to check with the **UILoader** component to divulge how much of the requested file has loaded.

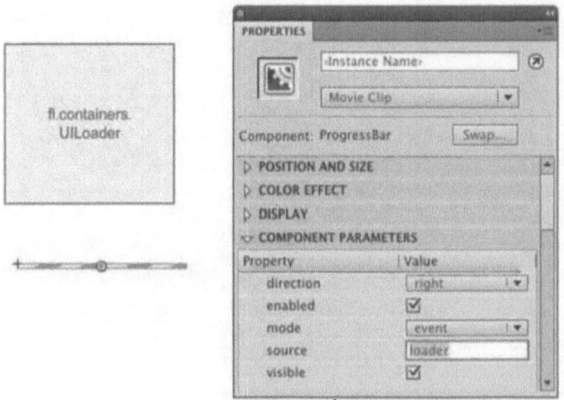

Figure 11-32. It's very easy to show the load progress for a **UILoader** instance.

7. Test your movie again.

8. In the SWF's menu bar, select **View ➤ Simulate Download** to see some super-easy preloading action.

9. Close the SWF.

10. To wrap up, let's add a teensy bit of ActionScript. (Don't worry, that half a worm we mentioned earlier was just a centipede—half a centipede.) To make sure ActionScript talks to the **ProgressBar** instance, give it an instance name. We're using `pb`. Click into frame 1 of the **scripts** layer, and type the following ActionScript:

```
pb.addEventListener(Event.COMPLETE, completeHandler);
function completeHandler(evt:Event):void {
  removeChild(pb);
};
```

11. Test the movie for the last time. You'll see what this ActionScript does: it makes the progress bar disappear when loading is complete.

UIScrollBar component

If you read any other sections of this chapter, you've probably already been introduced to the `UIScrollBar` component. This component is a humble but useful member of the team, because it allows other components to have scrollbars. `UIScrollBar` is skinnable by double-clicking any instance in the authoring environment. Styling doesn't make much sense, but it is possible as described in the "Button component" section.

> Using one or more instances of the `UIScrollBar` component in your movie will add 18KB to the SWF if no other components share the load.

So as to avoid repeating ourselves, we'll direct your attention to the "Using the UIScrollBar component" section in Chapter 6 to see this component in action.

What you have learned

In this chapter, you learned the following:

- How to use every one of the Flash CS5 UI components
- How to write the ActionScript that controls components
- How to skin a component
- How to manage components in a Flash movie

Clients are fickle. One day the black Times Roman they asked for is fabulous, and the next day it "just has to be" green Helvetica Narrow. This can be a huge waste of time. They start with one image and suddenly there are 100. You can spend hours opening Flash files and physically making the changes, or pawing through ActionScript looking for code that formats text or handles the images. Is there an easier way? XML. We have been talking about it throughout this book, and the time has arrived for you to explore XML's powerful relationship with Flash.

Intrigued? Turn the page.

Chapter 12

XML (Dynamic Data)

To this point in the book, we have dangled the use of XML in front of you with no real explanation of how it works. That time has arrived.

Flash is a social creature. Not only does it rub elbows with HTML—coexisting happily with text, JavaScript, images, audio, video, CSS, and more—but it can also reach out past its own SWF boundaries to collaborate with data hosted on a server.

In the hands of an experienced programmer, Flash can interact with database applications by way of the URLLoader and URLVariables classes, perform web service and Flash remoting calls, and even slap a secret handshake with Ajax, thanks to the ExternalInterface class. All this from a browser plug-in that began its life as a way to improve on animated GIFs! It's easy to see why Flash has become a widespread phenomenon, and its versatility makes equally social creatures of the countless designers and developers who end up warming their diverse mitts around the same campfire because of it.

This book isn't here to make programmers out of artists. We don't have the page count to delve into most of the concepts just mentioned, but we are going to introduce you to a markup language called XML that, with a bit of help from ActionScript, can make your SWFs dynamic.

Here's what we'll cover in this chapter:

- Retrieving and filtering XML data using E4X syntax
- Using retrieved data in collaboration with ActionScript

The following files are used in this chapter (located in Chapter13/ExerciseFiles_Ch13/Exercise/):

CHAPTER 12

- LoadXML.fla
- flashBooks.xml
- LoadXML-E4XBonusRound.fla
- CopyMotion.fla
- CopyMotion.xml
- XFLexercise.fla

The source files are available online at www.friendsofED.com/download.html?isbn=1430229940.

If you haven't already worked with XML, we bet our next single malt Scotch you've at least heard of it. The letters stand for eXtensible Markup Language, and extensibility—the ability to create your own HTML-like tags—is almost certainly the reason XML has become a towering champ in data communication. Countless markup languages and file formats are based on XML, including SMIL, RSS, XAML, MXML, RDF, WAP, SVG, SOAP, WSDL, OpenDocument, XHTML, and so on—truly more than would fit on this page. We'll leave the letter combinations to a Scrabble master.

"That's fine and dandy," you might be saying, "but, guys, *what is XML?*" Fair enough. The remarkable thing about this language is that it can basically be whatever you want it to be, provided you stick by its rules. The W3C defines the syntax recommendation for XML (XML 1.0, fifth edition, which is the latest at the time this book was written) at www.w3.org/TR/2008/REC-xml-20081126/.

The main purpose of XML is to let you share data. In fact, XML is so flexible that newcomers are often baffled about where to even begin. On paper—or rather, on the screen—XML looks a lot like another famous W3C specification: HTML. However, rather than using the predetermined tags and attributes supplied by HTML, XML lets you organize your content into descriptive tags of your own design. While HTML formats data for display, XML actually describes data. The combination of familiar, hierarchical format and completely custom tags generally makes XML content easy to read, both to computers and to humans. By separating your data from the movie, you give yourself the opportunity to change content from the outside, affecting SWFs without needing to republish them.

In a minute you are actually going to write the following XML:

```
<flashbooks>
   <book></book>
   <book></book>
   <book></book>
   <book></book>
   <book></book>
</flashbooks>
```

If you are new to this language, we'll bet you looked at it and thought, "Has something to do with a bunch of Flash books." You are correct, and that's the beauty and simplicity of XML. There is nothing here about formatting text or any other stuff. All it does is present data—a list of Flash books.

So, are you ready to write some XML?

Writing XML

Here's a typical scenario. One of the authors has a rather extensive collection of Flash books in his office. The collection expands and contracts based upon the current version of Flash, and he thinks it would be rather neat to keep a running inventory of his collection. Rather than list all 50 or 60 of them, he decides to start out with 5 core titles and grow from there. The reason for the 5 titles is simple: if he can get 5 books organized, then it is no big deal to get 50, 500, or even 5,000 books into the document.

The decision is to start with books from friends of ED, and he decides to start with: *ActionScript 3.0 Image Effects*, *Flash Applications for Mobile Devices*, *ActionScript for Animation*, *Foundation ActionScript 3.0*, and *Flash Math Creativity*. Each book has its own page count, author, and publisher. Where to begin? Let's take a look.

Every XML document must have at least one tag, which constitutes its **root element**. The root element should describe the document's contents. In this case, we're dealing with Flash books, so let's make that our root:

```
<flashbooks></flashbooks>
```

The rest of our elements will stack themselves inside this first one. Every title is its own book, so we'll add five custom <book> elements:

```
<flashbooks>
   <book></book>
   <book></book>
   <book></book>
   <book></book>
   <book></book>
</flashbooks>
```

Again, these tag names aren't things that exist in XML. It's up to you to decide which elements make sense for the data at hand, to name those elements accordingly, and then to use them.

Note that each opening tag has a closing tag partner (with a slash in it), which is a characteristic required by the XML standard. If an element doesn't contain further data inside it, that element can optionally serve as its own opening and closing tags. In such a case, the <book></book> pairing would look like this: <book />. But here, each book has a title, so these elements will remain as tag pairs.

The next step—adding a title—seems obvious enough:

```
<flashbooks>
  <book>
     <title> ActionScript 3.0 Image Effects </title>
  </book>
  <book>
     <title> Flash Applications for Mobile Devices </title>
  </book>
  <book>
     <title> ActionScript for Animation </title>
  </book>
  <book>
     <title> Foundation ActionScript 3.0</title>
  </book>
  <book>
     <title> Flash Math Creativity </title>
  </book>
</flashbooks>
```

The difference here is that the <title> tags contain textual data instead of additional elements, but you get the idea. Hold on a minute—*all* of these tags contain data! The <title> tags contain *text nodes* (that is, nonelement text content), and the <book> and <flashbooks> tags contain XML *element nodes* (that is, descriptive tags). It doesn't take much effort to connect the rest of the dots. An excerpt of the completed document might look something like this:

```
<flashbooks>
  <book>
    <title> Flash Applications for Mobile Devices </title>
    <publisher>friendsofED</publisher>
    <pageCount>663 pages</pageCount>
  </book>
  . . .</flashbooks>
```

Actually, that isn't complete after all, is it? The author is missing. The thing about these books is there may be one author on the cover or a number of authors on the cover. For that, another tier of elements is in order:

```
<flashbooks>
  <book>
     <title> Flash Applications for Mobile Devices </title>
    <publisher>friendsofED</publisher>
    <pageCount>514 pages</pageCount>
```

```
    <authors>
      <author>Richard Leggett</author>
      <author>Weyert de Boer</author>
      <author>Scott Janousek</author>
    </authors>
  </book>
  . . .
</flashbooks>
```

That would certainly do it. The tag names are meaningful, which is handy when it comes time to retrieve the data. The nested structure organizes each concept into a hierarchy that makes sense. Nicely done, but in a sizable collection, this particular arrangement might come across as bulky. Is there a way to trim it down? Sure thing. Remember that XML allows you to create your own attributes, so you have the option of rearranging the furniture along these lines:

```
<flashbooks>
  <book title=" Flash Applications for Mobile Devices " publisher="friendsofED"
pageCount ="514 pages">
    <authors>
      <author>Richard Leggett</author>
      <author>Weyert de Boer</author>
      <author>Scott Janousek</author>
    </authors>
  </book>
  . . .
</flashbooks>
```

The exact same information is conveyed. The only difference now is that some of the data has been shifted to tag attributes, or **attribute nodes**, rather than tags. HTML provides the same mechanism, by the way. Consider the src attribute of an <img> tag (`<img src="someImage.jpg" />`). All it does here is change how the data would be retrieved, as you'll see in the "Using E4X syntax" section of this chapter. Which approach is better? Honestly, the choice is yours. It's not so much a question of "better" as it is what best matches your sense of orderliness. Ironically, this open-ended quality, which is one of XML's strongest assets, is the one feature that is the hardest for those who are new to the subject to grasp. It doesn't have to make sense to anyone but you.

> *Working with and structuring an XML document follows the first principle of web development: "No one cares how you did it. They just care that it works." Find what works best for you, because in the final analysis, your client will never pick up the phone and say, "Dude, that was one sweetly structured XML document you put together." Having said that, if you are part of a collaborative work group, be sure that everyone involved agrees on terminology before you start.*

Folks, this is a bit like a ceramics class. As long as you're careful around the kiln, no one can tell you whose vase is art and whose isn't. Just work the clay between your fingers, let a number of shapes mull

CHAPTER 12

around your mind, and then form the clay into a structure that appeals to you. While you're at it, keep a few rules in mind:

- If you open a tag, close it (`<tag></tag>`).
- If a tag doesn't come in two parts—that is, if it contains only attributes, or nothing at all—make sure it closes itself (`<tag />`).
- Close nested tags in reciprocating order (`<a><b><c /></b></a>` is correct, but `<a><b><c /></a></b>` will "blow up").
- Wrap attribute values in quotation marks or single quotation marks (`<tag done="right" />`, `<tag done=wrong />`).

The `flashbooks` example we just discussed would be saved as a simple text file with the `.xml` file extension, as in `flashBooks.xml`. In fact, it isn't a bad idea, once you have finished writing your XML document, to open it in a browser like Firefox to see whether there are any problems.

Now that our introductions have been made, let's get social.

> *Feel free to use a text editor such as Notepad on Windows or TextEdit on the Mac to create your XML files. Just be sure you add the `.xml` extension to the file's name. If you have Dreamweaver CS5, that's even better, because it automatically writes the document declaration for you at the top, and it offers tools such as code completion to speed up your workflow. Also, keep in mind that manually writing XML is just one approach. As you start becoming more comfortable with using XML, you will eventually find yourself drifting toward server-side scripting—such as PHP—to handle complex data management.*

Loading an XML file

XML in Flash has had a rather rocky relationship simply because, until a couple of years ago, it was right up there with beating yourself in the head with a brick. Things have changed, significantly for the better.

The ActionScript required for loading an XML document isn't complicated. You'll need an instance of the `XML` and `URLLoader` classes, and, of course, an XML document. In our case, the document will always be an actual XML file, although XML documents can be built from scratch with ActionScript.

Open the `LoadXML.fla` file that accompanies this chapter. Click into frame 1 of the **scripts** layer, and open the **Actions** panel to see the following code:

```
var xmlDoc:XML = new XML();
var loader:URLLoader = new URLLoader();
var req:URLRequest = new URLRequest("flashBooks.xml");
loader.load(req);
```

XML (DYNAMIC DATA)

```
loader.addEventListener(Event.COMPLETE, completeHandler);
function completeHandler(evt:Event):void {
    loader.removeEventListener( Event.COMPLETE, completeHandler );
    xmlDoc = XML(evt.target.data);
    trace(xmlDoc);
};
```

Let's break it down. The first two lines declare a pair of variables: xmlDoc and loader, which point to instances of the XML and URLLoader classes, respectively. The third line declares a third variable, req, which points to an instance of the URLRequest class and specifies the location of the actual XML document.

Line 4 then invokes the URLLoader.load() method on the loader instance, specifying req as the parameter. The req parameter's value—"flashBooks.xml" in this example—is the name of your XML file, including a file path if necessary. This procedure starts the load process, but the data isn't available until the XML document has fully arrived from the server. For this reason, the final block attaches an Event.COMPLETE listener to the loader instance and then defines the associated function, completeHandler().

In response to a completely loaded document, the event handler function sets the value of the xmlDoc instance to the data property of the target property of the evt parameter passed into the function. That's a mouthful, but you'll understand it when we look at the expression in smaller chunks.

To begin with, we remove the event listener attached to the XML loader to keep our code clean. The incoming parameter, evt, is an instance of the Event class. As is possible with any other class, Event features properties, one of which is called target. The target property refers to the object that dispatched this event in the first place, which is xmlDoc. Being an instance of the XML class, xmlDoc features a data property, which refers to the text content of the flashBooks.xml file—in other words, the actual XML data. To let Flash know it should interpret this text content as XML, the expression evt.target.data is wrapped inside a pair of parentheses (()) and preceded by XML. This is called *casting*, where one data type (String) is converted to another compatible type (XML), and the expression is passed to the xmlDoc variable. At this point, the text file's XML tags become a "living XML object" inside the SWF, accessible via the xmlDoc variable.

To prove it with this sample, a trace(xmlDoc) function call sends the full set of book nodes to the Output panel. Test the movie, and compare the Output panel's content to the flashBooks.xml file itself, which you can open with Dreamweaver CS5 or any simple text editor.

The preceding sample code will serve as the basis for all loading for the rest of the chapter. It's really that simple. Even better, ActionScript 3.0 makes it just as easy to actually *use* XML, so let's jump right in.

Using E4X syntax

In ActionScript 2.0, interacting with an XML class instance was, as we said, like beating yourself on the head with a brick. This was because of the way XML nodes were accessed once loaded, which wasn't by the practical tag names supplied earlier in the chapter.

CHAPTER 12

Until Flash CS3 (and therefore ActionScript 3.0) arrived on the scene, XML in Flash was not up there on the list of "cool things I really need to do." In fact, many designers and developers (one of the authors among them) regarded the use of XML as being akin to slipping on ice and, on the way down, knowing you were in for a world of hurt.

Readers familiar with Flash XML prior to CS3 will doubtless groan to remember obtuse expressions, such as `xmlInstance.firstChild.firstChild.childNodes[2]`. Flash developers used properties like `firstChild` and `childNodes` because they had to, not because it was fun. Then there was the now defunct `XMLConnector` component, which complicated things more than it simplified the process. ActionScript 3.0 does away with this groping, thanks to something called E4X.

Dots and @s

What is E4X, and what makes it so good? Seemingly named after a military missile project, those three characters form a cutesy abbreviation of ECMAScript for XML. It's an ECMA International specification that has been around for a while, but it provides a completely new, simplified way to access data in an ActionScript 3.0 XML instance.

> *What's ECMA? The letters stand for European Computer Manufacturers Association, which was formed in 1961. They got together a few years back to devise the ECMAScript Language Specification, which is the basis for JavaScript and ActionScript. They have moved quite beyond their computer roots, and today the organization is officially known as Ecma International.*

In E4X, element nodes are referenced by the name you give them. Paths to nested elements and attributes are easily expressed by a neatly compact syntax of dots (.) and *at* symbols (@). This syntax closely matches the dot-notation pathing you're familiar with from the Twinkie example in Chapter 4.

Let's see how it works. If you haven't done so already, open the `LoadXML.fla` file in this chapter's Exercise folder. Click into frame 1 of the **scripts** layer, and open the **Actions** panel to reveal the ActionScript. The `trace()` function at line 9 is about to illustrate a number of dynamite E4X features.

Testing the movie as it stands puts the full XML document's contents into the **Output** panel, as shown here:

```
<flashbooks>
  <book title="Flash Applications for Mobile Devices" publisher="friendsofED" pageCount="514">
    <authors>
      <author>Richard Leggett</author>
      <author>Weyert de Boer</author>
      <author>Scott Janousek</author>
    </authors>
  </book>
```

```xml
    <book title="ActionScript 3.0 Image Effects" publisher="friendsofED"
pageCount="663">
        <authors>
            <author>Todd Yard</author>
        </authors>
    </book>
    <book title="ActionScript 3.0 Animation: Making Things Move"
publisher="friendsofED" pageCount="542">
        <authors>
            <author>Keith Peters</author>
        </authors>
    </book>
    <book title="Flash Math Creativity" publisher="friendsofED" pageCount="264">
        <authors>
            <author>David Hirmes</author>
            <author>JD Hooge</author>
            <author>Ken Jokol</author>
            <author>Pavel Kaluzhny</author>
            <author>Ty Lettau</author>
            <author>Lifaros</author>
            <author>Jamie MacDonald</author>
            <author>Gabriel Mulzer</author>
            <author>Kip Parker</author>
            <author>Keith Peters</author>
            <author>Paul Prudence</author>
            <author>Glen Rhodes</author>
            <author>Manny Tan</author>
            <author>Jared Tarbell</author>
            <author>Brandon Williams</author>
        </authors>
    </book>
    <book title="Foundation ActionScript 3.0" publisher="friendsofED" pageCount="566">
        <authors>
            <author>Steve Webster</author>
            <author>Todd Yard</author>
            <author>Sean McSharry</author>
        </authors>
    </book>
</flashbooks>
```

So far, so good. But if you don't care about the root element, `<flashbooks>`, and simply want to see the `<book>` elements, update the `trace()` line to read `trace(xmlDoc.book);`. Once you do that, test the movie again. This time, the `<flashbooks>` tag doesn't show, because you're accessing only its children.

To view <book> elements individually, use the array access operator, [], and specify the desired element, starting your count with 0:

```
trace(xmlDoc.book[0]);
// displays the first <book> element (Flash Applications for Mobile Devices)
// and its children

trace(xmlDoc.book[1]);
// displays the second <book> element (ActionScript 3.0 Image Effects)
// and its children
```

Now, what about attributes? To see those, just precede an attribute's name with the @ symbol as part of your dot-notation path reference. For example, if you want to see the title attribute of the first <book> element, type the following:

```
trace(xmlDoc.book[0].@title);
```

To see the second <book> element's title, substitute 0 with 1; to see the third, substitute 1 with 2; and so on. Based on this pattern, the last element's title attribute would be xmlDoc.book[4].@title. But we know to use the number 4 only because we're aware how many <book> elements there are. What if we didn't know? In that case, it helps to understand exactly what you're getting back from these E4X results. What you're getting are instances of the XMLList class, and that means you can invoke any of the methods that class provides on these expressions.

For example, you've already seen that the expression xmlDoc.book returns a list of all the <book> elements. That list is a bona fide XMLList instance. So, by appending an XMLList method—say, length()—to the expression, you get something useful (in this case, the length of the list, which is 5). We know that in this context counting starts with zero, so to see the title attribute of the last <book> element, put the following somewhat complex expression inside the array access operator ([]):

```
trace(xmlDoc.book[xmlDoc.book.length() - 1].@title);
```

It may look a little scary, but it isn't when you reduce it to its parts. The expression xmlDoc.book.length() - 1 evaluates to the number 4.

To see the title attribute of all <book> elements, drop the array access operator altogether:

```
trace(xmlDoc.book.@title);
```

In the Output panel, you'll see that the combined results run together, as shown in Figure 12-1. This is because these attributes don't have any innate formatting. They aren't elements in a nested hierarchy; they are just individual strings.

XML (DYNAMIC DATA)

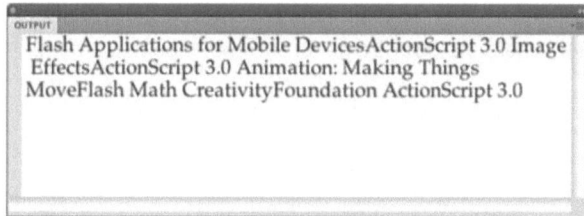

Figure 12-1. Unless they have their own line breaks, attributes will run together.

In this situation, another `XMLList` method can help you. To make each title appear on its own line, append `toXMLString()` to the existing expression:

`trace(xmlDoc.book.@title.toXMLString());`

Swap `title` for the `pageCount` attribute, as follows:

`trace(xmlDoc.book.@pageCount.toXMLString());`

As shown in Figure 12-2, you'll see page counts for each book instead of titles in the `Output` panel.

Figure 12-2. Any element's attributes can be retrieved.

What about looking at a list of the authors? Viewing individual authors is just as easy. Update the `trace()` function to look like this:

`trace(xmlDoc.book[0].authors .author [1]);`

This `trace()` function instructs Flash to look at the first `<book>` element's `<authors>` element and then pull out that node's second `<author>` element, which happens to be `Weyert De Boer`. For fun and to see how easy E4X makes things for you, contrast the preceding intuitive reference with its ActionScript 2.0 equivalent: `xmlDoc.firstChild.firstChild.firstChild.childNodes[1]`. Which would you rather use?

Moving back to the kinder, gentler world of ActionScript 3.0, update the `trace()` function as follows to see the whole 15-member cast of the fourth book:

`trace(xmlDoc.book[3].authors .author);`

This time, you get elements again, complete with their tag markup, as shown in Figure 12-3. This is just like tracing `xmlDoc.book` earlier, where the Output panel showed `<book>` elements and their descendants.

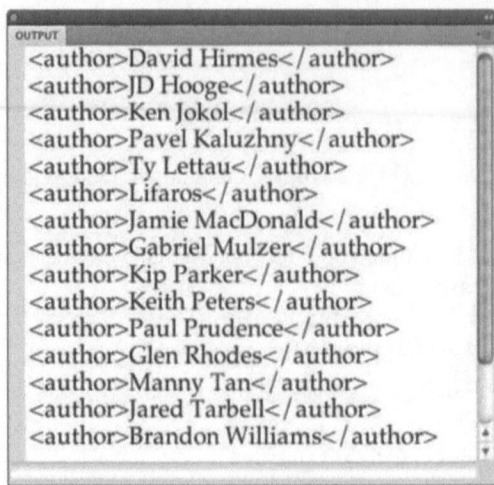

Figure 12-3. Accessing elements selects the elements themselves, as well as their children.

Node types

In the previous section, when you used the array access operator—`xmlDoc.book[0].authors.author[3]`—Flash gave you the immediate descendant of the `<author>` tag you specified, which was a text node (that is, just a string). Here, you're looking at a list of element nodes and their text node descendants. If you want just the text nodes, you can use another XMLList method, `descendants()`, to retrieve what you're after. You'll see an example in just a bit. First, make sure you grasp the idea that, when you see the expression `<author>Keith Peters</author>`, you're not just looking at one node; you're looking at two.

Both the tag (`<author>`) and its content (`Keith Peters`, in this case) comprise the element and text nodes mentioned earlier. The W3C XML recommendation actually specifies a dozen node types, but ActionScript 3.0 supports only a few of them: element, attribute, text, comment, and processing instruction. (And this is actually a relief, because knowing those few lets you easily pull out a tag's content.)

Add the `descendants()` method to the end of your E4X expression to see it in action:

```
trace(xmlDoc.book[4].authors .author .descendants());
```

Like attributes, text nodes don't have any inherent formatting. To put each string on its own line, slap the `toXMLString()` method on the end:

```
trace(xmlDoc.book[4].authors.author.descendants().toXMLString());
```

The result is exactly the sort of thing you might use to populate a text field, as shown in Figure 12-4.

Figure 12-4. Like attributes, text nodes are nothing more than strings.

> *Remember that we are dealing with text in this example. Although the results may look rather plain, you can format and manipulate them in a number of ways, as outlined in Chapters 6 and 13.*

To see how the `descendants()` method works, try it at the end of the expression `xmlDoc.book.authors`, like this:

`trace(xmlDoc.book[4].authors.descendants());`

The result might surprise you: not just immediate descendants, but all descendants are shown (see Figure 12-5). The first child, `<author>Steve Webster</author>`, appears at the top of the list. This includes the `<authors>` element along with its own "offspring," a text node. Next on display is the first grandchild, `Steve Webster` (the first child's child). After that comes the second child, the second child's child (that is, the second grandchild), and so on. The list makes sense, but if you were expecting only a list of immediate children, well, now you know better.

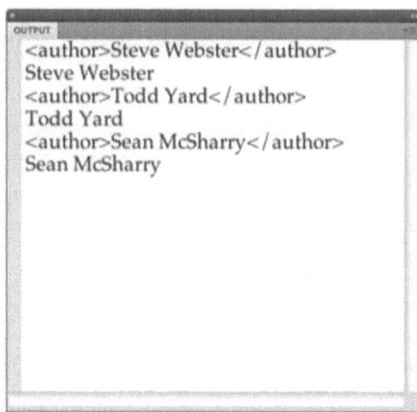

Figure 12-5. The `descendants()` method reveals all descendants.

E4X filtering

All right, we'll give you one more illustration of E4X (we've saved the best for last). The `flashBooks.xml` file included with this chapter's `Exercise` folder files has slightly different `pageCount` attributes from those shown earlier in the chapter. Instead of a whole phrase, such as `500 pages`, these attributes show only numbers. Why? It's because E4X allows you to evaluate comparisons so you can filter content based on specific criteria.

Let's say you want to know which books have a page count longer than 550 pages. Return again to our humble `trace()` function, and update its parameter to the following:

```
trace(xmlDoc.book.(@pageCount > 550));
```

The result is a list of the `<book>` elements whose `pageCount` attribute is greater than 550, along with all their children (see Figure 12-6).

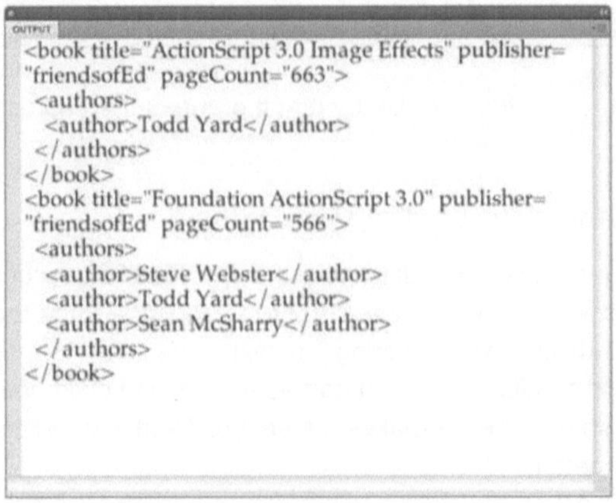

```
<book title="ActionScript 3.0 Image Effects" publisher=
"friendsofEd" pageCount="663">
  <authors>
    <author>Todd Yard</author>
  </authors>
</book>
<book title="Foundation ActionScript 3.0" publisher=
"friendsofEd" pageCount="566">
  <authors>
    <author>Steve Webster</author>
    <author>Todd Yard</author>
    <author>Sean McSharry</author>
  </authors>
</book>
```

Figure 12-6. E4X allows filtering by way of comparison operators.

The parentheses tell Flash that you're intending to filter the returned `XMLList` instance. Inside the parentheses, the expression is a simple comparison, `@pageCount> 550`, which in plain English would be, "Yo, dude, which `<book>` elements' `pageCount` attributes match this criterion?" Flash searches every `<book>` element in the bunch because nothing appears between the word `book` and the dot that begins the next expression.

What if you want only the title of these books? Try this:

```
trace(xmlDoc.book.(@pageCount > 550).@title.toXMLString());
```

The trick to understanding this expression, as always, is to break it into its parts. On its own, each concept is usually easy enough to understand. These concepts—these subexpressions—are separated by dots. A blow-by-blow account of the preceding `trace()` goes like this:

1. xmlDoc.book returns an XMLList instance composed of all the <book> elements in the xmlDoc instance.
2. Of this list, the expression .(@pageCount >550) filters only those <book> elements whose pageCount attribute is greater than the value 550.
3. The subexpression .@title refines the results further by pulling only the title attribute.
4. Finally, .toXMLString() invokes the XMLList.toXMLString() method to clean up the results.

Double dots and more

True, we already said "one more illustration of E4X," and that's the preceding one. If you're in a hurry to dispense with all this theory and jump head first into a practical application, we tip our fedoras and invite you to make a beeline for the next section. But we figure at least a handful of you are wondering whether it's possible to return book titles based upon who helped write the book. Dead simple.

Open the LoadXML-E4XBonusRound.fla file that accompanies this chapter, and click into frame 1 of the **scripts** layer. Most of the ActionScript should look familiar. The important part appears in lines 9 through 12, because it introduces three things: an operator called the descendant accessor (..), a new XML method called parent(), and the for each..in statement:

```
for each ( var node:XML in xmlDoc..author.(descendants() == "Keith Peters" ) )
{
        trace( node.parent().parent().@title );
}
```

The for each..in statement was introduced to ActionScript 3.0 thanks to the E4X specification. A similar ActionScript statement, for..in, has been available for quite some time. You point for..in at an object, and it loops through that object's properties—however many properties there happen to be. But note that a for..in statement loops on the properties' *names*, rather than the properties themselves. This can be either nifty or frustrating, depending on your needs. In contrast, the new for each..in statement loops on an object's actual properties, which is great for what we need in this particular endeavor.

To understand the mechanism of this E4X filtering, let's start with a skeleton and slowly build up to the skin. Here are the bones:

```
for each (someProperty in someObject) {
  // do something
}
```

The someObject in question is the hardest part of this equation, but based on what you've seen, it shouldn't be impenetrable. This object is an XMLList instance determined by the expression xmlDoc..author.(descendants() == "Keith Peters"). Up to this point, you would have used the longhand version to retrieve the same list. The longhand version looks like this:

```
xmlDoc.book.authors.author.(descendants() == "Keith Peters");
```

This version is still as valid as ever. But the descendant accessor (the double dots) lets you skip past the intermediate nodes—book and authors—straight to the element you're after. Pretty slick! Stepping through the subexpressions piece by piece, then, we get the following:

- xmlDoc..author: All <author> elements in the xmlDoc instance, no matter to which intermediate nodes they belong.
- .(descendants() == "Keith Peters"): Of that list, a comparison of the descendants of each <author> element against a particular string. These descendants are text nodes that happen to represent author names, and the comparison looks for a match with the string "Keith Peters". The returned XMLList instance is the someObject from our skeleton.

That gives us the following:

```
var node:XML;
for each (someProperty in xmlDoc..author.(descendants() == ↵
"Keith Peters")) {
  // do something
}
```

The replacement for our stand-in someProperty is an XML instance, stored in an arbitrarily named variable, node.

```
var node:XML;
for each (node in xmlDoc..author.(descendants() == "Keith Peters")) {
  // do something
}
```

All this means is that the for each..in statement is going to make laps around the node list returned by the comparison expression. On each lap, it will update the value of that node variable to the latest XML node it finds in that list. The node variable *becomes* the XML object in question. It's an XML reference, which means you can work your recently acquired E4X magic on it.

This is where the parent() method comes into play. Remember that at this point you're dealing with an element node (<author>) whose descendant matches the string "Keith Peters". As an XML instance, the <author> node has access to the XML.parent() method, which pretty much works in the same way as the MovieClip.parent property. The parent of <author> is <authors>, and the parent of <authors> is <book>. Given that point of view, the title attribute, referenced with the @ symbol, makes sense:

```
var node:XML;
for each (node in xml..author.(descendants() == "Keith Peters")) {
  trace(node.parent().parent().@title);
}
```

Namespaces

In spite of everything you've just seen, there will come a day when you pull on your E4X wizard hat, roll up your oversized E4X wizard sleeves, wave the wand...and nothing happens. You won't see anything in your `XMLList` instance. It won't be because you've done anything wrong, only that you've omitted something: the acknowledgment of an occasionally present XML *namespace*. In XML, namespaces are a way to filter or label certain elements in order to control their visibility. Namespaces basically give elements a secret handshake, and you can't see the elements unless you know it.

So, what's a namespace? The namespace concept is not unique to XML. It has been part of computer programming almost since there were computers. The idea behind a namespace is that, at any given time, a single name should refer to a single item regardless of whether it is a variable, function, or even a document. Think of your favorite sports team. Each player on that team wears a shirt with a number on it, and that number is unique to that player. No other player on the team can wear that number. When they play against the opposition, there may be someone on the other team wearing that same number, but, again, that number—or namespace—is used only by that player on that team.

XML documents don't require namespaces, but many use them, including iTunes playlists, ATOM and RSS feeds, and even Flash. In fact, let's use a bit of XML content that was generated by the **Commands ➤ Copy Motion as XML** command. The **Copy Motion as XML** command provides a way to encode certain kinds of motion tweens into XML data, and its root element contains three namespaces. Here's one example, which is available as `CopyMotion.xml` in the `Exercise` folder for this chapter:

```
<Motion duration="24" xmlns="fl.motion.*" xmlns:geom="flash.geom.*"
xmlns:filters="flash.filters.*">
  <source>
    <Source frameRate="24" x="150" y="120" scaleX="1" scaleY="1"
rotation="0" elementType="movie clip" symbolName="Symbol 1">
      <dimensions>
        <geom:Rectangle left="0" top="0" width="80" height="60"/>
      </dimensions>
      <transformationPoint>
        <geom:Point x="0.5" y="0.5"/>
      </transformationPoint>
    </Source>
  </source>

  <Keyframe index="0" tweenSync="true"/>
</Motion>
```

In XML, namespaces are defined by `xmlns` attributes—in this case, in the `<Motion>` element. Of the three defined, two have identifiers (`geom` and `filters`), and one doesn't, which means it's there but doesn't have a name. Given what you know and assuming the preceding XML is loaded into an `XML` instance named `xmlDoc`, you would expect to see the contents of the `<Source>` element with an E4X expression like this:

```
trace(xmlDoc..Source);
```

The problem is that if you test that—you can use CopyMotion.fla in the Exercise folder—you'll find that the Output panel does not display anything. To get your data back, you'll need to use the Namespace class, which is easy to do. Here's how:

1. In CopyMotion.fla, click into frame 1, and open the **Actions** panel to view the full code and trace() function:

```
var xmlDoc:XML = new XML();
var loader:URLLoader = new URLLoader();
var req:URLRequest = new URLRequest("CopyMotion.xml");
loader.load(req);

loader.addEventListener(Event.COMPLETE, completeHandler);
function completeHandler(evt:Event):void {
  xmlDoc = XML(evt.target.data);

  trace(xmlDoc..Source);
};
```

2. Enter the following new ActionScript just before the trace() function:

```
var ns:Namespace = new Namespace("fl.motion.*");
```

This declares a variable, ns, which is set to an instance of the Namespace class. This instance is fed the value portion of the XML document's first mxlns attribute ("fl.motion.*") as a parameter.

3. At this point, that ns variable gives you a prefix you can use to unlock your data. Use the name qualifier operator (::) between the ns variable, and the node will "unlock."

```
var ns:Namespace = new Namespace("fl.motion.*");
trace(xmlDoc..ns::Source);
```

4. Test the movie, and your <Source> element comes out of hiding, as shown in Figure 12-7.

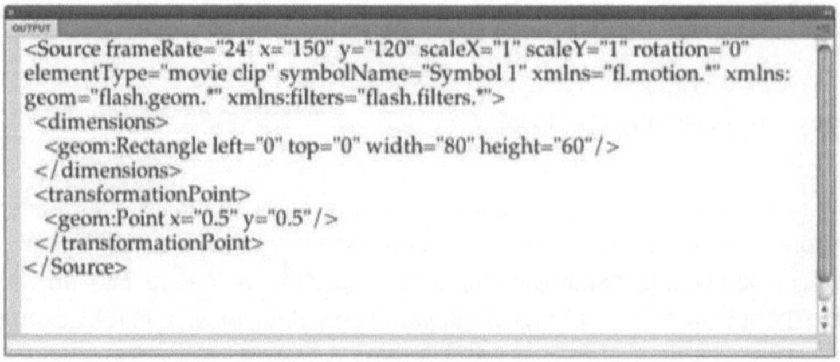

```
<Source frameRate="24" x="150" y="120" scaleX="1" scaleY="1" rotation="0"
elementType="movie clip" symbolName="Symbol 1" xmlns="fl.motion.*" xmlns:
geom="flash.geom.*" xmlns:filters="flash.filters.*">
  <dimensions>
    <geom:Rectangle left="0" top="0" width="80" height="60"/>
  </dimensions>
  <transformationPoint>
    <geom:Point x="0.5" y="0.5"/>
  </transformationPoint>
</Source>
```

Figure 12-7. Using a namespace instance can bring data back to light.

If you look carefully at the results in the `Output` panel, you'll see that the `<Source>` element now contains additional attributes not in the original XML document. Those are the namespaces. Why they show up here is one of the mysteries of life. But at least you won't be caught by surprise if you run into this sort of XML content.

5. If you don't know an `xmlns` attribute's value before writing your ActionScript, you can use the `XML.namespace()` method to grab the namespace currently in use. Replace the `"fl.motion.*"` parameter you entered just a moment ago with the following:

```
var ns:Namespace = new Namespace(xmlDoc.namespace());
trace(xmlDoc..ns::Source);
```

6. Test again, and you'll see the same `Output` panel content, even though ActionScript supplied the namespace information for you.

That's it for the fundamentals of the relationship between XML and Flash. When you reach Chapter 14, you will get a deeper understanding of how to use it and where it fits when you create a slide show, an MP3 player, and a video player that plays a sequence of videos based on an XML document. Next, though, we want to show you a new XML-based Flash file format called XFL that is going to have the codies drooling on their keyboards.

Your turn: time to explore XFL

To this point in the chapter you have seen how XML can be used to manage data in a Flash document. Now let's turn our attention to using XML to build and edit a Flash document without using Flash.

Over the past few years Adobe, at least to one of the authors, seemed to be developing a curious fascination with metadata and XML. Some of these efforts—the XMP engine—seemed to be rather esoteric and others, such as fixing how Flash worked with XML files, were downright useful. Phrases such as "interesting" and "curious" sort of disappeared when Adobe released the Flex and AIR technologies. Along the way, a new language, MXML, appeared and the phrase *Flash Platform* took on the trappings of a noun in much the same way that Photoshop became a verb.

If there was one issue that bedeviled developers, it was a way of getting all of the diverse applications comprising the platform to "play nice" with each other. This obviously didn't include designers because the only way of making this happen was to give the developers a way of changing things up or moving Flash files among the members of a workgroup without losing the integrity of the project.

The solution to that issue was handed to the community with the release of Flash CS4. This release introduced a new file format called XFL, which took an entire Flash movie broke it into its constituent elements and essentially "exposed" the structure of a Flash movie to an entire workgroup. The bottom line was the community was handed a method of working with Flash without working with Flash. One of the authors would make that statement in front of groups of developers, and inevitably he would see a lot of blank faces or hear muted mutterings of "Huh?" It shouldn't come as any great surprise then to say the format didn't gain the expected traction. That is all about to change.

What is XFL?

XFL isn't some sort of new arena football league. The XFL file format is a way to represent a Flash Professional document as an XML-based, open folder of files. Figure 12-8 shows an example of the XFL folder structure. You will notice that there is a file called `DOMDocument.xml`. This file is the key. Inside it you will see all of the information, presented as XML, for your document including timelines, actions, motion paths, and so on. When you first open it, the document won't seem to make much sense. We'll get you over that first impression because the code in this document can be edited and saved. When you do that, your changes will automatically take effect when you launch the file.

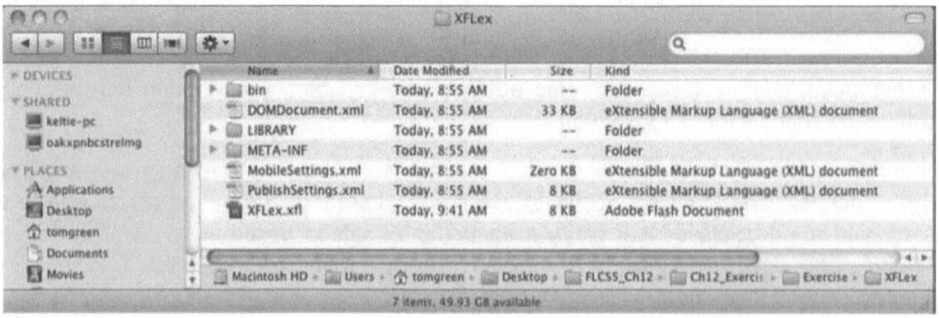

Figure 12-8. The XFL folder structure

Designers are also invited to the XFL party. The Library folder contains all the assets—images, audio, video, graphics and so on—contained in the document. These files can all be edited in Fireworks, Photoshop, InDesign, After Effects, Soundbooth, or whatever app is required to edit them and then can be saved and stuck back in the folder, and the changes will appear when the XFL file is opened in Flash.

Before we dig in, let's clearly understand that even though this is a massive change don't for a moment think that what we are going to present is easy. It isn't. You need to approach this new workflow with a high degree of organization and planning. Though we are going to show you how to change things in a Flash document based on this new format, don't for a minute think we are subliminally saying, "This is dead simple." Make one mistake, and you are essentially back to the drawing board. The exercise we are about to complete is designed more to show where stuff is and how these changes can be made than to hand you a hunting license. Still, this is pretty darn cool, and we think you will agree with that observation by the end of the exercise. Let's get started:

1. Open the `XFLexercise.fla` file found in the `XFL` folder in this chapter's `Exercise` folder. The reason for putting the `.fla` in a separate folder is to let you create an XFL document and not have to root around for the files created. When the file opens, you will see that there are some assets on the stage and in the **Library**. Also, note the layers and the `trace` statement contained in the **Actions** layer.

XML (DYNAMIC DATA)

2. Select **File ➤ Save As** to open the **Save As** dialog box. Open the **Format** drop-down menu, and select **Flash CS5 Uncompressed Document (*.xfl)**, as shown in Figure 12-9. The first two formats are the traditional .fla file format which we have been working with since Flash first appeared. Double-click an .fla, and Flash launches. The uncompressed document is an exploded view of the .fla. It will create a number of files and folders to hold the content which a developer, with serious coding chops, can use to change the Flash document without ever having to use Flash. The most important file, as you will see in a moment, is the .xfl document. Double-click it, and Flash will open. Conversely, it can be opened in Dreamweaver CS5 or other code editor, and the codie gets to play with XML. When the codie saves the document, the designer simply needs to double-click the .xfl document, and Flash will launch.

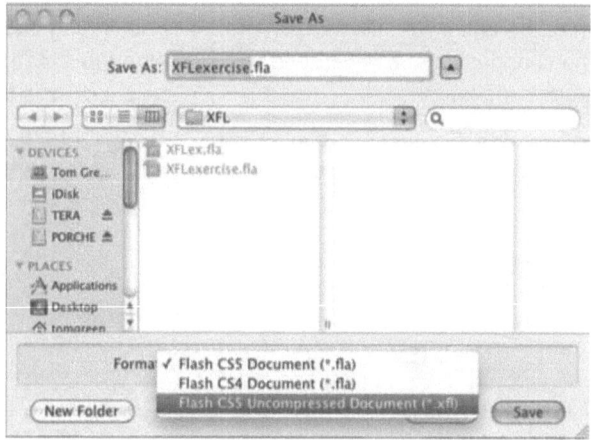

Figure 12-9. Creating an .xfl document

3. Minimize Flash, and navigate to the Exercise folder. Open the XFL folder, and you will see that a new project folder, bearing the name of the .fla, has been placed in the folder as well.

> *If you create external AS files, don't place them in this project folder. These files go in their usual place, alongside the .fla file in the root or top-level folder of the project.*

4. Open this new folder, and you will see three folders—bin, LIBRARY and META-INF—as well as three XML documents and the XFL document.

5. Open the LIBRARY folder. When the folder opens, you will see that all the files found in your Flash project's library are contained in this folder. This would also include any audio or video files, if they were a part of the project. There are a couple of things you need to know about this folder:

    - These are the contents of your library. Don't remove them.
    - All of the files are editable providing you don't change the name, and they are returned to this folder.
    - You can't add items to this folder. Any objects added to this folder must be loaded into the Flash library before they will appear.

6. Open the DOMDocument.xml file in Dreamweaver CS5 or a text editor. Take a minute to review the file. You will discover it is broken into sections that follow the structure of the Flash file. This file is at the heart of the entire XFL file format. The really neat thing about this document is it can be edited, and the changes can be saved and will appear in the .xfl document when you open it. Let's make some changes.

7. Scroll down the open code document and, as shown in Figure 12-10, locate the ActionScript used in the file. It has been decided that the trace statement needs to go and to be replaced with a stop(); action.

```
15          <DOMFrame index="0" keyMode="9728">
16            <Actionscript>
17              <script><![CDATA[trace("This is the XFL example.");]]></script>
18            </Actionscript>
19            <elements/>
20          </DOMFrame>
```

Figure 12-10. Changing a frame script

8. Select the code—trace("This is the XFL example.");—and replace it with stop();. Save the XML document. To see your change, return to Flash, close the open XFL document, and reopen it to load the changed XML file. Your code now has a stop(); action. What this tells you is that a developer can make changes to code on the timeline without needing a copy of Flash. Save the changes, and close the document.

9. Return to the XML file. Locate the color of the box found in the **Box** layer of the Flash file. It needs to change to an Olive color (#999900). Locate the section that starts with <DOMLayer name = "Box" ... and change the value of the hexadecimal color in the <SolidColor color ... /> tag to #999900, as shown in Figure 12-11. Save the file.

XML (DYNAMIC DATA)

```
52      <DOMLayer name="Box" color="#FF800A" autoNamed="false">
53          <frames>
54              <DOMFrame index="0" keyMode="9728">
55                  <elements>
56                      <DOMShape>
57                          <fills>
58                              <FillStyle index="1">
59 ▼                              <SolidColor color="#999900"/>
60                              </FillStyle>
61                          </fills>
62                          <edges>
```

Figure 12-11. Changing the color of a drawing object

10. Reopen the XFL document in Flash, and the box now has a green color.

11. Return to the XML document. Let's get rid of the author's photo and replace it with another in the **Library**.

12. Scroll down to the **Photo** layer in the XML document. Locate the <DOMBitmapInstance… > line shown in Figure 12-12, and change the libraryItemName from "Tom.jpg" to "OliverSeller.jpg". Save the XML file, and relaunch the XFL document. You now have an olive seller in the image.

```
52      <DOMLayer name="Box" color="#FF800A" autoNamed="false">
53          <frames>
54              <DOMFrame index="0" keyMode="9728">
55                  <elements>
56                      <DOMShape>
57                          <fills>
58                              <FillStyle index="1">
59 ▼                              <SolidColor color="#999900"/>
60                              </FillStyle>
61                          </fills>
62                          <edges>
```

Figure 12-12. Swapping an image

> Changing the **tx** and **ty** values shown in Figure 12-13 is how you change the **x** and **y** properties of an object in the document.

13. Return to the XML document. Let's wrap this up by changing both the title and the flag.

14. Locate the DOM reference to the Flag layer in the XML, and change the name from CanadaFlag.fxg to China.fxg.

15. The two text blocks are easy to locate. They are both TLF instances, meaning the XML document will be exposing all of their properties. Locate the name layer in the code, and in the properties found between the <markup> and </markup> tags, as shown in Figure 12-13, change the text from Tom Green to Olive Seller.

```
39            <DOMLayer name="Photo" color="#FF4FFF" autoNamed="false">
40              <frames>
41                <DOMFrame index="0" keyMode="9728">
42                  <elements>
43                    <DOMBitmapInstance name="" referenceID="" libraryItemName="OliveSeller.jpg">
44                      <matrix>
45                        <Matrix tx="306" ty="88"/>
46                      </matrix>
47                    </DOMBitmapInstance>
```

Figure 12-13. Editing text in the DOMDocument.xml file

16. Save the XML file, and relaunch the XFL document. The interface now sports a new flag and head line.

XFL bonus round

Having discovered how you can make changes to a Flash movie using the DOMDocument.xfl file is neat, but we just bet you are thinking, "Guys, what if I have to edit an image in the document? How do I put it back and get it to appear in the XFL file?" Great question. Here's how:

1. Open the OliveSeller.jpg image found in the XFL ➤ LIBRARY folder in an imaging application such as Photoshop or Fireworks.

2. "Flop" the folder by flipping it on the horizontal axis. Save the file, and don't change the name.

3. Reopen the XFL document. The image is facing in the opposite direction.

> *Here's an interesting little trick. Leave the XFL document open and make another change, like flipping it upside down, to the Oliverseller.jpg image. Save the image. Return to the XFL file and click it. The change is made.*

What you have learned

In this chapter, we gave you the absolute basics of XML use in Flash. On the surface, it may not seem like much. However, what we have presented in this chapter forms the foundation for complex Flash projects ranging from video pickers, MP3 players, and portfolio sites to e-commerce applications. In this chapter, you have discovered the following:

- The relationship between an XML document and Flash CS5
- How to retrieve and filter XML data using E4X syntax
- The creation of an XFL document and how to manipulate its contents.

The most important point you need to take away from this chapter is the sheer flexibility of XML in your Flash design and development efforts. You can make your movies expand or contract effortlessly by simply adding to or subtracting from the XML document being used by the movie. This is the true meaning of *dynamic*. Toss the new XFL format into the mix and a whole new world of Flash authoring and team dynamics opens up.

Now that you know how dynamic content is added to Flash, let's take a look at how you can dynamically change the "look" of a file using Cascading Style Sheets of CSS. Turn the page so we can get started.

Chapter 13

CSS

Cascading Style Sheets (CSS) refers to a World Wide Web Consortium (W3C) specification that, in the W3C's own words, provides "a simple mechanism for adding style (e.g., fonts, colors, spacing) to Web documents" (www.w3.org/Style/CSS/). The concept is simple, but as any web developer will tell you, CSS can be a behemoth when it comes to managing HTML. In other words, CSS is rugged and powerful and does a great job at making HTML behave. Obviously, this is a good thing. But CSS can also be a bit hard to work with, especially when you have Classic and TLF text in the same **Properties** panel.

In the world of HTML, a major issue with CSS is the wide variety of browsers (and versions of browsers) in use by the general public. Each browser supports CSS to a varying, and often buggy, degree. In Flash, you have a lot less to worry about, even though the use of CSS requires ActionScript. Why are things easier in a SWF? The answer is mainly that Flash supports only a very small subset of the full CSS specification. This means that there is less for you to worry about. As a Flash designer, you're not worried about half a dozen browsers but merely a single Flash Player plug-in. As an extra plus, the supported CSS subset hasn't really changed since the feature was introduced in Flash MX 2004 (Flash Player 7).

Here's what we'll cover in this chapter:

- Understanding the power and limitations of CSS in Flash
- Generating and applying CSS in ActionScript
- Using custom HTML tags
- Taking advantage of inheritance in CSS
- Styling anchor tag hyperlinks

CHAPTER 13

- Embedding fonts for CSS
- Loading styles from an external CSS file

The following files are used in this chapter (located in `Chapter12/ExerciseFiles_Ch12/Exercise/`):

- `Styling01.fla`
- `Styling02.fla`
- `Styling03.fla`
- `Styling04.fla`
- `ClassSelectors.fla`
- `ElementSelectors.fla`
- `Hyperlinks.fla`
- `HyperlinksVaried.fla`
- `Inheritance.fla`
- `StylingEmbeddedFonts01.fla`
- `styles.css`
- `StylingExternal.fla`

The source files are available online from either of the following sites:

- `www.FoundationFlashCS4.com`
- `www.friendsofED.com/download.html?isbn=1430229940`

In a nutshell, the power of CSS is that it allows you to separate styling from informational content. In Flash, we're essentially talking about text. You'll wrap text content in HTML tags—that's one side of the coin—and you'll style those HTML tags with CSS—that's the other side. Flip that coin as you see fit. If you change your mind about how the text should look—regarding font, color, indentation, spacing, and the like—you can change the CSS without affecting the text. The reverse is also true. Not only that, but styling can be applied to numerous text fields at once, and even managed from a convenient external file. As if that were not enough, this external style sheet can update a movie's styles without requiring you to recompile the SWF! Have we got your interest yet?

> *If you have little or no experience using CSS, then you may find this chapter to be a bit of a tough "slog" with a lot of terminology and techniques that will appear to be either mystifying or difficult to comprehend. If this describes you or your reaction to this chapter, then we suggest you either pick up a copy of* Getting StartED with CSS *by David Powers from friends of ED or that you head over to* `www.w3schools.com/` *and work your way through their excellent CSS tutorials.*

Styling with CSS

Before we turn you loose, it is important that you understand a couple of things. The first is the way CSS is handled by the Classic Text and TLF engines is different. You can't mix them up on the same stage. The other thing is Flash CS5 seems to have developed an unhealthy fascination with embedded fonts. Until further notice, ignore the messages in the Output panel.

The bulk of this chapter is going to be a focus on getting text styled. This means we will be using Classic Text, and the text will be added to the stage using dynamic text boxes with multiline behaviors assigned to them in the Properties panel.

> *Though we would dearly love to include how to style TLF text in this chapter, it became apparent rather early in the planning for this chapter that the technique for accomplishing this task is beyond the scope of this book. We simply did not have the space to do it justice, and the ActionScript required to make CSS work with TLF containers is in the realm of intermediate to advanced ActionScript coding.*

Before we start styling text, here are the available style properties:

- color: This property determines the color of text, specified as a hexadecimal value preceded by the # sign, as in #FFFFFF, rather than the 0xFFFFFF you would use in ActionScript.
- display: This property determines how the styled object is displayed. Values include inline (displayed without a built-in line break), block (includes a built-in line break), and none (not displayed at all).
- fontFamily: This property allows you to specify fonts for text content—either a single font or comma-separated collection of fonts listed in order of desirability.
- fontSize: This property is used for specifying font size in pixels. Only number values are accepted (units such as pt or px are ignored).
- fontStyle: This property optionally displays text content in italics, if the font in use supports it. Values include normal and italic.
- fontWeight: This property optionally displays text content in bold, if the font in use supports it. Values include normal and bold.
- kerning: This property, if specified as true, allows embedded fonts to be rendered with kerning, if the font supports it. *Kerning* is the removal of a bit of space between letters. It is applied only in SWF files generated in the Windows version of Flash. Once the SWF is published, the kerning is visible both in Windows and Mac.
- leading: This property determines the amount of space between lines of text. Negative values, which are allowed, condense lines. Only number values are accepted (units such as pt or px are ignored).

CHAPTER 13

- `letterSpacing`: Not to be confused with `kerning`, this property determines the amount of space distributed evenly between characters. Only number values are accepted (units such as `pt` or `px` are ignored).

- `marginLeft` and `marginRight`: These properties add marginal padding by the specified amount in pixels to the left and right. Only number values are accepted (units such as `pt` or `px` are ignored).

- `textAlign`: This property aligns text. Values include `left`, `center`, `right`, and `justify`.

- `textDecoration`: This property adds or removes underscoring by way of the `underline` and `none` values.

- `textIndent`: This property indents a text field by the specified amount in pixels. Only number values are accepted (units such as `pt` or `px` are ignored).

Now let's roll up our sleeves and use some of these properties:

1. Open the `Styling01.fla` file from the `Exercise` folder for this chapter. There are a few things already in place for you. Note the two dynamic text fields, side by side, with instance names `unstyledContent` and `styledContent`. There's also a bit of ActionScript in frame 1 of the **scripts** layer, which does nothing more than build a string of HTML tags and apply that string to the `TextField.htmlText` property of the two text fields. The image, banner, and headlines are found in the **TopPage** folder.

2. Test the movie to see two identical copies of the Street Food copy shown in Figure 13-1.

Figure 13-1. CSS is about to save you a lot of effort.

CSS

When you use CSS in Flash, the styling must be applied to a text field before any text is added to it. If you apply styling afterward, you'll get mixed results, or the styling won't work at all. We're going to leave the unstyledContent text field as is in order to let you see how the changes affect what you started with. The CSS that formats the styled text field will need to appear before the last line of ActionScript—styledContent.htmlText = str;—because the last line actually provides the HTML text.

3. Put your mouse pointer in front of the last line of code, and press Enter (Windows) or Return (Mac) three times. This is where the new ActionScript will go. Now, hold that thought.

How is this CSS thing going to work? That's a good question, and thankfully, the answer isn't especially complicated, even though the process takes a few steps. First, you're going to create an instance of the StyleSheet class. Next, you'll decide on a handful of style properties. You'll repeatedly use the StyleSheet.setStyle() method to associate those properties with an HTML tag. Finally, you'll associate the StyleSheet instance itself with a given text field and add HTML content to that text field.

The crafty thing is that there are a number of ways to handle the setStyle() part. We're going to step you through a wordy approach first, because we think it best summarizes, on a conceptual level, what's going on. When you've seen that, we'll steer you toward a more compact approach, which will eventually lead toward an external CSS file, which is the most versatile way to handle styling in Flash.

4. OK, still holding the thought? Good. Put your mouse pointer into the second of the three blank lines that precede the last line of code. Type the following ActionScript:

```
var css:StyleSheet = new StyleSheet();
var style:Object = new Object();

style.fontStyle = "italic";
style.color = "#FF0000";
style.leading = -"-2";

css.setStyle("li", style);
styledContent.styleSheet = css;
```

Let's review what you've done so far. The first line declares a variable, css, which points to an instance of the StyleSheet class. The StyleSheet class lets you create a StyleSheet object that contains text formatting rules for font size, color, and other styles.

The second line declares another variable, style, which points to an instance of the generic Object class—that's right, this is an Object object. The next three lines set arbitrary properties of this new object: fontStyle, color, and leading, each of which is set to a string value. The second-to-last line refers again to the css instance, using that instance to invoke StyleSheet.setStyle() with two parameters: an HTML tag to style and the object with which to style it. Quite simply, this line says, "Yo, any <li> tags in the house? If so, you're about to meet the style object, whose instructions are to render you in italics, in a red color #FF0000 and at a leading of -2." Finally, a text field whose instance name is styledContent has its styleSheet property associated with the css instance.

5. Test the movie so far to see a change in all the <li> content, as shown in Figure 13-2. You can save and close the movie if you want.

CHAPTER 13

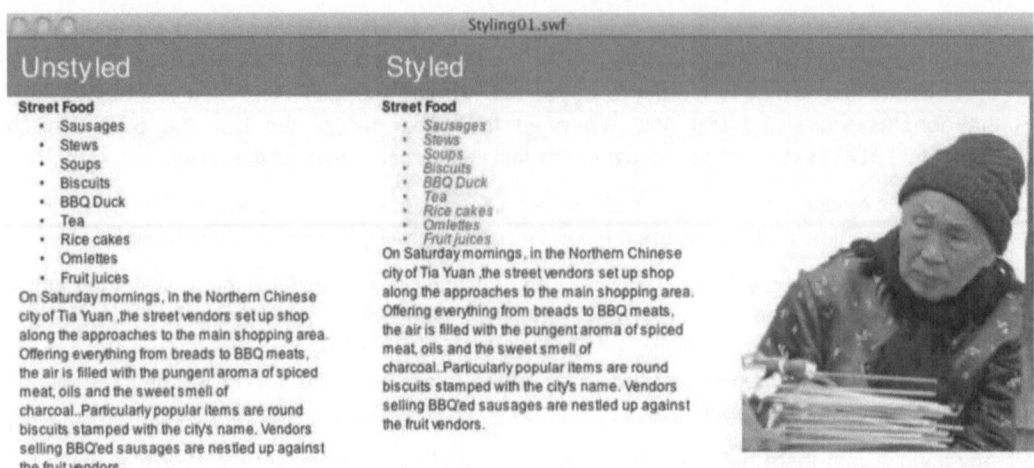

Figure 13-2. CSS styling applied to a series of `<li>` tags

Pretty nifty! Now, in case you thought that ActionScript was a lot to type, keep in mind that what you've seen is the most verbose of the styling approaches. It's possible to collapse five of those lines into one line, which we'll do in just a moment. First, let's take a look at how this might have happened without CSS—because once you see that catastrophe, even this version will seem a welcome relief.

Taking just the first `<li>` tag's content, how would you apply italics? That's easy enough. You'll remember from Chapter 6 that you do this with the `<li>` tag. So far, then, we have one nested pair:

`<li><i>Sausages</i></li>`

What about the coloring? That's the `<font>` tag. Combined, that makes this:

`<li><i><font color="#FF0000">Sausages</font></i></li>`

Almost done! The final style property is leading (the spacing between lines). In the HTML-only realm, that requires the proprietary Flash tag `<textformat>`. This brings the combined total of nested tags to the following example of spaghetti code:

`<li><i><font color="#FF0000"><textformat leading="-2">Sausages</textformat></font></i></li>`

Multiply that by the nine bullet points in this text block, and this exercise becomes a "feat of endurance"! If you decide later to change the text color, you'll need to revisit all nine nested `<font>` tags and either edit or remove them. It's a mess. Definitely, the CSS styling mechanism is the nicer pick—all the more so if we can reduce the amount of ActionScript code.

To accomplish that reduction, we're going to rely on a shortcut in creating our `Object` instance, involving the use of the curly braces (`{}`). Our `setStyle()` line will continue to use `"li"` as the first parameter, but

CSS

the second parameter will be composed of a single "shortcut" object that holds all three styling properties at once.

The actual ActionScript looks like this:

```
myCss.setStyle("li", {fontStyle: "italic", color: "#A2A2A2",leading: "-2"});
```

This brings the full ActionScript styling portion to a mere three lines:

```
var myCssStyleSheet = new StyleSheet();
myCss.setStyle("li", {fontStyle: "italic", color: "#A2A2A2",leading: "-2"});
styledContent.styleSheet = myCss;
```

Using this approach, let's style a few more HTML tags:

1. Open the Styling02.fla file in this chapter's Exercise folder. This file picks up where we left off. The same text fields are in place, and some styling has already been applied (see the **scripts** layer). What's there uses the shortened code version we just looked at.

2. Now, you'll style all the <p> tags. Position your mouse pointer after the setStyle() line, and press Enter (Windows) or Return (Mac) to make room for the new code. Update your ActionScript so that it includes the following new code (shown in bold):

```
var myCss:StyleSheet = new StyleSheet();
myCsssetStyle("li", {fontStyle: "italic", color: "#A2A2A2", leading: "-2"});
myCss.setStyle("p", {textAlign: "justify", leading: "6"});
styledContent.styleSheet = myCSS;
```

3. Test your movie to see the new formatting—justified and with a taller line height—below the bullet points at the bottom right (see Figure 13-3).

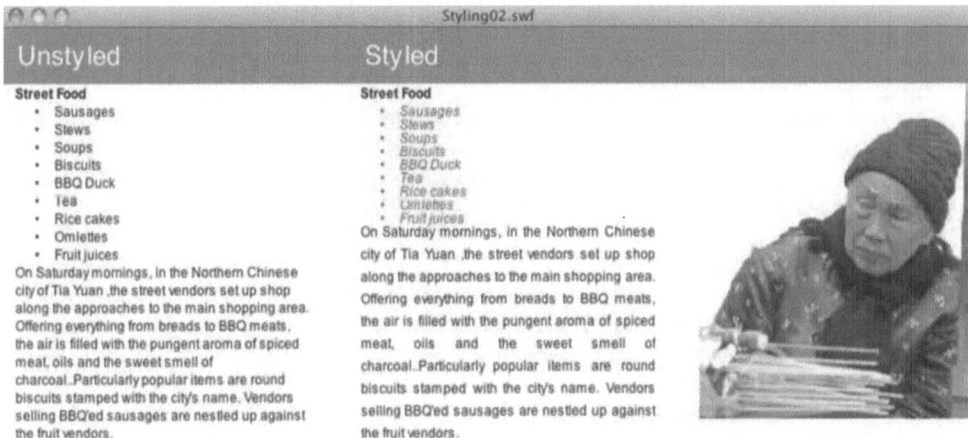

Figure 13-3. After the first style is in place, additional styles are a snap.

675

CHAPTER 13

Say, this is encouraging! Let's keep right on going. There really isn't enough space between the bullet points and the text below, so let's pad the bottom of the <ul> tag a bit. We also want the recipe's title to stand out more.

4. Enter the **scripts** layer again, and update the styling ActionScript so that it includes the following new code (shown in bold):

```
var myCss:StyleSheet = new StyleSheet();
myCss.setStyle("li", {fontStyle: "italic", color: "#FF0000",leading: -"-2"});
myCss.setStyle("p", {textAlign: "justify", leading: "6"});
myCss.setStyle("ul", {leading: "4"});
myCsssetStyle("b", {fontFamily: "Impact", fontSize: "18",color: "#339966"});
styledContent.styleSheet = myCss;
```

5. Test the movie to see the new styling—well, part of it.

Whoops! There's now space after the bullets—the additional 4 pixels of leading we wanted—but the title (the content) hasn't changed at all! What's going on? It is a matter of selectors, which we'll deal with in the next section.

6. Feel free to save the file or close it without saving the changes.

We're going to go off on a sizable tangent here, but don't worry. It all eventually leads back to the Street Food. The tangent...you know how to add styles, but what about loading a style sheet that already contains the styles?

Loading external CSS

If we had to pick our favorite aspect of CSS in Flash, it would undoubtedly be that CSS styling can be loaded from an external file. The existence of this feature brings the concept of separating style from content to its logical conclusion.

Given all you've learned so far in this chapter, you'll be happy to find that loading external CSS is a piece of cake. There's really only one snare to be aware of: some of the style properties we showed you in the beginning of the chapter are spelled just a tad differently when they appear in an external file. Single-word properties, such as `color` and `display`, are identical. Multiple-word properties, such as `fontFamily` and `fontSize`, are split into hyphenated parts: `font-family`, `font-size`, and so on.

To see how external CSS works, open the `StylingExternal.fla` file in this chapter's `Exercise` folder. You'll see a single text file with the instance name `styledContent`. Click into frame 1 of the **scripts** layer, and take a look at the ActionScript. The HTML portion is for a Wasabi Salmon recipe with a token hyperlink at the bottom. The new stuff is just below it:

```
var css:StyleSheet = new StyleSheet();
var loader:URLLoader = new URLLoader();
var req:URLRequest = new URLRequest("styles.css")
```

```
loader.load(req);
loader.addEventListener(Event.COMPLETE, completeHandler);

function completeHandler(evt:Event):void {
  css.parseCSS(evt.target.data);
  styledContent.styleSheet = css;
  styledContent.htmlText = str;
};
```

The first line creates our familiar StyleSheet instance. The next two lines are new. A variable, loader, is declared and set to an instance of the URLLoader class. This differs from the Loader class (covered in Chapter 14), which loads images or SWFs. What makes URLLoader different is that not only does it load files, but it also actually reads them, which is essential when the goal is to sift through external CSS. The third variable, req, points to an instance of the URLRequest class and specifies the location of the actual CSS document.

The URLLoader.load() method is invoked on the loader instance with req as the parameter. Finally, the Event.COMPLETE event is handled with a function that performs three straightforward tasks: it parses the loaded CSS, sets the text field's styleSheet property to the css instance, and sets its htmlText property to the prepared HTML string. You already know how the last two work, so let's pick apart the first line of this function.

The StyleSheet.parseCSS() method takes a single parameter, which in this case is the expression evt.target.data. That may look like a mouthful, but it's nothing more than a compact way of getting at the CSS styles themselves. The evt.target part refers to the loader instance. How? The evt variable is received as a parameter to the completeHandler() function and refers to the Event.COMPLETE event itself. In other words, evt is the event object dispatched by loader when the CSS file loads. The Event class features a target property, which refers to the object that dispatched the event—namely, loader. As an instance of the URLLoader class, loader features a data property that points to the CSS data stored inside the styles.css file.

Open the styles.css file in Dreamweaver CS5 or any simple text editor, such as Notepad on Windows or TextEdit on a Mac. (Although CSS files serve a special styling purpose, they are really just text files with a .css file extension.) The contents should be easily recognizable to you:

```
li {
    font-style: italic; color: #A2A2A2; leading: -2;
}
p {
    text-align: justify; leading: 6;
}
ul {
    leading: 6;
}
```

```
strong {
    font-family: Impact; font-size: 14; color: #339966;
}
a {
    font-family: Courier; font-weight: bold;
}
a:hover {
    color: #FF00FF;
}
```

Besides the hyphenated style properties and a few minor syntactical differences, these selectors represent the same styling approach you've seen throughout this chapter. The syntax differences to look out for are as follows:

- In this version, neither property names nor values are wrapped in a quotation mark or use camel cases, as they are in ActionScript. For example, we use `font-style: italic` instead of `fontStyle: "italic"`.

- Properties are separated by semicolons rather than commas, like this:

```
li { fontStyle: italic; color: #A2A2A2; leading: -2;
```

instead of this:
```
css.setStyle("li", { fontStyle: "italic", color: "#A2A2A2",
leading: -"-2" });
```

By the way, thanks to the semicolon punctuation, you have some leeway in how you arrange the properties, both in ActionScript and in the CSS file. Put them in a single line or spread them over several lines—it doesn't matter. As long as the required parts are present, Flash can figure out what you mean. So, go ahead and suit your fancy. For example, this line:

```
li { fontStyle: italic; color: #A2A2A2; leading: -2 }
```

is functionally the same as this:

```
li {
  fontStyle: italic;
  color: #A2A2A2;
  leading: -2;
}
```

And now we've arrived at the punch line. Test the movie to generate a SWF file, which should look something like Figure 13-4. Now close Flash. That's right, shut down the application. The rest is a matter between you, a SWF, and a CSS file.

CSS

Figure 13-4. CSS styles pulled from an external CSS file

Double-click your newly created `StylingExternal.swf` file to give it one last look. This is a bit like making sure the magician has nothing up either sleeve.

Now, open the `styles.css` document and make a few changes. If you are not sure where to start, update the `p` and `strong` styles as follows:

```
p {
  margin-left: 100; leading: 12;
}
strong {
  font-family: Impact; font-size: 40; color: #339966;
}
```

After you make your changes, save the CSS document. Then close `StylingExternal.swf`, and double-click it again to launch the SWF. Without republishing the SWF, you've updated its formatting (see Figure 13-5). That's no small feat!

Hey, did you catch that something is missing? What happened to that hyperlink? The increased leading in the p selector has pushed it off the stage! In fact, the phrase `Broil to taste` has also been shoved aside. No problem. All you need to do is to readjust the `leading` property or decrease the `strong` selector's `font-size` property until everything fits. This sort of tweaking is what CSS was made for.

> *We just love telling "war stories" to support what we are talking about. In this case, David Stiller, who was one of the coauthors in the CS4 version of this book, had recently completed a Flash-based training presentation for a U.S. government agency that featured more than 250 slides. At one point, David needed to change the color of one of the heading styles to a slightly different orange. He was able to make the change in a single CSS file. David tells us he is still smiling.*

679

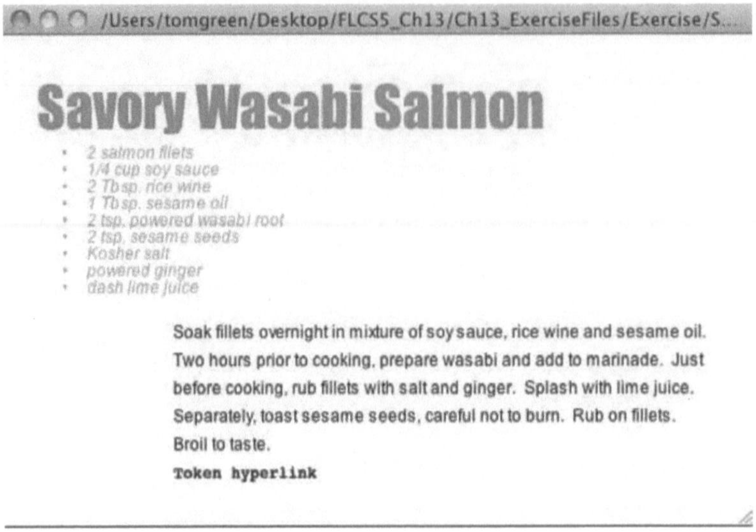

Figure 13-5. Look, ma—style changes without re-creating the SWF!

Block element styling

The authors spent a bit of time studying the tea leaves, and this is what we discovered: officially documented or not, the tags that support element selectors are all block elements, with the exception of the anchor tag (<a>). In other words, the rule of thumb is that, if the tag carries with it a built-in line break, then an element selector will do the trick. The special case is hyperlinks, which we'll cover in detail later in the chapter (hyperlinks are a special case in several ways).

For your reference, let's take a quick look at a "proof is in the pudding" sample file:

1. Open the ElementSelectors.fla file in this chapter's Exercise folder. You'll find a text field with the instance name styledContent. The ActionScript in the **scripts** layer shouldn't be any trouble for you by now. A string of HTML is created, element selectors are defined and then assigned to a StyleSheet instance, and finally, the HTML is supplied to the text field.

2. Test the movie to see the result in Figure 13-6. The output may not look all that interesting, but it is, because it demonstrates a few additional "gotchas" while verifying the block element principle.

Figure 13-6. Only block elements—and one exception, anchor tags—support element selectors.

3. Click into frame 1 of the `scripts` layer, and take a look at the ActionScript in the `Actions` panel.

Each line of HTML ends in a break tag (`<br />`), just to keep things visually neat. Every tag is given an element selector that alternates its color between #0000FF (blue) and #00FF00 (green). In normal HTML, most of these lines would display as either blue or green (`<img />` contains no actual text, so it wouldn't). In Flash, this holds true only for the block elements.

The `<a>` tag is not a block element, so it does not display an additional, built-in line break as some later tags do. But as the exception to the rule in question, the `<a>` tag does pick up the blue color (mid-gray, in Figure 13-6) from its element selector. The `<body>` and `<p>` (paragraph) tag contents carry their own additional line breaks—these are block elements—and both display the expected element selector color styling. The `<ul>` and `<li>` tags' content is combined. These are also block elements and therefore display a combined pair of extra line breaks, as well as the expected element selector styling.

4. Comment out the `body` and `li` element selectors in the ActionScript by preceding those lines with double slashes (`//`), as shown in Figure 13-7.

5. Test the movie again.

```
16  var css:StyleSheet = new StyleSheet();
17  css.setStyle("a", {color: "#0000FF"});
18  css.setStyle("b", {color: "#00FF00"});
19  //css.setStyle("body", {color: "#0000FF"});
20  css.setStyle("img", {color: "#00FF00"});
21  css.setStyle("font", {color: "#0000FF"});
22  css.setStyle("i", {color: "#00FF00"});
23  css.setStyle("ul", {color: "#0000FF"});
24  //css.setStyle("li", {color: "#00FF00"});
25  css.setStyle("p", {color: "#0000FF"});
26  css.setStyle("span", {color: "#00FF00"});
27  css.setStyle("textformat", {color: "#0000FF"});
28  css.setStyle("u", {color: "#00FF00"});
29
```

Figure 13-7. Commenting out the <body> and <li> selectors leads to a line-spacing quirk and the concept of inheritance.

It should come as no surprise that the <body> tag content is no longer styled. What may raise your eyebrows is that the extra line break is missing. This is a quirk involving only the <body> tag and will raise its head again in the "Custom tags" section of this chapter. The other thing to notice is that the <ul>/<li> content has changed color. This is because a distinct color style was applied to each tag (green for <ul> and blue for <li>). Blue won the wrestling match earlier because of a CSS concept called **inheritance** (covered in the "Style inheritance" section later in the chapter).

6. As a final experiment, uncomment the body element selector by removing the double slashes from that line. Instead, comment out the p element selector.

7. Test the movie a final time, and you'll see that the <p> content is still blue.

Why? Again, this is an example of inheritance, but in a really twisted way. Under normal circumstances, HTML documents feature most of their content inside a <body> tag. If a style is applied to the body, it will "trickle down" to tags inside that body if those inner tags happen to support the style properties at hand. Here in this Flash file, the <p> content is clearly not inside the <body> content, and yet some phantom inheritance seems to still hold sway. Comment out the body element selector one last time, and the <p> content finally turns black.

8. Close the file without saving the changes.

Every development platform has its quirks, and now you've seen a few of the ones that belong to Flash. Being aware of these, even if they aren't burned into your neurons, might just save your hide when something about CSS styling surprises you.

Now you've had some experience with block elements and the anchor tag, with the understanding that anchor tags still hold a bit of mystery, yet to be unfolded. Meanwhile, what remains of the other supported HTML tags? What's the opposite of a block element, and how can one be styled?

Inline element styling

In Flash, if a tag is not a block element, it is an inline element. There is no "in between," and all that means is that it doesn't carry its own line break with it. Examples include the <b> and <i> tags, which apply their own innate formatting—bold and italic, respectively—without otherwise interrupting the flow of text. As you've seen, inline elements in Flash do not support element selectors. Is there another option, then? Yes, there is. But it goes only so far.

Not to be confused with the classes discussed in Chapter 4, CSS features something called **class selectors**, which differ from element selectors in a significant way. Rather than apply their style to all tags of a specified type, class selectors look only for tags that have a class attribute whose value is set to the name of the class in question. We'll see an example of this in just a moment. In HTML documents, just about any tag can be given a class attribute, but this isn't the case in Flash. Actually, nothing *stops* you from giving an HTML tag such an attribute in Flash, but Flash applies class selector styling to only a few tags, and only one of those is an inline element.

Here's another "proof is in the pudding" exercise, which should make everything clear:

1. Open the ClassSelectors.fla file in this chapter's Exercise folder. At first glance, this file may look identical to ElementSelectors.fla, but click into frame 1 of the **scripts** layer to lay eyes on a different chunk of code.

You'll see that every HTML tag now has a class attribute, set either to blue or green, and the number of selectors has been reduced to two: the selfsame blue and green styles. Now, how can you tell that these are class selectors and not element selectors? The giveaway, which is easy to miss if you aren't looking for it, is the dot (.) in front of the style names, which is highlighted in Figure 13-8.

```
11   str += "<p class='blue'>Paragraph tag</p><br />";
12   str += "<span class='green'>Span tag</span><br />";
13   str += "<textformat class='blue'>Text format tag</textformat><br />";
14   str += "<u class='green'>Underline tag</u>";
15
16   var css:StyleSheet = new StyleSheet();
17   css.setStyle(".blue", {color: "#0000FF"});
18   css.setStyle(".green", {color: "#00FF00"});
19
```

Figure 13-8. Class selectors are much more selective than element selectors. You can spot them by their dot prefixes.

Those dots change everything, because at this point, CSS doesn't care which tag it's dealing with. It only cares if that tag has a class attribute set to blue, green, or whatever the style's name is.

> *Be careful where you put your dots! They belong only in the setStyle() method and never in the class attribute of any tag.*

2. Test the movie to see the result.

Remember that in the "real world" outside of Flash, every one of these tags would be affected by the relevant style. In the SWF, only the following tags do anything: `<a>`, `<li>`, `<p>`, and `<span>`. Unfortunately, we haven't found a way to memorize this list as neatly as the other, but if you can remember the block elements that go with element selectors, you need only swap the `<body>` tag for the `<span>` tag and drop `<ul>` to know the block and inline elements that go with class selectors. (Yeah, we agree, it's not especially intuitive.)

3. For the sake of completeness, comment out the `.green` class selector, and test the movie to verify the outcome. The `<ul>`/`<li>` content turns black, because class selectors don't apply to `<ul>` tags in Flash.

4. Close the movie without saving the changes.

Custom tags

Ready to head back to the street food? When we abandoned it to venture out on our educational tangent, our styling had been applied, with the exception of the `<b>` content, and now we know why. The `<b>` tag is not a block element, which means it simply doesn't support element selectors.

Element selectors affect all tags of a given type, and for the sake of illustration, let's say we want only this recipe's title to stand out, rather than all content that happens to be set in bold. An obvious solution, based on your current knowledge, is to swap the `<b>` tag for something that supports class selectors. Let's try it.

1. Open the `Styling03.fla` file in this chapter's `Exercise` folder to see an example of using a class selector. The key changes in the ActionScript from `Styling01.fla` are shown in bold in the following code:

```
var str:String = "";
str += "<p class='heading'>Savory Wasabi Salmon</p>";
str += "<ul>";
...
css.setStyle("ul", {leading: "6"});
css.setStyle(".heading", {fontFamily: "Impact", fontSize: "18",&#1048577;
color: "#339966"});
styled.styleSheet = css;
```

This mix-and-match approach is perfectly valid. In fact, it's a good basic methodology: use element selectors to sweep through the styling for most tags, and then cover the exceptions with class selectors. Alternatively, you can use custom tags, which provide a kind of hybrid mechanism. They save you from having to type `class='someStyleName'` throughout your HTML content. And the best part is that you can use familiar, genuine HTML tags from the "real world," if you like (think along the lines of `<h1>`, `<h2>`, `<strong>`, and so on). Flash happily accepts these as "custom" tags, because, in its skimpy repertoire, they are.

2. Open the Styling04.fla file to see a custom tag in action. Once again, this file is virtually identical to the previous one, except for the parts shown in bold:

```
var str:String = "";
str += "<strong>Street Food</strong>";
str += "<ul>";
...
css.setStyle("ul", {leading:"4"});
css.setStyle("strong", {fontFamily: "Impact", fontSize: "16", color: "#339966"});

styledContent.styleSheet = css;
```

Note the *absence* of a dot preceding the strong element selector, which means that this is *not* a class selector! If you put 50 <strong> tags full of content into your SWF, all 50 occurrences will pick up the style from this setStyle() method. That said—and we can't stress this enough—please understand that this is not a magical, undocumented way to squeeze additional tags out of Flash's limited HTML support. Flash has no idea what a <strong> tag is, much less that most browsers treat it like a tag. This is nothing more than a convenient hook for CSS—an excuse to dodge class selectors if you happen not to like them. In fact, to prove it and to reveal a limitation of the custom tag approach, proceed to step 3.

3. Replace the <strong> tag in the bolded ActionScript with the completely made-up <citrus> tag. There is no such tag in any of the W3C specifications (we looked). Your code will change in only three places:

```
var str:String = "";
str += "<citrus>Street Food</citrus>";
str += "<ul>";
...css.setStyle("ul", {leading: "6"});
css.setStyle("citrus", {fontFamily: "Impact", fontSize: "18", color: "#339966"});
styled.styleSheet = css;
```

4. In addition, find the word Fruit in the bulleted list, and wrap it with this new <citrus> tag:

```
str += "<li>Omelettes</li>";
str += "<li> <citrus>Fruit</citrus> juices</li>";
str +- "</ul>";
```

5. Test the movie. You should see the styling shown in Figure 13-9.

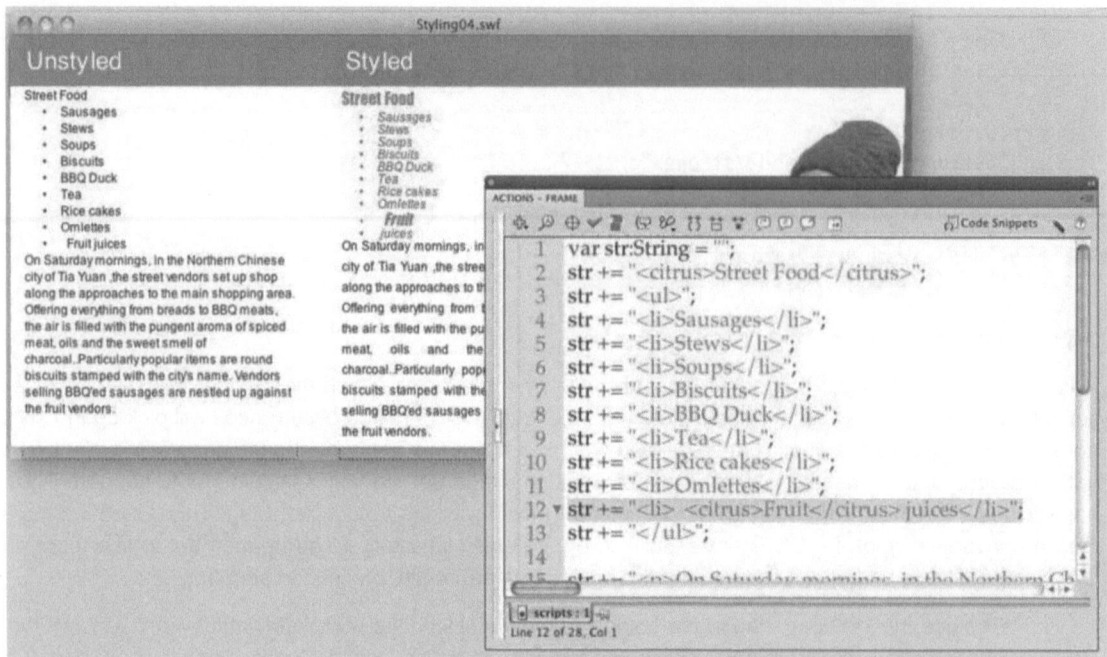

Figure 13-9. Whoops, something isn't right with the fruit juices.

Danger, Will Robinson! What do we learn from the broken `Fruit juice` line? A valuable lesson, that's what. The recipe's title is fine, but that's because it stands on its own. The `fruit juice` line breaks because custom tags become block elements when styled. In this case, the word `juice` has even been pushed past the extra line height given earlier to the `<ul>` tag.

We've spent the last several miles mulling over some pretty arcane rules and even hazier exceptions to them. CSS was supposed to be easier in Flash, right? If your head is spinning, take a break. While you wait, one of the authors will use a chant from the "L'Eglise CSS." It goes something like this: "To get the biggest bang for your buck, use element selectors first, then custom tags for headings and other short or specific blocks, and finally class selectors for special cases." (Take our word for, this sounds really great as a Gregorian chant.)

Style inheritance

In moving from `Object` instances to the object shortcut characters ({}) earlier in the chapter, we saw one way to trim CSS into a more compact form. There's another way to shrink things even further, but it's more conceptual than syntactical. The concept is called **inheritance**, and it basically means that styles applied "up the creek" tend to eventually flow down to lower waters.

Let's look at a concrete example. Open the `Inheritance.fla` file in this chapter's `Exercise` folder. You'll see a text field with the instance name `styledContent`. Click into frame 1 of the **scripts** layer to view the ActionScript. As with the other samples in this chapter, the code begins by building an HTML string. In this case, the structure of the HTML tags is important. Stripping out the text content, the structure of the tag hierarchy looks like this:

```
<body>
  <p>
  <outer>
    <mid>
      <inner><span class='big'></span></inner>
    </mid>
  </outer>
```

Styling is applied to the <body> tag, which sets its font to Courier. The tags nested inside this tag, <p> through <mid>, gain the same typeface thanks to inheritance. The custom <inner> tag would also inherit Courier, except that this particular tag bucks the trend by specifying its own font, Arial. This font overrides the inherited Courier and sets up its own new inheritance. Note that the <span> tag—which surrounds the word dignissim, whatever that means—lies within the <inner> tag. Because of this position, it displays in Arial, as its parent does (see Figure 13-10).

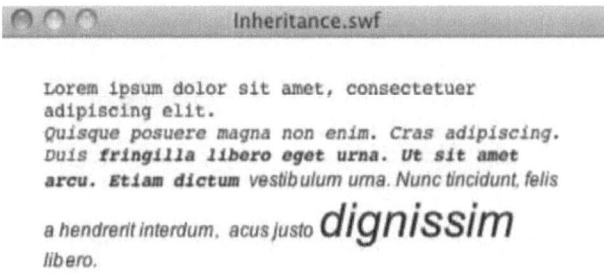

Figure 13-10. CSS inheritance in action

This sort of procedure can get fairly sophisticated. For example, the custom <outer> tag adds italics to the mix.

```
css.setStyle("outer", {fontStyle: "italic"});
```

In light of that, and because the flow goes downhill, <mid>, <inner>, and <span> inherit not only the font of <outer>'s parent but also its italics. Meanwhile, sibling tags (<p>) and parent tags (<body>) do not. And honestly, that makes good sense.

In the same vein, the custom <mid> tag introduces bold:

```
css.setStyle("mid", {fontWeight: "bold"});
```

If unopposed, <inner> and <span> would inherit that bold styling as well, but <inner> purposely overrides that by setting fontWeight to normal in its own element selector:

```
css.setStyle("inner", {fontFamily: "Arial", fontWeight: "normal"});
```

In turn, this causes `<span>` to inherit the override, because it too ignores the bold. Note, however, that `<span>` does inherit the italics, which were not overridden by a parent tag. The interesting thing is that the `<span>` content inherits styling applied to its parents, even though that styling is provided by element selectors. Why is this interesting? Remember that `<span>` is an inline element, and inline elements, as a rule, can't be styled with element selectors. Oh, the tangled web Flash weaves!

Use this inheritance phenomenon to your advantage. It saves you keystrokes. You don't need to specify font families for whole groups of related tags. In addition, inheritance gives you the opportunity to make sweeping changes from relatively few locations. As you've seen from the quirky exceptions, though, you'll want to experiment carefully before committing yourself to a particular styling scheme. But do make sure you experiment, because there's more to Flash CSS than first meets the eye.

Styling hyperlinks

Anchor tags are fun to style because of something called **pseudo-classes**. In CSS-speak, a pseudo-class corresponds to various possible states of an HTML element and is indicated by a colon (:) prefix. In Flash, the only supported pseudo-classes are associated with the anchor tag (`<a>`) and correspond to the following states:

- :link (an anchor tag that specifically contains an href attribute)
- :hover (triggered by a mouse rollover)
- :active (triggered by a mouse click)

The long and short of this is that you have the tools you need to create different anchor tag styles that update as the mouse moves and clicks your hyperlinks. Note that Flash does not support the :visited pseudo-class, which in normal CSS indicates that a hyperlink has already been clicked.

Think of pseudo-classes as a second tier of styles, not separated by hierarchy, as shown in the "Style inheritance" section, but instead separated by time or events.

Open the Hyperlinks.fla file in this chapter's Exercise folder to see an example in action. The ActionScript begins, as always, by establishing an HTML string:

```
var str:String = "";
str += "<ul>";
str += "<li><a href='http://www.apress.com/'>Hyperlink 1</a></li>";
str += "<li><a href='event:someFunction'>Hyperlink 2</a></li>";
str += "<li><a href='http://www.friendsofed.com/'>↵
Hyperlink 3</a></li>";
str += "</ul>";
```

These anchor tags happen to be nested within list items, but they don't need to be. The important part is that the anchor tags have href attributes actively in use. In these next three lines, the element selectors provide a style for all anchor tags in any state—that's the first bolded line—followed by distinct styles for the :hover and :active pseudo-classes.

```
var css:StyleSheet = new StyleSheet();

css.setStyle("li", {leading: "12"});
```
css.setStyle("a", {fontFamily: "Courier"});
css.setStyle("a:hover", {fontStyle: "italic"});
css.setStyle("a:active", -{text-decoration: "underline",color: "#FF0000"});
```
styledContent.styleSheet = css;
```

Test this movie to verify that hovering over hyperlinks puts them temporarily in italics, and that clicking omits the italics but additionally displays an underline and new color. The italic style isn't inherited by :active, because :active is not a child of :hover; they have a sibling relationship. The Courier typeface, however, appears for all states, because even the pseudo-classes are anchor tags.

What if you would like more than one style for your hyperlinks? The solution is to use a class selector. Open the HyperlinksVaried.fla file in this chapter's Exercise folder for an example. First, here's the new HTML (shown in bold):

```
var str:String = "";
str += "<ul>";
str += "<li><a href='http://www.apress.com/'>Hyperlink 1</a></li>";
str += "<li><a href='event:someFunction'>Hyperlink 2</a></li>";
str += "<li><a href='http://www.friendsofed.com/'>↵
Hyperlink 3</a></li>";
str += "</ul>";
str += "<ul>";
str += "<li><a class='oddball' href='http://www.apress.com/'>↵
Hyperlink 4</a></li>";
str += "<li><a class='oddball' href='event:someFunction'>↵
Hyperlink 5</a></li>";
str += "<li><a class='oddball' href='http://www.friendsofed.com/'>↵
Hyperlink 6</a></li>";
str += "</ul>";
```

Unfortunately, it isn't possible to create unique pseudo-classes for anchor tags with class attributes, but the following new class selector at least separates the new batch of hyperlinks in their default state (see Figure 13-11):

```
var css:StyleSheet = new StyleSheet();
css.setStyle("li", {leading: "12"});
css.setStyle("a", {fontFamily: "Courier"});
css.setStyle("a:hover", {fontStyle: "italic"});
css.setStyle("a:active", {textDecoration: "underline",↵
color: "#FF0000"});
```
css.setStyle(".oddball", {color: "#00FF00"});
```
styledContent.styleSheet = css;
```

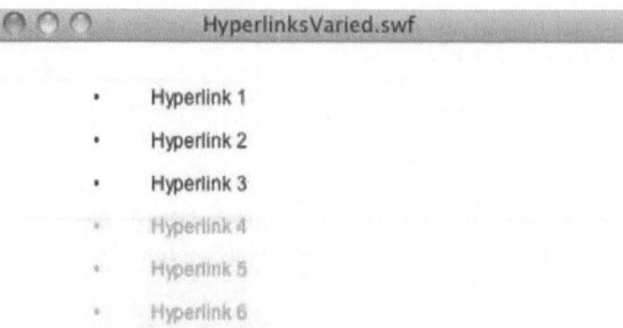

Figure 13-11. The last three hyperlinks are in a different color (gray here; green in real life).

Close the open files, and let's now look at embedding fonts.

Embedded fonts

Before we take what we've learned and nudge it all toward an external CSS file, let's make a quick stop as we buy a sausage on a stick to talk about embedded fonts. CSS in Flash requires HTML, which in turn requires a dynamic text field if you are using Classic Text. As you learned in Chapter 6, only static text fields embed font outlines by default, which explains why Flash has been chattering about embedding fonts in the Output panel. This means that unless you purposely embed your fonts—and the choice is yours—text in CSS-enhanced SWFs tends to have a jagged look.

Font symbols were introduced in Chapter 6, but there's a new twist in how they're used with CSS. To recap, the font-embedding process is as follows:

- Add a font symbol to the library and associate it with the desired font on your system.
- Enable the font symbol's linkage by exporting the symbol for ActionScript.
- Use the Font Embedding dialog, which is accessed through the Properties panel.

The new part—because Flash CSS usage requires ActionScript—is that you must refer to the font's actual name in your setStyle() method. The tricky part is how to reference the font's actual name, because neither its symbol name (in the library) nor its linkage class name necessarily provides any clues. Naturally, you can find out the font's actual name by consulting the Font Symbol Properties dialog box, but why rope yourself into something hard-coded? If you choose to associate your font symbol with another font, you'll need to change the font's name in your code, unless you use the Font.fontName property instead. Here's how:

1. Open the StylingEmbeddedFonts01.fla file in this chapter's Exercise folder. Test the movie, and you'll see jagged fonts. Let's change that.

2. Click into frame 1 of the **scripts** layer, and note the following pertinent lines of code:

```
var css:StyleSheet = new StyleSheet();
css.setStyle("li", {fontStyle: "italic", color: "#FF0000", leading: "-2"});
css.setStyle("p", {textAlign : "justify", leading:"6"});
css.setStyle("ul", {leading:"4"});
css.setStyle("strong", {fontFamily: "Impact", fontSize: "16", color: "#339966"});
styledContent.styleSheet = css;
styledContent.htmlText = str;
```

3. Look at the strong element selector, and you'll see that the fontFamily property is set to Impact, which is represented in the **Library** by a font symbol named **Impact**. Right-click (Windows) or Control+click (Mac) the **Impact** font symbol, and select **Properties** to open the **Font Embedding** dialog box.

4. In the **Font Embedding** dialog box, verify that the actual font selected is **Impact**. (If you don't have Impact on your system, choose some other suitable headline typeface.) Also verify that the font symbol is exported for ActionScript by clicking the **ActionScript** tab and that its linkage class name is **Impact**, as shown in Figure 13-12. Then click **OK** to close the dialog box.

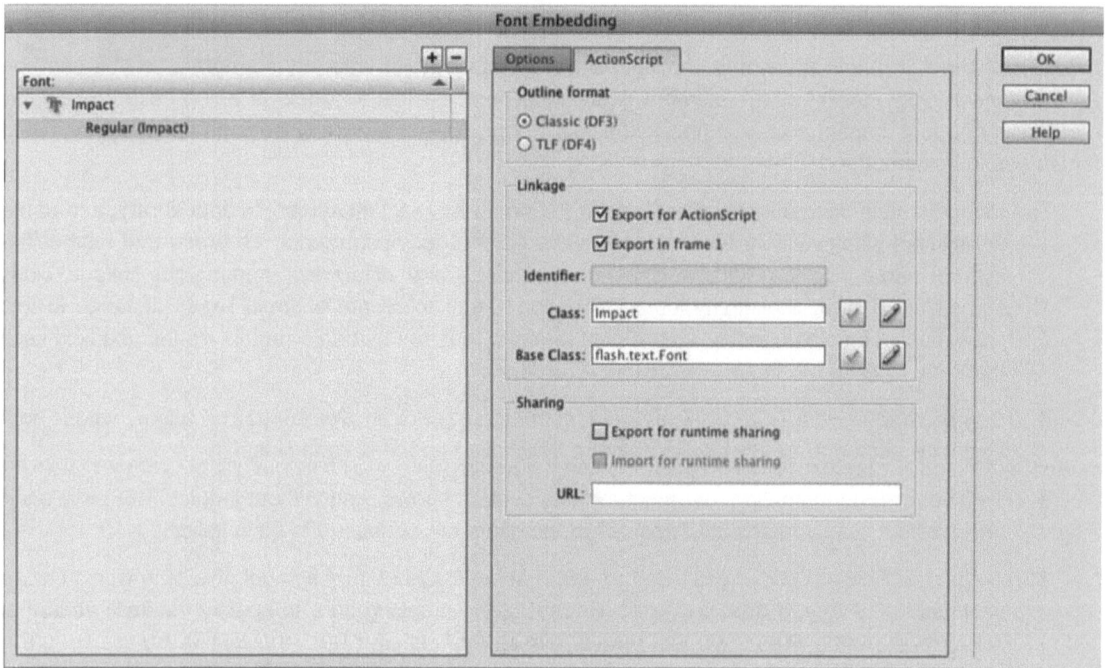

Figure 13-12. The font symbol's linkage class name is Impact.

CHAPTER 13

Referring to the actual font name—Impact (or your replacement)—will do, but you don't want to be tied to that changeable value. Instead, you're going to create an instance of this particular font—an instance of the custom `Impact` class—and reference that the `Font.fontName` property of that instance. You'll also set the `TextField.embedFonts` property of the `styledContent` instance to `true`.

5. Update the ActionScript as follows (new code in bold):

```
var embeddedFont:Impact = new Impact ();

var css:StyleSheet = new StyleSheet();
css.setStyle("li", {fontStyle: "italic", color: "#A2A2A2",↵
leading: -"-2"});
css.setStyle("p", {textAlign: "justify", leading: "6"});
css.setStyle("ul", {leading: "6"});
css.setStyle("strong", {fontFamily: embeddedFont.fontName,↵
fontSize: "18", color: "#339966"});

styledContent.embedFonts = true;
styledContent.styleSheet = css;
styledContent.htmlText = str;
```

6. Test your movie, and the text magically appears.

Oddly, only the `<strong>` element is showing! But hey...at least the lettering is smooth, as you can see from the inset. Only the `<strong>` element is showing because this text field is being asked to display more than one font: Impact and Arial (the text field's **Property inspector** settings specify Arial). Both fonts need to be embedded.

7. Using the technique described in Chapter 6, add an **Arial** font symbol to your library, and name the symbol whatever you like. Make sure to export it for ActionScript. To prove that neither the symbol name nor the linkage class name makes any difference, name your linkage class something absurd, like `HornyToads`. You don't need to create a `HornyToads` instance in this case, because nothing in the ActionScript refers to that font by name (again, it's the text field itself that's set to **Arial** in the **Properties inspector**).

8. Compare your work with `StylingEmbeddedFonts02.fla` in the `Complete` folder, whose font symbol is named **HornyToads** in both the **Library** and the linkage class.

9. Test your movie to confirm that all of the text content shows, and without jaggies. But there's still one problem. Can you spot it? Those `<li>` elements are supposed to be in italics!

10. To get the italics to show, you need to add a second **Arial** font symbol, this time with **Italic** selected in the **Style** drop-down list. Repeat step 7, making sure to specify the italic variant of Arial, and name your symbol (and class) something like **HornyToadsItalic**. The `StylingEmbeddedFonts02.fla` file in this chapter's `Complete` folder demonstrates this for you.

11. Test your movie, and you'll finally see everything, as shown in Figure 13-13, as it should be: all typefaces accounted for and smooth, including the italic variant.

CSS

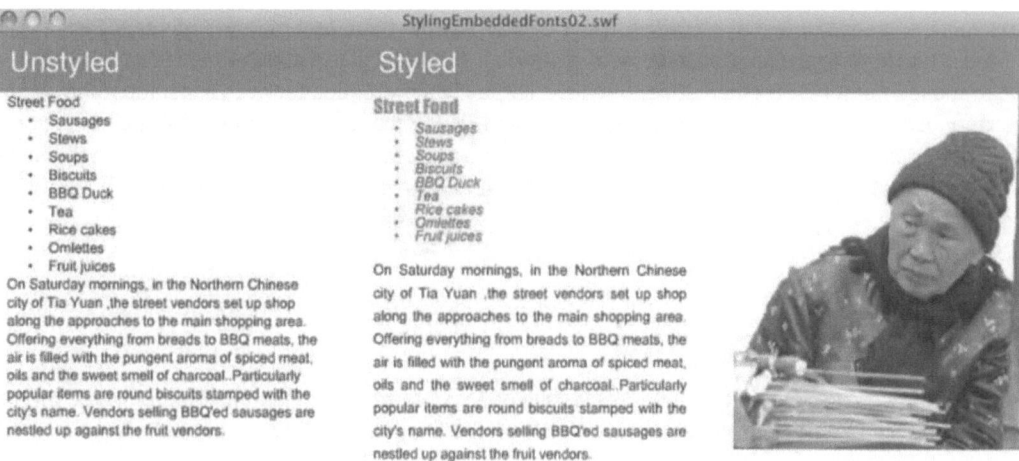

Figure 13-13. All the text is accounted for, and none of it suffers from the jaggies.

Selectors vs. the Properties panel

It's imperative that you understand how important the `Properties` panel settings are in the previous examples. The only reason you need to instantiate the custom `Impact` class—as opposed to both that and `HornyToads` (Arial)—is that Arial was already selected as the text field's font in the `Properties` panel.

Take a look at `StylingEmbeddedFonts03.fla` in this chapter's `Complete` folder for a working example of how to reference more than one font in the ActionScript. You'll see that the text field's `Properties` panel settings have been changed to **Times New Roman**. That means the Arial typeface (HornyToads), along with its italic variant (HornyToadsItalic) are present in the SWF but are not actually referenced anywhere. Here's the operative ActionScript to ensure that they do get referenced (new code in bold):

```
var embeddedImpact:ImpactNormal = new ImpactNormal();
var embeddedArial:HornyToads = new HornyToads();

var css:StyleSheet = new StyleSheet();
css.setStyle("li", {fontFamily: embeddedArial.fontName,↵
fontStyle: "italic", color: "#A2A2A2", leading: -"-2"});
css.setStyle("p", {fontFamily: embeddedArial.fontName,↵
textAlign: "justify", leading: "6"});
css.setStyle("ul", {leading: "6"});
css.setStyle("strong", {fontFamily: embeddedImpact.fontName,↵
fontSize: "18", color: "#339966"});

styledContent.embedFonts = true;
styledContent.styleSheet = css;
styledContent.htmlText = str;
```

In this version, the variable that holds the `Impact` instance has been renamed to `embeddedImpact`, just to differentiate it from the second scripted font reference, `HornyToads` (the `embeddedArial` variable). This solution makes use of CSS inheritance, because it specifies the `embeddedArial` instance only where it's necessary. Because the anchor tags (`<a>`) are nested inside the `<p>` tags, the p element selector takes care of both. The `li` element selector is needed because the `<li>` tags don't appear inside a tag styled for the embedded font. Note that, although some selectors call for a `fontStyle` of italic, Flash is smart enough to understand, without a third font variable, that HornyToadsItalic is the italic variant of the HornyToads font.

What you have learned

In this chapter, you discovered that the CSS techniques widely employed in the HTML universe are just as applicable to your Flash efforts. As you moved through the chapter, you learned the following:

- How to apply CSS styling through ActionScript
- The difference between an element selector and a class selector
- That you can create your own custom tags
- How to use the concept of inheritance to your advantage
- How to reference embedded fonts in your code and the fact that the **Properties** panel may help you avoid it
- How to use an external CSS style sheet in Flash

If there is one major theme running through this chapter, it is this: your CSS skills put a powerful tool in your arsenal. Speaking of powerful tools, let's build some stuff and give your new Flash skills a bit of a workout.

Chapter 14

Building Stuff

Up to this point in the book, you have created quite a few projects using images, text, audio, video, and other media. We bet you're feeling pretty good about what you've accomplished (you should!), and, like many who have reached your skill level, you are wondering, "How does all of this hang together?"

In this chapter, we will bring together the various skills and knowledge you have developed and use them to create some rather interesting projects. We are going to start slowly and show you how to build a preloader, and then we'll move through a slide show, MP3 player, and full-bore "Whack-A-Bunny" game designed for use on an Android device and as an AIR app. Some of these are quite complicated projects, but if you have reached this point in the book, you are ready to develop some Flash "chops" and explore what you can do with your newfound skills.

Here's what we'll cover in this chapter:

- Understanding how Flash movies are streamed to a web page
- Using the Bandwidth Profiler to turbo-charge movies
- Optimizing Flash movies
- Converting a Flash movie to a QuickTime video

CHAPTER 14

- Choosing web formats
- Publishing a SWF for web playback
- Dealing with remote content
- Using the new AIR for Android features

The following files are used in this chapter (located in Chapter14/ExerciseFiles_Ch14/Exercise/):

- preloader1.fla
- preloader2.fla
- 798_01.jpg-798_08.jpg
- slideshow.xml
- TinBangs.fla
- WhiteLies(Timekiller).mp3
- YoungLions.mp3
- YourSkyIsFalling.mp3
- Playlist.xml
- Whackabunny.fla
- 72X72Icon.png
- arfmoochikncheez.ttf
- Uni0563.ttf
- Build More Stuff

The source files are available at www.friendsofED.com/download.html?isbn=1430229940.

Before you start building some stuff, we must warn you that many of the projects don't include the extensive step-by-step instructions used throughout this book. This is not done to confuse you. It is done because many of the instructions involve much of what we have covered to this point in the book. Also, the time has arrived for you to start challenging yourself and seeing how the various bits and pieces of this book can combine to create some pretty cool stuff.

That last item—a folder named Build More Stuff—contains a bunch of projects that didn't make the cut for this chapter. They either were used in previous editions of this book or were things we thought you would find interesting but space requirements precluded us from fully documenting them in this chapter. What we have done is to provide you with heavily commented source code files. Feel free to study them, take them apart, dissect them, and adapt them for your personal use.

Loading content

Flash has a potentially bad habit that drives people crazy. In cases where everything in a movie is packed into the first few frames—and especially in single-frame movies—the SWF can take an awfully long time to display. Why? Because Flash Player loads content one frame at a time, and when a SWF's first frame is heavy, the rest of the movie suffers. It's even more interesting in cases where `Export for ActionScript` is selected for `Library` assets, because those items are included in the movie's first frame, in a behind-the-scenes way, even if you don't place them there yourself (Flash does it for you automatically). This should explain to you why, when you hit certain websites, you're slugged with an interminable wait, involving fingers drumming on the mouse or your desk and audible sighs as you wait for the movie to start.

One useful solution is to remove your heaviest assets—large images, audio, and video files—and use ActionScript to load them at runtime. This way, the rest of your content—the lighter stuff, including text and vector artwork—displays almost immediately, while the heavy stuff streams into the SWF from your server. Just keep in mind that even the light stuff may need a few seconds to load. But at least your audience will be looking at *something*, such as a preloader, and even the mere perception of at least *something happening* works wonders.

Are we there yet?

This first example is probably one of the most common preloaders in existence: the user is told how much of the SWF has loaded. In this example, a ribbon twirls while the numbers increase to show us loading progress. Let's get started:

1. To see how all of this works, open the `preloader1.fla` file in the Exercise/Preloader folder for this chapter. You'll see there's a single movie clip and a text box on the stage; this movie clip—`loaderAnim`—is the only one in the `Library`. The graphic symbol—gradientHalf—s the ribbon in the movie clip, and we have included a `Font symbol` for those of you who don't have the Impact font installed on your computers. The last symbol—`IMG_0098.jpg`—is a photograph of a dog. This is the content that will put the preloader to work.

2. Select frame 2 on the main timeline, and you will see the image of a rather large dog. The word *large* is important because, if you double-click the image in the `Library` to open the Bitmap Properties dialog box shown in Figure 14-1, you will see the image has a rather large file size, not to mention that its physical dimensions—1600 by 1200 pixels—are far larger than the stage.

Used as a starting point, this is a great example because it gets you to shift your thinking of the image in frame two from "Wow, that is a huge dog" to "Uh-oh, this content is going to be a problem." This image is going to take a lot of time to load. But don't think it's just images; that image could be anything from a video to an audio file to even another SWF, so it is not the dog that is the problem; it is the content.

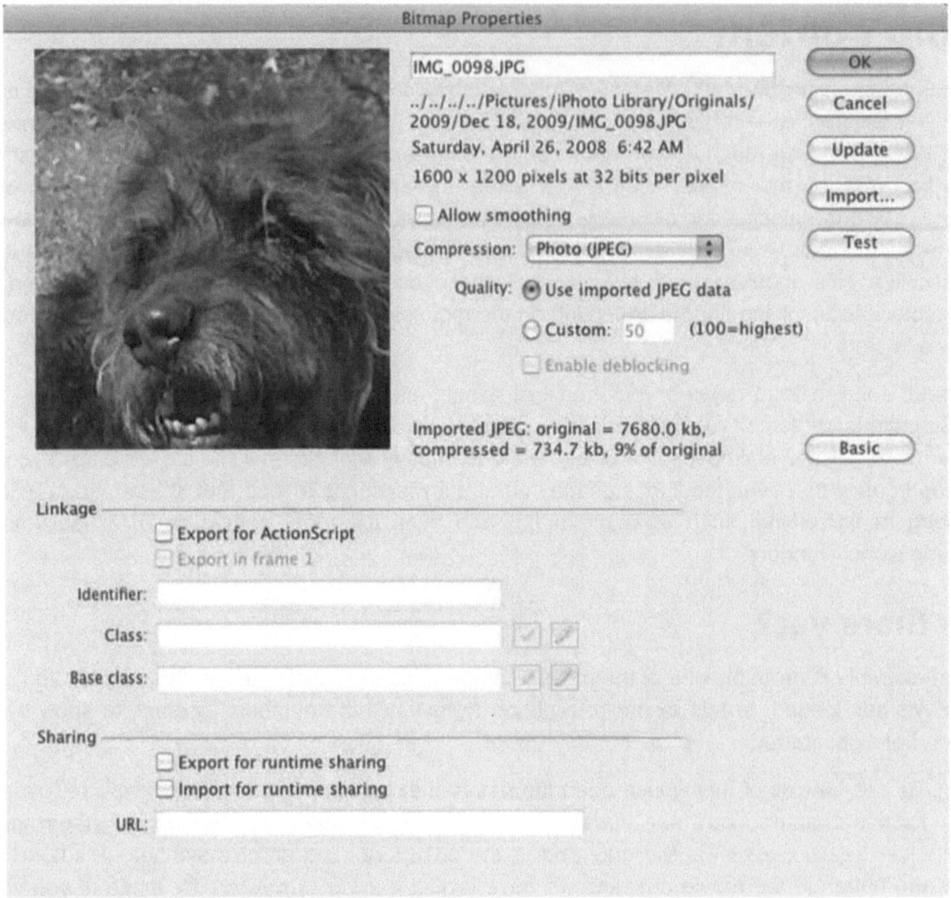

CHAPTER 14

Figure 14-1. If it's big, it needs time to load.

3. Open the `gradientHalf` graphic symbol in the Symbol Editor. This symbol was constructed by simply using the Pen tool to draw half of the shape and to fill it with a gradient. It was copied and "flipped" to make the ribbon. This object was then converted to the `loaderAnim` movie clip.

4. Open the `loaderAnim` movie clip in the Symbol Editor. The "twirl" was constructed by adding the keyframes and, using the Transform panel, rotated by 90 degrees, as shown in Figure 14-2, between the first two keyframes. The rotation amount was increase by 45 degrees between the keyframes at frames 11 and 15, which means the symbol rotates thorough 180 degrees over a span of 15 frames. Classic tweens were used because we were tweening a graphic symbol.

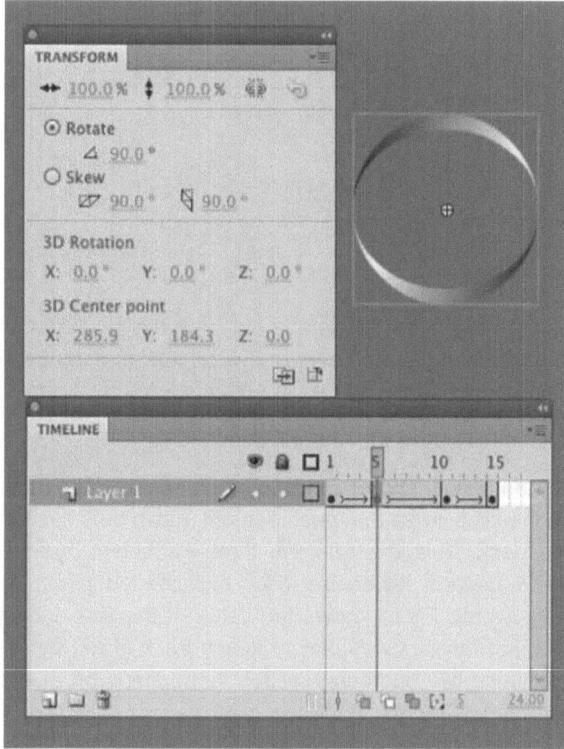

Figure 14-2. The preloader animation is created by using the Transform panel and a series of Classic tweens.

5. Click the Scene 1 link to return to the main timeline, and place the playhead at frame 1. Click once on the text block, and give it the Instance name of percentText in the Properties panel.

6. Select the first frame of the Actions layer, open the Actions panel, and add the following code:

```
import flash.events.Event;

stop();

addEventListener(Event.ENTER_FRAME, preloading);

function preloading(evt:Event)
{
    var bytestotal:int = stage.loaderInfo.bytesTotal;
    var bytesloaded:int = stage.loaderInfo.bytesLoaded;
```

```
        var percent:int = Math.round(bytesloaded*100/bytestotal);

        percentText.text = percent + "%";

        if (bytesloaded >= bytestotal)
        {
          gotoAndStop(2);
          removeEventListener(Event.ENTER_FRAME, preloading);
        }
}
```

The code starts off by loading in the Event class and stopping the playhead on frame 1. By stopping the playhead, you are going to give Flash time to keep an eye on how that image in frame 2 is loading and to let the user know what is going on. That process starts with the EventListener in line 3.

The function named preloading is where the "magic" happens.

When content loads it is not the image, sound or video that loads, it is the data in that content that loads. Though we traditionally use the kilobyte as the measurement, Flash gets even more granular and uses the bytes in the content as its base. This explains the three variables: bytestotal, bytesloaded, and percent (note that we have used a lowercase *l* for bytesloaded because the camel case version (bytesLoaded) is a Flash keyword). Flash knows the value of the first one—you saw it in the **Bitmap Properties** dialog box—and, as the movies play, it keeps track of the bytes loading into Flash Player. The percent variable takes those two numbers, divides them, strips off the decimals, and, in the fourth line, makes that number the value of the text in the text box.

The if () statement is there to tell Flash how to stop calculating and what to do when it has finished with the calculation. The parameter—bytesloaded>=bytestotal—is a little programming trick that tells Flash to do something when the bytesloaded value equals or exceeds the bytestotal value. We know the bytesloaded value can't exceed the bytestotal value, but adding the > (greater than) symbol makes sure this is the case.

The rest of the code tells Flash to hop over to frame 2, stay put, and forget about the EventListener.

   7. Test the movie.

You will most likely get a brief glimpse of the preloader, and then the image appears. Surely, that image didn't load that fast? In fact, it did, but what you may not know is the reason for it loading so fast is because you are testing the movie on your computer. Here's how to get a more accurate look at this project.

   8. With the SWF playing, select **View ▶ Simulate Download**, as shown in Figure 14-3. This choice allows you to simulate performance when content is delivered through a modem. You should now see the numbers start to change.

We are going to do a deep dive into Simulate Download in the next chapter. For now, just work along with us.

BUILDING STUFF

Figure 14-3. Use `Simulate Download` to check out performance through a modem.

Somebody stole my preloader

In Chapter 11 we showed you how to use the `ProgressBar` component. It is a useful component but contains very little "eye candy." This project shows how to "roll your own" progress bar but add a bit more jazz to the preloading process by replacing the bar with the animation of a thief fleeing from the scene of the crime. Here's how:

1. Open the `preloader2.fla` file.

   How this preloader works is rather simple. As the overly large cow image in frame 2 loads into the SWF, the thief runs from one side of the screen to the other. This preloader uses the width of the Flash stage as the width of the bar, and, as the content loads, the thief's horizontal position on the stage matched the percentage of the content that has loaded.

   The drawing of the thief was created in Adobe Illustrator, and Illustrator's layers were used for the various running positions. These positions were imported into Flash as movie clips, and if you open the runnerAnimation movie clip in the **Library**, as shown in Figure 14-4, you can see how the animation was created. The animation is in its own layer on the main timeline and has the instance name of `thief`.

   The streetscape was created using the Pen tool in Flash. What you can gather from this is that combining the tools and applications available to you is always an option.

   Though this is a rather interesting way of creating a preloader, always keep in mind that it, too, must be small for it to load fast. This means keeping everything as simple as possible.

CHAPTER 14

> The authors would like to thank Pascal Baumann for creating this exercise for use in the book. Pascal is a self-employed creative director from Zurich, Switzerland, currently living in Bangkok, Thailand. His work can be seen at www.pascalbaumann.com.

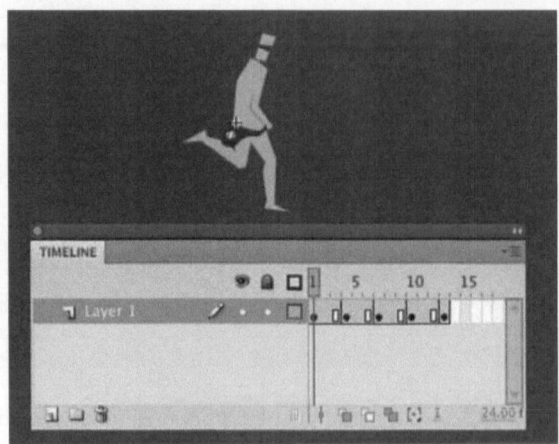

Figure 14-4. A simple animation can be used as an engaging preloader.

   2. Click once in frame 1 of the **Actions** layer, and enter the following code:

```
import flash.events.Event;

stop();

addEventListener(Event.ENTER_FRAME, myloading);

function myloading(evt:Event)
{
    var bytestotal:int = stage.loaderInfo.bytesTotal;
    var bytesloaded:int = stage.loaderInfo.bytesLoaded;
    var percent:int = Math.round(bytesloaded*100/bytestotal);

    thief.x  = stage.stageWidth / 100  * percent;

    if (bytesloaded >= bytestotal)
    {
      gotoAndStop(2);
      removeEventListener(Event.ENTER_FRAME, myloading);
    }
}
```

The myloading function is remarkably similar to the previous example. The major difference here is the movement of the thief across the stage

The thief instance's x property is determined by the width of the stage. Its position at any one time is simply set by multiplying the result of the percent variable by 100 and dividing the width of the stage by that number. Once that is determined, the thief instance is sent to that position on the x-axis.

3. Test the movie, and select **Simulate Download** while the SWF is playing. The thief, as shown in Figure 14-5, runs across the stage, and when he moves off the right side of the stage, the cow image appears.

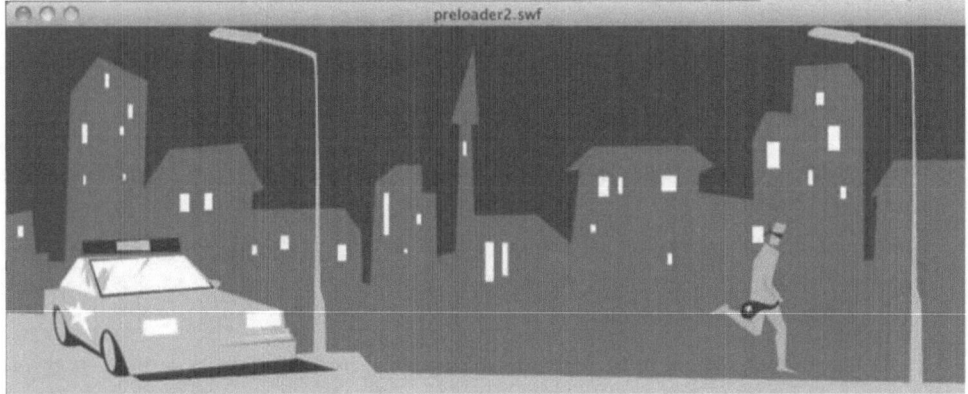

Figure 14-5. Preloading is almost complete.

Building a slide show with components and XML

The popularity of websites like Flickr and Photobucket prove that people like to share photos. Of course, this was true even before the Internet. But modern technology makes it easier than ever to whip out that tumbling, unfolding wallet and proudly show off all the kids, aunts, uncles, cousin Ed, and Finnegan, not only to friends but to every human on the planet. At the rate most people take pictures, photo collections just keep growing. So, if you were to make a photo slide show in Flash, you would want to be sure it was easy to update. With components and XML, that goal is closer than you may think.

To explore the concept, we'll start in an interesting location: the Quanjude Roast Duck Restaurant in Beijing, China. During the course of writing this book, one of the authors was in Beijing. One night, he was enjoying dinner in the company of a couple of Adobe engineers, John Zhang and Zhong Zhou. Naturally, one of the dishes was duck and, because of the restaurant's history, there was a particular way in which the duck was served and to be consumed. The author was struggling, and Zhong Zhou called the waitress over to demonstrate the proper (and complex!) procedure. It involved a wafer-thin wrap, duck meat, sauces, scallions, and a couple of other treats, which were to be added in a particular order. It took a

CHAPTER 14

couple of tries, but the grimacing author finally nailed it. When he thanked Zhong Zhu for the lesson, Zhong said, "It's really simple if you first master the process."

Mastering the creation of a Flash slide show is a lot like preparing that duck dish: it is all about process. We are going to show you two ways of creating a slide show, but the process is essentially the same for both. In fact, you'll be using some of the same process for the MP3 and video players later in the chapter.

A tour of the Beijing art district

To start, we're going to walk you through a self-contained, "hardwired" movie that displays a small collection of external JPEGs and their captions. The number of JPEGs and the order in which they appear are "baked in" to the SWF, which means the movie must be edited and republished to accommodate new images. This slide show features `ComboBox` and `Button` components to let people choose which JPEGs they want to see, and it even uses the `UILoader` and `ProgressBar` components to load the images, so this will be something of a cumulative exercise.

Once the test model is complete, we'll free the photo-specific data from its dungeon and move it to an XML file, where it can leap free in the fields like a shorn sheep or paddle merrily around a pond like a duck. Here we go!

1. Start a new Flash document, and save it as `Slideshow.fla` in this chapter's Exercise/Slideshow folder. Set the movie's dimensions to 320 × 480. Set the background color to whatever you like (we chose #336699).

2. Create the following five layers: `scripts`, `progress bar`, `loader`, `caption`, and `nav`. Lock the `scripts` layer to avoid accidentally placing content in this layer.

3. Open the `Components` panel (`Window ➤ Components` or click the `Components` button on the toolbar), and drag an instance of the `ProgressBar` component to the `progress bar` layer. Use the `Properties` panel to ensure its width is 150 and to set the height to 22, X position to 85, and Y position to 200. Give it the instance name `pb`.

4. Drag an instance of the `UILoader` component to the `loader` layer. Set its width to 300, height to 400, X position to 10, and Y position to 10. Give it the instance name `loader`.

5. Captions will be displayed with a text field. Use the `Text` tool to create a `TLF Text Selectable` text container in the `caption` layer. Set its width to 300, height to 28, X position to 10, and Y position to 416. Give this text field the instance name `caption`. Make the font `_sans`, 18pt, and `white` so that it shows over the blue background. We will leave the decision to embed the font up to you.

6. Drag an instance of the `ComboBox` component to the `nav` layer. Set its width to 220, X position to 10, and Y position to 450. Give it the instance name `images`.

7. Drag an instance of the `Button` component to the `nav` layer. Set its width to 70, X position 240, and Y position to 450. Give it the instance name `next`.

8. In the `Component Parameters` area of the `Properties` panel, set the button's `Label` parameter to `Next`. At this point, you have something like the scaffolding shown in Figure 14-6.

BUILDING STUFF

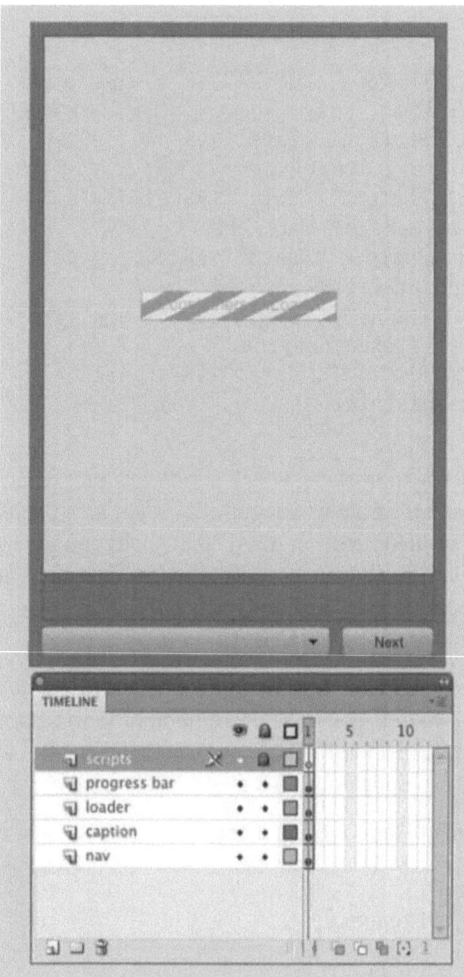

Figure 14-6. The parts are in place; time for the ActionScript.

Now it's time to bring these parts to life. For the most part, it's a matter of handling events for the components and populating the combo box.

9. Click into frame 1 of the **scripts** layer, and open the **Actions** panel. Here's the first chunk of code:

```
import fl.data.DataProvider;

var imageData:Array = new Array(
  {label:"798 Art District Photo 1", data:"798_01.jpg",
↵caption:"Lazy day on the street."},
```

705

```
    {label:"798 Art District Photo 2", data:"798_02.jpg",
↵caption:"Wall art."},
    {label:"798 Art District Photo 3", data:"798_03.jpg",
↵caption:"Angry and cute."},
    {label:"798 Art District Photo 4", data:"798_04.jpg",
↵caption:"The modern and the ancient!"},
    {label:"798 Art District Photo 5", data:"798_05.jpg",
↵caption:"Not sure what to make of this."},
    {label:"798 Art District Photo 6", data:"798_06.jpg",
↵caption:"The power of the artist?"},
    {label:"798 Art District Photo 7", data:"798_07.jpg",
↵caption:"Fashion shoot at a steam engine."},
    {label:"798 Art District Photo 8", data:"798_08.jpg",
↵caption:"A street in the district."}
);
```

The first line imports the DataProvider class, which is needed later when it's time to populate the combo box. After that, an arbitrarily named variable, imageData, is set to an instance of the Array class. Arrays are lists of whatever you put in them. You can use the Array.push() method on an instance to add elements to that instance, but you can also pass in the whole collection at once, which we've done here. This array has eight items, separated by commas, and each item is an instance of the generic Object class with three properties: caption, label, and data.

What, no new Object() statement? How are these objects being created? That's what the curly braces ({}) are for. It's a shortcut, and we're taking it. You'll remember from Chapter 11 that ComboBox instances can be supplied with **label** and **data** information, so that explains what those properties are in the array. The **caption** property is a custom addition.

10. Press Enter (Windows) or Return (Mac) a couple times, and type in the following:

```
var currentImage:int = 0;
var req:URLRequest = new URLRequest();

function changePicture(pict:int):void {
  pb.visible = true;
  caption.text = imageData[pict].caption;
  req.url = imageData[pict].data;
  loader.load(req);
}
changePicture(0);
```

The first line declares an integer variable, currentImage, and sets it to 0. This number will keep track of which image is being viewed. Next, a req variable holds an instance of the URLRequest class, which will be used to request the current image file. The next several lines declare a custom function, changePicture(), which accepts a single parameter, pict. This function does the following three things:

- Makes the `ProgressBar` instance visible (yes, it's already visible at this point, but because later code turns off its visibility when an image finishes loading, it needs to be set back).
- Makes the text field display the current caption. The incoming `pict` parameter determines which element to retrieve from the `imageData` array (`imageData[pict]`), and that element's `caption` property is retrieved. When the value of `pict` happens to be 0, the expression effectively says `imageData[0]`, which means, "Pull the first entry from the `imageData` list, please." Why start at zero? It's just one of those things; arrays start counting from zero rather than one.
- Makes the Loader instance load the current image. Here, again, the `imageData` array is consulted, but this time from the relevant item's `data` property, which is assigned to the `URLRequest.url` property of the `req` variable. In turn, `req` is fed to the `loader` instance by way of the `Loader.load()` method.

Immediately after its declaration, the `changePicture()` function is called, with 0 as its parameter. You're displaying the first image and its caption.

Now we just need to hook up the components.

11. Press Enter (Windows) or Return (Mac) a couple times, and type in the following:

```
pb.source = loader;

pb.addEventListener(Event.COMPLETE, completeHandler);
function completeHandler(evt:Event):void {
  pb.visible = false;
};
```

The first line associates the `ProgressBar` instance with the `Loader` instance. Thanks to the convenience of components, as the `Loader` component loads images, the progress bar will "automagically" know how to display load progress. The `completeHandler()` function makes the progress bar invisible when loading is complete.

12. Press Enter (Windows) or Return (Mac) a couple times, and type in the following:

```
images.dataProvider = new DataProvider(imageData);

images.addEventListener(Event.CHANGE, changeHandler);
function changeHandler(evt:Event):void {
  currentImage = images.selectedIndex;
  changePicture(currentImage);
};
```

The first line populates the combo box by setting its ComboBox.dataProvider property to a new DataProvider instance (this is why we need the import statement at the top). All the DataProvider instance needs is an array whose elements have label and data properties, which is exactly what we have in imageData. The caption properties are extra, but they don't hurt anything. That first line shoves the whole imageData array's content into the combo box in one swoop.

Next, the Event.CHANGE event is handled for the combo box. The handler function calls the custom changePicture() function and sets the currentImage variable to a number determined by the combo box's current selection. (The selectedIndex property doesn't care what data is *in* the selection; it only reports the index number of the current selection, and that's all the currentImage variable needs.) This variable is then used as the parameter to the changePicture() function, which updates the current photo.

13. Press Enter (Windows) or Return (Mac) a couple times, and type in the following:

```
next.addEventListener(MouseEvent.CLICK, clickHandler);
function clickHandler(evt:MouseEvent):void {
  currentImage++;
  if (currentImage == imageData.length) {
    currentImage = 0;
  }
  images.selectedIndex = currentImage;
  changePicture(currentImage);
};
```

Here, the MouseEvent.CLICK event is handled for the button. The handler function does the following:

- Increments the currentImage variable by one.
- Checks to see whether currentImage shares the same value as the expression imageData.length (the number of items in the imageData array). If so, it means the user has clicked often enough to progress through all the images, so currentImage is set back to 0.
- Sets the combo box's current selection to currentImage, to keep the combo box in sync with button clicks.
- Calls the custom changePicture() function and passes it currentImage as its parameter.

14. Test the movie. You'll be treated to a mini-tour of the 798 Art District in Beijing, China. Click the Next button to flip through the pictures in sequence, as shown in Figure 14-7, or use the combo box to skip around. If you like, try simulating download to see the progress bar at work and compare your work with the Slideshow.fla file in the Complete folder.

BUILDING STUFF

Figure 14-7. A few quick components and a bit of ActionScript, and you're off!

Extending the tour

As it turns out, wandering through the 798 Art District of Beijing makes for a decent metaphor for this exercise, because after all of this careful examination of the art in the galleries, we're about to uncover a treasure in a gallery just a few more paces up the street.

Save your file to keep everything safe. Now select **File ▶ Save As**, and save a copy as SlideshowXML.fla into the same folder. Click back into frame 1 of the **scripts** layer to make a few changes. Here's the first chunk of code, which replaces the Array, with revisions shown in bold.

```
import fl.data.DataProvider;

var xmlDoc:XML = new XML();
var xmlLoader:URLLoader = new URLLoader();
var xmlReq:URLRequest = new URLRequest("slideshow.xml");
xmlLoader.load(xmlReq);

xmlLoader.addEventListener(Event.COMPLETE, ↵
xmlCompleteHandler);
function xmlCompleteHandler (evt:Event):void {
  xmlDoc = XML(evt.target.data);
  images.dataProvider = new DataProvider(xmlDoc);
  changePicture(0);
};
```

CHAPTER 14

The `imageData` array is gone completely. In its place stands the familiar XML loading formula. The only differences here are the variable names. The `URLLoader` instance, for example, has been changed to `xmlLoader`, because `loader` is already in use as the instance name for the **UILoader** component. In the same way, the `URLRequest` instance is named `xmlReq`, because `req` is used later in the code, and the XML's `completeHandler()` function is named `xmlCompleteHandler()`.

This time, we're loading the file `slideshow.xml`, and that's where the former `imageData` content now resides. If you open the XML file, you will see not much has changed. It is practically the same as the previous array, except that this time, it's in a separate XML document instead of being hardwired into the ActionScript.

Let's take another look at the `Event.COMPLETE` event handler for the `xmlLoader` instance. The function runs as follows:

```
function xmlCompleteHandler(evt:Event):void {
  xmlDoc = XML(evt.target.data);
  images.dataProvider = new DataProvider(xmlDoc);
  changePicture(0);
};
```

Notice that the `DataProvider` handling has been moved here from its former position next to the combo box `Event.CHANGE` handler. Why? Because under the circumstances, the combo box can't be populated until the XML has loaded. Next, the `changePicture()` call has also been moved here from its earlier position. Why? Same reason: until the XML loads, the `changePicture()` has no reference for what image to summon.

Two more paces!

At or near line 21, you'll find the `changeFunction()` declaration. You'll need to tweak two lines (changes in bold):

```
function changePicture(pict:int):void {
  pb.visible = true;
  caption.text = xmlDoc.slide[pict].@caption;
  req.url = xmlDoc.slide[pict].@data;
  loader.load(req);
};
```

Instead of pulling from the old `imageData` array, the text field and **UILoader** component now draw their information from the xml instance, using E4X syntax to specify the relevant `<slide>` element attributes found in the XML file. Here, the function's incoming `pict` parameter serves the same purpose as it did before: it specifies which `<slide>` element to consult.

> Don't forget to delete what used to be the last line in this chunk: that is, *changePicture(0);*, which is now called inside the *xmlCompleteHandler()* function. It's easy to miss!

710

BUILDING STUFF

Here are the last touch-ups. There's a reward in sight! First, delete the following data provider line (which has been moved to the xmlCompleteHandler() function):
`images.dataProvider = new DataProvider(imageData);`

Finally, revise one reference in the button's event handler (new code in bold):

```
function clickHandler(evt:MouseEvent):void {
  currentImage++;
  if (currentImage == xmlDoc.slide.length()) {
    currentImage = 0;
  }
  images.selectedIndex = currentImage;
  changePicture(currentImage);
};
```

Since `imageData` is no more, that line depends on the number of `<slide>` elements, instead.

Test the movie and watch the show again. If you think you missed a step, compare your work to the `SlideshowXML.fla` work in this chapter's Complete folder.

Now that the movie has become XML-ified, you can have some fun editing the `slideshow.xml` file and running the SWF to see the changes. For example, delete the first three `<slide>` elements and test the movie again. Like magic, only the three remaining slides and captions display. Change the wording of one of the captions, and then run the SWF again. Change the order of the order of the `<slide>` elements or even add your own images into the show. With every edit or change you make, the SWF takes these changes effortlessly in stride.

Building an MP3 player with XML

When people get around to working with audio in Flash, one of the more common requests is, "Can I make my own MP3 player?" After reading Chapter 5, you already know the answer is yes.

> *Thanks again to Benjamin Taylor,, Bryan Dunlay, Philip Darling, and Robbie Butcher, of Tin Bangs (www.tinbangs.com) for the generous use of their music.*

There is going to be a lot going on here, so we suggest you set aside sufficient time to carefully follow along. You're about to be introduced to several new and fundamental concepts that will require your attention. Among them are the following:

- Creating buttons that go the previous or the next audio track
- Creating a seek slider that allows you to move through an audio selection
- Creating a volume slider that allows the user to adjust the audio volume
- Displaying an audio track's ID3 information

711

CHAPTER 14

The key to this exercise is understanding technique. Along the way, you will discover everything presented here builds upon what you have learned in the book. In the previous exercise, for example, the XML version of the slide show had a **Next** button. Here you'll have that too, along with the addition of a **Prev** button. And, again, the external files will be loaded from XML.

This exercise is designed to follow a fairly standard workflow, which is to assemble your assets first and then "wire them up" using ActionScript. This time, instead of components, you'll be creating some of your own controls.

Setting up the external playlist

The first order of business is to move the MP3 data to an XML file.

1. Open the `TinBangs.fla` file found in the `Exercise/MP3Player` folder for this chapter. This file is functionally identical to the one in the `Complete` folder for Chapter 5. The only difference is that the code comments have been made more obvious, like this:

```
/////////////////////////////////////
// Obvious code comment
/////////////////////////////////////
```

Why? This project is going to have a lot of ActionScript, and these striking "mile markers" help organize things visually. Why so many slashes? ActionScript ignores them after the first two in the line, so the rest are part of the comment.

The first task is to swap out the `Array` instance, `songList`, for an external XML document, just as you did for the Beijing slide show. Doing this will reacquaint you with the existing ActionScript in place.

2. Click info frame 1 of the **scripts** layer, open the **Actions** panel, and then locate the `songList` variable declaration on line 13, which looks like this:

```
var songList:Array = new Array(
  {label:"Select a song", data:""},
  {label:"White Lies (Timekiller)", data:"WhiteLies(Timekiller).mp3"},
  {label:"Young Lions", data:"YoungLions.mp3"},
  {label:"Your Sky is Falling", data:"YourSkyIsFalling.mp3"}
);
```

Delete those lines of code, and replace them with the following:

```
var songList:XML = new XML();
var loader:URLLoader = new URLLoader();
var xmlReq:URLRequest = new URLRequest("playlist.xml");
loader.load(xmlReq);
```

```
loader.addEventListener(Event.COMPLETE, completeHandler);
function completeHandler(evt:Event):void {
  songList = XML(evt.target.data);
  songsCB.dataProvider = new DataProvider(songList);
};
```

There's nothing new here. The XML instance is named `songList` in this case to minimize the impact on the rest of the code, which already refers to the song data by that name. A `URLRequest` instance already exists as `req`, so the new one here is named `xmlReq`. The requested file is now `playlist.xml`, whose contents are found in the XML file located in the `Exercise` folder. The `Event.COMPLETE` handler sets `songList` to the loaded XML document's data and then passes that to the `ComboBox.dataProvider` property of the `songsCB` combo box.

That last line inside the `completeHandler()` function—the one that refers to the data provider—originally appeared among the lines of code that configured the `ComboBox` instance, just before the line that reads `addChild(songsCB);`. You'll still see it there (should be at or near line 35 at this point), so delete it. (You only need to set the combo box's data provider once, and that needs to happen inside the `completeHandler()` function, after the XML has loaded.)

3. Test the movie so far. The **ComboBox** component created on line 30 of the code is added, and you can choose a song.

It's time to add the new stuff. But first, the authors would like to make a community service announcement.

Polishing up the symbols

We interrupt this program to introduce you to a fact of life that happens with collaborative Flash work. The controller bar—with its VCR buttons and slider control—was created in Adobe Illustrator and then imported into Flash. For the sake of demonstration, let's assume the designer didn't know how the controls would ultimately be used. If you don't think this will happen in your own Flash journeys, get ready to think again! In fact, count on it.

As a matter of good habit, you'll want to rename your `Library` assets to better suit their actual use in this project. In addition, to improve the user's interactive experience, you'll also want to use the drawing tools to give these VCR buttons—which are actually movie clips—a bigger clickable surface area. This is especially important for the `Pause` button, because without the fix, the mouse could easily slip between the two vertical bars of the pause icon.

Renaming Library assets

Renaming `Library` assets is the sort of work that seems like housekeeping. And it is. But don't underestimate its value! When deadlines loom and a manager is breathing down your neck, it helps to know your `Library` territory like the back of your hand. Take `VolumeSlider`, for example. In this MP3 player, that symbol is actually going to indicate how much of the audio has played. By dragging that slider, you'll be able to seek to various parts of the song. So, let's give it, and the other assets, better names.

1. Open the `Library` panel for the `TinBangs.fla` file. Locate the `Library`'s `AudioPlayer.ai Assets` folder, and you'll see a number of subfolders that ultimately contain the movie clips used for the controls in the `Player` layer of the `Timeline` panel. These include a handful of movie clips and subfolders whose names don't presently suit the purposes of this MP3 player: `FastForward`, `Layer 7`, `VolumeSlider`, `Rewind`, and `VolumeBar`.

2. Double-click the `FastForward` folder name, as shown in Figure 14-8, and rename it to `Next`. Do the same with the `FastForward` movie clip. This is, after all, a button that skips to the next song in the playlist, not a fast-forward button.

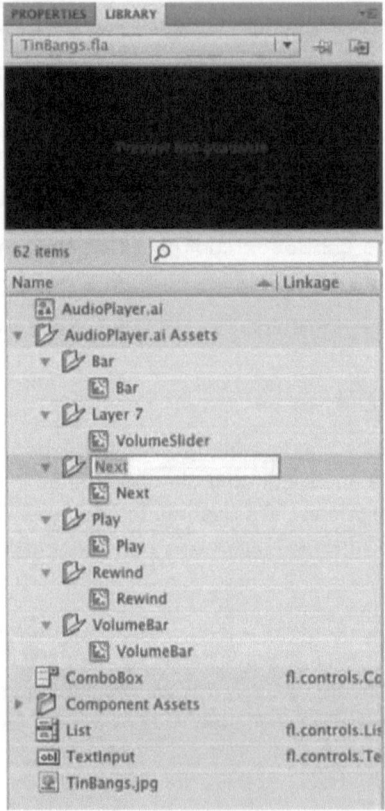

Figure 14-8. Appropriately naming `Library` assets helps when you resume work after a break.

3. Rename the `VolumeSlider` symbol to `SeekKnob`. Do the same with its containing folder, `Layer 7`.

4. Rename the `Rewind` symbol and its folder to `Prev`.

5. Complete your cleanup by renaming the `VolumeBar` symbol and its folder to `SeekBar`.

Improving the controls

The previous steps helped you as a designer/developer. Now it's time to help the user.

1. Double-click the **Play** symbol to enter its timeline. Drag the playhead to frame 2, and you'll see two vertical bars that represent "pause," as shown in Figure 14-9.

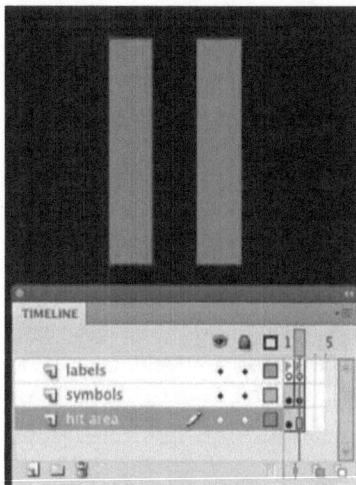

Figure 14-9. Be sure to keep your mouse-related assets mouse-friendly.

Granted, this symbol has been zoomed in quite a bit in the figure, but even at actual size, it's easy to see how the mouse can slip between the two bars, or accidentally miss the symbol altogether by slipping too far left or right. If this were a button symbol, the solution would be elementary: head to the **Hit** frame, and give the button a nice, sizable hit area. With movie clips, which don't have a **Hit** frame, you need to get creative. In this case, the solution happens in a layer named **hit area**.

2. Click frame 1 of the **hit area** layer, and you'll see a pixelated rectangle appear behind the "play" arrow icon, as shown in Figure 14-10.

This rectangle is a simple shape, drawn with the **Rectangle** tool. The reason you can't see it—until the shape is selected—is because the shape's fill color is set to 0% **Alpha**. From a visual standpoint, it's imperceptible, but when the user hovers a mouse over this symbol, even the invisible shape provides a larger clickable surface area.

Notice that the rectangle spans frames 1 and 2, so that it appears behind both the play and pause icons. This makes the hit area useful, regardless where this symbol's playhead appears.

CHAPTER 14

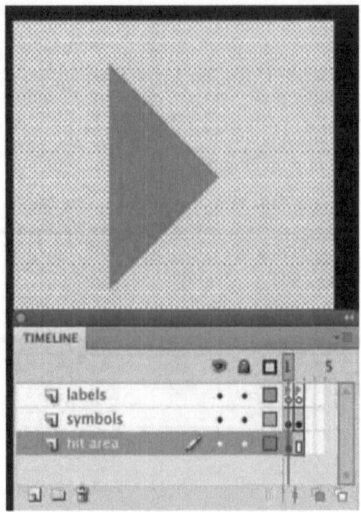

Figure 14-10. A low-alpha shape provides additional "surface area" for the mouse.

> *It is little things like this—giving a shape an opacity value of 0—that will separate you from the rest of the pack. This little trick takes maybe two to three minutes to accomplish. Someone who is unfamiliar with this will easily spend an hour trying to make the symbol "idiot-proof." This is a classic case of letting the software do the work instead of you overthinking it. In fact, the next step shows you how to do it yourself.*

The other VCR controls, and the `SeekKnob` symbol, need the same treatment. You can draw these shapes if you like, or you can let Flash do the work for you. Let's look at both ways.

3. Double-click the `Prev` symbol to enter its timeline. Rename the `Layer 1` layer to `arrows`, and then create a new layer named `hit area` beneath the first. In the `hit area` layer, use the `Rectangle` tool to draw a 20 × 20 pixel square with no stroke and a fill color of `#FFFFFF` (white) set to `0% Alpha`. Position the square so that it evenly fills the area behind the "prev" double arrows (we used an `X` position of `-2` and a `Y` position of `2`).

4. Right-click (Windows) or Control+click (Mac) frame 1 of the `hit area` layer, and select `Copy Frames` from the context menu. Now double-click the `Next` symbol to enter its timeline. Rename `Layer 1` to `arrows`, and then create a new layer beneath the first (no need to name it). Right-click (Windows) or Control+click (Mac) frame 1 of the new layer and select `Paste Frames` from the context menu. This accomplishes two things: it pastes the shape with the `0% Alpha` and also renames the layer to `hit area` for you. Pretty slick! Reposition the shape so that it evenly fills the area behind the "next" double arrows.

716

BUILDING STUFF

5. Using whichever approach you prefer, position a similar shape beneath the hollow rectangle in the `SeekKnob` symbol. In our case, we renamed that symbol's `Layer 1` layer to `knob` and then pasted the same shape into a new layer.

OK, so why two ways of doing the same thing? We are fond of telling anyone who will listen that there are usually 6,000 ways of doing anything in this business. What's the right way? Who cares? The only time someone cares is when it doesn't work.

As it turns out, the Illustrator designer forgot two widgets: a volume slider, which lets the user adjust volume, and a loading indicator, which tells the user an MP3 file is still loading. As often as not, you might need to create such assets yourself, but to speed things along, we've provided what you need in separate file named `controls.fla`. By using a technique we introduced in Chapter 3, you can quickly share the widgets from that FLA with your current working FLA.

6. Select `File ➤ Import ➤ Open External Library`, and browse to the `controls.fla` file in the `Exercise/MP3Player` folder for this chapter. Click the `Scene 1` link in `TinBangs.fla` to get back to the main timeline.

7. With the `Player` layer selected, drag the `LoadingDisplay` symbol from the newly opened `controls.fla Library` to the right side of the stage, as shown in Figure 14-11 (we used `X: 462, Y: 305`). Check the `TinBang.fla`'s own `Library`, and you'll see the movie clip there as well. As easy as that, you now have a loading indicator.

Figure 14-11. It's easy to drag in assets from another FLA's `Library`.

8. In the `TinBangs.fla Library`, double-click the `LoadingDisplay` movie clip to open it in the `Symbol Editor`. Scrub the timeline, and you'll see that the symbol is nothing more than a series of dots that seem to spin.

9. To make room for the volume slider, select the `SeekBar` symbol in the `Player` layer (the long red rectangle) and use the `Properties` panel to change its width to `138`.

10. With the `Player` layer selected, drag the `VolumeSlider` symbol from the controls.fla `Library` to the spot you just opened up—to the right of the other controls and just beneath the loading indicator.

When you drag the `VolumeSlider` symbol, an interesting thing happens in the TinBangs.fla `Library`: not only does `VolumeSlider` appear, but `VolumeBar` and `VolumeKnob` come along for the ride, as shown in Figure 14-12. This is nothing to be alarmed about. These other symbols show up because they're nested inside `VolumeSlider`, so they piggyback their way in.

Figure 14-12. Dragging in a nested asset carries with it the asset's children.

11. Drag the `volume icon` graphic symbol from the controls.fla `Library` to the stage, just to the left of the `VolumeSlider` symbol. This is nothing more than an icon that helps indicate the purpose of the slider next to it.

12. Double-click `VolumeSlider` in the TinBangs.fla `Library` to open it in the `Symbol Editor`.

This symbol is a bit more complicated than the circle of dots from the previous shared asset, but you've already been introduced to all the concepts. As Figure 14-13 shows, you'll find three layers: **knob**, **mask**, and **bar**. The **knob** layer contains a rectangular symbol, `VolumeKnob`, whose shape is composed of a `0% Alpha` fill. This is effectively an invisible button, like the hit area shape in step 2, except that the "button" is a movie clip. The **mask** layer contains five slanted columns, and the **bar** layer simply contains a red rectangle (this is the `VolumeBar` symbol). If you like, temporarily lock the **mask** and **bar** layers, and you'll see the masking in action. When this symbol is wired up, the user will be able to drag the invisible `VolumeKnob` symbol left and right. The `VolumeBar` symbol, partially hidden by the mask, will simply match the position of `VolumeKnob`, and the result will be an illusion: it will appear to the user that dragging left and right changes a red fill shared by the five slanted columns.

BUILDING STUFF

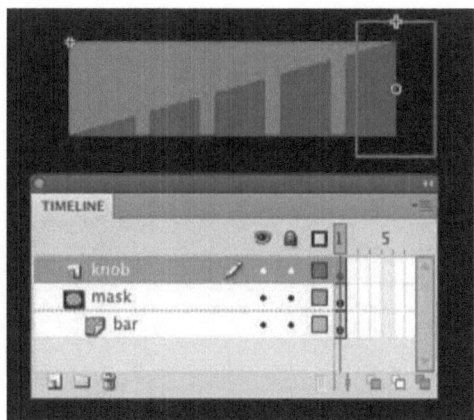

Figure 14-13. A low-alpha shape inside the rectangular movie clip provides "surface area" for the mouse.

13. Click the `Scene 1` link to return to the main timeline. Use the `Text` tool to draw a `Selectable TLF` text field in the `Player` layer, just to the left of the `LoadingDisplay` symbol. Configure the text field with whatever settings you like, but make sure the text field is dynamic and bears a light color, such as white.

With these assets in place, you're nearly ready to rock 'n' roll. Let's just make sure all the programmable assets have instance names, and then organize the timeline layers.

14. Open the `VolumeSlider` movie clip in the `Library`. Carefully select the `VolumeBar` and `VolumeKnob` symbols on the stage to verify that they've already been given instance names: `volumeBar` and `volumeKnob`, respectively.

15. Return to the main timeline and, moving left to right, select each button in turn and verify they have the following instance names: `btnPrev`, `btnPlay`, and `btnNext`.

16. Continuing toward the right, select the `SeekKnob` symbol, and give it the instance name `seekKnob`. Give the `SeekBar` symbol the instance name `seekBar`. For `VolumeSlider`, make it `volumeSlider`. Moving up, give `LoadingDisplay` the instance name `loadingDisplay`. Finally, moving left again, give the text field the instance name `songData`.

17. Select the `Player` layer by clicking its name. Now select `Modify` ➤ `Timeline` ➤ `Distribute to Layers`. Just like that—boom, you get a bunch of new timeline layers, named after the instance names of the symbols they contain.

18. The `Player` layer is still there, but it's now empty—so delete it. Rename the `Bar` layer to `player background` and the `interface` layer to `background image` (see Figure 14-14).

Now everything is tidy and much easier to locate.

CHAPTER 14

Figure 14-14. With everything neatly organized, you're well prepared for a smooth ride.

Wiring up the MP3 player controls

Now it's time to add the ActionScript. Fortunately, you have a leg up, because the `Play/Pause` button is already programmed. In order to proceed, we're going to tidy up the existing ActionScript, just as we did with the `Library` and timeline assets. We'll use the obvious code comments to help plot out our travel route.

Click into the `scripts` layer and review what's currently in place. This includes the revision you made earlier in this section, where `songList` became an XML instance (it had previously been an `Array` instance). Compare your work carefully. Nothing has changed since you last touched this code, but see if you can recognize what's going on. We'll meet you on the other side.

```
import fl.controls.ComboBox;
import fl.data.DataProvider;

/////////////////////////////////////////
// Variables
/////////////////////////////////////////

var song:Sound;
var channel:SoundChannel;
var req:URLRequest;
var pos:Number;

var songList:XML = new XML();
var loader:URLLoader = new URLLoader();
var xmlReq:URLRequest = new URLRequest("playlist.xml");
loader.load(xmlReq);
```

```
loader.addEventListener(Event.COMPLETE, completeHandler);
function completeHandler(evt:Event):void {
  songList = XML(evt.target.data);
  songsCB.dataProvider = new DataProvider(songList);
};

////////////////////////////////////////
// ComboBox
////////////////////////////////////////

// prep
var songsCB:ComboBox = new ComboBox();
songsCB.dropdownWidth = 200;
songsCB.width = 200;
songsCB.height = 24;
songsCB.x = 26;
songsCB.y = 68;
songsCB.dataProvider = new DataProvider(songList);
addChild(songsCB);

// events
songsCB.addEventListener(Event.CHANGE, changeHandler);

function changeHandler(evt:Event):void {
  if (songsCB.selectedItem.data != "") {
    req = new URLRequest(songsCB.selectedItem.data);
    if (channel != null) {
      channel.stop();
    }
    song = new Sound(req);
    channel = song.play();
    btnPlay.gotoAndStop("pause");
  }};

////////////////////////////////////////
// Buttons
////////////////////////////////////////

// prep
btnPlay.stop();
btnPlay.buttonMode = true;

// events
btnPlay.addEventListener(MouseEvent.CLICK, clickHandler);
```

```
function clickHandler(evt:MouseEvent):void {
  if (channel != null) {
    if (btnPlay.currentLabel == "play") {
      channel = song.play(pos);
      btnPlay.gotoAndStop("pause");
    } else {
      pos = channel.position;
      channel.stop();
      btnPlay.gotoAndStop("play");
    }
  }
};
```

It's worth noting that some of this code overlaps. (Don't worry if you didn't see it! That's a lot of ActionScript to pore through.) In the ComboBox block, for example, inside the changeHandler() function, notice that these two lines:

```
channel = song.play();
btnPlay.gotoAndStop("pause");
```

match these two lines in the Buttons block's clickHandler() function (relevant code in bold):

```
if (btnPlay.currentLabel == "play") {
  channel = song.play(pos);
  btnPlay.gotoAndStop("pause");
} else {
```

In simple projects, you don't need to lose any sleep over the occasional overlap. But it's definitely something you want to keep in mind. We've looked at some optimization already in this chapter (the preloader exercise), and there's more of that coming in Chapter 15. The concept of optimization applies as much to the structure of your ActionScript as it does to your assets. As we wire up the controls, you'll find that numerous event handlers are going to load, pause, or play a song, so it makes good sense to write custom functions to perform those actions. Then those functions can be reused by your various event handlers. Doing this makes your ActionScript easier to read and, ultimately, there's less of it to type. The result is code that is easier to deal with. We'll now make the revisions to get rid of the overlap.

Add the following new variables to the code inside your Variables block near the top (new code in bold):

```
////////////////////////////////////
// Variables
////////////////////////////////////

var song:Sound;
var channel:SoundChannel;
var xform:SoundTransform;
var req:URLRequest;
var pos:Number;
var currentSong:int;
var rect:Rectangle;
```

Like the existing variables, the three new ones are declared but not yet set to anything. The xform variable will be a SoundTransform instance for controlling audio volume. currentSong is just like the currentImage variable in the Beijing slide show (here, it's used to keep track of the currently playing song). rect will be a Rectangle instance, which is used later to control the draggable distance of the seek and volume slider knobs.

Skip down to the ComboBox block. Within the changeHandler() function, change what you see so that it looks like this (revision in bold):

```
function changeHandler(evt:Event):void {
  if (songsCB.selectedItem.data != "") {
    currentSong = songsCB.selectedIndex;
    loadSong(songsCB.selectedItem.data);
  }
};
```

This trims up the function quite a bit. Instead of dealing with the loading code here—URLRequest, checking if the channel instance is null, and so on—those lines have been moved to a set of new functions you're about to write. These new functions will fit between the ComboBox block and the Buttons block. Copy one of those code block commented headings and paste it after the changeHandler() function. Change its caption to Song Functions, like this:

```
/////////////////////////////////////
// Song Functions
/////////////////////////////////////
```

After this commented heading, type the following new function:

```
function loadSong(file:String):void {
  req = new URLRequest(file);
  pauseSong();
  song = new Sound(req);
  song.addEventListener(Event.OPEN, soundOpenHandler);
  song.addEventListener(Event.COMPLETE, soundCompleteHandler);
  song.addEventListener(Event.ID3, soundID3Handler);
  playSong();
};
```

This is an example of double-dipping, as far as code optimization is concerned. You might even call it "passing the buck." Just as we passed along the loading code earlier, we're passing along *some* of the ActionScript here again, this time to two additional custom functions: pauseSong() and playSong(). It's all in the name of keeping the ActionScript lean.

Notice that the loadSong() function accepts a string parameter, which will be referenced by the file variable by code inside the function. In the previous code, the value of this parameter was supplied by the expression songsCB.selectedItem.data, which retrieved the MP3's filename from the **ComboBox** component's current selection. In later code—namely, the **Prev** and **Next** button event handlers—you'll see this same value supplied in other ways.

The `req` variable, declared early on in the `Variables` block, is finally set to a new instance of the `URLRequest` class, which allows the MP3 file to be requested. If a song is currently playing, it's stopped by virtue of the `pauseSong()` function (you'll see how in the next block of code).

The `song` variable is set to a new `Sound` instance, and because the `req` variable is fed right into the expression new `Sound()`, we bypass the need for the `Sound.load()` method. With the new Sound instance in place, it's ready for three event listeners: one when the MP3 is loaded (`Event.OPEN`), one when loading is complete (`Event.COMPLETE`), and one when the MP3 file's ID3 tags are encountered (`Event.ID3`). The event handler functions are intuitively named, and you'll see how they're used shortly.

Finally, the custom `playSong()` function rolls the music—which makes this a good idea to write those functions.

Let's continue adding code. Press Enter (Windows) or Return (Mac) a couple times, and then type the following new ActionScript:

```
function playSong(pos:Number = 0):void {
  channel = song.play(pos);
  btnPlay.gotoAndStop("pause");
  seekKnob.addEventListener(Event.ENTER_FRAME, seekKnobUpdate);
};
function pauseSong():void {
  seekKnob.removeEventListener(Event.ENTER_FRAME, seekKnobUpdate);
  if (channel != null) {
    channel.stop();
  }
  btnPlay.gotoAndStop("play");
};
```

Most of this should seem familiar, but there's some new stuff, too. The `playSong()` function accepts a parameter, just like `loadSong()` does, but here, the parameter is already set to a value (`pos:Number = 0`)—so what's going on? New to ActionScript 3.0, this feature lets you provide default values for your parameters. What's it good for? Well, when referenced from the `loadSong()` function, `playSong()` isn't provided with a value; therefore, a default value of 0 is assumed. This will cause the song to play from the beginning when `pos` is passed into the first line inside this function: `channel = song.play(pos);`. As you'll see later, the **Pause/Play** button *does* pass in a value, because it lets you stop the music and resume from where you left off. In that case, the `pos` parameter *will be supplied* with a value, and the default 0 will be overruled.

So, when a song is played, it's assigned to the `channel` instance, and the `btnPlay` movie clip is sent to the **pause** label of its timeline. The other thing that needs to happen—and this is a glimpse ahead—is that the **SeekKnob** symbol needs to start moving along its track to indicate how much of the song has played. This is managed by way of an `Event.ENTER_FRAME` event, which triggers a `seekKnobUpdate()` function you'll write later in the exercise.

Once you understand the `playSong()` function, the `pauseSong()` function isn't hard to follow. It doesn't need a parameter. All it does is unhook the `seekKnobUpdate()` event handler, which halts the traveling of the `SeekKnob` symbol; determine whether the channel instance is null and, if not, stop its playback; and send btnPlay's timeline to the `play` label.

Earlier, we wired up three Sound-related event listeners. It's time to write the handler functions for two of those. Press Enter (Windows) or Return (Mac) a couple times, and type the following new ActionScript:

```
// events
function soundOpenHandler(evt:Event):void {
  loadingDisplay.visible = true;
  loadingDisplay.play();
};
function soundCompleteHandler(evt:Event):void {
  loadingDisplay.stop();
  loadingDisplay.visible = false;
};
```

These functions are straightforward. After a quick // events comment, the soundOpenHandler() function simply sets the visibility of the `LoadingDisplay` symbol to true (this is the spinning dots symbol, imported from the shared `Library`). To actually get the dots to spin, it invokes the MovieClip.play() method on the loadingDisplay instance name. This event handler function responds to the Event.OPEN event, which occurs whenever an MP3 file is loaded.

The soundCompleteHandler() function responds to the Event.COMPLETE event, which means a requested MP3 file has fully downloaded. As you can see, this handler stops the spinning dots and once again turns off the visibility of that movie clip.

Where's the Event.ID3 handler? It could certainly have been written here. Really, it's just a matter of organizational preference, and there's no arguing taste. To us, it makes sense to build out the rest of the code, which is composed entirely of event handlers, in the order in which the buttons and controls appear on the stage. We'll start with the buttons, move rightward to the sliders, then move up to the dots, and then move left again to the text field. It's the text field that does the two-step with the Event.ID3 event handler, so we'll meet it again at the end.

Ready for a quick intermission? Test the movie where it stands, and you'll see three error messages in the `Compiler Errors` panel. Those errors are because of three references to two event handler functions that don't exist yet. One of those is the Event.ID3 handler we just mentioned, located inside the loadSong() function. The other is the seekKnobUpdate() reference located in the playSong() and pauseSong() functions.

Find these addEventListener() and removeEventListener() references in the functions just mentioned, and comment them out, like this:

```
//song.addEventListener(Event.ID3, soundID3Handler);
//seekKnob.addEventListener(Event.ENTER_FRAME, seekKnobUpdatc);
//seekKnob.removeEventListener(Event.ENTER_FRAME, seekKnobUpdate);
```

Test the movie again. The errors disappear.

If you like, compare your work with TinBangsMilestone.fla in the Complete/MP3Player folder for this chapter. When you're ready to move on, you'll be wiring up the buttons.

But before you proceed, make sure to *uncomment those three lines again*!

Handling the button events

Remember that the `Play/Pause` button has already been programmed, which speeds things up a bit. Because we have the new playSong() and pauseSong() functions, you will need to make a few changes to what's there. Fortunately, this shortens the existing ActionScript, which is all part of the secondary plot for this exercise: code optimization. Let's do it.

In case you're not already there, click into frame 1 of the `scripts` layer again, and open the `Actions` panel. Find the Buttons code block and update what you see to the following new lines (new ActionScript in bold):

```
////////////////////////////////////////
// Buttons
////////////////////////////////////////

// prep
btnPlay.stop();
btnPlay.buttonMode = true;
btnPrev.buttonMode = true;
btnNext.buttonMode = true;

// events
btnPlay.addEventListener(MouseEvent.CLICK, playHandler);
btnPrev.addEventListener(MouseEvent.CLICK, prevHandler);
btnNext.addEventListener(MouseEvent.CLICK, nextHandler);
```

There's nothing difficult here. The `Prev` and `Next` buttons need their MovieClip.buttonMode properties set to true, simply because—like `Pause/Play`—they're movie clips that are masquerading as buttons. Following suit, they get assigned to their respective event handlers. Because there are now three click-related event handlers, the function originally assigned to the btnPlay instance has been renamed playHandler() (it was formerly clickHandler()).

Speaking of clickHandler(), you need to update it so that it reflects the following new code, making sure to rename it as shown (revisions in bold):

```
function playHandler (evt:MouseEvent):void {
  if (channel != null) {
    if (btnPlay.currentLabel == "play") {
      playSong(pos);
    } else {
      pos = channel.position;
      pauseSong();
  } }};
```

BUILDING STUFF

Here's where the custom functions begin to earn their keep. The behavior of the `playhandler()` function is intact, but thanks to the `playSong()` and `pauseSong()` functions, the actual lines of code have been reduced.

Notice, as before, that on one side of the `else` clause, the `pos` variable is set to the `SoundChannel.position` property of the `channel` instance. On the other side of that `else` clause, `pos` is passed into the `playSong()` function as a parameter. When you look at the `playSong()` function definition in the previous section, you'll see that the variable between the function's parentheses also happens to be called `pos`. That's a coincidence, and nothing more. Whether or not they're named the same, a value that represents the song's position is conveyed, and that's all that matters.

> *In real-world situations, you'll often find that project requirements change. In fact, it's rare when they don't! When this happens, you'll find yourself better equipped to respond to revisions when you're dealing with reusable functions. If the concept embodied by the playSong() function happens to change, you need to edit only one function in a single place, rather than needing to use a hunt-and-peck approach to touch up numerous blocks of code.*

The **Prev** and **Next** buttons are taken care of with one function apiece. Add the following two event handlers beneath the `playHandler()` function:

```
function prevHandler(evt:MouseEvent):void {
  currentSong--;
  if (currentSong < 1) {
    currentSong = songList.song.length() - 1;
  }
]songsCB.selectedIndex = currentSong;
  loadSong(songList.song[currentSong].@data);
};
function nextHandler(evt:MouseEvent):void {
  currentSong++;
  if (currentSong > songList.song.length() - 1) {
    currentSong = 1;
  }
  songsCB.selectedIndex = currentSong;
  loadSong(songList.song[currentSong].@data);
};
```

These should be reminiscent of the **Next** button in the Beijing slide show. Here, these two functions are metaphorically mirror images of each other. In `prevHandler()`, the value of the `currentSong` variable is decreased by 1 (`currentSong--`). If `currentSong` is less than 1—which it will be, eventually—then the variable is set to one less than the total number of `<song>` elements in the XML document (`songList.song.length() - 1`). Why one less than the total? Because arrays start with 0, rather than 1. Why aren't we checking whether `currentSong` is less than 0, then? Because the first entry in the XML,

727

and therefore the ComboBox component, is the "dead" entry without data—the one that says Select a song.

Once currentSong is updated, the selected index of the ComboBox component is configured to reflect that change, and the custom loadSong() function is instructed to load the new current selection. The parameter's expression happens to be based on the XML content, using a bit of E4X syntax—songList.song[currentSong].@data—but it could have just as easily be taken from the ComboBox component.

In contrast, the nextHandler() function increments the value of currentSong and then sets it back to 1 if it goes beyond one less than the total number of <song> nodes in the XML—in other words, the reverse. After that, the ComboBox component is updated, and once again, the loadSong() function is instructed to load the current selection.

> *Wait a minute! The last two lines of these functions overlap! Shouldn't they be folded into yet another function—maybe updateSong()? You could certainly do that. Optimization is as much an art as a science, and we encourage you to find your personal line in the sand.*

Programming the sliders

You're about to enter into the thickest part of the ActionScript for this project, so you may want to pull out your machete. Actually, it's not so bad, once you strike past the first bit of foliage. The mosquitoes are pretty big, true, but that makes it all the easier to swat them with the blade.

Joking aside, the ActionScript for the sliders isn't going to make your head explode. To understand it better, it helps to take a closer look at the way the slider-related symbols are laid out. Their registration points, in particular, are designed to make the math as easy as possible, so let's take a gander. Figure 14-15 shows these registration points.

Figure 14-15. The symbols' registration points are carefully chosen to make the code easier.

There are two parts to this slider: the **SeekKnob** symbol and the **SeekBar** symbol. When the knob is positioned on the bar's left edge, as shown in Figure 14-15, notice that the registration points of each symbol (the two pluses along each symbol's upper edges) are aligned.

Both of these symbols are positioned 260 pixels from the left side of the stage. If **SeekKnob**'s registration point was also in its own upper-left corner, it would have to be offset by several pixels to look as if it were hugging the left edge of `SeekBar`. As it is, however, the numbers are easy. To coordinate its movements with `SeekBar`, all `SeekKnob` has to do is know `SeekBar`'s horizontal position (seekBar.x) and take into consideration `SeekBar`'s width (seekBar.width).

To position the knob along the bar's left edge, all you need to do set its MovieClip.x property to the bar's MovieClip.x property. To slide it halfway across, set the knob's x property to the x property of the bar, plus half of the bar's width. To shove it all the way over, set its x property to bar's, plus the full width of the bar. Keep this principle in mind as we work through the seek slider ActionScript.

To begin, copy another one of the commented code block headers and paste it below the last bit of ActionScript (nextHandler(), from the Buttons section). Change the header's caption to Seek slider, and then type in the following ActionScript, so that your code looks like this:

```
////////////////////////////////////
// Seek slider
////////////////////////////////////

// prep
seekKnob.buttonMode = true;

// events
seekKnob.addEventListener(MouseEvent.MOUSE_DOWN, seekStartDrag);
```

Like the **Prev**, **Play/Pause**, and **Next** movie clip "buttons," the `seekKnob` instance needs to have its buttonMode property set to true. When the user clicks it, you want the user to be able to start dragging that knob, so the MouseEvent.MOUSE_DOWN event is associated with a custom function you're about to write, called seekStartDrag(). That function is triggered when the user clicks the mouse (MOUSE_DOWN) on the `seekKnob` instance. Type the following new ActionScript:

```
function seekStartDrag(evt:MouseEvent):void {
  if (song != null) {
    pauseSong();
    rect = new Rectangle(seekBar.x, seekKnob.y, seekBar.width, 0);
    seekKnob.startDrag(true, rect);
    stage.addEventListener(MouseEvent.MOUSE_UP, seekStopDrag);
  }
};
```

If the song instance isn't null— for example, it's null before a song is chosen from the combo box—then pause the song, in case it's playing. Next, define a Rectangle instance (stored in the rect variable), which will be used to constrain dragging to the desired location.

Rectangle instances are specified at a particular location (x and y) and at a particular width and height. In this case, we want the knob to be draggable only from the left side of the bar (seekBar.x, the first parameter) to the right side (seekBar.width, the third parameter). Its vertical position is fine where it is (seekKnob.y, the second parameter) and shouldn't vary from that, which means we set the rectangle to a height of 0 (the fourth parameter).

The MovieClip.startDrag() method, invoked on seekKnob, is fed two parameters: true, which snaps dragging to the symbol's registration point, and rect, which confines dragging to the dimensions just described.

Finally, a MouseEvent.MOUSE_UP event handler is associated with the stage, configured to trigger a custom seekStopDrag() function. Why is this association made with the stage, rather than with seekKnob? Because the user might just drag the mouse off the knob before releasing the mouse (MOUSE_UP). If the event handler were associated with seekKnob, then seekStopDrag() wouldn't be triggered. But when it's assigned to the stage, that pretty much means the mouse can be lifted anywhere, and the dragging routine will stop.

Here's the seekStopDrag() function. Type the following new ActionScript:

```
function seekStopDrag(evt:MouseEvent):void {
  seekKnob.stopDrag();
  playSong(song.length * (seekKnob.x - seekBar.x) / seekBar.width);
  stage.removeEventListener(MouseEvent.MOUSE_UP, seekStopDrag);
};
```

The first thing this function does is invoke MovieClip.stopDrag() on the **seekKnob** instance. That part is easy. The challenge comes in telling the song where to begin playing again, because it all depends on where the knob, as shown in Figure 14-16, is currently positioned along the bar.

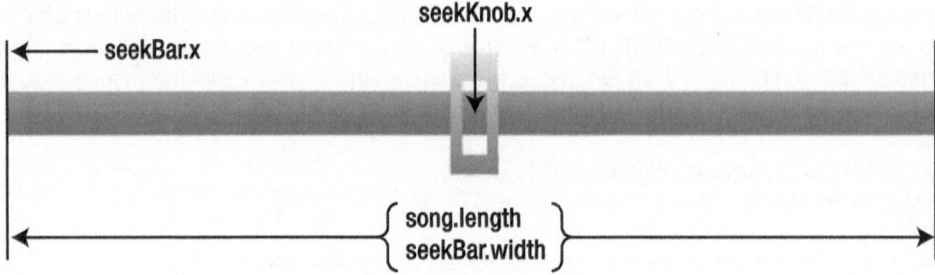

Figure 14-16. The variables used in the calculation to relate the position of the knob with a time in the song.

To illustrate, let's imagine the user dragged the knob right to the middle, and let's pretend the song is exactly 60 seconds long. Let's use those figures and run the math.

Here's the actual expression:

song.length * (seekKnob.x - seekBar.x) / seekBar.width

Using the numbers we just agreed on, that equates to this:

```
60 seconds × (knob's position-bar's position) / bar's width
60 * (329-260) / 138
```

60 multiplied by the difference between 329 and 260 (namely, 69) is 4,140. Divided by 138, the final number is 30 seconds, which is exactly what's expected when the knob is dropped halfway across.

The final total of the arithmetic equation is fed into the `playSong()` function, which starts the song from whatever value, in seconds, is provided.

The last thing this function does is to tell the stage to stop listening for the MOUSE_UP event, because the event obviously just occurred (since this function handles it).

In the `playSong()` function definition, seekKnob is associated with an Event.ENTER_FRAME event, which tells the knob to continuously update its position according to how much of the song has played. Here's that function. Type the following new ActionScript:

```
function seekKnobUpdate(evt:Event):void {
  var pos:Number = seekBar.width * channel.position / song.length;
  if (!isNaN(pos)) {
    seekKnob.x = seekBar.x + pos;
  } else {
    seekKnob.x = seekBar.x;
  }
};
```

Here's that pos variable again (a third one!). This one is unrelated to the other two, except in name. To the authors, pos just seems like an appropriate name for a variable for noting the *position* of something. In this case, pos is declared within the scope of this function and set to an expression that effectively does the opposite of the expression shown earlier. Let's run the numbers again, assuming that, at this very moment, our hypothetical -60-second song has played halfway through. Here's the actual expression:

```
seekBar.width * channel.position / song.length,
```

It equates to this:

```
bar's width × song's position / song's length
138 * 30 / 60
```

138 multiplied by 30 is 4,140 (sounds familiar, doesn't it?). 4,140 divided by 60 is 69. Hold that thought.

There may be times when neither channel nor song has a property value that yields a valid number when run through the math. To safeguard against that, an `if` statement uses the `isNaN()` function (is Not a Number) to prod the value of pos (which is hypothetically 69). If pos *is a valid number*—that is, if `!isNaN(pos)` evaluates to true—then it is added to the current MovieClip.x value of **seekBar**, the sum of which is bestowed upon **seekKnob**. Because **seekBar**'s position is 260, that (added to 69) puts **seekKnob** at 329, which is exactly halfway across the bar.

> The exclamation point (!) in front of the isNaN() function inverts whatever that function says, in the same way that the inequality operator (!=) means "is not equal to." If you want to find out if a value is not a valid number, check it against isNaN(). On the other hand, if you want to find out if a value is a valid number, check it against !isNaN().

The flip side of that if statement—meaning, pos is an unusable number—simply sets the knob's position to the position of the bar, which resets the knob to its original hug-the-left-side location.

As the song plays through, this seekKnobUpdate() function is triggered every time the timeline enters a frame, in other words, continuously. This causes the knob to indicate progress until the function is instructed to stop. Go ahead, test the SWF and give it a whirl.

The mechanics of the volume slider work in pretty much the same way. A similar knob symbol is instructed to drag within a constrained area. The difference is that the knob's position in relation to its bar is used to adjust the volume of the currently playing song. In addition, a separate symbol is instructed to follow the knob, whose movement either hides or reveals that symbol behind a mask. Let's add the code.

Continuing below the previous ActionScript, give yourself another code comment heading, this time captioned as Volume slider. Type in these additional new lines:

```
///////////////////////////////////////
// Volume slider
///////////////////////////////////////

// prep
volumeSlider.volumeKnob.buttonMode = true;

// events
volumeSlider.volumeKnob.addEventListener(MouseEvent.MOUSE_DOWN, ↵
volumeStartDrag);
```

The `volumeKnob` instance is nested inside `volumeSlider`, and that's because those movie clips are nested. Other than that, there is nothing remarkable about this addition. Let's keep rolling.

Enter the following new ActionScript, which defines the volumeStartDrag() function just referenced:

```
function volumeStartDrag(evt:MouseEvent):void {
  rect = new Rectangle(8, volumeSlider.volumeKnob.y, ↵
volumeSlider.volumeBar.width - 8, 0);
  volumeSlider.volumeKnob.startDrag(true, rect);
  volumeSlider.volumeKnob.addEventListener(MouseEvent.MOUSE_MOVE, ↵
volumeAdjust);
  stage.addEventListener(MouseEvent.MOUSE_UP, volumeStopDrag);
};
```

As with the other slider, `rect` is set to a new `Rectangle` instance when the knob is clicked and fed appropriate values. In this case, the values are purposefully tweaked to move the knob in from the left edge just a bit. Why? Because if the volume knob were dragged all the way to the left, it would completely obscure the red movie clip rectangle behind the slanted five-column mask. Letting it go *almost* all the way to the left—8 pixels shy, in this case—looks good visually.

> Where did the 8 come from? Even though it is an arbitrary figure, sometimes these numbers just appear, and you learn to live with them (but they still make you feel a bit weird because they don't quite adhere to the normal programmatic logic).

The `startDrag()` method is invoked on `volumeKnob`, and again the stage is associated with a MouseEvent.MOUSE_UP event to stop the dragging. This time, though, an additional event (MOUSE_MOVE) is associated with a custom function named `volumeAdjust()`. Let's look at both of those.

Enter the following new ActionScript:

```
function volumeStopDrag(evt:MouseEvent):void {
  volumeSlider.volumeKnob.stopDrag();
  stage.removeEventListener(MouseEvent.MOUSE_UP, volumeStopDrag);
  volumeSlider.volumeKnob.removeEventListener(MouseEvent.MOUSE_MOVE, ↵
volumeAdjust);
};
function volumeAdjust(evt:MouseEvent):void {
  volumeSlider.volumeBar.x = volumeSlider.volumeKnob.x;
  if (channel != null) {
    xform = channel.soundTransform;
    xform.volume = (volumeSlider.volumeKnob.x - 8) / ↵
(volumeSlider.volumeBar.width - 8);
    channel.soundTransform = xform;
  }
};
```

The `volumeStopDrag()` function is old hat by now. It stops the dragging and stops the MOUSE_MOVE handler. Let's break down the `volumeAdjust()` function.

First off, it sets the position of `volumeBar` to the position of `volumeKnob`. That hides and reveals the red rectangle behind its mask in concert with the knob's position. After that, assuming `channel` is not null, the `xform` variable—declared early on—is set to the `SoundChannel.soundTransform` property of the `channel` instance. This gives `xform` a `SoundTransform.volume` property, whose value is set in terms of `volumeKnob`'s position (accounting for that 8-pixel shy span) in relation to the width of `volumeBar`.

CHAPTER 14

The `VolumeBar` symbol happens to be 50 pixels wide, so let's run the numbers assuming the knob has been dragged halfway across the valid range. (Normally, halfway across would be 25, but we're adding half of that 8-pixel buffer, so half is 29 here.) Here's the actual expression:

`(volumeSlider.volumeKnob.x - 8) / (volumeSlider.volumeBar.width - 8)`

It equates to this:

```
knob's position - 8, divided by bar's width - 8
29 - 8 / 50 - 8
29 minus 8 is 21. 50 minus 8 is 42. 21 divided by 42 is 0.5, or 50%.
```

xform's volume property is set to 0.5, and then the final line reassigns xform to the channel.soundTransform property, which cuts the volume in half. Remember that this function is triggered every time the mouse moves, as it drags the knob.

Almost in the clear!

Finishing up the controls

The rest of the controls require barely a flick of the tail. All we need to do is hide the `LoadingDisplay` symbol (the spinning dots) by default and handle the `Event.ID3` event. Let's do it.

Add another block of code that looks like this:

```
//////////////////////////////////////
// Loading display
//////////////////////////////////////

loadingDisplay.stop();
loadingDisplay.visible = false;
```

This stops and hides the spinning dots. Now, enter your final block of code, and make it look like this:

```
//////////////////////////////////////
// Song Data
//////////////////////////////////////

function soundID3Handler(evt:Event):void {
  songData.text = song.id3.artist + ": " + song.id3.songName + "↵
(" + song.id3.year + ")";
};
```

This function is triggered whenever an MP3's ID3 tags are encountered. Tag information is retrieved from the `Sound.id3` property of the song instance—here, `song.id3.artist`, `.songName`, and `.year`—and concatenated into a string fed to the songData text field's `text` property.

> *ID3 tags have nothing to do with ActionScript 3.0 per se. The concept is part of the MP3 file format, and it just happens to be supported by ActionScript. On their own, ID3 tag names aren't especially easy to read. The tag intended for the artist's name, for example, is TPE1; the publication year is TYER, and so on. ActionScript provides friendly names for the most popular tags—comment, album, genre, songName, artist, track, and year—but the others are available by their less intuitive tag names. To see the full list, look up the Sound class in the ActionScript 3.0 Language and Components Reference, and then skim down the Properties heading until you come to id3. Click that listing.*

Test your MP3 player to give it a spin. Kick the tires a bit.

Evaluating and improving the MP3 player

Even with the best of planning, you might be surprised to find that some aspects of a project, including its faults, don't make themselves apparent until the work is done—or at least, until a first draft is done. (Some projects never do seem to end! Hey, at least it's a paycheck.) In Chapter 15, we discuss the idea of planning an FLA beforehand—the authors do believe in the practice, with a passion—but sometimes you can't tell how a car is going to handle until you actually wrap your fingers around the steering wheel and slam your boot on the gas pedal.

In this case, you may have noticed that every time a new song plays, the volume jumps back up to 100 percent, no matter where you drag the volume slider. Worse, when this happens, the volume is audibly at full, even though the slider might be positioned all the way to the left. That's a bug, and we're going to fix it.

In addition, you might want the player to cycle through the whole playlist, rather than simply stop after a song ends. You might also want the first song to start playing automatically. All of these options are possible, and thanks to the thoughtful arrangement of our existing ActionScript, they're easy to implement.

Let's tie up this MP3 player with a bow. First, let's address the volume bug. Locate the volumeAdjust() function, just above the Loading display block, and give its evt parameter a default value of null—like this (revision in bold):

```
function volumeAdjust(evt:MouseEvent = null):void {
```

What does this do? Without the addition, this function requires a MouseEvent parameter, which pretty much means it must be triggered in response to an event, which passes in the MouseEvent automatically. By giving the evt parameter a null value by default, you're making the parameter *optional*. This means the volumeAdjust() function can be triggered from anywhere, as an event handler or not.

Locate the playSong() function and update it to look like this (revision in bold):

```
function playSong(pos:Number = 0):void {
  channel = song.play(pos);
  volumeAdjust();
  btnPlay.gotoAndStop("pause");
  seekKnob.addEventListener(Event.ENTER_FRAME, seekKnobUpdate);
};
```

Just like that, the bug is fixed! The playSong() function actually sets the newly loaded song in motion, to speak, and associates the song instance with the channel instance. With channel updated, the xform variable, referenced inside volumeAdjust(), has what it needs to check the current position of the volume slider and adjust the volume accordingly.

Since we're in the playSong() function anyway, it's the perfect time to add a new event listener that will allow the player loop through its playlist. Update the playSong() function again to look like this (revision in bold):

```
function playSong(pos:Number = 0):void {
  channel = song.play(pos);
  channel.addEventListener(Event.SOUND_COMPLETE, nextHandler);
  volumeAdjust();
  btnPlay.gotoAndStop("pause");
  seekKnob.addEventListener(Event.ENTER_FRAME, seekKnobUpdate);
};
```

Once the channel variable is updated, it's associated with the already-written nextHandler() function in response to the Event.SOUND_COMPLETE event, which is dispatched when the sound channel of a currently playing sound reaches the end of the file.

Remember that the nextHandler() function is also associated with the MouseEvent.CLICK event, which is triggered when someone clicks the **Next** button. The MouseEvent class inherits some of its functionality from the Event class, and in this case, it's safe to strongly type the evt parameter inside the nextHandler() function as Event. This is because, at rock bottom, both Event and MouseEvent instances are ultimately instances of Event.

Locate the nextHandler() function and change it to look like this (revision in bold):

```
function nextHandler(evt:Event):void {
```

Finally, to make this MP3 player begin in "auto-play" mode, locate the completeHandler() function, just above the ComboBox block, and add the new lines shown in bold:

```
function completeHandler(evt:Event):void {
  songList = XML(evt.target.data);
  songsCB.dataProvider = new DataProvider(songList);
  loadSong(songList.song[1].@data);
  songsCB.selectedIndex = 1;
};
```

When the XML playlist fully loads, `completeHandler()` is triggered. It populates the `ComboBox` component. In addition to that, it now invokes the `loadSong()` function and feeds it the filename from the first `<song>` element that actually refers to an MP3 file (remember that the *very first* `<song>` element—`songList.song[0]`—doesn't contain file data). After that, the function updates the `ComboBox` component to its first song entry (the one after the filler `Select a song` entry), by setting its `selectedIndex` property to 1.

Test your movie again and, while you're tapping your feet, give yourself a pat on the back.

Going mobile

A year or so ago one of the authors, in response to a question around developing Flash projects for mobile devices, woke up the audience when he commented, "Not me. I'd rather drive chop sticks into my eyeballs." He didn't make this comment to be funny but to express to the audience that mobile is a frustrating and bewildering space fraught with competing operating systems, varying Flash Players requiring different versions of ActionScript with some playing video and others not, devices with varying screen sizes...we think you get the picture.

Just to make things even more interesting, Apple, in April 2010, dropped an atomic bomb on developers. They essentially told them they have to use Apple-approved development tools to create applications for the iPhone. Though widely regarded as a slap against Adobe and Flash, it became pretty clear that that if you wanted to play in Apple's sandbox, you had to use their toys. This was a rather interesting development because the "nobody cares how you did it they just care that you did it" approach to developing applications for the iPhone was no longer in play. This naturally had a rather major impact on us because the iPhone compiler—a choice in the `New Document` list—went out the window along with our plans for this chapter.

Over the weeks following this uproar the mobile community started looking for a new sandbox, which let them use their toys. As such there developed a loose consensus that the Google mobile OS, Android, might just be the place to go. Just to make sure that everyone knew that the Android sandbox was open for business Google announced, in May 2010, an updated version of the OS—code name Froyo—and Adobe, minutes later on that very same stage, made it crystal clear that Flash Player 10.1 was rock steady and ready to go to work with Froyo and practically every other smartphone on the planet (...elephant in the room excepted).

In this final section of the chapter, we are going to develop a small game—Whack-A-Bunny—that will be developed for play back on a Google Nexus One Android device, which is the test device used by Google and chipset manufacturer Qualcomm. To start, we need to take a stroll over to Device Central.

A quick tour of Device Central

Device Central has been around for while. Its purpose is to let you choose a variety of devices from a variety of manufacturers and test your project in an environment that emulates how a user would actually use the device and your application. When you install any of the Adobe Collections—we use the Master Collection—Device Central is installed with all of the other applications in the bundle. Let's go check it out:

CHAPTER 14

1. Launch Device Central. When it launches, you will see the `Start` page shown in Figure 14-17.

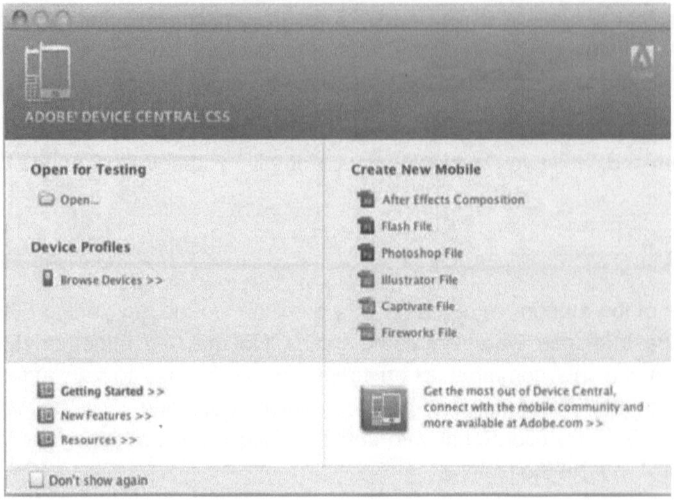

Figure 14-17. The Device Central `Start` page

As you can see, the page is quite similar to the Flash CS5 Start page in that it is divided into distinct sections:

- `Open for Testing`: Any files that you have tested in Device Central will be listed here, or you can click the `Browse` button to navigate to the file to be tested.

- `Device Profiles`: Click the `Browse Devices` button, and you will be taken to a list of every device resident in Device Central. There are quite a few of them, but don't let the list intimidate you. You get to choose which devices will be used. The listing lets you pick them.

- `Create New Mobile`: This area is new to Device Central CS5 and contains a listing of the applications that have a direct 'hook" into Device Central. Click an application, and Device Central doesn't launch the application; it opens the `New Document` panel in Device Central. When you are there, you can choose the player version, ActionScript version, and content type. From there, you choose your test player and click the Create button to launch the application chosen. We'll show you how in a couple of minutes.

2. Click the `Browse Devices` button to open a list of devices.

3. Scroll down the list and, as shown in Figure 14-18, locate the `Google Nexus One` device. The categories are self-explanatory. The device, if it has an image of the device, is an actual template of the device. The odd icon in the `Location` area—a globe over a handset—tells you the device is found on your hard drive. Just the globe indicates an online version will be used. You are also told the version of Flash Player that is used on the device, the screen size, and the `Creator` category that indicates who created the Device Profile, which, in this case, is Adobe.

BUILDING STUFF

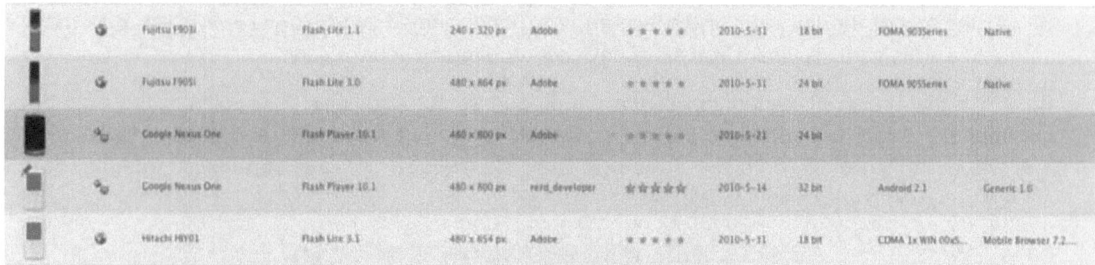

Figure 14-18. Device Central contains an extensive list of Flash-enabled devices.

4. Double click the device to open the full device profile shown in Figure 14-19.

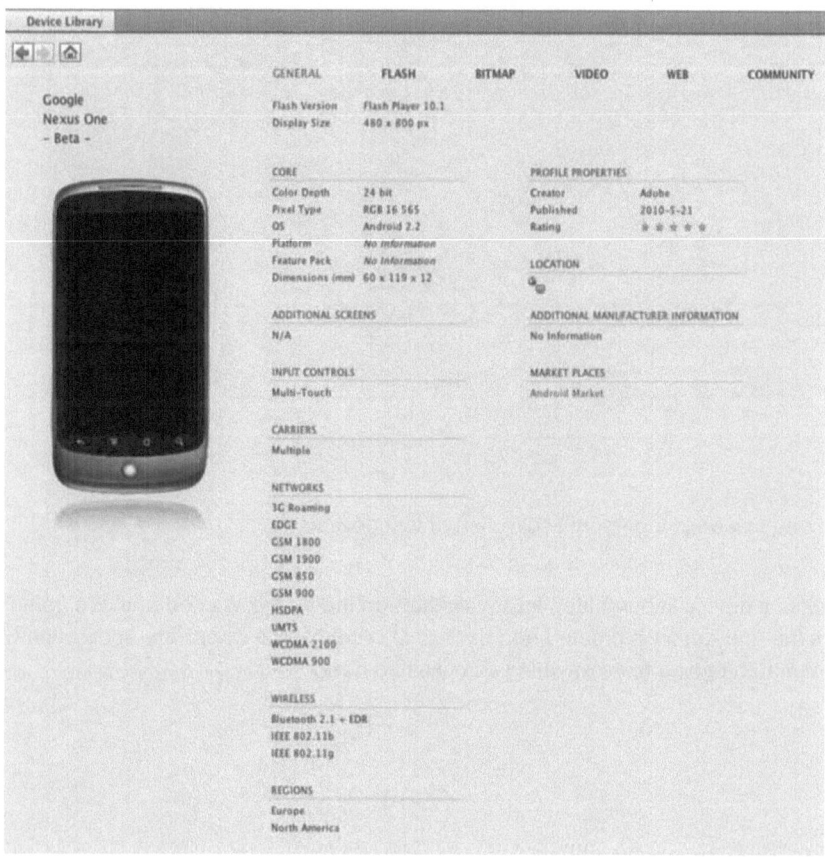

Figure 14-19. The device profile is quite extensive.

5. At the top of the left side of the screen is a panel named `Test Devices`. Click it to make it active. This panel is where you store devices targeting by your project.

6. Click the + sign at the bottom of the panel, and select `Add New Group` from the drop-down menu. A folder will appear in the panel. Double-click the folder name and change the name, as shown in Figure 14-20, to `My Devices`. Drag the `Google Nexus One` device from the device `Library` into your new folder.

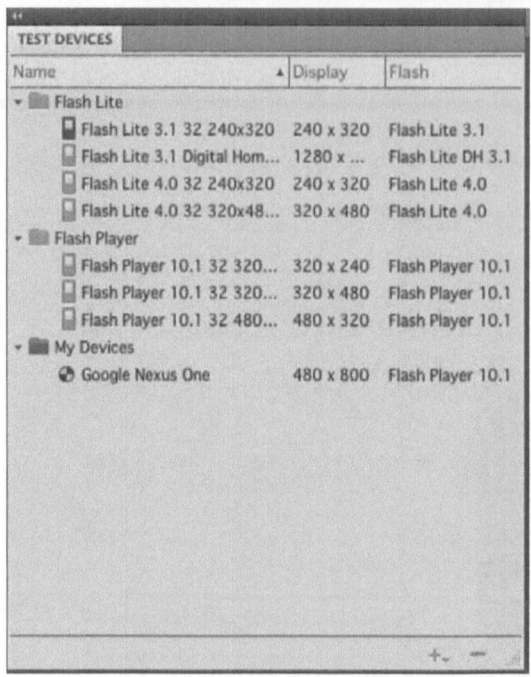

Figure 14-20. You can build a personal collection of test devices.

Now that we have a device in our folder, let's walk through the workflow used to move from Device Central to Flash where the application is created and back to Device Central where the application will be tried out in the device. We aren't going to do anything complicated here.

7. Click the **Create** button in the upper-right corner of Device Central. The **New Document** panel, shown in Figure 14-21, will open. Click the device in the **New Document** panel, and the options move from being grayed out to live.

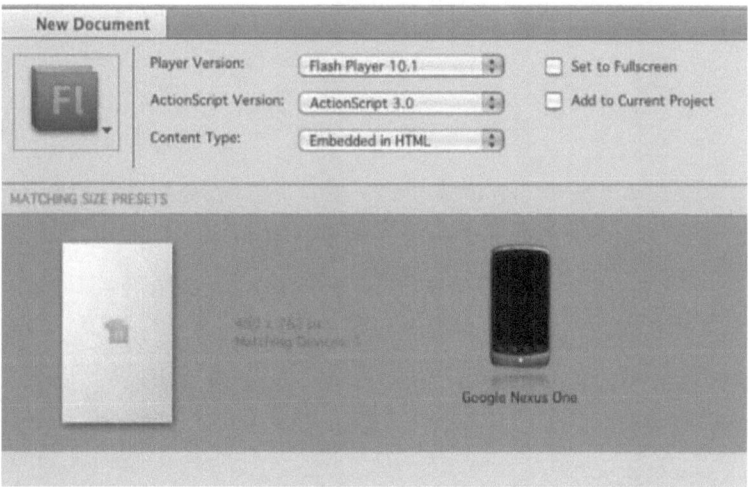

Figure 14-21. You get to choose how the Flash document will be configured to the device.

8. Click the **Create** button in the bottom-right corner of the **New Document** panel. This will launch Flash, and when it opens, the stage will match the screen dimension of the device.

9. Select the **Text** tool, and enter your name. We used **TLF text Read Only** as the format and set the text to 36-point Arial.

10. With the text container selected on the stage, open the **Motion Presets** panel, and apply the **spiral-3D** preset to your name. Save the file to your Exercise folder.

Follow these steps to see the animation play on your device:

11. Select **Control ➤ Test Movie ➤ in Device Central**. The SWF will be exported, and when the export finishes, as shown in Figure 14-22, Device Central opens, and your name is spinning on the screen of the Google Nexus One. If you look up in the upper-right corner of the window, you will see **Emulate Flash** has been selected. The panels on the right side of the device provide you with a number of options and configurations for the chosen device, and the buttons along the bottom allow you to play the SWF in the device, recode the movie in the device, take screen shots, and so on.

CHAPTER 14

Figure 14-22. You can test your work in the device chosen.

12. Close Device Central, and return to Flash. You will notice the `Output` panel has also given you a bit of information as to the status of the test.

13. Save the document and close it.

What you have just experienced is the bare-bones workflow between Device Central and Flash. This is about as far as we are going to go on this subject because mobile is a huge, emerging area that will grow to not only encompass smartphones but tablets and other Flash-enabled screen displays. We simply don't have the space to do a deep dive into the subject and the number of variables—screens, Flash Players, multitouch, and so on—are such that they are well out of the scope of this book. Even so, with this bar-bones workflow, you can do some amazing stuff. Let's give it a test drive and create a "Whack-A-Bunny" game for our Google Nexus One device.

BUILDING STUFF

"Wiring up" the game

This game is your standard "Whack-A-Mole" game, only in this case the mole is a bunny. The object of the game is to whack the bunnies popping out of the holes in the ground. The game will consist of two frames on the Flash timeline, and the code you will write will get the game started and then allow the user to play the game. The "end game" will be getting the game to work on the Google Nexus One device in Device Central. Let's get started.

1. Open the whackabunny.fla file in your Exercise folder. When the file opens, you will notice, as shown in Figure 14-23, we have included all of the game's assets in the Library.

Figure 14-23. All you need to do is to add the code.

2. Open the rabbitAnim movie clip in the Library's BunnyGraphics folder. You can see how the rabbit pops in and out of its hole—a mask is used—and the scripts in the Actions layer simply control the playhead during the animation. Click the Scene 1 link to return to the main timeline.

3. The game title, found in the StartScreen layer, simply has the title of the game grow out of a point on the horizon. To see how the title animation was created, open the title movie clip found in the Library's Intro folder. If you scrub the movie clip's timeline, you will see the title

743

is, as shown in Figure 14-24, nothing more than a tweened scale and alpha animation using a Classic Tween. Click the `Scene1` link to return to the main timeline.

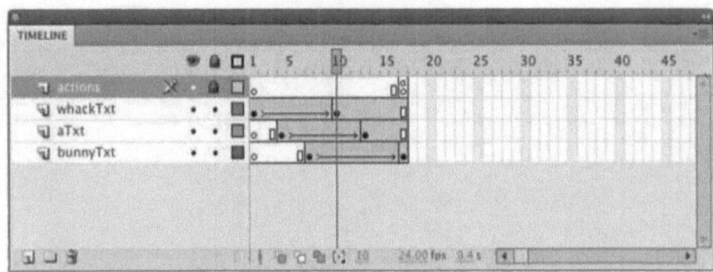

Figure 14-24. The Title sequence is a simple Classic Tween with an alpha fade.

The words **START**, **WHACK**, **A**, and **BUNNY** are used only once and use only 16 characters of the font. If you are using a custom font and don't want the user to access it, feel free to select each of the words, and using **Modify ➤ Break Apart**, you can "change" the text from a font to artwork. Just remember, this makes the text noneditable, so make sure everything is spelled correctly before doing the conversion.

4. Click the word `Start` on the stage. If you check the `Properties` panel, you will see we have given this movie clip the instance name `startBtn`. The user will have to click this button to start the game. Let's wire it up.

5. Click into frame 1 of the `Actions` layer, open the ActionScript panel, and enter the following code:

```
import flash.events.MouseEvent;

stop();

startBtn.addEventListener( MouseEvent.CLICK, startGame );
```

```
function startGame( evt:MouseEvent ):void
{
    nextFrame();
};
```

All this code does is to hold the playhead on frame 1 until the user clicks the **Start** button. When he or she does, the nextFrame() method is used to advance the movie to frame 2.

    6. Select frame 2 of the **Actions** layer, open the **ActionScript** panel, and enter the following variables:

```
var max:Number    = 8;
var min:Number    = 1;
var randNum:Number;
var timer:Timer;
var score:int;
```

There is going to be a lot going on in this game, and this is the place to anticipate and name values that will change on a regular basis. The first variable—max—is the maximum number of rabbits in the game, and the min variable determines the minimum number of rabbits. The randNum variable will be used to ensure there will always be between one and eight rabbits on the screen at any one time. The timer will be used to determine how often the number of rabbits on the screen will change, and the score variable will be used to change the number value in the scoreTxt text box on the stage.

    7. Press the Enter (Windows) or Return (Mac) key twice, and add the following:

```
init();

function init():void
{
    //Mouse.hide();

    //start timer with a callback of randomBunnyDisplay
    timer = new Timer( 2500 );
    timer.addEventListener( TimerEvent.TIMER, randomBunnyDisplay );
    timer.start();

addEventListener( MouseEvent.CLICK, checkHammer );
};
```

The init() function is where the "magic" happens. That first line, all by itself, is useless. It is the next line, where the init function is defined, that gets things going.

You may be wondering why the Mouse.hide() method is "commented out." It's because where the game will be played. To "whack" a bunny, you need to click it. If the game is being played on a computer, you will need to click a bunny, and to do this, you will need to see the mouse pointer. If this game is moving to the Nexus One device, there is no mouse pointer. The user will tap on a bunny with his or her finger. Seeing as how our first test of the game will be on your computer, the method is disabled.

CHAPTER 14

We start by determining that every 2.5 seconds—new `Timer(2500)`—something is going to happen. The next line determines that "something" is a function named `randomBunnyDisplay`. Having established that, the next line starts the clock running.

The final two lines listen for what happens when the playhead comes back into frame 2 and what happens when the mouse is clicked—figure out where the hammer should go, which is the next function you will need to add.

    8. Press the Enter (Windows) or Return (Mac) key twice, and add the following function to control the movement of the hammer:

```
function checkHammer( evt:MouseEvent ):void {
    for ( var i:int = 1; i < 8; ++i ){
        var mc:MovieClip = MovieClip( getChildByName( "bunny" + i ) );
        if( mc.hitTestPoint( mouseX, mouseY, true ) )
    {
        // mallet.x = mouseX - 40;
        //mallet.y = mouseY - 40;

        mallet.gotoAndPlay(2);
        mc.bunny.gotoAndPlay(81);
        mc.gotoAndPlay( 80 );
        score++;
        }
    }
};
```

The function starts by creating a number between one and eight and iterates the chosen number up to that maximum value. That number is then used to put the bunny movie clip on the stage and give it an instance name that is a combination of the word *bunny* and the number from the previous line. If you look on the stage in frame 2, you will see there are eight white dots, which are instances of the `rabbitAnim` movie clip in the **Library**. Each one of these has an instance name of the word bunny and a number. You can gather from this, the code line is how up to eight copies of the `rabbitAnim` movie clip get put into position on the stage.

Now that we know where the bunnies are, we have to get the mallet to their locations when the mouse is clicked or the screen is tapped. This is where the `hitTestPoint()` method comes into play. It makes sure that the point being clicked (`mouseX` and `mouseY`) intersects the bunny object on the screen, which is the True parameter.

The next two lines, which are commented, will only be used in the mobile version of the game and are there to ensure the mallet stays within the screen boundaries.

The final four lines are, in many respects, the "action" lines. If the cursor is on the bunny, thanks to the `hitTestPoint()` method, the hammer slams down because of the animation that starts in frame 2 of the **mallet** movie clip found in the **GameGraphics** folder. To show the user they have indeed "whacked a bunny," the bunny closes its eyes and stars appear over its head. This entire animation sequence kicks off in frame 81 of the `BunnyCharacter` movie clip found in the BunnyGraphics folder. Finally, the bunny goes back down its hole (frame 80 of the `rabbitAnim` movie clip), and the score increases.

You may have noticed there is nothing in this function telling the mallet where to move and how to change the score. Let's clean that up with the next function we'll name update.

   9. Press the Enter (Windows) or Return (Mac) key twice, and enter the following code:

```
function update( evt:Event ):void{
   mallet.x = this.mouseX - 40;
   mallet.y = this.mouseY - 40;
   scoreTxt.text = String( score );
   checkScore();
};
```

Other than the checkScore() function, which we will get to in a minute, there is nothing new here. What you do need to know is that the mallet.x and mallet.y properties need to be commented out if the game is destined to appear on a device.

Having dealt with the mallet movement and the changing score, it is time to turn our attention to populating the stage with randomly located bunnies.

   10. Press the Enter (Windows) or Return (Mac) key twice, and add the following function to the code:

```
function randomBunnyDisplay( evt:TimerEvent ):void {
   randNum = Math.floor( min + ( Math.random() * ( max - min ) ) );
   MovieClip( getChildByName( "bunny" + Math.floor( randNum ) ) ).gotoAndPlay( 2 );
};
```

This function determines which of the eight bunnies are on the stage at any given time. It starts by giving the randNum variable a number between 1 and 8 and tacks that number onto the instance name. For example, if the random number chosen is the number 2, the instance name is `bunny2`. With this information, Flash pulls the rabbitAnim movie clip and puts it on the stage where the `bunny2` instance is located. The gotoAndPlay(2) method keeps the playhead looping in frame 2, meaning the movie clips will constantly appear in a different location on the stage.

We only need to do one more thing. Use the checkScore() function from step 9 to introduce a bit of game play into the project.

   11. Press the Enter (Windows) or Return (Mac) key a couple of times, and let's finish the coding task. Enter this final function:

```
function checkScore():void {
    switch ( score )
      {
case 15:
         timer.delay = 2000;
         levelTxt.text = "02";
       break;
```

```
         case 30:
            timer.delay  = 1500;
           levelTxt.text = "03";
        break;

         case 40:
          timer.delay = 800;
           levelTxt.text = "04";
         break;
      }
};
```

The "game play" is located in the `case` statements. It won't take a user long to figure out that something happens every 2.5 seconds and the game becomes a bit tedious. The case statements check the score, and if it is at the number accompanying the case statement, things speed up because the `timer.delay` property reduces by a half-second. Also, when the timer reduces, the number in the `levelTxt` instance changes to let the user know they have advanced in the game.

12. Save and test the movie. As you can see in Figure 14-25, you can whack bunnies popping out of their holes.

Figure 14-25. Go ahead…whack a bunny.

BUILDING STUFF

Testing the game in Device Central

Now that we know the game works, let's give it a whirl on that Google Nexus One device we tried earlier. To start, though, we need to make a couple of changes to the code and then try it.

1. Close the SWF, and open the code.

2. Locate the Mouse.hide() line, around line 19, and remove the comment. Remember, the device is touch screen.

3. Locate the checkHammer function, and remove the comments for the mallet.x and mallet.y properties.

4. Finally, in the update function, comment out the mallet.x and mallet.y properties.

5. Select **Control ➤ Test Movie ➤ in Device Central**. Device Central will launch, and, as you can see in Figure 14-26, the game appears on the display. Of course, it looks all wrong because the game is laid out to play in landscape and not portrait mode. Let's fix that right now.

Figure 14-26. The game appears in the device but something is obviously very wrong.

6. On the right side of the Device Central interface are a number of tabs. Click the **Display** tab to bring it into focus. This panel is a godsend. Adjust the **Backlight** slider, and you can see the effect of the user turning down the brightness of the device. The **timeout** setting lets you put the device into timeout mode using a duration you set. The **Reflections** drop-down is really neat.

749

Select `Indoor` from the drop-down, and you get a look at what the game screen will look like if it is played indoors and a window was behind the user. Check out the other two settings—`Outdoor` and `Sunshine`. When you finish, reset the `Reflection` setting to `None`.

7. In the `Screen Mode` area, select `Landscape 90°` or `Landscape -90°`. Select `Full Screen`, and, as shown in Figure 14-27, the device revolves, and the game looks as it should. At this point, click the `Start` button, and begin whacking bunnies.

Figure 14-27. Change the `Screen Mode` setting to give yourself the proper device orientation.

Package the game as an Android AIR app

As we pointed out at the start of this section, the Android OS for mobile devices is poised to have a huge impact on the world of devices and tablets. This exercise is going to take you right out on to the bleeding edge of the technology—at least it was a bleeding edge when we were writing this—and show you how easy it is to turn a game destined for web delivery to a device to one that sits on the user's Android device or tablet and, for all intents and purposes, is a stand-alone application.

The technology that makes this possible is Adobe AIR—Adobe Integrated Runtime. Just so we all understand each other, creating pro-level AIR apps is well out of the scope of this book and involves some very highly developed code and design skills. What makes these things so cool is that they are browser independent. All they need is a connection to the Web—3G, WiFi, Ethernet—and they are good to go.

BUILDING STUFF

1. To get yourself started, you will need to install the AIR for Android extension. To get it, point your browser to http://labs.adobe.com/technologies/air2/android/, and click the `Sign Up` link. Adobe Labs is a site where public betas of new technologies are available for you to "kick the tires." Alternatively, go to www.adobe.com and search for *AIR for Android*.

2. Create an account, and you will be taken to the `AIR for Android Developer Prerelease` page. Click the `Download Software` link on the left side of the page to be taken to the downloads area.

3. Click the `Download AIR for Android Extension for Flash CS5` link, and the page shown in Figure 14-28 will open. Download both the extension and the documentation.

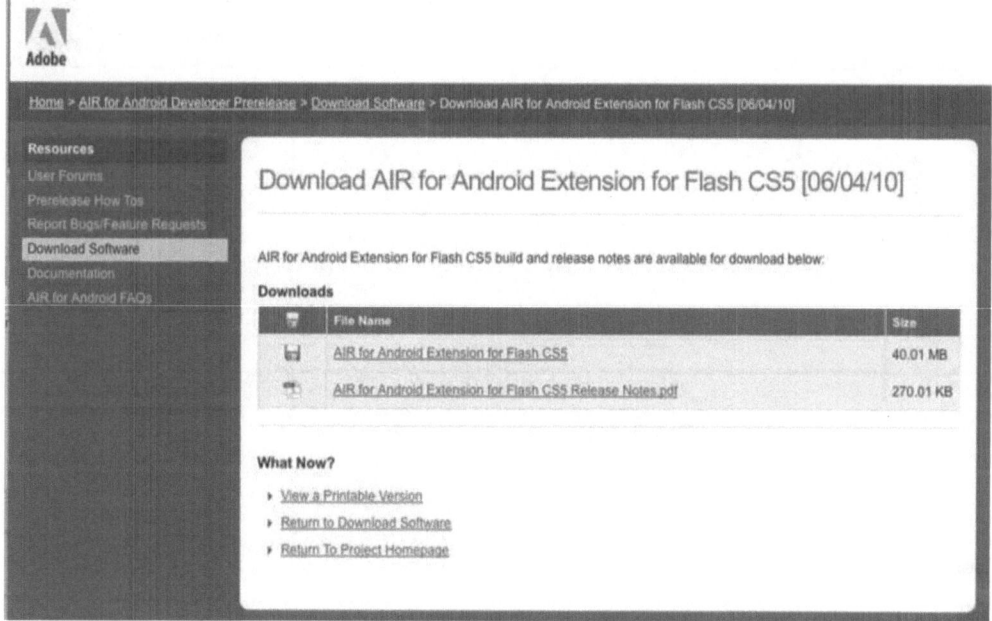

Figure 14-28. The AIR for Android Extension is available on the Adobe labs site.

4. When the file finishes downloading, double-click the `.zxp` file. This will open the `Adobe Extension Manager CS5`, and the extension will be automatically installed into Flash. When the process finishes, quit the `Extension Manager`.

5. Create a new folder in your Exercise folder, and name it AirForAndroid.

6. Open your whackabunny.fla file, rename it whackabunnyAndroid.fla, and save it to the folder you just created.

7. Open the WhackABunny folder in your Exercise folder, and move the file named 72x72Icon.png to the AirForAndroid folder.

751

CHAPTER 14

These last three steps aren't necessary. We added them to give you a clear idea of exactly what files get created and are needed when creating the application.

From Flash to AIR to Android

With the extension installed, follow these steps to create the AIR package:

1. Select `File` ➤ `AIR Android Settings` to open the `Application & Installer Settings` dialog box shown in Figure 14-29. As you may have guessed, the extension adds a new menu item to Flash.

> *There is another method of getting to the Android settings. Select* `File` ➤ `Publish Settings` *and click the* `Flash` *tab. Select* `AIR Android` *from the* `Player` *drop-down.*

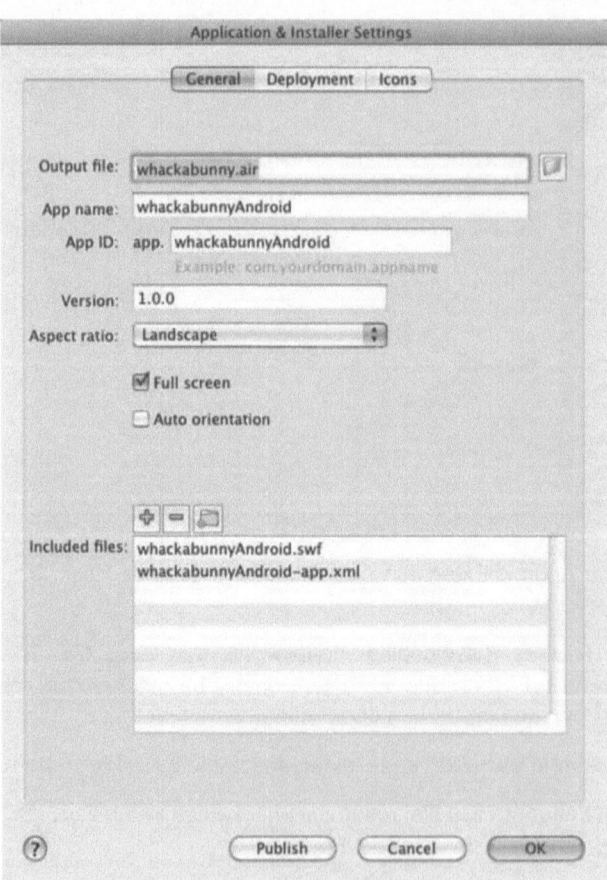

Figure 14-29. The AIR Android settings panel

BUILDING STUFF

This is not as intimidating as it looks, you really only need to make a couple of changes.

2. Change the Output filename to whackabunnyAndroid.air.

3. Select **Landscape** from the **Aspect ratio** drop-down, and select **Full Screen**. You saw why this needs to be done when you tested the game in Device Central.

4. Click the **Deployment** tab to open the deployment settings shown in Figure 14-30. This step is necessary to allow the creation of the AIR app, itself. All you will need to do here is to create the AIR certificate and assign a password to the certificate.

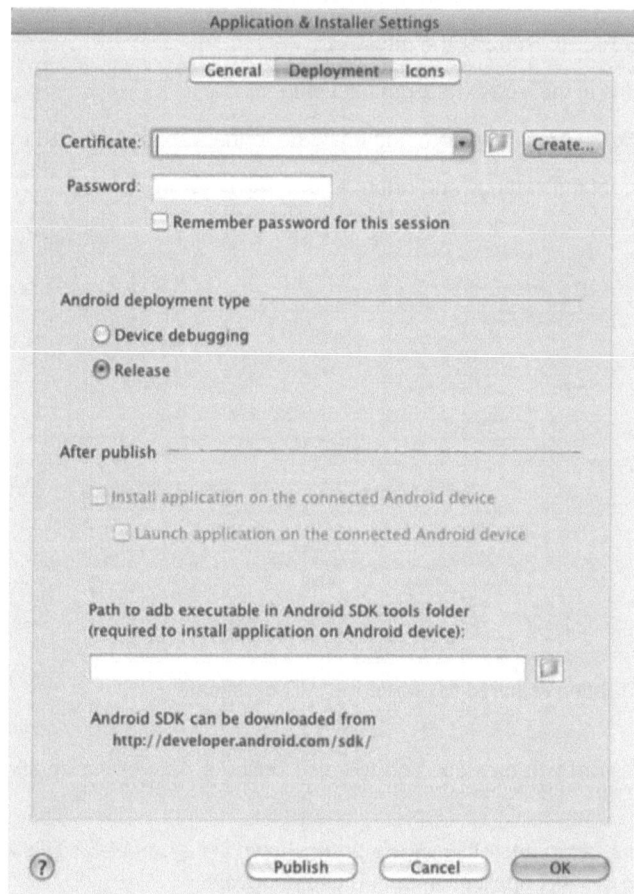

Figure 14-30. You need to use an existing AIR certificate or create one to enable AIR deployment to an Android device.

5. Click the **Create** button to open the certificate settings shown in Figure 14-31.

753

CHAPTER 14

This is not a spooky as it looks, but you need to complete all of the fields. Use these settings:

- `Publisher name`: Add your name.
- `Organization unit`: Self.
- `Organization name`: Use your company name.
- `Country`: Select your country code from the drop-down. Tom is in Canada, which explains the `CA`.
- `Password`: Enter an easily remembered password.
- `Confirm password`: Reenter the password.
- `Type`: Leave this at the `1024-RSA` default value.
- `Save as`: Click the browse button, and navigate to the `AirForAndroid` folder created earlier.

6. Click `OK` to accept the settings and return to the `Deployment` panel.

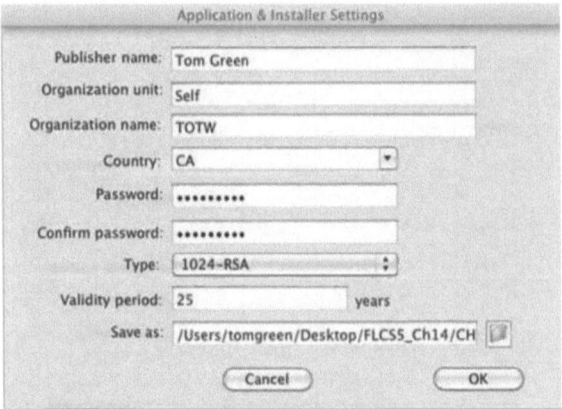

Figure 14-31. The information required to create the AIR certificate

7. Enter the password you created. You will also notice a path to the certificate has been added to the panel.

8. Click the `Icons` tab to open the `Icons` pane shown in Figure 14-32. This lets you choose the icon used to launch the AIR application on the user's device.

9. Select `icon 72 x 72` and click the `Browse` button. Navigate to the `AirForAndroid` folder and choose the `72x72Icon.png` file. Click `Open`, and a preview of the icon will appear in the pane.

BUILDING STUFF

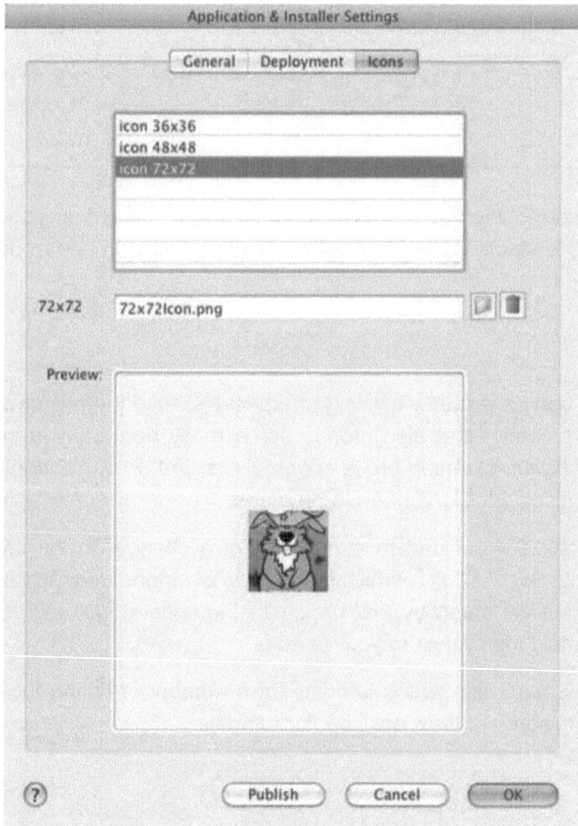

Figure 14-32. Choose the icon used to launch the application on the user's device.

Click the `Publish` button. The SWF will be created along with an HTML file (these are from the `Publish Settings` dialog box) and the whackabunnyAndroid.air file shown in Figure 14-33.

Figure 14-33. You get these files when you create the AIR application.

755

CHAPTER 14

> *If you are working with Flash Builder and plan to get this game onto an Android device, you will need to create an APK file. A very good and, we might add, intuitive packager is Package Assistant Pro from Serge Jespers at www.webkitchen.be/package-assistant-pro/.*

Finally, don't bother double-clicking the AIR installer package thinking that you can put the app on your computer. This application is strictly aimed at Android devices and won't open on anything but an Android device.

Build more stuff

Writing a new edition of a book is a rather exciting prospect because there is always a ton of new stuff that should be covered. Unfortunately, that also means some really neat stuff from the previous editions or ideas that cropped up during the planning process gets discarded. Physical copies of a book have a finite space requirement, and difficult decisions need to be made.

With this edition of the book, we decided to make a bit of a change. In the Exercise folder is another subfolder named Building More Stuff, which contains a few more ideas that are available to you on an "as is, where is" basis. What we mean by that phrase is the code is fully exposed, and you are going to have to figure out how to mold the project to your needs.

One of the authors, Tom Green, also writes tutorials for a number of online tutorial sites and, included in the folder, is a list of links to some of his more popular tutorials.

Enjoy!

What you have learned

Rather than list what we covered in this chapter, we think it is more important to take a broader view of that statement. Step back for a moment and think about what you knew when you first laid this book on your desk and flamed up Flash CS5. The answer, we suspect, is "Not a lot."

Now think about your working through this chapter. The odds are pretty good you were able to follow along, and we are willing to bet there were a couple of points where you may have asked us to "move along a little quicker." This says to us that we have done our job, and that you may just know a lot more than you are aware of. Congratulations.

We were also a little sneaky with this chapter. If you follow the flow from the start to the end, you will see it actually follows the structure of this book: each exercise is designed to add to your knowledge base by building upon what you learned in the preceding exercise and, as we kept pointing out, in preceding chapters.

Finally, this chapter expanded on practically every concept presented in this book. If you have completed the exercises, then you have quite a bit of practical experience using Flash CS5.

Now that you've learned the ropes and have practiced numerous techniques, let's concentrate on the end game of the Flash design and development process: publishing your file.

Chapter 15

Optimizing and Publishing Flash Movies

When it comes to Flash on the Web, a common user experience is sitting around waiting for the movie to start. From your perspective, as the artist who designed the site, this may seem odd. After all, when you tested the movie in the authoring environment, it was seriously fast and played flawlessly. What happened? To be succinct, the Web happened. Your movie may indeed be cool, but you made a fundamental mistake: you fell in love with the technology, not the user. In this chapter, we'll talk about how to improve the user experience.

Here's what we'll cover in this chapter:

- Understanding how Flash movies are streamed to a web page
- Using the Bandwidth Profiler to turbo-charge movies
- Optimizing Flash movies
- Converting a Flash movie to a QuickTime video
- Choosing web formats
- Publishing a SWF for web playback
- Dealing with remote content

CHAPTER 15

The following files are used in this chapter (located in `Chapter15/ExerciseFiles_Ch15/Exercise/`):

- `YawningParrot.fla`
- `BandwidthTest_01.fla`
- `BandwidthTest_02.fla`
- `Trillium.fla`
- `TrilliumSmall.fla`
- `BeefcakeDistributed2.fla`
- `ParrotFW.gif`
- `GardenFinal.fla`
- `TinBangs.fla`

The source files are available at `www.friendsofED.com/download.html?isbn=1430229940`.

Flash's love-hate Internet relationship

Back in the early days of Flash, when we really didn't know better, Flash designers would prepare these really "cool" intros to the site, which played while the rest of the site loaded. The problem was they were large; in many cases, the intro seemed to take almost as long to load as the site. The solution was the infamous `Skip Intro` button, as shown in Figure 15-1. The intro would start playing, and after a couple of seconds, the `Skip Intro` button would appear. The user would click it, only to discover the site hadn't quite loaded. Users were left to sit there, drumming their fingers on their desk. So, users began to see the button not as a `Skip Intro` option but as a "skip site" warning. This resulted in Flash gaining a rather nasty reputation for bloat, which it still has not shaken entirely.

> *Of course, the Flash community does have quite a sense of humor. One of the more popular Flash sites of the time was named "Skip Intro." You can watch it via Archive.org's Wayback Machine at* `http://web.archive.org/web/20011214005850/` `http://www.skipintro.nl/skipintro/skipintro98.htm`. *When you launch the site, make sure to click the phrase "Play Ball" (hip for "Enter this site") to start the never-ending Flash intro. Of course, some Flash people will take their sense of humor to outrageous levels. One of the best was a site that really was nothing more than one massive intro is* `www.zombo.com`.

To deal with the bloat issue, it is critical that you understand the underlying technology behind your Flash movie. This means we need to revisit what the Web really is so you can become familiar with many of the terms commonly used in the Flash design and developer community.

OPTIMIZING AND PUBLISHING FLASH MOVIES

Figure 15-1. Welcome to "Skip Intro" hell.

This "Internet" thing

The Internet's roots go back to the U.S. Department of Defense's need to create a bulletproof means of maintaining communications among computers. This involved such things as file transfers, messaging, and so on. At the time, computers were a virtual Tower of Babel, which meant different computer types and operating systems rarely, if ever, could talk to each other. As well, in battle conditions, the needed system would have to carry on even if a piece of it was knocked out, and it had to be accessible to everything from portable computers to the big, honking mainframes in "clean rooms" around the world.

The solution was an enabling technology called the **Internet Protocol suite**, though we know it by a far sexier name: **TCP/IP**. This is how data moves from your computer to our computers, or from your web server to our computers, and, as you may have guessed, the slash indicates that it comes in two parts:

- **IP (Internet Protocol)**: How data gets from here to there by using an address called the **IP address**. This address is a unique number used to identify any computer currently on the Internet. This protocol creates little bundles of information, called **packets**, which can then be shot out through the Internet to your computer. Obviously, the route is not a straight line. The packets pass through special computers called **routers**, and their job is to point those packets to your computer. Depending on the distance traveled, there could be any number of routers, which check your packets and send them either directly to your computer or to the next router along the line.

- **TCP (Transmission Control Protocol)**: The technology that verifies all the data packets got to your computer. The IP portion of the trip couldn't care less if packet 10 arrives at your computer before packet 1, or even that it got there at all. This is where TCP comes in. Its job is to ensure that all of the packets get to where they are supposed to go.

Once all of this got the kinks worked out, the U.S. military had quite the communications system on its hands.

CHAPTER 15

Enter the World Wide Web

Although straight data transmission was interesting, once the cool factor wore off, people started wondering how it would be possible to use this communication network to access files containing images, audio, and video. The solution was the World Wide Web—a network of networks, which is commonly seen as web pages and hyperlinks.

A web page is a simple text file, which uses HTML—a formatting language of tags and text—to define how a page should look and behave. This is important, because your Flash movies should always be found in an HTML wrapper.

> *The concept of hyperlinks and hypertext was around long before the Internet. The gentleman who managed the atomic bomb project for the United States during World War II, Vannevar Bush, wrote an article for the* Atlantic Monthly *in July 1945 that proposed a system of linking all information with all other information. The article was entitled "As We May Think," and you can still read it at www.theatlantic.com/doc/194507/bush.*

An HTML page may be nothing more than a text file, but it can contain links to other assets, such as CSS files, JPEGs, GIFs, and your Flash movies. These links take the form of a Uniform Resource Locator (URL) and specify the location of the assets requested by the HTML document. When Firefox, Internet Explorer, or any other graphical browser translates the page, those addresses are used to load the external assets and display them on your computer screen. Thus, the Web is really composed of two parts: browsers that request files and servers that store files and make them available when a browser asks for them.

As you can see, the infrastructure that moves your SWF files from a server to thousands of browsers is already in place. Where your pain and heartache arise is from something called **bandwidth**.

Bandwidth

In the early days of Flash, around 1999, one of the authors read an article written by a New York Flash designer, Hillman Curtis, and one phrase leaped out of the article and has been glued to the front of his cerebral cortex ever since. What's that phrase? "Keep an eye on the pipe."

The "pipe" is bandwidth. Bandwidth is a measure of how much data will move along a given path at a given time or how much information can be downloaded through a modem and how fast. One of the authors, when speaking on this topic at conferences or in class, uses a rather amusing analogy that will help you understand this topic. Imagine trying to push the amount of data contained in your favorite TV show through a modem. When that modem is connected to a telephone line, the effort is no different from "trying to push a watermelon through a worm."

Bandwidth is measured in bits per second (bps), usually in the thousands (Kbps) or millions (Mbps). A bit is either a one or a zero, so ultimately bandwidth is a measure of how many ones and zeros can be fed through a modem each second. The higher the number, the greater the bandwidth, and the faster things get from here to there. But bandwidth is not constant. It requires more bandwidth to move a video from here to there than it does to transfer a page of text. The issue is not "here to there." The issue is the modem's capacity to manage the data. This is the "pipe." Users with 56Kbps dial-up modems have a pipe that has the diameter of a garden hose. Users with cable modems have a pipe that has the diameter of a fire hose. Connect the tiny garden hose to the fire hydrant in front of your house, and you will get a graphic demonstration of data flow and the pipe when you turn on the hydrant.

As we pointed out earlier, the data packets sent to your computer get there eventually, and the route is never a straight line. Over time, TCP/IP ensures that the transmission rate averages to a more or less constant rate, but this is technology we're dealing with here. It is the prudent Flash designer who approaches technology with a dose of pragmatism and does not assume a constant flow. This has implications for your design efforts, and we will get into those implications shortly.

You need to regard the pipe and data transmission in much the same manner you regard your local highway. It may have six lanes for traffic and a posted speed limit of 60 mph (or 100 kph), but all of that becomes irrelevant during rush hour. Traffic moves at the pace of the slowest car. It is no different with the Internet. Servers can become overloaded.

A powerful example of this in recent history is the infamous event known as 9/11. On that day, the Internet essentially ground to a halt as it seemed like every computer on the planet was attempting to get the latest information on the tragedy. A more recent example is the day Michael Jackson died. The chart in Figure 15-2 from Google Trends shows Google Search traffic on that day. The sharp spike between 1 and 6 p.m. follows the news from the first reports around 1 p.m. and the reaction to the formal announcement a couple of hours later.

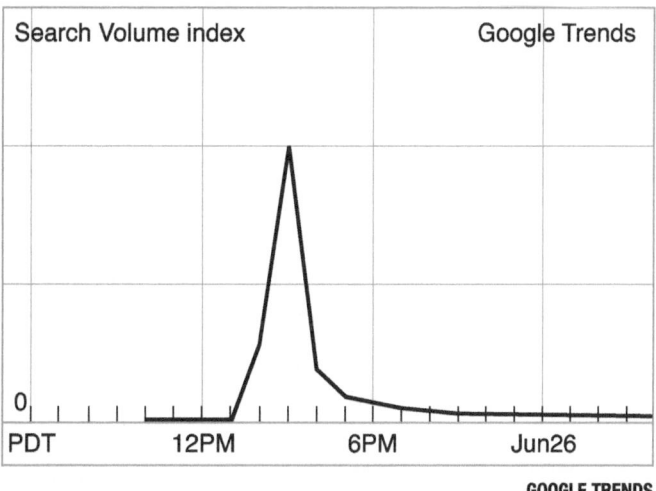

Figure 15-2. Google Search traffic when the world discovered Michael Jackson had died.

CHAPTER 15

What people overlooked on both days was that a server is only a computer, and it can only reply to a finite number of requests at a set rate. If the browser can't get the information, it will assume the assets are not there. As a consequence, the requested page either will not be displayed or will be displayed with information missing. It got so bad for CNN and the BBC on 9/11 that they were forced to post a message that essentially told people "come back later." Even the people lucky enough to make a connection experienced pauses in the download and frequent disconnects, which are the hallmarks of an overloaded server.

What you need to take away from these two stories is that the time it takes to download and play your Flash movie is totally dependent on the contents of your Flash movie and traffic flow on the Internet. This means you need to concentrate not only on what is in your movie but also on who wants to access it. This is where you fall in love with the user and not the technology.

So, who are these folks we call users?

The Flash community is an oddball collection of people, ranging from those who ride skateboards for entertainment to the classic nerd working in a corporate cubicle farm. This disparity, which actually is the strength of the Flash community, has resulted in a bit of a split between those who use supercharged pixel-spitting behemoths to develop their content and take a "Sucks to be you" attitude if you can't revel in their work and those who are corporate types and operate within strict standards set by their IT department. This standard is usually in the form of the following commandment:

> *Thou shalt develop to a Flash Player 8 standard, and may whatever god you worship have mercy upon your miserable soul if you step outside this stricture.*

So, what do you really need to know before putting your work out there? Here are some general guidelines:

- Small means fast. Studies show you have 15 seconds to hook the user. If nothing is happening or is appealing to your users, they're gone. Small SWFs mean fast download. The days of introductory eye candy for your Flash movies are over. If the content they see within that 15-second window is not relevant to the site or the experience, users leave.

- If a bleeding-edge Flash site isn't viewable on a two-year-old computer with a standard operating system and hardware, it's time to go back to the drawing board.

- For a commercial site, you may have to go back three years. Corporations are relatively slow to upgrade hardware because of the significant cost to do so. Old hardware means slower computers.

- If your target audience is urban and in a developed country, assume they have, at minimum, a cable connection.

- If your audience is the world, develop to the lowest common denominator, which is a dial-up modem.

Now that we have provided some background, let's look at how your Flash file actually gets from here to there.

Streaming

As you have discovered by this point in the book, simply tossing a bunch of audio, images, and video into your movie is not a good thing. They take an inordinate amount of time to download. In fact, toss all of that content into frame 1, and you can kiss your 15-second window of opportunity good-bye.

In the previous chapter, we looked at ways to prevent bulking up frame 1—by preloading the SWF itself and by externalizing assets and loading them at runtime. In this chapter, you'll learn how to optimize the rest of your timeline to help balance out and redistribute the load of a SWF's assets. Your goal will be to facilitate Flash Player's natural tendency to stream.

Please understand that streaming doesn't make things faster. What it does is give you the opportunity to intelligently organize the timeline so the movie starts playing in very short order. Used wisely, streaming can ensure that everything in the Flash movie is downloaded before it is needed. The result is a Flash movie that seems to start playing almost immediately and moves "as smooth as the hair on a frog's back."

So, what happens when a web page requests your movie? Two things are sent to the browser:

- The movie's timeline, including ActionScript and the stuff that is not in the `Library`, such as text and shapes that haven't been converted to symbols
- The `Library`, including audio, video, images, and symbols

When your Flash movie is shot through the Internet to the user's browser, the movie is received in frame-by-frame order. If the movie is split into scenes (a relatively rare practice today), the scenes will be sent in the order they appear in the `Scenes` panel, which is effectively in sequential order of the main timeline. The `Library` is also sent, but the `Library` items are not received in the order they appear in the `Library` panel. They are received in the sequence in which they appear on the timeline. To reinforce what we have just said, let's take a look at a typical file.

Open the `YawningParrot.fla` file in the `Exercise` folder for this chapter. As shown in Figure 15-3, the timeline is linear, but there are a lot of layers. Your first reaction might be, "Man, that is going to take a while to load." But that's not really the case.

Open the `Library` panel. You'll notice there is a lot less content in the panel than in the timeline layers—only 13 assets versus 22 layers. This is because the symbols in the `Library` are reused and repurposed. The "finger feathers," for example, all use the same `feather` asset. All six claws use the same `toe` symbol; they're just arranged differently (horizontal flips and tints, all performed on the stage). As we have said repeatedly throughout this book, Flash lives in a world of small, and using one symbol instead of six reduces the final size of the SWF. If you create advertising banners, for example, your "Small World" might just have a size of 30KB for the SWF. In that case, reusing content is critical.

CHAPTER 15

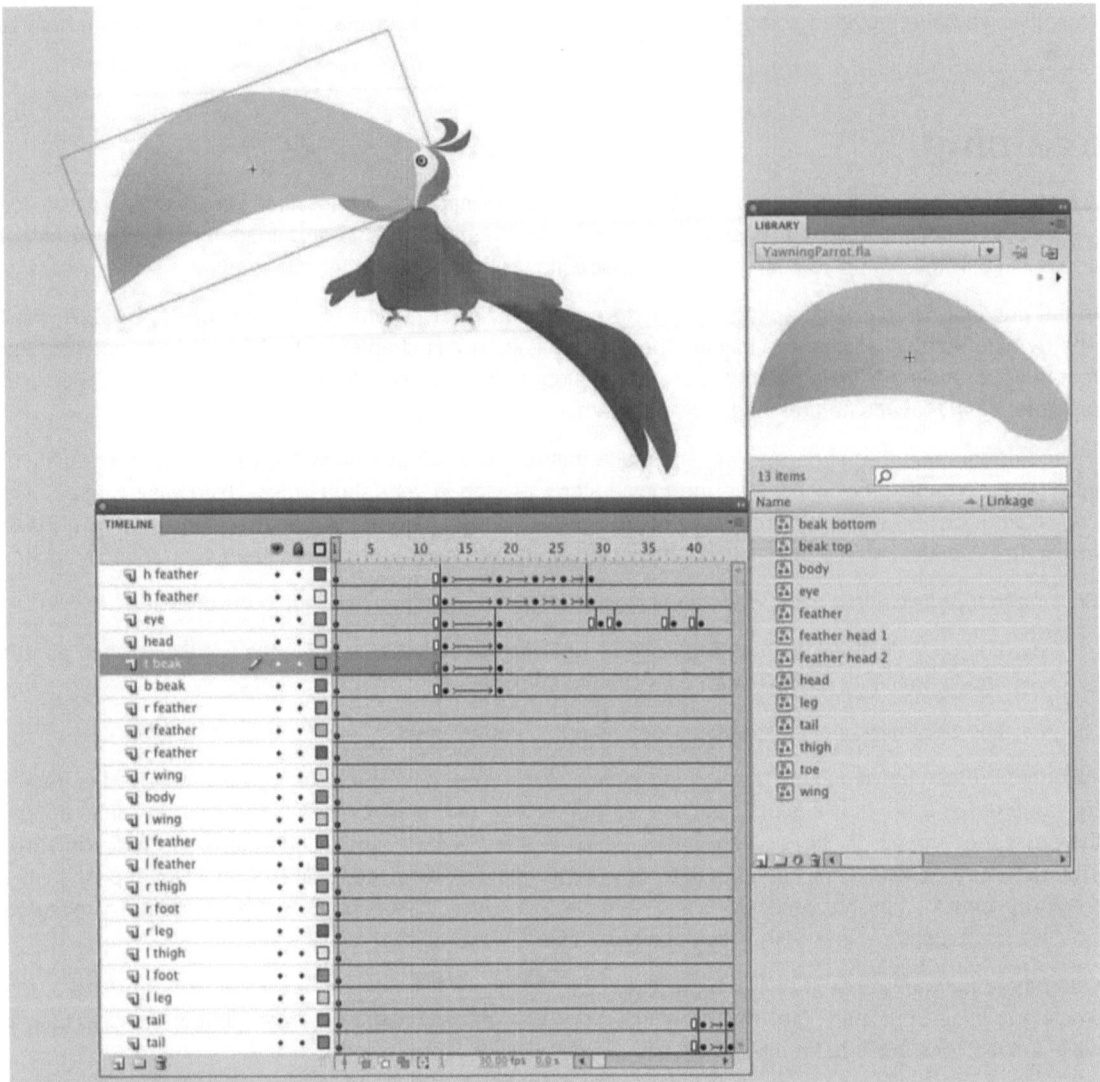

Figure 15-3. Streaming plays a movie in frame order and loads `Library` content in the order in which it appears on the timeline.

When this particular movie loads, because of how the parrot is constructed, all of its parts are loaded in frame 1 and composed of all the objects in the `Library`. These `Library` objects are purposely designed to be lightweight. They're vector shapes with few anchor points, which means they equate to a relatively small file size. As a result, little bandwidth is required to load them and get the movie playing.

To make sense of how this movie streams, consider adding an imaginary extra playhead to the timeline When the movie starts. Both playheads are in frame 1, but only one of them starts moving. That's the imaginary one. Let's call it the *streamhead* (just a made-up name), which advances ahead of the actual playhead. The streamhead's position on the timeline indicates how much of the movie has been downloaded. In contrast, the playhead indicates which frame is currently displayed on the stage. It should make sense that the playhead can never get ahead of the streamhead. That would be like writing a check for more money than you have in your account.

Now let's assume that you toss in a movie clip, containing a three-second FLV file embedded in the symbol's timeline, and this movie clip is added to frame 10. The odds are really good that the streamhead will stay put on frame 10 for a few seconds, while that frame's movie clip (complete with its video) loads. The playhead will catch up pretty quickly, especially with a default 24 fps frame rate. Until the embedded FLV loads, the playhead has no choice but to stay put. Essentially, the whole movie stops dead at frame 10, until the streamhead restarts its journey along the timeline.

To avoid this nastiness, you'll want to use a strategy called a **streaming buffer**. This could be in the form of a preloader or any other technique that keeps the playhead in place (in an interesting way) or smoothes out its path in order to let the streamhead do its job and load content.

In case you're having difficulty visualizing two heads on the timeline, Flash has a tool that lets you see how these two heads work and how the pipe can affect the delivery of your Flash movie to the browser. What is this tool? It's called the **Bandwidth Profiler**.

The Bandwidth Profiler

In many respects, the Bandwidth Profiler is similar to what you see in Device Central when you test a mobile movie. In Device Central, the movie opens in a mock device that emulates the performance of your movie in the chosen device. Likewise, the Bandwidth Profiler emulates how your movie will behave when it downloads from a remote server. Though the Bandwidth Profiler is an extremely useful tool, keep in mind that it is nothing more than an emulator. It won't mimic the real-life ebb and flow of network traffic, and it assumes a constant transfer rate into the browser. That noted, the Bandwidth Profiler can give you a good idea of where streaming bottlenecks are likely to occur. This can be an invaluable aid in relieving the "data jam" and solving a problem before it becomes a major one.

Simulating a download

Let's see how the Bandwidth Profiler works:

1. Open the `BandwidthTest_01.fla` file in the Chapter 15 `Exercise` folder. You will see that we have placed an audio file on the timeline, embedded an FLV into a movie clip, and placed the movie clip in frame 1. Scrub over to frame 2, and you will see that we have added some text to the stage. If you open the **Library**, you will see the text is actually a graphic symbol. Just by looking at the timeline, you can see that the movie clip with the FLV and the audio file will be the first pieces of content to load, and then the text will load.

2. Test the movie. When the SWF opens, select View ➤ Bandwidth Profiler from the SWF's File menu. A graph appears above the movie, as shown in Figure 15-4.

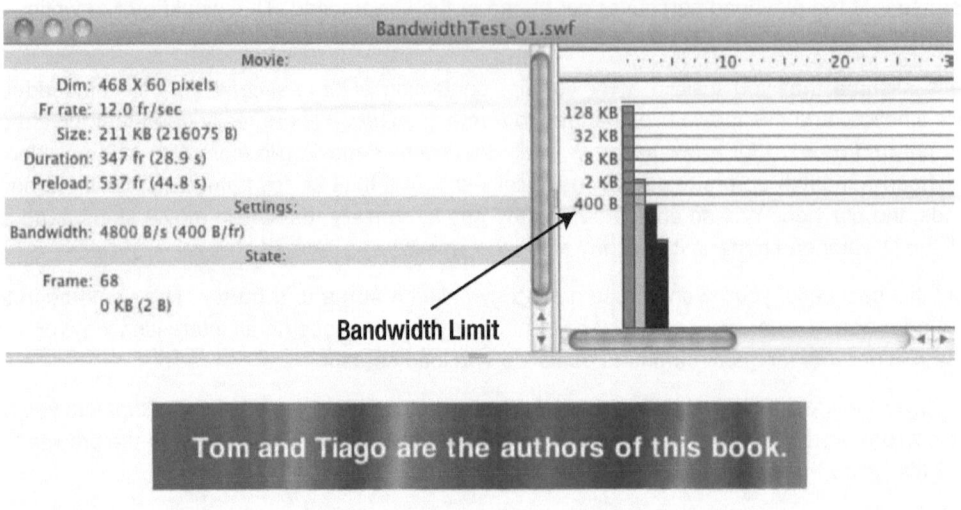

Figure 15-4. The Bandwidth Profiler

There are two main parts to the profiler. The first part is made up of three headings: Movie, Settings, and State. The second part is a frame-by-frame representation of the data downloading into each frame. Notice the spike in frame 1. This is understandable, because the audio file and the FLV need to load in this frame. The trouble is that this spike happens right at the beginning of the movie.

Under the Settings heading on the left, take a look at the Bandwidth entry: 4800 B/s (400 B/fr). Now look at the bottommost line on the right side. That red line is the **bandwidth limit** and represents the maximum throughput the selected modem emulation can handle. Notice that it matches the Bandwidth value on the left. Bars under the line are handled quickly. Bars that rise above the line indicate potential bottlenecks. The sooner you can stuff under that red line, the faster the movie will load and play.

3. Select View ➤ Download Settings. The drop-down menu you see allows you to choose from among various modem speeds, as shown in Figure 15-5.

OPTIMIZING AND PUBLISHING FLASH MOVIES

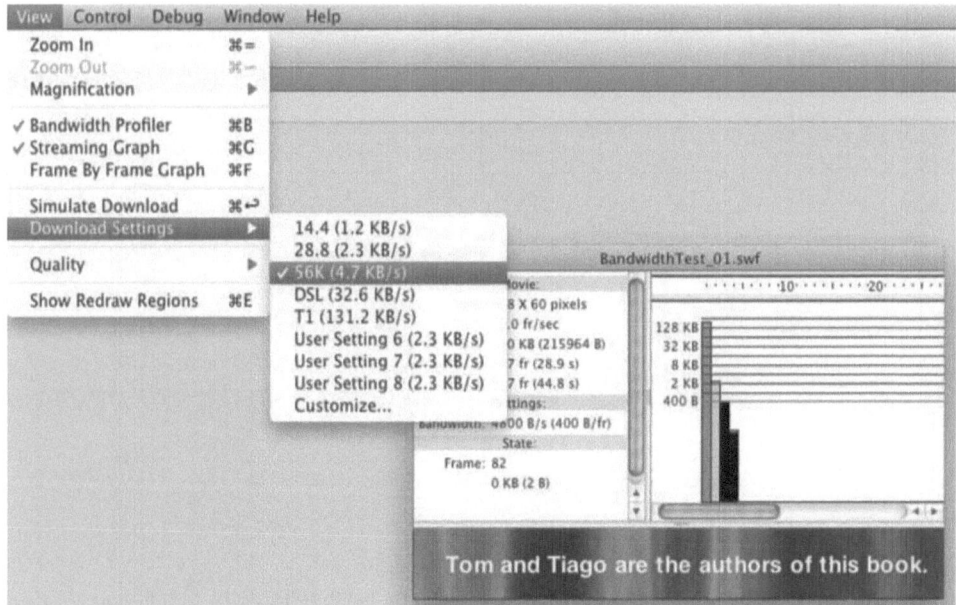

Figure 15-5. You can change the emulated modem speed.

4. Select the DSL (32.6 KB/s) choice from the drop-down menu, and scroll back to the start of the movie. You will notice the bandwidth limit has increased from 400 bytes to 2.78KB, and the markings on the graph have changed to reflect your selection.

You are most likely looking at that spike in the first frame and thinking, "Yeah, so? What's the deal?" Rather than having us explain it, we are going to let you experience it.

5. Change back to the 56Kbps modem choice, and this time select View ➤ Simulate Download.

Let us guess. You sat around for about 20 seconds waiting for the movie to start? What you have just experienced is the other, and most important, half of the Bandwidth Profiler. You just sat through what a person with a 56Kbps modem will experience—under ideal circumstances. Let's take a minute and talk about this.

When you selected Simulate Download, you essentially re-created how the movie will load into a 56Kbps modem. The other thing that happened is the profiler developed a green bar at the top of the graph, as shown in Figure 15-6, which held steady until the movie started to play.

767

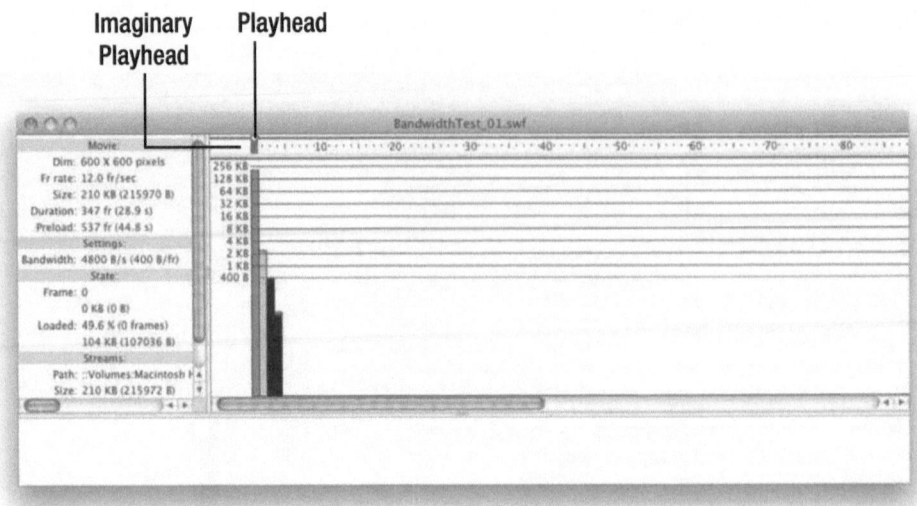

Figure 15-6. You can experience the user's issue with the movie's first frame by simulating the download.

The green bar is important. It's the imaginary streamhead we mentioned earlier. You are seeing what happens when the playhead catches up to the streamhead. If you wait long enough, the streamhead will suddenly rocket off to the right, and the playhead will follow behind, sticking to a rate no faster than the frame rate specified in the FLA (which happens to be 12 fps for this file). You can scrub that playhead, by the way. Drag it around as you would in the `Timeline` panel to view content on any of the frames.

On the left side of the Bandwidth Profiler, under the `Movie` heading, you'll see a value called `Preload`, which in this example is `537 fr` or `44.8 s`. When you started emulating the movie, the `Settings` area became active (to see this, you may need to increase the size of the Bandwidth Profiler window by dragging the bottom edge down). The `Preload` value tells you it will take about 45 seconds to load in all of the content in the first frame.

Change the `Download Settings` to `DSL`, and select `Simulate Download`.

You should find that you still had a short delay, but there was a marked decrease in how long you had to wait. The `Preload` setting should show you `76 fr (6.3 s)`. That's dramatically less than the almost 45 seconds you had to wait using a 56Kbps modem.

If you want to emulate a modem not represented in the list, choose Customize, which opens the Custom Download Settings dialog box, as shown in Figure 15-7. You can edit any of the existing entries, three of which are set aside for custom values. To return to the original values at any time, click the Reset button.

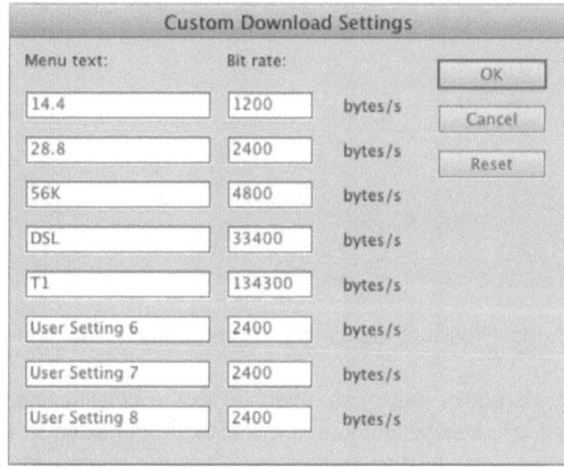

Figure 15-7. The Custom Download Settings dialog box lets you tailor your emulated modems.

As you can see, the Bandwidth Profiler is a rather powerful tool that you need to master. With it, you can tailor your movie to the bandwidth constraints of your user and ensure that you meet that 15-second window of opportunity that will open to you.

Pinpointing problem content

With the Download Settings option, not only do you get to see how bandwidth will affect your movie, but you also get to actually experience it, which isn't always fun. At this point, you may be thinking, "Shoot, I can cut back the preload value by using ActionScript to play the sound!" Doing that means the sound can be removed from the SWF altogether. Let's see if it works.

Open the BandwidthTest_02.fla file in this chapter's Exercise folder. Open the Library, and you will see the sound file is absent. Open the code in frame 3 of the Actions layer, and you will see we have added the ActionScript necessary to load to the sound from an external MP3.

Test the movie, and select Simulate Download. The graph has significantly changed, as shown in Figure 15-8. The overall size of the SWF has gone from 210KB—see the Size value in the Movie heading—down to 96KB, Yet the spike in frame 1 hasn't changed much at all, and the same nearly 20-second delay is still there. What gives?

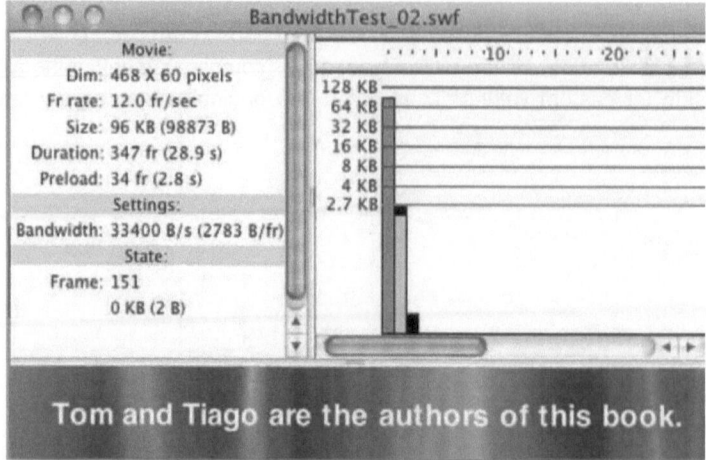

Figure 15-8. Use the Bandwidth Profiler to identify the content causing the delay.

Part of the answer is that the audio, previously attached to the timeline, had its `Sync` property set to `Stream`. Remember that the `Stream` setting keeps the audio from having to load all at once, as it does with, say, the `Event` setting. Because the audio's file size was spread out, only 1/300 of its weight appeared in frame 1 (because the timeline is roughly 300 frames long). This tells you the issue really isn't the sound in this case but rather the FLV embedded into the movie clip.

You have just discovered another use for the Bandwidth Profiler. Not only can it show you where the problem is, but it can even be used to isolate the content causing the delay.

> *How would we fix this? First off, bear in mind there will always be a spike in frame 1 of any movie you create. The goal is to get that spike to do the limbo—to get it as close to the red line as possible, if not below it. For this example, one approach would be to reduce the time of the curtain's effect from its current 46 frames seconds to 23 frames in the `background` movie clip. Do this, and the preload time drops to 1.2 seconds. Another approach would be to use a percentage-based preloader like the one demonstrated in Chapter 14.*

Can I get that in writing?

The Bandwidth Profiler's right graph gives you a quick bird's-eye view of your worst bandwidth offenders. If you want to dial in to the exact numbers, drag the playhead to any of your graph spikes and keep an eye on the `State` heading on the left side. The `Frame` value of that heading tells you which frame you're on and exactly how many bytes that frame contains.

If you really want to crunch the numbers, Flash will even create a log file for you. Head over to `File ➤ Publish Settings ➤ Flash` and select the `Generate size report` check box. When you next test your movie, look in the `Output` panel. You'll see a detailed analysis of the timeline, with columns for `Frame #`, `Frame Bytes` (per-frame bytes), `Total Bytes` (cumulative total), and more, including itemized byte weights at the bottom for fonts, shapes, and symbols. This report is also saved as a simple text file in the same folder as the FLA. In the case of BandwidthTest_02.fla, the report's name is BandwidthTest_02 Report.txt.

There is a new feature of Flash CS5 that is also an invaluable aid to tracking problematic content. At the bottom of the `Properties` panel is an area named `SWF History`. Every time you test the movie, this area will list the size of the SWF and the data and time that it was tested. If there is a large spike in the SWF, there will be an alert icon beside the entry.

Now that you know what the spikes mean, your goals are to minimize them when you can and to distribute their weight when possible. The next section tells you how.

Optimizing and fine-tuning your Flash movies

As you saw in the previous example, a simple thing like reducing the number of frames in an FLV can have a dramatic impact on how the movie loads. In this section, we'll outline a few tips, tricks, and techniques you can use to make your Flash movies leaner, meaner, and faster.

Surprisingly, the first mistake most people make often happens before a single pixel is lit up. That mistake is to not plan the movie.

Planning your project

That old adage "Plan your work and work your plan" is especially true when working with Flash. You can't make it up as you go along. You need to take the time before you start to think about what the user sees, and in what order, before you starting firing content into the `Library` and then onto the stage. For example, a video site that lets the user choose from a number of videos would probably involve the following:

- Preloader
- Intro screen
- Main movie screen where the videos are chosen and viewed
- A set of links to other video sites you may have created

CHAPTER 15

This means when users arrive at the site, they would usually proceed as follows:

1. See the preloader for a few seconds and then be taken to the Intro frame.
2. From there, choose to read the information and then move to the video picker screen by clicking a button. The video frame would load.
3. Click a series of buttons to view the videos associated with the buttons.
4. Choose to return to the Intro screen or go to a frame that contains a series of interactive links.

That is a simple example. Think about the process David Hogue and his team went through when planning the financial application presented in the "Fireworks + Flash: Rapid Prototyping for Rich Internet Applications" section. Now that you have an idea of what will happen, you might even want to put together a small flowchart that shows the purpose of each frame in the movie, as shown in Figure 15-9. Having one of these charts handy allows you to see how the user will move around the movie and provides a broad view of the content of each frame.

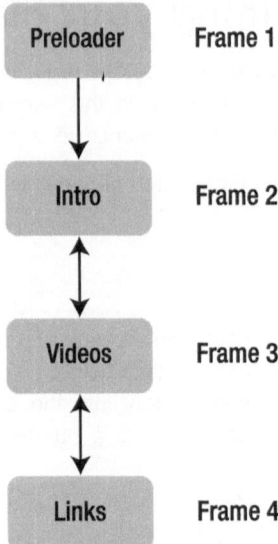

Figure 15-9. Map out your plan.

In fact, if you have arrived at Flash CS5 through the Adobe Web Premium Bundle, you have an ideal tool for this process at your disposal. Fireworks CS5 has been repositioned as a rapid prototyping tool. If you open that application and select `Window` ➤ `Common Library`, you will see bunch of folders that contain symbols for a variety of rapid prototyping tasks. The `Web & Application` symbols, shown in Figure 15-10, are ideal for planning a Flash or HTML project.

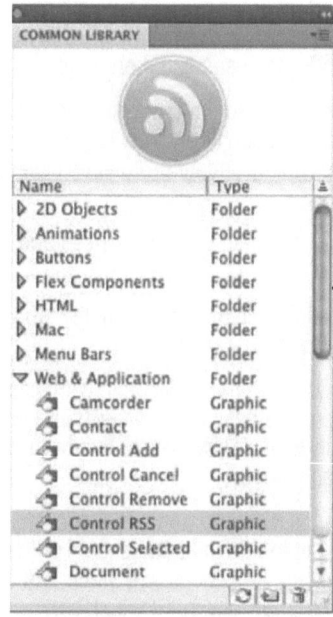

Figure 15-10. Use Fireworks CS5 as a planning aid.

By writing out what each frame does, you are ordering the content on the timeline. By "falling in love with the user" and streaming the content into the movie in that order, your site will meet the needs of your users. If you haphazardly place the content on the timeline, you have no way of ensuring it will load in any meaningful manner. The result is a site that must download in its entirety before the user can interact with it smoothly. If that happens, your users will leave…in a hurry.

Though many sites go the haphazard route, it is not considered a best practice within the Flash design community. Instead, you'll want to be mindful of balance.

CHAPTER 15

FIREWORKS + FLASH: RAPID PROTOTYPING FOR RICH INTERNET APPLICATIONS

By David M. Hogue

Crafting effective and engaging customer experiences is an iterative process. Concepts are refined, designs are created, and prototypes are tested. The information gathered from observing and speaking with actual customers and site visitors guides improvements made in each iteration. However, time to market is critical in the competitive world of web applications, and new ideas need to be tested, refined, and launched on a regular basis in order to keep customers engaged and to meet their needs.

Continuous design and development cycles require efficient processes and the ability to create designs and prototypes quickly. At Fluid, we use Adobe Fireworks, Flash, and Dreamweaver to move from concept to design to prototype and to rapidly update prototypes based on observations, feedback, and test results.

Begin the design process with Adobe Fireworks to capture ideas and concepts in sketches and wireframes.

When the core features have been defined, create higher fidelity storyboards in Adobe Fireworks to represent the steps and states of complex interactions.

Use the project team to test the flow through the application with simple click-throughs generated by Adobe Fireworks. After the application flow has been reviewed and improved, refine the appearance of the wireframes and storyboards using Adobe Fireworks to create the assets necessary to build a prototype with Adobe Flash and Dreamweaver.

Build a prototype web page and an application frame with Adobe Dreamweaver, and use Adobe Flash to assemble the graphics into screens and to add the functionality of the application (e.g., editable data grids, interactive charts, and form fields.) Transitions (e.g., fade and slide) and some effects (e.g., glow and shape changes) are added programmatically in Adobe Flash.

Prototypes often use locally simulated data and are not actually connected to a server-based data source. During testing the design team observes the flow and performance of the application. Although design and interaction improvements are made in the iterations after testing, sometimes opportunities or needs arise *during* a testing session to modify a prototype. For example, ambiguous labels can be clarified, subtle visual effects can be modified, and buttons can be moved, added, or deleted. The original graphics can be quickly edited in Adobe Fireworks and re-imported into Adobe Flash, and some functionality and behavior can be quickly modified in Adobe Flash. It is possible to modify a prototype during a testing session and have an updated prototype exported and available by the time the next test participant arrives for their session.

Figure 15-11 shows a financial application prototyped in Fireworks and assembled in Flash.

OPTIMIZING AND PUBLISHING FLASH MOVIES

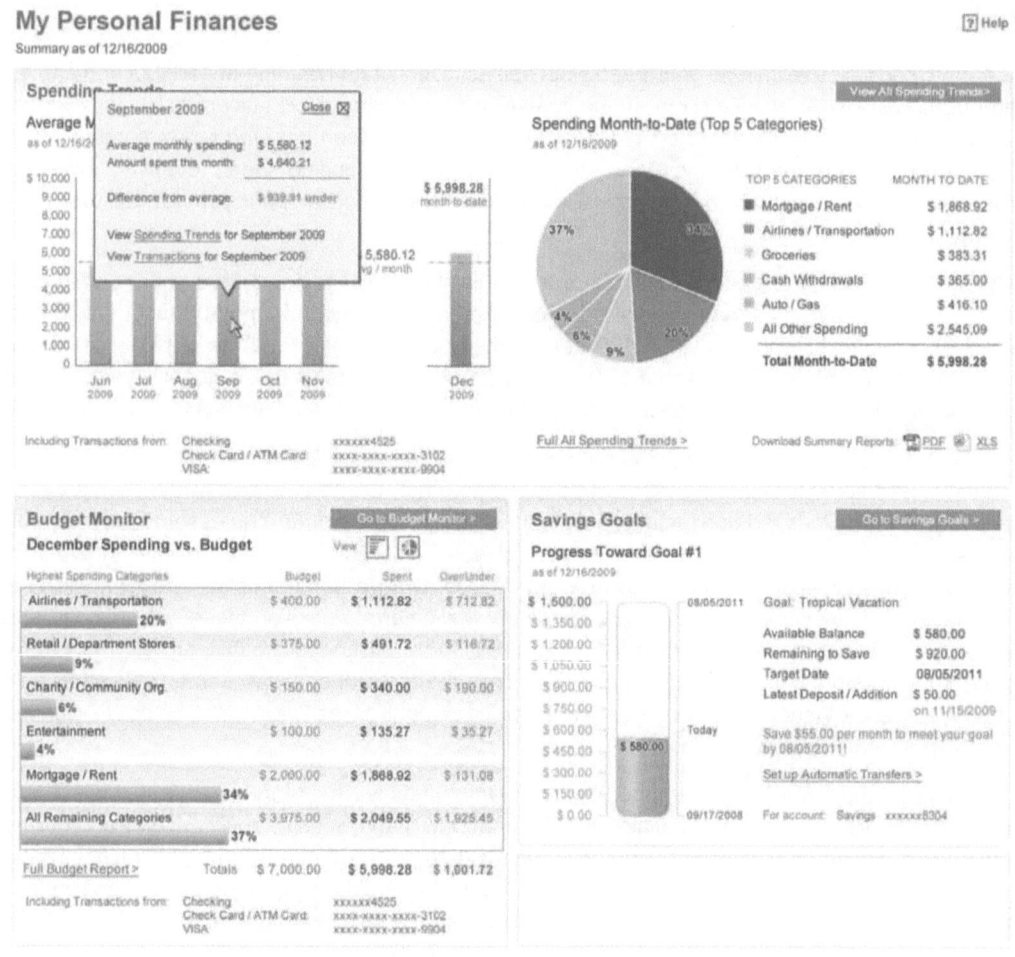

Figure 15-11. Financial application prototyped in Fireworks and assembled in Flash

David M. Hogue, PhD

Dave is the Director of Information Design & Usability at Fluid (www.fluid.com), a digital design and development firm in San Francisco specializing in e-commerce websites and RIAs. He uses his training in applied psychology and cognitive science to study how people learn and work in the digital world and develops workflow models and user interfaces that meet their needs and expectations effectively and efficiently. Dave has worked on projects for a diverse range of clients including Wells Fargo, Charles Schwab, Warner Bros., The North Face, Reebok, and Timberland. He also teaches information and interaction design classes in the Multimedia Studies Program at San Francisco State University and is a co-manager of Fire On The Bay (www.fireonthebay.org), an Adobe Users Group for Fireworks.

CHAPTER 15

Distributing the weight

It isn't always possible to eliminate your bandwidth spikes, even when planning ahead, but you can usually spread out the assets that cause them. If you've ever witnessed the sport known as curling—something like shuffleboard but on ice (celebrated in Canada)—then you've seen how the team members clear the way. They run ahead of the traveling stone as it glides across the curling sheet, feverishly sweeping the ice a few feet ahead, minimizing irregularities in the path. That's sort of what you can do with the main timeline.

Usually, it means making a few test runs with the Bandwidth Profiler to see where your culprits are. You might, for example, have a dozen symbols make their first appearance in frame 300, suddenly giving that frame a spike. Meanwhile, the previous 100 frames might be very lean in terms of bytes per frame. To diminish streamhead blockage on frame 300, you could place copies of those dozen symbols in earlier frames, just off the stage (on the pasteboard). Simply drag out another instance of each symbol as needed.

For example, let's say you're aiming for 56Kbps modems. That means your bandwidth limit, as indicated by the Bandwidth Profiler's red horizontal line, is set to 200 bytes per frame. You essentially have a budget of 200 bytes to spend per frame. To minimize the spike in frame 300, you could drag a couple 100-byte symbols from the **Library** and place them on frame 200. Drag a handful of 30-byte symbols to frame 220, another 180-byte symbol to frame 240, and so on. Make sure to position these symbols off the stage or use the **Properties** panel to set their **Alpha** property to **0%**. Arranged like this, each symbol makes its presence known before it is actually seen. By the time the streamhead hits frame 300, each of those symbols has already loaded, and the streamhead breezes right on by—the ice is smooth—clearing the path for the playhead.

How can you tell how much each symbol weighs? Unfortunately, the **Library** panel doesn't tell you, outside of the **Bitmap Properties** dialog box for imported graphics files. You'll need to do your best to distribute weight based on common sense and some trial and error with the Bandwidth Profiler. The extent to which you rearrange things depends on deadlines, budget, and your own personal predilection for anal-retentiveness. Just be aware of this strategy, because it really can make a difference.

Many Flash artists get their start creating banner ads. Depending on where they will appear, the average SWF size is somewhere between 30KB and 50KB. Add in the fact they have to play as soon as they hit the browser, weight distribution becomes a key skill to learn.

Sometimes your assets aren't so easy to redistribute. Consider an imported image. In cases like that, you'll need to get creative. To see what we mean, open the Trillium.fla file from the Exercise folder for this chapter. Test the movie and take a look at the Bandwidth Profiler. As Figure 15-12 shows, there's a massive spike at frame 50, right where the trillium photo appears. Any content after that frame will be delayed until that 2200KB has loaded. A possible solution is a preloader, displaying percent loaded of the SWF itself or percent loaded of the image as an external JPEG.

OPTIMIZING AND PUBLISHING FLASH MOVIES

Figure 15-12. There's a bandwidth bottleneck in frame 50.

If you look at the stage your first reaction is, "But …but… the image and the stage are really small. They are both 500 by 300!" To which we reply, "Oh really?" If you select the image in the **Library** and open its **Properties** panel, you will discover the image is actually 3872 pixels wide by 2592 high and weighs in at a hefty 2.2MB. The image you are looking at has been scaled, and the stage has been scaled to the dimensions of the scaled image. That spike is solely because of the image in the **Library** and should tell you that images really should be scaled to the dimensions needed before they hit the Flash **Library**.

Open the TrilliumSmall.fla to see what happens when images are scaled outside of Flash. If you test the movie, you will see that not only has the spike disappeared but it has actually sunk below the red line (Figure 15-13). This happens because, if you open the image's properties in the **Library**, you will see that it has sunk in size to just a hair above 60KB when Flash applies JPEG compression.

777

CHAPTER 15

Figure 15-13. Sometimes the best solution is the most obvious.

Optimizing elements in the movie

Every chapter in this book has directly or indirectly made it clear that Flash loves "small." After your experiences with the Bandwidth Profiler, we think you now understand why we are so adamant on this point. Small files mean fast loads. A fast load means short wait time. A short wait time means happy users. In various chapters, we have shown you several methods of keeping things small when it comes to images, sounds, fonts, and video. What about vectors?

We know Flash and vectors are bosom buddies. The thing about vectors is that they can be both small and large at the same time. Huh? Every time Flash encounters a vector point, it must load it into memory in order to draw the shape. If you create a vector with a large number of vector points, you may have a small file on your hands, but you have also increased the demand on memory to redraw the image, as you encountered with the American flag exercise in Chapter 9. The result is the inevitable spike in the Bandwidth Profiler. Here's one way of addressing this issue:

1. Create a new Flash document. Add three more keyframes to layer 1 in the `Timeline` panel. You now have four keyframes on the timeline.

2. Select the `Pencil` tool, and in frame 1, draw a curvy shape, like the one in Figure 15-14.

Figure 15-14. We start by drawing a shape containing a lot of vector points.

3. Copy your shape to the clipboard. Select each of the remaining three key frames in layer 1, and select **Edit ➤ Paste in Place**.

4. Select the shape in frame 2, and select **Modify ➤ Shape ➤ Advanced Smooth**. The new **Advanced Smooth** dialog box, shown in Figure 15-15, opens, and not a lot seems to happen. Make sure the **Preview** check box is selected, set the **Smoothing strength** to 100, and scrub across the **Smooth angle below** hot text. Note the changes to the object when you change the value to one greater than 90 degrees.

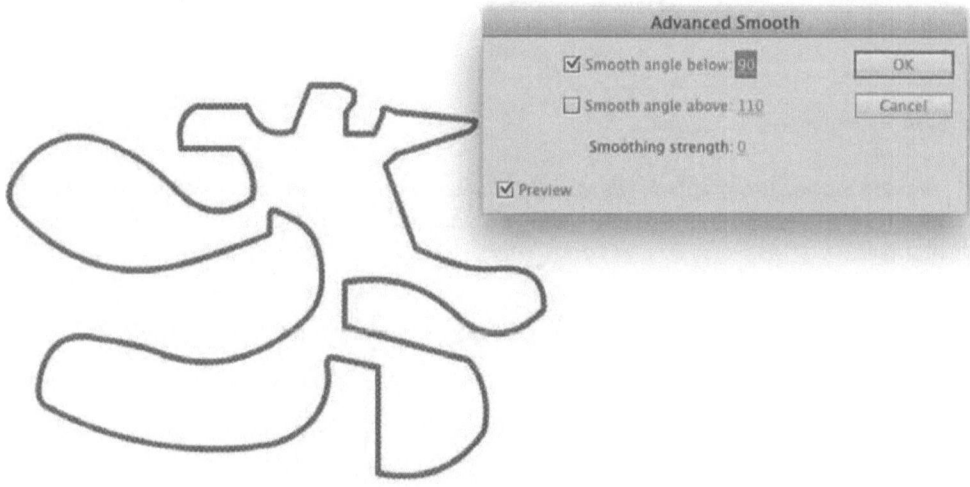

Figure 15-15. The new **Advanced Smooth** dialog box

5. Select the shape in frame 3, and select **Modify ➤ Shape ➤ Advanced Straighten** to open the **Advanced Straighten** dialog box. Scrub across the **Straighten strength** hot text, and the curves will start to come to attention as you increase the value.

6. Select the shape in frame 4, and select **Modify ➤ Shape ➤ Optimize**. This time, you are presented with the **Optimize Curves** dialog box.

   Select **Show totals message** and **Preview**. Move the slider all the way to the top, and click **OK**. The dialog box will close and be replaced by an alert box, telling you how many curves were found, how many were optimized, and the size of the reduction as a result of the optimization (see Figure 15-16).

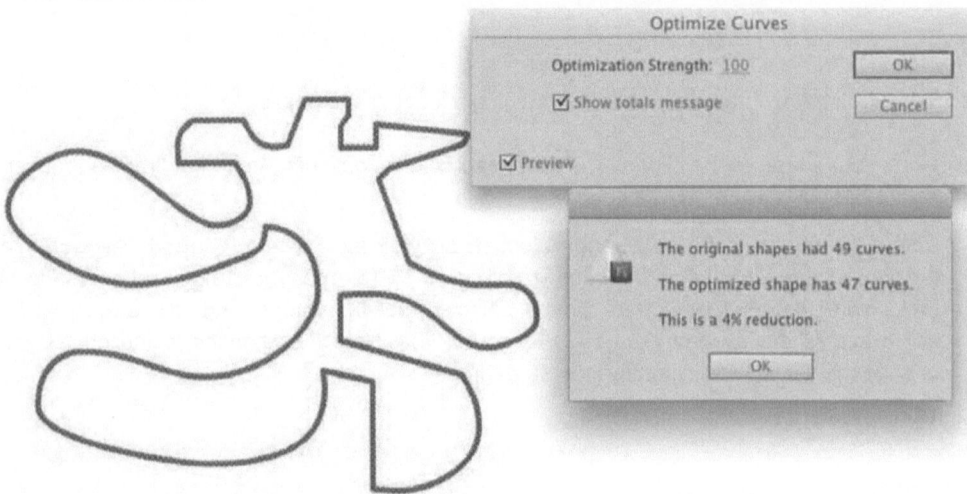

Figure 15-16. Using shape optimization

7. Test the movie. The graph shows you the file size of the content in each frame and the effect that modifying the shape has in each frame. As you can see in Figure 15-17, the results are quite dramatic.

OPTIMIZING AND PUBLISHING FLASH MOVIES

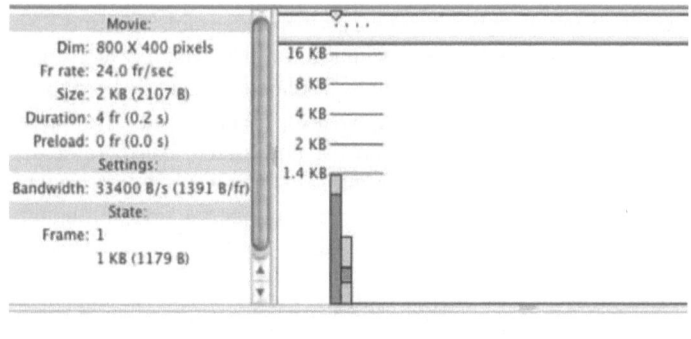

Figure 15-17. Smoothing, straightening, and optimizing curves can have a profound effect on download times.

You are most likely looking at the graph and thinking, "Wow, I am going to start optimizing all of my vector shapes!" Not so fast. Each of the three methods presented did a good thing and a bad thing. They did indeed reduce the bandwidth load. However, they also introduced distortions into the image. If you are happy with the distortions, fine. If you aren't, then you might want to consider doing the optimization manually, by selecting the shape with the **Subselection** tool and manipulating the shape and the points.

So, why was there such a drop in the graph between the object in frame 1 and its counterpart in frame 4? Remember that vector nodes require bandwidth. You removed a few of them using the **Optimize Curves** dialog box, which accounts for the drop in required bandwidth.

If you import vector artwork from outside sources, such as Illustrator files, you may find shape optimization quite challenging. Obviously, it depends on the intricacy of the artwork, but industrial-strength tools like Illustrator CS5 naturally have more complex features than the drawing tools provided by Flash. When Flash imports vectors from other tools, it does its best to "translate" those anchor points into the "language" it uses internally.

781

This can lead to some rather interesting missteps between Illustrator CS5 and Flash CS5. You can see this in Figure 15-18. The image on the left is the image, on the Illustrator CS5 page, as it was drawn in Illustrator CS5 using the Extrude filter and a couple of effects to create the splatter. The whole thing is vectors. The image on the right is the same image on the Flash stage. The top version is the result of importing the AI file into Flash. The bottom version is one saved in Illustrator as an FXG image. The difference is, when the FXG file was created, Illustrator rasterized the extrusion, which sort of defeats the purpose. Your "take away" from this is that all vectors are not equal, and, in certain instances, something could become "lost in translation."

Figure 15-18. Just because Illustrator CS5 draws vectors, don't get lulled into complacency.

Just be mindful of the pipe. If elaborate vector artwork seems to weigh more than you would expect, consider exporting it from the original application as a bitmap or FXG file and compare file sizes. If you don't have the original application, import the artwork into Flash, situate it on the timeline of a temporary stand-in FLA, and then use `File ➤ Export ➤ Export Image` to select a suitable raster format.

Aren't vectors supposed to be smaller? Generally speaking, yes. But every rule has its exception, and it goes both ways. Giulia Balladore (www.juniatwork.com), a self-taught artist featured on www.FlashGoddess.com, produces jaw-droppingly beautiful artwork directly in Flash. Her vector drawings rival the sort of detail that normally requires a camera and meticulous studio lighting. And yet, because she works in Flash and optimizes her vectors, images like "Sole" (see Figure 15-19) can be resized in the browser without ever getting pixelated. And the depicted SWF weighs a minuscule 23KB!

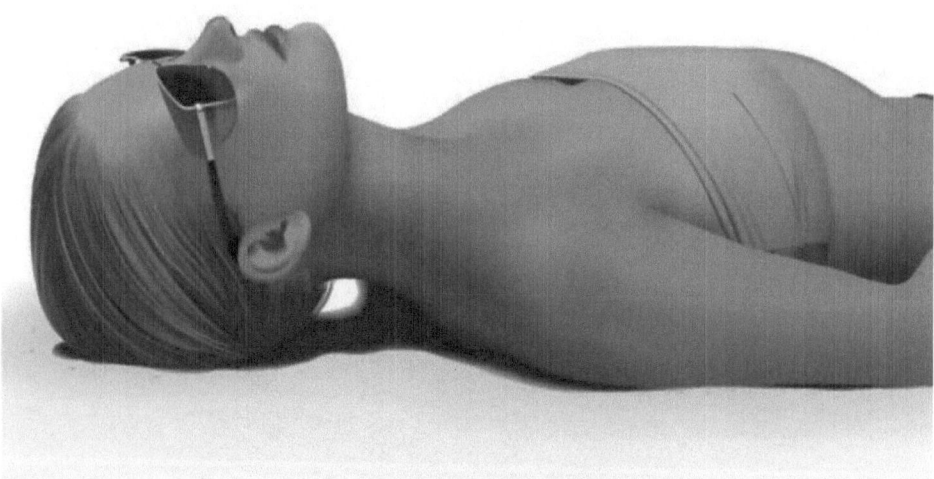

Figure 15-19. Yes, this image was drawn entirely with Flash's drawing tools, by Giulia Balladore (www.juniatwork.com/).

Publishing and web formats

Tattoo this to the inside of your left eyelid: *The SWF isn't a web document*.

Nothing drives us crazier than someone telling us, "Dudes, check out my Flash site," only to have that individual double-click a SWF on his computer's desktop. Flash SWFs should appear on the Web only if they are embedded into an HTML page. Why? Because you can use the HTML to control aspects of the SWF—scaling, context menu items, and more—that you can't do without the HTML wrapper. Thus, a "Flash site," to be precise, is composed of an HTML page that points to the SWF, along with any media—audio, video, images, text—that the SWF may need from external sources.

Creating the SWF is a bit more complicated than selecting `File ➤ Publish Preview` and merrily clicking away in the `Publish` panel. As we pointed out in the previous chapter, you need a solid grounding in what's under the hood before you create the car.

Again, as we have been saying since the first page of this book: *keep it small!* This is the reason for Flash's broad acceptance on the Web and where an understanding of the publishing process is invaluable. Up to this point, we have essentially created a bunch of FLA files and asked you to test them. The time has arrived to get off the test track and put the vehicle on the street.

When you publish your movie, Flash compresses the file, removes the redundant information in the FLA, and what you are left with—especially if you've been taking this chapter to heart—is one sleek, mean web presentation. The default output file format—yes, there is more than one—is the SWF. The SWF is wrapped in HTML through the use of `<object>` and/or `<embed>` tags, plus extra information about how the browser should play the SWF.

CHAPTER 15

> *Yes, you can link directly to a SWF without that bothersome HTML. Just be aware that the SWF will expand to the full size of the browser window, meaning all of the content on the stage will also enlarge. In many respects, linking directly to the SWF is rookie error number one.*

Before we move into actually publishing a movie, let's look at some of the more common file types used on the Web, listed here:

- Flash (.swf)
- HTML (.htm or .html)
- Images (.gif, .jpg, and .png)
- QuickTime (.mov)

Flash

Before there was Flash, there was Director. Though used primarily for interactive CDs, DVDs, and kiosks, it was at one time the main instrument employed to get animations to play on the Web. The technology developed by Macromedia to accomplish this was named Shockwave, and the file extension used was .dcr. Flash also made use of this technology, and in order to differentiate between them, it became known as Shockwave for Flash and used the .swf file extension. Flash Player is the technology that allows the SWF to play through a user's browser. Through a series of clever moves, Flash Player has become ubiquitous on the Web. In fact, Adobe can rightfully claim that Flash Player, regardless of version, can be found on 98 percent of all Internet-enabled computers on the planet. This means, in theory, that you can assume your movies are readily available to anyone who wants to watch them. But the reality gets a bit more complicated.

> *For you trivia buffs, the first couple of iterations of Shockwave for Director used a small application named Afterburner to create the DCR files. When Director developers prepared a presentation for the Web, they didn't just create the DCR; the movie was "shocked." One of the authors happened to be around on the night Macromedia quietly released Shockwave and Afterburner to the Director community. He still remembers the excitement generated by members of the group as they posted circles that moved across the page, and he remembers the "oohs" and "ahs" that followed as the circles moved up and down.*

Each new Flash Player version brings with it new functionality. Flash Player 8 introduced filter and blend effects, which can't be displayed in Flash Player 7. FLV video can't be played in Flash Player 5. Any movie you prepare using ActionScript 3.0 can be played only in Flash Player 9 or newer. Flash Player 9,0,115,0 was the first to display HD video content. The current version, 10.1, moves Flash onto practically any device, including smartphones, home television systems, and game systems found on the planet. Though you may initially think the Flash Player version is a nonissue, you would be making a gross miscalculation.

Corporations, through their IT departments, have strict policies regarding the addition or installation of software to corporate-owned computers. We personally know of one organization that isn't budging, and its Flash Player policy is Flash Player 6 or lower to this day. Shrewd Flash designers actually ask potential clients which versions of Flash Player are to be targeted for the project. The last thing you need is to find yourself rewriting every line of code and reworking the project, because you assumed the target was Flash Player 9, but corporate policy dictates Flash Player 7 or older.

> Flash Player 10 follows a tradition that each successive version of Flash Player will play content faster than its predecessors. When Flash Player 9 was released, Adobe claimed it provided a 75 percent speed increase over Flash Player 8, which was partly because of the support for ActionScript 3.0 introduced in Flash Player 9. This sort of increase is usually enough for most users to install the new version. Even so, in many instances, actually downloading and installing the plug-in is becoming a thing of the past. Flash Player has the ability to download and install in the background, but, as one of the authors is quick to point out: "It takes a programmer to make it work."

HTML

HTML is short for Hypertext Markup Language. Where HTML and ActionScript part company is that HTML is a formatting language, whereas ActionScript is a scripting language. This means HTML is composed of a set of specific instructions that tell the browser where content is placed on a web page and what it looks like. ActionScript has nothing to do with the browser. It tells Flash how the movie is to perform.

The HTML instructions, or **tags**, are both its strength and its weakness. HTML was originally developed to allow the presentation of text and simple graphics. As the Web matured, HTML found itself hard-pressed to stay current with a community that was becoming bored with static content on pages. The emerging version of HTML, HTML 5.0, deals with this in a rather fascinating manner, but it is still in its infancy, and we don't see it gaining broad adoption for a few more years.

The real problems with HTML start when you try to drop multimedia or interactive media into a web page. HTML simply wasn't designed for this sort of heavy lifting, which explains why JavaScript (a language that shares roots with ActionScript) is now so widely used.

For a Flash designer, knowledge of how HTML works is critical, because it is an enabling technology: it enables your movies to be played on the Web. Of course, this isn't as difficult as it once was. Today, through the use of Dreamweaver CS5 and even Flash, creating the HTML involves nothing more than a couple of mouse clicks. You will still need to play with the HTML—you saw this in Chapter 10 when you had to dig into the JavaScript code to enable full-screen playback of a Flash video—because your HTML document can do things that Flash can't. This would include such features as `alt` attributes for screen readers and keywords used to attract search engines.

The other thing to stick in the back of your mind is that Flash-only web pages aren't as common as they once were. Web pages consisting solely of one SWF are still around, but Flash is also becoming a medium of choice for the delivery of banner ads, videos, and other interactive content that are elements of an HTML web page. To see an example of this, you need look no further than our beloved publisher. If you hit the friends of ED home page at www.friendsofed.com, you will see a Flash banner at the top of the home page (see Figure 15-20), while the rest of the page is composed of HTML.

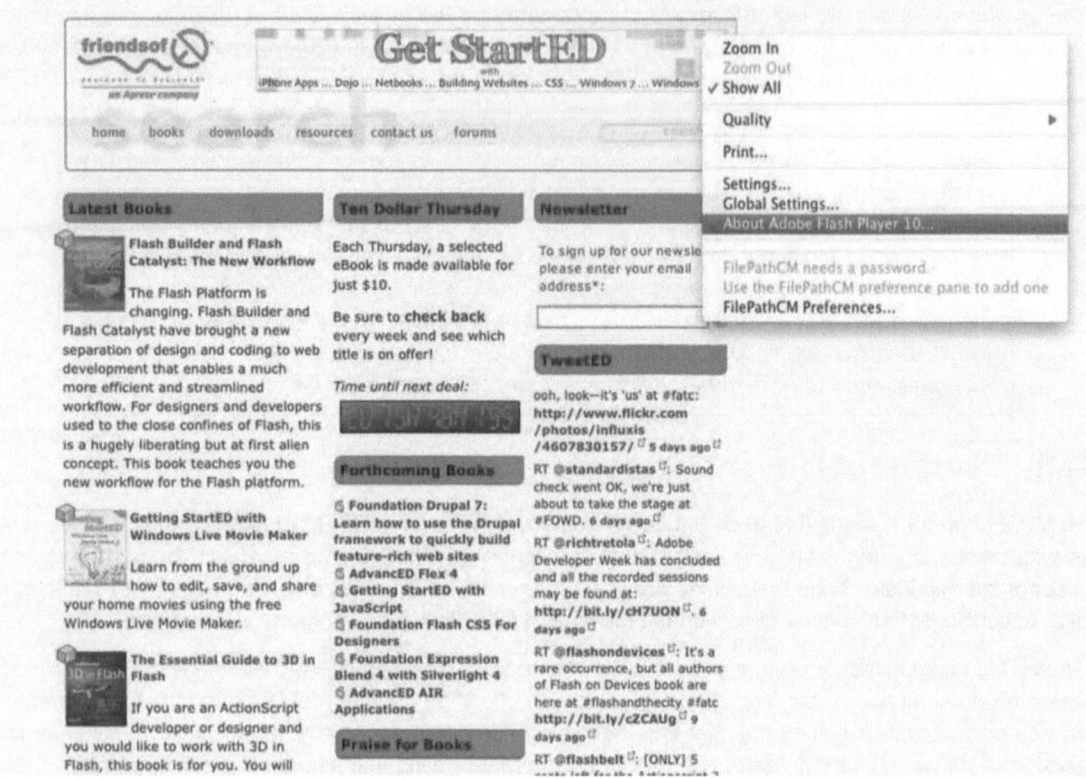

Figure 15-20. A typical Flash/HTML hybrid page

Animated GIFs

Before there was Shockwave, there was the infamous animated GIF file. These files were the original web animations, and you still can export your Flash movie as an animated GIF. Why would you want to do this if Flash Player is so ubiquitous? Because users don't need to install the Flash plug-in to view them. In fact, it is a two-way street: you can import a GIF animation into a Flash movie, and you can export a Flash movie as an animated GIF. In fact, it is not uncommon to encounter situations where the client wants both the SWF and a backup GIF animation.

OPTIMIZING AND PUBLISHING FLASH MOVIES

Exporting as an animated GIF

Let's reuse our now-familiar parrot to see how animated GIF exporting works:

1. Open the `YawningParrot.fla` file in this chapter's `Exercise` folder. This is the file to be exported as an animated GIF. Flash will convert each frame of the movie to a GIF image. There are 355 frames in this animation, meaning you should prepare yourself to create 355 separate GIF images.

> OK, web-heads, settle down. Creating an animated GIF consisting of 355 frames is, as our editor Ben Renow-Clarke would say, "Simply not done, old chap." We know that, but if you understand what happens—in a big way—you'll be more cautious in your efforts. Anyway, the parrot is pretty cool and makes for a rather interesting workout for Fireworks CS5.

2. Select **File** ➤ **Export** ➤ **Export Movie** (press Ctrl+Alt+Shift+S on Windows or Cmd+Option+Shift+S on a Mac) to open the **Export Movie** dialog box (see Figure 15-21). Navigate to the **Parrot** folder in the Chapter 15 `Exercise` folder, and select **GIF Sequence** in the **Format** drop-down menu. Then click **Save**.

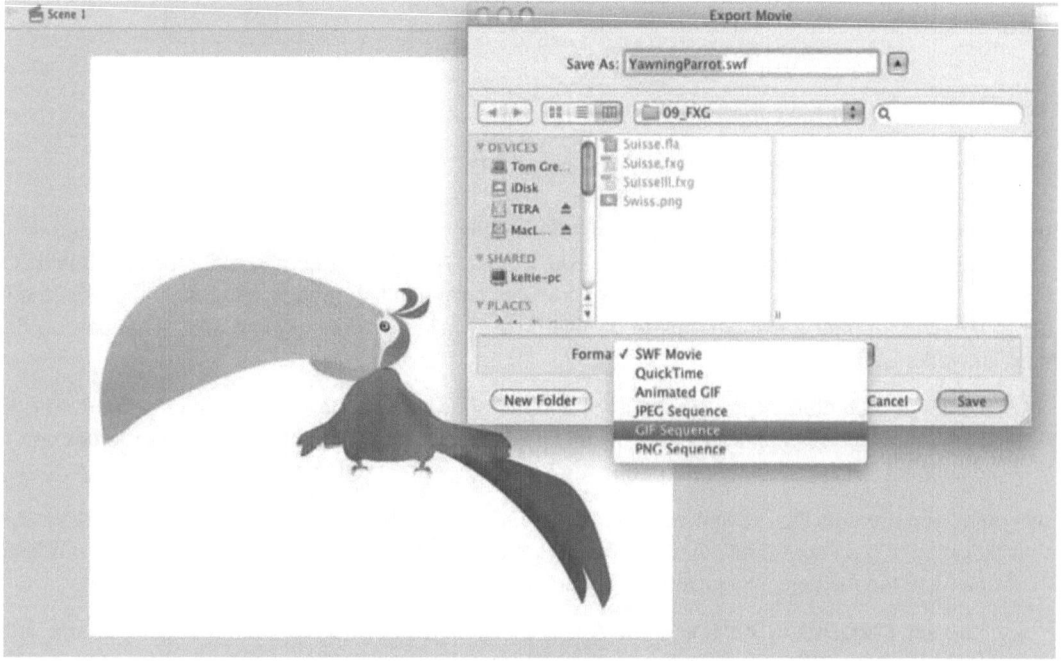

Figure 15-21. Select **GIF Sequence** as the export format.

787

3. In the `Export GIF` dialog box, specify these settings (see Figure 15-22):

   - **Dimensions**: 570 × 550 pixels
   - **Colors**: 256
   - **Smooth**: Selected

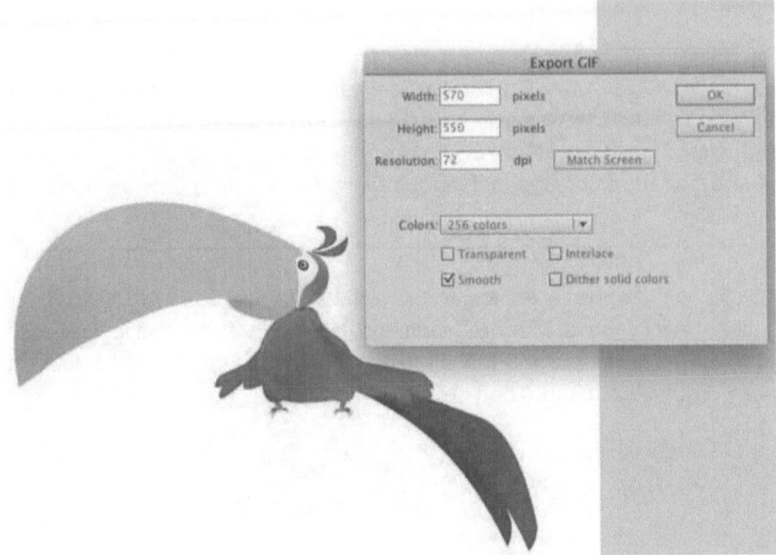

Figure 15-22. Preparing to export the Flash timeline as a GIF animation

You may notice that when you change the dimension settings, there is a corresponding reduction in the `Resolution` value. If you click the `Match Screen` button, you will be returned to the original settings for this image. The physical reduction of each frame and its corresponding reduction in resolution have the net effect of creating a rather small GIF image. In this case, you need to just ignore size. That can be dealt with in Fireworks CS5.

4. Click the `OK` button. A progress bar will appear, showing you the progress of the export. This is a fairly quick process and should take only a few seconds. When it finishes, the progress bar will disappear, and you will be returned to the Flash stage.

At this point, you are now the proud owner of the 355 GIF images that will be used to create the animation. We aren't going to get into the nitty-gritty of creating the GIF animation in Fireworks CS5. The process is fairly simple, and the next steps give you the general idea.

5. Launch Fireworks CS5, and then select `File ➤ Batch Process`. Navigate to the folder containing the GIF images and import all of them.

6. Scale the images to a size of 113 × 109, and save the scaled images to a new folder.

7. Still in Fireworks CS5, click the **Open** button on the Welcome screen, and navigate to the folder containing your GIF images. Select all of them in the **Open** dialog box, and select **Open as animation**, as shown in Figure 15-23. Then click the **Open** button.

8. When the animation appears on the Fireworks CS5 canvas, test it by clicking the **Play** button in the bottom-right corner of the canvas.

Fireworks will create the animated GIF by putting each image in a frame. You can then do what you need to do and export the file from Fireworks CS4 as an animated GIF.

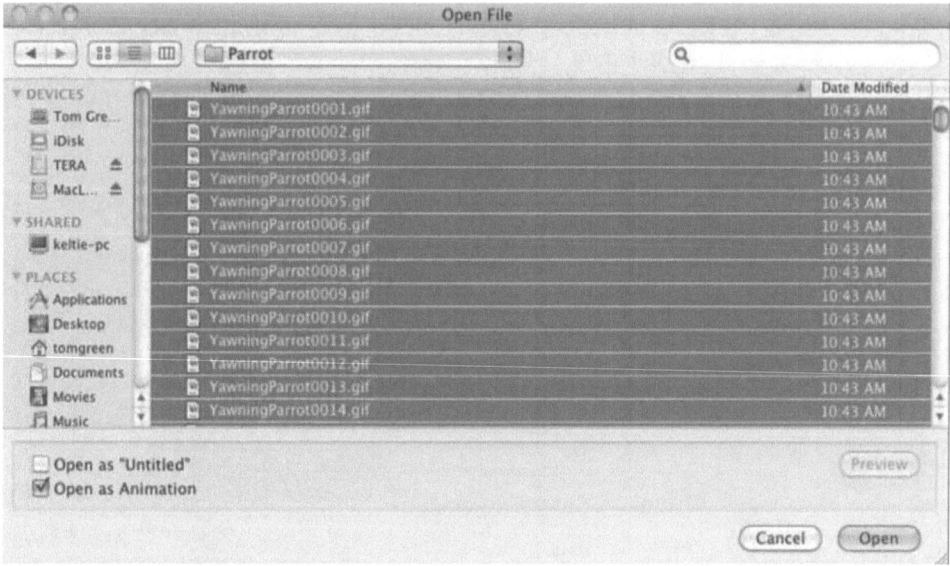

Figure 15-23. Importing the GIF files into Fireworks. The key is to select **Open as Animation**.

> *Only the main timeline is considered when Flash content is converted to an animated GIF. Nested movie clip timelines and ActionScript do not make it through the translation process. The simple rule of thumb is that if you can see it move while you manually scrub the timeline, the GIF can, too. If you can't, it won't show.*

Yes, we set you up. In Flash, if you select **File ➤ Export ➤ Export Movie**, you can bypass the need to restitch the GIF sequence in Fireworks by choosing **Animated GIF** from the **Export Movie** dialog box. Still, it's good to know where these things come from, how they are created, and your options!

Importing an animated GIF

Now that you know how to create a GIF animation in Flash, let's look at the reverse process. Here's how to import a GIF animation into Flash:

1. Open a new Flash CS5 document, and select `File ➤ Import ➤ Import to Library`.

2. Navigate to the `ParrotFW.gif` file in the `Exercise` folder for this chapter, and click `Import to Library`. When the process finishes, you will see that each image in the animation, along with a movie clip, has been added to the `Library`.

3. Drag the movie clip to the stage, and test the movie. You have a low-resolution version of the yawning parrot, as shown in Figure 15-24.

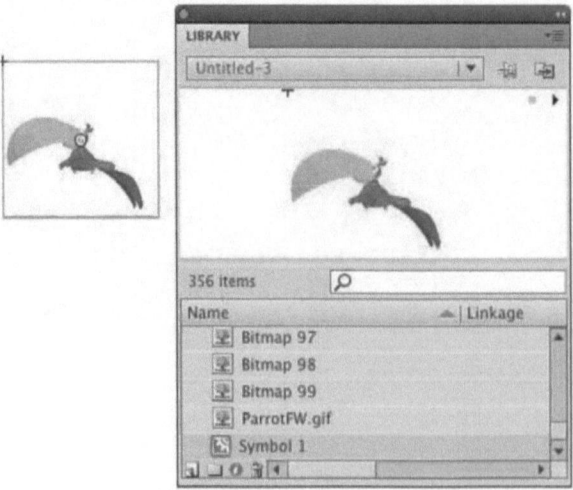

Figure 15-24. A yawning parrot in the GIF format

QuickTime

QuickTime is Apple's Internet streaming video technology. As we have pointed out throughout this book, QuickTime is losing its grip as the premiere web video technology. Even so, you have the ability to output your Flash animations as QuickTime movies—`File ➤ Export ➤ Export Movie ➤ QuickTime`—and use them in video projects. This isn't as farfetched as it sounds. The rise of motion graphics on the Web makes Flash an ideal tool for creating these things for web or broadcast. To prove it, Figure 15-25 is a screen capture from a video one of the authors did for activetutsplus (http://active.tutsplus.com/tutorials/screencasts/getting-to-grips-with-alpha-channel-video/), and you might recognize our pal Grotto in the bottom-left corner. He was output as a QuickTime movie and added to an AfterEffects project, which was then subsequently output as an F4V file.

OPTIMIZING AND PUBLISHING FLASH MOVIES

Figure 15-25. Flash animations can be output to video.

Flash is gaining ground as a broadcast animation technology, and no matter how you slice it, QuickTime is the way to go with digital video. Up until the previous release of Flash, QuickTime and Flash have had a rather uneasy relationship. It was extremely difficult to get Flash animations into QuickTime for editing in a video-editing application. Why? Because you couldn't use nested movie clips, nested timelines, or ActionScript. These impediments have been removed, and publishing a Flash document as a QuickTime movie is easier than it ever has been.

That raises this question: how do you publish a Flash movie for the Web?

It's showtime!

Everything works as it should. You have sweated buckets to optimize the movie, and the client has finally signed off on the project. It's showtime. The Flash movie is ready to hit the Web and dazzle the audience. Though you may think publishing a Flash movie involves nothing more than selecting `Publish` in the `File` menu, you would be seriously mistaken. The process is as follows:

1. Open the `Publish Settings` window to determine how the movie will be published.
2. Publish the movie and preview the SWF.
3. Upload the SWF and any support files to your web server.

Publish settings

We'll start by exploring the publish settings. Open GardenFinal.fla in this chapter's Exercise folder. It struck us as somehow appropriate that you finish the book by working with the file you created when you started the book.

> *We are going to concentrate on a movie headed for the Web and not a mobile device. We discuss the mobile process in greater detail in Chapter 14.*

Select File ➤ Publish Settings (Ctrl+Shift+F12 on Windows or Option+Shift+F12 on a Mac) to open the Publish Settings dialog box, as shown in Figure 15-26.

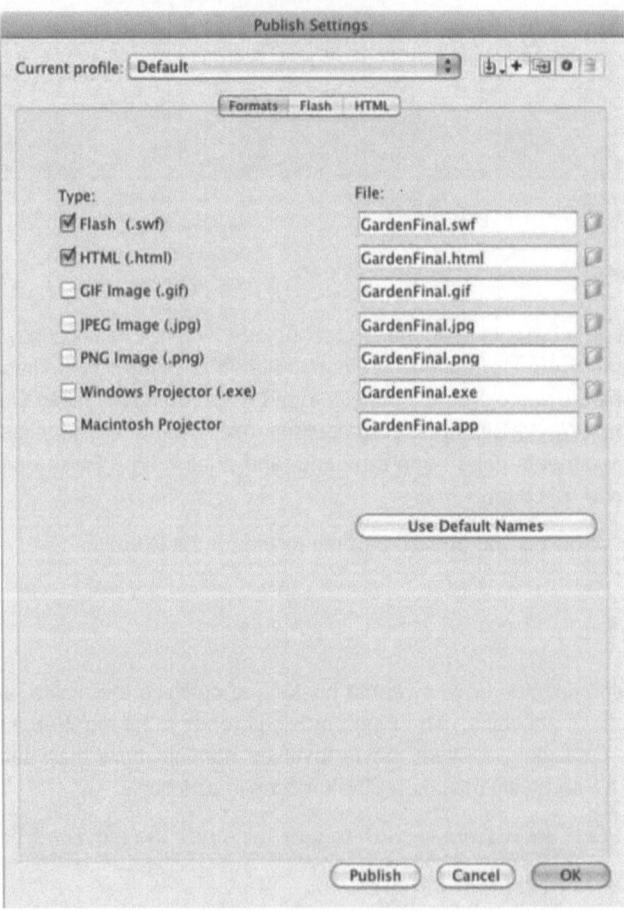

Figure 15-26. The Publish Settings dialog box

OPTIMIZING AND PUBLISHING FLASH MOVIES

> *You can also launch the* `Publish Settings` *dialog box by clicking the* `Edit` *button in the* `Profile` *area of the* `Publish` *section in the* `Properties` *panel. The one thing you don't want to do, unless you have a lot of Flash experience, is to select* `File ▶ Publish`. *Selecting this will publish the movie using whatever default settings are in place.*

As you can see, this dialog box is divided into three distinct sections: `Formats`, `Flash`, and `HTML`. In fact, that last tab (or tabs) will change depending on the format chosen. We'll get to that in a minute. The five buttons along the top, next to the drop-down menu, are the `Profile` buttons. These allow you to "tweak" your settings and then save them for future use.

Formats

The file types are as follows:

- `Flash (.swf)`: Select this, and you will create a SWF that uses the name in the `File` area unless you specify otherwise.

- `HTML (.html)`: The default publishing setting is that the Flash and HTML settings are both selected. This does not mean your SWF will be converted to an HTML document. It means Flash will generate the HTML file that will act as the wrapper for the SWF.

> *If you are a Dreamweaver CS5 user, you don't need to select the* `HTML (.html)` *option. Dreamweaver will write the necessary code for the SWF when it is imported into the Dreamweaver CS5 document.*

- `GIF Image (.gif)`: Select this, and the Flash animation will be output as an animated GIF, or the first frame of the movie will be output as a GIF image.

- `JPEG Image (.jpg)`: The first frame of the Flash movie will be output as a JPEG image.

- `PNG Image (.png)`: The first frame of the movie will be output as a PNG image. Be careful with this one, because not all browsers can handle a PNG image.

- `Windows Projector (.exe)`: Think of this as being a desktop SWF that is best suited to play back from a Windows desktop or CD, not from the browser.

- `Macintosh Projector`: This is the same idea as the Windows projector. Just be aware that a Mac projector won't play on a Windows machine, and vice versa.

The `Navigate` buttons (they look like folders and are located beside each file type) allow you to navigate to the folder where the SWF will be saved (see Figure 15-27). If you see a path, click the `Use Default Names` button to strip out the path from the file name.

CHAPTER 15

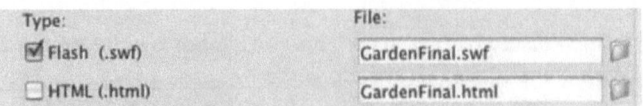

Figure 15-27. Strip out any paths in the file name to avoid problems.

Select all of the types. Notice how each file type kicks out its own tab. Deselect everything but the `Flash (.swf)` option before continuing.

Flash settings

Click the `Flash` tab to open the Flash settings, as shown in Figure 15-28.

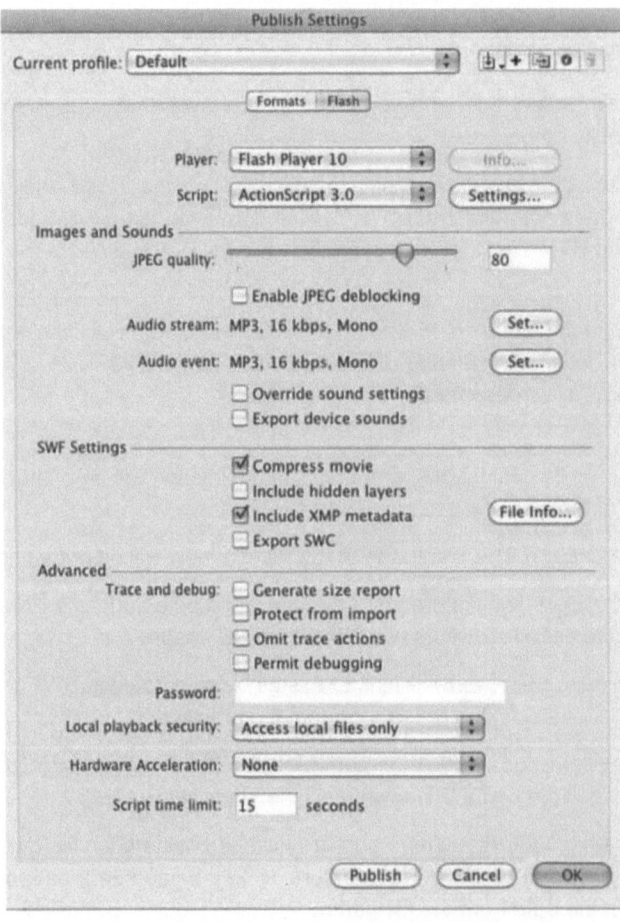

Figure 15-28. The `Flash` settings in the `Publish Settings` dialog box

OPTIMIZING AND PUBLISHING FLASH MOVIES

Let's review each of the areas in this panel:

- `Player`: This drop-down menu allows you to choose any version of Flash Player from versions 1 to 10.1 (the current version), AIR 2, and any version of Flash Lite Player from versions 1 to 4.0. If you have the `Properties` panel open, you will see the version chosen also appears there. It is extremely important for you understand that if you change your Flash Player version and are using features in the movie that aren't supported by the chosen Flash Player version, you will be greeted by the alert dialog box shown in Figure 15-29). In his case, we had used 3D tweens in the `GardenFinal` file, and that feature is not supported in our target player: Flash Player 6.

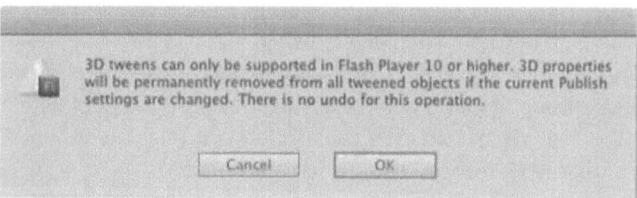

Figure 15-29. Flash will let you know you can't, when you try to do something that isn't supported by the version of Flash Player you have targeted.

- `Script`: There are three versions of the ActionScript language. If you are publishing to Flash Player 9 or newer, you are safe selecting `ActionScript 3.0`, `ActionScript 2.0`, or `ActionScript 1.0` (we recommend `ActionScript 3.0`). If you are publishing to Flash Player 8 through 6 or Flash Lite 2 or 2.1, `ActionScript 2.0` is your choice, though `ActionScript 1.0` will work. Everything else uses the `ActionScript 1.0` setting.

- `Images and Sounds`: This is where you control the compression of JPG images and sound quality. Your choices are as follows:

  - `JPEG quality`: This slider and text field combo specifies the amount of JPEG compression applied to bitmapped artwork in your movie. The value you set here will be applied to all settings in the `Bitmap Properties` area of the `Library`, unless you override it for individual bitmaps on a per-image basis.

  - `Audio stream`: Unless there is a compelling reason to do otherwise, leave this one alone. The value shown is the one applied to the `Stream` option for audio in the `Properties` panel.

  - `Audio event`: This comes with the same warning as the previous choice but for event sounds.

  - `Override sound settings`: Click this, and any settings—`Stream` or `Event`—you set in the `Sound Properties` area of the `Library` are, for all intents and purposes, gone.

  - `Export device sounds`: Use this only if you are using Flash Lite and publishing to a mobile device.

- **SWF Settings**: Use this area to tell Flash how to create the SWF. The following options are available:
  - **Compress movie**: Even though Flash compresses the FLA's assets when it creates the SWF, selecting this allows Flash to compress the SWF itself—usually text-heavy or ActionScript-heavy—to an even greater extent during the publish process. If you are publishing to Flash Player 5 or older, you can't use this option.
  - **Include hidden layers**: This option falls squarely in the category of "it's your call." All this means is that any timeline layer whose visibility icon is turned off will not be compiled into the SWF. Designers often like to keep reference layers handy during authoring, but in previous versions of Flash, such layers would show in the SWF, even if they were hidden in the FLA. An old trick to "really" hide them was to convert such layers to guide layers—but that can get tedious. If you really want those layers gone, just delete them. If you're a little lazy, use this feature instead. We tend to leave it unselected, but if there is a compelling reason to include your hidden layers, select this option.
  - **Include XMP metadata**: Select this option and click the **File Info** button, and the dialog box shown in Figure 15-30 will appear. Any text entered here will be added to the SWF's metadata. As you can see, the amount of metadata you can add is quite extensive. For more information about Extensible Metadata Platform (XMP), see www.adobe.com/products/xmp/.
  - **Export SWC**: Unless your name is Grant Skinner or you have been living and breathing Flash for most of your natural life, leave this one alone. It is used to create a component for Flash.
  - **Password**: This option works in conjunction with the **Debugger** workspace, but only for ActionScript 2.0. If you add a password to this text-entry box, whoever opens the ActionScript 2.0 **Debugger** panel will be prompted to enter the password if debugging the SWF in a browser. If the plan is to test and debug your Flash application remotely, this is a "must do." Just remember, this only allows you debug your code. It won't prevent people from maliciously "ripping" your def and decompiling the code.
- **Advanced**: You have a number of options regarding the treatment of the SWF available to you:
  - **Generate size report**: Select this, and Flash will generate a .txt document that shows you where potential bandwidth issues may be located. The .txt file is generated when you publish the SWF.
  - **Protect from import**: When this option is selected, the user will be prevented from opening your SWF in Flash.

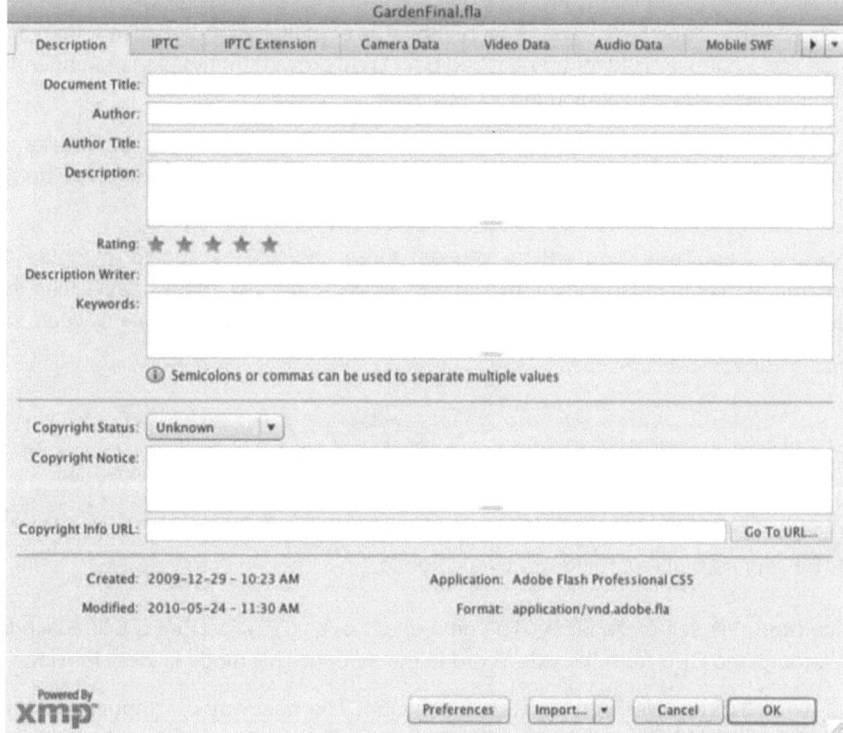

Figure 15-30. The ability to add metadata to a SWF is a major feature of practically every Adobe application.

- **Omit trace actions**: Flash will ignore any appearances of the trace() function you may have added to your ActionScript (they will actually be removed from the SWF). You use this function to track the value of a variable and display that value in the Output window. Tracing is great for debugging, but a ton of these common statements can affect performance.

- **Permit debugging**: Select this, and you have access to the Debugger workspace in Flash, even if the file is being viewed in a web browser. You really should turn this off before you make the movie public on the Web.

- **Local playback security**: The two options in this drop-down menu—Access local files only and Access network only—permit you control the SWF's network access. The important one is the network choice. Access networks only protects information on the user's computer from being accidentally uploaded to the network.

- **`Hardware Acceleration`**: This needs a bit of explanation because if you make the wrong choice, your user is in for a really bad day. We'll provide that explanation after the description of the next, and last, item in the `Flash` panel.
- **`Script time limit`**: Sometimes your scripts will get into a loop, sort of like a dog chasing its tail. This can go on for quite a long time before Flash sighs and gives up. Enter a value here, and you are telling Flash exactly when to give up.

For the `Hardware Acceleration` option, you get three choices, as shown in Figure 15-31. These choices are offered thanks to Flash Player 10.1 and its ability to do a lot more heavy-lifting than any Flash Player in history. By using hardware acceleration, Flash will work with the user's video card to render graphics and video more smoothly.

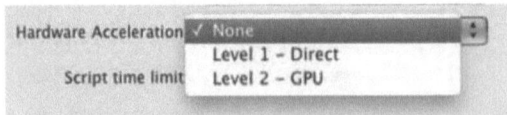

Figure 15-31. Be very careful regarding what you choose.

The first choice (`None`) is self-explanatory. The next one, `Level 1 - Direct`, tells Flash to look for the shortest path through the CPU from the video card to the screen. This mode is ideal for video.

The `Level 2 - GPU` option was introduced in Flash CS4. The best way of wrapping your mind around it is to consider how movieclips are rendered. They are essentially drawn on the screen using software, but they are rendered—think of the fly buzzing around the garden—with your graphics card, or GPU. Scaling is a great example of this, and full-screen HD video rendering is also done this way.

You probably read that last sentence and thought, "Well shucks, I'll do everything this way." Not so fast, bucko. As Flash engineer Tinic Uro points out in his blog (www.kaourantin.net/2008/05/what-does-gpu-acceleration-mean.html), "Just because the Flash Player is using the video card for rendering does not mean it will be faster. In the majority of cases your content will become slower."

Essentially, the `Level 2 - GPU` choice requires a minimum DirectX 9 card. If you are a Vista user, for example, and Aero Glass is a problem, you can bet that hardware rendering of Flash graphics will be equally problematic, because Aero has the same hardware requirements as the GPU choice.

Also, frame rate will be an issue, because the frame rate will max out to the screen refresh rate. This means if you have a Flash movie with a frame rate of 72 fps, you have exceeded the refresh rate of 60 times per second. In this case, your Flash movie's frame rate will downshift to 60 fps or, more realistically, 50 to 55 fps, thanks to dropped frames.

The bottom line here is that either `Hardware Acceleration` choice will result in a serious memory hit on the browser, to the point where the browser becomes either sluggish or unresponsive. If you must use this feature, limit yourself to one SWF per HTML page, and use `Level 1 - Direct` as your first choice. Both choices are tied directly to the video card manufacturers and their drivers. Over the next couple of years, this feature will become critical as Flash starts appearing on screens ranging from smartphones to your home entertainment unit.

HTML settings

Click the **Formats** tab, and select the **HTML (.html)** file type. When you do that, the **Publish Settings** dialog box sprouts an **HTML** tab. Click the **HTML** tab to see the HTML settings shown in Figure 15-32.

> *If you are a Dreamweaver CS5 user or prefer to "roll your own" HTML code, it still won't hurt to review this section, but be aware that Dreamweaver CS5 does this job for you.*

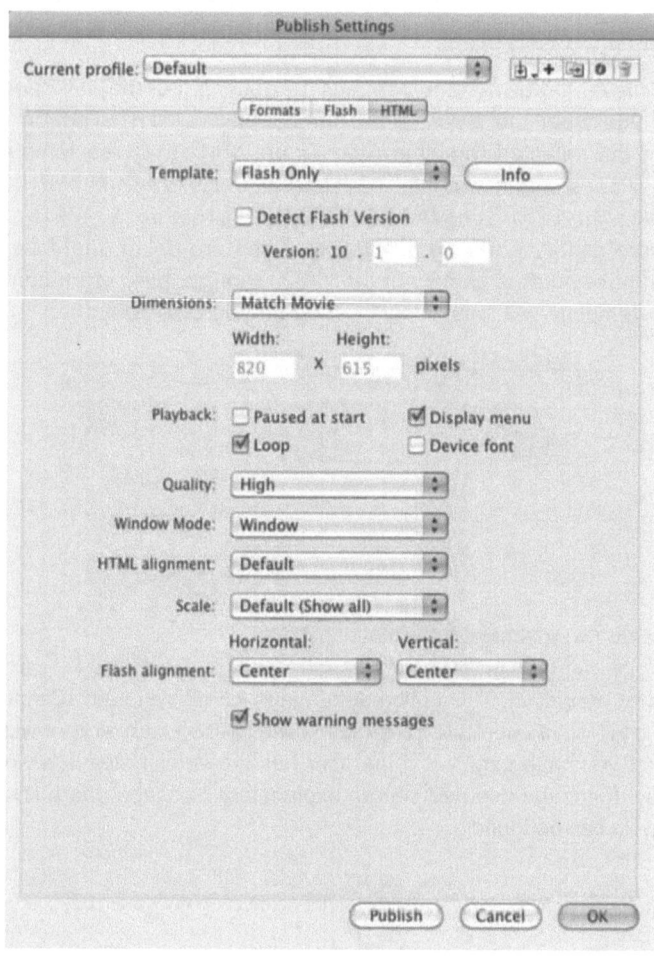

Figure 15-32. The **HTML** tab in the **Publish Settings** dialog box in Flash CS5

As we noted earlier, be aware that using this dialog box does not convert your SWF to HTML. The best way to consider this option is like buying a hamburger at a large international chain. When the hamburger is finally ready, it will be wrapped in paper or placed in a colored box that identifies the contents. For example, you have ordered the MegaBurger, and the burger is wrapped in blue paper that has "MegaBurger" printed on it. The HTML option performs the same job: it provides the wrapper that tells the browser what's inside.

> If the Flash movie is to appear in a CSS-based layout, a lot of the options in this dialog box will not be used by the coder. Still, the HTML page to be created is a good starting point for a code jockey.

Let's review the main features of this panel:

- **`Template`**: This drop-down menu contains 11 options, but they all specify the type of HTML file in which you want the SWF to be embedded. The `Info` button will give you a brief description of the selected template (see Figure 15-33). These templates can be found in `C:\Program Files\Adobe\Adobe Flash CS5\en\First Run\HTML` on your Windows machine or `HD:/Applications/Adobe Flash CS5/First Run/HTML` on your Mac. If you are a hard-core coder and know exactly what you are doing, feel free to change them (but only after you have made a backup of the files). Though there are a number of templates, the `Flash Only` template will most likely be the one you use most often.

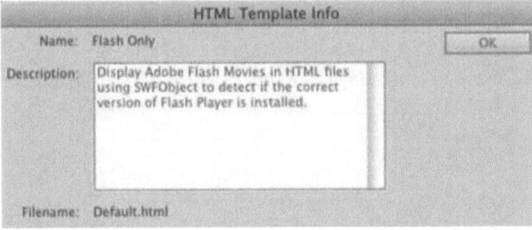

Figure 15-33. The `Flash Only` template description

- **`Detect Flash Version`**: This option determines whether the JavaScript code for this purpose is added to the HTML. It checks to see whether the user's Flash plug-in will work with the version of Flash Player you have targeted. If the user has the version, life is a wonderful thing, and the movie will play. If not, the user will see an explanatory message and a link to the location where the latest plug-in can be found.

> *If you are a JavaScript wizard, feel free to customize the detection JavaScript to react differently if the wrong plug-in version is detected. For instance, if the IT boys have decreed "Thou shalt not add software to our machines," you could rewrite the code to load and play an alternate version of the SWF instead of suggesting the user do something that is forbidden.*

- **Dimensions**: You get three choices in this drop-down menu: **Match Movie**, **Pixels**, or **Percent**. Select one of the last two options, and you can change the physical size of your movie. If you choose **Percent**, you will discover the one circumstance that allows content positioned outside the stage to possibly show.

- **Playback**: These four choices determine what happens when the movie starts playing:

    - **Paused at start**: This means the user gets things going. This is very common with banner ads, and you would need to provide a button to tell the playhead to start moving, or the user would have to be smart enough to right-click and use the plug-in's context menu to select **Play**. Our advice? Go with the button.

    - **Display menu**: This option is actually quite important. It has nothing to do with menus in the movie and everything to do with Flash Player. If you test GardenFinal.fla and right-click (Windows) or Control+click (Mac) the SWF, the menu shown in Figure 15-34 appears. This menu allows the user to modify how Flash Player displays the movie. Many Flash designers and developers turn this off because they don't want people switching to low-quality graphics or zooming in on the stage. Still, there is a very important use for this menu. If your site requires users to use a web camera or a microphone, clicking the **Settings** button will allow them to choose the devices to be used.

    - **Loop**: When selected, this option plays the movie loop again from the beginning. If it's not selected, it plays the loop only once. The key point here is any stop() actions you may have in your ActionScript will override this selection.

    - **Device font**: This selection replaces any static text in your movie with a system font—_sans, _serif, and _typewriter—which can result in a significant file-size reduction. The downside to this choice is that you have absolutely no control over which font is used. If the user doesn't have the three fonts installed, the machine will use one that is closest to the font, meaning the text may wrap or even change the look of your movie. Is this one of those things that falls into the category of "things you should never do"? Not really. It is your movie, and if you decide this is the way to go, you at least are aware of the potential hazards of the choice.

CHAPTER 15

Figure 15-34. The Flash menu that is displayed at runtime

- `Quality`: This drop-down menu contains the six choices shown in Figure 15-35. These specify the render quality at which your movie will play, and the choice you make determines the speed at which your movie runs on the user's machine or device. We suggest you start with `Auto High`, which permits Flash to automatically drop the quality to maintain the frame rate and synchronization if necessary. In many respects, this area is not one that should concern you, because if `Display menu` is selected, the user can change this setting at runtime.

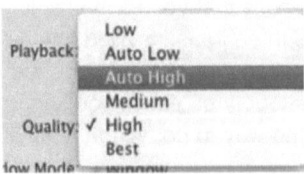

Figure 15-35. Try starting with the `Auto High` quality setting.

- `Window Mode`: The selection you make here will appear in the `wmode` settings in the `<object>` and `<embed>` tags used in the HTML. If you are unsure as to what the choices do, just leave the choice at the default, which is `Window`.

802

OPTIMIZING AND PUBLISHING FLASH MOVIES

- **HTML alignment**: This selection allows you to specify the position of your movie window inside the browser window. The default will place the SWF in the center of the browser window.

- **Scale**: If you have changed the dimensions of the movie using the **Dimensions** option, the choices in this drop-down menu determine how the movie is scaled to fit into the browser window.

- **Flash alignment**: These two options permit you to set the **Vertical** and **Horizontal** alignment of your movie in its window and how it will be cropped, if necessary.

- **Show warning messages**: If this box is selected, any errors discovered when the HTML file is loaded—missing images is a common error—are displayed as browser warnings when the user arrives on the page.

Publishing the butterfly garden

Now that we have reviewed the major points, let's publish the butterfly garden and look at it in a browser. Before you start, click the **OK** or **Cancel** button to close the **Publish Settings** dialog box and return to the Flash stage. Save the GardenFinal.fla to the Garden folder in your Chapter 15 Exercise folder. We'll explain why in a moment. Now open the **Publish Settings** dialog box, and let's get busy.

1. Click the **Formats** tab, and select the **Flash** and **HTML** formats.

2. Click the **Flash** tab, and specify these settings:
   - **Version**: Flash Player 10
   - **Script**: ActionScript 3.0
   - **Compress movie**: Selected
   - **Include hidden layers**: Deselected

3. Click the **HTML** tab, and specify these settings:
   - **Template**: Flash Only
   - **Dimension**: Match Movie
   - **Quality**: Auto High
   - **Flash alignment**: Center for both **Horizontal** and **Vertical**

4. Click the **Formats** tab. In this panel, click the **Use Default Names** button to strip off any paths that might be associated with this movie.

5. Click the **Publish** button. You will see a progress bar that follows the publishing process. Click **OK** to close the **Publish Settings** dialog box and return to your movie.

6. Minimize the Flash stage, and open the Garden folder in the Chapter 15 Exercise folder. You will see that Flash has created three files: the FLA file, the SWF file, and an HTML file (see Figure 15-36). The only file that doesn't need to get uploaded to the server is the FLA.

GardenFinal.fla   GardenFinal.html   GardenFinal.swf

Figure 15-36. The results of publishing the Flash movie

7. Open the GardenFinal.html file in a browser. The movie starts playing (see Figure 15-37). Congratulations!

Figure 15-37. Playing the movie in a browser

OPTIMIZING AND PUBLISHING FLASH MOVIES

> *Hang on. How did the background color of the browser page turn blue? There was nothing in the HTML settings for that one. If you publish a Flash movie and use the HTML option, the background color of the HTML document will change to the stage color of the Flash movie.*

Before we move on, we would like to talk about another option on the Flash `File` menu. As shown in Figure 15-38, the `Publish Preview` submenu contains the formats from the `Publish Settings` dialog box. Selecting this will publish the movie, and if you selected `Default - (HTML)`, you can launch the results in a browser. This menu reflects the choices made in the `Publishing Settings` dialog box, which explains why a lot of the options are grayed out. If you are a Dreamweaver CS5 or Fireworks CS5 user, this menu item is the same as being able to do a browser preview in both of those applications. In fact, they all use the same key, F12, to launch the preview. The browser that opens will be the default browser used by your computer's operating system.

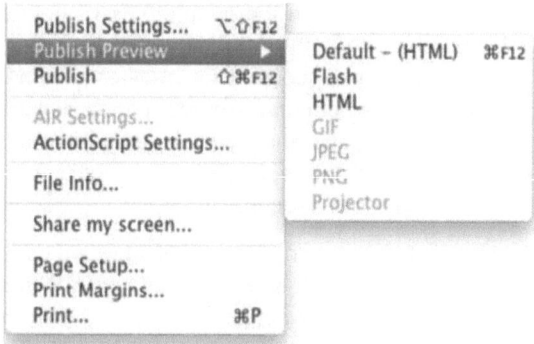

Figure 15-38. You can preview the movie in a browser without leaving the Flash interface.

Publishing Flash movies containing linked files

In Chapter 6 we showed you how to play a sound located outside of the SWF. Though you tested it locally, nothing beats testing on a remote server. Another aspect of that exercise is playing content located in another folder on the server. In the case of the MP3 files, this actually makes sense. Let's assume you are going to use the same MP3 soundtrack in five Flash movies over the coming year. If that MP3 is 5MB in size, you will have used up 25MB of server space if the file is slipped into the folder for each project that uses it. Doesn't it make more sense to upload it once and have the movies call it into the SWF from a single location?

In this example, we are going to assume the three audio files are located in a folder named Tunes in the mythical domain of mySite.com.

1. Open the TinBangs.fla file located in the Exercise folder for this chapter.

2. Open the **Actions** panel, and scroll down to the loadSong() function in line 56 of the **Script** pane.

3. The critical line in this function is line 47, which uses the load() method to get the song. Change this line to the following:

req = new URLRequest("http://www.mySite.com/Tunes/" + file);

That's all it takes. Of course, what you're seeing is just a sample URL, so if you test the file, you won't actually hear any music. The point is that you can add fully qualified paths to your URLRequest instances.

Everything is straightforward if you use absolute paths. Absolute paths contain the full domain name, which means they're accessible from anywhere on the Internet. That's both a plus and a minus. If you hard-code all your file references as absolute paths, you know they'll work—until you decide to change your domain name or until you repurpose your content for another project in another folder structure somewhere else. In cases like that, a relative path may suit your needs. Relative paths do not reference a domain name, and because of that, they depend entirely on a very particular point of view: the physical location of the file making the reference. (If this sounds familiar, that's because we touched on it in Chapter 10 in regard to video files. Consider this a recap.)

You would think that a SWF looking for MP3s (or any external files) would consider itself as the beginning of the path—"Where is that file in relation to *me*?"—but that's not how it works. When a SWF references external files with relative paths, its point of view is actually that of the HTML document that contains it. If the SWF and the HTML file are in the same folder, this is a moot point, but keep it in mind if you decide to put all your SWFs in one folder and your HTML files in another.

To make matters even more interesting, there's an exception: FLV files. If you are using the **FLVPlayback** component, the path to the video, if it is a relative path, takes its cue from the location of the SWF itself. The same thing goes for a video object using the NetStream class. That said, the **FLVPlayback** component optionally uses skins, and skins are SWF files. If your movie uses relative paths to reference an **FLVPlayback** skin, set your point of view to the HTML document that contains this movie, but when referencing the FLV, set your point of view to the movie itself.

This "gotcha" often raises its ugly head if you have a custom controller or video skin or are using a server that dynamically loads the content. Either make sure you understand the gotcha fully or enter the paths as absolute paths (see Figure 15-39).

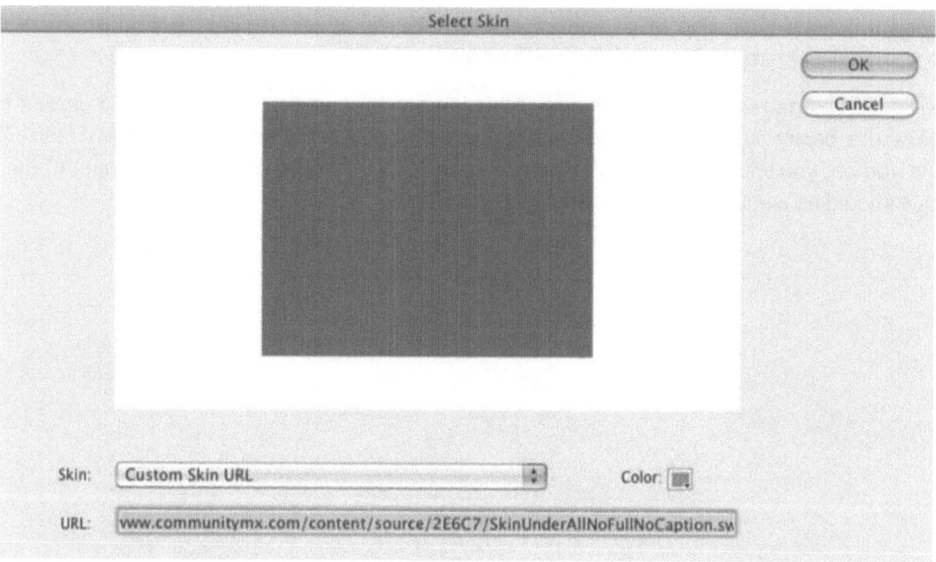

Figure 15-39. You can save FLV skins to remote sites as well.

What you have learned

There wasn't a lot of geeky or cool stuff in this chapter. Instead, the focus on this chapter was how to optimize your Flash movies for web playback. We examined how the data in your Flash movie gets from "here to there" and in what order. We reviewed several ways of using the Bandwidth Profiler, from identifying content bottlenecks to actually emulating the download of a bloated Flash movie into a dial-up modem. It wasn't pleasant, but we then showed you a number of ways to fine-tune your Flash movies in order to let you maximize that "15-second window of opportunity" you get when a user hits your site. The chapter wrapped up with a lengthy discussion about the publishing process. Along the way, you learned the following:

- How Flash movies are streamed to a web page
- A couple of ways of turning the Bandwidth Profiler into your new best friend
- Tips and tricks for optimizing content for fast download
- How to prepare a SWF for web playback
- How to export a Flash movie as a GIF animation and how to import a GIF animation into Flash
- How to deal with remote content needed by the SWF

This chapter dealt with the "end game" in Flash. We think you are now aware that preparing your Flash files for web output involves a lot more than simply selecting **Publish** in the **File** menu. There is a lot to consider, and those considerations range from what format will be used to output the file to a number of

CHAPTER 15

very important options that need to be addressed. We also dealt with remote content and how the SWF can grab it from elsewhere on your site and on the Web.

Speaking of the end game, we are at the end of this journey that started and ended at a garden filled with butterflies and a pesky fly. We hope you had fun and that you are inspired to explore Flash CS5 even further. As you do, you will discover a fundamental truth about this application: the amount of fun you can have with it should be illegal. We'll see you in jail.

Index

Special Characters and Numbers

+ button
    Flash Motion Editor panel, 444, 445
    Flash Values dialog box, 621
3D
    center point, 517–519
    depth limitations, 520–522
    overview, 495–498
    parallax effect, 512–517
    simulating photo cubes, 522–525
    tools
        Rotation, 501–506
        Translation, 506–511
    vanishing point, 498–501
3D Position and View area, Flash Properties panel, 209, 506, 512, 515, 523
3D Position and View strip, Flash Properties panel, 52
3D Position option, Flash, 510
3D Position property, Flash, 510
3D Position Z value, Flash, 524
3D Rotation area, Flash Transform panel, 209, 515, 523
3D Rotation tool, Flash, 70, 71, 499, 508, 516, 517, 518, 525
3D Rotation X value, Flash Properties panel, 524
3D Rotation Y value, Flash Properties panel, 524
3D Rotation Z value, Flash Properties panel, 525
3D Translation tool, Flash, 499, 521
3D Tween option, Flash, 518
3DCube.fla file, 523
9Scale movie clip, Flash, 163
9Slice2.swf file, 166
9Slice.fla file, 161
9SliceGotchas.fla file, 168

A

<a> tag, 586, 680, 681, 688, 694
AAC (Advanced Audio Coding), 281
actions layer, Flash, 39, 261, 269, 303, 342, 346, 420, 559, 702, 744
Actions menu option, Flash, 223
Actions toolbox, 217
ActionScript
    Actions panel
        Actions toolbox, 217
        versus Behaviors panel, 219–220
        overview, 216
        panel context menu, 218
        Script navigator, 217
        Script pane, 217
    Code snippets
        adding into Code Snippets panel, 269–271
        custom classes, 271–277
        overview, 266–268
    coding fundamentals
        capitalization matters, 233–234
        class files and document class, 251–253
        commenting code, 235–237
        conditional statements, 247–251
        data types, 241–243
        dot notation, 237–238
        operators, 244–247
        scope, 239–240
        semicolons mark end of line, 234
        syntax, 233, 253–257
        variables, 240–241
    copying motion as, 416–419
    creating random motion using, 421–426
    full-screen video, 574–576
    objects
        classes, 221–222
        overview, 220
        Properties, 222–225
    overview, 213–216, 555–557
    reading and Components Reference
        Help, 258
        overview, 257
        search tactics, 259–260
    setting properties via
        events, 229–233
        Methods, 226–229
        overview, 225
    snippets, 559–560
    timeline
        looping, 265
        pausing, 261–264

INDEX

using movie clips to control, 266
and TLF, 341–345
using, 260–261
ActionScript 3.0
adjusting volume with code, 304–305
overview, 298–299
playing sound from Library, 298–300
playing sound from outside of Flash, 301–302
turning remote sound on and off, 302–304
using button to play sound, 300–301
visualizing audio, 309–313
ActionScript menu option, Flash, 228, 234
ActionScript panel, Flash, 744, 745
ActionScript section, Flash, 218
ActionScript Settings area, Flash, 252
ActionScript Settings menu option, Flash, 252
ActionScript tab, Flash Font Embedding dialog box, 327, 691
:active pseudo-class, Flash, 689
:active tag, Flash, 688
Add a New Item to the Script button, Flash Script pane, 217
Add Anchor Point option, Pen tool, 103
Add blend mode, Flash, 180
Add Classic Motion Guide context menu option, Flash, 57, 411
Add Colors option, 117
Add Cue Point button, Adobe Media Encoder Export Settings window, 588
Add Filter button, Flash, 50, 176
Add panels to sets option, Flash, 8
Add Parameter button
Adobe Media Encoder Export Settings window, 588
Dreamweaver Parameters dialog box, 579
Add Shape Hint menu item, Flash, 374
Add Swatch option, 115
Add to Current frame button, Flash, 267, 268, 420, 559, 564
Add to Custom Colors button, 114
Add to swatches panel, 118
addASCuePoint( ) method, ActionScript, 583
addChild( ) method, ActionScript, 253, 351
addController( ) method, ActionScript, 341
addEventListener( ) method, ActionScript, 231, 262, 626, 630, 631, 725
Adjust Color filter, Flash, 175
Adobe AIR (Adobe Integrated Runtime), 750, 752–756
Adobe Community Help, 40

Adobe CoolType, 319–322
Adobe Extension Manager CS5, 751
Adobe Illustrator (AI) format, 124
Adobe Media Encoder
audio settings, 538
cropping videos, 539
overview, 532–533
previewing and trimming, 534–535
rendering process, 540–541
settings, 535–537
Adobe Sound Document (ASND), 281
Adobe TV link, 4
ADPCM compression option, Flash Sound Properties dialog box, 286
Advanced ActionScript 3.0 Settings panel, Flash Publish Settings dialog box, 252
Advanced Audio Coding (AAC), 281
Advanced button
Flash Convert to Symbol dialog box, 153
Flash Sound Properties dialog box, 59, 298
Advanced Character options area, Flash Properties panel, 349
Advanced Character properties, 334–335, 340
Advanced options, Flash Symbol Properties dialog box, 357
Advanced Options menu, 93
Advanced section
Flash Sound Properties dialog box, 298
Publish Settings dialog box, 796
Advanced Smooth dialog box, 779
Advanced Sound Properties dialog box, Flash, 300
Afterburner application, 784
AI (Adobe Illustrator) format, 124
AI File Importer, 145
AIFF (Audio Interchange File Format), 281
AIR (Adobe Integrated Runtime), 750, 752–756
AirForAndroid folder, 751, 754
AirheadMailAnimated.fla file, 522
AirheadMail.fla file, 520
Alert box, Dreamweaver, 592
align attribute, 587
Align Center option, Flash Paragraph properties, 336
Align Justify option, Flash Paragraph properties, 336
Align Left option, Flash Paragraph properties, 336
Align panel, Flash, 192–193, 456, 457, 523, 561
Align Right option, Flash Paragraph properties, 336
Align to stage button, Flash Align panel, 192

INDEX

Align to stage check box, Flash Align panel, 193
Align to stage feature, Flash, 193
Align Top Edge button, Flash Align panel, 194
Align Vertical Center button, Flash Alignment panel, 561
aligning objects
    aligning with guides, 188
    overview, 186
    snapping in guide layer and to pixels, 189
    snapping to grid, 187
AlignPanel.fla file, 193
Allow smoothing option, Bitmap Properties dialog box, 133
allowFullScreen attribute, HTML, 577
AllowFullScreen parameter, Dreamweaver Parameters dialog box, 579
allowMultipleSelection parameter, Flash List component, 624
allowMultipleSelections check box, Flash Properties panel, 625
Alpha blend mode, Flash, 180
Alpha property, Flash Color panel, 378
alpha video, 572–574, 593–596
AlphaEx.fla file, 574
Alpha.mov file, 573
Alsop, Will, 522
Always Show Markers option, Flash Timeline panel, 398, 399
Always update before publishing option, Flash Convert to Symbol dialog box, 154
Amsterdam.fla file, 500, 506
Anchor Onion option, Flash Timeline panel, 399
anchor points
    altering shapes, 371
    easing, 391–393
    shape IK and, 485–487
Android AIR apps, 750–756
Angle property, Flash bonex, 464
Angular setting, Flash Properties panel, 369
animated GIFs
    exporting, 787–789
    importing, 790
    overview, 786
animation
    classic tweening
        deforming, 382–384
        easing, 384–387, 395
        properties, 381–382
        rotation, 379–381
        scaling, 382–384
        stretching, 382–384

inspiration for, 492–493
inverse kinematics (IK)
    Bone tool, 459–468
    example, 487–492
    overview, 458
    Spring option for bones, 468, 492
modifying multiple frames, 400–402
Motion Editor panel
    easing with graphs, 437–445
    moving, 430–437
    overview, 428–429
    scaling, 430–437
motion guides, 408–411
motion paths
    advanced, 453–454
    manipulating, 450–454
    properties, 454–455
motion presets, 455–458
onion skinning, 397–399
overview, 361
programmatic
    copying motion as ActionScript, 416–419
    creating random motion using ActionScript, 421–426
    overview, 415
    using keyboard to control motion, 419–421
property keyframes, 445–450
shape tweening
    altering gradients, 377–378
    altering shapes, 369–373
    modifying, 368–369
    scaling, 363–368
    shape hints, 373–377
    stretching, 363–368
Timeline panel, 395–396
timelines, combining
    graphic symbols as mini-libraries, 406–407
    movie clip timelines versus graphic symbol timelines, 402–404
    nesting symbols, 404–406
tweening filter effects, 413–414
tweening masks
    animating masks, 411–412
    using motion guides with masks, 412–413
Animation category, Flash New Document dialog box, 422
Animation codec, Flash, 572
Animation folder, 269, 420

INDEX

Animation property, Flash Anti-alias drop-down menu, 333
antenna1 layer, Flash, 372
Ant.fla file, 372
Anti-alias menu, Flash, 323, 324, 325
Anti-alias property, Flash Properties panel, 333
anti-aliasing, 320
API (application programming interface), 217, 315
APK file, 756
Apparition.flv file, 580
Application & Installer Settings dialog box, Adobe AIR, 752
application programming interface (API), 217, 315
Apply Block Comment button, Flash Script pane, 218
Apply Line Comment button
    Flash Actions panel, 228
    Flash Script pane, 218
Armature_1 layer, Flash, 459, 468
Armature_2 layer, Flash, 462, 464
Arrange menu, Flash, 190
array access operator, ActionScript, 652, 654
Array class, ActionScript, 241, 706
Array.length property, ActionScript, 626
Array.push( ) method, ActionScript, 706
arrow class, ActionScript, 357
arrow movie clip, Flash, 356, 358
arrowLeft symbol, Flash, 170
arrows layer, Flash, 716
AS2Syntax.fla file, 253, 255
AS3Syntax.fla file, 254, 255
ASCuePoints.fla file, 562
ASND (Adobe Sound Document), 281
Aspect ratio drop-down menu, Adobe AIR, 753
assets, Library, 713–714
assignment operator (=), ActionScript, 606
at symbol (@), 650–654
attachSound( ) method, ActionScript 2.0, 300
attribute nodes, XML, 647
audio
    adding to button, 296–298
    adding to Flash movie, 59
    adjusting volume and pan, 293–296
    choosing sound type, 288–291
    controlling with ActionScript 3.0, 308
        adjusting volume with code, 304–305
        code snippet, 309–313
        playing sound from Library, 298–300
        playing sound from outside of Flash, 301–302
        turning remote sound on and off, 302–304
        using button to play sound, 300–301
    formats
        bit depth, 281–283
        MP3, 283–284
        overview, 280
        sample rates, 281–283
    importing, 284
    loopy, 291
    overview, 279
    removing file from timeline, 291
    setting sound properties, 285–288
    using in Flash, 288–296
Audio and Video folder, 564
Audio event option, Publish Settings dialog box, 287, 795
Audio folder, Flash, 43, 44
Audio Interchange File Format (AIFF), 281
Audio layer, Flash, 59, 60, 157, 289, 291, 293, 297, 519
Audio pane, Adobe Media Encoder Export Settings window, 538
Audio stream area, Flash Publish Settings panel, 287
Audio stream option, Publish Settings dialog box, 287, 795
Audio tab, Adobe Media Encoder Export Settings window, 537, 544, 573, 588
Audio Video Interleave (AVI), 530
Audio Visualizer snippet, Flash, 310
audio2 layer, Flash, 290
AudioPlayer.ai Assets folder, 714
AudioVisualization.fla file, 309
<author> elements, XML, 653, 655, 658
authortime feature, Flash, 187
Auto Format button, Flash Script pane, 218
Auto High quality setting, 802
Auto kern property, Flash Properties panel, 333
Auto Set Transformation Point option, Flash, 476, 477, 489
Auto-Collapse Icon Panels option, Flash Preferences dialog box, 31
Auto-fill button, Flash Create New Code Snippet dialog box, 269, 311
autoLayout parameter, Flash Properties panel, 570, 571
automatic class import feature, Flash CS5, 262

INDEX

autoPlay parameter, Flash Properties panel, 553, 554
AVI (Audio Video Interleave), 530

B

\<b> tag
   Flash, 684
   HTML, 586, 683
Background Color chip, Flash Properties panel, 27
Background color option, Flash Document Settings dialog box, 11
background image layer, Flash, 719
Background layer, Flash, 50, 51, 53, 54, 56, 500, 574
backgroundColor parameter, XML, 585
BackgroundImage layer, 148
Backlight slider, Device Central Display tab, 749
badBinding.fla file, 480
Balkan, Aral, 496
ball layer, Flash, 416
Balladore, Guilia, 782
bandwidth, 760–762
Bandwidth Profiler
   pinpointing problem content, 769–770
   reports, 770–771
   simulating download, 765–769
bang.fla file, 291
BannerEx.fla file, 149
Banner.png image, 138
bar layer, Flash, 718
BaseButton class, ActionScript, 606, 607
Baseline Shift setting, Flash Advanced character properties, 336
Basic Motion area, Flash Motion Editor panel, 21, 22, 54
Basic motion twirlie, Flash, 442
Basic Settings area, Adobe Media Encoder Export Settings window, 535
batch encoding, 541–542
Bateman, Rob, 496
Baumann, Pascal, 702
Behavior drop-down menu, Flash Properties panel, 338, 570
Behaviors panel, 219–220
Beijing art district, 704–711
betterBinding.fla file, 481
Bevel filter, Flash, 175, 595
Bezier curves, 102

Bind tool
   overview, 480–484
   shape IK and anchor points, 485–487
   shape IK and fills, 485
Bind.fla file, 481, 485
bit depth, 281–283
Bit rate setting, Flash Sound Properties dialog box, 286
Bitmap image with editable layer styles option, 148
bitmap images
   GIF files
      animations, 136
      images, 135
      overview, 134
   importing Fireworks CS5 documents, 137–139
   importing Illustrator CS5 documents, 140–145
   importing Photoshop CS5 documents, 146–150
   JPEG files, 131–132
   overview, 123–124, 125
   tracing, 127–130
Bitmap Properties dialog box, Flash, 132, 697, 700
Bitmaps object, Flash, 69
Bitrate [kbps] menu, Adobe Media Encoder Export Settings window, 537, 538
Bitrate Encoding area, Adobe Media Encoder Export Settings window, 537
Bitrate Encoding value, Adobe Media Encoder Export Settings window, 544
Bitrate Settings, Adobe Media Encoder Export Settings window, 537, 538, 573, 588
Bitrate value, Adobe Media Encoder Export Settings window, 544, 588
Black Borders option, Adobe Media Encoder, 539
Blam button, Flash Library panel, 297
Blam class, ActionScript, 300, 301
Blank Keyframe option, Flash, 17, 228, 230, 363
_blank setting, Flash Advanced character properties, 334
Blend menu, Flash Properties panel, 181, 369
Blend.fla file, 181
Blending drop-down menu, Flash Properties panel, 182, 582, 596
Blending option, Flash Properties panel, 581
blends, 180–181
BlobEffect.fla file, 582

813

INDEX

Blobs movie clip, Flash Library panel, 582
block elements, styling, 680–682
blockindent parameter, 587
Blossoms clip, 75
BlowUp button, Flash, 157
Blue layer, Flash, 451, 452
Blue Springs layer, Flash, 196
BlueMoon.fla file, 413
Blur filter, Flash, 50, 51, 56, 175
Blur pop-up menu option, Flash, 50
Blur property, Flash, 54
Body layer, Flash, 45, 410
Body movie clip, Flash, 45, 47
<body> tag, 681, 682, 687
bone chain, 459
Bone tool
    constraining joint rotation, 465–468
    deleting bones, 468
    overview, 459–461
    properties, 462–465
Bones.fla file, 465, 468
BonesRigged.fla file, 475
<book> elements, XML, 645, 651, 652, 654, 656, 657, 658
Boswell, Phoebe, 529, 571
BottomFlower movie clip, Flash, 49
Bounce context menu item, Flash, 441
Bounce ease, Flash, 442
bounce-smoosh preset, Flash, 455
Box layer, XML, 664
box.addEventListener method, ActionScript, 231

 tag, HTML, 586
Break Apart menu item, Flash, 744
Break setting, Flash Advanced character properties, 336
Bring Forward menu item, Flash, 190
Bring to Front option, Flash, 190, 524
Bringhurst, Robert, 315
Brown, Robert, 421
Browse button
    Adobe Media Encoder Import Video wizard, 546
    Device Central, 738
Browse for Folder dialog box, Adobe Media Encoder, 541
Browse for source file dialog box, Flash, 555
Brush Mode option, Brush tool, 87
Brush Shape option, Brush tool, 87
Brush Size option, Brush tool, 87
Brush tool, Flash, 71, 85–88
btnMute button, ActionScript, 305

btnPlay button, ActionScript, 301
btnPlay movie clip, Flash, 724, 725
Building Size value, 96
BunnyCharacter movie clip, Flash, 747
BunnyGraphics folder, 743, 747
Burns, Ken, 512
Butcher, Robbie, 711
Butterfly asset, Flash, 410
Butterfly button, Flash Symbol Editor, 45
Butterfly movie clip, 36, 37, 39, 47, 49
Button class, ActionScript, 609, 612
Button component
    adding button events, 606–608
    changing appearance
        skinning, 610–611
        styling components, 612–615
    considering component weight, 609
    referencing components in event handlers, 608–609
    using, 603–606
button events, 606–608, 726–728
button layer, Flash, 605
Button symbol, Flash, 157
Button01.fla file, 606
Button02.fla file, 606
buttonMode( ) method, ActionScript, 303
buttonMode property, ActionScript, 250
ButtonSound01.fla file, 298
ButtonSymbol.fla file, 157
ButtonTarget.fla file, 609
ByteArray( ) class, ActionScript, 311
bytesloaded>=bytestotal parameter, ActionScript, 700

C

Cab layer, Flash, 478
Cambridge movie clip, Flash, 268
campfire graphic example
    campfire movie, 108
    pine needles, 107
    pine tree, 106
    tree trunk, 104
CanadaFlag.fxg file, 666
CanoeBurnside.jpg file, 125
capitalization, ActionScript, 233–234
caption layer, Flash, 704
caption property, ActionScript, 706, 707
Captioning component, Dreamweaver, 592
Captioning component, Flash, 571

INDEX

CaptioningVideo folder, 569
captions, adding, 567–571
Captions layer, Flash, 570
captionTargetName parameter, Flash Properties panel, 570, 571
Car graphic symbol, Flash, 158
car1 movie clip, 266
car2 movie clip, 266
carRace.fla file, 266
Carter, Matthew, 324
Cascading Style Sheets. *See* CSS
Case drop-down menu, Flash, 335
Case setting, Flash Advanced character properties, 335
casting, ActionScript, 243, 649
Catalina Island example
    adding clouds, 206–207
    clouds in motion, 208–211
Category area, Flash Preferences dialog box, 9, 475, 488
CBR (constant bitrate), 537
CCW (counterclockwise), 454
CellRenderer class, ActionScript, 623
Center Frame button, Flash Timeline panel, 396, 398
Center point, 79, 517–519
Change Output Size option, Adobe Media Encoder, 539
changeHandler( ) function, ActionScript, 621, 626, 638, 722, 723
changePicture( ) function, ActionScript, 706, 707, 708, 710
Character area, Flash, 332, 340
Character properties, Flash, 332–334, 339, 358
Character range field, Flash Font Embedding dialog box, 326
Check Spelling dialog box, Flash, 354
Check Spelling option, Flash, 354
Check Syntax button
    Flash Actions panel toolbar, 234, 253, 257
    Flash Script pane, 217, 218, 253
CheckBox component, Flash, 606, 613, 615–616
CheckBox.fla file, 616
checkHammer function, ActionScript, 749
Checking options area, Flash Spelling Setup dialog box, 352
checking spelling, 352–354
checkPolicyFile attribute, 587
checkScore( ) function, ActionScript, 747
China.fxg file, 666

Chomyn, Jerry, 302
Circle movie clip, Flash, 160, 248
<citrus> tag, Flash, 685
Class area
    Flash Sound Properties dialog box, 300
    Flash Symbol Properties dialog box, 357
class attributes, 587, 683, 689
Class field, Flash Properties panel, 252
class files, ActionScript, 251–253
Classic Text option
    Flash Properties panel, 321
    Flash Text Engine drop-down menu, 328
    Flash Text Types drop-down menu, 330
classic tweening
    deforming, 382–384
    easing
        anchor points, 391–393
        multiple properties, 393–395
        overview, 384–390
    properties, 381–382
    rotation, 379–381
    scaling, 382–384
    stretching, 382–384
Classic Type text engine, Flash Properties panel, 570
ClassSelectors.fla file, 683
Clear button, Flash Properties panel, 24
Clear Guides menu item, Flash, 188
Clear Keyframe menu item, Flash, 363, 446
CLICK event, ActionScript, 566
Click to Go to Next Frame and Stop snippet, Flash, 269
Click to Seek to Cue Point snippet, Flash Code Snippets panel, 564
clickHandler( ) function, ActionScript, 231, 233, 301, 608, 609, 722, 726
clickHandler1( ) function, ActionScript, 609
clickHandler2( ) function, ActionScript, 609
clickHandler3( ) function, ActionScript, 609
clockwise (CW), 454
close( ) method, ActionScript, 559
Close option, Flash, 8
Close panels option, Flash, 8
Clouds layer, Flash, 206, 207, 208, 209
Clouds movie clip, Flash, 208, 209, 210
CloudsMask layer, Flash, 207
CMS (content management systems), 551
Code area, Flash Create New Code Snippet dialog box, 269
Code snippets
    adding into Code Snippets panel, 269–271

INDEX

custom classes, 271–277
overview, 266–268
Code Snippets button
   ActionScript, 267
   Flash toolbar, 455
Code Snippets menu option, Flash, 267
Code Snippets panel
   ActionScript, 267
   Flash, 268, 269, 270, 271, 310, 311, 420, 559, 564, 598
CodeButtonSound.fla file, 300
Codec area, Adobe Media Encoder Export Settings window, 536
CodeHint.fla file, 272
CodeSnippet folder, 309
coding fundamentals, ActionScript
   capitalization, 233–234
   class files and document class, 251–253
Collapse panels option, Flash, 6
color
   anti-aliasing, 320
   creating persistent custom colors, 115–117
   kuler color picker, 117–118
   overview, 110–111
color attribute, 586
Color chip, Flash filter, 414
Color Chip panel, ActionScript, 77
Color Effect area
   Flash Motion Editor panel, 21
   Flash Properties panel, 519
Color effect drop-down menu, Flash, 414
Color Effect properties, Flash Transform panel, 511
Color Matrix filter, ActionScript, 175
Color Modification grouping, Flash, 70, 71
Color palette, 112–114, 116
Color panels, Flash, 70, 378
Color Picker, 27, 112–114, 119, 414
Color Picker chip, Flash Properties panel, 27
Color property, Flash Properties panel, 332
Color Sliders button, 114
Color threshold setting, 128
Color window, 113
ColorPicker component, 617–618
ColorPicker.colors property, ActionScript, 618
ColorPicker.fla file, 617
ColorPicker.selectedColor property, ActionScript, 618
Colors area, Flash Tools panel, 29
Colors strip, Flash Motion Editor panel, 23
Columns category, Flash Properties panel, 338

CombineTimeline.fla file, 403
ComboBox component, 619–622, 624, 637, 704, 713, 723, 728, 737
ComboBox.dataProvider property, ActionScript, 708, 713
ComboBox.fla file, 620
ComboBox.selectedItem property, ActionScript, 621
commenting code, ActionScript, 235–237
comparison operator (==), ActionScript, 606
Compiler Errors panel
   ActionScript, 240
   Flash, 253, 254, 256, 257, 725
Compiler Errors tab, Flash Properties panel, 243
Compiler panel, Flash, 348
Complete folder, 348, 377, 387, 492, 500, 522, 609, 692, 693, 711
Completed status, Adobe Media Encoder, 541
completeHandler( ) function, ActionScript, 629, 649, 677, 707, 710, 713, 736, 737
Complete/MP3Player folder, 726
Component Assets folder, Flash, 604, 609, 619
Component Inspector panel, Flash, 562, 633, 636, 639
Component Parameters area, Flash Properties panel, 606, 621, 622, 623, 624, 626, 632, 634, 637, 639
Component Parameters option, Flash Properties panel, 570
Component Parameters tab, Flash Properties panel, 606, 616, 618, 620, 631, 635
components
   FLVPlayback, 552–555, 560–561
   FLVPlaybackCaptioning, adding captions with, 567–571
   slide shows with, and XML, 703–711
Components button, Flash toolbar, 604, 704
Components menu option, Flash, 355
Components panel, Flash, 355, 548, 552, 560, 604, 704
Components Reference
   Help, 258
   overview, 257
   search tactics, 259–260
Compress movie option, Publish Settings dialog box, 796
Compression drop-down menu
   Bitmap Properties dialog box, 133
   Flash Sound Properties dialog box, 286
computeSpectrum( ) method, ActionScript, 312
concatenation, ActionScript, 245

INDEX

conditional statements, ActionScript, 247–251
Configuration class, ActionScript, 341, 357
connecting rod symbol, Flash, 471
Constrain option
    Flash Properties panel, 465, 466, 490
    Flash Transform panel, 491
Constrain property, Flash, 464
Container and Flow options, Flash, 337, 339
ContainerController class, ActionScript, 357
containers, 337–338, 341
Containers.fla file, 337
content layer, Flash, 223
content management systems (CMS), 551
Content Path dialog box, Flash, 553, 554, 555
contents, loading, 697–703
Contents option, Flash Document Properties dialog box, 306
Contents radio button
    Flash Document Properties dialog box, 205
    Flash Document Settings dialog box, 10
Context menu, Flash, 219, 258, 365
Continue button
    Adobe Media Encoder Import Video wizard, 549
    Flash Import Vider wizard, 580
Controls layer, Flash, 561
controls, MP3 players with XML
    button events, 726–728
    improving, 715–719
    programming sliders, 728–734
Controls.fla file, 560, 717
controls.fla Library, Flash, 717, 718
Convert Anchor Point option, Pen tool, 103
Convert layers, 143
Convert to Symbol dialog box, Flash, 153, 155, 160
Convert to Symbol menu item, Flash, 153, 634
Convert To Symbol option, 105
Convolution filter, ActionScript, 175
Copy Frames context menu item, Flash, 177, 445, 716
Copy Motion context menu item, Flash, 457
copying motion
    as ActionScript, 416–419
    as XML command, 659
CopyMotion.fla file, 660
CopyMotion.xml file, 659
Corijn, Laurens, 497
Corner threshold setting, 128
counterclockwise (CCW), 454
Counterforce clip, 136

Counterforce.gif file, 136
crank movie clip, Flash, 474
crashing text, 333
Create a NetStream Video menu item, Flash, 559
Create area, Kuler panel, 118
Create Classic Tween context option, Flash, 18, 58, 367, 379
Create from Template category, 3
Create Motion Tween context option, Flash, 53, 199, 202, 227, 367, 431, 454
Create Motion Tween option, Flash, 208, 518
Create movie clip for this layer option, 148
Create movie clip option, 143
Create New area, 4, 5
Create New Code Snippet dialog box, Flash, 269, 310
Create New Code Snippet option, Flash, 269, 310
Create New Mobile section, Device Central, 738
Create New Symbol dialog box, Flash, 45, 47
Create Shape Tween context menu item, Flash, 365
Create video for use in Flash link, Flash Help panel, 41
Create Watch Folder menu item, Adobe Media Encoder, 541
CreateMotionAS3.fla file, 416
Creator category, Device Central, 738
Crop Proportions drop-down list, Adobe Media Encoder, 539
Crop Setting option, Adobe Media Encoder, 539
Crop tool, Adobe Media Encoder, 539
cropping videos, 539
crosshead bearing symbol, Flash, 471
CSS (Cascading Style Sheets)
    external, loading
        block element styling, 680–682
        custom tags, 684–686
        embedded fonts, 690–692
        inline element styling, 683–684
        overview, 676–679
        Selectors vs. Properties panel, 692–694
        style inheritance, 686–688
        styling hyperlinks, 688–690
    overview, 669–670
    styling with, 671–676
cue points
    creating XML captions, 588–592
    overview, 562–566
    XML format, 583–587

INDEX

Cue Points area
    Dreamweaver Properties panel, 592
    Flash Component Inspector panel, 562
    Flash Properties panel, 562, 584
Cue Points tab, Adobe Media Encoder, 583
<CuePoint> tag, XML, 585
CuePoints.xml file, 584, 591, 592
CuriousRabbit.fla file, 397
Current Frame area, Flash, 18
Current frame as movie clip option, 139
Current Frame indicator, Flash Timeline panel, 396
currentSong variable, ActionScript, 723
Curtis, Hillman, 760
Curve fit setting, 128
custom classes, Code snippets, 271–277
Custom Color boxes, 114
Custom context menu item, 444
Custom Download Settings dialog box, 769
Custom Ease In/Ease Out dialog box, Flash, 387, 388, 391, 395, 437
Custom Ease In/Ease Out editor, Flash, 384
Custom folder, Flash Code Snippets panel, 270
Custom graph, Flash Motion Editor panel, 444
Custom Presets folder, 456
Custom Skin URL setting, Flash, 551, 552
custom tags, 684–686
CustomEasingComparison.fla file, 388
CW (clockwise), 454
Cycle layer, Flash, 195, 196

D

Damping property, Flash bones, 464, 468
Damping value, Flash bones, 468
Dancing Fool symbol, Flash, 455, 456, 457, 458
DancingFool layer, Flash, 198, 199
DancingFool movie clip, Flash, 198
Darken blend mode, Flash, 180
Darling, Philip, 711
data parameter, Flash ComboBox component, 621
data property
    ActionScript, 677, 707, 708
    Flash ComboBox component, 621, 637
data types, ActionScript, 241–243
DataGrid component, 622–623
dataProvider area, Flash Properties panel, 625
DataProvider class, ActionScript, 706

dataProvider parameter
    Flash ComboBox component, 637
    Flash List component, 624, 626
    Flash Properties panel, 620
    Flash TileList component, 637
dataProvider row, Flash Properties panel, 625
DatatypeError.fla file, 242
Date class, ActionScript, 255
Davis, Joshua, 159
De Boer, Weyert, 653
Debug Options button, Flash Script pane, 218
Decision button, Flash Properties panel, 564
Deco tool, 88–97, 109
Deco02.fla file, 92
Deco03.fla file, 95
DecoCow.fla file, 91
DecoCow.swf file, 91
Deco.fla file, 89
Decorative drawing tools Group, Flash, 96
Default Presets folder, 455
Default Shape property, Spray Brush tool, 99
deforming classic tweening, 382–384
Delete Anchor Point option, Pen tool, 103
Delete Code Snippet menu option, Flash, 271
deleting bones, 468
Deployment panel, Adobe AIR, 754
Deployment tab, Adobe AIR, 753
depth limitations, 520–522
DeRaud, Cris, 520
descendant accessor (.), ActionScript, 657–658
descendants( ) method, ActionScript, 654, 655
Design View, Dreamweaver, 578
Destination layer, Flash, 181, 182, 183
Detect Flash Version option, 800
Device Central, 737–750
Device font option, 801
device fonts, 322–323
device Library, Device Central, 740
Device Profiles section, Device Central, 738
Device sound input field, Flash Sound Properties dialog box, 286
Dias, Tiago, 579
Difference blend mode, Flash, 180, 184
Digit Case setting, Flash Advanced character properties, 335
Digit Width setting, Flash Advanced character properties, 335
Dimensions drop-down menu, 801
Dimensions input area, Flash Document Settings dialog box, 10

INDEX

Dimensions setting, Flash Document Settings dialog box, 11
direction data, Bezier curve, 102
direction parameter, Flash Slider component, 634
Direction property, Flash Properties panel, 454
Displacement Map filter, ActionScript, 175
Display area, Flash Properties panel, 182, 596
Display icon, Flash Player dialog box, 597
Display menu option, 801
Display option, Flash Properties panel, 596
display property, 671
Display tab, Device Central, 749
displayAsPassword parameter, Flash TextInput component, 636
DisplayObject class, ActionScript, 222, 224, 629
DisplayObjectContainer class, ActionScript, 253
DisplayObject.localToGlobal( ) method, ActionScript, 474
Distort option, Flash, 365, 382, 501, 502
Distribute Horizontal Center button, Flash Align panel, 194
Distribute to Layers option, Flash, 37, 191, 192, 719
Distribute Top Edge button, Flash Align panel, 193
Distributive setting, Flash Properties panel, 369
document class, ActionScript, 251–253
Document menu option, Flash, 10
Document options area, Flash Spelling Setup dialog box, 352
Document Preferences, 9–10
Document Properties dialog box, Flash, 205, 306, 550
Document Settings, 10–11
document tab, Flash, 64
DOMDocument.xml file, 64, 662, 664, 666
Door Left layer, Flash, 517, 518
Door Right layer, Flash, 517, 518
dot layer, Flash, 412, 413
dot notation, ActionScript, 237–238
dots (.), 650–654
Down area, Flash Audio layer, 297
Down frame, Flash button component, 603
Download AIR for Android Extension for Flash CS5 link, Adobe web site, 751
Download Settings option
   Bandwidth Profiler, 769
   Flash, 629
Download Software link, Adobe web site, 751
downScroller function, ActionScript, 359
dragDude( ) function, ActionScript, 607
drawers, Flash, 7

Drawing category, 85
Drawing Effect area, 90, 92
Drawing Effect menu, 93, 95, 109
Drawing grouping, Flash, 70
Drawing objects, Flash, 69
Drawing option, Flash Preferences dialog box, 475, 488
Drawing section, Flash Preferences dialog box, 477
drawRect( ) method, ActionScript, 313
Dreamweaver CS5, 578–579
Drop Shadow filter
   applying, 175–177
   Flash, 178, 179, 596
   Symbol Editor Properties panel, 594
Dunlay, Bryan, 711
Duplicate Window menu option, Flash, 13
Dura, Josh, 496
Dynamic Text text type, Flash Properties panel, 570

E

E4X syntax
   descendant accessor (.), 657–658
   dots (.), 650–654
   filtering, 656–657
   namespaces, 659–661
   node types, 654–655
   overview, 649
   at symbol (@), 650–654
   XFL, 661–666
Ease hot text, Flash Properties panel, 368, 369, 385
Ease option, Flash Properties panel, 368
Ease property, Flash, 381, 388, 394, 454
Ease twirlie, Flash Properties panel, 436, 462
Eases area, Flash Motion Editor panel, 21, 22, 441, 442, 444, 445
Eases strip, Flash Motion Editor panel, 23
easing
   anchor points, 391–393
   custom, 387–390
   with graphs
      applying multiple eases, 444–445
      built-in eases, 438–443
      custom eases, 444
      overview, 437
   multiple properties, 393–395
   overview, 384–387

819

INDEX

ECMA (European Computer Manufacturers Association), 650
Ecma International, 650
ECMA-262 specification, 215
ECMAScript Language Specification, 650
Edit button
    Flash ActionScript Settings area, 252
    Flash Properties panel, 205, 293, 387, 388, 389, 391, 394
Edit Document menu item, Flash, 611, 627
Edit Envelope dialog box, Flash, 293, 294, 295
Edit Export Settings option, Adobe Media Encoder, 533
Edit Guides menu item, Flash, 188
Edit menu, Flash, 38
Edit Multiple Frames button, Flash Timeline panel, 396, 400
Edit Multiple Frames workflow, 457
Edit property, Flash Properties panel, 381
Edit stroke style button, 107, 108
Edit This Theme option, 118
Edit With option, Flash, 126
Editable text option, 147
Effect drop-down menu
    Flash Edit Envelope dialog box, 295
    Flash Properties panel, 293
Effect field, Flash Edit Envelope dialog box, 294
effects, parallax, 512–517
Elapsed Time area, Flash, 18
Elapsed Time indicator, Flash Timeline panel, 396, 397, 398
elements
    block, 680–682
    inline, 683–684
ElementSelectors.fla file, 680, 683
Embed button, Flash Font Embedding dialog box, 325
Embed FLV in SWF and play in timeline option
    Adobe Media Encoder Import Video wizard, 547
    Flash Import Video dialog box, 306
Embed video in SWF and play in timeline option, Flash Import Vider wizard, 580
<embed> tag, HTML, 577
Embeddable category, Font Book, 327
embedded fonts, 690–692
embeddedArial variable, ActionScript, 694
embedding
    fonts, 324–327
    video, 579–583

Embedding options, Flash Import Video dialog box, 306, 307
Embedding page, Flash Import Vider wizard, 580
Emulate Flash option, Device Central, 741
Enable check box, Flash Properties panel, 465, 469, 472
Enable guides for 9-slice scaling option
    Flash Convert to Symbol dialog box, 154
    Symbol Properties dialog box, 164
Enable hardware acceleration option, Flash Player dialog box, 597
Enable property, Flash bones, 464, 465
Enable Simple Buttons menu option, Flash, 157, 297
Enabled option, Flash Properties panel, 490
Encapsulated PostScript (EPS) format, 124
Encode Alpha Channel option, Adobe Media Encoder Export Settings window, 536, 573
Encoding Passes area, Adobe Media Encoder Export Settings window, 537, 544
end user license agreement (EULA), 327
endTime field, Adobe Media Encoder Export Settings window, 588
endTime property, XML, 585
engine layer, Flash, 473
Envelope option, Flash, 365, 382
EPS (Encapsulated PostScript) format, 124
EQ (equalization), 296
Erase blend mode, Flash, 180
Eraser Faucet modifier, Eraser tool, 101
Eraser Mode modifier, Eraser tool, 101
Eraser Shape modifier, Eraser tool, 101
Eraser tool, 71, 90, 91, 93, 100, 101
Errors dialog box, Adobe Media Encoder, 540
Essentials workspace, Flash, 8
Estimated glyphs total, Flash Font Embedding dialog box, 326
EULA (end user license agreement), 327
European Computer Manufacturers Association (ECMA), 650
Event class, ActionScript, 230, 609, 677, 700, 736
event handlers
    ActionScript, 229
    referencing components in, 608–609
Event keyframe, Flash, 297
event sound, Flash, 288
Event.CHANGE event, ActionScript, 618, 621, 626, 631, 634, 636, 708, 710

Event.COMPLETE event, ActionScript, 629, 649, 677, 710, 713, 725
Event.ENTER_FRAME event, ActionScript, 474, 724, 731
Event.fla file, 231
Event.ID3 event, ActionScript, 725, 734
Event.OPEN event, ActionScript, 725
events, 229–233, 288–291, 726–728
Events heading, ActionScript 3.0 Language and Components Reference, 607
Events.fla file, 230
Event.SOUND_COMPLETE event, ActionScript, 736
evt parameter, ActionScript, 233, 649
evt:MouseEvent expression, ActionScript, 232
evt.target expression, ActionScript, 609
evt.target.data expression, ActionScript, 649, 677
Exercise/MP3Player folder, 712, 717
Exercise/Preloader folder, 697
Exercise/Slideshow folder, 704
Exercise/YourTurn folder, 584
Existing folder radio button, Flash Move to folder dialog box, 154
Expand All button, Flash Script pane, 218
Expand timeline if needed check box, Flash Import Vider wizard, 580
Expanded Graph Size hot text, Flash, 436
Expanded Graph Size value, Flash, 22
Export for ActionScript option, Flash, 300, 357, 697
Export for runtime sharing option, Flash Symbol Properties dialog box, 171
Export formats available box, Adobe Media Encoder, 544
Export Settings window, Adobe Media Encoder, 533, 535, 539, 543, 544, 573, 588
Export SWC option, 796
exporting animated GIFs, 787–789
Extend link, 4
Extend option, Gradient Overflow tool, 120
Extensible Markup Language. *See* XML
external CSS, loading
    block element styling, 680–682
    custom tags, 684–686
    embedded fonts, 690–692
    inline element styling, 683–684
    overview, 676–679
    Selectors vs. Properties panel, 692–694
    style inheritance, 686–688
    styling hyperlinks, 688–690

external playlists, setting up, 712–713
Eyedropper tool, 117, 123

F

F4V files, creating, 542–544
f4v option, Adobe Media Encoder Export Settings dialog box, 543
face attribute, 586
Fade In a Movie Clip snippet, Flash, 269
Family drop-down menu, Flash, 335
Family property, Flash Properties panel, 332
FastForward folder, 714
FastForward movie clip, Flash, 714
FFTMode parameter, ActionScript computeSpectrum( ) method, 312
Figurine clip, 100
Figurine.jpg image, 503
Figurines image, 135
FigurineSmall.jpg file, 502
FigurinesNoTrans file, 135
File path area, Adobe Media Encoder Import Video wizard, 546
files
    F4V, creating, 542–544
    paths of, 551–552
Fill color chip, 78, 80, 115, 338
Fill color, Flash Properties panel, 338
Fill Color option, Flash Tools panel, 48
Fill property, Flash Properties panel, 346
fills, shape IK and, 485
FilmTV.mov file, 575
filter effects, tweening, 413–414
Filter layer, Flash, 203, 204
Filter.fla file, 175
filtering E4X, 656–657
filters
    applying, 174–177
    facts regarding, 179
    perspective, 177–179
Filters area
    Flash Motion Editor panel, 21, 23
    Flash Properties panel, 177, 179, 596
    Symbol Editor Properties panel, 594
Filters drop-down menu, Flash Properties panel, 176
Filters properties, Flash Properties panel, 394
Filters strip
    Flash Motion Editor panel, 23
    Flash Properties panel, 50

INDEX

Filters twirlie, Flash Properties panel, 175, 176
Find button, Flash Script pane, 217
Finish button
    Adobe Media Encoder Import Video wizard, 549
    Flash Import Vider wizard, 580
Finish Video Import dialog box, Flash, 308
Finish Video Import page
    Adobe Media Encoder Import Video wizard, 549
    Flash Import Video dialog box, 307
    Flash Import Vider wizard, 580
Fir layer, 106
Fire Animation Deco brush, 110
Fire Animation option, 109
Fire layer, 108, 109
Fireworks CS5, 137–139, 516–517
Fireworks import dialog box, 139
Fireworks Objects folder, 140, 513
Fireworks PNG Import Settings dialog box, 139
Fireworks, rapid prototyping for Rich Internet Applications, 774–775
First field, Flash Properties panel, 156, 403, 407
First input field, Flash Properties panel, 403
fl_NS_2.play method, ActionScript, 560
.fla file extension, 64
.fla format, 62
Flag layer, XML, 666
Flash (.swf) file format, 793
Flash alignment options, 803
Flash Color Set file, 117
Flash CS4 Document (*.fla) option, 63
Flash CS5 Document (*.fla) option, 63
Flash CS5, playing FLV in. *See also* full-screen video
    ActionScript, 555–560
    alpha channel video, 572–574
    cue points, 562–566
    FLVPlayback component, 552–555, 560–561
    FLVPlaybackCaptioning component, 567–571
    snippets, 559–560
    using wizard, 546–552
Flash CS5 Uncompressed Document (*xfl) option, 63
Flash documentation, 218
Flash Help menu option, Flash, 40, 258
Flash keyframes, 143
Flash movie
    adding audio, 59

animated fly project, 55–57
creating illusion of depth, 48–53
drawing fly, 47
nesting movie clips, 45
overview, 42–46
testing and saving, 61–65
Flash Only: Allow Full Screen HTML template, 598
Flash Only-Allow Full Screen option, Flash Publish Settings dialog box, 576
Flash option, Flash Publish Settings dialog box, 575
Flash Player dialog box, 597
Flash settings, publishing Flash movies, 794–799
Flash tab
    Adobe AIR, 752
    Flash Publish Options dialog box, 169
Flash Video (FLV). *See* FLV
<flashbooks> tag, XML, 646, 651
flashBooks.xml file, 649, 656
flashx.textLayout.elements.Configuration class, ActionScript, 342
fl.containers package, ActionScript, 614
fl.controls package, ActionScript, 614
Fleischer, Max, 588
Flick, Chris, 176
FliesBuzzing.mp3 file, 44, 59
fl.ik package, ActionScript, 473
"fl.motion.*" parameter, ActionScript, 661
flow, container and, 337–338
Flow icon, Flash, 338, 339
flutter by (motion guide) layer, Flash, 453
flutter by layer, 408, 454
FLV (Flash Video)
    encoding, 532–544. *See also* Adobe Media Encoder
    playing in Flash CS5. *See also* full-screen video
        ActionScript, 555–560
        alpha channel video, 572–574
        cue points, 562–566
        FLVPlayback component, 552–555, 560–561
        FLVPlaybackCaptioning component, 567–571
        snippets, 559–560
        using wizard, 546–552
FLV radio button, Adobe Media Encoder Export Settings window, 535
<FLVCoreCuePoints> tag, XML, 585

INDEX

FLVPlayback component, 552–555, 560–561
FLVPlaybackCaptioning component, adding captions with, 567–571
flvPlaybackname parameter, Flash Properties panel, 570
Fly layer, Flash, 56, 57, 58
Fly movie clip, Flash, 48, 56, 57, 58
Fly symbol, Flash, 47
FogMask layer, Flash, 206
Folder 1 folder, 40
Folder field, Flash Convert to Symbol dialog box, 154
Folder icon, Flash Layers panel, 40
Folder layer mode, Flash, 33
Font drop-down list, Flash, 332
Font Embedding dialog box, Flash, 325, 326, 327, 690, 691
font smoothing, 320
Font Symbol Properties dialog box, Flash, 690
<font> tag, HTML, 586, 674
fontFamily property, 671, 691
Font.fontName property, ActionScript, 692
fonts
    device, 322–323
    embedded, 690–692
    embedding, 324–327
    and typefaces, 316–318
fontSize property, 671, 679
fontStyle property, 671
fontWeight property, 671, 687
for constant bitrate (CBR), 537
for each..in statement, ActionScript, 657
for variable bitrate (VBR), 537
for..in statement, ActionScript, 657
Format drop-down menu
    Adobe Media Encoder, 533
    Flash, 63, 663
Format tab, Adobe Media Encoder Export Settings window, 535, 543, 573
formats
    audio
        bit depth, 281–283
        MP3, 283–284
        sample rates, 281–283
    video, 530–532
    XML, 584–587
fps (frames per second), 16, 537
Frame input field, Flash, 455
Frame menu item, Flash, 410
Frame movie clip, 164

Frame option, Flash Properties panel, 455
Frame Rate area, Adobe Media Encoder Export Settings window, 537
frame rate, Flash, 11, 16
Frame Rate indicator, Flash Timeline panel, 396
Frame Rate value, Adobe Media Encoder Export Settings dialog box, 544
frames, 5, 16–18
Frames button, Flash Edit Envelope dialog box, 294
frames per second (fps), 16, 537
Free Transform tool, Flash, 75–77, 165, 178, 365, 382, 410, 452, 477
FreeTransform.fla file, 75
FrogLoop.fla file, 292
FrogPan.fla file, 293
Front movie clip, Flash, 49, 51
FrontGarden layer, Flash, 49, 53, 59
Frutiger, Adrian, 324
Full Screen button
    Browser, 576, 578
    Dreamweaver, 579
FULL_SCREEN constant, ActionScript, 234
FullScreen folder, 574, 578
full-screen video
    ActionScript/HTML, 574–576
    Dreamweaver CS5, 578–579
    HD, 597–598
fullScreenRect.fla file, 598
fullScreenRect.html page, 598
FullScreenSkin.fla file, 575
Function class, ActionScript, 239
FutureSplash tool, 68

G

GameGraphics folder, 746
games, package as Android AIR apps, 750–756
Garden folder, 64
Garden layer, Flash, 34, 35, 37
Garden.fla file, 43, 49, 63
Garden.xfl file, 64
Gaussian Blur filter, Flash, 181
General category, Flash Preferences dialog box, 31
General option, Flash Preferences dialog box, 9
Generate size report option, 796
Georgenes, Chris, 404, 407, 408
ghost handle movie clip, Flash, 467, 468
ghost handle symbol, Flash, 467

INDEX

GIF (Graphic Interchange Format)
   animated
      exporting, 787–789
      importing, 790
      overview, 786
   animations, 136
   images, 135
   overview, 134
Glow effect, Flash, 220
Glow filter, Flash, 175, 413
goFullScreen function, ActionScript, 598
gotoAndPlay method, ActionScript, 229, 747
Grabber Hand tool, Flash, 71
Gradient Bevel filter, Flash, 175
Gradient Glow filter, Flash, 175, 204
Gradient Transform tool, 72, 77–80, 119, 121, 122, 377, 378
gradientHalf symbol, Flash, 697, 698
gradients, altering, 377–378
Graph Size hot text, Flash, 436
Graph Size value, Flash, 22
Graphic Interchange Format. *See* GIF
graphics
   bitmap images
      GIF files, 134–136
      importing Fireworks CS5 documents, 137–139
      importing Illustrator CS5 documents, 140–145
      importing Photoshop CS5 documents, 146–150
      JPEG files, 131–132
      overview, 123–125
      tracing, 127–130
   campfire example
      campfire movie, 108
      pine needles, 107
      pine tree, 106
      tree trunk, 104
   color
      Color palette, 112–114
      Color Picker, 112–114
      creating persistent custom colors, 115–117
      kuler color picker, 117–118
      overview, 110–111
   drawing
      Brush tool, 85–88
      Deco tool, 88–97
      Eraser tool, 101
      overview, 83–84

Pen tool, 102–104
Pencil tool, 83–84
Spray Brush tool, 98–100
   overview, 67–69
   symbols
      as mini-libraries, 406–407
      nesting, 404–406
      swapping, 401–402
      timelines, movie clip timelines versus, 402–404
   Tools panel
      Free Transform tool, 75–77
      Gradient Transform tool, 77–80
      Object Drawing mode, 80–82
      overview, 70–71
      Selection tool, 72–75
      Subselection tool, 72–75
graphs, easing with
   applying multiple eases, 444–445
   built-in eases, 438–443
   custom eases, 444
   overview, 437
Grden, John, 497
Green layer, Flash, 451, 452
Green, Tom, 579, 756
greensock-as3.zip file, 272
Grid area, Flash Custom Ease In/Ease Out dialog box, 388
Grid dialog box, Flash, 187, 188
Grid Fill option, 91, 95
Grid Fill properties, Deco tool, 90
Grid panel, Flash, 188
Grid Translation option, 93, 94
grotto movie clip icon, Flash, 406
grotto symbol, Flash, 406
grotto timeline, Flash, 406
Grotto.fla file, 404
groupName parameter, RadioButton component, 631
Guide context menu item, Flash, 408, 411, 453
Guide dialog box, Flash, 188
Guide layer mode, Flash, 34
guide mask layer, Flash, 413
Guide:Fly layer, Flash, 57, 58, 59
Guides dialog box, Flash, 188
guinness movie clip, Flash, 223, 224
Guinness symbol, 223
Guinness.jpg image, 223
Gutter Width field, Flash Properties panel, 338

INDEX

H

H (Height) property, Flash Properties panel, 454
hand symbol, Flash, 459, 476
handle symbol, Flash, 488, 492
Hanna, William, 302, 529
Hard Light blend mode, Flash, 180
Hardware Acceleration option, 798
Hauwert, Ralph, 497
HD (high-definition) video, 597–598
Head layer, 142
Head3 graphic symbol, Flash, 402
Head4 graphic symbol, Flash, 401, 402
Height (H) property, Flash Properties panel, 454
height attribute, 586
Height property, Flash Transform panel, 452
Height value, Symbol Editor Properties panel, 594
Help button
    Flash Actions panel, 258
    Flash Script pane, 218
Help feature, 40–42, 258
Help menu
    ActionScript, 175, 612
    Flash, 40, 258
Help panel, Flash, 40, 41, 243, 257
Henry, Kristin, 252
hertz, audio, 283
Hex edit box, 112
hexadecimal model, Flash, 111
Hide Object option, Flash, 178
high-definition (HD) video, 597–598
Highlight color list, Flash, 10
Highlight Color property, Flash Properties panel, 332
hit area layer, Flash, 715, 716
Hit frame
    button component, 603
    Flash, 715
hitTestPoint( ) method, ActionScript, 746
Hogue, David, 517, 772, 775
HornyToads class, 692, 693
HornyToadsItalic class, 692
Hosea, Birgitta, 529, 571
Household Door Wood Door Squeak 01.mp3 file, 519
:hover pseudo-class, Flash, 689
:hover tag, Flash, 688
href attribute
    Flash, 688
    HTML, 586
HSB model, Flash, 110

hspace attribute, 587
HTML (HyperText Markup Language)
    full-screen video, 574–576
    settings, publishing Flash movies, 799–803
    SWFs and, 783
    tags, 586–587
    web formats, 785–786
HTML option, Flash Publish Settings dialog box, 575
HTML tab, Flash Publish Settings dialog box, 550, 576, 799
hyperlinks
    styling, 688–690
    and TLF, 349–352
HyperText Markup Language. *See* HTML

I

<i> tag
    HTML, 587, 683
    XML, 585
Icons tab, Adobe AIR, 754
id attribute, 586
Identifier field, Flash Sound Properties dialog box, 299
if ( ) statement, ActionScript, 700
IFlowComposer( ) class, ActionScript, 341
IglooVillage.psd document, 146
IK (inverse kinematics)
    Bone tool
        constraining joint rotation, 465–468
        deleting bones, 468
        overview, 459–461
        properties, 462–465
    overview, 458
    Spring option for bones
        animating IK poses, 478–479
        applying joint translation, 470–475
        Bind tool, 480–487
        overview, 468–469
        preferences, 475–477
IK Bone symbol, Flash Properties panel, 472
IK Bone tool check box, Flash Preferences dialog box, 477
IK Bone tool: Flash Preferences dialog box, 475
IK Bone tool preference setting, Flash, 477
IK chain, 459
IK Node symbol, Flash Properties panel, 472
IK_Poses.fla file, 478
IKArmature class, ActionScript, 474

INDEX

IKBone class, ActionScript, 474
IKJoint class, ActionScript, 474
IKManager class, ActionScript, 474
IKMover class, ActionScript, 473, 474
Illustrator CS5 documents, importing, 140–145
Image layer, Flash, 305, 306, 517
imageData array, ActionScript, 707, 708, 710, 711
imageData variable, ActionScript, 706
imageData[pict] array, ActionScript, 707
ImageFill.fla file, 122
Images and Sounds settings, Flash Publish Settings panel, 287, 288, 795
Images layer, Flash, 267
IMG_0098.jpg symbol, Flash, 697
<img> tag
   HTML, 586
   XML, 647
Impact class, ActionScript, 692
Import ActionScript Cue Points button, Dreamweaver Properties panel, 592
Import as a single flattened bitmap option, Fireworks import dialog box, 139
Import Bitmap dialog box, 133
Import button
   Bitmap Properties dialog box, 133
   Flash, 286, 400
Import dialog box, Flash, 125, 142, 143, 145, 306, 581
Import option, Fireworks import dialog box, 139
Import to Library button, Flash, 44
Import to Library dialog box, 122
Import to Library menu option, Flash, 44
Import to Stage menu item, Flash, 490, 581
Import to Stage option, Flash, 284
Import unused symbols option, 143
Import Video dialog box, Flash, 306, 307
Import Video feature, Flash CS5, 308
Import Video menu option
   Adobe Media Encoder, 546
   Flash, 306
Import Video wizard
   Adobe Media Encoder, 546
   Flash, 579, 581
Imported JPEG Data check box, 133
importing
   animated GIFs, 790
   audio, 284
   Fireworks CS5 documents, 137–139
   Illustrator CS5 documents, 140–145
   Photoshop CS5 documents, 146–150

In point, Adobe Media Encoder, 534, 535
Include audio check box, Flash Import Vider wizard, 580
Include hidden layers option, 796
Include XMP metadata option, 796
Indent option, Flash Paragraph properties, 337
indent parameter, 587
inheritance, 682, 686–688
Inheritance.fla file, 686
init( ) function, ActionScript, 745
Ink Bottle tool, Flash, 71
Ink mode, Pencil tool, 84
inline elements, styling, 683–684
Inner shadow option, Flash, 179
<inner> tag, Flash, 687
Input Text type, Flash, 242
Insert a Target Path button, Flash Script pane, 217
Insert Frame context menu item, Flash, 478, 491
Insert Keyframe menu option, Flash, 17, 50, 446
Insert Pose context menu item, Flash, 478
Instance Name field, Flash Properties panel, 604
Instance3.fla file, 225
Instance4.fla file, 226
Instance.fla file, 223
InteractiveObject class, ActionScript, 222
interface
   creating new document, 5–6
   Document Preferences, 9–10
   Document Settings, 10–11
   Flash movie
      adding audio, 59
      animated fly project, 55–57
      creating illusion of depth, 48–53
      drawing fly, 47
      nesting movie clips, 45
      overview, 42–44
      testing and saving, 61–65
   layers
      adding content to, 36–37
      creating, 34
      grouping, 40
      Help feature, 40–42
      overview, 32
      properties, 33
      showing/hiding and locking, 38–39
   Library panel, 31
   managing workspace, 6–8
   overview, 2–4
   Properties panel, 23–26

INDEX

timeline
    frames, 16–18
    Motion Editor panel, 19–23
    overview, 14–15
  Tools panel, 29–31
  zooming stage, 11–13
International Standardization Organization (ISO), 531
Internet, optimizing and publishing Flash movies, 759
Internet Protocol (IP), 759
Internet Protocol suite, 759
Into option, Fireworks import dialog box, 139
Intro folder, Flash Library panel, 743
inverse kinematics. *See* IK
Invert blend mode, Flash, 180
IP (Internet Protocol), 759
IP address, 759
isNaN( ) function, ActionScript, 731, 732
ISO (International Standardization Organization), 531

J

jaggies, 319
Jeremiah, Andre, 301
Jespers, Serge, 756
jog controller, Adobe Media Encoder, 534
Joint Photographic Experts Group (JPEG), 124, 131–132
Joint: Rotation area, Flash Properties panel, 465, 466, 472, 490
joint rotation, constraining, 465–468
Joint: Rotation constraint, Flash, 466
Joint: Rotation property, Flash, 464, 467
joint translation, applying, 470–475
Joint: X and Y Translation property, Flash bones, 464
Joint: X Translation area, Flash Properties panel, 472
Jones, Tim, 493
JPEG (Joint Photographic Experts Group), 124, 131–132
JPEG quality option, 795
JPG Quality slider, 131
JPGCompression2.fla file, 132
JPGCompression.fla file, 131
JPGCompression.swf file, 132

K

kaboom.mp3 file, 289, 291, 296, 300
Kelly, Barry, 493
kerning property, 333, 671
Key frame interval area, Adobe Media Encoder Export Settings window, 537
Key frame placement selection, Adobe Media Encoder Export Settings window, 537
keyboard, using to control motion, 419–421
KeyboardControl.fla file, 419
Keyframe menu item, Flash, 363, 385
keyframes, Flash, 17, 143
keywords, ActionScript, 234
kilohertz, audio, 283
Knip, Tim, 497
knob layer, Flash, 717, 718
Kricfalusi, John, 424
kuler color picker, 117–118
Kuler panel, 118
kumimoji, 333

L

Label component, 624
label parameters
  Flash Button components, 608
  Flash ComboBox component, 621
label property
  ActionScript, 708
  Flash CheckBox component, 616
  Flash ComboBox component, 637
  Flash TileList component, 637
LabelButton.icon style
  ActionScript, 615
  Flash, 612
labelPlacement property, Flash CheckBox component, 616
Lasso tool, Flash, 70, 71
Layer 1 layer, Flash, 35, 36, 45, 191, 223, 239, 242, 248, 253, 254
Layer 2 layer, Flash, 35
Layer 3 layer, Flash, 35
Layer 7 folder, Flash, 714
Layer blend mode, Flash, 180
Layer context menu, Flash, 195
Layer height drop-down menu, Flash, 289
Layer Properties dialog box, Flash, 39, 289
Layer Visibility icon, Flash, 38, 39
Layer1 layer, Flash, 35

INDEX

layers
    adding content to, 36–37
    creating, 34
    grouping, 40
    Help feature, 40–42
    overview, 32
    properties, 33
    showing/hiding and locking, 38–39
Layers panel, Flash, 40
Layers.fla document, 34
LCD (liquid crystal display), 320
leading parameter, 587
Leading property
    ActionScript, 671, 679
    Flash Properties panel, 332, 358
Leaf layer, Flash, 16, 17, 19
Leaf.fla file, 16
Learn area, 4
Left Align button, Flash Align panel, 193
leftmargin parameter, 587
Leftwing layer, Flash, 45, 410
length( ) method, ActionScript, 652
Length property, Flash bones, 464
letter spacing option, Flash Paragraph properties, 333, 337
letterSpacing property, 672
<li> elements, Flash, 692
<li> SWF tag, 684
<li> tag
    Flash, 694
    HTML, 587, 674, 681, 682
Library assets, Flash, renaming, 713–714
Library drop-down menu
    Flash, 172, 555
    Symbol Editor, 594
LIBRARY folder, 663, 664, 666
Library icon, Flash, 31
Library menu option, Flash, 43
Library panel, 31, 122, 160, 763
Library Preview pane, 117
Library root link, Flash Convert to Symbol dialog box, 154
Library tab, Flash, 31
LibrarySound.fla file, 300
Ligature options, Flash Advanced character properties, 336
Ligatures drop-down menu, Flash, 335
Ligatures setting, Flash Advanced character properties, 335
Lighten blend mode, Flash, 180, 183

Line Numbers context menu option, Flash Actions panel, 219
Line tool, Flash, 106, 500
Link and Target areas, Flash Properties panel, 340
Link field, Flash Advanced character properties, 334
Link icon, Flash Properties panel, 338
Link property, Flash Advanced Character options, 349
Link setting
    Flash Advanced character properties, 334
    Flash Properties panel, 586
:link tag, Flash, 688
Linkage area
    Flash Advanced properties panel, 298
    Flash Font Embedding dialog box, 327
    Flash Symbol Properties dialog box, 171, 609
Linkage check boxes, Flash Convert to Symbol dialog box, 154
linkage class, ActionScript, 615
Linkage Properties dialog box, Flash, 171, 300
linked files, publishing Flash movies containing, 805–806
linkHoverFormat property, ActionScript TextFormat class, 347
Lip Synch menu item, Flash, 406
liquid crystal display (LCD), 320
List component, 619, 624–626, 638
List element, Flash, 619
liveDragging parameter, Flash Slider component, 634
Load Cue Points File dialog box, Adobe Media Encoder, 589
Load external video with playback component radio button, 546
load( ) method, ActionScript, 302
Loader class, ActionScript, 639, 677
loader layer, Flash, 704
loader variable, ActionScript, 677
loaderAnim movie clip, Flash, 697, 698
Loader.load( ) method, ActionScript, 707
loading XML files, 648–649
LoadingDisplay movie clip, Flash, 717
LoadingDisplay symbol
    ActionScript, 734
    Flash, 717, 719, 725
loadSong( ) function, ActionScript, 723, 724, 725, 728, 737
LoadXML-E4XBonusRound.fla file, 657

LoadXML.fla file, 648, 650
Local area, Flash Help panel, 40
Local playback security drop-down menu, 797
Locale setting, Flash Advanced character properties, 336
Location area, Device Central, 738
Lock Fill option, Brush tool, 87
Lock icon, Flash, 38, 196, 339
Log button, Flash Properties panel, 24
Log symbol, 105
LogoMorph.fla file, 377
LogoMorphNoHints.fla file, 373
Logs layer, 108, 109
loneliestNumber value, ActionScript, 240
Loop drop-down option, Flash, 455
Loop option
    Flash Properties panel, 407, 455
    HTML tab, Publish Settings dialog box, 801
Looping area, Flash Properties panel, 156, 292, 403, 455
Looping parameter, Flash Properties panel, 407
Looping properties, Flash, 404
looping timeline, 265
LoopTimeline.fla file, 265
looseChange variable, ActionScript, 246
Luminance slider, 113

M

Macintosh Projector file format, 793
Magnification drop-down menu, Flash, 12
Magnify.fla file, 13
Magnifying Glass tool, Flash, 47, 198, 478
MainArm symbol, Flash, 478
maintainAspectRatio parameter, Flash UILoader component, 639
maintainAspectRatio value, Flash Properties panel, 553
mallet movie clip, Flash, 746
MalletNoEasing.fla file, 384
MalletNormalEase.fla file, 387
mallet.x property, 747, 749
mallet.y property, 747, 749
Manage Workspaces menu option, Flash, 8
Mao symbol, Flash Library panel, 156
marginLeft property, 672
marginRight property, 672
Margins option
    Flash Paragraph properties, 336
    Flash Properties panel, 356

<markup> tag, XML, 666
Mascot layer, Flash, 457
Mascot symbol, Flash, 433
Mascot.ai file, 141, 142, 145
Mascot.ai.Assets folder, 145
MascotCustomEasing.fla file, 444
MascotMultipleEasing.fla file, 444
Mask context menu item, Flash, 195, 199, 412, 413
Mask layer, Flash, 33, 195, 196, 412, 718
Mask movie clip, Flash, 198, 199
Masked (or Mask) layer option, Flash, 196
Masked layer mode, Flash, 33
masks
    animating, 411–412
    simple, 194–199
    using motion guides with, 412–413
    using text as, 201–203
MaskTweenk.fla file, 413
MaskTweenMotionGuide.fla file, 413
Match area, Flash Document Settings dialog box, 10
Match source dimensions check box
    Flash Content Path dialog box, 555
    Flash Properties panel, 570
Math.round( ) method, ActionScript, 232, 423
Max hot text, Flash Properties panel, 466
Max property, Flash bones, 464
Max value, Flash Properties panel, 473
maximum parameter, Flash Slider component, 634
McCreedy, Shauna, 301
mercury movie clip, Flash, 628
Merge Layers button, 147
META-INF folder, 663
methods, 221, 226–229
<mid> tag, Flash, 687
MiddleGarden layer, Flash, 49, 54
Milbourne, Paul, 313
Min hot text, Flash Properties panel, 466
Min property, Flash bones, 464
Min value, Flash Properties panel, 473
MinimaFlatCustomColorPlayBackSeek.Counter Volume.swf file, 549
Minimize panels option, Flash, 7
Minimum area setting, 128
mobile devices
    Device Central, 737–750
    package games as Android AIR apps, 750–756
Modification grouping, Flash, 70, 71

INDEX

Modify a Document option, Flash Library panel, 306
Modify Onion Markers button, Flash Timeline panel, 396, 398
Modify Onion Markers menu, Flash Timeline panel, 398, 399
More Font Info button, Flash Font Embedding dialog box, 327
motion, copying
    as ActionScript, 416–419
    as XML command, 659
Motion Editor panel
    animating with, 428–430
    easing with graphs
        applying multiple eases, 444–445
        built-in eases, 438–443
        custom eases, 444
        overview, 437
    moving, 430–437
    overview, 19–23
    scaling, 430–437
motion guides
    overview, 408–411
    using with masks, 412–413
motion paths
    advanced, 453–454
    manipulating, 450–454
    properties, 454–455
motion presets, 455–458
Motion Presets panel
    Device Central, 741
    Flash, 455, 456, 457, 458
Motion Presets tab, Flash toolbar, 455
Motion Tween menu item, Flash, 431
motion tweens, 18, 430
<Motion> element, XML, 659
MotionGuide.fla file, 408
MotionGuideSimple.fla file, 451
MotionPreset.fla file, 455
MOUSE_MOVE handler, ActionScript, 733
MOUSE_UP event, ActionScript, 731
MouseEvent class, ActionScript, 609, 736
MouseEvent parameter, ActionScript, 735
MouseEvent.CLICK event, ActionScript, 231, 234, 301, 305, 607, 609, 708, 736
MouseEvent.MOUSE_DOWN event, ActionScript, 250, 607, 729
MouseEvent.MOUSE_MOVE event, ActionScript, 250
MouseEvent.MOUSE_OUT event, ActionScript, 231
MouseEvent.MOUSE_OVER event, ActionScript, 231
MouseEvent.MOUSE_UP event, ActionScript, 250, 607, 730, 733
Mouse.hide( ) function, ActionScript, 745, 749
mouseMoveHandler( ) function, ActionScript, 250
mouseOutHandler function, ActionScript, 231
mouseOverHandler function, ActionScript, 231, 232
mouseUpHandler( ) function, ActionScript, 301
mouth symbol, Flash, 405, 406, 407
Move to folder dialog box, Flash, 154
Move with Keyboard Arrows option, Animation folder, 420
moveAmount variable, ActionScript, 423
moveTo( ) method, ActionScript, 313
movie clip icon, 148
Movie Clip option, Flash Create New Symbol dialog box, 45
movie clips
    embedding video as, 581
    timelines, graphic symbol timelines versus, 402–404
MovieClip class, ActionScript, 221, 224, 225, 226, 234, 238, 239, 556, 629
MovieClip method, ActionScript, 227, 238
MovieClip properties, ActionScript, 225, 227
MovieClip.alpha property, ActionScript, 250
MovieClip.buttonMode properties, 608, 726
MovieClip.currentFrame property, ActionScript, 233
MovieClip.gotoAndPlay( ) method, ActionScript, 229
MovieClip.height property, ActionScript, 628
MovieClipLoader class, ActionScript, 226
MovieClip.mouseX property, ActionScript, 225
Movieclip.parent property, ActionScript, 238, 658
MovieClip.play( ) method, ActionScript, 263, 629, 725
MovieClip.rotation property, ActionScript, 474
MovieClips folder, Flash, 43, 45, 47, 48, 49
MovieClip.startDrag( ) method, ActionScript, 250, 607, 730
MovieClip.stop( ) method, ActionScript, 229, 230, 238, 263, 629
MovieClip.stopDrag( ) function, ActionScript, 730
MovieClip.totalFrames property, ActionScript, 225
MovieClip.x property, ActionScript, 224, 729
MovieClip.x value, ActionScript, 731

MovieClip.y property, ActionScript, 224
Moving Pictures Expert Group (MPEG), 530, 531
MP3 compression option, Flash Sound Properties dialog box, 286
MP3 players
   with Flash, 283–284
   with XML. *See also* controls, MP3 players with XML
      evaluating and improving, 735–737
      overview, 711
      renaming Library assets, 713–714
      setting up external playlists, 712–713
MPEG (Moving Pictures Expert Group), 530, 531
Multiply blend mode, Flash, 180, 182, 183
muteSound( ) function, ActionScript, 305
My Devices folder, 740
myFirstSet.clr file, 117

N

Name area
   Adobe Media Encoder Export Settings window, 588
   Bitmap Properties dialog box, 132
   Flash Convert to Symbol dialog box, 153
   Flash Create New Symbol dialog box, 45
Name drop-down menu, Flash Properties panel, 291
name qualifier operator (::), ActionScript, 660
<Name> tag, XML, 585
Namespace class, ActionScript, 660
namespaces, 659–661
Napierski, Steve, 487
nav layer, Flash, 704
Navigate button, Adobe Media Encoder Export Settings window, 589
Needles layer, 107
nesting
   graphic symbols, 404–406
   movie clips, 45
NetConnection class, ActionScript, 557
NetStream class, ActionScript, 557
NetStream.play( ) method, ActionScript, 558
New Document dialog box, Flash, 422
New Document panel, Device Central, 738, 741
New Folder icon, Flash Library panel, 43
New folder radio button, Flash Move to folder dialog box, 154

New from Template dialog box, 3
New Layer button, Flash, 35, 56
New Symbol button, Flash Library panel, 45, 47
New Symbol dialog box, 104
New Symbol menu option, Flash, 47
New Video, Flash Library panel, 555
New Workspace menu option, Flash, 8
Next button
   ActionScript, 723, 727, 736
   Adobe Media Encoder Import Video wizard, 547
   Flash, 726
Next symbol, Flash, 716
nextFrame( ) method, ActionScript, 745
nextHandler( ) function, ActionScript, 728, 729, 736
node types, 654–655
NONE constant, ActionScript, 347
Normal blend mode, Flash, 180, 182, 183
NORMAL constant, ActionScript, 234
Normal layer mode, Flash, 33, 196
NoSpring layer, Flash, 469
ns variable, ActionScript, 660
Number( ) function, ActionScript, 243
Number of Sides field, Flash Tool Settings dialog box, 346
Numeric column, Flash DataGrid component, 623
NumericStepper component, 626–628, 633
NumericStepper.fla file, 627
NuttyProfessor.fla file, 186

O

O1_Complete folder, 16
Object class, ActionScript, 673, 706
Object Drawing button
   ActionScript, 72
   Flash, 500, 501
Object Drawing mode, 80–82, 83, 87
Object Drawing option, Brush tool, 87
Object( ) statement, ActionScript, 706
Object Windows Library (OWL), 5
<object> tag, HTML, 577
ObjectDrawing.fla file, 82
objects
   classes, 221–222
   overview, 220
   properties, 222–225
Objects option, Fireworks import dialog box, 139

INDEX

OliverSeller.jpg file, 665, 666
Olives.fla file, 164, 166
Olsson, Richard, 496
O'Meara, Robert, 529
Omit trace actions option, 797
on( ) function, ActionScript, 219
On2 VP6 codec
    Adobe Media Encoder, 536, 573
    Flash, 572
onClipEvent function, ActionScript, 219
Onion All option, Flash Timeline panel, 399
Onion Skin button, Flash Timeline panel, 396, 398, 399
Onion Skin Outlines button, Flash Timeline panel, 396, 399
onion skinning, 386, 397–399
Online area, Flash Help panel, 40
Open a Recent Item category, 4
Open and close drawers option, Flash, 7
Open button, Adobe Media Encoder, 532
Open Code Snippets button, Flash Script pane, 218
Open dialog box, 126, 169, 532
Open External Library menu item, Flash, 169
Open for Testing section, Device Central, 738
Open in Device Central area, Adobe Media Encoder, 544
Open New Library buttons, Flash, 170
operators, ActionScript, 244–247
Optimize Curves dialog box, 130, 780
optimizing Flash movies
    bandwidth, 760–762
    Bandwidth Profiler
        pinpointing problem content, 769–770
        reports, 770–771
        simulating download, 765–769
    distributing weight, 776–777
    Internet, 759
    optimizing elements in movie, 778–782
    planning project, 771–777
    streaming, 763–765
    users, 762–763
    World Wide Web, 760
Options area
    ActionScript, 72
    Flash Font Embedding dialog box, 326
    Flash Properties panel, 156, 473
    Flash Tools panel, 29
Options button
    Flash Code Snippets panel, 310
    Flash Properties panel, 248

Flash Snippets panel, 269
Flash Tool Settings, 346
Options drop-down menu, Flash Properties panel, 403
Options grouping, Flash, 70, 71
Options twirlie, Flash Properties panel, 462
Orient to path check box, Flash Properties panel, 382, 409, 454
Orient to path option, Flash Properties panel, 454
Out point, Adobe Media Encoder, 534, 535
<outer> tag, Flash, 687
Outline format area, Flash Font Embedding dialog box, 327
Outline method, Flash Font Embedding dialog box, 327
Output Channels field, Adobe Media Encoder Export Settings window, 538
Output Channels option, Adobe Media Encoder Export Settings window, 573, 588
Output folder, Adobe Media Encoder, 542
Output Name field, Adobe Media Encoder Export Settings window, 535
Output pane
    Adobe Media Encoder, 539
    Flash Properties panel, 24
Output tab
    Adobe Media Encoder, 539
    Flash, 224
outPutArray parameter, ActionScript computeSpectrum( ) method, 312
Oval tool
    ActionScript, 77
    Flash, 82, 230, 248, 488
Over frame, Flash button component, 603
Over skin, Flash Button component, 619
Overlay mode, Flash, 180, 210, 583
Override sound settings, 287, 795
OWL (Object Windows Library), 5

P

<p> tag, 587, 675, 681, 687, 694
Package heading, ActionScript 3.0 Language and Components Reference, 614
packaging games, as Android AIR apps, 750–756
Padding area, Flash Properties panel, 338, 339
Padding option, Flash Properties panel, 356
pageCount attribute, XML, 656, 657

INDEX

pageCount attributes, flashBooks.xml file, 656
Pages feature, Fireworks, 517
Paint Behind modifier, 87
Paint Bucket tool, 48, 71, 78, 79, 105, 106, 107, 122, 123, 198, 206
Paint Fills modifier, 87
Paint Inside mode, 105
Paint Inside modifier, 87
Paint Normal modifier, 87
Paint Selection modifier, 87
pan, audio, 293–296
panel collapse process, Flash, 6
panel context menu, 218
panel set, Flash, 8
Panel tab, Flash, 6
Panels area, Flash, 6
Panels layer, Flash, 198, 199
panels, Selectors vs. Properties, 692–694
Paragraph properties, 336
Paragraph settings, Flash, 339, 570
parallax effect, 512–517
Parameters button, Dreamweaver, 578
Parameters dialog box, Dreamweaver, 578, 579
Parameters tab, Flash Component Inspector panel, 633, 636, 639, 640
parent( ) method, XML, 657, 658
_parent setting, Flash Advanced character properties, 334
Particle Movie Clip symbol, Flash, 422
Password option, 796
paste command, Flash, 38
Paste Frames context menu item, 177, 445, 716
Paste in Center command, Flash, 38
Paste in Place menu option, Flash, 37, 38, 177, 203, 454
Paste menu option, Flash, 354, 418
Paste Motion context menu item, Flash, 457
Paste using AI File Importer preferences choice, 144
Path, date, dimensions, Bitmap Properties dialog box, 132
Path options, Flash, 452
Pause and Loop exercise, 267
Pause button, Flash Library panel, 561
pause label, Flash Timeline panel, 724
pause( ) method, ActionScript, 559
Paused at start option, 801
Pause/Play button
    ActionScript, 724
    Flash, 726

pauseSong( ) function, ActionScript, 723, 724, 725, 726, 727
PauseTimeline.fla file, 262
pausing timeline, 261–264
PBS (Public Broadcasting Service), 512
PDF (Portable Document Format) format, 124
peaks, audio, 281
Pen tool, Flash, 102–104, 198, 206, 413, 444, 701
Pencil icon, Flash, 38
Pencil tool, Flash, 47, 57, 58, 83–84, 108
PepperShape.fla file, 369, 379
PepperSymbol.fla file, 379, 382
Permit debugging option, Publish Settings dialog box, 797
perspective, 177–179
Perspective Angle value, Flash, 510, 525
perspective layer, Flash, 500
Peters, Keith, 313, 415, 496, 654, 657, 658
Phillips, Adam, 492, 493
photo cubes, simulating, 522–525
Photo layer, XML, 665
Photoshop CS5 documents, importing, 146–150
Photoshop Drawing (PSD) format, 124
PICT format, 124
pict parameter, ActionScript, 706, 707
piston rod symbol, Flash, 471
pistonRod bone, Flash, 472
PixelDisposal.fla file, 445, 449, 450
Place instance on stage option, Flash Import Video dialog box, 307, 580
Place layers at original position option, 146
Play button
    ActionScript, 304
    Flash, 550, 562
    Flash component, 563
    Flash Edit Envelope dialog box, 294
    Flash Library panel, 284, 561
play label, Flash Timeline panel, 725
play( ) method, ActionScript, 300
Play Once option, Flash Properties panel, 455
Play Once setting, Flash Timeline panel, 403
Play symbol, Flash, 715
Playback options, 801
player background layer, Flash, 719
Player drop-down menu
    Adobe AIR, 752
    Publish Settings dialog box, 795
Player layer, Flash, 714, 717, 718, 719
playHandler( ) function, ActionScript, 726, 727
playhead, Flash, 6

INDEX

playlists, setting up external, 712–713
playlist.xml file, 713
Play/Pause button, Flash, 720
PlayPauseButton, Flash Library panel, 561, 726
playSong( ) function, ActionScript, 723, 724, 725, 726, 727, 731, 735, 736
Plocek, Mischa, 141
PNG (Portable Network Graphic) format, 124, 793
Point class, ActionScript, 473
Polystar tool, Flash, 248, 346
Poplar Tree option, 97
Portable Document Format (PDF) format, 124
Portable Network Graphic (PNG) format, 124, 793
pos variable, ActionScript, 731
Pose layers, Flash, 478, 490, 491, 492
Position and Size strip, Flash Properties panel, 46
Position area, Flash Properties panel, 28
Position context menu item, 445
Position properties
   ActionScript, 474
      Flash Properties panel, 394
      Flash text field, 331
Position X property, Flash, 464
Position Y property, Flash, 464
Powers, David, 670
PreachersAndThieves.aif file, 284
PreachersandThieves.mp3 file, 285, 290, 298
Preferences area, Flash, 8
Preferences context menu, Flash Actions panel, 234
Preferences dialog box, 9, 10, 72, 145, 475, 477
Preferences menu option, Flash, 9, 31, 475, 488
Preload setting, Bandwidth Profiler, 768
Preload value, Bandwidth Profiler, 768
preloader1.fla file, 697
preloader2.fla file, 701
preloaders, 701–703
preloading function, ActionScript, 700
Preprocessing area, Flash Sound Properties dialog box, 286
Preset area, Adobe Media Encoder, 533
Preset drop-down list, Adobe Media Encoder, 534
Prev button
   ActionScript, 723, 727
   Flash, 726
Prev symbol, Flash, 714, 716
prevHandler( ) function, ActionScript, 727

Preview area, Flash Custom Ease In/Ease Out dialog box, 388
Preview button, 128, 129
preview parameter, Flash Properties panel, 553
Preview play button, Flash, 393, 395
Primitive tool, Tools panel, 69
Primitives object, Flash, 69
procedural modeling, 89
Professor layer, Flash, 185
Professor movie clip, Flash, 185
ProgessBar component, Flash, 640
programmatic animation
   copying motion as ActionScript, 416–419
   creating random motion using ActionScript, 421–426
   overview, 415
   using keyboard to control motion, 419–421
programming sliders, 728–734
progress bar layer, Flash, 704
ProgressBar component, 628–630, 640, 704
ProgressBar.fla file, 629
ProgressBar.source property, ActionScript, 629
ProgressEvent.PROGRESS event, ActionScript, 630
prompt parameter, Flash ComboBox component, 622
Properties area, Flash, 8, 10
Properties context menu option
   Arrow movie clip, 356
   Flash, 33, 160, 164, 196, 289, 298, 400, 463, 531, 609
Properties dialog box, Flash, 160, 531
Properties inspector, Flash, 692
Properties menu item, Flash, 172
Properties panel, 5, 6, 10, 23–26, 77, 578, 592, 593, 594, 692–694
properties, setting via ActionScript
   events, 229–233
   methods, 226–229
   overview, 225
Properties tab, Flash, 51
Properties.fla file, 26, 31
Property area, Flash Custom Ease In/Ease Out dialog box, 388
Property drop-down menu, Flash Properties panel, 394
Property Inspector, Flash, 19, 692
property keyframes
   changing duration nonproportionally, 450
   changing duration proportionally, 449–450
   overview, 445–448

Property panel, Flash, 52
Protect from import option, Publish Settings dialog box, 796
prototyping, rapid for Rich Internet Applications, 774–775
PSD (Photoshop Drawing) format, 124
PSD File Importer, 146
pseudo-classes, 688
pt variable, ActionScript, 473
Public Broadcasting Service (PBS), 512
Publish area, Flash, 10, 252
Publish button
    Adobe AIR, 755
    Flash Publish Settings dialog box, 576
Publish dialog box, 132
Publish Options menu item, Flash, 169
Publish Settings dialog box, 252, 550, 575, 755, 792, 794
Publish Settings menu option, 287, 598, 752
publishing Flash movies
    bandwidth, 760–762
    containing linked files, 805–806
    Flash settings, 794–799
    formats, 793–794
    HTML settings, 799–803
    Internet, 759
    publishing butterfly garden, 803–805
    streaming, 763–765
    users, 762–763
    web formats
        animated GIFs, 786–790
        Flash, 784–785
        HTML, 785–786
        overview, 783
        QuickTime, 790–791
    World Wide Web, 760
Pukaskwa.jpg file, 305

Q

Quality drop-down menu
    Flash Blur filter parameters, 50
    Flash Sound Properties dialog box, 287
    HTML tab, Publish Settings dialog box, 802
Quality option, Bitmap Properties dialog box, 133
Quality setting, Flash Sound Properties dialog box, 286
Quality value, Adobe Media Encoder Export Settings dialog box, 544

quickTest( ) function, ActionScript, 239, 240
QuickTime, 281, 790–791

R

Rabbit movie clip, 397
Rabbit symbol, Flash, 403
rabbitAnim movie clip, Flash, 743, 746, 747
Rabbit.flv file, 546
Rabbit.mov file, 532
RabbitSwap.fla file, 401
Race movie clip, Flash, 158, 159
RadioButton class, ActionScript, 631
RadioButton component, 606, 630–632
RadioButton.fla file, 631
Radius handle control, 80
Rain layer, Flash, 305, 308
Rainfall.fla file, 581
Rain.flv file, 306, 308, 581
ramping technique, Flash, 19
randNum variable, ActionScript, 747
Random Building option, 96
Random Movement Brownian template, Flash New Document dialog box, 422
Random Rotation property, Spray Brush tool, 99
Random scaling property, Spray Brush tool, 99
randomBunnyDisplay function, ActionScript, 746
rapid prototyping, for Rich Internet Applications, 774–775
Raw compression option, Flash Sound Properties dialog box, 286
Read Only text field, Flash, 333
Readability Anti-alias option, Flash, 324, 355
Readability option, Flash Anti-alias drop-down menu, 325
Readability property, Flash Anti-alias drop-down menu, 333
Read-only text properties
    advanced character properties, 334–335
    character properties, 332–334
    overview, 331
    Paragraph properties, 336
Rear movie clip, Flash, 158
Recognize shapes menu, 85
Rectangle menu, ActionScript, 77
Rectangle tool
    ActionScript, 72
    Flash, 80, 157, 196, 248, 346, 501, 715, 716
    Tools panel, 69
Red cube symbol, Flash, 446

INDEX

Reflect Across Line option, 92, 93
Reflect Across Point option, 93
Reflect option, Gradient Overflow tool, 120
Reflection setting, Device Central Display tab, 750
Reflections drop-down, Device Central Display tab, 749
Registration field, Flash Convert to Symbol dialog box, 153
relative paths, 806
RemoteSound2.fla file, 302
RemoteSound3.fla file, 304
RemoteSound.fla file, 301
Remove Armature context menu item, Flash, 468
Remove button, Adobe Media Encoder, 541
Remove Comment button, Flash Script pane, 218
Remove Cue Point button, Adobe Media Encoder Export Settings window, 589
Remove Frames menu item, Flash, 391
Remove Transform button, Flash, 383, 505, 512
Remove Transform menu item, Flash, 381, 383
Remove Tween context menu item, Flash, 367, 432, 453
Remove Tween menu item, Flash, 368
removeEventListener( ) reference, ActionScript, 725
removing transformations, 77
renaming Library assets, 713–714
Render Queue, Adobe Media Encoder, 543
rendering videos, 540–541
Repeat drop-down list, Flash Properties panel, 292
Repeat option, Gradient Overflow tool, 120
Repeat property, Flash Properties panel, 292
req variable, ActionScript, 649, 677, 706, 707
reserved words, ActionScript, 234
Reset button, Flash Properties panel, 506, 512
Reset Essentials menu item, Flash, 8
Reset Status menu item, Adobe Media Encoder, 540, 541, 583
Reset Values button, Flash, 22
Resize handle control, 79
Resize values, Flash Transform panel, 508
Resize Video option, Adobe Media Encoder Export Settings window, 536, 588
resume( ) method, ActionScript, 559
Reverse Keyframes context menu item, 445
Revert button, Flash, 468, 477

Revert menu option, Flash, 36, 338, 468, 477
Rewind symbol, Flash, 714
Rewis, Greg, 517
RGB model, Flash, 110
RGB Sliders option, 114
Rich Internet Applications, rapid prototyping for, 774–775
Richard layer, Flash, 488, 490
Richard.fla file, 487, 492
Richardson, Darren, 313
rightmargin parameter, 587
RightWing layer, Flash, 45, 410
root element, XML, 645
root.loaderInfo reference, ActionScript, 629
Rosson, Allan, 493
Rotate [x] time(s) + [y]° property, Flash Properties panel, 454
Rotate and Skew option, Flash Tools panel, 383
Rotate area, Flash Transform panel, 386
Rotate Around option, 94
Rotate drop-down menu, Flash, 380, 454
Rotate handle control, 80
Rotate property, Flash, 381, 382
Rotate symbol property, Spray Brush tool, 99
Rotation area, Flash Transform panel, 386
rotation, classic tweening, 379–381
Rotation property
    Flash bones, 465
    Flash Properties panel, 333, 394
Rotation settings, Flash, 209, 382
Rotation tool, 501–506
Rotation Z graph, Flash Motion Editor panel, 441, 448
Rotation Z setting, Flash Motion Edior panel, 449
round-tripping feature, 126
routers, 759
rowCount parameter, Flash ComboBox component, 622
RSL (runtime shared library), 345
Rulers menu item, Flash, 188
runnerAnimation movie clip, Flash, 701
runtime shared library (RSL), 345

S

sample, audio, 281
sample rate, audio, 281
_sans font category, 322
Save As button, Flash, 64

INDEX

Save As dialog box
    Adobe Media Encoder, 535
    Flash, 63, 64, 663
Save As menu option, Flash, 63, 663
Save Colors option, 116
Save selection as preset button, Flash, 456
Save Theme button, 118
saving Flash movie, 61–65
Scale check box, Flash Properties panel, 382
Scale height property, Spray Brush tool, 99
Scale menu item, Flash, 202
Scale option, 803
Scale property, Flash Properties panel, 394
Scale setting, Flash Publish Settings dialog box, 550
Scale To Fit option, Adobe Media Encoder, 539
Scale width property, Spray Brush tool, 99
scaleContent parameter, Flash UILoader component, 639
scaleMode parameter, Flash Properties panel, 553
scaling
    classic tweening, 382–384
    Motion Editor panel, 430–437
    shape tweening, 363–368
Scene 1 link, Flash, 47, 48, 157, 160, 199, 230, 515, 611, 699, 719
scope, ActionScript, 239–240
Screen blend mode, Flash, 180
Screen Mode setting, Device Central Display tab, 750
Script Assist feature
    Flash Actions panel, 257
    Flash Script pane, 218
Script drop-down menu
    Flash Publish dialog box, 169
    Publish Settings dialog box, 795
Script navigator, 217
script navigator area, Flash Actions panel, 216
Script pane, 217
Script pane buttons, Flash, 218
Script pane, Flash Actions panel, 216, 217, 258, 311, 418
Script time limit option, Publish Settings dialog box, 798
scripts layer, Flash, 230, 239, 254, 265, 301, 473, 680, 681, 704, 705
scrollable text
    rolling scroller, 356–360
    UIScrollBar component, 355
ScrollBar component, ActionScript, 355

ScrollComponent.fla file, 355
ScrollPane component, 614, 632–633, 637
ScrollPane.fla file, 633
Scrubber button, Flash, 550
scrubbing technique, Flash, 6, 18, 21
scumSuckingPig variable, ActionScript, 241
Search and Replace feature, Dreamweaver, 592
Search button, Flash Help panel, 41
search tactics, 259–260
Seasons02.fla file, 203
Seasons.fla file, 201
second stop( ) method, ActionScript, 629
Seconds button, Flash Edit Envelope dialog box, 294
Seek control, Flash, 561
SeekBar symbol
    ActionScript, 731
    Flash, 714, 718, 719, 728, 729
seekBar.width parameter, ActionScript, 729
seekBar.width property, ActionScript, 729
seekBar.x parameter, ActionScript, 729
seekBar.x property, ActionScript, 729
SeekKnob symbol
    ActionScript, 731
    Flash, 714, 716, 717, 719, 724, 725, 728, 729
seekKnobUpdate( ) function, ActionScript, 724, 725, 732
seekKnob.y parameter, ActionScript, 729
seekStartDrag( ) function, ActionScript, 729
seekStopDrag( ) function, ActionScript, 730
seekToCuePoint function, ActionScript, 566
Select All menu item, Flash, 464, 490
Select Skin dialog box, Flash, 553
Select Swf dialog box, Dreamweaver, 578
Select Symbol dialog box, Deco tool, 90
Select Video page, Flash Import Vider wizard, 580
<select> element, HTML, 619
selectable text, 340
Selectable TLF text field, Flash, 719
selected property, Flash CheckBox component, 616
selectedColor property, Flash Properties panel, 618
selectedItems property, Flash List component, 626
Selecting grouping, Flash, 70
Selection tool, 72–75, 84, 105, 106, 491, 506, 509
Selectors panel, vs. Properties panel, 692–694

837

INDEX

_self setting, Flash Advanced character properties, 334
semicolons, ActionScript, 234
Send Backward menu item, Flash, 190, 521
Send to Back menu item, Flash, 190, 466
_serif font category, 322
Set button, Flash Publish Settings panel, 288
Set Key Frame Distance area, Adobe Media Encoder Export Settings window, 537
Set stage to same size as Photoshop canvas option, 146
setDate( ) method, ActionScript, 255
setFullYear( ) method, ActionScript, 255
setMillennium( ) method, ActionScript, 255, 256
setMilliseconds( ) method, ActionScript, 255
setStyle( ) method, ActionScript, 673, 683, 685, 690
Settings area, Bandwidth Profiler, 768
Settings button, Adobe Media Encoder, 541, 543
Settings ... option, Adobe Media Encoder, 573
shape hints, 373–377
shape IK
   anchor points and, 485–487
   fills and, 485
Shape Tween menu item, Flash, 368
shape tweening
   altering gradients, 377–378
   altering shapes
      anchor points, 371
      overview, 369–370
      shape changing, 372–373
   modifying, 368–369
   scaling, 363–368
   shape hints, 373–377
   stretching, 363–368
Shapes object, Flash, 69
SharedLibrary.fla file, 169, 170
Sharing area, Flash Convert to Symbol dialog box, 154
shiftKey property, ActionScript, 233
Shiman, Jennifer, 173
Shovelarm symbol, Flash, 478
Show All Layers As Outlines icon, Flash, 38, 39
Show Code Hint button, Flash Script pane, 218
Show collapsed panels as icons only option, Flash, 7
Show Font Info option, Font Book, 327
Show Guides menu item, Flash, 188
Show Info menu item, Flash, 530
Show Inherited Styles hyperlink, 607, 612
Show over objects option, Flash CS4, 188

Show Shape Hints menu item, Flash, 377
Show warning messages box, 803
showCaptions parameter, Flash Properties panel, 570, 571
Show/Hide Toolbox button, Flash Script pane, 218
showTextField parameter, Flash Properties panel, 618
Shroeder, Dave, 295
Sign Up link, Adobe web site, 751
Simple (Slow) ease, Flash, 22, 442, 444, 454
Simple (Slow) graph, Flash Motion Editor panel, 442
SimpleButton class, ActionScript, 612
simpleFormatting parameter, Flash Properties panel, 570
SimpleMask.fla file, 195
Simulate Download option
   Bandwidth Profiler, 767
   Flash, 629, 640, 700, 701, 703
Single Frame option
   Flash Properties panel, 455
   Flash Timeline panel, 403
Size area, Flash Properties panel, 28
size attribute, 586
Size property
   Flash Properties panel, 332
   Flash text field, 331
Skew property, Flash Transform panel, 452
Skew radio button, Flash Transform panel, 384
Skin drop-down menu, Adobe Media Encoder Import Video wizard, 547, 548, 549
skin parameter
   Flash FLVPlayback component, 575
   Flash Properties panel, 552, 553, 560, 570, 574
skinAutoHide parameter
   Flash FLVPlayback component, 575
   Flash Properties panel, 548, 553
skinBackgroundAlpha parameter, Flash Properties panel, 553
skinBackgroundColor parameter
   Flash FLVPlayback component, 575
   Flash Properties panel, 553, 554
SkinButton.fla file, 611
skinning, 610–611
Skinning page, Adobe Media Encoder Import Video wizard, 547
SkinOverAllNoCaption.swf file, 575
SkinUnderAllNoFullScreen.swf file, 591
SkinUnderAll.swf file, 548, 570

INDEX

Skip Intro button, Flash page, 214, 758
Skip status, Adobe Media Encoder, 540, 541
sky stuff layer, Flash, 248
slide shows, with components and XML, 703–711
Slider component, 633–634
Slider.fla file, 633
sliders, programming, 728–734
Slideshow.fla file, 704, 708
SlideshowXML.fla file, 709, 711
Smooth button, Tools panel, 85
Smooth mode, Pencil tool, 84, 85, 104
Smoothing button, Flash, 57
Smoothing option, 87
Smoothing slider, 130
Snap accuracy drop-down menu
    Flash Grid dialog box, 187
    Flash Guides dialog box, 188
Snap Align feature, Flash, 186, 187
Snap check box, Flash Properties panel, 382
Snap setting, Flash Properties panel, 409
Snap to Objects option, Flash, 189, 374, 489
snapInterval parameter, Flash Slider component, 634
snapping
    to grid, 187
    in guide layer, 189
    to pixels, 189
Snippet.fla file, 267
snippets, 559–560
Snippets panel, Flash, 269
Solid Color type, 115
song variable, ActionScript, 724
<song> elements, ActionScript, 711, 727, 728, 737
songData text field, ActionScript, 734
song.id3.artist property, ActionScript, 734
song.id3.songName property, ActionScript, 734
song.id3.year property, ActionScript, 734
songList variable, ActionScript, 712
songsCB combo box, ActionScript, 713
Sorenson Spark codec, Adobe Media Encoder, 536
Sound class, ActionScript, 300
sound on/off button, Flash pages, 296
Sound Properties dialog box, Flash, 59, 285, 287, 288, 298
Sound properties, Flash, 61
Sound twirlie, Flash, 61
Sound.attachSound( ) method, ActionScript, 298
SoundChannel class, ActionScript, 304

SoundChannel.position property, ActionScript, 727
SoundChannel.soundTransform property, ActionScript, 305
soundCompleteHandler( ) function, ActionScript, 725
Sound.id3 property, ActionScript, 734
Sound.load( ) method, ActionScript, 724
SoundMixer( ) class, ActionScript, 312
soundOpenHandler( ) function, ActionScript, 725
Sound.play( ) method, ActionScript, 301, 305
SoundTransform class, ActionScript, 305
SoundTransform.volume property, ActionScript, 733
Source area
    Flash Convert to Symbol dialog box, 154
    Flash Properties panel, 553
Source folder, Adobe Media Encoder, 542
Source layer, Flash, 181, 182, 183, 184
Source pane, Adobe Media Encoder, 539
source parameter
    Flash Component Inspector panel, 633
    Flash FLVPlayback component, 575
    Flash ProgressBar component, 640
    Flash Properties panel, 554, 560, 570, 571, 574, 591
    Flash UILoader component, 639
source property, Flash TileList component, 637
source row, Flash Component Inspector panel, 633, 639
<Source> element, XML, 659, 660, 661
Space options, Flash Align panel, 193
SpaceComposition movie clip, Fireworks Objects folder, 513
SpaceFinal.png image, 513
Space.fla file, 513
Spacing option, Flash Paragraph properties, 337
<span> tag
    Flash, 687, 688
    HTML, 587
Speech compression option, Flash Sound Properties dialog box, 286
speed data, Bezier curve, 102
Speed property, Flash bones, 464
Spelling Setup dialog box, Flash, 352, 353
SpellItOut.txt file, 354
spin( ) function, ActionScript, 474
spiral-3D preset, Device Central Motion Presets panel, 741
Spray Brush tool, 98–100, 108
SprayBrush.fla file, 98

INDEX

Spring ease, Flash, 445
Spring option
    animating IK poses, 478–479
    applying joint translation, 470–475
    Bind tool, 480–487
    overview, 468–469
    preferences, 475–477
Spring property, Flash bones, 464, 465
Springs.fla file, 468
Sprite class, ActionScript, 226, 252
Square layer, Flash, 196
src attribute, 586
stacking order, 189–193
Stacks.fla file, 189
stage area, Flash, 5
stage color (Stage) property, Flash, 11
StageDisplayState class, ActionScript, 234
stamp layer, Flash, 521
star asset, Flash, 615
Star layer, Flash, 345, 346
star movie clip, Flash, 248, 346
StarCircle.fla file, 371
Start button
    ActionScript, 302, 303
    Device Central, 750
    Flash, 745
Start page, 2, 3, 4, 5, 738
Start Queue button, Adobe Media Encoder, 540, 542, 544, 574, 591
startDrag( ) method, ActionScript, 733
StartingOut cue point, Flash, 563
StartScreen layer, Flash, 743
Static Text option, Flash Properties panel, 321
Status area, Adobe Media Encoder, 540, 541
SteamEngine.fla file, 470
Stiller, David, 214, 424, 679
Stop and Start (Medium) ease, Flash, 444, 445
Stop at this Frame snippet, Flash, 268
Stop button
    ActionScript, 302, 303, 304
    Flash Edit Envelope dialog box, 294
    Flash Sound Properties dialog box, 286
Stop keyframe, Flash, 291, 292
stop( ) method, ActionScript, 266, 304, 629, 664
Stop Queue button, Adobe Media Encoder, 540
Stories.f4v file, 570
str variable, ActionScript, 626
Straighten mode, Pencil tool, 84
Stream mode, Flash audio, 289
Stream option, Flash Sync drop-down menu, 61
Stream setting, Bandwidth Profiler, 770
Stream syncing, Flash Sound properties, 61
streaming, 763–765
Strength property, Flash bones, 464, 468
Strength value, Flash bones, 468
stretchFactor parameter, ActionScript computeSpectrum( ) method, 312
stretching
    classic tweening, 382–384
    shape tweening, 363–368
Strikethrough property, Flash Properties panel, 333
String data type, ActionScript, 243
Stroke color area, Flash Tools panel, 47
Stroke color chip, 107, 338
Stroke color, Flash Properties panel, 338
Stroke panel, ActionScript, 77
Stroke property, Flash Properties panel, 346
Stroke Style dialog box, 107
strong element selector, Flash, 691
strong selector, ActionScript, 679
<strong> tag
    Flash, 685, 692
    HTML, 586
Style drop-down menu, Flash, 248, 332, 339, 340, 346, 462, 511, 519, 692
Style property, Flash Properties panel, 332
style variable, ActionScript, 673
StyleComponents.fla file, 613
StyleManager class, ActionScript, 614
StyleManager.setComponentStyle( ) method, ActionScript, 614, 615
StyleManager.setStyle( ) method, 614, 615
Styles heading, ActionScript 3.0 Language and Components Reference, 612
styles.css file, 677, 679
StyleSheet class, ActionScript, 673
StyleSheet.parseCSS( ) method, ActionScript, 677
StyleSheet.setStyle( ) method, 673
styling
    block elements, 680–682
    components, 612–615
    with CSS, 671–676
    hyperlinks, 688–690
    inheritance, 686–688
    inline elements, 683–684
Styling01.fla file, 672, 684
Styling02.fla file, 675
Styling03.fla file, 684
Styling04.fla file, 685
StylingEmbeddedFonts01.fla file, 690

INDEX

StylingEmbeddedFonts02.fla file, 692
StylingEmbeddedFonts03.fla file, 693
StylingExternal.fla file, 676
StylingExternal.swf file, 679
subpixels, 320
Subscript property, Flash Properties panel, 333
Subselection tool, 72–75, 87, 104, 370, 372, 456, 482
Subtract blend mode, Flash, 180, 210
SupermanNoCuePoints.flv file, 592
Superman.xml file, 592
Superscript property, Flash Properties panel, 333
svg folder, 89
Swap button, Flash, 407
Swap Symbol dialog box, Flash, 401
swapping graphic symbols, 401–402
Swatches panel, 116, 117, 118
SWF History area, 24, 25, 771
SWF Settings section, 796
swingDoors.fla file, 519
Switch To Output toggle button, Adobe Media Encoder, 539
.swz file, 345
Symbol Editor, Flash, 45, 156, 158, 160, 164, 172, 198, 297, 582, 717
Symbol Properties dialog box, Flash, 164, 171, 356, 463, 609
Symbol Type drop-down menu, Flash Import Video wizard, 307, 580, 581
SymbolEdit.fla file, 160
symbols
    9-slice scaling
        function of, 161–163
        issues with, 166–169
        olive seller frame example, 163–166
        overview, 160
    blends, 180–181
    Catalina Island example
        adding clouds, 206–207
        clouds in motion, 208–211
    content management on stage
        Align panel, 192–193
        aligning objects, 186–189
        overview, 184–185
        stacking order, 189–193
    editing, 159–160
    filters
        applying, 174–177
        and blend modes, 174–181

        facts regarding, 179
        perspective, 177–179
    masks and masking
        simple mask, 194–199
        using text as mask, 201–203
    overview, 152–153
    sharing
        angryalien.com, 173
        overview, 169–170
        shared libraries, 171–173
    types of
        button symbols, 156–157
        graphic symbols, 155–156
        movie clip symbols, 158
Symmetry Brush option, Deco tool, 92
Sync area, Flash Properties panel, 290, 292
Sync drop-down menu, Flash, 61, 290, 297
Sync graphic symbols property, Flash Properteis panel, 454
Sync property
    Flash audio2 layer, 290, 291
    Flash Properties panel, 291, 292, 293, 382
Sync setting, Flash Properties panel, 290
syntax, ActionScript, 233, 253–257

T

tabstops parameter, 587
Tagged Image File Format (TIFF), 124
tags
    custom, 684–686
    HTML, 586–587, 785
tailJoint property, ActionScript, 474
TalkingPanda.fla file, 406
Tarbell, Jared, 421
Target field, Flash Advanced character properties, 334
target layer, Flash, 36
Target property
    ActionScript Event class, 677
    Flash Advanced Character options, 349
Target setting
    Flash Advanced character properties, 334
    Flash Properties panel, 586
    HTML, 586
Tayler, Benjamin, 711
TCP (Transmission Control Protocol), 759
Template drop-down menu
    Flash Publish Settings dialog box, 576
    HTML tab, Publish Settings dialog box, 800

INDEX

Template list, 138
Templates area, Flash New Document dialog box, 422
Templates button, 138, 422
Test button, Flash Sound Properties dialog box, 59, 60, 286, 287
Test Devices panel, Device Central, 740
Test Movie menu option, Flash, 62, 254, 377
testing, Flash movie, 61–65
text
    Adobe CoolType, 319–322
    checking spelling, 352–354
    Classic text engine, 328–330
    container and flow, 337–338
    device fonts, 322–323
    editable text, 340
    embedding fonts, 324–327
    fonts, 316–318
    hyperlinks and TLF, 349–352
    overview, 315
    Read-only text properties
        advanced character properties, 334–335
        character properties, 332–334
        overview, 331
        Paragraph properties, 336
    scrollable
        rolling your own scroller, 356–360
        using the UIScrollBar component, 355
    selectable, 340
    TLF and ActionScript
        creating column of text with ActionScript, 342–343
        import statements for this exercise, 344–345
        overview, 341
    TLF text engine, 328–330
    typefaces, 316–318
    using as mask, 201–203
    using TLF text as a button, 345–349
Text Engine drop-down menu, Flash, 324, 328
Text Engine option, Flash Properties panel, 570
text field layer, Flash, 242
Text Justify options, Flash Paragraph properties, 337
Text layer, Flash, 201, 202, 203, 560, 570, 582
Text Layout Framework. *See* TLF
Text option, Fireworks import dialog box, 139
text parameter, Flash TextArea component, 635
Text tool, Device Central, 741
Text tool, Flash, 201, 242, 321, 332, 333, 354, 570, 582, 704, 719

Text Type drop-down menu, Flash, 201, 324, 330, 570
Text type field, Flash Properties panel, 333, 340
textAlign property, 672
TextArea component, 635, 636
<textarea> element, HTML, 635
TextArea.fla file, 635
TextDecoration class, ActionScript, 347
textDecoration property, 672
TextDecoration.UNDERLINE constant, ActionScript, 347
TextField class, ActionScript, 226, 234
TextField.embedFonts property, ActionScript, 692
TextField.htmlText property, ActionScript text field, 672
TextField.text property, ActionScript, 243, 626
TextFlow( ) class, ActionScript, 341
textFlow container, ActionScript, 351
textFlowInitialFormat property, ActionScript Configuration class, 341
TextFormat class, ActionScript, 347, 587, 614
textFormat style, ActionScript, 614
<textformat> tag, HTML, 587, 674
TextFormat.color property, ActionScript, 618
textIndent property, 672
TextInput component, 619, 627, 636
TextInput.fla file, 636
textLayout_X.X.X.XXX.swz file, 345
TextLayoutFormat( ) class, ActionScript, 341, 342
theGreatStoneFace variable, ActionScript, 241
thermometer movie clip, 627
thermometer.mercury reference, ActionScript, 628
Thomas, Adam, 245
ThroughADoor.flv file, 555, 560
TIFF (Tagged Image File Format), 124
TileList component, 637–638
TileList.fla file, 637
Time area, Adobe Media Encoder Export Settings window, 590
Time parameter, Flash Properties panel, 562
<Time> tag, XML, 585
Timed Text (TT), 567
Timeline Navigation folder, 268, 269
Timeline panel, Flash, 5, 224, 395–396, 406, 433, 445, 449, 472
Timeline tab, Flash, 33, 54, 203
timelinePause variable, ActionScript, 262
timelinePause.start method, ActionScript, 263

INDEX

timelines
  combining
    graphic symbols as mini-libraries, 406–407
    movie clip timelines versus graphic symbol timelines, 402–404
    nesting symbols, 404–406
  frames, 16–18
  looping, 265
  Motion Editor panel, 19–23
  overview, 14–15
  pausing, 261–264
  removing audio file, 291
  using movie clips to control, 266
Timeline.swf file, 16
timeout setting, Device Central Display tab, 749
Timer class, ActionScript, 262
Timer.delay property, ActionScript, 264
TimerEvent.TIMER event, ActionScript, 262
timerHandler function, ActionScript, 262, 263
Timer.start method, ActionScript, 263
TinBangs.fla file, 712, 714, 717
TinBangs.fla Library, Flash, 717, 718
TinBangsMilestone.fla file, 726
Tinted Frames option, Flash Timeline panel, 366
Title area, Flash Create New Code Snippet dialog box, 269
title attribute, XML, 657
title movie clip, Flash, 743
<title> tags, XML, 646
TLF (Text Layout Framework)
  and ActionScript, 341–345
  and hyperlinks, 349–352
  text engine, 328–330
  text, using as button, 345–349
TLF Text option, 324, 328, 330, 333
TLF text Read Only format, Device Central Text tool, 741
TLF Text Selectable text container, Flash, 704
TLF_eventLink_AS.fla file, 345, 348
TLF_Hyperlink_AS.fla file, 350
TLF_scrollable_AS.fla file, 356
To stage option, Flash Alignment panel, 561
toggle parameter, Flash Properties panel, 605, 606
Tom.jpg file, 665
Tool Settings dialog box, Flash, 248, 346
Tool Settings, Flash, 346
tools
  Rotation, 501–506
  Translation, 506–511

Tools panel
  Free Transform tool, 75–77
  Gradient Transform tool, 77–80
  Object Drawing mode, 80–82
  overview, 29–31
  Selection tool, 72–75
  Subselection tool, 72–75
Tooltip area, Flash Create New Code Snippet dialog box, 269, 310
tooltips, 72
_top setting, Flash Advanced character properties, 334
TopPage folder, 672
torso symbol, Flash, 489
toXMLString( ) method, ActionScript, 653, 654, 657
Trace Bitmap dialog box, 127, 128, 129
trace( ) function, ActionScript, 224, 241, 650, 651, 653, 656, 660
Trace Image text, 127
Trace.fla file, 127
trace(theGreatStoneFace) function, ActionScript, 241
Tracking property, Flash Properties panel, 333
Transform menu item, Flash, 208, 383
Transform panel, Flash, 162, 209, 429, 491, 505, 511, 515, 518, 524, 699
Transform tool, Flash, 365
Transformation area, Flash Motion Editor panel, 21
transformation point, 365
Transformation twirlie, Flash, 442
transformations, removing, 77
Translation property, Flash bones, 465
Translation tool, 506–511
Transmission Control Protocol (TCP), 759
Trash Can icon, Flash, 35, 40, 179, 368
Trees layer, 108
Trees symbol, 108
trimming videos, 534–535
True parameter, ActionScript, 746
TT (Timed Text), 567
Tune class, ActionScript, 300
Turtle movie clip, Flash, 430
Turtle symbol, Flash, 458
Tween class, ActionScript, 348
tweening
  classic
    deforming, 382–384
    easing, 384–387, 395
    properties, 381–382

rotation, 379–381
scaling, 382–384
stretching, 382–384
filter effects, 413–414
masks
    animating, 411–412
    using motion guides with, 412–413
shape
    altering gradients, 377–378
    altering shapes, 369–373
    modifying, 368–369
    scaling, 363–368
    shape hints, 373–377
    stretching, 363–368
Tweening area, Flash Properties panel, 380, 381, 385, 387, 388, 391, 409
TweenMax class, ActionScript, 272, 273, 274, 275
TweenMax folder, 272
TweenMax.as file, 272
twinkie.fla file, 238
twirlies, After Effects, 20
Type drop-down menu
    Flash Create New Symbol dialog box, 45
    Flash Properties panel, 462, 464, 473
Type field, Flash Convert to Symbol dialog box, 153
Type property, Flash Symbol Properties dialog box, 463
<Type> tag, XML, 585, 592
_typewriter font category, 322

U

<u> tag, HTML, 587
UI components
    Button component
        adding button events, 606–608
        changing appearance, 610–615
        considering component weight, 609
        overview, 603–605
        referencing components in event handlers, 608–609
        using, 603–606
    CheckBox component, 615–616
    ColorPicker component, 617–618
    ComboBox component, 619–622
    DataGrid component, 622–623
    Label component, 624

List component, 624–626
NumericStepper component, 626–628
overview, 601–602
ProgressBar component, 628–630
RadioButton component, 630–632
ScrollPane component, 632–633
Slider component, 633–634
TextArea component, 635
TextInput component, 636
TileList component, 637–638
UILoader component, 638–640
UIScrollBar component, 641
what you have learned, 641
UIComponent.setStyle( ) method, ActionScript, 615
UIComponent.textFormat style, Flash, 612
UILoader component, 638–640, 704, 710
UILoader.fla file, 639
UIScrollBar component, 355–356, 635, 641
<ul> tag, 676, 681, 682, 684, 686
Ulloa, Carlos, 497
UNDERLINE constant, ActionScript, 351
Underline property, Flash Properties panel, 333
Undo Create Motion Tween menu item, Flash, 367
Undo Scale menu item, Flash, 364
Uniform Resource Locator (URL), 760
unmuteSound( ) function, ActionScript, 305
Untitled document, Flash, 422
Up frame, Flash button component, 603
up skin, Flash Button component, 610, 611, 619
Update button
    Bitmap Properties dialog box, 133
    Flash, 172, 286
Update context menu item, Flash, 172, 400
Update Library Items dialog box, Flash, 172
Update menu item, Flash, 172
updateSong( ) function, ActionScript, 728
upScroller function, ActionScript, 359
URL (Uniform Resource Locator), 760
URLLoader class, ActionScript, 648, 649, 677
URLLoader.load( ) method, ActionScript, 649, 677
URLRequest class, ActionScript, 302, 649, 677, 706
URLRequest.url property, ActionScript, 707
Use device fonts Anti-alias option, Flash, 355
Use Device Fonts option, Flash Anti-alias drop-down menu, 323, 324
Use device fonts property, Flash Anti-alias drop-down menu, 333

INDEX

Use Imported JPEG data option, Bitmap Properties dialog box, 133
Use one setting for all properties check box, Flash Properties panel, 394, 395
Use one setting for all properties option, Flash Custom Ease In/Ease Out dialog box, 388
Use Pressure option, Brush tool, 87
Use Tilt option, Brush tool, 87
User Interface components, Flash Components panel, 355
users, 762–763

V

Value area, Adobe Media Encoder Export Settings window, 588
value property, Flash Slider component, 634
Values dialog box, Flash, 621, 625
vanishing point, 498–501, 506, 512, 525
var keyword, ActionScript, 240
variables, ActionScript, 240–241
VBR (for variable bitrate), 537
VBR option, Adobe Media Encoder Export Settings window, 537
Vector images, 68
vectors, 778
Vertical Spacing button, Flash Align panel, 193
verticalScrollPosition property, ActionScript, 359
video
    adding cue points
        creating XML captions, 588–592
        HTML tags, 586–587
        overview, 583
        XML format, 584–587
    alpha video, 593–596
    embedding, 579–583
    FLV encoding. *See also* Adobe Media Encoder
        Adobe Media Encoder, 532–540
        batch encoding, 541–542
        creating F4V files, 542–544
    formats, 530–532
    full-screen video, HD, 597–598
    overview, 527–529
    playing FLV in Flash CS5. *See also* full-screen video
        ActionScript, 555–560
        alpha channel video, 572–574
        cue points, 562–566

        FLVPlayback component, 552–555, 560–561
        FLVPlaybackCaptioning component, 567–571
        snippets, 559–560
        using wizard, 546–552
    on web, 529
Video area, Flash Components panel, 548
Video category, Flash Components panel, 552
Video class, ActionScript, 556
Video components area, Flash Components panel, 560
Video Import dialog box, Flash, 567
Video layer
    Flash, 560, 570, 574, 581
    Symbol Editor, 594
Video pane, Adobe Media Encoder Export Settings window, 536
Video Properties dialog box
    Flash, 555
    Symbol Editor, 594
Video section, Flash Components panel, 552
Video tab, Adobe Media Encoder Export Settings window, 535, 543, 573, 588
VideoJam.fla file, 593
View ä Bandwidth Profiler option, Flash, 322
View area, Flash Tools panel, 29
View option, Flash, 510
View property, Flash, 510
Viewable Frames hot text, Flash, 436, 440
Viewable Frames value, Flash, 22
Viewing grouping, Flash, 70, 71
viking movie clip, Flash, 606
Virtual Reality Modeling Language (VRML), 495
:visited pseudo-class, Flash, 688
volume, audio, 293–296
volume icon graphic symbol, Flash, 718
volume parameter, Flash Properties panel, 553
volume property
    ActionScript, 305
    xform variable, 734
volumeAdjust( ) function, ActionScript, 733, 735, 736
VolumeBar symbol
    ActionScript, 733, 734
    Flash, 714, 718, 719
VolumeKnob symbol
    ActionScript, 733
    Flash, 718, 719
VolumeSlider movie clip, Flash, 719
VolumeSlider symbol, Flash, 714, 718, 719

845

INDEX

volumeStartDrag( ) function, ActionScript, 732
volumeStopDrag( ) function, ActionScript, 733
VRML (Virtual Reality Modeling Language), 495
vspace attribute, 587
Vultures.fla file, 555
Vultures.mp4 file, 543, 544

W

W (Width) property, Flash Properties panel, 454
W3C (World Wide Web Consortium), 216, 669
Wall.fla file, 198
WatchMe folder, 541
WAV format, 280
WaveAmerican.fla file, 486
waveform, audio, 281
WaveSwiss.fla file, 485
web formats
   animated GIFs
      exporting, 787–789
      importing, 790
      overview, 786
   Flash, 784–785
   HTML, 785–786
   overview, 783
   QuickTime, 790–791
web, video on, 529
Webster, Steve, 655
Weird Viking layer, Flash, 606
Welcome screen, Flash, 4, 9
WhackABunny folder, 751
whackabunnyAndroid.air file, 753, 755
whackabunnyAndroid.fla file, 751
whackabunny.fla file, 743, 751
What's new in Adobe Flash professional link, Flash Help panel, 41
wheel symbol, Flash, 474
wheel.crank.x property, ActionScript, 474
white dot, Free Transform tool, 76
widgets, 309
Width (W) property, Flash Properties panel, 454
width attribute, 586
Width property, Flash Transform panel, 452
Width value, Symbol Editor Properties panel, 594
Window menu, Flash, 8
Window Mode selelction, 802
Windows Media Video (WMV), 530
Windows Projector (.exe) file format, 793
WingL movie clip, Flash, 45, 46
WingR movie clip, Flash, 45
wings symbols, Flash, 410
WMV (Windows Media Video), 530
Wolfe, David, 493
word spacing option, Flash Paragraph properties, 337
workspace, managing, 6–8
World Wide Web Consortium (W3C), 216, 669

X

X [number] property, Flash Properties panel, 382
X property, Flash Properties panel, 454
.xfl file extension, 64
XFL file format, 64, 661–666
XFL folder, 662
XFL_Example folder, 63
XFLexercise.fla file, 662
xform variable, ActionScript, 305, 723, 733, 736
XML (Extensible Markup Language)
   captions, creating, 588–592
   E4X syntax
      descendant accessor (.), 657–658
      dots (.), 650–654
      filtering, 656–657
      namespaces, 659–661
      node types, 654–655
      overview, 649
      at symbol (@), 650–654
      XFL, 661–666
   formats, 584–587
   loading files, 648–649
   MP3 players with. *See also* controls, MP3 players with XML
      evaluating and improving, 735–737
      overview, 711
      renaming Library assets, 713–714
      setting up external playlists, 712–713
   overview, 643–647
   slide shows with components and, 703–711
   writing, 645–648
XML class, ActionScript, 648, 649
XML_Example folder, 64
xmlCompleteHandler( ) function, ActionScript, 710, 711
XMLConnector component, Flash, 650
xmlDoc variable, ActionScript, 649
xmlDoc.author subexpression, ActionScript, 658
xmlDoc.book class, ActionScript, 654, 657

INDEX

xmlDoc.book.authors expression, ActionScript, 655
xmlDoc.book.length( ) - 1 expression, ActionScript, 652
XMLList class, ActionScript, 652
XMLList method, ActionScript, 652, 653, 654
XMLList.toXMLString( ) method, ActionScript, 657
XML.namespace( ) method, XML, 661
xmlns attributes, XML, 659, 661
XML.parent( ) method, XML, 658

Y

Y property, Flash Properties panel, 454
Y Translation arm, Flash, 509
Y Translation arrow, Flash, 509
YourTurn folder, 591

Z

Zhang, John, 703
Zhou, Zhong, 703
Zoom drop-down menu, Flash Symbol Editor, 47
Zoom In menu option, Flash, 12
Zoom Out button, Flash Edit Envelope dialog box, 294
Zoom Out menu option, Flash, 12
Zoom tool, 71, 104, 108, 482
zooming stage, 11–13
zooming technique, Flash, 11
Zupko, Andy, 497